FUNDAMENTALISMS AND THE STATE

THE FUNDAMENTALISM PROJECT

VOLUME

3

FUNDAMENTALISMS AND THE STATE

Remaking Polities, Economies, and Militance

EDITED BY
Martin E. Marty and R. Scott Appleby

Sponsored by
The American Academy of Arts and Sciences

The University of Chicago Press
Chicago and London

MARTIN E. MARTY AND R. SCOTT APPLEBY direct the Fundamentalism Project.
Marty, the Fairfax M. Cone Distinguished Service Professor of the History of
Modern Christianity at the University of Chicago, is senior editor of *The Christian
Century* and the author of numerous books, including the multi-volume *Modern
American Religion,* also published by the University of Chicago Press. Appleby, a
research associate at the University of Chicago, is the author of *"Church and Age
Unite!" The Modernist Impulse in American Catholicism.*

The collection of essays in this volume is based on a project conducted under the
auspices of the American Academy of Arts and Sciences and supported by a grant
from the John D. and Catherine T. MacArthur Foundation. The opinions expressed
are those of the individual authors only, and do not necessarily reflect the views of
the American Academy or the supporting foundation.

The University of Chicago Press, Chicago 60637
The University of Chicago Press, Ltd., London
© 1993 by The University of Chicago
All rights reserved. Published 1993
Printed in the United States of America

02 01 00 99 98 97 96 95 94 93 5 4 3 2 1
ISBN (cloth): 0-226-50883-8

Library of Congress Cataloging-in-Publication Data

Fundamentalisms and the state : remaking polities, militance, and
    economies / edited by Martin E. Marty and R. Scott Appleby ;
    sponsored by the American Academy of Arts and Sciences.
        p.   cm. — (The Fundamentalism project ; v. 3)
    Includes index.
        1. Fundamentalism.   2. Religion and politics.   I. Marty, Martin
    E., 1928–   .   II. Appleby, R. Scott, 1956–   .   III. American
    Academy of Arts and Sciences.   IV. Series.
    BL238.F83 vol. 3
    291'.09'04 s—dc20   92-14582
    [291.1'77]   CIP

25747670

∞The paper used in this publication meets the minimum requirements of the
American National Standard for Information Sciences—Permanence of Paper for
Printed Library Materials, ANSI Z39,48—1984.

CONTENTS

Contents
vi

Part 2   Restructuring Economies

Part 3 Remaking the World through Militancy

ACKNOWLEDGMENTS

We thank first the advisers who began planning and conceptualizing this volume in meetings at the House of the American Academy of Arts and Sciences in Cambridge, Massachusetts. Gabriel Almond, Said A. Arjomand, Harvey Brooks, Gerhard Casper, Bruce Hoffman, Gerald Holton, Mohsin Khan, Daniel Levine, Şerif Mardin, Joel Orlen, David Rapoport, Susan Rose, Emmanuel Sivan, and Marvin Zonis participated in those sessions in November 1988.

Also contributing in significant ways to the process of identifying and recruiting scholars and clarifying themes for this volume were Nancy Ammerman, Daniel Brumberg, Stephen Graubard, Jeffrey Kaplan, Bruce Lawrence, Edward Levi, Frederic L. Pryor, and Martin Riesebrodt. Many other scholars contributed to this volume through written responses and criticisms of particular essays after they were presented during a public conference; those not mentioned by name here are acknowledged by the authors in the endnotes.

Joel Orlen, executive officer of the American Academy of Arts and Sciences, merits another word of thanks for his leadership and encouragement in advancing the project from stage to stage.

Alan Thomas of the University of Chicago Press made valuable recommendations and supervised the various phases of volume review and production. Randolph M. Petilos, Jennie Lightner, and Kathy Gohl also contributed to the editorial process in significant ways.

We thank the University of Chicago professors W. Clark Gilpin, dean of the Divinity School, and Bernard McGinn, director of the Institute for the Advanced Study of Religion, for providing intellectual stimulus, office space, and the semi-annual use of Swift Lecture Hall. The Divinity School also hosted a graduate seminar, led by the Project directors, during which students drawn from throughout the university discussed and dissected early drafts of the essays.

We are most grateful for the tireless efforts of the Project staff, who put in many hours of "overtime." Patricia A. Mitchell shared editorial responsibilities, compiled the index, and prepared the final manuscript for publication. Barbara A. Lockwood organized the conferences, coordinated research trips, and managed the office. We are happily in their debt.

Introduction

Martin E. Marty and R. Scott Appleby

In the early 1990s, pondering the collapse of communism across Eastern Europe and the unraveling of Marxist ideology even in the Soviet Union, American political commentators speculated at some length: Whence will come the new enemy? Who or what will replace the "evil empire" as the focus of American reaction and enmity? What ideology, fortified by military, economic, or political power, will be virulent and contagious enough to challenge the efforts of liberal Western democracies to direct the future course of global development?

"Religious fundamentalism" was the answer that came from some quarters.[1]

The delicate symbiosis by which the two great superpowers sustained their rivalry for four decades of the Cold War had produced an era of relative stability in the developed world. National borders were respected in principle, if not always in practice, as the postwar order was maintained along the NATO and Warsaw Pact axes. In the Third World, border disputes and civil wars, debilitating foreign debt, and ongoing economic crises only deepened the dependency of regimes on one of the two superpower patrons competing for global hegemony. With the diminishment of the Soviet player in this dangerous but effective game of deterrence and neutralization, political scientist John Mearsheimer warned that the era of world history dawning in the 1990s, contrary to widespread expectations, did not augur a splendid Pax Americana. The end of the Cold War would lead instead, in Europe at least, to a new factionalism, to sectarian strife and violent ethnic particularisms, to skirmishes spilling over into border disputes, civil wars, and battles of secession.[2]

In 1991, armed conflicts in "Yugoslavia," "Czechoslovakia," and the Baltic republics supported Mearsheimer's thesis, at least for the short term, while the splintering of what appeared increasingly to have been a poorly constructed national unity in India, Afghanistan, Sri Lanka, Algeria, the Sudan, Nigeria, and elsewhere suggested that in certain respects the Mearsheimer thesis may be applied beyond Europe. Once the Soviet Union was no longer able to act as a viable constructor and preserver of the (satellite) state, the full extent of the fragility and artifice of the postwar nation-state became painfully apparent to indigenous bureaucrats in these troubled regions and to their postcolonial patrons. Factionalism and disorder mocked earlier anticipations of an age of globalism, ecumenism, and one-worldism. Instead the world now seemed beset by an inward turning of peoples, by antipluralist particularisms, or by the open aggrandizement of more powerful states at the expense of the newly created states. Against this chaotic background, the forging of an American-led alliance to halt and reverse Saddam Hussein's aggression against Kuwait in the Gulf Crisis of 1990–91, and the subsequent American policy of respecting Iraqi borders, even at the expense of ethnic (Kurdish) and religious (Shi'ite) claims to autonomy, seemed to have more to do with preserving the old order than with establishing a "new world order."[3]

In this context religious fundamentalisms did seem poised to inherit the mantle of failed leftist and nationalist ideologies in some nations. Elsewhere, their influence seemed spent or at least diminished. Whether or not these movements attain a greater measure of power and influence in the years ahead, an examination of their impact in the 1970s and 1980s offers important lessons for those who seek to understand the fundamentalists' sociopolitical goals in various nations, and the strategies they have successfully or unsuccessfully pursued to attain these goals. We chose to do this in two companion volumes. One, *Fundamentalisms and Society,* assesses the progress of fundamentalist leaders and movements in their attempts to reorder scientific inquiry, to reclaim the patterns of "traditional" family life and interpersonal relations, and to reshape education and communications systems. Meanwhile, *Fundamentalisms and the State* examines and evaluates the ways in which fundamentalists have sought to influence the course of developments in politics, law, constitutionalism, and economic planning during the past twenty-five years.

One conclusion that will be immediately apparent to readers of both volumes is that "fundamentalism" has been much more in evidence in its extreme or unmodified form on certain levels of "society" than at the level of the "state." The three terms set off in quotation marks are central to this discussion and thus require early working definitions.

As a comparative construct encompassing movements within religious traditions as rich and diverse, and as different one from another, as are Islam, Judaism, Christianity, Hinduism, Sikhism, and Buddhism, "fundamentalism" is a useful analytical device. Objections to the use of the term are discussed in the first volume of this series, *Fundamentalisms Observed.*[4] The title of that volume, as of the project itself, is not meant to indicate that every movement examined within it equally "qualifies" as a fundamentalism. Rather, the project tests the hypothesis that there are "family resemblances" among disparate movements of religiously inspired reaction to aspects of the global processes of modernization and secularization in the twentieth century. In the concluding chapter of *Fundamentalisms Observed* the editors note and describe a pattern of traits recurring throughout the book's fourteen separate studies of fundamentalist-like movements in seven religious traditions and five continents. From those "family traits" the editors construct a working definition of fundamentalism that we repeat here to give readers of the present volume a general idea of how the term is understood by contributors.

Religious fundamentalism has appeared in the twentieth century as a tendency, a habit of mind, found within religious communities and paradigmatically embodied in certain representative individuals and movements, which manifests itself as a strategy, or set of strategies, by which beleaguered believers attempt to preserve their distinctive identity as a people or group. Feeling this identity to be at risk in the contemporary era, they fortify it by a selective retrieval of doctrines, beliefs, and practices from a sacred past. These retrieved "fundamentals" are refined, modified, and sanctioned in a spirit of shrewd pragmatism: they are to serve as a bulwark against the encroachment of outsiders who threaten to draw the believers into a syncretistic, areligious, or irreligious cultural milieu. Moreover, these fundamentals are accompanied in the new religious portfolio by unprecedented claims and doctrinal innovations. By the strength of these innovations and the new supporting doctrines, the retrieved and updated fundamentals are meant to regain the same charismatic intensity today by which they originally forged communal identity from the formative revelatory religious experiences long ago.

In this sense contemporary fundamentalism is at once both derivative and vitally original. In the effort to reclaim the efficacy of religious life, fundamentalists have more in common than not with other religious revivalists of past centuries. But fundamentalism intends neither an artificial imposition of archaic practices and lifestyles nor a simple return to a golden era, a sacred past, a bygone time of origins—although nostalgia for such an era is a hallmark of fundamentalist rhetoric. Instead, religious identity thus renewed becomes the exclusive and absolute basis for a re-created political and social order that is oriented to the future rather than the past. Selecting elements of tradition and modernity, fundamentalists seek to remake the world in the service of a dual commitment to the unfolding eschatological drama (by returning all things in submission to the divine) and to self-preservation (by neutralizing the threatening "Other"). Such an endeavor often requires charismatic and authoritarian leadership, depends upon a disciplined inner core of adherents, and promotes a rigorous sociomoral code for all followers. Boundaries are set, the enemy identified, converts sought, and institutions created and sustained in pursuit of a comprehensive reconstruction of society.

"Society" is understood here as the relationships among human beings as characterized by "the values [these relationships] embody, the individual and collective motivations they encourage, the incentives they inspire and sanction, and the ideals by which belief, attitude, and behavior are established and secured."[5] Fundamentalists pay special attention to the "values, motivations, incentives, and ideals" according to which the intimate zones of life are ordered. How best is one to marry, conduct sexual relations, order family life, raise children? How best is one to understand and teach others about creation and procreation, providence and scientific evidence, morality and spirituality? These perennial questions have generated religiolegal rulings, moral and behavioral codes, and scores of learned treatises by fundamentalist scholars and educators intent on sustaining, re-creating, or fortifying a religious enclave within a larger society that is perceived as invasive and threatening.

But because fundamentalists often live in close proximity to nonfundamental-ists—or to fundamentalists of a different religious tradition—a second question is inevitably raised when one examines "fundamentalist impact," as each author in this volume does. The observer must ask not only "How effective have fundamentalist movements been in influencing their own adherents?" but also "How much impact have they exercised in the lives of nonfundamentalists?" Inevitably this second question leads to a consideration of the fundamentalist social reformer's relationship to the "state," understood here as the "supreme public power within a sovereign political entity."[6]

Fundamentalists are boundary-setters: they excel in marking themselves off from others by distinctive dress, customs, and conduct. But they are also, in most cases, eager to expand their borders by attracting outsiders who will honor fundamentalist norms, or by requiring that nonfundamentalists observe fundamentalist codes. The state is the final arbiter of disputes within its borders. In cases in which the state is "fundamentalist" (e.g., Iran, Sudan) or has been influenced by fundamentalist socio-political agendas (Pakistan, Egypt, India, Israel), the fundamentalism of the enclave is encouraged or even empowered to spill over its natural boundaries and permeate the larger society. The impact in these instances is of a different order than in a society within which fundamentalists have been routed (Algeria, as of this writing), margin-alized (Iraq), or made to play by the rules of political compromise, as in developed democracies such as the United States and Great Britain.

By dividing this extensive study of "fundamentalist impact" into two volumes la-beled "state" and "society," we do not mean to imply that the two realms are distinct one from the other; rather, they overlap and interact in complex ways. Because the state regulates many aspects of social existence, and establishes the basic political and cultural conditions within which social life occurs, fundamentalists inevitably become involved in modern political life, even in the attempt to preserve their separateness (as in the case of the haredi Jews profiled by Ehud Sprinzak and Charles Liebman). In so doing they participate in a common discourse about modernization, development, political structures, and economic planning. Fundamentalists may nuance and modify the terms of that discourse—they may successfully or unsuccessfully try to redirect or reinvent aspects of it—but they are contained within it and find any hope of even a partial return to a pristine premodern world, much less the construction of a purely Islamic or Christian or Jewish or Hindu modern society or polity, well out of reach.

A Matter of Perspective and Allegiance

In a volume surveying and evaluating the impact of fundamentalists, who is doing the evaluating? Contributors to *Fundamentalisms and the State* include political scientists, legal scholars, sociologists, cultural anthropologists, historians of religion, and economists. None of the contributors claims to be a religious fundamentalist, although some are in greater sympathy with fundamentalism than others, and all draw heavily upon the writings, public pronouncements, and self-descriptions of fundamentalists. In most cases the author hails from the nation or religious tradition about which he or she is writing. Nonetheless the participants in this project are resolutely "of the Western academy," an institution and fellowship that radical fundamentalists everywhere oppose on principle and that moderate fundamentalists in the West have joined only recently and very selectively.[7]

If fundamentalisms, like other social phenomena, display a range of attitudes and behavioral responses to outsiders, it becomes possible to speak realistically of incorporating the ideas of moderate fundamentalists into studies such as this, just as it becomes possible to speak of moderate fundamentalists incorporating the ideas and procedures of the Western academy into their various worldviews. But can fundamentalism truly exist in a moderate form without being compromised in its essence? In the present volume fundamentalism is viewed as the struggle to assert or reassert the norms and beliefs of "traditional religion" in the public order. For fundamentalists these norms and beliefs, derived from a divinely revealed or otherwise absolute source of knowledge, establish a framework of limits within which development may occur and public officials may govern. Thus, the question for many fundamentalists and nonfundamentalists alike is whether the alternative modernization programs of fundamentalists can be pursued and implemented within a larger philosophical framework that does not privilege any particular religion and that respects the human and civil rights of nonfundamentalists and nonbelievers. Are fundamentalists destined to remain forceful, disruptive (and exceedingly shrewd) cultural critics, outside the pale of responsible political discourse? Or will fundamentalist religion become a viable basis for sociopolitical programs that compete democratically with nonfundamentalist and secular programs?

Answering this question is a matter not simply of semantics but of careful observation and definition. If fundamentalism is defined and understood by the utterances and actions of its most radical proponents, then one may conclude that fundamentalism is essentially antidemocratic, anti-accommodationist, and antipluralist and that it violates, *as a matter of principle,* the standards of human rights defended, if not always perfectly upheld, by Western democracies. By this reading of fundamentalism, the battle lines are drawn clearly between fundamentalist and nonfundamentalist, mutual understanding is unlikely or impossible, and public policy studies like the present one are inevitably devoted to the defense of principles and lifestyles under assault by the forces of resurgent religious radicalism.

Some influential opinion-makers and policy analysts have concluded that this reading of fundamentalism is accurate and sensible. They have turned their attentions, now that the evil empire is no more, to combating the spread and influence of fundamentalism. Several of the participants in the Fundamentalism Project share this view, although to varying degrees. But the directors and other participants in the project are devoted to exploring the possibilities of mutual understanding and dialogue, in the hope that these possibilities will not be abandoned prematurely, and in the apprehension that unnuanced policies may simply serve to radicalize potential fundamentalists and thus to polarize situations. A careful understanding of the differences between movements in several traditions and subtraditions labeled "fundamentalist," and of the complex role that religion plays, and may play, in these movements, leads one to resist sweeping generalizations like the following:

> Islamic fundamentalism of the Sunni or Shia variety in Iran, Iraq, Egypt, Jordan, the West Bank and Gaza, the Maghreb and also Algeria is not merely resistant to democracy but wholly contemptuous of and hostile to the entire democratic political culture. . . . [It] is an aggressive revolutionary movement as militant and violent as the Bolshevik, Fascist, and Nazi movements of the past.[8]

There is another way to define fundamentalism, namely, as a generalized tendency, a habit of mind, that may inspire a variety of specific activities. If it is said that the fundamentalist tendency is to rule, to gain power for the purpose of mandating divine or sacred law (and/or to serve the personal ambition of the ruler), it is equally true that the ways and means of pursuing power, and of enforcing the mandate, are many. These ways and means may run along a spectrum of possibilities from "radical" to "accommodationist." As the chapters in the present volume demonstrate, the nature and scope of fundamentalist impact are determined as much by the sociopolitical circumstances as by the zeal and skill of the fundamentalists in exploiting these circumstances. Furthermore, the tide of "influence" runs in both directions. The larger the stakes, the greater the risk for fundamentalists that their message and program may become compromised. In the attempts to order personal relations and family life, or to create alternative social and educational institutions on the local level, the arena of fundamentalist concern is often narrowly circumscribed for maximum effect and minimum compromise. When they play politics to influence the policies of the state, however, fundamentalisms are thus necessarily involved in some measure of compromise and accommodation. Political involvement may alter the original exclusivist, dogmatic, and confrontational mode of the fundamentalist to such a degree that the word "fundamentalist" no longer applies. Authors of *Fundamentalisms and Society* use words like "pragmatist" or "accommodationist" to describe their subjects less frequently than do authors of *Fundamentalisms and the State*.

Thus, we asked each contributor to consider the ways in which fundamentalist activism affected the fundamentalists themselves as well as nonfundamentalists within their sphere of influence. That is, in asking, "How and where did fundamentalists fail or succeed in achieving their goals?" authors were alert to the unintended as well as the intended consequences of fundamentalist activism. The various circumstances in which fundamentalists operated, and the complex repercussions of their activism, are summarized in the editors' conclusion to the volume.

The fact that nonfundamentalists do the writing guarantees that this volume, and the entire project, will reflect a particular orientation to foundational questions and will produce conclusions in keeping with that orientation. What are the sources of truth? What are the appropriate criteria for evaluating data and judging success or failure? From the perspective of a nonfundamentalist, fundamentalisms are often scandalous. They appear to stand in the way of individual self-determination, to violate basic human rights, and to impede material advancement, progress, and prosperity. But this is precisely the point of fundamentalisms: they and their God are not to be judged according to human standards. One cannot evaluate social behavior along strictly humanistic lines; behavior is good if it conforms to God's will. Critics who do not share the ethical and philosophical assumptions of fundamentalists cannot hope to "get it right."

But they have tried nonetheless. The editors asked the authors to put in brackets their own presuppositions, an approach which does not mean that they successfully leave them behind, but that they become aware of them, take them into consideration, and do some compensating for them. The goal in every case is to come up with essays in which the people described therein would recognize themselves in the portrait, even if they would almost inevitably disagree with the conclusions and evaluations of these nonfundamentalist authors. This seemed the best choice for a volume that seeks to measure fundamentalist impact upon outsiders as well as insiders, that asks, "What have religious fundamentalists 'accomplished' thus far that nonfundamentalists find significant?"

In mentioning this important matter of various perspectives on a controversial subject such as fundamentalism, it is important to state clearly that the positions or interpretations put forth in this collection of essays are those of the individual authors and do not necessarily reflect the views of the American Academy of Arts and Sciences. In undertaking this project, the principal purpose of the Academy is to bring together scholars with the best credentials in the several areas and cultures under study, and to ask them to present as inclusive and fair a presentation as possible.

By a swift glance at the table of contents, the reader will see that some important cases of fundamentalist influence are not examined. This is due to a number of considerations, not the least of which is the physical limitations of volumes which are already encyclopedic in length. Furthermore, the implications of recent developments such as the rapid dissolution of the Soviet Union for the spread of fundamentalisms were apparent only after these studies were commissioned and will be treated in subsequent volumes. The project does not attempt to chase the latest headlines; most of the chapters in this volume were completed in 1991, at a time when fundamentalisms worldwide seemed to be entering a new phase of intense activism in the aftermath of the Gulf War of 1990–91 and the collapse of the Soviet Union. Thus, the usefulness of these chapters lies not in up-to-the-minute reportage, but in their exemplification and analysis of patterns of fundamentalist activism that the reader may expect to discern in the headlines and news accounts for some time to come. In summarizing and elaborating these patterns in the concluding chapter, we were able to draw upon examples taken at the last possible moment (February 1992), but these are illustrative and not comprehensive.

Given the scope of the volume it was necessary to ask each author to identify the traits of "fundamentalism" present in the activities of the particular group or movement under consideration in the individual chapters. A subsequent volume in this series will focus upon comparative definitions of fundamentalism and deal explicitly with methodological problems, such as the decision to include Asian traditions in the project, but the authors of the important chapters in the present volume on Sikh, Hindu, and Buddhist "fundamentalisms" have succinctly provided their own reasons for using the construct to understand certain religiopolitical movements on the Indian subcontinent. The associate editors—John Garvey, Timur Kuran, and David Rapoport—also identify fundamentalist family resemblances and patterns across traditions and cultures in the introductory chapters opening each part of the volume.

Notes

1. See David Ignatius, "The West's Next Crusade: Fighting Fundamentalist Islamic Rule," *Washington Post National Weekly Edition*, 16–22 March 1992, pp. 23–24; "U. S. Official Calls Muslim Militants a Threat to Africa," *New York Times*, 1 January 1992, p. 3; "Islamic Fundamentalism: A Force to Be Reckoned With," *Chicago Tribune*, 20 January 1992, p. 13; "Mahatma vs. Rama," *Time*, 24 June 1991, p. 35; Benjamin J. Barber, "Jihad vs. McWorld," *The Atlantic* 269, no. 3 (March 1992): 53–55, 58–62, 64–65.

2. John J. Mearsheimer, "Why We Will Soon Miss the Cold War," *The Atlantic* 266, no. 2 (August 1990): 35–50.

3. See the discussion by Adeed Dawisha, "The United States in the Middle East: The Gulf War and Its Aftermath," *Current History* 91, no. 561 (January 1992): 1–5. Cf. Hermann Frederick Eilts, "The Persian Gulf Crisis: Perspectives and Prospects," *Middle East Journal* 45, no. 1 (Winter 1991): 22.

4. "Among the reasons for insistence on a single term are these: First, 'fundamentalism' is here to stay, since it serves to create a distinction over against cognate but not fully appropriate words such as 'traditionalism,' 'conservatism,' or 'orthodoxy' and 'orthopraxis.' If the term were to be rejected, the public would have to find some other word if it is to make sense of a set of global phenomena which urgently bid to be understood. However diverse the expressions are, they present themselves as movements which demand comparison even as they deserve fair separate treatment so that their special integrities will appear in bold relief. Second, when they must communicate across cultures, journalists, public officials, scholars, and publics in the parts of the world where these books have their first audience have settled on this term. Rather than seek an idiosyncratic and finally precious alternative, it seemed better for the team of scholars to try to inform inquiry with the word that is here to stay and to correct misuses. With those two reasons goes a third: all words have to come from somewhere and will be more appropriate in some contexts than in others. Words which have appeared in these paragraphs—'modern,' 'religious,' 'liberal,' and 'secular'—are examples. It is urgent in all cases that these terms be used in such ways that they do justice to the particularities of separate realities, something which we are confident readers will find the present authors responsibly undertaking to do. Fourth, having spent three of the five years set aside for research and study comparing 'fundamentalism' to alternatives, we have come to two conclusions. No other coordinating term was found to be as intelligible or serviceable. And attempts of particular essayists to provide distinctive but in the end confusing accurate alternatives led to the conclusion that they were describing something similar to what are here called fundamentalisms." See Martin E. Marty and R. Scott Appleby, "The Fundamentalism Project: A User's Guide" in Marty and Appleby, eds., *Fundamentalisms Observed* (Chicago: University of Chicago Press, 1991), pp. vii–xiii.

5. Walter H. Capps, "Society and Religion," in Mircea Eliade, ed., *Encyclopedia of Religion*, vol. 13 (New York: Macmillan and Free Press), p. 375.

6. *The American Heritage Dictionary,* 2d College ed. (Boston: Houghton Mifflin, 1985), p. 1190.

7. The academy is ostensibly a center of tolerance. Intolerance makes a good deal of sense when one believes that she possesses the sole and absolute truth not to be compromised through dialogue or give and take; why sully matters with a facile ecumenism?

But it is precisely this opinion that makes it difficult for fundamentalists to take part in a roundtable discussion in which their colleagues may privately or publicly adhere to a completely different set of revealed truths, or to none at all.

8. Amos Perlmutter, "Wishful Thinking about Islamic Fundamentalism," *Washington Post,* 22 January 1992, p. C7.

1

Remaking Polities

Introduction: Fundamentalism and Politics

John H. Garvey

There are many differences in the forms of religious fundamentalism discussed in part 1 of this volume. It would be remarkable if it were otherwise. We are treating movements within very different religious traditions. The relations between fundamentalism and politics are even more complex, because here we must take account of further differences in forms of government, international relations, economic organization, social mores, and the imprint of history. One is tempted to say that the only true similarity is the accident of contemporaneity. But I believe that we can say more than that.

There is a certain way of thinking about law and politics that is characteristic of modern industrial nations, and that religious fundamentalist movements invariably reject. I will call this habit of thought the public/private distinction. Its central premise is that social life can be divided into public and private realms. The function of government is to regulate behavior in the public sphere according to secular rules. Within the private sphere people are free to do as they like, in religious and other matters. Religious fundamentalists reject this method of political organization. They see the public/private distinction as artificial; they believe in particular that religion is inseparable from law and politics.[1]

This is the theme I want to develop below. I must add a note of caution before going on, though. The chapters in this part deal with only one facet of religious fundamentalism—its relation to politics. My remarks are limited in the same way. I do not say that certain modern political ideas account for the rise of fundamentalism—only that there is bad chemistry between the two. Nor does the chemistry always produce the same reaction. Evangelical Protestants in Ulster and Muslims in Nigeria both reject the public/private distinction, but they have different names for it and they are dealing with different problems.

I

I will begin by describing the public/private distinction—how it arose and what it means. In the most general terms it is a principle that is apt to accompany the phenomena of industrialism and nationalism, processes that occurred at different times in Europe and America but that have happened simultaneously in other parts of the world.[2] By industrialism I mean the change from an agrarian economy to an industrial one, marked by the division of labor, the use of modern production and distribution technologies, the aggregation of capital (whether in the hands of the state or of private entrepreneurs), and greater population concentration and mobility. This occurred in America during the nineteenth century, when we began building factories, railroads, stores, and cities on a large scale. As we became more industrialized the integral social unit became larger. Neither families nor local communities were economically self-sufficient. The states were too small to govern interstate commerce, and so the U.S. government was asked to regulate the railroads, monopolies, food and drugs, and so on.

Nationalism exerts a similar pull in the direction of a larger social unit. France treats millions of people who don't know each other as *enfants de la patrie*. Together they choose a common apparatus for making rules about defense, commerce, education, health policy, transportation, and numerous other matters of daily importance. They celebrate holidays and build monuments to commemorate significant people and events in the life of the national community.

Both of these forces unite very large numbers of people who, generally speaking, share the same culture and language. But the people are far from homogeneous. They eat, dress, and work differently, belong to different clubs and families, and believe in different gods. Most of them think, moreover, that these differences are what matter most. They are what define us as individuals, distinct from other members of the political community. This is the origin of the public/private distinction. It holds that the government should exercise authority over those matters that concern everyone in common (the public sphere) but should refrain from meddling in affairs that matter only to individuals, families, churches, etc. (the private sphere).

The line between the public and private spheres is maintained in legal systems through the concept of freedom. In constitutional democracies this notion is typically embodied in a constitution. In granting freedom to citizens, a constitution guarantees that the government will not interfere with choices about certain actions deemed particularly important. The American constitution, for example, provides that "Congress shall make no law . . . prohibiting the free exercise [of religion]."[3] The Indian constitution states that "all persons are equally entitled to freedom of conscience and the right freely to profess, practise and propagate religion."[4] These rules let people worship as they please. They also let people do other religiously motivated acts, like sending children to a religious school. In general terms, they ensure that the government will not coerce activity in the private sphere.

In the case of religion, modern societies often go further. In addition to keeping the government out of private life they ban religion from the public arena. This produces a clean separation: religion is a private affair; the public sphere is secular. In America this is done by the Establishment Clause, which speaks to the government: "Congress shall make no law . . . respecting an establishment of religion."[5] In Turkey the constitution speaks instead to individuals: "No one shall be allowed to exploit or abuse religion or religious feelings, or things held sacred by religion, in whatever manner, for the purpose of personal or political influence, or for even partially basing the fundamental, social, economic, political, and legal order of the State on religious tenets."[6]

To summarize, the combined forces of industrialism and nationalism lead to the organization of societies that embrace large numbers of people who inhabit a more or less extensive and well defined territory. The citizens of such societies are bound together by molar ties of economy and patriotism, but they are also bound in smaller groups by molecular ties of friendship, kinship, and religion. The more intimate bonds are protected by rules about freedom, which divide private life off from public. But there is also a fear that they will pull the larger society to pieces. This is particularly true of religion, which can win converts. So public life is also insulated from religion and made secular.

II

Religious fundamentalism fits uncomfortably into this world. This is not surprising, given the traits that characterize the movements we call fundamentalist. There are three of these that seem both typical and politically salient: fundamentalist movements are conservative, popular, and practical.

When I say that such movements are conservative, I do not refer (at least not directly) to a particular political slant. I do not mean, for example, that fundamentalist Baptists in America vote for right-wing candidates. Rather, fundamentalists try to conserve a particular religious heritage. They look to their religious traditions for guidance in dealing with modern problems. They do not propose new ideologies, nor do they want to revise their habits and beliefs to keep them in tune with the times. One symptom of this conservatism is an emphasis on literalism in the interpretation of sacred texts. The insistence upon biblical literalism and inerrancy may be the most frequently remarked trait of American Protestant fundamentalists. They believe that God created the world and Adam and Eve in just the way the Book of Genesis describes. Ann Mayer observes a similar tendency among Muslim fundamentalists in Iran, Pakistan, and the Sudan regarding their approach to the Qur'an. This kind of exegesis is a way of holding meaning steady in a moving current of scientific and social change.

Another conservative trait is the emphasis on "traditional values," a phrase that designates forms of behavior deemed virtuous within the speaker's tradition. Sexual continence is an example that one finds in most cultures and religions. Correct sexual behavior is not just a matter of good manners, prudent health policy, or wise psychology. It is a religious obligation. Fundamentalists look back to a time when people understood this.

It is not a coincidence that the religious traditions that fundamentalists reach back to typically antedate the public/private distinction. Samuel Heilman and Menachem Friedman have explained how haredi Jews, in their language, dress, and customs, maintain a connection with late-eighteenth-century Eastern European society. The traditional Jewish village of Eastern Europe still symbolizes their ideal past.[7] Such villages existed as separate Orthodox communities governed by the norms of *halakha* (Jewish law) and resisted the trend toward cultural integration, modernization, and secularization that was moving across Western Europe. Steve Bruce has pointed out that conservative Protestants in Ulster find a model for their political faith in the old Scots Covenants. The Covenanters believed that the civil state should enforce religious conformity by suppressing heresy, popery, and related forms of superstition.[8] The connection is strikingly similar to that which exists between American Protestant fundamentalists and the Puritans in seventeenth-century New England. In Nigeria the Maitatsine sect—the best known of the Islamic revivalist groups in recent years— drew upon the nineteenth-century Mahdist tradition in that region and upon the precolonial experience of theocratic government under the Sokoto caliphate.[9]

Religious fundamentalist movements are popular as well as conservative. By "popular" I do not mean "widely embraced" but, rather, the qualities that give fundamentalism the potential for mass appeal—its simplicity and its nonhierarchical style. The idea of simplicity is implicit in the very word "fundamentalist" that we use to describe such movements. The term comes from the American Protestant practice of listing a few beliefs (the fundamentals), like biblical inerrancy and the resurrection of Jesus, the acceptance of which is a sine qua non of Christian orthodoxy. This undertaking leads to a kind of stripped-down religion that travels light and fast. Ann Mayer points to a related kind of simplicity in Islamic fundamentalist movements. These generally call for reviving the *Shari'a* (Islamic law), but they simplify and stereotype its elaborate jurisprudence. Such simplification is politically wise, she argues, because it appeals to the nonspecialist and because greater detail means greater possibility of dissent.[10]

Doctrinal simplicity is related to the scriptural literalism discussed above. If sacred texts have a plain meaning, then the common man can understand them, just as he can remember the fundamentals of theology. This in turn is connected to a characteristic form of ecclesiastical polity. Believers in a system of this kind have no need of a hierarchy of religious ministers to mediate between them and God. Churches create complex ecclesiastical structures when they have to enforce doctrinal orthodoxy and provide religious services to their members. But these are not concerns for fundamentalist movements, which tend to assume a populist, loosely connected, nonhierarchial aspect.

This point is easily obscured by the prominent role that the Ayatollah Khomeini played in the Iranian Revolution and under the 1979 constitution, which made him the country's supreme ruler. But his authority derived more from personal charisma and the civil constitution than from religious office. Muslims in fact hold rather "protestant" ecclesiastical views.[11] They believe that individuals can get in touch with God through scripture and inner light, without the need to rely on spiritual intermediaries.

This seems to reinforce the public/private distinction by making religion a very personal affair. But it may have the opposite effect. If many people can come to the same beliefs on their own, there may be something to the idea of a collective will. And if there is, then it is possible to see religion as a molar rather than a molecular bond. It could unite a community as large as a nation.

The third principal characteristic of religious fundamentalism is its practical nature. Almost as though to compensate for their doctrinal simplicity, fundamentalists lay a heavy emphasis on right behavior. T. N. Madan has argued that "Sikh fundamentalism is orthoprax rather than orthodox." It stresses codes of conduct governing such matters as dress, smoking, and sexual intercourse with Muslim women. Scriptural exegesis is not a major concern.[12]

Robert Frykenberg makes a similar point about Hindu fundamentalists in India. The most visible contemporary force among them is the Rashtriya Swayamsevak Sangh (RSS), an organization that aims at creating a brotherhood of true believers through rigorous self-discipline. Young men who join RSS cadres are subjected to demanding daily schedules of physical, mental, and spiritual exercise.

My own essay in this chapter discusses American Protestant fundamentalists. Except for their millennial interests, they are not much concerned with theological speculation. Scripture is read for the light it sheds on daily living. And daily life is governed by a range of sexual taboos, family obligations, abstinence from drugs and liquor, and so on. A still more extreme example is the haredim in Israel. It is not quite accurate to say that their orthopraxis comes at the expense of belief, since haredi society, at least for males, is a society of scholars. But behavior in such communities is regulated to an almost unparalleled extent in matters of dress, diet, ritual, socialization, and contact with modern culture.

III

Religious fundamentalist groups with these characteristics resist the maintenance and expansion of the public/private distinction. Standing behind this resistance is the fundamentalists' conviction that God is active in the world. Thus, people act at cross-purposes to the divine will by fencing religion into a private arena.

It is characteristic of religions in modern societies to suppose that God deals with his faithful people in a spiritual way. He stores up rewards and punishments for the next life. This fits naturally with the notion that religion is a private matter. But fundamentalists reject this point of view. God doesn't just speak to the heart—God acts.

People tend to overlook some of God's actions because they blend so naturally into the mundane sequence of cause and effect. Homosexuality and drug abuse are the primary means for transmitting AIDS. But the fundamentalist would claim that the connection is more than biological: AIDS is God's way of punishing sinners. We shouldn't be surprised at this. On the contrary, we should admire his economy in harnessing natural causes for such a just purpose. Sometimes we are surprised at the course of events, as when bad things happen to good people. Here too, though, the notion of God's intervention proves useful. It allows us to suppose that there is a hidden divine purpose which we would appreciate if we could understand it. It is thus consoling to be able to say, "God wills it."

God's action is not always mundane. Sometimes it is miraculous. The original statement of the fundamentals by the Presbyterian General Assembly in 1910 is a telling instance of this fascination with miracles. In addition to the inerrancy of scripture the list included the virgin birth of Christ, his bodily resurrection, and the authenticity of the miracles recounted in the Bible.[13] Nor is this extraordinary kind of intervention just a thing of the past. Among Pentecostals it is frequently thought that God steps in to heal the sick.

Fundamentalists believe that it is possible to discern larger patterns in these divine actions. One typical pattern is God's choice of a certain group of people as his own. In the West the idea has its most familiar form in Jewish thought. The Jews are God's chosen people whom he sometimes favors and sometimes chastises, according to their faithfulness in keeping their covenant with him. The haredim see their own survival, in the face of the enticements of modern life, as a miracle attributable to God's grace in providing the Torah sages.[14] Protestant Christian Ian Paisley sees the experience of Free Presbyterians in Ulster in similar terms. "God has a people in this province. . . . This little province has had the peculiar preservation of divine Providence. You only have to read the history of Ulster to see that time after time when it seemed humanly impossible to extricate Ulster from seeming disaster, that God intervened."[15]

Another common pattern that fundamentalists have discerned in God's activity is a plan for the direction of history. Harjot Oberoi has pointed to the persistence of a millenarian tradition among the Sikhs. In recent times it was exemplified by the movement led by Sant Jarnail Singh Bhindranwale. A century ago the belief in God's plan found expression in terms like these: "A great battle will take place on the banks of the Jamna, and blood will flow like the waters of the Ravi, and no faringhi will be left alive. Insurrection will take place in the country in [1865]. The Khalsa will reign and the rajah and ryot will live in peace and comfort, and no one shall molest another. Day by day Ram Singh's rule will be enlarged. God has written this."[16] Those familiar with Christian fundamentalist literature cannot miss the similarity to descriptions of the battle of Armageddon, which will initiate the millennium that follows Jesus's second coming. The Gush Emunim, too, look for the coming of the messiah. These Jewish activists believe that they can hasten his arrival by the settlement of Judea and Samaria. Among Shi'ite Muslims the expectation is that the Imam Mahdi—the twelfth Imam who disappeared a millennium ago—will return to establish a rule of justice and equity.

The belief that God is active in the world has implications for politics. God is not a natural force like gravity or magnetism. His actions have a normative aspect. We would not say that it is "right," "good," or "just" that an apple falls to the earth. Gravity just pulls it there. But the fundamentalist could see justice in the fact that sodomy transmits AIDS. To put the point in Humean terms, a world in which God is active is a world that collapses the distinction between "is" and "ought." In a world run along these lines, natural events have a deeper level of meaning. Ann Mayer observes that, in the Middle East, Israel's defeat of Arab forces in 1967 "has been inter-preted as God's punishment [visited] on Muslim countries for having earlier discarded Islamic law."[17] Jerry Falwell interprets America's decline in a similar way: "God will not be mocked, for whatever an individual or a nation sows, that shall he also reap. America is not big enough to shake her fist in the face of a holy God and get away with it. Sodom and Gomorrah fell under the judgment of God, so did Israel, Babylon, Greece, Rome, and countless other civilizations as well."[18]

The connection between "is" and "ought" means that it is possible to have objec-tive knowledge about how we should behave. That would be a good foundation for making laws. People would then agree once they understood the facts, even in a pluralist democracy. This is not an argument for natural law or natural right. Funda-mentalists do not claim that we can reach political agreement through the use of reason alone. That belief is actually a form of idolatry, because it assumes that men and women can get along on their own. The real basis for hope in politics is that God is active in the world. I mentioned above a variety of ways in which his activity is manifest. But the most important from a political standpoint is this: he has given us, in writing, the foundation of a legal code.

Fundamentalists of nearly all persuasions hold this conviction. American Protes-tant fundamentalists argue that our law should be based on the Bible, which they look upon as the word of God. God intervened in human events by speaking his word to Moses and the evangelists. I explain in my essay how fundamentalists think that word should be transformed into rules of law governing contemporary society. In a large sense this has a parallel in the Ayatollah Khomeini's vision for Iran. As Said Arjomand and Ann Mayer explain, he believed that it was possible to base a legal system on nothing more than jurists' interpretations of Islamic sources: "The entire system of government and administration, together with the necessary laws, lies ready for you. . . . There is no need for you, after establishing a government, to sit down and draw up laws, or, like rulers who worship foreigners and are infatuated with the West, run after others to borrow their laws. Everything is ready and waiting. All that re-mains is to draw up ministerial programs."[19]

This system of law drawn from the Qur'an and the Sunna is the Shari'a. Umar Birai contends, in his essay in this part, that adoption of the Shari'a is the one point on which all observant Muslims in Nigeria agree.[20] The Muslim Brotherhood in Egypt has had the same ambition, according to Abdel Azim Ramadan.[21] Charles Lieb-man's essay observes that in Israel the declared goal of all the religious parties is a state ruled by *halakha*—rabbinic interpretations of biblical law.[22] The failure to press that demand reflects a degree of political prudence rather than a belief that there is a better system.[23]

The idea of drawing law from a sacred text is an obvious repudiation of the public/ private distinction. By relying on a religious document in the lawmaking process, it violates the principle of separation, which directs that the public sphere must be kept secular. If a society is serious about enacting revealed law, it might violate the secular understanding of freedom as well. The case of Salman Rushdie's *The Satanic Verses* is a good example. God's law imposes strict penalties for the sins of apostasy and blasphemy. In a society that keeps religion out of the public arena, by contrast, individuals are free to change their religious beliefs and to express insulting opinions about matters of faith without fear of government reprisals.

IV

I have argued that religious fundamentalists reject the public/private distinction because they believe that God is active in the world. As the essays in part 1 of this volume reveal, however, there is abundant variety in the phenomenon that we label "fundamentalism." We apply the term to movements within different religions in different societies. It is tempting to treat these various movements as facets of the same problem, because they all captured our attention at about the same time. In many regards, however, the differences overwhelm the similarities. In this section and the next I will argue that there are real and important distinctions, and some striking similarities, too, among the movements we address. Whether we are justified in our taxonomy I leave for the reader to decide. In the end the issue of naming follows rather than precedes understanding.

I will address the subject of differences (and similarities) by looking at two related topics. The first is, What causes fundamentalists to become politically active? The causes are not always the same, although they are fewer than one might suppose. The second is, What do politically active fundamentalists want? Here there is more variety.

In regard to the causes of fundamentalist political activism, we can divide the movements reviewed in this part into two groups. In the first are movements reacting to a change (or a threat of change) in national identity. These include the Sunni Muslims in Pakistan, the Sikhs in Punjab, the Free Presbyterians in Ulster, and (for separate reasons) both Gush Emunim and the haredim in Israel. In the second are movements reacting to government efforts to expand the public sphere in an existing nation-state. Here I would put American Protestant fundamentalists, the Muslim Brotherhood and Islamic groups in Egypt, the Nakshibendi activists in Turkey, the Islamic *tajdid* in Nigeria, and the popular revolution in Iran. Neither the Hindu groups in India nor Numayri's Islamization program in the Sudan fits neatly into either category. It is easy to understand why the threat of a change in national identity would be unsettling to people concerned with preserving a religious tradition. If the reconstituted society were dominated by some other faith, that society might submerge the tradition entirely. This is the outcome most feared by Free Presbyterians in Northern Ireland if Ulster were to merge with the largely Catholic Republic of Ireland. On the other hand, if the new society were to include people of several other faiths (or no faith), it might deal with the new pluralism by becoming more secular. This has been the case with the haredim in Israel. The haredim are remarkable among Jews for their anti-Zionism, but the basis for their opposition is their religious objection to the formation of a secular state that would wrest the redemption of the Jewish people from God's hands.

At times, though, the change in national identity presents itself as an opportunity rather than a threat. A partition (rather than a merger) could result in a society that is more religiously homogeneous. This is the situation in Pakistan, which was split off from India in 1947. The Islamization program there is an effort to create a national identity among people who are ethnically and linguistically divided. The one thing most members of the society have in common is their religion. The 1947 partition was also seen by some Hindu groups as a step toward making India more religiously homogeneous, though there are still very large non-Hindu elements in the population. The politics of *Hindutva* aims at reducing their significance, and at uniting the extended family of religious groups that we call Hindu.

Like a partition, a territorial acquisition can present an opportunity—the chance to extend the acquiring religion to a new domain. This is one way of describing the activities of the Gush Emunim in the occupied territories of Judea and Samaria.

It is natural that in most of these cases of merger, acquisition, and partition, religious fundamentalists are able to point to a discrete and well-defined group as the "enemy"—the force against which they react. In Ulster evangelical Protestantism defines itself by opposition to the Catholic church. In India the Bharatiya Janata Party (BJP) invites conflict with Muslims. In Israel the Gush Emunim is locked in struggle with the Arab population of the occupied territories. The case of Iran presents an interesting contrast. Khomeini's fundamentalist vision identified the United States (the Great Satan) as the enemy of his movement. But this conflict did not concern the territorial boundaries of Iran. It was in a sense proactive rather than reactive. As Ann Mayer puts it, the conflict was "prolonged because the regime thrived on having foreign devils to combat."[24]

The second class of movements comprises those that are reacting against internal change—efforts to enlarge the public sphere without changing territorial boundaries. This might occur, as it has in the United States, through an expansion of the welfare state. Since World War II the government, and in particular the federal government, has increasingly taken over the direction of such matters as education and family life. The federal courts have applied constitutional norms of separation to root out vestiges of religion in the public schools. They have used constitutional ideas of freedom and equality to change the rules of family life about inheritance, the bearing and rearing of children, and so on. The states have relaxed rules governing marriage, divorce, and living arrangements. Congress has affected many of the same matters through expenditures and tax policy. As these once private matters become more public and secular, religious fundamentalists fear that their traditional ways of life are being pushed aside.

In Iran the popular fundamentalist movement that led to the overthrow of the shah was preceded by several decades of modernization. The shah strove to create a capitalist high-technology economy, and to buttress it with educational and cultural policies that downplayed the Islamic aspects of Iranian religious identity.[25] In a similar way, the resurgence of Islam in Turkey since the 1950s can be seen as a reaction to Atatürk's secularization policy. Atatürk introduced the principle of secularism in the Turkish constitution. He disestablished Islam as the state religion, abolished the

Shari'a courts, and made all education secular. Şerif Mardin has said that, "like Durkheim, Atatürk believed . . . religion had only a secondary or marginal role to play [in the modern state]; it was relegated to the role of a personal value."[26]

In India the ideology that prevailed at the time of independence advocated a pluralist (and under Nehru, secular) democracy similar to those in the West. Recent unhappiness with that approach has given a push to fundamentalist political, cultural, and religious groups like the BJP, the Vishwa Hindu Parishad (VHP), and the RSS. These groups have successfully played upon a popular sense that the government has given special treatment to Muslim, Sikh, and other religious minorities.

It follows that in this class of cases religious fundamentalists focus their attention on issues of reform and revival—and on domestic rather than foreign policy. In the United States, for example, Protestant fundamentalists are concerned with questions of abortion, homosexuality, pornography, and public and private education. In Nigeria, Muslim traditionalists have focused on enforcement of the Shari'a, political appointments, and the role of religion in party politics.

It is common in reform efforts of this kind, as it is in the first class of cases, to identify an enemy against whom all believers should unite. But here the enemy is within. It is not a discrete religious or national group but, rather, a certain way of thinking that can affect anyone. Among American Protestant fundamentalists it is called "secular humanism." In Nigeria it is called "Euro-Christianity." In Turkey it is "Western Christian capitalism." In the ideology of the Muslim Brotherhood in Egypt it is "paganism." All these ideas have certain features in common, and the most important of them is the distinctively liberal notion that religion should be kept out of the public arena.

V

What do politically active fundamentalists want? There is a great variety in the demands they make, and this should not be surprising. Political programs vary with religious ideology, the nature of the surrounding society, its form of government, the size and prosperity of the religious group, its prospects for success, and many other factors. Although it would simplify things too much to say that religious fundamentalists all pursue the same objectives, there are several characteristic directions that they move in. I will look at three of these. The first I will call exit—the choice to withdraw from society. The second is union—the rejection of the idea of separation. The third is coercion—the rejection of religious freedom.

Exit is an attractive option for obvious reasons. If fundamentalists object to a social system that divides life artificially into public and private spheres, why not leave? It's a big step because it requires the group to start all over again, but it allows them to form a smaller and more homogeneous community governed by religious law.

There are, of course, less drastic ways of cutting ties with society. One extreme is to create a new state. This is what extremist Sikhs envision in the Punjab. As Master Tara Singh put it, "The Hindus got Hindustan, the Muslims got Pakistan, what did the Sikhs get?"[27] A less radical solution is to form an enclave within the secular society and cut off traffic in and out. This is what the Amish have done in America, and the haredim in Israel. More modest still is simple geographic concentration and isolation. In a country as large as the United States, particularly one governed along federalist lines, this option can allow a fair degree of flexibility for people to tinker with the social system. In the middle of this century evangelical Christians found that sort of isolation in many parts of the southern United States. Umar Birai suggests a greater emphasis on federalism as a way of accommodating Muslim demands in Nigeria.[28]

All of these solutions allow the rest of society to adopt whatever arrangements it deems fit in religious matters. And yet secularists tend to resist most forms of exit for a variety of reasons. Secession is out of the question because it conflicts with the ideology of nationalism. Religious dissenters today can't just leave their country and start a new one, as the Pilgrims did. They have to take some territory with them. Sikhs would need to take the Punjab away from India. Why nationalism requires territorial integrity and why the two are such strong forces are difficult questions. But it is clear that secession, as a solution to religious conflict, is a recipe for civil war.

Enclaves are unpopular for slightly different reasons. Advanced societies provide their citizens with a large number of public goods: national defense, roads, schools, even the system of government itself. Anchorites like the haredim or the Amish typically refuse to contribute to some of these goods, though they share in the benefits. The haredim decline to serve in the Israeli army, though they enjoy the security it affords them. The Amish do not pay social security taxes or serve in public office. In situations like these the general public may resent giving a free ride to members of a religious enclave. Of course the public may also resent the standing reproach that a religious community represents to its secular and materialistic habits. For these reasons it may be that such enclaves can only be maintained in liberal democracies where tolerance is legally enforced through a rule of freedom.

Even if society did not actively resist geographic isolationism, it would be hard to maintain in an industrial society in the face of improvements in communications and transportation technology. These forces break down the barriers and integrate the resisting group into the larger society.

The alternative to exit is union. Both reject the idea of separation, but unionists want to change the system rather than leave it. It is not clear what stimuli produce this reaction. I would make two apparently contradictory claims. One is that fundamentalists are more inclined to fight when they are losing. That is to say, they have become more politically active at times when their way of life is most threatened by the political process. The other is that they tend to make more radical demands when they have a chance of winning. In other words, the degree of union that fundamentalists seek varies inversely with the pluralism of the society.

Steve Bruce supports the first claim in his analysis of the New Christian Right (NCR) in America. He argues that the NCR moved from quietism to political activism in the last decade because secular policies formulated at the national level made it impossible to maintain a stance of geographic isolation.[29] Much of the fundamentalists' attack has focused on what Richard John Neuhaus has called the "naked public square."[30] They have tried to reintroduce an element of religion into public life: prayer and teaching about creation in the public schools, creches on public property, and so forth. But there is no society more pluralistic than America, and a straight-forward call for union of church and state would fall on deaf ears. For that reason fundamentalists have moderated their demands. As I explain in my essay for this part, they ask for neutrality rather than union—equal treatment of religion and secularism.[31]

The behavior of the haredim in Israel provides an illuminating comparison. They have been increasingly involved in electoral politics in the last few years, but as Charles Liebman points out, they have been motivated by fear of loss rather than hope of gain. Their politics has been defensive rather than aggressive.[32] Haredi parties, like American fundamentalists, have been concerned with the issue of separation, but the issue is inverted in a Jewish state. The controlling metaphor is not a "naked public square" but a "Jewish street." The public is willing to permit the conduct of public life in accordance with Jewish law so long as people can reject religion in their private lives. But the inversion of terms is not as important as one might think. For the ultimate question is how wide the Jewish street should be, and there the debate begins to look very much like its American counterpart. Like American fundamentalists the haredim have made modest demands: Sabbath closing laws, more power for rabbini-cal courts, more public money for religious schools, and an amendment to the Law of Return (a point they have not insisted on). This list is unimposing, in all likelihood because the haredim cannot hope for greater success. They are, in matters of religion, too out of step with their surrounding society.

The case is otherwise in Iran. Once again it is true that the fundamentalist move-ment arose because observant Muslims felt that they were losing their traditional way of life, in this case to the reforms of the shah's government. But their agenda was much more radical, and it succeeded to a degree. They have created an Islamic gov-ernment according to Khomeini's model of *velayat-e-faqih* (rule by the Islamic jurist). There are a number of plausible explanations for this success, but they must include popular support among the lower classes in urban areas for some of the fundamental-ists' goals and an even wider enthusiasm for Khomeini's charismatic leadership.

I turn now from the policy of union to the policy of coercion—the rejection of religious freedom. This is a more extreme approach than the last. It is possible for a society to establish an official religion for the conduct of its public affairs and yet permit individuals to dissent privately. Under such an arrangement the public religion would be supported by tax revenues, its ministers might be appointed (or conversely they might appoint the governors), its liturgy might be integrated into public cere-monies, and its creed might form the basis for some kinds of legislation. But it would still be possible for people to reject that creed, shun public ceremonies, worship in other ways, proselytize for other faiths, and in general live private lives at variance with the official religion. This is actually the situation in Israel. It is also true to some degree in England, whose established church is headed by the queen and supported with tax revenues.

The most ambitious fundamentalists would prefer to stamp out all forms of dissent. It might be useful, though, to distinguish between two kinds of coercion. The first forbids[33] behavior that people might object to for either religious or secular reasons. The campaign against pornography in America is a good example. Fundamentalists argue that we should control smut because it is a sin. Secular feminist groups support such laws too, not for religious reasons but because they think pornography offends the dignity of women. A society committed to the protection of freedom might accept such a law notwithstanding the fact that it was motivated in part by religious sentiments. If the secular arguments in its favor were strong enough, people could sensibly prefer good legislation over a good legislative process.

The second kind of coercion forbids behavior that people can only object to for religious reasons. Consider the case of the Baha'is in Iran: their faith has been deemed a form of apostasy from Islam, punishable by death. Or consider Ann Mayer's discussion of the fundamentalist campaign against the Ahmadi minority in Pakistan. A law passed in 1984 forbade them "to call themselves Muslims or their religion Islam, to use Islamic terminology, to use the Islamic call to prayer, to call their places of worship mosques, or to propagate their version of Islam."[34] Here it is not possible to judge the goodness of the law without making a religious judgment. Legislation of this kind is the ultimate rejection of the public/private distinction. It not only brings religion into public life but also eliminates the private sphere.

VI

I will not try to review the individual pieces in part 1 further than I have already done here. Instead I will close by offering two observations about the conclusions that they draw. The first is that most of them attribute relatively modest ambitions to the movements they study. Coercion (of the second kind) is not often mentioned. Union is much desired, but it is often a token or symbolic kind of union. The political programs advanced by fundamentalist movements have a sketchy quality about them. Talk about making the Shari'a (halakha, the Bible) the law of the land is usually phrased in the most general terms. Specific proposals and enactments tend to have a very limited focus. This may just be the nature of dissent. Criticism is easier than reconstruction. Or it may only reflect the novelty of the fundamentalist phenomenon. In time the programs might be better articulated.

There seems, though, to be a division almost along East/West lines on this first point. Movements in the more western, industrial states with strong national governments (United States, Ulster, Israel, Turkey, Egypt, Nigeria) seem less ambitious than those elsewhere (Iran, Pakistan, Sudan, India).

The second point is that most of the movements are thought to be unlikely to succeed in any impressive way. This point is explicitly made about movements in the United States and Israel; one may infer it in the cases of Egypt and Turkey. Whether the Free Presbyterians in Ulster and the Gush Emunim in Israel will achieve their nationalistic objectives are matters that lie largely within the control of other parties. Once again, however, this is a point that can be more confidently asserted of Western than of Eastern societies (Nigeria is a special case). The political future of fundamentalism in Iran, Pakistan, the Sudan, and India is more difficult to predict.

Notes

1. Those familiar with the role of organized religion in American public life will realize that I have simplified both sides of this dichotomy for the sake of clarity. A more nuanced statement would require several qualifications. On the one hand many religious liberals would tolerate, or even insist on, some overlap of the public and private spheres—religion has some implications for public policy. (Christian charity, as well as equal protection, requires us to combat racial discrimination.) On the other hand, American Protestant fundamentalists stop short of arguing for a full integration of religion, law, and politics. (They seldom claim that churches as such should have an influence on the state, and generally reject state interference with religion and promotion of doctrine.)

I omit discussion of these qualifications in part because I treat them more fully in chapter 3 and in part because what I have said in the text fairly conveys the difference in orientation between mainline religions and fundamentalism in America. Fundamentalists *do* contend that religious ideas, stated in religious terms, should play a more central part in public life than the rest of society is comfortable with.

2. E. Gellner, ed., *Islamic Dilemmas: Re-formers, Nationalists and Industrialization* (Berlin: Mouton Publishers, 1985), pp. 1–9.

3. U.S. Const. amend. I.

4. Constitution art. 25 (India).

5. U.S. Const. amend. I.

6. Constitution art. 24 (Turkey).

7. S. Heilman and M. Friedman, "Religious Fundamentalism and Religious Jews: The Case of the Haredim," in *Fundamentalisms Observed* (Chicago: University of Chicago Press, 1991), pp. 212–13.

8. S. Bruce, *God Save Ulster!* (Oxford: Clarendon Press, 1986), p. 146.

9. See P. Clarke, "The Maitatsine Movement in Northern Nigeria in Historical and Current Perspective," in R. Hackett, ed., *New Religious Movements in Nigeria* (Lewiston, N.Y.: E. Mellon Press, 1987), pp. 95–98.

10. A. Mayer, "The Fundamentalist Impact on Law, Politics, and Constitutions in Iran, Pakistan, and the Sudan," this volume.

11. Gellner, *Islamic Dilemmas*. The point is more obviously true of Sunnis than of Shi'ites.

12. T. N. Madan, "The Double-Edged Sword: Fundamentalism and the Sikh Religious Tradition," in *Fundamentalisms Observed* (Chicago: University of Chicago Press, 1991), p. 618.

13. G. Marsden, *Fundamentalism and American Culture* (New York: Oxford University Press, 1980), p. 117.

14. Heilman and Friedman, "Religious Fundamentalism and Religious Jews," pp. 207, 242–44.

15. Bruce, *God Save Ulster!* pp. 269–70.

16. "Two Poles of Akali Politics," *Sikh Review* 31 (1983): 45, 47.

17. Mayer, "The Fundamentalist Impact on Law, Politics, and Constitutions in Iran, Pakistan, and the Sudan."

18. J. Falwell, *Listen, America!* (Garden City, N.Y.: Doubleday and Company, 1980), pp. 249–50.

19. Mayer, "The Fundamentalist Impact on Law, Politics, and Constitutions in Iran, Pakistan, and the Sudan." See S. Arjomand, "Shi'ite Jurisprudence and Constitution Making in the Islamic Republic of Iran," this volume.

20. U. Birai, "Islamic Tajdid and the Political Process in Nigeria," this volume.

21. A. Ramadan, "Fundamentalist Influence in Egypt," this volume.

22. C. Liebman, "Jewish Fundamentalism and the Israeli Polity," this volume.

23. The situation among Hindus in India

is an interesting contrast to the examples given in the text. Muslims, Christians, and Jews are monotheists, each with a single sacred scripture that is the basis for religious law. Among Hindus the divine takes many forms and there are no texts accepted by all as authoritative. Hence, one does not hear of aspirations for the enactment of "Hindu law." But Hindu fundamentalists do oppose the enforcement of Muslim law, even in domestic disputes among Muslims. And they espouse some forms of legislation (e.g., protecting cows) for exclusively religious—Hindu—reasons.

24. Mayer, "The Fundamentalist Impact on Law, Politics, and Constitutions in Iran, Pakistan, and the Sudan."

25. A. Sachedina, "Activist Shi'ism in Iran, Iraq, and Lebanon," in *Fundamentalisms Observed* (Chicago: University of Chicago Press, 1991), pp. 417–20.

26. S. Mardin, "Religion and Politics in Modern Turkey," in J. Piscatori, ed., *Islam in the Political Process* (Cambridge: Cambridge University Press, 1983), pp. 142–43.

27. H. Oberoi, "From Punjab to 'Khalistan': Territoriality and Metacommentary," *Pacific Affairs* 60 (1987): 26, 38.

28. Birai, "Islamic Tajdid and the Political Process in Nigeria."

29. S. Bruce, "Fundamentalism, Ethnicity, and Enclave," this volume.

30. R. Neuhaus, *The Naked Public Square* (Grand Rapids, Mich.: Eerdmans, 1984).

31. J. Garvey, "Fundamentalism and American Law," this volume.

32. Liebman, "Jewish Fundamentalism and the Israeli Polity."

33. Or compels. For simplicity's sake I will talk just about prohibitions.

34. Mayer, "The Fundamentalist Impact on Law, Politics, and Constitutions in Iran, Pakistan, and the Sudan."

Fundamentalism and American Law

John H. Garvey

In the popular imagination, American Prot-
estant fundamentalists may seem an anachronism. Toting Bibles and preaching sobri-
ety and modesty, they look and sound like our Puritan forebears awakened from a
long sleep. In keeping with this image, they seem to reject the modern liberal society
they find around them.

This picture, though it contains elements of truth, is distorted. A close look at
their theology and politics shows that fundamentalists are committed to a number of
liberal ideals. Chief among them is a very modern form of individualism. They also
accept the related ideals of freedom and equality (though their religious beliefs give
these words a unique interpretation). As the popular image suggests, fundamentalists
do embrace some Puritan ideals as well. Most notable is their devotion to the Bible as
a source of political wisdom. But even though fundamentalists accept some blending
of church and state, they stop far short of prescribing the kind of biblical society that
prevailed in colonial Massachusetts.

In what follows I will try to bring fundamentalist politics into sharper focus. I
begin by looking at the fundamentalist view of religion. In order to explain the fundamentalist view of law in modern American society, and at considerable risk of over-
simplification, I stress two features—its "individualist" and its "biblical" character. I
conclude by evaluating the impact this view has had to date and is likely to have in
the near future.

Religion

The sociology and theology of the fundamentalist movement are treated at some
length in an earlier volume in this series and in a number of recent monographs.[1] I

will content myself with a brief account of the features that bear most directly on law and politics. For reasons that will become obvious, it is difficult to speak precisely about "what fundamentalists believe" as we might speak about "what Catholics believe." The account I offer is a model of typical beliefs to which most fundamentalists closely adhere. It is not a confessional statement.

Individualist Piety

Fundamentalists espouse a markedly individualist form of religiosity. Its best-known feature is the experience of being "born again" to a new life in Jesus Christ.[2] To be born again is to come to believe that one has been saved by Jesus. It often happens rather suddenly. Jerry Falwell recounts how it happened to him on 20 January 1952 as he sat in the kitchen eating breakfast.[3] But whether sudden or gradual, the experience is memorable. A person will know whether he has been saved. If the rebirth is real and sincere, it will change the way he lives. William Sheehan, chairman of the Division of Prayer in Falwell's church, testifies that he stopped cursing when, at the age of nineteen, he accepted Jesus as his savior.[4] Internal change is only the first step. The born-again Christian is moved to share his faith with others who are not so fortunate. A few years ago it was popular for people to wear buttons saying "I Found It!" I remember overhearing one of my students ask another what his button meant. "It means," he said, "I found a new life in Jesus Christ."

For our purposes the important point about this experience is its individual character. God saves individuals one by one—Jerry has been saved, Judy has not. This is not a belief that all Christians share. Consider the account, more typical of Catholic and liberal Protestant theology, given by Rudolf Bultmann: "Not the individual but the 'church' is called, to it belongs the promise. . . . The individual . . . finds deliverance, but only because he belongs to the . . . community."[5]

For the fundamentalist, furthermore, faith is not just a theological conviction. It is coupled with a commitment to personal virtue—chastity, fidelity, temperance, and piety. This is not just spiritual body building. It is an expression of the individual's submission to God. Consider the case of homosexuality:[6]

> Liberal churchmen not only betray their ignorance of and unbelief in the Word of God by their excessively lenient position on homosexuality, but they also reveal that they do not understand its true source. . . . Atheistic humanism . . . has come to deify man. Therefore, man owes no allegiance to anyone above him and ought to be permitted to lay aside all restraints on his behavior. Recall his favorite maxims—"Do your own thing," "Do what you feel like doing," or "Anything you want to do that doesn't hurt someone else is all right."

For fundamentalists there are no self-regarding actions or harmless immoralities. Homosexuality is a "sin against the body." It causes harm by "keep[ing] us from being 'joined unto the Lord.'"[7]

When it comes to living the virtuous life, "ought" implies "can." Many people today think that homosexuality is a natural sexual preference, not a choice, like being left-handed rather than right-handed. Fundamentalists disagree. If sin is that natural, then God is playing a cruel joke on us. Sin is learned behavior. When it becomes habitual it is hard to shake, but we can do it with God's help. That is why faith (being born again) is essential to virtue.[8]

Pornography and prostitution, like homosexuality, are sins against oneself and God. But they also have a wider significance. Fundamentalists find a special resonance in St. Paul's order of male-female relations. Sex is an activity that should be confined to marriage. And within marriage there are separate injunctions for husbands and wives: husbands should "love [their] wives"; wives should "submit [them]selves unto [their] husbands."[9] A woman should be an ornament to the home, a helpmate to her husband, and a loving mother to her children. This idea of sex-segregated roles is decidedly antimodern. It does, though, lead fundamentalists to make common cause with feminists in their opposition to pornography and prostitution. Both groups oppose treating women as objects for masculine wish fulfillment. For fundamentalists, that is wrong because it is inconsistent with the Christian ideal of chivalrous love.

Adultery and abortion spread harm in an even wider circle—to the family unit. Family life has an almost sacramental character for fundamentalists. The kitchen table is, in Nancy Ammerman's phrase, a kind of "family altar."[10] The home itself is a sanctuary that offers refuge from a world in which the believer is an alien. The love of husband and wife is an image of God's love for his church.[11] The result is that adultery doesn't just cause pain; it is a kind of apostasy. Because it tears apart the family, it strains the sinner's relation to his church. (This is even true of divorce.)[12] Abortion, which fundamentalists see as a form of infanticide, is the ultimate sin against family life.

Alcohol and drug abuse are other forms of private excess that fundamentalists try to avoid. There is nothing new about this; temperance has been a concern since the time of Dwight Moody.[13] Like chastity, it is a virtue closely tied to faith. People turn to drink and drugs out of anxiety and despair. Substance abuse provides a thrill, and finally a kind of amnesia, that is an inadequate stand-in for the love of God. Because it is ultimately unsatisfying, it is a descending spiral: people make attempts to remedy the deficiency. But the only real solution is faith in God. In the words of the song "Jesus Is Still the Answer": "Some men pretend that things of the world have brought them peace of mind / But with the dawn of each new day new thrills they try to find! Not until they meet the Prince of Peace can they ever hope to find release / For Jesus is still the answer for a world that's seeking for peace."[14]

The flip side of this preoccupation with personal virtue has been an apparent lack of interest in the larger concerns of social justice. Fundamentalists remain aloof from organized efforts to address poverty, hunger, environmental pollution, racial and sexual discrimination, peace among nations, and so on. This, too, is an attitude with a history. Early-twentieth-century fundamentalists reacted in the same way toward the Social Gospel preached by liberal Protestants. In one way this seems perverse. It would certainly be a good thing, from a Christian point of view, to wipe out poverty, hunger, war, pollution, and so on. Fundamentalists do not oppose this social agenda because of its intended results. (With this exception: the campaign against sexual discrimination is designed to produce results in conflict with the fundamentalist view of sex roles.) The explanation is more subtle. I will mention three factors.

One is a disagreement about the causes of social disorder. Socially active Christians tend to view sin, like salvation, as a group activity—a matter of society getting out of whack. The responsibility and the blame are corporate. Sin is a social pathology that we should treat with social science. Fundamentalists disagree. For them society is an aggregation of individuals and its problems are identical with the sum of their problems. It is individual sin that causes social disorder.

This naturally leads to distinct ideas about the solution of social ills. The way to address personal sin is to bring about individual conversions. The chief causes of poverty are drug and alcohol abuse, sloth, the breakdown of the family (itself a consequence of individual actions), and similar sins. Social programs like welfare treat the symptoms, not the disease; they make only cosmetic changes. Of course, sin is not the only cause. There are natural misfortunes too, like real sickness, economic dislocation, and old age. But the way to address these is private virtue—like the virtue of charity. The Good Samaritan "didn't check to see if the fellow had Blue Cross. Or, whether he was eligible for Medicare. He didn't go running to the county hospital or the welfare office to say, 'Hey, there's a guy back there by the side of the road.' He carried the victim to the inn and cared for him." [15]

Even if all this were true, one might ask why social action couldn't supplement faith and charity. The answer is that the Social Gospel has unintended consequences on the economy of effort. If we focus on social solutions, we will diminish our individual exertions proportionately.

The contrast I have drawn between individual and social action suggests that fundamentalists should be politically inert. This is not so, as I will explain in more detail below. Government action is quite consistent with fundamentalist aspirations when it addresses the real causes of social harm—when it leads people away from sin and toward lives of private virtue.

So far in the discussion of individual piety I have focused on the fundamentalist preoccupation with personal virtue (and the corresponding neglect of social action). I now want to say a word about the institutional features of fundamentalism. How do people who think this way get together, in churches and other organizations?

The most striking thing about Protestant fundamentalist ecclesiology is its voluntary and democratic character. Churches are voluntary associations of individuals. People join because the message appeals to them and leave when it does not. When Jerry Falwell decided to join a church, he asked his friends, "Does anybody know a church in Lynchburg that preaches what Dr. Fuller preaches on the radio?" [16] The minister is the leader of the group by virtue of his preaching authority. But he is subject to democratic control in this sense: he must carry a majority of his congregation with him or lose his position. "Almost everyone who has been part of a fundamentalist church for long has been through a full-scale church split over a pastor." [17]

In denominational terms most of these churches are independent Baptist, Bible, and Assemblies of God churches, or small fundamentalist sects. [18] They are *local* churches. In a sense they are like their members writ large. They exercise autonomy over their own affairs. When several churches join together, they affiliate, rather than unite in an episcopal or presbyterian fashion. The connection is often looser still—a common tie to a group of Bible institutes and colleges at which their pastors are educated.

Sometimes it has been more sensible to say that so-and-so is a fundamentalist in communion with Jerry Falwell's TV show (as he himself was a member of Dr. Fuller's radio congregation). Television and radio evangelists have played an important role in the definition and congruence of the fundamentalist movement. They are the ultimate form of private voluntary association. Members can tune in in their own homes and can switch churches by just changing the channel. The phenomenon of televangelism in turn has led to the creation of other parachurch organizations. The best known of these (Christian Voice, Moral Majority, Religious Roundtable) grew out of electronic ministries and used television and computerized mailings to communicate with their members.

There are also numerous other groups, less well known, that play important and distinctive roles in the fundamentalist movement. These groups, like the televangelists and their adherents, generally operate along nondenominational lines. Typical examples are Operation Rescue (a direct-action anti-abortion group), the Rutherford Institute (a legal organization concerned with abortion, school prayer and curricula, and government regulation of churches), and Theonomy (a group that promotes a radical program of laissez-faire capitalism and biblical law).[19]

Biblical Faith

It is difficult to understand the individual piety of fundamentalists apart from the faith in which it is rooted. That faith is biblical in a very strong sense.

Fundamentalists believe that God speaks directly to individuals in the Bible. This means, in the first place, that the Bible is literally the "Word of God." One need not believe that it was whispered line by line in the evangelist's ear. The inspiration might have been more subtle. But it came in terms sufficiently precise to preclude the possibility of error. The Bible is inerrant as God himself is.

When we talk about the fundamentalist belief in biblical inerrancy, we refer not just to its mode of authorship but also to a canon of construction. It is not just true; it is *literally* true. We should, whenever possible, understand it to mean exactly what it says. When Genesis says that God created the world in six days, it means six twenty-four-hour periods. One result of literalism is that the Bible says some surprising things about science, history, geography, and so on. Another is that we can foretell the future by looking into the prophetic books. This has led fundamentalists to expect (soon) the 1,000-year reign of Jesus Christ predicted in the book of Revelation.[20]

The combination of inerrancy and literalism makes the Bible accessible to the average person. This is not so true for people who approach it in a more sophisticated way. The principles of form criticism now accepted by scholars require the serious student to have a knowledge of languages, history, literary forms, and the work of other biblical experts. Fundamentalists reject those principles for a variety of reasons, among them a rather populist view of God: surely God would not speak to us in a language that only a few academics could understand. If God loves us all, his word must be addressed to us all. Reading the text can be difficult (particularly the King

James version favored by fundamentalists), but the only necessary study aids are prayer and the help of a minister.

The accessibility of the Bible has a central importance for fundamentalists because they use it as a guide to daily life. They consult it for advice about difficult decisions, for comfort in time of affliction, for words of praise and thanksgiving. One often hears how believers in search of guidance have opened their Bibles at random and lighted, like St. Augustine, on passages that spoke personally to them. People will often memorize their favorite passages and have them at their fingertips when the occasion arises. This frequent practice of reading and memorizing a common text naturally affects speech patterns. Fundamentalists have a distinctive biblical argot that sounds, not surprisingly, rather Jacobean to outsiders.[21]

So Bible study has a quotidian ethical significance. But it is also the principal form of religious observance. People read the Bible daily, even when they are not looking for personal advice, as a way of worshiping God. Sunday services are organized around a sermon, which is the preacher's explanation of a biblical text. "No Fundamentalist preacher would even dare enter the pulpit without an open Bible; it is an essential trapping of his authority. For a Fundamentalist congregation, the pastor's uplifted Bible is as ritually significant as is the elevated host for someone partaking of the eucharist. . . . The Bible is for Fundamentalists the very presence of God in their midst."[22]

Evangelization (spreading the gospel) is itself an important religious exercise. The true believer thinks that the most important thing one person can do for another is lead him to the faith, and that the best entrée is the Bible. There is a kind of circularity to this process: the unbeliever is asked to accept Christ on the authority of a book which he is told is the literal word of God. But the only way to enlighten the convert is to bring him to understand the faith from the inside, so he is taken there directly.

> From the first week after our conversions, Jack trained us to lead other people to Christ as we had just been led. We memorized the five or six Scriptures that outlined the simple plan of salvation. . . . We practiced reading and quoting them to each other. . . . We turned back and forth between the verses until the pages almost fell into place and the passages leapt out at us. We paired into teams with one member pretending to know nothing of the faith and the other acting as the evangelist-teacher.[23]

Fundamentalists do not have an elaborate theological system to supplement their devotion to the Bible. In fact they take their name from an early-twentieth-century effort to reduce Christian belief to its fundamentals.[24] Exactly how many fundamentals there are is not clear, because fundamentalists are not a denomination with an official creed approved by an authoritative body. But though there are various lists, they are all short. The first historian of the movement counted five points: the inerrancy of the Bible plus certain views about the birth, death, resurrection, and return of Jesus.[25]

This theological simplicity is quite natural, given other features of the fundamentalist movement. I have mentioned the individualism evident in both the conception of virtue and the reading of the Bible. A movement that allows each person to find her own truth in Scripture is not likely to develop a complex tradition binding all adherents to a particular set of views. The voluntary nature of the ties between member and church, and between one church and another, would make it impossible in any event to bind all fundamentalists to an elaborate creedal program. A simple set of five points (few enough to be counted on one hand) is just the thing for a movement of this kind. It is a theology that the individual can master on her own. It is accessible in the way that the Bible is.

Fundamentalist churches also put less stress than other Christian churches do on mediators (ministers and sacraments) between God and humans. This, too, fits with the features I have been examining. If theology is simple, we don't need a priestly caste to carry it on. If God speaks to each of us in the Bible, we also don't need an interpreter for his word. Sacraments are acts by which the church or its functionaries, as intermediaries, bring God's grace to individuals. They are thus out of keeping with an egalitarian faith that allows each individual to approach God on her own. (Baptism has a special place not because it is a sacrament, but because it is an initiation into the life of faith. It is a recognition that the believer has become liturgically self-sufficient.)

Law

The religious beliefs of fundamentalists affect their view of the law and their agenda for legal reform. In the first section I will argue that fundamentalists fit within the liberal tradition in their emphasis on individualism and freedom. But they shift these ideals to the right and use them to argue that the government should enforce rules of personal virtue. In the second section I will show that fundamentalists have a good deal of sympathy for the old Puritan religious establishment. But their devotion to freedom and equality puts them to the left of the Puritans on the political spectrum.

The Liberal Ideal

It is a working hypothesis of one strand of liberal theory that, because God is absent from the universe, humanity is sovereign. "If there is no master design, the challenge is to transcend all talk of good and evil and master the universe. If God is dead, everything is permitted."[26] This is the point of view that fundamentalists condemn, somewhat loosely, as "secular humanism." Actually it is a bit misleading to say that humanity is sovereign; it would be more accurate to say that individual human beings are sovereign.

We are not collectively heading in any particular direction. We are all going our separate ways, driven by our own desires. As Hobbes explains, "good" is nothing more than "the object of any man's appetite or desire . . . there being nothing simply and absolutely so."[27] It follows from these presuppositions that a legal system cannot be built around any particular idea about what is good. To do so would be unfair to the multitude of sovereign individuals who do not share that idea.[28] It would be inconsistent with liberal individualism.

Liberal political theory incorporates these presuppositions in the idea of rights, particularly the right to freedom. Freedom carves out an area where the individual is sovereign. It allows people to make choices. Consider the woman's freedom of choice on the issue of abortion: she can give birth or not give birth, as she wishes. The other freedoms in our Constitution have the same bilateral character. Freedom of speech protects the right to honor the flag or to burn it. Freedom of religion protects believers and atheists.[29]

Fundamentalism is a highly individualist form of religion. Its ethics stress individual piety. Its theology emphasizes unmediated access to God through Scripture. Its ecclesiology is atomistic.[30] Unlike liberals, however, fundamentalists believe that each person desires the same good—to do God's will in this world and to be united with him in the next. The problem with liberal theory is not its individualism but its views on human nature and the sovereignty of God.

Fundamentalists are also (like liberals) devoted to the ideal of freedom. Jerry Falwell's college is called Liberty University. Fundamentalist economic proposals always stress the free market.[31] Fundamentalist churches are voluntary organizations: members are free to come and go; individual churches retain their independence and reject larger ecclesiastical structures. Freedom also characterizes the individual's relation to God. The godly individual is one who obeys God's commands of his own free will. Fundamentalists believe, as Calvin did, that true freedom is voluntary submission to the will of God.[32]

This is where they part ways with the liberal tradition—because freedom is ultimately *submission*, even if it is voluntary submission. Fundamentalists argue that laws which drive us toward God's will are not inconsistent with freedom; indeed, they set us free. Conversely, true freedom must not be confused with license—with actions that are inconsistent with God's will. "Freedom of speech," Jerry Falwell says, "does not include perverting and sickening the moral appetites of men and women. . . . Liberty cannot be represented by sexual license."[33] In liberal theory the idea of freedom is bilateral, in the sense that it permits choices (to have an abortion/to give birth). For fundamentalists freedom is unilateral. The government must leave us free to do God's will, but it may properly close off other paths.

In some ways, then, fundamentalism is a peculiarly modern brand of religion that shares the ideals (individualism, freedom) of liberalism. But these are subordinate to a higher ideal: to get people to live as God commands. This peculiar blend of principles helps to explain various aspects of the fundamentalist political program.

Consider first the defensive side of the program. Like much of the American public, fundamentalists object to excessive government control over their private lives. The most common provocation has been the regulation of Christian day schools. From one angle this objection is a quintessentially liberal idea: people ought to be free to raise their children as they wish. That is a private matter to be decided on an individual or a family basis. But for fundamentalists the decision has a special poignancy, because Christian education accords with God's will.

The popular stereotype sees fundamentalists as law-abiding, conservative Republicans. In a conflict of this kind, however, civil disobedience is natural reaction. When man's law requires what God's law forbids, it is an obstacle to true freedom. Individuals are in a position to make that judgment for themselves because they can relate directly to God through Scripture. Moreover, to one who holds the key to biblical interpretation (literalism), questions about the conflict of law and Scripture are not questions about which reasonable people can differ. They are issues of black and white, good and evil. A number of fundamentalist parents and educators have shown their commitment to these principles by going to jail rather than complying with state laws designed to regulate Christian (and other private) schools.[34]

Those who engage in civil disobedience to protest abortion are motivated by some of the same principles. Members of Operation Rescue have been arrested repeatedly for blockading the doors of abortion clinics. These people are not defending their own freedom, but what they see as innocent lives. Like the Christian school protestors, they are unperturbed by their violation of social norms. As Francis Schaeffer put it, "If there is no final place for civil disobedience, then the government has been . . . put in the place of the living God."[35]

Freedom is not just the absence of governmental constraint. True freedom, fundamentalists believe, is willing submission to the will of God. This means that we can use the law to promote freedom by prodding people to do God's will. Here we turn from the defensive to the offensive side of the fundamentalist political program.

Fundamentalists think that we should use the law to promote true freedom in two ways. First, the law should condemn those who do evil. That is the essence of justice—to punish wrongdoers. The criminal law serves a retributive purpose. Most fundamentalists support vigorous efforts at crime control and the imposition of capital punishment.[36]

The law can also serve as a moral teacher. When Adam and Eve sinned, they brought confusion and a need for instruction. The law can help us to know right from wrong. This is why the political platform of the Christian right has emphasized personal moral reform. One central plank has been to undo the effects of the sexual revolution: to suppress pornography, discourage homosexuality, prevent heterosexual promiscuity, and (by overturning the Supreme Court's decision in *Roe v. Wade*) make abortion illegal. Another has been to control drug abuse—the modern-day equivalent of the temperance crusade.[37]

The Puritan Ideal

In our national mythology the Puritans are known for their devotion to personal virtue. They thought that the law should instruct us in God's law and punish those who violate it. They also distinguished between true liberty (what Governor Winthrop called the "liberty wherewith Christ hath made us free") and license (the "liberty for men to destroy themselves").[38] The Puritans thought of the social contract as a covenant with God: he would show us his favor if we did his will.[39]

This led to a second trait that we associate with Puritan society—the tendency to merge religion and government. Their government was not literally theocratic in the sense that it was run by church officials. Church and state were separate institutions, and neither was subordinate to the other. Their relation was fraternal, like Moses and Aaron.[40] Ministers could not hold public office. Magistrates could not intervene in most ecclesiastical matters. But the government existed to carry out a religious mission. The franchise was limited to church members, and there was close cooperation between the church and the state.[41] Public officials, no less than ministers, were doing God's work. They were just working in a different vineyard.

Public officials did God's work chiefly by enacting and enforcing laws based on God's law found in Scripture. This of course included rules against murder and theft, adultery, fornication, and sodomy. But it differed from our legal system in two notable ways. One was in the Puritan willingness to draw from the Bible fairly detailed rules for affairs (such as trade by the merchant class) that we might consider matters of religious indifference. The other was that Puritan law covered the first, as well as the second, table of the decalogue. The civil government punished blasphemy, heresy, vain swearing, and sabbath breaking. Baptists were banned from Massachusetts; several Quakers were hung. The General Court also made support for public worship obligatory. The Puritans saw no real distinction between "religion" and "morality"—between the first and the second tables of the law. Both were God's law, and if human governments were to enforce one they could enforce the other as well. Indeed, there would be some synergy in doing so, because pious citizens were more likely to be well behaved.[42]

Modern fundamentalists frequently say, as the Puritans did, that our law is based on the Bible.[43] They argue that the Founding Fathers wrote scriptural law into the Constitution.[44] Our common law has a similar provenance. Look at Blackstone's *Commentaries:* they begin by saying that human laws should not contradict revelation.[45] The Commonwealth of Kentucky adopted this version of history by statute in 1978. It passed a law requiring that the Ten Commandments be displayed in each public school classroom in the state, along with the following notation: "The secular application of the Ten Commandments is clearly seen in its adoption as the fundamental legal code of Western Civilization and the Common Law of the United States."[46]

And yet it is too simple to say that fundamentalism is just an effort to recover our Puritan heritage. Most fundamentalists hold beliefs that differ in significant ways from the picture I have just painted.[47] First, they demonstrate less enthusiasm than the Puritans did for enacting the second table of the law. Except for a few extreme groups, they have limited their efforts to the issues I addressed above. More radical change will only occur in units more intimate than society itself—the family, the school, and the church. This is why fundamentalists defend the traditional family (by proposing legislation like the Family Protection Act and by opposing the Equal Rights Amendment)[48] and Christian schools.[49]

Second, fundamentalist efforts to enforce the first table of the law (to merge church and state) have been tame by Puritan standards. Fundamentalists have pushed for prayer and curricular reform in the public schools. But in doing so they have usually appealed to the ideal of freedom. Proposals for school prayer call for noncoercive observance. During his first term, President Reagan urged passage of a constitutional amendment permitting voluntary school prayer.[50] Proposals for more religion usually appeal to the norm of equality as well. Consider the idea of a moment of silence, which students can use for prayer or some other form of thought.[51] A variation on this theme, supported by the National Council of Churches as well as evangelical groups, is the federal Equal Access Act of 1984. It guarantees religious groups the same right other voluntary student groups have to meet on secondary school premises during noninstructional time.[52] In the case of curricular reform, opposition to the teaching of evolution has taken such forms as Louisiana's Balanced Treatment Act, providing for the teaching of "creation science" alongside "evolution science."[53]

These appeals to freedom and equality are meant to be taken seriously. Fundamentalists believe that the public schools have established secular humanism as their own brand of religion. This, they say, is not neutrality about religion but a form of discrimination. The only way to remain neutral is to allow the Christian religion its place alongside its competitor so that it can compete for the attention of those who are willing to listen.

By comparison with historical Puritanism, then, the fundamentalist movement has been surprisingly modest in its view of what the law should accomplish. It is a mistake to suppose, as many do, that this is merely a tactical concession—a willingness to settle for what is possible rather than fight for what is ultimately desirable. Though they reject the value-neutrality of liberalism, fundamentalists are restrained by their own devotion to freedom and equality.

An Evaluation

The American Constitution provides two important directives concerning the connection between law and religion. One says that "Congress shall make no law . . . prohibiting the free exercise" of religion (the Free Exercise Clause). The other says that "Congress shall make no law respecting an establishment of religion" (the Establishment Clause). There is an apparent tension between these two rules. The Free Exercise Clause assumes that religion is special and gives it extra protection. The Establishment Clause seems to make religion taboo.

The liberal tradition resolves the tension by dividing the world into private and public spheres, and giving each clause its own sphere of influence. The private sphere includes the interior life (my thoughts, emotions, beliefs). It also includes my relations with people who share my thoughts, emotions, and beliefs: my family, my church, and so on. The public sphere is the larger society outside my private life—the world of government and the market.

In the liberal tradition religion is a private matter. We say that belief is "subjective," meaning that it can't be verified by other people. It is like (some would say it *is*) a dream. This view of the private life explains the characteristic liberal view of freedom. Freedom is a right that protects the private life against government interference. Religious freedom, like other freedoms, is bilateral (or perhaps multilateral)—it protects a variety of choices for and against religion. The reason, as we can now see, is that religious belief is subjective, unverifiable, incommensurable. There is no way of telling whether your religious belief is better or worse than mine. So the law treats us alike by giving us both a right to religious freedom.

On the other hand religion should have no part in public life. The Establishment Clause is not actually a condemnation of religion. It is a testimony to the fervency with which people hold their beliefs. Unless we forbid a religious establishment, liberals say, the dominant sect will want to impose its creed on everyone else. This will lead to civil strife and to restrictions on the freedom of dissenters. The Establishment Clause supports the Free Exercise Clause; it does not conflict with it.

That, at any rate, is the prevailing ideology in American politics, and the fundamentalist movement has made little headway against it. In the remainder of this chapter I look at the movement's successes and failures. As I will show, it has succeeded best with clearly religious claims in the private sphere. It has failed almost entirely in its attempts to introduce religious observance into the public sphere. The effort to regulate private morality falls somewhere in between, for reasons I will take up.

Let me begin my review by noting what I think should be obvious—that fundamentalists do not accept the division of life into private and public spheres. As to the private life, it is true that each of us has a direct and personal relation with God. And yet our several experiences are not unique. We are all cut from the same pattern (in the image and likeness of God). We all come with the same set of instructions (his commandments and the words of the Bible). Religion is not a dream life that only the dreamer experiences. It is rather like one loaf of bread—we all taste it separately, and yet we taste the same thing. This is why the fundamentalist conception of freedom is unilateral. Religion is not "subjective"; it is real, verifiable, and the same for everyone. We don't need to protect a variety of choices against government interference—only one.

As for the public life, it is a delusion to suppose that we can fence God out. Fundamentalists know that God is sovereign over all the world. That is the real point behind the evolution controversy. In the Genesis account, God is present and active, ordering the world according to his plan. There is a parallel to this in our legal system. God spoke his word to us in the Bible and thereby laid the foundation for our system of law. The Establishment Clause cannot require us to treat law and religion like unrelated phenomena.

These views have had a real influence on the fundamentalist political agenda. But let me first note one area where they have not mattered. This is what I have called the defensive part of the fundamentalists' program—the resistance to laws that restrict their own religious observance. I will offer two examples.

First, fundamentalists have objected to a variety of state laws governing private religious schools. These laws regulate curriculum, textbook selection, teacher certification, student testing and reporting, and such mundane concerns as fire prevention, health, and safety. Fundamentalists argue that these laws interfere with religious freedom and the freedom of parents to raise their children as they see fit. Both claims are consistent with liberal assumptions. Religion is a matter of private choice, and fundamentalist education is one legitimate way of exercising that choice. So, too, is child rearing a private matter, best left to the discretion of parents. It is thus natural that the legal system should offer some protection in this area. It has done so in several different ways.

The strongest form of protection is a holding that the federal or state constitution protects fundamentalist schools against government regulation. The state of Michigan requires preschool program directors to have certain educational qualifications, including at least sixty hours of credit from an accredited college. The Emmanuel Baptist Preschool objected that this rule would prevent it from hiring born-again Christians from Bob Jones University and Tennessee Temple University. The Michigan Supreme Court held that the rule violated the Free Exercise Clause of the federal Constitution.[54] The Kentucky Supreme Court held, at the request of the Kentucky Association of Christian Schools, that a similar rule violated the right of religious freedom guaranteed by section 5 of the Kentucky constitution.[55]

It is clear that federal and state constitutions—the freedom of religion and the right to privacy—cover fundamentalist schools. But there is a difference between the coverage and the protection of a right. (A suit of armor may cover me but not protect me against certain kinds of bullets.)[56] The government seldom sets out to restrict the freedom of religion as such. It usually interferes inadvertently, while pursuing some innocent secular interest. If the interest is important enough, courts will not stand in the government's way. Fire laws are a good example. And there are equally good, innocent, secular reasons for regulating curriculum, teachers, student attendance, and so on. The Supreme Court recently held that the freedom of religion guaranteed by the federal Constitution affords no special protection against such "neutral, generally applicable law[s]."[57]

Even if the freedom of religion is too weak to invalidate a law, it may be a strong enough reason for a legislative exemption. North Carolina's experience is illustrative. In 1978 a state court upheld, against constitutional claims, the existing scheme for regulating private schools. The next year the state legislature, in response to religious lobbying, enacted a law providing that "in matters of education . . . 'No human authority shall, in any case whatever, control or interfere with the rights of conscience.'" It eliminated the requirement of state approval for teachers and curriculum.[58] Where the demand for protection has been strong enough, this means of protection has proven more efficacious than resort to the courts.[59]

Where neither judicial nor legislative protection is available, the claim of religious freedom may still receive some protection from the executive branch, which can simply decline to enforce regulations that fundamentalist schools find too burdensome. It is, for obvious reasons, difficult to document the incidence of such inactivity. But there is good reason to believe that it occurs. In a recent case in Vermont, for example, a Department of Education official testified that "the Department conducts no on-site reviews to ensure that the report [discussing the school's hours, objectives, teachers, course of study] is accurate and has 'no authority to review whether, in fact, the private . . . school is . . . doing what they say they are doing.' There is no further intrusion by the State beyond the reporting."[60]

Let me now turn to a second example of the success of the fundamentalist defensive agenda. Given the crowded conditions of modern urban life, it is often necessary to provide a public forum for private activity. (Public parks are available for picnicking.) The liberal tradition holds, though, that religion is a private matter and has no place in public life. This might mean—and the government has sometimes argued—that we should exclude religious activity from public fora. For example, public schools that allow voluntary student groups to meet on the premises after school hours have often denied that privilege to religious groups.

In this kind of dispute, fundamentalists can appeal to widely accepted principles of equality and freedom to support their claim. If other private groups are free to meet, religious groups should be equally free. That is the principle behind the federal Equal Access Act. In *Board of Education v. Mergens* the Supreme Court upheld that act and rejected the argument that it violated the Establishment Clause by bringing religion into the public sphere.[61]

The fundamentalists' offensive program tries to engage the law in the reform of other people's behavior. Unlike the defensive program, this agenda rejects liberal assumptions about law and religion. Fundamentalists argue that the law is not a value-free process for accommodating private concerns. We cannot make public policy about abortion, for example, without making some judgments about the value of fetal life. And if convictions about value are to play a role in the legal system, there is no reason to exclude religious convictions. The Moral Majority and its successors have rightly insisted on their entitlement to proclaim that abortion, homosexuality, pornography, and other evils of modern life have been condemned by God.

The offensive agenda also rejects liberal assumptions about freedom and the private life. Recall that in liberal theory freedom is a bilateral right. It protects alternative choices: birth and abortion, sexual promiscuity and restraint, and so on. But if God has condemned some of those choices, then freedom is a one-way street. Laws against sexual misconduct do not restrict true freedom. Indeed, they promote it, by showing us the way to go.

In the pursuit of this agenda fundamentalists have had some modest success, but they remain, politically speaking, a third party rather than a "moral majority." Consider the three most visible issues in recent years: homosexuality, abortion, and government funding of controversial art.

The Supreme Court held in 1986 that the freedom guaranteed by the Due Process Clause does not protect homosexual sodomy. Speaking generally, this was a victory for fundamentalists. But the reasons the Court gave for its decision were by no means religious. Moral rules, it declared, could have their source elsewhere. They might just be matters of long-accepted social practice. We can forbid homosexuality because "proscriptions against that conduct have ancient roots."[62] Moreover, the Court did not hold that homosexual behavior must be forbidden; it merely freed the elected branches of government to deal with the issue as they like. And there the tide is running against the fundamentalist side. States are with increasing frequency repealing or refusing to enforce their laws against sodomy.[63]

The issue of abortion has followed a similar pattern. In the last few years the Supreme Court has taken three steps away from *Roe v. Wade*. It has indicated a dissatisfaction with the trimester rules laid down by *Roe* for regulating abortions. It has allowed the government to restrict public funding of abortions. And it has permitted states to require (subject to some exceptions) that adolescents notify their parents before having abortions.[64] But once again the Court has upheld these restrictions for nonreligious reasons. A limit on abortion, it has said, may be "as much a reflection of 'traditionalist' values towards abortion, as it is an embodiment of the views of any particular religion."[65] And here again the Court has not held that abortions must be forbidden, only that the elected branches of government may deal with the issue as they wish. In that forum fundamentalists—in conjunction with large numbers of Catholics, Mormons, and other religious (and nonreligious) conservatives—have had some successes. Louisiana and Utah have enacted restrictive laws which diverge from the trimester rules laid down in *Roe v. Wade*.[66] Iowa, Minnesota, and New York have restricted the use of public funds for abortion assistance.[67] Arizona, Arkansas, Michigan, Mississippi, North Dakota, Nebraska, Pennsylvania, South Carolina, and Tennessee have enacted laws designed to assure parental notice or consent for minors, or informed consent for adults.[68] On the other hand, legislative efforts to restrict abortions have failed in Alabama, Florida, Idaho, Illinois, and South Dakota. Connecticut and Maryland have passed laws designed to guarantee the right in the event *Roe v. Wade* should be overruled.[69]

In 1990 the funding for the National Endowment for the Arts (NEA) was jeopardized when it became known that the NEA had subsidized exhibitions of several controversial pieces. These included homoerotic photographs by Robert Mapplethorpe, a collage by David Wojnarowicz portraying Jesus as a drug addict, and a photograph by Andres Serrano of a crucifix submerged in urine. Fundamentalist groups like the American Family Association, Concerned Women for America, and the Rutherford Institute figured prominently among those who objected to such expenditures. Their arguments here had a broad appeal. This was, after all, not a simple effort to regulate offensive behavior. The government was using tax revenues (contributed in part by religious conservatives) to sponsor such behavior. The principle of equality seemed to say that if the government could not pay for religious art, neither should it pay for antireligious art. The principle of freedom seemed to say that people should not be taxed to support blasphemy and the glorification of sin.[70]

In the end, however, Congress reauthorized funding for the NEA with only a nod toward fundamentalist objections. The bill ultimately enacted approved a $174 million NEA budget. Its only concessions to the NEA's opponents were a requirement that the agency consider "general standards of decency" in awarding grants and a provision for recoupment of funds from recipients convicted of obscenity.[71]

Fundamentalists are losing the public debate on issues like these because most people think that God has expressed no opinion about them. The argument that American constitutional and common law are based on the Bible ignores the separatist aspect of eighteenth- (and twentieth-) century legal culture.[72] The claim that they *ought* to have a scriptural foundation overlooks two facts. One is that a large minority of Americans doubt that the Bible is the word of God. The other is that a majority of American Christians and Jews, who accept biblical authority, do not subscribe to literalism as a canon of interpretation. Many of these people will persist in differing with fundamentalists about the bearing of Scripture on issues of personal virtue.

Fundamentalists have had least success in their efforts to secure government support for specific acts of religious belief or observance. The Supreme Court has approved the government display of Christmas crèches, but more as cultural artifacts (like religious pictures in a museum) than as objects of devotion.[73] Proposals to amend the Constitution, or to restrict the Supreme Court's jurisdiction, in order to restore prayer to the public schools have failed in Congress.[74] The Supreme Court struck down Alabama's moment of silence law because it had an obviously religious purpose.[75] The Court also invalidated Louisiana's Balanced Treatment Act and indicated that it would have no further use for "creation science" in the public schools.[76]

This poor record might seem surprising, since these efforts have all respected the liberal icons of freedom and equality: they have called for voluntary prayer and balanced treatment. The problem is that the liberal tradition forbids us to introduce religion into public life even on those terms. There is no secular reason, comparable to "traditional morality," that we can offer to justify government-sponsored religious observance. The only possible explanation for such practices is that they carry out religious beliefs that many people do not share. It is only three decades since the Establishment Clause was first interpreted to forbid these observances,[77] but the rules are now widely accepted.

Conclusion

Discussions of the place of fundamentalism in the American legal system often have an unfortunate two-dimensional aspect. Enthusiastic portrayals tend to ignore the liberal and separatist strains in our constitutional history, and to characterize fundamentalist objectives as more congruent with our legal culture than they actually are. Legal writers typically fail to appreciate the depth and nuances of fundamentalist religious beliefs and the extent to which such believers share standard American legal assumptions and idioms.

I have tried to give an account that has a little more perspective and balance. I have argued that fundamentalists espouse individualism, freedom, and equality in religion and politics. These are ideals that occupy a prominent place in our legal system. It is not surprising that when fundamentalists have claimed to uphold these ideals (freedom for private schools, equal access to public fora), they have won popular support and a measure of success. They have even had some success in drawing the boundaries of these ideals. (The right to freedom does not extend to homosexual sodomy, drug abuse, some abortions, some pornography.)

I have also argued that fundamentalists espouse a biblical faith that shares some of the ideals of the seventeenth- and eighteenth-century Puritan establishment. In this, too, they are typically American, though more out of step with contemporary thought. Like the Puritans, fundamentalists find it hard to distinguish religion from morality and private from public life. They think that America should acknowledge its dependence on God and that our law should be based on the Bible. (Hence, they have supported school prayer, creation science, posting the Ten Commandments in public schools, and so on.) These efforts have been uniformly unsuccessful. But we should not exaggerate them. They have often been tempered by the beliefs I discussed above. School prayer would be voluntary (or even silent). Creation science would be given only balanced treatment. America Protestant fundamentalism is not just a revival of old-time religion. It is a modern (though, of course, conservative) way of thinking about modern problems.

Notes

1. N. Ammerman, "North American Protestant Fundamentalism," in Martin E. Marty and R. Scott Appleby, eds., *Fundamentalisms Observed* (Chicago: University of Chicago Press, 1991); S. Bruce, *The Rise and Fall of the New Christian Right* (Oxford: Clarendon Press, 1988); D. Bromley and A. Shupe, *New Christian Politics* (Macon: Mercer University Press, 1984); R. Liebman and R. Wuthnow, *The New Christian Right* (New York: Aldine Publishing Company, 1983); G. Marsden, ed., *Evangelicalism and Modern America* (Grand Rapids: William B. Eerdmans Publishing Company, 1984); R. Neuhaus and M. Cromartie, *Piety and Politics* (Washington, D.C.: Ethics and Public Policy Center, 1987).

2. The expression comes from a gospel passage where Jesus says, "Except a man be born again, he cannot see the kingdom of God." John 3:3.

3. J. Falwell, *Strength for the Journey* (New York: Simon and Schuster, 1987), p. 103.

4. F. Fitzgerald, "A Disciplined, Charging Army," *New Yorker,* 18 May 1981, pp. 53, 70.

5. R. Bultmann, *Jesus and the Word* (New York: Charles Scribner's Sons, 1958), p. 47.

6. T. LaHaye, *The Unhappy Gays* (Wheaton, Ill.: Tyndale House Publishers, Inc., 1978), pp. 145–46.

7. Ibid., p. 116.

8. LaHaye, *The Unhappy Gays,* chaps. 4–5; J. Falwell, *Listen, America!* (Garden City: Doubleday and Company, 1980), pp. 181–86; F. Schaeffer, *True Spirituality* (Wheaton, Ill.: Tyndale House Publishers, 1971).

9. 1 Cor. 6:18–20; Eph. 5:22–25.

10. N. Ammerman, *Bible Believers* (New Brunswick: Rutgers University Press, 1987), p. 139.

11. Eph. 5:22–25.

12. Ammerman, *Bible Believers,* pp. 144–45.

13. G. Marsden, *Fundamentalism and American Culture* (New York: Oxford University Press, 1980), pp. 66–68.

14. Falwell, *Listen, America!* p. 240.

15. R. Walton, *One Nation under God* (Washington, D.C.: Third Century Publishers, 1975), p. 175.

16. Falwell, *Strength for the Journey,* p. 105.

17. Ammerman, *Bible Believers,* p. 126.

18. J. Guth, "The New Christian Right," and R. Liebman, "Mobilizing the Moral Majority," in Liebman and Wuthnow, *The New Christian Right,* chaps. 2–3; P. Schwartz and J. McBride, "The Moral Majority in the U.S.A. as a New Religious Movement," in E. Barker, ed., *Of Gods and Men* (Macon: Mercer University Press, 1983), p. 127.

19. G. Wills, "Evangels of Abortion," *New York Review of Books,* 15 June 1989, p. 15; R. Pierard, "Religion and the New Right in the 1980s," in J. Wood, ed., *Religion and the State* (Waco: Baylor University Press, 1985), pp. 393, 407–10.

20. Most Protestant fundamentalists subscribe to a view of history known as "premillennialism." Premillennialists believe that the millennium will be ushered in by a period of great tribulation—God's judgment on the living who have rejected Jesus. Jesus will then return to earth and establish a millennial kingdom by his might. (Postmillennialists, by contrast, believe that the church will bring about the millennium peacefully, through its preaching of the gospel, and that Jesus will return at the end of the millennium.)

As to when all this will happen, many find the interpretive key in the founding of the state of Israel in 1948. That fulfilled God's prophecy to restore the Jews to their homeland. Fundamentalists understand the Bible to say that the rest of the prophetic scenario will be played out within a few years of that event. Matt. 24:32; P. Shriver, "Piety, Pluralism, and Politics," in R. Stone, ed., *Reformed Faith and Politics* (Washington, D.C.: University Press of America, 1983), pp. 48, 56.

21. Ammerman, *Bible Believers,* p. 87.

22. Ibid., p. 132.

23. Falwell, *Strength for the Journey,* p. 120.

24. *The Fundamentals: A Testimony of the Truth* (Chicago: Testimony Publishing Company, 1910–15).

25. S. Cole, *The History of Fundamentalism* (New York: R. R. Smith, 1931), p. 34. See the discussion in J. Pelikan, "Fundamentalism and/or Orthodoxy? Toward an Understanding of the Fundamentalist Phenomenon," in N. Cohen, ed., *The Fundamentalist Phenomenon* (Grand Rapids: William B. Eerdmans Publishing Company, 1990), p. 3. I should note, for the sake of clarity, that the theological simplicity I discuss in the text is partially compensated for by an elaborate, even intricate, system of biblical hermeneutics. A good example of this, still available on the shelves of large bookstores, is C. J. Scofield's annotated version of the King James Bible.

26. B. Ackerman, *Social Justice in the Liberal State* (New Haven: Yale University Press, 1980), p. 369.

27. T. Hobbes, *Leviathan,* M. Oakeshott, ed. (Oxford: Basil Blackwell), p. 32. See also D. Hume, *A Treatise on Human Nature* (Oxford: Clarendon, 1968), bk. 2, pt. 3, § 3; bk. 3, pt. 1, § 1.

28. Garvey, *A Comment on Religious Convictions and Lawmaking,* 84 Mich. L. Rev. 1288 (1986). In this discussion of what liberal theory believes, I have simplified even more drastically than I did above in my discussion of what fundamentalists believe. Here are some qualifications. First, there are many religious liberals who believe that God created and reigns over the universe. Their liberalism consists in the important role they assign human beings in working out their own salvation and in designing their own solutions to political problems. Second, there are those who remain agnostic about the existence of God and the objectivity of the good. They contend that that is the appropriate attitude to take in political life, because agreement on these questions is impossible. Third, some liberals (utilitarians like Mill) maintain that it is possible to speak about the good in objective terms, and hence possible for the state to play some role in promoting it. Their liberalism derives from their skepticism about the empirical likelihood of success when the state intervenes in certain areas of our lives.

29. *Texas v. Johnson,* 491 U.S. 397 (1989); *Torcaso v. Watkins,* 367 U.S. 488 (1961).

30. J. Whitehead, *An American Dream* (Westchester, Ill.: Crossway Books, 1987), p. 152.

31. Walton, *One Nation under God;* Falwell, *Listen, America!* pp. 12–13. See also the journal *Biblical Economics Today,* published by the Institute for Christian Economics.

32. D. Little, *Religion, Order, and Law* (New York: Harper and Row, 1969), pp. 41, 50–52.

33. *Listen, America!* p. 201. See also Walton, *One Nation under God,* chap. 3.

34. *Nagle v. Olin,* 64 Ohio St. 2d 341, 415 N.E. 2d 279 (Ohio 1980); *State v. Whisner,* 47 Ohio St. 2d 181, 351 N.E. 2d (Ohio 1976); *State v. Faith Baptist Church,*

207 Neb. 802, 301 N.W. 2d 571 (Neb. 1981), appeal dismissed, 454 U.S. 803 (1981).

35. Schaeffer, *A Christian Manifesto,* p. 130. The most noteworthy thing about these incidents is that they are so infrequent. Civil disobedience by fundamentalists has to date not approached in scale the religious lawbreaking of the 1960s civil rights movement. Nor is it likely to, for several reasons. First of all, Black civil rights activists saw themselves as a collective entity seeking a social structural change that would benefit the group to which they belonged. ("We shall overcome.") Fundamentalist civil disobedience is primarily motivated by the individual's desire to comply in his own actions with God's law, where civil law makes that impossible. The harm and the reaction are personal. There is not that element of group solidarity necessary to sustain large-scale illegal action. Anti-abortion demonstrations do not fit this pattern, but they are unique. They show a spirit of altruism, but no sense of solidarity. The demonstrators are concerned about harm to the unborn. Their reason for acting, however, is that the unborn are helpless, not that they have some special kinship with the demonstrators.

The second reason for the small scale of fundamentalist civil disobedience is that laws seldom conflict directly with Scripture (by requiring what is forbidden or forbidding what is required). The law may permit homosexual activity or the sale of pornography, but the godly can avoid both. Public schools may not conduct prayers, but pious children can still pray. In these circumstances the fundamentalist passion for order triumphs over the desire for reformation. Boycotts and other forms of legal pressure are desirable. But the licentious are ultimately responsible for their own souls; believers should not upset the legal order just to improve others' chances of salvation.

36. H. Brown, *The Reconstruction of the Republic* (New Rochelle, N.Y.: Arlington House, 1977), p. 192; W. Baker, "Capital Punishment," *Fundamentalist Journal* 7 (March 1988): 18; T. LaHaye, *The Battle for the Family* (Old Tappan, N.J.: Fleming H. Revell Company, 1982), pp. 66–80.

37. LaHaye, *The Battle for the Family;* Falwell, *Listen, America!;* J. Falwell, *The Fundamentalist Phenomenon* (Garden City: Doubleday and Company, 1981), pp. 186–212; F. Schaeffer, *A Christian Manifesto* (Westchester, Ill.: Crossway Books, 1981); Walton, *One Nation under God,* chaps. 5–6; J. Robison, *Attack on the Family* (Wheaton, Ill.: Tyndale House Publishers, 1980); *Moral Majority Report,* 20 July 1981.

38. T. Bozeman, *To Live Ancient Lives* (Chapel Hill: University of North Carolina Press, 1988); S. Ahlstrom, *A Religious History of the American People* (New Haven: Yale University Press, 1972), pp. 146–47.

39. T. Curry, *The First Freedoms* (New York: Oxford University Press, 1986), p. 6.

40. P. Miller, *Errand into the Wilderness* (Cambridge: Belknap Press of Harvard University Press, 1956), chap. 5; R. Hughes and C. Allen, *Illusions of Innocence* (Chicago: University of Chicago Press, 1988), p. 41 ("lyke unto Hippocrates twinnes").

41. Curry, *The First Freedoms,* pp. 3, 24.

42. Ibid., chap. 1; Ahlstrom, *A Religious History of the American People,* chaps. 9–10.

43. Falwell, *Listen, America!* p. 29; Brown, *The Reconstruction of the Republic,* p. 201; Schaeffer, *A Christian Manifesto,* pp. 28–29; R. Rushdoony, *The Institutes of Biblical Law* (Nutley, N.J.: Craig Press, 1973).

44. F. Schaeffer, *How Should We Then Live?* (Old Tappan, N.J.: Felming H. Revell Company, 1976), pp. 108–10; J. Whitehead, *The Second American Revolution* (Elgin, Ill.: David C. Cook Publishing Company, 1982), pp. 28–30; R. Rushdoony, *This Independent Republic* (Fairfax, Va.: Thoburn Press, 1964), p. 3. The historical assumptions underlying this version of events are severely criticized in M. Noll, G. Marsden, and N. Hatch, *The Search for Christian America* (Colorado Springs: Helmers and Howard Publishers, 1989); R. Pierard, "Schaeffer on History," in R. Rueg-segger, ed., *Reflections on Francis Schaeffer* (Grand Rapids: Zondervan Publishing House, 1986), p. 197.

45. W. Blackstone, *Commentaries on the Law of England* 42. See the discussion of

Blackstone's influence in H. Titus, *Moses, Blackstone, and the Law of the Land,* 1 C.L.S.Q. 5 (no. 4, 1980); J. Whitehead and J. Conlan, *The Establishment of the Religion of Secular Humanism and Its First Amendment Implications,* 10 Tex. Tech L. Rev. 1, 25–26 (1978); Whitehead, *The Second American Revolution,* pp. 30–32; Schaeffer, *A Christian Manifesto,* p. 38.

46. Ky. Rev. Stat. § 158.178 (1980). The Supreme Court held that the posting requirement violated the Establishment Clause, because its purpose was plainly religious. *Stone v. Graham,* 449 U.S. 39 (1980). For more elaborate statements of the connection between law and the Bible, see Whitehead, *The Second American Revolution;* Rushdoony, *The Institutes of Biblical Law.*

47. There is on the fringes of fundamentalism a small movement (Christian reconstruction) that self-consciously espouses a Puritan revival in America. See Rushdoony, *The Institutes of Biblical Law;* Rushdoony, *This Independent Republic;* G. Bahnsen, *Theonomy in Christian Ethics* (Oklahoma City, Okla.: Presbyterian and Reformed, 1977). The movement publishes various journals and newsletters, including the *Chalcedon Report, Christian Reconstruction, Covenant Renewal,* and *Dispensationalism in Transition.*

48. The bill proposing the Family Protection Act is S. 1808 (24 September 1979). See Falwell, *Listen, America!* p. 136; Walton, *One Nation under God,* chap. 5; LaHaye, *The Battle for the Family,* pp. 135–46.

49. *Bob Jones Univ. v. United States,* 461 U.S. 574 (1983); Devins, *State Regulation of Christian Schools,* 10 J. Legis. 363 (1983); J. Carper and N. Devins, "The State and the Christian Day School," in Wood, ed., *Religion and the State,* p. 211.

50. 18 Weekly Comp. Pres. Docs. 664 (17 May 1982). The Establishment Clause of the First Amendment is currently understood to forbid even voluntary prayers conducted by a public school. *Engel v. Vitale,* 370 U.S. 421 (1962); *School District of Abington Township v. Schempp,* 374 U.S. 203 (1963).

51. *Wallace v. Jaffree,* 472 U.S. 38 (1985).

52. 20 U.S.C. § 4071. The Supreme Court upheld the act in *Board of Education v. Mergens,* 496 U.S. 226 (1990).

53. The law was held invalid in *Edwards v. Aguillard,* 482 U.S. 578 (1987). Compare the arguments made by those who objected to the teaching of "secular humanism" in the public schools in *Smith v. Board of School Comm'rs,* 655 F. Supp. 939 (S.D. Ala.), rev'd, 827 F. 2d 684 (11th Cir. 1987); *Mozert v. Hawkins County Public Schools,* 647 F. Supp. 1194 (E.D. Tenn. 1986), rev'd, 827 F.2d 1058 (6th Cir. 1987), cert. denied, 484 U.S. 1066 (1988). Cf. *Grove v. Mead School District No. 354,* 753 F. 2d 1528 (9th Cir.), cert. denied, 474 U.S. 826 (1985).

54. *Michigan Dept. of Social Services v. Emmanuel Baptist Preschool,* 434 Mich. 390, 455 N.W. 2d 1 (1990). The court's holding is consistent with two lines of decisions by the United States Supreme Court. One protects parents' educational choices under the Free Exercise Clause of the First Amendment. *Wisconsin v. Yoder,* 406 U.S. 205 (1972) (excusing Amish children from compulsory attendance at public schools beyond the eighth grade). The other protects such choices as an exercise of liberty under the Due Process Clause of the Fourteenth Amendment. *Pierce v. Society of Sisters,* 268 U.S. 510 (1925) (right to operate a parochial school); *Farrington v. Tokushiage,* 273 U.S. 284 (1927) (striking down certain programmatic regulations of foreign language schools in the Territory of Hawaii).

For other recent examples involving fundamentalist schools, see *Bangor Baptist Church v. State of Maine, Department of Educational and Cultural Services,* 576 F. Supp. 1299 (D. Me. 1983); *Sumner v. First Baptist Church,* 97 Wash. 2d 1, 639 P. 2d 1358 (1982); *Nagle v. Olin,* 64 Ohio St. 2d 341, 415 N.E. 2d 279 (1980); *State v. Whisner,* 47 Ohio St. 2d 181, 351 N.E. 2d 750 (1976).

55. *Kentucky State Bd., Etc. v. Rudasill,* 589 S.W. 2d 877 (Ky. 1979). Section 5 provides: "Nor shall any man be compelled to

send his child to any school to which he may be conscientiously opposed."

56. F. Schauer, "Can Rights Be Abused?" *Philosophical Quarterly* 31 (1982): 225.

57. *Employment Div., Dept. of Human Res. v. Smith,* 494 U.S. 872 (1990). See also *Jimmy Swaggart Ministries v. Bd. of Equalization,* 493 U.S. 378 (1990); *Bob Jones University v. United States,* 461 U.S. 574 (1983).

For examples of cases applying this rule to fire, health, and safety regulations of fundamentalist schools, see *New Life Baptist Church Academy v. Town of East Longmeadow,* 885 F. 2d 940 (1st Cir. 1989); *Duro v. District Attorney,* 712 F. 2d 96 (4th Cir. 1983); *Antrim Faith Baptist Church v.Com., Dept. of Labor and Industry,* 75 Pa. Cmwlth. 61, 460 A. 2d 1228 (1983); *Hough v. North Star Baptist Church,* 109 Mich. App. 780, 312 N.W. 2d 158 (1981); *Douglas v. Faith Baptist Church,* 207 Neb. 802, 301 N.W. 2d 571 (1981); *State Fire Marshall v. Lee,* 101 Mich. App. 829, 300 N.W. 2d 748 (1980).

Many other cases have applied the same rule to programmatic issues—books, curricula, teacher certification, student reporting, and so on. *New Life Baptist Church Academy v. Town of East Longmeadow,* 885 F. 2d 940 (1st Cir. 1989); *Fellowship Baptist Church v. Benton,* 815 F. 2d 485 (8th Cir. (1987); *Blackwelder v. Safnauer,* 689 F. Supp. 106 (N.D.N.Y. 1988); *State v. Delabruere,* 1990 WL 75320 (Vt. 1990); *Care and Protection of Charles,* 399 Mass. 324, 504 N.E. 2d 592 (1987); *Johnson v. Charles City Community Schools Bd. of Educ.,* 368 N.W. 2d 74 (1985); *State v. Rivinius,* 328 N.W. 2d 220 (N.D. 1982); *New Jersey State Bd. of Higher Educ. v. Board of Directors of Shelton,* 90 N.J. 470, 448 A. 2d 988 (1982); *Attorney General v. Bailey,* 386 Mass. 367, 436 N.E. 2d 139 (1982); *State v. Shaver,* 294 N.W. 2d 883 (N.D. 1980).

Women employees of fundamentalist schools have often made sex discrimination claims about their pay and other terms of employment. The courts have been quite receptive to such claims even in cases where the schools have religious reasons for treating men and women differently. *Dole v.*

Shenandoah Baptist Church, 53 Empl. Prac. Dec. P 39,791, 59 Ed. Law Rep. 669 (4th Circ. 1986); *EEOC v. Fremont Christian School,* 791 F. 2d 1362 (9th Cir. 1986); *U.S. Dept. of Labor v. Shenandoah Baptist Church,* 707 F. Supp. 1450 (W.D. Va. 1989); *McLeod v. Providence Christian School,* 160 Mich. App. 333, 408 N.W. 2d 146 (1987). Such an issue was before the Supreme Court in *Ohio Civil Rights Comm'n v. Dayton Christian Schools, Inc.,* 477 U.S. 619 (1986), but the Court did not reach the merits.

58. N.C. Gen. Stat. § 115C, art. 39 (1987); *Delconte v. State,* 329 S.E. 2d 636 (N.C. 1985); Note, *The State and Sectarian Education: Regulation to Deregulation,* 1980 Duke L.J. 801.

59. Fla. Stat. Ann. § 232.01(b)1 (1989) ("Nothing in this section shall authorize the state or any school district to oversee or exercise control over the curricula or academic programs of nonpublic schools"); Tobak and Zirkel, *Home Instruction: An Analysis of the Statutes and Case Law,* 8 U. Dayton L. Rev. 1, 6–10 (1982) (Tabular Analysis of State Statutory Provisions concerning Home Instruction); N. Devins, ed., *Public Values, Private Schools* (Philadelphia: Falmer Press, 1989), pp. 5–7.

60. *State v. Delabruere,* 1990 WL 75320 (Vt.).

61. 496 U.S. 226 (1990).

62. *Bowers v. Hardwick,* 478 U.S. 186, 192 (1986).

63. Note, *Developments in the Law: Sexual Orientation and the Law,* 102 Harv. L. Rev. 1508, 1520–1521, 1536 (1989).

64. *Harris v. McRae,* 448 U.S. 297, 319 (1980) (public funding of abortions); *Webster v. Reproductive Health Services,* 492 U.S. 490 (1989) (use of public facilities; trimester system); *Hodgson v. Minnesota,* 497 U.S. 502 (1990) (parental notification); *Ohio v. Akron Center for Reproductive Health,* 110 S. Ct. 2972 (1990) (parental notification). Cf. *Rust v. Sullivan,* 111 S. Ct. 1759 (1991) (abortion counseling and referral by federally funded clinics).

As this volume was going to press the Supreme Court granted review in *Planned Parenthood of Southeastern Pennsylvania v. Casey,*

112 S.Ct. 931(21 January 1992). The case presented a variety of technical questions concerning such matters as spousal notice, parental consent, and informed consent by abortion patients. But some of the participants in the litigation, sensitive to charges in the Court's membership, urged the Court to reconsider the right of privacy recognized in *Roe v. Wade.*

65. *Harris v. McRae,* 448 U.S. at 319.

66. 1991 La. Acts 26; Utah Code Ann.§ 76-7-301.1 (Michie Supp. 1991).

67. 1991 Iowa Acts § 104, ch. 1270, sec. 2; Minn. Stat. § 145.925 (West 1989); 1991 N.Y. Laws 407.

68. Ariz. Rev. Stat. Ann. § 36-2152 (West Supp. 1991); Ark. Code Ann. § 20-16-801 (Michie 1991); Mich. Comp. Laws § 722.903 (West Supp. 1991); Miss. Code Ann. § 41-41-33 (West Supp. 1991); N.D. Cent. Code § 14-02.1-03 (Michie 1991); Neb. Rev. Stat. § 71-6901 to 6902 (Supp. 1991); 18 Pa. Cons. Stat. Ann. §§ 3204, 3205, 3211 (West 1991 Supp.); S.C. Code Ann. § 44-41-30 (Law. Co-op. Supp. 1991); Tenn. Code Ann. § 39-15-202 (Michie 1991).

69. Conn. Gen. Stat. §§ 19a-601 to -602 (West Supp. 1991); 1991 Md. Laws Ch. 1 (Senate Bill 162).

70. For accounts of such objections to NEA funding, see *Reauthorization of the National Foundation on the Arts and Humanities Act Institute of Museum Services: Hearings before the Subcomm. on Education, Arts and Humanities of the S. Comm. on Labor and Human Resources,* 101st Cong., 2nd Sess. 349-50 (1990) (testimony of Jane Chastain); Parachini, "Suit Revives Furor over NEA Grants," *Los Angeles Times,* 30 August 1990, p. F1; Bernstein, "Arts Endowment's Opponents Are Fighting Fire with Fire," *New York Times,* 30 May 1990, p. C13.

71. Department of the Interior and Related Agencies Appropriations Act, 1991, Pub. L. No. 101-512, 104 Stat. 1963, 1965 (1990).

72. *Everson v. Board of Education,* 330 U.S. 1 (1947).

73. On the issue of crèches, see *Lynch v. Donnelly,* 465 U.S. 668 (1984); *County of Allegheny v. American Civil Liberties Union,* 492 U.S. 573 (1989). On the issue of legislative chaplains, see *Marsh v. Chambers,* 463 U.S. 783 (1983).

74. E. Jorstad, *The New Christian Right* (Lewiston, N.Y.: Edwin Mellen Press, 1987), pp. 42–45. In *Lee v. Weisman,* cert. granted, 111 S.Ct. 1305 (18 March 1991), the Supreme Court considered the constitutionality of clerical benedictions at public school graduations. Counsel for Lee urged the Court to change the prevailing Establishment Clause rules and allow religious expression by the government so long as it did not coerce belief. The Court had not reached a decision when this volume went to press.

75. *Wallace v. Jaffree,* 472 U.S. 38 (1985).

76. *Edwards v. Aguillard,* 482 U.S. 578 (1987). In *Bowen v. Kendrick,* 487 U.S. 589 (1988), the Court upheld the federal Adolescent Family Life Act, which was designed to reduce adolescent sexual relations and pregnancy by funding the services of public and nonprofit private organizations. The Court indicated that religious organizations could receive funds but only if they refrained from delivering religious messages with their counseling services.

77. *Engel v. Vitale,* 370 U.S. 421 (1962); *School District of Abington Township v. Schempp,* 374 U.S. 203 (1963); *Epperson v. Arkansas,* 393 U.S. 97 (1968).

Fundamentalism, Ethnicity, and Enclave

Steve Bruce

Ulster Protestants and American Fundamentalists: Introductory Contrasts

A comparison of the politics of conservative Protestantism in Northern Ireland and America can be expressed as the contrast between the religion of politics and the politics of religion. Put briefly, the two settings are so different as to produce patterns of action which seem opposites. In Northern Ireland the basic structure of the ethnic conflict with Catholics means that, for Protestants, religion remains a vital part of their sense of identity, and even those people who are not committed "born-again" believers find themselves turning back to conservative Protestant ideologies and languages to make sense of their apparently beleaguered position in the north of Ireland and to give purpose to their political agenda, which is dominated by a desire to remain part of the United Kingdom of Great Britain and Northern Ireland. The nationalist Catholic threat to Ulster Protestants (using the term here politically rather than theologically) gives a political role to fundamentalism[1] and hence to its representatives, who are best exemplified by the Reverend Ian Paisley. Although American evangelicals have often spoken for America, and in places have come close to representing an American "ethnos" (The WASP—"white Anglo-Saxon Protestant"), American fundamentalists do not form an ethnic group under political threat. American fundamentalists are identified by their common religious culture and are only periodically mobilized to engage in electoral and pressure group politics by what they perceive to be threats to that culture and their ability to reproduce it. Here it is the desire to maintain a subculture (and occasionally the belief that they can once again dominate mainstream America) which produces the politics.

Being a minority in a culturally plural democracy forces American fundamentalists to attenuate the specifically religious elements in their program and to offer their agenda in "secular" form. Where the Northern Ireland situation gives even nonreligious Protestants good reason to support fundamentalists, the American setting makes religious fundamentalists masquerade as secular conservatives. In the former, secular parties appear religious; in the latter, religious groups appear secular.

Fundamentalism in the Northern Ireland Conflict

For most of its history, Ireland has been politically subordinate to Great Britain (the political unit containing England, Scotland, and Wales).[2] The conflict in Northern Ireland (or Ulster, as Protestants prefer) stems from attempts from the sixteenth century onward to use settlement to pacify a potentially troublesome neighbor. Those who settled the northeast of Ireland in the seventeenth and eighteenth centuries were Scots Protestants; the natives were Catholics. These are not simply two different religions; they are antithetical and have developed their identities in competition. Settlers and natives encountered each other at a time when people took religion seriously. They did not much intermarry, and each side used its religion to embody theodicies of success and failure in stereotypes. The settlers explained their privileges as the natural result of having the true religion: Catholics were poor because they had not been saved and were kept in bondage by their priests. Protestants were better off because they were hardworking, diligent, literate, and responsible. Religion also provided consolation for the subordinate population, whose Catholic church acted as the main repository of Irish identity.

Furthermore, the Scottish settlers were *Calvinist* Presbyterians. Although high theology requires that only individuals can be "elected" to salvation, there has always been a strong tendency for Calvinists to see themselves, in images drawn from the history of the Children of Israel, as an elect "collectivity," a tendency exaggerated when they are threatened by a large mass of "heathens." Although the 1859 revival in Ulster saw the import from America of an element of Arminian evangelicalism, the covenant motif remained powerful and is still periodically used by Ulster Protestants in political rhetoric.[3]

As I have argued at length elsewhere, secularization is a natural tendency of industrializing societies.[4] Only when religion does something other than mediate between man and God does it retain a high place in people's attentions and in their politics. That, from the point of settlement, the groups in competition were divided by religion meant that religion remained important. Nothing that has happened since settlement in the seventeenth and eighteenth centuries, since the rise of the nineteenth-century Irish nationalist home rule movement, or since the 1921 partition of Ireland into the Free State (later the Republic of Ireland) and Northern Ireland (remaining part of the United Kingdom of Great Britain and Northern Ireland) has reduced the importance of religion. Far from it. Once the south was established as a Catholic country, Protestants were bound to find the idea of a united Ireland abhorrent. Dispassionate observers might argue that the Protestants would be such a large block in any united Ireland that their religious identity could not be threatened by severing the link with Great Britain. Protestants do not see it that way. Instead, they point to the virtual disappearance of the Protestants in the Republic. At partition they were about 11 percent of the population; now they are under 4 percent.

As evidence of the hegemony of the Catholic church in the Republic, Protestants have been able to point to the failure of recent attempts to liberalize the Republic. Although organized with the intention of bringing the Irish Republic into line with other European countries, recent referenda on divorce (which remains illegal) and abortion (which before the referendum was illegal and is now unconstitutional) back-fired and confirmed the centrality of the Catholic church's teachings for the Republic's sociomoral climate.[5]

From 1921 to 1972, when the severity of the civil unrest persuaded the British government at Westminster to take direct control over the province, Northern Ireland was governed by a directly elected parliament at Stormont. While foreign policy, defense, and major taxation were controlled by Westminster, Stormont controlled policing, social policy, education, and the management of the local economy—precisely those areas which could be used to reward loyal Protestants and punish disloyal Catholics. Protestants undoubtedly enjoyed considerable material advantages over Catholics in Northern Ireland. More important for most of them, they enjoyed the privilege of having their symbols and culture accorded pride of place in the affairs of the state. But they explained these advantages to themselves as the natural consequences of having the true religion. Material and cultural interests combined in a complex manner so that material interests reinforced commitment to the religion. Furthermore, what is usually important in explaining behavior is not objective but *perceived* reality, and, far from feeling privileged, many Protestants have felt themselves relatively deprived, a paradox which is readily explained. One of the Catholic church's reasons for maintaining its own institutions—schools, hospitals, and colleges—is that those of the state are not genuinely secular. Some Protestants have seen the institutions of the Northern Ireland state as Protestant, as they ought to be, given that Catholics refused to embrace them. But many Protestants felt a strong sense of betrayal when the state proclaimed (however disingenuously) that its institutions were open to all. First, Catholics had already been given most of the island. Second, they were allowed their own institutions. Third, they could compete with Protestants in state institutions. Catholics could migrate to the Republic and teach in southern schools. They had a monopoly in Catholic schools. And they cried "discrimination" if they weren't given jobs in state schools.

Although the state was frequently seen by Catholics as "Protestant" (and often acted as though it were), it was sufficiently open-minded to appear so neutral that it inadvertently contributed to the sense of relative deprivation of the more nervous Protestants. For example, the Catholic Mater Infirmatorum happily displayed Catholic religious symbols and its staff were not shy in making it clear in the daily round of hospital work that it was a *Catholic* hospital. Yet in the early 1960s, gospel choirs were banned from a state hospital in Belfast after complaints from Catholics about religious offense. Especially under the reforming premiership of Terence O'Neill (1963–69), who put economic improvement before ethnic solidarity, many Protestants came to feel themselves threatened by Catholics (in the forms of both the Irish Republic and the minority in Ulster) and disprivileged by what should have been their own state.

Such reasoning may have taken scant regard of the objective status differences between Protestants and Catholics in Ulster, but it nonetheless explains why most Protestants did not feel themselves to be massively advantaged by the Stormont regime and why they were so hostile to Catholic campaigns for "civil rights." It also shows what is wrong with the still-popular reduction of Protestant antinationalism to a desire to maintain their socioeconomic advantages.

Religious and "Secular" Protestants

Theologically conservative Ulster Protestants see their opposition to a united Ireland as religious. Rome is the Antichrist, hell-bent on destroying Northern Ireland because it is the last bastion of evangelical Protestantism in Europe. Whatever the Catholic church says to the contrary and however often its bishops condemn the republican murder campaign, the militant republicanism of the IRA is simply doing the Church's work. But such people form only a small proportion of the unionists. There are no good surveys of Protestant theological distribution, but we can sensibly estimate it. At most, the conservative evangelical denominations are only 10 percent of the non-Catholic population. The Irish Presbyterian Church (to which a third of non-Catholics belong) is on the conservative wing of Presbyterianism; it recently voted against joining the new British ecumenical church organization because the Catholic church was involved. Perhaps a third of its members (with a bias to rural areas) see themselves as evangelicals and subscribe in some part to the view that a united Ireland has to be opposed on religious grounds. Members of the Episcopal Church of Ireland in Ulster are similarly more theologically conservative than Episcopalians elsewhere. Putting these estimates together and being generous, one can suppose that no more than a third of non-Catholics are evangelicals with a consciously religious view of the civil conflict.

Yet I want to suggest that religion has a considerable influence even on those who are not themselves evangelicals, and I will illustrate the argument by presenting some data on the religious composition of Ian Paisley's Democratic Unionist Party, data which are hard to explain without recognizing the central part played generally in unionist politics by religious beliefs and attitudes.[6]

For all its existence, the Stormont parliament was dominated by the Ulster Unionist Party, which had the unquestioned support of the vast majority of the Protestant people,[7] but there was always a critical "right-wing" fringe of two sometimes overlapping elements. There were working-class populists who were unsure of the UUP's willingness to favor Protestants, and there were evangelicals who wanted to turn the government's occasional use of religious rhetoric into a reality of preferential treatment for Protestant churches, ministers, and religious activity. In the 1950s Ian Paisley was active in both these milieu.

Paisley was the son of an independent Baptist minister in the town of Ballymena in North Antrim who, like his son, combined religious and political Protestantism. Kyle Paisley had resigned from the Baptist Union over its "liberal" trend. He had also been a member of the Ulster Volunteer Force, the militia which Sir Edward Carson raised in opposition to proposals for Irish independence. Ian Paisley studied for the ministry at the theological hall of the Reformed Presbyterian Church and at an evangelistic training college in Wales. During his time as a theology student, Paisley was active in Belfast's evangelical milieu and he was invited to preach to a small independent congregation on the Ravenhill Road in working-class east Belfast. This group had split from the local Presbyterian congregation and was in need of a Bible-believing gospel-preaching minister. Paisley was in need of a job.

Paisley worked hard to build his congregation and became well known as a loud street preacher of the gospel. He also became active in right-wing unionist circles. In both milieus his message was the same: the elites of the Irish Presbyterian Church and the Unionist Party could not be trusted to maintain the religious and political orthodoxy. "Sell out" and the "Romeward trend" were the order of the day. In the 1950s very few people paid much attention to Ian Paisley and his alarmist message, but the premiership of Terence O'Neill with its (albeit halfhearted) reforms and such gestures to the minority community as opening a Catholic school and inviting the Irish Republic's prime minister to Belfast made Paisley's paranoia seem like prescience.

Here is not the place to explain the rise of the civil rights movement or to describe the way in which first Terence O'Neill and then his successor, Major Chichester-Clark (1969–71), combined acquiescence and repression to alienate Protestants without satisfying Catholics. What is important for this story is the simple fact of political destablization. Regarding the civil rights movement as the old Irish republicanism wolf in democratic sheep's clothing, working-class Protestants attacked civil rights marches and Catholic areas. Catholics hit back. The local police could not control the violence (and indeed added their own tuppence worth). The government had to ask for British troops to be sent in to Belfast and Londonderry to keep the sides apart. As the army was under central London control, this meant Stormont was both admitting it could not control the trouble and allowing London some direct input. Although initially pleased to be protected from loyalists, the Catholics came to see the troops as defenders of the unacceptable "Protestant state" and support for the IRA increased. By 1971 the "troubles" had well and truly begun. It was against this background that Paisley's popularity and influence, both religious and political, grew.

In 1971, Paisley and a number of unionists unhappy about the apparent unwillingness of the Unionist government to defend itself against the twin threats of resurgent Irish nationalism and a compromising British government formed the Democratic Unionist Party. Since then the DUP has come first to rival the Ulster Unionist Party in electoral support and finally to be accepted by the UUP as an equal partner in various campaigns against British government policy. Since he won a seat in the Westminster parliament in June 1970, Ian Paisley has become easily the most popular unionist politician. In the 1984 elections to the European Community parliament, nearly a quarter of a million people—a sixth of the whole electorate—voted for him.[8]

In its early days, the DUP drew heavily on the membership of the Free Presbyterian Church of Ulster (FPC), as Paisley's first congregation had become as it gradually picked up other congregations of dissident Irish Presbyterians. When Paisley launched his first major foray into electoral politics in 1969, of six candidates, three

TABLE 4.1

DENOMINATION OF DUP ACTIVISTS

	Total	%FPC
1973 Assembly	17	47
1975 Constitutional Convention	18	78
1976 Local councillors	31	65
1978 Local councillors	75	61
1982 Assembly	35	77
1985 Local council candidates	218	57

were FPC ministers and one was an FPC elder. The denominations of DUP activists at various points since then are shown in table 4.1. FPs are massively overrepresented. Only 1 percent of non-Roman Catholics are FPs, but of the almost four hundred members of the six different groups of DUP activists, an average of 64 percent are FPs.

When DUP activists are not Free Presbyterians, what are they? Table 4.2 describes the 218 candidates for the 1985 local government elections. The picture is clear. Almost all of those who are not FPs are members of other conservative evangelical denominations. The three main denominations—the Irish Presbyterian Church, the Church of Ireland, and the Methodists—are all underrepresented. As if the evangelicalism of the DUP were not sufficiently attested to by these figures, many of the Irish Presbyterians and Baptists signified their place on the evangelical wing of their churches by adding to their election literature that they were "evangelical," "involved in mission work," or some such reference.

As the second column in table 4.2 shows, most Ulster Protestants are not conservative evangelicals or fundamentalists. The success of the DUP suggests that the many nonevangelical supporters of the DUP like being represented by fundamentalists. Of course, this may have nothing to do with religion. Nonbelievers might support fundamentalists because they believe them to be dogmatic, doctrinaire, and most likely to maintain an extreme unionist position. However, nonfundamentalist unionists have had the opportunity to support secular right-wingers every bit as resolute as the DUP. Between 1969 and 1975, when the Unionist Party was tearing itself apart, there were a number of able politicians, many of whom had the advantage over Paisley of position in the party and in such fraternal organizations as the Orange Order and the Apprentice Boys of Derry, who strove for the right vote. The best known was William Craig who had been sacked as minister for home affairs by O'Neill in 1969 for constant attacks on government policy. Craig led the Ulster Loyalist Association and the Vanguard movement (which became a fully fledged party in 1974) and was strongly supported by the paramilitary Ulster Defence Association. Even before he lost favor for suggesting that unionists form a temporary pact with the Catholic Social and Democratic Labor Party, Craig and his supporters were losing support to Paisley's DUP.[9] When given the choice between secular right-wingers and religious right-wingers, many working-class *secular* voters have preferred the fundamentalists of the DUP.

TABLE 4.2

DENOMINATION OF (a) 1985 DUP LOCAL GOVERNMENT ELECTION
CANDIDATES AND (b) NON-ROMAN CATHOLIC POPULATION (in %)

	(a)	(b)
Irish Presbyterian	10.6	35.7
Church of Ireland	3.7	29.6
Methodist	3.2	6.2
Baptist	4.6	1.8
Free Presbyterian	57.3	1.0
Congregational	1.8	0.9
Elim Pentecostal	1.8	0.4
Reformed Presbyterian	0.9	0.3
Independent Methodist	1.4	0.1
Church of God	0.9	0.1
Other evangelical/not known/none	23.3	23.9

Why this should be the case is clear if one considers the ideological foundations for ethnic identity. Ulster unionism needs evangelical Protestantism in a way in which Irish nationalism does not need Catholicism.[10] Nationalism is a popular modern creed supported by movements all over the world. Since partition, there has been a state in the south to serve as an encouragement to northern nationalists. Nationalism is a strong and stable ideology. In contrast, unionism is now precarious. Ulster has never been "just like" the rest of the United Kingdom, but until the 1960s many unionists were able to think of themselves as just "British." The "troubles" called into question the Britishness of Ulster by making clear to all parties the extent to which it differed from Great Britain and by giving many (even within the British establishment) a chance to challenge Ulster's constitutional connection with Britain. Furthermore, the majority of people in Great Britain have shown little interest in saving Protestant Ulster from the Roman Catholic Irish Republic.

The pressure on unionists to assert and defend their claims to be British has forced them to be clear about their identity, and this in turn has exposed the gulf between them and the British. The Britain to which unionists are loyal is the assertive Britain of the imperial monarchy. In part this reflects nostalgia for the Victorian and Edwardian periods, when Belfast's heavy engineering economy was booming (the Titanic and its sister ship, the Olympic, were built in Belfast) and the sons of Ulster were sacrificing themselves in the thousands in the trenches of World War I France. In part it represents the conservative religious, moral, and political climate of Ulster. Some 70 percent of Ulster people go to church; the comparable figure for present-day Britain—where abortion and homosexuality are legal and divorce rampant—is approximately 12 percent.

With the object of Ulster's romantic desires clearly unenthusiastic about the marriage, and, on close inspection, somewhat undesirable, what can serve as the ideological basis for unionist identity? The only thing which has sufficient presence in the history of Ulster is evangelical Protestantism, which is also the credo that makes the

Catholic Republic objectionable. If one is looking for a good reason to be opposed
to a united Ireland, one finds oneself being pushed back to fundamentalism.

Conservative members of the British parliament are big farmers, successful entrepreneurs, and lawyers. Conservative voters are not. Many people vote not for those
who *are like* them but for those who represent and embody the things which *they like*.
Representatives are exemplars, not averages. Secular Protestants want to support
evangelical Protestants—and there are plenty in unionist politics outside the DUP—
not because they themselves are evangelicals but because they recognize that evangelicals, although they may be spoilsports with their Sabbatarianism and total abstinence, embody what it means to be a unionist and a Protestant. The stereotypes that
Protestants have of themselves and of Catholics depend on evangelicalism for their
premises. Protestants are diligent, industrious, and independent but loyal and self-
sacrificing (the enormous toll of Ulster volunteers in the British armies of World War
I is often mentioned) lovers of democracy. Catholics are none of these things. Protestants and Catholics are as they are because they have, respectively, the true and the
false religion. Because a united Ireland would be a Catholic Ireland, it threatens religious truth and the attendant social and civil virtues.

What Is to Be Done?

The main purpose of Ulster conservative Protestants, in religion and in politics, is to
preserve their identity. Part of the threat to identity—the liberalism and ecumenism
of the mainstream churches—is found in other settings such as America. In Ulster,
Paisley has behaved as American conservatives did earlier in this century and has led
a schism from the main Presbyterian church. The centralized nature of British government gives far less opportunity than does America for the formation of specifically
fundamentalist institutions of education, mass media, and the like, but Paisley has
done his best. Because the Catholic church insists on maintaining its own schools, the
state schools are often called "Protestant" but Paisleyites find them insufficiently so
and, encouraged by the American model, the Free Presbyterian Church by 1991 had
some ten independent "Christian" schools. It has its own Bible College for ministerial,
missionary, and education students. It produces periodicals and tape recordings, and
organizes a round of social activities that form a distinct subculture.

Conservative Protestants have campaigned against legislative changes which are
seen as eroding the distinctively "Protestant" atmosphere of Northern Ireland: the
liberalizing of laws on homosexuality, public house licensing hours, Sunday trading
laws, and the like.

But for Ulster fundamentalists, such sociomoral crusades take second place to the
more pressing concern of maintaining citizenship. In contrast to the constitutional
stability of America, the issue of sovereignty in Northern Ireland remains open.
Through the direct political action of forming a party, fighting (and winning) elections, and mobilizing popular support, Paisley and his supporters have sought to keep
the iron in the soul of Ulster unionism and to prevent any sellout. Generally these
campaigns have been confined to conventional democratic politics. Many Protestants
convicted of terrorist offenses have blamed their actions on Paisley (and other politi-

cians who supposedly encouraged them), but Paisley has never actively promoted freelance violence. On the contrary, he has often insisted that loyalist murderers do not deserve the name of "Protestant." However, he is not a pacifist; periodically he has tried to form civilian militias to be ready to fight to defend Ulster if the British ever withdraw. But he is a constitutionalist who believes that the state should maintain its monopoly of force but should justify that monopoly by acting more vigorously against nationalist terrorism.[11] If the state forfeits its monopoly (by, for example, giving Ulster to the Irish Republic), then Protestants should fight and Paisley will lead them. Hence, periodically he has encouraged people to prepare for doomsday but has steered clear of illegality.

How successful Paisley has been is difficult to judge. Since the British government closed down the Stormont parliament and took over the direct running of the province in the early 1970s, there has been little or no opportunity for local politicians to govern or even to press detailed policy agendas in legislation. British government is peculiarly authoritarian. The cabinet of the party with a clear majority in the House of Commons formulates legislation and "whips" its members to vote for it. The House of Lords has little power to change legislation, and members of both houses have almost no power to initiate legislation. Under the present system of direct rule from Westminster, the British government imposes its will on Ulster and, when the party in power has a majority of over one hundred, there is nothing the seventeen Ulster members of parliament can do about it.

Furthermore, by an accident of fate, local government in Northern Ireland offers fewer possibilities for politics than it does in the rest of the UK. Because there was a regional parliament at Stormont to give "local" representation, the architect of the reform of local government in the early 1960s removed many powers from borough and county councils. The introduction of direct rule from London was not, of course, imagined even as a remote possibility. The consequence is that there is a marked lack of opportunities for politics.

Only in the search for a stable future political system for Northern Ireland—the constitutional issue—do local politicians have influence. Unionists want to remain British; nationalists want to become Irish. These are irreconcilable and non-negotiable goals. As the British government will not accept anything which is acceptable to unionists (because it would be unacceptable to nationalists), the best unionists can do is to stall political innovation. In this, Paisley and his movement have been extremely successful. From 1963 to 1972, three Unionist Party prime ministers— O'Neill, Chichester-Clark, and Faulkner—tried to mollify Catholics without alienating Protestants. Paisley and his associates played a major part in making sure that Protestants did feel alienated and that the reform strategy failed. In that sense, Paisley can reasonably claim to have "seen off" three prime ministers. Paisleyites were also involved in the general strike which brought down the 1974 "power-sharing" government, a constitutional experiment in which the constitutional nationalist party, liberal unionists, and the very small cross-confessional Alliance Party formed an executive to which powers were devolved.

That the DUP exists, ready to recruit defectors, ensures that the Unionist Party will never return to the reformist strategies of the O'Neill period. The Free Presbyterian Church plays a similar role in maintaining religious orthodoxy, acting as a brake on any liberal or ecumenical tendencies the Irish Presbyterians or the Church of Ireland might develop. Paisley succeeded in Ulster religion and politics not by innovating but by representing what many Ulster Protestants believed. So long as he enjoys the trust of a large part of the Protestant population, he will continue to exercise a veto on political and religious innovation.

The New Christian Right in America

In explaining the rise and nature of the New Christian Right (NCR),[12] there are two important points. First, the culture of the core constituency of the NCR—Sun Belt fundamentalists—has been increasingly encroached upon since the end of World War II. On many matters of social and moral policy, geographical and cultural peripheries have become increasingly subject to the core of cosmopolitan America. The reach of government has massively increased: in 1976 there were seventy-seven federal regulatory bodies, fifty of them created since 1960.[13] The sheer size, the diversity of ethnic groupings, and the federal system of American government have long permitted regions considerable autonomy, but the recent trend is for polity and culture to become more centralized (the mass media, for example, is becoming more centralized and homogeneous in output) and for the center to become more liberal. So fundamentalists have found themselves harder pressed by a more permissive culture. Where once two-thirds of the states were willing to vote for the prohibition of alcohol, there has been open campaigning for the legalization of marijuana. Conservative sexual mores have been openly questioned and sometimes publicly flouted. Abortion was made legal. A more aggressively secularist interpretation of the constitutional doctrine of separation of church and state has meant that school prayer is now forbidden.

A more subtle threat has been posed by the increasing frequency of claims to rights as a member of some previously disadvantaged *group* (a notion that is anathema to fundamentalists with their individualist Arminianism). First blacks, then women, and then homosexuals have claimed that social arrangements should be changed to improve their position. And the state has seemed willing not only to accept such claims but to impose new social patterns on subcultures which had previously been permitted to go their own way. Since the 1960s the southern states have been under constant political, judicial, and legislative pressure to promote racial integration and equality. All of these changes have appeared as threats to the lifestyle and sociomoral values of conservative Protestants and hence also as threats to the religious beliefs which fundamentalists hold and which legitimate such sociomoral positions.

The more prescient knew that electing conservative and fundamentalist councilmen in Greenville, South Carolina, had little influence where the important decisions were increasingly being made: the federal and Supreme courts, the presidency, and Congress. They were willing to listen to people who argued that fundamentalists had to become involved politically if they were to maintain (or restore) the Christian culture which had made America great.

At the same time as some fundamentalists were becoming more politically concerned, a number of professional conservative political activists were coming to see fundamentalists as an important bloc in a new populist conservative grouping which would differ from the old eastern establishment conservatism in mobilizing people around social and moral issues as well as around the more traditional concerns of foreign policy, the welfare state, the economy, and the regulation of business. They persuaded a number of leading fundamentalists to become politically active.

The key figures in the mobilization of the "New Christian Right" were televangelists. James Robison of Dallas and Pat Robertson of "The 700 Club" and the Christian Broadcasting Network played a part, but the most influential and consistently involved figure was Jerry Falwell of Lynchburg, Virginia. Falwell mobilized interest at two levels. Nationally, he used the audience for his televised church service, his computer mailing lists of supporters, and other lists of known sociomoral conservatives to create a base from which to raise funds and produce the appearance of a large united movement. At the same time, Falwell and other fundamentalist leaders used their ministerial networks to influence other independent fundamentalist Baptist pastors, who in turn mobilized their congregations.[14]

Pressure Group Politics

Falwell's Moral Majority and similar organizations such as Religious Roundtable, Christian Voice, and American Coalition for Traditional Values raised money to campaign as pressure groups on a range of public policy issues (such as abortion, homosexuality, the teaching of evolution in schools, the threat of "secular humanism," minority rights legislation, and prayer in public school). The campaigns had two related purposes. The first was to mobilize conservative opinion so that legislators, judges, journalists, and educators would temper their liberalism (either out of genuine respect for the opinions of conservatives or out of fear of retribution). The second was to turn that opinion into electoral clout. Legislators at the state and congressional level who had a record of voting the "wrong way" found themselves the targets of well-funded negative campaigns. Funds were also spent on behalf of acceptable conservative candidates.

Unlike the Protestants of Ulster, whose precarious position has meant a long history of sustained political involvement, American fundamentalists have tended to "quietist" retreat from the world. A major NCR tactic was voter registration, which seems to have succeeded in 1980 and 1984, although it would only have been significant if liberals had not also registered a similar number of new voters, if the new conservative voters had all voted the same way, and if their involvement had been sustained.[15]

For a variety of reasons (not least, the value of incumbency) third parties have a history of failure in America. Even if the fundamentalists had been sufficiently numerous to seriously attempt forming a party, the activists knew that such an attempt was doomed. So the effort to displace liberal politicians and mobilize conservative voters was accompanied by infiltration of the Republican Party at the local level.

To put it bluntly, none of this had any great lasting effect. Very few NCR sup-

porters were elected to national office, some of the few whose success was claimed by
the NCR repudiated that support, and a number of the successes (Senator Jeremiah
Denton, for example) failed to get reelected. Not surprisingly, given that only four or
five senators were ever "movement" conservatives and that the Democrats controlled
the House of Representatives, the NCR had no legislative success at the congressional
level. Although he made supporting noises, President Reagan conspicuously refused
to use his influence to mobilize congressional votes for NCR-promoted bills on
school prayer and abortion.[16] The NCR had some legislative success at the state level
in those states which had always had sizable fundamentalist populations, but even
these victories were often hollow. As in the case discussed below of the Arkansas
creation science bill, many NCR issues touched on basic constitutional rights and
thus could be challenged through the federal courts. The centripetal tendency of the
court system then allowed the more liberal and universalistic values of the cosmopolitan middle classes to overrule the particularisms of the NCR.[17]

If electoral and legislative politics failed to produce any major changes, were there
more subtle effects? Even the much vaunted shift to the right in the political agenda
which the NCR was supposed to have effected turned out to be candy floss. Measured
studies of attitude surveys during the Reagan era showed that the turn to the right
on defense and economic policy was not accompanied by any significant shift to the
right on sociomoral issues.[18] It might also be supposed that there is (or will be) a
long-term NCR effect through the training of large numbers of evangelicals and fundamentalists for conventional party politics. There is no doubt that many young conservative Protestants acquired an interest and some expertise in politics through NCR
involvement, but this would only be significant if the movement had not provoked a
similar and matching revival of interest among liberals and if it were the case that the
relative absence of religious or sociomoral concerns from the central interests of the
Republican Party was an *accident*, a condition to be rectified simply by the presence
of fundamentalists. It does not require much thought to realize that the relative neutrality of the Republican Party on sociomoral issues and its unwillingness to become
identified with a particular religious position is not an accident but a sensible response
to the problems of maximizing voter support in a culturally plural society.

Those NCR activists who remained most aggressively fundamentalist failed to get
anywhere. Those who got anywhere did so by compromising and becoming largely
indistinguishable from secular conservatives. Instead of following the eight years of
vacuous rhetoric of Reagan with the real support of Pat Robertson, the NCR got as
president George Bush, an old-fashioned eastern monied conservative.

The Courts

A minor but significant NCR tactic was the initiation of lawsuits (see chap. 3 of the
current volume). Although "unelected" judges were frequently a focus for conservatives' ire, having been largely responsible for many of the changes they most resented,
the NCR was willing to use the same avenues for change. When a number of courts
made it clear that the price to be paid for religious freedom was that the public arena
had to be free of religion, fundamentalists responded by trying to have "secular hu-

manism" (a catch-all label to cover anything which did not overtly recognize the supremacy of Christianity) judged to be a religion so that it, too, could be banned from schools.[19]

The presentation of Christianity and secular humanism as two "matching" religions had some initial success, but it was exposed as sleight of hand when it came to detailed discussion of the issues. In a major case in Alabama, Judge Brevard Hand found for Christian plaintiffs who wanted a range of textbooks banned for unconstitutionally promoting secular humanism, but the judgment was overturned by the Eleventh Circuit Court of Appeals, which ordered Hand to dismiss the case. The finality of the ruling was accepted by the National Legal Foundation, a right-wing pressure group, when it decided not to appeal the case to the Supreme Court.[20]

Fundamentalists in a Modern Democracy

The problem for the NCR is that fundamentalists are only a small minority of the American people. To have any national effect and to be able to claim national legitimacy, they have to work in alliance with conservative Catholics, Jews, black Protestants, Mormons, and secular conservatives. They have also to accept the rhetoric of the separation of church and state so that their crusades are promoted not on the basis of the superiority of fundamentalist religious beliefs and values but on the basis of a number of secular motifs. The limitation on this tactic is that their claims are then judged on *secular* criteria.

The Arkansas "equal time" bill is a good example. In the early 1970s, fundamentalists shifted the defense of the Genesis account of Creation from saying "we believe it because the Bible says so" to exploiting differences between evolutionary models to argue that creation *science* (as it was now called) fitted the facts as well as evolution. The Arkansas state legislature passed a bill to force schools which taught evolution to give "equal time" to the biblical creation account. The American Civil Liberties Union took the case to the courts, arguing that creationism was a religious belief, not a science, and that the bill meant that schools would be promoting a particular religion. The creationists had to give good reason why anyone who did not accept the Bible should believe in "special creation"; their presentation of such a case was dire. The judge decided for the ACLU.[21]

It is ironic, given fundamentalist dislike for the notion of group rights, that the NCR was most successful when it appealed to "fairness" and presented itself as a discriminated-against minority. Such very limited progress as was made was the result of appealing to the *secular* value of fairness rather than to theological rectitude. Attempts to go beyond a demand for a little more social space for their own culture to claiming some sort of hegemony were firmly opposed.

The problem was not only one of external opposition to fundamentalist aspirations. There was also an internal problem of motivation. The alliance with non-fundamentalist conservatives was precarious. The NCR asked fundamentalists to get involved in politics to defend their religiously inspired culture and then asked that, in order to do politics well, they leave behind their religion. On Sunday they believed

Catholics were not "saved"; on Monday they had to work with Catholics in defense of their "shared Judeo-Christian" heritage. But placing religion and politics in separate compartments governed by different criteria is exactly the feature of modern religion which they reject. My extensive interviewing in South Carolina and Virginia made it clear to me that fundamentalists cannot be pragmatic without conceding that which defines them and are themselves extremely uncertain, even troubled, by the issue. And even if they could abandon their anti-Semitism, racism, and anti-Catholicism, Catholics, blacks, and Jews had long enough memories to be suspicious. Additionally, there has always been an organizational block on Catholic participation in pressure groups: the Catholic church prefers its campaigning to be directed through church-controlled agencies.

Although organizations such as Moral Majority Inc. and the American Coalition for Traditional Values could always find a few black, Catholic, or Jewish figures to appear on their letterheads and platforms, such alliances were not successfully built at local levels, where NCR organizations remained primarily fundamentalist.

Pat Robertson for President?

Against those who saw Jerry Falwell's announced retirement from politics in November 1987 as the end of the NCR, some activists and some commentators construed the presidential campaign of Pat Robertson, presenter of "The 700 Club" and head of the Christian Broadcasting Network, as a major step forward for the NCR. It certainly represented an important increase in aspirations and inadvertently provided a mass of opinion poll data from which a number of general conclusions about the strength of the NCR can be drawn. These can only be sketched here but are discussed in detail elsewhere.[22]

To give the most sweeping characterization of Robertson's attempt at the highest political office, a well-organized and well-funded campaign backfired. The more people considered the issues raised by such a candidacy, the more anti-Robertson feeling outstripped pro-Robertson sentiment. Even those people who should have been most sympathetic were not mobilized. Contrary to the unwise predictions of some social scientists,[23] many fundamentalists were unhappy with such overt mixing of religion and politics. In one poll, even self-identified conservative Protestants said that Robertson's status as a former clergyman made them less rather than more likely to support him (by a margin of 42 to 25 percent). Many preferred a secular politician who had some of the "right" positions to a born-again televangelist who had them all (in a poll which was confirmed by the voting patterns in the southern states' primaries, southern fundamentalists and evangelicals divided 44 percent for George Bush, 30 percent for Bob Dole, and only 14 percent for Robertson).

General public sympathy for some NCR values did not translate into widespread support for NCR policies or politicians. Much of the mistake made in predicting the likely impact of the NCR came from misunderstanding survey data and the relation between attitudes and actions. An oft-cited indicator of likely NCR support is a study by John Simpson of 1977 NORC General Social Survey data.[24] Simpson claimed the data showed 30 percent of the public accepting the Moral Majority platform in its entirety and a further 42 percent being ideological fellow travelers. These claims were made on the basis of highly contestable assumptions about which responses to which questions represented a "Moral Majority" position. In an excellent reexamination of the same data, Sigelmann and Presser plausibly argue that the survey material gives no warrant for claiming widespread sympathy for the NCR platform.[25] Furthermore, as I have argued at length elsewhere,[26] even where there is a general sympathy for conservative sociomoral positions, one cannot assume that such sympathy translates into shared commitment to the particular *policies* of the NCR. It is one thing to be "against abortion"; it is quite another to actively support this or that measure to outlaw or severely limit abortion.

Nor can one assume that even shared policy commitments translate into a powerful sociopolitical movement; fundamentalists have other interests which divide them. Not all sociomoral conservatives place those interests at the top of their agendas, and anyway they are unlikely to be mobilized around those concerns unless the political circumstances allow or encourage choices on those issues. The main problem for the NCR has been its inability to keep its concerns to the forefront in political arguments.

Finally, we need to remember that the NCR has not had the field to itself. A large part of its very limited success was the result of surprise. Liberals took their political and cultural domination for granted and had forgotten that their values required active organized defense. Once natural scientists such as Stephen Jay Gould realized that they had to defend their evolutionist thinking, they did so extremely convincingly. I will give just two very different examples of successful liberal counterattack. Fundamentalists had exerted considerable influence over textbook content because of the legal structure of the Texas school book review procedure. Only books that had been approved by a committee could be bought from state funds. The review procedure permitted members of the public to criticize books, and for many years fundamentalists had dominated these hearings. It did not permit lay people to *defend* books against their critics. Rather than face the possibility of criticism and rejection, many publishers had taken to censoring their textbook offerings. People for the American Way successfully campaigned to have the procedure changed so that liberal lay groups could defend those works attacked for secular humanism, and fundamentalist influence was drastically reduced.

People for the American Way were also successful in countering Pat Robertson's attempts to shed his evangelist past. Like all good politicians, Robertson presented different faces to different audiences. To his religious following he continued to offer a born-again Christian view of political events; to the general public he presented himself as a conservative businessman whose business interests just happened to include running a Christian broadcasting network. People for the American Way prepared a video compilation of Robertson's utterances as an evangelist and circulated it free to hundreds of television stations so that Robertson's own publicity material was balanced by presentations of a self which he preferred to downplay.

Far more could be said. In this brief discussion I have argued that the NCR, although interesting, was not a particularly successful movement and that its failure was predictable from an examination of its own characteristics and from the characteristics of modern democratic societies.

Conclusion

Without wishing to imply support for grand evolutionary models of social development, I want to suggest that the role of religion in the Ulster conflict is in the historical sense "older" than what we see with the NCR in America and is of a type common in the early days of the formation of nation-states and the development of liberal democracies. Fundamentalism is important in Ulster because religion is central to ethnic identity, there is considerable ethnic conflict, and the basic political issues of national sovereignty and the alignment of ethnic and national boundaries have not been settled (conditions we see in large parts of the Third World and increasingly in the Second World as the communist hegemony collapses). In such circumstances the continuing conflict amplifies the importance of religion. That the other party to the conflicts is a Catholic people (and of a very conservative Catholicism) makes orthodoxy or "fundamentalism" appealing to Ulster Protestants.

In contrast, America is a stable democracy whose national boundaries are secure. In a religiously pluralistic democracy, religious particularisms have to be confined to the private world of the family and the home (Ulster shows what happens when this is not done). The only "religious" values which can be allowed in the public square are the most general and benign banalities which everyone can endorse. The federal and decentralized nature of American public administration allows subcultures a degree of autonomy unusual in Europe. This gave fundamentalists the platform from which to launch an attempt to turn America back to Christ, but the attempt failed, as it was bound to.

Notes

1. Although I accept the usefulness of the general characterization of fundamentalism given in the essays in volume 1 of this series, *Fundamentalisms Observed,* and its applicability to Paisleyism, there are considerable differences between the Ulster Protestant tradition of Calvinist Presbyterianism and North American fundamentalism. In addition to the point about covenants (see n. 3), the movements differ in that Ulster Protestantism is less Arminian, very unlikely to be Pentecostal, and is far less committed to Scofield premillennialism than American fundamentalism. See Martin E. Marty and

R. Scott Appleby, eds., *Fundamentalisms Observed* (Chicago: University of Chicago Press, 1991).

2. For good general accounts of the background to the Ulster "troubles," see P. Arthur and K. Jeffrey, *Northern Ireland since 1968* (Oxford, 1988), D. Harkness, *Northern Ireland since 1920* (Dublin, 1983), and A. J. Q. Stewart, *The Narrow Ground* (Belfast, 1988).

3. On the influence of Calvinism (especially the role of the idea of a "covenant" between God and his chosen people) on Protestant politics and parallels with South

Africa, see R. Wallis and Steve Bruce, *Sociological Theory, Religion and Collective Action* (Belfast, 1986), chap. 10.

4. Steve Bruce, *A House Divided: Protestantism, Schism and Secularization* (London, 1990). See also P. L. Berger, *The Social Reality of Religion* (Harmondworth, Middlesex, 1973), and B. R. Wilson, *Religion in Sociological Perspective* (Oxford, 1982).

5. On the influence of the Catholic church in the Republic of Ireland, see J. H. Whyte, *Church and State in Modern Ireland, 1923–1979* (Dublin, 1980), and T. Inglis, *Moral Monopoly* (Dublin, 1986).

6. What follows is argued at length in Steve Bruce, *God Save Ulster! The Religion and Politics of Paisleyism* (Oxford, 1986), and R. Wallis, Steve Bruce, and D. Taylor, *No Surrender! Paisley and the Politics of Ethnic Identity in Northern Ireland* (Belfast, 1986).

7. J. F. Harbison, *The Ulster Unionist Party* (Belfast, 1973).

8. Details of elections between 1968 and 1988 can be found in W. D. Flackes and S. Elliott, *Northern Ireland: A Political Directory, 1968–88* (Belfast, 1989).

9. Unlike Great Britain, which uses a "winner takes all," first-past-the-post system, elections in Northern Ireland use a single transferable vote system of proportional representation in order to allow the Catholic minority a voice they would otherwise be denied. This has the advantage that one can study detailed relationships between constituencies by examining the flows of second and third preference votes. Source details for such data are given in the appendix to Bruce, *God Save Ulster!*

10. My interpretation of Paisley's success and of unionism generally is challenged by A. Aughey, "Recent Interpretations of Unionism," *Political Quarterly* 61, no. 2 (1990): 188–99.

11. Steve Bruce, "Protestantism and Terrorism in Northern Ireland," in A. O'Day and Y. Alexander, eds., *Ireland's Terrorist Trauma* (London, 1989), pp. 13–33.

12. What follows is a very brief outline of parts of Steve Bruce, *The Rise and Fall of the New Christian Right: Conservative Protestant Politics in America, 1978–88* (Oxford, 1988).

See also R. Liebman and R. Wuthnow, eds., *The New Christian Right* (New York, 1983), and G. Peele, *Revival and Reaction: The Right in Contemporary America* (Oxford, 1984).

13. M. Janovitz, *The Last Half-Century: Societal Change and Politics in America* (Chicago, 1978), p. 368.

14. R. Liebman, "Mobilizing the Moral Majority," in Liebman and Wuthnow, eds., *The New Christian Right,* pp. 50–74.

15. C. Smidt, "Born Again Politics: The Political Behavior of Evangelical Christians in the South and the Non-South," in T. A. Baker, R. P. Steed, and L. W. Moreland, eds., *Religion and Politics in the South: Mass and Elite Perspectives* (New York, 1983), pp. 27–56.

16. Bruce, *The Rise and Fall of the New Christian Right,* pp. 133–39.

17. On the role of the courts in NCR-related matters, see R. A. Alley, *The Supreme Court on Church and State* (New York, 1988), and T. Robbins and R. Robertson, *Church-State Relations: Tensions and Transitions* (New Brunswick, 1987).

18. See, for example, T. Ferguson and J. Rogers, "The Myth of America's Turn to the Right," *The Atlantic,* May 1988, pp. 43–53.

19. *Birmingham Alabama News,* 30 November 1987.

20. For a detailed account of the Arkansas creation science trial, see Langdon Gilkey, *Creationism on Trial: Evolution and God at Little Rock* (Minneapolis, 1985).

21. The lessons of the Robertson campaign and the demise of the NCR are examined in detail in Steve Bruce, *Pray TV: Televangelism in America* (London, 1990).

22. For an embarrassingly mistaken assessment of the potential of the NCR and Pat Robertson's campaign, see Jeffrey K. Hadden and Anson Shupe, *Televangelism: Power and Politics on God's Frontier* (New York, 1988). What is argued here is presented in much greater detail in chaps. 8 and 9 of Bruce, *Pray TV.*

23. J. Simpson, "Moral Issues and Status Politics," pp. 187–205, in Liebman and Wuthnow, eds., *The New Christian Right.*

24. L. Sigelman and S. Presser, "Measuring Public Support for the New Christian Right: The Perils of Point Estimation," *Public Opinion Quarterly* 52 (1988): 325–37.

25. Bruce, *Pray TV,* chap. 9.

26. A lengthy sociological explanation of the difficulties of fundamentalist politics is presented in Steve Bruce, "Modernity and Fundamentalism: The New Christian Right in America," *British Journal of Sociology* 41 (1990): 477–96.

Jewish Fundamentalism and the Israeli Polity

Charles S. Liebman

The effort to understand Jewish fundamentalism and its impact on Israeli society is fraught with challenges.[1] Not the least is defining the subject in a manner which is both methodologically rigorous and politically relevant. Fundamentalist beliefs and aspirations are not the same as the beliefs and aspirations of other religiously serious people, but they aren't always distinguishable from them either. Moreover, religious beliefs and aspirations are sometimes hard to disentangle from national and ethnic beliefs and aspirations.

Israeli society has been profoundly influenced by Jewish religious symbols and ideas, especially since 1967, independently of the growth of Jewish religious fundamentalism.[2] In addition, Judaism, in Israel, has been increasingly interpreted in nationalistic and ethnically chauvinistic terms. This development has been influenced by the growth of religious fundamentalism but is not entirely accounted for by that growth. That is the subject of another study.[3] This essay is concerned with the direct impact of religious fundamentalism on the Israeli political system. Its primary purpose is to describe the demands which fundamentalist spokesmen have raised and the manner in which the nonfundamentalist sector has responded to these demands. What should be noted, however, is that social and cultural changes in the last twenty-five years within the secular public in general, but among the secular nationalists in particular, have generated a climate of sympathy for religion and a legitimacy to the airing of fundamentalist ideas which did not exist in the past.

The Subjects of This Study

According to most estimates, somewhat fewer than 20 percent of Israeli Jews define themselves as religious (*dati*). The last few years have seen the rise of fundamentalist or fundamentalistlike tendencies among them. These tendencies come from two directions. One tendency is the increased influence of the *haredim* (sg.: *haredi;* sometimes called ultra-Orthodox). Haredim look to the religious tradition as the exclusive source of legitimacy and are at least nominally hostile to Zionism, which they view as an ideology that conceives of the Jews as a people defined by a national, rather than a religious, essence and that aspires to the normalization of Jewish life.[4] (About one-third of Israel's religious population could be described as haredi, but in the absence of reliable surveys—haredim generally resist being surveyed—and precise definitions, this must remain a rough estimate.) The other strand of fundamentalism is associated in the public mind with Gush Emunim.[5] Gush Emunim was organized in 1974 to further Jewish settlement in the West Bank and Gaza Strip, areas that Israel occupied following the June 1967 war. Gush Emunim is led by religious Jews who hold diverse opinions on many religious matters but who share the conviction that the areas Israel occupied as a result of the 1967 war must be settled by Jews and must become an integral part of the State of Israel. This view has been associated with a theological position that not all Gush Emunim activists share—the position that we are living in a messianic age, i.e., a period of imminent Redemption; that the settlement of the occupied territories by Jews is a religious mandate, itself a stage in the coming Redemption; and that God will not forsake the State of Israel if it develops policies in accordance with these beliefs. We will use the term "Gush Emunim" as a shorthand label for this theological position because that is the way it is used in the media. In fact, it is more accurately ascribed to the theological disciples of the late Rabbi Zvi Yehuda Kook who were the founders of and continue to dominate the leadership of Gush Emunim but are a minority among its supporters.

Within these two strands of fundamentalism, the haredi and Gush Emunim, we can identify a variety of individuals and groups and a range of opinions.[6] If we focus on the more extreme elements in each strand—the most haredi, the most faithful to the tradition, the most vigorous in opposition to any innovation on the one hand and the most messianic and ultranationalist on the other—then we will find that the two strands have little in common. The most extreme haredim are hostile to the State of Israel. Their antagonism to any suggestion of Jewish nationalism has led a handful of them to favor dismantling the Jewish state. They constitute a tiny minority of haredim, but they fall within the camp of haredi fundamentalism. Even among less extreme haredim, those who define themselves as loyal citizens of Israel, there is a tradition of political passivity with respect to non-Jews, an anxiety about antagonizing the nations of the world, and a desire to find a peaceful accommodation with the Arabs, even if it requires surrendering territory which Israel has held since 1967.[7]

At the other extreme, among many of the most extreme ultranationalist messianists, opposition to any surrender of territory—and support for retaining the Greater Land of Israel under Jewish sovereignty and settling the length and breadth of the land with Jewish settlers—supersedes every other religious obligation. The belief of a few of them in the imminent coming of the Messiah encourages activity of the most extreme form. "I am not afraid of any death penalty, because the messiah will arrive shortly," proclaims Rafi Solomon, charged with the attempted random murder of two

Arabs.[8] Nationalism to them "is the highest form of religion."[9] Among individuals and groups at the extreme end of the ultranationalist continuum, we find those who are prepared to compromise on virtually every other religiopolitical demand. To further their cause they not only have formed alliances with secular Jewish nationalists but have justified this alliance as the fulfillment of a positive religious commandment. Religious Jews who are active in ultranationalist nonreligious parties—and they include a number of prominent rabbis—tend to be most moderate in raising "religious" (as opposed to "nationalist") demands on the Israeli polity. Indeed, these demands never exceed what the secular members of these parties have been willing to concede.

One could, therefore, make a rather convincing argument for distinguishing between two Israeli Jewish fundamentalistlike strands and arguing that they have virtually nothing in common with one another at the political level.

The argument I offer here is a different one. The emergence of militant fundamentalistlike groups on the Israeli scene in the last few decades needs to be assessed in terms of not only what the extremists and ideological purists have asserted but also how their emergence has effected that Israeli Jewish public which defines itself as dati. If Israeli-Jewish fundamentalism is treated in this way, one can point to the emergence of tendencies which integrate both fundamentalist strands, modifying and moderating them in the process. Viewed from this perspective one can discuss the political impact of Israeli-Jewish fundamentalism without necessarily distinguishing one type of fundamentalism from another.

There is justification for this approach in the growing usage of a label that was invented as a derogatory term less than ten years ago—*haredi-leumi* (a nationalist haredi). To the best of my knowledge, the term was first used by a moderate, anti-haredi leader of the religious-Zionist youth movement, Bnei Akiva. He was very concerned with the growth of haredi tendencies within his movement and unhappy, though perhaps less distressed, about the emergence of ultranationalist tendencies as well. The term *haredi-leumi* was certainly intended as a term of opprobrium. The term is now borne with pride by a growing number of religious schools, by a rapidly growing religious youth movement, Ezra, and by an increasing number of religious Jews who, according to a poll conducted by the religious weekly *Erev Shabbat*, decline to identify themselves as either haredi or religious-Zionist but prefer to be called haredi-leumi.

No less persuasive are developments among religious parties in Israel. In the elections to the 120-member Knesset in November 1988, the religious parties won 18 seats. These 18 seats were distributed as follows:

Shas 6
Agudat Israel 5
National Religious Party (NRP) 5
Degel Ha Torah 2

Agudat Israel and Degel Ha Torah are acknowledged haredi parties. Their constituents are predominantly Ashkenazic, that is, of European or American (primarily East European) descent. Shas is identified by the media as a haredi party and its leaders label themselves haredi[10] although, in this case, the label can be misleading.

Shas's constituents are overwhelmingly Sephardic, that is, of Asian or African (primarily North African) descent. Most Shas voters are not haredi but leaders of all three parties, Agudat Israel, Degel Ha Torah, and Shas are—at least nominally—anti-Zionist when the term "Zionism" is used in an ideological sense. Together, they won thirteen seats in 1988. The two largest parties of the three—Shas and Agudat Israel—appeared so much closer to the leading secular nationalist party of the right (Likud) than to the leading party of the more dovish left (Labor) that most observers dismissed the possibility that these religious parties would join a government led by Labor rather than Likud. (But they were proven wrong in 1992 when Yitzhak Rabin and the Labor Party succeeded in bringing Shas into a governing coalition.)

Leaders of Shas and Agudat Israel have been inconsistent on the issue of Israeli withdrawal from the West Bank and Gaza. Shas's premier religious leader reversed himself and adopted a dovish position in the early 1990s, but this came over the objections of his party's supporters, who constrained his activity in the political arena. Furthermore, what Shas lacks in territorial aggressiveness, it balances by ethnic xenophobia. Its television campaign in 1988 was critical of the Israeli government for not adopting harsher measures in the suppression of the Intifada. Agudat Israel's leaders are generally hawkish.[11] Degel Ha Torah, the smallest of the haredi parties, does espouse a dovish position. But as with the religious leadership of Shas, this position does not stem from an interest in the Palestinians or any belief in the legitimacy of their rights to the Land of Israel or for that matter out of any concern with the abuse of human rights that has accompanied Jewish rule over a recalcitrant national minority. The dovish position stems from the fear of antagonizing the non-Jewish world, the United States in particular, and from the possible outbreak of bloody warfare, which would result in the loss of Jewish lives. Those fundamentalists who object to surrendering territory, be they haredim or ultranationalists, do so primarily on the basis of religious salience. To the fundamentalists who have adopted dovish positions, such as the religious leaders of Shas and Degel Ha Torah, surrendering territory is an issue of secondary concern.

In the 1988 election the Likud won forty Knesset seats and Labor thirty-nine. Each of these two large parties then turned to the smaller parties in the hope of forming a governing alliance with some of them (i.e., control of at least sixty-one seats in the Knesset) and without the participation of the other major party. Shas won six seats compared to four in the previous election. Its leaders were tempted by generous promises from the Labor party with regard to religious legislation, especially promises of public funds and political appointments. However, demonstrations by Shas's own supporters and a reminder that the party leadership had explicitly promised, during the campaign, that it would not join with Labor rather than the Likud restrained the party leaders from taking this step.

The next largest haredi party, Agudat Israel, increased the number of its seats from two to five. Agudat Israel received support from two important groups whose religiously based opposition to any Israeli withdrawal from the occupied territories equals that of Gush Emunim. These two groups do not view the State of Israel in the same messianic and apocalyptic terms as does Gush Emunim, nor do they attribute the same metaphysical significance to events which began a century ago when nonreligious settlers initiated the present Zionist settlement of the land. But they are no less adamant about the religious imperative of maintaining Jewish sovereignty over the Territories.

The growth of support for haredi parties was an indication of their ability to attract voters from non-haredi segments of the population. This would have been unlikely had they not adopted a de facto nationalistic orientation and muted their opposition to Zionism.[12]

At the religious-Zionist end of the continuum, the National Religious Party (NRP) and its constituents—who until the 1970s were characterized by religious moderation, by an accommodationist rather than a rejectionist orientation toward modernity and secular culture—show increasing signs of rejecting modernity and adopting a rather reactionary interpretation of the religious tradition. This is evident in the increased allocation of school time to the study of sacred texts in religious-Zionist schools,[13] in an increasing insistence upon separating the sexes in institutions identified with religious Zionism, and in the more stringent standards of religious observance to which many religious-Zionists now adhere.[14] There are moderate elements in the NRP, but its foreign political platform has been increasingly radicalized and has come to resemble that of the Likud and even of secular parties to the right of the Likud. Its position on other, though not all, matters increasingly resembles that of the haredim. The counterpart to the nationalization of the haredim is, in some sense, haredization of the religious-Zionists. But this development has been accompanied by the toning down of messianic expectations. Thus, in 1989 a leading figure in circles which heretofore spoke of the imminent Redemption wrote that

> We don't know how much time will pass until we arrive completely at a state of rest and security. Perhaps many generations. "But I believe with full faith in the coming of the messiah, and even though he tarries," despite all the delays, "with all this," despite all the crises—"I await him each day that he may come."[15]

The author invokes, within his quotation marks, a traditional article of faith. It reminds the reader that belief in the coming of the Messiah is indeed basic to the tradition. But this very reminder tempers expectations for his immediate coming. Nothing is quite so religiously incendiary, or raises as many historically based suspicions of heresy among haredim, as the fear of "false messianism." But Jews always believed that the Messiah would come, "even though he tarries." The admission that "he tarries" integrates the writer's theology into that of traditional Judaism.

Statements by attempted murderer Rafi Solomon, cited above, and by the religio-nationalist "underground" movement uncovered in 1984[16] generated a counter reaction among religious-Zionist fundamentalists. It led them to moderate their messianic, though not their nationalist, doctrine. Growing numbers of Jews may continue to espouse acts of violence, and if Jewish-Arab relations continue to deteriorate we will find an escalation of terror and counterterror. However, these activities are no longer, for the most part, legitimated in theological terms.

These developments justify a conclusion that the growth of Jewish fundamentalism can be treated as a phenomenon that cuts across past differences between its Zionist and anti-Zionist strands. Elsewhere I have defined the spirit that is increasingly dominant in Israeli religious circles as an orientation toward ethnic particularism which includes suspicion of and hostility toward non-Jews, cultural isolationism including a suspicion of universalist moralist values, and, as already indicated, territorial irredentism.[17] We would expect these general orientations, which are admittedly more pronounced among some groups than among others, to find political expression in demands of the fundamentalistically oriented religious population. But before we turn to that subject, it is important to grasp the significance of the approach being urged here. According to this approach, the impact of Jewish fundamentalism on Israeli public policy is mediated by the larger religious public and the religious parties in particular. The religious public has certainly been influenced by the fundamentalistlike orientations of the haredim and Gush Emunim, but it has also moderated these tendencies and reformulated them in terms that are more acceptable to the general society. The National Religious Party has adopted much of the nationalist-political vision of Gush Emunim, (i.e., continued Jewish sovereignty over the Greater Land of Israel) but neutralized its radical religious (i.e., messianic) message. Opposition to any surrender of territory tends to be phrased in terms of Israeli security as much as in terms of Divine promises—and the relationship between Jewish settlement in the West Bank or Jewish sovereignty over the Greater Land of Israel and the imminent Redemption (i.e., the messianic vision of Gush Emunim) is generally absent. In the case of the haredim, anti-Zionism is muted and demands for expanding religious legislation are surrendered at the bargaining table without much resistance. Let us see how this has affected Israeli society at large.

Religious Demands on the Israeli Polity

One could make the case that the religio-nationalist demands of Gush Emunim and its supporters have successfully influenced Israeli society independently of the religious parties and even, perhaps, of the religious public.[18] Gush Emunim spearheaded the settlement of the occupied territories. In 1990 fewer than 20 percent of the estimated eighty thousand Jewish settlers in Judea, Samaria, and Gaza were thought to be active supporters of Gush Emunim (the political group, not the even smaller band of theological messianists), but its sympathizers dominated the local and regional councils in the Territories as well as its cultural life. In 1989, Gush Emunim enjoyed the deference of a group of thirty-one Knesset members calling itself the Land of Israel Lobby. That lobby is composed of members of right-wing as well as religious parties. At this writing (late 1991) it remains the spearhead of opposition to any Israeli concessions to the Palestinians. Hence, it might be argued that, in at least one area, the Jewish fundamentalists have achieved a great victory and have had a major impact on the Israeli political system independently of the religious parties.

But one can view the success of the religio-nationalist fundamentalists in this area in a different light. It is becoming increasingly difficult to distinguish the program of

Gush Emunim from the program of secular ultranationalists. As noted above, Gush Emunim itself resorts less frequently to religious rhetoric. From the very outset, its success depended on the sympathy and cooperation of nonreligious Jews. These secularists were not influenced by Gush Emunim's religious program or religious vision. Although they were impressed by the zeal and self-sacrifice of Gush Emunim members, what was most important was the coincidence of their goals and those of the religious nationalists. This is increasingly true in the 1990s. The intifada has led to rising Jewish-Arab tensions, and these, in turn, have strengthened the sense of many Israelis, especially of the ultranationalists, that any concession to the Arabs is dangerous, since their ultimate goal is the destruction of the Jews. In addition, the rise in tensions has triggered ethnic loyalties and xenophobic tendencies among many Jews that lead them to support any program which is anti-Arab. All of this leads to a conclusion that Gush Emunim has not succeeded in imposing a fundamentalist program on the Israeli political system but instead has succeeded through a coincidence between its objectives and those of nonreligious nationalists. Furthermore, the religionationalist fundamentalists have significantly modified their own religious message.

Rather than resolving whether Gush Emunim's success should or should not be treated as the success of religious fundamentalism, the remainder of this paper is devoted to an analysis of demands raised by fundamentalists which fall quite clearly into the category of religious demands at the domestic level, demands which set them apart from the remainder of the Jewish population.

Peculiarly enough, one demand that is not heard from the religious parties is for rule by Jewish law. All the religious parties pay lip service to this as an ultimate goal. A state ruled in accordance with Jewish law constitutes, to borrow a notion of Ann Mayer, a symbol and a focus of emotional commitment,[19] but it is not at all clear what "Jewish law" means. In fact, as critics have pointed out, in the unlikely event that the religious parties ever obtained enough votes to impose Jewish law upon the state, they would have trouble interpreting its consequences for the conduct of the state. Whereas religious leaders often proclaim that the Torah covers all aspects of life and, therefore, is suitable to serve as the law of the land, in practice, the application of Jewish law to a modern state would require so extensive an interpretive enterprise and so many changes that—with minor exceptions among ultranationalists—rabbinical leaders have been hesitant to undertake the groundwork necessary to transform their vision into a series of specific policies.[20]

As we noted, somewhat fewer than 20 percent of Israeli Jews define themselves as dati. The majority of Israeli Jews are not "religious" in belief or behavior. Many, probably most, of them harbor a feeling of sympathy for the religious tradition. Indeed, when asked about their religious identification between 35 and 40 percent prefer to define themselves as "traditional" rather than "secular." Many are distressed, though not to the point of doing much about it, by the increased ignorance of and alienation from religious rite and custom they find among their own children. But even this general mood is often accompanied by anticlerical feeling. Under the circumstances, religious leaders are reluctant to demand the imposition of Jewish law, even if they might hope for such an eventuality. What they have called for, in more outspoken terms, is the maintenance of what is called a "Jewish street," i.e., the conduct of public life in accordance with Jewish law. In fact, as we shall see, they have been more anxious to maintain victories they have already secured than to expand the scope of religious law.

It is far easier for many nonreligious Jews, especially political leaders anxious to form an alliance with religious parties, to acquiesce in demands of that sort—in part because they may be personally sympathetic to them and in part because such demands are not perceived as an infringement of freedom or as religious coercion. Yielding to them, in other words, requires no basic sacrifice of principle on the part of secular leaders. Political conflict over issues of religion and state in Israel is, in many respects, a conflict over what is public and what is private. What do religious parties and the religious public consider basic to maintaining the image of Israeli public life as Jewish, and what does the nonreligious public consider basic to the private rights of an individual?

It is remarkable how little all this has changed despite the new fundamentalist spirit which has penetrated the religious public. Part of the reason rests on the importance which some of the religious parties now place on their "nationalist" agenda—an agenda which by their definition is, of course, "religious." Nevertheless, they are sufficiently sensitive to the distinction between "national" and "religious" in the eyes of the secular public to avoid jeopardizing their "nationalist" agenda by emphasis on their "religious" one. Even if one accepts that settling and annexing, or at least refusing to surrender, parts of the Greater Land of Israel is a "religious" issue, the emphasis on this issue rather than others suggests an order of priorities. In addition, even the haredi parties now seek the support of nonreligious Jews and greater integration into the Israeli political system, if only to benefit from the spoils of office. Shas's success in this regard is attributable, at least in part, to its emphasis on Jewish ethnicity and the use of ethnic, rather than narrowly religious, symbols. This, as well as the decline of ideology among, for example, Agudat Israel and the increased weight it gives to pragmatic considerations, is reflected in the rather modest demands which even haredi parties make for expanding the scope of Jewish law.

Consequently, as already suggested, the key demands of the religious parties in the 1988 Knesset elections were defensive demands. In many instances, the religious parties simply sought to retain the fruits of legislative and administrative victories they had secured in the past. The most important of these included Sabbath closing laws passed by municipal councils which a 1988 court decision held invalid because the Knesset had never explicitly empowered local councils to pass such laws. Closely related was the demand for the expansion of the authority of rabbinical courts in matters of personal status (especially marriage and divorce), an authority which has been eroded as a result of decisions by secular courts. (The legal status of the latter is superior to that of the former.) However, for the haredi parties, two of the three in particular, the most important defensive demand was the continuing assurance that *yeshiva* (pl., *yeshivot*) students (students at schools for advanced religious study—which means virtually all haredi youth) would continue to benefit from draft exemptions as long as they were enrolled in yeshivot.

A second type of demand included increased benefits, or public funding for haredi educational and philanthropic institutions equal to what the non-haredi sector receives. The haredi parties also called for greater housing benefits for young couples, and Shas was especially interested in government recognition of its schools as an independent, administratively autonomous system eligible for public funding. These demands, while marginally burdensome to the Israeli taxpayer, hardly presaged a major shift in relations between religion and state.

An effort to expand religious influence in Israeli society was reflected in two types of demands. One was of a generally symbolic nature. For example, amending the "Law of Return" to preclude recognition by the State of Israel of non-Orthodox conversions performed abroad (popularly known as the "Who Is a Jew?" law) would have affected no more than a handful of Israelis but was of great symbolic importance because it would have established the authority of Orthodox rabbis in determining whom the State of Israel recognizes as a Jew. The second type of demand was in the area of culture and education. Proposals in this regard were rather vague. They included the demand that the government introduce more Jewish (read "religious") education. The NRP also talked about the need for more national (read "ultranationalist") education. There were also hints at the need to preserve Israeli culture against "negative influences" (an allusion to pornography and probably to antireligious and antinationalist expressions as well). Opposition to the construction of the "Mormon University" (in fact, a branch of Brigham Young University) on Mount Scopus in Jerusalem also falls into this category. These demands, it should be noted, were phrased very carefully, generally in a positive rather than a negative vein, under category headings that talked about the need for the unity of the Jewish people. Except for the proposal to amend the "Who Is a Jew?" law, these demands were quickly surrendered in the negotiations over the establishment of a coalition government following the election. Furthermore, although Agudat Israel and some leaders of the NRP did feel strongly about the need to amend the "Who Is a Jew?" law, neither of them conditioned their joining the government on a change in the law. Of course, once Likud and Labor agreed to form a "unity government" together, the bargaining position of all the smaller parties including the religious parties was severely weakened.

To conclude this point, despite the success of the fundamentalists in controlling the religious parties, the demands that these parties made upon the political system were relatively modest. How does one account for this?

Two types of factors ought to be mentioned. One set of factors is political. This includes the effort by at least two religious parties, Shas and Agudat Israel, to attract nonreligious voters. This means that their platform and campaign had to be phrased in religiously moderate terms. Both parties succeeded in attracting such nonreligious voters because, to some, these parties had become outlets for a display of ethnic pride and social protest during and immediately after the election campaign. In addition, the religious parties feared a secular backlash should their demands appear excessive. The religious parties are aware of their minority position in the society and are anxious to avoid confrontations with the nonreligious majority at both the political and the social level—confrontations which they can only lose. Indeed, the more the haredi parties in particular share in the benefits derived from participating in a government coalition, the more reluctant they are to jeopardize this participation by raising demands which the majority will refuse to meet.

A second set of factors is theological rather than political. It stems from the conviction which all but the most extreme fundamentalists share about the supreme importance of Jewish unity. This is not an empty slogan or even a tactical device. It is perceived, especially by the religio-nationalists, as a religious mandate and has led the more moderate among them to insist that, even though a course of action was both politically and religiously appropriate, it could not be imposed on a recalcitrant population lest it lead to conflict among Jews.[21]

The "Secular" Response

Despite the rather modest demands of the religious parties, the increase in the number of Knesset seats which they won in the 1988 elections (their number grew from thirteen to eighteen) evoked near hysteria. The assumption of virtually everyone, from political analyst to man in the street, was that the Likud would form a narrow coalition government with the religious parties and three small parties of the radical right. The images of the future reflected in various newspaper columns included religious control of the school system; increased expenditures for yeshivot at the expense of universities; greater censorship of the press, movies, and the theater; an expansion of the authority of religious courts; new laws restricting the opening of public places on the Sabbath; and amending the "Who Is a Jew?" law resulting in sharp conflict between Israel and Diaspora Jewry and the consequent reduction of political and financial support from the Diaspora.[22]

For example, on 3 November 1988 the *Jerusalem Post,* the only English-language daily newspaper, editorialized that the religious parties "will vie for the lead in wrenching Israel away from its commitment to the Declaration of Independence and into an undertaking to Halakha [Jewish law]." Headlines in *Haaretz,* Israel's most prestigious daily, referred to "extortion of the religious" or "parents [who] have reason to be anxious in the face of the possibility of the narrowing of our children's horizons." The more popular daily, *Maariv,* headlined stories with banners attributing such statements to religious Jews as "You didn't want the kosher law—now you'll get the supervision of our courts"; "You didn't want yeshivot, soon we will buy the buildings on Mount Scopus," a reference to the Hebrew University; or, "Now we are transforming democracy and a minority will rule over the majority."

A number of mass demonstrations took place in which two types of demands were heard. The first type was for revision of the electoral system. Proposals to revise the system were on the political agenda independently of the 1988 election results. What the election did was stimulate public demands for electoral change (for example, district elections or the direct election of the prime minister) that would limit the capacity of small parties in general and the religious parties in particular to form the balance of power in a government. Second, the backlash against the religious parties in general and the haredi parties in particular stimulated calls for the drafting of yeshiva students, who under the present law are exempt from military service. The fear of a Likud-led coalition dependent upon the support of religious parties for its existence strengthened the hands of a group within the Likud which favored a broader coalition with Labor. There were a number of reasons why this group favored such a coalition, but it is unlikely it would have succeeded in winning the support of the Likud's Central Committee if not for the public fear of a narrow government in which religious parties would have a major voice.

In this case, therefore, to further their own political agenda, politicians of the moderate right exploited the suspicions most Israelis harbor toward the religious parties and toward a growth of clericalism. The moderate left, as we shall see, has also sought to exploit the public's fear of religion—in its case, to unite secular Israelis in opposition to ultranationalism. The strategy of appealing to secular nationalists in an effort to turn them against religious nationalists will probably fail. The fact is that the secular right is more ultranationalist and antidove than it is anticlerical. Furthermore, what the secular left has never understood is that many of the fears it harbors about religion and clericalism are not shared as intensely by the secular right. The ultranationalist secularists perceive religion as an important part of the national heritage and a source of unity among Jews. They are less concerned than is the left over, for example, limiting freedom of expression. To their mind, a more important issue is protecting national values or what they call "the spiritual treasures of the nation" from defamation, thereby strengthening the "national will." But the point here is not whether the propaganda of the secular left is effective. Rather, the point is that the secular left believes that many other Israelis share their antipathy toward and fear of fundamentalistlike religion. They are at least partially correct in that assessment.

The final question, therefore, is, If religious demands on the body politic are as moderate as those portrayed above, how do we account for the grave concern the 1988 election returns generated or the effort by many intellectuals (see below) to exploit fears of religious extremism?

Religious Fundamentalism: Image and Reality

Religious fundamentalism in Israeli society has been portrayed in two ways. First, it is portrayed as demanding the imposition of Jewish law on all aspects of society. The Jewish religion, according to this point of view, is antidemocratic, and the rabbis seek to rule the entire population. "Khomeini-like" embraces the image that many secularists have of the political ambitions of the religious establishment. Second, the fundamentalists have been portrayed as successful. The forces of light, liberalism, modernity, and Jewish universalism are in constant retreat before the onslaught of fundamentalist Judaism, which means medievalism, close-mindedness, cultural isolation, and Jewish particularism.[23] We noted above that the moderate left has invoked the fears of fundamentalism in an effort to incite the secular ultranationalists against religious ultranationalists. Here, for example, is how world-famous author Amos Oz, generally considered a moderate leftist and by no means an extremist, describes the threat from the religio-nationalist fundamentalists such as Gush Emunim:

> A small sect, a cruel and obdurate sect, emerged several years ago from a dark corner of Judaism; and it is threatening to destroy all that is dear and holy to us, and to bring down upon us a savage and insane blood-cult.
>
> People think, mistakenly, that this sect is struggling for our sovereignty in Hebron and Nablus [Arab cities on the West Bank to which Jews have emotional ties dating from the Biblical period]. . . . But the truth is that, for this cult, the Greater Land of Israel is merely a sophisticated ploy to disguise its real aims: the imposition of an ugly and distorted version of Judaism on the State of Israel. . . .
>
> The real aim of this cult is the expulsion of the Arabs so as to oppress the Jews afterwards, to force us all to bow to the authority of their brutal false prophets.

Oz goes on to talk about

> the shocking success this cult has had in . . . pull[ing] the wool over the eyes of hundreds of thousands of Israelis who would quake with alarm were they to recognize . . . the face of the cruel and freedom-hating fanatic Jewish Hizbullah.[24]

Obviously such images, even if they fail to dampen the nationalist fervor of the secular right, reinforce the notion of the danger from fundamentalists. The media in general, and Israeli intellectuals, most of whom are identified with the political left, have always been antireligious, and the rise of religious fundamentalism feeds these antireligious sentiments and provides them with new elements to caricature. They are reinforced by a number of factors and given credibility by others. The reinforcing factors are, first, the activity of Khomeini, who posed a living model of what religious fundamentalism can lead to and showed that a fundamentalist group can take power. The second factor is the statements of the religious fundamentalists themselves which play directly into the fears of their opponents. This is not only true of statements by the extremists. Even the moderate fundamentalist rhetoric strengthens the suspicions of the nonreligious. In the case of the haredim, their nominal opposition to Zionism, even though it has no practical consequences today, is an irritant to the vast majority of Israelis to whom "Zionism" is a term which symbolizes their attachment to the Israeli state and society. The invoking of a messianic rhetoric by the religio-nationalist fundamentalists of Gush Emunim and their sympathizers strikes the nonreligious Jew as an indication of irrationality. Third, the fundamentalists' success—albeit a modest one—in attracting former secularists to their camp has generated enormous publicity and raises fears of children turning against their parents or of sons leaving the pursuits of this world to take up studies in religious institutions. Finally, there is a deep residue of resentment and hostility toward the haredim because of the refusal of so many of their young men to serve in the army.

In Israel, one's religious orientation is viewed as a total rather than a partial identity. Religious and nonreligious tend to lump the "others" into one stereotype and thereby assume that by defining them as religious or nonreligious, certainly as haredi or secular, they have identified all that is important about the other party. At the risk of oversimplifying, the dominant images each side has of the other are negative. Among the nonreligious, these include the haredi image (the image of the religious fanatic), the Gush Emunim image (the image of the nationalist fanatic), and the Shas image (the image of the poorly educated, superstitious Sephardim). Images and caricatures of the "other" also exist among religious Jews. They perceive the secular Jew as a political leftist, a person of relatively loose morals, one whose family relations are shaky, whose children are potential drug users, and who is distant and hostile to the Jewish tradition.[25]

Caricatures of religion and religious Jews can be maintained for a few reasons. The social distance between religious and nonreligious Jews in Israel is generally great. There are few occasions for intimate associations between most religious and nonreligious Jews. They are separated by play group and school from the earliest age. The army is one of the few places where these two publics are likely to meet in any kind of intimate relationship, and that relationship is limited by the fact that most religious girls do not serve in the army. Haredim do not generally serve in the army. If they do, they perform specialized functions of a religious nature, and many young religious men who do serve in the army undergo their basic training in units composed primarily of other religious soldiers. This is less true among the Sephardic segment of the population, and Sephardim, in the past, were far less affected by the negative images of religious Jews. But this too is changing. Social distance means that reports from the media and other secondary sources, anecdotes, and superficial impressions are likely to determine the images that each side has of the other.

Negative stereotyping is related to and reinforced by everything we know of public attitudes among Israeli Jews. Virtually every public issue—whether or not Israel should construct the Lavi airplane, extradite convicted killer William Nakash to France, negotiate with the PLO, surrender territory in exchange for peace, limit the rights of Israeli Arabs to vote or be elected, limit the freedom of the media, censor pornography—finds the same population groups arranged on the two sides of the issue. Those who are better educated, who are of Ashkenazic background, and who define themselves as nonreligious are likely to adopt one position, and those with the least formal education, of Sephardic background, and who define themselves as religious are likely to adopt the opposite position. (Haredim are generally omitted from such surveys. Pollsters don't often reach them, and when they do, haredim are less likely to respond.) There are two sets of related issues around which the Israeli polity is divided. These are the balance between a commitment to the Jewish historical and religious tradition and the security needs of the Jewish people on the one hand, and the extension of cultural, civil, and political liberties to every person and the risks one is willing to take in order to achieve a political settlement with the Arabs on the other. On this critical and highly emotional set of issues, the sociodemographic factors of education, ethnicity, and religious orientation do not overlap; they are cumulative. Obviously not all religious Jews lack extensive secular education, nor are all of them

Sephardim. Indeed, the majority of haredim are of Ashkenazic origin. It is equally clear that among the nonreligious not all are well-educated Ashkenazim. But when each side thinks of the other, they tend to think in stereotypes, and the image of religious and nonreligious is likely to accompany an attendant package with educational and ethnic components. In other words, the images of religious and nonreligious distinguish not only between groups with different beliefs and religious orientations but between two cultures, styles of life, forms of identity, and political values—and the image of the Other is threatening.

There is a danger in overstating this condition. It isn't true of all Israelis, and we don't have the in-depth attitude surveys to indicate how widespread these images really are. But these images are most prevalent not only among the secular and fundamentalist extremists but among the cultural elite of the nonreligious and the spiritual elite of the religious. Each in its own way, intellectuals among the secular and the rabbinical leaders of the religious, has much to lose from concessions to the other side. This is especially true of secular intellectuals, who feel far more threatened by fundamentalistlike tendencies, by any hint of censorship or religious coercion, than does the general public. The general public objects to inconveniences which religious parties might impose upon them. Among intellectuals, however, one finds a sense that their very way of life, and their deepest image of what constitutes a proper society, is threatened by the fundamentalists.

The Future of Fundamentalism as a Political Phenomenon

"Observers cannot predict future developments in the Middle East," one pundit has noted; "they can't even predict the present." This is especially true when the major actors in the drama include religiously motivated people whose ultimate commitments are to metapolitical beliefs and to the authority of spiritual leaders who are often insulated from political pressures. One can, however, reflect upon the future on the basis of the experience of the past. There is nothing in its recent history to suggest that fundamentalism will become a more significant factor in Israeli politics than it is today. To the contrary, it seems likely to become less significant. The haredi-oriented parties are becoming more rather than less involved in the political system. As their appetite for the spoils of office and the direct benefits of increased public funding grows, their demands for religious legislation of a far-reaching nature, the kind of legislation that would do more than inconvenience the nonreligious public, are likely to lessen. As long as Israel does not undergo a religious revival in which large numbers of Jews embrace a religious way of life, the ability of religious parties to retain power will depend on a modicum of goodwill on the part of nonreligious Jews. Nothing destroys that goodwill more than demands for increased religious legislation. There is no evidence that the nonreligious segment of the Israeli population has become any more observant of religious norms. On the contrary, there is evidence that the offspring of the nonreligious are totally indifferent to the Jewish religious tradition in their private lives and appallingly ignorant of its foundations.[26] As long as the religious fundamentalists are politically accountable to this population group in some way, they may continue to pay lip service to the demand for religious legislation but will satisfy themselves with a defense of their narrower communal interests. Democracy not only limits the achievements of the fundamentalists; it even moderates many of their demands. There is always a possibility that the haredi parties might resign from the ruling coalition. Infighting among haredim, an unstable structure of internal authority, and acute dissatisfaction with some symbolic act of the government could lead to this. But it has become extremely unlikely that any haredi party—or, for that matter, any religious party—would actually join in vigorous opposition to the government. Agudat Israel, incensed by Shamir's broken promises to them following the 1988 elections, did resign from the government, but this was interpreted as little more than a symbolic gesture of annoyance. Agudat Israel was confident that the Likud would not invoke retaliatory measures, and the Likud was confident that Agudat Israel would limit its critique to complaints against the integrity of the prime minister. No religious party today is prepared to remain in the political wilderness, bereft of the benefits that ties to the government bestow upon it.

The nationalist demands of the religious fundamentalists of Gush Emunim show no signs of moderation but are likely to be transformed more and more from messianic to secular nationalist demands. Less and less seems to distinguish the religious from the nonreligious ultranationalist. Should Israel reach an accommodation with the Palestinians involving its withdrawal from the presently occupied territories—a possibility that seemed more likely after the newly elected prime minister and head of the victorious Labor party, Yitzhak Rabin, took office in July 1992—civil disturbances among Jews are likely to follow. It is by no means clear whether the religious nationalists or the secular nationalists are more likely to engage in such disturbances, particularly if violent means are employed.

Postscript

Political developments between March and June of 1990 offered a test of the major conclusions of this chapter. In March 1990 the Labor party, in effect, resigned from the government. Its resignation was triggered by the opposition of Likud leader, Prime Minister Shamir, to a Cairo meeting between Israeli and Palestinian representatives. Labor, however, only resigned after its leader, Shimon Peres, became convinced that a majority of the Knesset would support a "no confidence" motion in the Shamir government and that a majority would support a new government under his leadership. On 15 March a majority did, indeed, pass a motion of "no confidence." Peres had a block of fifty-five members from Labor and secular parties to the left of Labor. Shamir had a block of forty-eight members from the Likud and secular parties to the right of the Likud. Peres, therefore, needed to secure six votes from among the eighteen members of the religious parties to form a "narrow" government (one without the Likud). Shamir, in turn, needed thirteen of the religious party votes to form a "narrow" government under his leadership. Peres failed to secure the necessary Knesset votes; Shamir succeeded.

For over a year preceding the fall of the Shamir government, Peres courted the haredi parties in his effort to overthrow the "unity" government of Shamir and to win support for a "narrow" government under his leadership. Peres received an unintended assist from the distrust which other party leaders harbor toward Shamir. In negotiations which preceded the formation of the 1988 government Shamir lied to virtually everyone, in some cases so blatantly and flagrantly that many party leaders, those of Agudat Israel in particular, felt that since nothing Shamir said was believable, it was preferable to negotiate a deal with the Labor party. Peres promised the haredi parties control of important ministries and generous funding for their educational and welfare institutions. But bearing in mind that Peres needed the support of Agudat Israel to form a government, the legislative promises which Agudat Israel extracted from him appear minor. Labor promised not to press for a civil liberties law, which the religious parties feared would be used by the courts to overturn existing religious legislation. It also promised to establish a radio channel devoted to strengthening Jewish consciousness, to make no changes in the electoral law without first consulting the leaders of Agudat Israel, to support passage of a law prohibiting the marketing or sale of pork products, to establish a joint committee to recommend laws that would outlaw "advertisements for abominations" (a reference to advertisements which the haredi public consider lewd), and to establish a joint committee to study ways of lessening Sabbath desecration (intended primarily to prohibit bus transportation on the Sabbath; at the present time buses are prohibited from operating on the Sabbath in all cities except Haifa, but they generally begin traveling an hour or two before the Sabbath ends; the proposal was aimed at prohibiting these early departures).

On the basis of these promises, Agudat Israel announced its readiness to join a Labor government, but Peres was unable to secure the support of any other religious party. The unwillingness of Degel Ha Torah to support a Labor government was most interesting since Degel Ha Torah's supreme religious leader, Rabbi Eliezer Schach, does not oppose surrender of the West Bank and Gaza strip. His ostensibly dovish views are, if anything, to the left of Peres's. Nevertheless, Schach adamantly refused to permit Degel Ha Torah to join a government led by Peres. In a major address to his party, which was aired live on Israeli television and provoked vigorous attacks from secular intellectuals and the president of Israel, Schach's position on the paramountcy of observing Jewish law, and his disdain for those who violate the law, was made clear. In this matter, the Labor party, by virtue of its behavior in the 1940s and 1950s, was deemed less trustworthy than the Likud. A view attributed to Rav Schach was that the "nations of the world" would force Israel to surrender the West Bank and Gaza regardless of who was in office. Therefore, peace and order within Israel could be maintained if it was the Likud rather than Labor that presided over the surrender of the Territories. This suggests how trivial in his opinion the issue of the Territories is from a religious perspective—more evidence of the fact that haredi parties march to tunes which are different from those of the non-haredim and another indication of the problematic of measuring them by their stance on issues which are critical to the non-haredi public.

In the case of the Sephardic haredi party, Shas, developments in 1990 paralleled those following the 1988 elections. The religious leader of Shas favored the formation of a Labor-led government. He himself was a dove, and the extravagant promises of money for Shas institutions and patronage for their political representatives—rumored to include the Ministry of the Treasury—were very tempting. This led Shas to abstain in the "no confidence" vote, which caused the collapse of the Shamir government. But pressure from Shas constituents, who are both hawkish and xenophobic, and from Rav Schach, who is revered by Shas's leaders, led to the party's refusal to support a Peres government. Shas itself was left badly scarred, and its own religious leader's authority was severely undermined.

Peres undertook fewer efforts to enlist the support of the NRP. It was assumed that its hawkish position precluded its joining a Labor government. However, when it looked as though Peres was going to succeed in forming a government, political observers predicted, and voices within the NRP demanded, that the NRP join the government after its confirmation by the Knesset.

The behavior of the NRP between March and June cast doubts on its radicalism. Once it became clear that Peres was unable to form a "narrow" government and the task of forming a government was transferred to Shamir, the NRP invested great effort in seeking to convince or even coerce Shamir into reviving a "unity" government with Labor. This seems surprising. After all, a "unity" government would not be as forthcoming as a "narrow" right-wing government in establishing Jewish settlements in the Territories; it might even agree to their surrender, in whole or in part, and it would certainly not annex them. The NRP, therefore, emerged from the political negotiations in the spring of 1990 as less radical than this chapter has suggested. But its behavior did confirm another point made in the chapter—the decline of messianic nationalism. The NRP understood that a "narrow" right-wing government in which radical secular nationalists such as Ariel Sharon held key positions would isolate Israel in the international arena. Under such conditions Israel would be in no position to effect any kind of nationalist program of any duration. Such thinking indicates that the NRP has effectively eschewed messianic expectations. It was no longer considered sufficient for Israel to do what was religiously proper and to anticipate God's help in the ensuing conflict.

In the last analysis, however, although all the religious parties preferred a "unity" government, they were prepared to join Shamir regardless of whether he succeeded in forming a "narrow" government without Labor or was forced to renew the broad coalition with Labor. The only difference between them was that Agudat Israel indicated that it would only join a "narrow" Shamir government some time after its formation. The price Agudat Israel extracted from Shamir was a bit more than what they had extracted from Peres. The munificent sums of money which Labor had showered on the haredi parties were retained but not enlarged. At the legislative level, Agudat Israel secured legislation tightening the present abortion laws but these, in fact, are quite liberal, and it is generally believed that the tightening will have little more than symbolic effect. Finally, the Likud sent an abject letter of apology to Agudat Israel for its broken promises.

In conclusion, events during the spring of 1990 placed the religious parties in a position of potential power which is unlikely ever again to be equaled. The religious parties responded like traditional conservative religious parties rather than radical fundamentalists. They were given the power to choose which of two major foreign policy alternatives would be followed. They sought to avoid making a choice. They had the power to determine which party was to rule the country, and they preferred to avoid even this decision. They translated their enormous power into more money for their educational, cultural, and welfare institutions, more positions in government for the party faithful, and incremental changes in legislation affecting the narrowest of religious interests—pornography, abortions, sale of pork products, and enforcing of laws against public transportation on the Sabbath. In the long run, the most important outcome of these developments may be the strengthening of popular demand for electoral reform as a secular backlash to the perception of religious party power. For example, the proposal for the direct election of the prime minister has become extremely popular. Its enactment would severely reduce the bargaining positions of the religious parties and, in turn, of the fundamentalists.

Notes

1. My colleague Professor Ilan Greilsammer read this paper with great care and offered a number of very helpful comments. We remain in disagreement over a few points.

2. On this development, see Charles S. Liebman and Eliezer Don Yehiya, *Civil Religion in Israel: Traditional Judaism and Political Culture in the Jewish State* (Berkeley: University of California Press, 1983).

3. Charles S. Liebman and Steven M. Cohen, *Two Worlds of Judaism: The Israeli and American Experiences* (New Haven: Yale University Press, 1990).

4. Samuel C. Heilman and Menachem Friedman, "Religious Fundamentalism and Religious Jews: The Case of the Haredim," in Martin E. Marty and R. Scott Appleby, eds., *Fundamentalisms Observed* (Chicago: University of Chicago Press, 1991).

5. On the history and present activity of Gush Emunim, see Ehud Sprinzak, *The Emergence of the Israeli Radical Right* (New York: Oxford University Press, 1990), and Gideon Aran, "Jewish Zionist Fundamentalism: On the Bloc of the Faithful (Gush Emunim)," in Marty and Appleby, eds., *Fundamentalisms Observed.*

6. Rabbi Meir Kahane and his party,

Kach, ruled ineligible to run in the 1988 elections because of its racist program, do not fit neatly into either of these categories although, as we shall see, the categories themselves are dissolving. In any event, Kahane's program of expelling the Arabs and conducting a campaign of collective punishment against all of them strikes a sympathetic chord among many Jews, high school students, the economically poorer groups, and Jews from Arab-speaking lands in particular. It deserves to be treated independently of a study of the political impact of religious fundamentalism. While Kahane is certainly a religious fundamentalist, it is not at all clear that his popularity is related to his fundamentalism. It would both lengthen and unduly complicate this study to add a consideration of Kahane and his movement. For a comprehensive discussion of Kahane within the framework of Israeli politics and the emergence of ultranationalism, see Sprinzak, *Israeli Radical Right.*

7. None of this is true of one haredi group, Habad, the followers of the Lubavitch rebbe. They are sui generis and merit separate treatment.

8. *Yediot Aharonot,* 6 July 1989, p. 17.

9. Gideon Aran, "From Religious Zionist

to a Zionist Religion: The Origin and Culture of Gush Emunim, a Messianic Movement in Modern Israel" (Ph.D. diss., Hebrew University, 1987, in Hebrew), p. 524.

10. For example, Arye De'eri, a leader of Shas, minister of the Interior at the time he was interviewed, and one known for his moderate rather than extremist position, is quoted as saying the following in an interview. "I never pretended to be something other than what I am. I am a representative of Shas. I am a haredi. I tried and I try to function in the public interest and not work only for the haredi public. We must take upon ourselves the burden of the state." *Yediot Aharonot,* Sabbath Supplement, 22 December 1989, p. 4.

11. For example, the head of Agudat Israel's Council of Torah Sages, the Gerer rebbe, who is the charismatic authority for the most important faction within Agudat Israel, announced that no part of the Land of Israel could be transferred to foreign rule. *Maariv,* 22 December 1989, p. 10.

12. Yosef Fund, "Agudat Israel Confronting Zionism and the State of Israel—Ideology and Policy" (Ph.D. diss., Bar-Ilan University, 1990, in Hebrew).

13. Michael Rosenak, "Jewish Fundamentalism in Israeli Education," in Martin E. Marty and R. Scott Appleby, eds., *Fundamentalisms and Society* (Chicago: University of Chicago Press, 1992), companion to this volume.

14. Aran finds these same tendencies in Merkaz Harav, the educational institution out of which Gush Emunim's leadership emerged. Aran, "From Religious Zionist to a Zionist Religion."

15. Rav Shlomo Aviner, "BaMidbar—Jerusalem Independence Day," *Shabat B'shabbato,* 2 June 1989, in Hebrew, p. 1.

16. For a description of the underground and its impact on Gush Emunim, see Sprinzak, *Israeli Political Right.*

17. Charles S. Liebman, "Jewish Ultra-Nationalism in Israel: Converging Strands," in William Frankel, ed., *Survey of Jewish Af-*

fairs 1985 (London: Associated University Presses, 1985), pp. 28–50.

18. See especially Ian Lustick, *For the Land and the Lord: Jewish Fundamentalism in Israel* (New York: Council on Foreign Relations, 1988).

19. Ann Elizabeth Mayer, "The Fundamentalist Impact on Law, Politics, and Constitutions in Iran, Pakistan, and the Sudan," chap. 7, this volume.

20. The point is frequently made by that outstanding polemicist and religious iconoclast Yeshayahu Leibowitz. It is made in more temperate terms in Moshe Samet, *The Conflict over the Institutionalization of Judaic Values in the State of Israel* (Jerusalem: Department of Sociology, Hebrew University, Studies in Sociology, 1979, in Hebrew). Evidence is to be found in a speech by Zerach Wharhaftig to the World Conference of Mizrachi in 1949. Wharhaftig, who served as minister of religion for many years, was one of those most active in the effort to integrate Jewish law into the law of Israel. His speech is summarized in Zerach Wharhaftig, *A Constitution for Israel: Religion and State* (Jerusalem: Mesilot, World Center of Mizrachi—Hapoel Hamizrachi, 1988, in Hebrew), pp. 351–57. But see especially pp. 356–57, and the refusal by the presidium to permit discussion of the topic, p. 357.

21. The point recurs constantly in articles written by moderate and even some of the less than moderate sympathizers with Gush Emunim on the pages of *Nekuda,* the monthly journal of the settlements in Judea, Samaria, and Gaza. In the case of such moderate fundamentalists as Yoel Bin-Nun, the desire for Jewish unity led finally to resignation from Gush Emunim. It is what led Rabbi Yehuda Amital, seven years earlier, to oppose the war in Lebanon.

22. For a study of how the Israeli press projected this image of the future, see Samuel C. Heilman, "Religious Jewry in the Secular Press: Aftermath of the 1988 Elections," in Charles S. Liebman, ed., *Religious and Secular: Conflict and Accommodation between Jews in Israel* (Jerusalem: Keter, 1990), pp. 45–56.

23. A good summary of this point of view is found in Uri Huppert's largely polemical work, *Back to the Ghetto: Zionism in Retreat* (Buffalo, N.Y.: Prometheus Books, 1988). For a more balanced presentation of this point of view, see Amnon Rubinstein, *The Zionist Dream Revisited: From Herzl to Gush Emunim and Back* (New York: Schocken Books, 1984), and for a scholarly presentation, see Gershon Weiler, *Jewish Theocracy* (Leiden: E. J. Brill, 1988).

24. The excerpt is from a speech delivered at a Peace Now rally on 3 June 1989.

The full text appeared in translation in the *Jerusalem Post*, 8 June 1989, p. 4.

25. This is even true among religious Sephardim, who, until recently, were distinguished by their greater understanding of and sympathy for the nonreligious. See, for example, Shlomo Deshen, "To Understand the Special Attraction of Religion for the Sephardim" (in Hebrew), *Politika* 24 (January 1989): 40–43.

26. Ephraim Tabory, "Living in a Mixed Neighborhood," in Liebman, ed., *Religious and Secular*, pp. 113–30.

Shi'ite Jurisprudence and Constitution Making in the Islamic Republic of Iran

Said Amir Arjomand

The Islamic revolution of 1979 in Iran is commonly seen as the most resounding triumph of religious fundamentalism in the contemporary world. Furthermore, its primary, and virtually immediate, impact was the remaking of the political order into a Shi'ite theocracy. The legal framework for this fundamental transformation has been constructed by clerical jurists who entered upon the distinctively modern enterprise of constitution making with the traditional methods of Shi'ite jurisprudence. Their ongoing efforts in the 1980s and early 1990s to reconcile the principles of Shi'ite jurisprudence and the public law of the Iranian state on the basis of Ayatollah Ruhollah Khomeini's idea of theocratic government have set in motion a legal revolution that is the subject of this chapter.

The Making of the Constitution of the Islamic Republic of Iran

While in exile in the late 1960s Khomeini began to consider the establishment of an Islamic theocratic government in place of the monarchy. By that time, a parliament had been in existence in Iran for over a half-century, a constitution was in force in theory, and constitutionalism was a staple of Iranian political culture held dear by the nationalist and Liberal opponents of the shah. Furthermore, the bureaucratic state which the Pahlavis had established on the Western model had made possible the division of governmental functions and the separation of powers. Khomeini and his followers among the *ulama* (religious scholars) had, however, given little thought to the character and functioning of this institutional apparatus. But when they seized it after the revolutionary overthrow of the Pahlavi regime, the question of the constitution of the new political order rose immediately. In this section, I shall analyze their reaction.

Constitutionalism had traveled from Western Europe to Iran through the Otto-man Empire, where a constitution had been promulgated in December 1876 and suspended less than two years later. The first modern Asian revolution occurred in Iran in 1906 and was soon labeled the "Constitutional Revolution" in view of its primary objective of establishing a parliament and subjecting absolute monarchy to the rule of law. That revolution produced the Fundamental Law of December 1906 and the Supplement of October 1907 which together made up the constitution of monarchical Iran until 1979.

Though based largely on the Belgian constitution of 1831, the Constitution of 1906–7 was not un-Islamic and included a number of articles proposed by the clerical leaders to safeguard Shi'ite Islam and hierocratic interests.[1] The Supplement of 1907 to the Fundamental Law represented a compromise between constitutionalism and Shi'ism in which some of the features of constitutional European law that were ob-viously inconsistent with the Shi'ite religiolegal tradition were modified.[2] But there was no attempt to create an Islamic constitution or a system of public law rigorously based on Shi'ite law. This was to be done after the Islamic revolution in the Funda-mental Law of 1979.

After the overthrow of the Pahlavi monarchy in 1979, Iran was declared an Islamic Republic. There had been virtually no discussion of Ayatollah Ruhollah Khomeini's idea of the "Mandate of the Jurist" (velayat-e-faqih) during the revolutionary turmoil of 1978–79.[3] In those days the vague term "Islamic government" enjoyed currency. But when the Assembly of Experts began its deliberations on the constitution of the Islamic Republic in the summer of 1979, the Mandate of the Jurist became the basis of the new Fundamental Law. This was a revolutionary change in Shi'ism itself and a radical transformation of the traditional Shi'ite theory of authority. Indeed, the revo-lution consists in the synthesis of the theocratic idea of the Mandate of the Jurist with the principles and organization of the modern nation-state.

According to the traditional theory, the political authority of the infallible imams fell into abeyance after the disappearance of the last of them in the ninth century. The authority of the imams as teachers in religion and the Sacred Law (Shari'a), on the other hand, was gradually transferred to the Shi'ite jurists. Khomeini took the radical step of claiming that the imams' right to rule also devolved upon the religious jurists and, further, that if one of them succeeded in setting up a government it was the duty of the other jurists to follow him. This last step was a sharp departure from the traditional Shi'ite principle that no religious jurist has any authority over other reli-gious jurists.[4] As such, it radically undermined the position of the other preeminent religious jurists, the sources of imitation (maraje'-e taqlid), who had been categorically independent according to the traditional Shi'ite theory of authority.

Khomeini himself, however, apparently did not grant much significance to consti-tution making at first. In declaring the formation of the Council of the Islamic Revo-lution on 12 January 1979, Khomeini specified as one of its tasks "the formation of a constituent assembly composed of the elected representatives of the people in order to approve the new constitution of the Islamic Republic."[5] There can be no doubt that this item in the declaration emanated from Bazargan and the other Liberals and

Islamic modernists in the revolutionary coalition. Faithful to this declaration, the Ba-zargan cabinet and the Council of the Islamic Revolution prepared a draft constitution during the spring of 1979. It was similar to the 1906–7 constitution in many respects, and especially with regard to the role of clerical authorities: it envisioned a Council of Guardians, consisting of five religious jurists, to be elected by the Majlis (Parliament) from a list supplied by the sources of imitation, with six lay legal experts in place of the committee of five religious jurists in the Supplement of 1907.[6] Apprehensive about the advances made by the leftist groups, Khomeini was reportedly prepared to accept this draft constitution in June 1979 with only minor changes. In fact, he proposed to bypass the promised constituent assembly and to submit the draft directly to a referendum.[7] It is highly significant that Bazargan and Bani-Sadr insisted on the election of a constituent assembly while Hojjatulislam[8] Hashemi Rafsanjani asked the latter, "Who do you think will be elected to a constituent assembly? A fistful of ignorant and fanatical fundamentalists who will do such damage that you will regret ever having convened them."[9] The lay modernists, Bazargan and Bani-Sadr, won their Pyrrhic victory. Elections for an assembly were to be held on 3 August 1979, but, for reasons to be discussed presently, Khomeini was by then on his guard and insisted on an Assembly of Experts instead of the promised constituent assembly.

The draft constitution instantly became the subject of debate by various secular parties, journals, and organizations. The most notable debate was generated by the commentaries of the Tehran University law professor Naser Katouziyan. Some of Katouziyan's strictures on a preliminary draft published in May were accepted by the provisional government, and the draft was modified accordingly.[10] These debates alarmed Khomeini. At the end of June, he told the clerics that their exclusive prerogative was the revision of the draft from an Islamic perspective:

> This right belongs to you. It is those knowledgeable in Islam who may express an opinion on the law of Islam. The constitution of the Islamic Republic means the constitution of Islam. Don't sit back while foreignized intellectuals, who have no faith in Islam, give their views and write the things they write. Pick up your pens and in the mosques, from the altars, in the streets and bazaars, speak of the things that in your view should be included in the constitution.[11]

And they did so, especially as elected members of the Assembly of Experts. At this point, a process largely independent of the personal inclinations of the participating ayatollahs was set in motion—that of working out, within the framework of the modern nation-state, the full logical and institutional implications of Khomeini's theocratic ideas. This impersonal process unfolded in the form of the constitution making of the clerically dominated Assembly of Experts.

Foremost among those who responded to Khomeini's charge were Ayatollahs Hossein 'Ali Montazeri and Mohammad Hosseini Beheshti. Beheshti seems to have been influenced by the constitutional ideas of the Iraqi Shi'ite thinker Mohammad Baqir al-Sadr in Iraq. In his jurisprudential commentary on the proposed Islamic constitution,[12] al-Sadr held that the function of Imamate had been fulfilled through the leadership of the sources of imitation during the Occultation. Accordingly, it would be proper for one of these sources of imitation to assume the position of the head of state and commander of the armed forces in the new Islamic regime and to nominate, or at any rate approve, a candidate for presidency to be popularly elected as the head of the executive branch of government. Mohammad Baqir al-Sadr had also suggested the institutionalization of an "assembly of the people of loosening and binding" whose members were to be those ulama and Islamic thinkers proposed for popular election by the source of imitation.[13] Beheshti appears to have adopted this suggestion by endorsing the form of the Assembly of Experts in preference to the promised constituent assembly. Ayatollah Montazeri wrote a commentary on the draft constitution of the provisional government which advanced the idea of the Mandate of the Jurist and refuted the separation of the three powers—all three were said to be subordinate to the just jurist.[14] He was prevailed upon by Khomeini to run for election to the Assembly of Experts from Tehran, and was elected president, with Ayatollah Beheshti serving as vice-president and playing a particularly important role in the making of the new constitution. The stage was set for the defeat of the proponents of national sovereignty and the unveiling of Khomeini's theocratic project.

In an important statement at the fortieth session of the Assembly of Experts on 9 October 1979, its president, Montazeri, presented as the major objective of the constitution making the removal of the traditional duality and contradiction between political and religious authority, or, in his words, between "customary government" and "hierocratic government." He distinguished between two kinds of ordinances, Qur'anic and jurisprudential ordinances derived from the Traditions, on one hand, and "governmental ordinances," on the other. The latter are not derived from the Qur'an and the Traditions by methods of jurisprudence but are based on generalities and the necessity of maintaining order. An example would be traffic regulations enacted by the Majlis.

> Such would be a governmental ordinance. If the ordinance is from the hierocratic authority/judge, it is incumbent on us to obey its authority and we are obliged to act upon it.[15]
>
> But if it does not rest on the Sacred Law, it would not be enforceable upon the conscience, which means that it would not be necessary for me personally to observe it. Many of the laws passed by the Majlis are of this kind. They are governmental laws, and so long as the religious jurists, whom we consider the appointees of the (Hidden) Imam albeit in a collective and general fashion, have not approved and endorsed them and have not commanded us to execute them, we are not obligated to execute them. Therefore, if we want to follow the Sacred Law, we must say that the enactments of the Consultative Assembly (Majlis) are not legal and enforceable without the approval of the religious jurists of the Council of Guardians.[16]

The establishment of the supervening hierocratic authority and veto of the clerical jurists of the Council of Guardians paved the way for the enthronement of the supreme hierocratic jurist as the Leader of the Islamic Republic. With Ayatollah Beheshti in the chair as vice-president, the militant clerics in the Assembly of Experts moved to establish Khomeini's idea of the Mandate of the Jurist. Hojjatulislam Rabbani Amlashi, for instance, argued that it was time to rescue the institution of the leadership of the sources of imitation from its present unsatisfactory condition by transforming it into the Mandate of the Jurist. He pointed out that if plans for doing so had been devised earlier, the Islamic revolution might have triumphed fifteen or sixteen years sooner.[17] The clerical makers of the constitution of 1979 then proceeded to institutionalize theocracy as described below. It is interesting to note that, in this matter, they refused to compromise with the norms of national sovereignty and, on 7 November 1979, rejected an article proposing that "the Leader and the members of the Leadership Council of the Islamic Republic of Iran must be Iranian citizens and [resident] in Iran."[18] The Assembly of Experts had entertained many other suggestions and altered the Bazargan government's draft beyond recognition. The new draft was no longer a republican constitution consistent with Shi'ite Islam, but a constitution that purported to be fundamentally Islamic and to incorporate specifically Shi'ite principles of government. To demonstrate this, Qur'anic verses and Traditions in support of many of the articles were cited in an "Appendix to the Fundamental Law." The Assembly concluded its deliberations shortly thereafter, in mid-November, and its draft constitution was ratified by the referendum of 2–3 December 1979.

The Fundamental Law of 1979

A comprehensive treatment of the contents of the Fundamental Law of 1979 has been offered elsewhere.[19] Here, it suffices to point out that, in comparison with the old constitution, it reflected many of the changes in the international political culture during the intervening eight decades.[20] These differences, however, were marginal in comparison to the features that set the Fundamental Law of 1979 apart from the constitution it superseded, and indeed from all modern constitutions. This was made amply clear by the Preamble to the Fundamental Law of 1979, which characterized it not only as emphatically ideological but also as distinctly and thoroughly Islamic.

The Preamble begins, in the name of God, with a historical sketch of the Islamic revolutionary movement. The Fundamental Law is then presented as an attempt by the nation to cleanse itself of the dust of godless government and foreign ideas, as a way to return to God and to the "authentic intellectual positions and worldview of Islam."

As an ideological constitution, the Fundamental Law of 1979 imposed severe restrictions on the civil rights of the individual. The vague qualification of the freedom of association in the previous constitution[21] was replaced by the much more restrictive one that parties and associations must not "violate the Islamic standards and the bases of the Islamic Republic." This could be and has been interpreted as outlawing secularist political parties and associations. Furthermore, in the manner of ideological constitutions,[22] the previously unqualified right to unarmed gatherings and demonstrations was virtually nullified by the qualification that they must "not be detrimental to the fundamental principles of Islam" (article 27).

More extraordinary and far-reaching in its implications than even this ideological character was the Islamic and theocratic nature of the 1979 constitution. Article 2 of the Fundamental Law explicitly established a theocracy by making sovereignty and legislation the exclusive possession of the One God (2.1), and by defining the Islamic order as an order based on belief in the five principal articles of faith in Shi'ite Islam. One of these principles, the Imamate, was extended, following Khomeini's theory, to establish the political authority of the clerical jurists (2.5 and 2.6). This amounted to a firm rejection of the separation of religion and the political order, the constitution of which is determined by the Fundamental Law of 1979. Thereafter, the underlying principles of the previous constitution such as national sovereignty, separation of the powers, and the legislative power of the Majlis are systematically reassessed and reformulated from this particular Islamic theocractic perspective.

Although chapter 5 of the Fundamental Law is entitled "The Right of Sovereignty of the Nation and the Powers Deriving Therefrom," there is no direct statement on national sovereignty that would correspond to article 26 of the Supplement of 1907. Instead, national sovereignty is delimited obliquely and in a manner devoid of clear legal implications. Article 56 declares: "Absolute sovereignty belongs to God, and it is He who has made man the governor of his social destiny." However, the idea of the separation of powers is retained, at least in principle, even though the legislative, executive, and judiciary powers are all subject to "the supervision of the [person invested with] the Mandate to Rule and the Imamate of the community of believers" (article 57).

The Majlis as the organ of national sovereignty is unquestionably the most important institution of the old constitution retained by the Fundamental Law of 1979. Its legislative power, however, is subjected to important new limitations. Article 72 specifies that "the National Consultative Assembly cannot enact laws contrary to the principles and ordinances of the established religion or the Fundamental Law," leaving the determination of this matter to the clerical jurists of the Council of Guardians. Article 93 further declares the Majlis devoid of legal validity in the absence of the Council of Guardians. These articles make the Council of Guardians a legislative body.[23] The Council of Guardians in effect emerges as an appointed upper house with veto power over all Majlis legislation. It consists of six plenipotentiary members (the clerical jurists) and six members with restricted powers (the lay lawyers) (article 91).

The organization of the judiciary power is laid down in chapter 11 of the Fundamental Law of 1979. Article 157 institutes a Supreme Judiciary Council, the highest judiciary organ, to reorganize the judiciary, recruit judges, and prepare laws appropriate for the Islamic Republic. It consists of its president, the prosecutor general, and three judges, all of whom must be religious jurists (articles 158 and 162). Article 163 states that the qualifications of the judges in accordance with the criteria of the Sacred Law will be determined by law, and article 167 requires that the judges must settle all disputes according to the laws, or if they be of no avail, on the basis of "valid Islamic sources or a valid injunction [of a clerical jurist]." There is also to be a minister of justice, but his function is that of coordination with the executive and legislative powers (article 160). Article 171, curiously, makes the judge personally responsible for damages in cases of willful miscarriage of justice. Thus, the traditional duality of the judiciary system of Shiʿite Iran, which was recognized in the old constitution, is replaced by a monistic theocratic one, and the judicial power is put exclusively under clerical control.

The centerpiece of the new Fundamental Law, however, is the Mandate of the Jurist. This idea is enunciated in the Preamble and translated into law in articles 5, 107, and 110:

> In keeping with the principle of the Mandate to Rule and the continuous Imamate, the Constitution provides for the establishment of leadership by a clerical jurist possessing the necessary qualifications and recognized as leader by the people. This is in accordance with the Tradition: "The conduct of affairs is to be in the hands of those who are trustworthy guardians of that which He has permitted and that which He has forbidden" (Preamble).

To extend the traditional connotation of the term "Imamate" in the novel revolutionary direction in the above passage, the unwonted qualification "continuous" (*mostamerr*) is added to Imamate just as it is coupled with the Mandate to Rule. Article 2.5 speaks of "Imamate and continuous leadership and *its* fundamental role in the continuation of the Islamic revolution" (emphasis added), thus equating Imamate with "continuous leadership." All the above is then juxtaposed with "continuous jurisprudential endeavor of the clerical jurists" in the following subsection, 2.6a. This paves the way for the transfer of the Imamate from the twelve infallible holy imams to the Jurist, whom the subsequent articles refer to as the Leader of the Islamic Republic:

> During the Occultation of the Lord of the Age . . . the Mandate to Rule and Imamate devolve upon the just and pious Jurist, who is acquainted with the circumstances of his age; courageous, resourceful, and possessed of administrative ability; and recognized and accepted as leader by the majority of the people. In the event that no Jurist should be recognized by the majority of the people, a Leadership Council, composed of jurists possessing the aforementioned qualifications, will assume these responsibilities in accordance with Article 107 (article 5).

Article 107 specifies being a source of imitation as a necessary qualification for the position of Leadership, or for membership in the Leadership Council, which is to consist of three or five sources of imitation. It also entrusts the selection of the Leader of the Leadership Council to popularly elected "experts" whose number and qualifications, according to the ensuing article 108, were first to be determined by the Council of Guardians and approved by the Leader, and thereafter by the Assembly of Experts itself. This body is, furthermore, entrusted with the important task of dismissing the Leader in cases of incapacitation and loss of qualifications in accordance with regulations to be laid down in its first session (article 111). Article 110 enumerates the extensive powers of the Leader, which include supreme command of the armed forces; appointment and dismissal of the chief of the general staff and of the commanders of the army, navy, air force, and the revolutionary guards; confirmation of the president of the republic and his dismissal upon either a verdict of the Supreme Court or a vote of "political incompetence" by the Majlis; and appointment of the highest judiciary authority and the jurists of the Council of Guardians.

The Majlis was given no jurisdiction over the election and constitution of the Assembly of Experts. These matters were regulated by laws passed by the Council of Guardians in October 1980 and October 1982, and by amendments in August and November of 1982. The most important qualification for the candidates was specified as either "competence in religious jurisprudence," established by the explicit or tacit approval of the Leader or by reputation in the learned circles, or preparation for it at the highest level of religious learning, as certified by three reputable professors.[24] The first Assembly of Experts was elected in December 1982 and was inaugurated on 14 July 1983. Four days later, the Assembly passed its internal constitution in accordance with article 108 of the Fundamental Law. During the elections for the second Assembly of Experts in October 1990, the clerical jurists of the Council of Guardians assumed the function of qualifying the candidates on the basis of their competence in religious jurisprudence.

Constitutional Crisis and the Amendment of the Fundamental Law

In the elections for the first Majlis after the revolution, the clerically led Islamic Republican Party won a solid majority against the Islamic modernists, nationalists, and Liberals who supported Bazargan and Bani-Sadr. By the first act it passed on 22 July 1980, the new Majlis changed its official name from National Consultative Assembly to Islamic Consultative Assembly. This was done, however, without amending the Fundamental Law accordingly.

From the very outset, the Majlis and President Abu'l-Hasan Bani-Sadr, who had been elected in January, were deadlocked in a political struggle that immediately became manifest in a prolonged disagreement over the choice first of the prime minister and then of the cabinet. In this power struggle the president was at a disadvantage, owing to the Fundamental Law of 1979. He did not have the power to dissolve the Majlis. In fact, no provision was made for the dissolution of the Majlis, not even by the Leader. Nor could he dismiss the prime minister. The one constitutional power he could and did use in this struggle was to withhold his signature from the enactments of the Majlis as required by article 123 of the Fundamental Law. By June 1981, the Majlis had decided to use and even exceed its constitutional powers against the president. It passed a law giving the president five days to sign the enactments; otherwise they would become law without his signature.[25] More important, on 17 June 1981, the Majlis passed a law expanding on the provision made in article 110.5 for the dismissal of the president on grounds of "political incompetence."

After the dismissal of Bani-Sadr, with the Islamic Republican Party in control of the presidency, the premiership, and the Majlis, constitutional conflict took a new form. Adhering to traditional Shiʿite principles of jurisprudence and using their power to determine the consistency of the enactments of the Majlis with Islamic standards, the jurists of the Council of Guardians vetoed several bills for land distribution, nationalization of foreign trade, labor, distribution, hoarding, and other economic measures. These had been found to be at variance with the rules of the Sacred Law, usually on grounds of infringement of the rights of private property and freedom of contract. As early as October 1981 and again in January 1983, Majlis speaker Hashemi Rafsanjani sought Khomeini's explicit intervention as the Jurist to overcome the veto of the Council of Guardians. The position taken by Hashemi Rafsanjani rested on a radically broadened interpretation of the Shi'ite jurisprudential principles of public "interest" and "overriding necessity." In the first instance, in 1981, when the Council of Guardians had vetoed a bill introducing qualifications to ownership of land within the limits of cities, Khomeini refused to intervene but issued an order delegating his authority as the Jurist to a majority of the deputies of the Majlis to determine overriding necessity and posit laws, on a temporary basis, as "secondary ordinances." The Council of Guardians, however, persisted in its veto, and it was not until four years later that Khomeini reaffirmed the delegation of his authority to determine overriding necessity to the Majlis, this time requiring a majority of two-thirds.[26] Even this qualified delegation of juristic authority stretched the principle of overriding necessity far beyond its stringent limitations in Shi'ite jurisprudence.[27] In the second instance, in 1983, too, Khomeini's intervention fell short of the explicit exercise of the legislative authority of the supreme jurist.[28]

In January 1988, Khomeini finally did what he had been reluctant to do earlier. On 6 January he reprimanded President Ayatollah Sayyid 'Ali Khamane'i for saying that the authority of Islamic government could only be exercised within the framework of the ordinances of the Sacred Law. This statement showed that President Khamane'i misunderstood and misrepresented Khomeini's views, and that he did not accept the Mandate of the Jurist. Government in the form of the God-given "absolute mandate" was "the most important of the divine commandments and has priority over all derivative divine commandments. . . . [It is] one of the primary commandments of Islam and has priority over all derivative commandments, even over prayer, fasting and pilgrimage to Mecca." Five days later, in another letter which set the tone for a chorus of affirmations and clarifications by the ruling clerical elite, Khomeini referred to the president as a brother who supported the Absolute Mandate of the Jurist.[29]

There immediately followed a campaign to promote the new elaboration of Khomeini's theory, which culminated in a seminar of the congregational prayer leaders on the clarification of the Absolute Mandate of the Jurist on 19–20 January 1988.[30] On 12 and 13 January, respectively, the spokesman and the secretary of the Council of Guardians, duly humbled, had visited Khomeini and declared their submission to his rulings. The spokesman, Hojjatulislam Emami Kashani, had announced that, in the eyes of the Council of Guardians, the Imam's injunctions constituted legal proof as required by the Sacred Law; and the bills rejected earlier could therefore be reconsidered with greater latitude. The Imam had taken the occasion of the visit by the conservative secretary of the Council, Ayatollah Lotfollah Safi, to issue a categorical statement of his revolutionary ruling which marked the final victory of "progressive" jurisprudence demanded by Hashemi Rafsanjani: the Mandate of the Jurist and the "governmental ordinance" were among the "primary ordinances" of God.[31]

Finally, on 22 January, a chastened President Khamane'i thus propounded the principles of the new theocratic absolutism:

> The commandments of the ruling jurist are primary commandments and are like the commandments of God. . . . The regulations of the Islamic Republic are Islamic regulations, and obedience to them is incumbent. . . . [They are all] governmental ordinances of the ruling jurist. . . . In reality, it is because of the legitimacy of the Mandate [of the Jurist] that they all acquire legitimacy.
> The Mandate of the Jurist is like the soul in the body of the regime. I will go further and say that the validity of the Fundamental Law, which is the basis, standard, and framework of all laws, is due to its acceptance and confirmation by the ruling jurist. Otherwise, what right do fifty or sixty or a hundred experts have? What right do the majority of people have to ratify a Fundamental Law and make it binding on all the people? The person who has the right to establish the Fundamental Law for society is the ruling jurist. . . .
> It is the ruling jurist who creates the order of the Islamic Republic as an order for the Islamic society and requires obedience to it. Opposing this order then becomes forbidden as one of the cardinal sins, and combating the opponents of this order becomes an incumbent religious duty.[32]

The downgrading of the Majlis in the president's statement, though more emphatic than ever before, was in line with the interpretation of the principle of consultation by the makers of the constitution of 1979. The explicit degradation of the constitution of the Islamic Republic, on the other hand, was new and clearly implied that the God-given Absolute Mandate of the Jurist no longer needed such man-made props as the Fundamental Law.

The matter did not rest with the statement of the principle of the Absolute Mandate of the Jurist, and Khomeini proceeded with its institutionalization. His intervention had also come against the background of the tightening of the government's grip on the private sector. In July 1987, Khomeini as the Jurist had delegated his authority to regulate prices and execute "governmental punishments" to the government in order to strengthen it in its fight against "economic terrorism."[33] On 6 February 1988, in order to determine "governmental ordinances" in cases of disagreement between the Majlis and the Council of Guardians,[34] he appointed a commission consisting of the six clerical jurists of the Council of Guardians, President Khamanei, Majlis speaker Hashemi Rafsanjani, Hojjatulislams Ardabili (president of the Supreme Judiciary Council), Tavassoli (a member of Khomeini's secretariat), Kho'iniha (prosecutor general), Prime Minister Musavi, and the minister concerned with the particular bill under discussion. Khomeini's son, Ahmad, would also participate in the meetings "so that the report of the sessions may reach me faster." The commission was to decide on the bills approved by the Majlis and rejected by the Council of Guardians by simple majority vote of those present at its meetings.[35] The Commission for the Determination of the Interest of the Islamic Order held its first meeting a week later, set its procedural rules, and elected President Khamane'i as its chairman.

The ruling clerics were not the only group to react to Khomeini's extraordinary rulings. In April 1988, Bazargan's Freedom Movement courageously issued a firm rejection of the Absolute Mandate of the Jurist. It was published as a book, together with the Arabic texts and Persian translations of the refutations of the idea of Mandate of the Jurist by three of the most eminent Shi'ite jurists of the nineteenth and early twentieth centuries. The book characterized the Absolute Mandate of the Jurist as exemplifying the cardinal sin of *shirk* (setting up partners for God) and considered the creation of the Commission for the Determination of Interest to be tantamount to burying the Fundamental Law and the traditional jurisprudence. The book also enumerated the contradictions between the new Absolute Mandate and the Fundamental Law of 1979.[36]

It is interesting to note that the controversy was revived after Khomeini's death by the proponents of traditional jurisprudence. In February 1990, both in a Friday sermon and in his newspaper, *Resalat,* Ayatollah Azari Qumi highlighted the contradictions between the Absolute Mandate of the Jurist and traditional Shi'ite jurisprudence and institutions. The Majlis speaker, Hojjatulislam Karrubi, and the Majlis deputies vehemently denounced Azari Qumi for sowing division and dissent, and for engaging in "Imam-obliteration" less than a year after the Imam's death. Khomeini's last rulings were resoundingly affirmed, and such "governmental ordinances" as Khomeini's order to execute the writer Salman Rushdie were hailed "as valid as Islam itself."[37]

The constitutional implications of the statements on the Absolute Mandate of the Jurist made in January and February 1988 remained unclear. In particular, it was not clear what would happen after Khomeini's death. On 28 March 1989, Khomeini's successor-designate, Ayatollah Montazeri, complied with the Imam's wish and resigned as his successor-designate. To the already pressing need for constitutional revision was added the urgency of a constitutional resolution of the problem of succession.

On 18 April 1988, 170 Majlis deputies, and the Supreme Judiciary Council separately, urged the Imam to order the revision of the Fundamental Law. He agreed within a week, assigning the task to a committee consisting of 18 clerics and 2 laymen, to which the Majlis was invited to add 5 of its members. They were given two months to complete a revision of the Fundamental Law with regard to the following questions: (1) leadership, (2) centralization of authority in the executive, (3) centralization of authority in the judiciary, (4) centralization of management of the radio and television network, (5) the number of Majlis deputies and the changing of its official designation to the National Islamic Assembly, (6) the place of the new Commission for the Determination of Interest, and finally (7) provisions for subsequent amendments of the Fundamental Law.

The committee met on 26 April and elected Ayatollah Meshkini, the president of the Assembly of Experts, as its president, with Khamane'i and Hashemi Rafsanjani as vice-presidents, and subsequently designated itself the Council for the Review of the Fundamental Law. The only recorded subsequent instructions from Khomeini came in a letter on 9 May advising that the requirement that the Leader be a source of imitation be dropped. In Khomeini's opinion, a "just religious jurist" recognized by the Assembly of Experts would suffice.

Khomeini died on 3 June 1989. The clerical elite acted decisively and without the slightest delay. The Assembly of Experts met the following morning and after a long session elected President Khamane'i as Khomeini's successor, the Leader of the Islamic Republic, by sixty out of seventy-four votes. Except for "Imam," all of Khomeini's political titles were transferred to Khamane'i, who was hailed as the Leader of the Revolution, Leader of the Islamic Republic, and holder of the Mandate to Rule over the Muslims. Even the revolutionary clerics must have concluded that the use of the title "Imam" was too much of an innovation in Shi'ism to be viable beyond Khomeini. However, the other titles transferred to the new Leader confirmed the authority given to him by the Fundamental Law and thereby clearly implied that he exercises the function of "continuous Imamate." Khomeini's son, Ahmad, declared his obedience to him as the new ruling jurist.[38] The Council of Guardians, the Central Bureau of the Congregational Prayer Leaders, and the humbled prime minister did the same. Within three weeks, the new Leader of the Islamic Republic had asserted his supreme authority as the jurist by confirming one of the last decrees issued by the deceased jurist, Imam Khomeini.[39] Khamane'i either confirmed Khomeini's representatives in various governmental and revolutionary organizations or appointed his own. These are now officially referred to as the representatives of the "ruling jurist."

The Council for the Review of the Fundamental Law continued its work at full speed, and held its thirty-eighth and last session on 8 July 1989. The most important revisions were made in the month after Khomeini's death. According to the official figures, the revised Fundamental Law was approved by over 97 percent of the votes in the referendum held alongside the presidential elections on 28 July 1989.

The council had faithfully carried out Khomeini's instructions. The name of the Majlis was now constitutionally changed to the Islamic Consultative Assembly throughout the revised Fundamental Law. A Council for the Review of the Fundamental Law was established. A new article established the Commission for the Determination of Interest as an organ of the state at the service of the Leader, its functions being to advise on any matter referred to it by the Leader and to arbitrate between the Majlis and the Council of Guardians. The Supreme Judiciary Council was replaced by a single head of the Judiciary Power, to be appointed by the Leader for five years.

The first and foremost task, and the most difficult one, had of course been the constitutional implementation of the Mandate of the Jurist, or the settlement of the Leadership issue. In accordance with Khomeini's instructions, the requirement that the Leader be a marja' was eliminated as a qualification for the office of the jurist in the amended article 109. Beyond this, some very important amendments were made after Khomeini's death. The amended article 111 gave the Assembly of Experts the power to dismiss the Leader upon incapacitation "or if it should become apparent that he had lacked one of the qualifications from the beginning." This new formulation appears to give the Assembly of Experts virtually unrestricted latitude, because the qualifications specified by article 109 include not only competence in religious jurisprudence but also a "correct political and social perspective, administrative and managerial competence, courage, and adequate power for Leadership." Last but not least, the provisions for a Leadership Council to fulfill the function of the jurist were eliminated in the amended articles 5 and 107.

Thus, the powers of Leadership were to be concentrated in a single person, as were the executive and judiciary powers. The legislative power, by contrast, became further diffused, even though in principle it emanated from Leadership. It could be exercised by all citizens, lay and clerical, through their participation in the Majlis, by the six clerical jurists of the Council of Guardians, all of whom were appointed by the Leader, and by the clerically dominated Commission for the Determination of Interest.

Theocratic Constitution Making and the Shi'ite Jurists' Law

Max Weber saw the modern state as the typical organization of rational-legal authority. Khomeini's project of Islamicization of the modern state into a Shi'ite theocracy required a drastic transformation of Shi'ite Sacred Law. From a "jurists' law" it had to be transformed into the law of the state. Shi'ite law had to be extended to cover public law fully; and law finding, the typical activity of the Shi'ite jurists, was supplemented, if not replaced, by legislation and codification. The purpose of this section is to analyze this transformation, which represents the impact of the takeover of the constitutional state by the Shi'ite legal tradition.

The Fundamental Law of 1979, the constitutional crisis of 1988, and the revised Fundamental Law ratified by a referendum in July 1989 can be viewed as a series of attempts to make Khomeini's theocratic idea, which was innovatively derived from Shi'ite jurisprudence, consistent with the legal framework of the modern nation-state. This would explain why the politics of constitution making during the 1980s centered around two issues: (1) the radical depreciation of the traditional Shi'ite institution of religious leadership, the paramount religious authority of the "sources of imitation," in order to make room for the new theory of theocratic government, and (2) the increasing centralization of authority in the postrevolutionary state. To arrive at this explanation, it might be helpful to examine the relation between the jurists' law and the public law of the state in ancient Rome, which supplies the prototypes of both types of law.

In the Roman Empire the jurists' law and the law of the state coexisted harmoniously. The four sources of ancient Roman law were custom (unwritten law), legislation by the popular assemblies, edicts of the magistrates, and *auctoritas prudentium* as embodied in the *responsa* of the jurists. By the end of the classical period (mid-third century C.E.) two new sources had been added to these: the resolutions of the Senate and the constitutions of the emperor.[40] The jurists' law that developed in Rome as the exercise of *auctoritas prudentium* by private jurists in their answers to legal questions and commentaries on *ius civile* was an integral component of Roman law. In fact, "in the creative period of early classical times the development of new law by *interpretatio* far exceeded in bulk and in significance the new law provided by statute."[41] It is important to note that the jurists completely dominated Roman private law but paid little or no attention to public and other fields of law. Consequently, the bulk of Roman private law consisted of the legal norms and principles of the jurists' law.[42]

Until the present century, Shi'ite Sacred Law remained very much a jurists' law. It never made the transition to law making that sets the canon law of Western Christianity apart from other sacred laws.[43] The Shi'ite hierocracy lacked the centralized organization of the Roman Catholic church,[44] and the Shi'ite religious jurists engaged exclusively in law finding, experiencing a last spurt of jurisprudential creativity as late as the nineteenth century. The fact that Shi'ite Sacred Law was a jurists' law also had important implications for the institutionalization of authority in Shi'ism: it produced the above-mentioned pluralism of religious authority at the highest level by assuring the equality of the sources of imitation.[45]

This pluralism in authority had striking parallels in Roman law and in Sunni Islam. In each case, the effect of this pluralism could be mitigated only through state intervention. In Rome, the fact that the authoritative private jurists could have different opinions on the same question required the intervention of the magistrate (*praetor*) or the emperor. The emperor often settled the controversial issue by rescript. Roman emperors were thus drawn into the jurisprudential process and would give free legal advice in response to a *libellus* (written petition) from a private citizen, and their legal service soon developed into the office *a libellis*. The records from the late second and third centuries show that this rescript office was manned by professional jurists who issued *responsa* in the emperor's name, whose perspective was that of private lawyers, and whose emphasis was on private law.[46] In the Ottoman Empire, the issue of disagreement among authoritative jurisconsults was resolved along similar lines through the appointment of the jurisconsults by the sultan as subordinates of the chief jurisconsult, the Shaykh al-Islam. A centralized office for issuing injunctions performed a function similar to that of the Roman rescript office.[47] In Shi'ite Iran, a parallel development had to await the Islamic revolution of 1979, but then it came with a vengeance.

The institutionalization of the Mandate of the Jurist into a monistic authority structure of the nation-state was directly detrimental to the traditional pluralism of the institution of the religious leadership of the sources of imitation. The latest stage of the constitutional implementation of the Mandate of the Jurist has entailed a shift in the foundation of hierocratic authority: a radical step back from the authority of the sources of imitation, and thus from acclamation by following, to competence in religious jurisprudence and qualification by formal training. This step was required for the *conciliar* institutionalization of hierocratic authority initiated by Khomeini and made definitive by the amended Fundamental Law of 1989.[48] A number of important tasks, most notably that of electing the Leader of the Islamic Republic, are entrusted to the clerical Assembly of Experts, whose members must be religious jurists by virtue of their formal training in religious jurisprudence. The importance of this clerical body is tremendously enhanced by amended article 111, which empowers it not only to elect but also to dismiss the Jurist.

The retention of the institution of religious leadership by the sources of imitation may not be due entirely to political expediency and in any event is revealing of the new paradoxical articulation of public and private law in the Islamic Republic of Iran. As there is no state office for issuing injunctions and rescripts and no state-appointed jurisconsults, a duality has come into existence within the realm of private law. There is the state-enforced private law, the bulk of which consists of secular contents of the modified codes and new Majlis enactments, and the totally unregulated Shiʿite jurists' law, which occupies the so-far-uncontested domain of religious duties and ritual observance. The paradox consists in the de facto secularization of private law that is due to the theocratic constitutional law.

Theocratic Constitution Making and the Nation-State

There can be no doubt that Khomeini sought to restore Shiʿite Islam as a religious tradition threatened by Western cultural and political domination. However, the clock can never be simply set back; every restoration is also a revolution. I have therefore characterized Khomeini's movement as "revolutionary traditionalism."[49] The initial impact of this revolutionary traditionalism on the constitution of the Iranian state was examined in section 2, and its impact on Shiʿite law was traced in section 4. In this concluding section, I shall focus on the absorption of revolutionary traditionalism by the state.

The revised Fundamental Law reconciles theocracy and the nation-state in four major ways. First, it centralizes authority in all three branches of government, invested in the Jurist on behalf of the Hidden Imam. Second, it establishes a fundamental distinction between a hierocratic elite, defined by their formal qualification as religious jurists, and the lay citizens. Eligibility for Leadership, headship of the judiciary power, membership in the Assembly of Experts, and the six consequential positions in the Council of Guardians is de jure reserved for the hierocratic elite. In addition, the ulama are certain to dominate the Council for the Determination of Interest and any future Council for the Revision of the Fundamental Law. The position of minister of information is also reserved for the hierocratic elite, though not in the Fundamental Law. Other offices, including membership in the Majlis, are open to lay citizens and clerics alike. Unlike the lay citizens, the hierocratic elite are not barred from any political, administrative, or judiciary office. Third, the Fundamental Law mandates the subordination of parliamentary legislation to clerical supervision through the Council of Guardians and, if necessary, the Commission for the Determination of Interest. Finally, legislation, codification, and systematic review of public law, as distinct from law finding (the derivation of the Sacred Law), have become institutionalized in the Shiʿite legal tradition.

This process began with the constitution making of the ayatollahs in 1979. As was pointed out, not only were Qur'anic verses and Traditions frequently cited in the body of the Fundamental Law, but a special Appendix consisting of additional verses and Traditions pertaining to specific Articles was added to the Fundamental Law. This was meant to demonstrate the consistency of the Fundamental Law with Shi'ite jurisprudence and, by implication, to present legislation by assemblies as an extension of the traditional jurisprudential methodology. Since then, throughout the 1980s and the early 1990s, the jurists of the Council of Guardians have participated in the legislative process regularly, as has the Assembly of Experts. The Commission for the Determination of Interest, the majority of which is composed of ulama, has also been established to exercise the legislative authority of the Jurist as the Leader of the Islamic Republic of Iran.

The constitutionalists who framed the Fundamental Law of 1906 and its Supplement of 1907 envisioned a distinct secular sphere to be subject to popular legislation. The Islamic revolutionary elite have vehemently denied this and have instead sought to extend the rule of the Sacred Law to all spheres of life by a series of institutional innovations that have extended the competence of the religious jurists from law finding to legislation. Nevertheless, their victory is more apparent than real. In practice, popular (parliamentary) legislation covers most areas of life. This legislation has now been "Islamicized" and can claim Islamic legitimacy as a result of the institutional innovations of the clerical constitution-makers.

These innovations have had two far-reaching and closely related consequences: a tremendous expansion of Shi'ite public law, and the accompanying absorption of an enormous amount of secular legal material. Although its legislation is subject to clerical supervision, the Majlis has shown great vigor and has enacted an impressive body of laws. These include the revision of the European-based commercial, civil, and other codes of the Pahlavi era, which now appear Islamicized as they bear the approval of the jurists of the Council of Guardians. In this fashion, an enormous amount of secular legal material has been appropriated as the public law of the Islamic Republic.

There is a surprising measure of agreement among Western Orientalists and Islamic fundamentalists that religion and politics are inseparable in Islam, that "church" and state are one.[50] Both claim that Islam is a total way of life and a total ideology. Against the authority of the former and the enthusiasm of the latter, however, I have sought to emphasize the paradox of the actual insignificance of political ethics in the Shi'ite Sacred Law—the paucity of its political provisions[51]—which is undoubtedly due to the fact that Shi'ite Sacred Law has hitherto been a jurists' law and not the state law or the "law of the land."

It is gratifying to have explicit confirmation of my thesis from unexpected quarters. Amid the confusion arising from the hasty campaign to clarify the Absolute Mandate of the Jurist, a number of very candid admissions were made, such as the one by Ayatollah Jannati, secretary of the Supreme Council for Islamic Propaganda and member of the Council of Guardians:

When we refer to books of applied jurisprudence, we see the discussion of purification, prayer, pilgrimage to Mecca, transactions and the like occupy the bulk of the contents—for instance, in our largest book, the *Jawaher* [*al-Kalam*] there are six volumes on rules of cleanliness and on impure substances, and eight volumes on prayer, whereas there are only a few pages about authority (*vilayat*)—while the topic of Islamic government is among the rare and forgotten topics in our centers of learning and books of law.[52]

Ayatollah 'Ali Meshkini, chairman of the Assembly of Experts, declared that, "in my opinion, the broad subject of this seminar [the Absolute Mandate of the Jurist] needs extensive time for research. . . . The problem of government has had no place in the books of jurisprudence and has not been properly worked on. . . . The issue of a nation liberating itself from tyranny and finding the power to form a state has not been posed in our books of law even at the hypothetical level."[53] The final attestation to Khomeini's revolutionary departure from the Shi'ite tradition is from Hashemi Rafsanjani's Friday sermon following Khomeini's death: "The writing of *The Mandate of the Jurist* itself at that time in Najaf was a great revolution: that he should come from the jurists and write on such an issue."[54]

For nearly nine years the clerical rulers of Iran denied the existence of this paradox in theory and sought to resolve it in practice by a variety of devices. The most important of these has been the legal distinction between "primary ordinances" and "secondary ordinances." The first derive from the sources of the Sacred Law, the second from expediency as the prerequisite for the implementation of the incumbent primary ordinances. Both categories were said to be binding on the believer as a religious duty. Through the principle of the public interest, *any* act could be considered necessary for the prevalence of Islam and the implementation of its primary ordinances. Then, for the first time in Shi'ite history, incumbency was claimed for a category of secondary ordinances comprising all state laws and government regulations, and this incumbency was derived *not* from the juristic competence of the religious jurists but from the alleged right of the supreme Jurist to rule. This radical departure from the Shi'ite tradition could not help but arouse the sarcasm even of one of the two Grand Ayatollahs who had explicitly acknowledged Khomeini's superior authority as the supreme jurist.[55]

In January 1988 the charade of the primary and secondary distinctions was definitively given up. Khomeini ruled that all governmental ordinances belong to the category of primary ordinances of the Sacred Law and are immediately incumbent upon all. But it became clear even to Khomeini's followers that this ruling created as many problems as it solved. By March 1990, a prominent member of the clerical elite, Hojjatulislam Taheri Khorramabadi, had concluded that Khomeini's division of the ordinances into primary and secondary was unworkable. He proposed that, "in view of the fact that under Islamic government law is posited by God and society is ruled by divine laws alone," there are three kinds of laws and ordinances for the administration of the country: "primary ordinances and laws," "secondary ordinances," and "governmental ordinances and regulations."[56] In this view, the traditional category of "secondary ordinances" reverts to its previous negligible status while a novel category of "governmental ordinances" is put forward to cover public law and is said to be binding on the consciences of the Muslims. This significant statement in a disquisition on Islamic government is an acknowledgment of the failure to create a consistent synthesis between Shi‘ite jurisprudence and the constitutional law of the Islamic Republic. The attempt to stretch the established categories of Shi‘ite jurisprudence had not worked, and only by setting up a novel category could contradiction be avoided.

Khomeini's statements on the Absolute Mandate of the Jurist would not only have created far greater latitude for regulation and legislation than was allowed by the traditional Shi‘ite jurisprudence; they would also have made the Shi‘ite state highly autocratic. The revised constitution contains no statement on the Absolute Mandate of the Jurist. But it does bureaucratize the legislative authority of the jurist and establishes the Commission for the Determination of Interest as the organ representing it. It therefore has the same consequence of removing the limitations on the exercise of governmental authority imposed by Shi‘ite Sacred Law and thus strengthens the authority of the state.

The story is not without irony. I believe that Khomeini, who had outsmarted all opponents, was eventually defeated by the cunning of history. The practical consequence of Khomeini's statements and of the amended constitution has been the strengthening of the actual authority of the bureaucratic state rather than the hypothetical authority of the jurist. To see the irony of this development, one need only be reminded of the declaration on executive power in the Preamble to the Fundamental Law of 1979: "The system of bureaucracy, the result and product of Godless forms of government, will be firmly cast away!" Nine years later we were told by Khomeini that obeying petty bureaucrats, who derive their authority from the sacred Mandate of the Jurist, is more important than prayer and fasting. Finally, the constitutional amendments of 1989 completed the translation of the Mandate of the Jurist into constitutional law of the bureaucratic state by compartmentalizing, conciliarizing, and bureaucratizing it.

Well over a century ago, de Tocqueville noted that, in France, the paradoxical consequence of revolution was the strengthening of the state it sought to destroy.[57] There can be little doubt that de Tocqueville has once more been vindicated. The reinterpretation of the Mandate of the Jurist in 1988 and the constitutional revisions of 1989 have made the state more autocratic. The state, which Khomeini initially intended to see wither, not only has grown enormously in size[58] but has expanded in the legal sphere too and has emerged as the unintended victor of the Islamic revolution, making its clerical masters also slaves to its logic.

Nevertheless, the absorptive capacity of the modern state should not be misconstrued. The state that has prevailed is not an essence. The modern state with its rational-legal legitimacy is capable of assuming many forms. Its components can occur in different configurations and be given enormously varying weights. Revolutionary traditionalism has transformed the Iranian nation-state as fundamentally as it has Shi‘ism. Though theocratic constitution making in Iran does bear the distinct imprint of the legal logic of the modern state, it has nonetheless transformed the latter into a veritable theocracy.

APPENDIX

GLOSSARY OF THE PERSIAN OR ARABIC EQUIVALENTS OF TECHNICAL TERMS

All but two or three technical terms have been translated into English
in order not to encumber the text with too many Persian or Arabic words.
This glossary is provided for readers who want to know the original expressions.

Absolute Mandate of the Jurist	velayat-e motlaqa-ye faqih
articles of faith	usul-e din
Assembly of Experts	shura-ye khobragan
clerical jurists	fuqaha'
Commission for the Determination of the Interest of the Islamic Order	majma'-e tashkish-e maslahat-e nezam-e eslami
competence in religious jurisprudence	ejtehad
Council for the Review of Constitution	shura-ye baznegari-ye qanun-e asasi
Council of Guardians	shura-ye negahban
customary government	hokumat-e 'orfi
Fundamental Law	qanun-e asasi
governmental ordinances	ahkam-e hokumati
governmental punishments	ta'zirat-e hokumati
hierocratic authority/judge	hakem-e shar'
hierocratic government	hokumat-e shar'i
injunction	fatva
(public) interest	maslahat
jurisconsult	mufti
(the) jurist	faqih
(the) Leader	rahbar
Leadership	rahbari
Mandate of the Jurist	velayat-e faqih
Mandate to Rule	velayat-e amr
ordinances	ahkam
overriding necessity	zarurat
people of loosening and binding	ahl al-hall wa'l-'aqd
primary ordinances	ahkam-e avvaliyya
religious jurist	mojtahed
ruling jurist	vali-ye faqih
Sacred Law	Shari'a
secondary ordinances	ahkam-e thanaviyya
sources of imitation	maraje'-e taqlid
sovereignty	hakemiyyat

Notes

1. Cf. *Encyclopaedia Iranica,* s.v. "Constitutional Laws of 1906–7" (1992).

2. There is one exception. The religious leaders had vehemently opposed the principle of equality of all citizens before the law (article 8), which they correctly perceived as contradictory to the provisions of the Sacred Law, but had eventually given in, reportedly because of both personal threats of violence and the restlessness of the Armenian minority. Cf. A. H. Hairi, *Shi'ism and Constitutionalism in Iran* (Leiden: E. J. Brill, 1977), pp. 232–33.

3. Ruhollah Khomeini, *Hokumat-e eslami* (Najaf and Tehran, 1971).

4. S. H. Modarressi, "Rationalism and

Traditionalism in Shi'i Jurisprudence: A Preliminary Survey," *Studia Islamica* 59 (1984): 143.

5. Hamid Algar, *Constitution of the Islamic Republic of Iran,* English trans. with a preface (Berkeley, Calif.: Mizan Press, 1980), p. 8.

6. N. Katouziyan, *Gozari bar engelab-e iran* (Tehran: Chapkhaneh-ye Daneshgah-e Tehran, 1981), p. 168.

7. Nahzat-e Azadi-ye Iran, *Velayat-e motlaqeh-ye faqih* (Tehran, n.d. [1988]), p. 12.

8. The term means "proof of Islam" and gained currency as an honorific title for Shi'ite ulama in the nineteenth century. See Said A. Arjomand, *The Shadow of God and the Hidden Imam: Religion, Political Order, and Societal Change in Shi'ite Iran from the Beginning to 1890* (Chicago: University of Chicago Press, 1984), pp. 238, 246. It underwent a process of gradual depreciation and is currently used for a religious leader who ranks below ayatollah. The latter term means the "sign of God" and is currently used to designate a member of the ulama who is authoritative in Shi'ite jurisprudence. The highest echelon of this category consists of the grand ayatollahs, who are considered the "sources of imitation" by their Shi'ite followers.

9. Shaul Bakhash, *The Reign of the Ayatollah* (New York: Basic Books, 1984), pp. 74–75.

10. Katouziyan, *Gozari bar engelab-e iran,* p. 132.

11. Bakhash, *The Reign of the Ayatollahs,* p. 78.

12. I am grateful to Mr. Ali al-Oraibi for bringing the importance of this document to my attention.

13. M. B. al-Sadr, "Lamha fiqhiyya tamhidiyya an mashru' dostur al-jomhuriyyat al-islamiyya fi iran," in *Al-Islam yaqud al-hayah,* 2d ed. (Tehran, 1403/1982–83), pp. 11–13.

14. M. Izadi, *Gozari bar zendeqi va andishehha-ye ayatollah montazeri* (Tehran: Nahzat-e Zanan-e Mosalman), pp. 272–78.

15. The play on the two senses of the term *hakem*—the older, more technical sense of judge, and the newer and more general sense of governor—is very significant in this attempt to extend hierocratic authority to government and transform it into a mandate to rule. The same is true of the substantive, "government" (*hokumat*), mentioned earlier.

16. Cited in S. J. Madani, *Hoquq-e asasi dar jomhuri-ye eslami-ye iran,* vol. 2 (Tehran: Sorush, 1985), pp. 177–78, n. 23.

17. Transcript in *Ettela'at,* 20 Sarhrivar 1363.

18. Madani, *Hoquq-e asasi,* vol. 2, p. 177, n. 14.

19. *Encyclopaedia Iranica,* s.v. "Constitutional Law of the Islamic Republic."

20. Notably the idea of the welfare state and the social and economic rights of the citizens, social and political participation of women, and the influence of the national liberation movements.

21. Article 21 of the Supplement of 1907 required that associations and gatherings "not give rise to religious and worldly sedition."

22. For instance, article 23 of the Soviet constitution of 1918, the world's first ideological constitution, gives the government the right to "deprive individuals and sections of the community of any rights used by them to the detriment of the interests of the Socialist revolution."

23. Katouziyan, *Gozari bar engelab-e iran,* pp. 259–61; Madani, *Hoquq-e asasi,* vol. 2, p. 133.

24. Madani, *Hoquq-e asasi,* vol. 2, pp. 87–92.

25. Ibid., pp. 192–93.

26. Nahzat-e Azadi, *Velayat-e motlaqeh-ye faqih,* pp. 8–9.

27. Ayatollah Azari Qumi knew this well and emphasized that overriding necessity could only be applied when chaos and dire danger threaten the lives and interests of the believers. Furthermore, "Some think that the Jurist (*vali-ye faqih*) and the Islamic government have the right to legislate and can delegate this right, for instance, to the Maj-

lis; and if so, the enactments of the Majlis would become divine ordinances. No! Not only is this not accepted by any of the Shi'ite jurists, but even the seminarians . . . know this to be wrong in Shi'ism." Cited in *Keyhan,* 28 February 1990.

28. S. Bakhash, "Islam and Social Justice in Iran," in Martin Kramer, ed., *Shi'ism, Resistance and Revolution* (Boulder, Colo.: Westview Press, 1987), pp. 104–5, 108.

29. *Jomhuri-ye Eslami,* 12 January 1988.

30. Said A. Arjomand, "The Rule of God in Iran," *Social Compass* 36, no. 4 (1989).

31. *Jomhuri-ye Eslami,* 13 and 14 January 1988.

32. *Kayhan-e Hava'i,* 27 January 1988. Compare this with the statement he made less than two months earlier: "The Fundamental Law is the crystallization of the revolution; the basis and foundation of the Fundamental Law are the Koran and the Sunna. . . . One of the aims of the Fundamental Law is to prevent the concentration of power in one place, because the concentration of power in one place [evokes] a very bitter experience." Cited in Nahzat-e Azadi, *Velayat-e motlaqa-ye faqih,* p. 20.

33. Nahzat-e Azadi, *Velayat-e motlaqa-ye faqih,* p. 11.

34. The request for such a determination, made in a letter by the president, the Majlis speaker, the president of the Supreme Judiciary Council, and two other signatories, was printed together with Khomeini's decree.

35. *Jomhuri-ye Eslami,* 7 February 1988.

36. Nahzat-e Azadi, *Velayat-e motlaqa-ye faqih,* pp. 4, 24, 113–18, 136–37. The contradictions with Khomeini's earlier promises and statements were also documented. See Nahzat-e Azadi, *Velayat-e motlaqeh-ye faqih,* pp. 106–13.

37. *Kayhan-e Hava'i,* 25 and 28 February 1990, p. 2.

38. Ibid., 14 June 1989.

39. Ibid., 28 June 1989.

40. H. F. Jolowicz and B. Nicholas, *Historical Introduction to the Study of Roman Law* (Cambridge: Cambridge University Press,

1972), esp. chap. 21; also, A. A. Schiller, "Jurists' Law," *Columbia Law Review* 58 (1958): 1230.

41. Schiller, "Jurists' Law," pp. 1227–28.

42. Ibid., pp. 1231, 1235.

43. Max Weber, *Economy and Society,* G. Roth and C. Wittich, eds. (Berkeley, Calif.: University of California Press, 1968), pp. 828–29.

44. Said A. Arjomand, *The Shadow of God and the Hidden Imam.*

45. Ibid., p. 9.

46. T. Honoré, *Emperors and Lawyers* (London: Duckworth, 1981), p. 102.

47. H. J. Liebesney, *The Law of the Near and Middle East: Readings, Cases, and Materials* (Albany: State University of New York Press, 1975), pp. 38–41.

48. Nevertheless, the clerical elite remained divided on this issue and found it prudent to compromise with the principle of following a source of imitation in view of public sentiment. They promoted a relatively obscure figure, Ayatollah Araki, into the position of a source of imitation. Their endorsement was accompanied by the advice to Khomeini's followers in law and ritual to imitate Araki, and by the promise to bring out the latter's own manual. Meanwhile, Araki advised them to continue following Khomeini's rulings. His own manual was eventually published in mid-August 1989. *Kayhan-e Hava'i,* 23 August 1989.

49. Said A. Arjomand, "Traditionalism in Twentieth Century Iran," in Said A. Arjomand, ed., *From Nationalism to Revolutionary Islam* (London: Macmillan, 1984).

50. Many examples can be given, but two should suffice. The distinguished Orientalist Gustav von Grunebaum insisted that for the Muslims Allah is not only spiritually supreme but "also the mundane head of his community which he not only rules but governs." The eminent fundamentalist thinker Ayatollah Mortaza Motahhari considered theocracy the essence of Islam and rejected the "colonialist idea of separation of religion from politics." Cf. G. von Grunebaum, *Medieval Islam* (Chicago: University of Chicago Press, 1954), p. 12; Motahhari's statement

is cited in Said A. Arjomand, *The Turban for the Crown: The Islamic Revolution in Iran* (New York: Oxford University Press, 1988), pp. 179–80.

51. Arjomand, *The Shadow of God and the Hidden Imam.*

52. *Jomhuri-ye Eslami,* 17 January 1988.

53. See *Jomhuri-ye Eslami,* 19 January 1988. His awareness of the urgent need for extensive research on and jurisprudential exploration of the topic of the Mandate of the Jurist would not make Ayatollah Meshkini hesitant in the least in proceeding to affirm that "the Mandate of the Imam upon society is different from the incumbency of the daily prayer upon society. They are both at the same level and are among the primary ordinances. But they very much differ in importance. The Mandate [of the Jurist] is the most important of the primary ordinances."

54. *Kayhan-e Hava'i,* 14 June 1989.

55. Mocking the passing of governmental laws and regulations as "secondary ordinances," Grand Ayatollah Mohammad Reza Golpaygani took the occasion of the reelection of President Khamane'i in 1985 to urge the implementation of the "primary ordinances of Islam" and complained of the implementation of "other than the primary ordinances." He further expressed the hope that the ruling elements would "be careful and be governed by the primary ordinances of Islam, not ordinances which God's servants [i.e., they themselves] wish to say are God's ordinances." See Shabrough Akhavi, "Elite Factionalism in the Islamic Republic of Iran," *Middle East Journal* 41, no. 2 (1987): 191–92.

56. *Kayhan,* 5 March 1990.

57. Alexis de Tocqueville, *Ancien Regime and the Revolution,* S. Gilbert, trans. (Berkeley, Calif.: Doubleday Anchor Books, 1955).

58. Arjomand, *The Turban for the Crown,* p. 173.

The Fundamentalist Impact on Law, Politics, and Constitutions in Iran, Pakistan, and the Sudan

Ann Elizabeth Mayer

In this paper I will be using the definition of fundamentalism that Martin Marty offered in a 1988 article.[1] I do this in the belief that the criteria that he has set forth can be meaningfully applied in the Islamic context and in the hope of facilitating comparisons, not to imply that Marty's is the only definition or the best definition of fundamentalism for use in the Islamic context. My focus will be limited to manifestations of Islamic fundamentalism after the 1967 Arab-Israeli war, the era of the so-called Islamic resurgence. In that period, there was a noticeable disenchantment in the Near and Middle East with the prevailing secular nationalist ideologies and a groundswell of support for policies of returning to Islamic values and Islamic law, the *Shari'a*.

Rather than treat the Shari'a as a body of specific and highly technical legal rules, contemporary Muslim fundamentalists tend to transform it into an ideology, thereby treating it as a scheme for reorganizing society that, because of its divine origins, can serve as a panacea for political, economic, and social ills. In its conversion for use as a political ideology, the Shari'a has inevitably become simplified and politicized; its elaborate jurisprudence and the complex and extensive rules worked out by the pre-modern jurists have been slighted in its fundamentalist formulations. In many areas, what reinstating the Shari'a might involve in practice is often left vague by the proponents of Islamization when they are seeking popular support. This vagueness is politically useful, since it allows Muslims who favor Islamization in the abstract to read into programs for reviving the Shari'a the content that they would like them to have. Were the goals of an Islamization program specifically enumerated, Muslims who were committed to a different vision of Islamization could be alienated. Where left vague, "Islamization" could be espoused by Muslims hoping to achieve a wide variety of goals, including goals that had little or nothing in common with those of fundamentalists. The deemphasis of specific legal rules is also a natural result of aspirations to garner mass political support, since the intended audiences could hardly be expected to be galvanized into action by discussing intricacies of Shari'a law, a law developed by and for Muslims with advanced legal educations and far beyond the grasp of nonspecialists.

A variety of ideological formulations of the Shari'a that range from the radical left to the reactionary right have been proposed in recent decades by Muslims with divergent philosophies and interests. In some cases, support for returning to the Shari'a could mean that Muslims are calling for the realization of political and economic goals such as honest and democratic government, accountability of public officials, social justice, and the redistribution of wealth, or the establishment of an egalitarian society. In another context, calls for Islamization could signify a pattern of hostile reactions to modernization measures and a commitment to buttressing the patriarchal family, expanding religious instruction in public schools, imposing discriminatory measures on religious minorities and Muslim dissidents, challenging the legality of land reform programs, or preventing women from working and serving in public office.

Governments that adopt programs of Islamization naturally propose ideological formulations that serve to consolidate their power while opposition groups appeal to ideological conceptions of Islamic requirements that justify their campaigns to unseat those in power. Islamization is also supported by Muslims who are convinced that, whatever its rules call for, the Shari'a can serve as a prophylactic against the West, which is viewed as bent on exploiting and oppressing Muslims. Muslims have been inclined to believe that Western-style law and legal systems, adopted everywhere except in Saudi Arabia, were imposed on Muslim countries by Western powers in an effort to undermine local sovereignty. This belief is prompted by the fact that Westernization of laws in the nineteenth and twentieth centuries coincided with the period in which Europeans colonized and subjugated most parts of the Near and Middle East. The borrowing of Western legal systems is perceived as a betrayal of Muslims' religious obligations leading to a corrosion of morals for which the punishment has been military vulnerability and political weakness. For example, the 1967 Arab defeat has been interpreted as God's punishment vested on Muslim countries for having earlier discarded Islamic law and morality. The assumption is made that the revival of Islamic law will automatically restore traditional morality and social order, which will in turn thwart neo-imperialist designs, protecting Muslim countries from ever again being subjugated and exploited by Western powers.[2]

In addition to being viewed as a bulwark against Western political influence, Islamization is seen a way of blocking Western cultural imperialism. Islam is associated with cultural authenticity, and demands for Islamization have resulted from a desire to define a cultural identity vis-à-vis the West at a time when Western cultural influences threatened to overwhelm the indigenous cultural identity. Islamization is, therefore, a complex phenomenon not necessarily prompted by fundamentalist attitudes. Moreover, even where Islamization involves a fundamentalist impulse, this may be combined with other factors.

In this chapter three fundamentalist governmental Islamization campaigns of the post–1967 period will be reviewed. To put them in perspective, one should first consider other responses that governments have had to the Islamic resurgence. One response has been official resistance to popular pressures for Islamization. Examples of this can be seen in Turkey, Syria, Iraq, and Iran under the shah. Egypt under Sadat and Mubarak and Pakistan under Zulfikar Ali Bhutto exemplify another type of response, by which governments following basically secular policies make limited, strategic concessions to groups demanding Islamization. A third and somewhat idiosyncratic approach to Islamization can be seen in the policies of Qaddafi in Libya. There Islamization was just one of the many symbolic measures originally adopted by Qaddafi to revive and glorify Arab culture and instill pride in indigenous institutions. Islamization was also exploited to legitimize the military regime that had replaced the venerable King Idris. Far from being an ally of fundamentalists or sharing their goals, Qaddafi proved after a few years in power to be more like Fidel Castro or Mao Tse-tung in his outlook and became the bitter foe of groups like al-Ikhwan al-Muslimun, or Muslim Brotherhood, the most powerful fundamentalist organization in the region. The thrust of his major initiatives affecting law and religion was actually designed to relegate Islam to a marginal role.

In Iran, Pakistan, and the Sudan, the philosophies shaping the governmental Islamization programs all represented a fundamentalist outlook. The legislative products of the programs indicate that the objectives were broadly similar in all three countries. Pakistan under President Zia ul-Haq and the Sudan under Presidents Jafar al-Numayri and Omar Hassan al-Bashir represent models of military regimes espousing Islamization as the central government policy, enacting Shariʿa rules into law, coopting members of fundamentalist groups, implementing aspects of their programs, and allowing them roles in the government, educational institutions, and the courts. Iran offers a distinctive model. The overthrow of the shah's government by a popular revolution was followed by a takeover of the new government by Shiʿite clerics, the force within the revolution that was most committed to implementing a fundamentalist Islamization policy.

What does it mean to say that these governmental programs fit into the category of "fundamentalism?" First, the legislative program in these cases was, at least in its initial phases, consistently reactive and in some cases reactionary. Where Islamic rules were enacted into law, they were ones designed to purge the societies of Western influences and to reimpose what was ostensibly an Islamic model of society, the Shariʿa being identified with the traditional social order and morality. The diversity of traditional Islamic jurisprudence was discounted: in official Islamization programs there could be only one version of Islamic law. To the fundamentalists in Iran, Pakistan, and the Sudan the Islamic sources had an objective and univocal meaning. Problematic Islamic texts were converted in literalist manner into codes of positive law, with no acknowledgment that these texts might be ambiguous or that they could be legitimately interpreted as stating moral principles incumbent on the individual believer's conscience or as having symbolic or allegorical meanings.

The Islamization programs were also exclusivist and oppositional. They were accompanied by repressive policies and censorship directed at silencing Muslim dissenters, some of whom were condemned to death as "hypocrites," "infidels," "heretics," or "apostates from Islam." The Islamization programs included harsh treatment of Muslim liberals and modernists and discrimination against local religious minorities that, according to the fundamentalists' perceptions, presented dangers to Islam. Enactments purporting to embody Shari'a criminal laws were effectively enshrined as the centerpieces of the Islamization programs. The priority given to criminal law was emblematic of the antipermissive outlook informing the programs. The corpus of Shari'a rules was selectively mined for means of punishing and deterring immoral conduct and eradicating decadence, while Western-inspired laws and institutions frequently remained intact in areas where the fight against vice was not implicated. The consistent stress on legal prohibitions of immoral conduct and the preoccupation with rules in the criminal justice sphere were in contrast with the orientation of premodern Islamic jurists, who had not been preoccupied with reacting against perceived decadence when they elaborated their multivolume works of legal principles. Premodern jurisprudence was more concerned with civil than with criminal matters. In drafting laws, interpreting them, and meting out punishments the contemporary fundamentalists have tended to construe Islamic prohibitions broadly, creating new categories of offenses that would justify condemning and prosecuting a wider range of conduct than was criminalized in the premodern Shari'a. In the Islamization programs in Pakistan, the Sudan, and Iran some Shari'a laws were directed against crimes like theft, apostasy, fornication, and alcohol use in the Muslim community—which were criminalized in the traditional Shari'a. But Islam was also presented as the rationale for prohibiting abortion, girls' and women's participation in sports, coeducational schooling, dancing and music (both modern and traditional folkloric), "immodest" and "un-Islamic" women's dress, women's use of cosmetics, women's participation in the professions and service in political positions, public school instruction not in accordance with Islamic values, and immorality and "obscenity"—very broadly defined—in books, movies, and television programs. In Iran and the Sudan, alcohol use became criminalized even outside the Muslim community.

An example of the reactive and antipermissive character of fundamentalist visions of Islamization can be seen in a statement by Maulana Maududi, the famous Pakistani fundamentalist whose ideas inspired the Pakistani model of Islamization, regarding the goals and duties of an Islamic state:

> Unlike a Secular state, its duty is not merely to maintain internal order, to defend the frontiers and to work for the material prosperity of the country. Rather its first and foremost obligation is to establish the system of *Salat* [prayer] and *Zakat* [alms tax], to propagate and establish those things which have been declared to be "virtues" by God and His Messenger, and to eradicate those things which have been declared to be "vices" by them. In other words, no state can be called Islamic if it does not fulfil this fundamental objective of an Islamic State. Thus a state which does not take interest in establishing virtue and eradicating vice and in which adultery, drinking, gambling, obscene literature, indecent films, vulgar songs, immoral display of beauty, promiscuous

mingling of men and women, co-education, etc. flourish without let or hindrance, cannot be called an Islamic State. An Islamic Constitution must declare
the above mentioned objective as the primary duty of the State.[3]

The three Islamization campaigns that have been classified here as fundamentalist
may be contrasted with the legal system of Saudi Arabia. Before 1992, although the
Saudi legal system had seen the introduction of some legal innovations in the form of
new institutions that were designed to regulate business activity and to resolve disputes in areas that the regime had decided would require modern expertise, formal
"law" remained the premodern jurisprudence contained in the treatises of Islamic
jurists, or *fuqaha*—that is, Shari'a law in the same form that was in use in the Muslim
world before the onset of Westernizing reforms. For this reason, Saudi Arabia had
had no constitution before the belated promulgation of one on 1 March 1992. In
theory at least, the system of jurists' law that the Saudis retained until the campaign
of legislative reform was launched in early 1992 could not be revised or controlled by
the government, and it left no room for human legislation. Instead, it was law interpreted and applied by fuqaha with traditional religious educations. Leaving aside the
areas where there had been "regulation" (not "law") designed to cope with some
pressing practical problems, what qualified as "law" in Saudi Arabia remained the kind
of premodern Islamic jurisprudence that had governed Muslim societies centuries
ago. Furthermore, the country remains governed by a traditional monarchy that until
March 1992 had resisted all demands for changes in governmental institutions. The
kind of dynastic rule exercised by the house of Ibn Saud has ancient antecedents. So
in terms of law and politics in Saudi Arabia one has, rather than fundamentalism,
conservatism, traditionalism, and orthodoxy. In countries like Iran, Pakistan, and the
Sudan, one sees the reactive character of fundamentalism in measures taken by the
regimes to implement fundamentalist policies to change the legal and political systems. But the insiders in the Saudi system had favored continuity and the maintenance
of the hoary status quo; they wanted to preserve premodern Islamic jurisprudence as
their law and the traditional monarchical form of government. Therefore, the official
Saudi policies in the areas of law and politics can hardly be labeled "fundamentalist"
as long as one sticks rigorously to Marty's categories. Many of the opponents of
the existing Saudi system might want to implement programs that would have a fundamentalist impact on law and politics, but they have so far had no opportunity
to do so.

A few points where there is possibility for confusion should be clarified, because
Saudi Arabia is so often called "fundamentalist" by people who are not discussing
questions of the impact of fundamentalism on contemporary law and politics or who
are not using Marty's definition.[4] Many people talk of Saudi fundamentalism in connection with the Wahhabi movement, which was an important impetus behind the
rise of the Saudi dynasty in the eighteenth century. Wahhabism was indeed a fundamentalist phenomenon.[5] However, since it made its impact on law and politics long
before the time framework of this essay, which only comprises events in the 1970s
and 1980s, the Wahhabi version of fundamentalism, which has lost its original, reac-

tive zeal after becoming entrenched in the Saudi system, is not considered here. People may be impressed by the fact that the Saudis are known to encourage and finance fundamentalist movements abroad.[6] This may lead them to infer, incorrectly, that the regime follows fundamentalist policies domestically. In reality the conservative Saudis have come under fire from some fundamentalists precisely because their form of Islam, which the Iranian regime dismissively calls "American Islam," is not serviceable for the fundamentalists' political agenda. In 1979 the Saudis even had to face a fundamentalist uprising in Mecca, the leader of which condemned the Saudis for religious laxity and corruption and called for a return to the model of Islamic society established in the era of the Prophet. In 1991 the Saudi regime was increasingly concerned about the threat posed by the domestic fundamentalist movement.[7]

Iran

The Goals of Islamization in Iran

Any examination of the goals of fundamentalism in Iran entails an analysis of the goals of the Iranian Revolution of 1978–79, a complex phenomenon beyond the scope of this paper. At the very least, however, it should be noted that in Iran fundamentalist leaders and the fundamentalist program were linked in a variety of ways to a strong popular movement that culminated in a broad-based revolution. This was not the case either in Pakistan or in the Sudan, where Islamization was imposed from above by military dictators.

Iranian fundamentalists insist that the Iranian Revolution was led by them and fought on behalf of their cause, so that Islamization can be said to have been the goal of the revolution. It seems more accurate, however, to say that there was a fundamentalist takeover of a revolution that was fought primarily for secular political and economic goals. There was doubtless popular support for some of the broader fundamentalist goals, particularly among the lower middle and lower classes in urban areas, but it would be hard to establish that the Iranian Revolution was widely understood to have been waged on behalf of the specifics of the legislative program that emerged after powerful clerics seized control. Indeed, Ayatollah Khomeini, before consolidating his control, was evasive and vague in pronouncements about his objectives.[8] It is possible that he realized that a candid revelation of the details of his fundamentalist agenda might weaken his position and undermine his popularity.

After the revolution the early focus of Iran's official Islamization program was on establishing an Islamic government, and one of the first tasks of the new regime was writing an Islamic constitution. This was a natural priority because of the prominence of Ayatollah Khomeini's leadership role in the struggle against the shah and his own preoccupation with setting up an Islamic government according to his model of *wilayat al-faqih,* or rule by the Islamic jurist. Khomeini's ideas for the Iranian constitution provoked much criticism by Iranians, including some prominent Shi'ite *ulama* who remained convinced that clerics should not play a role in governance. After a drafting process that was replete with disputes, in late 1979 Iran did succeed in promulgating a new constitution, in which the faqih was placed at the apex of the government (articles 5 and 107) and Islamic law was established as the supreme law of the land (article 4), which meant the law of the majority Twelver Shi'ite sect (article 12). Said Arjomand discusses the particular features of this constitution in his chapter of the current volume.

Once firmly ensconced in power, Ayatollah Khomeini and his allies worked toward a goal that they had not advertised prior to the revolution or even in its immediate aftermath: implementing a theocratic model of government in which Shi'ite clerics would play a dominant role in all important spheres and particularly in the legal domain.[9] Shi'ite clerics allied with Khomeini proved eager to take political positions and to supplant the Western-trained or Western-oriented judges and lawyers who had come to dominate the legal establishment under the Pahlavis, under whom law and the legal profession had been largely reformed along French lines. The revolution gave clerics the opportunity to assume the central roles that they had played in the courts and in legal education prior to the secularizing reforms of the 1920s. In addition, clerics began to play a new and unfamiliar role, that of the dominant force in the Majlis, or parliament, which had been a thoroughly secular institution during the reign of Muhammad Reza Shah.

One could see the clerics' dislodging of Westernized professionals and secular-minded technocrats from the dominant positions that they had occupied under the shah as just one facet of the populist, anti-elitist dynamic of the revolution. The Westernized elite of the shah's era had grown estranged from Iranian traditions and had little in common with the values and outlooks of less affluent Iranians. Clerics were more in touch with the traditional culture of the average Iranian than the elite of the Pahlavi era. Nonetheless, this does not mean that the Iranians would have chosen a theocratic form of government had they been given the opportunity to choose between theocracy and democracy in free elections.

As a result of clerical ascendancy, postrevolutionary fundamentalist policies in Iran have been articulated by Shi'ite clerics. Iran's fundamentalist clerics had two bêtes noires on the domestic scene. Not surprisingly, these were the groups most dramatically affected by the Islamization program. The first target was Iranian women who rejected their traditional cloistered and subjugated role and demanded full equality with men. As Shahla Haeri points out in volume 2 of this series, clerical ire had been aroused by the 1963 reform which granted women the right to vote and by the Iranian Family Protection Act of 1967, which significantly improved women's rights in the area of family law. The growing prominence of women in public roles and the professions in the last decades of the shah's regime was also profoundly disturbing to the clerics. A prime goal of the clerical regime was to discredit emancipated women as traitors to Islam, or "Western dolls," as they were often labeled. Once the clerics were in power, Islamic precepts were interpreted in ways that promoted sexual segregation and the exclusion of women from areas of education, employment, and public activity. Harsh criminal penalties were imposed to punish and deter any conduct by females that conservative clerics found indecent or immoral. Violating rules of modest dress was treated as a serious offense, with penalities such as seventy-four lashes being imposed on women if they appeared in public without proper veiling.[10]

The other nemesis of the clergy was the sizable Baha'i community, which, not coincidentally, was ecumenically oriented, espoused liberal and humanistic values, and accorded full equality to women. Baha'ism had originated in Iran in the nineteenth century and had won many converts among Iran's Muslims. Clerics deemed that converts to Baha'ism and their descendants were apostates from Islam and deserving of capital punishment, the apostasy penalty set in premodern Shari'a jurisprudence. Under the shah, despite intermittent persecutions, Baha'is had been able to achieve a measure of equality with Muslims. By neglecting to mention Baha'is as a recognized minority religion, the 1979 constitution denied them the measure of religious toleration that was accorded Zoroastrians, Jews, and Christians in article 13. To destroy Baha'ism and the values it stood for, the regime undertook persecutions, imprisonments, and executions of Baha'is and Baha'i institutions were dismantled. Enormous pressure was exerted on Baha'is to repent of their theological errors and return to the Islamic fold.[11] The reasons for the persecution of the Baha'is are complex, but some may relate closely to the kinds of reactions fundamentalists have to the modern world in general. One of the most distinguished scholars of Shi'ism and modern Iran has opined that Baha'is are seen by Iranians much as Jews were seen by European anti-Semites and that anti-Baha'ism is comparable to anti-Semitism. Like Jews they are viewed as being cosmopolitan types. "Baha'is are seen to symbolize threatening aspects of modernity. . . . They adopt modern education and modern science with alacrity, producing large numbers of intellectuals, physicians, engineers, and business people. If modernity menaces Iran's identity, they are surely accomplices."[12]

How Islamization Was Pursued

In Iran Islamization proceeded as a by-product of the clerical takeover of the government and the courts. The process entailed the unseating and eventual defeat of secular forces that were disposed to resist clerical rule. The regime was intolerant of criticism by dissident Shi'ite clerics, who risked being censored, harassed, and even placed under house arrest when they questioned the legitimacy of clerical rule or criticized the official Islamization line.[13] Claiming to represent "Islam," the regime treated its foes as if their opposition to the government was tantamount to declaring war on the Islamic religion. Ruthless persecution, incarceration, torture, and mass executions of the regime's critics withered the opposition. About two million Iranians, actual and potential opponents of the regime, fled to foreign havens and wound up as exiles in the West and in neighboring Turkey.

There was no way to challenge the regime's oppressive scheme of Islamization in the courts, which meted out an arbitrary form of summary justice from which any semblance of due process was banished. Among other secular institutions, the Iranian Bar Association was destroyed and with it the modern legal profession and its members' commitment to legality.[14]

Khomeini's Islamization policy was directed against various foreign devils, among which the United States was singled out for particularly strong vilification due to American support for the shah. In Khomeini's program the pursuit of Islamization became closely associated with a strident anti-Americanism, with the United States incessantly excoriated as the Great Satan and presented as the enemy of Islam. (This stands in remarkable contrast to the situation in Pakistan, where the United States was the primary backer of the Zia regime, and to the situation in the Sudan, where the United States was the sole foreign prop in the final stages of Numayri's regime.) Khomeini's demonizing of the regime of Iraqi president Saddam Hussein served a similar role within his Islamization program; the war with Iraq was in part a prolonged demonstration of revolutionary zeal against infidels on the doorstep. And once that war ended in the 1988 ceasefire, Khomeini kept the fires stoked by calling for the execution of Salman Rushdie as an apostate from Islam, while Iran's propagandists sought to tie Rushdie's work to an American and Israeli plot against Islam.

It is thus ironic that, while these battles were being fought, strikingly little lasting progress was made toward eradicating Western influences on the fundamental structure and institutions of the legal system. For example, in the 1979 Iranian constitution one finds borrowed Western institutions that lack Islamic antecedents such as the republican form of government, the division of the government into three separate branches, a directly elected president who functions as chief executive, a prime minister and a cabinet, the ideas of the independence of the judiciary and judicial review, the concept of legality, the notion of an elected legislative body, the need for the cabinet to obtain votes of confidence from the legislative branch, and the concept of national sovereignty. Even the distinctive institution of the faqih, as set forth in the 1979 constitution, is embedded in a matrix of relations with other, conventional Western governmental institutions. For example, according to article 110 the faqih's duties include appointing the chief of staff of Iran's armed forces, declaring war, organizing the Supreme Council for National Defense (the president, prime minister, minister of defense, and others), confirming the appointment of the president after his election, and dismissing the president in the interests of the country after a Supreme Court ruling that the president has violated his legal duties. Such principles have counterparts in Western political systems, but they have no relation to the traditional function of a Shi'ite faqih.

In many facets and in its general format, the Iranian constitution resembles the 1958 French constitution. The way Islamic content has been injected into provisions with French antecedents can be illustrated by comparing the treatment of national sovereignty in article 56 of the Iranian constitution with article 3 of the French constitution. The French version establishes that sovereignty rests on the will of the people as expressed through referendums and enjoins interference with the exercise of popular sovereignty. It begins: "National sovereignty belongs to the people, which shall exercise this sovereignty through its representatives by means of referendums. No section of the people, nor any individual, may attribute to themselves or himself the exercise thereof." In chapter 5 of the Iranian constitution under the heading "The Right of National Sovereignty and the Powers Derived from It" one sees in article 56 the Islamized version of the same provision, in which the theological tenet that God is the Supreme Ruler is inserted and the French provisions enjoining interference—this time with Divine Sovereignty—have been incongruously retained:

"Absolute sovereignty over the world and mankind is God's and He alone has determined the social destiny of human beings. None shall take away this God-given right from another person or make use of it to serve his special personal or group interests." Wanting to retain the provision for popular referendums, the authors of the Iranian constitution relegated it to article 59, by which placement the clash between the idea that national sovereignty is exercised by the people via referendums and the idea that sovereignty is the exclusive province of the deity has been rendered less obvious. The incongruity remains: there is no room for popular sovereignty exercised via referendums in a system based on the theological premise of divine rule, which at the very least should mean that God's laws are binding and not subject to modification by any human agency, such as popular referendums involve.

A similar pattern of borrowing Western constitutional principles and then modifying them can be seen in chapter 3 of the Iranian constitution, where there are provisions for rights principles that are of Western derivation but with Islamic qualifications added to circumscribe them. Thus, for example, article 20 provides for human rights, a Western concept, but Islamizes them by indicating that they are to be enjoyed "according to Islamic standards." Again, there is a resultant incongruity, since the philosophy of human rights precludes curbing rights by reference to the standards of a particular religion.

Even though the making of laws via human agency is barred under traditional Islamic legal theory, according to which all laws are to be found in and derived from the Islamic sources, Iran's Islamic constitution provided for lawmaking by the Majlis in article 58, and laws continued to be enacted by the Majlis just as they had been under the shah.

The Iranian approach to legislation thus differed markedly from the approach to law in Saudi Arabia, where, in deference to Islamic tradition, there was officially no man-made law.[15] Ayatollah Khomeini seems to have originally aspired to return to a similar system of jurists' law, asserting in 1970 in a speech: "The entire system of government and administration, together with the necessary laws, lies ready for you. There is no need for you, after establishing a government, to sit down and draw up laws, or, like rulers who worship foreigners and are infatuated with the West, run after others to borrow their laws. Everything is ready and waiting. All that remains is to draw up ministerial programs."[16] However, modern legal institutions on Western lines proved firmly rooted and survived the Islamic revolution largely intact.

The ultimate guarantee that laws would be in conformity with the Shari'a lay in the provision in article 4 that Islamic law would be supreme, overriding not only any laws in conflict with it but even the constitution itself. The article also provided that clerics on the Council of Guardians would make the decisions in this regard. This represented the achievement of a goal of Iran's clerics, who had been determined to ensure that there would be effective clerical review of proposed legislation in order to ensure conformity with Shari'a requirements.

In practice, the Council of Guardians reviewed and invalidated proposed laws with such stringency and zeal that acute embarrassment resulted at times for the government. For example, economic reforms such as land reform laws enacted by the Majlis were needed to retain the political support of the poorer classes but were repeatedly nullified by the Council of Guardians on the grounds that they violated Islamic law. For nine years Khomeini avoided challenging these "Islamic" vetos of legislation that the regime deemed politically essential. However, Khomeini finally ruled on 7 January 1988 that the Islamic state had absolute power—like the power enjoyed by the Prophet Muhammad—and was permitted to adopt such measures as it deemed necessary for the interests of the Islamic state *even where these might conflict with Islamic law or a fundamental religious obligation like the pilgrimage to Mecca.*[17] This ruling seemed to mean that measures passed by the Majlis and acceptable to the faqih would henceforth go into effect even if the Guardians believed that they contravened the requirements of the Shari'a. This ruling proved that fundamentalists were not actually concerned with restoring Shari'a law per se. As the Iranian experience showed, the commitment was actually to reinstate Shari'a rules insofar as they served fundamentalists' political agendas. Conversely, Shari'a rules could be discounted when they stood in the way of programs that served the fundamentalists' own political interests.

Thus, considerations of *raison d'état* were officially permitted to override Islamic criteria. This was, ultimately, embarrassing for a government officially committed to the implementation of Islamic law. A constitutional amendment adopted on 28 July 1989 attempted to deal with this problem by endorsing the establishment of a council that would mediate and consult when conflicts occurred between the Majlis and the Council of Guardians.[18] Since the new council's members were to be appointed by the faqih, it seemed unlikely that they would be disposed to contradict his views. It is too early to say what role the council will actually be able to play in resolving conflicts between legislation and Shari'a law, but its establishment suggests that the position of the Council of Guardians has been downgraded.

How Successful Has Islamization Been?

In terms of the scope of Islamization measures that have been formally enacted into law, it is in Iran that the fundamentalists have enjoyed their greatest successes. Islamization has gone far enough there that it is destined to have a long-term impact. The government itself has been reconstituted, and the constitution rewritten to institutionalize clerical authority and the supremacy of Islamic law (however it might be interpreted). In the 1980s and early 1990s fundamentalist clerics were firmly ensconced in powerful positions and dominated the country's legal system. Laws were enacted that embodied the fundamentalists' policies of combating the erosion of the traditional social structure and value system. Even if the application of criminal laws to enforce Islamic morality was relaxed somewhat, as it appeared to be in 1991, the impact of these laws on Iranian society remained considerable. Pre-revolution advances in women's status were rolled back, the 1967 Family Protection Act repealed, and women relegated to subservient roles caring for their husbands and children. The Baha'i religion has been virtually persecuted out of existence in Iran.[19]

At the same time, there have been detrimental side effects of fundamentalist policies that were not intended by the policymakers. In the wake of official efforts to confine women to domestic roles and encouraged by the regime's initial pronatalist policies, the birthrate soared to 3.9 percent a year. The population growth became so alarming that in 1990 fears were being publicly expressed in official circles that it could pose an obstacle to Iran's development. In a dramatic reversal, the regime began to support birth control measures. Another obstacle to development was the brain drain resulting from the mass exodus of highly trained professionals and technocrats who were alienated by the fundamentalist policies of the regime. By 1989 there was growing evidence that leaders of the regime felt that a policy of liberalization was essential to woo back members of the educated elite from exile. In hopes of attracting foreign investment and trade from Europe and Japan, a major project for a free-trade zone on Qeshm Island at the entrance to the Persian Gulf was approved by the Parliament in February of 1990, despite conservatives' vocal opposition to the plan for granting foreigners on Qeshm exemptions from Iranian law. In the prevailing climate of pragmatism, it was possible to hear a cleric, Hojjatulislam Hassan Ruhani, say openly in Parliament: "To install Islamic codes on Qeshm is in contradiction with reality. The more freedom we provide for investors, the more of them we can attract." [20] Thus, to attract badly needed foreign capital, the regime was prepared to lift the application of its version of Islamic law. Ironically, this meant replicating the kind of scheme of extraterritorial treatment for foreign nationals that had been negotiated by Americans under the shah, which Ayatollah Khomeini had excoriated in a famous speech in 1964 as the work of traitors.[21] Moreover, there were even some indications of official sentiment favoring liberalization of the veiling requirements for women.[22]

Iran's clerics remain uneasy with Iranian nationalism, which has been generally espoused by secular-minded politicians and intellectuals unsympathetic to clerical interests. The late shah gave Iran's clerics special reasons for opposing Iranian nationalism, since his version of Iranian nationalism sought to revive pride in Iran's pre-Islamic heritage as a means of denigrating the Islamic contribution to Iranian culture. In consequence, clerics have at various points since the revolution advocated measures like destroying the ancient ruins at Persepolis, banning the distinctive Iranian Nowruz (New Year) celebrations as pagan, and promoting Arabic as a replacement for Persian. That is, Iran's character as a nation-state, which survived the revolution, did so despite clerical and fundamentalist antipathy to aspects of Iranian nationalism.[23] The failure of the fundamentalists to carry out their plans for eradicating a separate Iranian national identity and setting up a supranational polity on a religious basis was due to the great resistance from Iranians, who are for the most part profoundly nationalistic and proud of their distinctive culture.

The Iranian model has not been emulated by other countries. In the eyes of many fundamentalists, the Islamic Republic of Iran is a failure as an Islamic polity, because it has a specific, Iranian national character. Islamic fundamentalists, including some in Iran, have tended to favor the concept that in Islam the only legitimate political entity is the *umma*, or community of believers, and that the nation-state and nationalism are inherently un-Islamic. One of the issues that had proved contentious during the drafting of the constitution was whether or not it was permissible for a self-proclaimed Islamic state to have a national territory, a national language, and citizenship requirements like those of other nation-states. Although the final version of the Iranian constitution affirms Iran's character as a nation-state, Islamic fundamentalists have persisted in challenging its legitimacy.

The Iranian fundamentalist version of Islam is not an inclusive, ecumenical one but is fraught with distinctive Twelver Shiʻite characteristics, and this bias in favor of Twelver Shiʻism may eventually have an untoward effect on the political loyalties of the Sunni Baluchis, Kurds, and Turkomans inside Iran. Outside Iran this same Shiʻite bias has sharply limited the appeal of Iran's Islamic revolution, which was originally intended to be a model that would be emulated throughout the Muslim world but which has inspired scant emulation except in Twelver Shiʻite communities in places like Lebanon.

Future Prospects

The fortunes of fundamentalism in Iran will be strongly affected by which factions are ultimately successful in the power struggles that ensued after Khomeini's death. Politically active clerics in 1990 and 1991 differed significantly in the degree to which they were actually committed to the fundamentalist cause.

Before the Rushdie affair of February 1989 there were indications that powerful figures in the government were ready to adopt more moderate and conciliatory policies toward the opposition and the West and that they had become disenchanted with fundamentalist extremism.[24] After the Rushdie affair exploded, the moderate Ayatollah Hossein Ali Montazeri, long Khomeini's chosen successor, came under siege. He was finally obliged to resign on 28 March after being attacked for having criticized government repression and for urging toleration of dissent. These manifestations of liberal sympathies led Montazeri to be characterized as one who had moved away from the Islamic system.[25]

The June 1989 death of Ayatollah Khomeini placed the viability of his concept of governance by the leading jurist in jeopardy. No successor of equivalent prestige and charisma was available to serve as faqih. After the disgrace of Ayatollah Montazeri and his elimination from the succession, no distinguished, high ranking clerics remained who could be trusted to follow Khomeini's political line. Articles 107 and 109 of the constitution were amended in July of 1989 to downgrade the requirements for serving the office of faqih in order to accommodate Ayatollah ʻAli Khameneʼi, a far less eminent cleric than Ayatollah Khomeini had been. In the aftermath of these changes, the importance of the office of faqih seemed destined to dwindle.

Constitutional amendments adopted in July of 1989 eliminated the office of prime minister and concentrated power in the presidency, a secular office, even though currently occupied by a cleric. Hojjatulislam Ali Akbar Hashemi Rafsanjani was able to win a pro forma election as president in July 1989. Rafsanjani's subsequent consolidation of his power signaled at least a temporary victory by a relatively moderate and pragmatic faction in the government at the expense of the fundamentalist hard-liners. The original Islamic scheme of government seemed to be in the process of being transformed into a mundane presidential one.

Under the leadership of President Rafsanjani it seems that Iran's policies are being significantly liberalized in the political, economic, and social domains. One suspects that, if he did not have to fear a backlash from militant fundamentalist forces and could follow his own personal inclinations, Rafsanjani might be moving even faster toward liberalization. In a brave move for a cleric, he has supported the idea of allowing women greater freedoms and participation in public life and the professions than they enjoyed under Khomeini.[26]

Like Prime Minister Nawaz Sharif of Pakistan, Rafsanjani seems to have little personal enthusiasm for the cultural dimensions of Islamization and appears primarily concerned with bold reforms to end his country's economic deterioration and to promote rapid development along free-market lines.[27] This liberalization program entails improving Iran's relations with Europe and Japan and institutions like the IMF, which in turn necessitate hewing to a moderate political line. The trends justified a tentative conclusion that under President Rafsanjani and the pragmatists allied with him, and in the face of overwhelming need to extricate the country from an economic morass, the fundamentalist impulse faded in the early 1990s—at least at the governmental level, where it would shape politics, laws, and the constitution.

Pakistan

The Goals of Islamization in Pakistan

In Pakistan one goal of President Zia's Islamization program was to establish Islam as an official, unifying ideology and to mine it as a source of national identity. Since fundamentalism is used, in Marty's words, "for setting boundaries, for attracting one's kind and alienating other kinds, for demarcating," one sees why Zia's government would adopt an ideology linked to a fundamentalist version of Islam.

Unlike Iran, a nation with roots in antiquity where today Persian culture is widely disseminated and the Persian majority has a strong cultural identity, Pakistan is a new and artificial entity, dating only from 1947. Pakistan's identity as a nation is negative, being defined against the map of India, out of which two areas were carved in regions where Muslims outnumbered Hindus in a last-minute compromise agreement worked out by the departing British colonizers. Domestically, Pakistan's leaders have had to cope with chronic regional rivalries and fissiparous tendencies caused by a lack of common ethnic or linguistic bonds among different groups in the population. The 1971 civil war that resulted in the loss of East Pakistan, now Bangladesh, was an ominous demonstration of the fragile nature of the polity. Against this background, Islamization in Pakistan can be seen as a program designed to reinforce an unstable polity and to create elements of a shared culture for a nation that suffers from an ongoing identity crisis.[28] One can see parallels between the official espousal of Islamic fundamentalism and the government's campaign launched in the early 1980s to spread the use of Urdu at the expense of the regional languages spoken by most Pakistanis and its insistence that bureaucrats wear uniform attire that was officially designated "national dress."[29]

The various players in the program also had specific agendas. From President Zia's standpoint, a central aim of Islamization was to provide legitimation for his protracted military dictatorship. Having overthrown the elected government of Zulfikar Ali Bhutto in 1977, Zia badly needed a justification for his repeated rebuffs to popular demands for a return to democracy. Zia, himself a devout Sunni whose personal piety was respected even by his foes, found in the Islamization campaign an ideal pretext for retaining power. Since the goal of achieving Islamization proved conveniently elusive, when demands for a return to democracy became embarrassingly loud, Zia was able to counter that he could not relinquish power, because the goal of Islamization had not been fully realized.[30]

Via Islamization, Zia forged alliances with Sunni clerics and fundamentalist groups. Very active and militant Sunni fundamentalist groups operate in Pakistan, including the Jamaat-i-Islami. Though originally opposed to the formation of Pakistan, since they believed the nation-state incompatible with Islam, Sunni fundamentalists like Maududi later decided to participate in Pakistan's political life. They hoped to gain enough power to implement their program of reimposing the Shari'a, which had been displaced by Anglo-Muhammadan law and British law during the period of British imperial rule. However, in Pakistan's occasional democratic elections, fundamentalist groups like Maududi's Jamaat-i-Islami consistently made poor showings.[31]

From the standpoint of the Sunni fundamentalists who made common cause with Zia, one goal was to exploit their alliance with him to expand opportunities for increasing their own participation in important institutions like the government, the courts, the schools, and the media. In return for their endorsement of his Islamization program, Zia gave them much more significant roles than they had been able to win previously.

It is worth remarking that, in contrast to Iran, the hotbed of Shi'ite fundamentalism, in Pakistan the large Shi'ite minority tended to be liberal, progressive, and bitterly opposed to fundamentalism. Some of the most vigorous criticism of Zia came from Shi'ite clerics. Benazir Bhutto's mother was a Shi'ite, and her opposition party was able to form alliances with Shi'ite forces. Quaid-i-Azam Mohammad Ali Jinnah, the revered founder of Pakistan, was himself a Shi'ite. Like other Pakistani liberals, Jinnah envisaged Pakistan as a basically secular political entity. In contrast, Sunni fundamentalists have argued that religion is the sole raison d'être for Pakistan and that the whole purpose of establishing Pakistan was to enable Muslims from the subcontinent to live under a government constituted according to Islamic principles and a society governed by Islamic law.[32]

Taking a page from the fundamentalist agenda, Zia sought to have the 1973 constitution of Pakistan replaced by an Islamic one. Naturally, Zia insisted on a constitution that would ratify his hold on power. However, this goal of producing an Islamic constitution was never achieved. All proposed drafts proved problematic, and it became obvious that adopting any version of an Islamic constitution was likely to cause such dissension and division that it would be politically counterproductive. Instead, Pakistani Islamization meant the reinstatement of various specific Islamic rules in what remained basically a common law system. The greatest emphasis was placed on reviving Islamic rules in the area of criminal law, preserving morality, and implementing some changes in tax and banking law designed to eliminate certain features deemed objectionable by proponents of Islamic economics. In addition, the educational system was reformed to ensure that Islam was studied and Islamic values inculcated, and clerics were accorded higher professional standing and a greater role in the legal system.[33]

Pakistan's fundamentalists also had ambitions to halt the progress of female emancipation. Fundamentalists had been outraged as more and more Pakistani women abandoned housebound roles, obtained higher educations, and moved into desirable professional and government jobs. While feminist ideas circulated among members of the elite, a backlash emerged among fundamentalists, who insisted that the traditional patriarchal order had been divinely ordained and sought to use Islamic law to relegate women to a segregated and subjugated status.[34] As will be discussed, several factors limited their successes.

A prime goal of the fundamentalists was to promote measures that would humiliate and discredit members of the large Ahmadi minority. This Islamic sect had long been excoriated by Pakistan's fundamentalists for what they saw as the Ahmadis' unorthodox beliefs, and Maududi and his followers had engaged in intense propaganda campaigns against the Ahmadis.[35] So intense had pressures grown for anti-Ahmadi measures that Zulfikar Ali Bhutto, no real friend to fundamentalism, had decided to make a gesture to appease the anti-Ahmadi sentiment in 1974 by having Ahmadis officially declared to be non-Muslims via an amendment to the constitution. Under Zia, the government winked at harassment of Ahmadis by fundamentalist groups, and additional stigmas were imposed on them by a 1984 law forbidding them to call themselves Muslims or their religion Islam, to use Islamic terminology, to use the Islamic call to prayer, to call their places of worship mosques, or to propagate their version of Islam. Under this law they became subject to criminal penalties for any conduct that "outrages" the religious feelings of a Muslim, making the subjective reactions of Muslims the gauge for what constituted a crime for which Ahmadis could be condemned to fines and jail. Criminal prosecutions and convictions of Ahmadis ensued.[36] The intrusive nature of the anti-Ahmadi campaign was shown when a group of Ahmadis were arrested and faced criminal charges for the offense of holding a prayer meeting in a private home.[37]

How Islamization Was Pursued

In Pakistan, President Zia was able to set the parameters of Islamization. He was a pragmatic and cautious man whose ultimate concern was holding on to power. Although it seems that he was genuinely committed to Islamization, he did not let his enthusiasm for Islamization lure him into attempting drastic or sudden changes until shortly before his death. In May of 1988 Zia dissolved Parliament and dismissed his government, alleging that there had been a failure to push for Islamization. This was followed by the sudden issuance of a presidential decree embodying a dramatic new Islamization initiative on 15 June 1988 according to which all government policies would have to guided by Islamic law and all laws contravening Islamic law were to be nullified. This Islamic Law Enforcement Ordinance was apparently designed to implement Islamic law across the board under clerical supervision and to make all laws, including the constitution, subordinate to the Shari'a, as had been provided in article 4 of the Iranian constitution. To avoid problems with foreign aid donors and institutional creditors, one exception was made for international economic and investment agreements. This Islamization decree was vigorously denounced by Pakistanis representing all parts of the political spectrum, who saw it as a fresh pretext for resisting demands for the restoration of democracy and for undermining the constitution. It seems likely that the decree was prompted by Zia's fears of upcoming elections that he had reluctantly scheduled for the autumn; he may have planned to exploit "Islamic" criteria to disqualify Benazir Bhutto, Zia's most formidable opponent, on the grounds that women serving in high political office contravened the Shari'a.[38] Zia's death on 17 August 1988, before the decree had been formally ratified, left it a dead letter.

Prior to the June decree, Islamization measures had been officially adopted only after consultative processes and input from groups that Zia felt the need to conciliate. Thus, even though he ruled under martial law from 1977 through 1985 and suspended all constitutional rights and freedoms in this period, Zia did not rush the Islamization process and took some pains to ensure that his Islamization proposals were well prepared and their consequences weighed before actually implementing them. The bureaucratic machinery for carrying them out was considered, as well. Through gradual, piecemeal enactments over several years, laws embodying some fundamentalist policies were extended to many areas without great disruption. Compromises were made when political realities made reforms inadvisable. As it turned out, Zia's cautious approach to Islamization provoked disillusionment on the part of some uncompromising fundamentalists, who objected to Zia's measures as halfhearted and inadequate.

Although Zia's regime engaged in repression and censorship of its foes, dissent was not as brutally or comprehensively quelled as it was in Iran, and Pakistanis could, within limits, express critical opinions. Civil society survived in the face of military dictatorship. Cynical assessments of Zia's Islamic laws were made by members of the educated elite, liberals, leftists, and secularists, who never accepted the validity of the premises of the Islamization program. Occasional public salvos at the Islamization program were fired by courageous clerics, journalists, lawyers, and politicians. There was enough political room for maneuver for the opposition on occasion to register protests over Islamization measures in ways that constituted political embarrassments for Zia, who had to be careful of running afoul of aid donors in the West. This inhibited him from attempting radical change—at least until June of 1988.

Zia tried to circumvent the concerns for legality on the part of the bar and the judiciary in Pakistan by exploiting the martial law regime and allowing military courts a major role in implementing "Islamic justice," which enabled the justice system to get around the niceties of due process. Harsh penalties like flogging were often imposed by military courts.[39] In contrast, the regular courts were disinclined to order floggings, much less amputations and stonings. The regular courts remained relatively strong and independent institutions, and there were instances in which Pakistan's courts agreed with lawyers who brought cases challenging the justifications for certain Islamization measures. Political prudence therefore dictated that the more extreme fundamentalist initiatives be abandoned or watered down.

Members of the large Shi'te minority were especially vehement in their attacks on Islamization, which embodied a Sunni fundamentalist perspective that was anathema to Pakistani Shi'ites. In July of 1980 the Shi'ite minority mustered a demonstration of hundreds of thousands in Islamabad that forced the government to revise an Islamic tax measure that was particularly offensive to the Shi'ite community, conflicting as it did with a central tenet of their jurisprudence. The relations between the Sunni majority and Shi'ite minority deteriorated sharply under Zia's rule due to frictions between the two sects that were traceable to the Sunni bias of the Islamization campaign.[40]

Zia was also confronted by organized opposition from women's groups when he sought to implement the fundamentalist agenda affecting their rights and status. Feminists had much to oppose, since fundamentalist groups kept pressuring the Zia regime for a wide range of curbs on women's rights and freedoms.[41] The Council of Islamic Ideology (CII), one of the institutions entrusted by Zia with the formulation of Islamization measures, was one of the targets of feminist ire. An illustration of the mentality of CII members can be seen in a leading question on a questionnaire that was ostensibly circulated by the CII to survey Pakistanis' views on women's proper role: "To satisfy their own lusts westernised individuals in Pakistan want to bring women out of their homes and make them the center of attraction in society in negation of Islamic instructions. They wish to thrust on women economic responsibilities in addition to family responsibilities. In your opinion, what weakness will result in an Islamic society because of this unnatural approach?"[42]

The message embodied in this phrasing illustrates how the CII served to spread the fundamentalists' view that women belonged in a domestic role. A number of discriminatory measures directed at women were enacted that were informed by the fundamentalist philosophy. The government also gave fundamentalists access to the media, which they used to broadcast claims that Westernized women were the source of decadence and immorality and that sexual segregation was essential for the preservation of virtue. However, fear of the embarrassment that women's groups kept the regime from adopting Islamization measures that too blatantly conflicted with international human rights norms. For example, while sharply curtailing the ability of Pakistani women to participate in international sporting events pursuant to fundamentalist claims that female athletes' participation in public sports violated Islamic norms of modesty, the government prudently decided to enact no law barring female participation in sports lest Pakistan be classified with South Africa as a country practicing discrimination, which could have led to Pakistan's male athletes being barred from international competitions.

The kind of bad publicity the regime feared occurred as women resorted to public protests in Lahore in February of 1983 to denounce a proposed law on evidence, which allowed a woman's testimony to be devalued in relation to a man's. These protests and the rough treatment meted out to the women protesters by the police were reported in the international press. Although the evidence law was enacted in 1984, the regime was chastened by the feminists' response. Thus, certain proposals for new laws, such as one that would have reinstated the Shari'a rule that in cases of killings the value of a woman's life was to be calculated as being worth one-half that of a man's, were never actually enacted, despite strong support from fundamentalists. Attempts by the fundamentalists to prohibit women from wearing saris—allegedly "un-Islamic"—foundered in the face of adamant resistance from Pakistani matrons who came from backgrounds in which wearing the sari was de rigueur for married women.[43]

In terms of practical consequences, Islamization had more impact in policies mandating an expanded role for clerics in the court system; in laws and regulations mandating religious instruction in schools and revising textbooks in accordance with Islamic standards; in the extensive restructuring of the operations of financial institutions to eliminate interest charges; and in changes in the tax system after the enactment of the law on *zakat,* or alms tax.[44]

How Successful Has Islamization Been?

While Zia was alive, Pakistan's fundamentalists, though not able to achieve all their goals, had reason to be pleased with the general direction developments had been taking. However, Zia's Islamization program may have better served his interests than it did the cause of fundamentalism. For Zia, Islamization offered a pretext for perpetuating his military rule and refusing to allow freely contested elections on a party basis, in which Bhutto's Pakistan People's Party would have been sure to emerge victorious.[45] But for fundamentalists the linkage of the fundamentalist program to Zia's continuation in office meant that their victories might be illusory, subject to cancellation with any change in regime. This was due to their inability to get a new Islamic constitution adopted that would have institutionalized the political gains they had won with Zia's support.

Perhaps the single most grievous failure of the fundamentalists was their inability to get laws enacted like those in Iran that would have demoted women to an inferior and subjugated status. They failed to obtain legislation to repeal the Muslim Family Laws Ordinance of 1961, which had introduced modest reforms improving the rights of women in the family and which fundamentalists condemned as a contravention of the Shari'a. They were also thwarted in their objectives of preventing women from working outside the home and of removing them from government jobs. The fundamentalist campaign against women's rights had the unintended effect of provoking counterpropaganda that offered feminist interpretations of the Islamic sources and arguments that the fundamentalist model of women's role was being shaped by reactionary interests and a retrograde clerical mentality, not by the true Islam of the Qur'an and the Prophet.[46]

One reason for the fundamentalists' failures in this area was that Pakistan's government was dominated by military officers and high-ranking members of the civil service bureaucracy. In these strata female participation in society and the work force was the norm, and women commonly obtained higher educations. In this regard the members of the Zia regime were very different from the postrevolutionary clerical elite in Iran, whose wives and female relatives seem to have accepted the *chador* (the black veil Iranian women must wear), seclusion, and loss of freedoms that they had enjoyed under the shah with little, if any, protest. Thus, with regard to the status of women, the goals of the fundamentalist allies of the military regime seem to have been at odds with the attitudes of the military and bureaucratic elite, which may account for many of the fundamentalist plans for curbing women's rights being thwarted.

As the election of Benazir Bhutto proved in 1988, the fundamentalists after enjoying twelve years of official sponsorship had not succeeded in adequately shaping public attitudes via their propaganda on the proper role for women in society to forestall a woman from acceding to the prime minister's office. To make matters worse, Bhutto, a vigorous critic of Islamization, embodied everything the fundamentalists especially abominated—she studied in the West, refused to settle down to a life of homemaking and child care, espoused leftist policies, and insisted on competing with men in the political arena.

Future Prospects

President Zia's death paved the way for the first relatively free elections held in Pakistan since his 1977 coup. Running on a secular platform, a woman who had attacked Zia's Islamization program emerged the winner. Benazir Bhutto, long Zia's most prominent political opponent, was able to win more votes than any other candidate and to become prime minister in December of 1988. This suggested that Zia's unwillingness to allow democratic elections had been based on a well-founded apprehension that his Islamization program had shallow popular support. Candidates who ran in the elections on fundamentalist platforms immediately after Zia's death generally fared poorly. Benazir Bhutto's strongest opponent was the Punjabi industrialist Nawaz Sharif, a friend of the powerful military forces overseeing the election and the leading candidate pledged to continue Zia's policies. Sharif did less well than Bhutto in 1988, even though the circumstances were advantageous for him, since oppositional political activity had been restricted for over a decade and a caretaker regime with ties to the military was in power during the elections.

During her tenure in office, Bhutto demonstrated little capacity to cure Pakistan's chronic political instability and did not manage to roll back the Islamization measures that she had criticized while in opposition. While trying to find her political footing, Bhutto seemed to fear risking an attempt to repeal Islamic laws, which could have provided her conservative opponents with a fresh issue to use against her. Given the exacerbated religious sensitivities stirred up by violent anti-Rushdie agitation encouraged by her political foes at the time she became prime minister, which continued into 1990, she had reason to proceed with great caution.[47]

As months passed without constructive initiatives, many of Bhutto's erstwhile supporters professed disenchantment over her inability to define and promote programs that would address the fundamental problems facing her troubled country. Her failure to take effective measures to end the turmoil and rising crime rate in her home province of Sind was also held against her. Exasperation was commonly expressed over her

toleration of egregious patterns of corruption that allegedly surrounded her, and her
husband was rumored to have profited spectacularly by exploiting his connection to
his powerful spouse. The exalted hopes originally entertained by Pakistanis that a
return to democracy would bring progress on the economic front, social justice, and
peace seem to have been dashed by Bhutto's lackluster performance at a time when
wise and forceful leadership was desperately needed.

Bhutto herself was abruptly dismissed from office on 6 August 1990 by the president. The move was officially justified on the grounds that her government had been
corrupt and nepotistic, but she claimed that her dismissal was a disguised military
coup mounted by the foes of democracy. While many charges were leveled against her
and criminal prosecutions of her family were threatened, as of two years later the
government had not substantiated its claims. Meanwhile, Bhutto had to contest the
24 October 1990 national elections under a cloud, not having had any chance to clear
herself in a court of law of the charges made against her and her family.

The low voter turnout seems to have resulted from the disillusioned and apathetic
state of the electorate. Amid charges of vote-rigging, Bhutto's party was able to win
only 45 seats to the 105 won by the loose eight-party coalition known as the Islamic
Democratic Alliance.[48] Of the three alliance leaders contending for the prime minister's office, the one chosen to lead the government was Nawaz Sharif, the favorite of
the military. The disappointing results of the restoration of democracy seem to have
made it easier for the military and their civilian allies to reassert control. But will this
mean the revival of a military and fundamentalist coalition along the lines of the one
relied on by Zia? It is possible that Nawaz Sharif made his alliance with fundamentalists only for reasons of political expediency. To date it remains unclear whether Prime
Minister Sharif will actively pursue a fundamentalist program or accord it priority in
the face of the enormous problems he faces in dealing with Pakistan's dramatically
worsening economic plight, the crisis in Kashmir, and the country's other ills. Unlike
Zia, he cannot count on the United States to bail him out or prop him up, because
improving U.S.–Soviet relations and a dwindling U.S. interest in the Afghan conflict
have led to a decrease in Pakistan's strategic value.

On 11 April 1991, when he introduced his own bill, the Enforcement of Shari'a
Act 1991, to make Shari'a law supreme in Pakistan, Prime Minister Nawaz Sharif
reportedly told a joint session of Parliament, "I am not a fundamentalist."[49] This
avowal could have been prompted by fears lest an association with Islamic fundamentalism should further damage his ties to the United States, which had already been
hurt by the American assessment that Pakistan's nuclear program was, contrary to
official assurances, aimed at developing nuclear weapons. However, the evidence suggests that he did not have a fundamentalist mentality. In his campaigns to attract
Western investment, he has tried to downplay Islamization and present himself to the
American business community as a pragmatic, technocratic reformer with a strong
pro-business, free-market orientation.[50] It seems likely that, given the existence of a
private bill calling for legislation to implement a fundamentalist version of Shari'a
law, the prime minister simply decided to preempt such proposals by putting forward
his own scheme for Islamization, one that he could control and that would not unduly

interfere with the conduct of his economic reform measures, his efforts to attract foreign investment, and his relations with international financial and aid institutions. In this connection, it is noteworthy that section 18 of his bill specifically provides that all of Pakistan's international financial obligations shall remain binding "till an alternative economic system is evolved." (One suspects that alternative system may be a very long time in coming.)

Many of the proposals in Nawaz Sharif's bill resemble measures pursued under President Zia—Islamization of education and the economy, promotion of Islamic values in the media, and the eradication of obscenity, immorality, and vice. Crucial provisions of the law were left sufficiently vague and abstract to allow the government great leeway in deciding how to implement them. For example, it would be hard to determine exactly what kind of action would be required to comply with section 5, which provides "All Muslim citizens of Pakistan shall order their lives according to the Shari'a." Members of religious parties in the Parliament denounced the bill as inadequate and "diluted," and they called for a constitutional amendment to make the Shari'a the supreme law.[51]

One got a sense of Prime Minister Sharif's mindset from the highly discursive and frequently repetitive speech he gave introducing his Shari'a bill.[52] The prime minister rambled, seeming uncomfortable talking about exactly what he envisaged Islamization would mean, repeatedly bringing up his Shari'a bill only to switch rapidly to other topics like rampant corruption, illegal arms, arrogant bureaucrats, delay in the courts, Pakistan's indebtedness, and the evils of poverty. One of the issues to which he kept returning was the amount of time and energy that had been diverted from concentrating on Pakistan's economic ills and development problems to deal with the recurrent debates on Islamization. He lamented that, "while the world is marching fast to meet the challenges [of] the twenty-first century, we are still to decide our direction of progress."[53] In the light of his comments, it seems probable that his putting forward his own Shari'a bill was not only a move designed to forestall the enactment of the more extreme private bill but also an attempt to end the divisive conflicts over Islamization measures that had been absorbing the attention of the government and to refocus attention on remedies for Pakistan's dire economic plight and the urgent need to revitalize the private sector.

A more sinister theme in the prime minister's speech lay in his reiterated threats of punishment for the vague crime of abusing or insulting Pakistan, which seemed to tie in with the call in section 16 of the Shari'a bill for laws protecting "the ideology, solidarity and integrity of Pakistan as an Islamic State." This arrogation of sweeping authority to penalize political opponents and critics of Islamization was ominous. Since under the new bill the Shari'a will override conflicting provisions in the constitution and since neither the Shari'a bill nor the Prime Minister's speech expressed any concern for respecting human rights or protecting individual freedoms, alarm for the future of civil liberties seemed warranted, particularly in view of the records of repression accumulated by other governments when pursuing Islamization.

Under the leadership of a businessman who publicly denies that he is a fundamentalist, Pakistan now seems embarked on a curious experiment of combining a seemingly perfunctory official commitment to Islamization with a determination to implement a program of far-reaching economic reform that would entail close cooperation with the West, Japan, and international institutions. Combining these policies will be difficult; Pakistan is in a state of mounting internal crisis, being beset by increasingly serious social turbulence, crime waves, and general lawlessness.[54]

The image of the fundamentalist-military alliance has been tarnished by two major financial scandals that erupted in 1991 in which both Nawaz Sharif's and Zia's regimes were implicated, scandals that were an acute source of embarrassment since charges of corruption had provided the pretext for removing Benazir Bhutto from the prime ministership. As the Bank of Credit and Commerce International (BCCI) collapsed amidst revelations of staggering levels of corruption and fraud, it turned out that many high-ranking members of the military, including former president Zia, had been involved in BCCI deals that were at best questionable. Nawaz Sharif also had to explain why, when the state cooperative societies had been going bankrupt, wiping out the savings of about 700,000 Pakistanis, they had been extending billions of rupees in loans to his family business.[55] Intriguing questions were raised by the facts that President Ghulam Ishaq Khan, who had sacked Benazir Bhutto, turned out to be closely tied to the BCCI, and Nawaz Sharif's family was shown to have benefited from a BCCI association—whereas both Benazir Bhutto and her father had, while in office, denied BCCI licenses to operate in Pakistan.[56]

In the light of Pakistan's deepening internal crisis, it is doubtful how much Prime Minister Sharif will be able to accomplish—or how much time he will have to try to stabilize the situation before the military decides that it is necessary to intervene directly.

The Sudan

The Goals of Islamization in the Sudan

When Sudanese president Jafar al-Numayri undertook Islamization in 1983, he was faced with a political and religious situation significantly at variance with the ones in Iran and Pakistan. He had ruled the country as its military dictator for fourteen years, managing to cling to power in the face of many hostile plots and attempted coups. By 1983 the political threat from secular and leftist political opposition forces like the Communists and Ba'thists had been exhausted, and Numayri's remaining major political rivals were ones who had strong Islamic credentials for leadership.

Sufism, Islamic mysticism, was an important component of religious life in the Sudan. Traditionally, the two major political parties had been organized by the Ansar and Khatmiyya Sufi orders. As of 1983 Numayri's most prominent political rival was Sadiq al-Mahdi, the leader of the Ummah Party, which corresponded to the Ansar order. But Numayri also had to deal with the political power of the Democratic Unionist Party, which corresponded to the Khatmiyya order. Sufi leaders like Sadiq al-Mahdi enjoyed both spiritual and political authority among their followers.

Compared to groups like the Ansar and the Khatmiyya orders, fundamentalists organized in groups like the Muslim Brotherhood were relative newcomers on the Sudanese political scene, but in a short time they grew into a potent force. A local branch of the Brotherhood was led by Sadiq al-Mahdi's brother-in-law, Hassan al-Turabi, who became internationally famous as an articulate spokesperson for the fundamentalist cause and assumed a prominent role in Sudanese politics in the 1970s.[57]

The role of Islam in the state and the place of the Shari'a in the legal system had been contentious issues in Sudanese politics ever since the Sudan became independent in 1956. There were recurring but inconclusive debates on whether the Sudan should have an Islamic constitution and whether Shari'a law should replace the common law system that had been inherited from the British, leaving the Shari'a applicable only in the area of personal status. As the country was wracked by political upheavals and attempted coups, resolution of the Islamization issue was repeatedly deferred.[58]

While politicians like Sadiq al-Mahdi wavered on what the role of Islam should be, the Muslim Brotherhood consistently campaigned for Islamization, including the adoption of an Islamic constitution. Although the Muslim Brotherhood has been hostile to Arab nationalism as a secular ideology incompatible with the universalist mission of Islam, in the Sudanese context fundamentalist calls for imposing Islamic law were associated with the imposition of an Arab and Islamic identity, an identity that was vigorously rejected by the southern Sudanese.

Like so many African nations, the Sudan is an artificial entity with boundaries that were drawn with flagrant disregard for natural ethnic, religious, or linguistic divisions. The most important single cleavage is the one dividing Arab Muslim northerners and African non-Muslim southerners. Southerners constitute approximately one-third of the population and adhere to Christianity or animist religions. From the beginning they have been suspicious of the governments in Khartoum and inclined to resent domination by northerners, characterizing their policies as racist and exploitative. Southerners have been insistent that their African heritage has to be accorded equal respect with the Arab one and that the government needs to be structured so that their interests are protected.

The northern disinclination to respect the sensitivities of the southern Sudanese was to have fateful consequences. Civil war broke out even before independence was formally proclaimed, and it continued until 1972. President Numayri, who had come to power via a coup in 1969, won considerable prestige as a statesman and conciliator by arranging the 1972 peace settlement, the Addis Ababa Agreement. The role of Islam was a major bone of contention, and, as a condition for ending the war, southerners demanded that no attempt be made to declare Islam the religion of the state.[59] The 1973 Sudanese Constitution recognized Islam, Christianity, and traditional religions and accorded each of these respect. To appease the southerners, the use of religion in constitutional or legal provisions to compromise the political and civil rights of any citizen was prohibited.[60]

When President Numayri in August of 1983 suddenly decided to co-opt the Islamic fundamentalist agenda and pursue a policy of Islamization, it was a startling turnabout. It signaled an abandonment of his policy of conciliating the South at a time when the country could ill afford the consequences.

The timing of the 1983 Sudanese Islamization program made little sense. A rational assessment of the country's needs would not have led to the conclusion that reform of the legal system should be given priority, for the existing legal system happened to be a good one for a country at the Sudan's stage of development. There were other much more pressing problems. The Sudan was in dire straits, because the country was so indebted and the economy had so deteriorated that the government was essentially bankrupt. There were serious scarcities of vital commodities like petrol and sorghum; the infrastructure had grievously deteriorated; a brain drain was leeching away the most able and best-educated Sudanese; devastating drought and famine afflicted much of the country; there was mass starvation afflicting several million Sudanese and Ethiopian refugees; and rapid desertification was causing displacement and misery for the population in the West. Most serious of all, politically disaffected southern Sudanese were already on the verge of renewing the civil war, a renewal of which would end crucial development projects in the South that were essential for any economic recovery. Concern for the reactions of the southerners by itself should have been sufficient to forestall any pursuit of Islamization. Numayri nonetheless proceeded, therewith ending any hopes of averting a full-scale civil war. Ever since that fateful decision, southerners have placed the abandonment of Numayri's Islamization policies and laws as the sine qua non for ending the war.[61]

Numayri's decision to adopt fundamentalist policies in the face of these counter-indications was improvident and quite difficult to explain in the light of his own character and political history. Earlier in his political career he had been closely allied with leftist groups and friendly with Sudanese communists, archfoes of the fundamentalists. Unlike the genuinely devout Zia, Numayri enjoyed no reputation as a pious Muslim. Numayri was a rough-hewn military man of loose morals who surrounded himself with corrupt cronies and had been notorious for his alcoholism.[62] To the extent that personal motives may have played a role in Numayri's decision to pose as a champion of Islamization, observers speculated that his newfound religious zeal in 1983 might have been connected to his declining health after major surgery. In this regard, it may be significant that by 1983 he had to forgo alcohol for medical reasons after years of heavy drinking.

Whatever increase in personal religious feeling Numayri may have experienced, it seems that some political calculations may have prompted his adoption of Islamization. It is possible that, after seeing the Iranian Revolution and the 1981 murder of Sadat by Egyptian fundamentalists, Numayri was anxious to forestall a political threat that he perceived to be coming from Sudanese fundamentalists. Perhaps the policy was also suggested by hopes that the fundamentalists, who enjoyed funding from Arabian sources, could serve as a useful political prop and source of funds for his faltering and impecunious regime.

There were Sudanese fundamentalists who abhorred Numayri and refused any collaboration lest they be tainted by association with his hated regime, such as members of the large minority faction of the Muslim Brotherhood who split off under the leadership of Sadiq 'Abd Allah 'Abd al-Majid. In contrast, fundamentalists belonging to the majority wing of the Ikhwan (Muslim Brotherhood) acclaimed his decision to

Islamize and quickly became his ardent supporters. As a reward, Numayri appointed cooperative fundamentalists to various government posts and particularly to the courts. For example, Hassan al-Turabi, the most prominent figure in the Sudanese Ikhwan, became attorney general and al-Makashfi Taha al-Kabbashi became a powerful judge.

In 1984 Numayri proclaimed himself the Sudan's Imam, meaning in this context the supreme religious and political leader. Although Numayri's fundamentalist allies proved willing to acknowledge him as their Imam, when Numayri in July of 1984 pressed the normally acquiescent Sudanese People's Assembly to amend the 1973 constitution to recognize his religious authority and establish an Islamic form of government, the assembly balked at endorsing his pretensions. Numayri had to abandon any plans to rewrite the constitution to ratify his status as supreme religious leader.

How Islamization Was Pursued

Numayri's Islamization program proceeded quite differently from Zia's. Apparently desirous of avoiding the need to share the credit for his Islamization program, Numayri did not allow the Muslim Brotherhood or qualified ulama to participate in the drafting of his Islamic laws, turning the task instead over to some of his ill-qualified cronies. In the last half of 1983 the latter were periodically assigned to produce on very short notice "Islamic" codes on various topics proposed by Numayri. The laws were thrown together in desperate attempts to meet Numayri's deadlines. To facilitate their task when drafting the longest and potentially most important law, the Civil Transactions Act, the drafters cribbed much of the "Islamic" law from the Jordanian Civil Code, which happened to be largely French in inspiration, inserting at points various opaque and ill-drafted "Islamic" provisions. Thus, with no preparation, Sudanese lawyers and judges, trained in the British common law system, were faced with having to use laws based on a dissimilar French tradition that contained various statements, often garbled ones, of "Islamic" rules. Since Numayri's Islamic laws were often unintelligible, lawyers were unable to guess how to structure civil transactions under the new and unsettled rules of the game. The confusion about what the laws meant and the threat of potential criminal liability for inadvertent violations discouraged business activity.[63] Because the economy was approaching a state of collapse, business activity was sparse in any event, so fewer transactions were affected than would otherwise have been the case.

In striking contrast to Iran and Pakistan, in the Sudan little attention was paid under Numayri to utilizing Islamic law as a device to force women into a traditional, subjugated role. The initial deemphasis of issues of women's status may have resulted from the fact that, as described, major fundamentalist figures were excluded from the process of drafting most of Numayri's Islamization measures. It was only after the new military junta seized power in 1989 and adopted a rigorous fundamentalist policy that measures along the lines of those adopted in Iran were taken to remove women from public life, to relegate them to domestic roles, and to restrict their freedoms.[64]

The Sudanese judiciary and bar strongly opposed Numayri's Islamization policy.

When cases involving Islamization measures arose, there was initially much foot-dragging by judges, and, in consequence, for some time the Islamic laws were virtually in abeyance. Infuriated by this judicial resistance, Numayri on 29 April 1984 declared an official state of emergency in order to effectuate Islamization without further delay. This entailed suspending all constitutional rights and freedoms, allowing the police great leeway in undertaking searches and making arrests, and setting up courts of decisive justice, the latter manned by new appointees who were enthusiastic partisans of Islamization. Under the new judges, penalties like executions, jailings, fines, floggings, and amputations were meted out not only to persons actually found in breach of the Islamic laws but to persons merely suspected of offenses or with some ties to persons who had violated Numayri's laws. The accused were convicted in summary, arbitrary proceedings.[65]

The revival and application of Shari'a penal law were treated as the centerpieces of Numayri's Islamization program. Residents of Khartoum were well informed of the rising toll of victims of Islamic justice since the criminal convictions were chronicled in reports on Khartoum television during prime time. Even when he put a formal end to the state of emergency on 29 September 1984, Numayri kept the emergency courts going, renaming them courts of decisive justice.

The operations of the criminal justice system in this period caused dismay and outrage. In general, criminal law was applied in a manner that reflected the nature of Numayri's government. Members of the regime and powerful and well-connected figures continued their blatantly corrupt practices unhindered.[66] Businesspersons in the private sector of the economy, toward which Numayri bore considerable animus, were common targets of criminal searches and prosecutions. Persons with influential enemies or helpless members of the poorer classes were frequently subjected to the harshest penalties. Although there are no accurate statistics on the race of the victims of Islamic justice in this period, there are indications that many of the victims of the floggings and amputations were non-Muslim southerners.[67]

Foreign governments that had formerly given aid to Numayri's regime abandoned him after seeing the way the economy was being mismanaged and out of disgust over his repressive policies, except for the United States, which wound up as the sole financial backer of his regime.[68] In return for generous financial aid, the United States found a staunch ally for pursuing its objectives in a strategic region and support for its anti-Qaddafi campaign. As mainstays of the faltering regime, the U.S. Embassy and Agency for International Development (AID) missions did in practice obtain certain exemptions from Islamic law, enabling these institutions to import and serve alcohol.[69] Although official U.S. State Department reports during the Islamization program did contain some accurate information on aspects of the human rights violations Numayri was perpetrating, the importance of the country for U.S. foreign policy seems to have inhibited the United States from giving Numayri an ultimatum warning of a cutoff of funding if he did not end the abuses caused by the Islamization program.[70]

Although the Islamization program was deeply resented and Numayri's versions of Islamic laws were viewed with contempt, while he was still in power the regime's punishment of dissent deterred many Sudanese from criticizing the laws in public. For the most part, it was in the demonstrations and after the popular revolution against Numayri that one saw the full depth of scorn and hatred that Sudanese felt for the dictator. With the lifting of censorship, his policies were pilloried in the newly free press and the media. However, even before Numayri was toppled and despite the dangers of speaking out, some Sudanese risked their lives to denounce the Islamization program. Among the most outspoken foes of the Islamization program were the Republican Brothers, a group of Muslims who supported liberal, modernist interpretations of Islam and demanded respect for human rights according to international standards. The Republicans advocated the cause of democratic pluralism, defending the rights of non-Muslim African Sudanese, who suffered under the new system of Islamic criminal justice, which represented values alien to sub-Saharan African culture.

In retaliation for their criticisms of Numayri's version of Islamization, prominent Republicans were jailed. Finally, Mahmud Muhammad Taha, the aged leader of the Republicans, was tried in January of 1985, convicted of apostasy, denied the chance to repent that the convicted apostate is given under the Shari'a, and sentenced to be hanged. This conviction took place even though there was no law on the books providing that apostasy was a criminal offense, much less one punishable by execution. Taha was publicly hanged in Khartoum on 18 January 1985, accompanied by great fanfare and acclaim on the part of Sudanese fundamentalists, who had long been hostile to the Republicans and their liberal ideas. To try to quiet further dissent and to intimidate Taha's followers, Numayri resorted to a publicly televised heresy trial of some of Taha's close associates, during which they were interrogated and berated and forced, under threat of execution, to repudiate formally their Republican beliefs.[71]

How Successful Has Islamization Been?

Numayri fell on 6 April 1985, less than three months after the judicial murder of Taha, which was widely perceived in Khartoum as an act of abject barbarism totally at variance with Sudanese values and tradition. Hanging Taha did not quell opposition but, rather, fueled outrage at the cruelty and arbitrariness with which criminal justice was being administered. Indeed, Numayri himself seems to have belatedly perceived that his sponsorship of the fundamentalist agenda, far from solving any problems or enhancing his tarnished image, had only aggravated his political woes. In the last months before he was overthrown, he sought to place the blame for the injustices of the Islamization program on his erstwhile fundamentalist allies, distancing himself from the Muslim Brotherhood and dismissing Turabi from the government in February of 1985 and then jailing him in March. However, Numayri's repudiation of fundamentalism came too late. Massive strikes and popular demonstrations in Khartoum convinced the military that Numayri's position was untenable. The military staged a coup and then set up a caretaker regime that was later followed by a civilian government in 1986.

An interim constitution was drawn up.[72] It stipulated that constitutional principles should prevail over all other laws. It also provided that the state should strive to "eradicate racial and religious fanaticism," that the state and each person should be subject to the rule of law as applied by the courts, that the judiciary should be independent, and that all persons should be equal under the law. In calling for restoring the rule of law, respecting constitutional rights protections, and ending discriminatory treatment, which southerners associated with Numayri's versions of Islamization and Islamic justice, it obviously was intended as a corrective to the abuses that had taken place under Numayri's Islamization policy.

By any terms, Numayri's Islamization campaign must be classified as the least successful of the three considered in this essay. It was short-lived and haphazard, and provoked a wave of revulsion that culminated in a popular revolution against the regime. Numayri's ill-considered initiatives led directly to his own downfall. Like others who had collaborated with him, fundamentalists associated with his policies discovered that their own credibility had been badly compromised. A further factor discrediting the Numayri regime was the revelation after censorship was lifted that, while he had been pouring resources into Islamization, he had been concealing from the public in the capital the horrors that had resulted from the devastating famine that had savaged many outlying regions. Indignation welled up as information and photographs showing the starvation and misery that Numayri had ignored and tried to conceal at last became available and Sudanese grasped the extent of the death and suffering that the Numayri regime had been covering up.

Deeply implicated in Taha's death, the fundamentalists were further embarrassed as Taha acquired the status of a martyr for the cause of human rights and the date of his execution was selected as the day for the annual celebration of Arab Human Rights Day. The honor that Taha received in death was a symbolic victory for the liberal and humanistic vision of Islam that the Sudanese fundamentalists had sought to have condemned as heretical.

Future Prospects

Long plagued by instability, the Sudanese political situation continued to be troubled after Numayri's overthrow. Dealing with the aftermath of Numayri's gross mismanagement of the economy, the disaffection of southerners, the ravages of war and famine, and other accumulated ills placed great strains on the newly democratized political system.[73] When free elections were held in 1986 at the end of the interim period of military rule, candidates representing the traditional Umma/Ansar and DUP/Khatmiyya groups did well, together garnering almost 70 percent of the total votes cast.[74] But Sadiq al-Mahdi, who became prime minister, proved a weak and indecisive leader who let the existing problems fester, including the contentious issue of how to deal with the legacy of Islamization measures left by Numayri. The civil war, carried out increasingly by irregular forces, continued to devastate the South.

In the free political atmosphere after the overthrow of Numayri, Sudanese lawyers and scholars outspokenly denounced the defects of his amateurishly drafted Islamic laws and criticized them as travesties of Islamic jurisprudence. Perhaps they assumed that they could pave the way for discarding Numayri's laws by demonstrating their flaws. However, they were to discover that proponents of Islamization were not as concerned with whether Numayri's laws correctly stated Shari'a principles as they were with upholding the general principle that Islamization should be pursued. Sudanese fundamentalists defended Numayri's laws and fought zealously for their retention, threatening a bloodbath if they were abandoned. At the most, they conceded that certain purifications of Numayri's laws might be in order.

Although fundamentalists did not do well in the democratic elections that followed Numayri's overthrow, the Muslim Brotherhood's strong, disciplined organization and single-minded zeal gave it disproportionate political weight. In particular, its members remained a force to be reckoned with in the capital, where they could stage disruptive demonstrations. Fear of the fundamentalists' political power prompted the shaky coalition governments that followed the interim period of military rule to seek some accommodations with the most influential fundamentalist party, Turabi's National Islamic Front (NIF). The attempts to placate the NIF complicated negotiations for settling the civil war.

John Garang, the leader of the Sudanese People's Liberation Army (SPLA), was adamant that the civil war would not end until a commitment was given to abandon Islamic law.[75] The SPLA and its civilian counterpart, the Sudanese People's Liberation Movement (SPLM), insisted that a secular government should be established with a legal system in which all Sudanese, regardless of race or religion, would be equal.[76] The drain of the civil war and pressures from the military prompted the government to accept a tentative agreement with the SPLA on 16 November 1988 which called for freezing Islamic law. A constitutional conference was to be held in September 1989, a move that was denounced by the NIF, which had been excluded from a new government formed in March 1989 that seemed to be moving toward a decision to roll back Islamization measures.

A military faction again intervened, overthrowing the civilian government on 30 June 1989. Lieutenant General Omar Hassan al-Bashir at first sought to disguise his ties to the NIF, but as the months wore on, it became obvious that the regime was closely allied with the NIF. However, Hassan al-Turabi was not formally a member of the government. The new regime showed no interest in alleviating the economic miseries of the population. The regime scuttled the tentative peace settlement, adopting an adamant position on retaining Shari'a law, which led to the collapse of a peace conference with the SPLA on 5 December 1989 in which former U.S. president Jimmy Carter was playing a central mediating role. On 7 December 1989, an official announcement was made that Shari'a law would again be enforced and its penalities imposed, but international pressures seem to have forestalled the executions of some amputation penalties that should have followed.

zeal and ruthlessness, declaring a state of emergency and resorting to drastic measures to stifle dissent and to intimidate and punish critics of NIF policies. Immediately after seizing power, Bashir imposed strict press censorship, threw political leaders and members of the professional elite into jail, and abrogated the interim constitution. The regime dissolved the Sudan Bar Association and the Sudan Human Rights Association, which had campaigned vigorously on behalf of human rights and peace in the South.[77] Bashir's government and security forces have compiled a record of egregious disregard for legality and systematic human rights violations in the course of campaigns of repression and persecution directed at political opponents and institutions that have in the past shown their capacity to mobilize resistance to military dictatorships. Civil society, long a prized feature of the Sudanese political landscape, disappeared under this onslaught.[78] Widespread purges have been undertaken to eliminate persons deemed unsympathetic to the fundamentalist cause from jobs in the public sector, jobs that have been turned over to fundamentalist loyalists. There have been arrests and protracted detentions without trial of hundreds of Sudanese human rights activists, doctors, lawyers, trade unionists, journalists, professors, diplomats, bankers, and civil servants, and the evidence is that many detentions have been accompanied by beatings, mistreatment, and torture. Several Sudanese have been executed after politically inspired prosecutions. In April of 1990 there was a documented case of a doctor being tortured to death by security forces. Twenty-eight army officers opposed to NIF policies were summarily executed, ostensibly as punishment for involvement in an attempted coup. Meanwhile, the regime tolerated and perhaps even encouraged militias and irregular forces that engaged in acts of wanton destruction and violence against southern Sudanese, which included a massacre of about six hundred civilians at El Jebelein on 28 December 1989.[79]

Before the universities were closed down by the regime, NIF members monitored the contents of university lectures to ensure that they accorded with fundamentalist tenets. Dr. Farouk Ibrahim el Nur of the Faculty of Science of Khartoum University was arrested in November of 1989, when the head of the security system expressed disapproval of his lectures, after which fundamentalist members of the security forces tortured him in an effort to force him to recant his belief in Darwinian evolution, which they stated was incompatible with Islam.[80]

Concerned and embarrassed about reports of atrocities in the South and repression in the North, the government imposed curbs on foreign visitors, restricting the activity of foreign relief workers and harassing and detaining foreign journalists. Mounting evidence in 1990 of an approaching famine of disastrous proportions gave the Bashir government a new motive for excluding foreign observers and relief workers, because the regime was determined to pretend that there was no food shortage. In this connection, many observers realized that one way for Sudanese fundamentalists to eliminate the major obstacle to their Islamization program would be to let southerners, the Sudanese most affected by the famine, simply starve to death out of view of the international community. Reports in 1991 suggested that between five and nine million lives were at risk from famine. The government was obviously angered by the complaints of foreign governments and international agencies that the government was blocking vital relief efforts and took the offensive against its foreign critics, stridently denouncing them. Only in March 1991 did it relent and allow in international aid and famine relief workers.[81]

On 31 December 1990, the government announced its decision to apply Islamic law, but only in the northern part of the country, where it would apply both to the

Muslim and to the non-Muslim populations. On 22 March 1991, the government enacted a new Islamic penal code designed by Hassan al-Turabi that included the premodern Shari'a rules discriminating against women and non-Muslims and requiring penalties like flogging, amputation, and stoning to death. It included a provision requiring the death penalty for apostasy for "any Muslim who advocates the rejection of Islamic beliefs or announces his own rejection of Islam by word or act."[82] On the basis of the record, one would expect that this would apply to dissident Muslims who criticized the government and its Islamization policy.

The enactment of the penal code seemed in context to be an act of defiance by a regime in the most parlous of circumstances, bankrupt and cut off from most sources of financial aid. By allying itself with Iraq during the Gulf Crisis, the Sudan had alienated all the countries in the U.S.–sponsored coalition, the members of which were not deceived by the regime's occasional propaganda efforts to portray its stance as one of principled neutrality. Estrangement from neighbors like Egypt and Saudi Arabia ensued. During the buildup before the war, Hassan al-Turabi was one of a number of prominent Islamic fundamentalists who identified the cause of Iraq with the cause of Islam despite Saddam Hussein's record of persecution of religious leaders and fundamentalist groups. It was not possible to gauge how many Sudanese agreed with Turabi's stance. By spring 1991 General Bashir's regime had become a pariah in most places, a rare exception being Libya, with which the Sudan was theoretically in the process of merging despite Qaddafi's well-known antipathy for Islamic fundamentalism and his executions of Muslim Brothers. The Sudan's need for oil and financial support and Qaddafi's eagerness to expand his influence apparently were behind the proposed merger. Qaddafi's record of pursuing numerous abortive union projects with other Arab countries, none of which had resulted in effective or stable unions, gave one reason to doubt that the Sudan-Libya merger would be successful. An announcement by the Bashir regime on 29 April 1991 that there would be a release of political prisoners suggested that the beleaguered regime might be trying to make a conciliatory gesture to the opposition and also to improve its standing in the international community.[83]

Ironies abounded in the shifts in alliances after the traumatic experiences of the Gulf War. After having sided with Saddam Hussein in late 1990 and early 1991, Bashir's regime began moving toward close cooperation with Saddam's nemesis, Iran, at the end of 1991. In return for substantial Iranian aid, Bashir allowed the Sudan to be used by Iran as a staging ground for various forces cooperating with the Iranian regime, including both Islamic fundamentalist groups and terrorist organizations.[84]

The policy of pursuing a fundamentalist program seemed to doom the Sudan to the perpetuation of a cruel military dictatorship, arbitrary criminal justice, and continued civil strife, accompanied by an increasing toll of human suffering and death. The future of Sudanese Islamization is uncertain, but the Bashir regime's adherence to the fundamentalist line has unquestionably had a disastrous impact on democratic freedoms and human rights and has dimmed the prospects for the Sudan's survival as a nation. In the case of the southern Sudanese, it may threaten their physical survival.

Conclusion

Iran, Pakistan, and the Sudan are noteworthy for being sites where field experiments in Islamization along fundamentalist lines have been carried out. By 1991 they were the only countries in which Islamic fundamentalist movements were able to gain enough power to attempt to remake laws, politics, and constitutions. Despite the dissimilarities in the specific reforms enacted in the three countries, there are common features that enable the observer to draw general conclusions about the impact of Islamic fundamentalism.

First and foremost, the ascendancy of fundamentalists did not mean a reversion to premodern Islamic law but instead a very selective revival of certain features of the Shari'a that fit the fundamentalists' immediate program and priorities—priorities which one could have predicted using Marty's definition of fundamentalism. By and large, the legal systems remained heavily influenced by Western models. On the basis of Iranian political developments and constitutional amendments in 1989, one might say that some of the central features of the 1979 constitution that were designed to make it Islamic have already been diluted or abandoned, having apparently been recognized as impractical.

From the examples of Iran and the Sudan, and to a lesser extent, Pakistan, one sees how, when Islamic fundamentalism is adopted as a government policy, it tends to accentuate the antidemocratic, authoritarian, and repressive tendencies in the local political systems. The absolutist spirit of fundamentalism pervades governments engaged in Islamization, which seem to feel that the divine mandate they enjoy can be used to justify any measures needed to keep their hold on power and to destroy their political enemies without any concern for legality. The local bar associations and judges with modern legal educations who are committed to certain principles of the rule of law have been perceived as constituting obstacles to implementing fundamentalists' version of Islamic justice. Special military courts or tribunals staffed with fundamentalists, which are permitted to mete out crude forms of summary justice, have had to be established. Egregious disregard for legality and human rights and an increase in arbitrariness and cruelty in the administration of criminal justice have correlated with fundamentalists' ascendancy. Among other things, fundamentalist ascendancy has meant the criminalization of certain nonconforming religious beliefs and the imposition of criminal penalties, including executions, on religious dissidents and religious minorities.

The evidence suggests that, while "Islam" and "the Shari'a" have highly positive connotations for Muslims, the specifics of the agendas pursued by fundamentalist groups in power do not enjoy wide popular support. Except where fundamentalists are able to associate their cause with popular protests against the existing order or the pursuit of broader social and political goals, fundamentalists seem unlikely to come to power in free elections. If ever they were successful in coming to power and then rigorously carried out fundamentalist policies, they would be unlikely to remain long in office under fully democratic conditions. The reactive oppositional bent of radical fundamentalists means that they concentrate on purging societies of immorality and fighting enemies, showing little capacity to pursue constructive programs to alleviate social ills or to eradicate pervasive economic problems.

The stunning victory won by the Algerian fundamentalist party known as the Islamic Salvation Front (FIS) in the first round of parliamentary elections in December of 1991 offered the prospect of testing this interpretation. But the FIS electoral success was not indisputably tied to the specifics of the FIS program. Indeed, during its campaign the FIS remained vague about the measures it would take if it won a majority. As significant as the FIS' gain of 188 of the total 430 seats in the first round was the fact that the ruling National Liberation Front (FLN) was able to win only 15 seats—or about 4 percent of the total. The vote was compelling testimony to Algerians' disillusionment with the repressive FLN regime, which had dominated the country since 1962, bringing Algeria to the brink of economic ruin while a small elite reaped the benefits of the FLN's stranglehold on power. Moreover, the secular political parties were fragmented and the FIS, as the only opposition party with a national base and a chance of unseating the FLN, seems to have become the beneficiary of pervasive anti-FLN sentiment. Voter dissatisfaction with the range of options being offered may account for the approximately 40 percent abstention rate in this, the first fully free election in Algeria's history. Those interested in learning more about how the FIS would fare once it had the opportunity to govern were thwarted when Algeria's bold democratic experiment was aborted by a thinly disguised military intervention on 11 January 1992 before the final round of elections were held, thereby robbing the FIS of its projected victory.

The examples to date show that fundamentalist domination survived in Iran by the systematic use of terror and recourse to harsh repression and censorship. Iran held periodic elections, but in circumstances in which there was no real test of voter approval of clerical rule. Since 1981, when President Bani-Sadr was forced to flee to exile, there has been no toleration of any political opposition to clerical rule except on the part of the small and beleaguered Freedom Movement led by former prime minister Mehdi Bazargan, which suffered constant harassment and threats. Since the Revolution voters have only been allowed to choose between candidates pledged to follow the official Islamic ideology, not to express disapproval by voting for candidates that oppose it. To demand a more open system has proved perilous. In June of 1990 an open letter by prominent political figures in Bazargan's Freedom Movement calling for more respect for constitutionally protected rights led to their arrest. Nine were kept in detention without charges being filed for over a year. They were then tried in secret, being punished with prison sentences from six months to three years and floggings of between ten and thirty lashes. Bazargan, whose proven moral courage and reputation for steadfast advocacy of human rights under the shah had long shielded him from the treatment meted out to other dissidents, was himself placed under house arrest.[85] Even the pleas of this small group for greater freedoms were seen as intolerably subversive. One important study of attitudes toward the clerical regime in an Iranian village suggests that disillusionment and disaffection among its inhabitants has been widespread.[86]

In Pakistan and the Sudan, the fundamentalists' political ascendancy owed a great deal to their willingness to forge alliances with the military or with military dictator-ships. When, after the experience of fundamentalist domination, the people of Paki-stan and the Sudan did have the chance to vote in relative freedom, the fundamentalists were unable to win elections. The October 1990 victory of the eight-party coalition that ultimately brought Nawaz Sharif to the prime ministership of Pakistan was a victory from which Pakistan's fundamentalists could initially take heart. However, it was something less than a clear mandate for fundamentalist government.

When does an entrenched fundamentalist regime cease to be fundamentalist? Funda-mentalism is oppositional and reactive in character, determined to purge society of corruption and restore a putative ideal Islamic model. But after a certain period in power, a government that is in its origins fundamentalist, like the Saudi regime, may become the kind of establishment against which new generations of fundamentalists are bound to react. Indeed, Saudi Arabia now faces serious trouble in the form of a burgeoning fundamentalist opposition. The indications are that in Iran and Pakistan, where fundamentalist policies dominated for over a decade, albeit with one interrup-tion in Pakistan under Bhutto, fundamentalist militance among the leaders of these regimes has significantly diminished.[87] In the Sudan, it is another story. The funda-mentalists of the NIF have had the upper hand only since the coup of June 1989, and their leaders' zeal to remake the world according to their fundamentalist agenda con-tinues unabated. This has meant that in an era when renewed concern for the prin-ciples of democracy, constitutionalism, and the rule of law is manifesting itself in most parts of the globe, the Sudan in 1992 seems to embody a society in which freedoms are abolished, rights are disregarded, and the reigning ideological absolutism elimi-nates any prospect of democratic pluralism.

Notes

1. Martin E. Marty, "Fundamentalism as a Social Phenomenon," *Bulletin of the American Academy of Arts and Sciences* 42 (November 1988): 15–29.

2. For background and analysis, consult Ali E. Hillal Dessouki, ed., *Islamic Resur-gence in the Arab World* (New York: Praeger, 1982); John L. Esposito, *Voices of Resurgent Islam* (New York: Oxford University Press, 1983); Shireen Hunter, ed., *The Politics of Islamic Revivalism: Diversity and Unity* (Bloo-mington: Indiana University Press, 1988); Bassam Tibi, *The Crisis of Modern Islam: A Preindustrial Culture in the Scientific-Techno-logical Age* (Salt Lake City: University of Utah, 1988).

3. Abul Ala Maududi, *The Islamic Law and Constitution* (Lahore: Islamic Publica-tions, 1980), p. 263.

4. Depending on the definition of funda-mentalism one is using, one might conclude that Saudi Arabia was the archetype of the fundamentalist state. For example, Dilip Hiro presents Saudi Arabia as "the oldest fundamentalist state," but he uses a defini-tion very dissimilar to Marty's. Hiro defines fundamentalism as "the term used for effort to define the fundamentals of a religious sys-tem and adhere to them." Dilip Hiro, *Is-lamic Fundamentalism* (London: Paladin, 1988), pp. 1–2.

5. For background, see Edward Mor-

timer, *Faith and Power: The Politics of Islam* (New York: Vintage Books, 1982), pp. 60–64.

6. Ibid., p. 179; Hiro, *Islamic Fundamentalism*, p. 141.

7. Mortimer, *Faith and Power*, pp. 180–85: Hiro, *Islamic Fundamentalism*, pp. 128–35; *New York Times*, 31 December 1991, p. A1; *New York Times*, 30 January 1992, p. A3.

8. In the period in which he was seeking to consolidate his leadership in exile just prior to the overthrow of the shah, Khomeini maintained a prudent silence on sensitive questions like his attitudes toward democracy, agrarian reform, the role of the ulama in politics, and the status of women. Hiro, *Islamic Fundamentalism*, p. 167.

9. Khomeini's aides downplayed the significance of his tract on the leadership of the jurist in the period before his ability to control the political scene had been established. Ibid., p. 170.

10. For background on the status of women and their treatment by Iran's theocratic government, see Azar Tabari and Nahid Yeganeh, *In the Shadow of Islam: The Women's Movement in Iran* (London: Zed Press, 1982); Eliz Sanasarian, *The Women's Rights Movement in Iran: Mutiny, Appeasement, and Repression from 1900 to Khomeini* (New York: Praeger, 1982), pp. 124–50.

11. Documentation of the persecutions of the Baha'is has been published by numerous authors and international organizations. A useful introduction to the subject is D. Martin, "The Persecution of the Baha'is of Iran, 1844–1984," *Baha'i Studies* 12/13 (1984).

12. Juan Cole, "The Baha'is of Iran," *History Today* 48 (March 1990): 28.

13. At the outset of Khomeini's regime, there was vigorous dissent from his policies voiced by many clerics, as discussed in Shahrough Akhavi, "Ideology and Praxis of Shi'ism in the Iranian Revolution," *Comparative Studies in Society and History* 25 (1983): 195–221. As the years went by, organized harassment of clerical critics increased. See Shahrough Akhavi, "Elite Factionalism in the Islamic Republic of Iran," *Middle East Journal* 41 (1987): 181–201. With the growth in repression, fewer clerics were willing to speak out in condemnation of the government. By 1988 the intolerance of dissident clerical voices had reached such a level that even clerics within the government entrusted with the responsibility of pronouncing on whether proposed laws were in conformity with Islamic law were ordered to cease expressing public disagreement with the government. Thus, declarations by the clerical members of the Council of Guardians that proposed legislation favored by the regime violated Islamic precepts provoked an admonition by the then speaker of the Majlis, Hashemi Rafsanjani, to the effect that "today the views of the leader are our final authority. . . . I beg the esteemed Council of Guardians . . . to pay serious heed to the imam's guidance, not to allow their own views or those of others to obstruct the implementation of the imam's guidelines. If they have a problem with a certain issue, they can meet with the imam privately and ask questions." *FBIS-NES-88-004*, 7 January 1988, p. 51.

14. A basic source for the effects of the collapse of the rule of law and the end of any respect for the principle of legality after the revolution is the reporting by Amnesty International contained in the Iranian sections of its annual reports beginning with the volume covering 1980.

15. On the official status of Islamic law in Saudi Arabia, see Hiro, *Islamic Fundamentalism*, pp. 120–21; Mortimer, *Faith and Power*, pp. 172–73; Farouk A. Sankari, "Islam and Politics in Saudi Arabia," in Dessouki, *Islamic Resurgence*, pp. 180–83. While theoretically the only law in force, in practice the Shari'a has been extensively supplemented by secular rules. See Bryant W. Seaman, "Islamic Law and Modern Government: Saudi Arabia Supplements the Shari'a to Regulate Development," *Columbia Journal of Transnational Law* 18 (1980): 413–81.

16. Imam [Ruhollah] Khomeini, *Islam*

and Revolution: Writings and Declarations of Imam Khomeini (Berkeley: Mizan, 1981), p. 137.

17. Khomeini's letter can be read in *FBIS-NES-88-004,* 7 January 1988, pp. 49–50.

18. *Iran Focus* 2 (July 1989): 5–6.

19. Officially, the religion no longer even exists. For example, in the chapter on religion in Iran in the 1987 official yearbook published by the Islamic Propagation Organization, various minority religions and communities are covered but Baha'ism is completely ignored. *Islamic Republic of Iran Today* (Tehran: Islamic Propagation Organization, 1987), pp. 109–27.

20. *New York Times,* 2 July 1991, p. A4.

21. Khomeini, *Islam and Revolution,* pp. 181–88.

22. See *Iran Focus* 2 (June 1989): 5; 3 (January 1990): 3; 3 (February 1990): 3.

23. See Shireen Hunter, "Islam in Power: The Case of Iran," in Hunter, *The Politics of Islamic Revivalism,* pp. 270–72.

24. A component of the dissatisfaction on the part of moderates was the record of human rights violations that the regime had accumulated since the revolution. Both Ayatollah Montazeri and Rafsanjani gave indications in 1987 that they wanted more respect for human rights in Iran. *Amnesty International Report,* 1988 (London: Amnesty International Publications), p. 234. Montazeri in the months before his forced resignation openly questioned whether these rights violations were not damaging to the revolution.

25. *Iran Focus* 2 (June 1989): 3–4.

26. For example, in a 1990 speech he said that women could be philosophers, scholars, teachers, jurists, and writers, and he supported their right to participate in international sporting events. He indicated approval of women being heard on television and on the radio, expressing disapproval of "fanatics" who thought that women's voices should not be heard. *FBIS-NES-90-167,* 28 August 1990, p. 67.

27. The urgency of economic improvement was brought home by arson and rioting in Tehran in July and August of 1991. Iran's own statistics indicated that 65 percent of the population was living under the official poverty line. *Financial Times,* 2 August 1991, p. 4.

28. Helpful general background is provided in Richard Nyrop, ed., *Pakistan: A Country Study* (Washington, D.C.: Government Printing Office, 1984), pp. 183–256.

29. Mortimer, *Faith and Power,* pp. 226–327.

30. Many critical accounts of Zia's tactics in this connection have been published. Examples may be found in Afzal Iqbal, *Islamisation of Pakistan* (Lahore: Vanguard Books, 1986), and the 1986 Supplement accompanying the Constitution of the Islamic Republic of Pakistan, in Albert Blaustein and Gisbert Flanz, eds., *Constitutions of the Countries of the World* (Dobbs Ferry: Oceana, 1986). For a laudatory account by an admirer of Zia's Islamization policy who views it as an attempted synthesis of Islamic and democratic values, see Golam W. Choudhury, *Pakistan: Transition from Military to Civilian Rule* (Essex: Scorpion Publishing, 1988).

31. For example, in the 1970 elections in West Pakistan, Zulfikar Ali Bhutto's leftist Pakistan People's Party (PPP) was condemned by clerics as anti-Islamic, but got 58.7 percent of the vote, as against 2.9 percent for the Jamaat-i-Islami and a total of 10.2 percent for two ulama-based parties. Mortimer, *Faith and Power,* p. 214. The election held under Zia in 1985 was boycotted by the major parties, which had been banned. Zia, who was not himself running as a candidate for office, had arrested hundreds of his opponents and had banned political campaign activity like rallies. Nonetheless, after eight years of fundamentalist propaganda, the Jamaat in these favorable circumstances won only eight of the sixty-three contested national seats. Likewise, the voters rejected almost all of the candidates who had been involved in the Zia government or closely associated with him. Iqbal, *Islamisation,* pp. 130–31. In the 1988 elections, the Jamaat-i-Islami was able to win three seats in parliament, while the party of Benazir Bhutto, the nemesis of the

Jamaat, got ninety-three. Malise Ruthven, *A Satanic Affair: Salman Rushdie and the Rage of Islam* (London: Chatto and Windus, 1990), p. 108.

32. Pervez Amirali Hoodbhoy and Abdul Hasmeed Nayyar, "Rewriting the History of Pakistan," in Mohammed Asghar Khan, ed., *Islam, Politics and the State: The Pakistan Experience* (London: Zed, 1985), pp. 164–77.

33. *Pakistan: A Country Study,* pp. 201–32, 225.

34. An excellent introduction to this topic is Khawar Mumtaz and Farida Shaheed's *Women of Pakistan: Two Steps Forward, One Step Back* (London: Zed Books, 1987).

35. An exceptionally thorough account of the disputes and conflicts between fundamentalists and the Ahmadis and the 1953 riots that these led to can be found in documents widely known as the Munir Report. It was published as *Report of the Court of Inquiry Constituted under Punjab Act II of 1954 to Enquire into the Punjab Disturbances of 1953* (Lahore: Government Printing, 1954).

36. Note, "Pakistan Ordinance XX of 1984: International Implications on Human Rights," *Loyola of Los Angeles International and Comparative Law Journal* 9 (1987): 667. By 1986 at least two Ahmadis had been sentenced to death under the Ordinance (p. 683).

37. The group was arrested in Abbotabad in January 1990. See *Amnesty International Report, 1991* (New York: Amnesty International, 1991), p. 176.

38. In this Zia would have had the support of the Jamaat-i-Islami. See Ruthven, *A Satanic Affair,* p. 108. However, in an earlier election, at a time when it served their political goals to support the candidacy of Jinnah's sister, the Jamaat had argued that there were no Islamic grounds for objecting to a female leader. Kalim Bahadur, *The Jama'at-i-Islami of Pakistan: Political Thought and Political Action* (New Delhi: Chetana Publications, 1977), pp. 106–10.

39. The annual reports of Amnesty International regularly criticized rights violations caused by the military courts and the brutality of the punishments that they meted out. In 1985 Amnesty published a special report, "The Trial and Treatment of Political Prisoners Convicted by Special Military Courts in Pakistan." The 1986 Amnesty International Report detailed the ways that the operations of the courts violated international legal standards, including their lack of independence from the military authorities, their unfair procedures, and their denial of the right to appeal. *Amnesty International Report,* 1986 (London: Amnesty International Publications), p. 248.

40. Mumtaz Ahmad, "Pakistan," in Hunter, *The Politics of Islamic Revivalism,* pp. 236–37; *Pakistan: A Country Study,* pp. 223–26.

41. An excellent survey of the conflicts between the proponents of Islamization and feminists can be found in Mumtaz and Shaheed, *Women of Pakistan,* pp. 71–162.

42. Rashda Patel, *Islamisation of Laws in Pakistan?* (Karachi: Faiza, 1986), p. 59.

43. Mumtaz and Shaheed, *Women of Pakistan,* pp. 77–78.

44. See Ann Elizabeth Mayer, "Islamization and Taxation in Pakistan," in Anita Weiss, ed., *Islamic Reassertion in Pakistan: The Application of Islamic Laws in a Modern State* (Syracuse: Syracuse University Press, 1986), pp. 59–77; Omar Asghar Khan, "Political and Economic Aspects of Islamisation," in Khan, *Islam, Politics and the State,* pp. 127–63.

45. Zia's mistrust of the level of popular support for Islamization and the public attitude toward his regime is evinced in the constitutional amendments that he imposed when he ended martial law in 1985. Clearly anticipating challenges to the legitimacy of his acts under martial law, Zia had added to the constitution provisions validating all actions of the martial law regime, including those of the martial law courts, and immunizing them from any kind of questioning on any grounds, as well as barring any prosecution or legal proceedings against persons acting on behalf of the martial law regime.

46. Materials in the book by Mumtaz and Shaheed provide good illustrations of femi-

nist reactions. See also Patel, *Islamisation,* pp. 78–82, 92–93, 120–27, 213–14.

47. Some background on the agitation, in which the Jamaat-i-Islami seems likely to have been involved, is given in Ruthven, *A Satanic Affair,* pp. 107–8.

48. *The London Times,* 26 October 1990, p. 13. Credible evidence that there had been vote rigging by Bhutto's foes belatedly surfaced. *New York Times,* 5 August 1991, p. A2.

49. *New York Times,* 11 April 1991, p. A5.

50. See the positive impression he conveyed in an interview with an Asian *Wall Street Journal* reporter, "Pakistan's Free Marketeer," *Wall Street Journal,* 11 July 1991, p. A10.

51. *FBIS-NES-91072,* 15 April 1991, pp. 71–72.

52. *FBIS-NES-91071,* 12 April 1991, pp. 54–59.

53. Ibid., p. 57.

54. The strife and breakdown in law and order are described in the *Wall Street Journal,* 31 July 1991, p. A1; *FBIS-NES-91,* 1 July 1991, pp. 52–55.

55. *Wall Street Journal,* 9 August 1991, p. A6; *New York Times,* 19 November 1991, p. A17.

56. *Wall Street Journal,* 23 October 1991, p. A1.

57. A helpful survey of the complicated religious background and the political orientations of different groups is in Khalid Duran, "The Centrifugal Force of Religion in Sudanese Politics," *Orient* 26 (1985): 572–600.

58. For background on this, see Abdullahi An-Na'im, "The Elusive Islamic Constitution: The Sudanese Experience," *Orient* 26 (1985): 329–40.

59. Gabriel Warburg, "Islam in Sudanese Politics," in Michael Curtis, ed., *Religion and Politics in the Middle East* (Boulder, Colo.: Westview, 1981), p. 315.

60. Bona Malwal, "The Roots of Current Contention," in Francis Deng and Prosser Gifford, eds., *The Search for Peace and Unity in the Sudan* (Washington, D.C.: Wilson Center Press, 1987), p. 14.

61. Bona Malwal, one of the most politically prominent Southerners, summarized the significance of the 1983 changes in policy as follows: "In 1983 The Addis Ababa Agreement was illegally revised by the action of one man supported by groups whose main aim was to return to the status quo before the agreement, partly to strengthen fundamentalist religious control and regulation of public life in the country and partly to weaken the autonomy in the south . . . security and military arrangements were changed, the language arrangement was canceled in an attempt to return to the original policies which promoted one language over others; the economic and financial arrangements were reviewed in the wake of the oil discovery in the south and significant financial powers were reassigned from the Southern Regional Government to the central government; the Shari'a law replaced a secular system of the life of the country." Malwal, *The Roots,* p. 14. (The "language arrangement" referred to was a retraction of the policies in place prior to the 1972 Addis accords, in which Arabic was promoted in lieu of local languages and English, which had become the lingua franca of the non-Muslim South.) Numayri's 1983 adoption of his Islamization policy coincided with a revival of the previous policy of official efforts to establish Arabic as the language of the Sudan. As already noted, Islamization in the Sudan has been associated with a policy of Arabization. In 1987 Francis Deng, a leading southern Sudanese intellectual, in discussing North-South tensions in the post–Numayri era, said that the most critical areas of debate were religion and, to a lesser extent, language and insisted that the Sudan be organized along secular lines because "to adopt an official religion or discriminate between religions in any way can only breed discontent, resentment, and hostility with the risk of endangering not only national unity, but indeed the very survival of the nation." Francis Mading Deng, "Myth and Reality in Sudanese Identity," in Deng and Prosser, *The Search for Peace,* pp. 67–68.

62. A scathingly negative portrait has been painted of Numayri by a disillusioned former colleague. See Mansour Khalid, *Nimeiry and the Revolution of Dis-May*

(London: KPI Limited, 1985). See also comments in Peter Woodward, *Sudan, 1898–1989: The Unstable State* (Boulder: Lynne Rienner Publishers, 1990), pp. 175–76, 186, 215, 254. In the period of his Islamization policy, Numayri was also closely associated with Adnan Khashoggi, the infamous Saudi Arabian middleman and arms dealer who has figured as a central personnage in several major international corruption scandals.

63. These comments are based on extensive interviews conducted by the author with members of the legal and business communities during research in Khartoum in December 1984–January 1985. Aspects of the laws and the predicament that they created are described in Ann Elizabeth Mayer, "Islamization: Business Is Definitely Not As Usual," *Middle East Executive Reports* 8 (March 1985): 8, 25–62. Among other things, the whole principle of limited liability seemed to be undermined by the new laws. There was risk of criminal liability being imposed by the courts of decisive justice for "offenses" in violation of Shari'a principles that were not stipulated as such in the penal laws. Thus, for example, in 1984 at a time when interest was not criminalized and was being routinely charged, a hapless Hindu merchant was suddenly singled out and arrested for charging interest in violation of Shari'a rules. He was sentenced to a flogging of ninety lashes, ten years in jail, confiscation of his personal property, and an $8 million fine. Ibid., pp. 25–26. A person connected to the Indian community in Khartoum told the author that the punishment of the merchant was inspired by motives of personal revenge.

64. "Sudan: Threat to Women's Status from Fundamentalist Regime," *News from Africa Watch,* 9 April 1990; "Women under Sudan's Fundamentalist Regime," *Middle East International,* 3 August 1990, p. 20.

65. The reports of Amnesty International covering the years 1983–85 provide many details of the collapse of legality and the rule of law in this period and the consequent human rights violations.

66. A striking example of the kind of deal that could be openly carried out was the public agreement Numayri made with Khashoggi in September of 1984 which gave Khashoggi 50 percent ownership of all the Sudan's natural resources—all for a filing fee of about $125. The assumption was widely made that millions of dollars had been passed under the table to government officials to obtain this extraordinary concession. This contract is discussed in Khalid, *Nimeiry,* pp. 380–82. It was immediately abrogated when Numayri was overthrown.

67. For example, hundreds of African women were flogged and imprisoned because they manufactured and sold a nutritious and mildly alcoholic beer, a staple of their traditional diet, the sale of which they used to obtain money to support their families. Alcohol had become prohibited to non-Muslims as well as Muslims under Numayri, with the result that Africans were punished for acts that fundamentalist Muslims considered crimes but that were innocuous according to African cultural and religious standards.

68. Woodward, *Sudan,* pp. 170–71.

69. The author attended the large and boisterous outdoor New Year's Eve party thrown by the U.S. Embassy in Khartoum on 30 December 1984. Alcohol flowed freely, but there was little risk of arrest, because the Sudanese government had placed guards around the premises to ensure that its American paymasters would not be disturbed by any zealous enforcers of Islamic morality.

70. Documentation of some of the policy considerations leading to U.S. support for Numayri, as well as some criticisms of the latter, can be found in the testimony in *Sudan: Problems and Prospects,* Hearing before the Subcommmitee on Africa of the Committee on Foreign Affairs, House of Representatives, Ninety-eighth Congress, 2d Session, 28 March 1984. Especially interesting are the Sudan sections of the Country Reports on Human Rights Practices issued in February of 1984, 1985, and 1986 by the U.S. Department of State, which report not just on the rights situation in the Sudan but provide statistics on the level of assistance being afforded by the U.S. government.

71. An account of this case by one of Ta-

ha's most prominent disciples can be found in Abdullahi Ahmed An-Na'im, "The Islamic Law of Apostasy and Its Modern Applicability to the Sudan," *Religion* 16 (1986): 197–224.

72. The text of this document along with an interesting survey of relevant historical and legal developments can be found in the "Transitional Constitution of the Republic of the Sudan" 1985, in Albert Blaustein and Gisbert Flanz, eds., *Constitutions of the Countries of the World* (Dobbs Ferry: Oceana, 1989). There was a stipulation that both the Shari'a and "custom" (which could potentially mean Arab or African custom) should be the main source of legislation, which had also been included in the 1973 constitution.

73. Woodward, *Sudan,* pp. 206–27.

74. Because of the ongoing civil war, there could be no voting in parts of the South affected by the conflict, so a large segment of the African Sudanese who would certainly have voted against the Islamic fundamentalists did not have their votes tallied. Antifundamentalist groups worked against the candidacy of Turabi, who lost his election. In the actual tally, the Ummah Party got 38.2 percent of the votes, the DUP 29.5 percent, and the NIF 18.4 percent. However, it is important to note that in the normal, geographically based voting districts, the NIF got twenty-eight of its total of fifty-one seats. The remaining twenty-three were obtained only through votes cast through the Sudan's oddly designed "graduate constituencies," which were tailor-made for control via the discipline and well-funded organization of the NIF. For details, see Woodward, *Sudan,* p. 207. The result of the NIF's ability to dominate the graduate constituencies meant that the NIF was probably substantially overrepresented in proportion to its numerical support among Sudanese voters.

75. His positions are outlined in Mansour Khalid, ed., *John Garang Speaks* (London: KPI, 1987).

76. See the statement by Lam Akol, one of the SPLM/SPLA leaders, at a conference in 1987: "The SPLM/SPLA is committed to the establishment of a democratic New Sudan. Democracy which embodies equality, freedom, economic and social justice, and respect for human rights, not as slogans but as concrete realities that have concrete content. . . . The SPLM/SPLA is committed to solving the nationality and religious questions . . . with a democratic and secular context . . . so that the Sudan belongs equally to all irrespective of race, religion, family background, or any other sectarian consideration." Lam Akol, "The Present War and Its Solution," in Deng and Prosser, *The Search for Peace,* p. 19.

77. "Sudan: Sudanese Human Rights Organizations," *News from Africa Watch,* 4 November 1991.

78. John Voll has pointed out how out of keeping with Sudanese democratic and egalitarian traditions the authoritarian, repressive policies of the Bashir regime are and how antithetical its intolerant attitude is to Sudanese political culture. John Voll, "Sudan: State and Society in Crisis," *Middle East Journal* 44 (1990): 575–95.

79. In addition to being based on information shared by Sudanese acquaintances of the author, this account rests on details supplied by Africa Watch, which has been regularly reporting on the deteriorating human rights situation under the Bashir government. Samples of the reports include "Sudan: Destruction of the Independent Secular Judiciary: Military Government Clamps Down on Press Freedom" (25 September 1989); "Political Detainees in the Sudan" (24 October 1989); "Sudan, Khartoum: Government to Execute Striking Doctors," "The Provinces: Militia Killings and Starvation Policy Return" (6 December 1989); "Sudan: Recent Developments in Khartoum, an Update" (13 December 1989); "Political Detainees in Sudan: Academics" (22 January 1990); "Sudan: The Massacre at al Jebelein" (23 January 1990). Many of the findings presented in these and other reports have been compiled in "Denying the Honor of Living," *Sudan: A Human Rights Disaster, an Africa Watch Report,* March 1990.

80. "Sudan: Suppression of Informa-

tion," *News from Africa Watch,* 30 August 1990, pp. 23–24. In actuality, the torturers were demonstrating how greatly the values and attitudes of fundamentalism had shaped their own understanding of what Islam permitted or forbade. American fundamentalist strictures against the teaching of evolution have until recently not had many counterparts in the Muslim world, as few Muslims have found any contradictions between the natural sciences and their religion.

81. See articles in the *New York Times,* 5 October 1990, p. A6; 31 October 1990, p. A3; 8 November 1990, p. A20; 11 December 1990, p. A15.

82. "Sudan: New Islamic Penal Code Violates Basic Human Rights," *News from Africa Watch,* 9 April 1991.

83. The announcement can be read in *FBIS-N-5-91-083,* 30 April 1991, p. 11. Not all prisoners were released.

84. *New York Times International,* 13 December 1991, p. A7; *New York Times International,* 26 January 1992, p. A12.

85. The new wave of repression in 1990 is discussed in *Iran: Violations of Human Rights, 1987–1990* (New York: Amnesty International, 1990). Reviewing the last three years, Amnesty International reported that in that period thousands of political prisoners had been executed, including a total of about twenty-five hundred in a few months of 1988. Reports of the cases of the nine persons imprisoned and later punished are

presented in "Iran: Political Dissidents, Held for over a Year, Are Reportedly Sentenced," *News from Middle East Watch,* 3 September 1991, and the September 1991 release from the Lawyers Committee for Human Rights, "Action Update: Islamic Republic of Iran, Ali Ardalan." See also *New York Times,* 12 September 1991, p. A9.

86. After presenting the opinions of his interviewees, the author summarizes aspects of their views as follows: "Nor can they find much Islam in the Islamic government. Such a government, they believe, should provide for the well-being of its subjects. Instead, there are warfare, bloodshed, refugees, economic decline, inflation, unemployment, inequality, injustice, repression, decline of education, and a general lack of care for the people's condition. . . . They condemn the regime's vengefulness against officials of the former government, the harsh punishment of moral offenders, and the enforcement of Islamic rules by violent means. They reject the clergy's dominant role in the affairs of the state, because they feel it causes the government's blatant failure." Reinhold Loeffler, *Islam in Practice: Religious Beliefs in a Persian Village* (Albany: SUNY, 1988), p. 226.

87. In Iran in late 1991 there were even hints that Ayatollah Montazeri, once vilified by fundamentalists and disgraced for being too moderate, might be being officially rehabilitated. See *FBIS-NES-91-233,* 4 December 1991, pp. 52–54.

Fundamentalist Influence in Egypt: The Strategies of the Muslim Brotherhood and the Takfir Groups

Abdel Azim Ramadan

Fundamentalism before 1970

"Fundamentalists" (rendered in Arabic as *usuliyyun*) is a Western term that the Arabic references and sources do not use.[1] Arabic references describe the Muslim Brotherhood's members simply as "radicals."[2] Hasan al-Banna, the founder of the Brotherhood, described his mission as a "*salafiyya* [traditional, or literally, 'ancestral'] mission."[3] He described his society as a "Qur'anic, Muhammadan, Islamic society, which follows the way of the Noble Qur'an, takes the path of the Great Prophet, does not deviate from what has come down to us in God's Book, his Messenger's Sunna, and the conduct of the venerable forefathers."[4] The name "fundamentalist" appeared in the Egyptian press with the rise of militant Islamic groups in the time of Sadat; it was used to *distinguish them from* the Muslim Brotherhood. The Egyptian press called these fundamentalists "Islamic groups" or "extremist religious groups." When they resorted to violence, the name "terrorist religious groups" was applied to them. Because they adopted the concepts of *jahiliyya* (pre-Islamic idolatrous society), *al-hakimiyya* (God's sovereignty), and *al-takfir* (branding with atheism), these groups were considered a part of the modern radical Islamic trend, while the Muslim Brotherhood was largely considered a part of the traditional Islamic trend.[5] For the purposes of this chapter, however, we will consider these as two forms of fundamentalism, the former a radical fundamentalism, the latter a moderate mainstream fundamentalism. Both large groupings were committed in the 1970s and 1980s to the implementation of Islamic law in Egypt, but they differed in important ways in their strategies for bringing this about.

The term "fundamentalist" in Islam, then, does not apply to those who wish to withdraw from secular life and return to earlier forms of religious life. Rather, it applies to those who wish to renew Islam by working to purify it from spurious beliefs, to return to its first principles, to reconcile Islam with the requirements of the modern age, to consider Islam as an appropriate instrument for government, and to insist on Islam's capacity to "push the wheels of progress" rather than to rely on Western secular political structures and laws. The Salafiyyin opposed the "Westernizers," who adopted secular Western thought and were influenced by the lure of the Western lifestyle.

After the modernization of Egypt during the reign of Muhammad 'Ali and Isma'il in the nineteenth century, the leadership of political and social life passed to the Westernizers. The changes in productive relationships during that period—shifts in land tenure from the system of *Iltizam* (tax-farming) to monopoly and to a system of private land ownership—led to the rise of a new social class. These changes in economic and social life were reflected in the intellectual life of Egyptian society, which had its first introduction to Western thought with the student missions to Europe and the translation movement. Education was transformed from the traditional system of *Kuttabs* (Qur'anic mosque schools) to a system of modern schools where students studied sciences and foreign languages. A new educated class influenced by European thought arose to contest with the men of religion (*ulama*) centered in the great Islamic university of al-Azhar in Cairo.[6]

In the beginning, the Salafiyyin sought to counter the Westernizing trend by tying religion to work and to *jihad* (used here in the sense of internal struggle), and by fighting the corruption and otherworldly mysticism of the Sufi orders. Shaykh Muhammad 'Abduh, leader of the reforming Salafiyyin, called for the introduction of modern sciences into the al-Azhar curriculum as part of its complete educational overhaul. He urged Muslims to learn European languages and use them to benefit the Islamic sciences.[7] Meanwhile, Shaykh 'Ali 'Abd al-Raziq was the first Muslim to attack the caliphate as the legitimate Islamic form of government; it had, he said, no textual basis in the Qur'an or the Prophet's Sunna. He condemned its role throughout Islamic history, saying that it was "a scourge on Islam and Muslims and a source of evil and corruption." Not a generation had passed without an attempt on the life of a caliph. In theory, the caliphate was based on elective consensus; in reality, 'Abd al-Raziq maintained, it rested only on arbitrary power. He called for the abolition of the caliphate and held that God had given Muslims the freedom to choose their political systems.[8] This reform movement also maintained that the decline in the conditions of Muslims derived from the stagnation of Islamic thought, the cessation of *ijtihad* (reinterpretation of the Qur'an in light of current needs), and the adoption of new beliefs alien to Islam's first principles which had paralyzed Muslims, preventing them from catching up with the modern age.[9]

After World War I, in the political climate created by the nationalist revolution of 1919, this reform movement entered a new stage. Copts and Muslims participated together in the revolt against the British occupation, and Atatürk's Turkey provided a model for secularization. Indeed, Turkey's turn toward the West followed its separation of religion from the state, its abolition of the caliphate, its Westernization of education, law, and literature, and its adoption of European dress. At the same time the Westernizing trend intensified in Egypt, under the belief that the only way to achieve what Western civilization has achieved was to adopt the substance and spirit of Western civilization. Hadn't modern Japan successfully taken on the essential aspects of Western civilization, and wasn't it now able to stand with it on an equal footing? During the 1920s Egyptian women abandoned the veil, entered the work force, acquired an education, even participated in politics, and began to criticize polygamy and call for elimination of the *Shari'a* (Islamic law) courts. Egyptian men turned to European lifestyles in their dress, customs, and thinking; youth turned from religious education at al-Azhar to modern sciences and embraced the principle of intellectual freedom.[10]

Naturally, this social transformation alarmed the religious fundamentalists in al-Azhar and Dar al-'Ulum, the Sufi orders, and the *Manar* magazine school of students of Shaykh Rashid Rida. These fundamentalists were descended from petite bourgeoisie, working class, and peasant roots; they were unable to bear the exorbitant educational expenses which British occupation had imposed and thus were forced to turn to the only type of education that was free at the time, the training colleges—Dar al-'Ulum and al-Azhar.[11]

The fundamentalist movement which arose in response to this wave of Westernization followed the path of confrontation and resistance to what was considered a movement of moral disintegration, a wave of "apostasy and obscenity." Hasan al-Banna, a teacher at an elementary school in Ismailiyya in 1927, challenged religious leaders to defend Islam from these encroachments: "If Islam [were] lost in this nation, al-Azhar and the ulama would disappear too, and you [wouldn't] find food to eat or money to spend."[12] In this early phase the fundamentalist movement commingled religion with the interests of a class fearing extinction under the advance of secularists. It had no well-defined ideology; the goal was merely to hold fast to the basic principles of Islam in the face of obscenity and apostasy. The first steps included the formation of Islamic societies, the publishing of Islamic newspapers, preaching, and providing guidance to the people. The Muslim Brotherhood, begun by Hasan al-Banna in Ismailiyya in March 1927, was thus a purely religious society, a reformist Islamic movement. Its goal was to bring up youth in accordance with proper Islamic ethics, and to disseminate the merits and purposes of Muhammadan prophecy, including the moral virtues of truthfulness, chastity, and good social relations.[13] With these simple principles, over which there was no disagreement, the Muslim Brotherhood was able to draw the attention of the masses of the people and to extend branches into other cities, like Port Said, Suez, Abu Suwair, and al-Bahr al-Saghir. Its headquarters was moved to Cairo in October 1932, and after one year there were fifty branches. In May 1933 its first newspaper, a weekly, appeared under the name *The Muslim Brotherhood*.[14]

With missionary work and the passage of time, it became necessary for the Brotherhood to define its ideological positions on a number of political issues. There is some evidence that al-Banna relied upon the *Manar* school in doing so.[15] The basic elements of al-Banna's ideology were the oneness of the religious world and the lay world, of religion and state; the belief in pan-Islamism in the face of Egyptian nationalism[16] (this accounts for the spread of the Muslim Brotherhood outside Egypt, particularly into the Sudan, Syria, and the Maghreb);[17] the adherence to the concept of the caliphate as a symbol of Islamic unity; and the establishment of an Islamic government as the final goal.[18]

The Muslim Brotherhood was thus the first Islamic association to appear in modern Egypt with the goal of seizing power. Hasan al-Banna considered noninvolvement in politics an "Islamic crime." The Brotherhood was also the first Islamic association to shift its activities from the traditional Islamic centers such as al-Azhar, the Sufi orders, and the uneducated popular classes over which religion had great spiritual sway to the secular universities and the educated classes influenced by Western culture.[19] The Brotherhood shifted the responsibility for establishing Islamic government from the religiously educated class to the Western incultured class, from the shaykhs to the lawyers, doctors, engineers, pharmacists, and army and police officers. This was a significant development in the history of contemporary Egypt because it linked pan-Islamic Egypt before World War I to nationalist Egypt after the war, just as it linked religion to modern science, and so prevented Egypt from joining Turkey in a headlong rush toward Westernization.

The political work of the Muslim Brotherhood soon led to clashes with the political powers in Egypt. The Brotherhood saw the royal palace as the force dominating Egyptian political life, and so avoided conflict with it and even bargained with it. This set the Brotherhood at odds with the major popular forces allied to the Wafd Party, which was struggling for independence, constitutional government, and the evacuation of British forces from Egypt. The Brotherhood also created a secret army to protect the movement from the hostility of the state (and in due time to seize power). This in turn set it at odds with the political system, which ruled the country according to a semiliberal constitution. In 1948 Egyptian Prime Minister Nuqrashi directed a preemptive blow against the Brotherhood by dissolving the organization and detaining its leaders. Both he and Hasan al-Banna paid with their lives for this clash. Al-Banna was succeeded as Supreme Guide of the Brotherhood by Hasan al-Hudaybi. Under his leadership the Brotherhood was the first to support the military officers of the July Revolution in order to strike a blow at liberalism. But amicable relations did not last long. The officers ordered the Brotherhood dissolved on 14 January 1954. The conflict reached a climax when the Brotherhood attempted to assassinate Abdel Nasser in Alexandria. Its leaders were jailed for terms of five to ten years.[20]

During this critical period for the Muslim Brotherhood, Egyptian society was undergoing profound social changes different from those that had produced the ideology of Hasan al-Banna. The older transformations had not touched the society's productive relations, the essence of which remained semifeudal-semicapitalist, despite the rapid movement toward capitalist production with the founding of the Bank of Egypt (Bank Misr) in 1920. Between 1952 and 1964, however, semifeudal-semicapitalist productive relations yielded to capitalist productive relations with the agrarian reform laws of 1952, then to socialist productive relations with the nationalization laws of July 1961. Owing to these changes, the semifeudal class, which had ruled before the July Revolution, was brought down by the agrarian reform laws. In 1961 there came the fall of the capitalist class, which had revived somewhat under the revolution, through the Egyptianization law of 1957. The petite bourgeoisie and the masses of workers and peasants thus came to the fore, but without exerting any influence on the government, owing to the complete control of the officers of the July Revolution over the country. Their imposition of dictatorship and their imprisoning of all political opposition, from the extreme Islamic right to the extreme communist left, prevented these emergent classes from taking any substantive role in the processes of government.

The reactionary, submissive social values characteristic of semifeudal societies faded with the semifeudal class. With industrialization and agricultural reform came modern values typical of industrial secular societies. The 1961 nationalization laws created a huge bureaucratic class, which grew even larger after the revolutionary leaders appointed university graduates to jobs in public factories or public administration whether their services were required or not. These changes were accompanied by the spread of secular socialist thought at the hands of the sole political organization of the revolution, the "Socialist Union." Nationalization was seen as equal to socialism. Egyptian communists and socialists encouraged this naive belief, and used the socialist press (which the revolution tolerated) to publish proper socialist thought. They also accepted the Socialist Union's invitations to deliver educational and ideological lectures in the Union's youth camps in Helwan and elsewhere. The media were filled with their writings and broadcasts; the weekly *al-Ahram* was an arena in which socialist writers vied for public acceptance.

Egypt established warmer relations with the Soviet Union, which provided arms in 1955, assistance in building the High Dam, and a promise of support to counter the West's arming of Israel. Egypt's pro-Soviet policies negatively affected its relations with the Islamic Arab states (most notably Saudi Arabia), which depended on the West in general and on the United States in particular. Egyptian-Saudi tensions reached a high point in 1962, when the two countries supported opposite sides during the revolution in North Yemen.

In the early 1960s, the Muslim Brothers anxiously watched these developments and concluded that Egyptian society had fallen into the hand of the communist atheists. The Brothers' long presence in the prisons had isolated them from society. [21] One such prisoner, Sayyid Qutb, forged a new ideology for the Brotherhood. He rejected Egyptian society completely, along with all other societies which he considered jahiliyya. Belief in God's divinity and belief in the Five Pillars were no longer sufficient defining marks of an Islamic society. It must also reject all laws and traditions made by humans. Muslim societies governed by human laws are in reality pagan. Qutb considered prayer and belief in God's divinity inadequate as long as a man conferred sovereignty (*hakimiyya*) upon other than God. Thus, he branded all Islamic societies with atheism and considered them *kafir* (atheist). This was unprecedented in the history of the Islamic movements in modern Egypt and constituted a break from the ideology of Hasan al-Banna.

Qutb drew many of his ideas and some of his terms from a book by the Pakistani thinker Abul Ala Maududi. Qutb's writings proved controversial even within the Brotherhood, which suffered a split when Hasan al-Hudaybi rejected them.[22] A violent youth movement espoused Qutb's cause, but he was executed in 1965 and his influence waned within the ranks of the Brotherhood. But other Islamic groups took up his cause: radicalism leading to armed violence passed from the Muslim Brotherhood itself, only to be taken up by takfir secret organizations. Thus, two major strands of fundamentalism developed in Egyptian society after 1965 with different strategies and levels of impact.

The Ideologies of the Takfir Organizations

Two years after the execution of Sayyid Qutb, in 1967, Egypt's defeat in the Six Day War ended the conflict between the July Revolution and the Muslim Brotherhood. The Israeli occupation of Sinai brought other political issues to the fore, especially after Abdel Nasser stirred nationalist feeling through what was known as the War of Attrition. There followed years of preparation for the 1973 October War. In this general context a number of secret Islamic organizations arose in Egypt.

The Military Technical College Organization

After 1967 the ideas of hakimiyya and takfir became more powerfully attractive to extremist youth groups emerging from the Muslim Brotherhood and to other more radical and violent religious groups. Some of them formed secret organizations aimed at overthrowing the state and establishing an Islamic government. The idea of takfir varied from one Islamic organization to another; interpretations ranged from branding the ruler alone with atheism to so branding the whole society with him. The first and most dangerous of these organizations appeared at the beginning of 1974 under the leadership of Salih Abd Allah Siriyya, a Palestinian. Siriyya began as a member of the Islamic Liberation Party, a group founded by Taqi al-Din al-Nabahani after the 1948 defeat of the allied Arab armies in Palestine. Al-Nabahani established branches of his party in Jordan, Syria, Lebanon, and Iraq. He sought to take power and establish an Islamic society by force.

Salih Siriyya wed the Islamic Liberation Party's idea of taking power by force with Qutb's (and Maududi's) ideas of hakimiyya and takfir. His notebook detailed his organization's principles, goals, and plan of action, as formed by his critical study of previous Islamic societies (including the Muslim Brotherhood) and the reasons for their failure. To Siriyya, his predecessors' most important mistake was their gradualist approach to seizing power—by first preparing the individual, then preparing the society, then ultimately establishing the Islamic state. This was the strategy adopted by the Supreme Guides of the Muslim Brotherhood and endorsed by Sayyid Qutb. Siriyya argued that the right course of action was first to seize control of the state through the overthrow of the Egyptian order. Muslims could then proceed directly to the task of creating a society shaped according to their own goals and beliefs.[23] Siriyya expanded the membership of his organization but failed in his attempt to take over the Military Technical College in April 1974 (the event from which his group took its name). The Muslim Brotherhood, on good terms with Sadat at the time, condemned the attempt.

The Society of the Muslims

The failure of Salih Siriyya's organization had an effect upon the Society of the Muslims, an organization founded by Shukri Mustafa and popularly known as al-Takfir w'al-Hijra (literally, "charging with atheism and emigration"). The Society of the Muslims dropped—at least temporarily—the idea of taking over the state first and adopted a new idea which Salih Ashmawi had introduced in 1954 during his struggle with al-Hudaybi for the leadership of the Muslim Brotherhood: the idea of emigration. This doctrine held that there must be an emigration of the good elements of society who work for God and His mission, and for Islam and its Shari'a, to a place suitable for the growth of the Islamic concept and the flourishing of the Muhammadan mission (much like the Prophet's own *hijra* to Medina in 622 C.E.).[24]

Shukri Mustafa broadened the historical connotation of emigration, dividing the concept into stages. He called on his followers to desert non-Muslim places of worship (i.e., all mosques in Egypt not under the society's control). True Muslims would then leave their homeland for another land in which God alone was worshiped, in which all would be exorcised of their polytheism.

> This having been done, retribution will descend upon them, and not fall upon us; mercy will descend upon us, and will not fall upon them, as there is no intermingling or assimilation or confusion between truth and falsehood, and as it cannot be that God would assist a society that pretends to support Islam, while its basic principles are still Jahiliyya principles, and its branches are intertwined with the branches of Jahiliyya.[25]

After the emigration from the land of Egypt—the land of atheism and the abode of war—Muslims would prepare to fight atheist society and attack the existing political system so as to take over the reins of authority. Thus, the movement would follow the same stages as the historical spread of Islam: Call, Emigration, Holy War (*da'wa, hijra, jihad*). The fighting would begin defensively and end offensively.[26]

Shukri Mustafa embellished the idea of takfir with the following assertions:

1. All sin is a kind of polytheism; everything which God forbade is an atrocious crime.
2. Because God imposed every religious imperative as a condition in Islam, it is necessary to perform them all. If one is missed, the rest are of no avail.
3. Every Muslim who is reached by the call of the Society of the Muslims and does not join is an infidel.[27]
4. Infidels deserve death, whether singly or as a group. The infidel's life's blood, his wealth, and his family honor are forfeit to the Muslim.
5. It is not permissible to name any mosque as a mosque of God unless all those who pray there believe in God and the day of judgment, perform prayer, give *zakat,* and fear only God.[28]

Mustafa's view of the exterior enemy, represented by Israel, was analogous to his view of the interior enemy, Egyptian society. He considered each a blasphemous society from which the faithful should emigrate to prepare and gather strength for the eventual jihad. When the Society of the Muslims was eventually brought to trial, the court questioned its members about their position in the event that Jewish forces should enter Egypt. They replied that their society would not fight in the ranks of the Egyptian army, but rather would flee to a place safe from both the incoming enemy and the local enemy.[29] For this reason, the society encouraged its members to avoid military conscription.[30]

Although the Society of the Muslims' plan was to emigrate first of all, the Egyptian government's unceasing pressure on it and the increased detention of its individual members led the society to abduct al-Shaykh al-Dhahabi (the former minister of *waqfs* [Islamic endowments]) on 4 July 1977, conditioning his release on the government's freeing of the society's detainees. When the government showed signs of evasion, the society killed al-Dhahabi. In a few days, the government arrested the perpetrators of the crime, as well as the rest of the members of the society. On 31 November 1977, Shukri Mustafa and four others were condemned to death.

The Jihad Organization

At the same time, another extremist takfir organization also came to trial, the Jihad Organization. Formed in Alexandria in 1975, the organization centered its activities in the province of al-Buhaira and in the town of Port Said. Ahmed Salih Amer, an engineer who had received his degree from University of al-Mansoura, led the group. It consisted primarily of students of the universities and higher institutes. This organization may be considered an extension of Salih Siriyya's group—both had the same goals and tactics, that is, overthrowing the infidel state as the first step toward the "Islamization" of the infidel society. The Jihad's leadership sprang from the freed leaders of Salih Siriyya's organization. Its tactical methods aimed primarily at overthrowing the state, and thus did not mirror those of the Society of the Muslims, which aimed at withdrawing from the society to prepare for future empowerment. An ideological conflict soon broke out between the two organizations.[31] Members of the Jihad were arrested and charged in November 1977 with participating "in an agreement of criminal aim to forcefully overthrow and change the constitution of the state, its republican system, and its form, in that they established a secret organization calling for Jihad against the existing regime, and its annihilation by force, on the pretext that the system is in conflict with the regulations of the Islamic Shari'a."[32]

This organization was the first to bear the name "Jihad," but the name was also applied to successive organizations. The first successor to the original Jihad appeared in Alexandria in 1979 and met the same fate as its predecessor in February 1980. That year one of its members who escaped arrest, Muhammad Abd al-Salam Faraj, an engineer in the administration of the University of Cairo, formed the third Jihad organization, the one that eventually killed Sadat. In *The Missing Ordinance* (i.e., the religious imperative of jihad), Faraj invoked the ideas of hakimiyya and takfir. But unlike Shukri Mustafa, Sayyid Qutb, and Salih Siriyya, each of whom had declared both the ruler and the society to be atheist, Faraj believed that the ruler alone was the infidel. Faraj cited a *fatwa* (legal religious opinion) by the great Damascene "literalist" scholar Shaykh al-Islam ibn Taymiyya (1263–1328), which he interpreted to mean: "Since the state is ruled by the judgments of atheism despite the fact that its people are Muslims; and since the laws which are raised over the Muslims today are the laws of atheism imposed on the Muslims by atheist rulers, hence there is peace for the Muslims, and *jihad* against the atheist state." This jihad to establish the Islamic state is a religious ordinance and an Islamic obligation, because God enjoined on all men duties and obligations which it is impossible to perform in the absence of the "Islamic state." The Islamic state is the nucleus from which to reestablish the "Islamic caliphate" to unite all Muslims anew.

Faraj believed that jihad was the religious duty for all Muslims whose country was occupied by the enemy—an enemy represented by the rulers holding the reins of government. Muslims cannot depose rulers who have forcefully imposed their absolutism upon their subjects without revolutionary violence; the tyrants of this earth will not be overthrown except by the sword. Fighting them is more appropriate than fighting the distant foreign enemy. The path to liberate Jerusalem, Faraj believed, must first pass through the liberation of our own countries from blasphemous rule. These blasphemous rulers are responsible for the colonialism in the countries of Islam. Through nationalistic ideas and nationalist battles, their store of power and blasphemy increases. So they must be eliminated as a prelude to the eruption of forces, under an Islamic leadership, for the liberation of the sacred places. In other words, rather than emigrate to another country in order to establish the state there and then return, Muslims should save their energy and establish the state of Islam in their own country and then go forth from it conquering. The only method validated by Shari'a for establishing the Islamic state is fighting.[33]

In the summer of 1980, Faraj decided to form nationwide an armed secret organization, thereby taking advantage of the political climate created by Sadat's game of balancing rival political forces in Egypt against each other. This gave the Islamic groups the necessary leeway to function as a counterweight to the socialists. By September of 1980 Jihad's secret organization had grown to the point where the security authorities felt constrained to arrest its members. Between 3 and 5 September a campaign to suppress Sadat's political adversaries took place. It included the detention of 1,536 people nationwide. Sheer coincidence, or the will of God, as Jihad adherents would have it, provided the opportunity for the organization to assassinate Sadat, when First Lieutenant Khalid al-Islambuli was selected to participate in the military parade review on 6 October 1981. The assassination was a success, but the members of the organization fell into the grasp of the state security organs after armed resistance in some of the provincial cities.[34]

The downfall of the last Jihad group did not, however, end the influence of radical fundamentalists in Egypt. President Mubarak's cautious democratization and liberalization policies nonetheless made possible a resurgence of the takfir organizations in the 1980s. The most widespread group was the Al-Jama'a al-Islamiyya (the Islamic Group).[35] This successor organization embraces the idea of takfir developed by its blind philosopher, Shaykh Umar 'Abd al-Rahman, in his statement for the defense in the Jihad court case, which Al-Jama'a published as a book. This collection of sophistries and misinterpretations uses a literal interpretation of Qur'anic verses to support the ideas of takfir and hakimiyya.[36] It is considered the manifesto of the Islamic groups in Egypt.

Al-Jama'a al-Islamiyya

Al-Jama'a al-Islamiyya (hereafter the Jama'a) was formed by leaders of Jihad who had been released from jail, and by members of the former Islamic groups in Cairo and Upper Egypt. The name was taken from the organization founded by the Pakistani thinker Maududi. Led by 'Abd al-Rahman, who had been acquitted of issuing a fatwa legitimizing the assassination of Sadat, the Jama'a covered a broad range of Egyptian society and a wide expanse of Egyptian geography, from Upper Egypt in the South to Alexandria in the North. Its main activities were in Upper Egypt and Cairo. This organization took up the mantle of Islamic fundamentalism from the Muslim Brotherhood, but in doing so made takfir a central concept.

'Abd al-Rahman worked out a practical policy for his organization that confined it to religious and social activity and, given the lesson of Sadat's assassination, relinquished any thought of political assassination or military coup d'etat. The new organization was centered in student environments and in working-class neighborhoods where the standard of living had deteriorated and people were open to the idea of an Islamic order and government.

According to 'Abd al-Rahman's interpretation of takfir, both ruler and society are pagan, but individuals are not necessarily so.[37] Although 'Abd al-Rahman and Shukri Mustafa differed in the proper scope of takfir, both agreed that it was based on the principle of the sovereignty of God. Under the motto of the Qur'anic verse "Fight against them until there is no *fitna* [polytheism], and the religion is entirely God's" (8:39), the Jama'a was built on the logic of resistance to and confrontation with whatever was seen as contrary to Islam in Egyptian society. It thus sought in all cases to implement the principle "Command what is right, and forbid what is wrong" as a duty imposed on Muslims by religious law. The organization took for itself the authority of the ruler on the pretext that the present ruling order was not committed to Islam. An Islamic ruling order should apply Shari'a systematically. Any ruler who governs without respect to divine revelation is pagan.[38] In this way of thinking, jahiliyya is not a historical period prior to the appearance of Islam but a condition that is found whenever its constituent elements are present in a situation or system—a state where rule and legislation are subject to human caprice rather than to Islamic law. People who are not under God's rule become the slaves of their legislator, whether it is an individual, a social class, a nation, or a group of nations. But when God legislates for the people, they are entirely free and equal because they bow only to God and serve only God.[39]

This ideology defined the Jama'a's political theory. It saw the Islamic caliphate as the ideal form of government for Islam. Any other political system was rejected.[40] This of course entailed the rejection of the liberal democratic experiment in Egypt. In the unwritten "social contract" between the Mubarak government and the Islamic groups, social and religious activity was permissible, as was a limited degree of political organization and participation (although not under the open banner of Islam). But the radical Jama'a saw the Muslim Brotherhood's participation in the 1984 parliamentary elections as a "great sin and offense." Parliament, after all, is based on positive civil laws and cannot, in consequence, promulgate Islamic religious law. The Parliament is worthy only of burning.[41]

In keeping with its opposition to the liberal democratic experiment, the Jama'a opposed a multiparty system for the simple reason that an Islamic society knows only two parties, the party of God and the party of Satan. Since the Jama'a alone represented the party of God, the remaining parties must represent the party of Satan. Some of the distinctive positions of the Jama'a on public questions were based on this dualistic worldview. From ancient Muslim society, for example, the Jama'a retrieved the requirement that non-Muslims pay tribute as compensation for being excused from jihad. The group also opposed a peace settlement with Israel and insisted on the military option of liberating Palestine. The Jama'a opposed the 1984 alliance of the Muslim Brotherhood with the Wafd party as an attempt to weaken the Islamic commitment to the Shari'a by assimilating Islam to liberalism. It resolutely rejected the suggestion that the Islamic movement might become part of the system instead of standing apart and towering above the system, as Sayyid Qutb had recommended.[42] The Jama'a also virulently opposed the participation of Muslims in the 1987 elections. Group members imprisoned in connection with the Sadat assassination directed a taped appeal from inside the prison to all Muslims, announcing their refusal to participate in the elections and calling for a boycott of them.[43]

The Jama'a believed that any Muslim who sees that his society is not ruled by God's legislation must launch a jihad.[44] But this mission must also include other obligations: the call to God and the recruitment of members; the publication of educational and instructive tracts; the conducting of Islamic social activities, such as aiding the poor with the *zakat* (alms) and *sadaqa* (donation) taxes and visiting the sick in hospitals.[45] The leadership of the Jama'a defined its activities around three axes: first, the call to God, whether in the mosques or in the coffeehouses, clubs, or train stations; second, "the commanding what is right and prohibiting what is wrong," beginning with notification and preaching, and ending with warning and rebuke, until all factories producing intoxicants were closed, until the tribute upon non-Muslims belonging to the "People of the Book" was imposed, and until the zakat was collected to be spent according to the Shari'a; and third, the waging of jihad until the rule of God was fully realized.[46]

Group members spoke in the mosques, and gave lessons and public meetings in various quarters and areas, and in villages, clubs, schools, and universities. Although the prevailing Islamic rule restricted using force to correct wrongdoing to the ruler, the Jama'a arrogated this right to itself in dealing with obvious perpetrators of sin—drunks on the street, truck drivers transporting intoxicants, and purveyors of sex videotapes. Another matter the group considered a clear sin was the wearing on the streets of immodest clothing and shorts by foreign female tourists. These clothes, they held, reveal parts of the female anatomy that "excite the feelings of Muslim youth."[47] Similarly, they considered the staging of plays in the cities and dramatic and musical shows in the colleges and universities to be sins. The Jama'a applied the principle of "prohibiting the wrong" to them. First they alerted the authorities to prevent the staging of such shows. If the staging of the shows went ahead, group members used force to shut them down. Naturally this led to clashes with the security forces. The Jama'a in this way inherited a legacy of violence once associated with the Muslim Brothers, but it was violence of a new type.

Group activity began in 1984 and 1985 with the publication of basic principles and the recruitment of members. At the beginning of 1986 the group entered a new phase when it sent its members to assault beer sellers, singers, and videotape clubs in the cities. On 24 August 1986 group members sat down across the Cairo-Aswan highway, blocking access to trucks carrying beer, and then arose and threw their cargos into the canals and on the road. The security forces intervened, and a violent confrontation took place at the al-Rahman mosque. A large number of the organization's leaders were arrested and brought before the courts by the state security prosecutor.[48] The most violent confrontation between the Jama'a and the security forces occurred in the 'Ayn Shams district of Cairo and in al-Fayyum. 'Ayn Shams, with its large university student population, became a staging ground for the Jihad Organization, which assassinated Sadat. Members of this group were prosecuted and acquitted, and made the Mosque of Adam in 'Ayn Shams their center of activity. On 12 August 1988 security forces threw a cordon around the Mosque of Adam. After the congregation set tires alight to use as barricades and threw blazing blocks and rocks at security forces, it was met with tear gas and water cannons. The Jama'a managed to set a police vehicle on fire with blazing torches and to demolish two other vehicles. But the police arrested 105 members.[49] Subsequently the Jama'a obtained explosives and planned to strike at tourism in the country under the pretext that tourism was a major source of corruption, inasmuch as the short dresses worn by female foreigners provoked the devout youth. Members of the Jama'a decided to intimidate the tourists by burning a tourist bus in front of the al-Salam Hotel on New Year's Eve in 1988, but they were arrested before they could commit this crime and subsequently prosecuted.[50] Finally, in al-Fayyum three members of the group tossed a bomb into a tent being used for the staging of a controversial play, wounding an officer. The group planned a demonstration for the following Friday led by 'Abd al-Rahman. Demonstrators carried firearms, heavy metal chains, and pieces of brick and rock, and clashed with security forces when the first hostile cries went up against the ruling order. Forty-nine demonstrators and their blind leader were arrested and brought before the State Security Court in 1989.[51]

The policy of the interior minister, Zaki Badr, was to deal with the Jama'a by repaying violence with violence, including lethal force. In January 1990, Badr was dismissed as interior minister. To test his successor, General Muhammad 'Abd al-Halim Musa, the Jama'a prepared to occupy three mosques in three separate provinces on 25 January 1990, the day of the police celebration. Demonstrations moved through the streets of Asyut, al-Fayyum, and Cairo. The Jama'a commander for Manfalut was to announce the organization's demands while President Mubarak was de-livering a political speech on the occasion of the Police Holiday. Among these demands was a call for release of Jama'a members who were imprisoned, and for the immediate prosecution of Zaki Badr, in return for evacuation from the three mosques. The demonstration actually took place in Asyut on Monday, 22 January: Jama'a dem-onstrators demolished a number of the prominent jewelry stores in the city's major streets along their way to occupy the Mosque of al-Khashabah. Security forces did not hesitate in dealing with the demonstrators. There was an exchange of fire; the Jama'a commander fell dead immediately, and six others were wounded. Security forces arrested thirteen members of the group.[52] In an interview published in the newspaper *al-Sha'b,* an organ of the Islamic movement in general and the Muslim Brotherhood in particular, 'Abd al-Rahman commented upon the meaning of these violent skirmishes: "There will be no room here for a discussion or mutual under-standing with the new minister unless or until he and his men return to the Truth."[53] The battle had been joined.

The Jama'a were the successors to the Muslim Brothers in other ways besides the resort to violent skirmishes with the security forces. They also sought and exercised authority over devout Egyptian youth in the universities, schools, villages, cities, and neighborhoods and clashed frequently with the political order after the Brothers had turned toward the liberal experiment. Nevertheless, the Muslim Brotherhood enjoyed a wider stage in Egypt for the propagation of its principles than the Jama'a, whose activity was centered in the cities of Upper Egypt and in certain poor, overcrowded neighborhoods in Cairo.[54] The undeniable limit to the appeal of 'Abd al-Rahman's takfir group was linked to its ideology: its principles were in fact too radical to be accepted and fully comprehended by the masses, and its demonstrations and riots never took root on a mass scale.

The New Muslim Brotherhood

Even as takfir groups such as the Jama'a attained a limited prominence in the 1980s, the Muslim Brotherhood was undergoing a transformation of some import. The Brotherhood had been renewed by Nasser's death and the appearance in the 1970s of new leaders ripened by years of imprisonment. Foremost among them were Mustafa Mashhur and Ma'mun al-Hudaybi, along with such traditional leaders as Farid Abd al-Khaliq, Abd al-Qadir Hilmi, the members of the Office of Supreme Guidance, and the Supreme Guide Hasan al-Hudaybi. The administrative agencies began to form in prison, and Sadat's victory over Nasser's supporters became a historic opportunity for the Brothers to resume their activities in more favorable conditions. The fallen group was the leftist group which the Soviet Union had supported. When Sadat overpow-ered them, he lost favor with the Soviets, who withdrew the support they had offered in Nasser's time. After Sadat expelled Soviet military advisers from the Egyptian army in July 1972, the Egyptian left began to intensify its criticism of him. Since the pretext Sadat offered for his conflict with the Nasserite group was its desire to set up a dictatorship (in contrast to his own enlightened support of democracy), Sadat did not risk vanquishing them as Nasser had done with his opponents. Instead he bolstered the political forces opposed to the left. One such force was the Muslim Brotherhood.

King Faisal of Saudi Arabia was at this time fighting the Soviet influence in the Arab world. He was thus attuned to Sadat's political situation. In the summer of 1971 King Faisal arranged a meeting between Sadat and the leaders of the Muslim Brotherhood who lived outside Egypt. During this meeting Sadat told Brotherhood leaders that he was facing problems comparable to theirs, and that he shared their objectives in opposing communism and blasphemy. He promised to help ease the return of the Brotherhood to public activity in Egypt.[55] Shortly thereafter he released the first group of imprisoned Brothers. Among them was Umar al-Telmsani, who later became the Supreme Guide upon the death of Hasan al-Hudaybi. Immediately after his release he went to the Abdin Palace to render his thanks to Sadat in the official visitors' book.[56]

The following year Sadat sought a meeting with certain Muslim Brotherhood leaders to "cooperate in the service of the country." Supreme Guide al-Hudaybi saw nothing objectionable in the idea if Sadat's intentions were good, and charged Umar al-Telmsani with continuing negotiations.[57] The release of the imprisoned Brothers was gradually completed, and crowned by a comprehensive pardon of all sentences that had been handed down in political cases before 15 May 1971. This was followed by a reorganization of Egypt's political party structure. Under the July Revolution only one political organization was recognized. It was known first as the Liberation Rally, then as the National Union, then as the Arab Socialist Union. Sadat transformed it into three "platforms"—right, center, and left. A decision to this effect was promulgated by the National General Conference in July 1975. The name "platforms" was later replaced by "organizations," then "parties."

The Muslim Brotherhood began to replenish its ranks under these favorable circumstances and discreetly to resume forming grassroots organizations throughout the country. Brotherhood leaders circulated rumors that they would seek permission to reconstitute the Brotherhood "as a religious Society," to be headed either by Kemal al-Din Husayn or by Husayn al-Shafi (Islamic personalities from among the Free Officers of the July Revolution). They of course denied the rumors. The Brotherhood then began to insinuate itself within the government by recruiting allies among public opinion shapers and political leaders capable of facilitating, or at least condoning, Brotherhood activity.[58]

Yet even as it sought to enter the political mainstream, the Brotherhood was divided about the proper approach to a new political role. One group wanted immediately to resume publishing the journal *Al-Da'wa* (*The Call*), in order to give the Brotherhood an organ to express its opinions and principles and announce the return of the Muslim Brothers in a practical and direct way. This might lead, it was hoped, to an increase in membership and a type of de facto political and legal existence. A second group called instead for a delay in publication and a revamping of *Al-Da'wa* to improve its journalistic quality. The first approach prevailed; *Al-Da'wa* reappeared in July 1976 with Salih al-Ashawi as editor-in-chief, under the management and supervision of Umar al-Telmsani. The Muslim Brotherhood reclaimed a public voice for the first time since 1954.

But the speed with which *Al-Da'wa* was published took an inevitable toll. It lacked a certain professionalism, and the subjects it treated did not necessarily appeal to Muslim youth or the Islamic masses. The lead articles resurrected the main old principles and policies that had formed the Muslim Brotherhood's original philosophy, that is, pan-Islamism, the demand for the application of the Shari'a, and a presentation of Islam as both religion and state. The single exception was a new treatment of the Islamic caliphate. The journal declared a truce with Sadat's regime in order to gain its confidence; it was hoped that the Brotherhood would be allowed to form as a legal party. The journal condemned Nasser and the communists in Egypt and elsewhere. The Brotherhood also opposed the United States, which had "an inclination which is hostile to Islam and disruptive of any kind of return to true Muslim life." The Brothers were skeptical of America's efforts to establish peace in the Middle East; they believed that it wanted to impose an American-Israeli settlement. But there were no objections to the economic "open-door" policy initiated by Sadat or to the return of Western capitalists to Egypt.[59]

The Brotherhood's approach to the economic, social, and political problems of Egyptian society was purely religious. It traced the causes of these problems to the "failure to apply the Islamic Shari'a." *Al-Da'wa* announced that a return to religion was the only way to salvation: "Return to the rule of God. Nothing else you have will ever save you, only this and nothing else." Consequently, the Brotherhood argued that only its legal return to the political field would lead to a revival of the Islamic nation and "fix the pillars of this religion in the souls of Muslims in a practical way."[60]

The official attitude toward the Muslim Brotherhood wavered at this time between two tendencies. The first tendency was to see it as the only society capable of opposing the communists, and therefore advocated its legal return as a political party; these politicians sought to have the Brotherhood lend them the authority of the Shari'a. Sayyid Mar'y, speaker of the People's Assembly, announced that "there is no sensibility here for the establishment of any sort of parties so long as they are committed to the national unity, the social peace and the inevitability of the socialist solution." But a second body of opinion argued that confrontation with the communists did not require paying this price. If the demand for Islamic Shari'a came from an officially sanctioned political party, this school argued, the government would be put in an awkward situation. To apply the Shari'a over the opposition of the Copts would be to risk the unity of the nation. There were external considerations as well: such a policy would in the end bring the government into collision with the Brotherhood, as the events of 1954 had demonstrated. President Sadat announced that the "establishment of a political party based on religion will never be permitted" and instead appointed Salih Abu Ruqayaq, a preeminent Brotherhood leader, to a leading position in the ruling Center Party. A number of others were co-opted in the same way.

On 28 October and 4 November 1976, the government held new (multiparty) elections for the People's Assembly. Ruqayaq waived his constituency in favor of the general secretary of the Center Party, which on 11 November 1976 was renamed the

Socialist Arab Party of Egypt. Six other members of the Brotherhood who had been attached to the party, however, entered the People's Assembly, and were chosen for leadership positions in both the party and the Assembly.[61] In a very short time the Muslim Brotherhood was able to become a major political power. It spread in the cities, the towns, the universities, and other institutions. Its importance was apparent during the elections. Campaign rallies to which its leaders were invited in the Sayyida Zaynab district in Cairo, in Damanhur, and in the universities attracted large numbers of students and young people who demanded the application of the Shari'a.[62]

Yet the Brotherhood was still, officially, an illegal society. It also faced the necessity of electing a Supreme Guide to succeed Hasan al-Hudaybi, who had died in 1973. There was some sentiment in favor of Salih Abu Ruqayaq, a member of the ruling party. But the leadership decided to choose their oldest member, Umar al-Telmsani, without any elections. He was already the Supreme Guide in all but name, particularly after his management of *Al-Da'wa* had given him effective power. The Egyptian authorities acknowledged this and held him answerable for the Brotherhood, though not in an organizational sense, "for had they been certain that an organization existed they would have delivered all of us up to the courts instantly." He accepted this situation, carried on his duties, and offered the authorities the Brotherhood's help in several situations. He considered this an implicit acknowledgment by the government of the Brotherhood's existence in the political arena, despite the order of 1954 that the Brotherhood dissolve.[63]

The Muslim Brotherhood served Sadat's regime by confronting the two political forces which threatened it—the forces of the political left (Marxists, Socialists, and Nasserites) which held the open-door policy responsible for the deepening economic crisis and the widening gap between the social classes, and the forces of the extreme right (the takfir organizations). The Brotherhood attacked communism, Nasserism, and socialism in each issue of *Al-Da'wa*. As for the extreme religious right, the Brotherhood did not hesitate to attack the takfir organizations, condemning their ideology and interpreting their movements as a revolt against true Islam. When Salih Siriyya confessed, in the course of the Military Technical Academy trial, that he had been in contact with certain leaders of the Muslim Brotherhood—including Hasan al-Hudaybi, Shaykh Muhammad al-Ghazali, and Zaynab al-Ghazali—the latter repudiated Siriyya and his militance. Shaykh al-Ghazali, an adviser to the Ministry of Waqf, denied meeting Salih Siriyya and vowed that he would never conspire against the believer-president, Sadat.[64] As for the Society of the Muslims, the Brothers condemned its thought as it branded its members with atheism, prohibited following their lead in prayer, and declared shedding their blood lawful.

Yet the Brotherhood also condemned the existing political order for prohibiting its work and for refusing to implement the Shari'a. The state needed the Brotherhood to control the extremist societies, the argument went, for the Brotherhood alone was in a position to inhibit the spread of takfir thought among young activists distraught over the corruption of society and searching for an Islamic solution.[65] In July 1977, for example, *Al-Da'wa* called the assassination of Shaykh al-Dhahabi "an awful crime, forbidden by religion and repugnant to custom; those who perpetrated this grievous crime did not have the least of religious knowledge. We condemn from the bottom of our hearts the crime, circumstances, and immediate causes of it."[66]

The honeymoon between the Brotherhood and Sadat's regime ended soon after the president's visit to Jerusalem. The Brotherhood did not make its opposition to the trip known at the time it was announced for a number of reasons, not the least of which was that the visit was well received by the masses and a significant number of religious personalities. To oppose the trip would also seem to place the Brotherhood in the same camp as the communists and Nasserites. Nevertheless, when the dispute over the peace terms arose and Sadat cut off links with Israel, the Brotherhood gained courage to oppose the policy. From February 1978 it was outspoken about Israel's greed for everything from the Euphrates River to the Nile, and warned against a peace that would sanction Israel's illegitimate position in the Arab area.[67] Umar al-Telmsani claimed that the Zionists had usurped the land of Palestine and must return it; the Jews might live in Palestine as fellow citizens but not as rulers. The Muslim Brotherhood was considering the visit to Jerusalem, he said, in light of the doctrine forbidding a Muslim to accept the attrition of his land.

The attitude of the Brotherhood entered a new phase with the Camp David accords. It announced its violent opposition to the agreement in October 1978:

> The religious Law of Islam states that if any part of the Land of the Muslims is seized and if they are able to recover it but do not, then they are sinners. And this is what has happened since the establishment of the State of Israel. It is incompatible with all divine laws to acknowledge a usurper's right to have what he has usurped. We need not, then, be afraid of war whatever its consequences would be![68]

Yet the same issue of *Al-Da'wa* called for deliberation to ease the conflict between Egypt and the other Arab states.

The opposition to the Camp David accords was clearly a crisis for the Muslim Brotherhood. Would it be content to use the channels Sadat's regime had opened for opposition, or would it resort to force? Some of the Islamic groups began to criticize the Brotherhood's attitude, suspecting it of weakness or fatigue. But the Brotherhood announced its opposition to the use of force. Umar al-Telmsani wrote that despite its opposition to the existing order—until such time as the law of God was applied—the Muslim Brotherhood was against burning means of transport, plundering stores, and wrecking government foundations; this would destroy the property of the people. The Brotherhood was similarly opposed to plotting against the regime; its ideologues explained that the Brotherhood (unlike the takfir groups) did not seek rule or care about those who ruled. It cared only about the sort of rule—its constitution, form, and regulations. Violent clashes with the authorities did little more than undermine the power of the people by wasting their efforts, ultimately benefiting only the enemies of the country.

Clearly a change in the attitude of the Muslim Brotherhood had taken place since the bitter confrontation with Nasser in 1954. It had learned from the ordeals of 1948,

1954, and 1965; in each case it had suffered profoundly from physical collisions with the political order in Egypt and was determined to avoid the same mistake again. A new pragmatism characterized the Brotherhood in the 1980s.

Sadat called on the religious scholars at al-Azhar Islamic establishment to vindicate the Camp David accords to counter the accusation that he had violated the principles of Islam by acknowledging the existence of an Israeli state in Palestine. This accusation was made in fatwa issued by the Muslim Brotherhood and a number of Arab states. Al-Azhar represented several establishments—the Islamic Research Academy, al-Azhar University, the Higher Council of al-Azhar, the Committee for Fatwa, the General Administration for Propaganda and Guidance, and the al-Azhar Institutes—and thus appealed as an authoritative Islamic voice to moderate Egyptian public opinion. Al-Azhar dutifully published an official statement in May 1979, announcing what it called the "Islamic Opinion" and the "Religious Legal Verdict" on the Egyptian-Israeli Treaty: Egypt was an Islamic country, and it was necessary for its ruler to support its affairs and to be vigilant for its protection. If he saw that the best interests of Muslims lay in reconciliation with their enemies and making peace with them, he could do so. The announcement compared the Egyptian-Israeli peace accords with the "Peace of al-Hudaybiya" and the "Pact of Ghatfan"—both drafted by the Prophet—and validated the agreement on the basis of Qur'an verse 8 (*Al-Anfal*): 61 ("If they incline to peace, make peace with them"). Contracting the Egyptian-Israeli accords stood religiously within the bounds of Islamic rule, for it was concluded out of strength after the victory of the October War, it realized the return of Islamic territory to Islamic people, and it did not surrender Jerusalem to the Israelis. The Muslim Brotherhood published two strong refutations in the July 1979 issue of *Al-Da'wa*.[69]

This struggle between the Brotherhood and al-Azhar did not, however, push the Brotherhood toward extremist Islam, which had begun to call for attacks on the Israeli Embassy and the assassination of Israeli diplomats and tourists (as well as Egyptians collaborating with them). *Al-Da'wa* continued to warn against such extremism in April 1980: "Now that disaster has befallen and Israel has an embassy in our country, what must we do? Do we blow up the Embassy? Do we seize the Jewish diplomats and kill them? No, a thousand times no! Blowing up the Israeli Embassy will never lead to any result but the reconstruction of another embassy at Egypt's expense." The magazine urged instead a boycott of everything Israeli.[70]

Despite these efforts at moderation, a collision with the regime began to seem inevitable. The January 1979 issue of *Al-Da'wa* had published a CIA report (an apparent forgery) asking the government of Egypt to destroy Islamic organizations—the Muslim Brotherhood foremost among them. The report was attributed to Richard Mitchell, professor of modern Near East and North African history at the University of Michigan and author of the book *The Society of Muslim Brothers*. This publication enraged Sadat, as it insinuated that his government received instructions from the United States. The Egyptian authorities for the first time confiscated an offending issue of the magazine.[71] Sadat publicly upbraided Umar al-Telmsani for publishing the forged CIA report, reminding him that it was within his authority as president of the republic to abolish the Muslim Brotherhood and its newspaper, neither of which had any basis in law. Sadat nevertheless said that "as a family elder" (a role in which he loved to imagine himself) he would not do this.[72]

Publication of the false CIA report was not the only thing to disturb relations between the Brotherhood and the regime. The Brotherhood had asked for a legal recognition of its existence, claiming that there was no official resolution dissolving it. The only relevant resolution was the one issued in 1948 by al-Nuqrashi prior to the July Revolution. The Wafd government had subsequently rescinded the resolution. But Sadat insisted that there was a resolution dissolving the society and added: "I've opened the jails and the concentration camps and restored to you all the respect that is yours. I have given the people complete freedom and restored the respect of the law; the proof of this lies in the fact that you publish a journal without anyone obstructing you, although this publication is on an extralegal basis. I just sent you the minister of the Interior to say to you: 'Shame on you!' "[73] Other incidents and recriminations followed.[74]

In the early 1980s the Muslim Brotherhood attempted to consolidate the Islamic groups in the universities under its leadership—a move the Sadat regime viewed as an attempt by the Brotherhood to recover the power and influence it had enjoyed prior to 1954. By the early 1980s every university in Egypt boasted an Islamic group with an emir over it. These Islamic groups fluctuated in their allegiance between the ideology of takfir and the ideology of the Muslim Brotherhood. *Al-Daʿwa* disseminated their news and encouraged their activities as a prelude to consolidating the various groups under Brotherhood leadership. The emirs of the groups elected a general emir over all of them. Then a coalition of Islamic groups outside the universities produced a general organizational framework known as the Permanent Islamic Congress for the Propagation of Islam, which elected al-Telmsani as its president.

The regime saw the establishment of this congress as a dangerous shift in the policy and attitude of the Brotherhood. The regime naturally preferred dealing with each group separately so as to play one off against another, and all of them against the Nasserites and communists. This new consolidated organizational framework meant that the Islamic groups had begun to work for their own specific objectives, not those of the regime.[75] This became evident as the congress began to organize against the regime's foreign policy and the Camp David accords. By various means the congress attempted to hinder Egypt from implementing the treaty, threatening to subvert Israeli-Egyptian relations and cancel the Israeli withdrawal from the Sinai. For example, the congress held a public meeting on 29 May 1981 immediately after the evening prayer at al-Azhar mosque to discuss ways of recovering Jerusalem. Tens of thousands of people attended. When Israel launched an unprovoked raid against the Iraqi nuclear plant less than a week later, the congress held a rally at the al-Nur mosque in the Abbasiya district of Cairo to discuss a response. Umar al-Telmsani, Shaykh Hafiz Salamah, and Salah Abu Ismaʿil spoke at the rally, as did the supreme commander (*emir*) of the Islamic groups, the physician Hilmi al-Jazzar. The rally drafted a declaration to Sadat asking him not only to condemn the Israeli raid but also to take "practical steps to deter Israel." The congress demanded abrogation of the process of normalization; a halt to the implementation of the Camp David accords; the withdrawal of the Egyptian ambassador from Tel Aviv; and the expulsion of the Israeli ambassador. The declaration summoned all young people to jihad for Jerusalem and demanded the lifting of all restrictions on Islamic groups and the opening of the mosques to independent Islamic preachers. Mosques, it stressed, are places not only for prayer but also for governing, consultation, legislation, and implementation. At another meeting in Alexandria the congress passed resolutions demanding the recovery of Jerusalem and Palestine, nonrecognition of the legitimacy of the Zionist seizure, and a proclamation of jihad as "an obligation remaining in force until Judgement Day."[76] In this atmosphere of rising Islamic militancy, sectarian clashes occurred in Zawiya al-Hamra, one of the poor neighborhoods of Cairo, on 17 June 1981. A riot between Muslims and Copts ensued. Dozens died and over a hundred people were wounded; a number of shops and dwellings were burned. The incident threatened to turn into a sectarian war.

Sadat's policy of balancing the political left had created a counterforce endangering his foreign policy and even threatening his regime. The success of the Muslim Brotherhood at integrating the Islamic groups under the banner of the congress alerted him to the danger of the Brotherhood's revival. Sadat came to believe that the Islamic groups represented the Brotherhood's secret organization:

> When they [the Muslim Brothers] became aware that there were seven to eight thousand boys [of the Islamic groups] including those who called themselves *emirs* of the Islamic groups, they fooled them and gave them weapons so as to frighten other students, and intimidation prevailed in all universities. The Islamic groups are the secret weapon of the Muslim Brothers, but instead of repeating their mistake and using them secretly, they used them openly! The Muslim Brothers did not immediately express themselves clearly; they took time.[77]

Sadat charged that the Muslim Brotherhood proclaimed the supremacy of God alone, idenitified the ruling authority as atheist and the society as pagan, and incited violence among the Islamic groups.[78]

Despite Sadat's accusations, the Muslim Brotherhood did not control all of the Islamic groups. A large proportion of these groups, as much as 20–30 percent, regarded the Brothers as enemies. Nor were all the leaders of the Brotherhood content with Umar al-Telmsani's policy of cooperation with the regime. Some of them would have preferred to form alliances with opposition parties—notably the leftist Unionist Party, the New Wafd Party, and the Labor Party. These dissidents believed that Umar al-Telmsani's policy was preventing the Brotherhood from gaining the support of a large portion of the Islamic forces and was permitting other emergent religious leaders to influence the public and gain fame. These new leaders included preachers in the larger mosques, notably Shaykh Muhammad al-Kahlawi (Imam and preacher at the al-Qa'id Ibrahim mosque in Alexandria), Shaykh 'Abd al-Hamid Kishk (Imam and preacher at the Dayr al-Malak mosque in Cairo), and Shaykh 'Abd al-Rashid Saqr (Imam and preacher at the mosque of Salah al-Din in Cairo).[79]

Sadat's conflation of the Muslim Brotherhood with the takfir groups was a great mistake, for the two were antithetical. Sadat did not understand that the congress was an attempt by the Brotherhood to absorb the extremism which embodied the real danger to the regime; he mistakenly feared that the congress would threaten the liberation of the Sinai. By focusing his concern on the Brotherhood alone, Sadat made the mistake that ultimately cost him his life, for the center and motivating force of Islamic extremism had passed from the Muslim Brotherhood into the hands of the takfir groups, of which the Jihad Organization was at the time the most dangerous.

This confusion of the Muslim Brotherhood with the extremists led Sadat to strike preemptively at the *political* forces blocking the path to the liberation of the Sinai from the Israeli forces. He feared that these Islamic forces in the political arena would give Israeli hard-liners an excuse to cancel the treaty. His intelligence apparatus warned him of preparations by the extremists to destabilize his regime, and he decided to launch a preemptive strike. On 3 September 1981 his security forces arrested 1,536 journalists, writers, politicians, and Muslim and Christian leaders representing various political currents. Umar al-Telmsani and other leaders of the Brotherhood were among them. Over one hundred were arrested from the traditional Islamic societies alone.[80]

The arrest of the Muslim Brothers represented a turning point in their relations with other opposition forces in Egypt. During their detention in Nasser's time it was customary to segregate the Brothers from other prisoners even during exercise periods. This practice actually led to the further radicalization of the organization. But in 1981 the Brothers were mingled with Wafd Party, Nasserite, and communist prisoners in the same cells and mixed with them in lunchrooms and at meetings.[81] Now in plain view of their rivals, whether from inside the regime or outside it, the Brothers entered a new phase in their relations with these political forces after the detention ended under the presidency of Husni Mubarak. Umar al-Telmsani even described his ideological rivals as "extremely charming," mentioning especially Doctor Isma'il Sabri Abdallah, the venerable communist, and Fu'ad Siraj al-Din Pasha, leader of the Wafd Party.[82]

Mubarak began his term of office after Sadat's assassination by releasing thirty-one detainees associated with various parties and political organizations on 25 November 1981. He received the detainees at the presidential palace immediately upon their release from prison. The prime minister announced the right of the released detainees to return to their professions and to practice their political activity.[83] Umar al-Telmsani and the leaders of the Muslim Brotherhood were released after having been moved from Tura prison to the Qasr al-Ayni hospital.[84]

The opposition journals began to reappear.[85] But because Sadat had died at the hand of an Islamic group member, the regime did not permit the return of the religious journals, forcing them to fall back on the courts.[86] Thus, the Muslim Brotherhood lost *Al-Da'wa*, formerly a powerful means of expressing its views. They retained only the magazine *Al-I'tisam*, with a small circulation and little impact. It did not represent their point of view completely but rather the opinions of a more extreme

Islamic organization, the Al-Jama'a al-Shar'iya (the Legal Group) founded by Shaykh Mahmud Khattab al-Subki.

In the three years between the release of the Brotherhood leaders and the 27 May 1984 elections, the Brotherhood resumed its attack on the rival ideology of takfir, which was in a sense responsible for Sadat's death. Umar al-Telmsani aided the political establishment by working among the prisoners from takfir organizations at Tura penitentiary, persuading them to abandon that ideology. He told the prisoners bluntly at a meeting held at Tura in August 1982 that what they were calling for "is not Islam, because Islam is an appeal to believe in God by means of wise and benevolent spiritual counsels." He reminded them that the regime was continuing to release them every few days; in one batch six hundred prisoners were released.[87]

Brotherhood relations with the communists in the Unionist Progressive Nationalist Party improved. In October 1982 the newspaper *Al-Ahali,* the Unionist Party organ, had published a series of interviews with Umar al-Telmsani which aroused attacks by rightist writers.[88] The Brotherhood leader responded that he distinguished between personal relations and his Islamic faith. Even the Prophet had visited his neighbor, the Jew. The Qasr al-Ayni prison, he said, brought together many different schools of thought and opinion: "There were those among the Communists who prayed with us."[89] Umar al-Telmsani maintained this stance. Asked four years later how he saw the possibilities for an alliance of Islamic and leftist forces in specific cases, he answered that "anyone who calls for freedom is my ally and I am his ally." He argued that fundamentalism (*salafiyya*) does not mean "backwardness"; it means progress: "Can any arrogant person advance a single proof that the Islamic fundamentalists did not welcome any discovery or invention for the good of the people? Did they call for segregation, isolation, or detachment from the people? They called in fact for diligent effort in all of life's objectives, in economics, society, politics, war and peace, in everything that benefits people in this world and the next."[90]

This significant change in attitude, the result of a political maturation over the course of three decades, enabled the Muslim Brotherhood to participate in the renewed life of parliamentary politics under the cloak of a secular party, the Wafd Party. The Brotherhood had failed in its attempts to recover its organizational headquarters and *Al-Da'wa.* Umar al-Telmsani also wrote an open letter to the interior minister demanding full legal existence for the Muslim Brotherhood like that allowed by the Mubarak regime to other parties. He cited the cooperation of the Brotherhood with the government in calming the students of the Islamic groups inside and outside the universities. He also referred to the Brotherhood's opposition to violence and condemnation of terrorism.[91] But once it became clear that the government would never return the Brotherhood's headquarters or magazine, or acknowledge its legal existence, the Brotherhood sought to enter the Parliament under the auspices of the Wafd Party. The Wafd was restored to political life by judicial decree in October 1983. In February 1984 the government returned political rights to the Wafd leaders. The Wafd began publishing its own weekly newspaper on 22 March 1984, took leadership of the opposition press, and prepared to plunge into the campaign for the elections scheduled for 27 May 1984.[92]

Meanwhile, the Muslim Brotherhood had concluded a detailed study of opposition political parties and chose to ally itself with the Wafd Party in order to take part in the elections. An alliance with the leftist Unionist Party was out of the question in view of doctrinal differences. The Liberal Party had no popular base of support. The Labor Party's recognition of Nasser ruled it out. This left only the Wafd Party, which had condemned Nasser's dictatorship and yielded to the forces pressing for application of the Shari'a. An agreement was reached by which the Wafd remained the Wafd, the Muslim Brotherhood retained its own character, and both would stand as opposition to the government. The Brotherhood deputies would attend the meetings held by the Wafdist members of Parliament. The Wafd and the Muslim Brothers were able to enter the elections in each electoral district jointly in such a way that in districts without Brotherhood nominees the Brothers would throw their support to the Wafd candidates.[93]

The alliance affected the reputation of the Wafd on the ideological level. The Wafd had previously stood for the separation of religion and state. It considered religion a personal matter, with the homeland open to all religions. The Wafd in its previous existence had no respect for nonconstitutional rule.[94] For these reasons the newer members of the party, as well as one of the older leaders, resigned over the alliance. Louis Awad, a major intellectual figure, criticized the party.[95] The newspapers of the ruling National Party accused the Brotherhood of political opportunism. The present author held the ruling party responsible for the alliance because it had not permitted the Muslim Brotherhood to form a legal party of its own.[96]

Not surprisingly, this alliance had a significant impact on the Wafd electoral program. Shaykh Salah abu Isma'il was among the architects of the party's first platform after a thirty-year absence from political life. Following a demand for democracy and a constitution, the platform called for the application of the Islamic Shari'a as "a main source of legislation."[97] Party propaganda held that Islam was both religion and state and demanded the Islamization of the mass media and educational institutions.[98]

Despite the political opposition of the regime, the alliance of the Muslim Brotherhood and the Wafd was immediately successful in increasing their share of seats in the People's Assembly. In a futile bid to impede this success, the administration intervened in favor of the ruling National Party's candidates. The proportional representation electoral system transferred votes for parties receiving less that 8 percent to the majority (government) party. Nonetheless the Wafd Party, now backed by the Brotherhood, received 15 percent of the vote, forfeited 2 percent by reason of the offset for small parties, but won 58 of 488 seats.[99]

By gaining entry into the Parliament in this fashion, the Muslim Brotherhood had become part of the ruling political system rather than part of the "Islamic Alternative"—the path taken by the takfir organizations. This situation was not entirely unprecedented, for some of the Brothers entered the October/November 1976 elections among the ranks of the ruling party. But they had done so on the basis of individual personal reputations rather than as representatives of their organization. The ruling authority accepted the entry of the Muslim Brotherhood into Parliament under the auspices of the Wafd because this seemed the best solution to the "Islamic problem."

The Brotherhood's undeniable popular strength was now recognized within the system notwithstanding the fact that the Brotherhood had no formal legal recognition. (Legal recognition would have led to resentment and riots by the Copts, the bitterest enemies of the Brotherhood in Egypt.)

Umar al-Telmsani died on 24 May 1986. Before his death he had formed a temporary Office for Supreme Guidance and made Mustafa Mashhur, the youngest Muslim Brother, his deputy, neglecting the established principle of seniority. Yet this did not make the choice of his successor any easier. Upon Telmsani's death the Brotherhood was divided into a number of factions. The first faction included a number of the "Qutabis" who had been imprisoned in the fifties and sixties after the dissolution of the secret Brotherhood organization and the execution of Sayyid Qutb. Under the leadership of Salah Shadi, a former police officer, they had called for the immediate election of a Supreme Guide. The second faction, led by Salih Abu Ruqayaq, insisted on the selection of someone detached from the former secret organization, such as Justice Ma'mun Hassan al-Hudaybi, the eldest son of the former Supreme Guide al-Hudaybi. A third faction, calling itself the "Bannawis and Qutbis," supported Mustafa Mashhur as a matter of self-interest. This faction was supported by the Brotherhood's new capitalism, which established telex, telephone, and telegraphic capacities to enhance rapid communication with organizations of Brothers in Europe and Kuwait. A fourth faction, made up of former Brothers, companions of al-Banna, and those intimate with him, demanded a return to Hasan al-Banna's original vision for the organization. They nominated Abd al-Rahman al-Banna, Hasan al-Banna's brother, who believed that the Brotherhood needed a mere "chief," not a Supreme Guide (a title which had historical connections and should only be carried by a reformer). Of course, the political situation prevented the group from convening in any legal form.[100] In the end, opinion came to settle upon Muhammad Hamid Abul Nasr as temporary Supreme Guide, on the basis that he was the oldest of the senior members.[101]

The Parliament of 1984 did not last long, because the opposition discredited it on constitutional bases. Mubarak decided to poll the Egyptian people on dissolving the People's Assembly, which meant advanced preparations for the new elections, leading to a new parliament to be entrusted with the election of a president of the republic by 1988.[102] Thus, the Muslim Brotherhood was faced in April 1987 with circumstances similar to those of 1984: they needed to enter the new parliament under the cover of another party.

The experience of their alliance with the Wafd convinced some factions of the Brotherhood that the Wafd was more dedicated to pursuing its secular politics than it was to the terms of the alliance. This led Shaykh Salah Abu Isma'il in February 1986 to resign from the Wafd and join the Liberal Party as vice-president.[103] He was able to achieve in the Liberal Party what he could not in the Wafd. He transferred Muhammad Amir (the Islamic writer for the newspaper *Al-Nur*) to the Liberal Party paper, *Al-Ahrar,* and made him chief editor.[104] The newspaper's policy then turned toward Islam, paving the way for another alliance between the Brotherhood and both the Liberal and Labor parties.

The Labor Party was a leftist party which belonged to the July Revolution—a fact that had prevented the Muslim Brotherhood from forming an alliance with it for the 1984 elections. Labor had gained 7 percent of the vote, less than the required 8 percent, and had forfeited its votes to the ruling National Party.[105] Ibrahim Shukri, Labor Party leader, had learned his lesson and began preparation for an alliance with the Muslim Brotherhood.[106] Given the Islamic transformations of the Liberal and Labor parties, the Muslim Brotherhood had a greater inclination to ally with them than with the Wafd. Salah Shadi and Ma'mun al-Hudaybi were commissioned to negotiate an alliance with the Labor Party leader on the understanding that Labor would receive 20 percent of the Assembly seats. Labor agreed. When the election results were announced, the Muslim Brotherhood had gained the lion's share of seats (thirty-six), while the Labor Party received twelve seats and the Liberals three seats.[107]

Just as the alliance of the Muslim Brotherhood with the Wafd Party had brought about the resignation of some of its members, so the alliance of the Brotherhood with the Labor Party led to a certain number of defections. Those with a social democratic orientation protested against the alliance, and three of them were dismissed from the party.[108] Two years later a major schism split Labor when the Social Democrats left with their leader following a defeat by their Islamic rivals in elections for the new executive committee. They announced that they represented the real Labor Party.[109] The Muslim Brotherhood, on the other hand, had in 1988 become the potent force in the alliance, with thirty-two seats in the People's Assembly and two newspapers, *Al-Sha'b* and *Al-Ahrar,* to publish their opinions. In the alliance with the Wafd they had been the smaller partner and weaker voice.

The new deputies from the Muslim Brotherhood hurried to announce that the Islamic Shari'a would once again be their primary issue and that they would begin by reintroducing the Islamic legislation they had supported in the previous session of the Assembly. These bills included the trade law, the maritime law, and the draft of a zakat law as first steps toward conformity with the Shari'a. Among the more provocative demands were a call by Shaykh Yusuf al-Badri to suspend sessions of the People's Assembly at the hours of prayer; an amendment of radio and television programming to suit the times of prayer during the month of Ramadan; and the delaying of recreational programming to make the performance of the *tarawih* prayers of Ramadan easier for the Muslims. (These prayers are not obligatory or performed by all Muslims.) Another unusual proposal came from Shaykh Yusuf al-Badri, leader of an Islamic group and attached to the Liberal Party. He lobbied for a declaration of a "renegade war" against Bulgaria and Spain since both had been Islamic states that lapsed from the Islamic religion.[110] Mukhtar Nuh announced that the Muslim Brotherhood would strive to restore the Islamic Caliphate as the only means of realizing unity.[111]

There were, however, some slightly more temperate voices among the Brotherhood politicians. Ma'mun al-Hudaybi announced that the Brotherhood would not seek to establish an Islamic state after the Iranian pattern, but only for the purpose of restoring the Shari'a.[112] Muhammad Hamid Abul Nasr, the new Supreme Guide of the Brotherhood, argued that the Shari'a must be applied gradually, just as the Shari'a itself had appeared gradually in the history of Islam. The prohibition of alcohol, for instance, came in three stages and the prohibition of slavery took many. Gradualism, he said, was the fundamental characteristic of the Shariʿa.[113]

In this way the Muslim Brotherhood transformed itself into a parliamentary political party with a unique place, existing and yet not existing on the political map. The political system does not acknowledge it in law but acknowledges it in fact. Its deputies enjoy parliamentary immunity, which enables them to legislate, to oversee the government, and to examine its accounts. But they cannot voice their opinions as members of the Muslim Brotherhood—only in their capacity as deputies of the alliance. They are a part of the political system, not an Islamic alternative to it, yet the system does not acknowledge legally that they are part of it. They attempt to shape public opinion on the pages of the two party newspapers, Al-Shaʿb and Al-Ahrar, but they are unable to confront it on the pages of a newspaper bearing their name.

Nonetheless the experience of entering Parliament and participating in the parliamentary process has been fruitful from the Brotherhood's point of view. As Muhammad al-Sheetani, one of its deputies, said, "It established the existence of the Brotherhood on the arena. The Brothers learned much from entering Parliament and acquired a long experience in political life. The Islamic partisans inside Egypt and abroad were assured that Islam has both a body and soldiers working for it."[114] The presence of the Brothers in Parliament gave them the opportunity at least to open debate on the issue of the Shariʿa and to present drafts of Islamic legislation.[115] Husni Abd al-Baqi argued that entering Parliament was indispensable in creating legitimacy for the Brotherhood in the popular arena, inasmuch as the law permits them to pursue political objectives only within parties. Similarly, Muhammad al-Maraghi noted that the Brotherhood presented more than two hundred noteworthy and significant questions and demands of interest to the people, but their activity did not appear in the political arena because they did not own a newspaper.[116]

Nevertheless, the Brotherhood's parliamentary experiment has not been crowned with success. They have been unable to realize the implementation of the Shariʿa and make good on their campaign slogan "Islam is the solution."[117] Husni Abd al-Baqi attributes this failure to the Brotherhood's lack of a parliamentary majority, explaining that "we tried to present drafts of Islamic legislation but the Assembly, supported by the majority opinion, began cleaning up the existing law instead of authorizing Islamic legislation."[118]

The actual accomplishments of the Muslim Brothers on the legislative level have amounted to very little indeed. Yet their very presence in the Parliament has pressed the issue of applying the Shariʿa on a national level for the first time in Egyptian history. Opponents of the Brotherhood argue that this is not a substantive issue because the entire civil law in Egypt is in agreement with the Shariʿa. The criminal code differs from Islamic law only in the matter of punishments for serious crimes (hudud).[119] These severe punishments could be, according to Supreme Guide al-Hudaybi, commuted by the ruler, for there are some crimes which constitute greater danger to society and yet are not included in hudud, such as bribery, espionage, embezzlement of public properties, forgery and falsification of official records, ravishment, narcotic crimes, and traffic crimes. Islamic jurisprudence held that it was within the rights of the ruler—that is, in modern times the legislator—to consider as a crime any action he sees as being dangerous to the society or disturbing its security, and to impose whatever punishments he wants. These punishments are *ta'azir* (castigations or punishments not based on Qur'anic texts). As for murder and disfigurement crimes, Islam allows the victim's family to accept blood money or to forgive, but there is no justification for this in modern times when immense wealth enables its owners to do injustices to people, killing and disfiguring, and to oblige them to accept blood money. Hence, the Egyptian legislation allows the victims of crimes or their families to reach compromise in civil rights cases, but not in criminal cases, which are left to the public prosecutor to take up on behalf of the society and, consequently, could not be given up.

Members of the Egyptian intelligentsia have made such arguments, but the Brothers have never been convinced by them.[120] When a journalist confronted Justice Ma'mun al-Hudaybi, one of the most prominent Muslim Brothers, with the fact that Shari'a was already applied in Egypt with the exception of criminal hudud, al-Hudaybi replied, "This is sophistry! For it is incumbent upon the ruler from the outset to promulgate laws which conform to the Shari'a and not to obstruct the command of God."[121] But of course this, too, is in the tradition of all politicians, who give justifications which do not correspond to the logic of things. The debate in the Parliament continues at this writing.[122]

Notes

1. This essay, an excerpt from a larger work by Professor Ramadan to be published as a separate book, was adapted for this volume by R. Scott Appleby.

2. Cf., for example, my book *Tatawwur al-Haraka al-Wataniyya fi Misr min sannat 1937 ila sanat 1948*, vol. 1 (Dar al-Watan al-'Arabi, 1973), p. 302. This constitutes the first academic study of the Muslim Brotherhood.

3. Hasan al-Banna, *Risalat al-Mu'tamar al-Khamis* (Dar al-I'tisam, Sislsilat sawt al-Haqq, no. 5, 1977), p. 18.

4. Hasan al-Banna's letter to the newspaper *al-Misri*, 26 July 1938.

5. Center for Strategic Studies, Egypt, *Religious Extremism* (limited and prohibited military edition: June 1987), pp. 103–4.

6. Dr. Abdel Azim Ramadan, *Tatawwur al-Haraka al-wataniyya fi Misr min 1918–1936* (Cairo; Daral-Kitab al-'Arabi, 1968), pp. 27–28.

7. Dr. Abdel Azim Ramadan, *Al-Fikr al-Thawri fi Misr qabl thawrat 23 Yulio* (Cairo Dar Madbuli, 1981), pp. 29–35.

8. Shaykh Ali Abd al-Raziq, *Al-'Islam wa-'Usul al-Hukm* (republished by Dr. Muhammad Ali 'Imara, Beirut, 1972).

9. Abd Allah al-Nadim attacked the mosque orators: "Had Europe taken it upon itself to kill the zeal and enthusiasm of the Muslims, and spent ages in devising a way to reach that end, it would not have hit upon what these orators have done." Quoted from *Al-'Ustadh*, 20 December 1892, in Dr. Muhammad Hussein, *Al'lttijahat al-Wataniyya fi-al-Adab al-Mu'asir*, part 1 (Cairo: Maktabat al-'Adab, 1956), p. 320.

10. Dr. Abdel Azim Ramadan, *Al-Ikhwan al-Muslimun wa'l-Tanzim al-Sirri* (Cairo: Dar Rosa'l Yusuf, 1982), p. 25.

11. Dr. Abdel Azim Ramadan, *Sira'a al-Tabaqat fi Misr* (Beirut, 1978), p. 149.

12. Hasan al-Banna, *Mudhakkirat al-*

Da'wa wa-l-Da'iya (Cairo: Dar al-Shehab, 1966), p. 50.

13. *Garidat al-Ikhwan al-Muslimin,* the fifth of Sha'ban, 1352 A.H. (1933).

14. Dr. Abdel Azim Ramadan, *Tatawwur al-Haraka al-Wataniyya fi Misr,* pp. 302–4.

15. According to his memoirs, he used to attend Rashid Rida's seminars and perused *Al-Manar* magazine. Hasan al-Banna, *Mudhakkirat al-Da'wa wa-l-Da'iya,* pp. 29, 49–50.

16. Hasan al-Banna asserted that "every piece of earth on which the banner of Islam is raised is a homeland for every Muslim to protect, work, and fight for" and that, "just as it is a belief and a worship, [Islam] is a homeland and a nationality. We consider all Muslims as one nation and the Islamic homeland as an integral whole." Hasan al-Banna, "*Qawmiyyat al-'Islam [The Nationalism of Islam],*" *Al-Ikhwan al-Muslimin* (8 Dhi'l-Qe'da, 1352 A.H. [1933]).

17. Branches of the association spread outside Egypt from early on. In *Risalat al-Mu'tamar al-Khamis [Message of the Fifth Congress]* (1938), p. 33. Hasan al-Banna said, "The mission has spread southward into the Sudan, eastward into Sham and its parts (Syria, Lebanon, Jordan, and Palestine), and westward into the Maghreb and its parts."

18. Ibid., pp. 39–40, 49.

19. Although the Society of Muslim Youth preceded the appearance of the Muslim Brotherhood in December of 1927, its activities were restricted to the social and religious fields and fighting Christian evangelism and apostasy, as well as to sports activities. It did not organize its followers for political work or for seizing political power. Hasan al-Banna, *Mudhakkirat al-Da'wa wa-l-Da'iya,* pp. 52–54; and Dr. Zakariya Sulayman Bayumi, *Al-Ikhwan al-Muslimun wa-l-Jama at al-'Islamiyya fi al-Hayat al-Siyasiyya al-Misriyya* (Cairo, 1979), pp. 68–71.

20. On these developments, cf. Dr. Abdel Azim Ramadan, *Al-Ikhwan al-Muslimun wa-l-Tanzim al-Sirri.*

21. For more details concerning the economic, social, and political changes in Egypt from 1928 to 1954, cf. Dr. Abdel Azim Ramadan, *al-Sira'a al-'Ijtima'i wa-l-Siyassi-fi Misr min thawrat 23 Yulio 'ila'azmat Maris 1954* (Cairo: Maktabat Madbouli, 1975); *Abd al-Nasir wa-Azmat Maris* (Cairo: Dar Roza'l Yusuf, 1976); *Al-Ikhwan al- Muslimun wa-l-Tanzim al-Sirri; Misr fi 'Asr al-Sadat,* vol. 2 (Cairo: Maktabat Madbouli 1986); *Misr fi Asr al-Sadat,* part 1 (Cairo: Maktabat Madbouli, 1989).

22. Sayyid Qutb gave "sovereignty" a broad range of meaning. The Supreme Guide said that the word was not mentioned in the verses of the Qur'an, nor in the Sunna. Hasan al-Hudaybi, *Du'a la Quda* (Preachers, not judges) (Cairo: Dar al-Tiba'a wa'l Nashr al-Islamiyya, 1977), pp. 63–65.

23. The doctrine to which Salih Siriyya and his organization subscribed was the doctrine of al-hakimiyya, which brands the society with infidelity. Supreme Court of State Security, *The Case Of Salih Abd Allah Siriyya and Others,* part 48.

24. Salih Ashmawi, *Hijra wa Tamyiz* (Emigration and segregation) (al-Da'wa, 18 September 1953).

25. Ragab Madkour, *Al-Takfir wa-l-Hijra wajhan liwajh* (Face to Face with al-takfir wa'l hijra), with a study and commentary by Dr. Ali Graisha, p. 160, quoting from a manuscript by Shukri Mustafa.

26. Dr. Hamid Hassan et al., *Muwajahat al-Fikr al-Mutatarrif fi-l-'Islam* (Confronting radical thought in Islam), p. 46, quoting from records of the court, p. 472.

27. Ibid., pp. 19–22.

28. Accordingly, there are only four mosques on earth in which the necessary conditions are met. They are al-Haram mosque in Mecca, the al-Aqsa mosque in Jerusalem, and in Medina the Quba'a Mosque and the al-Masjid al-Nabawi. With the exception of these four mosques and some of the privately owned mosques in Egypt, Shukri forbids prayer in all other mosques which he considered "harmful" (*derar*). Ragab Madkour, *Al-Takfir,* pp. 192–95; Dr. Hamid Hassan et al., *Muwajahat,* p. 90.

29. Dr. Hamid Hassan et al., *Muwajahat,* pp. 63–64.

30. The society's pretext for evading military service was that it is not appropriate for the individual Muslim to defend the pagan society. See the court proceedings in the murder case of Doctor al-Dhahabi, *Al-Ahram,* 1 November 1977. Not only did the society brand the society of Egypt as a whole with atheism but they considered all non-members to be atheist. Thus, according to the ideology of the society, every wife who joined the society without her husband was given sanction to leave him and to marry someone else without getting a divorce, on the condition that the new husband be a member of the society. Dr. Hamid Hassan et al., *Muwajahat,* pp. 66–67.

31. *Al-Ahram,* 17, 27, and 30 November 1977; and *Al-Akhbar,* 2 and 13 November 1977.

32. *Al-Akhbar,* 2 November 1977.

33. Dr. Muhammad 'Imara, *Al-Farida al-Gha'iba* (The missing ordinance: exposition, discussion and evaluation) (Cairo: Dar Thabit, June 1982).

34. "The court case of the Jihad organization, reasons for the sentence in the criminal case no. 48 for year 1982," Supreme State Security, prepared and presented by Advocate 'Abd al-'Aziz al-Sharqawi, pp. 66ff.

35. The security establishment in Egypt does not recognize this name. Rather, it calls the society the "Jihad Organization." It is the most important Islamic organization among the Islamic societies, which, according to security sources, amount to forty-four groups.

36. Dr. Umar 'Abd al-Rahman, *Kalimat haqq* (A word of truth: the testimony of Dr. Umar 'Abd al-Rahman in the Jihad case) (Cairo: Dar al-I'tisam).

37. He thereby opposed Shukri Mustafa, the leader of the Society of Muslims, who had labeled as pagan anyone guilty of disobedience or rejection of the society and thus subject to the seizure of his property and even death. Dr. Umar 'Abd al-Rahman, *Kalimat haqq* (A word of truth), pp. 103–4.

38. Ibid., pp. 42–47. This sort of paganism is a "major paganism" that expels a Muslim out of *al-millah* (religion).

39. Ibid., pp. 79–80.

40. Fahmi Huwaydi, "Al-Azma," *Al-Ahram,* 6 March 1986.

41. As was the al-Dirar (harmful) mosque built by the hypocrites in the time of the Prophet. Interview with Dr. Umar 'Abd al-Rahman published in the journal *Al-'Arab* (London), 26 June 1987.

42. Fahmi Huwaydi, "Al-Azma."

43. An article by Fahmi Huwaydi in *Al-Watan* (Kuwait), 12 May 1987.

44. Dr. Umar 'Abd al-Rahman, *Kalimat haqq,* pp. 110–11.

45. Interview with 'Ali 'Abd al-Fattah, emir of the Islamic Group in al-Minya, *Al-Sha'b,* 19 September 1987.

46. *Al-Ahram,* 9 October 1987.

47. Ali 'abd Al-Fattah interview.

48. "Truth of the Events in al-Minya," *Akhir Sa'a,* 11 November 1986.

49. *Al-Wafd,* 14 August 1988.

50. *Al-Akhbar,* 23 April 1989.

51. *Al-Ahram,* 5 June 1989.

52. In 'Ayn Shams, Cairo, the second pivot of their plans, Islamic group members tried to recapture the Mosque of Adam by force. But the security forces frustrated the attempt and made arrests. And in al-Fayyum, the third pivot, security forces surrounded the al-Shuhada Mosque, preventing group members from occupying it, and arrested sixty of them. *Al-Wafd,* 24 January 1990; *Al-Ahrar,* 29 January 1990.

53. *Al-Sha'b,* 30 January 1990.

54. The southern Egyptian cities where the Muslim group was most active were Asyut, al-Minya, Suhaj, al-Fayyum, and Bani Suef. In Cairo the group's activity centered on the neighborhoods of Bulaq al-Dakrur and on 'Ayn Shams. Asyut, capital of Upper Egypt, derives its special character from being the first to open a regional university, in 1957, which led to a heavy concentration of youth in its university area. These roughly seven thousand students are receptive to a variety of ideas, particularly to extremist religious thought, always most acceptable in a conservative environment. The Muslims of Asyut do not have a strong presence in the

economy or professions inasmuch as these fields are dominated by the Copts. But when the university opened, the majority of the poor Muslims were able to provide their sons with higher education free of charge and, accordingly, to change the social composition of the middle class. The new Islamic presence was associated with ever-intensifying Islamic feelings that was promising for the activities of the Islamic group. The group's teachings found a fertile ground in the hostel, which was crowded with students from the Upper Egyptian countryside. The students of the Al-Jama'a al-Islamiya swept the student union elections in nearly all the colleges, gaining all the seats (forty-eight) in all the colleges except the College of Commerce. In the elections for the all-university union they gained twenty-eight of thirty-eight seats. Fahmi Huwaydi, "Al-Azma."

55. Muhammad Hasanayn Haykal, *Kharif al-ghadab* (Beirut, 1983), pp. 269–70.

56. Adil Hammuda, *Al-Hijra ila l'unf* (Cairo: Dar Sina l'il-nashr, 1987), p. 59.

57. The negotiations reached a point at which al-Telmsani was asked to draw up a committee of Brothers to meet Sadat in Alexandria to place a final seal on the agreement, but Sadat saw fit to delay; the lines of communication were cut off suddenly. Umar al-Telmsani, *Dhikrayat la Mudhakkirat* (Cairo: Dar al-I'tisam, 1985), pp. 113–14.

58. Dr. Abdel Azim Ramadan, "Al-Tanzim al-jadid li'l-Ikhwan al-Muslimin," *Ruz al-Yusuf,* 13 September 1976; "Le nouvel élan des Frères Musulmins," *Le monde diplomatique,* August 1977, p. 10.

59. See the issues of the first year of publication of *Al-Da'wa,* June 1976–June 1977.

60. Ibid.

61. Among the six were Jamal Rabi, general assistant secretary of the ruling party and Salah Abu Isma'il, chairman of the Committee on Social Affairs, *Waqf* (Religious Endowments), and chairman of religious affairs of the People's Assembly.

62. Dr. Abdel Azim Ramadan, "Le nouvel élan."

63. Umar al-Telmsani, *Dhikrayat,* pp. 176–77.

64. Adil Hammuda, *Al-Hijra,* pp. 33–35.

65. Commentary in *Al-Da'wa,* January 1978, concerning the sentences to life imprisonment and the death sentence in the Takfir w'al-Hijra case.

66. *Al-Da'wa,* July 1977.

67. *Al-Da'wa,* February and April 1978.

68. *Al-Da'wa,* October 1978.

69. According to Umar al-Telmsani, the Israelis did not really incline to peace: they had established their state on Palestinian territory; they had persisted in building up settlements in the occupied territories; they had stated that Jerusalem would forever be their capital. Doctor Abd al'Azim al-Mata'ni tried to refute the basis upon which al-Azhar had built up its fatwa, through making distinctions between the Peace of al-Hudaybiya and the Pact of Ghatafan, contracted by the Prophet, on the one hand, and the peace which Sadat made with Israel, on the other. In a small pamphlet, "Documentation for the Statement," al-Azhar defended its opinion by stressing the permissibility of taking whatever measures for peace the well-being of the Muslims dictated. See the text of the al-Azhar statement in Kitab Hasanayn Krum, *The Muslim Brotherhood and the Peace with Israel* (Cairo: Sharikat Nadirku l'il-tiba'a w'al-nashr, 1985), pp. 145–54.

70. *Al-Da'wa,* April 1980.

71. Hasanayn Krum, *The Muslim Brotherhood,* p. 42; the American Embassy, as well as Professor Mitchell, responded to what was in the alleged document in *Al-Da'wa,* February 1979.

72. Umar al-Telmsani responded that he had refused to form a coalition with the Communists, "that the Muslim Brotherhood would never agree with them, ever." He "called on God to prolong the regime of Sadat for as long as possible, because under it we enjoy our freedom." *Al-Ahram,* 22 August 1979.

73. Ibid.

74. Ibid. The next incident was caused by the elections for the president of the Syndi-

cate of Barristers. The Muslim Brothers had united behind Abd al-Aziz al-Shurbaji, who attacked the Camp David accords and attacked Sadat personally, accusing him of dictatorship and suppressing freedom of opinion. Sadat responded to Umar al-Telmsani: "Shame on you! Did religion command the election of one who abuses the state and is insolent to the regime? Is it reasonable for the Muslim Brotherhood to join a coalition with the New Wafd party and the communists to support this candidate?" Umar al-Telmsani denied having ordered the Brotherhood lawyers to nominate al-Shurbaji. He said that he had refused invitations by the communists for him to attend a meeting they called, "because I know that Islam and Communism are enemies; I knew that they wanted to announce that Umar al-Telmsani sits with Communist leaders, that Muslim Brothers and Communists associate with one another. Muslim Brothers and Communists will never collaborate at any time in the future, will never associate with one another, ever."

75. Hasanayn Krum, *The Muslim Brotherhood*, p. 158.

76. Ibid., pp. 160–62.

77. Speech by Sadat, 14 September 1981 (*Al-Jumhuriya*, 15 September 1981).

78. Speech by Sadat, 5 September 1981 (*Al-Jumhuriya*, 6 September 1981).

79. Hasanayn Krum, *The Muslim Brotherhood*, pp. 163–64.

80. Two hundred thirty-five were taken from the Islamic groups and 469 from the takfir groups, according to the statistics cited by Sadat. Speech by Sadat, 14 September 1981 (*Al-Jumhuriya*, 15 September 1981).

81. Umar al-Telmsani, *Dhikrayat la Mudhakkirat*, pp. 220–22.

82. Ibid., p. 222.

83. *Al-Jumhuriya*, 26 November 1981.

84. Umar al-Telmsani, *Dhikrayat la Mudhakkirat*, p. 116. Their detention this time brought them under the close, kind care of the Interior Ministry, with special regard for Umar al-Telmsani, unlike the earlier detention under Abdel Nasser. In his memoirs, al-Telmsani states that the governor of Tura

prison "informed me continually of the interior minister's orders to see to my comfort."

85. The newspaper *Al-Sha'b*, organ of the Labor Party, began publishing in May 1982, followed by *Al-Ahali*, organ of the Unionist Progressive Nationalist Party.

86. The magazine *Al-I'tisam* reappeared, but the journal *Al-Da'wa*, according to article 49 of the law governing the press, lost the legal basis for its publication upon the death of its owner, Salih Ashmawi, on 12 December 1983. The text of article 49 states that "journals presently established and published by individuals remain the particular property of their owners, and continue to pursue their activities, until decease." In other words, the life of a publication ends with the death of its owner. Ramzi Mikha'il, *Azmat al-Dimuqratiya wa-ma'ziq al-sahafa al-qawmiya* (Cairo: Maktabat madbuli, 1987), p. 189.

87. *Al-Jumhuriya*, 25 August 1982.

88. *Al-Jumhuriya*, 28 October 1982.

89. *Al-Jumhuriya*, 4 December 1982.

90. *Al-Siyasa al-Kuwaytiya*, 3 April 1986.

91. *Akhbar al-Yawm*, 25 December 1982.

92. Ramzi Mikha'il, *Azmat al-Dimuqratiya*, p. 225.

93. Umar al-Telmsani, *Dhikrayat la Mudhakkirat*, pp. 184–85.

94. Dr. Abdel Azim Ramadan, *Tatawwur al-Haraka al-Wataniyya fi Misr*, part 2, pp. 192–93.

95. *Al-Musawwar*, 23 March 1984.

96. Dr. Abdel Azim Ramadan, "Al-Wafd w'al-Ikhwan al-Muslimun, lima kullu Hadhihi al-zawba'a?" ("The Wafd and the Brotherhood, What All This Noise For?"), *Al-Wafd*, 22 March 1984.

97. *Markaz al-dirasat al-siyasiyya w'al-istratijiya b'il-Ahram: Intikhabat majlis al-sha'b, 1984, dirasa wa-tahlil* (Cairo, 1986), p. 76.

98. *Markaz al-dirasat*, pp. 102–3; *Hizb al-Wafd al-Jadid, al-Bir namij* (The new Wafd Party, the program) (Cairo, 1984), p. 15.

99. Ibid., pp. 254–56; Ramzi Mikha'il, *Azmat al-Dimuqratiya*, p. 220.

100. "Mushkilat al-Ikhwan ba'd ghiyab al-Telmsani," *Al-Musawwar,* 30 May 1986.

101. This choice was made at an extremely restricted meeting attended by no more than three of the society's pillars—Muhammad Hamid Abul Nasr, Salih abu Ruqayaq, and Dr. Husayn Kamal al-Din.

102. *Al-watan al'arabi,* 3 April 1987.

103. *Al-Nur,* 19 November 1986. (This is the religious newspaper of the Liberal Party, edited by Hamza De'bis, vice-president of the party.)

104. Ibid.

105. Ramzi Mikha'il, *Azmat al-Dimuqratiya,* pp. 220, 236–37.

106. He replaced the former Nasserite editor of the party newspaper *Al-Sha'b* with Adil Husayn, the former Marxist writer who turned into an extreme Muslim and joined the Labor Party in December 1986, and the journal *Al-Sha'b* took on an Islamic political orientation. When the party held its fourth convention on 20 January 1987, Adil Husayn dropped the barrier that stood between the Labor Party and an alliance with the Muslim Brotherhood—that is, Nasserism—by modifying the party president's speech before the convention to include describing the period of rule by the July Revolution as a period of injustices and arbitrary political tyranny. This modification came suddenly because two months earlier the party had put forward a demand to join the Second Socialist International of the Labor and Socialist International. Earlier the party had proposed joining forces with African Socialism during Leopold Sanjur's visit to Cairo. "Asrar safqat al-tahaluf," *Akhir Sa'a,* 22 April 1987.

107. Ibid.

108. Ibid. These are Mamduh Qenawi, Husam al-Din Kamil, and Abd al-Majid Abu Zayd.

109. *Al-Sha'b,* 14 March 1989.

110. *Akhir Sa'a,* 22 April 1987.

111. "Qira'a fi fikr al-Ikhwan al-Barlamaniyin al-judud," *October,* 4 May 1987.

112. Interview with Judge Muhammad Ma'mun al-Hudaybi, *Al-Jumhuriya,* 23 April 1987.

113. Interview with the Supreme Guide after the election, *October,* 19 April 1987.

114. *Al-I'tisam,* April 1987.

115. Interview with Salah Abu Isma'il, *Al-I'tisam,* April 1987.

116. Interview with Muhammad al-Maraghi, *Al-I'tisam,* April 1987.

117. Election pamphlet for the Muslim Brotherhood; "Hadha Bayan l'il-nas, limadha yajib an tu'ti sawtak l'il-sawt al-Islami."

118. *Al-I'tisam,* April 1987.

119. These punishments, or hudud, are six: cutting off the hand for larceny; flogging for calumny (accusations of adultery in particular); flogging, or stoning till death for adultery; cutting off the hand for highway robbery; flogging for drinking intoxicants; death for apostasy.

120. See Abdel Azim Ramadan, *Al-Ikhwan al-Muslimun w'al-Tanzim al-Sirri,* pp. 302–3; "Qissat Tatbiq al-Shari'a al-Islamiya," *October,* 30 June 1985; "Al-tatarruf al-dini wa-muhakamat al-Shaykh Ali abd al-Raziq marratan ukhra," *October,* 31 January 1988; "Mahakim al-taftish marratan ukhra," *October,* 14 February 1988; "Ya fadilat al-Shaykh," *October,* 28 February 1988; "Bayn al-Shari'a al-Islamiya w'al-Qanun al-Misri," *October,* 25 December 1988. See also Muhammad Sa'id al-'Ashmawi, *Al-Shari'a al-Islamiya w'al-Qanun al-Misri* (Cairo: 1988).

121. Interview with Muhammad Ma'mun al-Hudaybi in *Al-Jumhuriya,* 24 April 1987.

122. January 1991.

Islamic Tajdid and the Political Process in Nigeria

Umar M. Birai

It is currently fashionable to apply the term "fundamentalism" to the religious revivals occurring in various Muslim societies. But there is a danger that the term may not "directly correspond to the cognitive reality that reflects the mood and moments of actual Muslims."[1] In this chapter I will attempt to examine the Islamic movement in Nigeria without recourse to the usual categories of thought. I adopt instead the viewpoint of one inside the movement. In collecting my data, I have interviewed a number of the leading shaykhs, and their perspective informs my own to a degree which the reader may judge.

The Islamic revival within Nigeria is best understood as a *tajdid* (renewal) movement.[2] Though the movement has obvious religious and cultural aspects, it has also assumed a political cast and has led to a "crisis of state and religion."[3] Muslims argue that the secular state perpetuates Euro-Christian culture and neocolonialism. There is a degree of factionalism within the Muslim *umma* (community), but the different voices are to an important degree united.[4] As Shaykh Ibrahim Saleh has said, though the "ideologies are different, our religion is one."[5] The Christian minority, on the side of the state, has defended the status quo. In that effort the Christian Association of Nigeria (CAN) has played a central role. Its activities have generated considerable opposition by Muslims. Indeed, its position as a common foe has done a good deal to bridge the gaps separating various Islamic groups.

Constitutionally, Nigeria is a federal republic. It has a strong central government which leaves little room for autonomy within the states. At present the country is ruled by a military regime, but it is preparing for a return to civil democracy. The final stage of this transition should occur in 1992. The military has been attempting to create a two-party system, in the hope of keeping religious, geographic, and tribal divisions out of the political process.

Nigeria was first brought together as a single political entity in 1914 by the British colonial authorities, who united the northern and southern areas for their own convenience. The north is larger in both population and territory. It was transformed socially, politically, and economically by the tajdid movement led by Shaykh Usman Dan Fodio in 1804. From then until the conquest of the Sokoto caliphate later in the nineteenth century, Islam was the official state religion. The north remains predominantly Muslim today. The south, by contrast, is divided between animists and Christians, though it is by no means homogeneous. In the southwest the ratio of Muslims to Christians is about fifty-fifty. And in some areas, such as Oyo State, Muslims hold a majority.

None of these figures is very precise, because the most reliable population data come from the 1963 census, and that was itself controversial. According to the 1963 figures, the population of fifty-five million was 47.2 percent Muslim and 35 percent Christian. The present population estimates put the percentage of Muslims at anywhere between 42 percent and 75 percent. The most probable figure lies somewhere around 55–60 percent.[6] The largest ethnic group in Nigeria is the Hausa-Fulani, a Muslim tribe located in the north. Next in size are the Yoruba in the southwest, about half of whom are Muslims.[7] The Ibo, a predominantly Catholic tribe in the east, are the third largest. Since the end of the civil war in 1970 a number of them have converted to Islam.

The country is thus divided religiously, geographically, and ethnically. But the religious factor had become the predominant one by the early 1990s. One sees, for example, increasing solidarity between the Muslims in the north and those in the south. This unity is stimulated by the efforts of various organizations: the Supreme Council for Islamic Affairs, the Council of Ulama, the Jama'atu Nasril Islam (JNI), and the powerful Muslim Students' Society (MSS), founded in 1954. In the same way, the formation of CAN in the mid-1970s has done much to unite the northern Christian minorities with Christians in the south.

Religious divisions were intensified during the civil war (1967–70) over the status of Biafra. In 1967, Ibos in the East-Central, South-Eastern, and Rivers states attempted to secede from Nigeria and to form their own country, which they proposed to call the Republic of Biafra. Those leading the rebellion argued that they were resisting an Islamic *jihad* (in this context, a "holy war") against the largely Christian eastern part of the country. Colonel Ojukwu, the leader of the rebellion, characterized it as "a resistance to Arab Muslim expansionism."[8] After the war, Islam did indeed begin to make modest inroads in the eastern states. It is now common there to hear such Muslim names as Alhaji Suleiman Onyeama (former chairman of the Anambra State Pilgrims Board) and Muhammad Aminu Kelechi (a radio broadcaster). To parry this effort, CAN has begun to oppose any manifestation of Islam in the area. Its efforts, though, may be counterproductive. Ibrahim Tahir, a professor of sociology and a former government minister, has made this observation:

> What is interesting is that CAN today is paradoxically the most effective instrument of propaganda for Islamic conversion among Christians because, if you constantly hear those who say they are protecting your interest bewailing the

success of those they oppose in maintaining the so-called Muslim domination and so-called Islamisation of the state, you would be [a] fool not to hurry up with your conversion.[9]

The Nigerian Islamic revival might seem to be just another in a series of such movements throughout Africa and the Middle East. But it is, at least in part, a response to conditions internal to the country. Since 1986, the government has been attempting to carry out (at the behest of World Bank and the International Monetary Fund) a Structural Adjustment Program (SAP) that has almost eliminated the middle class.[10] There is a crisis in the health care delivery system; hospitals are empty for lack of drugs and equipment. The educational system is on the verge of collapse. Murder and armed robbery are on the increase. There are among the symptoms of a deeper social malady whose cure can only be spiritual. Shaykh Abubakar Jibril has observed that revolution will erupt in Nigeria unless its leaders conform their attitudes to the teachings of Islam.[11] Professor Tahir has echoed this sentiment: "It is amazing given the present circumstances [that] a violent revolution has not yet occurred."[12] It is "almost a matter of consensus among [a] broad spectrum of Nigerians that this nation is in absolute need of an all-embracing transformation."[13] During the last decade there has been renewed intellectual interest in the historical jihad of Usman Dan Fodio. A number of seminars and conferences have been devoted to those events and their relevance to contemporary Nigerian affairs.

The Tajdid Movement

There are, of course, different ways of describing these activities among the umma. From a Christian point of view "the happenings in Nigeria can be [best explained as a kind] of modern Muslim fundamentalism . . . [the belief] that Muslim government and people should go back to practice primitive Islam."[14] From a Muslim point of view what is happening is a kind of tajdid—a spiritual reawakening at the individual level and within the larger umma. This process, begun in the 1970s, has now spilled over into the political arena.

The movement has not been entirely spontaneous. It has been spurred by the efforts of the ulama and various Islamic groups. As Muslims understand it, tajdid is a process of reawakening and reformation. It can be spread, as it has been in Nigeria, through teaching, preaching, and in print. But it can also take the form of jihad and *ijtihad* (independent reasoning and interpretation).[15]

The tajdid within Nigeria is essentially homegrown,[16] but it has not been unaffected by external forces. The ulama of the younger generation, for example, owe an obvious intellectual debt to Hasan al-Banna and Sayyid Qutb. The Islamic revolution in Iran has had an even more noticeable impact. Shaykh Abubakar Gumi, a leader of the Izala movement, has described the Ayatollah Khomeini as a respected scholar. Malam Adamu Ciroma—a former editor of *New Nigeria,* governor of the Central Bank of Nigeria, and minister and secretary-general of the National Party of Nigeria

(NPN)—has praised Khomeini's "boldness" in implementing the Shariʿa.[17] Ibrahim Gambari, the Nigerian ambassador to the United Nations, has suggested that the connection with Iran may go even further. There is some evidence that radical Muslim students in the north have been educated at Qom (in Iran) and have received financial support from Iran.[18] The affected groups deny the connection,[19] though they make no secret of their identification with the ideals of the Iranian revolution.

The debate over outside influence has overtones of conspiracy about it, but that is not the impression I want to convey. The idea of tajdid is firmly established in Islamic thought. Many connect it with the Prophet's saying that "Allah will raise at the head of each century such a people for this umma as will revive its religion for it."[20] And the movement within Nigeria is anything but overt. On university campuses many young women have adopted *hijab* (Islamic dress). (I would estimate that some 30 percent have done so.) The same is true in the secondary schools, particularly in the northern states. Indeed, one even notices it among older, Western-educated working women. Young men have adopted turbans and beards, and overflow the mosques.[21] The proponents of tajdid are not just numerous but often well known.[22]

Religion and Politics in Nigeria

For devout Muslims, it is difficult to keep the spirit of this religious revival out of the political sphere. In theory, at least, religion and politics are discontinuous in Nigeria. Political parties have not—at least not explicitly—defined themselves in religious terms, whether Christian or Muslim.[23] The constitution provides that "the government of the federation or of a state shall not adopt any religion as a state religion." The president, General Ibrahim Babangida, has reiterated the secular character of the state.[24] But as events occurring within since about 1985 have shown, it is becoming increasingly difficult to maintain the separation between religion and government. I will mention just four examples: Babangida's political appointments; Nigeria's membership in the Islamic Conference Organization; the Kafanchan crisis; and the attempted coup on 22 April 1990.

The government of General Babangida came to power by a coup on 27 August 1985. He replaced General Buhari, a man whom Christians suspected of planning to "advance the cause of Islam."[25] Under General Buhari the government's highest lawmaking body was the Supreme Military Council (SMC). It was composed of nineteen members: ten Muslims (Buhari and his deputy among them) and nine Christians. Buhari's Council of Ministers had twenty-one members: eleven Muslims and ten Christians. The National Council of States, made up of the military governors of the then nineteen states, had seven Muslims and twelve Christians.

During the first two years of Babangida's regime this balance shifted toward greater representation of the Christian minority. The SMC was replaced by the Armed Forces Ruling Council (AFRC), whose 28 members were evenly divided between Muslims and Christians. Of the 14 Christian members, 3 were from the Lantang group, a northern Christian ethnic group. Babangida's Council of Ministers had

22 members, only 9 of them Muslims. And of the 19 military governors in the National Council of States, only 5 were Muslims. All told, between Babangida's accession and December 1989, Christians had 204 members in the three major arms of government, Muslims only 138.[26] Since August 1991, there have been 30 military governors; 13 or so are Muslims.

Christians were initially encouraged by these appointments. Muslims, by contrast, began to feel uneasy. Shaykh Adam Al-Ilorin, the most widely known Muslim scholar in the south, expressed this feeling in confidence and kept a distance from the government.[27] In December 1989 the balance shifted slightly, and the Christian reaction was immediate. General Babangida relieved Lieutenant General Domkat Bali, a member of the Lantang group, of his posts as defense minister, member of the AFRC, and chairman of the Joint Chiefs of Staff. Babangida himself assumed the position of defense minister. He relinquished it soon after the changes. The AFRC was reduced to nineteen members: ten Muslims and nine Christians.[28] This change was accompanied by others in all three arms of government. In response, CAN organized demonstrations in a number of northern states. In a letter to General Babangida it charged that the changes were the last phase in the "ultimate promulgation of Nigeria as an Islamic state" and declared that Christians would resist that step at all costs:

> We wish to assure you, on behalf of all Christians, that our confidence in our security is neither in you nor even in the Christian population of the armed forces, but in God. Nobody goes to war with God and comes out victorious. We are confident that even if all the service chiefs remain Muslims and the entire armed forces Islamised, no single weapon or design against the people of God will prosper.[29]

Babangida felt compelled to respond. "There is," he said, "no north or south, no middle belt, no Christianity or Islam, there is a Nigerian nation. . . . The state is the unit of representation.[30]

It is obvious, despite Babangida's disclaimers, that religion is playing an increasingly important role in Nigerian political life. That fact has made the process of political appointments a contentious one, and neither Muslims nor Christians have been happy with the outcome. The same might be said of the government's decision to join the Islamic Conference Organization (OIC). Nigeria had been an observer at OIC meetings for a number of years, but in January 1986 it decided to become a full member. At that time the military government had been in office only a few months and was seeking a wider basis of legitimacy. Its decision to join OIC was seen as an effort to win the confidence and support of Muslims.

The immediate price of that effort was a loss of some Christian support. Babangida's deputy, a southern Christian, claimed that the matter had not been discussed by the AFRC or the Council of Ministers.[31] CAN threatened unrest and insisted that the decision was part of "a plan to Islamize the nation."[32] This was not entirely accurate. OIC has as members a number of Christian-dominated African countries: Gabon, Sierra Leone, Benin Republic, and Uganda are a few examples. But as is so often true in politics, what mattered was the perception, not the reality. The Muslim Council of Nigeria responded firmly to CAN's objections: "From now on we will demand and take effective steps to obtain our rights. Although we will be peace-loving, we will rebuff any threat or blackmail with the toughness that is historically characteristic of Muslims."[33] This incident, like the appointments process, shows the degree to which religion—excluded in theory from the structure of government—has come to permeate the practice of political life in Nigeria. It makes equally clear what a real and widening gap separates Muslim and Christian factions within the country.

The dispute has not been confined to exchanges of words. Kafanchan, a predominantly Christian city in north-central Nigeria, has a minority Muslim population, most of which is ethnically Hausa-Fulani. On 5 March 1987 a dispute began at the local College of Education between Muslim and Christian students. The immediate provocation seems to have been uncomplimentary remarks about the Qur'an and the Prophet by a minister.[34]

The dispute spread to the town, where it immediately took on ethnic and religious dimensions. A number of Muslim residents, regarded as settlers by the local population, were attacked and killed. Their properties were burned and two mosques were sacked. Many of the Muslims fled back to their old homes in Zaria, Katsina, and Funtua and spread the controversy with them. Several churches, bars, and movie theaters in those towns were burned down. (Bars and movie theaters are seen by the Muslim youth as symbols of the country's moral decay.)

The aftermath of the crisis fueled Muslim suspicions about the fairness of the state. The original (Christian) provocateur was still at large in 1991. Muslims in Kafanchan, Zaria, Katsina, Funtua, and Kaduna, however, were arrested, tortured, and sentenced to terms of four to twelve years by the Karibi Whyte Tribunal. (Justice Whyte is a Christian.) The Islamic Welfare Foundation in Lagos described the outcome as "kangaroo justice": "the tribunal placed a high[er] premium on the burning of churches than [on the] enormous loss of Muslim lives in the crisis. And no single Christian appeared before the tribunal throughout its sittings. It was [Christian] justice at its best."[35] The Council of Ulama has echoed these sentiments.[36] Each year since 1987 Muslim youths have come to Kaduna to commemorate the Kafanchan crisis. On 2 January 1988 there was a rally of unprecedented size which attracted Muslims from sects and groups around the country to raise funds for the victims of the crisis. Some Muslims even came across the border from Niger Republic. All Muslims jailed or detained were released in October 1990.

One can see in the events at Kafanchan some foreshadowing of the coup attempted against the national government on 22 April 1990. In each case there seems to have been apprehension or resentment, harbored by the Christian middle belt, toward Muslim ethnic groups from the north. And in each case the primary consequence of the crisis has been a worsening of relations between the two religious groups. The 22 April coup was led by a group of junior officers, all of them Christians, and many from the middle belt of the country. Major Gideon Orkah, the leader of the rebels, was both. In a broadcast at the time of the coup Orkah announced that he was suspending five predominantly Muslim and Hausa-Fulani states—Katsina, Sokoto, Borno, Kano, and Bauchi—from the Nigerian Federation. Citizens from those states were to be sacked from federal appointments and given seven days to leave other parts of the federation for their home states.[37] BBC London correctly perceived that the attempt was "a coup against the Muslim-dominated north" by the Christian middle belt.[38]

The forcible aspect of the coup was speedily put down, but the event left bitter feelings among even those peripherally involved. The northern zone coordinator of CAN, Jolly Tanko Yusuf, and his secretary were held in connection with the coup. CAN threatened public unrest if they were not released, renewed its demand that Nigeria withdraw from the OIC, and asked that the government once again make changes in the composition of the AFRC and the Council of Ministers. It insisted in particular on the removal of two Muslim ministers—Professor Jibril Aminu (Petroleum Resources) and Alhaji Rilwanu Lukman (External Affairs)—arguing that the government was trying to Islamize "all facets of public life including party politics [and] appointments to top political positions."[39]

The Council of Ulama reacted strongly to the CAN charges:

We wish to state categorically that the assumption by CAN that the present government is an Islamic one is untrue. Strictly speaking, the government has more to do with Christianity than Islam since secularism as practised by the government is an extension of the church concept of government. In Islam, politics and religion are inseparable. For a government to be Islamic, Allah has to be the legislator through the Qur'an and the Sunna of the Prophet.[40]

The National Council of Muslim Youth Organizations (NACOMYO) echoed these sentiments. It concluded, though, with the stronger message that it would not tolerate any attempt to intimidate Muslims: "The spirit of martyrdom that is characteristic of Muslims is burning in the veins of the Muslim youths [in Nigeria]."[41]

The coup and its aftermath cast a dark shadow over the transition from military to civilian rule, a process scheduled to conclude in 1992. The coup demonstrated that, like the rest of the country, the military is divided along religious, tribal, and regional lines.[42] The military government hopes to cut across these divisions by creating a secular two-party system. But the two parties—the National Republican Convention (NRC) and the Social Democratic Party (SDP)—themselves reflect the deeper social cleavage. The NRC is generally assumed to represent Islam and the north. The SDP is viewed as the representative of the south and of the northern Christian minority.[43] There are, to be sure, Muslims and Christians in both parties. But in northern areas where residents are mixed, the NRC is overwhelmingly Muslim in membership and Christians tend to join the SDP. The Samaru area in Kaduna State is a case in point: all officials and delegates to state and national conventions are Christian members of the SDP.[44]

The coup also drew attention to the settled assumption that federalism is the best approach to uniting the religiously diverse and ethnically plural Nigerian nation. It does appear that Nigerians in general still want to live together under one federal government. But what kind of federation? As the tajdid movement intensifies, and the nation finds it more difficult to keep religion out of the process and structure of government, a federation with greater state autonomy becomes more attractive. Such an arrangement—not unlike the system in effect in 1960–66—would allow the predominantly Muslim states more freedom to organize their societies according to the tenets of Islamic law. It is to a discussion of that ambition that I now turn.

The Shariʿa Debate

The most important and complex political issue dividing Muslims and Christians in Nigeria in the early 1990s is whether, and to what extent, the government should recognize and enforce the Shariʿa (Muslim religious law). To Muslims the issue is simply whether they too shall be able to enjoy the religious freedom guaranteed in theory to all citizens of Nigeria. As one Muslim leader put it, "While not a bit of the Constitution deprived the Christian from being Christian, every bit of the same Constitution can easily deprive the Muslim from being Muslim."[45] For Christians the call for enforcement of the Shariʿa awakens fears of a further "Islamization" of the country.

We cannot assess the views of either side without looking closely at the debate. There are, generally speaking, two issues. The first is whether Shariʿa in the limited form now applicable in the north shall be extended in practice to all parts of the federation. I will call this the "geographic" extension of Shariʿa. The second issue is whether Shariʿa, which today governs only questions of personal status (marriage and inheritance), should be enforced in all its particulars as a comprehensive legal system. I will call this the "legal" extension of Shariʿa. Let me up take these issues in the order in which I have mentioned them.

"Geographic" Extension

Nigeria became an independent country on 1 October 1960. It was then a federation of three regions, Northern, Western, and Eastern. In the Northern Region the courts of original jurisdiction in civil and criminal cases were the native courts. Appeals from the native courts lay to the High Court of the Region in ordinary cases, but in cases involving Muslim personal law (Shariʿa) appeals went to the Shariʿa Court of Appeal, which applied the law of the Maliki school as it was customarily interpreted in the area around the native court. Jurisdictional disputes between the High Court and the Shariʿa Court of Appeal were resolved by a Court of Resolution. Decisions of the Shariʿa Court of Appeal involving constitutional issues could be appealed further to the Federal Supreme Court.[46]

This constitutional system came to an end with a military coup in 1966. From then until 1979 Nigeria was ruled by a military government. It continued, after a fashion, the federal structure of control, though the country was redivided into twelve (later nineteen) states. The military regime determined in 1975 to prepare a new constitution (the Second Republic) and return power to a democratically elected civilian government. A partly elected, partly appointed Constituent Assembly met in 1977–78 to consider and approve a draft constitution. In those debates the issue of

Shari'a courts became a bone of contention between Muslims and Christians. The most expansive proposal would have provided for Shari'a courts in the states, and state and federal Shari'a courts of appeal. Jurisdiction within this system was to be limited to questions of Muslim customary law. This proposal met with strong opposition, however, and the military government intervened to impose a compromise. Within the states there would be Shari'a courts and state Shari'a courts of appeal. Further review of decisions that might conflict with federal law lay to a Federal Court of Appeal and, ultimately, the Federal Supreme Court.[47]

A new civilian government was installed in October 1979 and lasted until 31 December 1983, when it was overthrown by another military coup. The military again proposed relinquishing control to a democratically elected government under a new constitution (the Third Republic). To that end it created another Constituent Assembly for the purpose of reviewing and approving the revised constitution.

Here again the issue of Shari'a courts proved more controversial than any other. Debate that began before the Constituent Assembly continued in the two leading newspapers—the *New Nigerian* (owned by the federal government and based in Kaduna) and the *National Concord* (privately owned and based in Lagos). CAN argued in January 1986 that "the Shari'a debate was a prelude to ensuring that in any subsequent Constitutional arrangement in this country, Islam will be imposed."[48] In September of that year the Council of Ulama responded that Muslims in Nigeria "have vowed to reject any new political order that does not recognize the uninhibited application of Shari'a law in Nigeria."[49]

Some members of the Constituent Assembly were to be chosen through the machinery of local council elections. Those elections, in 1987, were carried out in religious terms in the north, particularly in Kaduna and Gongola states. With the help of CAN most members elected from the northern Christian minority areas subscribed to an anti-Shari'a platform. When the Assembly convened in 1989, Christian members proposed that the new constitution create no religious courts. If the AFRC "decides to rubber-stamp the desires of Muslims," they argued, "we shall reject the constitution and the AFRC must be ready to produce for Christians in this country a Christian constitution that recognizes ecclesiastical courts."[50] Muslims, on the other hand, insisted at a minimum on a continuation of the system in effect under the Second Republic: Shari'a courts of original and appellate jurisdiction in any state that desired them. They argued, though, that that system should be extended in practice as well as in theory to the southern part of the country, where Muslim requests for Shari'a courts had not been satisfied. The Muslim position in the Assembly was that the government had primary responsibility for establishing and funding religious courts. Indeed, some members were willing to support ecclesiastical courts as well as Shari'a courts if Christians actually wanted them.[51]

The Constituent Assembly was unable to reach a consensus. In the end the military government intervened and retained the system used during the Second Republic. This has hardly been satisfactory for opponents of the system. At the same time, it does not go far enough to satisfy Muslims, who would like to extend the legal, as well as the geographical, reach of Shari'a.

"Legal" Extension

In 1862 the British made Lagos a colony and established a court there. Until then, in most of the area now covered by the Northern states, the principal law was Muslim law of the Maliki school. For purposes of facilitating their own trade, and eventually in order to run their Nigerian colony, the British gradually displaced Shari'a with their own legal system. What was left of Islamic criminal law was eliminated on the eve of independence. The departing colonial administration threatened to withhold independence, impose economic sanctions, and prevent Nigeria's membership in the United Nations unless all vestiges of Shari'a were eradicated.[52] The only exception to this demand was the Muslim law of personal status, which deals with various aspects of marriage and inheritance.

Devout Muslims today view this secular legal system as essentially Christian. They argue that it has failed "to provide solutions to the country's problems."[53] The tajdid movement has highlighted their dissatisfaction with this system and evoked calls for its abandonment. According to Malam Ibrahim Suleiman, the "irreducible minimum" demand of the umma is

> that the Shari'a shall enjoy full application in areas where Muslims predomi-
> nate, and that it takes precedence over all other legal systems in Nigeria as the
> law that governs the majority of her people; that such other legal systems are
> accorded recognition in accordance with the extent of the following they com-
> mand. Equally significant, there must be a definite commitment by Nigeria to
> abolish all aspects of imposed laws which are inconsistent with [the] funda-
> mental values, norms and demands of our faith. In fact, the entire colonial
> enterprise must be abolished and be replaced with our authentic and legiti-
> mate laws.[54]

Suleiman's voice is not a solitary one. Muslims of all stripes generally concur with his program. As the Council of Ulama has put it, they seek "the uninhibited application of Shari'a law in Nigeria."[55]

It is important to note, however, that none of the ulama or Islamic groups whose views have stimulated the process of tajdid has developed very systematic views on law and politics. In that regard they are unlike revolutionaries such as the Ayatollah Khomeini or the Islamic theorist Sayyid Abul Ala Maududi. This should not be too surprising. In its origins the tajdid movement was an effort aimed at spiritual and moral rejuvenation, designed simply to address ignorance about the basic tenets of Islam.

Participants in the movement are aware of these limitations and have taken some steps to address them. For example, in May 1990 the Centre for Islamic Legal Studies at Ahmadu Bello University established a Fatwa (authoritative ruling) Commission. The commission is designed to be a "problem-solving body" which concerns itself with such issues as "the need for an economic order appropriate for . . . Muslims."[56]

It would be difficult to specify in exact terms the changes that would be entailed by the full implementation of the Shari'a. A number of examples should indicate the direction of change:

1. We can expect the enactment of sumptuary laws, particularly with respect to prostitution, alcohol, and gambling. Most of the older cities of the north already have such laws in place against the sale of alcohol.

2. We can also expect zakat (poor tax) to be revived and given a central place in the economy. Devout Muslims view zakat as the most effective means for the redistribution of wealth, the elimination of poverty, and the redress of social deprivation.

3. Land reform will be an important issue. Under the Shari'a, land belongs to society, which holds it in trust for Allah, to the end that we may realize justice and security for the weak and poor. In concrete terms this means that land will be retrieved from multinational corporations and given back to the peasants.

4. We can expect a variety of economic reforms. The IMF/World Bank Structural Adjustment Programme has been difficult to implement because the economy it is designed to restructure from the bondage of debts to make Nigeria economically independent has been in ruins for so long. In a related area, one hears various proposals for "Islamic" reform of the banking system. Some argue against the institution of *riba* (charging or collecting interest). The Kano State Foundation, a private organization, has floated a proposal for an Islamic bank. On a more modest level, the Nigeria Universal Bank Limited now provides separate counters for men and women in some of its branches, where that is in keeping with the religious attitude of the people.

5. Educational reform would proceed along fairly predictable lines. The Muslim Students' Society has called on the National Universities Commission and the Council of Legal Education to accord prominence to Shari'a in the curriculum.[57] This would require the creation of courses in Islamic economics, banking, political science, and so forth. It would also entail particular attention to the various faculties of law, which would be responsible for developing courses on the Islamic legal system. It would be erroneous to suppose, as some have suggested, that a legal system based on Shari'a must rely only on "common law" made by Islamic jurists. Muslims in Nigeria do not object to statutory and constitutional law. What they require is that all laws conform to the provisions of the Qur'an and the Sunna, making full allowance for the changing complexities of the human environment.

Division and Unity within the Umma

Though the tajdid movement now under way seems to be uniting Muslims in Nigeria, it is a gradual process and it has had to counteract a variety of divisions within the umma. In recent years we have seen three such divisions. The first two are what we might call "denominational." The third is a more philosophical dispute among the leaders of the tajdid movement about the proper pace and method of change. I will speak of this last at some length below. There is a fourth phenomenon which is sometimes, mistakenly, seen as a facet of the Islamic revival. This is the Maitatsine movement, which I will address at the end of this section.

The first "denominational" split worthy of mention was the rift between the Tijjaniyya and Qadiriyya sects that occurred during the 1950s and early 1960s. It mirrored, to some extent, a division within the political establishment. Most of the emirs were members of the Tijjaniyya sect. The emirs were traditional rulers governing defined territories (emirates) in the north. They traced their positions to the jihad of Usman Dan Fodio in the early nineteenth century. At one time the emirs were seen as custodians of the traditions of Islam. This is not as true today as it was forty years ago. Their loss of prestige among the young is attributable in part to the cooperation they have shown secular authorities since independence.[58] In any case for some years there was an acute schism between the two sects. Physical clashes were not uncommon, particularly in the north. The rift was healed through the efforts of organizations such as the Jama'atu Nasril Islam, founded in 1962 primarily for that purpose. Today the Tijjaniyya and Qadiriyya are more or less united in a group called Tariqa.

The denominational division currently most visible is between the Tariqa, on the one hand, and Jama'atu Izalatul Bidia Waikamatus Sunna (Izala), on the other. The Izala movement, begun in 1978, has been inspired by the teachings of Shaykh Abubakar Gumi.[59] Shaykh Ismail Idris, a student of Gumi, is its chief missioner. Some regard Izala as a kind of Wahabbism. Its leadership is certainly politically sympathetic to Saudi Arabia. Izala and Tariqa have clashed on a number of occasions, usually over the control of mosques or during preaching sessions. Their disagreements, though minor, are numerous. They concern such matters as naming ceremonies, discipline, celebration of the birthday of the Prophet, prayers for the dead and other forms of prayer, visits to the tombs of saints, even the mode of greetings between father and son. In all of these disputes Izala contends that Tariqa has tolerated innovations, and needs to return to the original teaching of the Qur'an and the Sunna.

I do not wish to overstate the degree of division within the Muslim umma. Perhaps as much as 65 percent of the total Muslim population belongs to neither Tariqa nor Izala. Many see the conflict as trivial and unnecessary. Moreover, both within and without these groups there is general agreement on matters of more substantive importance: *salat* (prayer), *zakat* (charity), *hajj* (pilgrimage), fasting, and the primacy of Shari'a as the law that should govern the Islamic community.

More relevant to our purposes than the "denominational" divisions I have mentioned is a philosophical difference over the means of bringing Shari'a into the political system. Here the opposing camps might be called gradualists and radicals.

The gradualists believe that, since Muslims are a majority within Nigeria, they can accomplish their aims by constitutional means through active participation in politics. What this calls for is active efforts at education and the exercise of numerical strength at the ballot box. For all their differences over minor doctrinal matters, both the Tariqa and the Izala groups generally favor this approach. Shaykh Idris has put the matter most succinctly. The conflict between Tariqa and Izala, he asserted, is simply an in-house matter that should not impede the larger effort to uproot secularism and institute the Shari'a. Shaykh Dahiru Bauchi, speaking for the Tariqa, agreed that a basis of unity exists (though he suggested that Izala must be "reasonable").[60]

Undoubtedly the most influential figure within the gradualist camp is Shaykh Gumi, the most politically articulate of the older generation of ulama. During the

First Republic he was the Grand Kadi of northern Nigeria (a kind of chief justice of the Shari'a Court of Appeal). Since then his influence has extended throughout the country. Since the 1970s, his daily exegeses of the Qur'an during the month of Ramadan, and his weekly *Hasken Musulunci* programs in the Sultan Bello mosque, have attracted huge crowds. The Ramadan exegeses are broadcast in Kaduna by the Federal Radio Corporation and the Nigerian Television Authority. One can gauge their impact from the fact that the military government tried (without success) to reduce the power of the Kaduna radio station in 1978.

For Gumi, politics is "rooted in the practice of Islam."[61] On the eve of the 1983 general elections he issued a controversial fatwa stating that in contemporary Nigeria "politics is more important than prayer" or going on pilgrimage, because politics ultimately controls the right to pray.[62] Gumi repeated the point in June 1990 as the country prepared for the elections for executive positions within the two political parties: "A Muslim who neglected [prayer] would have caused himself injury, but a Muslim who allowed the ship of state to sail anyhow, would have caused the whole society a major injury."[63] In his weekly *Hasken Musulunci* Shaykh Gumi has repeatedly urged Muslims, including women, to take part in the politics of transition from military to civilian rule, in order to determine who shall be the leaders of the Third Republic.

Shaykh Gumi believes that a country with a majority Muslim population should, except in extraordinary circumstances (e.g., a military regime), have Muslim leaders. He is certainly correct as a practical matter in saying that "it will be difficult for a non-Muslim to be [elected] leader in Nigeria." But he has caused considerable consternation by his willingness to carry these views to their logical conclusion. "If Christians do not accept Muslims as their leaders [and] Muslims cannot accept Christians as their leaders," he has said, then Nigeria will have to be divided.[64] Perhaps for that reason Gumi favors a one-party system; two parties will inevitably divide the country along religious lines.

Though he has urged women to play a role in the politics of transition, Shaykh Gumi believes that leadership is an affair exclusively for men. He has made it clear that he hopes not to see a woman leading Nigeria while he is alive. "Women can be very useful" in some aspects of politics, but "to make them mix [with men] like Europeans is not acceptable to Islam."[65]

There are those, particularly among the young, who reject the gradualism typified by Shaykh Gumi and favor more radical means of transforming the country along Islamic lines. The powerful MSS, the numerous Muslim youth organizations (including NACOMYO), and, perhaps most notably, the Islamic Movement argue that Muslims should reject the present secular order, including the constitution on which it is based. These groups contend that Muslims have spent too much time and attention on trivial disagreements—a tendency they think is exacerbated by petty jealousies among the older generation of ulama.

Typical of the groups that favor a radical approach is the Islamic Movement. Based in Zaria, the home of its leader, Malam Ibrahim El-Zak Zaky, it has attracted a wide following among university students and youths elsewhere. It is widely believed that

El-Zak Zaky engineered the "Islam Only" demonstrations that took place on 4 May 1980 in Zaria. The demonstrations were designed to raise political awareness among the Muslim population. Inscriptions from the event ("Islam Only") can still be seen on many public buildings in and around Zaria City. El-Zak Zaky was arrested that same year in Sokoto for allegedly burning the country's secular constitution.[66] In 1987 he was again arrested in the aftermath of the Kafanchan crisis, though he has been released.

The rhetoric of the Islamic Movement, as these activities might suggest, is confrontational. El-Zak Zaky has urged that "the state does not deserve worship." On the contrary, the custodians of the state have exploited the people and done little to eradicate alcoholism, prostitution, and other social maladies. "If the ummah in Nigeria is to establish the rule of Shari'a, it must start to hit at the appropriate area"—it must destroy the constitution first.[67] Malam Ture Muhammad, Zaky's deputy in the Islamic Movement, argues that a jihad is necessary until Shari'a is established as the governing law in Nigeria.[68]

Whether this rhetoric will be matched by an equally revolutionary program remains to be seen. As I have said, there are signs that the tajdid movement is leading to unity among the Nigerian Muslim population, and the effect of this may be to temper in some measure the approach of the radicals.

Maitatsine

Between 1980 and 1985 the northern states suffered massive outbreaks of violence. The disruptions began in Kano in 1980, where some five thousand people were killed.[69] They spread in 1982 to Bulunkutu in Borno State, and in 1984 and 1985 to Gombe in Bauchi State, Yola in Gongola State, and Kaduna City. The leader of these riots, Muhammadu Marwa (known as "Maitatsine"), is a mysterious figure.[70] He was born in Marwa, Cameroun. It is not clear what kind of Islamic education he received, though he seems to have had "an excessive belief in fetishism,"[71] and the Imam of Marwa declared him an infidel.[72] Maitatsine's own wife described him as a magician. After moving to Nigeria, he settled at Yan Awaki in Kano, where the violence began in 1980.

The motive force behind Maitatsine's movement is a matter of some uncertainty. According to one view, the violence was an expression of deepening class contradiction. This view has it that the protesting group was a marginalized class that took religion (in this case Islam) as a tool of protest.[73] The Kano state government, the emir of Kano, and the police all subscribed to something like this at the time of the riots—which they saw as an attempt to capture political power. The riddle that this explanation does not solve is Maitatsine's close connections with a number of prominent politicians, businessmen, and civil servants. These people patronized him for charms and other manifestations of spiritual power. If we take the "class conflict" thesis seriously, we have to suppose that Maitatsine was reacting against the very people who sustained him.

A second view about the Maitatsine movement holds that it was a form of "Islamic fundamentalism . . . a manifestation of Islamic resurgence aimed at reviving pristine Islamic practices."[74] This explanation is more difficult to credit than the above. As the federal government's report on the riots notes, Maitatsine proclaimed himself to be a prophet—a heretical position within Islam that is hardly designed to inspire support among the generality of Muslims.[75] Indeed, there is even evidence that Maitatsine's enclave at Yan Awaki engaged in "slaughtering . . . human beings by the neck as if they were rams or goats."[76]

Perhaps the most sensible comments on the Maitatsine affair were those of Professor Jibril Aminu. It is a mistake, he argued, to "vest [Maitatsine] with the stature of a misguided Muslim reformer, which he clearly was not. He was at best a Muslim deviant; at worst, a charlatan who took advantage of our societal weakness."[77] It is difficult to be certain that something like the Maitatsine movement will not occur again. But it is to be hoped, as the tajdid movement takes deeper roots and the umma becomes more sophisticated about its Islamic beliefs, that in the future such pretenders will be more speedily identified and rejected.

The Politics of Transition to Civil Rule

An important aspect of the transition program of General Babangida's military regime to civil rule is the attempt to undermine the potency of religion in the Third Republic. In the November 1991 census, an important item on the program, data regarding religious faith and ethnic origin of Nigerians, was not included in the questionnaire. The census has always been a controversial issue in Nigeria because of the weight of economic, geopolitical, and religious considerations.

On 27 August 1991 the country was fundamentally restructured from twenty-one to thirty states. Some of the states are now coterminous with geopolitical interests of the northern Christian minorities. This is an attempt to provide a structural balance for stability in the Third Republic.

The primaries for the nomination of governorship candidates in the two political parties (National Republican Convention and Social Democratic Party) were conducted in October 1991. There was some confusion and accusations of rigging in both parties from many states. This is the first time in the political history of Nigeria that primaries have been conducted before elections.

However, the fascinating aspect of the primaries was demonstrated in those states where the 1987 local council elections took on religious dimensions. Kaduna is an example. Observers expected that the SDP (rightly or wrongly identified generally as Christian-dominated) would nominate a Christian candidate for governor. But both the NRC and SDP nominated Muslim candidates. The NRC won the election. The result of the SDP primaries in the states of Kaduna and Adamawa may be taken as an indication of the numerical strength of the Muslims in the SDP in these states. It may also be an indication that the attempt by the military to reduce the role of religion in the political process has begun to yield results. However, in Benue and Taraba, two minority states in the north, ministers were elected as governors on the platform of the SDP. Ironically, however, the SDP lost the prestigious governorship of Lagos state to the NCR, largely because the SDP governorship candidate and his deputy were both Muslims.[78]

The tendency for geopolitical and religious considerations to be significant in the success of a presidential candidate from either of the parties is therefore still strong. The test of the extent to which the military government has effectively undermined the potency of religious interest in the politics of transition would seem to rest largely on the successful nomination of presidential candidates by the two parties. Presidential elections are scheduled for the end of 1992.

Two civil disturbances, probably motivated by political considerations, took place in 1991. The Bauchi riots of May 1991 and the Kano riots of October 1991 immediately assumed religious and ethnic dimensions. The Kano October 1991 disturbances were triggered by a visit of a German minister, Reinhard Bonnke, to Nigeria on an evangelical mission. Bonnke reportedly made uncomplimentary remarks about Islam in Kaduna on his way to Kano. This reminded Muslims of a previous slight that had seemed to indicate a double standard. In 1988 some Muslim organizations in Nigeria had invited a black American Muslim, Louis Farrakhan, and an international Muslim preacher, Shaykh Ahmed Deedat, to preach in Nigeria. But they were refused permission to preach. Several people were killed in the October 1991 riots, and property worth millions of naira was destroyed or looted by hoodlums and the army of unemployed youths. The large-scale destruction and looting of public and private properties has made the religious dimension difficult to understand. The massive involvement of an army of unemployed youth indicates the extent to which Structural Adjustment Programme has been unable to turn the economy around.

However, both CAN and some Muslim organizations blamed the government for the riots. NACOMYO's stand on the issue is suggestive that these kinds of problems are the result of the government's double standard and inequity in its treatment of religious organizations.[79] The riots are, in a real sense, an indication of the increasingly wide gap between Muslims and Christians in Nigeria.

Divisive religious tendencies within the Nigerian polity are not only on the increase but are also affecting sensitive institutions of government including the military establishment itself. A new organization called "Christian Fellowship of Uniformed People" is said to have penetrated the military establishment and other paramilitary organizations. The minister of defense and chairman of the Joint Chiefs of Staff called on soldiers to avoid religious bigotry in order to ensure the unity of the country.[80] The president, General Babangida, made similar references to the threat posed by divisive religious tendencies in the country.[81]

As the political dimension of the ensuing Tajdid process deepens, the Christian defense of the status quo will likely intensify. The crisis of state and religion will grow. Divisive religious tendencies will become clearer and more decisive in the competition for power in the Third Republic, perhaps leading to destabilization. How far the restructuring of the Nigerian Federation from twenty-two to thirty states may reduce this problem cannot be predicted. In early 1992 the economic and political atmosphere in Nigeria is clouded and in a state of flux.

It would be hazardous to predict what success the Third Republic will have in resolving Nigeria's religious divisions. If Christians continue to insist on a strict separation of religion and government, the gulf between Muslims and Christians is likely to grow wider. The primary objective of the tajdid movement is, after all, to extend the domain of Shariʻa as far as possible both geographically and legally. Given Nigeria's religious diversity, the federal system seems to be the most viable option for keeping the country intact. It might be necessary to allow the states more autonomy, in order to accommodate religious demands on a local level. But it is perhaps too much to hope that this alone will be enough to satisfy both sides.

Notes

1. Bruce Lawrence, "Muslim Fundamentalist Movements: Reflections towards a New Approach," in B. F. Stowasser, ed., *The Islamic Impulse* (Croom Helm, 1987), p. 13.

2. According to Shaykh Ibrahim Saleh, there can be a number of tajdid movements within the Muslim umma. Shaykh Ismail Idris, Shaykh Lawal Abubakar, and Professor Abdullahi Muhammed all agree that there is a tajdid movement under way within Nigeria today.

3. I. A. Gambari, *Nigeria and Islamic Revivalism: Home Grown or Externally Induced?* (Baltimore: Johns Hopkins Press, 1989).

4. *Newswatch*, Lagos, 10 October 1988.

5. Interview, *The Pen*, Kano, 29 September 1989.

6. See details in A. A. Mazrui, "African Islam and Competitive Religion between Revivalism and Expansion," *Third World Quarterly* 10, no. 2 (April 1988): 504–5.

7. *Western Nigeria Statistical Bulletin* 4, nos. 1–2 (1964): 11–12.

8. Ahira Declaration, 1967.

9. Interview, *New Nigerian*, 30 May 1990.

10. The national minimum wage is now N 250.00 per month ($31.20 at the current rate of exchange). That amount will just buy a 100 kg bag of maize, a staple of the Nigerian diet. The income of the middle class ranges between N 750 and N 1500 per month. This group is unable to afford basic requirements that less than N 350 would have bought in 1985, before introduction of the Structural Adjustment Programme. As Dr. Oni has observed, "By cutting down investments in social overheads and directed by IMF and the World Bank, Nigeria is destroying today, the human potentials required to build a sustained economic growth." Quoted in "Managers in Nigeria," *Journal of Nigerian Institute of Management* 24, no. 5 (September/October 1988): 7.

11. Interview, *Community Concord*, Sokoto, 9 February 1987. Professor Ogunsanwo describes the country's situation as "blatant enslavement." A. Ogunsanwo, "Nigeria's External Relations, 1960–1985," Public Service Lecture, Lagos, 1985.

12. Interview, *Megastar*, Lagos, March 1989.

13. *The Pen*, Kano, 29 September 1989.

14. D. Byang, *Shariʻa in Nigeria: A Christian Perspective* (n.p., 1988), p. 71.

15. H. I. Gwarzo, "The Principles of *Tajdid* (renewal) in the Contemporary Muslim World," *Unilorin*, 1980, 1989.

16. I. A. Gambari, "Nigeria and Islamic Revivalism."

17. A. Ciroma, Speech, Usmanu Dan Fodio University, 1989.

18. I. A. Gambari, "Nigeria and Islamic Revivalism."

19. *Newswatch,* Lagos, 10 October 1988. Nigerian law forbids political parties and trade unions from seeking or receiving financial or material assistance from outside the country.

20. This tradition is reported by Abu Hurryrah and recorded in the *Sunna* of Abu Dawud I. Sulaiman argues that "the concept of prophethood is synonymous with the philosophy of revolution or of *tajdid.* It implies that human society should not be left in darkness and corruption but be guided to righteousness." Sulaiman, *A Revolution in History: The Jihad of Usman Dan Fodio* (Mansell, 1986), p. 2.

21. "It is in these youths that one sees the *Jihad* proper: to dissipate that spirit is now virtually impossible." S. Lemu, "Remote and Immediate Causes of [the] Religious Crisis in Nigeria," memo, 31 August 1987.

22. Apart from the ulama, others include, Alhaji Maitama Sule (once Nigeria's Permanent Representative at the United Nations), Alhaji Aminu Dantata, and Chief M. K. O. Abiola (formerly vice-president of ITT and a well-known newspaper publisher).

23. Cf. H. Bienen, "Religion, Legitimacy and Conflict in Nigeria," ANNALS, *AAPSS,* 483, January 1986.

24. *New Nigerian,* Kaduna, 6 October 1989. .

25. *Newswatch,* Lagos, 24 February 1986.

26. *The Democrat,* Kaduna, 28 May 1990.

27. Informal discussion, June 1988.

28. *New Nigerian,* Kaduna, 3 January 1990.

29. CAN protest letter sent to General Babangida after the December 1989 changes.

30. Statement made at the swearing-in of a new minister of internal affairs in the wake of the December 1989 changes.

31. This was widely reported in the press. See *Guardian,* Lagos, 24 January 1986.

32. *Newswatch,* Lagos, 24 February 1986.

33. *Afkar Inquiry,* May 1986.

34. Details in B. Isyaku, *The Kafanchan Carnage* (n.p., 1991).

35. CAN's leadership analysis in "Nigeria: A Signpost of Danger," Islamic Welfare Foundation, Lagos, 1989.

36. Council of Ulama press conference, Kano, 31 May 1990. ("Innocent Muslims . . . were unjustly jailed. . . . Reverend Bako and his cohorts who murdered Muslims in cold blood must be brought to book.")

37. G. Orkah, broadcast, 22 April 1990.

38. BBC news bulletin, 22 April 1990.

39. Statement by CAN president, Archbishop Okogie, *The Democrat,* Kaduna, 28 May 1990.

40. Council of Ulama press conference, Kano, 31 May 1990.

41. NACOMYO press conference, Lagos, June 1990.

42. Appointments to top military and strategic command positions are made with an eye to religious and regional considerations. As of November 1991, three of the four division commanders are Christians; one is Muslim. Two of the Christians are from the north; one is a Yosuba from the south. The Muslim is a northerner. Recruitment into the various arms and levels of the military takes account of "federal character"—i.e., state representation. The danger in the event of a religious conflict is that the government might be unable to employ the military without splitting it into factions.

43. I have monitored the membership of the parties in a number of local government areas, particularly where the population is mixed.

44. Informal discussion with an insider from SDP, Kaduna State.

45. Interview with Ustaz Abdallah, deputy Grand Kadi of Kwara State, June 1990.

46. A. O. Obilade, *The Nigerian Legal System,* vols. 33–40 (London: Sweet and Maxwell, 1979).

47. B. Dudley, *An Introduction to Nigerian Government and Politics* (Bloomington: Indiana University Press, 1982), pp. 154–64.

48. CAN Enlightenment series 1, p. 36.

49. *New Nigeria,* 29 September 1986.

50. A. H. Yadudu, "The Prospects for Shari'a in Nigeria," Islam in Africa Conference, Abuja, November 1988.

51. Ibid.

52. A. Sir Bello, *My Life* (Cambridge: Cambridge University Press, 1962), p. 217.

53. P. Clark, "Islamic Reform in Contemporary Nigeria: Methods and Aims," *Third World Quarterly* 10, no. 2 (1988): 519–38.

54. I. Suleiman, "State and Religion in Nigeria: A Suggested Framework," Political Bureau, Lagos, 1986.

55. *New Nigerian,* Kaduna, 29 September 1986. See also *National Concord,* Lagos, 6 April 1988 (Supreme Council for Islamic Affairs); interview, 28 May 1990 (Shaykh Lawal Abubakar); I. El-Zak Zaky, "Reorientation by Deduction from History," lecture, Ahmadu Bello University, Zaria, 1987; *Gasklya Tafi Kobo,* Kaduna, 14 September 1989 (Shaykh Nasiur Kabara). As just one further example, consider the anonymous tract distributed in Kano on the day of Eid-El-Kabir, 13 July 1989. Written in the Hausa language, it reminded all Muslims that "it is time to rise up and go back to *Shari'a.*"

56. I. Suleiman, address at the inauguration of the Fatwa Commission.

57. MSS press conference, Kaduna, 27 June 1990.

58. In the late 1940s and early 1950s a Reformed Tijjaniyya tradition split off from the Tijjaniyya sect in Kano. The issues that divided them are not unlike the questions that have split denominations within American Protestantism. In 1954, for example, there was a disagreement over whether the Qur'an could be read on the radio. J. Paden, *Religion and Political Culture in Kano* (Berkeley and Los Angles: University of California Press, 1973).

59. Particularly important is Gumi's instructional pamphlet *Agigatul Sahihah be Muwafiqual Sharia* (The right path in accordance with the Shari'a) (n.p., n.d.).

60. Interview, 27 August 1989.

61. Interview, *Quality,* Lagos, October 1987.

62. On this point Gumi may be ahead of the majority of Muslims. There are some, like Shaykh Abubakar Jibril, who essentially agree. Jibril claims that "Islam without politics is like a man without a head." Interview, Sokoto, 1987. But others, though they agree with Gumi in principle, are uncomfortable with the claim that prayer is subordinate to politics within a secular regime. Shaykh Dahiru Bauchi typifies this position.

63. *Tafsir,* 29 March 1990.

64. Interview, *Quality,* Lagos, October 1987.

65. Ibid. Gumi is joined in this view by Shaykh Ibrahim Saleh. Interview, *The Pen,* Kano, September 1989.

66. Interview with El-Zak Zaky's wife. *Crescent International,* London, 16–31 August 1989.

67. I. El-Zak Zaky, "Reorientation by Deduction from History," lecture, Ahmadu Bello University, Zaria, 1987.

68. Interview, *Amana,* Zaria, July 1989.

69. Gambari, "Nigeria and Islamic Revivalism."

70. For treatment of the Maitatsine phenomenon see A. Na-Ayuba, "Yantatsine: An Analysis of the Gardawa Uprising in Kano, Niqeria, 1980–1985" (M.Sc. thesis, Department of Political Science, Bayero University, Kano, December 1986); B. Takaya, "The Foundation of Religious Intolerance in Nigeria: In Search of Background for Understanding the Maitatsine Phenomenon," conference proceedings, Department of Political Science, Ahmadu Bello University, Zaria (May 1987); S. Bako, "Maitatsine Revolts in Nigeria: Another Case of Class Struggle," NASA Conference, Port Harcourt (November 1985); Gambari, "Nigeria and Islamic Revivalism."

71. *New Niqerian,* Kaduna, 21 February 1982.

72. Na-Ayuba, *Yantatsine.*

73. See Takaya, "The Foundation of Religious Intolerance in Nigeria."

74. Na-Ayuba, *Yantatsine*.

75. "Federal Government Tribunal of Inquiry into Kano Disturbances," 1981, p. 25.

76. *New Nigerian,* Kaduna, 25 November 1981.

77. J. Aminn, *Observations,* Delta Publications, 1988, p. 64.

78. *Newswatch,* Lagos, 30 December 1991.

79. Press release, *Weekend Concord,* Lagos, 6 November 1991.

80. *Daily Sketch,* Ibadan, 18 October 1991.

81. General Babangida, press briefing, Calabar, 10 November 1991.

The Nakshibendi Order of Turkey

Şerif Mardin

Current works on Islamic fundamentalism approach the subject from a somewhat disingenuous perspective. Their time frame is that of the present progressive—i.e., fundamentalism is an ongoing process whose emergence is left unexplained. The oddity of this treatment emerges quite clearly when set against studies of Western Christian fundamentalism. In the pioneering studies of this latter genre, analysts, in order to clarify the conditions of the setting with which they have to work, do, at one time or another, invoke the Bible and its meaning, the Church Fathers, and the ideological characteristics of Protestantism.

Islamic fundamentalism is not accorded the same privilege due to a specific bias which sees Islamic history as a companion piece to Western history. According to this bias, Islamic fundamentalism can thus be understood only against the background of Western history. The point I make here has no originality, being the stock-in-trade of much recent writing about Islam (Amin, Djait, Fazlur Rahman, Said). However, it is important to state this point here, since the present chapter attempts to remedy such an optical illusion by studying a Turkish variant of modern Islamic fundamentalism, namely, the Nakshibendi Sufi order, which I will describe in relation to specific thresholds of Islamic history.

A major watershed in Islamic history separates Islamic fundamentalism in the premodern world from its modern version. The earlier frame is that of a world history with relatively little interaction between its component culture areas; the later historical frame, emerging in the late eighteenth century, is marked by the beginnings of a world communication network showing constant acceleration of the trend toward the formation of the "global village" of our days. The primary shift of emphasis, in this progression undergone by Islam, is the new saliency of modern organizational techniques emphasizing mass adherence to social-religious movements. This contrasts with an earlier structure of Islamic conventicles with limited membership. The new ideological component, introduced in tandem with new mass recruitment, also involves a basic shift in the nature of the "sounding board" in the elaboration of social identity. In the earlier stages, this resonance was acquired by setting oneself against heterodox Muslims; in the modern stage, the sounding board is the Western cultural "other."

Within the sphere of modernization I have discerned what may be termed "subthresholds." The first of these stages is the project of mobilizing the Islamic world and the policies of recruitment necessitated by it. The second is the attempt to capture instruments of modernization such as banks, newspapers, instructional books, and pamphlets. The third stage is the attempt to bring into one's orbit minds formed in modern schools, i.e., engineers, economists, and journalists. A final stage consists of attempts to emerge on the leading edge of modern political institutions. All of these important but subtle driving forces of modernization have, together, forced the Nakshibendi order to operate within the setting of a modern public.

In this sense, the discourse of the contemporary Nakshibendi is essentially modern. Nevertheless, the fact that even today the Nakshibendi order is wedded to the maintenance of an Islamic "canon" shows how in established cultures like Islam the idiom of tradition plays the role of a substantive core which maintains its value as a mode for self-placement in the universe. Sharing an Islamic "canon" means, in fact, sharing an Islamic idiom. The populist, democratic thrust of contemporary Islamic fundamentalisms is constructed through the ability of all Muslims to share this idiom. In turn, the possibility for such a sharing derives from the absence of an organized "church" in Islam.

The Nakshibendi Image in Modern Turkey

Asked what he would consider the darkest force of religious reaction in Turkey today, a Kemalist—a Turkish intellectual who identifies himself with the secular reforms of the Turkish Republic—would probably reply the "Nakshibendi [Sufi] order." This perception of the Nakshibendi order as fanatical and rigid fits one of the traits which has been attributed to fundamentalism. Nakshibendi are also fundamentalistlike insofar as they see "history and experience as diluting a basic religious canon."

Hidden behind the explicit denunciation of the Kemalist is an implication regarding the order's perennial opposition to the movement of modernization in Turkey throughout the twentieth century. Working back in time, our Turkish Jacobin would offer us the following arguments detailing incidents in which the Nakshibendi have, in his view, shown themselves to be foes of modernization.

On 13 April 1909, nine months after the Young Turks had carried out a revolution which reinstated the Ottoman constitution of 1876, a rebellion of Turkish privates led by noncommissioned officers took place in Istanbul. Soldiers, civilians, and students in religious seminaries as well as Muslim clerics laid siege to the Ottoman parliament, demanding the establishment of a state based on religious law. Encouragement to the rebels to take up cudgels was linked to the propaganda emanating from the newspaper *Volkan* (the Volcano) in the days preceding the rebellion. The movement itself was soon quelled; the editor of the *Volkan*—a Nakshibendi—and a number of other leaders were hanged. Modern Turkish republican history has consistently used the incident in schoolbooks to illustrate the dangers presented by religious fanaticism in Turkey.

A second incident which helped to link the Nakshibendi with "backwardness" was the Kurdish rebellion of 1925, also led by Nakshibendi shaykhs. The rebellion, occurring shortly after the founding of the Turkish Republic, led to the passing of draconian laws that clamped down on the expression of public criticism against the new regime.

Radical republican Turks also recall a movement against the republic in which the Nakshibendi were implicated, the little studied "Menemen Incident" of 1930. In a town next to Izmir, a shadowy Nakshibendi figure called Muslims to rally around the Green Flag of Islam and destroy the impious Republican regime. The person who stopped the rebels, a young officer by the name of Kubilay is rumored to have had his head cut off with a rusty saw when he fell into the hands of the rebels.

The resurgence of Nakshibendi influence in the 1980s among a number of educated Turks with a rural or provincial background—the origin of crypto-Nakshibendis in Turgut Özal's Motherland Party—renewed the suspicions of republican Turks.

These images of the Nakshibendi order emphasize its backwardness and unrelenting drive against secularization. While the role that the Nakshibendi order has played in Islamic history does confirm its stark orthodoxy, it also brings into relief a more varied set of characteristics than is offered by the order's Turkish Jacobin image. This richer set enables us to paint a more precise picture of its "fundamentalism." In a preliminary evaluation of our Kemalist's reaction to the Nakshibendi we may note that in at least two of the cases presented as evidence of Nakshibendi fanaticism, the events of 1909 and the Menemen Incident, reference is made to Nakshibendi purportedly operating within a framework of folk Islam. In fact, the main drift of Nakshibendi activity in history entails Muslim "high" culture. It is true, as we shall see, that the order's attempts at mass mobilization have been able to touch a historically sensitive nerve in Islamic societies, that of mass outbreaks led by religious leaders against the unjust ruler. But the direction has been one of bringing the masses into a better understanding of their religion rather than of exploiting mass volatility.

History of the Order

The Nakshibendi is a prominent order that originated in the twelfth century. It is characterized as "Sufi." Given the fact that Sufism is not usually understood as lending itself to activist configurations, I must emphasize an important preliminary distinction. The sober, inward-looking, disciplined spiritual practices of the Nakshibendi order brought it into the very center of orthodoxy and orthopraxy. This hardly fits with either received ideas about Sufism's ecstatic or cosmic aspects, or discussions about whether Sufism is induced by rules of mortification or by theosophical speculation.

Very early in its history the order acquired its characteristic tonality, its inward-looking attitude which shunned "show or distracting rites."[1] The soberness was structurally homologous with the spirit of the rule that prevailed in the Ottoman Empire. Indeed, the Ottomans relied on the Nakshibendi as one part of their policy of establishing law and order in the empire, especially in Anatolia. During the early years of their rise to power, the Ottomans were confronted by the heterodox beliefs and practices of the Turkic tribes that had entered Anatolia in great numbers from the thirteenth century onward. Ottoman hegemony depended on the pacification of tribes, and one way to achieve this was to integrate them with Sunni orthodoxy. From the fifteenth century onward, the Ottomans found in the Nakshibendi an excellent ally in achieving this goal. They were given the task of bringing the heterodox to heel. The order achieved considerable prestige in the empire, but the revival of its energies came somewhat later and from outside the empire.

Historical information about the Nakshibendi makes possible an analysis of the Nakshibendi operational code, the way in which the Nakshibendi, by activating and using some basic structures of Islamic society, are able to anchor their influence in the Islamic world and in Turkey. With this venue some of the characteristics of Nakshibendi "fundamentalism" may be unraveled.

Historical Dimensions of Muslim Fundamentalism

Let us start with the proposition that fundamentalism may be an episodic forum that any religion can assume. Fundamentalists have been characterized as "zealots" by Arnold Toynbee, who demonstrates that zealotry is a recurrent category of history.

One of the obstacles to an understanding of fundamentalism is that we study it almost exclusively as a contemporary issue. Our hasty attempt to classify what appears an unseemly throwback to a more primitive age should, but in fact does not, encourage its study in a diachronic rather than synchronic frame. Thus, relatively little is made of the possibility that fundamentalism could be a recurrent phenomenon. Yet even a superficial glance at its manifestation in Islamic culture enables us to distinguish a fundamentalism of the ninth century as well as fundamentalisms of the fourteenth, seventeenth, and twentieth centuries. Students of Muslim fundamentalism take up the background of the modern movement they are studying, but this is not quite the same thing as seeing modern Islamic fundamentalism as a historical emergent and the latest item in a series. I believe we need this perspective, which does not exclude that of "family resemblances," to achieve a more complete understanding of all forms of fundamentalism. Seen as a historical emergent, Islamic fundamentalism makes us fasten our gaze on intersecting historical trends and evaluate it as the constantly changing product of these forces rather than as an essence or a concept with ontological justification.

This view of Muslim fundamentalism as a historical emergent enables us to bring into play three long-term (longue durée) elements that have affected the process of religious change during modernization. One is the rationalization of the religious sphere, by which more abstract conceptions of the sacred have replaced the magical element in religion. The second element appears to be a demand for a more direct apprehension of the divine mysterium and its projection of the "everyday," where it takes the shape of a utopian attempt to build a seamless society. The problem of power in Islamic societies is a third vector to be taken into account in a study of Muslim fundamentalism.

Max Weber describes the displacement of the magical element in religion as follows: "The great historical process of the disenchantment of the world which began with the ancient Jewish prophets, and in conjunction with hellenic scientific thinking condemned all magical means of salvation as superstition and blasphemy, was here completed."[2] Although Weber speaks of the Lutheran ecclesiastical-sacramental salvation, all we have learned about Islam tells us that this religion too, with its condemnation of magic and idols, was also set on the road to rationalization and, ultimately, disenchantment. This characteristic of Islam provides a key to the struggle of Muslim sages against the magicalization of the relation between man and God and man and the world. The modern Muslim fundamentalist Sayyid Qutb's *jahiliyya*, the state of swinish ignorance of Muslims, gives us an example of this stance. For Qutb, jahiliyya is framed by the present magic of modern Western, "soulless" technological superiority as much as it is by the early magic practices of pre-Islamic Mecca.[3]

In the early history of Islam and in the ideas of the fundamentalist theologian Ahmad Ibn Hanbal (d. 855) the antimagical stance takes the form of keeping strictly to the Qur'an and the *Hadith* (traditions). This is also known as the pure, the old religion (*al-din al-atiq*). The same attitude appears in medieval thinker Ibn Taymiyya's lampooning of "popular manifestation of Shi'ism" and in his attack of the Shi'ite doctrine of the Hidden Iman, the anticipation of the return of which has produced "nothing but false hopes, sedition, and corrupt practices among certain groups of Muslims."[4] In the thought of seventeenth century Indian Muslim reformer Ahmad al-Sirhindi, the rationalizing component appears as a deep suspicion of the theosophy of Sufism and of the cosmological garden of Hinduism, the influence of which he was combating. A new element, which we may call "systematic activism," enters the picture of rationalization at that juncture.

The Role of Cultural Confrontation in the History of Islam

The history of Muslim fundamentalism underlines a major element of ambiguity in the propagation of Islam. Basically a product of Arabic-speaking areas, Islam soon expanded into new areas with independent, well-established cultural traditions. Islam acquired solid foundations in these regions and attempted their swift Islamization but did not fully assimilate the local cultures. Iran is a case in point, Central Asia another. Islam had a problem with non-Arab cultures. For Ibn Taymiyya, the problem was starker since he had to deal with a foreign and "heathen" culture. The same is true in the case of the Muslim Mughal's occupation of the Indian subcontinent. Here too was a resistant culture, Hinduism, which created problems for Islam. In the context of this latter confrontation Nakshibendism was fully activated as a proselytizing movement. Still another encounter with the invasive West was to constitute the background for greater Nakshibendi activism in the eighteenth and nineteenth centuries.

In India, cultural confrontation became a major problem for Islam in the seventeenth century. At that time, Indian culture was threatening both because of its natural power to offer a magical garden to Muslims and because a Mughal ruler, Akbar, was willing to listen to the siren's song of Hinduism. The consequence was the fundamentalism of Ahmad al-Sirhindi (d. 1624). Sirhindi found a secure mooring and organizational apparat for his views in the Nakshibendi order, whose framework makes up the particular stream of fundamentalism I take up here.

As a fundamentalist leader combating the diffuse effects on Islamic mysticism of Hindu culture in the Mughal empire, Ahmad al-Sirhindi seems to have been the first person who attempted to link the struggle against a new form of invasive magic, in this case the theosophy of Ibn al-Arabi, with an organization suited to this combat. Toward his middle years he joined the Nakshibendi order, which thereafter was infused with a renewed activism. He held a remarkable theory concerning the two *mims* (the Arabic letter "m") in the Prophet's name, which Friedman describes as follows:

> [The Prophet] Muhammad had in his lifetime two individuations (*ta'ayyun*), the bodily-human and the spiritual-angelic. These two individuations were symbolized by the loops of the two *mims* of his name. The bodily individuation guaranteed the uninterrupted relationship between the Prophet and his community and consequently ensure its spiritual well-being. The spiritual one, on the other hand, directed itself towards the Divine and received the continuous flow of inspiration emanating from that source. A proper balance was thus maintained between the worldly and the spiritual aspects of Muhammad's personality, and the Islamic community was continuously under guidance both prophetic and divine. Since the Prophet's death, however, his human individuation has been gradually weakening while the spiritual one has been steadily gaining strength. Within a thousand years the human individuation disappeared altogether. Its symbol, the first *mim* of Muhammad, disappeared along with it and was replaced by an *alef* standing for divinity. . . . Muhammad came to be Ahmad. He was transformed into a purely spiritual being, no longer interested in the affairs of the world. The disappearance of his human attributes . . . had . . . an adverse impact on his community which lost the lights of prophetic guidance emanating from Muhammad's human aspect.[5]

Sirhindi implied that he would fill this gap. His teachings gave new direction to the Nakshibendi order in India, which thereafter appears with a new name of "renewalist" (*mujaddidi*) Nakshibendism. These renewalists were for centuries to exert an influence, first in Indian Islam and then in the Ottoman Empire.

Renewalism was not an entirely new phenomenon since a tradition existed which stated that a renewer would appear in every century to revitalize Islam. But after

Sirhindi, the link established between a putative renewalist and a Nakshibendi leader gave the idea novel relevance. What enabled this idea to be fused with the Nakshibendi organizational structure at that point is not entirely clear. Like so many similar movements in Islam this renewalism might have eventually disappeared if a new ambient condition had not appeared, in this case the development of the world system of communication that institutionalized Nakshibendi activism.

Already as Islam entered the post-Renaissance era the sensitivity of Muslims to power arrangements was increasingly felt in regards to the decline of Muslim hegemony. The reactions to this perceived incapacity of Islam in the political order appear first in specific areas and then through a new self-consciousness of the Islamic world as a whole. The conquest of Kazan by the emerging Russian power in 1552 must have sent some echoes to the Islamic world. When Mughal power disintegrated in India after 1707, self-consciousness promoted the social utopia of Shah Waliullah working in the renewalist tradition. Here, once again, a return to origins and middle-of-the-road Sufism were combined, but Waliullah's extensive social project was something new.

Toward the end of the eighteenth century, Nakshibendi renewalism took another turn. This was the consequence of what may be described as the new "boundary conditions" promoted by the rise of the world communications system. Whether these new conditions are described as having prevailed with the hegemony of the nation-state or are depicted as emerging in a period of industrialism triumphant, the network now acquired world dimensions. This network was crucial in the evolution of Nakshibendi policies. One facet of the new system was the encroachment of the new Western states on Islamic areas—the Crimea, Egypt, the Caucasus. But a countervailing facet was the strengthening of linkages among Muslims. The facilitation of pilgrimages to Mecca and the enhanced role of Mecca and Medina as clearinghouses for ideas enhanced the weblike pattern of propagation of Nakshibendi teaching.

The traditional Nakshibendi emphasis on an "internal mobilizational of the soul" was now complemented by an increasing involvement in world history and by an external mobilization directed against Western imperialism and its cultural policy. Once more, this was accompanied by the Nakshibendi emphasis on a return to pristine Islam. The structural changes promoted by the new world system also promoted a more acute sense of the need for the masses to be deeply committed to the retrieval of their Islamic inheritance. The stark confrontation with the West brought about fundamental changes in the basic Nakshibendi project. These are best studied in relation to new recruitment practices and new identity models.

Identity Models and Social Change

The forging of personal identity among the Nakshibendi—the result of an "emptying" and "refilling"—figures in the relations established between the *Pir*, or Master, and the initiate. From what we know of Nakshibendi history this has been for centuries the foundation of the bond between teacher and pupil. In Nakshibendi treatises one of the first requirements for those who set out on the path for mystical knowledge is that of total identification with the Master. The first part of this surrender is one's surrender to the vocation as such, a step common to many Sufi orders.[6] A second level of surrender is *rabita,* which demands an integral concentration on the person and teaching of the Master. The close relation between Master and disciple expresses itself in *tawajjuh,* the concentration of the two partners upon each other resulting in experiences of spiritual unity, faith healing and many other phenomena.[7]

This type of bonding required special ambient conditions for its success, such as the preeminent role of the Master as compared to that of written commentaries. From the very beginning of "mujaddidism," rabita was given importance by the mujaddidi. A third element of bonding with the Master, *sohbet,* is the spiritual exchange through conversation between master and disciple. Together rabita and sohbet set parameters for a special form of interpersonal and intergroup communication, the "human chain." The three anchors of the mystical self establish a complex bond between Master and initiate. Two dimensions of this relation are the authoritarian bond established by the complete surrender to the higher authority of the master and the "libidinal" dimension of the bond with the Master. Sharabi has commented on a similar authoritarian social norm by subsuming it under the title of "patrimonialism," a characteristic which he sees pervading all social relations in the Middle East. But the authoritarian relation cannot be properly understood unless the symmetrical sentiment *ashk*— translated as "love" but better described by the Lacanian "desire"—is taken into consideration.[8] Ashk can be seen as a special form of a wider characteristic of Middle Eastern social formations, the central role of "persuasion" as the mode of general interpersonal discourse. However, as a result of the opening of the first stages of a new world communications network in the nineteenth century, the method for establishing the bond itself underwent changes. A long and demanding exercise placed the Nakshibendi in a disadvantageous position if they wanted to spread their creed. This situation had first become critical when, in the seventeenth century, the Nakshibendi began to encounter Catholic and Protestant missionaries whose influence they had to combat. In this situation the need for cadres led to a larger number of Nakshibendi completing their training faster.

These external forces forced the Nakshibendi to change their stance but the personal, one-to-one, relation retained its centrality and its potential for shaping the psyche of the follower. Nonetheless, a new form of training emerged, as evinced in the career of the mujaddidi Mir Dard, the "lyrical poet of Delhi," who became his father's first disciple and "spent the rest of his life propagating the doctrine of 'sincere Muhammadanism,' which was a fundamentalist interpretation of Islam, deepened by the mystical and ascetic techniques of the Naqshbandiyya."[9]

The costs of the new style of proselytism become evident in the accusation leveled against another Nakshibendi, Muhammad Mazhar Jan Janan.[10] A custodian of the "old" tradition was shocked by this bowdlerized version of the Nakshibendi initiation and commented: "Many came to him [when he lived in Mecca] and took the *khilafa* [succession] from him without being prepared for it: because we have seen several [of them] in Istanbul [*sic*] who have taken the *khilafa* and know nothing of the conditions [*ahval*] of the order. And our Shaikh Muhammad Jan was not unaware of that but his intention was to spread the order."[11]

In the process of rabita formation, identity is formed around the combating of heterodoxy, and is a reflection of the Master's identity and "lodge" identity. A number of changes occurred in this constellation of identity processes which correspond to the era of modernization and mass mobilization. These changes will become clearer in the perspective of some modern findings about identity formation. In modern social psychology and anthropology, group identity has been linked to a "resonating box," which we could describe as the "other," and the way in which the other is identified by stereotypical markers.[12] Confirming this finding, the Nakshibendi appeared on the modern scene with a violently antisecular and also anti-imperialistic stance. Accompanying this transformation was the shift of the traditional Nakshibendi "other," the magical garden of pantheism, onto Western European Christian culture. By the very nature of this confrontation a field which in the beginning was theological became cultural. The fact that the West was now perceived as an adversary culture and that this became the primary preoccupation of Islam, promoted the "ideological" use of Islam. Islam itself began to be seen as a culture, a development confirmed by the studies of W. C. Smith.

Thus, in the nineteenth century, the order became more clearly focused on the West as the "other" rather than on backsliders who had forgotten the orthodox Islamic emphasis on the unicity of God. This major transformation brought the order to see its mission in the world very differently than in the past. Running down pantheists was relegated to the back stage. An abstract project, the re-Islamization of the Islamic culture, took the place of a narrower identification with the order. In recent times the inroads of Western material culture among Turkish Muslims have prompted the themes of pantheism—now identified with the consumer society—to be disinterred once more. Indulgence in modern consumption patterns, to the extent that it has been identified with a sliding away from the eye of God, is considered to be a new form of pantheism and occupies an important place in the Nakshibendi critique of the West.

Mevlâna Halid and the Halidi Nakshibendi

This important change in training procedures allowed the Nakshibendi Mevlâna Halid (d. 1827)[13] to extend his influence in the Ottoman Empire. A mujaddidi Nakshibendi, Halid, working from Süleymaniye in the Kurdish region of Iraq and from Syria, was able to establish a network of Nakshibendi seminaries in Syria and eastern Anatolia. His followers, now known as "Halidi," organized protest movements based on religious affiliation. This new nineteenth-century political propellant of the Nakshibendi established a series of seminaries in the Kurdish region of Turkey (interposed on the path of the Protestant missions to eastern Turkey). From one of its graduates, we understand that they gave a type of instruction to the student body which prepared them to regain a preponderant position for Muslims chafing under the impious rule of colonialists or—what was not very different—under the yoke of impious Muslim regimes. The author of these recollections about Nakshibendi schooling, Bediüzzaman Said Nursi, had a part to play in the rebellion of 31 March 1909 and was to become one of the most painful thorns in the side of the Turkish Republic.

In the Caucasian and Chechen setting, where the Nakshibendi were most influential (1790s, 1830s), the movement was bolstered by a number of "overdetermining" influences. One was the pristine state of the Chechen tribes, which had been isolated from the Muslim world and therefore could be reconverted to an Islam that appeared as a civilizing, i.e., antimagical, influence. The second was the reverse factor of their long contiguity with Russian civilization. Just as in Indonesia, the sudden swift penetration of an alien culture which had stood in contiguity to the Chechen area but had not made a dent into it gave rise to a millennial form of Nakshibendi activity. This had not been true of Nakshibendi fundamentalism in less peripheral areas. In fact, in the Ottoman capital, in the 1820s, Nakshibendi activism took the form of a proposal for the reform of the empire, and the reinstatement of Islam as the guideline of reform. The Nakshibendi activists' promotion of a stricter use of the Shar'ia, however, was defeated by a Western-oriented reform known in Ottoman history as the "Tanzimat" (1839–76).

The more clearly political involvement of the Nakshibendi at this stage places them in the frame of "nativistic" movements. This transmutation was to a large extent unconscious. The Halidi Nakshibendi believed that they were doing what their spiritual ancestors, the mujaddidi Nakshibendi, had always done, namely, attempting to revitalize Islam. Having put down roots in the Ottoman capital during the early nineteenth century, they became increasingly involved in Ottoman politics. The first well-organized rebellion against the Westernizing reforms of the Tanzimat was led by a Nakshibendi, a certain Shaykh Ahmed of Süleymaniye, the very province from which Halid had emerged (1859). The conspiracy failed and the Nakshibendi came under suspicion.

The general climate of the 1860s in the Ottoman capital was not conducive to the continuation of the autonomous activities of the order. In these years part of the energy of the emerging conservative Muslim opposition to the Tanzimat was drawn into the wider net of the constitutionalist-liberal movement of the so-called Young Ottomans.[14] Nakshibendi activity did, however, surface during the Russo-Turkish War of 1877–78 when Nakshibendi shaykhs volunteered for military service. In these years, Süleyman Efendi of the Uzbek Sultantepe Nakshibendi lodge in Istanbul kept his links with Central Asia from where he had originated. He established a sort of intelligence service collecting information from Central Asian Muslims for the benefit of the Ottomans.[15] The leaders of this remarkable center of Nakshibendi activity were involved in many educational and social activities. It is reported that, for example, the head of the lodge, Ibrahim Ethem Efendi, a teacher in one of the newly established technical schools, built his own three-horsepower steam engine.[16]

Under these somewhat more routinized circumstances the next Halid Nakshibendi leader of importance surfaced. Ahmed Ziyaeddin, known as Gümüşhanevi (1812–93), was born on the Black Sea coast of Anatolia; he completed his religious studies in Istanbul and began to train followers and publish a number of works on religion between 1848 and 1875. He continued to spread the Halidi doctrine but with considerable caution since, at the time, the higher bureaucracy of the Ottoman state was proceeding briskly with a movement of reform inspired by Western Cameralism, the theory underpinning Western enlightened despotism. Gümüşhanevi trained a large number of men of religion who had come from all parts of the empire to study with him. A glance at the careers of these men shows that he was extending the scope of Mevlâna Halid's proselytization by targeting the Caucasus, the Crimea, Kazan Tatars, and China.

Gümüşhanevi's activism took the specific form of an appeal to citizens to harken to the sound of the mobilization of Ottoman defense forces during the Russo-Turkish War of 1877–78. But Gümüşhanevi also reacted to Ottoman modernist reformism. At the time when the first banks were established in Turkey he created his own "Loan Fund" for his disciples. He established four libraries, one each in Istanbul, Rize, Bayburt, and Of.[17] A pedagogic innovation he used was to "stream" his students according to their qualifications. This ability to respond in kind to modernization seems also to have been a quality found among more moderate Nakshibendi of the later nineteenth century. Taken together then, the totality of parameters which defined Nakshibendi social action had changed considerably by the nineteenth century. Gümüşhanevi's death in 1893 brought an interregnum in Nakshibendi influence.

The substance of the religious teachings of Gümüşhanevi provides a frame for an Islamic hermeneutic that depends both on textual interpretation proper and on a reading of prescribed Sufi interpersonal relations as paratext. The way in which this combination of text and Master-disciple relations led to a structuring of social action among Gümüşhanevi's followers can only be understood if we take the religious inner drive of his disciples as a legitimate datum in our analysis. At this point we have to remember some of the elements involved in the acquisition of knowledge in the Nakshibendi mode. In this method the items of book knowledge, the use of memory in propagating these themes, and one's positioning with regard to a mentor are all considered to be part of the substance of knowledge. Knowledge is defined as the pursuit of self-purification, and this is to be achieved not only by keeping closely to the central orthodox line but also, as we have seen, by establishing an intimate link between mentor and pupil. This bond, once established, is only the first link in what operates as a "chain" of linkages producing a network of Nakshibendi influences. To this basic frame we have to add a nineteenth-century innovation, the increased use of the traditions of the Prophet, the examples taken from his life, as a source of ethical guidance. This new element thereafter functioned as a template for the interpretive function of the mentor. This was an attempt to bring back the "original" meaning of Islam into the nineteenth century but by the use of a frame which allows considerable flexibility for interpretation. The central focus of one's belief now becomes the human example of the Prophet Muhammad. This development not only is associated with the Nakshibendi but is a characteristic one sees throughout the Islamic world in the nineteenth century. It is, together with the transmutation of the "other" from "pantheism" to "Western imperialism," one of the key parameters of the modernized Nakshibendi teaching.

The Operational Code of the Nakshibendi: Theoretical Considerations

In its history the Nakshibendi order has encountered and adapted to the many currents—both internal and external—that have shaped Islamic history. What remains unexplained is this seemingly serendipitous propensity for adaptation. One way of explaining the strength and historical breadth of Nakshibendi influence in the Ottoman Empire would be to make an argument for its continuity. Pareto's theory of the "persistence of aggregates" would do well here: the Nakshibendi had been involved with the fate of Turkey since the fifteenth century, and this in itself would provide an explanation for the persistence of their influence. But such general explanations do not tell us why the Kadiri order, with a similarly prestigious past, was unable to match the Nakshibendi. Surely the success of the Nakshibendi in adapting to ambient conditions since the fifteenth century has a better explanation than "persistence."

First, the Nakshibendi struggle against the "magical garden" of pantheism locked onto another structural component of Islamic societies which was basic, primordial. The one persistent form of popular participation in social concerns in Islam had been through a sharing of the common idiom of the divine message. There were many ways in which this sharing was, with time, restricted, but in the absence of a "church," the possibility—always present for Muslims of all walks of life—of invoking the Word of God for or against a view, an action, a stand could not be totally erased. The Nakshibendi tapped this patent legitimation for popular participation through setting a path for the righteous when taking sides against what they saw as "elitist," as well as godless, pantheism so that while they themselves had known for centuries how to manipulate the springs of political power, beginning with mujaddidism, they had means of drawing into their net a wider stratum of the population. This base for recruitment increased rather than decreased as modernization brought with it an alienating, secularizing policy on the part of the Ottoman Tanzimat and the further promotion of secularism by the Turkish Republic.

In the nineteenth century the Nakshibendi were helped by the new factors that promoted an already existing diffuse theory of populist legitimation. Among these were the popular revulsion against the special commercial privileges and de facto more favorable class position gained by non-Muslim minorities and foreign nationals in the Ottoman Empire. In a restricted sense, then, the success of the mujaddidi during the nineteenth century may be linked to a Muslim "democratizing" process, namely, the new, purely religious legitimation of politics underlined by the Nakshibendi, a novel element which emerged as the Ottoman population was gradually socially mobilized. On the other hand, aspects of Nakshibendi internal structure are also involved in this success.

M. van Bruinessen has alerted us to the idea that this success may be an outcome of the flexibility of the order in delegating powers to proselytizing shaykhs. I would propose that what we observe as the flexibility of the order is a consequence of other, internal ritualistic elements which had important consequences in the more clearly political stance that the order adopted following its mujaddidi stage of development. These are the extent to which it has been able to construct a social identity for its followers, a process the foundations of which I have described above.

Nakshibendi Political Impact in Turkey: Actual and Potential

Turkey is unique among countries with a majority Muslim population in having implemented a policy of radical secularization in modern times. Between 1923 and 1950 the attitude of the Turkish government could be characterized as that of Jacobin secularism and shows many parallels with the official Mexican attitude toward the Church during Mexico's revolutionary era. Following the establishment of the Turkish Republic in 1923, a number of laws redrew the foundation of Turkish society on a non-Islamic base. Among the most important of these was the abolition of the Caliphate (1924), the adoption of the Swiss Civil Code (1926), the Latinization of the alphabet (1928), and the striking out of the phrase in the Turkish constitution to the effect that the religion of Turkish state was Islam (1928). The same law which abolished the Caliphate also abolished the salaried position of all the upper-echelon "doctors of Islamic law," or *ulama*. In the following years, an official effort was made to promote a public image of the ulama as ignorant exploiters of the masses. Atheism was not encouraged; on the contrary, the Durkheimian view of religion as a stabilizing force for society had much currency among intellectuals and officials influenced by Durkheim. However, religion was seen in these quarters as a private belief with no claims on the political sphere and as an ancient and outmoded frame for the setting of social norms or the founding of social institutions.

This shift toward secularism in a society where Islam had occupied a central place in social relations had some success. It drew into its net three types of persons who became the "guardians" of the new Republican order: the ideologues who were instituting the new social system, the officials, and the upwardly mobile, including an important group of primary- and secondary-school teachers. "Kemalism," as the neo-ideology was named, left untouched large sections of the rural masses and many lower-class inhabitants of the three principal cities, Istanbul, Ankara, and Izmir. Mid-size towns did exhibit, in the center stage of official public life, the correct Republican rituals. But in the provinces, in the back stage, the old structures were maintained. Children were given private religious instruction, and religious feasts were celebrated; among a few provincials, religion was still a cement for a latent communal solidarity against what was seen as over-Westernization. This residual, private aspect of religion could well be misinterpreted by observers as the transformation of small-town Islam into "civil religion." The embers seem to have contained more fire than could be observed.

What transformed this glow into a flame seems best explained by theories of group identity. In the Ottoman Empire, group identity of the citizen in the widest sense had been structured by identification with a religious group—Islam in the case of Turkish-speaking Muslims, the Greek Orthodox church in the case of Greeks, etc. This type of social identity brought together all Muslims of the Ottoman Empire—Turks, Arabs, Kurds, and, to some extent, Albanians. The intrusion of a new focus of group identity, "Turkism," was a relatively recent innovation dating from the beginning of the twentieth century. The recent findings of social psychologists enable us to understand the many complications which enveloped Muslim Turks with the advent of secularization and nationalism. Tajfel found that group identity is structured in terms of cues of social comparison underlining differences.[18] The question for the Turk placed in the new secular social setting was, "If I am going to assume my identity by identifying with 'Turkishness,' who is the 'other'?" "Against whom do I have to measure myself to find the difference that will tell me who I am?" Whereas in the earlier circumstances the "other" had been a religious "other," this "other" had now been erased by secularism. Yet, there are a number of signs that even during the republic, in informal relations, Muslim Turks continued to identify as Turks not all the bearers of Turkish passports but only those who were Muslims.

What we would expect is that in a situation where the elaboration of social identity becomes problematic for want of "building blocks," a search for personal identity as well as "sporadic, idiosyncratic interpersonal behavior" would become more prevalent.[19] All of this then would result in a vacillation between a concentration on the building of personal identity and a diffuse search for social identity with a strong tendency to revitalize the old social moorings.

In the first stages of a multiparty system in Turkey in the 1950s it is the perception of this psychic instability among a pool of potential voters that drew the Demokrat Party to emphasize that it stood for a more tolerant attitude toward the practice of Islam than had its predecessor, the secularizing party (the Republican People's Party) of Atatürk.

Elected by a popular majority between 1950 and 1957, the Demokrat Party was removed from office in 1960 by a group in the military who believed that the pure ideals of the early republic had been cast off. The fear that the Demokrats were appealing to religious superstition also figured in the apprehensions of the military junta. But even the continued periodic interventions by the military between 1960 and 1980 could not destroy the foundations of democracy which had first been laid in 1950. In this period, Islam became increasingly visible as a force in Turkey. Part of this rise had a simple explanation: the new political parties that had appeared on the scene since 1950 had all been competing for the vote of an increasingly politically mobilized rural and lower-class population which between 1923 and 1950 had kept its Islamic values on the back burner but was far from having extinguished them. In addition, the parliamentary personnel was increasingly drawn from the provinces and often subtly appealed to the social concomitants of religious conservatism: family cohesiveness, honesty, and social order. Although the legal system of secularism, protected as it was by the figure of Atatürk, could not be subverted, religious conservatives worked through the infiltration of government departments. The Ministry of Education, with its many teaching and administrative-level positions and its suitability for the spreading of ideologies, was immediately targeted and infiltrated.

In the first years of religious liberalization after 1950, a number of events which could be classified as emanating from "fundamentalists" began to embarrass the Demokrat Party. One was the Tijani sect's widespread destruction of busts and portraits of Atatürk: these were considered "idols," which the republic worshiped. An attempt on the life of the journalist A. E. Yalman brought these fears to the forefront. In fact, the Demokrat Party, despite its tolerant view of the practice of Islam, strengthened the laws for the protection of the secular values of the republic during its incumbency. More important than this history of violence has been the continuing influence of the Nakshibendi order and its branches in the contemporary Turkish setting.

Bediüzzaman Said Nursi, a product of the Halidi seminaries, emerged as a Nakshibendi leader with his own autonomous organization during the Republican era. Said Nursi was implicated in the military rebellion of 1909, and though he protested his innocence he was sent into exile in Anatolia. After 1910 he was pardoned and began to collaborate with the Young Turks in their efforts to use Islam as a weapon against imperialism and colonialism. Taken prisoner by the Russians during World War I, he returned to find Istanbul occupied by Allied forces. The nationalistic brochures he wrote at the time put him in the good graces of the nationalist government in Ankara. But this prestige dissolved when he reminded the representatives to the assembly of the nationalist government that their success was not due simply to their own work but was the result of divine intervention. In self-exile in his native town of Bitlis, he was again accused of being implicated in the Kurdish rebellion of 1925, a movement which indeed was led by a Nakshibendi shaykh, a namesake of our man, Shaykh Said of Palu. Again, Said Nursi claimed total innocence but was exiled to a mountainous region in western Turkey. There he set out to build a clientele. His followers were local artisans and tradesmen, and the movement was spread among peasants of middling status.

The propagation of Said Nursi's writings, known collectively as the *Epistle of Light*, built up a network of persons who took spiritual sustenance from them. These were circulated clandestinely at first, but with the more tolerant attitude toward religious proselytization which followed the introduction of multiparty government in Turkey, they were accorded legitimacy (1956) and printed in the Latin alphabet, the only legal alphabet in Turkey since 1928. Said Nursi himself was imprisoned several times for activities aiming to undermine the secular foundation of the Turkish Republic. By the time he died in 1960 he had acquired a wide following which is still extremely active in Turkey.

When the first "clerical" party, the National Salvation party (NSP), emerged during the 1973 elections, the Nurcu, as the followers of Said Nursi are called, supported it. Although they later changed this political tack, claiming that the leader of the NSP had not met their expectation by his policies in parliament in the 1980s, their daily, *Yeni Nesil* (New Generation), still showed clear support for another political party, Mr. Demirel's "True Path" party.

The central directing institution among the contemporary Nurcu is the editorial board of the order which publishes both innumerable reprints of the *Epistle of Light* and also *Yeni Nesil*. Other activities of the board have been to publish a series of brochures which are popularizations of modern science and have titles such as *The Atom and the Universe*, *Cybernetics*, and *The Big Bang*. Each brochure is uncompromisingly "scientific" in its coverage but ends with a query as to whether the complexity of the system described can be reasonably attributed to chance. The contents of the *Epistle of Light,* on the other hand, are interesting in the sense that they present a contrast with the more militant themes one finds in the writings of such contemporary fundamentalists as Zahid Efendi (discussed below). Although the *Epistle of Light* has a helter-skelter structure which includes reminiscences, instructions, and copies of Said Nursi's correspondence, its bulk consists of commentaries on the Qur'an. An attempt is thus made to explain to an audience which knows no Arabic the layered context of meanings of the Qur'an. This attempt recalls the attempt by the nineteenth-century Egyptian-Syrian Salafiyya school to show that the teachings of the Qur'an are compatible with modern science. Said Nursi appears to have wanted to give to a large, relatively unlettered, but increasingly literate population an understanding of the bases of their religion.

The Nurcu's support of the existing democratic order in Turkey seems genuine, but the subtlety of this stand appears in a statement of Safa Mursel, a person who has been called the "ideologue" of the sect.

> In modern societies, government is either democratic or despotic. There is nothing more natural than choosing democracy, which is the libertarian form of government. The alternative to accepting the mechanism which brought to power the Demokrat Party, the Justice Party, and the True Path Party [the representatives of almost the same conservative constituency since 1950] is despotism. To determinedly support the libertarian parties against revolution [the military coups of 1960, 1971, and 1980] or anarchy [the Marxist social movements of the 1970s] does not mean that one is engaging in politics. The interest shown by Said Nursi to the Demokrat Party was due to the libertarian character of this party.[20]

The Nurcu group acquired prominence in the fall of 1990 by organizing a celebration of the birthday of the Prophet Muhammad on the day of Atatürk's death (10 November). The state prosecutor started proceedings against the group. Mehmet Kutlular, today the leader of a splinter group from Nurcu's original leadership, reacted by claiming that his group had no intention of undermining the fundamental principles of the state (i.e., secularism). According to him, the state monopoly of education established in 1924 had promised that the state itself would take up religious instruction but had never done so. What had been going on since the government of Özal had come to power, the widening of religious instruction in secondary schools, was simply an implementation of this promise. In fact, the time was one in which Turks could now support "minimum shared values" in which multiparty democracy figured up front.[21] Kutlular also stated that representation in parliament could substitute for the institution of the Caliphate.

With the Nurcu we begin to discern an aspect of the Turkish religious right shared by the Marxist left, the tendency to fragmentation of these wings. By 1990, the Nurcu had split into (1) the original publishers of *Yeni Nesil* and their rivals, who changed the daily's name to *Yeni Asya* (New Asia); (2) a dissident branch in Izmir led by

Fethullah Gulen which was rumored to have links with the intelligence component of the political establishment; (3) a younger group of "intellectual" Nurcu led by Mehmed Metiner, who, up to 1989, published his own periodical, *Girişim;* and (4) the "scriptarians," a dissident group which insisted on rescuing the authenticity of Said Nursi's thought by printing it in the Arabic alphabet, the script used by Said Nursi. This, of course, is illegal in modern Turkey.

Said Nursi's teachings also bear the stamp of the more esoteric teachings of the Sufis and often underline the subtlety of the meanings to be drawn from the Qur'an. The simplicity of some of his images, combined with an involuted style and vocabulary, has an undeniable power of attraction which gives a special gloss to his homiletics and also colors his more down-to-earth moralistic preachings. Like all Nakshibendi, he sends a message to all Muslims that shows a latent pan-Islamic flavor. Today, in about a hundred private homes, the followers of Said Nursi meet every Saturday to listen to comments on the *Epistle of Light*. The attendance often overflows onto the stairs. It consists primarily of young persons in their thirties or forties. One can discern that the audience comes from the more conservative Istanbul and takes in artisans, craftsmen, chauffeurs, laborers, minor officials, and university students. Leaders of the sessions have at least a secondary education. They stand in front of the congregation, open a page of the *Epistle* at random, and comment upon it. Questions are asked from the audience to which the leader responds. Tea is served, prayers are said, and the audience disperses. The influence of the Nurcu sect is thus a diffuse one: while the sect's newspaper disseminates the correct stand to take on current political, social, and economic issues, the effectiveness of the Nurcu is that of a freemasonry, of persons who establish social linkages and personal ties with each other, who support and promote people who think like themselves. But this diffuseness, among followers who may number a few hundred thousand, is an element to reckon with in the intellectual climate of contemporary Turkey.

While the Nurcu have primarily appealed to the provincial middle classes and have only recently gathered support from intellectuals, what may be called "main-line" Nakshibendism has stuck with the educated conservatives. One coup, that of the "conversion" of the modern Turkish poet Necip Fazil Kisakürek (1904–83), is especially interesting. Following a somewhat erratic course of studies in Paris in the late 1920s, Necip Fazil returned to Turkey and within a few years came under the spiritual influence of the Nakshibendi shaykh Ziyaeddin Arvasi, a development he has related in his autobiography, *O ve Ben*.[22] It may be assumed that it was the influence of the latter which led him to publish the periodical *Great East* in 1943. Necip Fazil's relation with his mentor and the gap which the latter's teaching filled in the poet's intellectual universe appear in the following description of his parents' household. True, this description came after the poet's "conversion," but this does not diminish its explanatory power:

> At the time when women's hair descended to their ankles, my grandmother, with her clipped hair reminiscent of women's fashions of today, with her grand demeanor, her jewels which were the envy of Istanbul, the parties she gave, with her mechanical piano and her baskets full of novels mostly translated from

the West, with her interior decoration that was a mix of every possible style, exhibited the model of the refined lady of Istanbul, a type passed on to the Young Turks by the preceding Hamidian era, a paste made of Eastern and Western condiments in equal proportions, a residue of the Tanzimat reforms, racked by neurotic fears, a person displaced from her own axis but who had found none to replace it.[23]

Also relevant is the poet's pronouncement on Western culture while he was a philosophy student in Paris in the 1920s:

Paris, which with its civilization symbolized the West, exhibited on its front stage designs of miraculous refinement which, however, turned out to be etched on a background of plastic, the latter in fact, attracting the eye to what it was disguising, namely, ruin and darkness, a civilization that was condemned to knock its head against one wall, against another and play hide-and-seek from one crisis to another.[24]

Kisakürek's *Memoirs* show the way in which a need for a cleansing moral gust drew him to Shaykh Arvasi. But the search for what I have described above as the seamless society is also a motive force in the poet's conversion. What Kisakürek searches for (he expresses it in French) is Rimbaud's *La vraie vie absente*.

In 1943 Kisakürek published *Great East*, a periodical whose promotion of Islamic culture led to its closure by the government in 1944. Kisakürek was the first Turkish secular intellectual of the Republican era to try to reevaluate and propagandize Islamic values. Though his periodic carousing diminished his moral influence, his literary production, his prestige as a modern author, and his articles attacking Western mores and promoting an Islamic renaissance have given younger fundamentalists a peg on which to hang their conservative thought.

Shaykh Mehmed Zahid Kotku (1897–1980), the premier Nakshibendi leader of our time, operated through somewhat different channels. Just as Shaykh Arvasi, he had to work in a setting in which Sufi orders had been outlawed (1925). He was in more ways than one the legitimate successor of Gümüşhanevi. Born in Bursa into a family of migrants from the Caucasus, a hotbed of Nakshibendi influence, Kotku at age twenty-one joined the circle first organized by Gümüşhanevi. At the age of twenty-seven he received authorization to carry on as an independent shaykh. When the Sufi orders were closed in 1925, he returned to Bursa and took over the mosque in the village of Izvat where his father had been officiating. Although the Sufi orders had been closed, as an Imam, Kotku was part of the lower hierarchy of the government's General Directorate of Religious Affairs. In this capacity, he was posted to Istanbul in 1952. At that time, he succeeded Abdülaziz Bekkine, the nominal leader of the Nakshibendi. This was a purely informal arrangement which had to be kept secret since the order operated underground. In Istanbul, he was first posted to the Çivizade Mosque and then in 1958 to the Iskenderpaşa Mosque where he remained until his death in 1980.

According to a recent biographer, the government was likely aware of Kotku's attempts to gather a circle around him but it considered these—as yet nonpolitical—activities of the shaykh preferable to those of the violent Tijani order.[25] At any rate, his predecessor had already established Nakshibendi influence among a number of prominent citizens in Istanbul. The social profile of these disciples was that of persons of provincial or rural origin who had come to Istanbul for university studies.

We now know from a notorious speech of Kotku's son-in-law and successor, Professor Esat Coşan, that Kotku was the architect of a many-sided strategy which included the organization of discussion groups throughout Turkey, the establishment of a Muslim-owned motor producing plant, the publication of the daily *Sabah* (established 1968), and last, but not least, the encouragement of political activities. According to Coşan, in 1970 Kotku encouraged the formation of the first religious political party in modern Turkey, the National Order party. When this party was dissolved by the Turkish Supreme Court, it was replaced by the National Salvation party. The advice of Kotku, Coşan implied, resulted in the selection of Professor Necmettin Erbakan to lead this party. Kotku kept a vigilant eye on the activities of the party, advising it to dissolve its youth branches because their members had become too violent.

Two of Kotku's collected sermons, *Cihad* (Jihad) [26] and *Mü'minin Vasiflari* (Qualities of the Believer),[27] enable us to reconstitute the themes he was promoting among his disciples:

1. Muslims do not practice their religion in private: Islam means being part of the Islamic community; where the Islamic community disappears, so does Islam.
2. To be religious is to be ready to engage in combat. Factories are not purveyors of consumer goods but places where this combat is to be elaborated. This combat demands that one get to know the worldly sciences, arts and commerce. This control will be the means of obtaining the "freedom" of Muslims.
3. Our greatest leaders have been *mujtahids,* who have taken upon themselves to reinterpret the Qur'an.
4. Our nation [interestingly enough, Turkey, not the Muslims] has been splintered by political parties. This is unfortunate.
5. To voyage to foreign countries simply to earn more money is irresponsible.
6. We think by imitating the West we too can go to the moon, but we have lost our most precious characteristic: through imitation we have conceded the core of our identity. As a consequence our country is ruled by the miniskirt, prostitution, drunkenness, bribery, adultery, gambling and the cinema. Such things didn't exist even in the days of darkest ignorance that preceded Islam.
7. We should forego consumption and encourage national identity. Every Turkish adult wears a watch. This means we are giving away 4 billion

liras to the Swiss. We must deliver ourselves from economic slavery to foreigners.

8. To convince followers, we should use a clear and friendly language. The believer establishes and cooperates with other believers.
9. The pure of heart are more learned than the people who have received the best education.
10. Muslims should try to capture the higher summits of social and political institutions in their country and establish control over the society.

Ersin Gündoğan, in 1990 a director of Faysal Finans, an Islamic bank operating in Turkey with Saudi funding, recently published his own account of the ways in which Kotku, known also as Zahid Efendi, was able to capture the minds of his disciples.[28]

Gündoğan's career is a model of the type of networking on which Nakshibendi influence is based. He was educated as a mechanical engineer. In 1968 he also completed a higher degree in management. His search for a job began with a visit to a teaching assistant at the Faculty of Engineering of Istanbul Technical University, presumably someone who shared his views. There he met an employee of the State Planning Organization (SPO). Through a chain of persons linked to this employee he was hired by the SPO and began work in its Projects Assessment Bureau. In 1968 this organization had been captured by a team known to its critics as the "clog wearers," denoting the clogs worn by Muslims during ablutions. Gündoğan is quite clear about the goals of this group: "We were trying to avoid the social and economic structure which the West was trying to impose on developing countries under the fallacious heading of 'modernization' or 'streamlining.'"[29] What he seems to have been advocating was an economic policy targeted to shifting away from possible links with the European Economic Community (EEC) and toward an eventual Muslim common market, a strategy which, in the long term, does not seem to have been able to get off the ground. Gündoğan met Kotku (Zahid Efendi) the first year that he began working for the SPO. In his words, "It was in the summer of 1968 that I had the pleasure of meeting our teacher for the first time; a person who, with his pioneering efforts kneaded and educated an army of intellectuals who were dreaming the great dream of protecting the selfhood, culture and identity of Muslims at a time when Turkey had entered an era of reconstruction."[30]

The concept of an era of restructuration is indeed interesting, in the sense that much of the renewed activity of Muslim conservatism in Turkey seems to have emerged in 1968. The Muslim daily *Sabah,* for instance, a sheet which is rumored to have been started with the encouragement of Kotku, began to appear that year. Whether it was a coincidence that the first Islamic Conference met the next year has still to be ascertained. What we perceive in Gündoğan's narrative of Kotku's influence is probably more important than conspiracy theories aiming to explain the takeoff of Islamic ideas in 1968. There exists a pattern in this revival that conspiracy theories habitually miss taking into account. In Gündoğan's narrative we see the way in which Kotku filled a void that was emotional, personal, and ideological. Gündoğan's narrative emphasizes closeness, friendship, face-to-face relations, sitting by the knee of the mentor who provides moral guidance. The lesson that Gündoğan draws from his contact with Kotku generalizes on this theme: he comes to understand the power of sohbet (conversation) in communicating with a Turkish audience. On the other hand, Kotku, the teacher, also broaches general ideas about the duties of Muslims as a collective. The mysterious attraction of the religious leader seems to originate in the intersecting of these two planes of individual and collective action.

The ambient, official nationalism of Republican Turkey that was the primary ideology from the 1930s through the 1960s left the "day-to-day" in a limbo. Even in the most stringently secular times of the republic, Islam filled in the void. The Republican strategy was a grievous error for, as a number of theoreticians of society from Alfred Shutz to Michel de Certeau have shown, no sociological theory can dispense with the "everyday." A theory that has no "everyday" is a theory of and for intellectuals, not a theory of social action. The presence in Kotku's "mix" of existential considerations about the meaning of life and death seems to have increased the potency of his teachings. Within these frames the role of sohbet as one of the operators now becomes clearer. The ways in which the Nakshibendi have expanded their influence should be analyzed from this vantage point, one which is closest to the *quotidien* as described by de Certeau. No item of Kemalism addressed itself to the "everyday," a failure in any social setting but one which cumulates in a setting where the personal as an aspect of the "everyday" is especially salient as community "cement." But Kotku also inherited the general ideological guidance he had received from Gümüşhanevi: to avoid consumerism, to boycott foreign products, not to buy comestibles imported from foreign countries, to prepare for combat, to infiltrate institutions. These themes are constantly reiterated. Nevertheless, a change comes about at the Gündoğan stage of the message: the rather simplistic economic ideas of Kotku are now interpreted in the wider cognitive frame that Gündoğan used in the SPO.

What, then, is the meaning—and the import—for sociological theory of the influence of Kotku insofar as he is an exemplar of Nakshibendi influence?

Let us note, first, the similarity between the message of Mevlâna Halid and that of Kotku. In both cases, identity, the self, is defined in contrast and in opposition to the "other," in this case the non-Muslim. What is remarkable is that this stance survives from the earliest Nakshibendi "renewalists" of the seventeenth century to the present, having taken the form of anti-imperialism in the late eighteenth and nineteenth centuries. In this sense of an uninterrupted ideological lineage, the stance is also different from that which we could impute to modern nationalism. It is in Gündoğan's ideas that, for the first time, we see a softening of this definition of the self. Here, the earlier emphasis on preparation for real war ("train your children to be sharpshooters") has been transformed into the necessity to be prepared to deflect the wiles of Western capitalism. In short, the main difference between Kotku and Gündoğan is the latter's more differentiated cognitive universe. Paradoxically, Gündoğan's mind was formed in the secular schools of the secular Turkish Republic. There are many other signs that Gündoğan's intellectual development is part of a much more general change which has affected fundamentalism and produced a new type in Turkey: the young Muslim intellectual.

Professor Esat Coşan, Kotku's successor, is an example of the new type of fundamentalist intellectual. He publishes magazines of information and analysis that copy the format of the highbrow Turkish reviews. Coşan was born in 1938. His great-grandfather was a disciple of Gümüşhanevi, and his father was a member of Kotku's circle. Graduating from the Faculty of Letters of the University of Istanbul, Coşan began his academic career at the Faculty of Theology in Ankara. In 1982 he became a full professor, and in 1987 he requested to be retired. In 1985 he started what was to become an extensive publishing career by founding the monthly, *Islâm*. In 1986 he added to this a new periodical, *Kadin ve Aile* (Woman and the Family). Both of these were current in 1991, and *Islâm* is said to have a circulation of 100,000. *Gül Çocuk*, a children's magazine, appeared between 1987 and 1990. *Ilim ve Sanat* (Science and Art), a sophisticated magazine covering history and current developments, was issued between 1985 and 1989. Vefa Yayincilik is the Nakshibendi corporation responsible for the magazines. Seha Neşriyat is the Nakshibendi company that publishes books such as Gümüşhanevi's biography.

Such fundamentalist publishing attempts to appropriate and transform secular discourse. This "capture of the secular discourse" exists among fundamentalists who are not necessarily Nakshibendi. For example, the autobiography of a young Muslim fundamentalist, Ismet Özel, bears the title *Waldo, Why Aren't You Here?* in reference to Ralph Waldo Emerson and his stand concerning freedom. An offshoot of the *Nurcu* published by the younger generation, the periodical *Girişm*, addresses questions that are more philosophical in nature than the parent group would have tackled.

To show that a qualitative change has occurred in the mindset of the more theoretically inclined younger generation of Muslim intellectuals is only the first step in the reconstitution of the extremely complex social background of modern Turkish fundamentalism. One must also study the meshing of the intellectual dimension of ideology with its social and psychological moorings. Islam, in this perspective, appears as a total sociocultural set. Here we are dealing with the life strategies of a social stratum which may be seen as of the periphery, i.e., the province.

Yet the operational mode of the province was and is that of networks based on personal contacts often channeled through what was left of *tarikat* structures after these had been banned in Turkey. These structures of communication retain their shape. Not only do these channels of communication continue to operate in secular Turkey, but they established the setting for a reenactment of the type of personal ties that, according to Kotku, informed collective relations in a Muslim community. As he rightly pointed out, it is in the community that the Muslim individual is formed; to remain a Muslim he must operate in and with the community. The ties that established the collectivity are personal ties; the community coalesces around them. It is this process which underlies the peculiar type of traditional Middle Eastern populism which one has such difficulty defining. Note that the Western conception which lies latent in many modern democratic theories—Adam Smith's idea that a collectivity is made into one by the forces of the market—is totally alien to this ideal Muslim community.

Nonetheless we must also take into consideration an aspect of Turkey in the 1990s which is eroding this foundation of Nakshibendi influence: as politics, the economy, and the world of communication become differentiated, Kotku's ideal Islamic society is undermined. Kotku was quite wary of democratic politics and the formation of adversary groups pitted against each other on turfs that have no meaning in a religious scheme. The differentiation of society, as seen in the emerging business class's promotion of its own class interests and in the unanticipated influence of secular education, unleashed processes that take us away from Kotku's Islamic utopia and into the present fragmentation of Turkish fundamentalism into many competing groups.

That Kotku's influence still prevailed in the 1970s and 1980s can be explained by the fact that the Turkish secular elite never understood that the periphery is a world of its own marked not only by a general "backwardness" but by an interlocking set of social characteristics. It is in effect a parallel society to the one the Kemalists characteristically were trying to establish. Secularization meant eliminating the invisible social boundaries of this parallel world, and this was a loss that the periphery refused to accept.

Nakshibendis Today

Turkish secularists have sounded the alarm with regard to the role of the Nakshibendi order in contemporary politics. These accusations appeared in scattered statements as a newly formed religious party, the National Salvation Party, emerged in the election of 1973. But these were vague reports that the NSP was using underground Nakshibendi groups as propagandists. With the emergence of the Motherland Party in the mid-1980s, the accusations found a target. The brother of the president of the republic, Turgut Özal (leader of the Motherland Party), was a disciple of Kotku, and his mother demanded to be buried near Kotku (which is where she rests today). Every Friday, the preaching of Professor Esat Coşan, the successor and son-in-law of Kotku, attracts a large constituency to the Iskenderpaşa Mosque in Istanbul, an audience that includes many professionals and what we might describe as Muslim intellectuals. A few years ago Professor Coşan was accused by a conservative Istanbul daily of having given then prime minister Özal a list of five candidates to be placed on the ticket of the Motherland Party, which held a majority in the Turkish parliament.[31] Even though he requested a correction of what he called this "unfounded rumor," Coşan made his own stand clear in a rebuttal published in *Islâm:* "I would gladly support the presence in parliament, in numbers sufficient to create a caucus or in larger numbers, of a party that would defend with sincerity our glorious past, our pure belief, and our higher national interests using party rules and an economic theory so drafted as to prevent our entrance into the European Community."[32]

Özal's Motherland Party was said to include many crypto-Nakshibendi, but it nevertheless applied for the acceptance of Turkey into the EEC. The EEC delay in responding to the application weakened Özal's position vis-à-vis the activists working for an alternative Islamic economic cooperation. Indeed, a constant theme in the Nakshibendi monthly *Islâm* is the implausibility of a Turkish adhesion to the European Community. In an article authored by Halil Necatioğlu, a pseudonym of Coşan, this theme was clear:

> Many Europeans in positions of responsibility are repeating that Turkey does not have a European identity. That country which is stated not to have a European identity is that country which for an entire century now has taken the most absurd measures for the sake of Westernization, namely Turkey. That state which every Tom, Dick, and Harry in the European parliament accuses of having failed with respect to human rights is not the Ottoman state; it is that entity which from the very date of its foundation to our day has engaged in many a somersault to "modernize" and to look appealing to the West and which has carried out practices regardless of the belief and culture of its people, namely the Republic of Turkey.[33]

The polemic nature of this article carries the marks of a discourse specific to a field that had not yet developed when the Nakshibendi began to be influential among Turkish intellectuals in the 1930s, namely, the field of public opinion. When the Nakshibendi agreed to operate in this field instead of continuing to work under cover, the element of prudence and discretion that characterized its earlier stance was profoundly affected. The Nakshibendi had now been drawn into a public debate and the eddies thereby created. By the same token, differences of opinion between the various factions of believers—Nakshibendi and conservative Muslims who saw Sufism as suspect—at one time could have been papered over, but now were projected onto the sphere of public opinion and envenomed by this exposure.

In fact, the first sign of a rift between the leaders of the Turkish clerical party, the Welfare Party, and the Nakshibendi appeared in January 1990 in a cryptic leading article of *Islâm* which, in its English version in the same issue, ran as follows:

> Throughout history Muslims have followed the pious, righteous and devout. They obeyed true Islamic scholars [i.e. the Nakshibendi] and pledged their allegiance to them. They worked under their orders and followed the path they showed to them. Thus they attained happiness in both worlds. The true caliphs of mankind are the blessed adepts and shaykhs joined in spirit with God; they are not oppressive and despotic politicians. How many faithful, just and intelligent government officials, commanders, ministers, even sultans pledged their allegiance to them, kissed their hands, requested their prayers, carried out their orders, took them as their guides, and performed services to them?[34]

Journalism, though it was seen by Kotku as a means of extending the order's influence, had brought with it unanticipated consequences, including disunity in the ranks of the Muslims.

In the months to follow, the Nakshibendi were gradually drawn into the establishment of a political party by the necessarily adversary position they took toward the

Welfare Party even though, paradoxically, the themes of brotherhood and together-ness occurred with increasing frequency in the pages of *Islâm*.[35] The declared goal of the Nakshibendi publishing firm, a "jihad [religious war] of love and affection," was presaged in a propaganda campaign launched in June 1990 in the article (in English) entitled "The Importance and Place of Politics in Islam," a passage of which follows:

> Muslims are responsible for conforming to the religious ordinances and com-mands in social-political matters just as much as they are in matters of worship and piety. . . . They cannot remain disinterested, uninformed, ineffective, care-less, detached and passive. If they do, they will be held responsible. . . . Reli-gion is a whole, one cannot fulfill some parts and turn one's back on others. . . . Political organization . . . is necessary because if governing by means of democracy and votes falls into the hands of the opposition, this can lead [to] the Muslims' most natural rights being violated.[36]

This entire issue of *Islâm* was devoted to the concept of *shura,* or Islamic political consultation. The rift with the Welfare Party was revealed clearly in the July issue of *Islâm* and was chronicled in the English translation of the leading article, an interview with Coşan, under the rubric "A Political Party and Us." In the Turkish version of the article, Professor Coşan indicated that in Central Asia a whole region was now open to Nakshibendi influence. He undoubtedly was aware that in Soviet Russia it was the Nakshibendi who were the architects of the Muslim revival.

Kotku, now dead for a decade, became, once more, a controversial figure when on 11 November 1990, the day Turkish secularists mourned Atatürk, the Nakshibendi chose to mourn their own shaykh. Possibly as a result of the general revulsion for the killing within a year of three Turkish personalities who had loudly proclaimed the dangers of fundamentalism, Professor Coşan had not taken the final step of establish-ing his own party by the date of this writing.

My excursus on Nakshibendi history has focused primarily on how external con-ditions have shaped Nakshibendi strategy. The core of Nakshibendi belief, its reviv-alistic aspect, has remained unchanged. The persistence of this common denominator could be explained by its influence as a principle of hope, a religious force not un-known to Christianity. But the deeper resonance of this principle, the effectiveness of the numinous, still remains a mystery to the nonparticipant observer, even though its recurrence as "fundamentalism" seems somewhat clearer once we have investigated the case of the Nakshibendi.

The Nakshibendi and Other Constellations of Turkish Revivalism

Nakshibendi "fundamentalism" is difficult enough to define: only in its ability to adapt to modern conditions while preserving a stable ideological core does its nature begin to emerge. But this is not the only difficulty one encounters in gauging its influence. The mujaddidi-Halidi-Nakshibendi "trunk" has given rise to a number of offshoots which have gone their own way. In Turkey in the early 1990s one finds a constellation of Nakshibendi subgroups. This constellation, however, is only one of the religious-revivalistic constellations in that country. It is true that what one could describe as the main Nakshibendi groups, those led by Kotku and Coşan, are the most influential, but one would lose much by not studying the whole gamut of revivalism.

Were one to take such a more general perspective, the larger picture to emerge would consist of three types of revivalist groups: some of these would be seen to retain a sect organization which they inherited from the past and also to operate within the networks that were adjuncts of this century-old organization. The Süleymanci Nakshibendi are representative of such an extremely conservative tendency. Some revivalist groups, the Nurcu and the Kotku-Coşan community, appear to be using both such traditional networks and the new mass media. These groups can be described as moderate-revivalistic. The third group, the more radical-revolutionary fundamentalists, would be seen to take their impetus purely from a set of ideological formulas, "slogans," as one recent author, Ruşen Çakir, has described them. These groups are totally focused on the journals which express their goals.

The Süleymanci group is the follower of Süleyman Hilmi Tunahan, born in Bulgaria in 1888. Constantly dodging prosecution during his lifetime, accused of collaboration with the Nazis during World War II, he established an absolute ascendancy over his followers. He died in 1959. His authority was inherited by his son-in-law, the former parliamentarian Kemal Kaçar, whose activities have scored phenomenal success among Turkish workers in Germany. Cemalettin Kaplan, the premier rabble-rouser among these Turkish guest workers, is the pole of another movement, which, paradoxically, suffers from a lack of clientele within the borders of the mother country, Turkey.

What becomes quite clear when one goes on to the second group is that here the basic structuring force of the community of believers as such has been transformed. It is now increasingly journals and periodicals published by these subgroups that constitute the fields where influence and ideas originate; these journals have assumed the role of organizational centers. A number of examples of this transformation, primarily from the Nurcu, which also seem particularly fissiparous, come to mind. First, Said Nursi's advice to his followers that they should study modern science has resulted in the creation of two dissident periodicals, *Sur* (Citadel Wall) and *Zafer* (Victory). *Sur* attempts to offer its readers an "objective" study of some of the burning religious issues of modern Turkey by opening its pages to intellectuals of the left and, at the same time, devoting each entire issue entirely to one problem. It shows its modernization in its proud command of modern theories of psychology and parapsychology, which it uses to its own ends.[37] In fact, its statistical studies of Qur'anic lettering have transformed a traditional obsession with numerology into a pseudoscientific project.

A Nurcu offshoot with real intellectual distinction was *Girişim*, published by Mehmet Metiner between 1985 and 1990. Its fare consisted of a mix of critical theory, radical rebellion against a "soft" Islam, and the percipient use of Western sociology, which gave it a prominent place among the younger generation of Muslim intellectuals.

Similarly radical in its tendencies but more conservative in its worldview has been

Dava (The Cause), whose main theme is that the Nurcu of the Yeni Asya–Yeni Nesil group have betrayed their Muslim principles by supporting political parties. For *Dava* there exists only one party, the party of the Qur'an, a party which will not compromise its principles by "politicking."

A third Nurcu offshoot is the so-called Erenköy group. This group, named after a suburb of Istanbul, is more interested in Sufism than in politics, but its ideas, once more, are expressed not in one-on-one encounters but in the pages of a magazine, *Altinoluk* (Golden Spout). Notice that all three of the cases cited above show that Sufi orders are not immune to the strongly differentiating tendencies of modern society. This is further evidence of the change which, unbeknownst to the sects themselves, has brought modernizing elements into the very foundation of traditional sects.

One of the most interesting constellations of revivalism is the set of groups which are both fundamentalist and revolutionary. These groups are interesting more in their failure to draw a clientele than in their extensive influence. *Girişim* and *Dava* are also radical in their critique of the immobilism of Turkish Islam but are not part of this last tendency since they do not promote revolution. The main revolutionary-radical group is the Turkish Hizbullah, modeled on their Lebanese namesakes. They follow in the wake of Ayatollah Khomeini, although from the beginning of their activities they have been hampered by the strongly Sunni quality of Turkish Islam.[38] Their organs *Istiklal* (Independence), *Şehadet* (Martyrdom), and *Tevhid* (Unity) have tried to bridge the Shi'ite-Sunni gap by running a series of interviews with Shi'ite leaders and panel discussions on Shi'ism. They have taken over Khomeini's formula of a "universal Islamic movement" in their attempt to bring Shi'ite and Sunni together. The most interesting development concerning this group is that it has been accused of having had a hand in the assassination of a prominent journalist in the spring of 1990. According to a commentator they have not had the courage either to confirm or to deny their involvement in the murder.

Fanatically opposed to the Shi'ites, but just as militant as the Hizbullah, are the publishers of the periodical *Ak-Doğuş* (White Birth). With no connections to the traditional Islamic world, they are young, disgruntled lower-middle-class youth whose social profile is strikingly similar to that of the bulk of the Turkish Marxist clientele of the 1970s. Their outlook can be summarized from random sentences taken out of *Ak-Doğuş:* "A strong construction can only be founded on destruction"; and "It is a spiritual truth that to kill has the value of a confirming act."[39] The Ak-Doğuş group was accused of planning the three assassinations of prominent citizens which shook Turkey in the spring of 1990, but their culpability could not be established.

Even taken together, these representatives of "fundamentalism" are mavericks whose influence can in no way rival that of "centrist" Nakshibendis who, as we saw, are themselves divided.

A summary of these influences would underline the fact that as long as Sufi orders and the many more recent spontaneous fundamentalist organizations continue to work as small conventicles, they have a strong ideological impact and gather a clientele of considerable solidarity. Once they appear on the field of national and international politics—which the majority of them have done by deciding to participate in open debate about national issues—they are obliged to bend to organizational imperatives that weaken them as religious organizations but do not transform them into partners on an equal footing with secular political parties.

Acknowledgments

I am especially grateful to Karl Barbir for the use of his study of organizational changes in the Nakshibendi order, as to Professor Irène Melikoff on whose work on the Ottoman Nakshibendi I rely.

Notes

1. J. Spencer Trimingham, *The Sufi Orders in Islam* (Oxford: Clarendon Press, 1971), p. 63.

2. Max Weber, *The Protestant Ethic and the Spirit of Capitalism,* translated by Talcott Parsons (New York: Scribner, 1958), p. 105.

3. Emmanuel Sivan, *Radical Islam* (New Haven and London: Yale University Press, 1985), pp. 24–25.

4. Hamid Enayat, *Modern Islamic Political Thought* (London: Macmillan, 1982), p. 35.

5. Johannan Friedman, *Shaikh Ahmad Sirhindi* (Montreal: McGill–Queens University Press, 1971), pp. 15–16.

6. Annemarie Schimmel, *Mystical Dimensions of Islam* (Chapel Hill: University of North Carolina Press, 1975), p. 117.

7. Ibid., p. 366.

8. Donald Schleifer, *Rhetoric and Death,* (Urbana: University of Illinois Press, 1990), p. 198.

9. Schimmel, *Mystical Dimensions of Islam,* p. 374.

10. Karl Barbir, "From the Muradis to Mawlana Khalid: Leadership Transition in the Naqshbandiyya in Syria, 1670–1827" (Paper presented at the Middle East Studies Association, Toronto, Canada, 1989), pp. 4–5.

11. Ibid., p. 5.

12. Frederik Barth, *Ethnic Groups and Boundaries* (Boston: Little Brown, 1969);

H. Tajfel, *Social Identity and Intergroup Relations* (London, 1982), cited in *Social Science Encyclopedia,* s.v. "Social Identity."

13. Butrus Abu Manneh, "The Naqshbandiyya Mujaddidiya in Ottoman Lands in the Early 19th Century," *Die Welt des Islams* 22, no. 5 (1982): 1–56.

14. Serif Mardin, *The Genesis of Young Ottoman Thought* (Princeton: Princeton University Press, 1962).

15. Gökhan Çetinsaya, "Il Abdülhamid Döneminin ilk Yillarinda 'Islam Birligi' Hareketi, 1876–1878" (M.A. thesis, Ankara Social Science Institute, University of Ankara, Turkey, 1983), p. 63.

16. Smith (1980), p. 136.

17. Irfan Gündüz, *Gümüşhanevi Ahmed Ziyaüddin* (Ankara: Seha Neşriyat, 1984).

18. H. Tajfel, *Differentiation between Social Groups* (London, 1978), cited in *Social Science Encyclopedia,* s.v. "Social Identity."

19. Ibid.

20. *Yeni Asya,* May 1987, cited in Ruşen Çakir, *Ayet ve Slogan* (Istanbul: Metis Yayinlari, 1990), p. 94.

21. *Nokta,* November 1990. It is almost impossible to follow the constant changes in the names of the newspapers published by various Nurcu splinter groups. The group which has adopted Yeni Asya as a name, for instance, has changed a number of times. In this case, personalities seem to be a more constant point of reference.

22. Necip Fazil Kisakürek, *O ve Ben* (Memoirs), 3d ed. (Istanbul: Büyük Dogü, 1978).

23. Ibid., p. 9.

24. Ibid., p. 64.

25. Çakir, *Ayet ve Slogan*, p. 18.

26. Shaykh Mehmed Zahid Kotku, *Cihad* (Jihad) (Istanbul: Seha, 1984).

27. Shaykh Mehmed Zahid Kotku, *Mu'minin Vasiflari* (Qualities of the Believer) (Ankara-Istanbul: Seha, 1984).

28. Ersin Gündoğan, *Gorünmeyen Universite* (Invisible University) (Ankara-Istanbul: Seha, 1989).

29. Ibid., p. 19.

30. Ibid.

31. *Tercüman*, 6 October 1987.

32. Such a party does exist in Turkey, the RP (Refah Partisi [Welfare Party]), but in the last national elections it could only achieve a small representation by forging alliances with other, smaller, parties on the right.

33. *Islâm*, November 1989, p. 32.

34. Halil Necatioğlu, "The Undisputable Value and Superiority of Islamic Scholars," *Islâm*, no. 77, January 1990, p. 6.

35. *Islâm*, April 1990, p. 17.

36. *Islâm*, June 1990, p. 7.

37. Çakir, *Ayet ve Slogan*, p. 114.

38. Ibid., p. 157.

39. Ibid., p. 176.

Hindu Fundamentalism and the Structural Stability of India

Robert Eric Frykenberg

Any discussion about the relationship between Hindu fundamentalism and India's political system as a modern state requires a clear working definition of the concepts "Hindu," "India," and "fundamentalism." Let us begin with the terms "Hindu" and "India." As employed in modern times, they are twins. Both trace their lineage (*vamsha*) from the "Raj"—the imperial system constructed by the East India Company during the late eighteenth and early nineteenth centuries upon foundations laid by the Mughals and rulers of earlier Indo-Islamic and still earlier indigenous empires. Two synchronized processes, structural integration and political mobilization, were involved in establishing the Raj, known as the "Indian Empire." Both required the employment or mobilization of indigenous ("Native" or "Hindu") peoples.

I

India possesses a political system whose structures cannot rest upon any single community, for no community is large or resourceful enough to construct even a regional state. The country has no single permanent majority community and is itself a mosaic of minorities. This being so, no structures with statelike properties can be maintained, and no government can rule over such a construction, which do not depend upon mutual collaboration by minorities. Even most villages, as political entities which endure, are ruled by coalitions of elite communities which are usually minorities. Without such collaboration and "contractual" arrangements (either implicit or explicit), no political system can survive for long.

Accordingly, no feature of the political systems of the subcontinent has been more decisive than the conflicting nature of primary loyalty and obligation. The loyalty of the ruled, including those who have served, or who have simply submitted to, powerful persons or institutions has often been severely circumscribed. Relationships of obligation to institutions and structures of "higher authority" have thus been exceedingly fragile. At its deepest level, this peculiar feature of Indian history and politics has arisen out of differing cultural, ethical, and religious convictions about the nature of reality and thus about the demands which can be made upon those who hold profoundly differing convictions. In India, the ultimate tests of obligation have been found in bonds of community and custom, which are seen as the embodiment of divine as well as domestic law. Obligation has also been formalized in the individual's relationship to basic sociopolitical institutions, especially in times of the construction of extensive state systems.

Tension has arisen continually between different kinds of loyalty and obligation—between bonds of blood, bonds of belief, and bonds of contract—with conflicting obligations and loyalties intermingling in intricate and complex ways. Family and community ties have maintained their own special kinds of cultural, ethnic, and ritual distinctiveness. Bonds of custom and contract have rarely been harmoniously integrated or linked together in larger structures so as to be taken for granted. Such linkages within political systems, no matter what their size, have never been stable features of Indian society. To the contrary, conditions of loyalty and obligation within power structures of increasing size or sophistication have become circumscribed and constrained, resting like a house of cards upon carefully balanced bonds of personal or "communal" contract.[1]

In the plural ethnic, ideological, political, and religious environments which make up India as a state, each birth group (caste or community) sees itself as unique and inherently distinct from thousands of other separate communities. Thus each birth group has gone to extraordinary lengths to preserve its own separateness and status in the world. For the sake of all that was sacred and treasured in their sense of identity and ritual purity, members of a given birth group were not allowed to intermarry (even to interdine) with members of other groups. No overlord or supreme ruler could afford to disregard this sense of primary identity and primary loyalty. To violate customs linked to "birth" or "caste" was to put one's entire regime at risk, especially in times of great upheaval and realignment. Crucial to the stability and the survival of any state, raj, or regime was the loyalty of its own retainers, servants, and tributary supporters. Such loyalty could be ensured only by paying scrupulous attention to those rituals by which each birth group preserved its distinct identity.

This situation is as prevalent within the subcontinent today as it was when Alexander marched into the Punjab in 326 B.C.E. The logic of loyalty is strikingly consistent whether one is studying the lessons of the great epics such as the Mahabharata and the Ramayana of North India, which reflect political relationships almost a thousand years before Alexander, or attempting to appreciate features underlying political campaigns conducted in the late 1980s and early 1990s by such national political parties as the Congress (I) or the Bharatiya Janata Party (BJP), or by regionally strong parties in Assam, Bengal, or Punjab. The issue of the limits of primary loyalty and the nature of obligation remains salient.

The Raj, as it evolved, was a carefully arranged hierarchy of ranked social, political, and religious contracts. The tiniest of dynastic domains, ruling over family members, retainers, and servants and holding sway over cultivated fields (or other tiny territorial resources), was subject to more powerful rulers whose domains covered larger territories; these larger domains in turn were subject to still larger and more powerful families whose rulers held principalities and kingdoms which were themselves subject to rajahs and maharajahs, each in turn more powerful and holding sway over wider and more vast territorial domains until, finally, somewhere at the top, there was some great overlord who ruled, or at least claimed to rule, over all. This was the kind of structure over which the Great Mughals held sway. The historical and metaphorical paradigm which neatly depicted this ordered pattern of interconnected contracts—or intricately arranged loyalties and obligations—dates back at least to the time of Emperor Ashoka and was caricatured in the administration, the alliances, and the architecture of Emperor Akbar. This paradigm, sculpted in stone at Konarak and Fatepur Sikri, was the Great Wheel (*Mahā-Chakra*), with its many spokes connecting central hub to surrounding rim. Another model was the Great Parasol (*Mahā-Chatra*), with its overarching canopy, like that of a vast banyan tree, casting its protecting shade across the length and breadth of the land.

Just has Akbar allied himself with elite families in North India, in effect making himself personal overlord of each important caste and community, so the Company's Raj (and, later, that of the Crown and the Congress) entered a matrix of contractual arrangements, making itself into the corporate overlord of each important dynastic or elite community in India. Within these arrangements, conflicts over questions of precedence or rank, over social distinction, over social distance, and over ritual or social purity (and sacred space) are a recurring theme in virtually all the source materials. Reports from various localities throughout India during the last two centuries tell much the same story. Local sources, especially those which probe the incredibly complex varieties of bonding in administrative, military, and political service (as reflected in land grants, bureaucratic appointments, military titles, or religious endowments), are loaded with details of controversies which put stress upon the limits of loyalty and obligation. Such stresses often resulted from too rapid changes in the political culture and the social order that threatened the security and well-being of some small community, or set of communities. The Great Mutiny of 1857 and the assassinations of Mohandas K. Gandhi, Indira Gandhi, and Rajiv Gandhi—events so different in other regards—serve as stark reminders of what happens when contractual bonds holding together the complex social elements composing the body politic are broken and when the logic of political obligation is violated.

The types of issues that have stretched political loyalties beyond their limits are locally perceived grievances, "wrongful actions," that have served to violate bonds of contract held in deeds, engagements, titles, or treaties. These grievances are of incredible and marvelous variety. Any violation of social custom or sacred ritual, especially if its implications might have cosmic or divine significance, could invite dire political consequences. Hence, any change in the use of buildings, conveyances, drinks, foods, garments, hostels, roads, schools, temples, or other kinds of facilities could quickly transgress the limits of loyalty to a regime and put the political stability of an entire state structure into jeopardy. Once limits of loyalty have been transgressed and bonds of obligation broken, events have quickly escalated into protests and these, in turn, have quickly become flash points for explosions of outrage and carnage. Heedless officials have often found it convenient to gloss over such events. Never bothering to explain what happened, they have merely used words like "spontaneous" or "unexpected" in their reportage about the causes of civic and political unrest.

During the Company's Raj, old bonds of loyalty and obligation were undermined by a number of developments, including the consolidation of modern military establishments; the reification of modern religious institutions, including the emergence of an increasingly self-conscious "Hinduism," partly as a by-product of official policies; the development of modern education, together with a vast infrastructure of communication networks (e.g., news, printing, postal/telegraph, and transportation systems); and the evolution of "representative" interests, voluntary associations, and political parties. The Indian National Congress ultimately assumed the role of a third "corporate dynasty" of the Raj (succeeding Company and Crown). Among the significant reactions to the shifts of loyalty and obligation ensuing upon these developments, the one that most concerns us here is the rise of a competitive "communalism" assuming the existence of an ostensible "majority" community, in contradistinction to "minority" communities, and the consequent rise of fundamentalist movements.

Communalism in the contemporary Indian context is a deep, almost visceral form of antagonism and antipathy between communities of differing cultural, ethnic, linguistic, and/or religious identities. Based in part on fear and ignorance of the Other, communalism often gives rise to conflict and violence between Hindus and Muslim or between caste communities and outcaste communities (e.g., Untouchables). Communal troubles between Hindus and Muslims, Hindus and Sikhs, Hindus and Christians, Hindus and Buddhists, and even between different Untouchable communities (striving against each other for the smallest crumbs of precedence in claims to purity) have been common during this century. But no single form of communalist conflict has cost so many lives as that between Muslims and Hindus. "Fundamentalism" thrives within this system as a distinctively extreme reaction to threats to communal identity. It is a militant form of religious separatism in radical opposition to forces of "Falsehood" or "Impurity" which are perceived as undermining the very foundations or "fundamentals" of received "Truth."

Beneath the surface of many conflicts occurring in India today, then, one finds that bonds of political loyalty and obligation, upon which depend the substructures holding the state together, are most at issue. The substructures of the state rest, in the final analysis, upon the confidence inspired by promises. Crucial to the stability of the state system is its role in balancing and mediating relationships between thousands of separate communities. Such balancing and mediating calls for measured degrees of impartiality, neutrality, syncretism, and tolerance. In a land where there had never existed a consciousness of anything vaguely resembling a single "majority community" and where the entire body politic consisted of an intricately arranged mosaic of separate and separately competing minority communities, the role of the modern state has been to ensure that no special favoritism or coalition of interests could become so powerful as to tip the delicate balance of competing interests and thereby threaten the stability of the whole.

Parallel to the development of an all-encompassing state has been the fortification of the notion of an inclusive Hinduism. Romila Thapar, writing about pre-modern India, points out the fallacy of assuming that some sort of inclusive Hinduism existed when "the reality perhaps lay in looking at it as a cluster of distinctive sects and cults, observing common civilizational symbols, but with belief and ritual ranging from atheism to animism and a variety of religious organizations identifying themselves by location, language, and caste."[2] No common sense of community bound the entire population together. Small communities, birth groups, and religious sects—now explained in terms like Brahmanism, Shaktism, Puranic Shaivism and Vaishnavism, and Bhaktism—ranged from "high" or textual cultures to innumerable "low" or popular religious cultures: "Hinduism" was a "mosaic of distinct cults, deities, sects and ideas" adjusting to and distancing themselves from each other. In other words, what bound communities to each other, if at all and then only inadvertently, were the manufactured mechanisms and structures of statecraft. These structures, while supportive of local religious and sectarian institutions, had to remain "impartial," "neutral," or "secular."

II

India's first universal modern state required the construction of a common political identity, something capable of cutting across the countless parochial identities, each hierarchically stratified and each based upon profound convictions about its own inherent uniqueness in purity of birth (sacred blood) and sanctity of earth (sacred soil). The political systems of modern India are more potent than those which preceded them precisely because they are so much more potentially all-embracing—thanks to the advent of technologies leading to systems of mass social communication and rapid transportation. In their range and speed, accuracy, and accessibility, these systems have enabled massive mobilizations on a scale hitherto unimagined. Mobilizations engendered by successive communications revolutions cut across the segmental identities of local elites, enabling appeals (whether based on true or false information) to various sentiments.

The "Hinduism" promulgated by mass mobilizations—the rising ideal of an all-embracing, monolithic "Hindu community"—is, accordingly, a recent development. The notion of one Hindu community became necessary, in Thapar's view, "when there was competition for political and economic resources between various groups in a colonial situation" and "a need to change from a segmental identity to a community which cut across caste, sect and religion."[3] From a tide of socioeconomic, political, and religious reform movements in the nineteenth century emerged a "community" that is increasingly self-conscious about its fears and aggressively militant about its "sacred destiny." It claims the status of sole representative of India's "majority community" and demands loyalty or submission from all other communities in India. This "Hindu community" is the twin of "India" as a state. Both were constructed at about the same time. The new system of loyalty, initially used for the construction of what became an imperial state, has more recently served to buttress what is now a national state. But this system has turned upon its creators in that it has also come to threaten the structures and contracts of obligation that made possible the construction of modern India.

The integrative institutions and processes represented by the terms "Hindu" and "India" first began to take shape during the early years of the Company's Raj, between 1770 and 1820. During the Raj of the British Crown, serious disjunctions began to develop between these parallel sets of processes. Processes of political mobilization accelerated beyond processes of structural integration. The structural strength of the huge imperial/national state was undermined by this clashing disjunction of processes. Fissures in the body politic began to appear in the late nineteenth century.

Three parallel processes contributed to the shaping of the modern religious community known as "Hinduism." One of these was institutional; another was ideological; and yet another was sociopolitical. The first came by government fiat in 1810, just when the term "Hindu" was coming into vogue as a way to describe all things indigenous to India. The Raj, then becoming the first "universal" or "All-India" state ever to hold sway over the entire subcontinent, decided that all religious institutions, endowments, and properties, including all maintenance and ceremonial functions, should be brought under the care, protection, and purview of the state. Thereafter, during the nineteenth century and down to our day, the state administered and maintained all "Hindu" (or "native") religious endowments and charitable institutions—"pukka" temples and temple events, "monastic" academies (*matths*), pilgrimage sites, sacred places, ceremonies, festivals, and much more. The Raj became a de facto "Hindu" (and heavily Brahmanical) Raj.

The second process was scholarly. Inspired by Warren Hastings, the Company's first governor-general (1772–86), "Orientalism" was a joint enterprise of discovery, in which learned Europeans and Indians (Brahman pandits, Muslim hakims, Buddhists, Jains, and others) collaborated. They worked together in recovering and preserving India's cultural heritage, rescuing it from the obscurity and near extinction into which some of it had fallen. This gigantic enterprise, marked by Max Müller's editing of the fifty-volume series *Sacred Books of the East*,[4] found its ultimate apotheosis in the life, scholarship, and political career of Dr. Sarvapalli Radhakrishnan (president of India from 1962 to 1967). Orientalism lent to the newly emerging "Hinduism" an aura of intellectual and philosophical respectability, and, through cultivating the eclectic and syncretistic impulses necessary for the imperial (and national) integration of the state, also provided doctrinally attractive elements, such as tolerance and nonviolence. These elements, unveiled at the 1893 Parliament of World Religions in Chicago, enabled "Hinduism" to gain formal recognition as a world religion.

The third potent process was a mobilizing of local resistance to radical conversion movements begun by Christian missionaries in the eighteenth century. Radical conversion movements became potent and contagious. Reinforced by the two parallel processes described above, radical conversion had a catalytic effect. It inspired the first glimmerings of a fundamentalistic reaction and marked the emergence of a more fully self-conscious "Hinduism" distinct from other religions.[5]

Two more institutional innovations during the late nineteenth century further hastened the social mobilization of a self-consciously Hindu identity. The All-India Census of 1871 introduced a vocabulary of communal, social, and religious categorizations, and conveyed two messages: (1) that all peoples who were not Muslims, Sikhs, Christians, Jains, Jews, or Parsis were, ipso facto, "Hindus"—still a vague label which could be taken to mean either a native of India or someone belonging to the "Hindu" religion (whether a sublime Vishishtadvaita philosopher, a gypsy Banjara, an untouchable Mala, or a head-hunting Sema Naga)—and (2) that "twice-born" communities of "clean" or "pure" birth (i.e., "Aryans") made up little more than 15 percent of the entire population. The Census found that Muslim and Untouchable communities together accounted for nearly half of the population of the Indian Empire (roughly 25 and 20 percent, respectively). Considering that the disabilities of untouchability were so strong—witnessed in economic thralldom verging upon perpetual slavery and in the denial of entry to ritually pure temples—there were grounds for Arya Samaj and other propagandists to raise cries of alarm. The Census clearly showed that to be Aryan might not be enough, in itself, to give these elite communities any clear assurance that the positions of strength which they occupied would be safe in the future. They began to feel that they desperately needed to occupy places of dominance in the top ranks of a permanent Hindu-majority community.

The prospects for democratic and representative local self-government increased after the 1870s, further deepening the fears of a possible future subjection of the "high born." Native Indians were beginning to take seats in parliament and on benches of the High Courts. Generating political strength by mobilizing voter constituencies seemed, to some traditional elites, a threatening wave of the future.

III

The first sign of an openly fundamentalistic Hinduism came with the Hindu Sabha, an association "ardent and watchful in the interest of the Hindu community" that began in the Punjab in 1907. An All-India Hindu Mahasabha came into being in 1915, perhaps partly in reaction to the Muslim League and as an adjunct of the Indian National Congress (which initially allowed dual memberships).[6] By 1920, dismay at the Lucknow Pact (1916) and at Congress concessions on separate electorates, coupled with alarm at the declaration of a pan-Islamic *jihad* by Muslim activists, made the Mahasabha increasingly militant. Gandhi's calling off of his *satyagraha,* or campaign of nonviolent civil disobedience, after the mob killing of police in early 1922 brought further disenchantment. At Benares, Pandit Madan Mohan Malaviya called for "means to arrest the deterioration and decline of Hindus and to effect an improvement of the Hindus as a community." He encouraged Hindus to adopt the martial (*kshatriya*) model of valor and to form martial gymnasiums (*akharas*) for both men and women. Lala Lajpat Rai later declared that Gandhi's tactics could only weaken Hindu solidarity and engender a "slave mentality." As energies were directed increasingly against the Muslim community, Mahasabha activities did little to discourage the spiral of Hindu-Muslim riots which kept mounting in scale, intensity, and violence throughout the 1920s.

Perhaps no single work was more influential upon rising fundamentalistic militancy than that of Vinayak Damodar Savarkar. Entitled *Hindutva* and originally penned at the Ratnagiri jail, his booklet of 1923/24, with its later printings and its English version of 1942, contained the essentials of Hindu fundamentalism. Savarkar proclaimed that Hindus were the original indigenous people of the land and that this people, formed out of the intermingling of Aryan and non-Aryan blood and culture, constituted one single nation (*rashtra*). Whatever a person's community or caste, culture or language, region or sect, a Hindu was one who felt common ties of sacred "birth" and "earth." The "fundamentals" of *Hindutva* were imprinted in genetic codes linking sacred blood and sacred soil (and, indeed, sacred cosmic sound, all knowledge of this stemming from the Rig Veda). Any person was Hindu so long as he could feel the pulse of its timeless "antiquity" and "unity" (*sanghatan*). It was this heritage, this "inner text" as it were, which bound India's people to their sacred fatherland (*pitrubhu*) and their divine country (*punyabhu*). The subcontinent was a "holy land" stretching from the encompassing eternal rivers (Indus, Ganges, and Brahmaputra) which, originating beyond the snow ridges of the Himalayas, watered the sacred soil and flowed down to the meeting of seas at Kanya Kumari. Here, indeed, was the basis for fundamentalism in classic form.[7]

Parallel to the Hindu Mahasabha (in which Savarkar became a central figure, if not cult hero) was the Rashtriya Swayamsevak Sangh (RSS), founded by Kesnav Baliram Hedgewar. A Brahman who had already been involved in national politics for some time, Hedgewar had become disturbed by the lack of any overarching institutions or national solidarity in India and by the deep regional, linguistic, and social divisions which, in his view, had opened the subcontinent to Muslim and British subjugation. He had also become profoundly disillusioned and frustrated by Gandhi's tactics of nonviolent noncooperation and by the principles (*ahimsa* and *satyagraha*) underlying Gandhi's campaigns.

Savarkar's ideas so captivated Hedgewar that he decided to devote his life to restoring the "essential unity" of Hindutva. The only way in which this could be done, he decided, would be to bring about a profound psychological change within individuals. What was required was a movement of total inner transformation, involving each person in a radical conversion of outlook and commitment.[8] A "brotherhood" of true believers, of individuals who could transcend petty antagonisms and parochial disorders, had to be built from scratch. With a cadre of such totally transformed and committed persons, he could then begin to build a totally new organization, something truly revolutionary. The building of such a cadre would depend, he believed, upon the awakening of a self-consciousness and sense of community in young people through rigorous self-discipline.

To that end, special "enlightened" *swayamsevaks* (literally, "self-servants") were carefully selected and recruited. These self-dedicated voluntary participants, chosen before they reached adolescence, were sworn in and trained to serve the cause. Utter *loyalty* and ultimate *obligation* required special "character-building" exercises. Ideological indoctrination and orientation was to be completed at adolescence. Imbued with the Sanskritic ideals of the warrior (*kshatriya*), these young men were to subject themselves to demanding daily schedules of physical, mental, and spiritual exercise. Beyond self-regimentation and self-examination, paramilitary drills (involving *lathi* or quarterstaff training), public indoctrinations, and social services, members were bound by oaths, prayers, and salutes. (Only a relatively small proportion were ever judged fit for a "life oath.") Rituals of fealty were made to the Supreme Sangh Director, to the Sangh's saffron-colored banner, to the Maruti Deva (Hanuman), and to Ramdas Swami (and other saints). Organized into tight *shakhas,* or regimented "branches," swayamsevaks were continually involved in activities: forest camps, weekly discussions, special events, holidays, and other exercises designed to generate devotion to the cause.

The new movement was formally launched in September 1925, at the annual festival of Dasara, which celebrated Rama's victory over Ravana. The first *sevaks,* drawn from an *akhara* (fencing academy/gymnasium) in Nagpur, were Brahmins. Brahmins in that part of India had long been conspicuous as rulers and soldiers. The number of akharas in the area, institutions known for kshatriya lifestyles, jumped during the mid-1920s from 230 to 570.[9] To make sure that the RSS message captured wide attention, uniformed volunteers of the first shakha appeared at the Ram-Navami festival of 1926, singing verses from Ramdas, providing drinking water, and driving away corrupt pandits and priests. When communal rioting broke out in 1927, sixteen RSS squads moved into various neighborhoods to provide protection. Uniformed RSS members then journeyed to Bombay for a session of the Hindu Mahasabha. In subsequent years, networks of RSS branches rapidly expanded, swayamsevak numbers multiplied, and rituals proliferated. Between 1931 and 1939, the number of shakhas grew from 60 to 500, with 60,000 active members (roughly half were Marathi-speakers). By 1929, an elaborate hierarchy of RSS leaders and officials began to emerge. These ranged upward from humble levels of swayamsevaks, ranked by age and tenure, to group or squad leaders, chief teachers, secretaries, celibate staff workers, and city and regional directors. All looked up to the Supreme Guide for ultimate direction and leadership.

Yet, for all his earlier political activism and his regimental style, Hedgewar scrupulously kept the RSS out of politics. His policy of refraining from overt political activities, a feature which did not disappear until after independence, brought consternation, criticism, and disappointment from many Hindu partisans. Savarkar denounced this "purely cultural" emphasis, predicting that the RSS would never accomplish anything significant. Anna Sohani withdrew from the RSS when its uniformed squads were told not to provoke unnecessary violence by marching in front of mosques on Fridays. After all, Muslim paramilitary groups, such as the Khaksars, were also being provocative, as were Sikh and other militant communities. The RSS general secretary, G. M. Huddar, was reprimanded for funding antigovernment activities by means of armed robbery (which landed him in prison); he drifted away from the RSS. While RSS individuals could take part in political actions in their private capacities, they could not do so as members of the RSS. The RSS even refused to support the Hindu Mahasabha's 1938–39 agitations against Hyderabad. As a consequence, relations between the Mahasabha and the RSS cooled and they gradually drifted apart. Refusing to participate in anti-British actions during World War II, even refraining from schemes to militarize Hindus or undermine the loyalty of Hindus within the Indian army, the RSS eventually severed its links with the Hindu Mahasabha.

Hedgewar died in 1940, after a long illness. His place as Supreme Leader was taken over by Madhav Sadashiv Golwalkar. Golwalkar, an ascetic ex-teacher whom Hedgewar had brought into the movement and made general secretary in 1939, was even less political than his mentor. His apolitical style convinced some that he was otherworldly. Yet, blunt and innocent of protocol as he was, it was he who first gave the RSS a systematic ideology. His *We, or Our Nationhood Defined*, published in 1938 (abridging Savarkar's *Rashtra Mimansa*), exemplified the degree of intolerance in RSS fundamentalism that worried other communities:

> The non-Hindu peoples in Hindustan must adopt the Hindu culture and language, must learn to respect and hold in reverence Hindu religion, must entertain no idea but glorification of the Hindu race and culture: i.e., they must not only give up their attitude of intolerance and ungratefulness towards this land and its age-old traditions, but must also cultivate a positive attitude of love and devotion instead. . . . in a word, they must cease to be foreigners, or must stay in this country wholly subordinated to the Hindu nation, claiming nothing, deserving no privileges, far less any preferential treatment, not even citizen's rights.[10]

Since independence, membership in the RSS has grown enormously, despite its being outlawed twice—once for being implicated in the Gandhi assassination (some twenty thousand members were jailed) and again, during the 1975 Emergency, for subversive activities. Gandhi's assassination by a former sevak (Nathuram Vinayak Godse) left the RSS tainted.[11] But Golwalkar devoted his energies to restoring the RSS image. RSS volunteers rendered succor to thousands of refugees after the Partition and after India's wars with Pakistan (1950, 1965, 1971) and China (1962). RSS staff workers were assigned to help Vinobha Bhave in a sacrificial land donation program aimed at getting landlords to give some of their land to the landless. Later, RSS networks were to organize resistance against Indira Gandhi's government during the Emergency. After riding the enormous wave of Hindu revivalism in the 1970s and 1980s that they had helped to generate, the RSS could boast in 1989 that it commanded the loyalty of over 1.8 million dedicated and trained sevaks, bound within approximately 25,000 branches and located in some 18,800 urban and rural centers.

IV

RSS members showed clear signs of frustration at the organization's apolitical stance. This frustration increased with the ban imposed in the wake of Gandhi's assassination (lifted on 11 July 1949). Many felt that, had the RSS possessed political muscle, such a ban would not have been possible. Many also believed that, had the RSS been more active politically, the Partition might never have happened. RSS members blamed the Congress for destroying India's political unity. Thus, after their release from jail in 1948–49, a few elite RSS leaders—Eknath Ranade, Vasant Rao Oke, M. D. Deores, Deendayal Upadhyaya, and others—talked to Syma Prasad Mookerjee about forming a new party. Dr. Mookerjee, then a disgruntled member of the cabinet, already differed with Nehru over relations with Pakistan. A former member and president of the Hindu Mahasabha, he had recently resigned, partly over policy differences in the wake of the Gandhi assassination. Instead of joining Patel and the anti-Nehru forces within the Congress, he resigned from the Cabinet in April 1950 (in protest to the Indo-Pakistan Delhi Agreement) and, in May 1951, joined a large segment of RSS leadership to inaugurate the political party Bharatiya Jana Sangh, becoming its president.[12]

Thus, while the RSS itself stayed discreetly out of politics, at least officially, and strove to recruit and train converts to the Hindu cause, the new party entered the lists to engage in political combat. From the very first, the Jana Sangh, as it soon became known, caught the public eye. This was due, in part, to the personal popularity of Mookerjee but also, in part, to disciplined efficiency, experience, vigor, and organizational skills drawn from the combined ranks of the Arya Samaj, the Hindu Mahasabha, and RSS leaders who entered the political arena as Jana Sangh workers. At no time, it should be noted, was there any formal arrangement between the RSS and the BJS. But, in its roots, the Jana Sangh was a composite creation. Neither the Arya Samaj, the Hindu Mahasabha, the Ram Rajya Parishad, nor the RSS, by itself, in Mookerjee's view, could generate an appeal broad enough to build an alternative to the Congress. But the possibility that a merger of Hindu parties could provide such an alternative ended with Mookerjee's premature death (May 1953) in Kashmir. For the next quarter century, until the Emergency, the Jana Sangh was led into a narrower and more militant path. Its efforts to impose Hindi upon the rest of India and its focus on concerns restricted to the northern heartland provoked regional alienation. Amid ever-shifting alliances and coalitions, the Jana Sangh vision of Hinduism, "inspired by an activist version of Hindu nationalism and, indirectly, by the values of Brahmanism rather than the quietist values of popular Hinduism," was too exclusive and restrictive to appeal to a "national" constituency.[13]

During the late 1960s and early 1970s, the Jana Sangh softened its Hindu voice and turned its appeal toward populism. The "grand alliance" it joined in 1971 was not very successful. Indira Gandhi, victorious in the Bangladesh War, seemed invincible. Moreover, with tactical wizardry, she was able to co-opt opposition appeals on behalf of the poor and to adroitly combine vast patronage powers with the organizational apparatus of the Congress. Eventually, however, arrogance, corruption, and scandal accomplished what no combined opposition had been able to do. In 1974, the Jana Sangh and RSS cadres joined Jaya Prakash Narayan's well-orchestrated "total revolution." The ultimate showdown was precipitated by, among other events, a High Court decision invalidating Indira Gandhi's seat in parliament and Narayan's call (on behalf of a newly formed directorate) for the military to stop obeying "illegal orders." The government cracked down on opposition, declared a state of emergency, and imposed censorship, placing all "subversive elements" under "preventive detention."

Hindu fundamentalism gained strength during the 1975–77 Emergency. Indeed, the RSS underground set the stage for what was to follow. No sooner had the Emergency ended than elections brought India's first non-Congress government to power. This Janata government, formed by Moraji Desai, contained three Jana Sangh members: Atal Behari Vajpayee (External Affairs), Lal Krishan Advani (Information and Broadcasting), and Brij Lal Varma (Industry). From its very beginnings, however, the fragile and factionalized Janata coalition was doomed. RSS influence within the Jana Sangh became an issue. Since Jana Sangh leaders were RSS and since the RSS had made huge gains in membership and public respect during the Emergency, other groups within the Janata Party protested the holding of dual memberships and loyalties by party members. The dual membership controversy, along with petty infighting, contributed to the Janata's disastrous defeat in the general elections of January 1980. Moreover, by blaming the Jana Sangh for its defeat and, in consequence, outlawing dual membership, the Janata Party drove many Jana Sangh members and their allies into forming a new party. Only a rump of the old Jana Sangh, extreme anti-Muslim supporters of Hindu Rashtra, remained behind. The new party, formed by over thirty-five hundred delegates on 5 April 1980, became the Bharatiya Janata Party, or the BJP.

Quite clearly leaders of the new BJP wanted to draw upon the mobilization capabilities of the disciplined RSS cadres. At the same time, however, they did not wish to isolate the party from any potentially broader appeal and thus prevent it from becoming a national alternative to the Congress (I). There was, in consequence, a curious and ironic reversal of roles. Gone was the fiery "abolish poverty" slogan of the pre-Emergency Indira Gandhi. While the new Indira Gandhi and her government became ever more deeply embroiled in the communalism and separatist troubles of Assam, Kashmir, and Punjab, the BJP sought to portray itself, at this time, as less closely linked to the RSS. It was Indira who played the "Hindu card" by inviting a jet-setting sadhu to be her spiritual guide, by making pilgrimages to sacred rivers, shrines, and temples across the country, and by speaking about "Hindu hegemony" in the Hindi heartland. She fomented anti-Muslim fears in Kashmir and turned a deaf ear to Sikh pleas that the constitutional definition of them as Hindus should be corrected. At the same time, she tried to gain control over the Punjab by allowing the release of Sant Jarnail Singh Bhindranwale from prison (October 1981). Unwittingly, in courting Bhindranwale, the militant leader of the Damdami Taksal, she was also courting her own destruction. Bhindranwale took control of the Golden Temple in Amritsar (July 1982), and the incidence of killing escalated. While Sikh swayamsevaks were dispatched to Punjab to convince Sikh militants that the RSS considered them to be part of the "Hindu community," Bhindranwale sought to polarize relations by having gruesome parts of cow carcasses left in temples. For him, Sikhs "could neither live in or with India."[14]

The intensification of the religiopolitical crisis during Indira Gandhi's administration, in part the result of some of her policies, dealt heavy blows to the structural stability of India's political system. The government's anxiety to win "Hindu support," coupled with its failure to satisfy Sikh demands for autonomy, even in a limited way, resulted in turmoil and an increase in terrorism. This in turn led to the strengthening of radical factions within Sikh as well as Hindu fundamentalisms.[15] The Operation Blue Star storming of the Golden Temple at Amritsar on 5 June 1984, for example, led to a spiral of retaliatory violence in which the prime minister herself was assassinated by two Sikh bodyguards (31 October), and over three thousand Delhi Sikhs were in turn massacred at the hands of Congress supporters and "Hindu nationalists." The parliamentary elections held in the aftermath of these events "communalized" the issue of national unity; a blatant form of "competitive communalism" between major parties and a flagrant exploitation of communal "vote banks" contributed to Rajiv Gandhi's landslide victory a few weeks later.[16] The Congress party had effectively co-opted BJP issues and had encroached upon BJP constituencies. Congress even won support from RSS leaders who were worried about ways to check India's disintegration. Clearly, the BJP defeat of 1984 and the advent of Lal Krishnan Advani as BJP president pushed the party into an all-out effort to pursue and reach "Hindu" voters. This strategy required closer relations with other "Hindu" agencies which were part of the rising Hindu tide, agencies such as the RSS and Vishwa Hindu Parishad (or VHP, the World Hindu Party).

V

The Sikhs were by no means the only community to rethink its loyalty to "India." In the 1980s other major communities and segments of the population raised serious challenges and provocations, and Hindu revivalism (*Hindutva Jagaran*) became the most pervasive single political presence in India. But this presence entailed inherent contradictions between reality and rhetoric, between inclusive claims and exclusive demands.[17] Among the organizations which took this contradiction to its farthest limit, none was more persistent in seeking to create a permanent Hindu religious establishment for all of India than the Vishwa Hindu Parishad. The VHP, founded in 1964 by Golwalkar, was yet another sister affiliate belonging to the RSS family. Led by former RSS staffers, it was dedicated to molding a unified Hindu society. It worked mainly through educational, ecclesiastical, and missionary channels, striving to abolish "foreign" ideologies, influences, and institutions and to thwart separatist movements in the country. Prior to 1980, its main activities—setting up schools, clinics, temples, and other vehicles for proselytization—were among "backward," tribal, and untouchable communities. The purpose of the VHP was to block and reverse non-Hindu (Muslim, Christian, Buddhist, or other) influences. In 1981–82, however, an incident occurred which focused attention, aroused concern, provoked consternation, and concentrated minds all over India. This event took place at Meenakshipuram.

Some fifteen hundred Dalits in Tamil Nadu, untouchables who despaired of ever escaping from their centuries of servitude to "clean-caste" overlords, turned to Islam. Their bold and desperate action, widely publicized by the media, was furiously debated. If all of India's tribals and untouchables, amounting perhaps to three hundred million people, were ever to turn Muslim or Christian, the dangers to Hindu Dharm could be incalculable. VHP proponents raised the alarm of "Hinduism in Danger!" and warned that, unless conversions were immediately nipped in the bud and reversed, Hindus might become a minority in their own country. The Meenakshipuram Affair became a symbol of the need to generate Hindu solidarity. A huge campaign under the slogan of "*Ekamata Yajna*" ("Sacrifice for Unity [One Mother]") was launched. Great processions were organized to raise fifty million rupees for the cause, and for reconversion. The month-long campaign, conducted between mid-November and mid-December 1983, mobilized sixty million people and covered 85,000 kilometers, the VHP claimed. Urns of water from the sacred Ganges, mixed with waters from other rivers (all being sacred), were sold to temples along the way. The message of the campaign was clear: Hinduism was in danger, and no danger was more sinister than the possibility of a concerted movement of Muslim and untouchable communities working together.

The next campaign against the "common enemy" was in the north. Few popular symbols possessed more potential for arousing fear, generating hostility, and mobilizing Hindu masses than the "birthplace of Rama" at Ayodhya. The focal point of hostility was the Babri Masjid. This mosque had been built in 1528 with funds contributed by Babur, the first Mughal ruler. Ever since 1853, the site had been an object of contention. In 1859, the government had erected a fence to separate Hindu and Muslim places of worship within the compound. Legal actions by the Mahant in 1885 and 1886 aimed at constructing a temple on the platform. Sporadic attacks and incidents, year by year since 1912, had culminated on the night of 22–23 December 1949: an idol of the Hindu god Lord Rama was installed inside the mosque, riots erupted, and the gates to the disputed premises were locked by the government. In 1955, the Allahabad High Court confirmed a 1951 order from the civil judge allowing the idols to remain. Justice Deoki Nandan Agarwal had declared: "The continued existence of such a mosque-like structure is galling to the Hindu psyche and a matter of national shame."[18] Further suits by Muslim *waqf* (religious endowments) officials asking for removal of the idols failed. The gates remained locked.

The time had come, as VHP leaders saw it in the early 1980s, to convert the mosque into a temple: Lord Rama was still "behind bars" and his place for receiving worship not yet purified. In April 1984, the VHP Dharma Sansad meeting at Vidyan Bhavan in New Delhi issued a clarion call to action. Another gigantic campaign was to be launched: the Sri Ramajanmabhumi Mukti Yajna. Six months later, a huge chariot-cavalcade—actually a motorcade of trucks carrying images of "Lord Rama behind Bars," accompanied by thousands of dedicated *kar sevaks* (official service givers) armed with swords and tridents—left Bihar and slowly approached Ayodhya. The cavalcade was on the point of reaching its destination when the assassination of Indira Gandhi interrupted its progress. Again, early in 1986, matters came to a head. A court refusal to lift restrictions on puja in the mosque was reversed: the Faizabad district judge, on 1 February, ordered the gates to the mosque to be unlocked and, at the same time, forbade Muslims from using the mosque for prayers.

As if the Meenakshipuram and Ayodhya confrontations were not enough, the highest judicial tribunal of the land reached a decision in the controversial Shah Bano case.[19] This case, seemingly so trivial on its surface, stirred deep and explosive emotions. In 1978, the Muslim Ahmed Shah had divorced Shah Bano, his wife of forty-four years, returning her 3,000 rupee (then $300) dowry as required by Muslim community law (Shari'a). This was common practice. But then, the crusty old lady, perhaps instigated by her sons, sued for maintenance. Under section 25 of the Criminal Procedure Code, a magistrate awarded her only 25 rupees per month. When a higher court raised this amount to 180 rupees, her former husband appealed the matter to the Supreme Court of India.

At issue was a conflict between substantive and procedural law. When the legal system of modern India was constructed by European and Indian officials of the East India Company in the 1780s, indigenous substance and alien procedure had been grafted together. Each community's own (civic and domestic) customs and laws were to be respected so long as the general "civic peace" was not endangered and the security of the state not undermined (at which point, as under the Mughals or any previous state regime, the substance of an issue became a criminal matter). But the procedures for determining facts in any court, whether civil or criminal, were to conform to the hallowed principles of English law. There had, however, also been occasions of intrusion into the substance of a community's domestic law, with precedents going back to the early nineteenth century. Various forms of communal or "domestic" violence (infanticide, human sacrifice, the burning of widows, and so forth), for example, had been deemed criminal offenses.

The Supreme Court of India, a bench of five judges whose task was to pronounce on matters of law, ruled that the ex-husband was required to provide support for a wife without other means, and raised Shah Bano's award to 500 rupees. Yet, in pronouncing the law in this case, Chief Justice Chandrachud went beyond his authority and offered an opinion on the meaning of the domestic law of the Muslim community. He declared that the Supreme Court of India's ruling was more in keeping with the Qur'an than were traditional interpretations of the Qur'an made by Muslim *ulama* (religious scholars), as found in the Shari'a. Moreover, the chief justice suggested, the time had come for all communities, irrespective of their own particular beliefs or customs, to be subject to one common code. Clearly, his gratuitous remarks went beyond a mere judicial interpretation of public law.

Muslims of India were not slow to show their distress. Even those Muslims who felt it was time for "progressive" reforms, and who wanted to see modest advances in the rights of Muslim women, were incensed. If agencies and instruments of the state were now going to start interfering with matters intrinsic to the internal government of various communities, something neither the Mughals nor the British had dared and then only at their own peril, then surely the social contract between each community and the state would be weakened, if not negated. The very grounds of loyalty and obligation to India might become null and void. Surely the entire contractual structure of the body politic, as epitomized in constitutional emphasis upon India's secular nature, required more than this. It was one thing to impose a single, uniform "law of the land" and quite another, in so doing, to question the accumulated wisdom of a community's highest religious authorities, as the home minister (Arif Khan) had done in parliament.

The old alliance between the Congress and orthodox Muslims, members of the orthodox Jamiyyat-ul-Ulama (clerics linked to the famous scholars of Deoband), was now in danger. Moreover, Muslims held nearly 150 out of a total of 542 seats in parliament. As VHP extremists spoke of eradicating mosques and erecting temples in their place, and as violence in Ayodhya sparked Hindu-Muslim riots in Old Delhi, Kashmir, and Gujarat, laments about the serious weakening of the Muslim community grew louder. Late in March 1986, a huge rally was held at New Delhi's Boat Club. Nearly a half million Muslims gathered to hear fiery declamations, air their grievances, and voice demands for action.

The Congress-led government was not slow to get the message. As protests grew louder and more massive, Prime Minister Rajiv Gandhi reversed himself and, faced with political realities, introduced the Muslim Women's (Protection of Rights on Divorce) Bill. But this piece of legislation raised another storm. The controversy became remarkable for the careful, penetrating, and sophisticated debate which it evoked. With so much at stake—the essentials of the social order undergirding the political stability of India—the public discourse was impressive and wide ranging. Madhu Kishore, editor of *Manushi* and the most radical and vocal feminist in India, saw the sudden concern for Muslim women by upper-class Hindus as a form of condescension and contempt for Muslim backwardness. Muslim opponents of the bill, orthodox and liberal alike, joined to resist Hindu bigotry and "colonialism." Yet, ironically, when the bill was finally passed a year later (on 6 May 1987), it essentially incorporated the substance of the Shari'a provisions: a divorced Muslim woman would have no right to support from her ex-husband but should receive support either from her own family and relatives or, failing that, from the waqf (local tax-free endowments maintained for charitable or pious purposes). In the meanwhile, the imam of Indore had long since persuaded Shah Bano to withdraw her claim: no individual's opinion had a right to prevail over the accumulated consensus of the community.[20]

VI

The politics of the ensuing five years, from 1987 through 1991, were marked by increasing pressures from Hindu fundamentalists on the political structures of the state. In the forefront of this movement have been the interlinked forces of the BJP, the VHP, and the RSS, with other militant groups such as the regional Bajrang Dal and Shiv Sena also throwing themselves into the fray. Each element in this sometimes awkward BJP-VHP-RSS axis (political party, missionary agency, and training institution) has had its own part to play in a concerted bid to take control of the country in the name of Hindutva. After Advani became BJP president in 1986, there was a grass-roots effort to generate a massive Hindu backlash in response to the escalating violence in Punjab and Kashmir. With attacks upon Hindus and with Hindu refugees fleeing for their lives, the "communal card" was played more blatantly than ever. In political campaigns for the general elections of 1989 and 1991, mounting conflicts and violence over the Babri Masjid–Ramjanmabhumi site and over the "multidimensional challenge of Mandalism" became decisive.

The symbol used by the BJP in the 1989 elections was the Rama Shila Puja. This massive campaign, organized by the VHP and manned by the RSS cadres, aimed to bring "sacred bricks" (*ramshilas*) from every city, town, and village in India, each carrying the Hindu message that the Ram Janmasthan Mandir (Temple of Ram's Birth Place) was being constructed. This huge temple—270 feet long, 126 feet wide, and 132 feet high, with 34,000 feet of floor space, costing fifty-five crores ($5.5 million)—was to have its sanctum sanctorum where the image of Ram now stood, within the mosque. After months of backroom maneuvering and court action, the Shila Puja took place on 30 September 1989. On 9–10 November, a ceremonial brick consecration was held and foundations for the temple were dug. The very next day, however, a delay in construction was announced by the VHP. The general election had been called (for 22–26 November), and a populist National Front manifesto had tacit BJP-VHP-RSS approval. The new government headed by V. P. (Vishvanath Pranab) Singh was a fragile coalition of the Janata Dal with extreme left- and right-wing parties. It could not survive without BJP support. The BJP, with 86 of 545 seats in the Lok Sabha (making it the third largest party), played a pivotal role but remained outside the government.

The BJP's final rupture with V. P. Singh came ten months later. The issues on which they split were Singh's attempt to build a political base out of the alienated, backward, and excluded communities and his unwillingness to consistently support the BJP-VHP-RSS (Hindutva) agitations in Ayodhya. Singh's announcement on 9 August 1990 that he would implement the Mandal Commission recommendations, reserving 27 percent of all government positions for other backward castes (OBCs: untouchables), alarmed struggling elements within the urban upper class. Singh's action seriously challenged the BJP's position. The BJP's Advani faced a major dilemma—oppose Mandal and lose the rural, backward poor or endorse Mandal and lose the urban, upwardly mobile support. His response was to resort to the BJP's most tried and trusty weapon: Hindutva.

The BJP-VHP-RSS syndicate heated up the Ayodhya controversy as never before. The demolition of the Babri Masjid and construction of the Rama Mandir were announced for 30 October 1990. A giant *Rath Yatra* would bring this about by force. Larger than ever, processions throughout the "Hindi heartland" rallied support.

Thirty-six organizations under VHP-RSS flags sent ranks of volunteers to march on Ayodhya. As the "grand progress" entered its final phase, leaving Bihar and approaching eastern Uttar Pradesh, the government attempted to block the caravan. Uttar Pradesh's chief minister, Myalayam Singh Yadav, ordered state security forces into action. Arrests increased each mile, with nearly 200,000, including BJP legislators and party figures, taken into custody, thousands injured, and many killed. On the day of the takeover, tens of thousands broke through police barriers, swept into the site's compound, and planted victory flags on top of the mosque's dome. The police, retaliating with rubber bullets and tear gas, eventually drove the militants away. But public confidence was severely shaken by a "crisis of near unmanageable dimensions, the dreadful fall-out of which [would] affect not just the leadership of the country but the very well-being and stability of the nation."[21]

Singh's uncompromising stand on the issue precipitated his downfall. No sooner had Advani been arrested (on 23 October) than the BJP withdrew its support of Singh. The BJP, VHP, and RSS now refused to have anything to do with him. Someone had to be chosen to defuse the increasingly dangerous situation and to quell explosive forces before matters got completely out of hand. When Congress (I) leaders offered to support a breakaway group, minus V. P. Singh, a group of 60 MPs renamed themselves the Janata Dal (S) and crossed over to join 211 MPs of the Congress (I). Their leader, Chandra Shekar, was asked to form a new government. But this arrangement also was too unstable. It was only a question of time before shifting political sands brought down this shaky coalition. Chandra Shekar resigned on 7 March 1991. Soon thereafter the president of India dissolved parliament and called for a midterm general election.

The time had come, at last, for Hindu fundamentalism to make its national move. If ever the BJP was to have its opportunity to take control, surely it was now. Pictures of "Lord Ram behind Bars" again symbolized the campaign message. A half million supporters gathered in New Delhi on 4 April 1991, and the VHP and RSS publicly proclaimed their full participation, in the name of Hindutva and Ram Mandir. Along Advani's campaign trail, RSS workers set up thousands of banners and posters, manned stalls giving out water, provided jeeps and cars, and organized rallies. BJP slogans called for "Ram, Bread, and Justice!" and large numbers of seat tickets were given to "OBC" and "Harijan" candidates. Concerned about its need to expand its base beyond the "cow belt" of the Hindi heartland, BJP volunteers went into the south, contesting parliamentary seats and seeking support. Playing up polls showing that voters were fed up with corruption and petty squabbles, BJP billboards cried: "You have tested everyone. Give us a chance too!!" At the same time, knowing that the violence at Ayodhya in October had frightened the whole country, the BJP toned down its rhetoric of Hindutva. Emphasizing the unifying role of "Hindu nationalism" as superior to a 'bogus pseudosecularism," the BJP accused the Congress of currying the favor of "minorities," especially Muslims, as exemplified in the Muslim Women's Bill.

The 1991 elections were conducted, however, in the ominous shadow of the assassination of Rajiv Gandhi (by Tamil militants). Again, the BJP failed to gain power over the state. Once more, as in the post-Emergency poll, voters across the land showed a remarkable caution, restraint, and practical common sense. No single party was able to win a clear majority: Congress won 225 seats; the BJP, 115; and Janata Dal, 55. While the Congress "Old Guard," led by P. V. Narasimha Rao, cobbled together another coalition government, however, the BJP's base in the Hindi heartland and Gujarat expanded (at the expense of the Janata Dal), giving the party 33 more seats and 8.5 percent more votes than in 1989. More than that, the BJP gained control of state governments in Uttar Pradesh, Madhya Pradesh, Himachel Pradesh, and Rajasthan.

Clearly, with cohesive and disciplined cadre organization and with support from the VHP and RSS organizations, the BJP is at this writing (mid-1992) in a stronger position than ever. It must prove itself worthy, however, to moderate or "common" voters if it is to be awarded worthy custody of the structural stability of the state. The inability to project an image of political moderation was a factor inhibiting BJP popularity in late 1991 polls. When, in November, the extremely militant wing of the VHP, the Bajrang Dal, stormed the Babri Masjid and began to demolish some of its rooms, this image was damaged. This defiance on the part of BJP leadership, resulting in the arrest of more than three hundred activists, came when the Uttar Pradesh government, under BJP chief minister Kalayan Singh, dragged its feet: a court order forbade the government to turn over three acres at the disputed site to any private group and forbade any new construction thereon. This quarrel within the BJP "family" served to demonstrate that the fiery tonic of Hindutva is potent but can be diluted by inner strife. Quite clearly, the last chapter in the saga of Hindu fundamentalism and its influence upon India's political structures has yet to be written.

VII

The presence of Hindu fundamentalism in India, as epitomized by the BJP-VHP-RSS "family," entails a contradiction between reality and rhetoric.[22] The insistence of these fundamentalists that the concepts "Hindu" and "Indian" are synonymous and interchangeable, and that "Hindutva" alone encompasses all matters—religious or political, social or cultural—lies at the heart of this contradiction. To insist on holding to the original meaning of "Hindu" as "native of India" or "Hindustani,"[23] and to advance the view that all religious associations, beliefs, or customs in India which do not adopt the norms of Hindutva (i.e., Brahmanic, Puranic, Sanskritic, or Vedic norms) are "alien" and "not native to India," is to insist upon something which, on its very face, is not possible. By such reasoning, hundreds of millions of peoples who are Hindus (*adivasis:* aboriginal natives) in one sense are non-Hindus (*adharma:* "irreligious" or "lawless"; and *mlechcha:* "barbarian") in another sense. In this regard dogmatic and exclusivistic inflexibility belies claims to eclectic or syncretistic tolerance. The religious definition of "Hindu" excludes any culture or group in India whose "religious" ("*dharmic*") positions are not properly "Hindutva," as defined by Sanskritic norms.

The political strategy of Hindu fundamentalism's "majoritarian appeal" is a calculation that has paid dividends in a time of economic and communal crisis: it largely accounts for the considerable influence of the BJP-VHS-RSS contingent in electoral politics in the 1980s and early 1990s. By this strategy India's native Muslims, Christians, Sikhs, Buddhists, Jains, Parsis, and numberless other communities (e.g., untouchable communities and tribal peoples) cannot be counted as loyal and true citizens of India. Of course these "non-Hindus," numbering in the hundreds of millions, have lived on the subcontinent and have become a part of its general culture, even though, by dint of birth, they have been seen as impure, inferior, or subject. Majoritarian politics, as exploited by the BJP-VHS-RSS, is thus a recipe for division, suffering, and tragedy. No less than the future structural stability of the political system is at stake in the current debate about India's "destiny."

If we ask what is new about the type of influence exerted by Hindu fundamentalism or about the impact of the BJP-RSS-VHP upon India's structural stability, we can see what is happening either as an attempt to forge a new contractual framework for loyalties and obligations between communities, or as an attempt to impose subservience of all communities to the will of one powerful minority by means of force, intimidation, and terror. The BJP-RSS-VHP position on caste and untouchability suggests that the latter interpretation is closer to the mark. The promise contained in the provisions of the Mandala Commission recommendations would have given "affirmative action" openings to the backward and lowest communities. The consequence of V. P. Singh's support of these recommendations was, as we have seen, an outburst of indignation from upwardly mobile, urban, and middle class communities from the "high born" old elites. After violent demonstrations in which some of their offspring immolated themselves, these elites turned to the BJP-RSS-VHP to help them sustain the traditional places of their communities within the upper ranks and stratas of the traditional social structure of each region. The "fundamentalist message" was filled with menace for any untouchables who might have the temerity to opt for conversion into a religion whose worldview is more egalitarian (e.g., Christianity or Islam) and for any people who might strive to implement the recommendations of the Mandala Commission. But the message was often conveyed in a pious rhetoric implying that there is a *"proper"* place within "Hindutva" for all whose birth is rooted to the sacred earth of India.

The turmoil at Ayodhya brought down the government of Singh. But this might not have happened had the government been strong in the first place. However, because corruption weakened the inner machinery of the once powerful Congress party—the Congress party itself had violated the "logic of power" by which structures of loyalty and obligation are forged within India—it has ceased to be the "corporate dynasty" that it once was (when it took control of India from the British). Until some new, dynamic, and shrewd political leader comes along who can do what Akbar did, what the Company did, and what the early Congress did, structural stability in India will be in jeopardy. All that stands between India and chaotic disintegration is the Constitution—the Rule of Law. But if this structure of laws is now to be increasingly violated, not just in letter but in spirit, one can only begin to imagine how frightening may be the future of communal (and religious) strife. It may simply hasten the tearing apart of the body-politic.

To many in India, the BJP-RSS-VHP position and influence has been disruptive of everything which has provided balance and security to the political system. By its appeal to "Hindutva," to "one nation," to "religion" over "secularity," and to "majority community" dominance, Hindu fundamentalism is more than a militantly defensive reaction in the name of "fundamentals." It is a raw bid for power which, by breaking the delicate balance of contractual support for the political system, risks the destruction of India itself.

While this kind of action may not be unprecedented, the massive scale of communalism being unleashed by the BJP-RSS-VHP axis most certainly is. Moreover, because of this scale of action and of rhetoric released through technologies of mass communication (both through the public media and through the private sale and distribution of audio- and video-cassettes), defensive reactions have come from all communities (religious, ethnic, or regional) which feel threatened. A massive government-supported and taxpayer-subsidized propaganda blitz occurred when the "Hindutva" worldview imbedded within the Sunday-morning "soap-opera" productions of the two popular epics, the Ramayana and then the Mahabharata, was broadcast week after week. This troubled non-Hindutva communities in India, for it hardly seemed to be the impartial action of a government committed to maintaining a delicate balance between many communities.

Election strategies will continue to depend upon which constituencies are being courted. In the Hindi Heartland, fundamentalism may be expected to play well, especially in Bihar or Gujarat or other places in which communal feelings can be inflamed. In Assam, Kashmir, and Punjab, however, this rhetoric is a recipe for disaster, insurgency, and terrorism. Indeed, competitive forms of fundamentalism have been evoked by and are nourished by Hindu fundamentalism. Sikh fundamentalism in Punjab has led to the struggle for an independent Khalistan; Muslim fundamentalism in Kashmir, after long provocation, has led to the driving out of Kashmir of the Brahman and other Hindu communities from its valley; and Christian fundamentalism in South India or in Nagaland, while not yet strident, has also come into being. Communal troubles evoked between clashing Hindu-Muslim fundamentalisms have brought an escalating chain of increasingly violent and widespread riots during the past dozen years. Should any single fundamentalism ever succeed in galvanizing the two hundred million people who have been counted as "untouchable" rather than "Hindutva" for so long, the results would be as tumultuous as they would be unpredictable. The structures of India, like spokes of contractual loyalty and mutual obligation between communities, need to be balanced if the Wheel of State is to remain strong.

Notes

1. Thus, by tradition, to accuse any person, whether prince or peasant, of "*namakharam!!*" (of being "false-to-salt," in breach of contract, or disloyal) was to question that person's integrity and sense of worth. To do so "publicly"—that is to say, in the presence of others, especially in the presence of notables and notables who were "strangers"—

was to inflict mortal insult, disgrace, and shame ("loss of face") not only upon an individual but also upon his family, his caste, and his community or religion. Yet, conversely, to acclaim any person or community as possessing and practicing *"namak-hallal!"* was to offer praise and tribute, if not worship, to truth, integrity, and loyalty.

2. Romila Thapar, "Imagine Religious Communities? Ancient History and the Modern Search for Hindu Identity," *Modern Asian Studies* 23, no. 2 (1989): 229.

3. Romila Thapar, "Historical Realities," in Ramjilal, ed., *Communal Problems in India—A Symposium* (Gwalior, 1988), pp. 82–83.

4. Max Müller, *Sacred Books of the East* (Oxford: Clarendon Press, 1984).

5. The first glimmers of this catalytic reaction can be seen in the 1820s, with the appearance of the Vibuthi Sangam (Ashes Society) in Tirunelveli, the Chatur Veda Siddhanta Sabha (or Salay Street Society) of Madras, and the Dharma Sabha of Bengal. Later in the century, long after the rise of Raja Ram Mohan Roy's Brahmo Samaj (a reform movement strongly influenced by Christian thought) and Ranade's Prarthana Samaj, came much more aggressive movements, such as the Arya Samaj of Swami Dayanand Saraswati and the Nagari Pracharini Sabha—the latter being a militant movement to replace Urdu with Hindi (and Perso-Arabic with Deva Nagari script) in all "public" discourse, but especially in courts of law. These movements, along with the Ramakrishna Society, led by Swami Vivekananda, and the Theosophical Society, founded by Europeans but energized by Brahmin pandits of Adyar and Mylapore, in turn set the stage for more radical "revivalist" movements and militant anti-cow-killing campaigns in Bengal, Maharashtra, and Punjab. By then, in the name of swaraj, some adherents of these movements were turning to terrorism.

6. For those who, all along, felt that the Hindu Mahasabha was not "orthodox" enough or who felt offended by the reformist appeals of the Arya Samaj, there was the Sanathana Dharm Sabha or, later on, the Ram Rajya Parishad (RRP).

7. Here is a radical and militant reaction to certain elements of change and perceived threats from an alien, hostile, modernist, secularistic world which are seen to be inherently contradictory to "the Truth" as found in a literal or strict interpretation of an inerrant body of scriptural text, imprinted in genomes and cosmic sounds of Brahma (stemming from the *Rig Veda,* as conveyed from the mouths of sages or prophets). See Walter K. Andersen and Sridhar D. Damlé, *The Brotherhood in Saffron: The Rashtriya Swayamsevak Sandh and Hindu Revivalism* (Boulder, Colo: Westview Press, 1987), p. 76.

8. For the anatomy of conversion, see Robert E. Frykenberg, "On the Study of Conversion Movements: A Review Article and a Research Note," *Indian Economic and Social History Review* 18, no. 1 (January–March 1980): 121–38.

9. Andersen and Damlé, *The Brotherhood in Saffron,* p. 35.

10. Mahadev Sadashiv Golwalkar, *We, or Our Nationhood Defined* (Nagpur: Bharat Prakashan, 1939, 1947 edition), pp. 55–56.

11. Godse felt that Gandhi had insulted the Hindu Nation, weakened it by advocating *ahimsa,* and, by his fasts, catered to Muslim fanatics. Andersen and Damlé, *The Brotherhood in Saffron,* p. 51 (from a 1969 interview with Gopal Godse by Damlé.)

12. Myron Weiner, *Party Politics in India: The Development of a Multi-Party System* (Princeton: 1957), pp. 190–94 (164–).

13. Bruce D. Graham, *Hindu Nationalism and Indian Politics: The Origin and Development of the Bharatiya Jana Sangh* (Cambridge: Cambridge University Press, 1990), p. 256.

14. Mark Tully and Satish Jacob, *Amritsar: Mrs. Gandhi's Last Battle* (London: Cape, 1985), p. 50.

15. Atul Kohli, *Democracy and Discontent: India's Growing Crisis of Government*

(Cambridge: Cambridge University Press, 1990), p. 4.

16. Ashgar Ali Engineer, "Lok Sabha Elections and Communalism in Politics," *Economic and Political Weekly*, 6–13 July 1991, p. 1649; idem, "The Causes of Communal Riots in the Post-Partition Period in India," in Engineer, ed., *Communal Riots in Post-Independence India* (Hyderbad: Sangam Books, 1984), pp. 33–41; idem, "Old Delhi in Grip of Communal Frenzy," *Economic and Political Weekly*, 27 June 1987, pp. 1649–52.

17. Paul R. Brass, *The Politics of India since Independence* (Cambridge: Cambridge University Press, 1990). *The New Cambridge History of India*, vol. 4, no. 1, pp. 16–17.

18. A. G. Noorani, in Sarvepalli Gopal, ed. *Anatomy of a Confrontation: The Babri Masjid–Ramjanmabhumi Issue* (New Delhi: Viking [Penguin], 1990), p. 59.

19. Engineer, "Old Delhi in Grip of Communal Frenzy."

20. Ainslee T. Embree, *Utopias in Conflict: Religion and Nationalism in Modern India* (Berkeley: University of California Press, 1990), pp. 93–110.

21. *India Today*, 15 November 1990.

22. Brass, *The Politics of India*, pp. 16–17.

23. Robert Eric Frykenberg, "The Emergence of Modern Hinduism as a Concept and as an Institution," in Günther D. Sontheimer and Hermann Kulke, eds., *Hinduism Reconsidered* (Delhi: Manohar, 1989), pp. 30–33.

12

Sikh Fundamentalism: Translating History into Theory

Harjot Oberoi

> There exists a scholastic and academic historico-political outlook which
> sees as real and worthwhile only such movements of revolt as are one
> hundred per cent conscious, i.e., movements that are governed by plans
> worked out in advance to the last detail or in line with abstract theory.
> But reality produces a wealth of most bizarre combinations. It is up
> to the theoretician to unravel these in order to discover fresh proof of
> his theory, to "translate" into theoretical language the elements
> of historical life.
>
> Antonio Gramsci, *Prison Note Books*

> Meanings—whether embodied in actions, institutions, products of labor,
> words, networks of cooperation, or documents—can be made accessible
> *only from the inside.* Symbolically prestructured reality forms a universe
> that is hermetically sealed to the view of observers incapable of commu-
> nicating; that is, it would have to remain incomprehensible to them. The
> lifeworld is open to only subjects who make use of their competence to
> speak and act. They gain access to it by participating, at least virtually, in
> the communication of members and thus becoming at least potential
> members themselves.
>
> Jürgen Habermas, *The Theory of Communicative Action*

Fundamentalism among the Sikhs today is primarily a movement of resistance. While Sikh fundamentalists certainly envision a separate nation-state in the Indian subcontinent, in the last decade much of their energies have been spent in assailing and battling the Indian state. Denied political authority and engaged in constant struggle for survival and legitimacy, Sikh fundamentalists have not succeeded in articulating their vision of the world in any great detail. This lack of an elaborate model, say on the lines of Iranian clerics, of what the world should look like is closely tied to the social origins of Sikh activists. A great majority of them come from the countryside and would be classified as peasants by social anthropologists. Historically, peasants have not been known to come up with grand paradigms of social transformation. Peasant societies are by definition made up of little communities, and their cosmos is invariably parochial rather than universal. To speak of Sikh fundamentalism and its impact is to enter a universe that until recently was largely characterized by marginality, incoherence, and disorder. But as the comforting epigraph from Antonio Gramsci suggests, it is for the social scientist to "translate" what appears to be bizarre and meaningless into "historical life" and theory.

In the present context any efforts to grapple with the raw and embryonic universe of Sikh fundamentalism will be considerably shaped by how we define and deploy the term fundamentalism. I use the term not out of any ethnocentrism or lack of understanding of the historical specificities that made it current in the United States at the turn of the century.[1] The current debate surrounding the term fundamentalism is hardly unique in the conceptual history of social sciences. In the past there have been similar discussions regarding the cross-cultural applicability of terms like feudalism, millenarianism, religion, class, state, madness, and so on. Interestingly, the arguments proffered in defense or rejection have not been dissimilar to the recent intellectual exchanges surrounding the term fundamentalism. Those keen on defending these terms have often argued that there was little scope for cross-cultural comparisons if we did not possess a common pool of conceptual vocabulary. Others opposed to the enterprise retorted that the history of the world should not be inscribed in terms of the Euro-American experience alone, for in doing so one would further enhance the hegemony of Euro-American intellectual discourse.

With this background to the contested nature of our conceptual vocabulary, and keenly aware of how loaded and tainted the term fundamentalism can be, I would like to defend my usage of the term Sikh fundamentalism on three grounds. First, in the Punjabi word *mulvad*, Sikhs possess a term that exactly corresponds to fundamentalism and stands in stark opposition to *adharma*, a Punjabi word for secularism. Although the term mulvad is of recent coinage, resulting from the need to have a Punjabi counterpart to fundamentalism, Sikh journalists, essayists, and politicians, in discussing contemporary religious and political movements, now constantly use the term mulvad, connoting a polity and society organized on the basis of religious (particularly scriptural) authority.[2] Thus, in the Sikh case the commonly voiced objection, that non-Christian religious groups to which the term fundamentalism is applied have no such equivalent in their own lexicon, does not fully hold.

Second, there are strong cultural reasons for adopting the term "Sikh fundamentalism." Much like Protestant church groups in the United States that at the turn of the century insisted on the inerrancy of the Bible and opposed liberal theology, Sikh fundamentalists have no patience for hermeneutic or critical readings of Sikh scriptures. Their scriptural absolutism precludes any secular or rational interpretation of what they consider to be a revealed text. K. S. Mann, a secretary of the Institute of Sikh studies in Chandigarh, notes: "Nobody who has any regard for feelings of the Sikhs, should take liberties to indulge in exercises with the Guru Granth Sahib [the Sikh scripture], literary or otherwise."[3] Similarly, a recent book written by a group of Sikh civil servants questions the use of Western historiography and textual analysis for the study of Sikh history and sacred texts.[4] It is their firm belief that only those scholars who can strengthen the faith and espouse its "fundamentals" should study Sikhism. Daljeet Singh, a Sikh writer who for many years has opposed the study of Sikh religion and history within the academy, protests: "From the point of view of the men of religion, such studies would be limited in their scope, partial in their vision and inadequate as a study of man in the totality of his being and functioning, i.e., of his spiritual and empirical life."[5]

Critical scholarship among the Sikhs is under attack, and those who dare to practice it are under constant pressure to relent or face elimination. On 22 February 1984, Summet Singh, the thirty-one-year-old editor of Punjab's oldest literary journal, *Preet-Larhi,* was gunned down outside Amritsar. His main fault was his independent-minded interpretation of Sikh theology and tradition. More recent targets have been university professors, poets, artists, and journalists. Theoretically, the Sikh community should be guided divinely in all matters and this divine direction is seen to come from the Sikh scripture, which is perceived as normative for all time and in all places. A critical textual analysis of the Sikh scriptures that may introduce an element of historicity and plurality of interpretations, thus undermining scripturalism, would certainly be construed as an affront—one that would bring quick retribution. Jarnail Singh Bhindranwale (1947–84), a key figure in the rise of Sikh fundamentalism, repeatedly reminded his audience that they should not tolerate any form of insult toward the Sikh scriptures and that, where required, Sikhs were morally obliged to kill an individual who dared to show disrespect toward the holy book.

Third, the current Sikh movement, as will become apparent in this chapter, amply manifests many tendencies like millenarianism, a prophetic vision, puritanism, and antipluralism, trends that have been commonly associated with fundamentalism.[6] For these three reasons—linguistic, cultural, and associative—I think we are justified in speaking and thinking in terms of Sikh fundamentalism.

Having said this, I must stress that in Foucault's terms there is no archaeology to Sikh fundamentalism. It is an episteme that is still in the making, and its canon, ideology, objectives, and practices are being gradually defined. In this sense, for all those who are interested in fundamentalism, the Sikh case is of particular value, for here we can clearly see how a group of fundamentalists invent and reproduce themselves in the late twentieth century. Given its relatively recent origins, the success of Sikh fundamentalism has been staggering. In less than a decade Sikh fundamentalists not only established a multitude of relationships with ethnicity, political economy, and nationalism but also eventually came to encompass these materially and conceptually varied conditions. To speak of Sikh fundamentalism is therefore to address simultaneously issues of Sikh identity, the crisis of agrarian development, class antagonisms, and the process of state formation in India, including popular resistance to this process. All this can be phrased in another way: When today large segments of the Sikh population consider who they are, how to live and die, and how to construct the universe they live in, the answers flow out of what may be termed the discourse and ideology of fundamentalism. Why is this discourse so attractive and powerful? What does this cultural innovation promise? I grapple with these issues in this chapter.

The chapter is divided into two parts. The first examines the background of Sikh fundamentalism. What shapes it? While probing the political, religious, and structural conjunctures of fundamentalism, I simultaneously seek a social profile of individuals, organizations, and support groups that are called fundamentalist. As Bruce Lawrence observes in his seminal work on comparative fundamentalism, "There is no fundamentalist movement apart from it constituent members."[7] Having looked at the theoreticians and practitioners of Sikh fundamentalism, particularly in the institutional setting of the Damdami Taksal, I turn in the second part to the vision of Sikh fundamentalists. Here I address two themes: the demand for a new personal law for the Sikhs, and the famous Anandpur Sahib resolution—a document that may be considered the magna carta of Sikh activists. By addressing these two themes we get a glimpse of the world in which Sikh fundamentalists want to live.[8]

The Background

Despite the powerful normative notion of a Sikh collectivity, popularly known in the Punjabi language by the term *panth,* Sikhs are not a monolithic religious community. Much like other religious communities, the Sikhs are divided by geography, ethnicity, social hierarchy, sects, ritual practices, and individual preferences. Consequently, when it comes to political participation, Sikhs have never been represented by a single political party. They have always opted for a wide variety of political platforms, ranging from archconservative to ultraradical.

The first explicitly Sikh political party—the Central Sikh League—was formally established in Amritsar in December 1919. Before the end of the following year the Sikhs had founded two new organizations: the Shiromani Gurdwara Parbandhak Committee (henceforth SGPC) and the Shiromani Akali Dal (henceforth Akali Dal). While the former was technically only supposed to administer major Sikh shrines, it soon turned into an arena within which to wage political battles and to garner social prestige and patronage. Its offshoot, the Akali Dal, initially formed as a body to coordinate Sikh religious volunteers, gradually matured as a political party. By actively participating in the anticolonial nationalist struggle, the Akali Dal gained pan-Indian recognition. Mahatma Gandhi, impressed by the nonviolent agitation of the Akalis, congratulated them for winning the first decisive battle in India's struggle for freedom.[9] Although the growing political influence of the Akalis was often challenged by the Central Sikh League, several breakaway groups, and newly founded Sikh political parties, by the 1940s the Akalis had succeeded in establishing their hegemony among Sikhs.[10] Master Tara Singh (1885–1967), an Akali Dal leader, emerged as the chief spokesman of the Sikhs and formulated Sikh positions on a variety of issues like India's participation in World War II, the demand of the Muslim League for a separate state of Pakistan, and the constitutional parleys when the British decided to pull out of India. When in 1947 the colonial government decided to partition the subcontinent, the Akalis aligned themselves with the Indian National Congress. Thus emerged East Punjab, an entity that was to crystallize into the province of Punjab, one of the twenty-five states of India.

In the euphoria of independence many Akalis decided that their party had outlived its historic usefulness and that it should merge with the Congress, India's national party. However, the merger did not secure every Akali Dal member a place in the sun. The Congress had to take care of its own constituency and could not provide the Akalis with all that they aspired to in terms of policies and political power. Disappointed, many Akali Dal leaders, never shy of hyperbole, incessantly inquired: "The Hindus got Hindustan [out of independence], the Muslims got Pakistan [out of partition], what did the Sikhs get [out of independence or the partition]?"[11]

One dominant response was the call to set up a "Punjabi Suba," a state within the Indian republic where the Punjabi-speaking Sikh population would be a majority. The story of how the Punjabi Suba was finally attained in 1966 despite massive opposition is too well known to be repeated here.[12] What must be noted is that the establishment of the Punjabi Suba completely transformed the religious demography of the Punjab. Overnight, due to a redistribution of territories, the Sikhs turned from a minority into a majority in the Punjab. In the older, larger Punjab from 1947 to 1966, compared to a 63.7 percent Hindu majority the Sikhs constituted only 33.3 percent of the population. The new state of Punjab reversed the older equations. Now the Hindus, with 44 percent of the population, became a minority and the Sikhs a majority with 54 percent of the population of the new state. The Akalis never had it so good. With such a large Sikh electoral base, Akali strategists thought political power was going to be theirs for the asking. After all, they had been the "natural" political party of the Sikhs since the 1920s. In their reading they had always tried to secure the interests of the panth; now it was time for the panth to reward them. Master Tara Singh's oft-repeated claim that "Sikhs were either rulers or rebels" now seemed to have a ring of truth to it. The Sikhs were going to crown the Akalis as the rulers of the new Punjab.

Unfortunately for the Akali Dal, realpolitik proved to be different from the theory of politics. The Congress party, which had governed the Punjab since independence, was not about to let the Akalis walk away with the province. Punjab was too close to the national capital, New Delhi, and invariably what happened in the province had an impact on the neighboring states of Haryana, Himachal Pradesh, and Rajasthan. From 1967 to 1990, a total of twenty-three years, an Akali-led government ruled the province roughly for one-third of the time (approximately eight years and two months). For the other fifteen years the Punjab was either ruled directly by the Congress or put under president's rule. This in practice amounted to unfettered governance by the Congress, since it was the federal ruling party, and it decided on all the policies and key administrative appointments in the province. Two other brief observations need to be added to all this to understand the political process that was eventually to empower Sikh fundamentalists in the Punjab.

First, an Akali-led government in the Punjab could stay in power on an average for only a year and four months.[13] The Akalis' best tenure was from June 1977 to March 1980, a little over two and a half years. This pales in comparison to the Congress. From 1972 to 1977 the Congress, under its leader Giani Zail Singh, enjoyed uninterrupted control over the state. This solid performance by a non-Sikh political party in a Sikh majority state naturally did not enhance the Akali reputation. Second, the Akalis have never secured more than 38.5 percent of the total vote, whereas the

Congress tally in the post–1967 period has been as high as 45.2 percent. Clearly, for some Sikhs the Akalis had badly failed in translating the Sikh demography of Punjab into a permanent political power for Sikhs. In their eyes the democratic option had only further weakened Sikhs, by making them susceptible to factionalism, political manipulation, and extended rule by the Congress. A further complaint was that even when an Akali government ruled the Punjab, it failed to advance Sikh religious interests, because the Akalis almost always had alliances with other political parties, particularly the Jana Sangh, an overtly Hindu political party. A position of compromise and consensus among the Akalis was for some a sure sign of political failure. Disillusioned and angered, some Sikhs were ready to teach the Akalis a few political lessons. After all, the Sikhs had a kingdom of their own in the early nineteenth century and this historical acumen could be once again put to use. The first sign of this came in April 1978, when a group of young Sikh men assembled in Chandigarh and founded the Dal Khalsa.[14]

The founders of the Dal Khalsa justified the founding of the new body by claiming that the government of India had cleverly duped the Sikhs in the name of secularism, when actually all that had happened since India had attained its independence in 1947 from the British was the further extension of "Hindu imperialism" and the enslavement of Sikhs.[15] In support of this thesis Dal Khalsa activists pointed to a series of abuses: Sikhs were not allowed to freely practice their religion, the sanctity of their holy places had been often violated, Akali governments in the Punjab were never allowed to last for the period of their constitutional term, and Sikhs were being economically discriminated against by the federal government, particularly in areas of employment and budget allocations. Harjinder Singh Dilgeer, a founding member of the Dal Khalsa, writes:

It is merely in name that the Akali Dal formed the provincial government in the Punjab several times between 1967 and 1978. In reality the conditions of the Sikhs were getting worse day by day. Sikhs were being discriminated against on every front: religious, political, and economic. Schemes were being devised to destroy Sikh heritage and culture. Every opponent and enemy of the Sikh community received patronage from the Hindus. Everything that would have favored the Sikhs was forcefully opposed by the Hindus. Surprisingly, the Hindus were willing to see improvements in Russia or China, but not so for the Sikhs. When it came to the Sikhs, the Hindus keenly awaited their eventual destruction. Much like the Sikhs, the Punjab province, too, was discriminated against because it was a Sikh majority state. Punjab was denied its capital, Chandigarh, and other Punjabi-speaking areas that duly belonged to it. Power plants belonging to the province were seized by the Congress-led federal government. There exists a virtual moratorium on industrial development in the state. The price control mechanism ensured that everything produced in Punjab sold for less and everything produced outside the province sold for more. The recruitment of Punjabis into the army was reduced, and similarly a concerted effort was made to reduce the proportion of Punjabi speakers in Punjab by sending in large numbers of Hindu migrants. . . . In short, Hindu India used Punjab like a colony. All this was done not for any profound reasons but simply because Punjab is a Sikh-majority state.[16]

For the Dal Khalsa there was from the beginning only one solution to right all wrongs, imagined or real: the establishment of a sovereign Sikh state called "Khalistan." This state was to be a "final solution" for all the political, economic, and religious problems affecting the Sikhs. Except for a few quixotic youth bodies, there were not many Sikhs who wanted to buy into the Dal Khalsa's final solution. This may have dawned on the Dal Khalsa leadership when all twenty of its candidates lost badly in the 1979 SGPC elections. The SGPC had always been considered the first grand step toward power among the Sikhs. What rankled the Dal Khalsa most was the fact that the Akali Dal it so badly detested won 133 out of 140 seats it contested for the general house of the SGPC.[17] The Akali Dal's hegemony over the SGPC was secure. Those who had set out to teach the Akalis a few political lessons demonstrated that they themselves needed some.

While the Dal Khalsa came to contest the Akali Dal's power over the Sikhs from a largely political-secular context, another body, the Damdami Taksal, sought to humble the Akalis on religious grounds. Although the Damdami Taksal was not as miserable a failure as the Dal Khalsa, it succeeded in getting only four of its contestants elected. Its most prominent candidate, Bhai Amrik Singh, who was in the near future to play a significant role in the politics of the Sikhs, lost to a leader of the Akalis.

The spring of 1979 was a moment of pride for the Akalis. Not only had they attained a resounding success in the SGPC elections, but for the past year they had been governing in the Punjab and at last two of their members were ministers in the federal government. But it took less than a year for this sweet success to turn bitter. In early 1980 the people of India voted Mrs. Gandhi back to power at the federal level, and soon thereafter she dismissed the Akali Dal government in the Punjab. When new elections were called in the state, the Akalis lost to Mrs. Gandhi's Congress party. This dramatic reversal in Akali Dal's political fortunes was followed by another serious blow. The Damdami Taksal was on its path to power and by mid-1983 it had its old foe, the Akali Dal, and its leaders on their knees. Month after month, old and tested members of the Akali Dal were deserting their party to swell the ranks of Jarnail Singh Bhindranwale, the charismatic leader of the Damdami Taksal. Political observers are still trying to solve this puzzle. There is nothing within the paradigm of institutional politics that can convincingly explain why an established political party with a history of sixty years would come to the brink of collapse within two years. What is more, besides wrecking the Akali Dal, Bhindranwale also made Punjab ungovernable. The Congress party that was at the time ruling Punjab proved to be totally inept at dealing with the storm troopers inspired by Bhindranwale.

There is an almost obvious nexus between the success of Bhindranwale and the rise of Sikh fundamentalism. To account for this success is to explain Sikh fundamentalism. And any explanation of Sikh fundamentalism has to be made up of two ingredients: the crisis in Punjab's political economy and its articulation by the Damdami Taksal. Before I turn to these two, it would be appropriate to say something about the linkages between fundamentalism and political economy. Those who study fundamentalism in the metropolis, let us say the United States, find the economy to play no role in its contemporary formulations. Anyone who proposes correlations between the economy and fundamentalism sounds almost naive. But fundamentalism in peripheral societies, almost all of them agrarian or only partially industrialized, is certainly different. There it begins to address predicaments that in the metropolis are routinely addressed by the welfare state and its socioeconomic programs. If fundamentalism is to be concretized as an analytical category, it will, much like other social science concepts, apply differently to those on the other side of the North-South divide. The Sikh case is a good illustration of this point.

Political Economy and Sikh Subjectivity

There is no denying the fact that the nature of the contemporary Sikh polity is closely tied to the social and economic transformations undergone by the province of Punjab over the last three decades. Punjab, one of the smallest states in the Indian union, is primarily an agrarian economy, and almost 80 percent of the Sikh population lives here. In 1988–89 over 48.6 percent of the state domestic product was derived from agriculture and livestock, and the same sector generated employment for 59.1 percent of the total labor force.[18] Following the capitalist path of development, the accelerated growth in the agrarian sector made Punjab the first region in South Asia to experience what is commonly known as the "Green Revolution." The social costs of such agrarian innovation have been extremely high, and Punjabi society over the last two decades has become highly polarized.

The benefits of agrarian development have primarily accrued to those sectors of rural society which already possessed substantial resources like land and capital.[19] By successfully harnessing their resources to high-yielding varieties (HYV) of seeds and modern technology, the rich cultivators were able to produce large surpluses and further expand their resources, particularly land, the key economic input in Punjab. In 1970–71, rich cultivators having more than twenty-five acres of land constituted 5.01 percent of the total peasantry and operated approximately 27 percent of the land. Within a decade their proportion of land use increased to 29.17 percent.[20] In contrast to rich cultivators, small and marginal farmers have fared poorly in the Green Revolution. They are faced with a situation where their small land holdings, ranging from two to five acres, have increasingly become less viable. A recent study of agrarian conditions in Punjab points out that while small farmers were faced with an annual loss of 125 rupees per capita, farmers with land holdings between five and ten acres were earning a profit of 50 rupees per capita, while substantial farmers with twenty acres of land or more were producing a profit of 1,200 rupees per capita.[21] The negative returns have made it hard for the small and marginal farmers to sustain their family farms. Consequently, in recent years a large number of small holdings have disappeared. According to agricultural census data, from 1970–71 to 1980–81 operational holdings in Punjab declined by 25.3 percent.[22]

Suffering this decline were countless Sikh peasants from the small and marginal sector. As yet it is not clear what exactly has been their fate. In classical models of development those who are dispossessed either join the ranks of the agrarian labor force or turn to jobs in the burgeoning industrial sector. In Punjab there is no such simple transition. The bulk of the small and marginal farmers are from the high-status Jat caste, and even when they find themselves without land to cultivate they are most unwilling to become agricultural laborers. This would imply working in the midst of low-caste Harijans, a clear loss of face for the status-conscious Jats. (The strong sense of egalitarianism of the Sikhs does not easily extend to others, particularly non-Sikhs.) The other alternative—working in the industrial sector—is equally difficult, for two reasons. First, Punjab does not have the large-scale industries which could absorb the depeasantized Sikh cultivators. Second, even where such jobs exist, particularly in medium- and small-scale industries, the work force is made up of migratory labor from the poorer areas of northern India. Given their already depressed conditions, these nonunionized worker are willing to work for subsistence wages for long hours, a prospect which Sikh peasants stoutly resist. Consequently, it is hardly surprising that a recent economic survey found that 24 percent of the small farmers and 31 percent of the marginal farmers in Punjab live below the poverty line.[23] Capitalist agriculture since 1965–66 has not only enhanced differentiation in the countryside but also left those who have been impoverished with what they perceive as nonviable options. They must either descend in the rural social hierarchy or become willing proletarians.

In entering the final quarter of the twentieth century, the Akali Dal, led almost exclusively by rich kulaks, had no solution for the crisis in Punjab's political economy. Parkash Singh Badal, who for a second time became a chief minister of Punjab in 1978 in an Akali Dal–led government, was one of the wealthiest farmers in the whole of India. Many of his cabinet colleagues came from highly privileged backgrounds. For the most part the Akali Dal leadership had prospered from the Green Revolution, and they were unconcerned about those who had lost out in the process.[24] Ronald Herring is quite correct when in analyzing the issue of redistributive justice in rural India he observes: "How can fundamental structural change be effected through the very institutions that service and reproduce the existing society and reflect the existing distribution of power and privilege?"[25] However, in all fairness to the Akali Dal, it must be acknowledged that the Akalis are part of the general political malaise in the country. India, a social democracy enamored of socialism, has never jettisoned capitalism. This hybrid model of development has only exacerbated poverty and social unrest. In this context the Akali failure to deal with the social inequities in Punjab was perhaps no greater than, say, that of Congress regimes in other provinces across northern India. But while provincial governments in the rest of the country could more easily gloss over the pervasive socioeconomic problems and their long-term failure to alter the situation, the Akalis had no such luck. They were faced with a rural electorate that had often been mobilized and had a bloody history of radical, religious solutions.

The rising tide of inequalities in the Punjab did not easily blend with the dominant ethos of Sikh religious tradition, which demands a just moral economy based on an equitable distribution of wealth and resources. From its inception in the early sixteenth century, Sikh discourse has sought the creation of an egalitarian society where all men, if not all women, would be equal and share the ritual, sacred, profane, and economic resources collectively. The appeal of such teachings was considerable in a society where the organizing ideology gave open recognition to principles of human inequality, expressed in the caste system. Over a period of roughly three centuries the Sikh movement launched an offensive against the theory and practice of the "Hindu" social structure, particularly its acceptance of the notion that inequality was inherent in the human condition. It set up the institution of the *sangat* (congregation) and *langar* (communal consumption) to combat social distinctions and molded a collectivity called the *panth*. The practitioner of faith had equal access to the holy scripture, and there was no institutional priesthood that could act as the sole custodian of the Sikh holy book. During the eighteenth century, Sikh militants further sought to implement the egalitarian paradigm of Sikhism. The Sikh movement attracted the rural poor, the urban underprivileged, and others who persisted on the margins of Punjabi society. No efforts were spared by the peasant armies of the Sikhs to destroy all modes of authority, all order, and all mechanisms of social control. They succeeded in doing away with a whole range of intermediaries, those who extracted the much-hated land revenues for the state and often acted as instruments of oppression. Large estates were dissolved, and the lands distributed to the peasantry.

Only by recognizing this egalitarian impulse within the Sikh tradition can we make sense out of statements like that of the British historian Prinsep that, in the late eighteenth century, Punjab was "ruled by seventy thousand sovereigns."[26] The statement is suggestive of intense notions of equality within the Sikh tradition, where each man considered himself equal to the rest and was unwilling to acknowledge any social superiors. George Forster, who toured the Punjab in the late eighteenth century, mentions in his travelogue an incident in which a Sikh told him "he disdained an earthly superior and acknowledged no other master but his prophet."[27] This egalitarian tradition is not confined to the past. Joyce Pettigrew, a Scottish social anthropologist who has lived a long time in the Punjab, in a widely read monograph on the politics of Jat Sikhs, noted among them a strong cultural tradition whereby "they did not regard themselves as subordinate to another person."[28] Obeisance, if any, was owed only to God.

Whenever this egalitarian thrust within Sikhism has been ably voiced, it has demonstrated an immense power to mobilize the faithful and lead them toward the inversion of the status quo, in order to establish a society free of religious and social inequalities. Such an ideology becomes most attractive in periods of intense social change. During the nineteenth and early twentieth centuries under British colonial rule, there were numerous movements within the Sikh community, like the Kukas,

Ghadarites, and Babbar Akalis, which sought to recover the original message of Sikhism and establish a society relatively free of human distinctions. The Sikh past endowed its constituents with a highly developed vocabulary of social justice, and the community had a long experience of social movements that fought for greater social equality.

By the early 1970s then there was a serious crisis in Punjab's political economy that polarized class distinctions. The scope of this crisis was further enhanced by the nature of the Indian nation-state in general and the pro-rich policies of the Akali Dal in particular. While the crisis may have been more easily accommodated in the rest of India, the egalitarian impulse within the Sikh tradition was to make the voice of redistributive justice more compelling in Punjab. All those who perceived their lived experience in this sequence began increasingly to search for solutions. Some were readily convinced of the veracity of the Dal Khalsa's "final solution." Others kept looking. Eventually in the late 1970s they were to shape a body—the Damdami Taksal—that was to articulate their aspirations forcefully and, by challenging the status quo, to turn the 1980s into a decade of Sikh fundamentalism.

Damdami Taksal

Much as the history of modern Sikh politics is tied to the Akali Dal, so the tenor of contemporary Sikh fundamentalism is most forcefully represented by the Damdami Taksal. Earlier in their history the Sikhs went the way of orthodoxy, traditionalism, reformation, and nativism, but it is only with the Damdami Taksal in the late 1970s, almost at the same time as the Islamic revolution in Iran, that a considerable segment of the Sikh population, particularly young males, seized on the powerful discourse of fundamentalism. Given the centrality of Damdami Taksal in forging Sikh fundamentalism, this section examines, first, the history of this organization; second, its worldview, particularly its nexus with a millenarian ideology; and, finally, its social makeup.

Until the early 1970s few Sikhs had heard of the Damdami Taksal (hereafter Taksal). No major work on Sikh religion, society, or history alludes to this body. This obscurity seems to have helped Taksal leaders invent an impressive genealogy. They trace their origins to Guru Gobind Singh, the tenth and final preceptor of the Sikhs who founded the Khalsa order, which, doctrinally and numerically, is today the dominant sector within the Sikh community. In 1706, when Gobind Singh was encamped at Sabo Ki Talwandi (more recently known as Damdama Sahib), he is said to have founded a distinguished school of exegesis. Among those who graduated from this school, in the class of 1706, was one Deep Singh. When within two years the Guru died, Deep Singh kept his instruction alive by establishing the Damdami Taksal. There is much in this putative history that could be correct, but for the moment there is no firm evidence to back it.

For all practical purposes the Taksal comes to the fore early this century under Sant Sunder Singh (1883–1930), a figure of great piety and traditional learning. As if almost to foreclose the rapid socioreligious transformation undergone by the Sikhs during this period of British colonial rule, Sunder Singh like many of his contemporaries set out to purge diversity in Sikh doctrine, ritual, and practice, hoping thereby to engender a uniform religious community. Given his special skills in exegesis, Sunder Singh's strategy to negate differentiation among Sikhs was quite simple: abolish all polysemous interpretations of Sikh scriptures and cultivate a univocal reading of texts, in order to shape a more homogeneous community. Accompanying this strategy was the insistence on a standardized Khalsa code of conduct, or *rahit*. Since many others at this juncture—including the leadership of the influential Singh Sabha and the Akali movement—were engaged in a similar task, the Damdami Taksal under Sunder Singh and his two successors, Sant Kartar Singh (1932–37) and Sant Gurbachan Singh (1902–69), continued to be a minor player in this project to manufacture a monolithic Sikh community.

Eclipsed by history, the Damdami Taksal and its cadres were rescued from potential oblivion by three factors: the political failures of the Akali Dal in post–1966 Punjab, the crisis induced by the Green Revolution in Punjab's political economy, and the zealous teachings of Sant Jarnail Singh Bhindranwale, the new head of Damdami Taksal. The first two of these factors have been addressed at some length earlier in this chapter. The teachings of Bhindranwale have been recently handled with great skill by Joyce Pettigrew, Mark Juergensmeyer, and T. N. Madan.[29] For that reason I will focus on the millenarian element in the oppositional movement sponsored by Bhindranwale, a theme that as yet has attracted no attention in the analysis of contemporary Sikh politics.

Millenarianism is hardly new to Sikhism. Of all the indigenous religious communities in India, Sikhism possesses the most advanced paradigm of millennial thought and practice. For much of their history, at least since the rise of the Khalsa, Sikhs have opted to deal with major social crises—state oppression, economic upheavals, colonialism, collapse of semiotic categories—by invoking the millenarian paradigm. Central to this entire model has been a prophetic figure of extraordinary charisma with the will to establish an alternative social system in which oppression would cease and people would lead a life of harmony, purity, and good deeds. Bhindranwale was heir to this cultural tradition. Perhaps nothing would have come of it without the Green Revolution and the social processes it unleashed. In hindsight it is possible to see how the Sikh past, an expanding network of communications, mechanized farming, and the Sikh identity became inextricably linked in the Punjab of the 1970s. As the first people to experience the Green Revolution in South Asia, Sikhs were confronted with unprecedented change in economy, lived experience, and social relationships. No one had prepared them to handle so much change in so little time. Failed by established political parties, they turned to a messianic leader and his seminary to make sense of a world they had helped create, but one they no longer fully grasped or controlled.

Bhindranwale knew little about economics or parliamentary politics. He turned the complex problems faced by the Sikhs into simple homilies. In his worldview, what I shall call the "Sikh impasse" resulted from the prevalent religious depravity among the Sikhs and the ever-increasing Hindu domination over the Sikhs. As had happened with earlier social movements within the community, Bhindranwale sought a resolution to this new Sikh impasse by invoking the millenarian charter. In 1982 he agreed to participate in the *dharma yuddh,* or righteous battle, earlier launched by the Akalis. Unlike the Akalis, who viewed the dharma yuddh as a politically expedient campaign, Bhindranwale characterized it as an epic war where good was pitted against evil and only one side was to be victorious. His participation in the campaign was fired by the cultural logic of Sikh millenarianism.

During the eighteenth century many a Sikh activist had chanted the following quatrain: "The army of the Guru will sit on the throne of Delhi/Over its head will be carried the umbrella of royalty, and its will shall be done/The Khalsa will rule, their enemies will be vanquished/ Only those that seek refuge will be saved." In February 1984 Bhindranwale echoed that sentiment when he informed a visiting journalist: "I do not want to rule. I would like the Sikhs to rule; rule Delhi, rule the world: Raj karega khalsa, baaqi rahe na koe [The Khalsa will rule, their enemies will be vanquished]. . . . In the next ten years Sikhs will get their liberation. This will definitely happen."[30] Many similar quotes from the speeches of Bhindranwale underscore his unflinching confidence in divine intervention and strong identification with apocalyptic thinking. How else could he believe that the Sikhs, with less than 2 percent of India's population, would rule Delhi or attain liberation within a decade? His refrain, "This will certainly happen," is a hallmark of messianic leaders. As Yonina Talmon notes in a review essay on millenarian movements:

> Perhaps the most important thing about millenarism is its *attitude towards time.* It views time as a linear process which leads to a final future. . . . The transition from the present into the final future is not a gradual process of progressive approximations to the final goal. It is a sudden and revolutionary leap onto a totally different level of existence. . . . The apocalyptic victory will be won by means of a prodigious and final struggle which will destroy the agents of corruption, purge the sinful world and prepare it for its final redemption. Millenarism is thus basically a merger between an historical and non-historical conception of time. Historical change leads to a cessation of all change.[31]

The Damdami Taksal is rooted in the metahistorical time to which Talmon alludes. According to its own version of history, the organization was founded by a cultural hero during the golden age of the Sikhs, the eighteenth century. Similarly, its new cultural hero, Bhindranwale, anticipated a "decisive phase," a new redemptive age for the Sikhs to be dramatically ushered in with the foundation of Khalistan. By casting this new utopia in a religious idiom, Bhindranwale recruited to his ranks a wide variety of people from different economic, cultural, and political backgrounds. But the bulk of his following from 1978 to 1984 was made up of those who were at the bottom of the social ladder. Such a constituency confirms a commonplace in the literature on millenarian movements: in class terms they invariably appeal to the disinherited, the marginalized, and the subordinate. Millennial aspirations are a cultural mode for securing self-respect, social dignity, and economic well-being for all those who lack it, particularly in preindustrial agrarian societies. This too is fully supported by Sikh fundamentalism.

On 26 January 1986, when the Panthic Committee[32] announced the formation of a Sikh homeland called "Khalistan," it issued a short document that stated:

> No individual will be allowed to exploit others [either economically or socially], particularly the backward village community. Profiteering, black-marketing, adulteration and all such other offences and social inequalities will not be tolerated by the Khalsa, which will also not allow mental retardation of any individual. . . . The policy of Khalistan will be as per the Guru's wish of "Sarbat Da Bhala" [welfare of all] and a policy of encouraging a civilized life, of promoting the sense of brotherhood of mankind and a sense of involvement. The segregation of humanity based upon caste, jati [subcaste], birth, locality and colour will not be permitted, and such divisions will be abolished by the use of political power. Likewise, such other cruel and distasteful practices ascribed to social inequality, especially between Sikh males and females, will be removed through the use of political power.[33]

Clearly, Sikh fundamentalists are responding to prevailing socioeconomic conditions in the Punjab and envision a society free of distinctions based on birth, gender, and class. Their social program seeks to invert the existing hierarchies of power and advance the rights of the subaltern over the elite. In the late 1980s and early 1990s Sikh fundamentalist organizations, particularly the Damdami Taksal, convened large public meetings which collectively endorsed resolutions in support of an alternative society. One such popular meeting was held in the spring of 1986 under the auspices of the Damdami Taksal and the All-India Sikh Students Federation.[34] The assembled public enthusiastically supported a *gurmatta* (a collective resolution of the congregation):

> If the hard-earned income of the people or the natural resources of any nation or the region are forcibly plundered; the goods produced by them are paid at arbitrarily determined prices while the goods bought by them are sold at high prices and in order to carry this process of economic exploitation to its logical conclusion, the human rights of people or of a nation are crushed, then these are the indices of slavery of that nation, region or people. Today, the Sikhs are shackled by the chains of slavery. This type of slavery is thrust upon the states and 80 percent of India's population of poor people and minorities. . . . The practice of high and low, casteism and to [sic] orientation towards exploitation and appropriation of other's labour should be stopped in general life and specially in Sikh society. The poor, the weak, the old people, women and children should be fully respected.[35]

Even if this was rhetoric for public consumption, such resolutions endorsed by tens of thousands of Sikhs are a powerful critique of the existing social norms and distribution of resources. The vision of an alternative universe has often proven to be incentive for a people to expend all in pursuit of it, particularly when the world to be ushered in will have none of the drawbacks of the old.

The Vision

The utopia that fundamentalists envision is not a secular one. Its identity is to be defined in terms of Sikh religious tradition. The 1986 *Declaration of Khalistan* stipulates: "The Sikh religion will be the official creed of Khalistan. Further, it will be a paramount duty of the Government to see that Sikhism must flourish unhindered in Khalistan." [36] By proclaiming an official religion for the state of Khalistan, Sikh fundamentalists stand in direct opposition to the present secular constitution of India that guarantees freedom of religious practice. Sikh militants are dismayed by several aspects of that constitution. One is its secular content. Another is its association of Sikhs with Hindus. Article 25, section 2b, states that all public Hindu shrines must be open to all Hindus, irrespective of their caste. [37] The clause includes under the category "Hindu" all "persons professing the Sikh, Jain or Buddhist religion." For Sikh fundamentalists there can be no greater affront than being included among the Hindus. In their view Sikhism and Hinduism are two diametrically opposed religions; there is no common ground between them. Angered by the insensitivity shown to them by the constitution, Sikh leaders in February 1984 took to the streets of major cities in Punjab and publicly defaced copies of the Indian constitution in order to protest article 25, section 2b. Behind this act of defiance stretches a long history of Sikh search for a personal law.

Fortunately or unfortunately, the first principles of Sikhism were never explicitly codified. The little that was formalized during the formative phases of the Sikh movement under the gurus or preceptors could hardly be enforced in the absence of an organized clerical hierarchy. Here a comparison with Islam, the other "great" tradition in the Punjab, may be illuminating. Sikhism has no equivalent to the Islamic Shari'a, which spells out what is permissible and what is prohibited for a devout Muslim. If we may carry the comparison further, in Sikhism there is also no counterpart to the Islamic *ulama,* which always had both a personal and a moral stake in enforcing a Muslim code of conduct and punishing its violation. The closest we come to something corresponding to the Shari'a within Sikhism is the *rahit,* a distinctive code of conduct constructed from oral and scriptural sources and expressed in what has come to be known as the *rahit-nama* (manuals of conduct) texts. These manuals visualized a considerably purified Sikhism, shorn of polytheism, idolatry, and Brahmanical dominance. In addition, they laid down ritual observances, sumptuary codes, and social behavior.

While the Sikh tradition sees the rahit as having evolved from the writings of the Sikh gurus, with additions made by Guru Gobind Singh to its corpus in 1699, recent historical research points in a radically different direction. [38] The bulk of the extant versions of the rahit all appear to date from the nineteenth century, not from the late seventeenth or early eighteenth century as tradition would have us believe. The only exception is the *Chaupa Singh rahit-nama,* which dates back to the middle of the eighteenth century. The complexity of the Sikh rahit is further compounded by the fact that there are, according to one account, eighteen works that qualify as principal texts expounding the rahit.[39] Even when this list has been purged by a rigorous historian, we are left with nine different manuals of the rahit.[40] While they all share certain normative premises, they are by no means a uniform body of literature establishing what may amount to a standard code of behavior. In addition, there is the question of how representative of the Sikh panth these works were. It is not clear in what ways Sikhs over the nineteenth century fashioned their everyday lives according to the precepts laid out in the rahit manuals.

What we have here are different subtraditions evolving within Sikhism, each claiming allegiance and constituents for its own version. The rahit-nama textual materials reflect only the aspirations and worldview of the hegemonic Khalsa tradition and not of the entire Sikh tradition. A single orthodoxy for the entire Sikh community was not articulated until the late nineteenth century; many observers have mistakenly accepted this as the orthodoxy for all times and phases of the Sikh movement. Given the pluralistic nature of the Sikh tradition in the nineteenth century and the absence of a powerful orthodoxy, Sikh cultural, social, and economic transactions were based on Punjabi customary law and, more recently, on Anglo-Saxon law as it evolved during the colonial and postcolonial periods.

This ambiguity is not to the liking of Sikh fundamentalists. They have demanded a Shari'a-like personal law for the Sikhs. Such a demand was put forward in the Akali Dal's forty-five-point charter of demands submitted to the federal government in September 1981. What exactly is to be covered under the rubric of Sikh personal law (hereafter SPL) is still largely undecided. Though there is no agreement, it is possible to gain some idea of what its scope and nature would be from the sermons of Sikh leaders like Bhindranwale and Darshan Singh Ragi, a former head of Sri Akal Takhat Sahib.[41]

The major thrust of the proposed SPL would be to define who is a Sikh. Although such definitions have been attempted in the past, particularly in the Sikh Gurdwaras Act of 1925 and the *Sikh Rahit Maryada* (Sikh personal code) of 1950, these enactments were ambiguous.[42] A liberal reading of them would permit a person to consider him- or herself Sikh without undergoing initiation (the Khalsa *amrit* ceremony) and maintaining the famous five K's.[43] To Bhindranwale one could not be a Sikh without undergoing initiation and upholding the five K's. As head of the Damdami Taksal, Bhindranwale spent much of his time touring the villages of Punjab and exhorting Sikh youth to take *amrit* (baptismal nectar) and be loyal to the external insignia of the faith. He constantly reiterated in his sermons, "Only people without ambiguity in their heart have the right to call themselves Khalsa." The ambiguity Bhindranwale was seeking to redress had to do with contemporary Sikh identity. Under the growing influence of a secular culture many Sikhs in the 1960s and 1970s turned indifferent toward their religious identity. To counter this trend, preachers like Bhindranwale advocated a stricter definition of Sikh identity. A more rigorous definition would clearly distinguish the true believers from nonbelievers, and help prevent Sikh assimilation into Hinduism.

In 1971 when the government introduced new legislation for the management of Sikh shrines in Delhi, the new definition of a Sikh came closer to the ideals of Sikh fundamentalism. Ironically, despite being out of power, Sikh preachers had cast a long shadow on the legal epistemology of the federal government. The 1971 legislation, unlike earlier enactments, identified a Sikh as one who had unshorn hair (called a *Keshadhari*).[44] But a Sikh with unshorn hair is still not close enough to the ideal of a Khalsa Sikh, one who has undergone the initiation ceremony (*amrit sanskar*) and committed himself to live by the rahit. If SPL were introduced, it would do away with the ambiguities.

SPL would also include legislation on marriage and inheritance. At present both are covered by laws that apply equally to Hindus. For instance, although Sikhs have a distinct marriage ritual, for a civil marriage Sikhs are still governed by what is called the "Hindu Marriage Act." Inheritance among Sikhs is decided by the Hindu Succession Act. Sikh fundamentalists do not take governance by Hindu personal laws lightly, as the case of article 25, section 2b, illustrates. They feel their independent religious identity is threatened when they are lumped together with Hindus. A common refrain in Bhindranwale's speeches was that Sikhs had been enslaved by "Hindu imperialism." To support his thesis of Hindu dominance he would often speak about how Sikhs could only be married under statutes meant for the Hindus and how Sikhs had no right to inheritance without Hindu legal precedents.

In addition to distancing Sikhs from Hindus, SPL would also prohibit the use of tobacco and intoxicants like alcohol and opium. If the legacy of Bhindranwale were to fully assert itself, consumption of meat, too, would be stopped. However, not all restrictions would apply equally. The burden of some would be exclusively carried by women. Sikh women would be barred from the use of jewelry, cosmetics, and clothing that exposes the body. In the absence of a *purdah* among Sikhs, the logic of these injunctions seems to be to subject female images and sexuality to patriarchal social control.

The search for a highly univocal identity brought Sikh fundamentalists into direct conflict with groups like the Nirankaris, who have a more ambivalent attitude towards their Sikh heritage. This conflict is not very different from the travails of the Ahmadis in Pakistan or the tragedy of the Baha'is in Iran. Nirankari associations with the Sikh tradition go back to the mid-nineteenth century when their founder, Baba Dayal, tried to introduce a series of reforms in Sikh religious practices and doctrines.[45] He did not make much headway, and, by the time he died in 1855, the Nirankaris had emerged as a sort of sect within the larger Sikh tradition. Their firm belief in a living guru or preceptor, as distinct from the orthodox Sikh belief in a scriptural guru, resulted in an uneasy relationship among Sikhs and Nirankaris. But since their number was small and they never sought to occupy center stage, the Nirankaris were tolerated. Things began to change dramatically in the late 1960s when a breakaway guru lineage among the Nirankaris (popularly known as the Sant Nirankaris) suddenly began to attract large number of followers and the head of the Sant Nirankaris started circulating works that many orthodox Sikhs considered blasphemous. The Sant Nirankaris paid no heed to Sikh injunctions against image worship. They took to worshiping the sandals of Baba Gurbachan Singh, their spiritual head.[46] For Sikh fundamentalists, who were just beginning to assert themselves, the Sant Nirankari issue provided a cause that would bring them public recognition. Sikh preachers began to publicly denounce the Sant Nirankaris as false Sikhs. Some demanded that Sant Nirankari centers be closed and the Sant Nirankaris themselves not be allowed into the Punjab.[47]

Matters came to a head when in April 1978 the Sant Nirankaris met in the Sikh holy city of Amritsar for an annual convention. For men like Bhindranwale, this was the supreme insult. How could the Sant Nirankaris, a reprobate sect, dare to congregate in Amritsar, the center of Sikh orthodoxy? Inflammatory speeches by Sikh religious leaders, particularly Bhindranwale, prompted many among their congregations to take direct action. They marched down to the Sant Nirankari convention center to forcibly stop the proceedings. In the ensuing melee twelve Sikhs and three Sant Nirankaris were killed.[48] Many observers of Sikh fundamentalism date its rise to this bloody clash in Amritsar. Two developments after the clash are worthy of note. First, in 1978 an encyclical (*hukamnama*) was issued from Sri Akal Takhat Sahib prohibiting all Sikhs from any dealings with Sant Nirankaris.[49] In other words, Sant Nirankaris were no longer to be considered Sikhs. Second, the spiritual head of the Sant Nirankaris, Baba Gurbachan Singh, was shot dead in April 1980. His death was followed with the mass killings of Sant Nirankaris in Punjab.

The writings of Edward Said and Johannes Fabian have made us sensitive to the fact that power groups in all societies require an image of the Other in order to bolster their own identity and further their sociopolitical interests.[50] It is by cultivating a profound sense of Otherness that cultural groups promote their notions of superiority, insularity, and incompatibility. Secular and fundamentalist thought does not seem to be very different when it comes to distinguishing "us" from the "others." Fundamentalists, be they Sikh, Shi'ite, or Hindu, always require the Other to sharpen their self-identity and appropriate a higher moral ground relative to their adversaries. A discourse of heightened religious boundaries helps religious groups to gain or retain power.

I have been arguing that the vision of Sikh fundamentalists is closely related to the problem of Sikh identity. Secular public culture in their view erodes morality and religion. To counter this threat, Sikh fundamentalists seek to inscribe their religious identity on all possible cultural resources: constitutions, dietary habits, and the environment of the body. The objective of all this is to leave no lacuna in definition. For Sikh fundamentalists it is ambiguity that breeds atheism, immorality, and denial of tradition. The following statement is representative of such a worldview:

> Retreat from religious and absolute moral values is a world-wide phenomenon and permissiveness, sex-promiscuity, moral laxity and social disintegration is by no means peculiar to India today; the phenomenon is world-wide and ecu-

menical, the reasons for which are deep-seated and historical. Nor is this phenomenon exceptional to modern times. It erupts whenever there is an onset of
decay and deterioration in social cohesiveness and moral vitality of culture or
civilization.[51]

The World to Come: The Anandpur Sahib Resolution

An hour's drive from Le Corbusier's city of Chandigarh, the capital of the Indian state
of Punjab, is the tiny town of Anandpur. Here in 1699, according to tradition, the
tenth and last preceptor of the Sikhs, Gobind Singh, transformed Sikh religion by
founding the Khalsa order. Ever since, Anandpur has been a major center of pilgrimage for the Sikhs; it is one of the five centers of temporal/spiritual authority for the
community. According to the Akali Dal, in the autumn of 1973 the party's working
committee met at Anandpur and approved the draft of a new policy program that had
been earlier prepared by a special subcommittee. This draft proposal was later approved in the form of twelve resolutions at a massive conference of the Akali Dal held
in Ludhiana on 28–29 October 1978 and came to be popularly known as the Anandpur Sahib Resolution (hereafter ASR).[52]

Perhaps no other "text" in independent India has caused so much contention and
turmoil as the ten-page ASR.[53] There are two reasons for this controversy. One concerns the provenance, the other the message, of the ASR. The two are in fact related.
Of the several versions of the ASR in circulation, some are more radical—that is to
say, secessionist—in their implications than others.

Most writers accept the official Akali line on the origins of the ASR.[54] A few are
deeply suspicious. Robin Jeffrey, a political scientist who recently wrote a major monograph on the Punjab, searched in daily newspapers like the Chandigarh *Tribune* back
to 1973 for a reference to the ASR. He found none.[55] This is, to put it mildly, rather
odd, since the Akalis are a leading political party in the Punjab. One would expect a
major party meeting, particularly one which was going to endorse the draft of a new
program, to be reported. These doubts have led some to believe that the ASR was
actually drawn up by the late Kapur Singh (1909–86), long considered the Rahmat
Ali of Khalistan.[56] (Rahmat Ali, a Muslim student at Cambridge, is commonly considered to have been the brain behind the original proposal for Pakistan, a Muslim
nation-state.) Kapur Singh, an Oxford alumnus cashiered from the Indian Civil Service, was the most systematic ideologue behind the idea of a Sikh homeland called
Khalistan. The mystery surrounding the ASR, however, does not end with its origins.

By late 1970s there existed several different versions of the ASR in Punjabi and in
English.[57] The most controverted of these was the one associated with the enigmatic
Kapur Singh. Central to this version was a five-word Punjabi sentence in the political
preamble: "Khalsa ji de bol bale." According to Kahn Singh's authoritative *Encyclopedia of Sikh Literature*, this famous sentence translates as: "The sovereignty of the
Khalsa."[58] Kapur Singh often spoke and wrote that "political sovereignty is the true
desideratum of the Khalsa. Sovereignty is the divine Commandment for the Khalsa,

which might be disobeyed by the renegades, neglected by the weaklings and compromised by the traitors, but which cannot be abrogated or annulled by the mortals. All such powers or organizations that seek so to do commit an act of War against the Khalsa."[59] As far as Kapur Singh was concerned, if the doctrine of Khalsa sovereignty could be fully enunciated and made to gain public recognition, the rest—protection of Sikh religious interests, Sikh separatism, personal law, nation-state—would simply follow. As an avid reader of Lewis Carroll's fables, he was well aware of the following exchange between Alice and Humpty Dumpty:

> "When I use a word," Humpty Dumpty said, in a rather scornful tone, "it means just what I choose it to mean—neither more or less."
>
> "The question is," said Alice, "whether you can make words mean so many different things."
>
> "The question is," said Humpty Dumpty, "which is to be master—that's all."[60]

Kapur Singh, a veteran of Sikh politics, would have heartily agreed with Humpty Dumpty. The agenda for the Sikhs was "to be master—that's all."

Another ASR version, viewed by some as the *Urtext,* demands a "geographic entity" for the Khalsa Sikhs and a "political constitution." Mysteriously this text also had a Kapur Singh inscription—the phrase "Khalsa ji de bol bale." But here the English rendering calls for "the supremacy of the Khalsa" as distinct from "the sovereignty of the Khalsa." This Urtext is much shorter than its subsequent incarnations.

Scholars may have the patience to reason about Urtexten, but others, particularly the political opposition to the Akalis, had no such patience. The federal government was beginning to see the ASR as a document of secession, and no one was sure what the Akalis meant when they said that the goal of their dharma yuddh was the full implementation of the ASR. It slowly began to dawn on the Akali leadership that they had a major credibility problem and they had to do something to settle the controversies that had begun to simmer around the ASR. On 11 November 1982 Sant Harchand Singh Longowal, the president of the Akali Dal, released what has come to be known as the authenticated version of the ASR. Fortunately, the new version was in English, but once again its authors had to grapple with the dilemma posed by Kapur Singh: How were they to render "Khalsa ji de bol bale?" This time the words were rendered as "preeminence of the Khalsa." But this diluted translation was not of much avail in dousing the fires lighted by the older versions of the ASR. In the public mind, particularly outside the Punjab, the political opposition to the Akalis had made sure that the ASR would be seen and read as a secessionist text. On their part the Akalis kept insisting that the ASR embodied the hopes and aspirations of the Sikh people, and simply sought devolution of power by demanding a truly federal system in India.

In 1982, when Bhindranwale became active in the dharma yuddh, he insisted that his major objective was the full implementation of the ASR. Since Sikh fundamentalist groups are still far from capturing political power, it is hard to say how seriously they would take the ASR if they were to become the political rulers of Punjab. If their past pronouncements are any indication, it would play a key role. Thus any discussion of the goals of Sikh fundamentalism would be incomplete without a review of the demands of the ASR.[61] I will refer to the so-called authenticated version released by Sant Harchand Singh Longowal.

In its structure and demands the ASR is hardly different from the election manifesto of a political party in India or any other part of the world. The document is made up of three parts: one religious, one political, and one economic. By categorically separating the religious from the political, the authors of the ASR seem to have been implicitly acknowledging the impact of secular thought. In fact there is little in the ASR that by any definition could be classified as fundamentalist. It primarily seeks a redistribution of powers between the federal and provincial governments so that people at the provincial level can decide for themselves what kind of economic development they want and how best to further their cultural and religious interests.[62] The first resolution of the ASR states:

> The Shiromani Akali Dal realizes that India is a federal and republican geographical entity of different languages, religions and cultures. To safeguard the fundamental rights of the religious and linguistic minorities, to fulfil the demands of the democratic traditions and to pave the way for economic progress, it has become imperative that the Indian constitutional infrastructure should be given a real federal shape by redefining the central and state relations and rights on the lines of aforesaid principles and objectives . . . . The climax of the process of centralization of powers of states through repeated amendments of the Constitution during the Congress regime came before the countrymen in the form of the Emergency, when all fundamental rights of all citizens were usurped. It was then that the programme of decentralization of powers ever advocated by Shiromani Akali Dal was openly accepted and adopted by other political parties. . . . Shiromani Akali Dal has ever stood firm on this principle and that is why after very careful considerations it unanimously adopted a resolution to this effect first at all India Akali Conference, Batala, then at Sri Anandpur Sahib which has endorsed the principle of state autonomy in keeping with the concept of Federalism.[63]

In the economic domain the ASR seeks to rectify the terms of trade that have historically gone against the agrarian sector. It also promises housing for all, an unemployment allowance, an old-age pension, and a minimum wage for agrarian and industrial workers. In short, it seeks to "create means to fulfil all those necessities of a civilized life without which life appears incomplete."[64] Although not hostile to the idea of industrialization, the ASR prefers that all heavy industries be under state control. Similarly, it demands that the entire trade in food grains should be nationalized. With the bulk of the Sikhs engaged in agrarian production, the agrarian bias of ASR is understandable.

In its religious objectives ASR simply seeks the better propagation of Sikhism, a more streamlined administration of Sikh shrines, and the quality training of preachers.

In line with a stricter definition of who qualifies to be a Sikh, the ASR calls for large-scale campaigns to administer *amrit* (Khalsa baptism) and greater emphasis on *rahit* (the Sikh code of conduct). In India the federal government has a monopoly over radio and television broadcasts. Resolution number nine of the ASR seeks permission to install a broadcasting station at the Golden Temple, Amritsar, for the broadcast of religious music and readings from Sikh scriptures. The proposed broadcasting station would be underwritten by the Sikh community.

The world the ASR seeks to construct and for which Sikh militants have been battling since 1982, except for its overt religious diacritics, is not radically different from that of many other groups. In seeking a more decentralized polity, the ASR is in league with many others around the globe who have already articulated a similar disenchantment with all-powerful nation-states. Indeed, a major inspiration behind the ASR seems to be the tensions between the civil society and the state. For the authors of the ASR and tens of thousands who endorsed it, the Indian state has become too powerful and repressive, and there is an urgent need to press for the rights of the people over the exactions of the state. In seeking a greater devolution of power, the ASR embodies emancipatory objectives, and Sikh fundamentalists expect that it will play a key role in recasting federal-provincial relations.

In a way this impact has already been felt. The Memorandum of Settlement signed by Rajiv Gandhi and Harchand Singh Longowal in July 1985, required that the sections of the ASR that deal with center-state relations be forwarded to the Justice Sarkaria commission looking into federal-provincial relations in India. Sikh fundamentalists view this as a triumph for their cause, for the federal government had repeatedly stated that the ASR was a secessionist text and as such could not even be the subject of discussion.

Implementing the ASR, however, is only the first milestone in the world Sikh fundamentalists seek to establish. To fully grasp its nature and underlying logic, we need to turn to other oral and written texts, like the speeches of Bhindranwale and the 1986 Declaration of Khalistan. There is a fundamental chasm between the worldview of Sikh fundamentalists and what Habermas has described as the "project of modernity." A key element in the "project of modernity" has been its separation of the domain of politics from the sphere of religion. It was this differentiation across "cultural value spheres" that Max Weber convincingly used to distinguish modern from premodern polities. This distinction between the political and religious domains is anathema to Sikh fundamentalists. For them religion and politics are inseparable.

In the last decade all shades of Sikh politics—accommodative, intransigent, and millenarian—have been formulated within the walls of *gurdwaras,* or Sikh religious shrines. Sikh ideologues have justified this by invoking the long hand of history. When the sixth Sikh preceptor, Guru Hargobind (1595–1644), was faced with oppression from the all-powerful Mughal state, he proposed two stratagems. First, he commissioned the construction of an imposing tower, Akal Takhat (the eternal throne). This new building was just across from the central Sikh shrine, Harimandir (the Golden Temple), in Amritsar. Guru Hargobind made the Akal Takhat his political headquarters, from which he challenged the hegemony of the Mughal state. The architecture of the holiest Sikh shrine combined the temporal and the spiritual. Second, Hargobind also broke with the convention that the guru should concern himself solely with spiritual pursuits. He tied around his waist two swords, one to symbolize *miri* (politics) and the other *piri* (spirituality). These precedents are constantly invoked by Sikh leaders to justify their practice of the religion of politics. Joyce Pettigrew writes:

> It is the Sikh doctrine of *miri-piri,* the indivisibility of religious and political power, and of the spiritual and the temporal, that gave legitimacy to the political action organized from within Darbar Sahib (the Golden Temple), and which was indeed the organizing principle for that action. . . . *Miri-piri* is indeed so fundamental that it receives material concretization in the *nishan,* or Sikh emblem, in which the double-edged sword representing the purity of faith is shielded by two protecting *Kirpans* (swords).[65]

In the early 1980s Bhindranwale waged his battle against the Indian state from the Akal Takhat. When the government of India finally decided to launch a counterattack in June 1984 the army operation, named Operation Blue Star, succeeded only after blowing up the Akal Takhat. The tragedy in no way altered Sikh perceptions concerning the relation between religion and politics. Possibly, the army action only further strengthened the Sikh resolve to articulate their politics in the idiom of religion. Indeed, the Sikhs have never known a truly secular movement of dissent. Opposition to political authority and the various institutions of the state has always been articulated in religious terms.[66] Whether dealing with the oppression of the Mughal state in the eighteenth century or the economic exploitation of British colonial rule, the Sikhs have always responded with social movements mediated through religion.

Thus the Sikhs have no language of politics free of religion. The categories of thought, the heroic figures, the symbols, the costumes which have motivated Sikhs to react to the demands of the state or come to grips with ongoing social transformations have been of a purely religious nature. The most important qualification for a political leader among the Sikhs is his understanding of Sikh scriptures and his ability to expound on their meaning. It is no coincidence that Bhindranwale, the most important political leader of the Sikhs in the 1980s, belonged to a seminary which instructed Sikh students in the art of exegesis. Politics among the Sikhs is always explained and internalized by referring to the religious history of the panth or by quoting from the writings of the Sikh masters. The vocabulary of political discourse and the goals of society are rooted in perceived Sikh experience. What happens outside that experience is unimportant. It is not from classical models of structural change—the French or the Russian revolution—that inspiration is sought. Nor is there an echo of the Indian struggle for freedom from colonial rule. Rather, political mobilization and the search for justice is solely based on Sikh texts and semantics. In recasting the world, Sikh militants today look to the emergence and consolidation of the Sikh movement for their theory and practice.

But it would be wrong to draw from all this the conclusion that the rise of Sikh fundamentalism was inevitable and a logical result of the Sikh past. Much as it would be oversimplistic to ascribe the rise of Nazism to German tradition, similarly Sikh tradition by itself is no explanation for the formation of Sikh fundamentalism. Fundamentalism is a modern ideology, and while it voraciously appropriates the past, the success of Sikh fundamentalism is to be traced to the massive crisis in contemporary Indian society.

Conclusion: The Impact of Sikh Fundamentalism

I am writing the conclusion to this chapter in late 1991, when the influence of Sikh fundamentalism seems to be stronger than ever before. The last decade in the Punjab belonged in many ways to Sikh fundamentalists. Not only did they define the public agenda within the province, but their impact was felt all across India. One of the main planks in the Congress party's electoral strategy during the 1984 parliamentary elections addressed the threat posed by Sikh fundamentalists to India's security and nationhood. After winning the elections the Congress spent its term in office grappling with the issue throughout the 1980s.

The appeal of Sikh fundamentalism was demonstrated during the December 1989 parliamentary elections. Of the thirteen candidates elected from the Punjab, six were from the Akali Dal (the Mann faction) and two others, elected from Amritsar and Ferozepur, were closely aligned to this party. These eight candidates won largely because of the efforts of the All-India Sikh Students Federation (hereafter AISSF). The AISSF is closely tied to the Damdami Taksal and has served as its political front in the late 1980s and early 1990s. The legitimacy conferred by the fundamentalist Taksal enabled Akali Dal (Mann) candidates to trounce the contestants from the Congress party and from the other two Akali factions—the Badal and Longowal groups.

As the election demonstrated, fundamentalism has become an autonomous and an authoritative discourse in the Punjab; it has subsumed other ideologies, particularly Sikh ethnonationalism. What once was the exclusive preserve of the state and conventional political parties is now being increasingly usurped by fundamentalists. With the broad policy outlines of the ASR as their framework, Sikh fundamentalists take positions on a variety of issues ranging from political economy to federal-provincial relations. In 1991 Sikhs all over Punjab, in increasing numbers, turn to fundamentalist organizations to settle land claims, labor disputes, marital discord, and numerous other collective and personal problems.

The discourse of Sikh fundamentalism is no longer simply rooted in the material conditions of the Punjab. Although these conditions continue to sustain it, fundamentalism is quickly maturing as an ideology and now offers seemingly attractive solutions for the everyday life of both the weak and the powerful. In relating to contemporary struggles fundamentalism tackles lasting questions of freedom, responsibility, morality, will, faith, righteousness, and collective discipline. It envisions a state of its own, where it would reign supreme in both the private and the public sphere and remake polity, economy, and society. Nonfundamentalist Sikh organizations do not possess a grand paradigm of transformation to challenge the religious idealism of the Sikh radicals.

Moreover, the extensive coverage given to Sikh fundamentalists by the print and the broadcast media made people all over India familiar with Bhindranwale and his cause. What registered the most about him and his allies, perhaps, was their ability to bring India under a state of siege. Fundamentalist Sikhs presented a powerful model for those who wanted the attention of the Indian establishment. When one day a definitive study is written on the history of fundamentalisms in India, it will show ample connections between Sikh fundamentalism and similar ideologies among Hindu and Muslim populations. There is an obvious connection, for example, between the Sikh case and the upsurge in Muslim fundamentalism in Jammu and Kashmir, a province neighboring Punjab.

As long as Sikh fundamentalism embodies the resistance of a significant Sikh population to the Indian nation-state, it will remain a powerful discourse. However, fundamentalists themselves have not fared quite as well politically as the message they promote, and radical fundamentalists have poisoned the waters by sporadic acts of violence and the threatened disruption of the electoral process. As mentioned at the beginning of this chapter, much of the dynamism of Sikh fundamentalism to date has been generated by an oppositional stance rather than by the construction of specific programs to remedy the economic plight of dispossessed Sikh workers. The active membership of the Damdami Taksal has always been miniscule, and even today, when it is at the height of its popularity, its cadres do not exceed a few thousand. The 1989 parliamentary election results demonstrated the influence of the fundamentalists, but did not assure their political hegemony. Sikhs voted for Akali Dal (Mann) because it most effectively articulated their resistance to the ruling Congress party and its model of what the Indian nation-state should look like. But only one among the thirteen candidates who won these elections belonged to the Damdami Taksal. Moreover, the Akali Dal (Mann) secured only 30.47 percent of the total votes polled in the elections. Its archrival, the Congress party, was not far behind, with 26.49 percent of the votes.[67] In Rajasthan, where Akali Dal (Mann) contested the provincial elections, all nine of its candidates lost.[68] Numerically, Sikh fundamentalists remain a minority by any count.

What empowers this minority is its trenchant opposition to the Indian state and all those who defy its project, including secularists, communists, collaborators, and those Sikhs who are suspect in their morality. While ideologues of Sikh fundamentalism are still in the process of formulating Sikh "fundamentals," their firm advocacy of scriptural inerrancy makes them quickly attack anyone who proposes a critical textual analysis of Sikh sacred writings. These are now deemed revealed and thus beyond rational discourse. The continued fortification of an absolutist rendering of Sikhism may be necessary for a movement that remains oppositional in nature, but it remains to be seen if such a rendering will inspire the formulation of concrete economic and political reforms.

Acknowledgments

In seeking to understand the nature and dynamic of the Sikh universe under fundamentalist rule, I have tried as far as possible to base my essay on tape-recorded speeches and discourses of Sikh preachers like Sant Jarnail Singh Bhindranwale and Darshan Singh Ragi. Much of this material is only available in Punjabi. Since these speeches were not systematically recorded, they are cited here without any detailed references. But I have all the primary materials cited here on audio- and videotapes. I am grateful to John Garvey, Bruce Lawrence, R. Scott Appleby, Mark Juergensmeyer, Susana Devalle, Gerald Larson, Gurudharm Singh, Joyce Pettigrew, W. H. McLeod, Jerry Barrier, Gene Thursby, and Barbara Jung for their thoughtful suggestions and demanding criticisms. The usual disclaimers apply.

Notes

1. On how the term "fundamentalism" came to be used in the United States and what it encompasses, see George M. Marsden, *Fundamentalism and American Culture: The Shaping of Twentieth-Century Evangelicalism* (New York: Oxford University Press, 1980).

2. For instance, see Kirpal Singh Azad, *Sikh Mulvad Bare* (Regarding Sikh Fundamentalism) (Chandigarh, 1988).

3. K. S. Mann, "Compilation of Punjabi Poetry," *Sikh Review* 37 (1989): 57.

4. Gurdev Singh, ed., *Perspectives on the Sikh Tradition* (Patiala: Siddharth Publications, 1986), especially pp. 3–11. In a review supporting the conclusions of this book, Trilochan Singh states: "The Sikhs are very tolerant and liberal in all matters but they are not so insensitive and stupid dunces as to go on remaining silent in the face of such nasty and malevolent attacks on Sikh historical traditions, doctrines and scriptures on the basis of . . . compulsive skepticism [read critical historical and textual scholarship]." Trilochan Singh, "A Critique of W. H. McLeod's Books on Sikh History, Religion and Traditions," *Sikh Review* 36 (May 1988): 5–18.

5. Daljeet Singh, "Issues of Sikh Studies," in Jasbir Singh Mann and Harbans Singh Saron, eds., *Advanced Studies in Sikhism* (Irvine, Calif.: Sikh Community of North America, 1989), p. 21.

6. I first explored the millenarian and prophetic aspects of current Sikh fundamentalism in my article "Two Poles of Akali Politics," *Times of India,* 1 June 1983, p. 5.

7. Bruce B. Lawrence, *Defenders of God* (New York: Harper and Row, 1989), p. 105.

8. I have avoided the subject of violence, not because it is irrelevant to a study of Sikh fundamentalism but simply because I want to focus on the motives and objectives of the movement rather than its (and its opponents') tactics. Those interested in the problem may wish to consult Mark Juergensmeyer, "The Logic of Religious Violence: The Case of the Punjab," *Contributions to Indian Sociology* 22 (1988): 65–88.

9. Ganda Singh, ed., *Some Confidential Papers of the Akali Movement* (Amritsar: Shiromani Gurdwara Parbandhak Committee, 1965), p. 11.

10. For background on Sikh politics during this period, see K. L. Tuteja, *Sikh Politics (1920–40)* (Kurukshetra: Vishal Publications, 1984).

11. This puzzle is generally attributed to Master Tara Singh. See *Spokesman* 11, no. 27 (1961): 10, quoted in B. R. Nayar, *Minority Politics in the Punjab* (Princeton: Princeton University Press, 1966), p. 102.

12. For details, see Paul Brass, *Language, Religion and Politics in North India* (Cambridge: Cambridge University Press, 1974), pp. 277–366; Joyce Pettigrew, "The Growth of Sikh Community Consciousness, 1947–66," *South Asia* 3 (1980): 42–62; and Robin Jeffrey, *What's Happening to India?* (London: Macmillan, 1986), pp. 36–45.

13. On how the Congress high command has persistently sought to split the Akali Dal and wreck Akali-led governments in the Punjab, see Paul R. Brass, "The Punjab Crisis and Unity of India," in Atul Kohli, ed., *India's Democracy* (Princeton: Princeton University Press, 1988), pp. 169–213.

14. So far two theories have been put forward to account for the foundation of the Dal Khalsa. According to Mark Tully, in *Amritsar, Mrs. Gandhi's Last Battle* (London: Pan Books, 1985), p. 60, and Kuldip Nayar, in *Tragedy of Punjab* (New Delhi: Vision Books, 1984), p. 32, the Dal Khalsa was set up by Giani Zail Singh, a longtime chief minister of the Punjab and later a federal home minister, to harass the Akalis. The other view is that the Dal Khalsa was inspired by Kapur Singh, a veteran of Sikh politics and a leading advocate for a Sikh state. For this theory, see Harjinder Singh Dilgeer, *Khalistan di Tawarikh* (The History of Khalistan) (Oslo: Guru Nanak Institute of Sikh Studies, 1988), p. 307. Although some members of the Dal Khalsa may have been under the influence of the Congress, the later history of the organization does not support the Congress thesis. By the early 1980s the Dal Khalsa was closely aligned with Bhindranwale, and several of its members were involved in hijacking an Indian Airlines plane in order to have Bhindranwale released from prison.

15. I base this statement, and the following observations on Dal Khalsa thinking, on my reading of Satnam Singh's deposition before a Pakistani judge in the case of a hijacking of a plane to Lahore on 29 September 1981. Satnam Singh was a founding member of the Dal Khalsa and also a member of its executive committee. The transcript of his lengthy deposition is reproduced in Harjinder Singh Dilgeer, *Sikh Hijacker* (in Punjabi) (Oslo: Guru Nanak Institute of Sikh Studies, 1989), pp. 130–96.

16. Harjinder Singh Dilgeer, *Khalistan di Tawarikh,* p. 301.

17. For an excellent analysis of the 1979 SGPC elections, see Surinder Suri and Narinder Dogra, "A Study of the SGPC Elections, March 1979," in Paul Wallace and Surendara Chopra, eds., *Political Dynamics and Crisis in Punjab* (Amritsar: Guru Nanak Dev University, 1988), pp. 123–34; and Robin Jeffrey, *What's Happening to India?* p. 138.

18. Figures from *Link,* 10 August 1990; and Sucha Singh Gill, "Contradictions of Punjab Model of Growth and Search for an Alternative," *Economic and Political Weekly* 23 (1988): 2167.

19. How the Green Revolution further enriched rich cultivators is by now well established. There is a vast literature on this theme. For instance, see S. S. Johl, "Gains of Green Revolution: How They Have Been Shared in the Punjab," *Journal of Development Studies* 11 (1975): 178–89; and T. J. Byres, "The New Technology, Class Formation and Class Action in the Indian Countryside," *Journal of Peasant Studies* 8 (1981): 405–54.

20. These figures are based on Sucha Singh Gill, "Contradictions of Punjab Model of Growth," p. 2168.

21. *Punjab da Kisani Masla* (in Punjabi), 13 March 1984, cited in Sucha Singh Gill, "Contradictions of Punjab Model of Growth," p. 2167.

22. Sucha Singh Gill, "Development Crisis in Agriculture and Its Political Implications—an Enquiry into the Punjab Problem," in Paul Wallace and Surendara Chopra, eds., *Political Dynamics and Crisis in Punjab,* pp. 441–42.

23. G. S. Bhalla, and G. K. Chadha, "Green Revolution and the Small Peasants: A Study of Income Distribution in the Punjab," in 2 parts, *Economic and Political Weekly* 17 (1982): 826–33, 870–77.

24. On how the Akali Dal favored rich peasants, see A. S. Narang, *Storm over the Sutlej: The Akali Politics* (New Delhi: Gitan-

jali Publishing House, 1983), pp. 198–99.

25. Ronald J. Herring, *Land to the Tiller: The Political Economy of Agrarian Reform in South Asia* (New Haven: Yale University Press, 1983), p. 2.

26. H. T. Prinsep, *Origin of the Sikh Power in the Punjab* (Patiala: Languages Department, 1970, first published Calcutta, 1834), p. 17.

27. G. Forster, *A Journey from Bengal to England through North India, Kashmir, Afghanistan and Persia into Russia, 1783–84*, 2 vols. (London: R. Faulder, 1798), p. 286.

28. Joyce Pettigrew, *Robber Noblemen* (New Delhi: Ambika Publications, 1978), p. 57.

29. Joyce Pettigrew, "In Search of a New Kingdom of Lahore," *Pacific Affairs* 60 (1987): 1–25; Mark Juergensmeyer, "The Logic of Religious Violence: The Case of the Punjab," *Contributions to Indian Sociology* 22 (1988): 65–88; and T. N. Madan, "The Double-Edged Sword: Fundamentalism and the Sikh Religious Tradition," in Martin E. Marty and R. Scott Appleby, eds., *Fundamentalisms Observed* (Chicago: University of Chicago Press, 1991), pp. 594–627.

30. Interview with M. J. Akbar, cited in his book, *India: The Siege Within* (Harmondsworth: Penguin Books, 1985), p. 185.

31. Yonina Talmon, "Pursuit of the Millennium: The Relation between Religious and Social Change," in Norman Birnbaum and Gertrud Lenzer, eds., *Sociology and Religion* (New Jersey: Prentice Hall, 1969), p. 240.

32. The Panthic Committee, a leading organization within the Sikh resistance movement, was set up in January 1986. Its original leadership was made up of a five-member collective, among whom the most well known is Gurbachan Singh Manochahal. The armed wing of the older Panthic Committee is known as the Bhindranwale Tiger Force. The Panthic Committee also has the support of the Khalistan Commando Force. Sometime in mid-1989 the Panthic Committee split and a new faction emerged under Dr. Sohan Singh, a retired director of health services in the Punjab. This group is widely known as the Panthic Committee (Sohan) and has the support of the powerful and well-armed Babbar Khalsa.

33. Panthic Committee, "Document of the Declaration of Khalistan," reproduced and translated from Punjabi in Gopal Singh, ed., *Punjab Today* (New Delhi: Intellectual Publishing House, 1987), pp. 389–91.

34. The All-India Sikh Student Federation was founded in 1944. Almost from its inception it functioned as a student wing of the Akali Dal. Dormant during the 1970s, it shot into fame in the early 1980s under Bhai Amrik Singh, a close associate of Bhindranwale. Since then it has been very active in Sikh politics, and at the moment there are at least four major factions: (1) Mehta-Chawla, (2) Manjit Singh, (3) Daljit-Bittoo, (4) Gurjit Singh.

35. Quoted in Pritam Singh, "Two Facets of Revivalism: A Defence," in Gopal Singh, ed., *Punjab Today*, pp. 173–74.

36. "Document of the Declaration of Khalistan," in Gopal Singh, ed., *Punjab Today*, p. 390.

37. Article 25 of the Indian constitution stipulates the following:
1. Subject to public order, morality and health and to other provisions of this Part, all persons are equally entitled to freedom of conscience and the right freely to profess, practise and propagate religion.
2. Nothing in this article shall affect the operation of any existing law or prevent the state from making any law—
(a) regulating or restricting any economic, financial, political or other secular activity which may be associated with religious practice;
(b) providing for social welfare and reform or the throwing open of Hindu religious institutions of a public character to all classes and sections of Hindus.
Explanation I—The wearing and carrying of Kirpans shall be deemed to be included in the profession of the Sikh religion.
Explanation II—In sub-clause (b) of clause 2, the reference to Hindus shall be constructed as including a reference to persons professing the Sikh, Jaina or Buddhist reli-

gion, and reference to Hindu religious institutions shall be construed accordingly.

38. For a seminal article on the origin and evolution of the rahit-nama literature, see W. H. McLeod, "The Problem of the Panjabi Rahit-namas," in S. N. Mukherjee, ed., *India, History and Thought: Essays in Honour of A. L. Basham* (Calcutta: Subarnarekha, 1982), pp. 103–26.

39. Kahn Singh, *Gursabad Ratanakar Mahan Kosh,* 4th ed. (Patiala: Languages Department, 1981), p. 1015.

40. W. H. McLeod, "The Problem of the Panjabi Rahit-namas," pp. 110–11.

41. At present there are five seats of religious/temporal authority among the Sikhs. Sri Akal Takhat Sahib at the Golden Temple in Amritsar is one of them. The other four are Harimandir in Patna, Kesgarh Sahib in Anandpur, Hazur Sahib in Nander, and Damdama Sahib in Bhatinda.

42. For a concise examination of these ambiguities, see W. H. McLeod, *Who Is a Sikh?* (Oxford: Clarendon Press, 1989), pp. 93–97.

43. The five K's are: *kesa* (unshorn hair), *kanga* (a comb), *kara* (a steel bracelet), *kachh* (short breeches), and *kirpan* (a sword). Since all the five external symbols begin with the letter K, they are collectively termed the five K's. They are considered mandatory for Khalsa Sikhs.

44. For background to the 1971 legislation and the new definition, see Attar Singh, "The Shiromani Gurdwara Prabandhak Committee and the Politicization of the Sikhs," in Joseph T. O'Connell et al., eds., *Sikh History and Religion in the Twentieth Century* (Toronto: Center for South Asian Studies, 1988), pp. 226–32; and Jatinder Kaur, *The Politics of Sikhs: A Study of Delhi Sikh Gurdwara Management Committee* (New Delhi: National Book Organization, 1986), p. 242.

45. The best work on the Nirankaris in the nineteenth century is John C. B. Webster, *The Nirankari Sikhs* (Delhi: Macmillan, 1979). Also see Surjit Kaur Jolly, *Sikh Revivalist Movements* (New Delhi: Gitanjali Publishing House, 1988).

46. For an eleven-point list of Sant Nirankari religious practices and doctrines that orthodox Sikhs find objectionable, see *Sikhism and the Nirankari Movement* (Patiala: Guru Nanak Dev Mission, n.d.), pp. 45–50.

47. Sikh fundamentalists were not alone in wanting to put an end to the Sant Nirankaris' practicing their religious traditions in the Punjab. A prominent Sikh historian, Fauja Singh, had this to say of the Sant Nirankaris: "Whatever may be [their] principles on paper, in actual practice the Sant Nirankaris Dal [Nakli Nirankari] has become a challenge to all right thinking Indians. In the name of spiritualism and brotherhood of man, all moral values which are the bedrock of human society, particularly Indian society, have been thrown to the winds. Naturally this is causing heavy damage to our society, to our whole value system and it is high time that effective steps were taken by the Government as well as by the people to ban all these objectionable activities of these Nakli Nirankaris. *"Sikhism and the Nirankari Movement,"* p. 31.

48. For a journalistic account of this clash, see Mark Tully and Satish Jacob, *Amritsar, Mrs. Gandhi's Last Battle,* pp. 58–60. The orthodox Sikh position on this clash is put forward in *Sikhism and the Nirankari Movement,* pp. 32–35.

49. The entire text of this encyclical is reproduced in Satinderpaul Singh Kapur, *Bhindranwale* (Jalandar: Bharti Publishers, 1984; first published, 1983), pp. 173–74.

50. See Edward Said, *Orientalism* (New York: Vintage Books, 1979), and Johannes Fabian, *Time and the Other: How Anthropology Makes Its Object* (New York: Columbia University Press, 1983).

51. *Sikhism and the Nirankari Movement,* p. 40.

52. For this official history, see "Anandpur Sahib Resolution Authenticated by Sant Harchand Singh Longowal," in Government of India's *White Paper on the Punjab Agitation,* n.d., pp. 70–71.

53. Ronald Barthes defines a text as "a work conceived, perceived and received in its integrally symbolic nature," in "From

Work to Text," *Image-Music-Text* (London: Fontana, 1984), p. 159.

54. For instance, see M. J. Akbar, *India: The Siege Within* (Harmondsworth: Penguin Books, 1985), pp. 178–79, and Rajiv A. Kapur, *Sikh Separatism* (London: Allen and Unwin, 1986), p. 219.

55. Robin Jeffrey, *What's Happening to India?* pp. 126–27.

56. This view, for instance, is advanced by Kulwant Singh in *S. Kapur Singh* (Patiala: Punjabi University, 1988), p. 10.

57. The following discussion of the various versions of the ASR is based on personal interviews with Sikh political leaders and on Sukhdev Singh, "Many Faces of a Resolution," *Tribune,* 13 September 1982; article reproduced in Ghani Jafar, *The Sikh Volcano* (Lahore: Vanguard, 1987), pp. 460–65.

58. See the entry for the compound word *bolbala* in Kahn Singh, *Gursabad Ratankar Mahan Kos* (Patiala: Languages Department, 1981), p. 892. A Punjabi-English dictionary dating back to 1895, however, interprets the word *bolbale* somewhat differently. It provides three English equivalents: "prosperity, success, superiority," and also states that the word was much used by faqirs and Brahmans as a mode of benediction. See Maya Singh, *The Panjabi Dictionary,* reprint (Patiala: Languages Department, 1972), p. 165.

59. Press statement made by Kapur Singh on 27 April 1969 at Jullundur, cited in Gur Rattan Paul Singh, *The Illustrated History of the Sikhs* (Chandigarh: published by the author, 1979), pp. 109–10.

60. *The Works of Lewis Carroll* (Feltham: Spring Books, 1965), p. 174.

61. In a speech delivered at the Golden Temple, Bhindranwale stated, "You people come and offer me money, love and support. And if the Akali leaders try to compromise on the Anandpur Sahib resolution I'm not going to forgive them. I will be your watch dog but I tell you as watch dog that you will have to force the Akalis! But don't think as in the past, leaders can settle everything in Delhi or by taking a glass of juice on their own [a reference to Master Tara Singh abandoning his fast unto death in 1961]. This time they can't give up by taking a glass of juice. Either the full implementation of the Anandpur Sahib resolution or their heads." Cited in Joyce Pettigrew, "In Search of a New Kingdom of Lahore," p. 12, n. 36.

62. For a detailed survey and refreshing analysis of the political conditions and backstage center-state relations that prompted the ASR, see Paul R. Brass, "The Punjab Crisis and Unity of India," in Atul Kohli, ed., *India's Democracy,* pp. 169–213. A close legal reading of the ASR is to be found in R. S. Narula, "Anandpur Saheb Resolution," in Patwant Singh and Harji Malik, ed., *Punjab: The Fatal Miscalculation* (New Delhi: published by the author, 1985), pp. 63–77.

63. "Anandpur Sahib Resolution Authenticated by Sant Harchand Singh Longowal," in Government of India's *White Paper on the Punjab Agitation,* n.d., pp. 72–73.

64. Ibid., p. 85.

65. Joyce Pettigrew, "In Search of a New Kingdom of Lahore," pp. 4–5.

66. For the following observations I am indebted to Bernard Lewis, "Islamic Revolution," *New York Review of Books* 34 (1988): 46–50.

67. Figures based on *General Elections, 1989, to the 9th Lok Sabha,* Press Information Bureau, Government of India, p. 72.

68. *Times of India,* 9 July 1990, p. 1.

2

Restructuring Economies

CHAPTER
13

Fundamentalisms and the Economy

Timur Kuran

Many fundamentalist movements have an economic agenda. This means not that their participants want to enrich themselves—which they might and often do—but that they wish to restructure economic systems to conform with the stipulations of their respective religions. So it is that we hear of Christian economics, Buddhist socialism, and Islamic banking.

To the untrained eye, the economic agendas of the major fundamentalisms will seem worlds apart. After all, each agenda draws on a distinct philosophical heritage and features a unique mode of discourse. And the involved fundamentalisms engage in almost no interchange of ideas or methods. One can read thousands of pages of Islamic economics without encountering a single reference to Christian economics, and vice versa. Yet such economic doctrines share the objective of supplanting secular economic thought.

This mutual isolation is rooted in two factors. First, each fundamentalist economic doctrine takes for granted the correctness and unrivaled superiority of its own religion. Thus, no Christian economist would try to resolve biblical ambiguities by consulting Deendayal Upadhyaya's *Integral Humanism,* a cornerstone of Hindu economics. Second, each doctrine employs a distinct form of expression that outsiders can penetrate only with training. A Christian economist who chooses to leaf through *Integral Humanism* would be overwhelmed by its esoteric terminology and symbolism. The mutual insularity of these doctrines stands in sharp contrast to the acknowledged awareness and manifest openness of each to secular economic thought. As the following essays demonstrate, fundamentalist economic doctrines borrow heavily from the very intellectual traditions they ostensibly aim to supplant: Marxian socialism and diverse secular traditions that promote a market order.

In terms of substance, the economic blueprints contained in these doctrines exhibit some important differences. The elimination of interest is a supreme objective of Islamic economics but is hardly an issue in Hindu economics. Buddhist economics encourages the construction of shrines, a matter alien to Christian economics. Against such substantive differences, there are major commonalities in their messages, rhetorical tendencies, and pragmatic adaptations. A sketch of these commonalities will help place in context the essays of part 2 and sensitize the reader to their shared themes.

Two of the following four essays deal with the fundamentalist doctrines of Islam and Protestant Christianity, faiths that rest upon authoritative scriptural foundations. The other two essays analyze the fundamentalist doctrines of Buddhism and Hinduism, faiths less dependent on canonized scripture but firmly rooted in traditional belief and behavior.

I shall refer to these doctrines collectively as "fundamentalist economics." The use of this term is not meant to obscure the particularities of its variants. The term "neoclassical economics" groups together various economic traditions that share a common set of concerns, assumptions, and methods. In the same spirit, the term "fundamentalist economics" may serve as a generic name for a rather diverse cluster of doctrines that are formally unrelated but share a professed, though not necessarily exercised, opposition to secular economic ideals and practices—an opposition based, moreover, on a common aspiration to ground economic prescriptions in normative religious sources. Nor does the term encompass all economic thinking linked to religion. While fundamentalist economics is necessarily religious economics, the converse does not hold. By implication, a "fundamentalist economist" is not merely an economist whose work draws inspiration from religion or one who is religious. So when I use the term "Buddhist economist," I mean an economist who subscribes to Buddhist fundamentalist economics, not just any economist of the Buddhist faith or one influenced by Buddhist teachings.

Before we set out to characterize fundamentalist economics, one more clarification is in order as to what it is not. Fundamentalist economics is not the creation of backward-looking theologians who see and seek nothing but the glories of some past utopia. Although its rhetoric may convey a desire to restore lost social virtues, it is driven, as we shall see, by concerns related to contemporary phenomena. Fundamentalist economics does not oppose mastery over the physical universe, discourage temporal prosperity, or glorify poverty. It is not the economics of renunciation, asceticism, stoicism, or monasticism. Tertullian (160–223 C.E.) and other Christian Fathers may have denounced the acquisitive instinct as the sin of covetousness,[1] but Christian economics is no revolt against property and no conspiracy against economic growth. Nor does fundamentalist economics stand for the leveling of economic achievements. While there is an egalitarian streak in each of its variants, none goes so far as to oppose earthly rewards for effort or demonstrated talent. Finally, fundamentalist economics does not preach that faith alone will put bread on our tables, operate our factories, and build our highways. Islamic economics treats faith as essential to both worldly and otherworldly happiness, but it does not view praying five times a day as the key to material prosperity.

Fundamentalist economics is largely a reaction to perceived injustices in existing economic systems and to transformations engendered by the industrial revolution, the expansion of government, and the information revolution. The perception is commonplace in both rich and poor societies—and not simply in their segments left behind economically—that modernization has corrupted individuals, torn apart communities, compartmentalized human knowledge, and replaced the fraternal atmosphere of the premodern economy with either the ruthless competition of the marketplace or the equally bitter competition over public resources. The propensity to view the latter form of competition as the prime cause for alarm is especially pronounced in Protestant Christian economics, whose American exponents identify closely with the ideals of the American republic. The Christian economists of America tend to be troubled by many new forms of economic regulation, which they see as endangering cherished market freedoms. The contrary tendency to see market competition as a threat, as opposed to a fading virtue, is most apparent in Hindu economics and in the Burmese variant of Buddhist economics.

The books, articles, and pamphlets that constitute the corpus of fundamentalist economic thought do not always capture the full spectrum of factors instrumental to its development. One needs to know the historical context to understand the motives of fundamentalist writers in all their complexity. As Deepak Lal's essay explains, Hindu economics is driven by a desire to keep India's traditionally closed economy highly protected from foreign competition. This policy serves the interests of the shopkeepers, professionals, and civil servants with a stake in perpetuating the status quo, but it hurts the broader mass of consumers. Islamic economics is just one component of a wider revivalist movement that aims to break the domination of Western thought over Muslim minds and thus restore the Islamic community's sense of superiority. Many recent contributions to Islamic economics obscure this elementary motivation, creating the impression that it aims simply to promote justice and efficiency. Buddhist economics features, as the essay by Charles Keyes demonstrates, a host of stipulations that protect the socioeconomic status of Buddhist monks. Its stated goal is more noble: to liberate the individual from the shackles of materialism. Finally, Protestant Christian economics is distinct from libertarian economics, although some writings give the impression that the two are equivalent. Laurence Iannaccone's essay indicates that Christian economists are opposed not to government per se but, more specifically, to un-Christian government. Their embrace of libertarian ideals is a strategic move aimed partly at coalition building and partly at weakening the incumbent secular state's economic base.

However they differ in their misgivings about recent economic trends, fundamentalist economists all believe that the ills of modern civilization are rooted in moral degeneration. Irreligious government and secular education have left the individual's selfishness untamed, his ambitions unchartered, and his noble instincts uncultivated. Accordingly, behavioral reform through moral uplift figures prominently on the agenda of every variant of fundamentalist economics. In one form or another, each encourages people to bring the social interest into their economic calculations, promotes the display of generosity, and insists on the individual's obligation to refrain from waste.

Modern economics, which grew out of the works of David Hume, Adam Smith, and other luminaries of the eighteenth-century Scottish Enlightenment, puts little emphasis on morally or socially motivated individual behavior. Its most celebrated proposition is that people who are free to pursue their own economic objectives make choices beneficial not just to themselves but also to the wider community. It posits that economic activities fueled by selfishness, greed, avarice, and even ostentation yield substantial social gains, though as unintended and often unforeseen by-products. Fundamentalist economics takes a radically different view. In the belief that modern economic thought exaggerates the social returns from economic pursuits motivated by the baser instincts and greatly underestimates the social losses, it asserts that the collective good requires the individual to subordinate his own interests to those of the wider community.

This position rests implicitly, but critically, on the assumption that the individual can easily identify the collectively optimal course of action. No one would deny the existence of choices where this condition is met. If you have your finger on the detonator of a nuclear bomb, you can figure out effortlessly that it is in society's interest for you to refrain from pressing the button. But in everyday life we face many decisions where the collectively optimal choice is hardly self-evident. Suppose you are considering whether to build a new synthetic fertilizer factory in some large city. If you construct the factory, you will create new jobs and probably enrich yourself; but the fumes emitted by the factory might cause some deaths, and existing fertilizer plants might be forced to lay-off workers. Here, the collectively optimal course of action is not obvious: however well intentioned and altruistic you are, your judgment may conflict with those of others who are equally well meaning and unselfish.

Fundamentalist economics denies the existence, or at least downplays the significance, of complex economic choices of the latter type. It asserts that on ordinary economic matters people can easily figure out what is socially optimal, provided they have noble intentions and the right frame of mind. It insists, moreover, that these crucial characteristics are cultivated only through strict adherence to divinely revealed and authoritatively interpreted religion. The wellspring of economic legitimacy is thus the divine will, as embodied in revelation and in faculties acquired through faith and devotion.

Implicit in this view is the notion of a unique legitimate choice, as opposed to many, equally legitimate choices. Right, just, and good are absolute concepts, not relative ones over which informed, reasonable, benevolent people might disagree. Thus, where modern economics attempts to compensate for the individual's informational deficiencies by absolving him of the need to forecast the social consequences of his possible actions, fundamentalist economics does so by pointing to religious texts or traditions as the appropriate behavioral blueprint.

Within each variant of fundamentalist economics one can find positions and specific statements that blur this contrast. Most strikingly, Christian economics holds in high regard various secular writings on the market's role as mediator among competing individual claims, notably the works of Friedrich Hayek and Ludwig von Mises. This is not to say that Christian economics concedes the deficiency of Christian teachings as a guide to economic behavior. It has not come to terms with the inconsistency between its claim that the Bible offers solutions to complex economic problems and its embrace of the market as an institution that obviates the need to find these solutions. There are such unresolved tensions in every variant of fundamentalist economics, a point to which I shall return.

Simplification is common to all thought, religious and secular. And every intellectual current features thinkers convinced of the correctness of their answers, solutions, and interpretations. A neoclassical economist exploring how to improve government efficiency starts from a set of simplifying assumptions supplied by his discipline. Combining these with observations and logic, he concludes that one should restrict the government's ability to run budget deficits. How does this neoclassical economist's approach to the world differ, if at all, from that of a Christian economist who happens to offer the very same prescription? Each proposes a distinct course of action on the basis of a thought process that begins from vast simplifications. The neoclassical economist keeps his proposal open to modification, assuming, of course, that he is a faithful adherent to the central scientific principle of his school of thought, namely, the obligation to abandon hypotheses, analytical procedures, and conclusions discredited by new findings. For his part, a Christian economist loyal to the spirit of his own school treats his conclusions as fixed whenever he considers these to be rooted in the Bible, God's inerrant guide to the correct economic order.

It would appear, then, that fundamentalist economics differs from its secular alternatives in terms of its responsiveness to information inconsistent with adopted positions. Where a neoclassical economist might come to recognize that the benefits from budget deficits sometimes outweigh their costs, his Christian fundamentalist counterpart, if he considers the Bible to speak to the issue and thus to provide inflexible boundaries for analysis, is less prepared to change his mind, even in the face of highly inhospitable empirical evidence.

Once again, the contrast between the two schools of economics gets blurred in practice. Christian economics is unchangeable only in theory. As a practical matter, developments of the kind that influence the evolution of neoclassical economics also influence that of Christian economics. So the key difference is not that one system of thought is dynamic and the other static. It is that changes acknowledged openly and unabashedly in neoclassical economics can only be made surreptitiously in Christian economics, lest a clear acknowledgment contradict the Bible's assumed inerrancy. After all, if the truths embodied in Christian economics are absolute, they cannot be subject to erosion or change over time. It is also true, no doubt, that the typical neoclassical economist is hardly a paragon of responsiveness to empirical evidence. Most practicing neoclassical economists, like their peers in other secular disciplines, abandon only with great difficulty the assumptions, methods, and ideas on which they have staked their careers and reputations. New secular paradigms triumph less by converting the old guard than by outliving it.

To sum up thus far, what renders Islamic, Christian, Hindu, and Buddhist economics *fundamentalist* is their commitment to the idea of unchanging fundamentals on which a just economy must rest, not simply their insistence on giving religion a role in economic matters. One can believe that religious values promote cooperation in the work team or that religious traditions harbor valuable economic lessons—even prescriptions and proscriptions—without being a fundamentalist. One enters the realm of fundamentalism by insisting that the relevant teachings and injunctions are absolutely fixed—never subject to disagreement or adaptation—and equally binding on believers and unbelievers alike. Accordingly, it is not a manifestation of fundamentalism to draw inspiration from the economic experiences of the earliest Muslims in seventh-century Arabia. Such an interest in early Islam approximates fundamentalism only to the extent that the known record is assumed to escape the limitations of historical knowledge and thus to provide a timeless normative basis for economic practice. To take another example, in their 1986 pastoral letter on the U.S. economy, the American Catholic bishops keyed their teachings and the binding authority of their words to the heterogeneity of their audience. They held Christians to a higher standard than non-Christians. Likewise, on spiritual and economic matters they held practicing Catholics to a higher standard than the general public, including nonpracticing Catholics. These economic teachings are obviously Christian teachings, but they do not constitute fundamentalist economics.[2] By contrast, Christian fundamentalism considers its economic injunctions to be equally binding on everyone.

Divided as it is on the merits of market competition and on the competitive instincts in need of disciplining, fundamentalist economics is also divided on the identity of the social groups particularly in need of moral and behavioral reform. In variants that condemn market competition, the prime villains of society include the trader, the middleman, and the speculator. In those that glorify competition, they are the bureaucrat, the social engineer, and the regulator.

But we must be cautious in drawing such categories, for no variant of fundamentalist economics forms a logically tight and fully consistent system of thought. Like all social thought, fundamentalist economics partitions what it perceives as reality, simply because no writer's or reader's mind has the capacity to incorporate all the diverse variables and relationships that bear on human existence into one comprehensive model. Just as neoclassical economics segments its domain of analysis using different models in microeconomics than in macroeconomics, and in labor economics than in industrial organization, so, too, fundamentalist economics applies to issues disparate clusters of facts and principles. We have already seen how Christian economics promotes both the market and biblical commandments as guides to socially useful economic behavior, but without recognizing the possibility of conflict, let alone prescribing how conflict is to be resolved. In the same vein, some texts in Islamic economics feature long passages on the virtues of the market mechanism which suggest that price movements are vital to the equilibration of supply and demand. These same texts contain other passages that instruct traders to refrain from taking advantage of anticipated shortages through unjust price increases. There is an inconsistency between these two classes of passages, which is that the equilibration lauded in the first is obviated by the principle of the "just price" promoted by the second. Such inconsistencies point to the futility of trying to place Islamic economics squarely in the pro- or antimarket camps. Islamic economics puts two faces on the market process, although one or the other may be more prominent in any particular text. Likewise, the list of immoral economic activities varies from text to text. We will return to such divisions.

If competition is one major theme to which fundamentalist economics links the issue of individual morality, another is scarcity. The typical modern textbook on economic principles treats human wants as unbounded. Recognizing the boundedness of physical resources, it argues that potential demand inevitably exceeds the possible supply. The challenge, it then informs, is to maximize some index of social satisfaction subject to resource constraints. Large segments of fundamentalist economics reject this amoral approach to the economic problem in favor of one centered on individual morality. Where the standard textbook treats the unboundedness of human wants as a fact of life, fundamentalist economics tends to view it as a problem rooted partly in modern civilization's failure to control individual acquisitiveness. The obvious solution is to couple efforts to supply more consumables with efforts aimed at curbing the demand for them. The latter objective would involve inculcating the individual with a sense of moderation.

The fundamentalist emphasis on tempering the individual's wants may be characterized as a utopian agenda, for no known society has managed to dampen its members' consumptive and acquisitive ambitions sufficiently to eliminate the problem of nonsatiation. Every society features some individuals committed to a frugal lifestyle. In South Asia ascetics, and in Christendom monks, offer prominent cases in point. But nowhere has self-denial been the rule.

This observation has a major implication: the objective of forming a temperate society provides the basis for a permanent critique of the economic order. Indeed, the futility of trying to eliminate all unsatisfied wants gives fundamentalist economics an irremovable justification for demanding moral reform. For the sake of comparison, neoclassical economics denies itself the authority to judge, let alone to criticize, individual wants. By treating individual preferences as immutable, it shifts the burden of economic performance entirely onto resource availability, production, and distribution.

To blame society's ills on excessive wants is to claim an ability to distinguish between moderation and immoderation. In a static economy with a population, technology, and menu of goods that are all fixed, a lasting consensus on the limits of temperance is not out of the question. But in a dynamic economy where economic possibilities are in flux, a consensus would be outdated almost from its inception. By the time the morally acceptable number of radios per household settled at one, the invention of the transistor would render this limit meaningless. A further complication lies in the enormity of the variety of goods. People living beyond subsistence enjoy a vast selection of spending outlets, including diverse learning opportunities, countless forms of leisure, a huge array of medical services, and a panoply of social and political causes. So consumption patterns may vary substantially among individuals of similar means, and with regard to any particular good one individual may consume more than the norm. Such heterogeneity of lifestyles constitutes an insurmountable obstacle to achieving a true consensus on the limits of moderation, even under the most favorable condition where the goal of promoting moderation is very widely shared.

Like the notion of "just price" and the treatment of middlemen as exploiters, the search for limits of moderation rests on a value system that predates the industrial revolution. As a general objective it is realistic only in the context of an economy far less differentiated and far less changeable than any in existence—even less than the poorest and the most stagnant. In view of this, the tendency within fundamentalist economics to treat moderation as a major instrument for economic betterment should be seen as an atavism—a longing for the cosy certainties of a slower and simpler age. This theme receives further attention in Lal's essay on Hindu economics.

By no means is fundamentalist economics the only branch of social thought that places emphasis on individual moderation. Secular economic discourse is replete with calls for resource conservation and frugal living. Such calls are not uniformly meaningless or necessarily harmful. Drawing attention to inefficient consumption patterns, they keep vitally important economic issues on the public agenda. The point remains that consumptive inefficiencies cannot be eliminated only through individual moderation. Realistically, one needs to rely heavily on the price system.

Fundamentalist economics berates secular economic doctrines for their indifference to the moral content of individual economic choices. The individual must be prevented, it insists, from pursuing an immoral lifestyle, both for his own good and for the welfare of the community. But what if indoctrination fails to eliminate the behaviors identified as immoral? Apart from redoubling its educational efforts, fundamentalist economics may respond in one of several ways.

Most obviously, it may resort to repression, eliciting moral behavior on pain of punishment. A movement's coercive capacity depends, of course, on its political influence. An indoctrination campaign backed by the state's coercive apparatus is generally more effective than one undertaken in opposition to the state. This is one reason why fundamentalists advocating an economically limited state are anything but averse to taking control of the reins of government. Thus, Christian economists who oppose the welfare state and much industrial regulation see government, now an obstacle to their designs, as a potential vehicle for restructuring the American economy according to their own morality. Political power would serve, of course, other objectives as well. As Iannaccone argues, noneconomic objectives like banning abortion constitute complementary, if not more basic, motives for seeking control over the state's coercive apparatus.

If repression is one possible response to failure to eliminate practices identified as immoral, another is to look the other way, and yet another to redefine the nefarious practices as moral. Social movements finding their aspirations thwarted by the cold facts of human nature have routinely chosen to accommodate reality. In medieval Christianity, for instance, violations of the usury doctrine were either legalized through clever stratagems or simply tolerated.[3] And in the twentieth century the absurdity of trading at prices determined according to the Marxian "labor theory of value" has led communist countries to trade with one another at prices established in capitalist-dominated outside markets.[4] Generally speaking, whenever rules are impossible or impractical to follow, even by a committed believer, they will yield to reality in one manner or another. They will either cease to be enforced or be brought under the law through semantic twists. My essay on Islamic economics shows how the revival of ancient legal fictions aimed at getting around Islam's ostensible ban on interest, and the production of new variants, is a thriving pursuit in Islamic banking.

Redistribution is a persistent theme in social discourse. Not surprisingly, it is a prominent concern of fundamentalist economics. All of its variants encourage the materially well-off to assist the less fortunate. Yet none insists on full equality, although there are differences in the forms and grades of inequality considered tolerable. There are also differences in the degree of coercion deemed necessary to bring about the desired redistribution. Islamic economics promotes the use of state power to enforce the collection of a religious tax whose proceeds are, by tradition, reserved largely for the poor. Buddhist economics enjoins individuals to support monks through alms and to help finance the construction and maintenance of shrines; the notion of redistribution within the laity is a matter of controversy. Hindu economics espouses a populist egalitarianism that features protection against foreign competition and the promotion of small-scale industry. Protestant Christian economics stands out as the one variant whose current focus is on preventing redistribution: it advocates the curtailment or abandonment of many of the forced transfer programs instituted in recent decades, on the grounds that they have failed to alleviate poverty. Nevertheless, it teaches that society has a responsibility toward its poor. And it asserts that obeying God's commands regarding tithing and charity would go a long way toward alleviating poverty and inequality.

It is one thing to articulate a preference regarding the distribution of income or wealth, quite another to formulate a policy package capable of generating the ostensibly desired distribution. Proposed policies are not necessarily consistent with the goals they are supposed to serve. As Iannaccone demonstrates, Protestant Christian fundamentalists have taken few concrete steps to reverse the transfer policies they profess to oppose. I argue in my own essay that the redistribution schemes instituted in the name of Islam have reduced neither poverty nor inequality. In the same vein, Lal argues that the fierce nationalism and strident populism of the Hindu revivalists serve to perpetuate the economic status quo, benefiting the politically well connected at the expense of consumers and start-up producers. I have already touched on how the Buddhist traditions of almsgiving and shrine building serve the purpose of distributing wealth to the religious establishment.

While each variant of fundamentalist economics has dominant positions on specific issues, these are subject to change over time. And at any one time, no variant presents a united front on every issue. On the proper economic role of government, for instance, all feature the same ideological cleavages found in secular discourse. Thus, Buddhist economics espouses a form of socialism in Burma (Myanmar) but mild liberalism in Thailand. The Hindu support of India's long-standing protectionism has been challenged by some prominent Hindu revivalists, although the discordant voices remain in the minority. Within the American wing of Protestant Christian fundamentalism, a large portion of the leadership currently subscribes to the ideals of free enterprise. But the rank and file is as divided as the American nation is as a whole. Revealingly, Christianity is also the ostensible fountainhead of liberation theology, which promotes the view that capitalism betrays the Bible, and encourages massive redistribution in favor of the poor.[5] Finally, Islamic economics has featured, from the very beginning, divisions on the domain of government control and intervention. These divisions are evident even in the careers of its individual promoters. In Pakistan some of today's champions of an "Islamic market economy" were until recently leading advocates of "Islamic socialism."[6]

The observed internal divisions within the variants of fundamentalist economics stem from a combination of two factors. First, each religion harbors tensions among its various objectives. It is incumbent on us to help the downtrodden, but people ought to take responsibility for their own actions. We must fight evil, yet whatever exists is a manifestation of a humanly unfathomable divine plan. In view of such tensions, it is hardly surprising that each variant of fundamentalist economics features, to use the most common social taxonomy of our time, a right wing and a left wing. Which one dominates will depend on circumstances. Keyes argues that the basic variations between the Burmese and Thai versions of Buddhist economics reflect historical particularities: whereas the former served as an ideological weapon against colonialism, the latter was co-opted by the local political establishment. This brings us to the second source of internal divisions. Each of the great religions has a rich heritage that can be used to justify just about any economic policy. Its scriptures and traditions provide a wealth of precedents in favor of measures now identified with capitalism, innumerable others in favor of ones identified with socialism. Under the circumstances, any fundamentalist with a modicum of talent can rationalize, through appropriate appeals to scripture or interpretations of religious tradition, just about any economic agenda from strict isolationism to unencumbered liberalism.

What I am suggesting is that fundamentalist economics is shaped heavily by the very secular forces from which its proponents claim immunity. Like nonfundamentalists, fundamentalists become socialists or capitalists, protectionists or free-traders, and regulators or deregulators for reasons that lie largely beyond their respective religions. Having taken particular positions, they buttress these through selective religious appeals. Thus, they accept some texts literally, others only metaphorically. And they designate some events and statements as profoundly and eternally significant, dismissing others as meaningless, unrepresentative, or irrelevant. From this perspective, fundamentalist economics is less a distinctive economic doctrine than a method for shoring up economic agendas that may or may not be rooted in religion.

This is not to say that the exponents of fundamentalist economics engage in this process of selective retrieval self-consciously or in bad faith. Nor are they prepared to concede the dependence of their cherished "fundamentals" on transient social factors. On the contrary, individual theoreticians, practitioners, and supporters insist on the correctness of their own interpretations and by implication, if not in word, on the mis-guidedness of their cofundamentalists who subscribe to radically different interpreta-tions. The process of selective retrieval is not unique to fundamentalists. The works of Karl Marx and the deeds of the Founding Fathers of the United States, to give just two examples, have each provided ideological ammunition to a wide variety of social movements.[7] But the parallel with nonfundamentalist thought stops there. Whereas secular and nonfundamentalist religious scholarship harbors numerous traditions that emphasize the fluidity and multiplicity of historical interpretation, fundamentalisms deny the ambiguities of their guiding texts and traditions.

Fundamentalist economists differ from nonfundamentalist economists in another crucial aspect: they insist on the inseparability of economics from other realms of human activity. At least in principle, the fundamentalist view of the world is not compartmentalized. It is holistic and integrationist. Accordingly, economics is not to be developed in isolation from social, moral, and political concerns, and most impor-tant, it is to be subordinate to religious principles.

It is one thing to set out to provide a comprehensive guide to economic activity, quite another to achieve this ambitious goal. In practice, fundamentalist economics pays attention to a select subset of the economic issues that enter public discourse. There are major economic issues on which fundamentalist economics is quiet, if not silent. For instance, Islamic economics has little to say on public finance—beyond, that is, its preoccupation with reviving Islam's traditional scheme of redistribution. Many Islamic economists acknowledge the need for a flexible taxation system to fi-nance expenditures that fall outside the purview of the traditional scheme, but they are generally mute on the specifics of the additional taxes. This is all the more remark-able given the ongoing dependence of every Muslim government on various taxes collected under schemes lacking religious significance.

A salient difference among the variants of fundamentalist economics that are dis-cussed in the following essays lies in their concrete achievements to date. Islamic economics has brought into being some widely publicized economic institutions, in-cluding Islamic banks in dozens of countries and state-administered redistribution schemes in several. The other variants have no comparable achievements. Hindu and Buddhist economics have lent their support to existing practices and institutions, such as protectionism in the former case and almsgiving in the latter; they have not created new institutions or revived ones in disuse. Likewise, the Protestant Christian variant has had no tangible influence on the economy; it has merely lent political support to a free-market agenda spearheaded by secular thinkers and lobbies. These other vari-ants may, of course, follow the lead of Islamic economics and take concrete steps to reshape the economic order in the name of their respective religions. But if the short history of Islamic economics provides any indication, it is doubtful that such steps would have a major impact on resource allocation or the distribution of wealth. Their main accomplishment would probably be to bolster the appeal of measures desired for nonreligious reasons.

Conspicuously absent from the list of religions covered here is the oldest scriptural religion, Judaism. It so happens that economic restructuring has not been a major objective of Jewish fundamentalism, which is preoccupied with the issue of redefining Jewish identity and other such issues generated by the establishment of Israel. In Judaism's intellectually rich heritage there is no lack of motifs capable of spawning a Judaic variant of fundamentalist economics. There is the ancient tithing system, which could form the basis of a redistribution scheme similar to its now-revived Islamic counterpart.[8] There are the anti-usury laws of the Torah, on whose authority Jewish fundamentalists could set out to reform Israel's financial system.[9] The Torah and a host of rabbinic decisions offer abundant material on which to build a blueprint for Jewish economic conduct.[10] As yet another example, there are biblical commandments to observe every seventh year as a "Sabbatical Year," when contracted debt is to be remitted and land left fallow, and the close of every seventh seven-year cycle as a "Jubilee Year," when, in addition, expropriated land is to be returned to its original owner. These commandments could form the linchpin of a distributional agenda. They were a source of controversy as late as 1910, when Abraham Isaac Kook, the chief rabbi of Jaffa, led a movement to make Jews refrain from acquisitive dealings during the Sabbatical Year. Kook went so far as to encourage the preemptive sale of Jewish-owned lands to Muslims. His campaign faltered in the face of opposition from other prominent rabbis, many of whom were busy laying the groundwork for a modern Jewish state.[11]

For our purposes here, the significance of this episode is twofold. The campaign itself demonstrates the potency of scripture as a source of far-reaching economic policy. And its failure lends support to one of my earlier points: the outcome of competition among rival religious interpretations depends substantially on the prevailing social, political, and economic winds.

Also absent from the religions covered here is Sikhism, which has given rise to a powerful fundamentalist movement. Motivated in part by the perception that India's Sikh-populated regions are economically exploited, this movement endeavors to establish an independent country run by Sikhs. But while its goals include improving the Sikh nation's economic fortunes, it has not articulated a coherent economic program. Nor has it produced a body of economic thought that draws on Sikh motifs.[12]

The Jewish and Sikh cases suggest that, for fundamentalisms, the development of a distinct economic doctrine is a goal of second-order importance. In the presence of serious concerns about national independence or survival, this goal may be shelved indefinitely. Such concerns are muted, if not absent altogether, in the birthplaces of the fundamentalist doctrines explored in the following four essays.

Acknowledgments

This essay was written during a sabbatical at the Institute for Advanced Study at Princeton, financed partly by a fellowship of the National Endowment for the Humanities. I am indebted to R. Scott Appleby, Ekkehart Schlicht, and Laurence Iannaccone for some helpful comments.

Notes

1. For an overview of the economic doctrines of early Christianity, see Barry Gordon, "Biblical and Early Judeo-Christian Thought," in S. Todd Lowry, ed., *Pre-Classical Economic Thought: From the Greeks to the Scottish Enlightenment* (Boston: Kluwer Academic Publishers, 1987), pp. 43–67. A fuller account is provided by Jacob Viner, in Jacques Melitz and Donald Winch, eds., *Religious Thought and Economic Society* (Durham, N.C.: Duke University Press, 1978), chap. 1.

2. *Economic Justice for All: Pastoral Letter on Catholic Social Teaching and the U.S. Economy* (Washington, D.C.: United States Catholic Conference, 1986).

3. *Dictionary of the History of Ideas: Studies of Selected Pivotal Ideas*, s.v. "Casuistry."

4. For many other examples from diverse times and places, see E. L. Jones, *Growth Recurring: Economic Change in World History* (Oxford: Clarendon Press, 1988), chap. 5.

5. See Michael Novak, ed., *Liberation Theology and the Liberal Society* (Washington, D.C.: American Enterprise Institute for Public Policy Research, 1987), especially William P. Glade, Jr., "A Dialectic between Liberationism and Liberalism," pp. 4–20; and Arturo Fontaine, "It Is Not Easy to Argue with Liberation Theologians," pp. 164–77.

6. Based on discussions with Shahid Zahid and Tanzil-ur-Rahman, Karachi, November 1989.

7. For more examples and many pertinent insights, see Bernard Lewis, *History—Remembered, Recovered, Invented* (Princeton, N.J.: Princeton University Press, 1975); and David Lowenthal, *The Past Is a Foreign Country* (New York: Cambridge University Press, 1985).

8. *Encyclopaedia Judaica*, s.v. "Tithe."

9. *Jewish Encyclopedia*, s.v. "Usury."

10. For one such attempt, see Meir Tamari, *"With All Your Possessions": Jewish Ethics and Economic Life* (New York: Free Press, 1987). Tamari, an Israeli, is not affiliated with any organized fundamentalist movement.

11. *Encyclopaedia Judaica*, s.v. "Sabbatical Year and Jubilee."

12. See Harjot Oberoi, "Sikh Fundamentalism: Translating History into Theory," in this volume.

The Economic Impact of Islamic Fundamentalism

Timur Kuran

The Islamic Economy

In 1979 Pakistan took some major steps to give its economy an Islamic character. To satisfy the presumed Qur'anic ban on interest, banks were ordered to offer an interest-free alternative to the conventional savings account and to purge interest from all their operations within five years. Although the wider objective has not yet been met, the interest-bearing savings account is no longer an option for new depositors. Another highlight of the 1979 program was *zakat,* Islam's tax on wealth and income. Voluntary until then, zakat was made a legal obligation. The Pakistani government now collects zakat from several sources, notably bank deposits and farm output. Every year thousands of local committees distribute the proceeds to designated groups.[1]

Pakistan has not been alone in trying to restructure its economy according to ostensibly Islamic stipulations. Zakat is now compulsory for certain groups in Malaysia, Saudi Arabia, and the Sudan. In some other predominantly Muslim countries, the establishment of a state-run zakat system is under consideration. The impact of Islamization is especially widespread in banking. Banks claiming an Islamic identity are in operation in most countries of North Africa, the Middle East, and South Asia. In some of these they hold more than 10 percent of the commercial deposits.[2] The leading Islamic banks have also established a presence in countries where Muslims form a small minority. New Zealand now has an "Islamic Finance Corporation," and Pasadena, California, an "Al Baraka Bankcorp."

These developments are not occurring in an intellectual vacuum. There is a rapidly growing literature known as "Islamic economics" that seeks to guide and justify the ongoing reforms.[3] The prescriptions in this literature rest partly on economic logic and partly on the Qur'an and the Sunna, the latter consisting of recollections of the words and deeds of Prophet Muhammad and his companions. Several research centers have been established to promote Islamic economics. Some of these, including the International Center for Research in Islamic Economics at King Abdulaziz University in Jeddah, the International Association for Islamic Economics in Leicester, and the Kulliyah of Economics at the International Islamic University in Kuala Lumpur, publish journals devoted to the discipline. There are also several specialized periodicals, such as the *Journal of Islamic Banking and Finance,* a quarterly published in Karachi.

The exponents of this discipline, who call themselves "Islamic economists," emphasize that it covers far more than zakat and interest-free banking. The discipline aims, they say, to provide a comprehensive blueprint for all economic activity. Accordingly, a list of suggested research topics published by the International Center for Research in Islamic Economics covers every major category of research recognized by the American Economic Association, including consumer behavior, market structure, central planning, industrial relations, international trade, and economic development.[4] Some Islamic economists are quick to admit that in most of these realms the nascent discipline has yet to make a significant contribution. But they generally agree that the fundamental sources of Islam harbor clear and definitive solutions to every conceivable economic problem. To find these, they suggest, we must turn to the Qur'an and to the wisdom of the earliest Islamic community in seventh-century Arabia, drawing wherever necessary on modern tools and concepts.

Islamic Economics as Fundamentalist Doctrine

The classical sources of Islam contain numerous prescriptions that lend themselves to the construction of economic norms, and the religion's early history offers an array of lessons concerning economic behavior and institutions. But the notion of an economics discipline that is distinctly and self-consciously Islamic is very new. The great philosophers of Medieval Islam wandered freely beyond the intellectual confines of the Islamic scriptures. And none of their works, not even the celebrated *Prolegomena* of Ibn Khaldun (1332–1406 C.E.), gave rise to an independent discipline of economics.[5] The origins of Islamic economics lie in the works of Sayyid Abul-A'la Maududi (1903–79), a Pakistani social thinker who sought to turn Islam into a "complete way of life." In his voluminous writings Maududi exhorted that Islam is much more than a set of rituals. It encompasses, he argued, all domains of human existence, including education, medicine, art, law, politics, and economics. To support this assertion, he laid the foundations of several Islamic disciplines, among them Islamic economics.[6] Other seminal contributions to Islamic economics were made by Sayyid Qutb (1906–66), an Egyptian, and Muhammad Baqir Sadr (1931–80), an Iraqi.[7]

There are major substantive differences among the teachings of these pioneers. Maududi is quite sympathetic to the market process, though he insists that market behavior must be constrained by behavioral norms found in the classical sources of Islam. Generally less trusting of the market, Qutb and Sadr favor supplementing norm-guided self-regulation by state-enforced controls. A related difference is that Qutb and Sadr are less tolerant of economic inequality. These variations among the pioneers of Islamic economics are reflected in the writings of their followers, which offer a wide spectrum of views concerning government, markets, and property rights. But they have not given rise to sharply differentiated subschools. The substantive divisions within Islamic economics are more amorphous than, say, those between neoclassical economics and Marxian economics. Thus, the followers of Maududi tend to hold Qutb's and Sadr's works in high esteem. Moreover, their key positions often bear the influence of these other pioneers.

Whatever its internal divisions, Islamic economics has always presented a united front in justifying its own existence. The dominant economic systems of our time, virtually every major text asserts, are responsible for severe injustices, inefficiencies, and moral failures. In capitalism interest promotes callousness and exploitation, while in socialism the suppression of trade breeds tyranny and monstrous disequilibria.[8] The fundamental sources of Islam prohibit interest but allow trade; hence, a properly Islamic economy would possess the virtues of these two systems without their defects. Typically, this claim is supported by references to Islam's Golden Age, the period 622–61 C.E., which spans the latter part of Prophet Muhammad's helmsmanship of the Muslim community and the tenure of the "rightly guided" caliphs.[9] During the Golden Age, it is suggested, the Islamic code of economic behavior enjoyed widespread adherence, the prevailing spirit being one of brotherly cooperation. With everyone "subject to the same laws" and "burdened with the same obligations," injustices were minimized.[10] And resources were allocated very efficiently, ensuring a rapid rise in living standards. After the Golden Age, so the belief goes, the Muslim community's attachment to the precepts of Islam weakened, setting the stage for a painful and protracted decline in its global economic standing.

The case for restructuring economies according to Islamic principles thus rests on two claims. First, the prevailing systems have failed us. And second, the history of early Islam proves the Islamic system's unrivaled superiority over its alternatives.

To put in perspective the latter claim, we must recognize that by modern standards the seventh-century economy of the Arabian peninsula was very primitive. It produced few commodities, using uniformly simple technologies. It was essentially free of the major physical externalities that afflict modern economies, like air and water pollution. And it featured only the most rudimentary division of labor. The specific economic injunctions found in the Islamic scriptures—mostly in the Sunna—are responses to problems that arose in this ancient setting. Some of these injunctions were perceived as eternally valid. But many others were seen as changeable. Thus, rules and regulations were altered openly and unabashedly in response to new conditions. As a case in point, the scope and rates of zakat underwent many modifications during the Golden Age.

The historical record also calls into question some of the virtues attributed to the Golden Age. The notion that the early Islamic community was a paragon of brotherly unity conflicts with the fact that it was plagued by disagreements and also with the fact that force played an important role in its internal governance. Significantly, three of the four "rightly guided" caliphs met their ends at the hands of fellow Muslims. Nor was the Golden Age free of the corrupt practices attributed to contemporary capitalism and socialism. Officials of the Islamic state, including the caliphs themselves, were often accused of nepotism and misjudgment.[11] During part of this period the state did indeed enforce the collection of zakat, and a substantial portion of the proceeds must have gone to various disadvantaged groups. We possess no reliable evidence, however, on whether this redistribution brought about a major reduction in inequality.

Still, the literature is replete with calls for the immediate implementation of the holy laws of Islam (Shari'a) in the form they are believed to have taken almost a millennium and a half ago, in one locality. In issuing such calls, Islamic economics denies that certain economic problems of the modern age had no counterparts in the past. It also denies that once-beneficial institutions might now be dysfunctional, even harmful. Some of the rhetoric of Islamic economics thus conveys the impression that it seeks to rediscover and restore the economy of a distant past.

At the same time, it draws heavily on modern concepts and methods, including many that originated outside the Islamic world. And it pursues such modern objectives as growth, employment creation, and efficiency.[12] It would be wrong, therefore, to characterize the discipline's intense preoccupation with the economy of seventh-century Arabia merely as a scholastic search for ancient solutions to ancient problems—although this representation does fit certain writings. Islamic economics applies ancient solutions to perceived problems of the *present;* and where such solutions are lacking, it seeks scriptural justification for its favored reforms. Accordingly, Islamic economics shows interest in only some features of the seventh-century Arabian economic order. Having identified the prohibition of interest as the sine qua non of Islamic reform, it is engrossed in Qur'anic verses concerning lending and borrowing. It devotes comparatively little effort to exploring whether the Golden Age offers useful prescriptions against environmental pollution, having chosen, if only by default, to refrain from making the environment a major issue.

So Islamic economics is as much a response to contemporary grievances as it is a nostalgic escape into the imagined simplicity, harmony, and prosperity of an ancient social order. Notwithstanding much of its rhetoric, in its applications it seeks to revive only bits and pieces of the seventh-century Arabian economy, not to restore it in toto. In practice it thus exhibits more willingness to accept economic realities than it does in theory.

Islamic economics is appropriately categorized as a "fundamentalist doctrine," because it claims to be based on a set of immutable principles drawn from the traditional sources of Islam. By no means does its flexibility in practice negate this label's descriptive power. All doctrines labeled "fundamentalist" claim to rest on fundamentals set in stone, yet in application these prove remarkably malleable. Moreover, such doctrines assert a monopoly over knowledge and good judgment, even as they show receptivity to outside influences.[13]

Having billed itself as a superior alternative to all other economic traditions, Islamic economics has drawn sharp criticism from two quarters. A number of scholars, including this writer, have drawn attention to the literature's empirical and logical flaws, arguing that the proposed institutions are either unworkable or inherently inefficient.[14] Other scholars, notably Seyyed Vali Reza Nasr, have observed that Islamic economics has invited all this criticism by presenting itself not as a faith or philosophy to be understood on its own terms, but as a positive science that lives up to established scientific standards. In this view, Islamic economics has been drawn into the game of utilitarian social science and it is trying to prove its worth by beating the materialistic economic traditions of the West on Western turf. The mission of Islamic economics, maintains Nasr, should be to create a worldview that brings man's material goals into harmony with his spiritual yearnings. It should get on with this mission without apology—without offering excuses, that is, for pursuing nonutilitarian objectives. If it concentrates on its own agenda, it will eventually prove its superiority, but according to its own standards as opposed to those of the non-Muslim West.[15]

Nasr would thus have Islamic economics withdraw into its own shell in order to avoid being sidetracked by Western priorities. The logic behind this call to self-imposed isolation parallels Maududi's apparent motivation for establishing the discipline. What propelled Maududi to establish distinctly Islamic disciplines was a desire to defend Islam "against the inroads of foreign political and intellectual domination." He wanted to establish Islam's authority in domains where Muslims had come to rely on the West's guidance, in order to restore the Islamic community's self-confidence and enable it to face the world proudly, as in the days before the economic and military rise of the West.[16] Thus, for Maududi Islamic economics was primarily a vehicle for reasserting the primacy of Islam and secondarily an instrument for radical economic change. Like Maududi, many other supporters of Islamic economics have subordinated it to wider objectives. For example, the Ayatollah Khomeini made a point of denying that the revolution he spearheaded in Iran was motivated by economics. It was not made, he once quipped, to make watermelons more plentiful.[17] He meant that the revolution was spawned primarily by noneconomic factors—most importantly, a threat to Islam's role in providing cultural identity, social cohesion, and moral guidance—and so it should not be judged by its economic impact. Khomeini repeatedly spoke out, of course, against poverty and exploitation, and he supported certain economic reforms, including the ostensible elimination of interest. But he always subordinated economic objectives to the general goal of restoring the centrality of Islam in private and public life—even to particular objectives such as eliminating the consumption of alcohol and ensuring feminine modesty.

Just as Khomeini's aides included activists for whom economic concerns were paramount, the expositors, practitioners, and sympathizers of Islamic economics include people drawn to the discipline's substantive goals. Many undoubtedly see it as an antidote to exploitation and expect it to bring prosperity. For some, the attraction of Islamic economics lies in its promise to solve heretofore intractable economic problems. To them, the raison d'être of Islamic economics is its ability to improve economic performance, defined in materialistic terms. But the point remains that Islamic economics also serves, and is perceived as serving, as an instrument of legitimation and power. By advancing the view that an Islamic economy will promote harmony, growth, and justice simultaneously, Islamic economics enhances the appeal of an Islamic *political* order. And it bolsters the case for a pan-Islamic union within which Muslims can enjoy the benefits of cross-continental trade without having to compromise their religious principles.[18]

Each of the two principal institutions engendered by Islamic economics, zakat and Islamic banking, provides sources of funding for fundamentalist causes. Islamic banks channel a portion of their profits into religious education, publishing, networking, and other activities that foster the spread of fundamentalism. Likewise, in countries with obligatory zakat, a significant portion of the proceeds are allocated to religious schools dedicated to the dissemination of fundamentalist views. Islamic institutions also constitute a channel of upward mobility for fundamentalists and potential fundamentalists. In Turkey, for example, Islamic banks provide career opportunities to relatively religious youths whose cultural backgrounds might otherwise handicap them in the corporate world.[19] Another attraction of Islamic economics, then, is the economic basis it provides for expanding the influence of fundamentalism.

Not everyone who voices support for Islamic economics is at heart a fundamentalist. Both the discipline and its applications enjoy the public support of intellectuals, politicians, and laymen who are committed neither to Islamization in general nor to Islamic economics in particular. Their reason for falsifying their preferences lies in the identification of Islamic economics with core Islamic values. Because of this identification, it has become prudent in some societies to be known as sympathetic to its objectives. In Pakistan, for instance, a politician who fails to endorse Islamic banking may find his aspirations thwarted. Significantly, Islamic banking is on the platform of every major political party.[20] Yet it is known to seasoned observers of Pakistani politics that many politicians have a low opinion of Islamic economics. Indeed, politicians who lend public support to its goals are apt to do little of practical significance to promote it, once in power.[21]

All this goes to show that Islamic economics owes its support only in part to the real and imagined successes of its past and present applications. While one would hardly know this from studying theoretical expositions, there exists a range of reasons why people find Islamic economics appealing. The merits of Islamic economics lie for some fundamentalists primarily in its *Islamic* character but for others mostly in the substance of its *economics*. For still others, it is an instrument for advancing the political agenda of Islamic fundamentalism. Finally, there are nonfundamentalists who lend it support simply to avoid being stigmatized as bad Muslims.

It is important to keep this diversity of motivations in mind as we turn to an analysis of the discipline's practical accomplishments. I argue below that there are vast incongruities between the rhetoric of Islamic economics and its practice. Specifically, I demonstrate that the impact of Islamic banking has been anything but revolutionary, that obligatory zakat has nowhere become a significant vehicle for reducing inequality, and, lastly, that the renewed emphasis on economic morality has had no appreciable effect on economic behavior. My evaluation thus indicates that by its own lofty yardstick Islamic economics is a failure. This assessment needs to be qualified by the fact that the strictly economic impact of Islamic economics is not the only measure of its achievements. Some of its promoters may well consider the shortcomings I describe to be outstripped, from the standpoint of the wider fundamentalist cause, by political and cultural consequences that lie beyond this essay's purview.

Banking and Finance

Islamic Banking

Suppose you lend $100 to an industrialist, at 5 percent interest for a period of one year. Since you stand to receive exactly $105 at the end of the year, your return is predetermined. But the industrialist's return depends on the success of his business. If his revenue exceeds $105, he will make a profit. If it falls short of $105, he will incur a loss. An interest-based loan thus places the risk of loss entirely on the borrower. Under the prevalent interpretation of Islam, this is prohibited as unfair.

The literature is replete with additional reasons why interest is best avoided. "Interest," writes one Islamic economist, "inculcates love for money and the desire to accumulate wealth for its own sake. It makes men selfish, miserly, narrow-minded and stone-hearted."[22] Another evil attributed to interest is that it "transfers wealth from the poor to the rich, increasing the inequality in the distribution of wealth."[23] And yet another: it draws people's energies away from productive enterprise.[24]

The purpose of Islamic banking is to prevent such inefficiencies, moral failures, and injustices by allowing people to borrow and lend without having to deal in interest. In theory, an Islamic bank accepts only two types of deposits: transaction deposits, which are risk free but yield no return, and investment deposits, which carry the risk of capital loss for the promise of a variable return. Deliberately ruled out are the insured savings deposits of conventional banks, which provide a predetermined return. An Islamic bank's lending operations are based on the same principle of risk sharing. In lending money to a firm, it agrees to share in the losses of the underwritten business activities in return for a share of any profits.

Since Islamic banks and their depositors are allowed to profit from their monetary assets only by carrying some risk of loss, Islamic economics treats the mechanics of profit-and-loss sharing as a topic of paramount importance. Two profit-and-loss-sharing techniques, each utilized in early Islam and discussed in classical Islamic jurisprudence, receive the bulk of attention: *mudaraba* and *musharaka*. Under mudaraba, an investor or group of investors entrusts capital to an entrepreneur, who puts this into production or trade, and then returns to the investor(s) a prespecified share of his revenues. The remaining share is kept by the entrepreneur as a reward for his time and effort. If the business fails, the capital loss is borne entirely by the investor(s), the entrepreneur's loss being his expended labor. Under musharaka, the entrepreneur adds some of his own capital to that supplied by the investor(s), exposing himself to a risk of capital loss. The key difference between the two mechanisms lies in the entrepreneur's own financial commitment.

Mudaraba and musharaka have been likened to the financing techniques used by the venture capital industries of today's advanced economies.[25] Three factors differentiate a venture capitalist from a conventional bank. First, while the bank bases its loan decisions primarily on the creditworthiness of its applicants, the venture capitalist focuses on the potential profitability of the proposed projects. Thus, an applicant with no collateral but an economically promising project may fail to secure an ordinary bank loan yet succeed in obtaining venture capital. Second, the conventional bank earns interest on its loans, whereas the venture capitalist receives shares of profits. Third, unlike the bank, the venture capitalist often participates in the execution of the projects he underwrites, sometimes by supplying managerial know-how. The second and third differences are obviously linked. The venture capitalist's closer involvement in project execution reflects his greater stake in the project's profitability.

In advanced economies the venture capital industry has fostered the rise of many new enterprises, most recently the high-technology sector. Islamic banking, say its proponents, can make an equally significant contribution to the Muslim world's economic development. The logic that sustains this claim is simple. A banking system that bases its loan decisions on project profitability does not turn down projects with excellent long-term prospects but lengthy gestation periods. Nor does it deny support to entrepreneurs merely for lack of a track record. It thus allocates credit more efficiently than one which insists on demonstrated creditworthiness. The result is faster development, with everyone benefiting: entrepreneurs, who find it easier to finance their projects; owners of banks, who share in the profits of the projects they underwrite; and depositors, whose investment accounts earn greater returns.

The first Islamic bank offering a range of commercial services opened in Dubai in 1975, and there now exist Islamic banks in about fifty countries.[26] Many of these banks have been secretive about the composition of their assets. Knowledgeable observers generally agree, however, that neither mudaraba nor musharaka has ever absorbed a dominant share of the Islamic banks' assets. According to figures supplied by the Central Bank of Iran, in 1986 mudaraba and musharaka accounted for 38 percent of the assets of Iranian banks.[27] Two years earlier, when the Islamization of Pakistan's state-owned banking system was ostensibly nearing completion, only 14 percent of that country's bank assets were in mudaraba or musharaka, according to official reports.[28] Moreover, most of the contracts categorized as mudaraba or musharaka were actually based on thinly disguised interest. In violation of the spirit of profit-and-loss sharing the bank would set a target return on its loans, agreeing in advance to reimburse the entrepreneur for any "excess profit."[29] In the Pakistani banking community it is widely believed that the share of legitimate mudaraba and musharaka never rose above a few percentage points and that it quickly fell to under 1 percent. In Turkey, where, in contrast to Pakistan and Iran, the banking sector remains heavily dominated by conventional banks, profit-and-loss sharing is similarly unpopular. The privately owned Islamic "finance houses" place at most 8 percent of their funds in mudaraba and musharaka.[30]

By far the most popular financing mode of the Islamic banks is *murabaha*, which works as follows.[31] A producer or trader submits to his Islamic bank a list of goods that he wishes to purchase, let us say a ton of steel. The bank buys the steel, marks up its price as compensation for this service, and then transfers ownership of the steel to the client. Along with his steel, the client receives a bill at the inflated price, to be paid at some jointly determined date in the future. What makes this transaction legitimate from an Islamic standpoint is that the bank takes ownership of the steel for some time, exposing itself to risk. Indeed, if the steel were stolen while under the bank's ownership, the loss would fall not on the client but on the bank. But the involved risk could be negligible, because there is no minimum to the duration of the bank's ownership; a millisecond suffices to make the transaction legitimate. From an economic standpoint, of course, an infinitesimal ownership period makes murabaha equivalent to an interest-based loan: the bank bears no risk, and the client pays for the time-value of money. There remains merely a semantic difference, which is that the client's payment is called a "service charge" or "markup" in one case and "interest" in the other.

In their applications of murabaha, the Islamic banks are keeping their ownership periods very short. Banks whose declared mission is to stamp out interest are thus making extensive use of a technique that is nothing but interest concealed in Islamic garb. In defense of Islamic banking it could be said that under murabaha there is no penalty for late payment, as there is under interest. This is true in principle, but in practice the Islamic banks have devised an ingenious method for penalizing accounts past due. They simply charge *in advance* for late payment, offering the client a rebate for payment on time.[32] In implementation, therefore, murabaha differs only cosmetically from the interest-based financing practices of the merchant banks and trading firms of the West. Not surprisingly, Pakistani bankers routinely tell their clients that murabaha is equivalent to interest.[33] There is actually a precedent for treating the two terms as synonymous: an Ottoman ruling of 1887 that pegged interest rates at 9 percent was named the "murabaha ordinance."[34]

The second most popular financing mechanism is lease financing, known in some countries as *ijara*. Under this mechanism, the bank rents some asset, let us say a truck, to an end user for a specified period of time, at a mutually agreed upon rental that reflects the truck's cost as well as the time-value of money. The end user may have the option of purchasing the truck. In theory, at least, lease financing satisfies the requirement of risk sharing, since the bank owns the asset for some period. If the truck suffers damage during the leasing period, the resulting loss would be borne by the bank.[35] In practice, however, the bank shifts such risk onto others by requiring the user to put up collateral and to pay for insuring the asset.[36] From an economic standpoint, therefore, the lease-financing practices of the Islamic banks do not differ from those of the interest-laden, risk-averse leasing firms that have long existed throughout the world, including many Muslim countries.

Murabaha and lease financing are well suited to trade and commodity financing, but neither is applicable to the provision of working capital. A start-up firm that needs to finance its day-to-day operations will receive no help from an Islamic bank that has chosen to specialize in murabaha and lease financing. Nor are these mechanisms of use to a firm with a cash-flow problem: a company facing a pile of unpaid bills needs not merchandise but money. So, at least in its current form, Islamic banking does not qualify as a full-fledged substitute for conventional banking, if only because it offers a limited range of financing services.

On the whole, the sectoral composition of the Islamic banks' investments does not differ significantly from that of conventional commercial banks. Their clients tend to be established producers and merchants, as opposed to newcomers. They generally favor urbanites, as opposed to villagers, who in many parts of the Muslim world remain dependent for credit on moneylenders charging notoriously high rates. The banks have shown no inclination to favor labor-intensive firms. Many have invested in real estate, and a few have speculated in the international currency and commodity markets. With few exceptions, they have preferred trade financing to project financing. Insofar as they have engaged in project financing, they have favored safe short-term projects over long-term projects fraught with uncertainty.

Even the Islamic Development Bank, an intergovernmental organization established in 1975 to promote economic development using Islamic financial instruments, has evolved into an export-import bank. It uses the funds at its disposal largely to finance international trade, in particular, oil exports to poor countries of the Muslim world. Revealingly, from 1975 to 1986 the portion of profit-and-loss sharing in the Islamic Development Bank's portfolio fell from 55 percent to 1 percent, while that of murabaha rose from nil to over 80 percent. Lease financing has also increased sharply, although this mode of business is not even mentioned in the bank's charter.[37] Like its commercial counterparts, the Islamic Development Bank now goes to great lengths to avoid risk. Through governmental guarantees and client-financed private insurance, it absolves itself of risk, in violation of its own principles. If a machine purchased on behalf of a Bangladeshi company is damaged in transit, the loss falls on the company, or some insurance agency, or the government of Bangladesh—but never the bank itself.[38]

None of this implies that the financing operations of the Islamic banks are harmful to social welfare. They do no damage by refraining from carrying bona fide risk. The promotion of international trade is an economically valuable service, especially in countries featuring severe allocational distortions caused by long-standing protectionism. Lease and commodity financing stimulates economic production. At least with respect to countries where the Islamic banks compete with conventional commercial banks, it is fair to say that they would not have survived were they not meeting some previously unfulfilled need. My basic point is simply that the lending practices of the Islamic banks do not conform in the least to the stipulations of Islamic economics.

The Resilience of Interest

Why, it behooves us to ask, does the practice of Islamic banking diverge so critically from the underlying theory? Why, specifically, are banks that were established to revolutionize the world of finance sticking so closely to the techniques of conventional banks?

One reason has to do with the ongoing presence of conventional banks in all countries with Islamic banks, except Iran and Pakistan. By allowing entrepreneurs to choose between interest and profit-and-loss sharing, conventional banks create an "adverse selection" problem for the Islamic banks: entrepreneurs with below-average profit expectations prefer profit-and-loss sharing in order to minimize their losses in the likely event of failure, while those with above-average expectations prefer interest in order to maximize their gains in the likely event of success. The upshot is that the Islamic banks receive a disproportionately large share of the bad risks.[39] Implicit in this observation are the following two points. First, an entrepreneur who knows that his project is very risky is likely to conceal this from the Islamic banking community. And second, no bank possesses a fail-proof method for determining a project's riskiness.

Through training, of course, bankers can become reasonably adept at identifying bad deals. Were the attainment of such skills impossible there would be no venture capitalism in the West. But the required skills are in short supply in the Muslim world, which is a factor in the Islamic banks' reluctance to engage in genuine profit-and-loss sharing. To remedy this recognized deficiency an institute was established in 1982 in northern Cyprus for the training of personnel to screen projects. But it closed in 1984, leaving the Islamic banking system without a training center.[40] If one factor in this closing was the curriculum's shortcomings, another was a lack of enthusiasm on the part of the Islamic banks for genuine profit-and-loss sharing. Even the banks of Iran and Pakistan, which are shielded by law from having to compete with conventional banks, have been reluctant, as we saw above, to commit substantial funds to mudaraba or musharaka.

So the adverse selection problem caused by conventional banking cannot be the only reason why the Islamic banks are extremely reticent to abide by their own principles. A more fundamental factor is the widespread practice of double bookkeeping. Firms habitually understate their revenues and overstate their costs to conceal their profits from the tax collector, generally getting away with it because of inadequate government audits.[41] Under the circumstances, bankers are reluctant to lend on the basis of profit-and-loss sharing, unless they can sit on the recipient's board. But the typical firm will let no banker monitor its operations, for fear that information about its true profitability will find its way to the government. In sum, there is a mutual distrust between the providers and users of funds. This makes interest, a compensation mechanism that requires no monitoring, mutually preferable to profit-and-loss sharing. Some Islamic economists are beginning to realize that profit-and-loss sharing is unworkable in the presence of rampant dishonesty.[42] They continue to believe, however, that it is possible to lower dishonesty to a level where *all* borrowers and lenders will happily substitute profit-and-loss sharing for interest.

An additional reason why the practice of Islamic banking conflicts with the underlying theory has to do with the profitability and relative risklessness of trade and commodity financing. In many parts of the Muslim world certain goods are routinely in short supply, due to production controls, import restrictions, and price ceilings. The firms that acquire these scarce goods for resale or production tend to profit handsomely, which makes financing their operations ordinarily quite safe. Understandably, many Islamic banks would rather finance such commercial ventures than sink funds into long-term development projects with very uncertain outcomes. In so doing they seek, like the typical business enterprise, to avoid unnecessary risks. What needs recognition here is that the abundance of low-risk, yet lucrative, opportunities in trade and commodity financing reduces the appeal of long-term development financing.

A Historical Perspective

To put in perspective all these incongruities between theory and practice, it may be noted that Islamic banking is a very recent creation. Neither classical nor medieval Islamic civilization featured banks in the modern sense, let alone "Islamic" banks. Classical Islamic jurisprudence produced elaborate rules to regulate financial transactions among individuals. Yet, as noted by Murat Çizakça, these rules did not give rise to a system of banking.[43] Medieval Islamic civilization produced no organizations that could pool thousands of people's funds, administer them collectively, and then survive the death of their managers. The financial rules of Islam remained frozen up to modern times, precluding the formation, except outside of Islamic law, of durable partnerships involving large numbers of individuals. It was the Europeans who, probably starting from Middle Eastern financial practices, developed a complex financial system centered on banks.[44] Given this, it is not surprising that the banks now operating in the name of Islam look more like other modern financial institutions than like anything in Islam's heritage.

In the 1930s there were some abortive attempts in India to establish interest-free banks. But the first successful forerunner of Islamic banking was a savings bank established in 1963 in the Egyptian town of Mit Ghamr. This bank was modeled after some of West Germany's local savings banks. It paid no interest on deposits and charged no interest on loans, borrowing and lending on the basis of profit-and-loss sharing. On account of these features, the bank claimed an Islamic identity, partly to distinguish itself from government banks and partly to enhance its attractiveness in the eyes of pious Egyptian peasants. The Mit Ghamr Savings Bank rapidly gained popularity and began making a substantial contribution to the local economy. Nonetheless, it was closed in 1968 by a government hostile to private initiative and suspicious of religion, under the pretext that it was in violation of the country's banking laws.[45] The significant point is that Mit Ghamr was not modeled after some Islamic institution of the past. Although it assumed a religious identity as a public relations ploy, its essential features were copied from a non-Islamic source, with no attempt to disguise this appropriation.[46] A fundamentally different claim is made on behalf of the commercial banks chartered as Islamic institutions since 1975, under the watchful eyes of clerics. They have all been billed as inherently Islamic creations. Yet, as we have seen, there is nothing distinctly Islamic about their operations. The contrast could not be more striking. Mit Ghamr shunned interest and actively promoted long-term development; today's Islamic banks pay and receive interest as a matter of course, and their primary activity is the promotion of trade.

Not that it is particularly Islamic to favor profit-and-loss sharing over interest. Profit-and-loss sharing predates Islam, and since the seventh century it has been practiced continually by diverse non-Muslim societies. Like the venture capital industry, the world's stock markets operate on the basis of profit-and-loss sharing. In any case, it is not clear that the Qur'anic prohibition of interest was originally understood to encompass the institution of interest as we know it today. What the Qur'an bans unambiguously is the pre-Islamic Arabian institution of *riba,* whereby a borrower saw his debt double following a default and redouble if he defaulted again. Because it tended to push defaulters into enslavement, riba had long been a source of communal friction. The purpose of the ban was undoubtedly to forestall communal disharmony by curbing, in the spirit of a modern bankruptcy law, the penalty for default. This is supported by the fact that the Qur'anic verses banning riba tend to be accompanied by calls for charity. The Qur'an enjoins lenders to show compassion toward borrowers in distress and to refrain from taking advantage of their misfortunes. The ban on riba may be interpreted, then, as an injunction against kicking a person when he is down.[47]

Many early Muslims subscribed to this interpretation, and they clashed with their contemporaries who read into the ban not an injunction against exploitation but a general prohibition of interest.[48] While the broader interpretation eventually gained dominance, this did not deter Muslims from continuing to borrow and lend at interest.[49] They went on doing so through various ruses, such as the following practice which leading jurists endowed with legitimacy: A wants to lend B $100 at 5 percent interest, without violating the ban. So he buys a chair from B in return for $100 and then promptly returns it for $105, payable in one year. The chair's ownership remains unchanged; B receives $100 now; and A stands to receive $105 in a year. While none of the individual transactions involve interest, together they are equivalent to a single transaction whereby A lends $100 to B at 5 percent per annum.

Murabaha, the most popular lending mechanism of the Islamic banks, is a similarly ancient ruse, which consists of several interest-free transactions that together amount to interest. Not surprisingly, murabaha was a source of controversy in the early days of Islamic banking. In 1980 Pakistan's Council of Islamic Ideology took a cautious view on its legitimacy, stating that although it was "permissible under the Shari'a, it would not be advisable to use it widely or indiscriminately."[50] Another common ruse takes the form of redefining as Y what everyone knows to be X. In Iran, for instance, the government has decreed that when a financial transaction between two public agencies takes place at a fixed rate of return, the charge involved is not called interest—as it would be if one of the parties were a private citizen. So agencies freely borrow from each other at interest, liberated by the twist of a definition from having to acknowledge their violation of what passes as a sacred Islamic tenet.[51]

While there is a consensus among both the theorists and practitioners of Islamic economics that interest is sinful, there is no consensus as to what is meant by an "interest-free" loan. Under inflation, is it the nominal rate of return that must be zero, or the real? In other words, must loans be indexed to the rate of inflation to protect their purchasing power? A few writers argue that indexation is not only legitimate but a requirement of justice, although the dominant view is that indexation is un-Islamic.[52] Two international conferences on indexation, one held in Islamabad in 1986 and the other in Jeddah in 1987, reached the conclusion that indexation is incompatible with Islam.[53] Nonetheless, the Islamic banks index their markups, commissions, and service charges to inflation. In Turkey, where in the mid-1980s the rate of inflation was about five times higher than in Pakistan, the markup under murabaha was also about five times higher.

Denunciations of the Anti-Interest Campaign and the Fundamentalist Defense

The controversy over interest rages on. Expositors without practical experience in banking tend to insist on the necessity of eliminating interest, but they are divided as to whether what goes as Islamic banking is genuinely Islamic. While many are comfortable with the ruses that provide ways around the prohibition, others see these as a manifestation of the Muslim community's moral degradation.[54]

Each of these positions has drawn fire from Süleyman Uludağ in a 1988 treatise that employs an Islamic form of expression and draws heavily on Islamic classics. Those who insist on banning interest are ignorant, he says, of Islamic history and guilty of misinterpreting the Qur'an, which bans not interest but usury, or exorbitant interest. And those who appreciate the impossibility of doing business without interest and who, for this reason, tolerate an array of ruses are guilty, in addition, of promoting dishonesty and hypocrisy. This, he says, is a serious crime against Islam, a religion that stands for truthfulness. It is also a grave offense against God: even if interest were unlawful, it would be a lesser sin to deal in interest openly than to cloak it in practices aimed at deceiving Him.[55] Uludağ's suggestion that Islamic banking promotes dishonesty is highly significant in view of the argument, mentioned earlier, that the diffusion of veritable profit-and-loss sharing must await the improvement of business morality. If so, Islamic banking is its own worst enemy: by fostering trickery and duplicity, it hinders the task of imbuing businessmen with norms of truthfulness and trustworthiness.

Another broad attack on the prevalent opinion concerning the legitimacy of interest came in 1989 through a legal opinion *(fatwa)* of Muhammad Sayyid Tantawi, mufti of Egypt. Interest-based banking instruments are not necessarily corrupt, says Tantawi, because they may benefit everyone involved, including third parties. Generally beneficial and, hence, legitimate intruments include, he says, high-yielding government bonds and interest-bearing savings accounts.[56] But Tantawi's position is a minority position within the Islamic establishment. The dominant position remains that all interest, regardless of the benefits it confers to borrowers, lenders, and third parties, violates both the spirit and the letter of Islam.

The proceedings of recent conferences on Islamic banking and statements by leading fundamentalists show that it is now a generally accepted view in fundamentalist circles that the Islamic banks in existence are not quite the intended interest-free institutions. Khurshid Ahmad, a prolific writer who has held influential positions on key governmental commissions charged with steering the Islamization of Pakistan's economy, has publicly criticized his country's Islamic banks, saying that "99 percent" of their business is still based on interest.[57] Many Islamic economists believe nonetheless that for all their identified shortcomings the Islamic banks are superior to conventional banks.

For one thing, they say, even if the Islamic banks lend at interest, they generally avoid paying interest to their depositors. Indeed, the dividends paid to depositors are not predetermined, in that they fluctuate. But the same can be said of the bond funds in operation throughout the Western world. A bond fund holds interest-bearing assets, its yield on any given day being the day's average interest income, minus a managerial commission. This average may vary from one day to the next because of changes in the fund's holdings. Yet the dividends paid to the fund's depositors are financed by pure interest. Similarly, the dividends the Islamic banks pay to their depositors originate, as we saw earlier, in thinly disguised forms of interest. The fact that these dividends fluctuate makes an Islamic bank no more "Islamic" than an ordinary bond fund in Korea or Switzerland.

The second line of defense against the shortcomings of Islamic banking hinges on its allegedly superior profitability. Independent observers have found, in fact, that in the late 1970s and early 1980s the Islamic banks made huge profits. But generally speaking their profit rates have subsequently fallen below the domestic norms. In a recent comparative study Clement Henry Moore finds that between 1984 and 1986 the Islamic banks in Bahrain, Tunisia, and Turkey earned higher returns on total assets than their conventional competitors, while those in Egypt, Jordan, Kuwait, Qatar, and the Sudan achieved substantially lower returns. Outside of Bahrain, only the younger Islamic banks seem to be enjoying returns above the norm. The star performers in this period were two Islamic banks in Turkey, the Al Baraka Turkish Finance House and the Faisal Finance Institution, both established in the mid-1980s.[58]

It is not surprising that certain Islamic banks have done very well, because they enjoy some special advantages. The existence of a small but significant group of savers who feel uncomfortable with interest has given the Islamic banks a ready-made source of deposits. Thus, with a handful of branches Turkey's Islamic banks managed in a few months to attract about 1 percent of the country's total bank deposits. After this initial surge, however, they found that for further expansion they must open more branches. The resulting rise in their overhead will most likely reduce their profitability. Still, they could remain more profitable than their conventional rivals because, like many of their counterparts elsewhere, the Turkish Islamic banks enjoy some important legal privileges. They enjoy tax breaks. They have lower-than-usual reserve requirements, which means that, relative to their rivals, they transfer a smaller fraction of their deposits to the Central Bank. And, unlike ordinary banks, they are allowed to engage in real estate transactions and in foreign trade.[59]

What is surprising, in view of all this, is that the older Islamic banks have tended to suffer a fall in profitability. A major reason is that they made careless loans during the oil boom of the 1970s, which are now taking a toll on their profits. The fact that some of these bad loans were made under profit-and-loss sharing helps explain why the Islamic banks are now lending almost exclusively on the basis of interest. It also supports my contention that these banks face a shortage of the skills required to make profit-and-loss sharing viable.[60] Interestingly, in terms of profitability Turkey's spectacular performers of the mid-1980s had by the late 1980s fallen below the Turkish norm.[61] While this slip is attributable in part to the expenses of establishing new branches, it calls for added caution in accepting the claim that Islamic banking is inherently more profitable.

Yet another defense of Islamic banking is that it enhances economic stability. In an interest-based system macroeconomic shocks may lower bank revenues, causing them to aggravate the crisis by defaulting on their interest obligations. This source of instability allegedly disappears when returns to depositors are variable, because any decline in bank revenues is then matched by a fall in bank obligations.[62] There is a flaw in this argument which stems from the implicit assumption that an Islamic bank whose revenues fall will not suffer a withdrawal of deposits. One would expect, on the contrary, deposits to move away from banks performing poorly and into those performing relatively well. There is, in fact, some evidence that the depositors in Islamic institutions are just as fickle as their counterparts in conventional banks. In Egypt, news in 1986 that the al-Rayan Islamic investment company lost $100 million speculating in gold provoked massive withdrawals. Depositors who were happy to hold al-Rayan's shares when high returns seemed assured were apparently unwilling to do so once the downside risk became appreciable.[63]

As Volker Nienhaus observes, Islamic banks losing funds must reduce the credit they supply to their clients.[64] So in any case it is not obvious that the replacement of interest by profit-and-loss sharing enhances macroeconomic stability. The opposite may well be true, and the Iranian and Pakistani governments take this danger seriously. Accordingly, Iran requires banks to share a single rate of return, while Pakistan forces rates to stay within a narrow band.[65] Thus, there is no necessary relationship in either Iran or Pakistan between a depositor's rate of return and the actual profitability of his own bank's operations. Since a common rate of return effectively does away with profit-and-loss sharing, one may infer that the Iranian and Pakistani authorities regard genuinely Islamic banking as destabilizing.

The Responses of Conventional Banks

We have seen in several contexts that attempts to establish interest-free banks or banking systems have failed to replace interest by its much heralded alternative, profit-and-loss sharing. In no country and in no sense has the anti-interest movement revolutionized banking, let alone the entire economic system. Perhaps this is why the secular financial community shows no sign of alarm. On the contrary, secular banks see the campaign against interest as having created an exploitable opportunity. In Egypt and elsewhere many conventional banks, even those under non-Muslim ownership, have established interest-free branches or windows, and some investment companies have begun touting their operations as "Islamic." Even Wall Street has become a player: Citicorp and other large American banks have devised financial instruments acceptable to their customers who prefer not to deal in interest. And where interest is illegal, European, American, and Far Eastern banks have had no trouble abiding formally by this ban. The Pakistani branches of Chase Manhattan and Deutsche Bank now do only interest-free business, although it is widely recognized that there is nothing fundamentally new about their operations.

Redistribution

Zakat

Like other major religions, Islam stands opposed to great inequalities in the distribution of resources. From the very beginning, therefore, it has featured mechanisms aimed at reducing, though not necessarily eliminating altogether, social inequalities. These include an inheritance law that specifies in intricate detail how a person's estate is to be divided among his relatives.[66] A more celebrated mechanism is *zakat,* an annual tax on wealth and income generally understood to incorporate certain levies that have been collected under other names, like the agricultural tax, *'ushr.* The proceeds of zakat are earmarked mostly for assistance to specific categories of impoverished and disadvantaged individuals. Mentioned explicitly in the Qur'an, zakat is viewed as one of the Five Pillars of Islam, along with belief in the unity of God, obligatory prayers, fasting during Ramadan, and pilgrimage to Mecca for those who can afford the trip.

The Qur'an provides only the broadest guidelines on zakat's coverage, and it leaves open the issue of rates. By tradition, it is levied on agricultural output, livestock, minerals, and precious metals—the major sources of income and wealth in seventh-century Arabia. The rate varies between 2.5 and 20 percent, depending on the source and on the conditions of production, although there are various exclusions and exemptions. Wealth held in the form of precious metals is subject to a 2.5 percent levy, while mining income is subject to the highest rate, 20 percent. For another illustration, the rate on agricultural output is 5 percent if the land is irrigated by the owner but 10 percent if it is irrigated naturally. Again by tradition, the beneficiaries of zakat include the poor, the handicapped, travelers in difficulty, debtors, dependents of prisoners, and the zakat collectors themselves. The proceeds are also used to free slaves and to assist people serving the cause of Islam.[67]

We do not know how zakat affected inequality in the Arabian economy of early Islam. It has been claimed that the scheme was progressive in collection, which is to say that its burden fell disproportionately on the rich.[68] This claim is plausible, but to determine the scheme's overall impact we would need to know not just the intended pattern of collection but also the actual patterns of collection and disbursement. If evasion was especially prevalent with respect to certain sources of income or if the proceeds went primarily to the well-to-do, the overall effect might have been unequalizing. In any case, the purpose of zakat was not only to reduce inequality but also to raise revenue for the Islamic state. The state was empowered, as already noted, to channel funds to "people serving the cause of Islam," which allowed it to spend zakat revenue on public works and territorial expansion. Such objectives need not have been compatible with the goal of inequality reduction.

But whatever the impact of zakat in seventh-century Arabia, in a modern economy the effect of a traditional zakat scheme is unlikely to be equalizing. For one thing, the involved rates are generally lower than those of the prevailing secular taxation systems; even the 20 percent levy on mining income falls short of the marginal income tax in most modern economies. For another, the commodities covered by the traditional scheme play a considerably less important role today than they did more than a millennium ago. In any economy, even a very undeveloped economy like that of the Sudan, a substantial portion of income originates in industry and the services, two sectors the traditional scheme exempts by default. And a substantial share of wealth is in forms not covered by the traditional scheme, such as oil wells and corporate equity.

Yet some expositors of Islamic economics consider the forms and rates used in the seventh century to be applicable, with similarly beneficial results, to any modern economy. They believe, moreover, that a restructuring of zakat would do violence to Islam's spirit.[69] This attachment to ancient specifics has drawn fire from the modernist school of Islamic thought. A luminary of this school, the late Fazlur Rahman, once wrote: "It is surely this kind of attitude which gives point to the communist maxim, 'religion is the opium of the poor people,' since it effectively throws dust in their eyes."[70] The modernists want the sources of collection to include new commodities and activities, and they favor varying the rates according to society's changing needs. They also wish to redefine the categories of expenditure.

The modernist position now has the support of most Islamic economists.[71] But among the reformists there is yet no consensus on what reform should entail. There are disagreements on rates, exemption limits, and disbursements. Another source of controversy is the seventh-century principle that property is taxable if it is apparent *(zahir)* but not if it is hidden *(batin)*. On the basis of this principle, some would exempt bank deposits, equities, and other financial assets. Others hold that because of advances in accounting and record keeping the distinction between apparent and hidden property has become obsolete.[72]

Voluntary versus Obligatory Zakat

Two of the zakat systems in operation, those of Pakistan and Saudi Arabia, feature major innovations concerning coverage and rates. While traditionally zakat was levied only on individuals, these countries have extended the obligation to companies, on the grounds that companies are juristic persons. In addition, they have imposed a flat levy on certain types of bank deposits. Saudi Arabia levies zakat on imports, at rates varying from commodity to commodity. Pakistan allows farmers to deduct their expenses on fertilizers and insecticides, items for which classical law makes no allowance. Another Pakistani innovation is that the levy is 5 percent on all farm output, regardless of the mode of irrigation.[73] In contrast to Pakistan and Saudi Arabia, Malaysia has in place a collection system that departs minimally from traditional stipulations. Thus, each farmer is granted a fixed exemption, but no deductions are allowed for modern production costs. Another striking aspect of the Malaysian system is that it effectively exempts industrial workers, bureaucrats, businessmen, and shopkeepers, as well as the growers of rubber, coconuts, and other tropical cash crops, none of whom are mentioned explicitly in classical texts.[74]

As one might expect, these systems vary greatly in terms of yield and incidence. Pakistani figures for 1987–88 show that revenue stood at 0.35 percent of Gross Domestic Product. A mere 8 percent of the total came from agriculture, which is explained partly by the difficulty of compelling rich and powerful landlords to pay their dues.[75] Saudi Arabian figures for the 1970s show that revenue hovered between 0.01 and 0.04 percent of Gross Domestic Product.[76] Given that per capita income in Saudi Arabia is much higher than in Pakistan, this is prima facie evidence of restrictive coverage and extensive loopholes. In fact, certain commodities of great economic importance, like housing, are exempt from zakat. There is also evidence of widespread evasion.[77] In Malaysia, too, the yield is constrained by extremely restrictive coverage and also by substantial evasion. As of 1988, the rate of compliance was just 8 percent.[78] More interestingly, however, the zakat burden falls almost exclusively on rice growers, a large share of whom lie below the country's poverty line. In the state of Perlis, for instance, rice growers accounted for 93 percent of the zakat collection in 1985.[79] If nothing else, this finding shows that zakat does not necessarily transfer resources *to* the poor; it may transfer resources *away* from them. It is also significant that in sharp contrast to Pakistan the agricultural sector carries a huge share of the burden. Within the agricultural sector, zakat is progressive at the lower end of the income scale because of the traditional exemptions. But it is regressive at the upper end, apparently because the wealthier farmers are more prone to evasion.[80] In one village in the state of Kedah, for which we have a detailed study by the political scientist James Scott, the rate of compliance between 1977 and 1979 was merely 15 percent—which means that the farmers evaded 85 percent of their obligations. Evasion took a variety of forms: disguising or underdeclaring one's cultivated acreage, underreporting one's crops, and handing over to the zakat collector spoiled or adulterated grain.[81]

Malaysia, Saudi Arabia, and Pakistan are among a handful of countries where zakat is administered by the state. In most of the Muslim world individuals have discretion over whether and how to pay zakat.[82] The Qur'an itself is mute on the issues of administration and enforcement, ruling out neither the centralized, obligatory mode nor the decentralized, voluntary mode. Yet each mode has a basis in historical precedent. In the earliest years of Islam, when the Muslim community lived in Mecca, assistance to the poor was unregulated and strictly voluntary. Zakat became a formal and compulsory transfer system shortly after the community's relocation to Medina (*hijra*), at a time when it was expanding very rapidly. Thus, during Prophet Muhammad's last few years zakat came to be administered by state-appointed agents and enforced, as necessary, by military might.[83] Barely two decades after his death, however, the Islamic state's ability to administer zakat crumbled as a result of violent leadership struggles.[84] From then on, zakat was up to the individual Muslim's discretion, although in certain times and places local bodies played a role in collection and disbursement. In sum, while zakat was a centrally administered, obligatory system during a brief but important segment of early Islamic history, for most of the religion's life it has been administered in a decentralized manner, the agents of enforcement being peer pressure, fear of God, and the individual's own conscience.

Distressingly little research has gone into the voluntary system in operation. But the available studies suggest that only a fraction of the nonimpoverished population pays regularly. A 1978 survey of educated middle-class Muslims in Karachi showed that while almost all had heard of zakat, fewer than a quarter made regular payments themselves.[85] Under the present system in Pakistan, Muslim citizens must themselves assess their dues on their precious metals and deposit these voluntarily into the national zakat fund. According to an internal document of the Permanent Commission on Islamisation of Economy, such deposits have been negligible.[86] Revealingly, the zakat tables in the *Pakistan Statistical Yearbook* contain no entry for precious metals. Yet a study on the zakat potential of another country, Turkey, suggests that the dues on precious metals may be substantial. On gold and diamonds alone, the study found, this potential is around 5.5 percent of Turkey's annual savings.[87] But it would be very difficult to enforce payments on precious metals, since they are easily hidden. In any case, an enforcement campaign would most certainly cause people to shift their wealth from precious metals into assets exempt from zakat, like real estate.

Another important finding is that charity is not the only impetus for making voluntary payments. Other common motives are the encouragement of worker loyalty and the promotion of social conformity. In the Kedah village studied by Scott, where payment was essentially voluntary until 1955, it was customary for landowners to make, under the rubric of zakat, a small gift to their workers, over and above wages. This gift, which the workers came to expect, helped ensure the loyalty of the landowner's work force during times of peak labor demand. Typically, the size of a worker's gift depended on his "respectability," as judged by the landowner. A worker whose comportment, manners, or political views gave him an unfavorable reputation received a relatively small gift. In addition to reputable workers the major beneficiaries appear to have been the village's religious functionaries, such as the teacher of religion and the caretaker of the local mosque.[88]

If the system that existed in Kedah is any indication, the voluntary mode does not treat the needy equitably. Apart from the religious establishment, it benefits primarily those with connections, tending to pass over the truly destitute, the unemployed, and the handicapped. This observation is bolstered by the common fact that the Muslim world has long featured, even in relatively prosperous localities, many desperately poor people who receive little, if any, charity. Against this background, the ongoing fundamentalist campaign to recentralize the administration of zakat is, if not reasonable, at least understandable. The proponents of obligatory zakat argue that this mode will augment the funds available for distribution and prevent their disbursement on the basis of personal ties. They remind us that the Prophet himself made zakat obligatory and also that the currently dominant voluntary mode took hold *after* the Prophet's death.

State-Administered Zakat in Operation

How, then, are the recently instituted state-administered systems performing? Are they more successful than their decentralized counterparts at channeling resources to the poor? Have they overcome the role of personal connections? Given the sparseness of the pertinent documentation and research, these questions can only be answered in a tentative manner. But we shall see clearly that the high hopes of the architects of obligatory zakat have not materialized.

In Pakistan, zakat revenues are channeled by the Zakat Administration to thousands of local committees that decide whom in their communities to support. The funds are allocated among the committees roughly according to the populations they represent, which means that relatively poor communities generally receive more than their contributions to the national fund.[89] According to official records, during the 1980–88 period 58 percent of the zakat funds went as subsistence allowances to people unable to work, including widows, orphans, and the handicapped.[90] But the grants involved were much too small to make a significant difference in the living standards of such groups. In the 1980s, when an individual needed an estimated $22 a month just to survive, most zakat payments varied between $4 and $8 per individual, and in some regions the typical payment was as low as $1.[91] The system has one million beneficiaries, which represents about 10 percent of the Pakistanis situated below the country's poverty line. An official report notes in this connection that in its eight years of operation Pakistan's state-administered zakat system has had little visible impact on inequality. There has been no noticeable decline, it says, in the number of beggars and no discernible alleviation of poverty. Under the circumstances, "people are losing faith not only in the system, but also in the belief that Islam offers a better economic order."[92]

It would be a gross error, the report goes on to say, to attribute the system's failure merely to a shortage of resources. The funds set aside for subsistence aid and rehabilitation should have been enough to provide around $8 per month to every person below the poverty line. While the assumptions that underlie this assertion are open to question, the figure is suggestive, as the report itself indicates, of serious mismanagement and corruption.[93] In fact, ever since the system's inception Pakistan has been awash in rumors and newspaper reports of arbitrariness, favoritism, nepotism, and embezzlement. The zakat recipients apparently include "orphans" with two living parents, "impoverished women" wearing rows of gold bracelets, and "old people" long under the ground. Zakat resources have also been used by influential people as a slush fund for programs benefiting primarily the rich.[94]

Ever since the beginning, Pakistan's Zakat Administration has been allocating about 20 percent of its funds to rehabilitation. Under this program, many poor women have received a sewing machine. Unfortunately, the earning ability of these women is hampered by their lack of training and materials.[95] Still, there is a growing feeling in official circles that properly managed rehabilitation and public works programs would constitute more effective antidotes to poverty than subsistence allowances. Accordingly, the Zakat Administration is now building seventy-five thousand houses for the poor and various public works schemes are under discussion.[96] Ironically, it was a modernist, Fazlur Rahman, who launched the debate on whether zakat funds could be used on public health, housing, and education. When in the 1960s he pushed for a program-oriented expenditure pattern, he was denounced by fundamentalists for promoting a scheme not anchored in Islamic tradition. Since then the widely recognized failures of the subsistence-oriented expenditure pattern have made many fundamentalists increasingly receptive to innovative alternatives.

Malaysia's federal structure assigns the administration of zakat to an office at the state level. In each state, collected funds are forwarded to the zakat office for disbursement. Here is how the zakat office in Alor Setar, the capital of Kedah, allocated its proceeds in 1970, according to its own official report. Of the total, 53 percent went toward "commendable measures" (which generally means religious education), 6 percent to people making a pilgrimage to Mecca, 2 percent to converts, 22 percent as commissions to the zakat collectors and central administration, leaving a mere 15 percent for the poor.[97] Figures from the early 1980s show that disbursements to the poor ranged between 11 and 13 percent, with zakat officials and various religious causes claiming much of the rest.[98] In Perlis, likewise, about 12 percent of the annual zakat revenue was going to the poor, the lion's share being set aside for zakat officials, the faculty and students of Islamic schools, and pilgrims.[99] The amounts given to the indigent were minuscule. Those included in the list of recipients received between $3 and $19 (U.S.) a year—for many, a sum less than the cost of traveling to the zakat office to collect the money.[100]

As in Pakistan, funds collected in one locality are often spent in another. Thus, an impoverished rice-growing village that supplies funds to the system will not necessarily receive anything in return. In the village studied by Scott, in fact, not a single poor peasant had ever received aid through the zakat office, at least as of 1980. Apparently, the only recipient of official aid was the university-student son of the zakat collector, one of the wealthiest men in the village.[101] Many Malaysian Islamic economists now recognize that the established system is an embarrassment to those who have touted it as a supremely effective measure against poverty. Some are now advocating a drastic reorientation of expenditures toward rehabilitation. One proposal is to use zakat funds for providing the very poor with resources to start their own businesses. Another is to divert a portion of the funds into a program to help urban prostitutes find new jobs.[102]

As we saw earlier, decentralized, voluntary zakat was criticized for its bias against poor people without proper connections and its failure to alleviate poverty. The Pakistani and Malaysian records suggest that the same flaws may also afflict obligatory zakat administered by the state. The two modes do differ, of course, in their effects, but the essential difference lies neither in fairness nor in ability to reduce poverty. It lies, rather, in the connections to which they confer value. Decentralized zakat confers value to economic connections, especially ones based on employment; state-administered zakat confers value to political connections, particularly ones touching on religion. Thus, under Malaysia's old decentralized system, the surest way to obtain regular zakat payments was to work loyally for a wealthy landlord; under the current centralized system, it is to enroll in a religious school or to work for the zakat office.

A major difference between the current Pakistani and Malaysian systems lies in the source of compensation for officials of the zakat administration. In Malaysia officials are paid out of zakat revenues, in accordance with scripture. In Pakistan they are paid out of general government funds, apparently to enhance the system's appeal by fostering the illusion that the system operates costlessly.[103] Even in Pakistan, of course, the religious establishment benefits from the system. Some religious functionaries receive compensation for collection and administration, and in addition, a portion of zakat revenue is channeled into religious education.[104] But the religious establishment's stake in zakat has been far greater in Malaysia, where helping the poor appears as a convenient pretext for advancing broad Islamic objectives and for lining the pockets of religious officials. It is important to recognize that the official Malaysian figures underestimate the actual take of the officials. There are various irregularities in collection that benefit the collectors personally. For instance, collectors are known to under-invoice their collections, presumably embezzling the differences.[105]

Malaysia's state-administered zakat system has generated resentment among the peasantry, which tends to view it as just another tax. What may be surprising is that many ordinary Pakistanis harbor similar feelings. One cause of their resentment is the impression of widespread corruption. As in Malaysia, another factor is that the payer does not see, much less determine, how his personal contribution is spent.[106] Not only does this deny him the satisfaction of observing his contribution's impact, but it opens up the possibility of disagreement over spending priorities and decisions. A zakat payer whose needy acquaintances are passed over by a fund known to support distant students may well consider the system inequitable, as apparently many contributors do. Some telling evidence on people's dislike of governmental involvement is that almost no contributions were made to a voluntary zakat fund established by the Pakistani government in the 1950s.[107] More recent evidence comes from a Malaysian survey conducted in 1987 by Aidit bin Ghazali. About 60 percent of this survey's participants indicated that they prefer to choose the beneficiaries of their zakat payments on their own, as opposed to leaving the decision to the government.[108]

A significant source of friction in Pakistan has been the Shi'ite minority's unwillingness to pay zakat to a Sunni-dominated government.[109] In its original form, the zakat law obliged all Muslims to contribute to the government-administered fund, but when the Shi'ites took to the street in protest, the law was amended to give members of minority sects the option of exemption. To exercise this option a Shi'ite would simply have to submit an affidavit to his bank or the rural zakat collector.[110] Many Shi'ite depositors have opted to exempt themselves, and it is known that a small number of Sunni depositors are passing as Shi'ites simply to avoid the automatic annual deductions.

Yet another cause of frustration lies in the compulsory nature of the payments. In each of these countries, some individual Muslims feel that obligatory payments leave their religious obligations unmet. Accordingly, they make additional payments to people of their own choice.[111] In Malaysia there is even a terminological distinction between the two types of zakat. Payments to the government are referred to by a pejorative term, *zakat raja*, literally the "ruler's zakat," while voluntary payments made as acts of charity are called *zakat peribadi*, or "personal zakat." Because some Pakistanis and Malaysians make zakat payments over and above their obligatory payments, zakat transfers more wealth to the poor than shown by the official records. But while I know of no systematic research on the additional transfers, they do not seem to be large. In neither Pakistan nor Malaysia can the typical indigent count on significant support from the well-to-do.

Evaluation

Underlying all the problems of the recently established zakat systems—public opposition to government involvement, widespread evasion, nepotism, and the diversion of extensive resources to the religious establishment—are two basic characteristics of human nature. People's perceptions of justice and efficiency are colored by their personal experiences and circumstances. And people seek to influence the allocation of resources as a means of promoting their own priorities. Thus, no society is without citizens opposed to government spending patterns; charges of favoritism, fraud, and misuse are as ubiquitous as government itself. In general, moreover, government officials are more sympathetic than ordinary citizens to centralized redistribution and relatively less trusting of private decision making. In view of these observations, the recorded frictions over zakat are merely another manifestation of the universal struggle to control resource allocation. This should not be obscured by the religious character of zakat. Neither Islam nor any other religion has overcome the human impulse to control economic outcomes.

Earlier I concluded that Islamic banking has not revolutionized the way Muslims save and invest. Now I can add that zakat has not made a major dent in Muslim poverty and inequality. While it has obviously redistributed some income and wealth, it has not conferred substantial benefits on the poor as a group. One must recognize in this connection that in its fundamentalist interpretation zakat constitutes a rather conservative means of redistribution. Touching neither on productive assets like land and physical capital nor on consumptive goods like housing and furniture, it is a vehicle for limited transfers involving a restricted menu of goods and assets. Even in the best of circumstances the distributional impact of such a scheme would be modest. Under poor management it has been downright disappointing.

In response to this assessment one might reiterate that by extending its coverage to new forms of income and wealth zakat may be turned into a highly significant instrument of redistribution. The potential yield is indeed considerable. Islamic economists have shown that it can exceed 3 percent of Gross National Product.[112] But this estimate overlooks the huge problem of evasion. In any case, to turn zakat into a major equalizer it is not enough to raise its yield. It is necessary also to increase the share of the proceeds channeled to the poor. This will require the development of auditing systems and the establishment of social and legal sanctions that counter the motivation to divert funds away from the poor.

The existing state-administered systems might be defended on the grounds that many other official transfer programs are afflicted by the same problems. But remember that Islamic economics aspires to vastly superior standards. It promises not that zakat will do as well as other systems of redistribution but that it will do markedly better.

Economic Development: The Role of Islamic Morality

Islamic economics claims, as mentioned, that Islamic scripture harbors solutions to every conceivable economic problem. Many problems are to be solved by curbing selfishness through injunctions concerning consumption, production, and exchange. If these injunctions are followed, the pace of economic development will allegedly quicken, while taking on a fairer, more balanced, and less disruptive form. This assertion turns on its head the long-standing Western suspicion that Islam is an obstacle to modernization.[113] Rejecting the notion that Islam is inimical to economic development, Islamic economics affirms it to be a principal source of growth and harmony.

In their most general form the advocated economic injunctions consist of moral guidelines common to many value systems, both religious and secular. The individual is encouraged to enjoy the bounties of civilization, but he must be willing to share his possessions with others, particularly with the less fortunate. He must refrain from abusing the goods at his disposal and from keeping them unutilized. As a producer or trader, he is free to seek personal profit. But in exercising this freedom he must avoid harming others. Nor must he earn more than his efforts justify; he must pay "fair" wages to his employees and charge "just" prices to his customers. Remaining honest in his economic dealings, he must admit his mistakes and avoid false advertising. He must work hard and strive to fulfill his commitments.[114]

In the early centuries of Islam these general injunctions were applied to a panoply of situations, generating multitudes of specific injunctions. For example, the requirement to earn no more than one's fair share was taken to imply that Islam prohibits the sale or purchase of a fruit tree in blossom. The logic: since the traders cannot predict the tree's yield with certainty, the selected price could cause an unearned gain for one party and an undeserved loss for the other.[115] Some Islamic economists consider such ancient interpretations to retain validity in the modern world, even though some are contradictory and classical Islamic jurisprudence provides several different interpretations of many individual cases.[116] Feeling less constrained by classical applications, other Islamic economists call for fresh interpretations.[117]

But regardless of where they stand on the applicability of ancient interpretations, the Islamic economists generally agree that if the moral guidelines of Islam are observed and enforced the economic performance of Muslim societies will improve dramatically. People will readily sacrifice their own material pleasures for society's interests. They will find their economic activities more fulfilling. Even their jobs will become more satisfying, as they take on the character of worship. Some writers observe such changes already in countries that have committed themselves to Islamization. Here is a striking statement by a Turkish writer in a 1987 volume on economic development and Islam.

In February 1982, I was in a bus on the way to Tehran airport, at dawn, during the time of morning prayers. We passed a middle aged, bearded street sweeper, who was cleaning the sidewalk on one of the main avenues. That one glimpse gave me the impression that in this hour of prayer he was sweeping with devotion and ecstasy. The glow on his face affected me deeply, and I conveyed my feelings to the young Iranian sitting beside me. He explained: "At various levels of our society there are Muslims for whom diligent, effective work is like worship, like a service to religion and community. This street sweeper must know that to devote oneself to cleaning the streets of an Islamic state is a form of worship.[118]

The central point of the article to which this quote belongs is that successful development requires imbuing society with a communitarian morality of self-sacrifice, altruism, and brotherhood. This is not an isolated view. The literature is replete with statements such as, "[Islam] deals with all aspects of economic development but always in the framework of total human development and never in a form divorced from this perspective."[119]

In accordance with this view, a major, if not the primary, source of the Muslim world's underdevelopment is held to be its moral degeneration. The standard of morality began falling when the "rightly guided" caliphs of the seventh century were succeeded by a string of increasingly corrupt leaders. But this degeneration has taken a calamitous form only in recent centuries, through the influence of the West. Declining morality, say Islamic economists, has sapped productivity and reduced the effectiveness of government. Moreover, by weakening the ties of Islamic brotherhood, it has made Muslims oblivious to one another's needs. As a sad consequence, Muslims are divided on key issues and their rivalries are keeping them from cooperating toward common objectives. Low morality is also held substantially responsible for the practical shortcomings of zakat and Islamic banking. The misuse of zakat funds is attributed to the moral deficiencies of local officials. Likewise, the continuing prevalence of interest-based lending is ascribed, as we saw, to rampant dishonesty in the business community.

All this is taken to mean that moral education must be accorded a crucial role in the process of economic development. Through family and school instruction, people must be molded to fit the requirements of a just, harmonious, and efficient society. They must be imbued with the notion that they belong to a community of Muslims, the *umma*, whose interest takes precedence over their interests as individuals. One may reform the institutions of society, as opposed to the people who live by them. Many students of development would argue that underdevelopment is caused primarily—though not exclusively—by institutional inefficiency, in other words, by the unsuitability of a society's institutions to its particular needs and circumstances. As far as I know, no Islamic economist denies that social institutions matter; after all, they attach great importance to the institution of zakat. The distinctiveness of their position lies in the primacy it gives to the restructuring of individuals. Throughout the Muslim world, of course, massive efforts have been made since the beginnings of Islam to instill in individuals an Islamic morality. Have these efforts influenced work effort, generosity, and market behavior? If so, how? Islamic economics has undertaken no serious investigation of such matters, treating it as self-evident that Islamic education furthers growth and justice simultaneously.

Much of Islamic economics conveys the impression that a communitarian ethic is a prerequisite for economic development. But certain writers hold that such an ethic is an objective in its own right. This objective takes precedence, they say, over economic development, recognizing explicitly that moral imperatives may in certain contexts conflict with growth.[120] But the two camps are united in the belief that Islamic morality is a crucial ingredient of healthy economic development. Accordingly, they agree that Muslim societies have been held back by an individualistic ethic that keeps them from working together toward common objectives.

A striking aspect of this emphasis on the inculcation of a communitarian ethic is that it draws no distinction between numerically small and large groups. The Islamic morality of self-sacrifice, altruism, and brotherhood is expected to work with equal effectiveness and beneficence in a populous modern nation as among Prophet Muhammad's first group of companions. Let us be clear about what this means. The development of a country committed to an Islamic way of life is expected to be driven substantially by Muslims' efforts to meet one another's observable needs and by their mutual cooperation toward jointly held and commonly perceived goals.

There are two serious flaws in this thinking. First, it implicitly attributes to the individual an infinite ability to receive, store, retrieve, and process information. In fact, even in a small city no individual can handle more than a minuscule fraction of the information relevant to local interests. Consequently, no member of a modern nation can be aware of the wants of more than a tiny fraction of his fellow citizens. He may understand the needs of his acquaintances and have some feel for the wants of strangers. But in general not even a pure altruist can be expected to be capable of identifying the socially optimal course of action. The argument's second flaw is that it overlooks the difficulty of generating common goals. In a large society, environmental heterogeneities and the division of labor make individuals experience different joys and frustrations and develop different conceptions of reality. As a result, they tend to form different judgments concerning justice and efficiency. A common Islamic education might mitigate these differences but never eliminate them.

This argument is supported by recent applications of Islamic economics. Islamic banks are supposed to commit a portion of their assets to making interest-free loans to the needy *(qard hasana)*. By and large they make such loans only to their own employees, in the form of advances on their salaries. Evidently, Islamic bankers are more sensitive to the needs of their acquaintances than to those of strangers. The same can be said about officials charged with distributing society's zakat funds. The pervasive irregularities in their operations indicate that they are inclined to differentiate among the needs of their fellow Muslims.

In an isolated group numbering at most in the low hundreds and whose members perform similar tasks, the range of experiences may be sufficiently narrow and the volume of relevant information sufficiently small to enable a veritable agreement on objectives. Moreover, the individual members of such a group may possess adequate knowledge of one another's needs. But it is sheer romanticism to expect such traits to characterize a population running into the millions. In a large society, sustained cooperation toward jointly held and commonly understood ends is possible only in small subgroups like the family, the work team, and tightly knit partnerships.

If economics has taught us anything over the past two centuries, it is that the institution of the market allows traders pursuing *different,* rather than *similar,* ends to achieve mutually satisfying outcomes. As an unrivaled economizer of information, the market permits traders to serve the needs of others while pursuing nothing but their own selfish objectives. True, the viability of the market mechanism depends on the existence of certain constraints on people's actions, such as property rights, sanctions against dishonesty, regulations to curb harmful externalities, and contracting rules. And cooperative production in firms is a source of immense social gain. Still, a large society's economic viability is ensured not simply, or even mainly, by altruism or joint-ness of purpose. A crucial role is played by institutions that make traders, whether lone individuals or firms, serve society as a by-product of personal pursuits based on personal knowledge. Put differently, prosperity does not require the commonality of all knowledge, in the sense of each person knowing the needs of every other person. Nor does it require general conformity to joint objectives. Given people's very limited informational abilities, it always requires some division of knowledge and labor.

Friedrich Hayek, the most forceful modern exponent of these insights, traces the common misperception that the economic viability of a large society depends on jointness of both knowledge and purpose to Aristotle's teachings on household man-agement and individual enterprise. These teachings showed no comprehension of the market order in which Aristotle lived, yet they set the pattern over the following two thousand years for religious and philosophical thinking on the social order. General-izing erroneously from the household to the wider economy, later thinkers such as Thomas Aquinas propagated the notion that only actions aiming at known benefits to others are morally justified and, hence, economically desirable. Not until the eigh-teenth century would it be recognized that the market makes it possible "to do a service to another without bearing him a real kindness," or even knowing him.[121]

But habits of thought do not die easily. Socialism, arguably the most influential social doctrine of the twentieth century, promotes the notion that a classless society is possible, even inevitable, where selfish greed has given way to benevolence. Hayek calls this the "fatal conceit" of our time, the fundamental error that has led dozens of countries to unbearable inefficiency and tyranny. The supremely efficient, just, and harmonious society promised by socialism has existed nowhere but in murals of bliss-ful workers resolutely serving socialism.

This brings us back to the Iranian street sweeper. The apparent glow on his face was taken to imply that Islam can generate widespread benevolence and, further, that this benevolence can propel a large, complex economy like that of modern Iran. This thinking obviously betrays the Aristotelian influences on Islamic philosophy. Like other derivatives of Aristotelian thought, such as socialism, this philosophy rests to a substantial degree on empirically untenable assumptions concerning human inclina-tions and capabilities.[122]

Given the preeminence of morality in Islamic thinking on economic development, one might expect some consensus of opinion on the proper domain of government and on the need for central planning. In fact, there is none. The literature harbors various arguments in favor of government ownership and central planning, and many others in favor of private property and the market mechanism, all supported by reve-lation and tradition.[123] Significantly, the term "Islamic" has been juxtaposed both with "socialism" and with "capitalism." And however tolerant or intolerant of market pro-cesses, regimes have had no trouble finding an Islamic basis for their policies. This point is seldom appreciated by the exponents of Islamic economics, who claim rou-tinely that their own particular positions are rooted in a well-articulated divine law that admits a single, unambiguous meaning.

It was not lost on Hashemi Rafsanjani, who as speaker of the Iranian Parliament observed during a heated debate on the economic role of government that some of his colleagues favored more control over the economy, others less. Describing the disagreements as "differences among experts, not over matters of religion," he said that "Islam can accommodate all these views." It is desirable, he went on, that the rival camps reach a consensus. But if a consensus cannot be reached, then the majority view will have to prevail, and "if in practice the majority view yields no results, then the community will obviously revert to the other view."[124] As Shaul Bakhash observes, "To say that the government will try one policy and, if it fails, it will go back and try another is . . . very different from asserting that Islam requires that economic and property relations be ordered on the basis of divine law."[125]

Islamic economics features divisions on numerous other concerns of the field we call "development economics," like trade protection and industrial promotion. Many such issues have no counterparts in early Islam. In seventh-century Arabia central planning was not a possibility, industrialization not an issue. The economy being mostly nonmonetized, there was no monetary policy in the modern sense. It is even doubtful that the notion of economic development was present. The early Muslims had a sense of the ideal economy: one which treats its participants fairly and minimizes inequality. And they clearly felt that the attainment of this ideal depends on curbing selfishness and dishonesty. There is no evidence, however, that they conceived of self-sustaining economic growth, let alone that they reflected and agreed on how best to attain it. In view of all this, it is not surprising that Islamic economics is as divided on the institutional context of development as it is united on the primacy of morality.

Prognosis

It is time to pull together the threads of a long argument. In practice, not to mention doctrine, Islamic economics is hardly as comprehensive as its proponents apparently believe. Its concrete applications have been limited essentially to redistribution and banking. Not even in Pakistan, which has undertaken the most carefully planned attempt to reorder an economy according to Islamic precepts, and which has a population emotionally committed to Islam, has the scope of reform gone much beyond these two areas. Like the underlying theory, the implemented modifications lack coherence. Islamic redistribution and banking have involved two separate agendas, and neither has been reconciled with other institutions and practices serving related or similar goals. As a case in point the Pakistani zakat scheme exists side by side with a plethora of price controls and indirect taxes which counteract, if not offset, the intended redistribution. Nor have the specific reforms been revolutionary in their consequences. The advent of Islamic banking has altered only the cosmetics of banking and finance, and zakat has nowhere led to a perceptible reduction in poverty or inequality. Finally, the Islamic economic agenda remains poorly defined. It is not yet clear, for instance, whether the ban on interest precludes the indexation of monetary commitments. And while there is agreement on the desirability of imbuing Muslims with an Islamic morality, no consensus has emerged on what this implies for govern-ment activity.

In trying to explain why Islamic economics has had no major impact, one identifies several classes of causes. First, its many ambiguities allow the prevailing political forces to give it whatever meaning seems least threatening to the status quo. Second, certain elements of the Islamic economic agenda conflict with human nature. Thus, Muslims are required to accept financial risk, whereas they prefer to avoid it. And they are supposed to pay zakat on their precious metals, but they prefer not to. Third, the Islamic reforms have been impeded by social realities that their promoters have ex-pected religious sentiment to overcome. We saw, for instance, how the continuing prevalence of tax evasion has made it imprudent for bankers to engage in profit-and-loss sharing. And fourth, the Islamic reforms have suffered from poor organization and a shortage of skills. While there is some demand in every society for profit-and-loss sharing, the Islamic banks do not yet possess the skills necessary to make this financing technique viable. Likewise, the established zakat systems suffer from a lack of effective monitoring.

What does the future hold for Islamic economics, and what of its continuing im-pact? The myth that the reforms undertaken in the name of Islam represent radical departures from preexisting practices probably cannot be sustained for much longer. But they can be recognized as ineffective without causing the abandonment of basic objectives like the elimination of interest. People do not modify their ideologies at the first sign that they conflict with reality. As Albert Hirschman suggests, mental resis-tance is especially pronounced where the fit between ideology and reality was poor to begin with. Given the initial disparity, new facts that contradict the ideology do not worsen the fit appreciably and are therefore disregarded or else easily rationalized.[126] In any event, even when an individual becomes disillusioned with the prevailing ideology, real or imagined social pressures might make him refrain from publicizing his doubts.

Yet, as long as some individuals have the will to voice their misgivings, there is reason to expect the eventual mobilization of an organized opposition, even in coun-tries where the wisdom of Islamization is now seldom questioned in public. How long, then, will it take for the emergence of broad-based dissent? And what will be the response of committed fundamentalists? Forecasting is a difficult task, especially, it has been said, when it is about the future. A social scientist can detect instabilities but not predict when these will give way to order, recognize sources of conflict but not specify how these will be resolved, and identify ranges of future possibilities but not provide a definitive account of impending evolution. While historical circum-stances delimit the possible evolutionary paths, historical accidents determine the paths actually followed.

One possible scenario is for the ongoing quest for a moral order to become an obsession that makes power holders try earnestly to perfect the individual Muslim. Since there is vast room for disagreement on the nature of moral perfection, a consen-sus that the human impulses of Muslims need no further organizing would never emerge. But if the history of socialism is any indication, it could take decades for a broad segment of society to wonder why the desired benevolence is so difficult to elicit. Failures along the way could easily be taken to mean that educational efforts need to be redoubled and non-Islamic influences curbed further. In this vain search for the Islamic utopia the political establishment would become increasingly repressive, making it treacherous to suggest that Islam does not offer clear and definitive answers to all economic problems. Meanwhile, the discipline of Islamic economics could feed on itself for decades, mistaking apologetics for serious reflection and cosmetics for genuine reform. The twenty-first century could thus become for Islam what the twentieth was for socialism: a period of infinite hope and promise, followed by disappointment, repression, disillusionment, and despair. Identified with failed policies, Islam would lose its authority as a wellspring of sound economic policy. The sequence could end with a flight from Islam into other sources of spiritual and moral inspiration.

An alternative scenario is for Islamic economics which emerged as a movement to restore idealized economic relationships of the past to turn into a major innovative force. After all, the Protestant Reformation started as a backward-looking movement, only gradually assuming a forward-looking character. As the historian R. H. Tawney has documented, Luther and other leaders of the Reformation fought for the reestablishment of virtues they thought had been abandoned; yet, paradoxically, their attacks on ecclesiastical corruption weakened Church authority, thereby accelerating the developments they tried to reverse. The Reformation thus set the stage for the Industrial Revolution.[127] Such a scenario could be replayed within the Islamic world. Here is a possible sequence of events. The current preoccupation with economic morality turns the spotlight on incumbent political establishments, heightening the perception that they are corrupt. Thus delegitimized and weakened, the existing regimes are replaced by fundamentalist regimes which promise to rid society of its major social and economic problems by restoring properly Islamic values and practices. Alas, problems do not just yield to the new order. Disillusionment sets in, the fundamentalist regimes split into discordant factions, and the ensuing power struggles force the traditionally interventionist governments of the Muslim world to loosen their controls on private economic activity. By the time central governments regain their lost authority, market institutions are firmly entrenched and private enterprise very influential. These developments leave the promoters of an Aristotelian morality with no significant base of support.

Just as the rise of European capitalism coincided with the emergence of new social philosophies, so, too, political and economic liberalization in the Islamic world could be accompanied by a far-reaching transformation of Islamic economics. The Islamic banks become genuine venture capital organizations, and zakat evolves into a bona fide social security system. Meanwhile, it becomes commonplace that feelings of altruism and solidarity carry less significance in a large, complex economy than in a small, simple one. And the notion that the Islamic scriptures offer limited help in the realm of economic policy gains increasing recognition. There are, in fact, precedents within Islam's heritage for accepting the limitations of the traditional sources. As a case in point, the religious establishment eventually released army commanders from the requirement to abide by Islam's rules of warfare, permitting Muslim armies to act as their commanders saw fit.

In a less tumultuous and less circuitous variant of the second scenario, the key players are the practitioners of Islamic economics. Endeavoring to implement Islamic economics, they recognize the unattainability of its key objectives. As we have seen, this point has already been reached in Islamic banking, where bankers instructed to lend on the basis of profit-and-loss sharing have discovered that under current circumstances this yields more loss than profit. Sensing that it may never be practical to do away with interest, that zakat requires much new thinking to become an effective instrument of redistribution, and that the envisaged moral transformation is a mirage, onetime believers in Islamic economics begin chipping away at its edifice. At first they transform only the practice, resorting to many ruses. Then they begin altering the theory openly—for example, by redefining interest and reformulating the mechanics of zakat. Their endeavors meet with the approval of individuals with a stake in common practices, including fundamentalists who have prospered doing "interest-laden" business. In this scenario the practitioners of Islamic economics serve as hidden agents of secularization, arbiters between the discipline's goals and the secular practices it still condemns.

Acknowledgments

In conducting the research that underlies this essay, I benefited from the assistance of many people, who shared with me their knowledge and insights, put at my disposal important texts, and critiqued earlier drafts. I am indebted especially to Anjum Altaf, Muhammad Anwar, R. Scott Appleby, Sohrab Behdad, Ruşen Çakır, Murat Çizakça, Nazif Gürdoğan, S. M. Hasanuzzaman, Abdul Jabbar Khan, Daniel Klein, Jomo K. S., Ann Mayer, Anthony Milner, Clement Henry Moore, Jeffrey Nugent, Frederic Pryor, D. M. Qureshi, Tanzil-ur-Rahman, Yusuf Rahme, and Shahid Zahid. My interpretations do not necessarily conform to the opinions of these individuals, which in any case are diverse. The essay was composed partly during a sabbatical at the Institute for Advanced Study, Princeton, where I held a fellowship of the National Endowment for the Humanities. Part of my research was supported by the Faculty Research and Innovation Fund of the University of Southern California.

Notes

1. For further details, see Afzal Iqbal, *Islamisation of Pakistan* (Delhi: Idarah-i Adabiyat-i Delli, 1984), chap. 10.

2. Clement Henry Moore, "Islamic Banks: Financial and Political Intermediation in Arab Countries," *Orient* 29 (1988): 45–57.

3. For a sympathetic survey of this literature and a useful, though dated, bibliography, see Muhammad Nejatullah Siddiqi, *Muslim Economic Thinking: A Survey of Contemporary Literature* (Leicester: Islamic Foundation, 1981). Among the influential contributions in English are Mohammad

Abdul Mannan, *Islamic Economics: Theory and Practice* (Lahore: Sh. Muhammad Ashraf, 1970); Khurshid Ahmad, ed., *Studies in Islamic Economics* (Jeddah: International Center for Research in Islamic Economics, 1980); Syed Nawab Haider Naqvi, *Ethics and Economics: An Islamic Synthesis* (Leicester: Islamic Foundation, 1981); Ziauddin Ahmed, Munawar Iqbal, and M. Fahim Khan, eds., *Fiscal Policy and Resource Allocation in Islam* (Jeddah: International Center for Research in Islamic Economics, 1983); Ziauddin Ahmed, Munawar Iqbal, and M. Fahim Khan, eds., *Money and Banking in Islam* (Jeddah: International Center for Research in Islamic Economics, 1983); and Mohsin S. Khan and Abbas Mirakhor, eds., *Theoretical Studies in Islamic Banking and Finance* (Houston: Institute for Research and Islamic Studies, 1987).

4. "Announcement on Research Proposals," revised 4th ed. (Jeddah: International Center for Research in Islamic Economics, 1983).

5. For a sampling of Ibn Khaldun's writings, see *An Arab Philosophy of History: Selections from the "Prolegomena" of Ibn Khaldun of Tunis (1332–1406)*, translated and arranged by Charles Issawi (Princeton, N.J.: Darwin Press, 1987; 1st ed., 1950).

6. A representative economic work by Maududi is *The Economic Problem of Man and Its Islamic Solution* (Lahore: Islamic Publications, 1975; 1st Urdu ed., 1947).

7. Qutb's most relevant work is *Social Justice in Islam,* J. D. Hardie, trans. (New York: American Council of Learned Societies, 1970; 1st Arabic ed., 1948). Sadr's masterwork is *Iqtisaduna: Our Economics,* 4 vols. (Tehran: World Organization for Islamic Services, 1982–84; 1st Arabic ed., 1961).

8. See, for instance, Yusuf al-Qardawi, *Economic Security in Islam,* Muhammad Iqbal Siddiqi, trans. (Lahore: Kazi Publications, 1981; 1st Arabic ed., 1966), chap. 2; Mannan, *Islamic Economics,* chap. 3; Muhammad Abdul Mannan, *The Frontiers of Islamic Economics: Theory and Practice* (Delhi: Idarah-i Adabiyat-i Delli, 1984), chap. 5; and Syed Nawab Haider Naqvi, *Ethics and Economics:*

An Islamic Synthesis (Leicester, U.K.: Islamic Foundation, 1981), chap. 4.

9. Strictly speaking, only the Sunnis subscribe to this conception of the Golden Age. The Shi'ites believe that the Islamic social order performed ideally only during the Prophet's lifetime and the five-year tenure of the fourth caliph, 'Ali.

10. Muhammad Hussain, *Development Planning in an Islamic State* (Karachi: Royal Book Company, 1987), p. 14.

11. For the history of this period, see Marshall G. S. Hodgson, *The Venture of Islam: Conscience and History in a World Civilization,* vol. 1 (Chicago: University of Chicago Press, 1974), pp. 187–217; and M. A. Shaban, *Islamic History: A New Interpretation,* vol. 1 (Cambridge, U.K.: Cambridge University Press, 1971), chaps. 2–4.

12. See, for example, M. Umer Chapra, *Towards a Just Monetary System: A Discussion of Money, Banking and Monetary Policy in the Light of Islamic Teachings* (Leicester, U.K.: Islamic Foundation, 1985), chap. 8.

13. These themes are developed by Martin E. Marty and R. Scott Appleby, "Conclusion: An Interim Report on a Hypothetical Family," in Marty and Appleby, eds., *Fundamentalisms Observed* (Chicago: University of Chicago Press, 1991), pp. 814–42.

14. Detailed critiques of Islamic economics include Fazlur Rahman, "Riba and Interest," *Islamic Studies* 3 (1964): 1–43; Fazlur Rahman, "Islam and the Problem of Economic Justice," *Pakistan Economist* 14 (24 August 1974): 14–39; Timur Kuran, "Behavioral Norms in the Islamic Doctrine of Economics: A Critique," *Journal of Economic Behavior and Organization* 4 (1983): 353–79; Frederic L. Pryor, "The Islamic Economic System," *Journal of Comparative Economics* 9 (1985): 197–223; Timur Kuran, "The Economic System in Contemporary Islamic Thought: Interpretation and Assessment," *International Journal of Middle East Studies* 18 (1986): 135–64; Timur Kuran, "On the Notion of Economic Justice in Contemporary Islamic Thought," *International Journal of Middle East Studies* 21 (1989): 171–91; and Thomas Philipp, "The Idea of

Islamic Economics," *Die Welt des Islams* 30 (1990): 117–39.

15. Seyyed Vali Reza Nasr, "Whither Islamic Economics?" *Islamic Quarterly* 30 (1988): 211–20. For references to other statements along these lines, see Seyyed Vali Reza Nasr, "Islamic Economics: Novel Perspectives," *Middle Eastern Studies* 25 (1989): esp. n. 30.

16. Mumtaz Ahmad, "Islamic Fundamentalism in South Asia: The Jamaat-i-Islami and the Tablighi Jamaat," in Marty and Appleby, eds., *Fundamentalisms Observed*, pp. 457–530.

17. Shaul Bakhash, "What Khomeini Did," *New York Review of Books* 36 (20 July 1989): 16.

18. A detailed economic argument in favor of a pan-Islamic union is provided by Masudul Alam Choudhury, *Islamic Economic Co-operation* (New York: St. Martin's Press, 1989).

19. This is not to say that these banks are hiring exclusively from among the non-Westernized segment of the population. Each has made a point of keeping its ranks open to Westernized bankers, even to non-Muslims from the West.

20. The Islamization of economic life was an issue even before Islamic economics achieved recognition as a discipline. Muhammad Ali Jinnah, Pakistan's founding father, spoke soon after independence of the need for creating an economy compatible with Islamic teachings. See Jamil-ud-din Ahmad, ed., *Speeches and Writings of Mr. Jinnah*, vol. 2 (Lahore: Sh. Muhammad Ashraf, 1952), pp. 565–68.

21. These observations are based on discussions with several Pakistanis with excellent connections to leading politicians. I ought to point out that the act of preference falsification is by no means a preserve of Pakistanis. For a general analysis of the phenomenon, and evidence from various times and places, see Timur Kuran, "Private and Public Preferences," *Economics and Philosophy* 6 (1990): 1–26.

22. Afzal-ur-Rahman, *Economic Doctrines of Islam*, vol. 3 (Lahore: Islamic Publications, 1976), p. 55.

23. Siddiqi, *Muslim Economic Thinking*, p. 63.

24. Ibid., p. 63.

25. Murat Çizakça, "Rise of Islamic Banks and the Potential for Venture Capital in the Middle East," in Erol Manisalı, ed., *The Middle East and Eastern Mediterranean: Recent Economic and Political Developments* (Istanbul: Middle East Business and Banking, 1987), pp. 74–90.

26. Some of these countries feature only subsidiaries of Islamic banks headquartered elsewhere.

27. As cited by Mohsin S. Khan and Abbas Mirakhor, "Islamic Banking: Experiences in the Islamic Republic of Iran and Pakistan," *Economic Development and Cultural Change* 38 (1990), table 3.

28. Khan and Mirakhor, "Islamic Banking," table 6.

29. Tim Ingram, "Islamic Banking: A Foreign Bank's View," in Butterworths Editorial Staff, *Islamic Banking and Finance* (London: Butterworths, 1986), pp. 58–60. Other ruses commonly employed to make interest-based loans appear like musharaka are discussed in a report by a group of bank executives entitled "Elimination of Elements at Variance with Shari'ah Injunctions from 'Mark-Up' and Musharaka Modes of Financing under Non-Interest Banking System in Pakistan." Drafted in Karachi, this photocopied report was submitted in November 1988 to the Permanent Commission on Islamisation of Economy.

30. Tansu Çiller and Murat Çizakça, *Türk Finans Kesiminde Sorunlar ve Reform Önerileri* (Istanbul: Istanbul Sanayi Odası, 1989), p. 76; and Clement Henry Moore, "Islamic Banks and Competitive Politics in the Arab World and Turkey," *Middle East Journal* 44 (Spring 1990): 248–49.

31. For a detailed illustration, see Terrence L. Carlson, "Trade Finance under Islamic Principles: A Case Study," *Middle East Executive Reports* 9 (December 1986): 9, 15–16.

32. Ingram, "Islamic Banking," p. 57; and Mohamed Ariff, "Islamic Banking," *Asian-Pacific Economic Literature* 2 (Septem-

ber 1988): 58. The existing practice of rebates is criticized in the 1988 report on banking to Pakistan's Permanent Commission on Islamisation of Economy, "Elimination of Elements at Variance with Shari'ah Injunctions," annex A, pp. 3–4, 10. Interestingly, the report stops short of recommending a ban on rebates, proposing only that income derived from penalties be channeled into welfare activities.

33. See the 1988 report on banking to the Permanent Commission on Islamisation of the Economy, pp. 2–3. Some bankers, while admitting that Pakistani institutions continue to charge interest, point out that banks no longer earn compound interest.

34. Çiller and Çizakça, *Türk Finans Kesimi*, p. 77.

35. Luay Allawi, "Leasing: An Islamic Financial Instrument," in Butterworths Editorial Staff, *Islamic Banking and Finance*, pp. 120–27.

36. Barbaros Ceylan, "Finansal Kiralama ve Uygulamaya İlişkin Sorunlar," in *Özel Finans Kurumları ve Türkiye Uygulaması Sempozyumu* (Istanbul: Marmara Üniversitesi Ortadoğu ve İslam Ülkeleri Ekonomik Araştırma Merkezi, 1988), pp. 212–28. My interviews with Islamic bankers suggest that this practice of risk shifting is common to Islamic banks throughout the world.

37. Islamic Development Bank, *Eleventh Annual Report (1985–1986)* (Jeddah: IDB, 1987), pp. xviii–xix. Amazingly, few Islamic economists show an awareness of these statistics. In fact, they continue to characterize the IDB's operations as distinctly "Islamic." As a case in point, in 1988 Ariff, "Islamic Banking," p. 48, wrote: "The IDB operations are free of interest and are explicitly based on *Shariah* principles."

38. S. A. Meenai, *The Islamic Development Bank: A Case Study of Islamic Co-operation* (London: Kegan Paul International, 1989), esp. chaps. 7–10.

39. I owe this observation to Volker Nienhaus, "Islamic Economics, Finance and Banking: Theory and Practice," *Journal of Islamic Banking and Finance* 3 (1986): 43.

40. As of 1990, the Islamic Development Bank was planning to establish a new training center in its skyscraper under construction in Jeddah.

41. There are no reliable statistics on the extent of dishonesty and fraud. But anyone who has done business in, say, Pakistan, Egypt, or Morocco knows that many more transactions go unreported than in the developed economies of Europe and North America. Significantly, the first *Directory of Islamic Financial Institutions,* John R. Presley, ed. (London: Croom Helm for the International Centre for Islamic Studies, 1988), points out that "shortcomings in business ethics make it difficult to establish closer bank-client relationships." It goes on to say that "clients either do not keep adequate records or keep fraudulent records of their operations" (p. 300).

42. See, for instance, Waqar Masood Khan, "Towards an Interest-Free Islamic Economic System," *Journal of King Abdulaziz University: Islamic Economics* 1 (1989): 3–37. Several architects of Pakistan's Islamic banking system have suggested to me in private conversations that genuinely Islamic banking must await a major improvement in the "moral fiber" of Pakistanis.

43. Murat Çizakça, "Origins and Evolution of Islamic Banks," unpublished paper presented at the First General Conference of Islamic Banks, Istanbul, October 1986, sect. 6.

44. Abraham L. Udovitch, "At the Origins of the Western Commenda: Islam, Israel, Byzantium?" *Speculum* 37 (1962): 198–207.

45. For further observations, see Ann Elizabeth Mayer, "Islamic Banking and Credit Policies in the Sadat Era: The Social Origins of Islamic Banking in Egypt," *Arab Law Quarterly* 1 (1985): 36–40.

46. Reversing this interpretation, Islamic economists now claim that although Mit Ghamr was designed according to Islamic principles, the Nasser regime's opposition to Islam forced its founder, Ahmed al-Naggar, to disguise his source of inspiration. Accordingly, the public relations ploy was to package Mit Ghamr as an Egyptian replica of Germany's local savings banks. This interpretation enjoys the endorsement of al-

Naggar himself, who went on to become a prominent Islamic banker. See Ahmed Abdel-Fattah El-Ashker, *The Islamic Business Enterprise* (London: Croom Helm, 1987), pp. 155–59.

47. Rahman, "Riba and Interest," pp. 30–37. Many other predominantly agricultural communities operating close to subsistence are known to have restricted interest, particularly on loans to people in distress. Invariably the rationale has been to bolster the individual's sense of security, thus reinforcing the community's viability. For evidence and an elaborate argument, see Richard A. Posner, "A Theory of Primitive Society with Special Reference to Law," *Journal of Law and Economics* 23 (1980): 1–53.

48. Rahman, "Riba and Interest," esp. pp. 12–30.

49. Maxime Rodinson, *Islam and Capitalism*, Brian Pearce, trans. (New York: Pantheon, 1973; orig. French ed., 1966), chap. 3. For evidence on the prevalence of interest in later times, see Jon E. Mandaville, "Usurious Piety: The Cash Waqf Controversy in the Ottoman Empire," *International Journal of Middle East Studies* 10 (1979): 289–308. The Arabic term for ruse is *hila* (plur., *hiyal*).

50. *Report of the Council of Islamic Ideology on the Elimination of Interest from the Economy* (Islamabad: CII, June 1980), pp. 15–16. The report refers to murabaha as "bai muajjal."

51. Presley, *Directory of Islamic Financial Institutions*, p. 300.

52. For the pro-indexation argument, see Mohammad Abdul Mannan, *The Making of an Islamic Economic Society: Islamic Dimensions in Economic Analysis* (Cairo: International Association of Islamic Banks, 1984), chap. 14a. The rationale against indexation is developed by S. M. Hasanuz Zaman, "Indexation—An Islamic Evaluation," *Journal of Research in Islamic Economics* 2 (1985): 31–53. Additional references and a critical survey of the relevant arguments are offered by Ziauddin Ahmed, "Currency Notes and Loan Indexation," *Islamic Studies* 28 (1989): 39–53.

53. Muhammad Arif, "Islamic Economics: Challenges and Potentials," in Abdullah

Omar Naseef, ed., *Today's Problems, Tomorrow's Solutions: The Future Structure of Muslim Societies* (London: Mansell Publishing, 1988), p. 87.

54. I encountered both positions in discussions with fundamentalist leaders in Pakistan.

55. Süleyman Uludağ, *İslamda Faiz Meselesine Yeni Bir Bakış* (Istanbul: Dergah Yayınları, 1988), esp. pp. 287–90.

56. *Economist,* 16 September 1989, p. 42. Similar positions were taken by earlier Egyptian religious leaders of this century. See Chibli Mallat, "The Debate on Riba and Interest in Twentieth Century Jurisprudence," in Mallat, ed., *Islamic Law and Finance* (London: Graham and Totman, 1988), pp. 69–88.

57. Rashida Patel, *Islamisation of Laws in Pakistan?* (Karachi: Faiza Publishers, 1986), p. 74. Influential fundamentalists whom I interviewed in November 1989 cited figures between 95 and 99.9 percent.

58. Moore, "Islamic Banks and Competitive Politics in the Arab World and Turkey," table 2 and pp. 235–42. Some complementary figures pertaining to the early to mid-1980s are provided by Volker Nienhaus, "Lectures on Islamic Economics and Banking," Faculty of Economics Discussion Paper no. 6, University of Bochum, December 1988, pp. 24–30.

59. For an English translation of the relevant laws and regulations in Turkey, see *Özel Finans Kurumları,* pp. 73–135. An additional advantage enjoyed by Turkey's Islamic banks is that they are permitted to advertise on television, whereas most of their rivals are not. The privileges granted to the Islamic banks are outlined by Uğur Mumcu, *Tarikat, Siyaset, Ticaret* (Istanbul: Tekin Yayınevi, 1988). Islamic bankers complain that they are denied one major right taken for granted by their non-Islamic rivals: the right to the trademark of one's choice. Indeed, Turkey's Islamic banks are barred from identifying themselves as such.

60. Meenai, *The Islamic Development Bank,* p. 74, reports that, like the commercial Islamic banks, the Islamic Development Bank made an unusually large number of bad

loans in its early years. Moreover, the losses were associated primarily with equity investments. The bank's return on equity was apparently lower even than its modest "service fee" on ordinary loans.

61. Clement Henry Moore, "La Place des Banques Islamiques dans un Système Politique d'Ouverture: Comparaison des Cas Turc et Égyptien," unpublished paper presented to the Fondation Nationale des Sciences Politiques, Paris, March 1990, table 2.

62. Mohsin S. Khan, "Islamic Interest-Free Banking: A Theoretical Analysis," in Khan and Mirakhor, eds., *Theoretical Studies in Islamic Banking and Finance,* chap. 2; and Zubair Iqbal and Abbas Mirakhor, "Islamic Banking," International Monetary Fund Occasional Paper no. 49, 1987.

63. On the al-Rayan crisis, see Robert Springborg, *Mubarak's Egypt: Fragmentation of the Political Order* (Boulder, Colo.: Westview Press, 1989), pp. 45–61.

64. Volker Nienhaus, "Lectures on Islamic Economics and Banking," pp. 33–49.

65. On Iran, Iqbal and Mirakhor, "Islamic Banking," p. 25; on Pakistan, Khan and Mirakhor, "Islamic Banking," pp. 370–71.

66. For a comprehensive survey of Islam's traditional means of redistribution, see Muhammad Anas Zarqa, "Islamic Distributive Schemes," in Munawar Iqbal, ed., *Distributive Justice and Need Fulfilment in an Islamic Economy* (Islamabad: International Institute of Islamic Economics, 1986).

67. For traditional expositions, see Afzal-ur-Rahman, *Economic Doctrines of Islam,* vol. 3 (Lahore: Islamic Publications, 1976), chaps. 14–18; and Abdur Rahman Shad, *Zakat and 'Ushr* (Lahore: Kazi Publications, 1986).

68. See, for instance, Ahmad Oran and Salim Rashid, "Fiscal Policy in Early Islam," *Public Finance* 44 (1989): 75–101.

69. For explicit statements, see Afzal-ur-Rahman, *Economic Doctrines of Islam,* vol. 3, p. 197; and Shad, *Zakat and 'Ushr,* p. 100.

70. Rahman, "Islam and the Problem of Economic Justice," p. 33.

71. For several more or less reformist positions, see Ziauddin Ahmed, Munawar Iqbal, and M. Fahim Khan, eds., *Fiscal Policy and Resource Allocation in Islam* (Islamabad: Institute of Policy Studies, 1983), chaps. 1–4.

72. On this controversy, see Tanzil-ur-Rahman, *Introduction of Zakat in Pakistan* (Islamabad: Council of Islamic Ideology, 1981), pp. 15–21.

73. Ann Elizabeth Mayer, "Islamization and Taxation in Pakistan," in Anita M. Weiss, ed., *Islamic Reassertion in Pakistan: The Application of Islamic Laws in a Modern State* (Syracuse, N.Y.: Syracuse University Press, 1986), esp. pp. 67–69, 73–75; and Abdin Ahmed Salama, "Fiscal Analysis of Zakah with Special Reference to Saudi Arabia's Experience in Zakah," in Mohammed Ariff, ed., *Monetary and Fiscal Economics of Islam* (Jeddah: International Center for Research in Islamic Economics, 1982), esp. pp. 349–54. Pakistan's Zakat Ordinance is reproduced in Tanzil-ur-Rahman, *Introduction of Zakat in Pakistan,* pp. 27–85. The ordinance has been amended several times.

74. Ismail Muhd Salleh and Rogayah Ngah, "Distribution of the Zakat Burden on Padi Producers in Malaysia," in M. Raqibuz Zaman, ed., *Some Aspects of the Economics of Zakah* (Plainfield, Ind.: Association of Muslim Social Scientists, 1980), esp. pp. 81–84.

75. *Pakistan Statistical Yearbook, 1989* (Islamabad: Federal Bureau of Statistics, 1989), pp. 451–52, 507.

76. Salama, "Fiscal Analysis of Zakah with Special Reference to Saudi Arabia's Experience in Zakah," table 1.

77. Ibid., p. 351.

78. Aidit bin Ghazali et al., "Zakat: A Case Study of Malaysia" (Unpublished paper presented to the Third International Zakat Conference, Kuala Lumpur, May 1990), p. 49.

79. Nik Mustapha Bin Hj. Nik Hasan, "Zakat in Malaysia—Present and Future Status," *Journal of Islamic Economics* 1 (1987): 57. The figure excludes *zakat al-fitr,* which is paid by most practicing Muslims at the end of the month of Ramadan. It amounts to about $1 (U.S.) per person.

80. Salleh and Ngah, "Distribution of the Zakat Burden on Padi Producers in Malaysia," pp. 86–110.

81. James C. Scott, "Resistance without Protest and without Organization: Peasant Opposition to the Islamic Zakat and the Christian Tithe," *Comparative Studies in Society and History* 29 (1987): 426–27.

82. Thirteen countries have enacted zakat laws or regulations. But as a practical matter in most of these countries the payment of zakat is still voluntary. See Fuad Abdullah al-Omar, "A Comparative Study of Zakat Systems: The General, Administrative, and Organizational Aspects" (Unpublished paper presented to the Third International Zakat Conference, Kuala Lumpur, May 1990).

83. *Encyclopedia of Islam*, s.v. "Zakat."

84. See Mohammad Akhtar Saeed Siddiqi, *Early Development of Zakat Law and Ijtihad* (Karachi: Islamic Research Academy, 1983), chaps. 4–5.

85. M. A. Sabzwari, *A Study of Zakat and 'Ushr with Special Reference to Pakistan* (Karachi: Industries Printing Press, 1979).

86. "Improvement in the Nizam-e Zakat and Ushr for Achieving Its Declared Objectives of Removing Abject Poverty and Eradication of Beggary from the Country," p. 4. This photocopied report was submitted to the Permanent Commission on Islamisation of Economy in February 1989.

87. Beşir Hamitoğulları, "Türkiye'de Altın-Gümüş Gibi Varlıklarda Zekat Potansiyeli," in *Türkiye'de Zekat Potansiyeli* (Istanbul: İslami İlimler Araştırma Vakfi, 1988), pp. 27–51.

88. James C. Scott, *Weapons of the Weak: Everyday Forms of Peasant Resistance* (New Haven: Yale University Press, 1985), pp. 121–22, 169–78.

89. For further details, see the Zakat and 'Ushr Ordinance, reprinted in Tanzil-ur-Rahman, *Introduction of Zakat in Pakistan*. The disbursement system is also described by Grace Clark, "Pakistan's Zakat and 'Ushr as a Welfare System," in Weiss, ed., *Islamic Reassertion in Pakistan*, pp. 83–91.

90. *Pakistan Statistical Yearbook, 1989*, pp. 453–59.

91. Clark, "Pakistan's Zakat and 'Ushr as a Welfare System," p. 89.

92. "Improvement in the Nizam-e-Zakat and Ushr," p. 5.

93. Ibid., pp. 5–6.

94. Various irregularities are documented in a report prepared by Shahid N. Zahid for the World Bank, "The Zakat and Ushr System in Pakistan," Karachi, August 1989. According to a small survey included in this report, the official roster of zakat recipients includes poor people who deny having received assistance.

95. Clark, "Pakistan's Zakat and 'Ushr as a Welfare System," p. 90.

96. *Dawn* (Karachi), 11 November 1989.

97. Scott, "Resistance without Protest and without Organization," p. 433.

98. Mustapha, "Zakat in Malaysia," pp. 60–62.

99. Ibid., p. 62.

100. Ibid., pp. 63–64.

101. Scott, "Resistance without Protest and without Organization," pp. 433–34.

102. *New Straits Times* (Kuala Lumpur), 6 March 1990.

103. Mayer, "Islamization and Taxation in Pakistan," p. 69.

104. Official figures show that in the 1980–88 period 8.6 percent of the disbursements went to religious education (*Pakistan Statistical Yearbook, 1989*, pp. 453–59).

105. Scott, "Resistance without Protest and without Organization," pp. 431–32.

106. See Richard Kurin, "Islamization: A View from the Countryside," in Weiss, ed., *Islamic Reassertion in Pakistan*, pp. 123–24.

107. Tanzil-ur-Rahman, *Introduction of Zakat in Pakistan*, p. 9.

108. Ghazali et al., "Zakat," pp. 47–48 and table 13.

109. The Shi'ites base their objection on a precedent set by rebellious tribes in early Islam that refused to pay zakat to the first caliph, considered by Shi'ites a usurper. See Munir Morad, "Current Thought on Islamic Taxation: A Critical Synthesis," in Mallat, ed., *Islamic Law and Finance*, pp. 120–22.

110. Patel, *Islamisation of Laws in Pakistan?* pp. 63–64.

111. On Pakistan, see Mayer, "Islamization and Taxation in Pakistan," p. 64; on Malaysia, see Scott, "Resistance without Protest and without Organization," pp. 431–35.

112. Zarqa, "Islamic Distributive Schemes," pp. 201–2.

113. For a highly influential argument to this effect, see Max Weber, *Economy and Society: An Outline of Interpretive Sociology,* 3 vols., Guenther Roth and Claus Wittich, eds. (New York: Bedminster Press, 1968; 1st German ed., 1922). Weber's scattered remarks on Islam are synthesized and critiqued by Bryan S. Turner, *Weber and Islam: A Critical Study* (London: Routledge and Kegan Paul, 1974).

114. These injunctions are discussed in detail by M. Umar Chapra, "The Islamic System of Islam: A Discussion of Its Goals and Nature," parts 1–3, *Islamic Quarterly* 14 (1970): 3–18, 91–96, 143–56; Muhammad Abdul-Rauf, "The Islamic Doctrine of Economics and Contemporary Economic Thought," in Michael Novak, ed., *Capitalism and Socialism: A Theological Inquiry* (Washington, D.C.: American Enterprise Institute, 1979), pp. 4–12; Syed N. H. Naqvi, *Ethics and Economics;* and Seyyed Hossein Nasr, "Islamic Work Ethics," in Jaroslav Pelikan, Joseph Kitagawa, and Seyyed Hossein Nasr, eds., *Comparative Work Ethics: Judeo-Christian, Islamic, and Eastern* (Washington, D.C.: Library of Congress, 1985), pp. 49–62.

115. Afzal-ur-Rahman, *Economic Doctrines of Islam,* vol. 2, 2d. ed. (Lahore: Islamic Publications, 1980), p. 47.

116. For other examples, see Muhammad Nejatullah Siddiqi, *The Economic Enterprise in Islam* (Lahore: Islamic Publications, 1972), pp. 57–60.

117. See, for instance, S. Waqar Ahmed Husaini, *Islamic Environmental Systems Engineering* (London: Macmillan, 1980), pp. 79–81.

118. Beşir Atalay, "İktisadi Kalkınmada Geleneksel Değerlerin Yeri (Japon Örneği)," in Ahmet Tabakoğlu and İsmail Kurt, eds., *İktisadi Kalkınma ve İslam* (Istanbul: İslami İlimler Araştırma Vakfı), p. 97.

119. Khurshid Ahmad, "Economic Development in an Islamic Framework," in Ahmad, ed., *Studies in Islamic Economics,* p. 178. For additional such statements and many more references, see Muhammad A. al-Buraey, *Administrative Development: An Islamic Perspective* (London: Kegan Paul International, 1985); Aidit Ghazali, *Development: An Islamic Perspective* (Petaling Jaya, Malaysia: Pelanduk Publications, 1990); and Abul Hasan Muhammad Sadeq, *Economic Development in Islam* (Petaling Jaya, Malaysia: Pelanduk Publications, 1990).

120. See, for instance, Naqvi, *Ethics and Economics,* esp. p. 63. On the finer points of this view, see Seyyed Vali Reza Nasr, "Toward a Philosophy of Islamic Economics," *Muslim World* 77 (1987): 175–96.

121. Friedrich A. Hayek, *The Fatal Conceit: The Errors of Socialism* (Chicago: University of Chicago Press, 1988), pp. 45–47. The quote, recorded by Hayek, belongs to David Hume. On Hayek's views concerning the basis of modern civilization, see the remainder of this book, esp. chaps. 1–5. A more detailed presentation may be found in his *Law, Legislation and Liberty,* 3 vols. (Chicago: University of Chicago Press, 1973–79).

122. This is not to suggest the absence of currents within Islamic philosophy which conflict with Aristotelian perceptions. From the very beginning Islamic philosophy has featured traditions that glorify the market, commerce, and the trader. See Bernard Lewis, "Sources for the Economic History of the Middle East," in M. A. Cook, ed., *Studies in the Economic History of the Middle East* (London: Oxford University Press, 1970), pp. 78–92. But to this day these traditions have failed to generate a sustained overt reaction against Islam's communitarian vision.

123. As an example of the former class, see Syed S. H. Naqvi, *Individual Freedom, Social Welfare and Islamic Economic Order* (Islamabad: Pakistan Institute of Development Economics, 1981), chaps. 4–5; for the latter, see Chapra, "The Economic System of Islam," pt. 2. A detailed comparison is offered by Sohrab Behdad, "Property Rights in Contemporary Islamic Economic

Thought: A Critical Perspective," *Review of Social Economy* 47 (1989): 185–211.

124. Shaul Bakhash, "Islam and Social Justice in Iran," in Martin Kramer, ed., *Shi'ism, Resistance, and Revolution* (Boulder, Colo.: Westview Press, 1987), p. 113. The debate in question took place in 1984.

125. Ibid.

126. Albert O. Hirschman, "Underdevelopment, Obstacles to the Perception of Change, and Leadership," *Daedalus* 97 (1968): 925–37.

127. R. H. Tawney, *Religion and the Rise of Capitalism* (Gloucester, Mass.: Peter Smith, 1962; first published, 1926).

Heirs to the Protestant Ethic? The Economics of American Fundamentalists

Laurence R. Iannaccone

If the average American were to choose a single word summarizing the economic views of fundamentalists, the word probably would be "conservative." Asked to defend this choice, he or she might well reply as follows: "Theological and economic conservatism go hand in hand. Theologically conservative Protestants are staunch defenders of market capitalism. They denounce every form of socialism, reject paternalistic government spending programs, and advocate free enterprise as the solution to virtually every economic problem."

This image is largely a myth. The reality is both different and more complex. Theologically conservative Protestant leaders espouse a variety of economic positions. A free-market consensus is at best a prospect for the future, and an unlikely prospect at that. Most rank and file evangelical-fundamentalists are not economic conservatives and would probably reject any free-market consensus that did emerge from their leaders. And, despite well-publicized and extensive lobbying on social and moral issues, even such avowedly conservative groups as the Moral Majority have never seriously attempted to implement an *economic* agenda. This essay attempts to document and explain this surprising state of affairs.

The Scope of the Study

The word "economics" has many meanings in everyday speech. This study concerns what might be termed "formal economics." It investigates what theologically conservative Protestants have to say about the production of commodities, the nature of markets, the economic impact of government, and the growth and distribution of a society's income. The informal aspects of everyday financial activity, the specific problems associated with running a business or managing one's money, are of secondary concern. Hence, this study does *not* review sermons and writings that counsel Christians against personal indebtedness, admonish them to contribute liberally, or instruct them on spiritual guidelines for money management.[1] These are omitted, not because they are insignificant, but simply because they are, in the words of one Christian economist, "light years from the mainstream" of formal economic thinking.[2]

The word "fundamentalism," like the word "economics," means different things to different people. Studies that presume one meaning arrive at conclusions inapplicable to the other meanings. To avoid confusion, I must therefore explain how the term "fundamentalism" is used, and why it is often avoided, throughout this study.

Theologians and religious historians typically define "fundamentalism" as a specific religious movement that emerged from the controversies raging within mainstream American Protestantism around the turn of the century. In the face of attempts to adapt and modernize traditional Christian beliefs, the members of this movement fought to defend what they viewed as the "fundamentals" of the Christian faith and so styled themselves "fundamentalists." The origins of historical fundamentalism, the thought and actions of its leaders, and the development of its churches and institutions have been chronicled by Sandeen, Marsden, Ammerman, and others and need not be repeated here.[3] It suffices to note that historical fundamentalists share not only a common past but also a particular theology and social orientation. As one scholar observes:

> Fundamentalist . . . Christians [are those] who believe in the total errorlessness—inerrancy—of the Bible in all its assertions, of whatever kind; who believe that the present penultimate dispensation of history will end in utter disaster, as have all of its predecessors; who expect the imminent, public return of Christ in a second advent that will usher in the final dispensation of history; and who feel bound by faithfulness in an inerrant scripture to anathematize, and to separate themselves from, those who take a different view, whether they be Christians or others.[4]

Despite its value to theologians and religious historians, this definition of fundamentalism proves unsuited to many social scientific investigations. Sociologists, political scientists, and economists—particularly those who employ population surveys and large-scale data analysis—adopt broader definitions which subsume "fundamentalism" under the heading of "evangelicalism." ("Evangelicalism" here refers to the many churches and denominations that insist that salvation comes only through personal faith in Jesus Christ as Savior, that affirm the need to proselytize, and that accept the Bible as the inerrant Word of God.) For example, in a recent book entitled *The Fundamentalist Phenomenon,* the noted political scientist James Reichley concludes that "for political analysis, the older and more inclusive term, 'evangelical' in many ways works better" than the narrower term, "fundamentalist."[5] In a similar manner, Susan Rose analyzes the educational impact of fundamentalism entirely within the context of evangelicalism. She does so, not because she chooses to ignore the fundamentalist/evangelical distinction, but rather because maintaining that distinction is impractical. She finds it "difficult to assess how many of the Christian schools are 'strictly' fundamentalist, for fundamentalist and charismatic schools may belong to the same Christian school associations and the distinction among types is not necessarily made."[6]

Similar difficulties plague economic studies of fundamentalism. Three of these deserve special mention: (1) A substantial fraction of all self-styled "fundamentalists," those belonging to the more strict and separatist wing of the historical movement, have expressed no real interest in economic issues. A study of their economic thought would be brief indeed but also misleading, since it is their very lack of attention to economic issues that is most noteworthy. (2) Those self-styled fundamentalists who *are* interested in economic issues have developed their ideas and pursued their goals jointly with other evangelicals. As a practical matter, neither their orientation nor their impact can be separated from that of the other evangelicals with whom they routinely interact. (3) There is no reliable way to isolate the economic attitudes or behavior of rank and file fundamentalists. It simply is not possible to survey a representative sample of fundamentalists as distinct from other theologically conservative Protestants.[7]

In light of these problems, this study explores the attitudes and actions of fundamentalists within the larger context of evangelicalism. It surveys the economic attitudes of a broad evangelical-fundamentalist population, and it investigates the economic teachings of a variety of theologically conservative Protestant leaders. Some of these leaders call themselves fundamentalists, some evangelicals. Some, though by no means all, have been associated with Jerry Falwell's Moral Majority or other organizations of the so-called New Christian Right. Despite these differences, however, all share a distinctive view of economics and religion. They not only accept the Bible as the inerrant Word of God but also look to it for specific solutions to economic problems. Most have considered the economic implications of Scripture at length and have emerged with something substantive to say about economics, not just personal finances or Christian charity. In other words, they have seriously considered the kind of issues that economists actually address and have arrived at conclusions that they insist are consistent with biblical principles and justifiable in terms of specific biblical texts. Though they are by no means in complete agreement, most are aware of each other's work and take it seriously. Many have interacted face to face, and most acknowledge the others as co-contributors to a growing body of thought that they often call "Christian economics."

The Spectrum of Evangelical Economic Thought

Evangelical economic attitudes are anything but unanimous. Though it is fair to characterize the typical evangelical as supportive of capitalism and opposed to communism—an attitude shared by most Americans—there is wide variation of thought within the movement's religious and intellectual leadership. At one extreme, Christians reconstructionists and the New Christian Right enthusiastically embrace free markets and decry virtually all forms of government intervention. At the opposite extreme, self-styled "radical evangelicals" brand capitalism as hopelessly decadent and espouse a quasi-Marxist theology of liberation. The majority fall between these extremes, some calling for greater government intervention and larger social welfare programs and others advocating more free enterprise and a smaller government sector.

Strict, Self-Styled Fundamentalists

Historical fundamentalism has always advocated separation from the corrupting influences of secularism and liberal Christianity. Even so, the *degree* of separatism has been a subject of frequent dispute. The original fundamentalist movement split in the 1940s and 1950s, with Billy Graham and others leading the more accommodating wing that came to call itself "evangelical," and Carl McIntire leading the strict separatists who retained the "fundamentalist" label.[8] Today's self-styled fundamentalists are similarly divided, with a more accommodating, or "open," wing epitomized by Jerry Falwell and his associates at Thomas Road Baptist Church and Liberty University, and a more strictly separatist wing epitomized by institutions like Bob Jones University.

Strict fundamentalists exist within the American economy and in that sense cannot help but participate in it, but they have never sought to understand or critique its workings from a religious perspective. Their major periodical, *Sword of the Lord,* has little to say about economics, only occasional praise for capitalism (typically within the context of attacks on communism).[9] Their largest colleges, Bob Jones University, Tennessee Temple, Baptist Bible College of Missouri, and Baptist Bible College of Pennsylvania, devote no resources to economic studies. None has a department of economics, none offers an economics major, and with just one exception none even offers courses in economics.[10] Indeed, it appears that there is not a single member of the American Economic Association among the ranks of strict fundamentalists.[11] Not surprisingly, therefore, strict fundamentalists have not participated in the economic discussions and debates that have occurred in other theologically conservative circles, nor have they generated their own body of economic teachings. It is this very lack of attention to economic issues that best characterizes their economic orientation. Extreme separatists appear suspicious of all economic systems, rejecting the possibility of any truly Godly outcomes from any secular institution, political or economic. The attitudes of the fundamentalist congregation studied by Nancy Ammerman are probably typical: "They accept the division of the world into sacred and secular, private and public. The structures of the economy are not expected to run by God's rules. . . . When profit comes first, ahead of God, corruption and dishonesty are only to be expected."[12] Such fundamentalists are as likely to view themselves as victims of the marketplace as its beneficiaries.[13]

The New Christian Right

In contrast to their strictly separatist brethren, members of fundamentalism's more accommodating wing have expressed interest in economic issues. Falwell, for example, has often praised the virtues of free enterprise while also condemning social welfare programs and state control of the economy. Falwell's Liberty University in Lynchburg, Virginia, has a department of economics, offers an economics major, and teaches a full range of undergraduate economics courses. Its four-person economics department ranks as one of the largest in any Christian college, fundamentalist or evangelical.[14] Liberty University is also the site of a public policy center, the Contemporary Economics and Business Association (CEBA), established in 1987. However, as CEBA's own president, Robert Mateer, has emphasized, none of these activities should be viewed as distinctly fundamentalist. Most of the people featured in CEBA's conferences and publications label themselves "evangelical" rather than "fundamentalist" and some are not even Protestant.[15] Moreover, many of them contribute to economic discussion and debate occurring in mainstream evangelical circles, at universities such as Wheaton, in organizations such as the Coalition on Revival,[16] and through activities such as the Oxford Conference.[17] It is therefore impossible to isolate the economic thought and economic activities of fundamentalist leaders, such as Falwell and Mateer, from those of other evangelicals who share their political and social agenda. The natural unit of analysis is the entire group of leaders who promote this agenda, both evangelical and fundamentalist, a group known as the New Christian Right.

The New Christian Right, or NCR, is a generic term applied by social scientists and the media to the collection of theologically and socially conservative Christian organizations that gained prominence in American politics in the late 1970s and early 1980s.[18] In the popular press and public sentiment, the NCR has always been epitomized by Jerry Falwell and his now disbanded Moral Majority.[19] The "fundamentalist" label, which Falwell embraced and certainly deserved, therefore is often applied to the entire NCR, and many Americans now routinely equate fundamentalism with religiously motivated conservative political action. The equation is erroneous, however. The NCR should not be viewed as the embodiment of fundamentalism but rather as a broad coalition of evangelicals drawn together by their conservative social and political agenda. The NCR has always included nonfundamentalists—moderate evangelicals, charismatics, and even some mainline Protestants and Catholics. Moreover, many self-styled fundamentalists, those I have called strict separatists, utterly reject the goals and methods of the NCR. They remain firmly isolationist and repudiate political activism. Their position is epitomized by Bob Jones, Jr., who denounced Falwell as the "most dangerous man in America today as far as Biblical Christianity is concerned."[20]

Leaders of NCR organizations share a conservative economic outlook that they have often voiced in sermons, newspaper interviews, popular books, and journal and newspaper articles. Regarding the economy as a whole, they applaud the free-market system, criticize the welfare state, and oppose any form of socialism. The following passage from "The Christian World View of Economics," a position paper published by an evangelical association called the Coalition on Revival, is representative:

> We affirm that a free market economy is the closest approximation man has yet devised in this fallen world to the economy set forth in the Bible, and that, of

all the economies known to man, it is the most conducive to producing a free, just, and prosperous society for all people (p. 19).

We deny that central planning and other coercive interferences with personal choice can increase the productivity of society; that the civil government has authority to set the value of property; and that the Bible teaches any "just" price other than that resulting from the interaction of supply and demand in a marketplace of free people (p. 15).

Although statements like this have characterized the New Christian Right since its inception in the late 1970s, serious attempts to defend them are relatively recent.[21]

The intellectual and biblical defense of free enterprise "Christian economics" is the primary goal of the Contemporary Economics and Business Association. CEBA publishes a journal called *Christian Perspectives: A Journal of Free Enterprise,* sponsors conferences featuring noted conservative Christian economists and free-market apologists, and has produced a videotaped series along the lines of Milton Friedman's "Free To Choose" television series.[22] Through the energetic efforts of its president, CEBA has financed its continually expanding activities with private industry donations and has aimed for professional respectability by building its conferences, publications, and videotapes around respected authors, economists, and businessmen.[23] The cover page of a recent issue of CEBA's *Christian Perspectives* journal states:

The economics faculty of the school [of Business and Government at Liberty University] and the staff of CEBA . . . believe:

1. that the combination of democracy and our capitalistic economy (free enterprise) is the philosophical foundation upon which the practical solutions to almost all political-economy problems and issues must be based,

2. that the economic development and progress of nations is directly related to the extent to which they have applied, in practice, the principles of free-enterprise economics,

3. that even a free-enterprise-based system of political economy can only be successful in Western civilization if it has the underpinning of the Judeo-Christian moral value system, the value system which has been the basis for most of our great achievements.[24]

The NCR has been influenced by libertarian ideology associated with the Chicago and Austria schools of economic thought. Libertarians like Milton Friedman and Friedrich Hayek provide Christian economists with a body of carefully worked, highly respectable research that defends free markets, private property, and minimal government on theoretical and empirical grounds. Thus, in an extended discussion of economic issues, Jerry Falwell cites Friedman repeatedly[25] and Robert Mateer recommends Friedman's *Capitalism and Freedom* as one of three books "virtually essential to an understanding of capitalism, freedom, and the role of government."[26]

Although the proponents of conservative Christian economics freely acknowledge their debt to secular conservatives like Friedman, they also emphasize that their views remain grounded in God's Word. They argue that free enterprise and respect for private property is advocated throughout the Bible. Moreover, they insist that free enterprise yields its benefits only when coupled with ethical structures that maintain and promote the Bible's moral principles. The CEBA statement quoted above is in this respect completely typical. It is echoed by Pat Robertson's observation that "communism and capitalism in their most extreme, secular manifestations are equally doomed to failure. . . . When greed and materialism displace all spiritual and moral values, capitalism breaks down into ugliness."[27] The NCR's economic agenda thus links the rehabilitation of American capitalism to the restoration of traditional American values. James Kennedy, one of the Moral Majority's founders, argues that America's economic problems will be solved "only when we get back to the Protestant or Biblical work ethic."[28]

The Christian Reconstructionists

No group of theologically conservative Protestants has spelled out its view of the economy in as much detail as the Christian reconstructionists. Its two most prolific leaders, Rousas Rushdoony and Gary North, have written numerous books and articles defending a free market as the only economic system compatible with God's Word. The following statements, from Rushdoony's *Politics of Guilt and Pity*, are typical of their overall economic views:

> Social progress comes with the accumulation and development of *wealth*. Wealth comes, in a free economy, as a product of *work and thrift*—in short, of character. Capital is often accumulated by inheritance, a God-given right which is strongly stressed in the Bible. . . . In a free economy, *property* is freed from the restrictions of the state because it is under the restrictions of the family and of a religiously oriented community. . . . The security of a man in his property, and in his inheritance, means a stability in the social order which is productive progress.[29]

Reconstructionist policy recommendations are in many cases identical to those of the Austrian school of economic thought. And there is no doubt that North, at least, has been directly influenced by Austrian writings.[30] Nevertheless, it is biblical texts that the reconstructionists use to justify their positions. The biblical tithe is said to demand a flat tax; God's authority as the world's creator and ultimate owner prohibits centralized planning; the Old Testament's metallic currencies illustrate that "honest money" is based on tangible commodities, not government fiat; and the eighth commandment ("Thou shalt not steal") condemns income redistribution as nothing more than institutionalized theft.

As these examples illustrate, the reconstructionists reject any distinction between secular and religious truth. Rushdoony claims that the "roots of the free market . . . rest in the doctrine of God."[31] "Economics cannot be seen in isolation from ethics, theology, and much, much more. . . . Economics does not exist in a vacuum, nor is it separate from morality, the family, and vocation."[32] Economic revival and spiritual renewal are ultimately inseparable. "The battle for the free market is but one facet of a battle against idolatry."[33]

Outsiders sometimes refer to the reconstructionists as fundamentalists, but the reconstructionists themselves reject the label on both historical and theological grounds. The movement grew out of the Calvinist Dutch Reformed wing of Protestant evangelicalism, which is historically distinct from that which gave rise to traditional fundamentalism.

Reconstructionists also reject the critical fundamentalist doctrine known as "premillennialism," the belief that Christ must return *before* God's Kingdom (the millennium) can be established. True to their Calvinist roots, reconstructionists are "postmillennialists," believing that Christ will return only *after* Christian efforts help to bring about God's millennial Kingdom.[34] The practical significance of this apparently esoteric distinction is great. Premillennial theology sees the world going from bad to worse, only to be redeemed through God's sudden intervention at the Second Coming of Christ. Any efforts, including those of Christians, to reform secular society are therefore ultimately futile. The logical Christian response to the evils of the world is therefore defensive isolationism, holding the fort until God's cavalry arrives. Premillennial theology thus tends to undermine arguments for political activism and so is something of an albatross about the NCR's neck. In contrast, postmillennial theology calls Christians out of isolation. A Christian society can and will be achieved. It is incumbent upon Christians to dig in and fight since Christ is literally waiting for them to finish the job that He began.

Dominion theology is increasingly filtering into the mainstream of the New Christian Right. It has, for example, shaped some of Pat Robertson's economic positions[35] and underpins many of the economic views and goals of at least one major NCR organization, the Coalition on Revival.[36] Put off by the reconstructionists' militant rhetoric and occasional *ad hominem* attacks, most members of the NCR hesitate to be openly associated with them. But as one interviewee said, "Though we hide their books under the bed, we read them just the same."

The Evangelical Left

The New Christian Right has garnered so much attention in recent years that its positions are sometimes taken as typical of all evangelicals. To do so is a mistake. There are other evangelicals whose economic positions are as far to the left as the NCR and reconstructionists are to the right. Moreover, the right's economics cannot be fully appreciated apart from the contrasting views of Ron Sider, Jim Wallis, and other leaders of the evangelical left. When Gary North named his series of books "Biblical Blueprints," he was self-consciously rejecting Ronald Sider's claim that "we do not find a comprehensive blueprint for a new economic order in Scripture."[37] When another reconstructionist, David Chilton, wrote a book on economics, it was framed as a refutation of Sider's *Rich Christians in an Age of Hunger,* and titled *Productive Christians in an Age of Guilt Manipulators.* In a recent review of Calvin Beisner's *Prosperity and Poverty,* Liberty University's Mark Clauson makes a point of noting that "Beisner responds to the Siderite interpretations of Scripture" and espouses "a concept of justice that is directly opposed to the ideas of many evangelicals in the mold of Ronald Sider."[38] This fascination with Sider and his associates is revealing. The evangelical right has made no analogous attempt to refute Catholic and mainline Protestant teachings, which are at least as liberal as those of Sider and which have received far more attention in the secular press. Leaders of the evangelical right are well aware that both they and their counterparts on the left contend for the same evangelical Christian audience.

Ronald Sider is a philosopher at Eastern Baptist Theological Seminary and prob-ably the most influential leader of the evangelical left.[39] Sider sees issues of poverty, inequality, and economic justice as central to biblical morality. He condemns fellow evangelicals for "ignoring the central Biblical teaching that God is on the side of the poor"[40] and repeatedly draws attention to the vast disparities in wealth and living standards that exist in the modern world. The scriptural solution, according to Sider, is basically one of redistribution. Christians in the world's developed countries must consume less, contribute more to the poor, and demand that their countries enact trade policies that benefit less-developed countries. Although Sider and other evan-gelicals of the left concede the biblical "legitimacy of private property," they are quick to add that "the right of private property in not absolute."[41] It is not surprising, therefore, that market intervention is implicit in many of their specific proposals, such as the call for a "national food policy," increased foreign aid (channeled through organizations like the United Nations), "just" international trade, and guaranteed wages.[42]

A handful of evangelical leaders flatly reject capitalism in favor of socialism. Most of these are self-styled "radical evangelicals" whose thinking has been influenced by the secular left, the 1960s counterculture, and communitarian Christian groups such as the Hutterites, Mennonites, and Amish. Adopting a Marxist formulation of socie-ty's problems, they argue that "the system which creates and sustains much of the hunger, underdevelopment, and other social ills in the world today is capitalism. Capi-talism is by its very nature a system which promotes individualism, competition, and profit-making with little or no regard for social costs. It puts profits and private gain before social service and human needs. As such it is an unjust system which should be replaced."[43] These sentiments find their strongest expression in the writings of Jim Wallis, the radical left's most influential leader. His *Agenda for Biblical People*[44] insists that American "overconsumption is theft from the poor" and that "the people of the nonindustrialized world are poor *because* we are rich; the poverty of the masses is maintained and perpetuated by our [economic, political, and military] systems and institutions and by the way we live our lives." He calls for the rejection of consumer-ism and the "redistribution of wealth and power on a global scale."[45]

Fundamentalist Attributes and Economic Orientations

Our overview of a variety of theologically conservative Protestants—strict fundamen-talists, the NCR, Christian reconstructionists, and the evangelical left—illustrates why right-to-left variation in religious economic thought cannot be linked to corresponding variation in theological beliefs or social attributes. It is simply not true that "conservative" economic views are the consequence of "conservative" theology or other "fundamentalistlike" attributes. Premillennialism, a characteristically fundamentalist doctrine, is not the key to economic conservatism, since the most radically right-wing group of evangelicals, the reconstructionists, utterly reject that doctrine. Separatism also fails to predict economic conservatism—the strict separatists associated with Bob Jones University appear suspicious of *all* economic systems and utterly repudiate the goals of the New Christian Right. Belief in biblical inerrancy likewise fails to predict economic outlook. Ronald Sider and other economic liberals of the evangelical left are defenders of biblical inerrancy, and Sider's writings are packed with scriptural quotations interpreted literally. Yet Sider embraces government intervention and argues that "laissez-faire economics . . . reflects a modern, secularized outlook rather than a biblical perspective."[46]

This record of diversity underscores a crucial fact: there is no generally accepted biblical standard for economic conduct. Different evangelical leaders with similar theologies and similar views of Scripture have little trouble finding biblical justification for radically different economic teachings. Some emphasize that the early Christian church "had everything in common" (Acts 4:32); others invoke the eighth and tenth commandments, which prohibit stealing or coveting another's property, as mandating respect for private property; and yet others justify income redistribution and poverty programs with reference to the Jubilee laws (Leviticus 25:8–55), which mandate the periodic freeing of slaves and return of land to its original owners.[47] In fact, different people sometimes defend radically different economic policies with exactly the same scriptures. The founders of virtually every Christian commune quote Acts 4:32 as proof that private property is contrary to the Christian ideal. Sider and Wallis likewise see in this text a "model" for Christians' "common use and consumption" of economic resources.[48] But others use the same passage as evidence that communism proved unworkable even in the golden age of the Apostles. They claim that the experiment was short-lived and was never repeated "because it obviously didn't work." They even interpret Paul's subsequent efforts to collect funds for the Jerusalem church as proof that "the poor saints at Jerusalem . . . bankrupted themselves though their experiment in communal living."[49] Most evangelicals say that the biblical tithe requires Christians to contribute a tenth of their income to the church. But the reconstructionists also interpret the tithe as limiting government revenue to a flat 10 percent tax.[50] Christians on all sides agree that the Bible commands charity toward the poor. But those on the left invoke these scriptures to justify income redistribution and social welfare programs, whereas those on the right argue that biblical charity and mandated redistribution are in fact antithetical, since true charity must be freely given.

Statistical data provide further proof that economic thinking often varies independent of theological beliefs. Consider, for example, a 1981 survey of over a thousand faculty members at 198 seminaries and theological schools drawn from the full range of Christian denominations. The faculty were asked numerous questions about their religious, political, and economic beliefs. The results showed that conservative theology—belief in biblical inerrancy, the divinity of Jesus, the promise of immortality, and the threat of Hell—did *not* lead to economic conservatism. Theologically conservative professors displayed tremendous variation in their attitudes toward social welfare programs. Whereas theologically liberal professors seem to have attained a liberal consensus on such issues as welfare spending, income redistribution, reducing the role of government, and aid to poor countries, theologically conservative professors range all over the map. There was no evidence of an economic consensus, conservative or otherwise, among the professors in this latter category. Likewise, when analyzing results by school type, the economic views of professors at evangelical and fundamentalist schools showed substantially greater variation than those of professors at mainline Protestant schools. Interestingly, the situation was reversed on issues of sexual conduct. Professors at fundamentalist and evangelical schools responded far more consistently and conservatively to questions about abortion, homosexuality, and premarital sex than did professors at mainline Protestant schools. Hence, it is incorrect to attribute the economic results to some greater underlying diversity in the evangelical-fundamentalist (as opposed to mainline) population. Evangelicals and fundamentalists *are* capable of consensus. But this consensus is moral rather than economic.[51]

In short, there is little relation between standard fundamentalist attributes and economic orientation. Unless one plays with tautologies—for example, by equating fundamentalism with Falwell and the New Christian Right—it is impossible to argue that all fundamentalists, much less all evangelicals, are ardent supporters of laissez-faire capitalism or other conservative economic policies. Rather, one must acknowledge that fundamentalist and evangelical leaders with similar theological beliefs and social traits subscribe to a wide range of economic views.

Impact

The economic teachings of evangelical leaders appear to have had little impact on rank and file members or on national debate, economic policies, and economic institutions. Moreover, the evidence below gives no indication that this situation will change any time soon.

The Rank and File

If one were to compare the economic views of the typical evangelical or fundamentalist to those of the typical American and then summarize the comparison in a single phrase, the phrase would be "no difference worth mentioning." This fact so contradicts the conventional wisdom that it demands both evidence and explanation.

As already noted, the widespread image of fundamentalists and evangelicals as economic conservatives is partly due to the media's extensive coverage of Falwell and the New Christian Right throughout the 1980s. But it is also due to the fallacious notion that all forms of conservatism—religious, moral, economic, and so forth—go hand in hand. Rank and file fundamentalists and evangelicals do indeed stand out as religious and moral conservatives, but their economic views are largely indistinguishable from those of other Americans. In this respect they are much like their theology school counterparts, whose diverse economic views but consistent moral views have already been noted.

Consider, for example, a recent study by Ted Jelen comparing the attitudes of more than one thousand Catholics, mainline Protestants, and evangelical Protestants on issues concerning sexual morality, abortion, feminism, school prayer, communism, arms spending, and government welfare programs.[52] On all issues except the last, evangelicals proved significantly more conservative than Catholics and mainline Protestants. But their attitude toward welfare spending was virtually the same as (and indeed slightly more liberal than) other Christians'.

Although Jelen's study addressed only one economic issue and employed a very loose, denominational definition of evangelicalism, the same result holds for stricter definitions and many other issues. We see this in tables 15.1 and 15.2, which summarize the moral and economic attitudes of white Protestants in the 1987, 1988, and 1989 General Social Surveys. In these tables, I have classified more than four thousand respondents on the basis of their denomination *and* their personal religious beliefs. Respondents have been labeled "evangelical-fundamentalist" if (1) they belong to an evangelical or fundamentalist denomination[53] and, (2) they also accept the Bible as God's Word, "to be taken literally, word for word."[54]

Table 15.1 shows that evangelical-fundamentalists are far more likely to espouse traditional moral standards than are other white Protestants. Eighty-two percent of them (but only 57 percent of other Protestants) oppose laws that "permit abortion for any reason." Ninety-five percent of them (but only 78 percent of others) believe that "extramarital sex is always wrong." Sixty-three percent of them (but only 23 percent of others) believe that "premarital sex is always wrong." Their condemnation

TABLE 15.1

MORAL ISSUES

	Evangelical-Fundamentalists (%)	Other Protestants (%)
Opposes laws that permit abortion for any reason	82	57
Favors laws prohibiting the distribution of pornography to persons of any age	63	43
Believes that homosexual sex is always wrong	95	72
Believes that premarital sex is always wrong	62	23
Believes that extramarital sex is always wrong	94	78

Source: General Social Surveys, 1987 through 1989.

TABLE 15.2

ECONOMIC ISSUES

	Evangelical-Fundamentalists (%)	Other Protestants (%)
Believes that we currently spend too little on solving the problems of big cities	24	27
Believes that we currently spend too little on welfare	41	43
Believes that we currently spend too little on improving the condition of blacks	22	19
Believes that we currently spend too little on improving and protecting the nation's health	64	66
Believes that we currently spend too little on improving the nation's education system	59	64
Believes that we currently spend too little on improving and protecting the environment	54	66
Believes that we currently spend too little on foreign aid	4	4
Believes that we currently spend too little on the military, armaments, and defense	16	16
Believes that we currently spend too little on halting the rising crime rate	65	61

Source: General Social Surveys, 1987 through 1989.

of pornography and homosexuality is no less emphatic. On each of these moral issues, the differences between evangelical-fundamentalists and other Protestants is strong, striking, and statistically significant. Moreover, these differences remain after controlling for background characteristics.[55] The distinctive attitudes cannot be traced to income, education, age, gender, or marital status. Fundamentalists and evangelicals truly are moral conservatives.

Even so, they are *not* economic conservatives. Table 15.2 shows this quite clearly. When asked about government spending on health, poverty, education, the environment, and the problems of blacks and large cities, evangelical-fundamentalists are nearly as likely as others to advocate increased expenditures. For virtually every economic item, the difference between them and nonevangelical Protestants is small, on the order of a few percentage points, and statistically insignificant.[56] The NCR notwithstanding, fundamentalists and evangelicals seem just as comfortable with big government as everyone else.

This last statement can be taken even farther. Recent research by Burton, Johnson, and Tamney indicates that when it comes to "economic restructuring" (income redistribution and job and income guarantees), fundamentalists are actually *more* liberal than others. Viewing fundamentalism as a matter of degree, Burton, Johnson, and Tamney surveyed people to determine the extent to which they believed in strict biblical inerrancy, the second coming of Christ, human sinfulness, and God's control over every aspect of life.[57] Their surveys also investigated political, sexual, and economic attitudes.[58] The results show that, although fundamentalism correlates positively with conservative political attitudes and traditional sexual attitudes, it also correlates positively with support for economic restructuring.[59] Indeed, even when focusing on supporters of the Moral Majority, they could find no evidence of a conservative economic orientation.[60] Burton, Johnson, and Tamney attribute their results to the continuing influence of values embodied in the Populist and Prohibitionist parties of the late nineteenth and early twentieth century, two movements closely associated with traditional, conservative Protestantism. They conclude that William Jennings Bryan "seems a more apt personification of Protestant Fundamentalism than does Jerry Falwell."[61]

It is difficult to know whether the economic views of fundamentalists and evangelicals really stem from populism. Other explanations certainly are possible. (For example, one might attribute the rank and file's lack of economic conservatism to their leaders' lack of economic consensus. Or one might argue that there really is nothing to explain since their economic attitudes are not much different from anyone else's.) Nevertheless, the legacy of populism is cited by both leaders on the inside and researchers on the outside. Gary North has blamed Bryan for turning fundamentalist Christians against the gold standard, free trade, and free markets. "Bryan radicalized a substantial segment of Christian voters in the United States. . . . Thus, American Christian thinking on economics is muddled. Christian's 'populist' instincts are anti-bank, yet pro-paper money. Christians are patriotic, but with this has come a suspicion of foreigners and foreign imports."[62] Political scientist James Reichley raises the same points while discussing evangelicals' historic allegiance to the Democratic Party. He observes that

> evangelicals, while for the most part socially conservative . . . have by no means given up all the other attitudes and dispositions that for many years kept them loyal to the Democrats. . . . As the evangelicals have begun to acquire political confidence, some have shown signs of doubting that there is a necessary connection between traditional morality and, say, supply-side economics or an aggressively interventionist foreign policy. Older themes of economic populism and foreign policy noninterventionism, even isolationism, have begun to reappear.[63]

In any case, whether or not populism is the key, most evangelicals are neither libertarians nor free-market ideologues at heart. In the final analysis, they seem more at home with a "Christian" government that fosters and even imposes "Christian" values than a truly nonintrusive, minimal state. Just as conservative Protestants supported prohibition around the turn of the century, so contemporary evangelicals have sought a constitutional ban on abortion, restrictions on drugs, pornography, and sexual conduct, and laws that require school texts to teach "creation science" as an alternative to evolutionary theory. The majority of evangelicals likewise look to the state for relief from poverty, reductions in economic inequality, and solutions to racial conflict, urban decay, and environmental pollution. They fear the growth of government insofar as it serves the interests of "secular humanists," but by no means do they oppose all restrictions on personal liberty. One suspects that when rank and file evangelicals claim to support "free" and "open" markets, they mean markets free of communism and open to the influence of Christian values. Though it might come as a surprise, their middle-of-the-road sentiments were aptly summarized by Falwell himself:

> I believe in the free enterprise system. . . . I look on socialism as mutually shared poverty. But I also believe that we must continue to struggle to bring justice, equality and a fuller measure of mercy and generosity through our free enterprise system. The exploitation of workers, the misuse and abuse of power and wealth, the unequal and discriminatory distribution of profits should have no place in America's practice of capitalism.[64]

Impact on Public Policy

If evangelical leaders have failed to impress their members with a distinctive economic ethic, they have had even less effect on governmental policies. Indeed, it appears that for all practical purposes they have never even tried to change current economic policy.

Consider, for example, the track record of the New Christian Right. If any group of evangelicals was in the position to have policy impact in the 1980s it was the NCR. Yet, for all its pro-capitalist rhetoric, the NCR never lobbied seriously for or against any economic bills. One searches in vain for instances in which NCR leaders and organizations directed significant time or money toward the passage of specific free-market legislation—such as laws to reduce agricultural price supports, eliminate quotas and tariffs, scale back the minimum wage, or cut social spending and poverty programs.

The NCR's lack of support for economic legislation contrasts sharply with its approach to moral and educational issues such as abortion, school prayer, the teaching of creationism, tuition tax credits, and gay rights.[65] On abortion, for example, the NCR actively supported constitutional amendments designed to overturn the *Roe v. Wade* Supreme Court ruling. It also supported statutory proposals to strip the Court of its jurisdiction over the abortion issue. The NCR's approach to school prayer was likewise characterized by support for constitutional amendments, statutory restrictions, and special legislation aimed at getting around the Court's rulings. Bills mandating the teaching of "creation science" were introduced and in some cases passed in state legislatures.[66] The NCR also supported tuition tax credits, but for reasons more educational than economic. By reducing the cost of private Christian schooling, the NCR simply sought to facilitate the inculcation of fundamentalist values.

The NCR's political effectiveness was debated throughout the 1980s, and it continues to be debated today. Some have noted that despite tremendous media coverage, extensive lobbying, and eight years of a president committed publicly to much of its agenda, virtually none of its policy objectives were realized.[67] While conceding the lack of legislative victories, others contend that it was a major achievement merely to get Congress to debate school prayer, abortion, and tuition tax credits.[68] By either standard, however, the NCR's *economic* impact must be judged as virtually nonexistent. For all intents, economic issues were never even on the NCR agenda. In this respect, Falwell's 1981 "Agenda for the Eighties" was entirely typical. Its ten-item list of the Moral Majority's "vital issues" included abortion, homosexuality, drugs, pornography, women's rights, ERA, national defense, support for Israel, church-state separation, and the autonomy of the Moral Majority state organizations.[69] Economics was never even mentioned. Falwell's 1980 "Biblical Plan Of Action" likewise lists abortion, homosexuality, pornography, humanism, and the fractured family as the five major moral-political problems "that moral Americans need to be ready to face."[70]

The NCR's failure to pursue, let alone attain, specific economic goals is easy to understand given the statistical evidence described above. Rank and file evangelicals are no more enamored of free markets than are other Americans, nor are they any more opposed to government intervention. The NCR's legislative activities, which attacked moral issues but avoided economic ones, accurately reflected the interests of its constituency and thus accord with standard political theory. What needs to be explained, therefore, is not why the NCR failed to lobby for economic change but rather why it even raised the issue of free markets.

Beyond Rhetoric

The economic rhetoric of Falwell and company defies explanation only as long as we focus on the NCR's own constituency. The paradox is resolved when we broaden our perspective and recognize that the New Christian Right was from its inception just one side of a new right-wing political coalition. This fact, though often ignored by the press and the public, has been documented by both political scientists and sociologists. Recounting the history of the NCR, Richard Pierard notes that the coalition got its start in the mid-1970s, when *secular* conservative activists, most notably Richard Viguerie, Howard Phillips, and Paul Weyrich,

> set out to build a broad coalition that would be autonomous from the political parties and possess a comprehensive set of political organizations. . . . The leaders of the so-called New Right were careful to emphasize the vital nature of the social issues that interested the evangelical conservatives. In 1979, they assisted in creating the three groups the media most closely identified with the New Christian Right: the Moral Majority, (Religious) Roundtable, and Christian Voice.[71]

Pierard's interpretation is echoed by other scholars, such as Reichley:[72]

> In its early stages, the religious new right was tutored and even to some extent created[73] by a cadre of secular conservative organizers and publicists who for

some years had been seeking to mobilize a right-wing coalition in national politics. . . . Up to 1976, the chief preoccupations of the far right had been resistance against the growth of the welfare state and hardline opposition to the Soviet Union. After the 1976 election, Weyrich in particular spotted the social agenda of the religious right, with which he was in personal sympathy, as a new source of major electoral strength for a broad right-wing coalition.[74]

The New Christian Right would probably never have arisen, much less captured public attention, had it not from the start allied itself with secular conservatives. In turn, that alliance would never have formed had not both sides conceded the issues most cherished by the other. The secular conservatives embraced the evangelical-fundamentalist moral agenda, and the NCR in turn embraced the secular conservatives' economic agenda. However, for many leaders, and perhaps most followers, that embrace was less than loving. In the words of one scholar, "Many traditional Republicans are uncomfortable with the emotionally charged moral agenda of the Christian right." Hence, as the fundamentalists and evangelicals loudly lamented, the very conservatives that they worked to elect, most notably Ronald Reagan, failed to pursue their moral agenda with the vigor that they had anticipated.[75] For its part, the NCR gave only nominal support to the economic goals of the secular conservatives. The NCR leaders' apparently paradoxical failure to lobby for their economic goals is thus explained by the fact that the goals were never really "theirs" in the first place.

The politics of coalitions helps to explain not only why evangelicals and fundamentalists have done so little to affect economic policies directly but also how they might have had some *indirect* impact. Insofar as the NCR coalition succeeded, it helped elect Republicans whose economic orientation was relatively conservative. The economic effect of the NCR in the 1980s thus hinges on the answers to two questions: Was the support of fundamentalists and evangelicals critical for the election of conservatives, and did the election of these conservatives lead to conservative economic outcomes? The future must be the judge of these questions. To date, scholars remain deeply divided over the political impact of Falwell, the Moral Majority, and the rest of the New Christian Right. On the one hand, it seems clear that the 1980s saw a substantial increase in the political activity of evangelicals and fundamentalists.[76] On the other hand, the NCR often antagonized many more people than it attracted, and thus may have mobilized more opposition than support.[77]

The future political effectiveness of evangelicals is also unclear. On the one hand, evangelical support for Republican candidates continues to coalesce. The evangelical vote for Republican presidential candidates has risen from 55 percent in 1976, to 63 percent in 1980, to 76 percent in 1984, and 81 percent in 1988. As Hadden observes, "Evangelical Christians seem to be moving toward a consensus that their best chance for achieving [their] goals is through the Republican party. Their allegiance to the Republican party is now approaching" that of blacks to the Democratic Party.[78] The Republican Party likewise recognizes that "they need evangelical Christians if they are to build a majority party. . . . Thus from a pragmatic perspective, the moralist Christians and the traditional pro-business Republicans are a likely alliance."[79] On the other hand, this coalition remains "an uncomfortable . . . marriage of convenience."[80] According to Reichley, the religious right is now showing less enthusiasm for Republican economics and foreign policy than it did when it first joined the Reagan coalition of the early 1980s.[81] And as evangelical leaders have gained more political clout, they have also displayed a greater tendency to fragment, as they did in the 1988 Republican primary when some supported Robertson, others (including Falwell) supported Bush, and still others backed Dole or Kemp. All in all, there is little doubt that the New Christian Right will continue to make *some* contribution to political conservatism. But the magnitude of that contribution and its relevance to specific policy areas, particularly economics, remain open questions.

Interestingly, the most ardent evangelical proponents of economic conservatism— people like Gary North, Calvin Beisner, and Robert Mateer—set their sights well beyond the Republican Party and the immediate future. They disavow lobbying for legislative change on both practical and theoretical grounds. They know full well that most evangelicals do not share their positions. Striving for immediate change is therefore premature. They also recognize the hazards of coalition politics. Gary North, who once worked for the libertarian presidential candidate Ron Paul, is said to have remarked that "anyone who goes to Washington expecting to change things is in for disillusionment." Rather than enter into the process of compromise and concession that inevitably characterizes political activity, they have instead chosen to embark on a long-term program of education. The reconstructionists in particular emphasize that theirs is an educational movement with a "bottom up" rather than "top down" plan of action. For North, Beisner, Mateer, and many others, the immediate goal is to teach fellow Christians the biblical mandate for free markets founded on Christian moral values. They express confidence that their grass-roots methods will eventually affect economic policies, but they anticipate waiting decades or longer for tangible results. Though not always articulated, their plan of action really has four distinct steps: (1) developing a systematic, Christian view of economics; (2) converting other evangelical educators and leaders to this view; (3) teaching this new economic orthodoxy to rank and file Christians; and finally (4) democratically altering America's economic system, bringing it into line with biblical principles. By their own admission, they have yet to go past the first two steps.[82] Still, in religion as in politics, progress and consensus can arrive unexpectedly. And as the Bible itself states "with God all things are possible" (Matthew 19:26).

Conclusions

This essay has reviewed the economic positions of evangelical leaders and has investigated the impact that these positions have had upon the attitudes of rank and file evangelicals and national economic policies. The positions espoused by evangelical leaders were found to be far more diverse than the platforms of specific groups, such as the Moral Majority, would suggest. A strong free-market consensus remains at best a prospect for the future. Moreover, rank and file evangelicals show no signs whatsoever of embracing a distinctive, religiously motivated economic ethic. They are just as open to income redistribution as other Americans and just as supportive of government programs to promote health, education, and urban renewal, and to alleviate the problems of race, poverty, and the environment. This contrasts sharply with their attitudes toward many moral issues, which are indeed different from and more conservative than those of other Americans. Thus, the conservative economic rhetoric of the New Christian Right appears to be a concession to its secular, political allies, not an expression of the concerns of its rank and file members. This in turn helps to explain why Falwell and other leaders of the NCR never attempted to move from "free enterprise" talk to specific free-market legislation. The only immediate impact that fundamentalists are likely to have on the economy is via their support for conservative Republicans. The importance of that support remains a subject of debate. Moreover, even where their support may have been or may yet become decisive, its primary economic effect will have been to promote an economic agenda that is not really theirs. Evangelical leaders with a serious, religiously-oriented commitment to conservative economic principles remain few, their best hopes a distant prospect.

Some tentative conclusions emerge from this study that may apply to fundamentalism as a generic phenomenon. The first is that the diversity of economic thought within Protestant fundamentalism and the even greater diversity within Protestant evangelicalism may not be exceptional. This study has found no evidence that the logic of fundamentalism drives people toward a particular view of the economy, much less particular economic policies. Rather, we observed examples of the "selective retrieval" that Martin Marty describes as common to all fundamentalisms.[83] Selective retrieval, "picking and choosing . . . from some earlier . . . stages in one's own sacred history," aptly describes the way in which fundamentalists and evangelicals have arrived at biblical justifications for everything from a flat tax to communal living, from income redistribution to the gold standard. Fundamentalists and evangelicals have no difficulty advocating virtually any reasonable economic orientation, as well as many unreasonable ones, with reference to their traditions and written authorities. Hence, where consensus does ever emerge among fundamentalists and evangelicals on the relative merits of capitalism versus socialism or economic efficiency versus equity, it more than likely reflects the working of external forces, such as the dictates of political coalitions or the perceived failure of communist economies. Such an externally induced consensus may indeed have impact upon both rank and file members and the society in which they live, but it is an impact that is no less shaped by secular circumstances than it is by the internal logic of a particular religious form or tradition.

This leads to a second point. Fundamentalism may ultimately relate to economics in much the same way that it relates to technology. Observers are always surprised to see how quickly the so-called antiscientific fundamentalists embrace new technology and how readily they adapt it to their own purposes. The secular medium of television becomes the basis for televangelism; the notebook computer gives rise to the "on-line" Bible. Fundamentalists appear to appropriate economic concepts in much the same way: picking and choosing, paying little attention to an item's original source, and above all using everything they can as an instrument to further their religious (and perhaps ultimately social) agenda. From time to time, academics must pinch themselves to recall that most people are not terribly concerned with nor constrained by logical consistency. In the final analysis, a fundamentalist "worldview" may indeed limit one's attitudes toward technology, education, economics, and politics. But more often than not a fundamentalist's primary concern with each of these is the same as everyone else's: using them as effectively as possible to pursue their larger goals. This could well be the most important lesson that emerges from the messy world of evangelical-fundamentalist economics.

Notes

1. So, too, this study does not concern itself with promises of material gain as God's reward for personal piety, such as those embodied in the teachings that have come to be called "prosperity theology."

2. Kenneth Elzinga, "What Is Christian Economics?" in Robert N. Mateer, ed., *Christian Perspectives on Economics* (Lynchburg, Va.: Christian Economics and Business Association, 1989), p. 9.

3. Ernest R. Sandeen, *The Roots of Fundamentalism* (Chicago: University of Chicago Press, 1970); George M. Marsden, *Fundamentalism and American Culture* (Oxford: Oxford University Press, 1980); Nancy T. Ammerman, *Bible Believers: Fundamentalists in the Modern World* (New Brunswick, N.J.: Rutgers University Press, 1987).

4. Lloyd J. Averill, *Religious Right, Religious Wrong* (New York: Pilgrim Press, 1989), pp. 178–79.

5. A. James Reichley, "Pietist Politics," in Norman J. Cohen, ed., *The Fundamentalist Phenomenon: A View from Within, a Response from Without* (Grand Rapids, Mich.: Eerdmans, 1990), pp. 76–79.

6. Susan Rose, "The Impact of Fundamentalism on North American Education," in Martin E. Marty and R. Scott Appleby, eds., *Fundamentalisms and Society* (Chicago: University of Chicago Press, 1993).

7. National surveys provide researchers their best tool for determining the economic, political, and social attitudes of religious groups in America. Unfortunately, such surveys fail to distinguish between fundamentalists and evangelicals. This failure stems not from inadequate survey design but rather from the nature of fundamentalism itself. The negative connotations of the term "fundamentalist" are so great that many people refuse to identify themselves as such when asked "Are you a fundamentalist?" Fundamentalism cannot be inferred from a respondent's denominational affiliation, since many fundamentalists belong to independent congregations not affiliated with any denomination and most others belong to denominations like the Southern Baptist Convention that also house many nonfundamentalist evangelicals. It is likewise impossible to identify fundamentalist respondents on the basis of their theological beliefs, since these are shared by many evangelicals. The esoteric theological distinctions that scholars use to differentiate fundamentalism and evangelicalism, such as "dispensational premillennialism" versus "historic premillennialism," are lost on the typical survey taker. For example, Ted Jelen finds that survey takers do not discriminate between biblical literalism and biblical inerrancy in "Biblical Literalism and Inerrancy: Does the Difference Make a Difference?" *Sociological Analysis* 49, no. 4 (1989): 421–29. Distinctions based on social attitudes such as separatism or militancy are no less problematic, since these attitudes are shared by evangelicals in the Holiness and Pentecostal traditions. Marsden makes this point in "Defining American Fundamentalism," in Cohen, ed., *The Fundamentalist Phenomenon,* p. 26. In short, a survey researcher has little choice but to accept Rei-

chley's conclusion that "there is . . . no reliable statistical tool for distinguishing within evangelical ranks between fundamentalists and nonfundamentalists." Reichley, "Pietist Politics," p. 79.

8. For details on this split, see Nancy T. Ammerman, "North American Protestant Fundamentalism," in Martin E. Marty and R. Scott Appleby, eds., *Fundamentalisms Observed* (Chicago: University of Chicago Press, 1991), pp. 1–65.

9. See, for example, "Communism: Corruption of a Dream of Freedom," *Sword of the Lord,* 25 May 1990, p. 11, which states that "Soviet Republics must have the freedom to solve their own ethnic and economic problems—a chance at free enterprise."

10. The exception is Tennessee Temple, which teaches a standard two-course introduction to economics. For catalog information on all these schools see *College Catalog Index: 1990–1991,* Career Guidance Foundation, vol. 17, 1990.

11. According to the latest AEA directory, no association member is currently affiliated with any of the previously noted fundamentalist colleges. See *American Economic Review* 79 (December 1989): 6.

12. Ammerman, *Bible Believers,* p. 207.

13. This view appears to be shared by the Jehovah's Witnesses, a Christian sect which manifests many "fundamentalistlike" attributes including strict separatism, belief in biblical inerrancy, emphasis on evangelism, and belief in the Lord's immanent return. See, for example, "Big Business—What It Does for You . . . and to You" in the Jehovah's Witnesses newsletter *Awake!* 65, no. 2 (22 January 1984): 3–10.

14. One must note, however, that a four-person economics department is minuscule by the standards of most secular universities and thus serves to underscore the relative lack of attention that all evangelical schools have given to the subject.

15. In private interviews, August 1989 and November 1990, Mateer refused even to label himself "a fundamentalist" although he emphasized his commitment to "the fundamentals" of the faith.

16. The Coalition on Revival is an organization of socially, politically, and theologically conservative evangelicals. E. Calvin Beisner, the principal author of COR's statement on "The Christian World View of Economics," is a regular contributor to CEBA's conferences, publications, and videos. Like Mateer, he rejects the fundamentalist label, preferring instead to be known as "a doctrinally, ethically, politically, and economically conservative evangelical, not a fundamentalist." Letter dated 29 June 1990.

17. The Oxford Conference, a group of more than one hundred evangelical leaders from all over the globe, met January 1990 in Oxford, England, to draft a formal statement on Christian faith and economics. The statement, entitled the "Oxford Declaration on Christian Faith and Economics," is reprinted and reviewed in *Bulletin of the Association of Christian Economists* 15 (Spring 1990): 7–22.

18. For extended definition and discussion of the NCR, see Steve Bruce, *The Rise and Fall of the New Christian Right* (Oxford: Clarendon Press, 1988), and Richard V. Pierard, "Religion and the New Right in the 1980's," in James E. Wood, Jr., ed., *Religion and the State* (Waco, Tex.: Baylor University Press, 1985), pp. 392–417.

19. Falwell officially dissolved the Moral Majority in August of 1989. For the most part, however, the organization ceased its activities upon being absorbed into Falwell's Liberty Federation in 1986. See "Falwell Claims Victory, Dissolves Moral Majority," *Christianity Today,* 14 July 1989, pp. 58–59.

20. The Baptist pastor James E. Singleton published two booklets of statements from fundamentalists around the country condemning Falwell and the Moral Majority for their alleged compromises. See *The Moral Majority: An Assessment of a Movement by Leading Fundamentalists* and *The Fundamentalist Phenomenon or Fundamentalist Betrayal?* (Tempe, Ariz.: Fundamentalist Baptist Press, n.d.).

21. See, for example, the chapter entitled "A Look at Our Government Today," in Jerry Falwell's *Listen America!* (New York: Doubleday, 1980), pp. 69–81.

22. This continuing series, entitled "Perspectives: A Judeo-Christian View of Economic Issues," currently includes programs entitled "Collapsing Socialism," "The Creation of Wealth," "The Immorality of Our Welfare State," and "Economics—Values."

23. These include Nobel laureate James Buchanan, Catholic theologian and political commentator Michael Novak, political commentator Paul Craig Roberts, and noted black economist Walter Williams.

24. *Christian Perspectives: A Journal of Free Enterprise* 2, no. 3 (Winter 1989): 1.

25. Falwell, "A Look at Our Government Today," *Listen America!* pp. 69–81.

26. Mateer, *Christian Perspectives on Economics,* p. 152.

27. Pat Robertson, *The Secret Kingdom* (Nashville: Thomas Nelson, 1982), p. 151.

28. D. James Kennedy, "The Spiritual State of the Union—1989," *Christian Perspectives* 3, no. 1 (Fall 1989): 7.

29. Rousas J. Rushdoony, *The Politics of Guilt and Pity* (Fairfax, Va.: Thoburn Press, 1978), pp. 236–37.

30. For example, in *Honest Money* and *Inherit the Earth,* North cites Hayek's *The Road to Serfdom,* von Mises's *The Theory of Money and Credit,* and Dolan's *The Foundations of Modern Austrian Economics.*

31. Rousas J. Rushdoony, "The Philosophy of the Free Market," *Journal of Christian Reconstruction* 10, no. 2 (1984): 35.

32. Rousas J. Rushdoony, "How the Christian Will Recover through Economics: The Problem and the Very Great Hope," *Journal of Christian Reconstruction* 10, no. 2 (1984): 41.

33. Rousas J. Rushdoony, "The Philosophy of the Free Market," p. 38.

34. Ammerman, "North American Protestant Fundamentalism," discusses the pre-postmillennial distinction in greater detail.

35. Robertson's *Secret Kingdom* contains repeated references to "dominion."

36. North, Rushdoony, and several other prominent reconstructionists are members of COR's steering committee.

37. In *Honest Money,* p. 161, North asks his readers, "How many times have you heard . . . 'The Bible doesn't provide blueprints'. . . . The odd fact is that some of the people who assure you of this are Christians." North is alluding to Ronald Sider, *Rich Christians in an Age of Hunger* (Downers Grove, Ill.: Intervarsity Press, 1977), p. 205.

38. *Christian Perspectives* 2, no. 4 (Spring 1989): 11.

39. Other intellectual leaders include Samuel Escobar of Eastern Baptist Theological Seminary, Robert Goudzwaard of Free University of Amsterdam, Andrew Kirk, C. René Padilla, Waldron Scott, and Jim Wallis, editor of *Sojourners* magazine, and the *Sojourners* Christian community.

40. Ronald Sider, "An Evangelical Theology of Liberation," in Richard J. Neuhaus and Michael Cromartie, eds., *Piety and Politics: Evangelicals and Fundamentalists Confront the World* (Washington, D.C.: Ethics and Public Policy Center, 1987), p. 158.

41. Sider, *Rich Christians in an Age of Hunger,* p. 114.

42. Sider's discussion of trade policies is especially noteworthy. Though it begins with a call for the "sweeping elimination of tariff barriers," it quickly moves to alternative restrictions on free trade: "As developed nations eliminate trade barriers to products from developing countries, two things will be necessary. Developed nations will need to grant trade preference to developing nations and also permit them to protect their infant industries with tariffs for a time. Developed nations will also need to have some mechanism (such as a guaranteed job or guaranteed annual income for all) so that the small number of U.S. citizens thrown out of work by cheaper foreign imports do not bear this burden alone. . . . Commodity agreements may be another way to increase the export earnings of poor nations by stabilizing prices [above their market levels]." Sider, *Rich Christians in an Age of Hunger,* p. 212.

Statements like these underscore the left's deep distrust of unregulated markets. The evangelical right accepts classical economic arguments, dating back to Adam Smith, that voluntary trade is *mutually* advantageous in practice no less than in theory and that the "wealth of nations" therefore derives from free trade and free markets. Evangelicals on the left adopt a more Marxian view. They take it as axiomatic that real markets tend to exploit the disadvantaged. Free trade favors the wealthy and the powerful. Economic activity is often a zero-sum game, taking from the poor and giving to the rich. Biblically mandated solutions reverse this process: "More just international trade patterns will cost affluent consumers a good deal." Christians must therefore "inform their elected officials that they are willing to pay the cost of international justice." Sider, *Rich Christians,* pp. 213–14.

43. Eugene Toland, Thomas Fenton, and Lawrence McCulloch, "World Justice and Peace: A Radical Analysis for American Christians," *Other Side* 12 (January–February 1976): 50, quoted in Craig Gay, "Recent Evangelical Appraisals of Capitalism and American Class Culture" (Ph.D. diss., Stanford University, 1989), p. 62.

44. Jim Wallis, "The Powerful and the Powerless," in Richard J. Neuhaus and Michael Cromartie, eds., *Piety and Politics,* pp. 189–202.

45. Ibid., p. 189.

46. Sider, *Rich Christians in an Age of Hunger,* pp. 114–15.

47. *The Encyclopedia of the Jewish Religion* describes the Jubilee as follows: "According to the bible every fiftieth year is to be proclaimed a Jubilee. . . . All slaves were released and all land reverted to the original owner. . . . [Thus,] only such possession of land as has been obtained through inheritance is permanent in Jewish law. Land obtained in any other way (including land mortgaged for debt) reverts to its original owner with the advent of the J[ubilee]. This institution prevents the alienation of an inherited share of the land and converts all sales or gifts (Bek. 52b) of land into leases

for a known, fixed, and limited period (Lev. 25:28)." R. J. Zwi Werblowsky and Geoffrey Wigoder, *The Encyclopedia of the Jewish Religion* (New York: Holt, Rinehart, and Winston, 1966), p. 216.

48. Wallis, "The Powerful and the Powerless," pp. 200–202. Sider describes several Christian communes in *Rich Christians,* pp. 180–81, 200–202.

49. Kennedy, "The Spiritual State of the Union—1989," p. 6. These brief comments do not do justice to the extensive and serious treatment that evangelicals have given to Acts 4 and 5. They do, however, convey the extremely divergent interpretations that have been drawn from it.

50. Gary North, *Inherit the Earth, Biblical Principles for Economics* (Fort Worth, Tex.: Dominion Press, 1987), p. 46.

51. The statements in this paragraph are based on Daniel Olson and Jackson Carroll's "Theological and Political Orthodoxy among American Theological Faculty" (Paper presented to the Society for the Scientific Study of Religion, Salt Lake City, 1989).

52. Jelen's data are taken from the 1988 General Social Survey. He classifies Protestant respondents as either "mainline" or "evangelical" on the basis of their denominational affiliation. Ted Jelen, "Religious Belief and Attitude Constraint," *Journal for the Scientific Study of Religion* 29, no. 1 (March 1990): 118–25.

53. The evangelical-fundamentalist denominations include Southern Baptists, Missouri Synod Lutherans, Churches of Christ, Nazarenes, Pentecostal and Holiness, Assemblies of God, and Churches of God. The nonevangelical-nonfundamentalist Protestant denominations include Episcopalians, United Church of Christ, Presbyterians, Methodists, non-Southern Baptists, non-Missouri Synod Lutherans, Disciples of Christ, and Reformed. Several empirical studies, most notably Rodney Stark and Charles Glock's *American Piety* (Berkeley, Calif.: University of California Press, 1968) and Wade Clark Roof and William McKinney's *American Mainline Religion* (New Brunswick, N.J.: Rutgers

University Press, 1987), have demonstrated the validity of this categorization.

54. Researchers and fundamentalists both agree that belief in strict biblical inerrancy is a critical, and perhaps even *the* critical, fundamentalist doctrine. See Ronald Burton, Stephen Johnson, and Joseph Tamney, "Education and Fundamentalism," *Review of Religious Research* 30, no. 4 (June 1989).

55. In regressions that take account of respondents' age, gender, marital status, income, and education, the evangelical-fundamentalist effect remains statistically significant at the .001 level.

56. The differences between evangelical-fundamentalists and other Protestants become even smaller after controlling for respondents' background characteristics.

57. See Ronald Burton, Stephen Johnson, and Joseph Tamney, "Education and Fundamentalism." See also Joseph B. Tamney, Ronald Burton, and Stephen D. Johnson, "Fundamentalism and Economic Restructuring," in Ted Jelen, ed., *Religion and Political Behavior in the United States* (New York: Praeger, 1989).

58. The economic questions asked respondents how strongly they agreed with statements like "the government should guarantee a job to everyone willing to work," "we must create a society in which goods and services are distributed more or less equally among all people," "employers have an obligation to provide jobs that people enjoy doing," and "personal income should not be determined solely by one's work; rather, everybody should get what he or she needs." Burton, Johnson, and Tamney, "Education and Fundamentalism," p. 349.

59. My analysis of data from the 1987 through 1989 General Social Surveys produced a similar finding. Fundamentalists, whether defined in terms of denominational affiliation or religious belief or both, were significantly more likely than other Protestants to agree that "government in Washington ought to reduce income differences between rich and poor."

60. See Joseph Tamney and Stephen

Johnson, "Explaining Support for the Moral Majority," *Sociological Forum* 3, no. 2 (1988): 234–55. A similar finding emerged in Clyde Wilcox's analysis of a 1982 survey of Ohio Moral Majority members. Wilcox found that whereas the vast majority of Moral Majority members attributed their position on abortion and the ERA to their religious beliefs, only half felt that their religious beliefs strongly influenced their position on a balanced budget or social service spending. See Clyde Wilcox, "Seeing the Connection: Religion and Politics in the Ohio Moral Majority," *Review of Religious Research* 30, no. 1 (1988): 50.

61. Tamney and Johnson, "Explaining Support for the Moral Majority," p. 92.

62. North, *Honest Money,* pp. 133–34.

63. Reichley, "Pietist Politics," pp. 75–76.

64. Jerry Falwell, *Strength for the Journey* (New York: Simon and Schuster, 1987), p. 372.

65. The NCR's program is discussed by Matthew C. Moen, *The Christian Right and Congress* (Tuscaloosa, Ala.: University of Alabama Press, 1989), pp. 83–92, and Bruce, *The Rise and Fall of the New Christian Right,* chap. 5.

66. The Louisiana and Arkansas state legislatures passed bills requiring that creation science be taught as an alternative to evolution. Both laws were ultimately struck down by federal courts. See Bruce, *The Rise and Fall of the New Christian Right,* pp. 114–23, for a discussion of creationist legislation in the 1980s.

67. Bruce, *The Rise and Fall of the New Christian Right.*

68. Moen, *The Christian Right and Congress.*

69. Ed Dobson, Ed Hindson, and Jerry Falwell, *The Fundamentalist Phenomenon* (Grand Rapids, Mich.: Baker Book House, 1986), pp. 189–90.

70. Falwell, *Listen America!* pp. 252–54.

71. Pierard, "Religion and the New Right in the 1980's," pp. 396–97.

72. See also Bruce, *The Rise and Fall of the New Christian Right,* and Jeffrey K. Had-

den, "Conservative Christians, Televangelism, and Politics: Taking Stock a Decade after the Founding of the Moral Majority," in Thomas Robbins and Dick Anthony, eds., *In Gods We Trust*, 2d ed., (New Brunswick: Transaction Publishers, 1990), pp. 463–72. Falwell himself traces the founding of the Moral Majority to a 1979 meeting with "a group of conservative leaders," and he attributes the phrase "moral majority" to Paul Weyrich. Falwell, *Strength for the Journey*, pp. 358–59.

73. For an example of this creative process, see Pierard's description of how "New Christian Rightist Howard Phillips . . . was placed in contact with Jerry Falwell . . . [and at] a meeting in 1979 . . . persuaded Falwell to form a religiopolitical movement called the Moral Majority." Richard V. Pierard, "Religion and the 1984 Election Campaign," *Review of Religious Research* 27, no. 2: (December 1985): 99.

74. James A. Reichley, "Religion and the Future of American Politics," *Political Science Quarterly* 101, no. 1 (1986): 25–26.

75. Bruce, *The Rise and Fall of the New Christian Right*.

76. Reichley, "Religion and the Future of American Politics."

77. Bruce, *The Rise and Fall of the New Christian Right*; Clyde Wilcox, "The New Christian Right and the Mobilization of Evangelicals," in *Religion and Political Behavior in the United States*, pp. 139–55.

78. Hadden, "Conservative Christians, Televangelism, and Politics: Taking Stock a Decade after the Founding of the Moral Majority," p. 467.

79. Ibid, pp. 468–69.

80. Ibid, p. 468.

81. Reichley, "Pietist Politics," p. 75.

82. This paragraph is based on Gary North's essay "What Are Biblical Blueprints?" in *Honest Money*; E. Calvin Beisner's "Christian Economics: A System Whose Time Has Come," in *Christian Perspectives on Economics*; and telephone interviews with Robert Mateer, E. Calvin Beisner, and Bruce Barron in March of 1990.

83. Martin E. Marty, "Fundamentalism as a Social Phenomenon," *Bulletin: The American Academy of Arts and Sciences* 42, no. 2: (November 1988): 20.

Buddhist Economics and Buddhist Fundamentalism in Burma and Thailand

Charles F. Keyes

Buddhism and the Political Economies of Burma and Thailand

In his widely read book *Small Is Beautiful* E. F. Schumacher argued that there is a "Buddhist economics" which contrasts with the "materialist economics" of the post-Christian and communist West.[1] While modern economics is centered on commodities and the product of labor, Buddhist economics is centered on work and the worker. "Modern economics . . . tries to maximize human satisfactions by the optimal pattern of consumption, while [Buddhist economics] tries to maximize consumption by the optimal pattern of productive effort."[2] In the same vein, "While the materialist is mainly interested in goods, the Buddhist is mainly interested in liberation"[3] and production is the means to this end. Buddhist economics is best pursued within self-sufficient societies: "From the point of view of Buddhist economics, therefore, production from local resources for local need is the most rational way of economic life, while dependence on imports from afar and the consequent need to produce for export to unknown and distant peoples is highly uneconomic and justifiable only in exceptional cases and on a small scale."[4]

Burma,[5] a country with which Schumacher had firsthand familiarity and which figures prominently in his discussion, has sought to institute an economic order based on "Buddhist socialism" or "the Burmese way to socialism." This concept is essentially what Schumacher terms "Buddhist economics." Modern Burmese Buddhist economics has its origins in what can only be termed a "fundamentalist" variant of Buddhism that emerged in the first half of the twentieth century.

The Burmese, like the Thai, the Lao, the Khmer or Cambodians, and the Sinhalese in South Asia, trace their Buddhist traditions to the interpretation of texts written in Pāli which became authoritative in the fourth century C.E. in Sri Lanka. In this interpretation, which became known as Theravāda Buddhism, or the "way of the elders,"

the *sangha,* or Buddhist order of monks, is seen as the exemplar, teacher, and embodiment of the *dhamma,* the message of the Buddha. Through following the discipline (*vinaya*), monks emulate the ideal of the *arahant,* the saint who has achieved
the liberation which lies at the end of the path established by the Buddha. Through
sermons and ritual acts, monks make the path known to others. As "fields of merit,"
especially for the offering of alms (*dāna*), monks make it possible for lay people to
gain "merit" (*puñña*) which advances them on the path.[6]

From the eleventh through the fifteenth centuries, some Theravādin monks joined
a purification movement begun at the Mahāvihāra monastery in Anurādhapura (the
medieval capital of Sri Lanka). These monks enjoyed the patronage of most rulers of
principalities and kingdoms located in what is today Burma, Thailand, Laos, and
Cambodia. By the end of the period, temple-monasteries had also been established in
most villages throughout the region. Theravāda Buddhism thus became the basis for
the social orders in these societies.

In the nineteenth century, the proselytizing efforts of Protestant missionaries, coupled with the expansion of colonial power, were perceived by some in Ceylon (as Sri
Lanka was known during the colonial period) and Southeast Asia as posing serious
threats to traditional Theravādin orders. In response to these threats, some leading
members of the sangha in Ceylon, Siam (as Thailand was known until World War II),
and Burma[7] called for a new "purification" of the religion. This move entailed new
exegesis of the Tripitaka, the Buddhist scriptures, and a stricter adherence by monks
to the "discipline."

The reforms instituted in Theravāda Buddhist thought in the nineteenth century
constitute the basis for what can be termed "Buddhist fundamentalism" because, like
fundamentalisms elsewhere,[8] these reforms led to a retrieval from scriptural sources
of "essential truths" stripped of traditional trappings. The reforms did not in and of
themselves produce Buddhist fundamentalism. For this to occur, these reforms first
had to be popularized so that adherents were not restricted to a small religious elite;
in other words, reformed Buddhism had to attract significant followings from among
lay people as well as from among monks. The precipitating factor in this development in the Theravāda Buddhist societies was reaction to radical restructuring of the
social order.

In Burma (as in Ceylon)[9] the establishment of a colonial order by the British made
the question of the relationship of a "Burmese" community to the state intensely
problematic. Among Burmans (but not among the Shan, Karen, Karenni, Chin, and
other upland peoples, to whom the British colonial government accorded separate
recognition), the emergence of nationalism—a vision of a moral community whose
interests could be served by a state ruled not by a colonial government but by an
indigenous one—was inextricably linked to reformist Buddhist ideas. Buddhist nationalism, in other words, made reformed Buddhism a popular ideology in Burma.
Because Burmese nationalist movements in the 1920s and 1930s looked to reform
Buddhism for the ideological rationale for radical opposition not only to the colonial
state but also to the secularist premises of the state, the nationalist movements assumed a recognizably fundamentalist character.

In the immediate post–World War II period, after Burma had gained its independence from Britain, Buddhist fundamentalist ideas were incorporated into the ideology of the dominant elite. Since the 1962 coup which brought General Ne Win, the military, and the Burma Socialist Programme Party to power, the Burmese political economy has been structured on assumptions derived from a Buddhist fundamentalism linked to an explicitly non-communist interpretation of Marxism.[10]

By the 1980s the socialist experiment in Burma proved to have been a failure of catastrophic proportions, and the deep disillusionment with the guidance provided by the Burmese military and the Burma Socialist Programme Party precipitated a crisis at least the equal to that of a half century earlier. Many Burmese have again turned to Buddhism for inspiration and to the sangha for organizational support in their opposition to the government. The new political Buddhism of the late 1980s and early 1990s in Burma has some clear fundamentalist characteristics: it is explicitly nontraditional (even antitraditional); it is intensely moralistic; it is impelled by a quest for an all-inclusive communal identity; and it is in opposition to the authority of a would-be secular state. The new political Buddhism of Burma is unlike the fundamentalist Buddhism of an earlier era, however, in that it is not associated with a socialist program.

That a fundamentalist turn in Theravāda Buddhism does not lead inevitably to the embracing of Buddhist socialism is also demonstrated by the case of Thailand. Although Siam was never brought under colonial rule, the Siamese governments of the late nineteenth and early twentieth centuries undertook a restructuring of the Siamese polity in direct emulation of neighboring colonial orders. Some peoples outside the core of Siam experienced this restructuring as a form of colonial domination, and protonationalist movements—again strongly rooted in popular Buddhism—emerged among Lao in northeastern Thailand and Khonmuang in northern Thailand. The Siamese court was ultimately able, however, to assume the role of shaping a new national community that would subsume diverse ethnic groups, each of which adhered to Buddhism within the same order. The most significant political change in Siam in the pre–World War II period—the imposition in 1932 of a constitution on the king by a group of nonroyalist bureaucrats—was not backed by any popular movement, fundamentalist or otherwise.

It was not until much later in the twentieth century, after the effects of rapid economic growth manifested themselves in Thai society, that the question of community was to become a burning one in Thailand. Since the 1960s many new popular movements have emerged to challenge in one way or another the increasingly secular pro-capitalist governments that have ruled the country. A number of these movements have also assumed characteristics which are associated with fundamentalisms elsewhere. They have found in the reformist interpretation of Buddhist doctrines the sources for their raison d'être; they advocate adoption of strict ethical discipline to overcome the temptations and evils of secularized materialism; they offer their followers a strong sense of identity with a moral community; and they promote opposition to those in power who do not share their moral vision. Although several of these movements have entered into public debates about specific economic policies, and although the follower of one has become the governor of Bangkok, none is ever likely be in a position to have exclusive control over the formulation of the basic economic policies of Thailand. Rather, all these movements give greater emphasis to the importance of cultivating individual detachment from worldly desires by those who live in a highly materialistic society. In other words, none appears likely to be in a position of instituting any form of Buddhist socialism in Thailand.

The very different approaches to economic life linked to interpretations of Buddhism in Burma and Thailand do not mean that Buddhist thought is infinitely plastic and that Buddhism is ultimately irrelevant to the actual structure of economies. As I will seek to show, the development of self-consciousness about what constitutes the fundamental doctrines of Buddhism in both countries has been inextricably intertwined with the economic transformations of the two countries. My focus will first be on Burma, and then I will turn to Thailand to consider the contrasts between these two Buddhist societies.[11]

Salvation and Economic Culture in Theravāda Buddhism

The adherents of the historic religions—Judaism, Islam, Christianity, Hinduism, and Buddhism—understand everyday life to be disvalued with reference to some ultimate reality. This ultimate or, to use Max Weber's term, "other-worldly" reality is not a place or a state of being—heaven or *nibbāna*, for example[12]—but is understood as being an absolute power or will with reference to which it is possible to make sense of certain experiences. This absolute assumed different forms in different historic religions although, as Weber observed, a fundamental contrast obtains between those religions that emerged in the Middle East and those that arose in India. In the former, the absolute is conceived of as a transcendental volitional being—Yahweh, God, or Allah. In the latter, it is understood as an impersonal immanent force—*kamma*. Having accepted as unquestioned truth a particular notion of the absolute, it follows that one must also engage in certain actions or refrain from others if one is to ensure a positive relationship to this absolute. The result of achieving such a positive relationship is *salvation*. It is the way in which the quest for salvation is understood that gives an economic culture its distinctive religious cast. Wealth is valued differently when viewed from the perspective of salvation goals than when it is viewed with reference to immediate, this-worldly goals.

The absolute in Theravāda Buddhism, as in Hinduism, is understood as an impersonal principle of cause and effect, the law of kamma, which determines the consequences of the actions of sentient beings. While the world is experienced as constantly changing and impermanent, the law of kamma is inexorable and eternal. If one's actions, as understood according to Buddhist teachings, are positive, one will acquire "merit" (Pāli *puñña*), which is realized as enhanced well-being. If one's actions are negative, one will acquire "demerit" (*pāpa*), which is experienced as heightened "suffering" (*dukkha*).[13] The kamma one acquires during a lifetime is not dissipated after death but attaches itself to the "consciousness" (*viññāna*) that connects one life with the next. Every person is thus born with a kammic legacy that situates him or her within the world in a particular status and with particular abilities and disabilities. This kammic legacy is not absolutely determinative of one's place in life but leaves one free within certain generalized constraints to assume responsibility for actions which will in turn have future kammic consequences. Buddhist traditions, like Hindu traditions which also posit kamma as an absolute, accord differential significance to the effects of previous kamma which determine the constraints on present action as against the freedom to act to produce new kamma.[14] There are significant differences in Buddhist practice in Burma, Thailand, and other Theravāda Buddhist societies depending on the relative emphasis given to retrospective and prospective kamma and on the interpretation of how much time must elapse between an action and its consequence.

The Theravādin salvation ethic is not restricted to the quest for merit since so long as one is bound by the law of kamma one can never fully escape from actions which will lead to some suffering. Theravāda Buddhism also offers a way to achieve a state, nibbāna, in which one has transcended kamma forever. The way to nibbāna is also not wholly independent of the quest for merit since one must have a sufficient store of merit before one is able to aspire to nibbāna. Nonetheless, the quest for nibbāna does entail a distinctive form of action, one that generates neither positive nor negative merit, but results instead in "detachment" from the world ordered by the law of kamma.[15]

All Theravāda Buddhists ascribe the origin of teaching of the way to salvation, the dhamma, to Gotama Buddha. Although Buddha has achieved nibbāna, he still remains a presence in this world in the form of "reminders" (cetiya), including stupas (pagodas), images, and artistic and ritual reenactments of the life of the Buddha and of the Boddhisattvas (future Buddhas) in which the Buddha-to-be achieved the "perfections" necessary for Buddhahood. By relating to the reminders of the Buddha or recollecting the Buddha through ritual, sermon, and art, one puts oneself in close proximity to the source of the dhamma. Devotion to the Buddha brings, at the very least, merit, and some believe that in exceptional circumstances it may bring one to nibbāna itself.

The dhamma is both taught and practiced in an exemplary way by the sangha, or order of monks. The sangha comprises those men who follow a way of life most in keeping with the teachings of the Buddha and who are responsible for the preservation, transmission, and dissemination of the dhamma. To enter the sangha is to launch oneself on the path toward nibbāna. To offer alms (dāna) to the members of the sangha is considered throughout the Buddhist world as a primary way for laity to gain merit.[16]

The basic dogmas of Theravāda Buddhism—kamma, dukkha, nibbāna—do not determine an invariant economic ethic for those who accept them as religious truths. Variant interpretations of these fundamental premises of Theravāda Buddhism by practicing Buddhists in different societies and, especially since the late nineteenth century, within the same society, have led to quite different stances toward economic life, all of which are in some sense Buddhist.

Traditional Religious Uses of Wealth in Burma

The rulers of Pagan, the great Burmese kingdom that flourished from the eleventh to the thirteenth centuries, established a distinctive pattern of Buddhist practice perpetuated, albeit in somewhat altered form, until the present day.[17] For the rulers of Pagan, and the nobles and wealthy commoners who emulated them, the supreme religious act assuring salvation was the building of a pagoda or temple that served as a reminder of the Buddha. The act of building a shrine was of such great soteriological significance that the builder could see it as providing salvation for others as well as him- or herself. An early-thirteenth-century inscription by a noblewoman who dedicated a temple contains a formula common to most such inscriptions: "By the benefit of the work of merit done by that wife [the sponsor who built the temple for her deceased husband], may all creatures reach *nirapān* [nibbāna]."[18] Such shrines typically were erected as funerary monuments, either dedicated to the memory of the deceased or built by a person in anticipation of his or her own death. The building of a shrine related this world to the cosmos, assured the immortality of the sponsor or of the sponsor's deceased relative, and generated such great merit as to make possible the aspirations for attainment of nibbāna not only of the sponsor but also of all who rejoiced in the merit making.

Aung-Thwin[19] estimates that during the period from the beginning of the eleventh to the end of the thirteenth century, three to four thousand shrines were built at the capital. Even the remains at Pagan that one can see today astound the visitor. In the post-Pagan period, the building of a shrine—albeit on a scale much more modest than great monuments—became a goal not only for the rulers but for commoners as well. The individual who was able to amass sufficient wealth to build a pagoda not only gained merit of such magnitude as to render it a shortcut to Nibbāna but also acquired great prestige in the eyes of his or her fellows.[20] The pattern has persisted to the present. Research carried out in villages in the Mandalay area in the late 1950s and early 1960s found that great prestige was still attached to one who was a "pagoda builder" or "monastery builder."[21] The numerous recently built shrines observed by visitors to Burma in the 1970s and 1980s bear witness to the continued salience of the ideal of becoming a sponsor of a pagoda or monastery. The costs for the man or woman who aspires to be a *payā-dagā* by building a shrine of any significance are immense relative to the local economy.[22]

Pagoda building is not the only religious activity that necessitates the expenditure of vast wealth. The other act which Burmans believe to generate extraordinary merit is the *shin-byu,* the ordination of a boy into the sangha as a novice. Just when the shin-byu became an initiation rite through which almost every boy passes is uncertain. Since Buddhism's early years in India ordination into the sangha has been believed to generate merit not only for the person ordained but more importantly for the sponsor of the ordination. The sponsor, typically a parent or parents, reaps great merit from the act. In Burma, as well as elsewhere in Theravādin Southeast Asia—but not in Sri Lanka—it became the ideal in about the fifteenth century for every man to be ordained for at least a temporary period. Although in other Southeast Asian Buddhist societies it became the custom for men to enter the monkhood once they turned twenty as well as for younger boys to enter the novitiate, in Burma only the practice of temporary ordination as a novice was established.

In the late nineteenth century ordination was considered "the most important event in the life of a Burman [male], since only under the role of the recluse and in the abandonment of the world can he completely fulfill the law and hope to find the way to eventual deliverance from the misery of ever-recurring existences."[23] Colonial domination may have even contributed to the significance of the shin-byu in Burmese life. After the British abolished the monarchy, the shin-byu ritual provided a means for the reenactment of some symbolic aspects of court life, thereby investing it with a significance it had not had in the precolonial period.[24] In 1960 the shin-byu was still considered *the* central Buddhist ceremony. "Almost without exception, every Burmese male has this nuclear and prototypical Buddhist experience of abandoning the world and donning the yellow robe."[25] The ceremony has lost none of its significance; I noted dozens of shin-byus in villages in upper Burma and in Mandalay in early 1985 and again in early 1987.

There has been, however, a change over the past hundred years in the way in which the pattern is observed. At the end of the nineteenth century the introduction of government schools had the effect of lowering the age at which boys were ordained as *shin* or *koyin* from the ideal of fifteen to an average of about twelve.[26] This downward shift in the age of ordination continued in the twentieth century. In 1960 Spiro found that the eldest among those who had recently gone through ordination in a village in upper Burma was only twelve.[27] In a shin-byu I saw in 1985, also in rural upper Burma, at least one of the boys appeared to be no more than three or four years of age. The lowering of the age for ordination has been associated with elaboration of the ceremony at the expense of the training and religious disciplining that a member of the sangha is supposed to receive. Even for the purpose of seeing a boy ordained for a very short period of time, parents or other sponsors expend as much or more money on an ordination as they might in becoming a pagoda builder.[28]

While the willingness of a family to expend as much money as possible on a shin-byu can be ascribed, in part, to their desire to gain prestige through a sort of Buddhist potlatch in the eyes of their fellows, the underlying motivation must still be seen as religious. One is moved through the merit generated from the act upward on the kammic hierarchy, thus ensuring reduced suffering in a future existence. While sponsoring an ordination or attaining the status of a pagoda builder are the greatest religious acts a Burman can engage in, one can also gain lesser merit by sponsoring a number of other types of rites, called *ahlu* (lit., "offering"), at which gifts of food, clothing, shelter, and medicine are given to members of the sangha.

Toward a Buddhist Socialism

Has the great expenditure on pagoda building and ordinations as well as on other alms giving been a hindrance or a stimulus to the production and accumulation of wealth in Burma? Aung-Thwin maintains that the religious impulse that led so many at Pagan, especially among the royalty, to expend vast amounts of wealth to build shrines served as a stimulus, not a drain, to the economy.[29] If the laborers who built and maintained these temples were paid rather than forced to work, production may have been stimulated by the need for large amounts of surplus wealth. It must be added, however, that the labor expended to build these monuments was not employed in the production of additional capital.

Spiro has argued that because Burmese need wealth to attain salvation, they are motivated in a way similar to the Calvinists to whom Max Weber ascribed the "Protestant Ethic."[30] There is another side to the picture, however. While salvation goals may stimulate the production of surplus wealth, if the wealth thus produced is invested primarily in conspicuous displays seen as indicative of attainment of salvation goals, little is left to put into this-worldly enterprises that could generate even more wealth. As Sarkisyanz has observed, "Though 'works of Merit' continued to some reduced extent as motivation for economic activity, Buddhist values remained an obstacle to purely economic goals of rational accumulation and profit."[31]

Prior to the advent of British rule there was little impetus toward using capital to expand the economy. The British instituted free-trade policies predicated in part on the assumption that these would stimulate economic growth. Initially they did result in significant growth as peasants saw the selling of produce, especially rice, as an opportunity to garner additional wealth. Through taxation, the colonial government used part of the generated surplus wealth to create an infrastructure—roads, railways, port facilities, and so on—that would, it was held, promote further development. The colonial government also enabled farmers to obtain credit that, it was assumed, would also be used to expand production. By the first decades of the twentieth century, however, the indebtedness of Burmese farmers was growing more rapidly than their income.[32]

This situation was explained in two different ways by British officials of the time. Some argued that the farmers were victims of economic forces beyond their control. Some officials stressed, however, what they saw as the "'improvidence" of the Burmese peasants and their failure to understand the modern, market-oriented economic system. In this view agriculturalists borrowed too much and spent a high proportion of their earnings and loans on religious ceremonies, festivals, jewelry, gambling, and other "nonproductive" pursuits. Even more, officials listed the cost of ceremonies such as ahlus and shin-byus as a major, even the main, cause of debt in the early twentieth century.[33] Although the former explanation was certainly valid to a degree, the fact remains that even after Burma was incorporated into a world economy most Burmese were motivated to accumulate wealth by a salvation ethic that entailed expending wealth on nonproductive ceremonies and edifices.

At the same time the institution of British rule caused such a radical disruption in the social order that the world as experienced could no longer be viewed as in harmony with a cosmic moral hierarchy. Many Burmese, especially when faced with the severe economic hardships of the Great Depression and the resulting loss of their agricultural land to moneylenders, turned to millenarian movements in the hope of restoring this harmony. Those involved in such movements, such as the Saya San rebellion of 1930–32,[34] believed that through manipulation of sacred objects and

performance of innovative rituals, the British could be ousted and the Buddhist monarchy restored. Other Burmese, especially among the elite, were attracted to new
perspectives on Buddhism. Their perspectives can, I believe, be termed "fundamentalist," although this term has not previously been applied to the transformation of
Buddhism in Burma. Central to this transformation was a self-consciousness about
being Buddhist and a recognition that the quest for salvation must entail actions
whose consequences would be realized not only in a future life but also in *saṃsāra,* or
this world.[35]

One of the most significant sources for this transformation was a monk from upper
Burma known as the Ledi Sayadaw (1846–1923).[36] Early in his career he distinguished himself as a student and then as a Pāli scholar. After the British conquered
upper Burma and eliminated the monarchy in 1885, he abandoned a career as a religious scholar, leaving the monastic college in Mandalay where he had been residing.
Thenceforth, he pursued a mission of moral renewal, seeking through popular sermons and tracts to persuade people to become conscious of the ethical implications
of Buddhist teachings. Instead of merit making, he promoted the practice of meditation and the study of metaphysical doctrines contained in the Abhidhamma, the most
philosophical part of the Buddhist scriptures.[37]

The Ledi Sayadaw's renown led the Government of India to honor him through
the title of Agga-Mahāpandita in 1911.[38] The recognition made him a powerful advocate for protesting the violation of the sacred space of Buddhist pagodas and monasteries by British officials who refused to remove their shoes and socks on entering
such places. During the "foot-wearing" controversy of 1916, the Ledi Sayadaw circulated a booklet in Burmese, *On the Impropriety of Wearing Shoes on Pagoda Platforms,*
which provided the religious authority for the protest.[39] This incident marked the
beginning of involvement of Burmese monks in the nationalist movement.

The initial protests gave way to much more forceful agitation which was meant to
provoke police action, and Ledi Sayadaw was replaced by U Ottama, whom many
acclaim as a Buddhist saint and others as the Gandhi of Burma.[40] U Ottama's militant
Buddhist nationalism had a distinctive fundamentalist caste.[41] Born in 1879 near Ak-
yab in Arakan in northwestern Burma, he was first educated in an Anglo-Burmese
school and then became a novice at the age of fifteen. A year later, with support from
a wealthy Shan woman, he went to Calcutta and, although still a Buddhist novice,
took a further three years of Western education. For the next thirteen years he traveled
between India, Burma, and Japan and visited many other countries in Asia. During
these travels, his encounters with other variants of Buddhism as well as other religions
led him to reflect deeply on his own tradition. An accomplished student and teacher
of Pāli as well as Sanskrit, he approached the scriptures with the perspective of one
living in a pluralistic world. In India he became involved in the Indian nationalist
movement and determined to work for Burmese nationalism.

After his return to Burma from Japan in 1919, he formulated in writings, in
speeches, and in his actions a Buddhist fundamentalist attack on British rule. He saw
no contradiction between being a monk and being a political activist. On the contrary,
he argued that for people to attain the ultimate goal of nibbāna they must first free

themselves from enslavement by an alien government. "When the Lord Buddha was alive, man had a predilection for Nirvana. There is nothing left now. The reason why it is so is because the government is English. . . . Pongyis pray for Nirvana but slaves can never obtain it, therefore they must pray for release from slavery in this life."[42]

The "political monks" who followed U Ottama became the vanguard of the nascent nationalist movement, and were particularly effective in broadening the base of support for the movement from a small Anglicized educated group to include villagers. "The pongyi was the most important instrument by which the independence movement reached the rural masses and gained the adherence of the bulk of the people."[43] The movement led by U Ottama was fundamentalist not only in its opposition to an "evil" political order but also in its critique of traditional religious practice. Sayadaw Zeyawadi U Thilasara, a leading political monk, argued that monks should devote themselves to efforts to bring about changes in political and economic life rather than participate in traditional ceremonies or offer conventional moral guidance.[44] Although the political monks sought the "restoration" of a Buddhist society, their vision was of a society based on ethical premises rather than a court-centered cosmological order.[45] Unlike the millenarian followers of Saya San, who turned to magical means to achieve the restoration, the political monks employed as tools political agitation and resistance.

In the 1920s U Ottama and others initiated a series of demonstrations of civil disobedience, modeled in part on those led by Gandhi in India. The goals were the boycott of foreign goods, the denial of tax revenues to the government, the avoidance of the colonial courts, and the creation of schools run by Burmese Buddhists rather than foreign Christians. Significant attention was given to promoting abstinence from liquor, an action that was in accord with Buddhist morality and also lowered government excise revenues.[46]

U Ottama's leadership of demonstrations led to his arrest in 1921 and subsequent imprisonment for a year. Arrested again in 1924, he was imprisoned for three years. Less than a year after his release, he was back in prison and was to remain there until his death in 1939. Although he had an immense influence on the nationalist movement in the 1920s, by the 1930s leadership of the movement had shifted from political monks to lay people.

Many lay nationalist leaders found appealing a Buddhism that emphasized the cultivation through meditation and ethical reflection of detachment from personal desires. Although the ultimate goal of such detachment is the attainment of nibbāna, it also served a more mundane purpose for many lay Burmese practitioners. Through the attainment of "dispassionateness, objectivity, and concentration in *everything*" one does,[47] it was believed that one could act effectively in the world without self-interest. The tying of the spiritual discipline of meditation to realization of a Buddhist vision of a social order that would ensure a generalized reduction of suffering gave Burmese Buddhism a fundamentalist turn.

During the 1930s the lay Buddhist nationalist leaders began to adapt their vision of a Buddhist utopia to socialist ideas borrowed from the West. A critical figure in the development of this "Buddhist socialism" was U Ba Swe. Born in Tavoy in southern Burma in 1915, Ba Swe entered Rangoon University in the mid-1930s. There he became acquainted with Marxism and initially aligned himself with others who were to join the Communist Party of Burma. He gained prominence as the general secretary of the All-Burma Student Union and as a leader of the effort to organize labor protests in 1938. Even in this radical phase, his Buddhist roots were still evident; he referred, for example, to Stalin as "builder of Lokka Nibban," nibbāna on earth.[48] The notion of nibbāna on earth was Buddhist, not Marxist, in origin. It linked him directly with U Ottama and his followers, who had in the 1920s made the attainment of political and social goals prerequisites for the state of nibbāna.[49]

Over the critical years between 1938 and 1948, as a major leader of the nationalist movement, U Ba Swe advocated an ideology that synthesized Buddhism and Marxism. For him, Marxism provided an understanding of the political economic conditions of suffering that must precede the Buddhist quest for ultimate liberation from suffering. In a widely cited speech to military officers in 1951, he proclaimed: "Marxist theory is not antagonistic to Buddhist philosophy. The two are . . . not merely similar. In fact they are the same in concept."[50] He saw Marxism as providing the worldly counterpart to Buddhist metaphysics. By following Marxist tenets to effect the elimination of injustice and poverty in the world, humans can be freed to follow the Path to ultimate liberation, that is, to nibbāna.[51] In the 1930s U Ba Swe imbued the borrowed Marxist methods with a Buddhist interpretation. This was apparent in a strike of petrol workers he organized in 1938. "The very terminology for Strike [thabeit hmauk] and Strikers [thabeit hmauk-thu] was borrowed . . . from a traditional term for refusal of Buddhist monks to accept alms [by inverting their bowls as protest against the givers]."[52] The refusal to accept alms carries a religious, not a political, sanction; if one cannot offer alms, one is, in effect, excommunicated from the Buddhist community.

From the time of Burmese independence in 1948 until 1958, U Ba Swe held a number of high government posts.[53] The prime minister for most of the period, U Nu, shared the same ideology as U Ba Swe, although they eventually differed regarding practical politics. U Nu and Ba Swe both worked to create a Buddhist socialist order, one which was termed Pyidawtha, or "welfare state."[54] Pyidawtha was socialist because the state was to assume dominance over the economy; it was Buddhist because it was to create the conditions by which people could pursue the path toward ultimate salvation. Their efforts were frustrated, however, by immense problems.[55]

The authority of governments in the period from 1948 to 1962 was challenged by powerful insurgents associated with the Communist Party of Burma and with the Karen National Defense Organization. The economy was in extreme disarray during World War II, for more infrastructure was destroyed in Burma than in any other country in Southeast Asia. Moreover, much of the productive land of the country was in the hands of absentee landlords, many of whom were Indians who did not hold Burmese citizenship.[56] The problems proved more than the governments of the period, most of which were led by U Nu, could cope with.

Indeed, as early as the mid-1950s U Nu seemed to be turning away from Buddhist socialism and toward a traditional model of the Buddhist kingship with himself as the de facto monarch. He organized a world council of monks to purify the Buddhist scriptures in conjunction with the celebration in 1957 of the twenty-five hundredth anniversary of the Buddha's death. He also built the Peace Pagoda at Kaba Aye on the outskirts of Rangoon in direct emulation of the rulers of Pagan who had sought to harmonize worldly and cosmic orders through the construction of pagodas and temples. Finally, he attempted to establish Buddhism as the state religion, a move that would have accorded preeminence to a neotraditional Burman Buddhism over both socialist and ethnic types of Buddhism as well as over non-Buddhist religions. The protests that emerged in opposition to this move provided the pretext for a coup which launched Burma on the road to autarchic socialism.

Failure of the Burmese Way to Socialism

On 2 March 1962 the Burmese military under General Ne Win staged a coup against the elected government of Prime Minister U Nu. A Revolutionary Council, composed entirely of senior military officers, assumed power and began ruling by decree. Military coups were not exceptional in Southeast Asia at the time. One had been staged in neighboring Thailand in 1957, another would occur five years later in South Vietnam, and yet another three years later in Indonesia. The coup in Rangoon, however, launched Burma on a very different trajectory than other countries in Southeast Asia.

Within a few months of the coup, the new government laid down the ideological premises of the revolution it sought to create in Burma. These were contained in two publications, *The Burmese Road to Socialism* and *The System of Correlation of Man and His Environment*,[57] the latter providing the philosophical underpinnings for the former. *System* "was an eclectic mixture of Marxism and Buddhism, and distinctly Burmese."[58] The key terms used in *System* are taken from Theravāda Buddhist philosophy,[59] and it adopts a Buddhist view of human nature in which the individual is motivated by egocentric desires. If left to his or her own impulses, the individual will not develop "right livelihood." "*Aware as we are of such human frailties* we must make our way of life a reality, i.e., a *socialist way of democratic life* that can constantly check and control this evil tendency to lapse. Only then can everyone have the right of using his own creative labor and initiative."[60] The discipline of socialism would bring out the altruistic side of human nature.

Although the ideology espoused by the new government had unmistakable roots in the Buddhist socialism of U Ba Swe and through him in the fundamentalist Buddhism of monks like U Ottama, the government that promoted this ideology made a fundamental break with Burmese Buddhism in assigning the task of instructing the populace in moral discipline not to the sangha but to the cadre of a new party, the Burma Socialist Programme Party (BSPP). This cadre was expected to lead society "by a 'reorientation of views' to eradicate 'fraudulent practices, profit motive, easy living, parasitism, shrinking, and selfishness.'"[61] Unlike Pol Pot in Cambodia, Ne Win did not attempt to replace the Buddhist monks by party cadres through the destruction of the sangha. The Ne Win government was not anti-Buddhist even though it rescinded the laws and promulgations of the previous regime designed to make Buddhism the state religion. Monks were not, however, to be allowed to play any role in politics, as many in the order had done prior to 1962. In 1964 Ne Win made a distinction between the legitimate religious role of the sangha and an illegitimate political one: "The Revolutionary council . . . desires the purity of religion, especially of Buddhism, the religion of the majority of the people of the country, and believes that this task of keeping the Buddha *sasana* [religion] pure should be borne solely by the sanghas. For this purpose of keeping the Buddha sasana pure, the Revolutionary Council said, the sanghas' sanctity is besmirched by dabbling with the mundane affair of politics."[62]

No U Ottamas were allowed to emerge; monks who engaged in political action were arrested. The arrests of those who in 1965 protested the controls instituted over the sangha by the state and those involved in 1974 in demonstrations associated with the funeral of U Thant, former secretary general of the United Nations, served as warnings to others. At the same time monks were allowed to continue to occupy highly respected places in local society. For the period between 1962 and the 1980s monks were in a "legal limbo" in relation to the state.[63]

Denied a political role, the sangha was also excluded from playing a constructive role in the pursuit of the Burmese Road to Socialism. Left to themselves, most in the sangha over the next twenty-five years perpetuated a traditional cosmological Buddhism. The consequence for Burmese society was "an uneasy sense of contradiction between two extremes: radicalism in economic change and conservatism in cultural change."[64] This reversion to tradition was encouraged by the xenophobic policies of the Ne Win government, which closed Burma to external influences. Ne Win's intent to make Burma entirely independent of the outside world reflected a commitment to self-sufficiency that Schumacher noted as a hallmark of Buddhist economics, but under Ne Win, Buddhist socialism was no longer associated with the sangha.

After 1962 foreign as well local firms and banks were nationalized; cultural connections, such as those promoted by the British Council, the Ford Foundation, and foreign magazines and newspapers, were severed; tourism was effectively ended by restricting tourist visas to twenty-four hours; foreign nationals, including missionaries, were denied permission to remain in the country. In the mid-1960s approximately 200,000 Indians and Pakistanis, many of whom had been born and raised in Burma and who constituted a large percentage of the country's traders, managers, and technicians, were deported.[65] Although they were not allowed to take away any of their capital—indeed, they were often stripped of personal wealth such as jewelry as well—they took with them much of Burma's commercial and managerial expertise.

Although the new government's extreme chauvinism appealed to the many Burmans who blamed the former British rulers for most of the problems inherited by an independent Burma, it alienated many of the indigenous minority peoples, some of whom had benefited from British support. The Ne Win government not only failed to eliminate the long-running rebellion by Karen but also faced a proliferation of rebel movements seeking autonomy for groups such as the Shan and Kachin.[66] Although none of the ethnic rebellions have ever posed a serious threat to the Burmese state,[67] they have had a major effect on the economy. The persistence of the minority group rebellions has required the Burmese government to maintain and provision one of the largest standing armies in non-communist Asia. In addition, communist, Karen, Shan, and some other rebels have controlled much of the trade across the frontiers of Burma with China, Thailand, and, to a lesser extent, India, and have used the revenues generated from this trade primarily to support their military efforts. The ethnic rebellions have resulted, thus, in the expenditure of much of Burma's official and unofficial foreign exchange for arms produced outside the country rather than in productive activities within the country.

The nationalization of all industry, banking, and trade, coupled with the institution of centralized planning, failed to stimulate significant economic development in Burma. In the first decade following the 1962 coup, the Ne Win government gave little attention to agriculture, traditionally the mainstay of the economy. In 1972 the government admitted that its policies had not been successful and moved to reorient its economic policies to emphasize agriculture, forestry, fisheries, and mining.[68] The government procurement price for rice was increased, although still kept low compared to world market prices. Although some significant increases in average yields resulted from technological changes introduced in the 1970s, rice exports, long the country's major source of foreign exchange, still remained far below pre–World War II levels.[69] The stagnation in the export sector was evident in the fact that, although rice exports almost disappeared by the early 1970s, they still continued to be the major foreign exchange earner.[70]

The government eventually admitted that even the new policies instituted in 1972 had resulted in little economic growth. In June 1987 Burma applied to the United Nations for Least-Developed Country (LDC) status. To qualify for this status, Burma had to demonstrate that it met three criteria: (1) that per capita income was less than $200; (2) that the manufacturing component of the economy accounted for less than 10 percent of the GDP; and (3) that the literacy rate was less than 20 percent.[71] In meeting the last criterion, the government of Burma had to pretend that the country's much higher literacy rate was an illusion. The government claimed that most literacy in Burma in the 1980s had been gained through study in monastic schools (this, after forty years of state-sponsored universal education) and was not effective literacy. Yet, while the deception on the question of level of literacy was most troubling, the economic situation did appear to justify the application which Burma had made for LDC status. In its application the government admitted that per capita GDP had been essentially flat since 1970. Since that year, "the annual growth rate was about 2.5 percent, while the population growth rate for the same period was 2 percent. 'Hence,' the government's report concluded, 'there has practically been no increase in the real per-capita GDP for the people of Burma.'"[72]

In fact, the government's estimate of per capita GDP did not take into account the real economy of Burma. The black market economy, much of which remains in the hands of insurgents on the country's borders, grew much more rapidly than the official economy, especially in the 1980s. In November 1985 the government, realizing that it had lost control of the economy, attempted to reassert itself by demonetizing the highest denomination banknotes. The result was a slight disruption in economic activity, but the black market continued much as before. On 5 September 1987, the government once again attempted to gain control through demonetization; the very commonly used 25-, 35-, and 75-kyat banknotes were demonetized.[73] Estimates of how much of the currency was rendered valueless vary between 60 percent and 80 percent.[74]

These demonetizations, like previous ones, were aimed as much at eliminating a burgeoning entrepreneurial class as they were at controlling the black market. The one in September 1987, however, had a marked negative impact on much of the population. Almost everyone—government officials as well as farmers, workers in the state trading firms as well as private entrepreneurs, ethnic Burmans as well as minorities—experienced a rapid decline in standard of living. Although the government had instituted a number of economic reforms such as privatizing the rice trade just before the second demonetization, these were too few and too late. An economic crisis soon gave way to a political crisis. On the day the demonetization was announced, students organized the first significant protest rallies since the mid-1970s. The government moved quickly to suppress these protests but did little to meet the underlying economic concerns which had prompted them.

The modest student protests of September 1987 proved to be the harbinger of massive protests in 1988, each of which brought harsh responses from the military. There was outrage at the government's violent actions, which resulted in the death or injury of hundreds of people. The protesters literally seized the high ground. In June 1988 students aligned with Buddhist monks set up a protest center at the Shwe Dagon Pagoda in Rangoon, the shrine which could truly be said to be the sacred center of Burmese society.[75] The demonstration brought to the fore a new breed of "political monks" who broke with the conservative position adopted by most monks during the Ne Win period.

Between June and September 1988 the crisis deepened despite promises made by the government, under a succession of surrogates for Ne Win, to institute economic and political reforms. The demonstrations grew even larger and drew participation from increasingly wider sectors of society, including many in the civil service. Students provided the main leadership for the protests, but monks were conspicuous as well. Spokesmen for the opposition made connections between their protests and those of the 1920s and 1930s in which an earlier generation of political monks had been active. The effective government in several towns and cities was in the hands of committees of students and monks.[76]

The opposition eventually turned for its leadership to Aung San Suu Kyi, the daughter of General Aung San, who had led Burma in its struggle to free itself of British rule. Aung San has become a hero of mythological proportions to the Burmese, in part because of his tragic death at the hand of an assassin on the eve of Burma's independence, and something of this mythological aura surrounds his daughter. She has lent her charisma to a movement seeking to reinstitute a democratic system and reestablish links with the outside world.

In September 1988, the army openly took over the control of the state under a junta called the State Law and Order Restoration Council (SLORC). The new military government also issued a ban on demonstrations and, when protests continued, deployed forces with orders to use whatever force was necessary to restore order. In the next few weeks, thousands of protestors (mainly students) were killed. SLORC also ordered all workers in state agencies to return to work or lose their jobs. The prospect of losing even minimal pay after a long period of near total collapse of the economy coupled with fear of the use of force brought most government employees back to their jobs.

Even with the military willing to shoot anyone judged to be a rebel, the crisis was not over. Rather, it has moved into a new phase with a very uncertain future. What is certain is that military rule can be sustained only by force; the military-run government lacks legitimacy. SLORC acknowledged the existence of a legitimacy crisis by promising elections. The elections, postponed several times and finally held on 27 May 1990, were the first since the coup of 1962 in which a number of parties were allowed to compete. The Burma Socialist Programme Party was officially abolished in 1988, and although it was re-formed as the National Unity Party, it no longer could make any credible claim to providing the moral leadership for the country. SLORC attempted to ensure that opposition parties would not win the election by imprisoning the leaders, including Aung San Suu Kyi, the general secretary of the National League for Democracy (the major opposition party). Nonetheless, the opposition still won an overwhelming majority in the election. Despite the clear rejection of its mandate to rule the country, the army refused to transfer power to the opposition; instead, it instituted even more repressive rule. Aung San Suu Kyi, who remained under house arrest and who was allowed no contact with the outside world, became a symbol of the moral bankruptcy of SLORC. The choice in late 1991 of Suu Kyi as the recipient for the Nobel Prize for peace underscored the fact that the crisis of legitimacy in Burma had not yet ended.

Buddhism and the End of the Burmese Way to Socialism

The deep-rooted character of the crisis stimulated a reconsideration on the part of many Burmese of Buddhist premises for political and economic order. A growing realization from the early 1980s that government policies were failing to bring about increasing benefits for all led Ne Win to turn away from the socialist ideals of his revolution. He appeared to look for alternatives not in the Buddhist fundamentalism of the 1920s and 1930s, but in a more traditional Buddhism that emphasizes association with a purified sangha and the building of pagodas as means to ensure the attainment of liberation from the vale of woes in which humans find themselves. In 1980, emulating the great Buddhist monarchs of history and, ironically, U Nu, whom he forced from the premiership in 1962, Ne Win called together a Congregation of the Sangha of All Orders for Purification, Perpetuation, and Propagation of the Sasana (religion). Representatives of all sects of Buddhist monks gathered "to clarify scriptural problems, to weed out bogus monks, and to solve doctrinal disputes." Ne Win, as the convener, "earned great Buddhist merit and was able to gain approval to register the monks, a long-term goal."[77] Although it gave the state greater control over the sangha, the convening of this Congregation and a subsequent one in 1985 brought the sangha back to center stage in Burma.

One unintended consequence of state support for sangha reform was an increase in the amount of surplus wealth used for religious purposes. Despite the faltering economy, public donations for support of monks and shrines actually increased in the 1970s and 1980s.[78] Among the most conspicuous of ad hoc projects was the construction of the "great victory" pagoda (Maha Wizaya Zedi) on a hillock in Rangoon near the Shwe Dagon pagoda, the national shrine of Burma. Officially undertaken to commemorate the convening of the Congregation of All Orders, the project was Ne Win's own memorial,[79] and was very expensive in wealth and labor.[80] The relative size of investment in this shrine, 50 million kyats, can be grasped by comparing it to the government budget for public health which in 1977–78 was about 288 million kyats.[81]

In emulating the Buddhist monarchs of the past, Ne Win also made the political crisis of the late 1980s into a traditional one of succession. The line of succession in the Burmese monarchy was never fixed because any son of any king could assert a claim; thus, the death of a monarch often ushered in a bloody conflict between potential successors and their supporters, a conflict which was resolved only when one claimant was able to mount the throne, have himself crowned, and clothe himself, literally, in the raiment of state.

The recent effort of the government to reassert a traditional relationship between state and sangha is indicative of the failure of party cadres and army officers to assume the moral leadership roles which they had been expected to do. Even before the events of 1987–88 the Party had been discredited and now the army has been as well. By stepping into the moral vacuum the sangha has reemerged as a major arbiter of legitimacy. A number of the monks who became involved in the demonstrations of 1987–88 formed the Yanhapyo, or Young Monks. Even after the crackdown of September 1988, Yanhapyo monks and some of their supporters continued to provide moral leadership to the opposition, especially in Mandalay and northern Burma.[82] These monks became the vanguard for a new, albeit short-lived, fundamentalist Buddhist movement in Burma. Politically this new movement resembled the one that had developed in the 1920s under U Ottama and his associates. Like their predecessors, the Young Monks set themselves apart from the majority of monks in Burma, who continued to reproduce a traditional cosmological Buddhism centered on the important rituals of shin-byu and pagoda building. The new political monks even more clearly set themselves against monks associated with the millennial version of cosmological Buddhism embraced recently by Ne Win. The new political monks also set themselves against those monks coopted by the government in a rather belated effort to create an establishment form of Buddhism.

While the new political monks in Burma adopted similar political tactics to their predecessors of the 1920s and 1930s, they did not share the same vision of new order as that held by an earlier generation of Buddhist activists. The socialist experiment in Burma, which evolved from vague ideas of social welfare put forth by monks in the late nineteenth and early twentieth century into a synthesis of Buddhism and Marxism and then into the Buddhist-inspired ideology of the Burma Socialist Programme Party, has been so deeply discredited that no political faction in Burma today could advocate its continuation in any form. The Young Monks had little time to develop a coherent stance toward economic action, but they were aligned with the National League for Democracy, which has advocated capitalistic development but with attention given to the conservation of natural resources.[83]

The primary goal of the Young Monks was to effect a transfer of power from the military to the parties that had won the mandate of the people in the May 1990 election. The Young Monks' political agenda called for the military to acknowledge the moral supremacy of the sangha. In mid-1990, the SLORC moved to render impotent the National League for Democracy, which had won the May elections by a landslide, by arresting its leaders. At that point monks moved to the forefront of the opposition. In September 1990 thousands of monks, mainly in Mandalay and northern Burma, began a protest which directly echoed those of the 1930s. They refused to accept alms offered by soldiers and their families, "in effect excommunicating anyone associated with the military."[84] Monks would also "bow down in front of passing soldiers in insulting irony."[85]

The highly dramatic and public rejection of the moral authority of the military by an increasing number of monks was obviously very threatening to SLORC. In late October 1990, the military moved against the monks, storming 133 monasteries and arresting scores of monks.[86] The Young Monk organization was banned. Despite the shocking sight of army men seizing control of monasteries and forcing monks to accept their superior power, the public reaction was very subdued. In a very short time, SLORC demonstrated that it was firmly in control of the country.

In the wake of this direct assault on the sangha, SLORC immediately encouraged a return to cosmological Buddhist practices by permitting traditional ritual activity to continue; it has also sought to restore its patronage of establishment Buddhism.[87] A "fundamentalist" Buddhism championed by the new political monks had failed not because it lacked popular support but because it was insufficiently militant. This lack of militancy is evident in the observation of "a well-educated woman in Rangoon" in the wake of the suppression of the boycott by monks of the military. "'Our tradition and our religion prevent us from getting things done.' . . . Reflecting on the revolutionary zeal of Vietnamese monks who used self-immolation as a weapon against the Saigon regimes of the 1960s, she stresses the differences. 'Our kind of Buddhism . . . does not allow that.'"[88]

As of late 1991, the future of fundamentalist Buddhism in Burma is uncertain. With a regime so obviously lacking in moral authority in power, the sangha remains an obvious alternative source of legitimacy. At the same time, those in the sangha who reject cosmological or establishment forms of the religion as the basis for the social order appear to lack the ability to mount an effective opposition to SLORC. The ethnic insurgents, who have long carried the major burden of the struggle against a military-dominated Burma, are also very wary of fundamentalist Buddhism because many of their leaders are Christian. Yet, given the role which fundamentalist Buddhism has played in the shaping of modern Burma, it is unlikely that it can be counted out in a post–Ne Win order.

Buddhist Reform and Establishment Buddhism in Thailand

Although Buddhist movements exhibiting certain "family resemblances" to fundamentalisms have appeared in Thailand in recent years, the conditions that have fostered such movements have been very different from those in Burma. In Thailand, these movements have developed as part of a wider Buddhist critique of capitalism.

The Thai[89] have long shared with Burmans the same basic premises about the fundamental nature of the world which are derived from Theravāda Buddhism. Their ethical interpretations of these premises are, however, significantly different from those of the Burmese. Some of these differences have their roots in premodern practice, but most derive from fundamentalist reforms instituted in Thai Buddhism beginning in the mid-nineteenth century which had very different social implications from the comparable ones in Burma.

In premodern Buddhist practice, the Thai, like the Burmans, took refuge in the Three Gems—the Buddha, the dhamma, and the sangha—and committed themselves to actions which would result in "merit" in order to ensure their enhanced well-being in a future existence. The religious acts of the Thai were believed to situate one within the same basic Buddhist cosmological realm as did comparable acts among the Burmans. Many of the traditional merit-making rites of the Thai are very similar, and often related, to the ahlus of the Burmans.[90] The Thai also "worshiped" the Buddha in the form of "reminders," although most tended to accord less attention than Burmans to stupas and more attention to images as "reminders" of the Buddha.[91] The Thai, like the Burmans, also sponsored the ordination of males mainly for temporary but sometimes for permanent service within the sangha, although the custom of most Thai again differed from that of the Burmans. Among all but the northern Thai (who had been under Burmese control for part of their history), temporary ordination into the monkhood as young adults was more important than ordination of boys into the novitiate. Finally, the Thai, like the Burmans, offered alms of food, clothing, shelter, or medicine to members of the sangha, although again there were some variations in practice. Such differences notwithstanding, the Thai shared in the premodern era the same basic economic ethic as that of the Burmans. In the wake of religious reforms in Siam which followed a very different path to the reforms in Burma, some of the differences in premodern religious practice took on new significance and have contributed to the formation of the contrastive ethics which can be observed today.

Buddhist reform in Siam began, as in Burma, as a consequence of a confrontation with the West.[92] This confrontation was, however, quite different in Siam than in Burma; it began earlier in Siam and was not the result of a political upheaval brought about by colonial domination. In 1824, a young Siamese prince—later known to the world as Mongkut—who had entered the monkhood for a temporary period, found it politically expedient to remain in the order when his father, the king, died suddenly and an uncle ascended to the throne. Guided by monks who were either well versed in Buddhist scriptures or adept at the practice of meditation, Mongkut set out to become an exemplary monk. He began to acquire a critical perspective of Buddhism as currently practiced through his own study of the tradition and through his extended conversations and study sessions with the few Westerners in the country, most of whom were Protestant missionaries. Mongkut learned of the distinction made in the West between natural and divine law. From missionaries trained in medicine, he acquired some knowledge of Western science as well as of Christian theology. Through correspondence with monks in Sri Lanka, Mongkut became aware of the effects of Western rule on that predominantly Buddhist country. The British conquest of lower Burma in 1824 gave him a more proximate example of the power commanded by Westerners. His encounters with Western thought and power together with his own studies of Buddhist scriptures led Mongkut to develop over the period he was in monkhood (1824–51) the basis for a radical reorientation in Buddhist practice. The reform of Buddhism he set in motion was given the authority of the throne after he became king in 1851; it reached full florescence during the reign of his son and successor, King Chulalongkorn.

Mongkut was disdainful of many popular myths from which people drew their ideas of Buddhist cosmology and he also criticized many traditional socially centered merit-making rituals, seeing both as historical accretions which detracted from the fundamental message of the Buddha. Buddhism, he maintained, was concerned more with the individual cultivation of detachment from the desires which lead to suffering than with the acquisition of merit through unreflective participation in traditional rituals. This shift in emphasis preceded but was parallel to that which occurred in Burmese Buddhism. In Siam, however, the fundamental rethinking of Buddhist doctrine and practice became the basis for state-sponsored reform of the Buddhist sangha whereas the transformation of Buddhist practice in Burma was inextricably linked to opposition to a colonial order established by the British.

Official Buddhism under King Mongkut (1851–68) and especially under King Chulalongkorn (1868–1910) contributed indirectly to enhanced individualism through the stress placed on the responsibility of each person for his or her own actions. Whereas traditional Buddhist practice had accentuated merit-making rituals, most of which were carried out as communal efforts, this reformed practice emphasized the individual's pursuit of detachment from the desires conducing to suffering. Initially, this new approach was restricted to a relatively small number of royalty and nobility, but by the end of the nineteenth century it was promoted more widely by the strict Thammayut order of monks, which established branches throughout the country. At the turn of the century all members of the Buddhist clergy in the kingdom were placed under the authority of a Thammayut-headed sangha.

By the first three decades of the twentieth century, the state-sponsored sangha organization had marshaled all segments of the Buddhist order under its jurisdiction and implemented a uniform system of clerical education. Some monks, especially in northern Thailand, encouraged resistance to the challenge from the state-supported sangha to distinctive local traditions.[93] By the late 1930s, however, most monks in the country had been brought under the jurisdiction of a state-supported sangha hierarchy. Through its control of clerical education, the hierarchy was able to institute an "establishment" Buddhism that promoted the perspective on practice and doctrine developed first by Mongkut and later by his son, Prince Wachirayān (Vajirañāṇa), who was successively the head of the Thammayut order and then Prince Patriarch with jurisdiction over all monks. Prince Wachirayān wrote the basic texts which are still in use for clerical education in Thailand. Like his father, he emphasized a rational interpretation of Buddhist doctrine over the myths which had shaped traditional cosmological Buddhist thought. He also was responsible for bringing monks throughout the country under the jurisdiction of the state-sponsored sangha.[94]

Capitalist Development in Thailand

During the period when a state Buddhist church was being created, the foundation was laid for the reorientation of the economy of Siam toward a world capitalist system. In the latter half of the nineteenth century, the economy of Siam was "opened" as a consequence of the adoption of a free trade policy dictated by the British. In Siam as in Burma, the policy encouraged agricultural production for an export market and discouraged manufacturing and even the production of goods by traditional crafts in order to stimulate demand for finished goods produced in Great Britain and other European countries. The major export from Siam, as from Burma, was rice, and in both cases the expansion of rice production to meet market demand was undertaken primarily by indigenous peoples. Siam, however, lagged far behind Burma in total exports of rice prior to World War II.[95] In the years just prior to World War II rice exports constituted a lower percentage of the total in Burma than in Siam, but in total tonnage the rice exports of Burma were almost double those of Siam.[96] The fact that rice exports accounted for an average of 44.6 percent of total exports in Burma for the period 1937–41 as compared to an average of 53.5 percent for Siam for 1935–39 suggests that the Burmese economy was also somewhat more diversified than the Siamese.[97]

In general, then, economic growth was much slower in Siam than in Burma during the first four decades of the twentieth century. Whereas the Siamese government followed conservative fiscal policies, in part to avoid giving the colonial powers a pretext for extending their rule over their country, the British colonial government in Burma promoted economic expansion. Because of too rapid reorientation of the Burmese economy to the world economy, the Burmese suffered much more from the Great Depression than did the Thai.

While the expansion of commercial rice production was carried out by native peoples in Siam as in Burma, the development of other sectors of the economy created a demand for labor which was met in Siam, again as in Burma, by immigrants from other Asian countries—Chinese in Siam and Indians in Burma. Slower growth notwithstanding, the influx of alien labor was much higher in Siam than in Burma.[98] Chinese and Indian immigrants not only filled low-paid laboring jobs but also came to dominate many of the middleman roles in processing and marketing. Despite the greater numbers of aliens in Siam as compared with Burma, Siam was far less divided as a society by the beginning of World War II. Whereas the Indians in Burma rarely assimilated to Burmese Buddhist culture, a large percentage of the descendants of the Chinese who settled in Thailand became adherents to Thai Buddhism.

While Siam was relatively less integrated into a capitalist world economy than Burma prior to World War II, after the war the situation was reversed. Thailand experienced economic growth rates among the highest of any Third World country, while Burma's economy stagnated. This reversal was partly a consequence of the far greater problems of postwar economic development faced by the two countries. Burma suffered much more damage to its infrastructure than had Thailand during the war and was not, mainly for political reasons, able to acquire the necessary capital to restore the infrastructure to prewar levels until into the 1960s. What damage was inflicted on Thailand could also have taken longer to repair if Thailand had been forced to pay the heavy reparations demanded mainly by the British because of Thailand's alliance during the war with Japan. The intervention of the United States, however, not only led to a significant reduction in these reparations but also laid the basis for significant foreign investment, especially for building roads and irrigation projects in Thailand during and after the 1950s.

A more serious consequence of the war for Burma than the destruction of roads, shipyards, airports, and so on was the loss at the outset of the war of a large percentage of the people, mainly British and Indians, with managerial and technical skills.[99] The British and Indians who left in 1942 did not return after the war, as the Burmese government which was to take power in 1948 was committed to policies of economic nationalism. Very few Chinese who played important roles in the economy in Thailand left during the war; indeed, some even prospered. And when the Thai government which came to power in 1947 also adopted economic nationalist policies, the Chinese who still played a major role in the Thai economy maintained their position by developing alliances with high-ranking members of the military.

By the late 1950s the Thai government had abandoned economic nationalist policies and had begun to encourage private investment, most of it foreign, in almost every sector of the economy. In contrast, the Burmese government which was installed in 1962 by Ne Win instituted even more restrictive economic nationalist policies than had its predecessors. These changes in policy are primarily responsible for the different economic histories of the two countries over the past three decades.

During this period Thailand experienced very high economic growth rates. In the 1950s the Thai GNP grew an average of 4.7 percent per year; in the 1960s it grew at a remarkable average of 8.6 percent per year; in the 1970s the rate was slower, but still a very strong average of 6.9 percent per year; and the strong growth continued throughout the 1980s, averaging probably above 6.0 percent.[100] The contrasts with Burma are striking. By 1980 per capita income in Thailand was about $670 as compared with $150 for 1978 in Burma.[101] Today Thailand has a far more diversified economy than Burma. While rice continues to be Burma's major export, other significant sources of foreign exchange for Thailand include tourism, rubber, tin, cassava and kenaf, and, increasingly, manufactured goods, especially textiles and electronics. Although a majority of the people in both countries continue to be employed in agriculture, there has been a much more significant movement of people from rural to urban areas in Thailand than in Burma. In both countries immigrant minorities no longer predominate in financial, middleman, and urban labor occupations, although the reasons for this change are radically different for the two countries. Almost all Indians were forced to leave Burma permanently after the country gained its independence from Great Britain in 1948 and especially after 1962. The Chinese in Thailand, on the other hand, have been assimilated to a remarkable degree, and it is difficult today to distinguish among the middle class those of Sino-Thai and those of ethnic Thai descent.

Establishment Buddhism and Buddhist Economics in Thailand

Buddhism not only has proven not to be an impediment to rapid capitalistic development in Thailand but also has contributed to this development.[102] Through "strategies of compromise, ambiguity, and silence" similar to those adopted by Buddhist sects in Japan,[103] establishment Buddhism in Thailand has proven to be a "passive enabler" of capitalist development. No critique of capitalistic development has come from the Buddhist establishment because most recent governments have exerted very tight control over the sangha[104] and because the religion has clearly benefited materially—in the form of new buildings and shrines and consumer goods such as refrigerators, electric fans, and so on permitted for monks[105]—from the new wealth in the society. Governments in power since 1957 have explicitly rejected the Buddhist socialist and Buddhist-based economic nationalist programs of some earlier political leaders.[106]

The elaboration of the traditional rite of offering robes to monks at the end of Buddhist rains—retreat or lent—a rite called *thọt kathin* in Thai,[107] is indicative of the relationship between establishment Buddhism and capitalism. In its traditional form, the ritual was quite simple and served as a way a community could honor those who had spent the three months of lent in the monastery. Beginning in the late 1950s, the rite was given new significance when King Bhumipol Adulyadej,[108] with the support of the government of Prime Minister Sarit Thanarat, restored an old royal tradition of offering kathin robes at temple-monasteries which had been designated as being under royal patronage.[109] Very quickly others moved to emulate the king, and by the mid-1960s the rite had been significantly transformed. The robes have become an almost incidental portion of an offering (much of which is now typically in the form of cash) made by charitable organizations (many organized for this purpose alone), government agencies, political parties, and especially corporations and financial institutions to temple-monasteries typically located in areas quite distant from the site of the sponsoring institution. Some sponsors hope in return for their offerings to gain the support of a temple-monastery's congregation in the form of votes, bank deposits, or purchase of products.

While the wealth spent on thột kathin rites today is unquestionably greater in proportion to what was spent in the past, the investment is rarely today exclusively or even primarily for realization of a salvation goal; rather, it has become a means for promotion of this-worldly ends and can be better compared with monies spent on advertisement in the West than with those spent on building stupas in Burma.

The co-opting of establishment Buddhism has not been the only way in which Buddhism has contributed to capitalistic development in Thailand. Some laymen have also acquired through their practice of Buddhism the discipline that enables them to refrain from using their wealth for immediate purposes. Wealth thus accumulated has become available for investment. Two groups in particular in Thailand include members who have developed the Buddhist equivalent of the Protestant work ethic as described by Weber.[110]

The first can be found among those rural Thai, especially the Thai-Lao in northeastern Thailand, where the ideal of young adult men spending at least one lenten period in the monkhood is still adhered to. In subjecting oneself as an adult to the "discipline," one cultivates the virtue of "detachment" to a more intense degree than one does as a novice, for in addition to separating oneself from the warmth of one's family and forgoing sexual intimacy, the monk learns to minimize his material wants. He eats only two meals a day and owns no more than the robes he wears and a very few utensils such as a begging bowl and razor. Traditionally, the reward for a man who demonstrated his ability to control his passions for at least a rains-retreat of three months was a title which indicated prestige in the local community. Since one's prestige increased after having spent even longer in the sangha, many men would spend two or three years before returning to the world. Today, the reward, although rarely conceived of as such, may be economic success. Ex-monks, who know how to forgo gratification (*ot thon*), have been in the vanguard of rural entrepreneurs in northeastern Thailand[111] and may well have been so elsewhere.

The second group is found among the Sino-Thai. Although the Sino-Thai became adherents of Theravāda Buddhism, they have retained the pragmatism rooted in the Sinitic tradition of their ancestors. This pragmatism, linked to the worldview of establishment Buddhism, contributed to the development of an ethic of tolerance, one which is well adapted to laissez-faire capitalism.[112] The Sino-Thai ethic of tolerance has become the dominant ethic of Thailand's middle class today, including those in the middle class who are not of Sino-Thai descent. As the middle class has assumed increasing political importance, this ethic has influenced policy formation in the country. This ethic of tolerance is manifest in the fact that while Buddhism is the established religion in Thailand, there has been very little pressure to use the law to enforce moral tenets specific to Buddhism comparable to the use of law in some Islamic countries to enforce Islamic morality. While avoidance of greed, for example, is one of the five basic precepts to which all Buddhists are to adhere, the ethic of establishment Buddhism in Thailand places the ultimate responsibility for repressing greed on the individual more than on the state or society at large. Similarly, alms are an individual matter and are not mandated by law, as is the case in some societies for Islamic *zakat*.

Buddhist Debates about Capitalistic Development and the Rise of Buddhist "Fundamentalism" in Thailand

Although the dominant economic ethic of contemporary Thai is unabashedly capitalistic whether still linked explicitly, as it is for most, to Buddhist roots or expressed in secular form, there have been countertendencies as well.[113] Over the past two decades, the number of critics of excessive materialism and of the legitimation of capitalistic development by establishment Buddhism has grown significantly. While some criticism has come from secular groups, mainly on the left, since the late 1970s the voices having the widest appeal have been those drawing their ideas from Buddhist sources.

The highly respected monk Phutthathāt Phikkhu (Buddhadāsa Bhikkhu)[114] has provided an articulate defense of an ethic that would foster suppression of personal greed in favor of redistribution of wealth to alleviate suffering more generally.[115] Phutthathāt celebrated his eighty-fourth birthday in 1990 (a most auspicious birth date because it marked his completion of a seventh twelve-year cycle). He "appears to have been strongly influenced by the rationalist aspects of the religious reforms of Prince Mongkut"[116] but has set himself apart from the Buddhist establishment. For most of his life he has lived in Chaiya in southern Thailand, far from the center of both secular and ecclesiastical power. At his "Garden of Liberation" in Chaiya, Phutthathāt has developed, taught, and put into practice through meditation and his "spiritual theater" a theology that centers on the premise that "in *saṃsāra* exists *Nibbāna.*"[117] This theology, which he acknowledges seems contradictory, makes detachment from the passions a goal to seek even in the midst of intense activity in the world. In the 1960s and 1970s he began to develop a "dhammic socialist" critique of the growing materialism in Thai society. Unlike the Buddhist socialism of the Burmese, Phutthathāt's dhammic socialism looks not to the state to control natural proclivities to greed, anger, and delusion but to the enlightened individual working together with other such individuals.

Some lay followers of Phutthathāt have attempted to create community organizations dedicated to dhammic socialism. A leading figure in this effort has been Sulak Sivaraksa, a prolific social critic and promoter of groups committed to the Buddhist equivalent of the Social Gospel.[118] In the essay "Buddhism and Development: Is Small Beautiful?"[119] inspired by both Phutthathāt and Schumacher, Sulak argues that the premises of "development" promoted by economists and politicians entail accentuating the very desires that Buddhism considers the major impediments to the attainment of nibbāna:

> For economists see development in terms of increasing currency and things, thus fostering greed (*lobha*). Politicians see development in terms of increased power thus fostering ill-will (*dosa*). Both then work together, hand in glove, and measure the results in terms of quantity, thus fostering ignorance (*moha*), and completing the Buddhist triad of evils.[120]

Sulak looks to Sarvodaya, a Buddhist-inspired movement in Sri Lanka, for an alternative perspective on development. This village-level movement, he observes, is derived from the Buddha's teaching of the Four Wheels. "As a cart moves steadily on four wheels, likewise human development should rest on the four *dhammas,* namely Sharing, Pleasant Speech, Constructive Action, and Equality.[121] "Sharing" (*dāna*) entails not just the offerings given to monks but all giving—of "goods, money, knowledge, time, labor"—to others. "Pleasant Speech" is not limited as in traditional Buddhism to words from the teachings of the Buddha but to all talk which is devoid of deceit. "Constructive Action" is not only the rituals which have traditionally been deemed to generate "merit" but all "working for each other's benefit." Finally, "equality" should not be restricted only to those who have become members of the sangha but should mean that no group will exploit another.[122]

Groups committed to the ideals of dhammic socialism have proliferated in the past two decades. They include the Coordinating Group for Religion and Society, the Thai Development Support Group, and the Asian Cultural Forum on Development (ACFOD), in which Sulak has played a key role.[123] They also include a growing number linked to "development monks" (*phra phatthānā*) whose idea of "development" is very different from the "development monks" of the 1960s and early 1970s who had been recruited by the government.[124]

Neither Phutthathāt nor the groups which have sought to promote the equivalent of a Social Gospel for Thai Buddhism can be considered "fundamentalist," for they remain committed to a pluralistic or ecumenical vision of Thai society, one which includes not only adherents of different types of Buddhism but Muslims, Christians, and other non-Buddhists as well. Their critique of capitalism has, however, had a strong influence on groups which are indeed exclusionary and antipluralist.

A movement that emerged in the 1970s led by a monk known as Phra Kittiwuttho (Kittivuddho) manifested the "reactive, reactionary" character of fundamentalist movements elsewhere.[125] Kittiwuttho became a monk in 1957 at the age of twenty. He shares with Phutthathāt the view that Buddhists must give attention to the conditions of the world because these are prerequisites to the pursuit of religious goals. He differs from Phutthathāt in his assuming an active leadership role in the effort to transform society in accord with his religious vision. This role is predicated on his view of himself as a saint who has forgone attainment of nibbāna in order to help others improve conditions in the world.[126]

Kittiwuttho's major endeavor has been Cittaphāwan College, which he founded in 1965 and continues to direct. The college, which has become all but independent of the sangha establishment, provides its own distinctive form of education for novices and training in religious and social action for monks.[127] Its "Program for Spiritual Development" is predicated on the assumption that "the prosperity of Buddhism . . . depends on a healthy economy; . . . if the people are poor, Buddhism will deteriorate."[128] The curriculum of the college includes secular as well as religious subjects, and students also acquire skills such as carpentry and farming.

The reasons given for teaching secular subjects and offering practical training . . . are that the monks or novices must have an understanding of all aspects of society, if the propagation of Buddhism is to be carried out successfully.

Second, the practical work and training is vocational preparation for those students who may leave the monkhood for the secular world.[129]

The novices and monks who have been trained at the college—numbering in the tens of thousands—have formed a cadre both within the sangha and in lay organizations for the promotion of Kittiwuttho's message.

In the mid-1970s Kittiwuttho caused a furor by advocating that the killing of communists does not result in the demerit that one would expect from the Buddhist injunction against the taking of life. He justified this position by maintaining that communists are not persons but are the embodiment of Māra, the Buddhist devil. This ideological position provided legitimacy for a right-wing political organization backed by many in the military which is thought to have supported death squads sent out to kill leaders of left-wing movements. Kittiwuttho's "militant Buddhism" provided a moral justification of violence in Buddhism similar to that espoused by some movements in contemporary Sri Lanka.[130] But it did not remain a major factor in Thai politics. His message lost appeal after the installation of a more liberal government in the late 1970s.

In the wake of the political changes and because of a need to improve his reputation after he became embroiled in a scandal involving the import of Volvo automobiles without the payment of proper taxes, Kittiwuttho moved toward a closer association with establishment Buddhism and away from militancy. In the late 1980s, two ranking monks in the Council of Elders sought to have Kittiwuttho appointed abbot of a famous and wealthy temple, Wat Rakhang, in Bangkok. In such ways monks aligned with the political establishment seek to "entrench their clique's position and influence both financially and politically."[131]

Despite Kittiwuttho's association with the establishment, Cittaphāwan College remains semi-independent and through it he advances an economic ethic that is in some ways similar to that advocated by Phutthathāt. Kittiwuttho promotes "improved efficiency in work practices and socioeconomic development through the application of dhamma; a strengthening of Buddhist morality to fight corruption; and self-sacrifice for the common good."[132] He couples this economic message with a conservative political one, insisting that "a strong but benevolent central government composed of representatives of the establishment can benefit the people and best promote both development and social welfare."[133]

A Buddhist approach to politics and economics similar to that of Kittiwuttho has been adopted by another movement which became significant in Thailand in the 1980s. This movement, centered in Wat Thammakāi on the outskirts of Bangkok, promotes spiritual renewal through the practice of a simplified form of meditation.[134] The name of the temple and of the movement, Thammakāi (Pāli *dhammakāya*), points to the central tenet of the movement, namely, that the dhammic "body" (*kāya*) of the Buddha can be found within the body of every person through meditation. By meditating on the seat of consciousness, located "two finger-breadths above the navel,"[135] an effort that is assisted by visualizing this place as a crystal sphere, one is supposed to discover the Buddha in oneself. The creation of this method is credited to a monk, usually known as Luang Phǭ ("revered father") Wat Pāknām after the monastery where he resided, who died in 1959; it has been perpetuated by two of his disciples, Phra Thammachayō (Dhammajayo) and Phra Thattachīwō (Dhattajīvo), who founded Wat Thammakāi. Having transformed oneself spiritually through this method, one is prepared to return to the world and act without the desires that lead to suffering. Like the teachings of Phutthathāt, Thammakāi emphasizes that nibbāna is to be sought within the world, not through withdrawal from the world.

The typical Thammakāi follower is a lay person who combines spiritual retreat on the weekends with work or study in the everyday world during the rest of the week. Many of the followers are the "conservative Thai equivalent of Western 'yuppies'"[136] although some are also "senior members of the Thai establishment."[137] For these people, Thammakāi offers religious legitimation for inequalities in wealth since success in the world is held to be a reward for spiritual attainment. After practicing the meditation method taught by the monks who lead the movement, it is believed that "students will study better and people will be more successful in their businesses."[138]

The Thammakāi movement has adopted an aggressive evangelical program to extend its form of Buddhist nationalism throughout Thai society. For its evangelical activities—including issuing glossy publications, holding international conferences, and supporting monks traveling both within and outside the country—and for the maintenance of its architecturally striking and elaborate facilities, Thammakāi depends on sizable donations from its followers. The temple-monastery itself is estimated to have assets of about $32 million.[139] Insofar as it emphasizes evangelism over maintenance of a form of spiritual purity by a community which sets itself off from society, it differs from the typical fundamentalist movement. There is, however, a fundamentalist tendency in the movement, one most clearly evident in the student groups which the movement has spawned.

Each hot season when universities are closed, Wat Thammakāi sponsors for students the Thammathāyot—heirs of the dhamma—program which entails both physical and spiritual exercises. Male participants in the program are ordained into the monkhood while female participants assume the roles of lay ascetics. The numbers involved increased rapidly in the 1980s, with sixty male students ordained in 1979, the first year of the program, and over one thousand ordained in 1986.[140] Like those ordained at Kittiwuttho's Cittaphāwan College, those who have taken the Thammathāyot program at Thammakāi have become a cadre of religious activists in the world. In the case of Thammakāi, this cadre is restricted almost completely to university students. A very interesting comparison could be drawn between the Thammakāi students and the Malay students who have become affiliated with *dakwah* (Islamic missionary) movements in Malaysia. Just as dakwah followers have gained control of student associations in Malaysia, so Thammakāi followers now dominate most of the Buddhist associations on university campuses in Thailand. Here they advocate a more exclusivist Buddhism than do the nonstudent leaders of Thammakāi.[141]

Thammakāi has come under criticism for what some consider to be a rather heterodox approach to spirituality. Phra Thepwēthi (Devavedhi), a theologian who is highly respected both within the sangha establishment and by the followers of Phutthathāt,[142] has observed that orthodox Theravāda Buddhism (by which is meant the authoritative exegesis of the scriptures by the fourth-century monk Buddhaghosa) sees the type of meditation practiced by Thammakāi as inadequate for attainment of spiritual liberation because it can become an end in itself, producing a spiritual high rather than true understanding of self and the world.[143] The movement has been criticized for its dogmatic insistence on the superiority of its meditation system, for the intolerance shown by student followers of other perspectives on Buddhism, and for its apparent political aspirations.[144] Kukrit Pramoj, a former prime minister and an influential commentator on the relationship between religion, politics, and economics in contemporary Thailand, has questioned whether Thammakāi is offering spirituality or "religious pleasure" comparable to that of recreation clubs and fishing parks.[145] The criticisms have not been only verbal; some villagers, upset about the loss of their lands to both the main temple complex and a branch in northern Thailand, damaged a Buddha image belonging to the movement, threatened to set fire to the temple, and attacked Thammakāi monks.[146] The controversy surrounding Thammakāi has not, however, been as intense as that relating to another movement, Santi Asoke.

The Santi Asoke sect, its religious center on the outskirts of Bangkok, most closely fits the fundamentalistic mold of any of the movements in contemporary Thailand. The founder of Santi Asoke, known mainly by his clerical name, Phra Phōthirak (Bodhiraksa), typifies the stance which the movements have taken toward capitalism in Thailand.[147] In the 1960s he was a highly visible television personality who led the life of a playboy. Not finding satisfaction in materialism, he turned in his thirties to more spiritual endeavors. In 1970 he was ordained a monk and soon began to practice a more strict form of Buddhism than was typical of most monks. As a monk, Phōthirak became a vegetarian, breaking with the established interpretation in Theravāda Buddhism that meat eating is permissible. He also became critical of most ritual practices, which he saw as distractions from the main purpose of Buddhist endeavor— achieving detachment from worldly desires. When he was denied by the abbot of the monastery of the Thammayut sect into which he had been ordained the right to create his own following among members of the sangha, he left the order and was re-ordained in the Mahanikai sect. In 1975, he separated completely from the sangha hierarchy and established his own religious center. Subsequently, he began to ordain monks himself even though he had not been delegated this authority by sangha officials. He further alienated himself from the sangha by claiming to be an incarnation of Sariputra, one of the Buddha's chief disciples, thereby claiming religious authority higher than that of the most senior member of the sangha.

Phōthirak's message has been widely characterized in Thailand as "fundamentalist." He requires all followers—lay as well as clerical—to abandon traditional religious practices since they involve Buddha images and ritualized acts that he considers a hindrance to achieving detachment. Instead, they must practice meditation on a daily basis and, for lay followers, undertake spiritual retreats periodically. All followers must adhere strictly to a vegetarian diet, and even lay followers should eat only two meals a day. The true adherent must eventually give up sexual activity even if married. While lay followers continue to hold positions in the world, they are not to pursue their activities to satisfy their desires for wealth or power. Rather, they are to approach their activities with a detachment which has been cultivated through their adherence to the strict version of the Buddhist precepts. The ideal follower is one who is successful in the world, even in business, while still maintaining a very simple lifestyle.

Phōthirak's message has appealed to the younger generation—predominantly professionals, middle-class to lower-class—who have become disenchanted with the commercialism, ritualism, and animism "which have overtaken our mainstream order and which have been misinterpreted as the true essence of Buddhism."[148] His followers are found not only in Bangkok but also up-country, especially in his native northeastern Thailand. By far the most prominent of the followers of Santi Asoke, and the man who has brought the sect great visibility, is Major General Chamlong Srimuang.[149]

Chamlong was converted (and conversion is, I believe, the appropriate term) in the 1970s while still active in the military. After leaving the military, he entered politics, first as an adviser to the prime minister and then as a candidate for the governorship of Bangkok. His image as someone who was the antithesis of the typical politician, whose pursuit of office is impelled by the quest for power and wealth, gave him a charismatic appeal in the gubernatorial election held in 1985. He won by a landslide. Chamlong's position probably protected Phōthirak from official condemnation for a period of time. As early as 1982 a commission was set up by the Sangha Council to investigate Phōthirak, but nothing happened until 1989 when after public attacks by one of the most distinguished Buddhist theologians in the country (Phra Rātchawaramunī, that is, Thepwēthī today), by a former prime minister (Kukrit Pramoj), and even by sympathetic liberals (Prawase Wasi and Sulak Sivaraksa), the Sangha Council finally determined that Phōthirak was in violation of both the discipline of the order and Thai law relating to the sangha. He was ordered to be defrocked, and legal charges were brought against him.

On 19 June 1989, Phōthirak was arrested, but almost immediately the government instituted a ban on media coverage of the aftermath of the arrest. His trial began in September of that year and was given almost no attention in the press and none at all on radio and television. Despite—or perhaps because of—the controversy, Chamlong has remained very popular. He was reelected governor of Bangkok in early January 1990 in a resounding landslide, and his party, Palang Dhamma (lit., power of the dhamma), took most seats on the city and district councils in related elections.

The controversy over Santi Asoke has spurred considerable debate in Thailand about whether establishment Buddhism has failed to address itself to the problems of too rapid development and of excessive consumerism. Social critics, such as Sulak Sivaraksa, have echoed Phōthirak in denouncing the tolerance for magical-animistic practices by members of the clergy: "The emergence of [the] Santi Asoke fundamentalist movement, [Sulak] says, reflects the inefficiency of the clergy in dealing with the pains of alienation among the younger generation, instead confining itself to performing rites and rituals, and concerning itself too greatly with materialism and capitalism."[150]

Throughout 1990 and 1991 very little appeared in the press about Phōthirak or Santi Asoke and the case remained unresolved. The major stories concerning the sangha were about a popular monk who was charged with having had an affair with a woman who claimed to have given birth to his son. A succession of legal proceedings by sangha authorities had found the woman's charges to be valid, and the monk was ordered to defrock. The case provided additional reason for the younger generation to feel alienated from the sangha.

In February 1991, the military staged a coup in Thailand and abolished the constitution. The National Peacekeeping Committee, whose members include the heads of all branches of the armed forces and the police, justified the coup on moral grounds, claiming that the previous parliamentary-based government had been excessively corrupt. They also said the "dictatorship" of a parliament controlled by the parties which were most successful in buying votes had led to the undermining of "national" institutions. These institutions include not only the monarchy and the military, which were referred to extensively in the pronouncements of the coup leaders, but also the (established) sangha. Shortly after the coup, the leaders demonstrated visible public support for establishment Buddhism by appearing on a live television broadcast in an audience with the Supreme Patriarch. Critics of establishment Buddhism, whether liberals or fundamentalists, are unlikely to be allowed much freedom so long as the military retains ultimate power in Thailand. While on the surface there seems to be a marked similarity in the stance of the military governments in both Thailand and Burma toward Buddhism,[151] some fundamental differences between the two countries still remain.

Conclusions

While the debate in Thailand about the appropriate stance for Buddhists toward capitalistic development may be subdued for a period, it will continue. Although most in the society have benefited to some degree from economic growth, there is widespread unease about its ill consequences: unequal distribution of benefits; deterioration of the quality of life, especially in Bangkok, because of pollution and congested streets; significant increase in injuries from car accidents; destruction of forests, which will have long-term environmental consequences; high rates of prostitution; and so on. This unease has spurred many to look to their Buddhist culture for alternative ideas about economic activity and about policies which shape such activity.

Although some in Thailand have intensified traditional patterns of "merit-making," seeking to translate increased wealth through alms into a higher position on the kammic ladder of relative suffering, cosmological Buddhism today holds far less appeal for the Thai than it does for the Burmese. The major reason for this is that establishment Buddhism in Thailand—the Buddhism which both is controlled by the state and serves to legitimate the political order—has been so shaped by the reformist rationalizing of Buddhist thought undertaken by Mongkut and his successors in the sangha as to undermine the premodern view of the world as ordered hierarchically according to the distribution of inherited "merit." Cosmological Buddhism has not disappeared from contemporary Thai life, as some state-sponsored rituals—especially those involving the king or other members of the royal family—are designed to evoke positive responses from those, living mainly in villages, for whom traditional ideas remain salient. Even for villagers, however, given their education in a state school system which emphasizes rational control of life, such rituals appeal less as evocations of the sacred than as dramatic theater.[152]

The greater salience today of cosmological Buddhism in Burma than in Thailand is due to two factors. First, the rationalizing reforms of Buddhism were never as fully incorporated into an establishment form of Buddhism in Burma as they were in Thailand. Under the British the state did not sponsor the creation of a statewide sangha comparable to that in Thailand, and without such a sangha there was no authority to enforce the institution of reformed Buddhist thought. Second, leaders of postcolonial governments in Burma have, when confronted by serious political crises, turned themselves to traditional ideas about the relationships between ruler and the Buddha as manifest in a stupa and between ruler and the sangha. In these cases, traditional ideas have been backed by the authority of the state in a millenarianlike effort to restore harmony between social and cosmic orders.

Even in Burma cosmological Buddhism has not been the primary source of reflection about the relevance of Buddhist values for the modern political economy. In Burma as in Thailand, it was the reforms instituted in Buddhist thought and practice beginning in the nineteenth century that has spawned debates about Buddhist economics and Buddhist politics. Although the reform movements in the two countries have different histories, they share a common feature, one they also share with fundamentalist thought in other countries. The reforms initiated by Prince Mongkut in Thailand and Ledi Sayadaw in Burma entailed identifying the "basic" or "essential" doctrines of Buddhism through a new critical examination of Buddhist teachings.[153]

Whereas Buddhist reforms in Burma became the basis of fundamentalist movements in the 1920s because they were linked to opposition to the state and to the goal of national independence, those in Thailand were adopted by a state-sponsored sangha and were linked, thus, to establishment Buddhism. It was not until the 1970s that the fundamentalist potential in reformed Thai Buddhism reemerged. By the early 1970s, an increasing number of Thai, mainly from the middle classes, had become disillusioned both with a patently corrupt political order that promoted development with little regard for the social or cultural consequences and with an establishment sangha which could not be counted on for support against government policies and actions. They turned instead to a variety of movements, some radically secular, such as the Communist Party of Thailand, but others associated with members of the sangha who set themselves apart in one way or another from establishment Buddhism.

Although most of the Buddhist movements which rose to prominence in Thailand in the 1970s resemble fundamentalist movements elsewhere in their separation from established religion and in their selective emphasis on the "essentials" of Buddhist doctrine and practice, they do not all share other characteristics typical of fundamentalist movements. Those groups associated with the dhammic socialist teachings of Phutthathāt Phikkhu and the Thammakāi movement are nonexclusivist, the former because they are ecumenical and the latter because it is evangelical. Other movements, most notably the militant Buddhist movement under Kittiwuttho in the 1970s and the ethically strict Santi Asoke sect under Phōthirak in the 1980s, have adopted exclusivist stances which resemble those of fundamentalisms elsewhere.

In one way or another, all these movements have addressed themselves to economic concerns which have intensified in the 1970s and 1980s as the disrupting consequences of rapid growth have become more apparent. The dhammic socialist groups and Santi Asoke both advocate the pursuit of a "small is beautiful" philosophy, but see this as being implemented through individual commitment to ethical premises about the common good rather than through government imposition of socialist policies. Kittiwuttho, through his Cittaphāwan College, and the Thammakāi movement have taken a different stance, seeing economic growth as good for the society; but both insist that spiritual training is essential if people are to be uncorrupted by materialism.

Although Buddhist fundamentalism was an important factor in Burma in the 1920s and 1930s, it all but disappeared when the political and economic program envisioned by the early fundamentalists—a welfare state run by Burmese nationalists—was adopted by those who came to power in independent Burma. The growing realization in the 1980s that the pursuit of the vision of a socialist Burma had resulted in political and economic stagnation prompted the Burmans to look to some Buddhist leaders for a new vision. Those monks who have assumed roles in the opposition to the military-run government of Burma oppose not only the state but also those in the sangha who have associated themselves with the military. Although the ideas of the political monks which led a new fundamentalist movement in Burma in 1990 are not known in any detail and may not be known because of their suppression, it appears they advocated a stance toward economic behavior which contrasted to that of the Burmese Socialist Programme Party. Instead of the BSPP view that the state is needed to control the base passions of humans, the new fundamentalists seemed, like their Thai counterparts, to advocate placing responsibility for cultivating detachment from one's passions on the individual. Such a position, however, is not conducive to the militancy which seems to be needed in the struggle against military rule.

Buddhist fundamentalism in both Burma and Thailand, as elsewhere, has been a concomitant of severe political and economic crises. But these crises do not determine the character of fundamentalism. Rather, that character must be sought in the distinctive way in which any religious tradition formulates salvation goals and defines appropriate action within the world to attain such goals. In both Burma and Thailand, fundamentalism has been shaped by reflection—intensified since the reforms of the nineteenth century—on the basic Buddhist doctrines of the moral consequences of action (kamma) for both self and others and on the capacity of humans to cultivate detachment from desire (tanhā) in order to achieve transcendence (nibbāna) from suffering (dukkha).

Buddhist fundamentalists in both Burma and Thailand have sought to shape debates about the relationship of the economies of these countries to a global system dominated by capitalism. They have not, however, been notably successful in acquiring the power which would make it possible to translate their positions into effective public policy. This lack of success demonstrates how difficult it has been to make sufficiently militant a religion which stresses individual responsibility and nonviolence. Herein may lie a major difference between Buddhist "fundamentalism" and fundamentalisms associated with other religions.

Notes

1. Although I have not always adopted their suggestions, I have very much benefited from comments made on previous versions of this paper by Robert Hefner, Michael Adas, Robert Taylor, Timur Kuran, Chao Tsang Yawnghwe, Jane Keyes, and R. Scott Appleby. The paper is part of a larger project on Buddhist ethics and economic action in which I have been intermittently involved over the past several years. See Charles F. Keyes, "Buddhist Economics in Action," in *Visakha Puja B.E. 2522* (Bangkok: Buddhist Association of Thailand, Annual Publication, 1979), pp. 19–25; Introduction to "Peasant Strategies in Asian Societies: Moral and Rational Economic Approaches—a Symposium," *Journal of Asian Studies* 42, no. 4 (1983): 753–68; "Economic Action and Buddhist Morality in a Thai Village," *Journal of Asian Studies* 42, no. 4 (1983): 851–68; and "Buddhist Practical Morality in a Changing Agrarian World: A Case from Northeastern Thailand," in Donald K. Swearer and Russell Sizemore, eds., *Attitudes toward Wealth and Poverty in Theravada Buddhism* (Columbia: University of South Carolina Press, 1990), pp. 170–89.

2. E. F. Schumacher, "Buddhist Economics," in *Small Is Beautiful* (New York: Harper and Row, 1973; originally published in *Asia: A Handbook,* Guy Wint, ed. [London: Anthony Blond, 1966]), p. 58.

3. Ibid., p. 57.

4. Ibid., p. 59. For other reflections on the economic implications of Buddhist teachings as contained in the Pāli scriptures, see the following: Serge-Christophe Kolm,

"La philosophie bouddhiste et les hommes economiques," *Information sur les sciences sociales* 18 (1979): 489–598; Chaiwat Satha-Anand and Suwanna Wongwaisayawan, "Buddhist Economics Revisited," *Asian Culture Quarterly* (Taipei) 7 (1979): 37–45; and Andreas Buss, "Buddhism and Rational Economic Activity," *Internationales Asienforum* 13 (1982): 211–31.

5. In 1989 the government of Burma declared that the official name of the country was Myanmar. The older name has, however, remained the preferred one in most writings on the country, and I use "Burma" throughout in this paper.

6. For a general overview of Theravāda Buddhism, see Frank E. Reynolds and Regina T. Clifford, *The Encyclopedia of Religion,* s.v. "Theravāda."

7. The reform movements that developed in Cambodia and Laos were both derivative of the one begun in Siam.

8. In characterizing Buddhist fundamentalism, I have drawn on Martin E. Marty's "Fundamentalism as a Social Phenomenon," *Bulletin of the American Academy of Arts and Sciences* 42 (1988): 15–29; and Martin E. Marty and R. Scott Appleby, "Conclusion: An Interim Report on a Hypothetical Family," in Martin E. Marty and R. Scott Appleby, eds., *Fundamentalisms Observed* (Chicago: University of Chicago Press, 1991), pp. 814–42.

9. The development of Buddhist fundamentalism in Ceylon parallels its development in Burma.

10. Buddhist socialist ideas have also been promoted by many of the leaders of Sri

Lanka, and while the leaders of the Lao People's Democratic Republic are explicitly committed to orthodox Marxist-Leninist dogmas, a case might also be made that the socialism of that small country has been adapted to the Buddhism of the majority of the population. The Burmese revolution begun in 1962 has certain similarities to that attempted by Pol Pot in Cambodia from 1975 to 1978; I believe it can be shown that the ideology of the Khmer Rouge also has significant Buddhist roots. See, in this regard, my "Buddhism and Revolution in Cambodia," *Cultural Survival Quarterly* 14, no. 3 (1990): 60–63. In Burma, however, socialism has been most distinctively Buddhist in character.

11. By emphasizing Burma in this paper, I also seek to complement Donald K. Swearer's paper for the first volume in the Fundamentalism Project. Swearer gave primary emphasis to Thailand with comparisons drawn to Sri Lanka. "Fundamentalistic Movements in Theravāda Buddhism," in Martin E. Marty and R. Scott Appleby, eds., *Fundamentalisms Observed*, pp. 628–90.

12. As Theravāda Buddhist traditions derive their religious language from Pāli texts, I employ Pāli rather than Sanskrit forms of Buddhist terms. Thus, I use *kamma* instead of *karma, nibbāna* instead of *nirvāṇa,* and so on.

13. The Buddhist doctrine of dukkha subsumes the experiences of both well-being and suffering since states of well-being are never permanent and when they end, the experience is painful. In practice, however, Burmese and Thai Buddhists contrast well-being with suffering.

14. See, in this regard, Charles F. Keyes, "Introduction: The Study of Popular Ideas of Karma," in Charles F. Keyes and E. Valentine Daniel, eds., *Karma: An Anthropological Inquiry* (Berkeley: University of California Press, 1983), pp. 1–26.

15. Detachment from the world cannot be equated with "renunciation" of the world since one seeks in cultivating detachment to transcend the passions that lead to attachments to the world rather than to reject the world as such.

16. Dāna is similar to the Christian "tithe" in that it is a donation impelled by a religious motive. Dāna is not, however, determined as a percentage of produce or income; rather, the donor gives according to her or his own wishes. The most common types of dāna are the "four requisites"—food, clothing, medicine, and shelter—offered to members of the sangha.

17. I am concerned here primarily with the dominant people of Burma, the ethnic Burmans. The discussion applies, to a great extent, to ethnic Mons and Arakanese as well, and the term "Burmese" as I use it subsumes Burmans, Mons, and Arakanese. The analysis does not, however, apply to Shans, Buddhist Karen, and some other smaller groups whose members also adhere to Buddhism.

18. Quoted in Michael Aung-Thwin, *Pagan: The Origins of Modern Burma* (Honolulu: University of Hawaii Press, 1985), p. 173.

19. Ibid., p. 169.

20. Sir James George Scott characterizes well the pattern as it existed in the late nineteenth century: "It is certainly marvelous how many pagodas there are in the country, far exceeding the number raised in the sacred island of Ceylon, or by the Thibetans [or] Chinese. . . . No work of merit is so richly paid as the building of a pagoda. The Pāyataga [donor of a pagoda] is regarded as a saint on earth, and when he dies he obtains the last release; for him there are no more deaths." Shway Yoe [pseud. for James George Scott], *The Burman: His Life and Notions* (New York: W. W. Norton, Norton Library, 1963; originally published in 1882; revised edition in 1909), p. 153.

21. Cf. Melford E. Spiro, *Buddhism and Society: A Great Tradition and Its Burmese Vicissitudes* (New York: Harper and Row, 1970), p. 455; cf. Manning Nash, *The Golden Road to Modernity: Village Life in Contemporary Burma* (New York: John Wiley and Sons, 1965), pp. 116–17.

22. In the Mandalay-area village of Yeigyi in 1960 one villager was sufficiently wealthy to have sponsored the construction of a monastery at a total cost of 10,000 kyats,

which at the official rate of exchange was equal to $2,100, or more than twenty times the annual per capita cash income. Nash, *The Golden Road to Modernity*, p. 118. The rate of exchange from 1948 to 1971 was 4.76 kyats to the dollar. See David I. Steinberg, *Burma's Road toward Development: Growth and Ideology under Military Rule* (Boulder: Westview Press, 1981), p. xix.

23. Shway Yoe, *The Burman*, p. 22.

24. I am indebted for this insight to an unpublished paper by Nancy Pollock.

25. Spiro, *Buddhism and Society*, p. 234; also see Nash, *The Golden Road to Modernity*, p. 131.

26. Shway Yoe, *The Burman*, pp. 22–23.

27. Spiro, *Buddhism and Society*, p. 235.

28. In a village in upper Burma in 1960 in which the average annual income per family was approximately K1,000, the costs of a shin-byu ranged from K200 to K5,000. Cf. Spiro, *Buddhism and Society*, p. 237. Nash, *The Golden Road to Modernity*, p. 126, gives similar figures. In 1987, a tour group under my leadership came across a shin-byu in a village between Meiktila and Mandalay. We stopped for a time at the village to join the roughly one thousand people who had joined the festivities prior to the actual ordination. There were five boys being ordained, all appearing to be between seven to nine. The ceremony was being sponsored by one boy's parents. Through our Tourist Burma guide, we learned that the sponsors of the ceremony had spent 14,000 kyats. This is equivalent to $2,090 at the then official rate of exchange. It should be noted that official rates of exchange have not, ever since Burma gained its independence, corresponded to the real buying power of the kyat in Burma. In the 1980s, the black market rate for the kyat was between 30 and 34 kyats to the dollar as compared to an official rate of 6.69. The difference between official and black market rates in the late 1950s and early 1960s was not so great. Thus, the 5,000 kyats which Nash and Spiro report as having been expended for shin-byus when they carried out their fieldwork in 1959–60 may have been roughly equal in buying power to the 14,000 kyats which was spent in the rite in 1987 which I observed.

29. "Pagan stands as an example of religious endowments and temple buildings that acted as stimulants to agricultural production and a variety of related 'industries'; people were attracted into the kingdom where the religion flourished, the culture was exquisite, and festivities and work were plentiful." Aung-Thwin, *Pagan*, p. 170.

30. Spiro, *Buddhism and Society*, p. 454; also see Melford E. Spiro, "Buddhism and Economic Saving in Burma," *American Anthropologist* 68 (1966): 1163–73.

31. E. Sarkisyanz, *Buddhist Backgrounds of the Burmese Revolution* (The Hague: Martinus Nijhoff, 1965), p. 142.

32. For an analysis of the transformation of the Burmese political economy during the colonial period, see John Sydenham Furnivall, *Colonial Policy and Practice: A Comparative Study of Burma and Netherlands India* (New York: New York University Press, 1956; first published in 1948).

33. Michael Adas, *The Burma Delta: Economic Development and Social Challenge on an Asian Rice Frontier, 1852–1941* (Madison: University of Wisconsin Press, 1974), pp. 140–41.

34. See Sarkisyanz, *Buddhist Backgrounds of the Burmese Revolution*, pp. 160–65; Robert L. Solomon, *Saya San and the Burmese Rebellion* (Santa Monica, Calif.: Rand Corporation, Rand Corporation Papers P-4004, 1969); Michael Adas, *Prophets of Rebellion: Millenarian Protest Movements against the European Colonial Order* (Chapel Hill: University of North Carolina Press, 1979), pp. 185ff.; James C. Scott, *The Moral Economy of the Peasant: Rebellion and Subsistence and South-east Asia* (New Haven: Yale University Press, 1976), pp. 149–57; U Maung Maung, *From Sangha to Laity: Nationalist Movements of Burma, 1920–1940* (Columbia, Mo.: South Asia Books, Australian National University Monographs on South Asia, no. 4, 1980), pp. 83–107; and Patricia Herbert, *The Hsaya San Rebellion (1930–1932) Reappraised* (Melbourne: Monash University, Centre of Southeast

Asian Studies, Working Papers, no. 27, 1992).

35. Winston L. King, "Contemporary Burmese Buddhism," in Heinrich Dumoulin and John C. Maraldo, eds., *Buddhism in the Modern World* (New York: Collier Books, 1976), p. 90; also see Winston L. King, *In Hope of Nibbana: An Essay on Theravada Buddhist Ethics* (LaSalle, Ill.: Open Court, 1964), and Winston L. King, "Saṃsāra Revalued," in Robert Sakai, ed., *Studies on Asia* (Lincoln: University of Nebraska Press, 1965), pp. 201–9.

36. *Sayadaw,* from *saya* (teacher) is a term of respect accorded to a monk who has become a senior elder by virtue of spending ten years in the monkhood and who has achieved a reputation for knowledge or practice of religion. The term typically is used in association with the name of the monastery or community where the monk resides. The Ledi Sayadaw was a highly respected monk who resided at the Ledi-tawya monastery in upper Burma. See "A Life Sketch of the Venerable Ledi Sayadaw," in Ledi Sayadaw, *The Manual of Insight: Vipassanā Dīpanī,* translated by U Nyāṇa Mahā-Thera (Kandy, Ceylon: Buddhist Publication Society, Wheel Publication no. 31/32, 1961), p. 86. Although some of the Ledi Sayadaw's writings on Buddhist meditation have been translated into English, his life is only sketchily recorded in a number of scattered sources in English. See Ledi Sayadaw, *The Manual of Insight,* and Ledi Sayadaw, *The Requisites of Enlightenment: Bodhipakkhiya Dīpanī,* translated by Sein Nyo Tun (Kandy, Ceylon: Buddhist Publication Society, Wheel Publication no. 171/74, 1971).

37. Maung Htin Aung, *A History of Bunna* (New York: Columbia University Press, 1967), p. 278; "A Life Sketch," p. 86.

38. "A Life Sketch," p. 86.

39. Donald Eugene Smith, *Religion and Politics in Burma* (Princeton: Princeton University Press, 1965), p. 88.

40. All English accounts of U Ottama cite as their source *Sayadaw U Ottama: Lutlatye Seikdat Myozicha thu* (Sayadaw U Ottama: he who sowed the seeds of in-dependence) by Bama Khit U Ba Yin (Rangoon: Thamamitta, Djambatam, n.d.). The most extended account in English is to be found in E. Michael Mendelson, *Sangha and State in Burma: A Study of Monastic Sectarianism and Leadership* (Ithaca, N.Y.: Cornell University Press), pp. 200–206.

41. See Maung Maung, *From Sangha to Laity,* p. 14.

42. U Ottama, *Rangoon Gazette Weekly Budget,* 11 July and 19 September 1921. Quoted in Smith, *Religion and Politics in Burma,* p. 96.

43. Burma Police Department, *Report on the Police Administration in Burma, 1922,* quoted in Albert D. Moscotti, *British Policy and the Nationalist Movement in Burma, 1917–1937* (Honolulu: University Press of Hawaii, 1974), p. 36.

44. Sarkisyanz, *Buddhist Backgrounds of the Burmese Revolution,* p. 126.

45. Mendelsohn, *Sangha and State in Burma,* pp. 223–24.

46. Smith, *Religion and Politics in Burma,* p. 101.

47. King, "Saṃsāra Revalued," p. 207 (emphasis in original).

48. Sarkisyanz, *Buddhist Backgrounds of the Burmese Revolution,* pp. 168–69.

49. Ibid., p. 170.

50. Josef Silverstein, *Burma: Military Rule and the Politics of Stagnation* (Ithaca: Cornell University Press, 1977), pp. 86–87; quotations from U Ba Swe, *The Burmese Revolution* (Rangoon: Information Office, 1952), pp. 10, 14, 17; see also Smith, *Religion and Politics in Burma,* pp. 128–29.

51. Sarkisyanz, *Buddhist Backgrounds of the Burmese Revolution,* p. 197.

52. Ibid., p. 169.

53. He was minister of defense and mines, deputy prime minister, and even prime minister for a year. See Smith, *Religion and Politics in Burma,* p. 128; Frank N. Trager, *Burma from Kingdom to Republic: A Historical and Political Analysis* (New York: Praeger, 1966), pp. 131–32, 173. Both Robert Taylor (personal communication, 7 January 1990) and Chao Tzang Yawnghwe

(personal communication, 2 March 1990) have suggested, although for quite different reasons, that I may have overemphasized U Ba Swe's role in the development of political culture in Burma. I agree with Taylor that U Nu and Thakin Soe were of at least equal importance to Ba Swe. I have focused on Ba Swe because his thought appears to be an important link between the Buddhist socialism of the U Nu period and the Burmese Road to Socialism of the Ne Win era.

54. "*Pyidawtha* has been freely translated as 'welfare state' but 'co-operation between people and government for the happiness of the country' is probably nearer the true meaning." John F. Cady, *A History of Modern Burma* (Ithaca: Cornell University Press, 1958), p. 616. The Pyidawtha program was first set forward in 1952.

55. After Ne Win took power in 1962, Ba Swe was imprisoned along with U Nu and other politicians of the 1950s. When he was released after a short time, he went into retirement. Steinberg, *Burma's Road toward Development,* pp. 127–28. Robert Taylor reports that when he was in Burma in 1982 "Ba Swe used to lead a large parade of laymen around the streets of east Rangoon where I lived soliciting alms." Personal communication, 7 January 1990.

56. In 1948, 42 percent of the cultivated land in lower Burma was in the hands of nonresident landlords. Although absentee landlordism was not significant in upper Burma (only 7.5 percent of the land was owned by nonresident landlords), lower Burma was the rice basket of the country and the source of most of the rice exported. See Robert H. Taylor, *The State in Burma* (Honolulu: University of Hawaii Press, 1987), p. 276.

57. Burma Socialist Programme Party, *The System of Correlation of Man and His Environment* (Rangoon: Burma Socialist Programme Party, 1963).

58. Steinberg, *Burma: A Socialist Nation of Southeast Asia,* p. 76. Wiant says that although this work, apparently written by U Chit Hlaing, a Marxist active in the pre-revolution National United Front, "draws extensively on Marxist teaching in explain-

ing material developments, its central concerns are as much related to traditional notions of Burmese authority and the laws of Buddhist causation." See Jon Wiant, "Tradition in the Service of Revolution: The Political Symbolism of Taw-hlan-ye-khit," in F. K. Lehman, ed., *Military Rule in Burma since 1962* (Singapore: Maruzen Asia, 1981), p. 62.

59. Taylor, *The State in Burma,* p. 361.

60. Quoted in Silverstein, *Burma: Military Rule and the Politics of Stagnation,* p. 82; emphasis in original.

61. Taylor, *The State in Burma, p.* 363; Taylor is here quoting from the Burma Socialist Programme Party's *The System of Correlation of Man and His Environment.*

62. *The Guardian* (Rangoon), 19 April 1964; quoted in King, "Saṃsāra Revalued," p. 206.

63. Taylor, *The State of Burma,* p. 358.

64. Mya Maung, "Cultural Values and Economic Changes in Burma," *Asian Survey* 4 (1964): 763.

65. Steinberg, *Burma's Road toward Development,* p. 35; Taylor, *The State in Burma,* p. 341, places the number of Indian and Pakistani refugees from Burma between 125,000 and 300,000.

66. Beginning in the early nineteenth century, Christian (American Baptist Mission and Catholic) missionaries met with considerable success in their efforts to convert tribal Karen. By the end of the colonial period, the large Karen Christian population was found mainly in lowland village and towns. Christian Karen have provided the main leadership of the Karen National Defense Organization, an organization committed to obtaining for Karen either independence or considerable autonomy within the Burmese state. Shan—who are related to the Thai and who live in northeastern and northern Burma—were relatively autonomous under both the precolonial Burma state and under the colonial state. After 1962, however, the Burmese government jailed many of the Shan leaders and eliminated most aspects of Shan autonomy. Kachin tribal people, living in

northern Burma, also have been converted to Christianity in large numbers, although much more recently than were the Karen. Many Kachin also have felt threatened by the assimilationist policies of the Burmese state since the 1960s. On the history of ethnic rebellions in Burma, see Martin Smith, *Burma: Insurgency and the Politics of Ethnicity* (London: Zed, 1991).

67. Taylor, *The State in Burma*, p. 334. Ethnic insurgencies may, however, have an important influence on the shape of Burmese nationalism in the post–Ne Win period. See Smith, *Burma*.

68. Steinberg, *Burma's Road toward Development*, p. 4.

69. In 1940/41 rice exports had totaled 3,123,000 tons. In 1974–75 they had declined to 166,000 tons. In the subsequent years they increased some, but still only reached an estimated 700,000 tons in 1979–80. Ibid., p. 113.

70. Hal Hill and Sisira Jayasuriya, *An Inward-Looking Economy in Transition: Economic Development in Burma since the 1960s* (Singapore: Institute of Southeast Asian Studies, Occasional Paper no. 80, 1986), p. 31.

71. Ted Morello, "Forlorn Conclusion: Burma Nears the Expected UN Approval for LDC Status," *Far Eastern Economic Review*, 22 October 1987, p. 101.

72. Ibid.

73. Paisal Sricharatchanya, "Riots over Kyats," *Far Eastern Economic Review*, 17 September 1987, p. 13.

74. Denis Gray, "Burma Violence Reflects Disillusionment with Socialist System," *The Nation* (Bangkok), 26 June 1988, and Margaret Scott, "Fear Is the Key to Burmese Docility," *Far Eastern Economic Review*, 5 November 1987, p. 50.

75. *Bangkok Post*, 25 June 1988; *The Nation* (Bangkok), 26 June 1988. Also see Bertil Lintner, *Outrage: Burma's Struggle for Democracy* (Hong Kong: Review Publishing Company, 1989), pp. 122–23. Lintner, whose book and articles in the *Far Eastern Economic Review* provide the most detailed account of the events of 1987–89, docu-ments the involvement of monks in the demonstrations. See *Outrage*, pp. 132, 141, 151, 178, 217.

76. See Lintner, *Outrage*, pp. 163–64.

77. Ibid., p. 89; also see Taylor, *The State in Burma*, p. 358, Lintner, *Outrage*, p. 91; and, for a detailed description, Tin Maung Maung Than, "The *Sangha* and *Sasana* in Socialist Burma," *Sojourn* 3 (1988): 26–61.

78. Tin Maung Maung Than, "The *Sangha* and *Sasana*," p. 50.

79. See Andrew Sullivan, "Burmese Daze," *New Republic*, 2 November 1987, p. 19. Also see Lintner, *Outrage*, pp. 93–94.

80. "Paid for by public donations (estimated at more than 50 million kyats), supervised by a central committee chaired by the chairman of the Rangoon Division People's Council, and supported by nine working committees, it took more than five-and-a-half years before the Hti or Golden Umbrella could be hoisted to its pinnacle on 28 February 1986," Sullivan, "Burmese Daze," p. 49.

81. Steinberg, *Burma's Road toward Socialism*, p. 86.

82. See Lintner, *Outrage*, pp. 113, 166. By 1988 there was also at least one sangha opposition grouping, the Union of Young Monks, operating in territory controlled by ethnic insurgents. See "Reflections from a Buddhist Perspective: Problems of Buddhist Monks under the Single-Party System of Ne Win," *Seeds of Peace* (Bangkok) 6.1 (1990): 7.

83. SLORC has attempted to finance purchases of arms and salaries for a large army by selling concessions to non-Burmese firms for exploitation of forests, fisheries, and oil reserves.

84. Bertil Lintner, "Saffron Sanctions," *Far Eastern Economic Review*, 8 November 1990.

85. *The Nation* (Bangkok), 2 October 1990.

86. See *The Nation* and the *Bangkok Post*, 23 and 24 October 1990. In December Major General Khin Nyunt, the first secretary of SLORC, said that the government had ar-

rested seventy-seven monks. *The Nation,* 8 December 1990. *Time* magazine, in a feature article on Burma, 19 November 1990, estimated the total arrested was about two hundred.

87. See *Time,* 19 November 1990, and *Bangkok Post,* 4 and 5 February 1991.

88. *Time,* 19 November 1990.

89. I use the term "Thai" here to include the major Tai-speaking peoples—the central Thai or Siamese, northern Thai or Yuan, northeastern Thai or Lao, southern Thai or Khon Pak Thai, and those of Chinese descent who have assimilated to Thai culture (sometimes called Sino-Thai)—who today constitute 85–90 percent of the population of Thailand. Although these peoples today still retain some distinctive characteristics from their premodern traditions, all have adapted over the past century to the same political economic conditions. Other Tai-speaking groups outside of Thailand—e.g., the Lao of Laos, the Shan of Burma, and the Lue of southwestern China—have, on the other hand, evolved contrasting patterns of cultural practice that stem from adapting to very different political economic conditions. I have not taken into account in the discussion that follows the approximately 5 percent of the population of Thailand who do not belong to Tai-speaking groups but are still Buddhist. Most of these non-Thai Buddhists are Khmer (Cambodians) or members of groups related to the Khmer.

90. All of the traditions of Theravādin Southeast Asia, for example, give great ritual significance to the presentation of the *Vessantara-jātaka,* the story of the life of the Buddha in his incarnation in which he achieved the last of the virtues—that of "generosity"—necessary to attain Buddhahood.

91. There is nothing quite equivalent in Burma to the "Emerald Buddha," an image that has successively served as the palladium of the kingdoms of Lanna Thai (northern Thailand), Lan Xang (Laos), and Siam/Thailand. See Frank E. Reynolds, "The Holy Emerald Jewel: Some Aspects of Buddhist Symbolism and Political Legitimation in Thailand and Laos," in *Religion and Legitima-*

tion of Power in Thailand, Laos, and Burma, Bardwell L. Smith, ed., (Chambersburg, Pa.: Anima Books, 1978), pp. 175–93. In Thailand today one sees far more gargantuan images of recent construction than one does in Burma. Somewhat ironically, these images stand as indicators of the greater economic development of Thailand than Burma since their construction requires more sophisticated technology and architectural skills than are currently available in Burma.

92. The major study of the Buddhist reforms initiated by Mongkut is by Craig Reynolds, "The Buddhist Monkhood in Nineteenth Century Thailand" (Ph.D. diss., Cornell University, 1973). I have also discussed these reforms at some length in my "Buddhist Politics and Their Revolutionary Origin in Thailand," in S. N. Eisenstadt, ed., *Structure and History,* a special issue of the *International Political Science Review* 10 (1989): 121–42.

93. See, in this regard, my "Buddhism and National Integration in Thailand," *Journal of Asian Studies* 30, no.3 (1971): 551–68.

94. On the role of Prince Wachirayān, see, especially, Reynolds, "The Buddhist Monkhood in Nineteenth Century Thailand," and *Autobiography: The Life of Prince-Patriarch Vajirañāṇa of Siam, 1860–1921,* translated, edited, and introduced by Craig J. Reynolds (Athens: Ohio University Press, 1979). Names and titles for Buddhist monks, ranks in the Sangha, and names of many monasteries are derived from Pāli forms; they are, however, pronounced differently in Thai. I give the Thai phonetic form first with the Pāli form in parentheses.

95. Total exports from Burma were, on the average, about double those from Siam for the period. For figures, see Charles A. Fisher, *Southeast Asia: A Social, Economic and Political Geography* (London: Methuen and Co., 1964), pp. 436, 507.

96. For 1937–39 exports of rice from Burma averaged 6,585 million pounds compared to an average of 3,349 million pounds for 1935–39 for Siam.

97. Statistics for Burma are from J. Russell Andrus, *Burmese Economic Life* (Stan-

ford: Stanford University Press, issued under the auspices of the American Council, Institute of Pacific Relations, 1948), p. 164, table 23, while those for Siam are from James C. Ingram, *Economic Change in Thailand, 1950–1970* (Stanford: Stanford University Press, 1971), p. 38, table III and p. 94, table VIII.

98. The total number of all Chinese in Thailand in 1932 has been estimated at 1.6 million, accounting for 12.2 percent of the total population. By contrast, in 1931 Indians constituted 6.95 percent of the total population of Burma. For Thailand, see G. William Skinner, *Chinese Society in Thailand: An Analytical History* (Ithaca: Cornell University Press, 1957), p. 183, table 8. For Burma, see Furnivall, *Colonial Policy and Practice*, p. 117.

99. Taylor, *The State in Burma*, p. 271.

100. Sources for these figures can be found in Charles F. Keyes, *Thailand: Buddhist Kingdom as Modern Nation-State* (Boulder: Westview Press, 1987), pp. 153 and 175n.

101. Statistics for Thailand are from Keyes, *Thailand*, p. 119, and for Burma are from Steinberg, *Burma's Road toward Development*, p. 130.

102. For an overview of the relationship between the dominant Buddhist culture and the political economy of Thailand, also see A. Thomas Kirsch, "Economy, Polity, and Religion in Thailand," in G. William Skinner and A. Thomas Kirsch, eds., *Change and Persistence in Thai Society.* (Ithaca: Cornell University Press, 1975), pp. 172–96.

103. Winston Davis, "Buddhism and the Modernization of Japan," *History of Religions* 28 (1989): 306.

104. See, in this regard, Somboon Suksamran, *Political Buddhism in Southeast Asia: The Role of the Sangha in the Modernization of Thailand* (New York: St. Martin's Press, 1976), and Somboon Suksamran, *Buddhism and Politics in Thailand* (Singapore: Institute for Southeast Asian Studies, 1982).

105. Many temple-monasteries also have televisions even though such would seem to pose some potential problems for monks

required to adhere to a precept against viewing entertainments. More wealthy temple-monasteries also have automobiles, vans, and other vehicles. On the wealth of urban temple-monasteries, see Richard Allan O'Connor, "Urbanism and Religion: Community, Hierarchy and Sanctity in Urban Thai Buddhist Temples" (Ph.D. diss., Cornell University, 1978).

106. In the 1930s and 1940s, Pridi Phanomyong, one of the leaders of the group which established a constitutional monarchy in 1932 and also a former prime minister, advocated a form of Buddhist socialism. Phibun Songkhram, who was prime minister of Thailand from 1938 to 1944 and again from 1947 to 1957, promoted a type of economic nationalism which he justified in vaguely Buddhist terms.

107. *Thọt kathin* literally means laying down the *kathina*, or frame for making robes for monks. It refers to an ancient custom whereby the robes for monks were woven especially for this ritual action.

108. This is the official spelling of the king's name. It is pronounced Phūmiphon Adunlayadēt.

109. See Christine Gray, "Thailand: The Soteriological State in the 1970s" (Ph.D. diss., University of Chicago, 1985), pp. 442ff. In this work, Gray provides a detailed, insightful, and provocative analysis of the economic culture of Thailand with reference to the monarchy, the ruling elite of the constitutional period, and the emergent middle class.

110. Max Weber, *The Protestant Ethic and the Spirit of Capitalism,* translated by Talcott Parsons (New York: Charles Scribner's Sons, 1958; originally published in German in 1904–5, and in English translation in 1930).

111. Keyes, "Economic Action and Buddhist Morality in a Thai Village."

112. On the Sino-Thai work ethic, see Frederic Deyo, "Ethnicity and Work Culture in Thailand: A Comparison of Thai and Thai-Chinese White-Collar Workers," *Journal of Asian Studies* 34, no. 4 (1973): 955–1015.

113. There is now a substantial literature in English on contemporary religious movements in Thailand. See Somboon Suksamran, *Buddhism and Politics in Thailand;* Charles F. Keyes, "Political Crisis and Militant Buddhism in Contemporary Thailand," in Bardwell L. Smith, ed., *Religion and Legitimation of Power in Thailand, Laos, and Burma* (Chambersburg, Pa.: Anima, 1978), pp. 147–64; Keyes, "Buddhist Politics"; Peter A. Jackson, *Buddhism, Legitimation, and Conflict: The Political Functions of Urban Thai Buddhism* (Singapore: Institute of Southeast Asian Studies, 1989); Suwanna Satha-Anand, "Religious Movements in Contemporary Thailand," *Asian Survey* 30, no. 4 (1990): 395–408; and Swearer, "Fundamentalistic Movements."

114. The names of Thai monks are often rather confusing to Westerners. When a man is ordained, he assumes a new religious name. "Phutthathāt," meaning literally "servant of the Buddha," was assumed by a young man whose name at birth had been Ngyam when he entered the monkhood. Unlike other monks, he has preferred not to be known by a title associated with his rank in the ecclesiastical hierarchy. While the names of most monks in Thailand is prefaced by the Thai honorific *phra*, meaning "venerable," his name is typically coupled with the word, phikkhu (Pāli *bhikkhu*), meaning "monk."

115. See Buddhadāsa Bhikkhu (Phutthathāt Phikkhu), *Thammikasangkhomniyom/ Dhammic Socialism*, edited and translated by Donald K. Swearer (Bangkok: Munnithi Komonkhimthong, 1986); Donald K. Swearer, ed., *Me and Mine: Selected Essays of Bhikku Buddhadāsa* (Albany: State University of New York Press, 1989); Peter Jackson, *Buddhadasa—A Buddhist Thinker for the Modern World* (Bangkok: Siam Society, 1988); *Radical Conservatism: Buddhism in the Contemporary World—Articles in Honour of Bhikku Buddhadasa's 84th Birthday Anniversary* (Bangkok: Thai Inter-Religious Commission for Development and International Network of Engaged Buddhists, 1990).

116. Jackson, *Buddhism, Legitimation, and Conflict,* p. 126.

117. This is the title of one of his sermons. See Buddhadāsa Bhikkhu, *In Samsāra Exists Nibbāna,* translated by Thawee Sribunruang (Bangkok: Sublime Mission, 1970); also see *Me and Mine,* chap. 8.

118. The allusion here to Christianity is purposeful since although Sulak is a strongly committed Buddhist, many of the groups he has worked with are also supported by Christians and, more rarely, by Muslims.

119. Sulak Sivaraksa, *A Buddhist Vision for Renewing Society* (Bangkok: Thai Watana Panich Co., 1981), pp. 52–78.

120. Ibid., p. 57.

121. Ibid., p. 77.

122. Ibid., pp. 77–78.

123. See Robert Bobilin, *Revolution from Below: Buddhist and Christian Movements for Justice in Asia—Four Case Studies from Thailand and Sri Lanka* (Lanham, Md.: University Press of America, 1988), chaps. 5 and 6.

124. Seri Phongphit, *Religion in a Changing Society: Buddhism, Reform and the Role of Monks in Community Development in Thailand* (Hong Kong: Arena Press, 1988). This book, by a Catholic, is dedicated to Buddhadāsa.

125. As Kittiwuttho first came to prominence when known by this name, it is the one still most commonly used, although he is sometimes referred to by the title Rāchathamphanī (Rajadhammabhani) associated with his ecclesiastical rank. For discussions in English of the role of Kittiwuttho, see Somboon Suksamran, *Buddhism and Politics in Thailand,* pp. 92–99 and 132–57; Keyes, "Political Crisis"; and Jackson, *Buddhism, Legitimation and Conflict,* pp. 147–54.

126. Keyes, "Political Crisis," pp. 155–56; Somboon Suksamran, *Buddhism and Politics in Thailand,* p. 92. As I note in my article, he sought to plant the idea of his being a saint in people's minds without actually making an explicit claim that could constitute a fundamental violation of the disciplinary code of the Sangha.

127. Somboon Suksamran, *Buddhism and Politics in Thailand,* p. 93.

128. Ibid., p. 93. Somboon is here paraphrasing a passage from a booklet in Thai by Kittiwuttho, "Buddhism in Daily Life."

129. Ibid.

130. Keyes, "Political Crisis."

131. Jackson, *Buddhism, Legitimation and Conflict*, p. 150.

132. Ibid., pp. 150–51.

133. Ibid., p. 151.

134. See Swearer, "Fundamentalistic Movements in Theravada Buddhism"; Jackson, *Buddhism, Legitimation and Conflict*, pp. 199–221; my "Buddhist Politics," pp. 134–35; and Suwanna Satha-Anand, "Religious Movements," pp. 400–402, for discussions of the Thammakāi movement.

135. Rawi Bhawilai, "Buddhism in Thailand: Description and Analysis," paper presented to the International Conference on Thai Studies, Australian National University, Canberra, July 1987, p. 4; quoted in Jackson, *Buddhism, Legitimation and Conflict*, p. 201.

136. Jackson, *Buddhism, Legitimation and Conflict*, p. 203.

137. Ibid., p. 199.

138. Nithinan Yorsaengrat as quoted in Jackson, *Buddhism, Legitimation and Conflict*, p. 213.

139. Suwanna Satha-Anand, "Religious Movements," pp. 395–408.

140. Jackson, *Buddhism, Legitimation and Conflict*, p. 210.

141. Ibid., pp. 209–14.

142. Phra Thepwēthī is better known under his old title, Rātchawaramunī (Rajavaramuni).

143. Phra Rajavaramuni's critique is discussed in Jackson, *Buddhism, Legitimation and Conflict*, pp. 202–4.

144. Ibid., p. 215.

145. *Bangkok Post*, 20 July 1988; quoted in Suwanna Satha-Anand, "Religious Movements," p. 402.

146. Ibid.

147. In the following account of Phra Phōthirak, I draw on an article in *The Nation* (Bangkok), 28 May 1989, and for the tenets of the movement on Prawēt Wasi's (Prawase Wasi's) *Suanmōk, Thammakāi, Santiasōk* (Suan Moksa, Dhammakaya, Santi Asoke) (Bangkok: Chāo Bān Publishers, 1987).

148. *Bangkok Post*, 27 May 1989.

149. See my "Buddhist Politics," pp. 121–22.

150. Sanitsuda Ekachai, "Santi Asoke: Symptom, Not Sickness," *Bangkok Post*, 23 July 1988. Also see S[ulak] Sivaraksa, *Panhā lae thāng ǫk kǫranī Santi asōk* (The Question and Resolution of the Santi Asoke Case) (Bangkok: Committee for Religion and Development, 1989).

151. General Sunthorn Kongsompong, the Thai commander-in-chief who heads the National Peacekeeping Committee, led a military delegation to Burma just the day before the coup. The name of the Thai junta also echoes, especially in Thai, that of its counterpart in Burma, the State Law and Order Restoration Committee.

152. See, in this regard, my "The Proposed World of the School: Thai Villagers' Entry into a Bureaucratic State System," in Charles F. Keyes, ed., *Reshaping Local Worlds: Rural Education and Cultural Change in Southeast Asia* (New Haven: Yale University Southeast Asia Studies, 1991), pp. 89–130. I have said little in this paper about religious movements which are primarily rural-based. There has been very little research on contemporary rural movements in Thailand as distinct from those of earlier in the century, which were clearly millennial in character. The conventional view is that villagers are still traditional, but my own work in rural northeastern Thailand leads me to question this view. More research needs to be done on the question of religious change in rural Thailand.

153. I am here following Marty ("Fundamentalism as a Social Phenomenon," p. 20) in my use of the terms "basic" and "essential."

The Economic Impact of Hindu Revivalism

Deepak Lal

There has been no distinctive impact of Hindu fundamentalism on Indian economic policy, apart from the protection of village and small-scale industries advocated by Gandhi. Beginning with an outline of Gandhi's attempt to resurrect the old Hindu equilibrium based on autarkic village communities and the reasons that attempt failed, this paper traces the changing economic policies, vague and incoherent as they are, advocated by the major fundamentalist Hindu party, the Jana Sangh (now the Bharatiya Janata Party [BJP]). It argues that economics has been secondary to that party's aim of establishing a Hindu nation-state. The economic nationalism this entails is shared by all postindependence parties except the Swatantra. Because of its tactical alliance with the Swatantra party in the 1960s, the Jana Sangh advocated free enterprise policies, but this did not imply any ideological commitment to the free market on its part like that of the Swatantra. Similarly, the party's espousal of a populist egalitarianism is tactical, as it goes against the maintenance of *Homo Hierarchus* which remains a cornerstone of the Hindu culture the party seeks to revive.[1] When briefly in power in the Janata coalition in the 1970s, it embraced the consensual inward-looking dirigisme which has characterized Indian economic policy, with only a greater emphasis on protecting urban small-scale producers and rural kulaks. But it did not seek the dismantling of the Permit Raj. This paper argues that this is not surprising, as the party draws much of its support from shopkeepers, traders, and lower-level civil servants and police, all of whom have benefited from the "rent seeking" bred by controls.

Being a Hindu has always meant adherence to a way of life (that is, a particular social system) rather than to any specific religious philosophy. With no central church or central dogma, Hinduism has no religious fundamentals which can be used to identify or organize a Hindu fundamentalist movement. As many current leaders of the Hindu nationalist party (the BJP, which is a successor of the Jana Sangh) have emphasized, Hindu fundamentalism is a contradiction in terms.[2] However, as the term "fundamentalism" is being used in this series mean "fundamentalist-like,"[3] the terms "revivalism," which I have adopted, and "fundamentalism" should be seen as interchangeable in the context of this series.

Equally, there is nothing in Hindu symbolism to link economics and religion. There is a famous ancient text, the Arthashastra, written by Kautilya in the fourth century B.C.E., on statecraft. It is a Machiavellian manual for an absolute ruler. "It deals exhaustively with all topics connected with internal foreign relations, and sets before a ruler the goal of conquest of the world and describes way of attaining that goal."[4] But Hindu revivalists have not used this text as a source for any of their economic policies.

The current wave of support for the BJP is better described, therefore, as representing Hindu nationalism. This in turn follows a long line of descent from various socioreligious movements which have sought to revive Hinduism in the face of perceived assaults by alien cultural influences associated with the foreign rule under which the Hindus have lived since 1000 C.E., first under the Muslims and more recently under the British. These revivalist movements have by and large sought to cleanse Hinduism of what have been perceived by the reformers as unjustified accretions to its core social practices, thereby making the Hindu social system resilient to more radical demands for change. In modern India it was primarily Mahatma Gandhi who sought such a Hindu revival. It is his ideas (however attenuated), particularly on the economy, which continue to resonate in the minds of the Hindu revivalists and are (at least rhetorically) embodied in their current policy programs.[5]

In assessing the economic impact of Hindu revivalism in modern India, I first briefly outline the characteristics of the Hindu socioeconomic system which was established in the ancient Hindu monarchies beginning in about 500 B.C.E. Second, I discuss how Gandhi sought to refurbish what I have elsewhere characterized as the Hindu equilibrium[6] (particularly its economic aspects) and why his ideas failed to carry the day in the economic policy of independent India. This allows me to move to the third and major section, which traces the vague and essentially incoherent economic policies advocated by the major Hindu revivalist political party—the Jana Sangh and its successor, the BJP. This section also attempts to explain why Hindu revivalism has had no distinctive impact on Indian economic policy, even when the Jana Sangh was briefly in power as part of the Janata coalition in the mid-1970s.

At the outset it may be useful to provide a brief outline of the evolution, platforms, and constituency of the Jana Sangh and its successor, the BJP. The Jana Sangh was founded in 1951 with support from a Hindu revivalist voluntary organization, the Rashtriya Swayamsevak Sangh (RSS).[7] The Jana Sangh's principal leader was S. P. Mukherjee, who had left the Hindu Mahasabha (also an affiliate of the RSS) because it did not allow Muslims to become members. In 1977 the Jana Sangh became a partner in the Janata coalition which defeated Mrs. Gandhi's Congress party at the polls called after the ending of the state of emergency (imposed in 1975). With the disintegration of the Janata, most but not all of the ex–Jana Sangh elements formed the BJP. Among those from the old Jana Sangh who remained in the greatly attenuated Janata Party was Dr. Subramanian Swamy. There has thus by and large been a continuity in the personnel and platforms of the Jana Sangh and the BJP. The Jana Sangh's main constituency is in the north Indian Hindi-speaking states, though more recently it has established important beachheads in the southern state of Kerala and the eastern state of West Bengal. Its social bases of support are to be found among urban shop-keepers and small businessmen, big rural landlords, and some middle-income and rich peasants. Its party manifestos have emphasized the maintenance of the traditional Hindu institutions of family, caste structure, and law. They have demanded the displacement of English by Hindi as the sole official language of the country and have opposed concessions to the Muslim minority on matters of language and education.[8] On economic issues, they have opposed excessive state control over the economy and the development of heavy industry, but have been against foreign aid and foreign investment and in favor of small-scale local business.

The Hindu Socioeconomic System

The twin pillars of the ancient Hindu socioeconomic system were the caste hierarchy and the village community. It was a decentralized social system which did not require either a centralized political power or a church for its perpetuation.[9] The village communities were not completely autarkic,[10] but their trading links were fairly localized. The social system consisted of numerous endogenous hierarchically ranked occupation- and often region-specific subcastes (*jatis*). They were subsumed under the fourfold *varna* classification, under which there were four broad varnas (castes): Brahmins (priests), Kshatriyas (warriors), Vaishyas (merchants), and Shudras (workers and the rural peasantry). Although this scheme is usually identified as the caste system, it merely provided the broad theoretical framework for Hindu society, with the inter-weaving of the hierarchically arranged subcastes being the real fabric of the Indian social system. Within the village economy, the relationship between the different caste groups took a particular form. This patron-client relationship, called *jajmani* in the North, continues to this day. In writing about the social structure of modern-day Indian villages, Srinivas states:

> The essential artisan and servicing castes are paid annually in grain at harvest. In some parts of India. the artisans and the servicing castes are also provided with free food, clothing, fodder and a residential site. On such occasions as birth, marriage and death, these castes perform extra duties for which they are paid a customary sum of money and some gifts of land. . . . Although, primar-ily, an economic or ritual tie, [the caste system] has a tendency to spread to other fields and become a patron-client relationship. The relationship is gener-ally stable and usually inherited. The right to serve is hereditary, transferable, saleable, mortgageable and partible. The jajmani system bound together the different castes living in a group of neighboring villages. The caste-wise divi-sion of labour and the consequent linking up of different castes in enduring and pervasive relationships provided a pattern which cut across the ties of caste.[11]

One aspect of the caste system, the third of our elements defining the ancient Hindu socioeconomic system, was a set of distinctive social beliefs which influenced Indian rulers' attitudes toward trade and commerce. This is the Brahminical tradition, which has looked down upon the merchants (*vaisyas*) and has been suspicious of the self-interested pursuit of profit which underlies operations in markets.

The final element in the ancient Hindu socioeconomic system was a tradition of paying a certain customary share of the village output as revenue to the current over-lord, which meant that any new political victor had a ready and willing source of tribute already in place. Given the endemic political instability of ancient and medieval India, the caste system's vocational segregation meant that war was a game for the professionals, which saved the mass of the populace from being inducted into the deadly disputes of changing rulers. For the latter, however, the ready availability of revenue from customary local arrangements greatly reduced the effort required to finance their armies and court. The village communities on their part bought relative peace and quiet and could carry on their daily business more or less undisturbed by the continuing aristocratic conflict.

Thus, the relatively autarkic and decentralized village community came to be the primary economic unit of the Indian economy. Together with the caste system it provided stability to a common society over the millennia, in the wake of political instability, foreign invasions, and the periodic ravages of pestilence and famine. But above all:

> the institution of caste, independent of the government and with social ostra-cism as its most severe sanction, was a powerful factor in the survival of Hin-duism. The Hindu, living under an alien political order imposed from above, retained his cultural individuality largely through his caste, which received most of the loyalty elsewhere felt towards king, nation and city. Caste was so strong that, until recent years, all attempts at breaking it down have ended in failure.[12]

Various religious reformers like Kabir[13] have tried. The Sikhs, despite the specific injunctions of their religion, never overcame caste feelings. The Roman Catholic and other converts to Christianity brought and perpetuated their caste prejudices, and even the Muslims with their egalitarian religion, once settled in India, organized themselves into castes.[14] The notion of caste has thus formed the framework for the material life of all the peoples in the subcontinent.

This socioeconomic system succeeded in maintaining an agrarian revenue econ-omy (in the sense of Hicks)[15] which, though stagnant, provided for nearly two thou-sand years an average standard of living probably unparalleled in most other regions and countries over such a long period. India's economic "failure" is only relative when, from the sixteenth century onward, its technological and economic stagnation is compared with what has come to be called the European miracle.[16] By the nine-teenth century this relative decline had undoubtedly left India a "backward" country, and it is to the Hindu attempt (initially under British prodding) to overcome this backwardness that we now turn.

Gandhi, *Hind Swaraj,* and Nehruvian Planning

There were two types of responses to the seeming threat posed by the British Raj to the Hindu social system. One was a rejection on rationalist grounds of the whole structure of Hinduism, as epitomized by a young nineteenth-century Anglo-Indian called Derozio. The Nehruvian modernists, Westernized elites who have by and large governed India since its independence, are of the same lineage. The other response was to reform Hinduism in keeping with the sacred texts. Raja Ram Mohun Roy and his new Brahmo Samaj sect sought to combine the best features of Hinduism with Christianity. By contrast, Swami Dayananda, who founded the Arya Samaj mission, and Swami Vivekananda, who founded the Ramakrishna mission, "sought to return to the past on more orthodox and more drastic lines."[17] It is from this more orthodox revivalism that current Hindu revivalism stems.

The purpose of these reformers was to assert a distinct Hindu identity in which Hinduism was to be reformed to cope with the modern world. But there was disagreement about how drastic that reform should be and what should be its primary direction: personal, political, or social.[18]

Gandhi provided the most clear-cut outline of a refurbished Hindu society and is, therefore, of interest for our purposes. Like Vivekananda and Dayananda he sought to revive Hinduism against the onslaught on caste and Hindu society that had been launched by the Christian missionaries and utilitarian reformers in the early part of the nineteenth century. Like them, he sought to affirm the caste system while purging it of certain evils.[19] But for him, even the great curse of untouchability was a matter which Hindu society had to deal with internally and in which other communities had no business. By redefining untouchables as Harijans (children of God), Gandhi effectively co-opted and annexed these groups (which had been outside the Hindu pale) into Hinduism.[20]

It was in his little book called *Hind Swaraj,* written in 1909, that Gandhi most clearly set forth his program for maintaining the ancient Hindu equilibrium.[21] This work is an uncompromising attack on Western civilization and an agenda for maintaining the traditional, albeit refurbished, Hindu socioeconomic system. Gandhi saw *swaraj* (self-rule) "not as a question of who held the reins of government." Swaraj was a quality or state of life which could only exist where Indians followed their traditional civilization, uncorrupted by modern innovations. The means to this end was "truthforce" (*sataygraha*).[22] He was implacably opposed to Western education, industrialization, and those other "modern" forces which could undermine the ancient Hindu equilibrium. Above all, even though he was unequivocally against untouchability, he nevertheless upheld the caste system and its central feature of endogamy.[23] He wished to see a revival of the ancient and largely self-sufficient village communities which were an essential part of the Hindu equilibrium.

It is surely not accidental that, in *Hind Swaraj,* Gandhi launches a diatribe against what he saw as the three major agents of Western civilization destroying India—railways, lawyers, and doctors. The railways, of course, destroyed village autarky; the lawyers symbolized the rule of law, which led to the replacement of custom by contract; the doctors, by reducing the mortality rate, caused the population explosion of the twentieth century. Because of the population explosion, labor was no longer scarce, and the labor control embodied in the caste system was increasingly redundant. Thus, all three Western "agents" were changing the basic parameters of the Hindu equilibrium. Small wonder Gandhi should have been opposed to them!

Gandhian economics is not a systematic body of thought. Gandhi's views on society and the economy were influenced by Tolstoy and Ruskin. Like them he believed that the economy should be founded on morality rather than on conventionally accepted economic principles.[24] He was hostile to modern industrialization and urbanization. He was also against large-scale production, except of goods that could not be produced on a small scale within relatively self-sufficient village communities. He promoted what would now be called intermediate technology, which would use India's most abundant resource—labor—particularly in village industries. Due to his advocacy, hand-spun cloth (*khadi*), became the uniform of the Indian National congressmen and the spinning wheel (*charkha*) became their emblem. Where the use of heavy machinery was unavoidable, Gandhi wanted the relevant industries to be state-owned for the public benefit. Though he claimed he was a socialist, much to the chagrin of those who were inspired by the theories of Marx and Lenin, Gandhi disavowed the notions of class and revolution central to those theories. He eschewed the equality of outcomes sought by many socialists, and instead sought an equality of respect for the necessarily unequal but functionally interdependent members of a society represented by the traditional caste system. He was against collectivism, for it suppressed the individual. In its place he hoped to promote his notion of socialist equality by improving the moral fiber of individuals through truth-force. He was in favor of private property and against the redistribution of income and wealth. Rather, he wanted the rich and capitalists to look upon themselves as trustees for society of the wealth their inherent talents (which, he maintained, must always be unequal) had allowed them to acquire. Determined to curb what he saw as the repugnant mass consumption of the West, Gandhi favored a self-imposed austerity whereby individuals would learn not to crave for goods beyond the requirements of their basic needs.

The resulting Gandhian panaceas have formed an important part of the Hindu revivalist economic programs. These include revitalizing the village economy and deemphasizing industrialization; promoting *swadeshi* (indigenous) technology and relative autarky in relations with the outside world; and accepting the wealthy as society's ushers who have a moral obligation to help the poor.

The Westernized Indians who formed an important part of the polity, while showing some sympathy with Gandhi's desire to uphold the traditional system, did not accept his wholesale attack on Western civilization and education. As long as Gandhi's novel methods of mass mobilization (through *sataygraha,* that is, nonviolent civil disobedience) were seen to be successful in challenging the Raj, his socioeconomic views were tolerated. However, with time, as noncooperation penetrated the localities, the clash of interests, particularly of caste and community, was sharpened rather than softened by Gandhi's tactics.[25] The double-edged nature of Gandhi's political technique of mass mobilization became apparent. As the political leaders discarded sataygraha, Gandhi's hope of achieving his ideals through political action faded. His political party, the Congress, was thereafter taken over by the "modernizers" under Nehru.

Another revivalist strand runs through the Arya Samaj to the Hindu Mahasabha (HM) (founded in 1921), which absorbed it, and the RSS (a youth wing created by the HM) with its own political affiliates: the contemporary revivalist parties, the Jana Sangh and BJP. Unlike the Congress party, which sought to retain its all-inclusive national character by incorporating the Muslims, the Hindu Mahasabha became a political conduit of Hindu communal interests much like the Indian Muslim League.[26]

The RSS under its leader, K. B. Hedgewar, came to be based on a more inward vision. What the Hindus needed according to Hedgewar was not a political party of their own, but communal discipline and revitalization.[27] The RSS and its political affiliates, the Jana Sangh and BJP, have espoused a cultural nationalism which identifies Indian-ness with the culture of the Hindus. Given the doctrinal pluralism inherent in Hinduism, the RSS cleverly absorbed some broad ideological understandings: ideas about hierarchy, pollution, and transmigration of Hinduism with "nationalistic concepts adopted from Western political thought."[28]

By emphasizing that many of the Indic religions—Jainism, Sikhism, Buddhism—arose as offshoots of Hinduism, and as such are part of the Hindu culture, the "alien" was identified as the Muslims and Christians in India. This cultural nationalism also looked upon the Hindu nation as an organic whole, where different castes serve complementary functions but where "the ideal of caste is revised to emphasize all functions as *equal* in the sense of being necessary for the social organism."[29] Thus, the revivalist political parties have been against reserving jobs for the lower castes, which have burgeoned in the secular Indian state since independence.

By separating religion from culture, the Hindu revivalists have sought to incorporate even Muslims into their notion of "Hindu-ness" and have argued against according the Muslims (and other minorities) special treatment. This emphasis on Indian-ness, subsuming the various pluralisms in the subcontinent, has led the political parties of the revivalists to move from the purely communal Hindu Mahasabha toward the more national Jana Sangh and BJP, which admit non-Hindus. The practical goals of the revivalist political parties have "usually included a strong defense, entailing a nuclear arsenal, Indian control of industry, and the removal of preferential quotas for depressed castes as a step towards ending 'casteism' in general."[30] The parties have been critical of Western ideologies, both of the liberal, capitalist variety and of the socialist variety, as being divisive and leading to the concentration of power in the hands of either capitalists or the state, and thus destroying that unique organic wholeness that is purported to be the core of Indian cultural nationalism.

At independence, the "modernizers" in the nationalist movement triumphed, with Nehru—Gandhi's political heir—becoming prime minister. He was the leader of the secular Western-educated Indians who espoused a modern ideology, Fabian socialism. But this Western import ironically provided a new underpinning for India's atavistic attitudes toward commerce and the market. India set up one of the most dirigiste systems of economic controls,[31] with a large expansion of the public sector, ostensibly to foster "socialism." Slightly more than lip service was paid to some Gandhian economic panaceas—such as the special protection offered to hand-spun cloth and to small-scale industries. We cannot here go into the details of the economic impact of the resulting Permit Raj. All that we need to outline are the basic features of postindependence economic policy.

First, the model of development adopted by Stalinist Russia and an extremely pessimistic assumption about Indian export prospects led India to promote the domestic production of previously imported commodities. In particular, the policy sought the rapid development of heavy industries such as steel, chemicals, and machine tools. This heavy industry-biased import substitution strategy was and remains the centerpiece of Indian industrial planning. Second, as agriculture with its myriad producers and spatial dispersion was not easily amenable to the planners' desires, it was industry that bore the brunt of the control system that was set up. Third, the instruments used to legislate the investment and output targets laid down in the plans (themselves of doubtful provenance) were a complex system of industrial licensing and foreign exchange, price, and distributional controls. Independent India is thus best characterized as the Permit Raj. Fourth, an expansion of the public sector to include the so-called commanding heights of the economy, taken to lie in producing "basic goods" (such as steel, chemicals, machinery), became an important aspect of public policy.

There has been a virtual consensus on these fundamental aspects of economic policy across the political spectrum—except during the brief period in the 1960s when the Swatantra party[32] argued against them on free market lines. But the Swatantra's virtual elimination at the polls in 1971 has meant that there has been no political party since then to espouse the free market in India, even though it is now generally recognized that planning has not delivered the promised economic results. Growth has been well below potential and not based on labor-intensive industrialization. Hence, the alleviation of absolute poverty has been meager while the dirigiste system of controls has bred corruption and black markets on a scale that has put the democratic political process (increasingly based on the distribution of spoils) into disrepute.

As one recent political historian sums up the current Indian political scene: "It would be folly . . . to be sanguine about the future of India. to consider that the country is only going through a 'stage' in its development, and to fail to recognize that a grave systemic crisis is in progress."[33]

The Economic Policies of the Jana Sangh and BJP

The Hindu revivalists have always claimed that the so-called Nehruvian strategy of secular socialism which leads to the concentration of power in the hands of the state, and which state functionaries will inevitably misuse, would lead to such a crisis. What have been their panaceas, particularly in the economic sphere? The most important single feature of the political movements spawned by revivalism since the nineteenth century has been the desire to revitalize Hindu traditions and culture by defining and advocating a form of Hindu nationalism. Today the major revivalist organizations and movements include the following:

> The Rashtriya Swayamsevak Sangh (RSS), a Hindu 'cultural' organization organized into cells, whose members practice martial arts, and which promotes also an exclusively Hindu definition of the Indian nation; the Jana Sangh, originally the main political party off-shoot of the RSS, but now a rump of quite extreme anti-Muslim supporters of Hindu nationalism; the Bharatiya Janata party (BJP), the more broadly based descendant of the early Jana Sangh; and such other organizations as the Vishwa Hindu Parishad [VHP], which is currently engaged in a campaign to 'liberate' alleged Hindu religious sites from their occupation by Muslim mosques built upon them.[34]

The Jana Sangh, BJP, and VHP have all had links with the RSS, and they share a common ideology. Their major aim is to implant the notion that Hindu and India are virtually interchangeable categories and that India should be identified as the nation of Hindus.[35] It is claimed that propagating this sentiment has electoral payoffs, as was shown by Rajiv Gandhi's playing of the Hindu card in the 1984 election after his mother's assassination and by the BJP's strong performance in the 1989 elections (so that it emerged as a power broker in V. P. Singh's coalition government founded in 1989).

What of their economic policies? Only the Jana Sangh and subsequently its successor, the BJP, have made some attempt to define their economic policies. The major elements in these policies are an extreme form of economic nationalism combined with elements from Gandhian panaceas and Poujadism.[36] But the differences between the resultant economic policies and those pursued by secular postindependence governments are slight, as we shall see. This is hardly surprising, for economics has been secondary to the Jana Sangh–BJP's primary aim of establishing a Hindu nation-state. The revivalists presume that the establishment of such a nation-state will occur not by the articulation and implementation of a specific economic program, but by less precise sociopolitical means. So the rather general formulation of "economic nationalism" is simply accepted as an all-purpose means to this end.

The economic ideas underlying Jana Sangh–BJP policies are close to those espoused by Gandhi, with the major difference being that unlike him they do not want to completely reject the modern world. This has led to a degree of incoherence unlike Gandhi's more clearheaded desire to establish a refurbished version of the ancient Hindu equilibrium. The major thinker on Jana Sangh–BJP economic issues was Deendayal Upadhyaya. Unfortunately, his ideas were never set down in any systematic fashion. They were set out in a brief volume, *Integral Humanism,* published in 1965.[37] But as Atal Behari Vajpayee (past president of the BJP) and Dr. Subramanian Swamy (until recently a leading thinker in the Jana Sangh) testify,[38] it is Deendayal's ideas of "integral humanism" which underlie the Jana Sangh–BJP position on economic policy. As Vajpayee has put it:

Jan Sangh as a political party had to examine the two existing systems. Jan Sangh as a political party rejected both capitalism and communism because these systems though opposed to each other, lead to similar results, in the sense that both result in the concentration of economic power. In capitalism economic power is concentrated in the hands of a few and in communism it is concentrated in the hands of the state . . . and concentration of economic power leads to dangerous results.

Deendayal's integral humanism seeks to provide a third path in consonance with ancient Hindu notions of *dharma* (social order).[39] His panacea: "Swadeshi and decentralization are the two words which briefly summarize the economic policy suitable for the present circumstances."[40] He advocates the development of Bharatiya (Indian) technology, which is very similar to Gandhi's desire for a Swadeshi (home-spun) technology. Both are terms for an indigenous technology. But by contrast with Gandhi, who wanted to turn his back on modern technology, Deendayal seems to be arguing for what today would be called appropriate technology, that is, machines adapted to the factor endowments of India, with its preponderance of unskilled labor. He also seems to accept Gandhi's notion of trusteeship. "In [Deendayal's] terms, man must be encouraged to save and acquire wealth, but then it must be made socially prestigious to give away his wealth or manage it as a 'trustee' for society."[41] Finally, he wishes to add to the normal democratic rights enshrined in the Indian constitution the rights to food, to work, to education, and to free medical care.[42]

There is nothing said about the organizational or institutional framework within which such policies could be adopted. Yet it is not difficult to see that the ancient Hindu system of relatively self-sufficient village communities with their patron-client relationships ensuring the rights adumbrated by the above (at the village level) would be one of the viable organizational forms for establishing Deendayal's vision. It is thus fairly close to Gandhi's vision. But as with Gandhi, it had limited appeal to the growing Westernized middle classes which influenced policy.[43]

It was left to a young Harvard-trained economist, Subramanian Swamy, to try and marry the old to the new. In 1969 he prepared a "Swadeshi Plan," which was introduced by the Jana Sangh leader, A. B. Vajpayee, in the budget session of the Lok Sabha (the lower house of the Indian parliament) in 1970 as an alternative to the official plan. Swamy openly stated that his plan was based on economic nationalism. It had five objectives: "(1) A 10 percent rate of growth; (2) full employment; (3) guaranteed minimum acceptable consumption for all citizens; (4) total and immediate self reliance; and (5) full defense preparedness including the manufacture of nuclear weapons." His main targets were foreign aid and foreign investment, which he wanted to cease. But many of his other economic suggestions were sensible. He advocated relying on flexibility in exchange rates to deal with the balance of payments, thereby eliminating import controls; shifting the emphasis in industry away from heavy capital-intensive to "small" labor-intensive industries; reducing high marginal tax rates to encourage savings and to increase tax revenues; and emphasizing agriculture. All these are now recognized by mainstream economists as the essential ingredients of a development policy which promotes economic growth with equity in developing countries where labor is abundant.

But the Swadeshi Plan had little impact on policy. Like most professional observers, Mrs. Gandhi dismissed it, as devised by a Santa Claus![44] Subsequently (after the collapse of the Janata party coalition in the late 1970s) Swamy left the Jana Sangh–BJP and is now one of their trenchant critics, but he has not given up on devising economic policies which would lead to a revival of the Hindu nation—on which more later.

In the 1960s, the Jana Sangh came to be thought of as a party with right-wing economic policies. This was due to its tactical alliance with the Swatantra party. Both opposed the Congress party's proposals for agrarian reform, particularly after the so-called Nagpur Resolution, adopted by the party, which endorsed a program for cooperative farming. "Although the Jan Sangh advocated economic policies that were little different from the free enterprise program advocated by Swatantra, the party nevertheless adopted a populist rhetoric in calling for a more equitable distribution of wealth."[45] This alliance did well in the 1962 and 1967 elections. But its electoral eclipse in the late 1960s taught the Jana Sangh that it could not be seen to be associated with a party whose free market ideology was considered by the electorate to favor the haves against the have-nots.[46] In a poor country with universal suffrage and large disparities in income, being charged with being against the poor can be electorally disastrous. Hence the populist rhetoric now espoused by all Indian political parties. The Jana Sangh's brief flirtation with free enterprise in the 1960s was thus motivated more by tactical electoral considerations than by any ideological commitment. When electoral tactics demanded its abandonment, it was jettisoned—particularly as it conflicted with the critique of capitalism embodied in *Integral Humanism.*

With the Jana Sangh's entry into the Janata party coalition in 1977, some of the distinctive elements of its quasi-Gandhian populism could be discerned in Indian economic policy. But as the constituents of the Janata coalition were professed Gandhians of some sort who had been brought together by the Gandhian and former socialist J. P. Narayan, it is difficult to say that the Janata party's policies represented those of its Hindu revivalist component, the Jana Sangh. In fact, even though the Jana Sangh was the largest faction (with 30 percent of the Janata's parliamentary seats), the economic ideas and policies of the Janata were based mostly on the ideas of Charan Singh, the leader of the rural peasants. He advocated the promotion of agriculture rather than large-scale industry, a self-sufficient peasantry, and labor-intensive small-scale industry.[47] The congruence of Janata policies with some of the policies the Jana Sangh had espoused merely reflects the continuing resonance of Gandhian ideas across the Indian political spectrum (excluding the communists).[48]

The Jana Sangh while part of the Janata coalition also learned the uses of a broader constituency and thus moderated its communal image further when it reemerged as the BJP. It now had a Muslim as a general secretary, and Gandhian socialism replaced integral humanism as the party's articulated first principle.[49]

The Janata party also sought (mostly rhetorically) to reverse the Nehruvian industrial strategy. The main practical manifestation of this desire was policies to protect the small-scale and something called the "tiny" sector. This resulted in a policy-induced fragmentation of the industrial sector which created in effect an industrial caste system whose economic merits were far from obvious.[50] The implementation of the new industrial strategy did not, moreover, involve any dismantling of the Nehruvian panoply of controls and licenses. The Jana Sangh as part of the Janata coalition thus seemed to embrace the consensual inward-looking dirigisme which has characterized Indian economic policy. The only added nuance was a greater emphasis on protecting urban small scale producers and rural kulaks through further dirigisme.

The other "new" element of Janata economic policies was the institution of various direct programs (such as an employment guarantee scheme in Maharashta and "food for work" programs) to deal with rural underemployment. These again can hardly be described as marked departures from the Nehruvian programs. The latter have, at least rhetorically, promised to implement various populist policies to meet so-called basic needs, and have claimed to have a poverty and employment focus since at least the fifth Five-Year Plan of Mrs. Gandhi's government in the early 1970s.

It was Mrs. Gandhi's son, Rajiv, who tried unsuccessfully to initiate a more radical break with the Nehru model. His stated desire (soon after his large electoral victory in 1984) was to dismantle the Permit Raj and tackle the political corruption it had engendered. His embroilment in his own corruption scandals stalled this brief attempt at liberalization.

What of the new BJP (the successor to the Jana Sangh)? Does it have any distinctive economic policies? Apparently not. There is an emerging consensus in India for economic liberalization, but no party has advocated a dash for the free market as has happened, for instance, in Eastern Europe. When asked why not, Mr. Advani, the president of the BJP, honestly stated that there were still no votes in it.[51] The party wants a reduction in the role of the public sector, but it wants to restrict foreign investment to high-technology areas. At the same time it supports populist measures, such as the right to work, and the forgiveness of rural debt. The espousal of this populist egalitarianism is largely tactical, to the extent that it goes against the maintenance of a social system based on *Homo Hierarchus,*[52] which remains a cornerstone of the Hindu culture virtually all Hindu revivalists have sought to revive.

The BJP's current economic policies and its justifications for them thus seem very much part of the continuing Nehruvian economic policy consensus in India, namely, to move hesitantly toward some liberalization of the economy but with a predominant role for the state and the bureaucracy. The differences in policy with the Nehruvian model lie essentially in a greater emphasis on the Gandhian features which are already contained in the consensus strategy.

There is, however, one politician, Dr. Swamy (an ex–Jana Sangh), currently president of the Janata party, who has produced an agenda for the revival of the Hindu nation whose cornerstone is the creation of a market economy.[53] He argues that

the adoption of policies which foster rapid economic growth and increasing social justice is vital for national renaissance. . . . The Hindu ethos is based on individualism. If an individualistic democracy is to be strong, which is an important dimension of national renaissance, then the economic philosophy of such a society should accord the highest priority to self-employment and secure jobs to foster the spirit of self-reliance. Since the ethos of the Hindus who are nearly eighty-two percent is individualistic, the correct economic policy is one that is largely based on the use of the market mechanism. The government [in such a polity] would have a role, no doubt, but it will be primarily to correct market malfunction, promote minimum standards of living, and generally act as an umpire in the interaction between consumers and producers in the market place. The government would also have the right to intervene in the market to give protection to those who cannot survive unfair competition, give cheap credit to small producers and arrange marketing facilities for farmers and small industrialists. In such an economy, the government will have no right to occupy the "commanding heights," the concept favoured by Nehru and the Leftists. Overall, the government's major role would be to levy taxation and set interest rates which induce investments that promote employment, to modernize agriculture, and to encourage small industries, such as the government did in Japan. Such an economic policy is not capitalistic or socialist but is the modern update of Gandhian ideas.

Whether Gandhi would have agreed with this is dubious. Nor will most revivalists accept the individualism Swamy espouses. Moreover, Swamy's agenda still pays lip service to finding a middle way:

> The world over, socialism has failed, while capitalism has produced exploitation and social unrest. Thus, we must reject both. Instead we need to rely not on the power of the government, nor on that of capitalists, but to focus power of the human initiative and enterprise to develop by providing the proper freedom and opportunity. . . . The sixth item on the agenda for national Renaissance is the acceptance of an economic philosophy that is liberal and in which the economic role of the government is limited to providing the physical and policy infrastructure for the market to function efficiently.

Any free market economist would wholeheartedly concur with this. But it seems a long way from the Hindu revivalist economic program that Gandhi laid out in *Hind Swaraj*. Nor does the individualism Swamy extols seem consonant with the traditional hierarchical social system based on caste. But if the purpose of Hindu revivalism is to create a powerful Hindu nation-state, then Swamy is right in realizing that the most efficient means to that end is a full-fledged market economy.[54]

However, having left the Jana Sangh, he is unlikely to see his ideas adopted by the BJP in the near future. What his *Agenda for Hindu Renaissance* does illustrate, however, is the absorptive quality of "Hinduism . . . [and] the continued indefiniteness of its religious, social and political boundaries."[55] Though beginning with the revivalist dream of setting boundaries and purifying Hinduism, the revivalists have steadily moved toward the consensual policies they find have electoral appeal. Once the desire to refurbish the ancient Hindu equilibrium is recognized as impractical, as it increasingly has become with the spread of the modern economy and the expansion of the middle class, there is no distinctive set of economic policies left to distinguish a Hindu revivalist program from any other program which seeks to adopt "policies which foster rapid economic growth and increasing social justice . . . vital for national renaissance."[56]

Elsewhere I have argued[57] that many of the parameters which have sustained the ancient Hindu equilibrium have decisively shifted during the past century. Population growth has ended India's ancient demographic stability and the need to tie labor down to the land; the Green Revolution has ended village autarky; even the modest industrial growth since independence has replaced custom with the contract in many situations, particularly in the labor market. Meanwhile the growth of Western education and social legislation—which has picked up where Bentinck left off—and the gradual movement of the literary castes into business and commerce are slowly changing long-standing casteist attitudes. The ancient Hindu revenue economy is thus now being undermined. The impracticality of a full-scale reestablishment of the Hindu equilibrium makes Gandhian economic panaceas look more and more antediluvian and romantic to the electorate. Hindu revivalist parties, therefore, while seeking to uphold Hindu culture, are unlikely to seek a return to ancient economic ways. Thus, I would argue that, just as there has been no distinctive impact of Hindu revivalism on Indian economic *policy* in the past, there is unlikely to be a major impact in the future. Nevertheless, the indirect economic consequences of the violence resulting from unleashing religious passions can be dire. As the recent revivalist agitation surrounding the building of a temple on the site of a mosque in Ayodhya attests, when law and order—the basic public good—is threatened, there is a grave danger that the economic framework will also unravel.

Acknowledgments

I have benefited from personal interviews with Mr. L. K. Advani and Dr. Subramanian Swamy concerning the economic policies of Hindu revivalist political parties. While thanking them for their help, I absolve them of any responsibility for anything said in this paper! I am also grateful for detailed comments by R. Scott Appleby and Timur Kuran on a draft of the paper.

Notes

1. *Homo Hierarchus* is the title of Lewis Dumont's important book on the Hindu caste system. It described a social system which has hierarchy as its central organizing principle. L. Dumont, *Homo Hierarchus* (Weidenfeld and Nicholson, 1970).

2. This was emphasized in a personal interview with Mr. L. K. Advani, current president of the BJP.

3. See Martin E. Marty and R. Scott Appleby, eds., *Fundamentalisms Observed* (Chicago: University of Chicago Press, 1991).

4. R. P. Kangle, *The Kautilya Arthashastra* (University of Bombay, 1965), part 3, p. 20.

5. Gandhi is not self-consciously appropriated by the revivalists, who object to what they see as the appeasement by him and the Congress party (of which he was a leader) of the Muslims. Gandhi's motives had more to do with his desire to see a united India than did the principled stand of the Nehruvian modernists who captured Congress and for whom secularism was an essential part of the modernizing ideology they espoused.

6. See Deepak Lal, *The Hindu Equilibrium*, 2 vols. (Oxford: Clarendon Press, 1988, 1989).

7. See Daniel Gold, "Organized Hinduisms—From Vedic Truth to Hindu Nation," in Marty and Appleby, eds., *Fundamentalisms Observed*, for a detailed discussion of the evolution and ideology of the RSS.

8. P. R. Brass, *The New Cambridge History of India: The Politics of India since Independence* (Cambridge, 1990).

9. For details and an economic explanation for the rise and stability of this socioeconomic system, see Lal, *Hindu Equilibrium*, vol. 1. This and the following section are based on this work.

10. That is, with no trade links outside the village.

11. M. N. Srinivas, "Social Structure," *The Gazetter of India*, vol. 1, *Country and People* (New Delhi), p. 511.

12. A. L. Basham, *The Wonder That Was India* (London, 1967), p. 152.

13. Kabir (1440–1518) was a leader of the Bhakti movement, which was a devotional cult combining elements of both Hinduism and Islam. "By and large its adherents were from the lower castes. Institutionalized religion and objects of worship were attacked, caste disregarded, women were encouraged to join in the gatherings, and the teaching was entirely in the local vernacular language." Like Nanak (the founder of the Sikhs), Kabir was against caste and the distinctions between Hindus and Muslims as expressed in organized religion. See R. Thapar, *A History of India*, vol. 1 (London), pp. 308–11.

14. See Robert E. Frykenberg, "Caste,

Morality and Western Religion under the Raj," *Modern Asian Studies* 19, no. 2 (1985), for a review of recent work which shows how the British, having failed to alter the caste system, adapted to it. On caste among the Muslim, see I. Ahmad, "The Ashraf-Ailaf Dichotomy in Muslim Social Structure in India," *Indian Economic Social History Review* 3, no. 3 (1966); and Thapar, *A History of India*, vol. 1, pp. 301, 320.

15. J. R. Hicks, *A Theory of Economic History* (Oxford: Clarendon Press).

16. E. L. Jones, *The European Miracle* (Cambridge, 1981).

17. T. G. P. Spear, *A History of India*, vol. 2 (London), p. 164. Also see C. A. Bayly, *The New Cambridge History of India: Indian Society and the Making of the British Empire* (Cambridge, 1988).

18. Gold, "Organized Hinduisms."

19. See D. B. Forrester, *Caste and Christianity* (New Jersey, 1980).

20. As Frykenberg in "Caste, Morality and Western Religion under the Raj" notes: "Yet, if anything, it was this very unprecedented action itself, this annexation of untouchability into Hinduism, this arbitrary co-option by definition, which was so profoundly offensive to Ambedkar and other leaders of the 'untouchables'" (p. 326). In secular postindependence India, various forms of affirmative action have been instituted (largely through job reservation) to improve the socioeconomic status of the harijans. More recently this form of reservation (largely for government jobs and higher education institutions) has been extended to other backward castes. This has aroused a backlash against all job reservations from higher-caste youths. Whether these job reservations have markedly improved the socioeconomic status of the harijans is dubious.

21. M. K. Gandhi, *The Collected Works of Mahatma Gandhi*, vol. 10 (Delhi, 1958), pp. 6–68.

22. Judith Brown, *Gandhi's Rise to Power: Indian Politics, 1915–1922* (Cambridge, 1972), p. 2. *Satyagraha* for Gandhi meant self-knowledge, self-sacrifice in nonviolent civil disobedience.

23. Ibid., p. 46.

24. Ibid., p. 79.

25. Brown, *Gandhi's Rise to Power*, p. 328.

26. See Gold, "Organized Hinduisms."

27. Ibid.

28. Ibid.

29. Ibid.

30. Ibid.

31. These included direct and discretionary bureaucratic controls of the allocation of industrial investments, foreign exchange, and commercial credit, along with controls on the prices and distribution of commodities.

32. The Swatantra party was "a coalition of urban big business and rural aristocratic and landlord elements in which the latter were dominant." Paul R. Brass, *The New Cambridge History of India: The Politics of India since Independence* (Cambridge, 1990), p. 70. Founded in 1959, it reached its height in 1967 as the second largest party in Parliament. But soon after its decimation at the polls in 1971 it became defunct.

33. Brass, *The New Cambridge History of India*, p. 336.

34. Ibid., p. 16.

35. See, for instance, Balraj Madhok, *Indianization?* (Delhi: S. Chand and Co., 1970).

36. Poujadism was the political movement of small shopkeepers and peasants organized by the French politician Poujade in the 1950s.

37. Deendayal Upadhyaya, *Integral Humanism* (Delhi: Navchetan Press, 1965).

38. A. B. Vajpayee, "A Memorial Lecture," and S. Subramaniam, "Economic Perspectives in Integral Humanism," in M. J. Mehta, ed., *Upadhyaya's Integral Humanism—the Concept and Application* (New Jersey: Deendayal Upadhyaya Committee of America, 1980).

39. The concept of dharma systematizes the doctrine of karma (action). The latter embodies the notion of transmigration of souls and "the theory that souls were born to happiness or to sorrow according to conduct in their previous life. . . . The doctrine of Karma also provided a philosophical justification for caste. One's birth into a high or low caste was also dependent on one's actions in a previous life, and this led to the hope of social improvement in one's next incarnation. The doctrine of Karma came to be systematized in the broader concept of Dharma: the word defies translation into English, but in this context can perhaps be best described as the natural law. The natural law of society was the maintaining of the social order, in fact, the caste laws." Thapar, *A History of India*, vol. 1, p. 46. The only aspect of dharma of relevance for economic policy is possibly the injunction for charity toward the indigent, particularly Brahmins, and those who are living on alms in the last stages of the ideal life, which involves renunciation of the worldly life of the householder.

40. Upadhyaya, *Integral Humanism*, p. 78.

41. Swamy, "Agenda for National Renaissance," mimeo, Janata Party (New Delhi, April 1990), p. 58.

42. Ibid., p. 55.

43. These revivalist groups appeal to the many Hindus, particularly in the North, with communal sentiments. As Brass notes: "There is also presumed to exist a Hindu 'vote' in India which can be mobilized for the sake of national unity against the secessionist or otherwise excessive demands of minorities such as Sikhs and Muslims." But he also notes "there remains in India today considerable ambiguity concerning the use of the word 'Hindus' to define any clearly demarcated group of people in the subcontinent and considerable doubt about the existence of a Hindu political community . . . [because of] the continued indefiniteness of [Hinduism's] religious, social and political boundaries." Brass, *The New Cambridge History of India*, p. 16.

44. Because its targets were completely infeasible, given existing resources and technology.

45. F. Frankel, *India's Political Economy, 1947–77* (Princeton, 1978), p. 207.

46. Personal interview with L. K. Advani, April 1990.

47. Brass, *The New Cambridge History of India*.

48. As L. Rudolph and S. Rudolph note: "Two of the triumvirate who became Janata's leaders, Morarji Desai and Charan Singh, were professed Gandhians. . . . The Jan Sangh faction too declared itself to be deeply committed to JP's interpretation of Mohandas Gandhi's ideas and practices. The appreciable socialist component of the new party included many doctrinal orientations and organizational legacies. Not least among them was Gandhian socialism, an orientation that trade union socialists (e.g., George Fernandez) and 'Sorellian' Lohia socialists (e.g., Raj Narain) if not Popular Front socialists (e.g., Madhu Limaye) could appreciate and support because of the redistributional thrusts of its employment oriented growth strategy and its concern for social justice." L. I. Rudolph and S. H. Rudolph, *In Pursuit of Lakshmi: The Political Economy of the Indian State* (Chicago, 1987), p. 166.

49. Gold, *Organized Hindusims*.

50. See Deepak Lal, "Janata's Industrial Policies," *Times of India,* 9 and 10 January 1978; and I. M. D. Little, "Small Manufacturing Enterprises in Developing Countries," *World Bank Economic Review,* January 1987.

51. Personal interview, April 1990.

52. See Dumont, *Homo Hierarchus.*

53. Swamy, "Agenda for National Renaissance."

54. For detailed arguments in favor of this case, see Lal, *Hindu Equilibrium,* vol. 1, chaps. 13 and 14.

55. Brass, *The New Cambridge History of India,* p. 16.

56. Swamy, "Agenda for National Resistance," p. 57.

57. Lal, *Hindu Equilibrium.*

3

Remaking the World through Militancy

Comparing Militant Fundamentalist Movements and Groups

David C. Rapoport

In this chapter I will introduce the six case studies discussed in part 3, address common themes, comment on ideas which need more discussion, and develop categories for comparing the materials. The conclusions are my own, but they are implied by, or at least are not inconsistent with, the studies. When authors differ or when I disagree with a writer, I have made the reader aware that a conflict exists.

Three articles are devoted to Islamic groups and movements (Keddie and Monian, Roy, and Kramer), and one each to Jewish (Sprinzak), Buddhist (Tambiah), and Christian (Ginsburg) entities. Each treats a particular country: Iran, Afghanistan, Lebanon, Israel, Sri Lanka, and the United States. In the cases of Lebanon and the United States, detailed studies of Hizbullah (the Party of God) and Operation Rescue are offered. And because the Iranian revolution had an enormous influence on Shi'ite communities in the Arab world, a theme in several of the conferences held by this project, I have extended the discussion to include materials on Iraq and the Persian Gulf states of Saudi Arabia, Kuwait, Qatar, and Bahrain.[1]

A group is characterized as militant because it pursues causes so aggressively that it breaks laws made by the state. In the name of a sacred law, each group or movement considered in this part of the volume has used violence. Although they have conspicuously different origins, doctrines, practices, and institutions, each group wants to establish or protect communities based on divine authority.

Arguing that the changing moral, political, and legal standards derived from human secular authority create rampant and incurable disorders and injustices, fundamentalists address themselves to what they perceive as a crisis in existing standards of legitimacy. The secular view, most fundamentalists contend, draws its greatest strength from a world outside their civilizations; thus, they understand themselves to be reviving authentic native traditions. Their aggressiveness is defensive, springing largely from fears that secularization will destroy the authority of the sacred, that traditional religious establishments lack confidence in the truth or viability of divine principles, and that time is running out.

The leaders of these movements have diverse backgrounds. Islam provides two different pictures. Sunni fundamentalist leaders are laymen. University graduates but autodidactic in religious studies, they tend to oppose the *ulama* (learned sages), who depend on the state for their livelihood. Shi'ite fundamentalist movements, on the other hand, spring from new cleavages within the largely autonomous clerical hierarchy. The young clerics of Hizbullah, Kramer notes, come from a narrow age group whose educational careers were interrupted when Saddam Hussein expelled them from Shi'ism's major shrine cities and educational centers in the 1970s. Khomeini's followers in Iran, strengthened by a similar element, were initially opposed by the clerical establishment. Although laymen lead Operation Rescue, Jewish rabbis and Buddhist monks dominate their respective fundamentalist groups. More important than the vocation of group leaders, however, is the fact that the relationship of these leaders to those in the religious mainstream reflects the decentralization of authority characteristic of each religion.

The hostility to secularization is not unmitigated. When they come to power, as in Iran or Sri Lanka, fundamentalists find that creating contemporary institutions from sacred authority alone is beyond the capacity of their political imagination. They need the electoral and legislative forms associated with secularism. A similar pattern seemed to be emerging in the early 1990s among groups attempting to achieve power for the first time, such as the Sunni fundamentalists and Hizbullah.

Fundamentalists also recognize that the secularization process produces potential benefits. Modern technology often evokes admiration, and some fundamentalists are confident that they can use it without succumbing to the cultural mentality which produced it. Furthermore, much like the liberation theologians of Latin America, major fundamentalist leaders and writers in Iran, Afghanistan, and Sri Lanka have appropriated one secular product extensively: Marxist doctrine. Although fundamentalists cooperated with Marxists in the three countries indicated, they ultimately destroyed Marxist groups which had been allies.

The Gush Emunim (the Bloc of the Faithful), the best-known Israeli fundamentalist group, has no Marxist element yet expresses its ambivalence toward secularization in a unique, almost Hegelian, manner. Secularization is a necessary stage in the historical process and the "inadequacy" of secularism will be revealed fully only after it has served its purpose in the unfolding of the divine plan for messianic redemption.

Operation Rescue has deliberately refused to engage in theoretical and theological discussions in order to concentrate on tactics—tactics which, ironically, were borrowed from the secular left. "We learn[ed] the lessons of history which show how the labor movement, the civil rights movement, Vietnam protest, and gay liberation all occurred because a group of people created social tension."[2]

There are two major fundamentalist responses to secularism. A total withdrawal from the existing society may be recommended, but more often fundamentalists become preoccupied with politics in order to transform the society so that the benefits of secularism may be absorbed without assimilating its evils. All of our examples except the Jewish *haredi* (God-Fearing) groups—popularly known as the "ultra-Orthodox" in the English-speaking world—have taken the second, or political, route. But in the 1988 national and the 1989 municipal elections and again in the 1992 elections, some haredi groups broke with long-standing traditions to move closer to an activist fundamentalist pattern. Their purpose, paradoxically, was to preserve their isolation, a condition which partly depends upon securing economic benefits from the state. How far their involvement in Israeli politics will extend is unclear.

Individual fundamentalist movements or groups perceive the concrete expressions of secularism differently, but they tend to agree that secularism exhibits two dimensions simultaneously, one internal, or domestic, and the other external, or international.[3] With regard to the domestic scene, fundamentalists believe that the spirit of secularism is manifested simultaneously in different guises, not only in government and political parties but also in alien cultural influences or bodies (e.g., the Hindus and Muslims in Sri Lanka; the Christians in Lebanon). In every case, fundamentalists also accuse existing religious establishments of having succumbed to secularist influences. The international character of secularism assumes various forms in fundamentalist polemics, with a foreign civilization (most often the West) or a foreign state (the United States, the Soviet Union, and, in the case of Sri Lanka, India) looming as the threat to indigenous religiopolitical sovereignty. Foreign political ideologies such as imperialism and Marxism are perceived as even more invasive and insidious.

Strategies for dealing with these two dimensions of secularism vary. Some groups believe that they must engage the internal enemy first, while others give the international one priority. In either case, the international foe is always more difficult to eliminate, and fundamentalists believe that the foreigner who once made their land a colonial or neocolonial appendage intends to do so again. In Afghanistan and Lebanon, the presence of foreign troops gave these beliefs concerning colonial intentions a very compelling force.[4]

Religious enemies are important. Fundamentalists normally divide existing religious communities; Hizbullah and Amal, for example, have battled furiously for ascendancy within the Lebanese Shi'ite community. Theravada Buddhists fear Hindus and loathe Christian missionary activity, an activity which also upsets Jewish fundamentalists. Shi'ites believe that the Sunni governments in the Persian Gulf, which claim Islamic principles as the basis for legitimacy, are agents of Western civilization, and they regard the Christian Maronites of Lebanon in the same light. The significance of these enemies also differs considerably over time, even in the same community. Buddhist anxieties about Christians and the West, for example, have diminished, while those about Hindus and India have become more prominent.

To discuss fundamentalist militancy I shall focus on four overlapping themes in the studies: (1) the political contexts which help explain differences in the intensity, scope and rationale of the violence, (2) the impact of violence on other religious and ethnic elements within the respective states, (3) the international implications of the violence, and, finally, (4) the distinctively religious features of the violence.

Two Political Contexts

The essays which follow treat particular movements and focus on the process of militancy rather than its causes. While no statistical data reflecting precise comparisons of movements is offered, the ample evidence supplied establishes a central point. The declared purposes of violent acts—as well as the scale, persistence, intensity, and impact—vary enormously. How do we explain these differences?

The varieties of fundamentalist militancy described relate specifically to two political contexts, one being the "sectarian state" and the other the secular, or nation-state. Iran, Sri Lanka, Afghanistan, Lebanon, Saudi Arabia, Bahrain, Qatar, Kuwait, and the United Arab Emirates are sectarian states. Iraq under Saddam Hussein professes secular principles but exhibits a volatile sectarian undercurrent. The United States and, to a lesser extent, Israel are secular, or nation-states.[5]

When fundamentalist violence occurs in a sectarian state, it normally aims at revolution and the expulsion of a foreign presence. The objectives and the organized resistance encountered indicate that once violence is initiated, it persists for prolonged periods and much blood is shed.

In nation-states, however, the immediate purpose of militant fundamentalist activity is to change government policy. Compared to the experiences of the sectarian states, Jewish violence has been limited in time and space. The most significant Jewish accomplishments—the West Bank (Judea-Samaria) settlements—were manifestly extralegal but were not directly the result of violence. By the standards of militancy displayed in the other instances, the extralegal actions of Operation Rescue are negligible.

The Sectarian State

The distinctive characteristic of the sectarian state is that its territory contains several *partial* and sometimes mutually exclusive communities. The major communities are religious, as the term sectarian suggests, but fundamentalists have become important in recent times only. The term "sect" refers also to ethnic and tribal communities, and each type of community is important here.

The concept of a nation exists in sectarian states but only in the sense of a partial community, one more significant among social elements normally associated with the government. Furthermore, several concepts of nation may exist simultaneously in the same state, for example, the Iraqi nation and the Arab nation in Iraq. In all cases, the identity of the nation appears volatile and contested. Iran, for example, shows a persistent but unsuccessful effort throughout its history to establish a preeminent national secular identity.[6] Most Sri Lankans, Tambiah indicates, reject the secular idea of nation (perceived as a part of their colonial inheritance), believing instead that their nation is inseparable from Theravada Buddhism, which means that they fear that the Tamil ties with Hindu coreligionists in India could eventually end Sri Lanka's independence.

Nationalism in the Arab world, a world dominated by sectarian states, became a slogan which grew stale by repetition and could no longer gather ideas around [it] into a powerful constellation, mobilize social forces for action, or turn power into legitimate authority. . . . It could always exist as an immediate and natural reaction to a threat from the outside as during the war between Iraq and Iran when parts of the Iraqi population which might have been considered hostile to the government gave it support. . . . In general, the function of Arabism was as a weapon in conflicts between Arab states, and as a pretext for the interference of one state in the affairs of others.[7]

Roy's description of the significance of Islam for Afghanistan is telling.

Everyday life revolves around religious practice. . . . Although there never has been such a thing as an Afghan nation, there is certainly an Afghan state whose history can be traced. How do Afghans themselves see their [country for which] . . . they have no name? There are two possible interpretations: the first, a territorial and dynastic view identified Afghanistan with the area ruled by the Amir of Kabul [a reference to tribal origin]. The other . . . identified the country with the area which remained Muslim, surrounded . . . by the infidels or the heretics [the Shi'ites in Persia].[8]

Indeed, religious identity is such a crucial ingredient of politics in the Muslim world that no revolutionary ever felt willing or capable of renouncing Islam![9]

In a sectarian state the major religious communities, the initial source of fundamentalist symbols and values, have enormous resources which fundamentalists may be able to capture. Although a fundamentalist group always begins as a peripheral element, in sectarian states there is a "sort of indeterminate area around it [the fundamentalist group] which enables it to maintain ties with society as a whole and serves as a channel for recruiting sympathizers, and ultimately adherents, with varying degrees of commitment. . . . The periphery shares basic beliefs with the hardcore and collaborates with it in various realms of life. It represents the proverbial water in which the militant fish can swim."[10] To continue the metaphor: In specific bywaters secular elements, like Marxists and ethnic communities, may offer crucial havens, but the mainstream religious communities provide daily nutrients.

Patterns of militancy and violence are related initially to whether or not the state contains a dominant religious community. Iran, Afghanistan, and Sri Lanka have such a community, and it is no surprise that in each case fundamentalists have shed much blood to create a new political order and have had some success in doing so, though the struggles have had different forms and outcomes. The Iranian Shi'ite fundamentalists have overthrown a government and remained in firm control ever since; their example has had enormous influence beyond Iran's borders. The Theravada Buddhists of Sri Lanka are closer than the Afghans to achieving the domestic preeminence the Iranian Shi'ites obtained. Since the 1956 election the extralegal actions of the Buddhist monks enabled them to determine an increasing portion of the state's agenda for some thirty-five years, but still they do not govern. Moreover, as successive governments inched closer toward a Theravada Buddhist state, the resistance of the largely Hindu Tamil population grew, so that they now want to secede.

The Afghans provide a third picture. The resistance to a Marxist government (1978) and then to a Soviet invasion (1979) was impressive, but the traditional Sunni ulama, though riven by ethnic cleavages, were crucial to success. When the Soviets arrived, fundamentalists attempted to unify the community, and their influence kept growing as long as the Soviets remained. But the customary religious and ethnic divisions did not disappear, and the fundamentalists themselves developed mutually hostile organizations based on ethnic loyalties. As the Soviets withdrew, the precarious Islamic unity began to dissolve and fundamentalists declined in influence. Roy believes that a "Lebanonization" of Afghanistan may occur.

Though violence in Iran, Sri Lanka, and Afghanistan has been spasmodic, occurring in several phases involving different domestic and international targets, it has persisted for decades. The Iranian cycle alone may be complete. It began in 1946 with the Fida'iyan-Islam's assassination campaign, which appeared to yield no immediate political fruit. An initial turning point occurred in 1962 when the head of the clerical establishment, Ayatollah Burujirdi, generally a government supporter and hostile to Shi'ite political participation, died. His successor, Ayatollah Khomeini, expressed radically different views so forcefully that he was soon arrested. Hundreds of unarmed demonstrators protesting the arrest were killed, an event which broadened the fundamentalist religious base enormously because it brought support from virtually all the major religious leaders, and for the Shi'ites the disposition of the clergy is paramount.

The event spawned various guerrilla and terrorist groups, but it was another series of demonstrations led by the ulama which brought the shah down. During those final upheavals, Khomeini understood that the army's resistance would melt if the demonstrators were prepared to keep taking casualties, that sometimes one gained more by dying than by killing. Once in power he became less restrained, as his regime became beleaguered by international and domestic enemies. Among the latter were many groups, especially Marxist ones, which had helped bring the shah down. The recourse to state terror after power is achieved is a familiar development, reminiscent of the secular revolutionary experiences of France, Russia, and Cuba. As the earlier revolutionaries had discovered, however, the political and economic costs of sustaining state terror became too great; and in Khomeini's final years he moved slowly toward a more "pragmatic fundamentalism," which became more striking under his successor, President Rafsanjani.[11] A dramatic illustration of this policy occurred in the immediate aftermath of Iraq's defeat in the Gulf War, when Iran did not aid an uprising by the Iraqi Shi'ites even in the face of a grave threat to the most holy sites in the Shi'ite world. The most recent manifestation (November 1991) was Iran's role in persuading Lebanese Shi'ites to release American and British hostages.

Revolutionary rage still persists in Iran. Rafsanjani increased the bounty which Khomeini had placed on the head of the British author Salman Rushdie for writing *The Satanic Verses*. In August 1991 the Japanese and the Italian translators of the book were stabbed to death.[12] In that month also, the shah's last premier, Shahpur Bakhtiar, was assassinated in Paris. Again daggers were used, and a French court determined that Iranian officials had directed the assassins. Subsequently, a decision by the Swiss government to extradite to France one of Bakhtiar's suspected assassins who had taken refuge in the Iranian embassy provoked threats from Tehran.[13] Iran's hostility toward Arab and Palestinian moves toward a peace treaty with Israel also suggests the continued importance of revolutionary rage.

In Sri Lanka, according to Tambiah, the cycle of violence has not yet run its course. The 1956 riots instigated by Sinhalese and Tamil extremists destroyed a compromise on a national language that was meant to resolve the growing tensions. The weakness of subsequent successive governments contributed to an intensifying spiral of violence, a seemingly unending series of mutual atrocities where every new attack has been justified by a previous injury received.

Afghan fundamentalists first took up arms in 1975 in a vain effort to organize rural areas against the Republican coup of President Daud. The lay leaders of the revolt, Roy notes, seemed more Marxist than Islamic to the peasants. Once the Soviets withdrew (1989) and the ulama-led traditionalist parties returned to their tribal ways, fundamentalists became more interested in the spoils of war than in a blueprint for a new Islamic state.

Hizbullah (Party of God), Lebanon's most notorious Shi'ite terrorist body, hoped to create an Islamic Republic after the model of Iran's. But although the Shi'ites are Lebanon's largest and most aggrieved religious element, their goal seems chimerical because power has been divided among Lebanon's several mutually hostile armed confessional groups. Indeed, perhaps because the aim seemed so impossible, Hizbullah's statements often affirmed a belief, Kramer points out, that the situation required even grander aspirations. "We do not work or think within the borders of Lebanon, this little geometric box which is one of the legacies of imperialism. Rather we seek to defend Muslims throughout the world." The establishment of an Islamic state in Lebanon "is not our demand"; rather, it is an "all-encompassing Islamic state" which would absorb Lebanon and "liberate Jerusalem."

Hizbullah appeared initially in 1982, when it broke off from Amal (Hope), a Shi'ite group allied with Syria. Amal began in the first year of Lebanon's civil war (1975), proclaiming aims reasonably consistent with the bewildering array of confessional and international forces in Lebanon. Nonetheless a truly active Shi'ite community emerged only after the Iranian revolution and tensions with the Palestinian Liberation Organization (PLO) occurred in 1979. The Israeli invasion of 1982 and the subsequent landing of the multinational Western peacekeeping forces precipitated the birth of Hizbullah, which identified with Iran and opened up a spectacular suicide or self-martyrdom bombing campaign against foreign troops. The campaign killed hundreds, driving American and French troops out of the country and confining the Israelis to a narrow zone in the south. Thereafter, Hizbullah's assassination campaign against Western civilians led to the taking of more than one hundred hostages over the course of a decade. To support Iran in its war against Iraq, Hizbullah struck targets in Kuwait and France, a major Iraqi arms supplier. Finally, in 1988, when very few foreign targets were available in Lebanon, it began a war against Amal which caused thousands of Shi'ite casualties before the Syrians and Iranians stepped in to mediate a truce in 1990.

With the development of Iran's "pragmatic fundamentalism," which led to the freeing of most foreign hostages and the pacification of Lebanon by Syria in the wake of the Gulf War, Hizbullah's activities moved in a different direction, and it argued for a referendum on the issue of an Islamic state. Hizbullah, Kramer says, then appeared as "a champion of democracy . . . and began to evolve into a political party . . . whose clerics spoke more like candidates." But in 1992 Hizbullah still had the most heavily armed militia in Lebanon and its struggle against the Israelis persisted. Hizbullah was no closer to achieving its goals of an Islamic state, spreading Iran's revolution, and liberating Jerusalem. But driving foreign troops out of Lebanon and gaining the loyalty of Shi'ites in Lebanon and Iran were not insignificant feats. Hizbullah's most significant achievement, in Kramer's judgment, has been its success in promoting a return to Islam, "a gradual process of internal transformation, whose results no one could predict."

The Shi'ite community is the majority in Iraq, and the Da'wa party, intially concerned with preventing Shi'ites from becoming Marxists, has revolutionary aspirations. In the wake of the Gulf crisis it hoped to create an Islamic Republic independent from Iran, one that would bridge Sunni and Shi'ite differences. But Sunni hostility was unrelenting,[14] and the secular Arab Baath Party, buoyed by Saddam Hussein's policy of sticks and carrots, was sustained.[15] Militant Shi'ite fundamentalists were driven abroad to operate from Iran. Although the defeat of Saddam Hussein in the Gulf War provided new potentially significant opportunities for Shi'ite militancy, the initial postwar uprising failed.

The Arab states of the Persian Gulf have Shi'ite communities with a history of intermittent militancy, a militancy intensified by the Iranian revolution and the attempts of Iranian governments to organize Shi'ite discontent. In these states the Shi'ite experience of being a persecuted minority is reinforced by the hostile and potentially dangerous environments controlled largely by the Sunni, a problem further complicated by Shi'ite ethnic divisions and invidious economic or class disadvantages. In states where the Shi'ites are most numerous, fundamentalist groups have been extremely ambitious. In Bahrain, where the Shi'ites constitute 60 percent of the population, the most extensive effort was an abortive plot in 1981 to set up an Islamic Republic.

In the remaining Persian Gulf states Shi'ite numbers are too small to mount a revolution without outside aid. But in Saudi Arabia, the Shi'ites are considered a threat. Though only 5 percent of the population, Shi'ites are concentrated in an oil-rich eastern province close to Iraq and Iran, and thus are under constant police surveillance. Equally important is the two centuries of animosity between Shi'ites and the Wahhabis, the oldest Sunni fundamentalist sect and the religious base of the Saudi government.[16] Since the establishment of the Saudi state after World War I, serious demonstrations have occurred during the pilgrimage (*hajj*) seasons, upsetting relations between various Iranian and Saudi governments, the latter fearing that the demonstrations would undermine the principal religious rationale for Saudi govern-ments—their role as guardians of the holy sites. The persistent tension between Iran and Saudi Arabia led several times to breaches in diplomatic relations. Conceivably, many Saudi Shi'ites may be satisfied with political reform, but the community has produced several revolutionary terror groups supported by Iran.

Serious tensions between the Sunni and Shi'ites in Kuwait were evident in the early decades of the century, and the Shi'ites were excluded from representative assem-blies. The rift grew in the 1980s when the Shi'ites, mostly guest workers and nearly a quarter of the population, were not allowed to become Kuwaiti citizens. Most im-migrants came from Iran and Lebanon, and in the aftermath of the upheavals in those countries, terrorist activity, often directed against Western targets, became a feature of Kuwaiti life. Thousands of Shi'ite immigrants were subsequently expelled. Only two Persian Gulf states have been free of Shi'ite violence: the United Arab Emirates, where the Shi'ite element is only 5 percent, and Qatar, which maintained good rela-tions with Iran throughout the Iran-Iraq war.

In most of the Arab states where significant Shi'ite communities exist, the open physical terrain ensures that if violence materializes, it will quickly reach a climax. In Lebanon, the principal exception, the geography is comparable to that of Sri Lanka; it provides advantages for minorities to maintain prolonged struggles. Iraq has moun-tains and would also seem to be an exception, but the Shi'ites do not live in the mountainous regions.

The Nation-State

When the nation as a secular entity is the primary source of legitimacy, the major religious communities, which provide fundamentalists with sympathizers and recruits, have less political potential than their counterparts in sectarian states. Success for fundamentalists, therefore, depends upon a willingness to pursue limited concerns, which secular elements may support, albeit for different reasons. Both nation-states examined here exhibit this pattern, though their circumstances are quite different.

The Israeli concept of nation is tied to its origin in religion. Israelis do not have to be Jewish, but it is much easier for a Jew to become an Israeli. If one is not a Jew by birth (ethnicity), a religious conversion to Judaism is necessary to claim Israeli citizen-ship under the Law of Return. By the same token, a Jew who converts to another religion loses the right to claim Israeli citizenship.[17] In May 1991, when the Israelis evacuated some fourteen thousand Falashas (Ethiopian Jews), many who had con-verted to Christianity were left behind. The concern of Israel to be a Jewish state obviously has a variety of implications for Israeli Arabs, who have increasingly iden-tified with the Palestinians in the years of the Intifada.

Fundamentalist militancy vexes Israel much more than it does the United States, no matter what criteria (purpose, scale, impact, and persistence) are applied. Many Israelis find credible the claim of Gush Emunim that it is fulfilling the original Zionist mission of settling the land of Israel, a mission largely abandoned by a secular move-ment apprehensive of risks. The ability of Gush members to set up extralegal settle-ments starting in 1967, largely without resorting to large-scale violence, is a fact of capital political importance which immeasurably strengthened those secular elements in Israel which wish to keep the West Bank for other reasons.

Jewish fundamentalists ultimately want to preside over the erosion or destruction of Israel's secular character; but they are deeply divided on how and when that might occur, and no violence has yet been directed at overthrowing the government. Only the haredi Jews attack other Jews regularly, but they have *never* killed anyone. Their purpose is to protect the geographic and cultural boundaries of their community. Jews who violate the sacred law blatantly in or near haredi communities are the targets of stone-throwers who fear erosion of their enclave, the incurring of divine wrath, and the possible delay of the messianic redemption. Other victims are haredis themselves, the by-product of intense interharedi competition.

Gush Emunim and Kach (Thus), the newest fundamentalist group, sponsor activities of a wholly different order. Crucial distinctions must be made between these two latter groups. Both seek to create conditions favorable for incorporating the West Bank. Besides their extraordinarily important work in creating settlements on the West Bank (Judea-Samaria), Gush members engaged in anti-Palestinian vigilante activity in the late 1970s, activity which they claimed was necessitated by inadequate state protection. The fact that the Gush settlers perform frontier defense duties, and are thus issued arms, makes them more difficult to control. The Karp Report (1981) found that the state did not punish most criminal assaults by Gush members.[18]

Influential members of the Gush also organized terrorist attacks against Palestinians in 1980, and some created, but lacked the authority to implement, the Temple Mount Plot in 1984. The Plot's purpose was to destroy the Dome of the Rock, a sacred Islamic shrine, which would make possible the building of the Third Temple, a condition believed necessary for the coming of the Messiah.

The Gush has been less conspicuous during the Intifada. It could not persuade the government to use harsher methods of violence against the Palestinians, and sporadic vigilante activity created tensions between the army and the settlers. The public sided with the army, which helped dissipate vigilante activity and contributed also to the decision of some to abandon the Gush.

Kach is an amorphous entity which may have been seriously damaged when its founder, Rabbi Meir Kahane, was assassinated in November 1990. Much of its violence is symbolic, though it is the only Jewish fundamentalist group which has threatened to kill Jews, those who are "left-wing, secular, and dovish."[19] So far the hostility toward other Jews has taken the form of an intimidating pernicious harassment campaign. Kach's principal concern is to intimidate Palestinians and provoke them to leave the West Bank, for Kach repudiates the Gush Emunim's view that two peoples can inhabit the same land.

Thus far the violence of the three Jewish fundamentalist groups has been limited, but the potentialities and consequences are great. One such consequence, Sprinzak notes, is the gradual raising of Israel's threshold for violence as a means of coping with political conflict and the potential deterioration of democracy as a result.

American politics encourages single-issue campaigns. When Protestant fundamentalists began Operation Rescue in 1988, they naturally sought support from other Christians, Jews, and various secular elements. The organization's direct-action tactics have two dimensions. Members assault others and at the same time seek to become victims or martyrs themselves in what might be called a "sacrificial war." The two kinds of tactics are not unique to Operation Rescue, but it has developed its own style. With regard to the first tactic, militants systematically harass highly vulnerable pregnant women. They organize sit-ins which block access to abortion clinics; threaten physicians and clinic personnel; and damage property. This has led, Ginsburg observes, to a situation in which private guards, bomb checks, and escorts for patients are now considered essential for most facilities. The hostility these actions create is partly disarmed by the willingness of Operation Rescue militants to become "victims" themselves, in imitation of the martyred Christ. Thus, members generate sympathy while simultaneously reinforcing their own commitment to the cause. "Being dragged by the neck to a paddy wagon is an epiphany."[20]

Although Operation Rescue claims that secular groups, particularly the civil rights movement, provided models for its tactics, American fundamentalists earlier employed similar tactics, particularly in the temperance movements of the late nineteenth and early twentieth centuries.[21] The pattern is a familiar form of protest in the history of religions.

To resist the "undeclared war" on fetal life, Operation Rescue leader Randall Terry employs a fierce rhetoric. He believes, Ginsburg indicates, that the organization's activities will be the spearhead of a drive to return America to its religious roots. "This is going to be the seedbed of revival in the church, the locomotive to bring reformation in our culture. When the Lord put the vision in my heart, it was not just to rescue babies and mothers but to rescue the country. This is just the first domino to fall." Nonetheless, by the standards of fundamentalist violence described in these essays or by those articulated elsewhere, the scale and object of Operation Rescue's militance so far have remained quite limited. Only haredi activities are more restricted and their purposes less ambitious.

In the first three years of Operation Rescue's life, its assaults on abortion clinics were effective.[22] In 1990 signs of disintegration appeared as the organization reeled from a double blow—denunciation by major religious communities, and the cumulative impact of legal costs and arrests. "Phase II," a new strategy, began in June 1990, when the national group altered the timing and geography of its assaults. Instead of encouraging local groups to attack clinics for a few days at a time, it concentrated resources for the purpose of laying siege to individual clinics for long periods. By uniting pro-life and rescue forces into one mighty army with one specific focus, it hoped to wage "an all-out holy war on the child-killing industry—one mill at a time." Significantly, its targets were clinics in the "heartland" and smaller towns, where public sentiment was more supportive. Dobbs Ferry, New York, was besieged for six months (1990), and the next year hundreds of rescuers from all parts of the country gathered in Wichita, Kansas, to close abortion clinics for three months, producing considerable national interest and inducing some three thousand arrests.

Among the unintended consequences of its activism, Operation Rescue clearly helped to rejuvenate pro-choice movements, which had become relatively dormant after *Roe v. Wade*, a revival which was stimulated as well by the impact of successive conservative appointments to the Supreme Court. Those movements have tied Operation Rescue up in damaging legal suits. Although the balance of forces within the political community has not yet been changed, Operation Rescue has helped to polarize Americans more strongly on both sides of the abortion issue, and this may be a critical achievement. The passions evoked concerning what one side calls "murder" and "holocaust" and the other deems a "fundamental right" militate against a political resolution of the problem. Unless a resolution of this sort occurs, the issue could have an enormously destructive impact on the American party system and even the nation's constitutional life. One thing seems certain: those who raise an issue with such deep emotional resonance for the community will not be deeply or permanently affected by legal barriers and penalties. Organizations may be destroyed, but new and more ingenious ones will take their place.

The Impact on Other Religious and Ethnic Communities

The effort to redefine or reestablish a political identity based on religion is inspired by the conviction that social harmony will result, but social harmony rarely occurs—certainly not in the short run. Instead, divisions within the parent religious community often become greater, and ancient hostilities between religious communities are revived or serious new ones are created. Ethnic cleavages are rarely overcome. Even when they do not treat the subject directly, the essays in this part of the volume reveal such a pattern.

Tambiah (whose subject, Sri Lanka, is a multireligious society) and Roy (who is concerned with Afghanistan, where only Islam is relevant) treat the theme explicitly and at length. Theravada Buddhist fundamentalism in Sri Lanka began in the late nineteenth century as a protest against giving Christians special privileges. In a pattern reminiscent of the growth of fundamentalism in other multireligious societies, the oppressed gradually became oppressors; an initial reaction against legal and political exclusivism was transformed into a pursuit of exclusivist policies favoring Sinhalese Buddhists. The dynamic seemed to boomerang, however. Hindus and Muslims became even more hostile to the Buddhists, and violence within Buddhist ranks emerged. One example was the decimation of many of the older monks by the younger ones. Simultaneously, the number of Tamil rebel groups, many of whom are hostile to each other, also grew, the latest count being thirty-five.[23] The conflict has stimulated a new Muslim self-consciousness, and the Sri Lanka Muslim Congress has asked for an autonomous region separate from Buddhist and Hindu areas. The original vision of harmony becomes more and more obscure.

The Afghan dynamic is similar and demonstrates that a community with one religious identity may experience intense hostilities.[24] Rifts between Sunni and Shi'ites have intensified. Roy chronicles the inability of Sunni and Shi'ite fundamentalists to cooperate even for limited military purposes against the Soviets. Shi'ites follow Iran's lead while Sunni fundamentalists associate themselves with Iran's antagonist, Saudi Arabia. Fundamentalists have added at least three new cleavages to those ancient rivalries of the traditional Sunni communities, further splitting the seven-party alliance, which in 1991 was still unable to accomplish its purpose of ousting the government the Soviets left behind.

In Iran the size of the Shi'ite community is overwhelming and the clerical establishment has prevented the fragmentation visible in Afghanistan, let alone the gruesome bitter strife between Shi'ite groups in Lebanon. Nonetheless, Iran's largest religious minority, the Baha'i, whose history since the birth of the religion in the nineteenth century has been punctuated by savage Shi'ite pogroms, has suffered enormously since the revolution. The Baha'i may be a special case because Shi'ites consider them to be apostates, which in Islam is punishable by death. In other cases, the regime has pledged to follow a "generous policy" based on 'Ali's precedents, though Jews, Christians, and Zoroastrians remain apprehensive.[25] The efforts to convert the Sunni of Iran are bitterly resented and have alarmed neighboring Muslim countries. It is clear that the new Shi'ite common identity has worked to enable Iranian Persians to dominate more thoroughly the non-Persian communities—Azerbaijani Turks, Kurds, Arabs, Baluchis, and Turkomans. Moves by Azerbaijani Turks and Kurds to gain ethnic autonomy have been crushed. At the very minimum, ethnic hostilities in the new Iran seem as great as they were in its predecessor.

After achieving power, Khomeini tried to export the revolution as an Islamic one, but the Sunni could not be persuaded. Even Sunni fundamentalists who shared political aspirations grew increasingly hostile. One problem was the unanticipated consequences of employing ancient doctrines, for the ideological sources of the Sunni radicals are inextricably linked to a fierce anti-Shi'ite sentiment. On the Shi'ite's side, the renewed concern with the beginnings of their sect resuscitated memories of Sunni persecution.[26]

Kramer notes interesting exceptions. The Tawhid movement of Lebanon is the only Sunni fundamentalist movement that "unashamedly embraced Iran as its model," and the Tunisian "Renaissance" Islamic party and the Palestinian Islamic Jihad expressed sympathy for Iran's revolution. Despite these counterexamples, so often does Shi'ite fundamentalism increase tensions with the Sunni that one is tempted to say that where a Sunni fundamentalist movement did not already exist, it would be a natural response to a Shi'ite one, and vice-versa. (En passant, one might note that the development of Hindu fundamentalism in the late nineteenth century was a crucial condition in similar developments among Indian Muslims and Sikhs.)

Israeli fundamentalist groups share a common hostility to Christian missionary activity in Israel, but each expresses it differently. The haredim have developed a formal structure (the "Brotherhood") to combat Christian missionary activity. (They have nothing comparable to combat secularism.) The Brotherhood organizes constant spying, frequent demonstrations, and occasional assaults on church property. Christians were the targets of Rabbi Kahane's most ferocious rhetoric: he argued that God established Israel to punish the Gentiles. Gush Emunim's animosity toward Christians is deep, but the movement is concerned more with the Palestinians, as is Kahane's Kach party.

In the Middle East, Christians have been deeply affected by the growth of Islamic and Jewish fundamentalism. In Lebanon and in Egypt (which have the largest Christian populations, 45 and 12 percent, respectively) Christians have become militant. Throughout the entire region Christian emigration has been great. On both sides of the Jordan the Christian population has declined from 400,000 to 170,000. Jerusalem may soon be "bereft of Christianity as a living religion," housing only sacred churches and icons.[27]

Operation Rescue's initial aim of uniting Protestants, Catholics, and Jews in a common effort is not entirely without success. Still, Protestants greatly dominate the organization, and even though a Catholic element played an important role in Wichita (1991), the much more important fact is that Catholics, who initiated direct-action tactics on the abortion issue, are less attracted to such tactics now. Moreover, if the larger agenda of Operation Rescue of "Christianizing America" was a topic for discussion, the organization would likely lose the little ecumenical appeal it now has. Operation Rescue's tactics have also split the much larger pro-life movement, and provoked considerable ire from both conservative and liberal Protestants outside the movement. Nonetheless, the pro-life movement has become much more Protestant; and this in part is attributable to reactions which Operation Rescue activities have produced, signifying, Ginsburg believes, an acceleration of the trend away from separatism, a traditional feature of American fundamentalism until the 1970s.

International Implications

With the exception of Operation Rescue, each example demonstrates that militant fundamentalist activity can produce important international consequences. Fundamentalists usually see themselves engaged in an international struggle. Prolonged domestic violence and violence which occasions the collapse of a government produce significant international results, especially if the state has a strategic international location or is an important international actor.

Struggles in the sectarian state have a special international significance also because the boundaries of its partial communities often transcend those of the state. The simplest example which involves only two major state actors is Sri Lanka, where the plight of the Hindu Tamils and the large number of refugees in India inevitably brought India, with its massive Hindu population, deeply into Sri Lankan politics. No other state felt sufficiently affected and had enough power to become so deeply involved. Initially, India supported the Tamil rebels and gave them indispensable sanctuaries. But India did not want a separate Tamil state, which eventually became the objective of the rebels; and as a result of the 1987 Indo–Sri Lanka accord India dispatched 50,000 soldiers to help terminate the insurrection. Three years later some 1,250 Indian soldiers had been killed, and in May 1991 a disastrous repercussion of

Indian involvement occurred when Rajiv Gandhi was assassinated by Tamil separatists who felt betrayed by the 1987 accord with Sri Lanka, which Gandhi had authored.

A less dramatic fact is that all the Tamil militant groups (there are perhaps thirty-five) have international links with various terrorist groups, usually groups within the PLO. The government, in its turn, has received assistance from Belgium, China, Singapore, Pakistan, Israel, South Africa, the United States, and Britain. Sri Lankan Tamils have responded by some successful lobbying in the Western states to cut off this aid.

When the identity of a community is being altered, an inevitable consequence of a major revolution, the international impact is magnified further. The Iranian constitution of 1979 gives some indication of this new identity. Its preamble states that sovereignty "belongs to God," not the people.[28] The fifth article stipulates that the constitution will remain in force until the Mahdi (Messiah) arrives. The National Assembly became the Islamic Assembly. Neither citizenship nor residency is a requirement for membership on the Leadership Council. A twelve-man Council of Guardians, six of whom are drawn from the clergy, has the power to veto legislation found to be contrary to Islamic law.

Iran's enormous domestic upheaval seriously shook the Middle East, and with it the world. American support of the shah gave Shi'ite fundamentalists reasons to believe that they had to oppose the United States (the "Great Satan") everywhere. They reversed all of Iran's existing international commitments, pulled Iran out of CENTO, and recognized the PLO, describing the struggle against Israel as a "religious and political duty." A "war against the West" was launched, one carried on through new alliances, terrorist activity, and ferocious language. Normally during the Cold War, when a Middle Eastern state (e.g., Egypt or Iraq) broke with one side, it always became identified with the other. Iran was different; it remained hostile to the Soviet Union, and its hostility intensified in the wake of a new Iranian concern for Soviet Muslims, the Iran-Iraq war (the Soviets armed their Iraqi ally), the Soviet invasion of Afghanistan, and the crackdown on Iranian Marxist elements.

The policy of hostility to both East and West was meant to demonstrate that Iran could stand alone and could unify Islam, or at least its radical fundamentalist elements. Tensions between international aspirations and domestic concerns plagued Iran as it does most revolutionary states. Iran's self-declared international mission as the leader of a radically aggressive new Islam was everywhere compromised by its domestic reconstitution as a Shi'ite state, and its activities struck a responsive chord only in some states with Shi'ite populations. But even here Iran was often disappointed.

In neighboring Iraq, where a Shi'ite majority exists, Iranian hopes, despite an initial favorable response, were frustrated most. Sunni elements, having good historic reasons to feel threatened, backed Saddam's vigorous measures. One surprising result was that Saddam, made anxious by Iranian efforts and greedy by the prospect of gain which the spectacle of the apparent weakness of a neighbor undergoing revolution always produces, launched the Iran-Iraq war. The war did much to drive home the cost of revolutionary policies to the Iranians, and Shi'ites in Iraq remained loyal as differences between Persian and Arab Shi'ites endured.[29] Some Iraqi Shi'ite militants who immigrated to Iran became instruments of Iranian policy, mounting attacks against Sunni and Western states.

Iran's effort, Kramer notes, "had its greatest impact in Lebanon, the most westward and remote outpost of the Shi'ite world." There were many reasons for this paradoxical result. Lebanon had no government to help organize resistance to Iran's intrigues, and unlike Iraq, Lebanon had no memory of recent Shi'ite uprisings which could have been the incentive for preventive measures. On the Shi'ite side, strife in Lebanon had increased the suffering and dislocation far beyond that of other Shi'ites in the Arab world. The Shi'ites, moreover, had been active before the Iranian revolution and the foreign enemy, the West, could be identified unmistakably after the Israeli invasion and the multinational force arrived. Accordingly, many of Hizbullah's attacks were planned to support Iran during the Iran-Iraq war. Initially, Iraqi interests in Lebanon were attacked, then the campaign spread to Kuwait to compel Kuwait to withdraw support for Iraq, and finally (1986) Hizbullah launched a series of terrorist bombings in Paris to force France to stop supplying Iraq with arms.

In the other Arab states, Iranian efforts produced more difficulties than advantages. Although Iran excited the hopes of Shi'ite populations and often supplied rebels with material aid, Sunni resistance did not melt and the anxiety about Iranian influence over the Shi'ites undoubtedly contributed to the enormous financial help the Persian Gulf states gave Iraq in its long war against Iran. The attempted coup by Shi'ite elements in Bahrain led to the creation of the Gulf Cooperation Council, a body set up to coordinate security and intelligence matters among Arab states of the Gulf, which later ironically played an important role in mobilizing those states against the Iraqi invasion of Kuwait.

The Iranian revolution made the struggle for the loyalty of the Shi'ite populations much more significant in the international life of the Muslim world, but it did not create the phenomenon. The shah financed Shi'ite opposition to Saddam Hussein and gave refuge to Iraqi Shi'ite exiles and fugitives. Roy says that the Afghani Shi'ites always took their lead from Iranian governments. Until 1971 the shah claimed sovereign rights over Bahrain, which gave a familiar ring to a 1979 announcement by a prominent Iranian cleric, Ayatollah Ruhani, that he would lead a revolutionary movement to annex Bahrain unless it adopted an "Islamic form of government."[30]

From the very inception of the Saudi dynasty after World War I, Sunni reactions to Shi'ites during the pilgrimage periods created profound diplomatic problems. In 1927 Iran refused to recognize the Saudi government, would not allow Iranians to participate in the annual pilgrimage, and even supported a call for a Shi'ite conference in India to rally all Muslims to expel Ibn Sa'ud by force from the holy places. In 1943 Iran broke relations with Saudi Arabia over the same issue, and when demonstrations led to a second break in 1988, it seemed as though nothing new had occurred except that this time Iranians had helped organize the demonstrations to "profess a unity of purpose with the Sunni," a novel purpose indeed, and one which backfired.[31]

If Iran's experience demonstrates that great international changes may occur in the wake of radical domestic transformations, the Afghan experience illustrates something else, for here great international developments materialized without significant domestic transformation. The armies of a superpower were involved directly and, therefore, when Soviet troops experienced their first defeat since the 1920s, the event had enormous significance, making a vital contribution to the end of the Cold War, to the initiation of perestroika, and most of all to the loss of belief in the cause, which was the source of Soviet international aspirations and domestic legitimacy. The Islamic forces in Afghanistan mounted the first successful resistance to a foreign power which was not based on either nationalist or socialist principles. The pride it generated among Muslims, and the Afghan efforts to increase Islamic solidarity, contributed to the growth of Islamic fundamentalism in the Soviet Union, Central Asia, and the Indian subcontinent. The Saudis, who largely financed the Afghanis, gained important leverage over Sunni fundamentalist movements in the non-Arab world. Because Afghan internal divisions persist, foreign powers (Pakistan, Saudi Arabia, the United States, and Iran) became deeply involved in the crosscurrents of Afghan domestic politics.

The international implications of haredi Jewish fundamentalism are much less apparent. Still, haredi communities do extend overseas, and because the Israeli elements are not economically self-sufficient, foreign financial support is sought to reduce the dependence on the government, a dependence which always undermines haredi claims that they have withdrawn from the state. (Indeed, sometimes the violence against other Jews seems designed to attract economic support.) In 1988 overseas supporters got conspicuously involved in one parliamentary election.

Kach and Gush Emunim activities could have much more serious consequences. Kach wants to remake Israel into a wholly Jewish state by forcing the government to either expel the Arab population or allow it to be expelled, and Kach has proposed an international terrorist organization modeled after that of the PLO! Gush Emunim finds such policies quite distasteful, but agrees that the reestablishment of Israel's biblical boundaries is essential and inevitable. The aggressive Gush settlement policies in the West Bank, which the Israeli government subsequently accepted and expanded, is a provocative and persistent international issue, one which is a special irritation for Israel's major ally, the United States. Israel's ability to deal with the Palestinian question is hampered by the very real possibility of a violent response from the two groups, which, as members of the military, have weapons. In view of secular sympathies for retaining the land, this situation could under certain circumstances spark a civil war. An unlikely, but yet conceivable, Israeli move to annex the West Bank would throw the gauntlet down to the international community and could provoke sanctions. Sprinzak's conclusion, based largely on the negligible casualty statistics, that the influence of fundamentalists is marginal now, seems warranted only in the absence of efforts to change the status of the land.

Religious Features of the Violence

Islam has received disproportionate attention because recently violence in the name of Islam has been very extensive, and Islamic communities are located in volatile and politically significant areas of the world. Many might wonder whether Islamic fundamentalists, compared to those of other religions, are more likely to be violent. Keddie and Monian speak directly to the issue, at least as far as it concerns the Shi'ites, reminding us that the Twelvers, who are Shi'ism's mainstream and dominant in Iran, have a long history of passivity which is often overlooked when we discuss recent episodes of violence. The martyrdom of Husayn, the grandson of Muhammad, probably the decisive act in establishing the sect, and often seen as the source for the legion of self-martyrs associated with Shi'ism, say Keddie and Monian, has produced no greater militancy within Shi'ism than Christ's martyrdom did in Christianity.

There is much truth in this last claim. Richardson and Wilkinson, our best students of comparative war statistics, note that every major religion has its peaceful and violent periods, and that Christian religious wars have occurred more often, been more intense, and been more internecine in character than those waged by any other religious community! Islam is second on their index of religious militancy; Buddhism is at the bottom of the scale.[32] Although these statistics refer to events before 1950 and the violence described in our volume concerns a later period, the statistics should make one cautious in generalizing about host religions from the very limited sample of fundamentalist experiences available here.

All major religions have enormous potentialities for creating and directing violence, which is why wars of religion are exceedingly ferocious and difficult to resolve. When a religious justification is offered for a cause which might otherwise be justified in political or economic terms, the struggle is intensified and complicated enormously. There are many reasons why this happens, perhaps the most important being that religious conflict involves fundamental values and self-definition; and struggles involving questions of identity, notoriously, are the most difficult to compromise because they release our greatest passions.[33]

Some religions may have a higher propensity for violence, but nothing in the experiences discussed here sheds light on the issue. The case studies do indicate that fundamentalists can exploit the violence a religion contains, even when that religion is rarely perceived as having a violent potential. Thus, the depressing scenes in Sri Lanka for nearly forty years conflict radically with the reputation Buddhism has earned as a religion of peace. "Nationalist demagogues" and "democratic politicians" anxious to forge a new "collective identity" and "win elections" have, Tambiah laments, corrupted a great religion, the mainspring of a civilization whose greatest emperor, Asoka, purportedly made nonviolence and a multireligious society the basis of his state. The principal participants in that violence are monks who "traditionally are required by disciplinary rules not only to refrain from killing but also to be nowhere near marching armies and the traffic of arms."

In a secular world, violence is normally understood as a means to an end whereby participants strive to increase efficiency wherever possible by discarding less productive structures and methods. That propensity exists among fundamentalist groups; to Keddie and Monian that seems the only relevant feature. But Kramer notes that there is another dimension. Hizbullah aims to implement Islamic law, and its actions have to be made consistent with the Islamic law of war which distinguishes legitimate targets and methods. Clerics can interpret that law, but they cannot make it infinitely elastic. Obviously the furies violence releases cannot always be governed, and Kramer elaborates different reasons for this loss of control. Still, he notes that the firm religious direction of Hizbullah distinguishes its violence from that of the other sectarian militias of Lebanon. Kramer's thesis that the violence of religious groups often has a sacred dimension is one which the literature rarely addresses, but it is one which is both correct and critical.[34] The fundamentalist groups described here use violence in ways which exhibit that sacred dimension, one derived from the symbols, rites, and precedents of the parent religious communities.

The other contributors to part 3 of this volume do not refer directly to sacred violence or sacred war; nonetheless, information contained in their accounts enables readers to make relevant differentiations. Of the various possible distinctions, I will mention four: religious justifications or purposes,[35] occasions, objects, and methods. The distinctions overlap, because the same theological source justifying violence, for example, may suggest appropriate occasions and methods as well. The Shi'ite account of Husayn's death is a good example; during the 1960s, the annual mourning ceremonies became common occasions for violence, culminating in a "sacrificial war" appealing directly to Husayn's example to stimulate appetites for martyrdom.

Two principal religious sources are used to justify violence: the "founding myth" (to borrow a term from political theory)[36] and millenarian or messianic expectations. The first source reflects a belief that a return to a community's origins will renew its initial vitality, while the second refers to divine promises concerning the future.

In most cases, both themes are likely to be important. But the individual essays here focus on one or the other. Tambiah highlights the founding myth of the Theravada Buddhists contained in the fifth-century chronicle Mahavamsa, which describes the settlement of Sri Lanka as a refuge for Buddhists and their subsequent bloody struggles against Hindus wishing to destroy Buddhism.[37] Since the tenth century, this myth has been invoked periodically to mobilize Buddhist masses. Normally, the terms of a myth are sufficiently general to enable believers to apply them to many different enemies; but a striking and unusual feature of this myth is that the same contending parties are still on the island.[38]

Unlike the Sinhalese myth, the Shi'ite one traditionally induces believers to turn their violence from others toward themselves. Astonishing outbursts of weeping and self-flagellation occur in the vast annual processions during Ashura to commemorate "the martyr who was not given a proper burial and his [Husayn's] ideals which were never implemented." The most common interpretation of his death was that Shi'ites should accept their lot and submit to illegitimate powers even if that required them to conceal their identity as Shi'ites (taqiyya).[39] Until the Twelfth Imam (the Mahdi, or messiah) called the community to arm itself and establish universal justice, nothing could be done.

In the new 1960s interpretation, action became the most appropriate response to this event and the Iranian masses began to see the shah as Yazid, the archtyrant and assassin of Husayn.[40] Thus, the "ideological key" was cut for the revolution and for the altered self-perceptions of Shi'ites elsewhere. In Lebanon the mourning ceremonies became occasions for extensive teachings on the "activist postures" of Shi'ite ideology in special buildings constructed for the purpose, known appropriately as *husaniyya*.

Keddie and Monian contend that this new interpretation "diluted, even negated," Shi'ism. But passivity and militancy are requisites for any community's survival; and all major religious traditions necessarily have conflicting models, or conflicting interpretations of the same model, for action. (It is also true, as the discussion below indicates, that Ashura was considered a moment of potential violence even when the the Shi'ite community was not militant.)

Because traditions necessarily depend upon interpretations rather than legislation for change, precedents cannot be annulled. Precedents can be put aside, but only temporarily; later generations will always revive them, a fact which lies behind Bernard Lewis's characterization of the history of the Shi'ites as exhibiting intermittent periods of activism and quietism.[41]

This pattern is a typical one for messianic religions.[42] In its founding period, Shi'ism was a collection of millenarian and often violent sects known as the Ghulat (Exaggerators),[43] whose interpretations of Husayn's death resemble those of the 1960s.[44] Subsequently, a quietist dimension became the dominant one through the innovations of the Sixth Imam, Ja'far al-Sadiq (d. 765), who provided a coherent order which enabled the community to survive and to cope with sporadic messianic outbursts.[45]

Sunni fundamentalists believe that a truly Islamic society existed only in the period of the Prophet and the first four Caliphs and that their revolt is a jihad to recover the spirit of Islam's original enterprises. In *Islam and Resistance in Afghanistan,* Roy notes that "the return to first things makes it possible not only to circumvent the accretion of tradition but also the social stratum which manipulates that tradition, namely the clergy."[46] Their anticlerical view, he says, makes it easier for Sunni fundamentalists to incorporate critical modern conceptions into an Islamic idiom.

The traditional clergy-led Afghan jihad—a repeated activity in the last few centuries—always began as a struggle to unify the tribes, but ultimate unification was impossible because the military strategy kept the tribal bonds intact. The fundamentalist jihad has a different character because it aims to destroy old structures and create new ones, leading Roy to argue that the Afghan fundamentalist military strategy must be an expression of Marxist revolutionary war theory. This last point is only partially true, because the classical jihad of Islam's founding period is very different from the traditional Afghan jihad. Classical jihad has a revolutionary purpose,[47] The founding myth of Islam also imposes serious restraints because its model for constitutional forms, the Caliphate, is no longer viable. This weakness contributes to an inability to create constitutional structures that plagues Sunni fundamentalists throughout the Muslim world.[48]

Messianism inspires Jewish fundamentalists, Sprinzak emphasizes. Compared to mainstream Orthodox Jews, who are also messianists, fundamentalists live in heightened expectation of the Messiah's appearance. Yet each of the Jewish fundamentalist elements understands the role of human action differently. The haredim wish to protect the boundaries of the "righteous remnant," for the survival of that community is seen as the precondition for fulfilling the messianic promise. Because Jews are not supposed to shape history, violence against the state cannot be justified. This is so even though the Zionists who established a state without the messiah are often described as "Amalekites," the traditional archetype of pure evil in the Jewish tradition. (The Amalekites were a desert tribe which treacherously attacked Israel as the exodus from Egypt began, and there is a rabbinic tradition that in every generation Amalekites try to destroy Israel.)[49]

Gush Emunim, on the other hand, stresses the decisive role of action, and the particular requirement to resettle the biblical lands, Judea and Samaria (the West Bank), to complete the messianic process. Because the secular state has been committed to regaining the land, it views that state as legitimate, even in some respects divine.

The Gush sometimes perceives the Palestinians as Amalekites. Kach is more emphatic and emphasizes violence as a purifying source reflecting a traditional messianic theme that sustained antinomian activity creates the "new Jew."[50] But Kach's messianism, Sprinzak makes clear, is so idiosyncratic that one has difficulty verifying its sources within the Jewish messianic tradition. Repeated references to Amalekites by all Jewish fundamentalists indicate that a complete picture of the messianic process requires more attention to a group's founding myth than is provided here. The model forthe haredi is the outraged action of the High Priest Pinchas, Aaron's successor, who killed two persons, blatantly defiling Israel's most holy site, a deed enabling Israel to enter the Promised Land. Gush Emunim has its own founding precedents, namely, the conquest and settlement of the Promised Land[51] (the books of Joshua and Judges).

Messianism was manifestly present in the Iranian revolution.[52] A clause in Iran's constitution anticipates the coming of the Hidden Imam, and his birthday has always been one of the four major holy days in Iran's calendar, along with Ashura and the birthdays of 'Ali and Husayn, dates all connected to the founding myth. After the 1960s Khomeini served as *marja'*, whose authority represents a guardianship on behalf of the Hidden Imam, and as such he was able to give a strictly religious institution a crucial political function.[53] Khomeini was called Imam, which has the connotation of a messianic precursor. Abdulaziz Sachedina's personal account of the revolution's early days indicates that a sense of the Mahdi's imminence was widespread, greatly influencing the revolution's flavor.[54] Arjomand stresses that the ability of the Iranian clergy to use messianic exaltation without losing control of it was a decisive and unusual feature of the revolution.[55] Kramer links Hizbullah's vision of an all embracing Islamic state to messianic expectations.

Sunni millenarianism is rare. But it does occur and is important, as the startling attack on the Grand Mosque of Mecca in 1979 made clear.[56] Two years earlier, the Egyptian group Takfir wa-Hijara declared its leader to be the Mahdi. Afghan Sunni tribesmen are no strangers to millenarian enthusiasms. Roy notes that "Afghanistan is different from North Africa in that Sufism, fundamentalism, millenarianism, and the anti-colonialist struggle go hand in hand. . . . The fundamentalists aim at the total reconstruction of political relations on the lines of the first Muslim political community. No longer state and law but utopia, the millennium and revolution."[57] Paradoxically, millenarianism is associated with the traditional Afghan jihad, a phenomenon which the new breed of Islamic radicals find inappropriate to the contemporary situation, and hence an anomaly worth exploring.[58]

In Sri Lanka the belief that the millenarian promise (leading to the expulsion of the Tamils) would be fulfilled in the twenty-five hundredth year of the Buddhist era "seems to have been well established by the fifteenth century." The extensive preparations for that date (1956) were crucial in precipitating the initial entry of Theravada Buddhist monks into politics and in the subsequent riots—the major modern turning point in Sri Lanka's history.[59]

Elsewhere in this volume, Harjot Oberoi writes of the critical importance of millenarianism for Sikh fundamentalists, who produced some of the most gruesome terrorist episodes in the 1980s. "Of all the indigenous religious communities in India, Sikhism possesses the most advanced paradigm of millennial thought and practice. For much of their history . . . Sikhs have opted to deal with major social crises—state oppression, economic upheavals, colonialism, collapse of semiotic categories—by invoking the millenarian paradigm."[60]

Millenarian expectations sometimes fuel violence and most fundamentalist groups have a millenarian component. Even when they do not have an explicit millenarian claim, fundamentalist groups usually want to return to themes expressed in the founding of the larger religious community, a point at which millenarian expectations usually loom large.

Millenarian justifications do not oblige specific actions, but they are related to a likely range of activities. Normally, millenarian themes induce passivity. Among Christians this often became pacifism. Orthodox Jews in the Diaspora accepted the legitimacy of existing governments in all matters except those involving denial of religious commitment, while Shi'ites normally believed that a denial of one's faith to escape persecution was appropriate. One Shi'ite messianic offshoot, the Baha'i, is a pacifist community, a rare product in Islam, one which began as a terrorist body, the Babis, in nineteenth-century Iran. The common element in these contradictory positions of passivity and activism is the extreme response produced in either manifestation. Less clear are the conditions under which one or the other predominate.

In American fundamentalist movements, millenarianism has always been a major theme.[61] Operation Rescue uses apocalyptic language extensively, but serious discussions of the millenarian theme are avoided as "playing church games when the Lord's business is to be done in the real world of struggle."[62] The avoidance of the millenarian discussions in Operation Rescue has a political rationale; it helps attract the broadest possible secular and religious support base. Authority for the organization's view on abortion comes from Scripture,[63] and Proverbs 24:11 provides its mission and a name: "Rescue those who are unjustly sentenced to death: don't stand back and let them die." But one of the organization's striking characteristics is its apparent indifference to developing a coherent theological doctrine.

Besides providing justifications, religious traditions may influence the occasions, targets, and methods for violence. All religions hallow moments of time and sanctify points of space, objects, and actions. Sacred times and sacred sites are commemorated with rites and ceremonies attracting large numbers of people. At such times and in such places, the community is expressing its distinctive identity. Powerful passions will be evoked; and when trouble strikes, those passions are susceptible to manipulation and may even explode spontaneously, or without conscious design. References to the importance of such happenings abound in the essays.

The two most important events in the Iranian revolution that aroused public consciousness and involved great numbers of participants occurred during Ashura ceremonies. The arrest of Khomeini (1963) set off great demonstrations, resulting in the massacre of hundreds of unarmed persons. Fifteen years later, clerical elements transformed the ceremonies into massive political demonstrations. In daily marches, a "sacrificial war" was waged where the willingness, indeed the eagerness, of the demonstrators to martyr themselves dissolved the army's morale and broke the back of the shah's government. During the 1960s, the determination of the religious community was immensely inspired and even fortified by strikes against its most important symbols—for example, a government campaign highlighted by the imposition of a new calendar, making the pre-Islamic Persian state the basis of Iranian identity.

Ashura, the highest emotional moment in the Shi'ite calendar, commemorates the martyrdom of Husayn at Karbala. Ever since Europeans first witnessed these ceremonies in the seventeenth century, Kippenberg tells us, they have noted that the state employed force to keep the demonstrations from erupting into violent episodes.[64] Outside Iran, a similar expectation exists. During Ashura, fighting broke out in Bahrain (1923 and 1953), Iraq (1972, 1974, and 1979),[65] Lebanon (1974), and Saudi Arabia (1979 and 1980). In the vast Ottoman Empire, Ashura ceremonies were proscribed for centuries. In at least one successor state (Saudi Arabia), similar restrictions prevail; and in another, Lebanon, until the 1940s Ashura was observed "out of public view in order to avoid offending intersectarian harmony."[66] In October 1983 an Israeli convoy inadvertently interrupted an Ashura ceremony in southern Lebanon and casualties resulted. The next day a Shi'ite cleric ruled that a "comprehensive civil opposition" against Israeli forces was required and the Israeli failure in Lebanon was sealed.[67]

Messianic myths lead believers to anticipate special moments in time. It is believed that the Mahdi will come when a new Islamic century begins. Nineteen seventy-nine was the Islamic year 1400, and the millenarian attack on Islam's holiest shrine occurred in the first hour of the first day of that century! Earlier, the prominent Sudanese Mahdi had staked his claim on the first day of the Islamic century 1300; simultaneously, a number of violent millenarian movements in Africa emerged appealing to the same dating tradition. In the 1970s the pattern repeated itself in the Middle East, and it is quite plausible that the expectation had some influence in the Iranian revolution.

Although unique dates in various messianic myths have unrivaled special significance, the most frequent occasions for violence are associated, of course, with regularly repeated ceremonies. In Israel, for example, one always expects that crowds emerging from Friday mosque services will be in an ugly mood and that the aftermath of Jewish holy days might also produce encounters. For Operation Rescue, the symbolism of the Easter weekend provides a propitious opportunity for blocking abortion clinics, but a nonreligious date, the anniversary of the *Roe v. Wade* decision, which made abortion legal and is, thus, a symbol of secularism, is the most emotionally favorable moment for its biggest and most aggressive assaults.

Normally, in Islam the respective symbols of opposing elements invite attack. Ottoman successor states aimed at putting Ashura out of public view in order to disarm Sunni hostility and muffle Shi'ite resentments. When those ceremonies happen in full view of the public, the Sunni are likely to find them obnoxious for a variety of reasons, not the least of which is that they are meant to commemorate Sunni villainy.

A similar pattern may be observed in numerous and very different religious contexts. Davis's illuminating study of sixteenth-century French Catholic and Protestant riots observes that "the occasion for most religious violence was during the time of religious worship. . . . Much of the religious riot is timed to ritual, and the violence seems often a continuation of the rite. Almost every type of public religious event has violence associated with it. . . . A Catholic mass is the occasion for an attack on the host or the interruption of a sermon, which then leads to a riot."[68] Josephus reports that the Passover pilgrimage season was the time when violence between Jew and Roman was most common.[69]

In the struggle between two religious groups, what is sacred to one is likely to be obscene to the other. Desecrations of the enemy's sacred symbols are attempts to demean identity, express contempt, and show that the symbols are really empty, that they have no power, and that no power can protect those symbols. One should expect that attacks of this sort will provoke outrage and cries for vengeance. Clearly, each religious community has its own array of vulnerable points to attack and defend. In Sri Lanka, Sinhalese civilians were attacked near Theravada Buddhism's most sacred site, the Bo Tree, in the historic pilgrimage city of Anuradhapura, immortalized in the Mahavamsa. Hindu and Buddhist temples were desecrated, Hindu priests were murdered, and a bus carrying Buddhist monks was blown up. The Wahhabi, the mainstay of the Saudi state and generally considered the first Islamic fundamentalists, have always regarded the Shi'ite veneration of the Imams and their tombs as idolatry. In the early nineteenth century they sacked Karbala, the major Shi'ite shrine city, and desecrated Husayn's tomb, and several times since they have been involved in similar incidents.

In Israel the most striking events occur in situations when two groups regard the same space as sacred and each wishes to use that space for its own particular purposes, a problem which is always present in a land which the three revealed religions regard as holy. Hence, the first violent clashes between Gush Emunim and Palestinians occurred in Hebron at the tomb of Abraham, a holy site for both Islam and Judaism and a persistent source of religious tensions. Ever since 1929 (two decades before the birth of the Israeli state) violent clashes have occurred intermittently during religious holidays at the Temple Mount (*al-haram al-sharif*), the most sacred site for both Jews and Muslims in the Holy Land,[70] where a mosque was built to commemorate a feat of Muhammad on the rock where Abraham intended to sacrifice Isaac, and this rock is within the remains of the Jewish Temple. Since 1986, three fundamentalist groups, the Gush Emunim, Kach, and an Islamic one, Hamas, regularly demonstrate at the site on important religious holy days.

A strikingly comparable situation exists in the Indian town of Ayodhya, where a Hindu temple commemorating the birthplace of the demigod King Ram, the "human incarnation of Lord Vishnu and the prime exemplar of orthodox Hindu virtues,"[71] was purportedly destroyed by conquering Muslims in the sixteenth century. On the site of the desecrated temple, a mosque, it is believed, was built. Repeated bloody clashes have occurred there, and most recently those riots have resulted in the fall of two national governments and the death of thousands.

Predictable objects of haredi violence are archaeological digs, which are always likely to disturb burial sites. The haredim are provoked because they believe that the process of messianic deliverance may be impeded by an interference with remains, for the Messiah will resurrect the dead only if their bodies—the bones—are intact. This belief explains, too, why some haredi desecrate the graves of "evil Jews"—reform rabbis and prominent Zionists—though their attacks in this regard are largely symbolic since they are careful not to disturb the bones.

Religions often sanctify methods, as the preoccupation with martyrdom among the Shi'ites indicates, where an initially successful pattern of seeking to become a victim of the shah (without necessarily resorting to violence) gave way to costly, ineffective "suicide attacks" in the Iran-Iraq war and, finally, to extraordinarily effective suicide bombings in Lebanon. But suicide is forbidden in Islam, and the Lebanese practice raised serious questions among the Shi'ite clergy who, Kramer notes, ultimately banned the practice.[72]

When the enemy is a Muslim or purports to be one, Shi'ite militants seem to have a strong propensity for assassination. The pattern is conspicuous in contemporary Iran, and outside it, too, as the practices of the Jund al-Haqq (Soldiers of Truth) in Saudi Arabia indicate. Keddie and Monian argue that the practice is instrumental or expedient; and they note that secular terror groups in Iran in the recent past used assassination more often than religious ones did. Still, this deeply rooted practice has an undeniable early ritual basis.

In early Shi'ism, some messianic groups expressed their resistance through assassination with ritual weapons designed to humiliate (desanctify?) their victims. Thus, the Khunnag strangled their victims with scarves, the Kaysaniyya beat them to death with wooden cudgels, and the Assassins employed daggers. In each case, the necessity to get to close range to complete the deed precluded escape, which in effect made assassination a prelude to martyrdom.

We do not know the rationale for the practice of assassination with ritual weapons, but it may derive from precedents in Islam's founding period, when methods appropriate for a jihad against members in the community who pretended to be Muslims were distinguished from those appropriate against persons outside the community. Although not as strong among the Sunni, the pattern can be found there as well.

When the Afghan group Hizb-i-Islami broke with its partners in the resistance, it initiated an assassination campaign. The assassins of the Egyptian Anwar Sadat justified their deed by citing precedents which came from the life of the Prophet distinguishing the types of jihad. A puzzling feature of that assassination was the assassins' refusal to make plans either for their escape or for measures to consolidate gains achieved by the assassination.[73]

The Shi'ite practice of setting movie houses and banks on fire in Iranian towns appears as a dramatic form of ritual violence, one which ultimately played a major role in bringing the shah's government down. The movie houses and banks were seen as polluted objects, symbols of secularism and the West. Fire, of course, is a traditional method of purification, one often prescribed for hated symbols and a practice which lies deep in history of the revealed religions.[74] Normally, the site was empty when it was set alight, but one movie house was full and some four hundred died. The event was crucial in unseating the shah, because Khomeini was successful in getting the enraged population to hold the government culpable. In fact, as Keddie and Monian show, the fire was set by Khomeini supporters, who may or may not have been authorized to do so.

For the haredi, as for Muslims, stoning has ritual significance. Zealous acts of violence in rabbinic law are supposedly expressions of the whole community, so individuals qua individuals refrain from violence and acts of violent zeal normally occur at night, when the anonymity this ritual requires is more likely to be protected. The rabbinic tradition allows zealous killing only in three cases and permits the potential victim to kill in self-defense, which may explain why the violence does not produce death.[75]

Conclusions

The initial element in explaining variations in the purpose, intensity, impact, and persistence of the violence exhibited by fundamentalists is the domestic political context, and the sectarian and the secular, or nation-state, are the two kinds of political context represented here. The first contains several partial communities, the most important being the religious ones, which generally justify their institutions as divinely sanctioned. The ethnic and national partial communities of the sectarian state also have significance. In the secular or nation-state, the community embraces all persons and its institutions are justified as human creations.

Because fundamentalists develop or elaborate the core values of larger religious communities, their potentialities are maximized in the sectarian state where a predominant religious community exists, for example, Iran, Sri Lanka, and Afghanistan. In these cases, the *immediate* objective is revolution and the violence has persisted, sometimes intermittently, for considerable periods of time. Only in Iran, where a revolution was achieved and its international ambitions apparently curbed, is it possible to believe that the cycle of violence might have run its current course. Still, there is no clear resolution in the Iranian case, as the circumstances surrounding the publication of *The Satanic Verses* in various countries and the assassination of former premier Bakhtiar in France suggest.

The following chapters indicate that the critical variables shaping the different processes and outcomes of militancy are: the strength of traditional religious leaders and their willingness to support or resist fundamentalist activities, the responses of other religious communities, the perceptions of the external enemy, and the ways in which violence was actually used. The essays do not investigate these matters systematically, but they do provide much information which others could use for that purpose. Critical variables not discussed here are the power and self-confidence of secular groups.

Revolutionary aspirations also inspire fundamentalist violence from the weaker religious communities in a sectarian state, and quite obviously the resulting patterns differ from those stemming from a dominant religious community. All our examples of the weaker religious communities derive from the Shi'ites in the Arab world facing governments firmly controlled either by antagonistic confessional elements (Saudi Arabia, Kuwait, Bahrain) or by a cohesive secular-Sunni element (Iraq). The resulting violence in these states has persisted for generations, but it has not been very intense. The extraordinary weakness of Shi'ite fundamentalists in the Persian Gulf states makes them more vulnerable to Iranian influence. They cannot operate in their own countries. They are compelled to seek international targets, but this activity may seem more natural because a striking ideological feature of Shi'ite fundamentalism is that the enemy has a prominent external dimension.

In Lebanon interconfessional violence originated in the wake of the state's breakdown and in the persistent competitive involvement of foreign powers. But the free hand given Syria in the wake of the Gulf War may allow that power to restore the government's powers and disarm various confessional militia. In Iraq much depends upon whether the center, or more specifically Saddam Hussein, can survive. If not, a "Lebanonization of politics" could develop too; but the major relevant foreign powers do not want and, therefore, may be able to avoid that outcome. "Lebanonization" seems most likely in situations where a predominant religious community is absent, but if existing ethnic divisions are as hostile as they appear to be in Afghanistan it could occur even when a religious community is dominant.

In the nation-state, the restraints governing the violence of fundamentalists are much greater, because efforts to capture governments are simply not credible. Militant fundamentalists may still have a revolutionary mission, but their immediate political objective is to find issues which secular parties support, albeit for secular reasons. Those issues will be much narrower in scope than they would be for militants in a sectarian state. Nonetheless, if the issues raised resonate, as they do in Israel, where they are crucial to the way the community perceives itself, the potentialities of fundamentalism in a secular state could be enormous. In the United States, Operation Rescue has helped to polarize the community further on an important issue and has made the abortion controversy even more difficult to resolve.

Although fundamentalists perceive secularism as the chief threat, militancy increases hostility within and between confessional and ethnic groups. In a sense, this always happens when a revolution is aborted, regardless of whether its purpose is secular or religious. As the Iranian experience demonstrates, it may occur even when a revolution has apparently been consummated. Violence which fails to achieve its purpose leaves very bitter legacies; and because of the baggage they must carry, fundamentalists who engage in revolution have some distinctive problems. In exhuming critical founding precedents in the parent religion, fundamentalists, whatever their intentions, find that they cannot divorce those precedents from others associated with ancient hostilities. Going back to Shi'ite and Sunni roots, hence, seems to exacerbate differences between the sects, and especially between their respective fundamentalist elements. This denouement does not always happen, but it occurs very often and it is easy to understand why.

One can expect serious international consequences when domestic violence is prolonged, particularly if the state has a strategic location or has experienced a significant revolution or transformation of identity. An additional special complicating factor is that the various communities of a sectarian state normally extend beyond its borders. In all our examples, with the exception of the United States, where none of these factors applies, a critical international impact occurred. Iran and Afghanistan produced the most significant consequences. By transforming its identity, Iran was able to cut itself loose from the Cold War and make fundamentalism a critical feature of Middle Eastern and world politics. Its aspiration to become the leader of a renewed Islam was undermined by the necessity to reconstitute Iran as a Shi'ite or a very special kind of Islamic state, one inimical to the dominant Muslim community. The impact of Afghan resistance may be more profound because it is hard to imagine anything in our time more critical than the Soviet domestic and international transformations which that resistance helped precipitate.

Organized violence has an instrumental character—it is a means to an end—or it is driven by desires to discard less efficient elements and structures. Violence for religious ends, however, has its own distinguishing characteristics, and the militancy of fundamentalists displays a paramount concern to defend their sacred symbols and to desanctify those of secular communities and other religious ones, a practice at least as old as Deuteronomy. "And ye shall overthrow their altars, and break their pillars, and burn their groves with fire; and ye shall hew down the graven images of their gods, and destroy the names of them out of that place."

Theological concerns shape violence by providing justifications, occasions, objects, and methods. The primary sources for these distinctions are the "founding myths" and millenarian expectations of the major religious traditions, which define the cause and the enemy, mandate appropriate methods of struggle, and specify holy sites and times. Within particular traditions, variations of these themes exist, and each may nourish a different kind of militancy.

The abundant information and analyses presented in the following chapters demonstrate that there is much to know about how traditions compare with one another, how the variations within religious traditions are expressed, and how fundamentalist violence is distinctive. These chapters represent an important beginning in the quest for that knowledge.

Notes

1. For these states, I have drawn from Abdulaziz A. Sachedina's "Activist Shi'ism in Iran, Iraq, and Lebanon," in the first volume of this series, Martin E. Marty and R. Scott Appleby, eds., *Fundamentalisms Observed* (Chicago: University of Chicago Press, 1991), pp. 403–56, and Augustus R. Norton, "The Shi'ites at the Margins of the Arab World" (manuscript, 1991).

2. Faye Ginsburg, "Saving America's Souls: Operation Rescue's Crusade against Abortion," this volume.

3. Only Operation Rescue, which is different from the other groups in most respects, does not talk about an external enemy. Belief in an external enemy (Zionism) is critical to the tiny violent American millenarian communities subscribing to "identity theology," such as the Aryan Nation, Posse Comitatus, the Covenant, Sword, and Arm of the Lord, and the Order. The American Fundamentalist movement, created in 1919 by the World's Christian Fundamentals Association, lasted some thirty years. Michael Barkun has provided the best discussion of the theological character of these groups, which derive from the Victorian group, the British Israelites. See "Millenarian Aspects of 'White Supremacist' Movements," *Terrorism and Political Violence* I, 4 (October 1989): 410–34. The groups were portrayed in the popular film "Betrayed." Also see James Aho, *The Politics of Righteousness* (Seattle: University of Washington Press, 1991).

4. Anxiety concerning an international conspiracy, William O. Beeman argues, is a characteristic of traditional Shi'ism. Still, all but one of our cases exhibit that feature too, though the parent religions are not described this way. See "Images of the Great Satan: Representations of the United States in the Iranian Revolution," in Nikki Keddie, ed., *Religion and Politics in Iran* (New Haven: Yale University Press, 1983), p. 19.

5. The nation may not be the only political entity conceivable for a secular world, but it has been the dominant form in the past and is likely to be so in the future.

6. See Azar Tabari, "The Role of the Clergy in Iranian Politics," in Keddie, *Religion and Politics in Iran,* esp. pp. 54–56; Abdul Hadi Hairi, *Shi'ism and Constitutionalism in Iran* (Leiden: Brill, 1977); and Charles W. Gallagher, "Contemporary Islam: The Plateau of Particularism, Problems of Religion and Nationalism in Iran," (New York: American Universities Field Service Reports, 1966).

7. Albert Hourani, *A History of the Arab Peoples* (London: Faber and Faber, 1991), pp. 454–55.

8. Olivier Roy, *Islam and Resistance in Afghanistan,* 2d ed. (Cambridge: Cambridge University Press, 1990), pp. 4, 12, and 16.

9. Mostofa Reja and Kay Phillips, *Leaders of Revolution* (Beverly Hills: Sage, 1979), p. 72. The study covers three hundred years ending in 1968; but as the religious demands have been more compelling since 1968, I have assumed that the observations in the book are still accurate. In states of European origin, by way of contrast, more than half of the revolutionaries studied abandoned their religions.

10. Emmanuel Sivan, *Radical Islam, Medieval Theology, and Modern Politics* (New Haven: Yale University Press, 1985), p. 130.

11. Said A. Arjomand, "A Victory for the Pragmatists: The Islamic Fundamentalist Reaction in Iran," in James Piscatori, ed., *Islamic Fundamentalisms and the Gulf Crisis* (Chicago: American Academy of Arts and Sciences, 1991).

12. *New York Times,* 12 December 1991. The previous day, Rushdie delivered a blistering attack on Iran's human rights record and announced the impending publication of a paperback edition of *The Satanic Verses,* and so the tension could escalate even further. For an interesting discussion of the international dimensions of the struggle, see Mehdi Mozaffari, "The Rushdie Affair: Blasphemy as a New Form of International Conflict and Crisis," *Terrorism and Political Violence II,* 3 (Autumn, 1990): 415–41.

13. *Los Angeles Times,* 29 December 1991, p. A11.

14. Amatzia Baram, "The Radical Shi'ite

Opposition Movements in Iraq," in Emmanuel Sivan and Menachem Friedman, eds., *Religious Radicalism and Politics in the Middle East* (Albany: State University of New York Press, 1990), pp. 95–125.

15. Saddam executed major Shi'ite fundamentalist leaders. Simultaneously, he rebuilt sacred shrines, poured money into the Shi'ite community, gave the Baath Party a more Islamic cast, and denounced Mu'awiya, the Caliph who dispossessed 'Ali. The last step was the most remarkable, and perhaps it is significant that Saddam's reputation as a believer has been suspect. When the Gulf War broke out, he went even further and invoked the memory of Hussain, the major figure in the Shi'ite fundamentalist tradition.

16. Martin Kramer, "Khomeini's Messenger: The Disputed Pilgrimage of Islam," in Sivan and Friedman, *Religious Radicalism*, p. 180. Kramer cites Ibn Sa'ud, the founder of the Saudi dynasty, who said in 1918, "I would raise no objection if you demolished the whole lot of them [Shi'ite shrines], and I would demolish them myself if I had the chance."

17. For an illuminating discussion of the problem, see Zalman Abramov, *Perpetual Dilemma: Jewish Religion in the Jewish State* (Rutherford, N.J.: Farleigh Dickenson Press, 1976). See also Yoav Peled, "Retreat from Modernity: The Ascendance of Jewish Nationalism in the Jewish State" (paper, American Political Science Association annual meeting, 1990).

18. Sprinzak notes that Rabbi Kahane initiated vigilante activity, but Gush settlers were responsible for most incidents. See his *The Ascendance of Irael's Radical Right* (New York: Oxford University Press, 1991), p. 88.

19. "It is this foreign body, this malignancy of gentilized [*sic*] foreign culture concepts and values that must be dealt with and erased from our midst. . . . These are born-by-accident Jews [and they] . . . not the PLO represent the real threat to the Jewish state and people. . . . They corrupt the country from within. . . . We must kill the Jew deserving of death in a humane way." Rabbi Meir Kahane, in A. Ravitsky, "Religious Radicalism and Political Messianism," in Sivan and Friedman, *Religious Radicalism*, p. 84. See also Ehud Sprinzak's discussion of other comments in *The Ascendance*, esp. pp. 230–31.

20. Cited by Ginsburg, "Saving America's Souls."

21. Neither Terry nor Ginsburg acknowledges that earlier fundamentalists used "direct-action" tactics. Carry Nation's career, in particular, is worth studying. See Barbara Leslie Epstein, *The Politics of Domesticity: Women, Evangelism, and Temperance in Nineteenth Century America* (Middletown, Conn.: Wesleyan University Press, 1981); and Robert Lewis Taylor, *Vessel of Wrath: The Life and Times of Carry Nation* (New York: New American Library, 1966).

22. Ginsburg believes the tactics reflect a "male" influence. The irony is that women used them earlier both in the temperance crusades and in the suffragette movements, when they were known as "tactics of the weak," i.e., "women's tactics."

23. Gamini Samaranayake, "Ethnic Conflict in Sri Lanka and Prospects of Management: An Empirical Inquiry," *Terrorism and Political Violence III*, 1 (Summer 1991), p. 80.

24. Sachedina uses a striking example to make the same point. When the Shi'ite shrine city of Najaf rose against the Turks in 1915, "the four quarters of the city, organized on tribal lines, established independent and autonomous city-states and would remain as such until the British occupation of 1917." Sachedina, "Activist Shi'ism," p. 438.

25. J. Douglas Martin, *The Persecution of the Baha'is of Iran: 1844–1984* (Ottawa: Association for Bahai Studies, 1984). See Michael Fischer's discussion of the uneasy status of the other religious minorities in the early days of the revolution, *Iran: From Religious Dispute to Revolution* (Cambridge: Harvard University Press, 1980).

26. "Anti Shi'ite sentiment was ten times greater among new radicals whose revolutionary theory was based entirely on Ibn

Taymiyya," Emmanuel Sivan, "Islamic Radicalism," *Religious Radicalism,* p. 55.

27. "In the Mideast, a Christian Exodus," *Los Angeles Times,* 10 August 1991, p. A16. Fundamentalism is not the only cause for emigration, but it is a very significant factor.

28. Said Amir Arjomand, "Shi'ite Jurisprudence and Constitution-Making in the Islamic Republic of Iran," this volume.

29. Saddam portrayed the war as a nationalist struggle against Persian imperialism.

30. R. K. Ramazani, "Shi'ism in the Persian Gulf," in Juan Cole and Nikki Keddie, eds., *Shi'ism and Social Protest* (New Haven: Yale University Press, 1986), p. 48.

31. Kramer, "Khomeini's Messengers," p. 183.

32. See David Wilkinson's interesting analysis of the Richardson data, *Deadly Quarrels: Lewis F. Richardson and the Statistical Studies of Wars* (Berkeley: University of California Press, 1980), particularly pp. 87–91, 112. As far as I know, this is the only systematic study of the warlike propensity of particular religions.

33. See my "Some General Observations on Religion and Violence," *Journal of Terrorism and Political Violence III,* 3 (Autumn 1991): 118–40.

34. See my "Sacred Terror: A Contemporary Case from Islam," in Walter Reich, *Origins of Terrorism: Psychologies, Theologies, States of Mind* (Cambridge: Cambridge University Press, 1990), pp. 131–60, which deals largely with rebel violence. Various sacred war patterns are discussed by James A. Aho, *Religious Mythology and the Art of War* (Westport, Conn.: Greenwood Press, 1981). see also Natalie Zemon Davis, "The Rites of Violence," in her *Society and Culture of Early Modern France* (Stanford: Stanford University Press, 1975). Originally appearing in *Past and Present* 59 (May 1973), it analyzes sixteenth-century Catholic and Protestant riots.

35. By this standard, the violence in Northern Ireland is not religious, because the issue there is how many secular states should exist on the island. Obviously, the violence could be religious by other criteria, i.e., each side draws its recruits from a particular religious group, etc.

36. Machiavelli introduces the concept though not the term. "For as all religions, republics and monarchies must have within themselves some goodness, by means of which they obtain their first growth and reputation, and as in the process of time this goodness becomes corrupted, it will of necessity destroy the body unless something intervenes to bring it back to its normal condition. And the best proof of this is furnished by our own [religion] which would have been entirely lost had it not been brought back to its pristine principles and purity by Saint Francis and Saint Dominick." *Discourses* I: 1.

37. Heinz Bechert, "The Beginnings of Buddhist Historiography: Mahavamsa and Political Thinking," in Bardwell L. Smith, ed., *Religion and Legitimation of Power in Sri Lanka* (Chambersberg, Pa.: Anima Books, 1978), pp. 1–12.

38. Tambiah argues that the "Sinhalese tensions . . . in the form we know them today are of relatively recent manufacture . . . owing more to polemics of nationalist ideologues and the politics of nation-making and election winning than to the earlier concerns and processes." *Sri-Lanka: Ethnic Fratricide and the Dismantling of Democracy* (Chicago: University of Chicago Press, 1986), p. 7.

39. Michael Fischer, *Iran: From Religious Dispute to Revolution,* p. 176.

40. Ibid., p. 7.

41. Bernard Lewis, "The Shi'a in Islamic History," in Martin Kramer, ed., *Shi'ism, Resistance, and Revolution* (Boulder, Colo: Westview Press, 1987), pp. 29–30.

42. See my "Messianic Sanctions for Terror," *Comparative Politics* 20 (January 1988): 195–213.

43. Marshall G. S. Hodgson, "How Did the Early Shi'a Become Sectarian?" *Journal of the American Oriental Society* 75 (1955): 1. One could argue that a model for quietism exists in the founding period itself. Hasan, Hussain's elder brother, renounced his claim to the Caliphate in return for a

pension. See S. H. Jafri, *The Origins and Early Development of Shiʻa Islam* (Beirut: Libraieri du Liban, 1979), pp. 141–47. I am grateful to R. Scott Appleby for providing some bibliographic help on this question.

44. Mary Hegland says that Shiʻite fundamentalists ascribe different political functions for the two interpretations. "When a strong repressive government controls Shiʻis, Islam counsels acquiescence, for survival is of primary importance . . . resistance is passive, merely taking the form of weeping . . . and keeping the memory of Husain alive. When, however, conditions allow hope that struggle will not be in vain, Islam provides an inspiration for rising against tyranny and injustice. Each of the two views depends for its existence on the other, and Islam itself can survive only with the help of both world views and strategies." "Two Images of Husain: Accommodation and Revolution in an Iranian Village," in Keddie, *Religion and Politics,* p. 231.

45. See Said Amir Arjomand, *The Shadow of God and the Hidden Imam: Religion and Political Order and Societal Change in Shiʻite Iran from the Beginnings to 1890* (Chicago: University of Chicago Press, 1984), esp. parts 1 and 2.

46. *Islam and Resistance in Afghanistan,* 2d ed. (Cambridge: Cambridge University Press, 1990), p. 7. The foundation myth is described in chaps. 1 and 4.

47. The dominant modern conception, until the development of Sunni fundamentalism, was that jihad referred only to defensive struggles or intense moral striving. See Rudolph Peters, *Islam and Colonialism: The Doctrine of Jihad in Modern History* (The Hague: Mouton, 1979). Discussions of the revival of the classic doctrine appear in Sivan, *Radical Islam;* Gilles Kepel, *Muslim Extremism in Egypt: The Prophet and the Pharaoh* (Berkeley: University of California Press, 1985); Bernard Lewis, *The Political Language of Islam* (Chicago: University of Chicago Press, 1988); and my "Sacred Terror." For a penetrating discussion of the classical jihad as a military doctrine, see James A. Aho, *Religious Mythology.*

48. In this respect, the clerical disposition

of the Shiʻites which Roy finds too constricting may be more useful.

49. Secular communities probably have more difficulty in defining and using such archetypes. But in the Gulf War, President Bush's ability to rally support depended partly on his ability to identify Saddam Hussein with Hitler.

50. See my "Messianic Sanctions," pp. 205–6.

51. See Haim H. Cohn, "Holy Terror," *Violence, Aggression and Terror I,* no. 2 (1987): 1–11, and Menachem Friedman's essay, "Religious Zealotry in Israeli Society," in Solomon Poll and Ernest Krausz, eds., *Ethnic and Religious Diversity in Israel* (Ramat Gan: Bar Ilan University, 1975), pp. 91–111. Though he lacked legal authority and Moses' endorsement, Pinchas received a divine covenant after committing the act, the only biblical covenant given as a reward. Paradoxically, Pinchas was also a model for the Zealots, a messianic group in the first century whose indiscriminate violence against Romans and Jews led to the destruction of the Second Temple, Masada, and the Diaspora. The ultra-Orthodox, however, follow rabbinic traditions in limiting the meaning of this model, a matter elaborated below.

52. In an unpublished essay, Keddie argues that messianism is a principal source for justifying revolt. "Islam, Politics, and Revolt" (Los Angeles: UCLA Religion and Conflict Conference, April 1991). When the Iranian revolution is not treated in the context of the Shiʻite messianic tradition, its violence appears more novel than it really is.

53. Emmanuel Sivan, "Islamic Radicalism," *Religious Radicalism,* p. 54.

54. Abdulaziz Sachedina, "Activist Shiʻism in Iran," p. 403.

55. Said A. Arjomand, "Iran's Revolution in Comparative Perspective," *World Politics,* April 1986, p. 412.

56. See Joseph Kechichian, "Islamic Revivalism and Change in Saudi Arabia: Juhayman al-Utaybi's 'Letters' to the Saudi People," *Muslim World* 80, no. 1 (January 1990): 1.

57. Roy, *Islam,* pp. 6–7.

58. Akbar Ahmed, *Millennium and Charisma among the Swat Pathans* (London: Routledge and Kegan Paul, 1979).

59. Kitsiri Malaboda, "Millennialism in Relation to Buddhism," *Comparative Studies in Society and History* 12, no. 4 (1970): 438.

60. Harjot Oberoi, "Sikh Fundamentalism: Translating History into Theory," this volume.

61. The millenarian theme was the driving force in the development of British and American fundamentalism, Ernest Sandeen's classic work has maintained. *The Roots of Fundamentalism: British and American Millenarianism, 1880–1930* (Chicago: University of Chicago Press, 1970).

62. Garry Wills, "Evangels of Abortion," *New York Review of Books,* 15 June 1989, p. 21.

63. See Paul G. Fowler, *Abortion: Towards an Evangelical Consensus* (Portland: Multnomah Press, 1987). Garry Wills provides a brief critical view of the appropriate passages in "Evangels," p. 20.

64. See Hans G. Kippenberg's fascinating "Jeder Tag' Ashura, jede Grab Kerbala: Zur Ritualisierung der Strassekampfe im Iran," in Kurt Greussing, ed., *Religion und Politik im Iran* (Frankfurt A.M.: Syndikat, 1981). It seems strange that the government did not understand the danger of arresting Khomeini at this moment in 1963, but such blunders are common in the sociology of revolution.

65. Baram, "The Radical Shi'ite Opposition," p. 103.

66. Norton, "The Shi'ites," p. 23.

67. Augustus Richard Norton, *Amal and the Shi'a: Struggle for the Soul of Lebanon* (Austin: University of Texas Press, 1987), pp. 113–14.

68. "The Rites of Violence," pp. 170–71.

69. See my "Terror and the Messiah," in David C. Rapoport and Yonah Alexander, eds., *The Morality of Terrorism,* 2d ed. (New York: Columbia University Press, 1988), pp. 13–43.

70. Roger Friedland and Richard Hecht provide an extremely informative history of the struggle in "The Politics of Sacred Space: Jerusalem's Temple Mount/*al-haram al-sharif*," in J. S. Scott and P. Simpson-Housley, eds., *Sacred Spaces and Profane Places: Essays in the Geographics of Judaism, Christianity, and Islam* (Westport, Conn.: Greenwood Press, 1991), pp. 22–61.

71. Daniel Gold, "Organized Hinduisms: From Vedic Truth to Hindu Nation," in Marty and Appleby, *Fundamentalisms Observed,* p. 581. On 4 April 1991 the largest demonstration (some 500,000) since the birth of Indian independence occurred. *Los Angeles Times,* 5 April 1991, p. 1.

72. See Stephen Frederick Dale, "Religious Suicide in Islamic Asia: Anticolonial Terrorism in India, Indonesia and the Philippines," *Journal of Conflict Resolution* 32, no. 1 (March 1988): 37–59.

73. I discuss the ritual dimension in ancient religious terrorism in "Fear and Trembling: Terrorism in Three Religious Traditions," *American Political Science Review* 78, no. 3 (September 84): 658–77. Subsequently, I tried to show how that ritual is reflected in the justifications and precedents cited by the assassins of Anwar Sadat. See my "Sacred Terror." Possibly, the prolonged series of knife attacks on Israeli Jews after the killings at the Temple Mount in October 1990 has ritual meaning.

74. Deuteronomy 12:3.

75. Haim Cohn discusses rabbinic restrictions on zealotry in "Holy Terror."

Three Models of Religious Violence: The Case of Jewish Fundamentalism in Israel

Ehud Sprinzak

The Middle East has recently been associated with a dramatic rise in religious radicalism and extremist fundamentalism. Khomeini's revolution in Iran, the assassination of President Sadat in Egypt, and the violent eruption of Shi'ite terrorism in Lebanon have all contributed to the identification of the region with religious violence and fanatic terrorism. For years, however, there was one exception to this turbulent image—the State of Israel. The Jewish state was perceived as an isolated island of democracy, secularism, pragmatism, and nonviolence. But events of the late 1980s and early 1990s raised the question of whether, within its borders, Israel was in fact isolated from the atmosphere of religious violence that prevailed in most of its neighboring countries.

Thousands of young *yeshiva* (Jewish Orthodox seminary) students took to the streets during this period in order to fight the establishment of a Mormon university in Jerusalem, in order to stop archaeological digs all over the country, in order to burn bus stations where "obscene" commercial advertisements had been posted, and in order to stop the screening of movies on Friday nights in Jerusalem. Such incidents were reminiscent of fanatical street demonstrations in Tehran or Beirut. The vigilante violence of the young messianic settlers of Gush Emunim (the Bloc of the Faithful) in the West Bank approximated recognized forms of the type of religious terrorism which is highly visible in the region. And the 4–6 percent of support of Kach, the violent quasi-fascist party of the late Rabbi Meir Kahane (disqualified for the 1988 and 1992 elections by the Supreme Court), especially among soldiers and youth, indicated that for many Israelis anti-Arab violence in the name of God was no longer an unacceptable practice by the late 1980s.

There are, in fact, many other warning signals regarding the growth of religious violence in Israel. Not a day passes—certainly not a weekend—without a new press report of harassment of a secular citizen, Jewish or non-Jewish, by a group of excited yeshiva students or aggressive settlers in Jerusalem, Bnei Brak, Safad, Netania, Tiberias, or a West Bank settlement. The intensive interreligious clashes which dominated the campaign of many religious parties in the 1988 national elections did not damage the image of these parties in Israel. On the contrary, these parties fared extremely well. They increased their electoral power in the Knesset (Israel's parliament) by 50 percent. Many observers who have been following other Middle Eastern radicalization processes cannot but wonder where it all will lead.

The purpose of this chapter is to describe and explain the violence practiced by Jewish fundamentalists in Israel in the late 1980s and early 1990s and its sociopolitical impact. Comparative observation of fundamentalist movements suggests that, contrary to their popular image, not all such groups are violent and that the forms of violence resorted to by those that are vary significantly. This observation suggests further that the likelihood, degree, and shape of the fundamentalist violence depend especially on the following variables: (1) the ideology and self-perception of the movement, and its attitude toward the powers that be; (2) the nature of the enemy of the movement and its perceived threat; and (3) the nature of the leadership of the movement and its form of organization.

The present study is less interested in the magnitude of religious violence in Israel than in its cultural and institutional structure. It suggests that even within the small fundamentalist minority in Israel it is possible to identify *several* forms of Jewish extremism and that at least three distinctive models of violence presently exist: the defensive and enforcement violence of the haredi society; the offensive yet restrained anti-Arab violence of Gush Emunim; and the offensive, unrestrained, and ideologically motivated anti-Arab violence of Kach, the movement founded by the late Rabbi Meir Kahane. The study also shows that, while extremism and militancy are attitudes shared by the entire fundamentalist milieu, only a small fraction of the members of the religious movement involved are actually engaged in violence.

Defensive and Enforcement Violence: The Case of the Haredi Society

The haredi (ultra-Orthodox) community is the oldest fundamentalist segment of the Jews of Israel. Its roots go back to the Old Settlement (Jews who lived in Palestine before the beginning of the Zionist immigration) and to the traditional East European Jewish Ghetto. As a social phenomenon, the haredim are not a homogeneous social movement or a single theological school. They make up a whole Israeli social segment and a variegated subculture which bring together several ultra-Orthodox traditions, Hasidic courts, religious seminaries, and prominent rabbis and religious thinkers. While they are united by their lifestyle and several common beliefs, they are divided along theological interpretations, countries of origin and communal traditions.[1] The more extreme among them, members of the Eda Haredit (pious community), are middle- and lower-middle-class people who live in relative poverty and are led by very old and conservative rabbis.

What brings most of the haredim together are two fundamental existential elements: (1) an extremist interpretation of Jewish Orthodoxy which insists upon a strict observation of all the injunctions of Jewish law; and (2) a theological negation of Zionism which is the guiding ideology of secular Israel. These two themes are so important that they overshadow all the internal divisions among the ultra-Orthodox and separate the haredi society from the rest of the nation spiritually and socially. Most of the haredim are different in appearance from other Israelis, behave differently, and even live in separate cities or neighborhoods. They have a world of their own, which is largely separated from Israel's secular culture.

The haredim have various conceptions of the virtuous Jewish life, but almost all of them believe that the people of Israel are still in exile and that Zionism and the State of Israel are meaningless at best and terrible sins at worst. The destruction of the Second Temple in 70 C.E. and the ensuing exile (*Galut*) of the Jewish nation are not, according to all haredi schools, just historical tragic events that happened to the nation. They amount to a divine punishment of the people of Israel and to a clear sign from heaven that the Jews who do not follow God do not deserve a state of their own.[2] Only a full Jewish repentance and a strict observance of God's commandments will bring about God's forgiveness and redemption. Heavenly redemption (and real national independence) according to the ultra-Orthodox understanding will take place miraculously through the coming of a Messiah, a metahistorical redeemer who will remove at once all the miseries and agonies of the Jews.

The main sources of haredi militancy are animosity, fear, and suspicion of Zionism in particular and modern secular culture in general. According to the ultra-Orthodox, ever since its early pronouncement in the late nineteenth century, Zionism was a direct revolt against God, a religious sin of the first degree. Secular Jews who desecrated the name of God in their countries of origin dared come to Eretz Yisrael on their own to establish a secular society and struggle for national independence. Not only was the act erroneous and hopeless in the first place; it was also a clear apostasy, a most outrageous affront, an abrogation of God's direct instructions. God, according to the ultra-Orthodox version, made it very clear to His people that they were supposed to wait patiently until He decided they were deserving of redemption. He instructed them not to "rebel" against the nations of the world and not to initiate massive Jewish settlement in Eretz Yisrael. Jews were traditionally permitted to come to Eretz Yisrael to die and to be buried in its holy soil. They were never allowed to revive it and establish a state on their own.[3]

Many haredi schools have moderated their attitude toward Zionism and the Zionists over the years and have expressed a de facto recognition of the Israeli body politic.[4] But for the most extreme sects among them, the radical members of the Eda Haredit, the campaign against Zionism is still understood in terms of religious struggle and a fight against profanity. These sects include today the divided community of Neturei Karta (Guardians of the City), Toldot Aharon, and the followers of the Hassidic Rabbi of Satmar. They live in Jerusalem and Bnei Brak, with several branches in New York and London, and see themselves as the only legitimate Jews, the gatekeepers of the entire nation. "God is our king and we are His servants. It is our obligation and calling to preserve His teaching, and since we do not recognize the rule of the infidels, because they are rebels against the kingdom of our Creator-King be blessed, it is forbidden to obey and work for a rebellious regime. Our Torah is our constitution and . . . under no conditions can we respect their laws."[5]

Since the Jewish people is seen by all haredim as a corporate body whose individuals are part of an organic whole, the existence of a sinful majority is a great disaster for them for it implies that no redemption is likely to take place in the near future. Heavenly redemption would come either when a miraculous collective repentance takes place or when the entire infidel society is destroyed by God.

Despite their self-perception of living in the midst of a sinful community, the extremist haredim direct a large measure of their militancy at other haredim and exercise much of it within the ultra-Orthodox society. There are three reasons for the containment of haredi militancy. First, there is a conviction that Jews in exile (and all the people of Israel) are in no position to change history and take initiatives in this direction, including the application of offensive violence against the powers that be.[6] Second, a sense of physical powerlessness and inability to challenge the law enforcement agencies of the State of Israel pervades haredi sensibilities. Finally, the existence of internal threats to the integrity of the haredi order makes it necessary to enforce strict uniformity inside the ultra-Orthodox groups. The most common type of haredi violence is therefore an *enforcement violence* aimed at enforcing the haredi lifestyle over deviant individuals and groups threatening to bring in secular ideas and practices. Though people join the haredi society voluntarily, it is a totalitarian system which does not recognize privacy. Everything that happens to the individual member of the community, including his most personal matters, has a public and communal side.[7] Those who do not conform to the strict norms imposed by the rabbis are exposed to legitimate violent sanctions. Hence, it is not surprising that perhaps the most important institution in this regard is Miahmarot Hatzniut (the Chastity Guards), whose main job is to make sure that no sexual deviance takes place within the community. Since due process of law is not known or recognized by the haredi society, although the community has a very orderly *halakhic* court system, many acts of violent punishment take place on the basis of hearsay and rumors. Individuals who are said to be violating the moral norms of the group become highly vulnerable. It is very hard to tell how effective the Chastity Guards have been in curtailing deviant behavior within the ultra-Orthodox community, although it seems that all of its members are aware of their existence and their ability to hit hard. Other acts of violence are triggered by rabbis' heated sermons that either mention the sinners by name or point clearly in their direction.[8]

The variety of haredi communities and schools by no means implies a normative pluralism or a principled recognition of the right of the individual haredi to disagree or do his own thing. The haredi epistemological world is monistic; there is no question about the existence of a single truth. Consequently, many internal conflicts within the haredi society, especially conflicts between rabbinical courts and yeshivot, which involve theological or personal debates end up in violence. Scuffles, fist fights, beatings, trashing, and property damage are very common. A "raid" against the wrongdoers is usually conducted by the young yeshiva students whose loyalty to their rabbis and yeshivot knows no limits. Studying at the yeshiva for sixteen to eighteen hours a day creates emotional and physical tensions which are greatly relieved by a good scuffle.[9] The yeshivot are thus the main source of haredi soldiers and militants.

An example of haredi violence involving "intercourt" struggle was the beating of Knesset member Menachem Porush in June 1984. Porush, a well-known haredi politician in his late sixties and the owner of a hotel in Jerusalem, was praying one Saturday evening in the hotel's synagogue when nearly fifty yeshiva students from Yeshivat Sefat Emet, of the Gur Hassidics, all wearing black dresses, broke in. They brutally attacked the old man, hitting his ribs, pulling his beard, breaking his eyeglasses, trampling his holiday dress, and letting him bleed. Porush's sons and friends, who were also present, were beaten too. The "Geralachs" (a nickname for the Gur Hassidics) did not leave the place until they had torn it apart, breaking chairs, tables, lamps, and windows. Porush, who was rushed to the hospital and placed in intensive care, stayed there for a full two weeks.

Every Israeli who read *Ha'aretz* (Israel's most respected daily) of the day previous to the brutal attack discovered why it had taken place. A few weeks earlier, Porush had been ordered by the Rabbi of Gur to give up his Knesset seat and to resign from the house prematurely. In the newspaper, Porush was quoted as saying that the eighty-six-year-old rabbi, by virtue of his advanced age, was no longer compentent enough or in any position to tell Porush what or what not to do in the Knesset. What Menachem Porush had apparently forgotten was that the Rabbi of Gur was not just another distinguished Torah authority. The old rabbi happened to be the leader of Israel's largest Hassidic court and was for the thousands of his followers an admired guru with unparalleled spiritual power. Several followers of the rabbi found Porush's statement intolerably humiliating and during the Sabbath prayer recalled a similar case which took place in Poland many years earlier and which ended up in a Hassidic assault on the home of the disloyal politician. The hot-blooded yeshiva students who heard the prayer did not wait long. Upon the termination of the Sabbath services they moved in, in full force.[10]

As long as the haredi violence is conducted within the ultra-Orthodox community, as most of it is, it rarely gets more than scant attention in the secular community. The haredim do all they can to maintain their pious self-image of disinterested true believers. Their press hardly reports in-group violence.

Cases of haredi aggression and violence which are highly publicized in the secular media are usually the acts conducted against the non-haredi secular society. *What is important about this violence is that, although it looks very offensive to most nonreligious Israelis, it is in fact defensive.* The haredim rarely attack others in order to directly expand their sphere of influence or power. They live in constant fear of losing ground to the forces of secularization, and their aggressive operations are conducted in order to stop what they see as a disastrous erosion of their status and control.[11] The haredim have two major enemies which have to be acted against when their threat exceeds certain limits: (1) the Christian Mission in Israel and (2) the aggressive Jewish secularists. For Jewish ultra-Orthodoxy, Christianity remains the greatest enemy of the nation, the bastard religion which has been trying to destroy Judaism by all means since the days of Christ. The haredim are certain that nothing has changed in this area, and that the theological and physical battle is still going on. Not forgetting for a single moment the halakhic injunction of "be killed rather than sin" regarding religious conversion, they cannot stand still in front of the Christian presence in the Holy Land and especially in front of Christian missionary activities.[12] There is constant action on that plane, and on occasions it reaches intense violence. Given the legal status of most Christian denominations in Israel, much of this activity, which is handled by a very sophisticated organization, "Yad Leachim" (the Brotherhood), is conducted in secrecy. It involves a constant spying on the Christian Mission and preventive operations against the conversion of Jews.[13] But on occasions there are unexpected eruptions which result in a burned church, a blown-up monastery, or a hasty escape of a frightened group of nuns.

If not for the Israeli police, the extremist haredi sects would undoubtedly be considerably more aggressive and dangerous. Yet a number of factors explain the relative quiet on the "front" between secular and haredi Jews. The haredim's theological orientation makes them exceedingly pessimistic regarding their ability to bring about a collective repentance of the nation. They are unable to cope with the Israeli regime but are socioeconomically vulnerable to it. Finally, the advanced age and conservatism of their leaders inhibit haredi violence. These factors also explain why the struggle against the secular Jewish society has no formal organization.

But there are exceptions to that. When the haredim perceive an outstanding danger to the corporate life of the Jewish community in Eretz Yisrael, a gross violation of the very unsatisfactory status quo they live in, they go to the streets in full force, taking all the risks involved. An archaeological dig which is conducted in an ancient Jewish cemetery is, from a haredi perspective, an abominable crime justifying violent protest at all costs. Such was the city-supported construction of a Mormon "missionary" academic center in Jerusalem. The placing of "obscene posters" (girls advertising bikini swimming suits) in bus stations, including stations used by young yeshiva students, likewise deserves a strong reaction. The opening of a new road into or adjacent to an Orthodox neighborhood which is not closed on the Sabbath, as the Torah commands, may be a cause for months of Sabbath demonstrations and intense rock throwing. The secular authorities responsible for these acts are thus symbolically equated with the worst historical enemies of the Jewish people: the Amalekites (the ancient treacherous Canaanite tribe whom the Jews were ordered to destroy completely), the Inquisition (of the Catholic church, which was responsible in the Middle Ages for the massive forced conversion of the Jews), and the Nazis.[14] Thus, while not being partner to any "status quo" agreement with the secular Israelis, the haredim have an acute sense of the status quo regarding their living conditions and the nation's in general. When they sense an abrogation of this unwritten agreement, they go out in protest. In doing so, the most extremist among them follow the ruling of one of their great late leaders, Rabbi Amram Blau, who said, after the establishment of the State of Israel, that despite their weakness there were still two ways to confront the Zionists, "to self-isolate and to protest."[15] There are no signs that the self-isolation and protest of the radical haredim will disappear in the foreseeable future.

One of the most intense antisecular campaigns conducted in the 1980s was the haredi struggle against the archaeological digs carried out in the ancient City of David, in Jerusalem. The haredim have never been interested in the scientific study of the past, including the most glorious biblical times of the nation, but the reason they attacked the archaeologists digging the City of David had nothing to do with this general disdain. One of the upper layers at the cite of the ancient city was used, according to the haredim, as a cemetery, and its removal in the service of archaeology involved the desecration of the dead. It was, consequently, *Hillul Hashem,* a desecration of the name of God, a secular sin no loyal servant of God could ignore. The campaign over the City of David involved a powerful struggle of will. Neither the archaeologists backed by the entire Israeli scientific community nor the haredim would give in.

The ultra-Orthodox demonstrations and protests took months and involved typical antisecular haredi operations. The hundreds of demonstrators (thousands on special occasions) who participated in any such event were mostly young yeshiva students belonging to the Eda Haredit and closer circles. Mobilization for the big operation was not conducted by any formal organization. It was very effectively carried out by dramatic rabbinical sermons made in their yeshivot and by *Pashkevils*—wall posters, spread all over the haredi neighborhoods, calling the pious, in the name of the great rabbis, to protest the calamity. The young yeshiva students would usually come in groups. Sometimes they were led by their rabbis, and on occasions by the most daring and committed among themselves. They would stand at the site, pray, cry, scream, and tear their dresses in grief. Although no violence was planned in advance, many of these occasions ended in bloodshed. Violence sometimes erupted as a result of rock throwing, attempts to interfere with the archaeological work, clashes with the police, and large crowds which ran out of control. Part of the campaign against the digging of the City of David involved the personal struggle of the haredim against the chief archaeologist of the city, Professor Yigal Shilo. Shilo, who argued that no ancient cemetery was involved and that his was a purely scientific work, was determined to complete his mission. He was consequently excommunicated by the entire rabbinical leadership of the Eda Haredit, which also prayed that he be punished by God. When he died in 1987 of cancer, the ultra-Orthodox were certain that their prayer had been answered and that Shilo had been punished by Almighty God Himself.

It is important to stress that while the haredim do not kill, they are very militant.[16] In addition to being ideo-theologically exclusivist and confrontational with the forces of modernization and secularism, their militancy is greatly enhanced by their siege mentality and sense of fighting a perennial uphill battle. While the siege mentality of most Israelis has to do with the Arabs and with the military threat to their country, the haredi siege mentality is cultural and spiritual. And unlike the siege mentality of the secular Israelis, which can be extremely exaggerated, the haredi sense of being isolated in a hostile environment is fully justified. Not only are the haredim really surrounded by an unfriendly secular culture, but they are politically and economically very weak. Their survival dictates an almost total dependency on the Zionist authorities and the State of Israel, about which they can do very little. This dependency may dictate restraint but is, on occasion, the root cause of very bitter and violent eruptions.

Restrained Intercommunal Violence: The Case of Gush Emunim

Gush Emunim (the Bloc of the Faithful), the movement of the settlers in the West Bank and Gaza, is by far the most recognized Israeli fundamentalist movement. In its short history it has been a subject of great interest in Israel and abroad.[17] It is not surprising that, given its intense involvement in national politics and its controversial presence in the West Bank (occupied by Israel since 1967), Gush Emunim has acquired the image of the most militant fundamentalist movement in the Jewish state. In the perspective of the present essay, however, the real story of Gush Emunim's militancy is not what the movement's activists have done but, rather, what they have not done. While Gush Emunim has certainly had a role in intensifying the religious violence of post–1967 Israel, it has done much less than is usually assumed. And the reason for that has to do with the parameters within which Gush Emunim has been operating since its establishment: its ideology and self-perception, the nature of its leadership and organization, and its perception of the enemy.

There are many dissimilarities between Gush Emunim and the haredim. The latter are an old society which brings together over two hundred and fifty thousand ultra-Orthodox middle- and lower-middle-class Ashkenazi settlers under the leadership of very old and conservative rabbis. Most of them are poorly educated and are doing their best not to be exposed to the intellectual and technological temptations of the modern world. Gush Emunim, on the other hand, is a young and small movement of middle- and upper-middle-class Ashkenazic Jews and yeshiva students whose members and close adherents do not exceed twenty thousand. The leaders and rabbis of the movement are in their mid-forties and early fifties and are energetic and innovative. Many members of the movement hold academic degrees from Israel's secular universities and are in favor of taking all possible advantage of modern science and technology. Indeed, in the context of the present study the most important difference between the two communities is Gush Emunim's positive and optimistic attitude toward the outside world and the powers that be. Gush Emunim tries to maintain as Orthodox and traditional a Jewish lifestyle as the haredi society, but unlike the haredim it is rather pleased with the modern world. Unlike the haredi society, the roots of which go back to the eighteenth-century ultra-Orthodox struggle against the impact of the Enlightenment on European Jewry, Gush Emunim is very young. Whereas it was officially established only in 1974, its ideological and social articulation started to take shape after the 1967 Six Day War. The future members of Gush Emunim were thrilled about the war and gave it a profound theological meaning. The great Israeli victory was for them a clear sign that Jehovah, the God of Israel, did not desert His people in their worst moment. Not only did He save the nation from what appeared in May 1967 as a certain disaster, but also He gave the Israelis huge territories which the nation had not controlled since the days of Kings David and Solomon. The mira-

cle that happened to the people of Israel was so clear that the excited religious youngsters convinced themselves that heavenly redemption was just around the corner.[18]

Gush Emunim's optimistic attitude toward the world derives from two sources,
the ideo-theology of the movement and the post-1967 Israeli reality. Long before
Gush Emunim became a social and political movement, its future leaders were part of
a unique Jerusalem yeshiva, Yeshiva Mercaz Harav. The spirit of this yeshiva was
shaped by the teaching of its founder, Rabbi Abraham Itzhak Hacohen Kook
(1866–1935), the first chief rabbi of the Jewish settlement in Palestine. It was later
augmented by Rabbi Zvi Yehuda Kook, the son of the founder of the school and the
mentor of Gush Emunim. Unlike many other religious thinkers, Kook the Elder believed that the secular Zionist movement was holy and that its rise was an indication
of the beginning of heavenly redemption. He saw signs of redemption in the very
establishment of the Zionist movement in the late nineteenth century, in the 1917
Balfour Declaration, which promised the Jews the establishment of a national home
in Palestine, and in the success of the Zionist venture in Palestine, which had expressed itself most substantially in the return of the Jews to their land and their ability
to develop it and reap its fruits. Since the Zionist movement was initiated as, among
other things, a secular reaction to the Orthodox Judaism of the Diaspora, Rav Kook's
proposition had been revolutionary and unconventional. It allotted a sacred role in
the messianic process to secular Jews, who did not even believe in the coming of the
Messiah. His theology conferred upon secular Zionism a legitimacy it had never had
before. Historically, Kook the Elder was able to bridge many differences between
secular and Orthodox Zionists in the pre-State period, a precedent that later helped
Gush Emunim in its contacts with secular elements in Israel.[19]

Rav Kook's historical and theological conceptions explain a great deal about Gush
Emunim's understanding of the present state of affairs. According to this understanding, the Six Day War, in which Judea and Samaria were conquered and Jerusalem
reunited, was no chance turn of events. It was a major step forward in the messianic
process that started with the birth of modern Zionism. Further, Gush Emunim's
tremendous confidence in its cause is derived from its unshakable conviction that the
empirical reality of the last century has verified Rav Kook's grand reading of history,
including the stages that took place long after his 1935 death: the 1948 establishment
of the State of Israel, the ingathering of exiles from all corners of earth, the blooming
of the desert, and the 1967 glorious military victory.[20] There is little doubt in the
mind of the believers that Rav Kook the Elder and his son Rabbi Zvi Yehuda were
bestowed with heavenly illumination and prophesy. There is, consequently, no reason
not to be optimistic about the future or to suspect the coming of the next stage, full
redemption.

> I could come up with . . . plenty of quotations from authoritative sources,
> according to which we are living in an era of redemption, but I prefer to ob-
> serve reality. After two thousand years Jews return to their homeland; the
> desolate land is being continuously built; there is a unique process of the in-
> gathering of the exiles; we have won independence and sovereignty which we

did not have even during the era of the Second Temple. What would you call this reality if not a reality of redemption?[21]

The optimistic perspective which characterized the formation of Gush Emunim did not leave much room for destructive militancy. Unlike many modern fundamentalist movements which have emerged in a reaction to communal crisis or national disaster, and were formed by bitter and angry activists, the Gush leaders started their career with a strikingly positive attitude toward the world. The secular government of Israel, which was instrumental in bringing about the victory of the Six Day War, was highly commendable. Even the Arabs, the traditional enemies of the Jews, were no longer seen as an ominous threat. This Gush Emunim optimism was thus instrumental in producing in the movement a rather "liberal" orientation toward the secular Jews and the Muslim Arabs. While the former were seen as equal partners in the evolving heavenly redemption, the latter were looked upon as a harmless part of the landscape and as potential nonpolitical neighbors. The Palestinians of the West Bank and Gaza—territories destined, according to Gush Emunim, to be annexed to Israel soon—were consequently offered three alternatives: to announce their complete loyalty to the Zionist State of Israel (and serve in the Israeli army) and become full and equal citizens of the enlarged Jewish state; to remain nonpolitical residents (without having to declare allegiance to Israeli Zionism) and to retain full personal rights; or to emigrate to the Arab world with compensations.[22] None of the alternatives implied heated conflict or anti-Arab violence, and all three were considered operational.

The first significant militant acts of Gush Emunim were committed after the Yom Kippur War. They were focused on two issues, the intention of the government to return territories in Sinai and the Golan Heights to the Egyptians and Syrians, and the demand to settle the West Bank. The Israeli government was greatly weakened by the 1973 war and was not as prestigious as the victorious administration of 1967. Gush Emunim did not lose its complete conviction in the coming of redemption but felt it had to strengthen the "positive" forces in Israel, all those who were still determined to keep and settle all the occupied territories. Because the post-1974 Rabin administration was determined to reduce the tension with Egypt and Syria at the expense of small territorial concessions, and its opposition to free settlement in the occupied territories was firm, Gush Emunim's position soon led to conflict and extralegal behavior on behalf of its members. Gush Emunim's most illustrious illicit settlement attempts in the West Bank took place in the mid-1970s. But they involved only relatively mild confrontation with the government. Loyal to its Kookist doctrine of the sacredness of the state, Gush Emunim used methods of nonviolent demonstrations and passive disobedience. Its members were aggressive, but their militancy was quite restrained.[23] Even the Gush's most extreme confrontation with the regime, the 1982 struggle to stop the retreat in northern Sinai and to prevent the actual destruction of Jewish settlements, was conducted within the parameters of civil disobedience.[24]

But even in the early days of the "coexistence" there was one place on the West Bank which caused a great deal of Jewish-Arab friction. This was Hebron. The bone of contention was the Cave of the Patriarchs (the Machpela), the traditional burial place of Abraham, Isaac, Jacob, and their wives. Immediately following the Six Day War, the Israeli military government opened the shrine, traditionally the second holiest place for Jews, for regular prayers and visits. Since the site had been for many generations a holy Muslim mosque, special arrangements were made to secure Jewish access without infringing on the rights of the Arabs and without desecrating the large worship halls. The general policy of Moshe Dayan, Israel's minister of defense, was to respect freedom of religion and to make as few changes as possible in the pre-1967 status quo.[25] The practical consequence of this policy in Hebron was that most of the Cave of the Patriarchs was left in Muslim hands and Jewish worshipers were allowed to pray only during certain hours. This arrangement worked for a short time. The Jewish settlers in Hebron under the zealous leadership of Rabbi Moshe Levinger were extremely unhappy with the situation and did not care a great deal about the *status quo ante*. Levinger and his followers believed that all of Hebron was Jewish land by right and that the shrine had been dedicated to their holy forefathers since time immemorial. The fact that Jews had not had control of the Cave of the Patriarchs for generations was, according to them, a result of historical injustice. They were consequently determined to change the status quo whenever possible and pushed incessantly for more space and longer prayer hours in the shrine.

The Jewish expansion in the Cave of the Patriarchs was to lead to growing Arab hostility and conflict. Unlike other early settler demands, the Jewish aggrandizement into the Machpela involved a zero-sum game. Every space won by the Jews meant an Arab loss. Rabbi Levinger and his followers were interested in achieving control of the holy shrine without causing open conflict with the military government. The tactic chosen was extremely effective. The settlers would refuse, for example, to leave on Friday in time to let Muslim worshipers in. On other occasions they would leave the halls but block the main entrance. When early Jewish demands regarding prayer were fulfilled, Kiryat Arba settlers started to push for Kiddush in the cave—the rite of taking wine after the conclusion of services on the Sabbath and holidays as well as during marriage, circumcision, and other ceremonies. They also demanded that the Israeli flag be flown over the shrine on Israel's Independence Day.[26] All these encroachments were extremely insulting to the Muslims, especially the taking of wine. Islam strictly forbids alcohol, and the introduction of wine into the mosque was seen as an intended humiliation. This conflict and friction led directly to violence in the Cave itself and in the area as a whole. In 1968, a hand grenade was thrown at a group of Jewish visitors in front of the mosque. This was followed by the placement of a special military guard in the area. After the summer of 1975, the situation around the Machpela became extremely tense and Jewish-Muslim skirmishes became routine.[27] A more intense conflict erupted in 1976, when a Muslim crowd reacted violently to the theft of Qur'an scriptures by a Kiryat Arba resident. Arabs stormed the Jewish part of the building, expelled the worshipers, and set Jewish scrolls and ceremonial objects on fire.[28] Only prompt military intervention prevented a large-scale and bloody escalation of violence.

While most of Gush Emunim settlers were able to restrain their militancy vis-à-vis the government of Israel, this early moderate attitude toward the Palestinians of the West Bank began to deteriorate in the 1970s. The change had to do with the post–1974 reappearance of the Arab threat to Israel and with the growing friction between Jewish settlers and Arabs in the West Bank.[29] The Arab military success in the Yom Kippur War destroyed the post–1967 Israeli superiority complex. Even optimistic movements like Gush Emunim had to recognize that the existence of the State of Israel was still in danger and that the relative passivity of the Palestinians of the West Bank could not be counted upon.

The growing skepticism of Gush Emunim regarding the likelihood of an Arab-Jewish coexistence under a benevolent Israeli rule was greatly intensified by the increasing friction between the Jewish settlers and the local Palestinians in the West Bank. As long as the number of Jewish settlements was small and the settlers lived under the strict control of the cautious Labor administration, the level of conflict was low. But the 1977 rise of Likud (Israel's right-wing party) to power changed this situation at once. The entire West Bank was opened to Jewish settlement, and thousands of Israelis flocked in. Frightened and unsure of their future, the local Palestinians began to resort to violent means and the friction and low-level communal violence rose dramatically.[30]

The kind of militancy adopted by Gush Emunim toward the Palestinian challenge was *settler vigilantism*. The activists of the Gush developed a vigilante theory which maintained that, if the government of Israel was unable or unwilling to provide the settlers with the same security the residents of Tel Aviv were provided, it was their obligation to defend themselves and their families. Every act of Arab defiance and sabotage had to be responded to in kind, demonstrating thereby settler force and resolve. This was translated into action through settler raids of Arab villages suspected of hosting Arab saboteurs, through the breaking of windows of dozens of Arab cars whenever a Jewish car was attacked on the road, and on occasions through the killing of Arab civilians in response to previous acts of Arab terrorism.[31] The individuals participating in the raids were all highly trained officers and soldiers in reserve in the Israeli army. The most dramatic such operation was the 1980 blowing up of the cars of several Arab mayors suspected by Gush Emunim of masterminding the murder of six yeshiva students in Hebron a month earlier. The plan was to injure these people severely without killing them. The crippled leaders were to become living symbols of the consequences of anti-Jewish terrorism.[32] The "mayors' affair" was only a partial success. Two of the leaders involved, Mayor Bassam Shak'a of Nablus and Mayor Karim Khalef of Ramalla, were instantly crippled. Two mayors escaped injury when the demolition teams failed to wire their cars.[33]

Elaborating on the vigilante philosophy of the settlers, one of the leaders of the Jewish underground responsible for the act said:

> Planning and executing the attack on the murder chieftains took only one month of my life, one month that started with the assassination night of six boys in Hebron, and ended up in conducting this operation. I insist that this operation was right. So right in fact, that to the best of my understanding . . .

even the law that prevails in the State of Israel could recognize its justice or ought to have recognized it as a pure act of self defense. . . . It is unquestionable that in our present reality . . . the reality of the sovereign State of Israel . . . the defense forces of the state had to take care of this matter, quickly, neatly, and effectively, so that nobody could have, in his right mind, thought about such an operation. I, furthermore, do not deny that it was a clear case of undue excess. But the situation at stake was a case in which the "policeman" responsible for the matter, not only stepped aside . . . not only ignored the gravity of the case, and the fact that the murderers were allowed to act freely . . . but developed with them a friendly relationship. . . . This situation, Sirs, was a case of no choice, a condition that created a need to act in the full sense of the word, for the very sake of the preservation of life.[34]

What Yehuda Etzion so eloquently told the court was that he had devoted one month of his life to becoming a vigilante terrorist. A vigilante movement, we should recall, never sees itself in a state of principled conflict, either with the government or with the prevailing *concept* of law. It is not revolutionary and does not try to destroy authority. Rather, what characterizes the vigilante state of mind is the profound conviction that the government, or some of its agencies, has failed to enforce the law or to establish order in an area under its jurisdiction. Backed by the fundamental norm of self-defense and speaking in the name of what they believe to be the valid law of the land, vigilantes in effect enforce the law and execute justice.[35] Due process is thus the least of their concerns.

The vigilantism of Gush Emunim, which is marked by an emotional quasiloyalty to the nation, may also be explained by the movement's profound sense of belonging. In spite of their growing illegality, the members of Gush Emunim believe that they are the pioneering spearhead of the entire nation and that in due time all Israelis will discover this truth. Given the power of the governing camp in Israel, this is not simple daydreaming. From 1977 to 1992 Israel was under the dominance of the rightist Likud. Menachem Begin, Likud's first leader, used to refer to Gush Emunim as "my dear children" and considered them the best and the brightest. In spite of the growing involvement of Gush members in anti-Arab violence, this attitude among the Israeli right has persisted to this very day. In fact, it would not be an exaggeration to suggest that Gush Emunim has become the "kibbutz movement" of the entire Israeli right, the exemplary pioneering elite that sets the standards of nationalism and patriotism. It is very telling that, despite the great epistemological differences between the members of Gush Emunim and the rest of the Israeli right, the former refer to themselves as the "Eretz Yisrael camp." Thus, the vigilantism of the Gush has been tacitly tolerated by over 50 percent of the Israelis who vote for religious parties and by the right.

Another part of the unofficial support system of the Gush Emunim vigilantism has been provided by the army and the military government of the occupied territories. Almost from the beginning of the occupation there were security problems in the West Bank. Because of anti-Jewish terrorist and guerrilla attacks, the settlements were designated "confrontation settlements" and special military orders authorized their guards to defend them with force. Many Jewish residents of the West Bank are, in fact, soldiers "on extended leave," mainly religious students combining military service with Talmudic study. In every settlement, one settler is appointed "security officer" and receives a salary from the Ministry of Defense or the Israeli police. The result is the direct involvement of the settler community in defense and security matters that were originally handled by the military government.

In 1978, Israel's chief of staff, General Raphael Eitan, initiated a new policy under which the settler community in the West Bank was assigned complete responsibility for securing the area and defending itself. Hundreds of settlers were transferred from their regular army units to the West Bank, where, in addition to securing their own settlements, they were to secure cultivated fields, access roads, and commercial and general community facilities. Every settlement was required to have an allotted number of fit combatants, including officers. These combatants were to perform their active duty on a part-time basis while leading normal civilian lives. In addition, regional mobile forces equipped with armored personnel carriers were established to police the Palestinian population. Large quantities of military equipment, including sophisticated weapons, have been stored in the settlements under the complete control of the local commanders. Most of the members of Yehuda Etzion's group were part of this regional defense system, including a captain on active duty.

One type of violence which the same Gush Emunim group was involved in, but which was fortunately never consummated, was *messianic violence,* the attempt to trigger a catastrophe of large magnitude in the hope of facilitating the coming of the Messiah. The plan involved the blowing up of the "abomination," the Muslim Dome of the Rock situated on the Temple Mount in Jerusalem. The idea of obliterating the third holiest Muslim shrine on earth was a response to the 1978 Camp David accords and to the readiness of Israel's prime minister, Menachem Begin, to return Jewish sacred territories to the Arabs in exchange for a "phony" peace. The idea was conceived by Yehuda Etzion and another exceptional individual, Yeshua Ben-Shoashan. Both men, although closely affiliated with Gush Emunim and its settlement drive, were nevertheless not typical members. More than most of their colleagues they were intensely preoccupied with the mysteries of the process of regeneration that was about to bring the Jewish people, perhaps in their own lifetime, to its redemption. Literally messianic, the two convinced themselves that the historical setback of Camp David must have had a deeper cause than Begin's simple weakness. It may have been a direct signal from Heaven that a major national offense had been committed, a mistake that was responsible for the political disaster. Only one prominent act of desecration could match the magnitude of the setback: the presence, sanctioned by the government of Israel, of the "infidels" and their shrine on Temple Mount, the holiest Jewish site, the sacred place of the first, second, and third (future) temple.[36]

Students of messianic movements have long noticed that millenarian types are driven to extreme and antinomian acts when the imminent process of redemption is suddenly stalled. Such types become convinced that an exceptional operation is needed in order to calm the Lord's anger. Only such an action can restore the messianic process and ensure its consummation.[37] This psychological mechanism was probably involved in the Temple Mount plan. But the plan had an additional goal. Its perpetrators believed that it would ruin the peace treaty between Israel and Egypt and stop the final evacuation of Sinai.[38] Following several tête-à-tête meetings between Etzion and Ben-Shoshan, in which they cautiously studied the possibility of an operation on Temple Mount, the two decided to extend the circle. They brought in several trusted friends. Three years were devoted to preparing the operation, and in 1982, just prior to the final Israeli retreat from Sinai, everything was ready. The plan was shelved, however, because none of the rabbis consulted approved of the idea and because most of the members of the group were unwilling to act without a rabbinical green light.

In December 1987 a new stage in the Jewish-Arab violence in the West Bank was opened with the Intifada, the Palestinian uprising in the occupied territories. The Intifada dealt Gush Emunim a serious blow. The rabbis and leaders of this movement had never credited the Palestinian Arabs with the capacity to conduct a successful and sophisticated anti-Israeli struggle, or to maintain the pressure for a long time. And the setback has been conceptual and theological just as it was practical and concrete. The overall effect of the uprising on Israeli society has been a significant increase in the price it has been asked to pay for keeping the West Bank and Gaza. Gush Emunim's activists, who have argued all along that Judea, Samaria, and Gaza, in addition to being integral parts of the holy Eretz Yisrael, are profitable territories economically, had to recognize painfully that this was no longer the case. And they had to admit that most Israelis "voted with their feet" against settling the territories. In addition, they were anxious about the safety of their families, especially children, traveling daily to school through Arab villages.

The Intifada has undoubtedly drawn more Gush Emunim activists into the cycle of violence. Settler vigilantism has become the order of the day and was sanctioned by the movement's rabbis on religious grounds. Perhaps the most dramatic case of such action involved Gush Emunim's most prominent settler, Rabbi Moshe Levinger, who in 1968 initiated the first Gush settlement in the West Bank. In 1989 Levinger shot and killed an innocent Arab bystander in Hebron. In court he argued that his was an act of self-defense but was nevertheless sent to five months in prison.[39]

It is significant to note, however, that despite the hardships of the time, the majority of Gush Emunim settlers have not actively joined the growing violence. There are a number of reasons for this restraint, not the least of which is Gush's tactical preference for creating or aggravating a crisis situation and then relying on the armed intervention of the Israeli Defense Force to resolve it. The middle-class mentality of the movement has also served to restrain members from life-threatening involvement in vigilantism. Add to this the high level of discipline of most Gush members, coupled with the high degree of control exposed by the movement's leaders, and it becomes evident that the active involvement of settlers in direct acts of violence is inhibited, if not undermined altogether, in a number of ways.

The members of Gush Emunim have lived under greater stress than most of Rabbi Meir Kahane's followers but nevertheless have demonstrated a much greater restraint. Despite the movement's growing suspicion of the long-range intentions of the Palestinians of the West Bank and the removal of its earlier offer to grant full political rights to loyal Arabs, most of its leaders have remained reluctant to preach unmitigated violence. Refusing to recognize the legitimacy of the Palestinian cause, they have consistently stated they are willing to let the peaceful Arabs stay. Anti-Arab violence has been legitimized only in cases of self-defense.[40] Thus, while the idealistic and nonviolent posture of Gush Emunim's early days has certainly vanished, the movement remains cautious and relatively restrained in its attitude toward the Arabs.

Unrestrained Intercommunal Violence:
The Case of Rabbi Kahane and Kach

Unlike the ultra-Orthodox society, which is a large conglomerate of pious communities that live a full haredi life, or Gush Emunim, which is a small but cohesive social movement made up of settlements and active settlers, Kach (Thus!) is basically a right-wing backlash movement organized politically. From its founding in New York in 1968 the movement was led, inspired, and controlled by one man, Rabbi Meir Kahane. Kahane, who was assasinated in New York City on 5 November 1991, had written all the movement's theoretical tracts as well as its popular pamphlets. He had been the movement's only director, public speaker, fund raiser, and public relations person. The growing appeal of Kahane's message in the 1980s among Israelis of all descriptions was an indication that Kach had been expressing a broader sentiment than that of its founder, yet Kahane's ideological and political monopoly of the movement was so complete that in his lifetime he *was* the movement.[41]

The public career of Rabbi Kahane started in 1968, when he and a few friends established the Jewish Defense League (JDL) in New York. The original intention of the group was to provide American Jews with a defense against criminal and anti-Semitic groups in the urban centers of the eastern United States. But its unexpected success, especially in the media, led Kahane to change the nature of the organization. Instead of remaining a local defense group, the JDL became an offensive movement of the first degree. It made itself the self-appointed representative of Jewish misery all over the world and concentrated especially on the plight of Russian Jewry. Although most JDL activities until 1969 included symbolic violence permitted by the law, the League was soon involved in actual violence and illegal acts. Following an attack on an anti-Semitic radio station, JDL members began to be imprisoned. In January 1970 they disrupted a concert of the Moscow Philharmonic Orchestra in Brooklyn, and in June almost thirty members were arrested when they invaded the Soviet trading company Amtorg. Many violent anti-Russian activities followed.[42]

Rabbi Kahane arrived in Israel in September 1971 and declared that he had come to stay. His official explanation was that all Jews should emigrate to Israel since it is the only safe place for Jews in the world. A less favorable interpretation maintains that by 1971 Kahane had come to a dead end in the United States: in the spirit of détente, the American administration was by then determined to rein in extreme anti-Soviet activity and the FBI made it clear to Kahane that it had sufficient evidence to send him to prison. Just prior to his departure from the United States, he was given a suspended sentence of five years' imprisonment with five years probation. Unready to face the consequent decline of his movement, he decided to leave his followers and emigrate to Israel, seemingly on ideological grounds. Upon his arrival in Israel Kahane declared that he had no intention of becoming involved in national politics, but only of devoting himself to education. But less than a year later the small Israeli JDL was back on the streets. Surrounded by a handful of young American supporters who had followed him to Israel and by a smaller group of young Russian émigrés, Kahane came out on the streets demonstrating against the Christian Mission in Israel and against the Arabs. While specializing in symbolic action, Kahane and his followers did not abstain from involvement in planning and executing acts of violence, for which they were sent, on occasion, to jail. Kahane also opted for the electoral alternative and attempted to get elected to the Knesset. In 1973, 1977, and 1981, he did very poorly. His call for the expulsion of all Arabs from the State of Israel and for its complete "Judaization" was too radical for most Israelis.[43]

The situation changed dramatically during the 1982–85 war in Lebanon. The nation was polarized along ideological lines, and Kahane's right-wing radicalism became popular. In 1984 he was elected to the Knesset with the support of 1.3 percent of the nation. In 1984 a new term, "Kahanism," was coined in Israel to denote a blend of ultranationalism, strong anti-Arab sentiment, religiosity, and a demand to respond in kind to Arab terrorism irrespective of the law. Kahanism has outgrown Kahane and has become the ideological denominator of a large group which does not necessarily vote for Kach on election day.[44]

Kahane's ideology is a strange mélange of haredi and Gush Emunim thinking. Like the haredim and very much unlike Gush Emunim, the secular State of Israel is for Kahane a sinful state. There is no holiness in the manners and behavior of the Israeli leaders, who do not respect God and behave according to non-Jewish norms. They should and will in due time be punished by God. In fact, many of the problems faced by Israel are caused, according to Kahane, by the refusal of these leaders to follow the right path, i.e., to repent and establish in Israel a full and complete Jewish state. But unlike the haredi version, the sinful life of the Jewish state does not imply its illegitimacy. The State of Israel was not established, according to Kahane, by the secular Zionists although they think it was. It was created by God, and it is therefore holy no matter how corrupt its present leadership is. Kahane may not have been happy about secular Zionism, but there is no question that like Gush Emunim he was part of the Zionist camp. And just like Gush Emunim, Kahane did not believe in an individual Messiah, a metahistorical redeemer who would save the nation in an unnatural way. The people of Israel could bring about redemption by their very acts. They only had to repent and respect the fundamental laws of the Torah, exactly as these laws were handed down to the nation three thousand years ago.[45]

Kahane's belief in unrestrained violence stemmed from his profound animosity and mistrust of the *goyim* (Gentiles). Many Jews have expressed since time immemorial the Jewish antagonism toward the cruel Gentile nations, which have repeatedly harassed the Jews, persecuted them, and been responsible for their mass murder. But

Kahane was by far the most extreme representative of this school in modern times. And what was unique about his approach was that *he openly sought revenge*. There is not a single essay or book in which this enmity and drive for revenge does not surface. Kahane's emotional reaction to the Gentiles is so profound that *they, not the Jews, are paradoxically responsible for the establishment of the State of Israel*. The State of Israel was established, according to Kahane, not because the Zionists (who did not repent!) deserved it but as a result of the actions of the Gentiles. The perennial humiliation of the Jew by the Gentile world was, by this strange theory, also a humiliation of God since his chosen people were repeatedly being persecuted.[46] Following the Holocaust, God had the State of Israel established as his revenge against the Gentiles.

While his revenge theory was only fully developed in the 1980s, it was already noticeable in an essay Kahane wrote after the 1976 terrorist attack on a school in Kiryat Shmone that took the lives of more than twenty children. In that essay, "Hillul Hashem" (the desecration of the name of God), Kahane developed his answer to the Kookist theology of Gush Emunim regarding the process of modern redemption and the origins of the State of Israel:

> The debate about the religious legitimacy of the State of Israel and its place in our history has gone on within religious circles for a long time. It has focused on the penetrating and real question; How can a religious Jew see the hand of God in a state that was established by Jews who not only do not follow the paths of God but reject Him openly or, at best, are passive to His blessed existence? . . . The State of Israel was established not because the Jew deserved it, for the Jew is as he has been before, rejecting God, deviating from his paths and ignoring His Torah—but all this is immaterial to the case. God created this state not for the Jew and not as a reward for his justice and good deeds. It is because He, be blessed, decided that He could no longer take the desecration of His Name and the laughter, the disgrace and the persecution of the people that were named after Him, so He ordered the State of Israel to be, which is a total contradiction to the Diaspora.
>
> If the Diaspora with its humiliations, defeats, persecutions, second-class status of minorites . . . means Hillul Hashem, then a sovereign Jewish state— which provides the Jew a home, majority status, a land of his own, a military of his own, and a victory over the defeated Gentile in the battlefield—*is exactly the opposite,* Kidush Hashem (the sanctification of the name of God). It is the reassertion, the proof, the testimony for the existence of God and his government.[47]

Thus, Kahane's State of Israel is not a reward but a punishment. It is not the Jews who deserve it but the Gentiles! The specific Gentiles may not be the same, but they are always there: the Nazis, the blacks, the Christian Church, the Russians, and, of course, the Arabs. Kahane's intense radicalism, immense passion, and irrevocable commitment to his special political struggle seemed to be exclusively rooted in this one element, the insatiable urge to beat the *goy,* to respond in kind for the two millennia-old vilification of the Jews. However, since he claims to be more than an individual Jew who seeks revenge, and is rather expressing the halakha opinion and the voice of God, it is not surprising that the vengeance the Jews are supposed to take is not simply a personal act but the revenge of God for the humiliation he suffered through the desecration of his people.

> Do you want to know how the Name of G-d is desecrated in the eyes of the mocking and sneering nations? It is when the *Jew*, His people, His chosen, is desecrated! When the *Jew* is beaten, G-d is profaned! When the *Jew* is humiliated—G-d is shamed! When the *Jew* is attacked—it is an assault upon the Name of God! . . .
>
> Every pogrom is a desecration of the Name. Every Auschwitz and expulsion and murder and rape of a Jew is the humiliation of G-d. Every time a Jew is beaten by a gentile because he is a Jew, this is the essence of Hillul Hashem! . . . An end to Exile—that is Kidush Hashem. An end to the shame and beatings and the monuments to our murdered and our martyrized. An end to Kaddish and prayers for the dead . . . An end to the Gentile fist upon a Jewish face. . . .
>
> A Jewish fist in the face of an astonished gentile world that had not seen it for two millennia, this is Kidush Hashem. Jewish dominion over the Christian holy places while the Church that sucked our blood vomits its rage and frustration. This is Kidush Hashem. A Jewish Air Force that is better than any other and that forces a Lebanese airliner down so that we can imprison murderers of Jews rather than having to repeat the centuries old pattern of begging the gentile to do it for us. This is Kidush Hashem. . . . Reading angry editorials about Jewish "aggression" and "violations" rather than flowery eulogies over dead Jewish victims. That is Kidush Hashem.[48]

Kahane's use of the formal halakhic terminology of "Hillul Hashem" (the desecration of the name of God) and "Kidush Hashem" (the sanctification of the name of God) should not mislead the reader to believe that this is an ordinary halakhic argumentation. What really comes out of these emotional statements is Kahane's idiosyncratic conviction that the very definition of Jewish freedom implies the ability to humiliate the Gentile. The stronger the Jew is, the more violent and aggressive, the freer he becomes. Kahane may not have gone as far as George Sorel and Frantz Fanon in claiming that violence is a moral force in history or that violence sets one free, but he does share many similarities with the two, especially Fanon. In a sense what he is proposing is that a Jewish independence and a Jewish state are not enough. Jewish sovereignty does not provide a full and satisfactory solution of the Jewish problem, for it only solves the misery of exile. There is, however, another wound which has to be healed, the pain of humiliation, the misery of thousands of years of discrimination and victimization, the bleeding memories of generations of vilified Jews, killed for their religion.

Kahane, it is important to stress, did not concentrate solely on the Holocaust, though his profound reaction to the Nazi genocide of the Jews during World War II was a dominant theme in his actions and writings from the days of the American JDL.[49] The Holocaust was a natural product of anti-Semitism which could develop in any "normal" nation and is still a historical possibility. According to Kahane the Holocaust, and the countless pogroms that preceded it have left in the nation's collective psyche an almost irreparable damage. Jewish independence alone cannot redress the damage, only a concrete revenge, a physical humiliation of the Gentile. Therefore, Kahane, just like Frantz Fanon, is not satisfied with a peaceful liberation. A military force that astonishes the world is needed, "a fist in the face of the Gentile."

Kahane's penchant for violence, which he later expanded to a full-fledged ideology of violence, did not develop out of his experience with the Arabs. Already in the days of the American JDL, Kahane was emphasizing the importance of physical force. One of the pillars of the JDL's operative ideology was the notion of "Jewish iron." Kahane, it is true, did not invent either the idea or the metaphor: he adapted it from the secular ideology of Vladimir Jabotinsky, the founder of Revisionist Zionism, who said that, in the Diaspora or under foreign rule, Jews were no longer to bow to their oppressors but were called upon to respond to them in kind and with physical force, if necessary. Kahane was so impressed with the notion of "iron," and the application of physical force for self-defense, that he divided the JDL in America into two groups, the Chaya groups and the Scholar groups. *Chaya* in Hebrew means "animal," and Chaya squads were in charge of the use of violence against the League's rivals.[50] When he was brought to trial in New York in 1971, one of the main charges against Kahane was illegal possession of guns, ammunition, and explosives. The leader of the JDL, who did not hesitate to ally himself with the Mafia boss Joseph Colombo (himself the founder of the ersatz Italian–American Civil Rights Association in New York), had no problem translating the idea of "Iron Israel" into the actual use of firearms against the enemies of the Jews. Some of his followers, members of the JDL and probably of a Chaya squad, planted a bomb in the offices of Sol Hurok, the Jewish producer who used to bring Russian artists to America. The bomb that set the place ablaze killed a young Jewish secretary who worked for Hurok.[51] It was the beginning of a series of terrorist acts which characterized the behavior of the JDL and its splinter groups long after Kahane left the United States.

Kahane had never denied his penchant for violence and in his own account of the story of the Jewish Defense League devoted a whole chapter to the justification and rationalization of JDL's violence. While making the usual argument that "violence against *evil* is not the same as violence against good" and that violence for self-defense is fully legitimate, Kahane reaches his famous conclusion that, since Jews have been victimized for so long, "Jewish violence in defense of Jewish interest is *never* bad." According to this theory Jewish violence is nothing but an extension of Jewish love, *Ahavat Isroel.*[52]

In Israel, there was no place for further expression of "Jewish iron," since from 1948 the country had been sovereign and Jabotinsky's notion had been realized in the Israel Defence Forces (IDF). But unlike Jabotinsky's recognized successors, Meir Kahane had apparently not been satisfied. Though he did not establish Chaya teams in Israel, he maintained that, if the state was incapable or unready to react in kind against those who spilled "so much as one drop of Jewish blood," then it was the duty of individual Israelis to do so. Thus, Kahane took to legitimizing anti-Arab terror, a message fully absorbed and acted upon by his followers. In 1974, Kahane first came up with the idea of TNT (Hebrew acronym for Terror Neqed Terror, i.e., Jewish terrorism against Arab terrorism). In *The Jewish Idea,* he suggested that a "world-wide Jewish anti-terror group" be established and that "this group must be organized and aided in *exactly the same way as the terrorists are aided by the Arab governments.* With a totally serious face, the government of Israel must deny any connection with the group, even while allowing the *same* training bases on its soil as the Arab states allow the terrorists." [53] Kahane even recommended at the time the application of indiscriminate terrorism against the population of the Arab countries which provide the PLO with financial, political, and military support.

Kahane's idea to apply brutal Jewish counterterrorism did not change much over the years, and in his last book he vowed to establish, upon assuming the leadership of Israel, special Jewish antiterror groups that would operate all over the world and help Jews wherever there was trouble, disregarding the local authorities and their laws. [54] Since the government of Israel was not receptive to Kahane's notions, his followers and other individuals inspired by his idea soon started to act on their own. Out of fear of the Israeli police and secret services, they did not try to establish permanent terror organizations but rather engaged in occasional anti-Arab atrocities, using the symbol of TNT. Kahane's devotees were actively involved in the intensification of the conflict between Jews and Arabs in Hebron in the 1970s. Yossi Dayan, a student of Kahane and later the secretary general of Kach, has been caught and arrested several times for provoking the Arabs in the Cave of the Patriarchs. In an interview he once bragged, "I had more trials than the number of stars on the American flag." [55] Before the Intifada, which has changed all the rules of public conduct in the West Bank, it was Kahane's followers who usually acted in response to Arab attacks, although by the middle of the 1980s such pretexts as acting only in reaction to Arab violence were decreasingly needed. Craig Leitner, a Kahane student, described a typical mid-1980s operation:

> One day towards the end of July 1984, I agreed with Mike Gozovsky and Yehuda Richter to operate against the Arabs. We left Kiriyat Arba in a hired car, headed towards Jerusalem. . . . That night around 23:00, we went to the Neve Yaacov area. Yehuda was driving. Around midnight, we saw an Arab in his twenties walking along the road. I said, "Lets stop the car." I went out and hit the Arab with my fist on the shoulder. I also kicked him. He escaped into the night. We continued to Hebron and it was decided—I don't remember by whom—to burn Arab cars. We had in our car two plastic bottles containing four and a half liters of gasoline. In Hebron Yehuda stopped the car. Mike took the gasoline and poured it under several cars, maybe three. Following the burning of the cars by Yehuda, we moved, not waiting to see what would happen. Dogs were around and I was afraid that they would wake up the neighbors, or perhaps bite us and we would get rabies. [56]

When asked for his reaction to the activities of Leitner and his friends, who later fired on an Arab bus wounding several passengers, Kahane expressed total approval.

He said that he was sorry they would have to spend years in prison and added that, in his eyes, they were Maccabees. Later, Kahane placed Yehuda Richter, the main suspect in the operation, second on his list for the Knesset. Had Kach won two seats in 1984, Richter would have been released due to the immunity of Israel's members of the Knesset. When asked once by a journalist whether he would be willing to instruct his followers not to hit innocent Arabs who happened to be near the location of a terrorist incident, Kahane responded bluntly by saying, "No, I would not. As long as they are here we are lost. I have no way of knowing if this Arab or another is innocent. The real danger is the demographics."[57]

Kach was intensely violent before the Palestinian uprising. Its entire posture, the yellow shirts with the black clenched fists, the attacks on Arab families from within the Green Line (the pre–1967 Israeli border) that move into Jewish neighborhoods, the chasing of innocent Arab workers for the fun of it, the anti-Arab "victory parades," the attempts to break up leftist meetings in a style reminiscent of the Italian and German Fascists of the 1920s , have all spelled out hooliganism and violence. Especially violent has been Kach's most aggressive local stronghold, the Kiryat Arba branch in the West Bank. Kahane's devoted followers, who are legally armed by the army like the rest of the settlers in the occupied territories, have initiated since the mid-1970s countless violent operations against the local Arabs. Unlike the Gush Emunim activists who have usually resorted to anti-Arab violence in response to previous Arab attacks and who have said all along that they were ready to tolerate a peaceful Arab presence in the area, Kach people have never concealed their hope for a massive emigration. The only reason for their relative restraint has been their fear of the security forces. In 1986 and following the intensification of Arab-Jewish violence, they established the "Committee for the Preservation of Security," which was to patrol the roads in the area. But the committee that was established as a defensive instrument against Arab rock throwing became during the intifada a most aggressive vigilante group. Its notorious commander, Shmuel Ben-Yishai, publicly declared that any incident involving a harassment of Jewish traffic would make him shoot to kill without warning. "I do not shoot in the air, I shoot to kill. . . . It is stupid to fire the entire magazine in the air! Only the Jews speak about the 'purity of the arms.' Just a minute! Listen who is talking about morality: Shamir, the biggest terrorist? Rabin who killed Jews on Altalena? The Americans who murdered the Indians?"[58]

By 1988, Ben-Yishai's statement was no longer an exception among the settlers of Judea and Samaria and the larger non-Kach radical right. Palestinian violence in the occupied territories had "confirmed" what Kahane had been saying about the Arabs (and the Gentiles in general) all along. It was another attempt to "humiliate" the Jews and to "kill" them if possible. For most of these people it has been an indication that the decisive battle for Eretz Yisrael has already started.

The vast majority of Kahane supporters, including the activists of his movement, have not read his books and do not understand his ideo-theology, especially his idiosyncratic explanation of the establishment of the State of Israel. Many of them do not even qualify as Orthodox Jews. There are nevertheless three reasons for their support of the rabbi and readiness to follow his brutal way: the "halakhic" legitimation he provides to their hidden desires to respond to Arab terrorism in kind; their anxieties about Arab competition in the low-paying job market and the threatening presence of West Bank Arab workers in their neighborhoods;[59] and their immense antiestablishment sentiment and resentment of the old Ashkenazic elite of Israel. Kach's ideological violence is nourished, in this respect, by the low self-esteem of most of its adherents and by their inferior socioeconomic status. It took the American-born rabbi many years to reach the poor and downtrodden of Israeli society, most of whom are Sephardic Jews (Jews who came to Israel from Oriental countries), but since the mid-1980s he has become their authentic spokesman. Thus, the lower-class penchant for violence, the sense of social alienation and failure, and the sophisticated halakhic theory of violence have created a very explosive Israeli force which was hardly expected just several years earlier.

The Sociopolitical Consequences of Fundamentalist Violence

Any discussion of the impact of fundamentalist violence on nonfundamentalist society must start with the recognition that fundamentalist violence is an integral part of the larger fundamentalist milieu. This evaluation, therefore, cannot be separated from the general issue of the interaction of the respective fundamentalist movements, the West Bank Arabs, and the Israeli society. In this perspective, there has always been a great difference between the impact of haredi society and its mores on the general Israeli society and the impact of religious Zionism. The doctrine of haredi separation, the practice of haredi ghettoization, and the relatively low intensity of haredi antisecular violence have produced a situation of minimal friction and little impact. Most secular Israelis have not been very pleased with the politics of the ultra-Orthodox parties, but have learned to live with the sporadic antisecular eruptions and tolerate them without changing their own nonviolent behavior. With very few exceptions haredi violence directed at the secular society has been taken care of by the police without spilling over to the external secular world.

The West Bank Arabs, who are the targeted community of the fundamentalist violence of Gush Emunim and Kach, have never bothered to understand the settlers' point of view, their motivation, or the difference between the two movements. The main issue for them was, and remains, the *occupation*. From their perspective the settlers are none other than the spearhead of the Israeli occupation which started in 1967, and the effort to annex the territories and evict all their Arab residents. Arab violence is seen in this context as part of a legitimate national liberation struggle while Jewish violence is obviously an illegitimate repression. The fact that all settlers are armed by the government to the teeth, and that many of them are soldiers in reserve, serves as full proof for the Palestinian argument that the government of Israel is secretly supporting all settlers irrespective of their theological affiliation. The violence inflicted by the fundamentalist settlers is seen in the same way. It makes no difference to the local Arab resident whether he was shot at by a settler with a skullcap or by a soldier trying to maintain law and order.

It is very hard to determine whether the the vigilante violence of Gush Emunim has been helpful in curtailing Arab antisettler activities and to what extent, but there is no doubt about its contribution to the Arab-Jewish cycle of violence in the occupied territories. This is especially true of the ideologically motivated violence of the members of Kach. Kahane's people may not have reached their goal of enticing the Palestinians of the occupied territories to leave, out of fear of what would be done to them when Kahane takes over, but they have been instrumental in putting the intercommunal violence within the framework of a self-fulfilling prophesy. Jewish extremists, just like Arab extremists, are certain today that the other side is out to kill them and are doing their best to strike first. There is consequently a vicious circle of violence and counterviolence in the occupied territories which plays directly into the hands of the extremists of both sides.

Unlike the case of haredi fundamentalism, the impact of the Zionist fundamentalists on post-1967 Israeli society has been significant. Zionist fundamentalism, especially the Gush Emunim version, has become popular not so much because of its fundamentalist message as because of the movement's ability to manipulate skillfully national symbols such as "pioneering," "settlement," and even "Zionism." The same has been true of the Kahane movement, although its message and symbolic action have been directed at different public and social strata.

Before his assassination in November 1990, Rabbi Kahane had become popular with larger nonfundamentalist circles not because of his idiosyncratic theology but because of his aggressive attitude toward the Palestinians and his radical solution to the Israeli-Arab conflict. As part of their larger endorsement of Gush Emunim and Kach, many Israelis have come to identify with the militant posture of the two movements and with their intercommunal violence. The large questions that have to be asked in this perspective pertain less to the direct impact of fundamentalist violence than to the general influence of Zionist fundamentalism on Israel's regime and civic culture. Does Zionist fundamentalism presently pose a real threat to Israeli democracy? Is the rise of the new mélange of militant fundamentalism, Jewish ultranationalism, and anti-Arab sentiment an indication that the State of Israel stands in danger of losing its traditional attachment to humanism, rationalism, and an open secular society?

Given the relatively small number of Israeli Zionist fundamentalists and the absence, among most of them, of a clear antidemocratic model of action, the answer to these questions seems to involve two time perspectives. Thus, it appears that in the short run the militant practices of Gush Emunim and Kach do not challenge the entire paradigm of Israeli politics and consequently cannot be considered an immediate threat to the system. There is, in other words, no danger of a fundamentalist takeover in Israel, and the likelihood that the violent practices described in this study will be extended to wider circles is minimal.

Things are different in the long run, for the major issue in this time perspective is the *slow but steady* penetration of the civic culture of the nation by fundamentalist militancy and violence. It is important to maintain that even those "moderate" Gush Emunim radicals who say that present-day Zionist democracy is holy do not conceal their conviction that democracy ought to be inferior to many higher political norms: the integrity of the land, the supremacy of many religious laws, and the *a priori* superiority of the Jewish citizens of the state. The fundamentalists of Gush Emunim and Kach are today part of a larger political camp, the Israeli radical right, which is thriving. The vast majority of spokespersons and members of this camp, which amounts to 15–20 percent of the nation, do not participate in the anti-Arab vigilante operations conducted by Gush Emunim but approve of them. Not a few of these are also "Kahanists," those who like both Kahane's theory and practice. It is evident that this endorsement, although not directly antithetical to democracy, has an incremental corrupting influence on Israel's civic culture.[60]

It may be worthwhile to stress that the magnitude of fundamentalist violence in Israel and its intensity have been, in a comparative perspective, rather low. Jewish fundamentalists themselves since 1967 have not killed more than two dozen Arabs (they have wounded a few thousand), and have greatly "trailed" in this respect many Muslim, Buddhist, and Hindu fundamentalists in Lebanon, Iran, India, and Sri Lanka. But the issue, of course, is not statistical. A visitor to the Jewish state who has not been in the country for twenty years is unlikely to find there the civic style he had become familiar with in the past. In present-day Israel, discussions turn into debates, debates into physical clashes, and anti-Arab demonstrations into violent raids on Arab villages. There is no question that a major contribution to this growing extremism has been made by Arabs, PLO terrorists, supporters of PLO terrorism, and Palestinians opposed to an independent and secure Israel.

But the issue discussed here is not Arab extremism but the new Jewish radicalism. For the first twenty years of their state the Israelis were able to cope with the Arab desire to destroy their country at almost no cost to their civic culture. This is no longer the case. The growth of militant fundamentalism and ultranationalism is a most serious indication that the culture of Israeli democracy has started to pay a very dear price for the continuation of the conflict and a heavier price may yet come.

It is important to note that no democracy on earth is devoid of tensions, conflicts, corruption, and some degree of violence. But if the majority of the conflicting parties respect a certain set of democratic ideals and cultural tenets, these tensions do not become pathological and the system can cope. If, on the other hand, the conflicts evolve without an overall respect for these values, the system is in trouble. For a democracy to survive decently, it is not enough that all the partners to the regime formally respect its institutions. A respect for its values and a positive orientation toward its legal order are also necessary. This is today the Achilles' heel of Israel's democracy and the problem with the new religious radicalism. Even those ultranationalists and fundamentalists who say they are committed to democracy in their own way are a serious danger because their commitment is instrumental and their allegiance is conditional. The threat of their anti-Arab violence may not be immediate, but it is not negligible either. No one can afford to forget that ten, twenty, or thirty years of *cultural* erosion of a troubled democracy can finally reach the hard core of the regime and turn to an *institutional* breakdown.[61] In this respect, the experience of the growth of militant Zionist fundamentalism in the last two decades is not very encouraging.

Notes

1. On the haredim in general, see Samuel C. Heilman and Menachem Friedman, "Religious Fundamentalism and Religious Jews: The Case of the Haredim," in Martin E. Marty and R. Scott Appleby, eds., *Fundamentalisms Observed* (Chicago: University of Chicago Press, 1991).

2. Cf. Aviezer Ravitzky, "The Expected—and the Possible: Messianism, Zionism and the Future of Israel in the Divided Religious Schools in Israel," in Alouph Hareven, ed., *Israel towards the 21st Century* (Jerusalem: Van Leer Foundation, 1984, in Hebrew), pp 140–46.

3. See the discussion of the haredi position in Menachem Friedman, "The State of Israel as a Theological Dilemma," in Baruch Kimmerling, ed., *The Israeli State and Society: Boundaries and Frontiers* (Albany: SUNY Press, 1989).

4. On the evolution of the political and ideological relationships between Agudat Israel (the political party of the haredim), the Zionist movement, and the State of Israel, see Yoseph Fund, "Agudat Israel Confronting Zionism and the State of Israel—Ideology and Politics" (Ph.D. diss., Bar Ilan University, 1989).

5. Cf. A. Yehuda Cohen, "Under Examination," *Om Ani Homa* (Jerusalem: Neturei Karta, 1950, in Hebrew), part 2, p. 70.

6. Cf. Samuel C. Heilman and Menachem Friedman, "Religious Fundamentalism and Religious Jews: The Case of the Haredim," in Marty and Appleby, *Fundamentalisms Observed.*

7. Cf. Amnon Levy, *The Ultra-Orthodox* (Jerusalem: Keter, 1988, in Hebrew), p. 13.

8. Ibid., chap. 14.

9. Ibid., pp. 9–11.

10. Ibid., pp. 9–10.

11. Cf. Yosef Shilhav and Menachem Friedman, *Expansion within Seclusion: The Haredi Community in Jerusalem* (Jerusalem: Jerusalem Institute for the Study of Israel, 1985, in Hebrew), p. 9.

12. See, for example, *The Mormon Fraud* (Jerusalem: Yad Leachim pamphlet, March 1986).

13. Cf. Amnon Levy, *The Ultra-Orthodox*, chap. 15.

14. The most extreme denunciations of the secular authorities including references to the "Nazis" appear in wall posters and announcements, which are called *Pashkevils.* The Pashkevils may be seen as instruments of both communication and political mobilization. The individual haredi is informed about exceptional events which pertain to the community and is called, on occasions, to demonstrate and react to a severe "desecration of the Name."

15. For a general discussion of religious extremism and militancy, and its relevance to the Jewish ultra-Orthodox, see Charles S. Liebman, "Extremism as a Religious Norm," *Journal of the Scientific Study of Religion* 22, no. 1 (1983): 75–86.

16. For an interesting account of the militancy of the haredim from the perspective of the secular victims, see Abraham Ferver, "Patterns of Haredi Attacks on non-Haredi Inhabitants in North-West Jerusalem as Part of the Struggle for the Area" (M.A. thesis, Institute of Criminology, Hebrew University of Jerusalem, 1987, in Hebrew).

17. On Gush Emunim, see Gideon Aran, "From Religious Zionism to Zionist Religion: The Roots of Gush Emunim and Its Culture" (Ph.D. diss., Hebrew University of Jerusalem, 1987, in Hebrew); David Newman, ed., *The Impact of Gush Emunim* (London: Croom Helm, 1985); Zvi Raanan,

Gush Emunim (Tel Aviv: Sifriyat Poalim, 1980, in Hebrew); Danny Rubinstein, *On the Lord's Side: Gush Emunim* (Tel Aviv: Hakibbutz Hameuchad, 1982, in Hebrew); Ehud Sprinzak, "Gush Emunim: The Iceberg Model of Political Extremism," *Medina Mimshal Yeyehasim Beinleumiim*, no. 17 (Fall 1981, in Hebrew); "Gush Emunim: The Politics of Zionist Fundamentalism in Israel" (New York: American Jewish Committee, 1986). For a recent review of Gush Emunim literature, see Eliezer Don-Yehiya, "Jewish Messianism, Religious Zionism and Israeli Politics: The Impact and Origins of Gush Emunim," *Middle Eastern Studies* 23, no. 2 (April 1987).

18. Cf. Tsvi Raanan, *Gush Emunim*, chap. 2; Danny Rubinstein, *On the Lord's Side*, chaps. 4–5.

19. Cf. Gideon Aran, "From Religious Zionism to Zionist Religion: The Roots of Gush Emunim and Its Culture," chap. 2; Zvi Yaron, *The Philosophy of Rabbi Kook* (Jerusalem: Jewish Agency, 1979, in Hebrew), chap. 10.

20. Cf. Tsvi Raanan, *Gush Emunim*, pp. 60–73.

21. Rabbi Haim Drukman, quoted in Gideon Aran, "From Religious Zionism to Zionist Religion: The Roots of Gush Emunim and Its Culture," p. 444.

22. Cf. Ehud Sprinzak, "Gush Emunim: The Politics of Zionist Fundamentalism in Israel," p. 11.

23. Cf. Ehud Sprinzak, "Gush Emunim: The Iceberg Model of Political Extremism."

24. Cf. Gideon Aran, *Eretz Israel: Between Politics and Religion* (Jerusalem: Jerusalem Institute for the Study of Israel, 1985, in Hebrew).

25. Cf. Moshe Dayan, *Milestones* (Jerusalem: Edanim, 1976, in Hebrew), pp. 497–504. Cf. Moshe Dayan, *Story of My Life* (London: Sphere Books, 1976), pp. 372–74.

26. Cf. Michael Roman, *Jewish Kiryat Arba versus Arab Hebron* (Jerusalem: West Bank Data Project, 1986), pp. 57–58.

27. Cf. Peter Robert Demant, "Swords into Plowshares: Israeli Settlement Policy in the Occupied Territories, 1967–1977" (Ph.D. diss., University of Amsterdam, 1988), pp. 369–71.

28. Ibid., pp. 59–62; see also Danny Rubinstein, *On the Lord's Side*, pp. 96–97.

29. The only exception to the rather peaceful relations between Gush Emunim settlers and Arabs in the West Bank until 1974 occurred at the Cave of the Patriarchs in Hebron, a shrine holy to both Jews and Muslims, where a constant settler drive to extend the Jewish presence produced occasional skirmishes and fights. Cf. Michael Roman, *Jewish Kiryat Arba versus Arab Hebron* (Jerusalem: West Bank Data Project, 1985), pp. 55–68.

30. Cf. Meron Benvenisti, *1987 Report: Demographic, Economic, Legal, Social and Political Developments in the West Bank* (Jerusalem: West Bank Data Project, 1987), pp. 40–44.

31. Cf. David Weisburd and Vered Vinitzky, "Vigilantism as Rational Social Control: The Case of the Gush Emunim Settlers," in M. Aronoff, ed., *Cross Currents in Israeli Culture and Politics*, Political Anthropology, vol. 4 (New Brunswick, N.J.: Transaction Books, 1984).

32. Menachem Livni, *Interrogation*, 18 May 1984 (Court documents, the Jewish Underground trial).

33. Cf. Haggai Segal, *Dear Brothers* (Jerusalem: Keter, 1987, in Hebrew), pp. 77–78.

34. Yehuda Etzion, "I Felt an Obligation to Expurgate the Temple Mount," *Nekuda* 88 (24 June 1985): 24–25.

35. Cf. Richard Maxwell Brown, "The American Vigilante Tradition," in Hugh Graham and Ted Gur, eds., *Violence in America* (New York: Signet Books, 1969), pp. 144–46; John H. Rosenbaum and Carl Sederberg, "Vigilantism: An Analysis of Establishment Violence," *Comparative Politics* 6 (1974).

36. Cf. Haggai Segal, *Dear Brothers*, pp. 47–57.

37. Cf. David Rapoport, "Messianic Sanctions for Terror," *Comparative Politics* 20, no. 2 (January 1988): 204–5.

38. Haggai Segal, *Dear Brothers,* p. 55; Ehud Sprinzak, "From Messianic Pioneering to Vigilante Terrorism: The Case of Gush Emunim Underground," *Journal of Strategic Studies* 10, no. 4 (December 1987): 200.

39. Cf. Ehud Sprinzak, *The Ascendance of Israel's Radical Right* (New York: Oxford University Press, 1991), pp. 164–65.

40. Although there has been a constant erosion of Gush Emunim's "liberal" attitude toward its Arab neighbors, it appears that most of the leaders of the movement do not favor either a Kahane-like expulsion of the Arabs or the more "moderate" demand currently heard in Israel to "transfer" them to the neighboring Arab states.

41. On Rabbi Kahane and Kach, see Ehud Sprinzak, *The Ascendance of Israel's Radical Right,* chap. 6.

42. Janet L. Dolgin, *Jewish Identity and the JDL* (Princeton: Princeton University Press, 1977), pp. 33–37.

43. Cf. Ehud Sprinzak, "Kach and Meir Kahane: The Emergence of Jewish Quasi-Fascism," *Patterns of Prejudice* 19, nos. 3–4 (1985): 5–6.

44. Cf. Gerald Cromer, "The Debate about Kahanism in Israeli Society, 1984–1988," *Occasional Papers* (New York: Harry Frank Guggenheim Foundation, 1988).

45. On the various components of the Kahane ideology, see Aviezer Ravitzky, "The Roots of Kahanism: Consciousness and Political Reality," *Jerusalem Quarterly* 39 (1986).

46. Ibid.

47. Rabbi Meir Kahane, "Hillul Hashem" (a Kach mimeographed article, n.d., in Hebrew).

48. Rabbi Meir Kahane, *Listen World, Listen Jew* (Tucson, Ariz.: Institute of Jewish Ideas, 1975), pp. 121–22.

49. Cf. Gerald Cromer, "Negotiating the Meaning of the Holocaust: An Observation on the Debate about Kahanism in Israeli Society," *Holocaust and Genocide Studies* 2.2 (1987).

50. Cf. Janet L. Dolgin, *Jewish Identity and the JDL,* chap. 3.

51. Cf. Yair Kotler, *Heil Kahane* (Tel Aviv: Modan, 1985, in Hebrew), pp. 103–8. Kahane has never bothered to apologize for the killing of the innocent secretary. Instead, he complains in his book on the JDL about the refusal of the Jewish establishment to bail out the three JDL youngsters accused of "Jewish political crime." Cf. Rabbi Meir Kahane, *The Story of the Jewish Defense League,* p. 191.

52. Ibid., pp. 141–42, 75–80.

53. Rabbi Meir Kahane, *The Jewish Idea* (Jerusalem: Institute of Jewish Ideas, 1974), p. 14.

54. Cf. Rabbi Meir Kahane, *Uncomfortable Questions for Comfortable Jews* (Secaucus, N.J.: Lyle Stuart, 1987), p. 285.

55. Quoted in Yair Kotler, *Heil Kahane,* p. 257.

56. Quoted in Nadav Shragai, "Going for the Action," *Ha'aretz,* 27 November 1984.

57. Quoted in Haim Shibi, "Wherever There Is Blood Spilled You Find Kahane," *Yediot Achronot,* 2 August 1985.

58. Quoted in Yair Avituv, "All Is Well in the Kasba," *Kol Hair,* 12 August 1988. Itzhak Shamir, Israel's prime minister, was the commander of the Lehi terrorist underground during the 1940s. Altalena was a 1948 arms ship brought to Israel without official permission by the Irgun underground and destroyed by an army unit under the command of young Itzhak Rabin, Israel's present-day minister of defense.

59. On the Kach social composition and the attraction to Kahane, see Gershon Shafir and Yoav Peled, "Thorns in Your Eyes: The Socioeconomic Basis of the Kahane Vote," in Asher Arian and Michal Shamir, eds., *The Elections in Israel, 1984* (Tel Aviv: Ramot Publishing Company, 1986).

60. The Jerusalem van Leer Foundation has conducted since the summer of 1984 three surveys of the political attitudes of Israel's high school generation (the fifteen- to eighteen-year-olds). The September 1984 study found out that 60 percent of the respondents thought the Arabs did not deserve full equality and 42 percent were in

favor of restricting the political rights of non-Jews. The following survey, conducted in May 1985, showed that 40 percent agreed with Kahane's opinions and 11 percent were ready to vote for him. A further breakdown of the results indicated exceptionally strong support for Kahane's ideas among the religious youth (59 percent) and among young people of Oriental origin (50 percent). The April 1986 survey, which was conducted after an intense anti-Kahane campaign throughout most of the political system, showed a small decline in support for the rabbi's positions. Only one-third of the respondents thought Kahane's opinions

were right, and 75 percent said they would not vote for him. Fifty percent, however, were still favorable to the idea of restricting the rights of the Arabs and 56 percent opposed equal rights for non-Jews. For a further description of the growth of Israeli ultranationalism, see Charles S. Liebman, "Jewish Ultra-Nationalism in Israel: Converging Strands," in William Frankel, ed., *Survey of Jewish Affairs* (London: Associated Universities Press, 1985).

61. Cf. Juan J. Linz, *The Breakdown of Democratic Regimes: Crisis, Breakdown and Requilibrium* (Baltimore: John Hopkins University Press, 1978), pp. 27–38.

Afghanistan: An Islamic War of Resistance

Olivier Roy

O_n 27 April 1978, a successful communist coup took place in a landlocked, little-known, and mountainous country, Afghanistan, without arousing great concern all over the world. On 27 December 1979, the Soviet army launched a large-scale invasion of Afghanistan to save the communist regime from a probable collapse in face of an increasing Muslim resistance. This time the world took notice, but most of the experts thought that the Soviet army would not withdraw from Afghanistan until as the insurgents were crushed. On 15 February 1989, the last Soviet soldier crossed the border back to the Soviet Union. On the surrounding hills, bearded and triumphant Muslim fighters, or Mujahidin, kept watch before trying to topple the remains of the communist regime or plunging into internecine feuds.

The Afghan war is the first war since World War II in which Soviet troops have been defeated. It is also the first liberation war won by a movement which proclaims Islam, not nationalism or socialism, as its goal. Of course, it is not the first time that a guerrilla movement has taken power in a Muslim country, but the movements in Algeria and South Yemen adopted both their ideology and their political organization from Western models like Marxism and nationalism. The last purely Muslim upheavals go back to the ill-fated anticolonial revolts in the Sudan (the Mahdist movement) and Central Asia (Basmachis), doomed to fail for lack of adaptation to the modern world. Since World War II, it seemed as if only a modern one-party system, based on a secular ideology, could achieve some success against a colonial power.

Yet the Afghan Mujahidin, discarding the one-party system and advocating Islam as their political ideology, were able to thwart the Soviet invasion. The Afghan war reflected both the decline of the Soviet Empire and the rise of Muslim radicalism. Is there a link between the two historic events? Is the Afghan war an exception or the beginning of a new trend among Third World countries by which secular ideologies are yielding ground to religious ones? Answers to these questions may be revealed over the next few years in the evolution of the domestic situation in Afghanistan and the consequences of the Afghan war among the Soviet Muslims of Central Asia.

It has often been said that it is the weaponry, especially the famous Stinger anti-aircraft missiles, that allowed the Mujahidin to expel the Soviets. But history shows that a guerrilla movement can win only if it has political roots among the peasantry. If it does not, weaponry is of little use, as has been obvious in Nicaragua. This observation raises questions central to this essay. If the Afghan Mujahidin movement has little in common, in both ideology and political organization, with the contemporary liberation movements, how was it able to achieve such an unexpected success against the Soviet army? And why was it unable to transform this initial success into the establishment of a new stable central government?

The answers emerge only when one analyzes the Afghan Mujahidin on two different levels, for the movement is the expression both of the contemporary Islamic radicalism of young educated and urban laymen,[1] and of the traditional segment of Afghan society, which could be and was mobilized only temporarily under the banner of an Islamic *jihad*. Traditionalist Islamic religious scholars (*ulama*) were able to enlist the support of this latter group only under the dire circumstances occasioned by the Soviet invasion and then only to defend Islam against a specific external threat.[2]

This explains the great originality and ambiguity of the Afghan war: it was at the same time a war of liberation, a traditional jihad, and a modern revolutionary movement to establish an Islamic state. Nationalism, traditionalism, and revolutionary fundamentalism (which elsewhere I prefer to call Islamism) merged together, at least as long as the Soviets remained in Afghanistan. Once the Soviets withdrew, however, and with them the strongest justification for a jihad, this tenuous coalition unraveled. Nonetheless Afghanistan is the only contemporary Sunni Muslim country in which a radical Islamic movement has taken roots among the peasantry and in which young Islamist militants have sided with at least a segment of the traditionalist ulama. Once the different elements of the coalition were separated and even became antagonists after the Soviet withdrawal, the fragile nature of the coalition did not preclude the distinct possibility that the pattern might be repeated in Soviet Central Asia. Indeed, the tumultuous events of late 1990 and 1991, including the Soviet acknowledgment of Islamic revivalism in the USSR, indicated that fundamentalist Islam might once again find itself in an uneasy but profitable partnership with traditionalist elements.

Jihad and Fundamentalism in Afghanistan

Religious violence is not a new phenomenon in Afghanistan. From the beginning of the nineteenth century, uprisings and wars in the name of religion have been conducted either to oppose a foreign non-Muslim invader (Sikhs and then British) or, from 1924, to thwart a state endeavor to modernize the country. None of these campaigns, however, resulted in an attempt to establish a new social and political order. These wars were fought largely for the purpose of preserving the social framework of Afghanistan and waged according to traditional patterns of violence, that is, employing the concept of jihad under the leadership of the ulama. Yet it would be wrong to assume that these movements were purely traditionalist and reactive. In fact most of the jihad leaders proclaimed that a tepid commitment to the Islamic faith was making Afghans vulnerable to foreign influence and thus raising the necessity of fighting secularization and foreign encroachments. The jihad movements in Afghanistan advocated cultural and judicial reform (that is, the increasing implementation of the *Shari'a*, or Islamic law) in society, but did so without calling the political or economic framework into question. Jihad wars waged from 1879 into the 1930s against foreigners were generally led by clerics who, although not drawn from the dominant tribal establishment, were able to enlist traditional groups, like tribes, which were headed by their traditional local leaders.[3] Strategy and tactics were the same as in traditional tribal warfare. Organization and administration followed the traditional local patterns, and, at the upper level, a medieval model: the leader, or *emir*, was assisted by some "secretaries," or *monshi*, in charge of the main departments (finance). But this kind of organization lasted no longer than the military campaign and always gave place to a traditional sovereign.

The point is this: jihad has so little to do with "revolution" in modern Afghan history that the Afghan sovereigns, from the eighteenth century to 1919, never hesitated to call a jihad and to enlist the high-ranking ulama in defense of the country. Moreover, reference to jihad and Shari'a bestowed religious legitimacy upon rulers who took the power by the sword. Indeed, *"Zia-ul Millat wa Din"* ("Protector of the Nation and of the Religion") was the title adopted by the founder of the modern Afghan state, Emir Abdurrahman, who reigned from 1880 to 1901.[4] There was, in the eyes of most of the ulama, no discrepancy between the true tenets of Islam and a monarchial and traditional government. The only contention was about law: does the Shari'a supersede the tribal common law? In order to strengthen the central power against the tribes, authoritarian rulers like Abdurrahman, although from tribal origin, advocated the implementation of the Shari'a instead of tribal common law and enlisted the high-ranking ulama as a way of legitimizing the central power.

In these circumstances, even when the religious leaders were advocating reforms to bring back "true Islam," jihad was never used to legitimate a subversive political movement. Although they were seen as subversive by the British colonial Raj in India, in fact the upheavals against British troops in the "frontier" area were the expression of tribal irredentism, legitimized by jihad, and not of the will to subvert the British Raj or to convert infidels.[5]

This traditional understanding of jihad explains why the Afghan peasantry took up arms against the communist regime in 1978, as it had against King Amanullah's reforms in 1928,[6] and why the whole countryside arose against the Soviet invasion in 1979, much as they had when the British invaded Afghanistan in the nineteenth century. But this tradition does not account for the political forms taken by the contemporary resistance movement. If the Mujahidin had stuck solely to the traditional patterns of jihad, they would never have been able to check the Soviet army. Even if many local leaders and many Mujahidin rank and file did not see the difference between their anti-Soviet upheavals and the traditional jihad against the British, there were some definitive new patterns in the Afghan resistance movement: a new leadership, a new "Islamic" ideology, and, to a lesser extent, new forms of organization. The main political and military leaders of the Afghan resistance were members of militant Islamic movements which had been involved in politics before the communist coup and which were committed to ideology and political organizations alien to the Afghan tradition of jihad; these people are in fact typical representatives of the new Islamic movement which pervades the contemporary Sunni Muslim world. They come from the intelligentsia, not from the ulama; they were educated in the modern, government-sponsored schools, not in the religious *madrasa;* they are schooled in twentieth-century political ideologies rather than in the centuries-old religious controversies; they see Islam as a political ideology.[7]

The Ulama and the Fundamentalists

The leadership of the resistance movement in Afghanistan is composed of (1) traditional petty notables, (2) ulama, educated mainly in private traditional theological schools, and (3) young educated people. The notables and ulama generally behave according to the traditional patterns of leadership in the Muslim peasant, sometimes also tribal, society. The ulama, as we have seen, advocate the implementation of the Shari'a but do not care who is in charge of the state, provided that he supports the Shari'a and protects the religion. In this sense they are traditionalists; that is, they want a return to the fundamental tenets of the religion, understood as a code of conduct both in private and in public life, but they do not advocate a specific political system.

A new political trend emerged in the 1960s, however, among students who advocated a return to religion. Influenced by the Pakistani political activist Maududi, by the Egyptian Muslim Brother theorist Sayyid Qutb, and by the Iranian Shi'ite thinker 'Ali Shari'ati, these students saw in Islam more a political ideology than a mere religion. They became convinced that the condition for a true return to religion was not so much a change in individual or collective practices but rather the establishment of an "Islamic state." This could only be achieved, they felt, through an "Islamic revolution." They used Islamic references, including quotations from Qur'an, but fit them within the framework of modern ideologies like Marxism. They advocated the building of a vanguard party, whose task was to lead the masses in the path of the revolution. Although the individual practices of these students were generally devout, few of them had a real religious background. They were mainly educated in science or engineering high schools, or in teacher training schools. To distinguish them from the ulama, I use the word "Islamists" or, as in this essay, "fundamentalists."[8]

Thus, in Afghanistan, as in most of the other Muslim countries, there was a widening gap, turning sometimes to antagonism, between the traditional clerics and the lay-religious radicals. Each group adopted a different meaning for the word "jihad." For the ulama it was understood as a defensive action designed to protect a threatened religion from foreign encroachments or from secularization initiated by the state; for the new fundamentalists it was interpreted as an offensive action designed to topple an illegitimate secular state, whatever its policy toward religion might be. For the ulama, accommodation with the existing power was seen as desirable. For the fundamentalists, no compromise could be struck with any state whose foundations were not thoroughly Islamic.[9]

The History of the Fundamentalist Movement

The problem for the fundamentalists before the communist coup was that they did not have the religious legitimacy to call for a jihad; this privilege and responsibility traditionally belongs to the ulama or to the sovereign. And most of the ulama did not see the need to call for a jihad against rulers, who, whatever their secular trends, were avowed Afghan Muslims. The activities of the fundamentalists in the sixties were thus confined to student and intellectual circles in Kabul campuses. The inner circle was made up of professors of the State Faculty of Theology, such as Gholam Mohammad Niyazi and Burhanuddin Rabbani, who both sojourned for a long time in Cairo at the prestigious religious university of al-Azhar. Even if the teachers at the university were conformists, the stay in Cairo was an opportunity for such fundamentalists to enter the circles of the Muslim Brothers. In Kabul, this nucleus of university teachers gave birth to a more militant wing, which recruited, among younger and lay students of the State Faculty of Sciences or Polytechnic School, men such as Gulbuddin Hikmatyar and Ahmed Shah Masud. This wing was called the "Muslim Youth"; its members spent most of their time battling their Marxist fellows. The most brilliant military commanders of the resistance came from the ranks of the Muslim Youth.

But unlike the fundamentalists in the other Muslim countries, the Afghani fundamentalists chose to implement their "revolution" through an armed upheaval of the peasantry, and not through a coup d'etat or terrorist activities in Kabul and the other big cities. There were two reasons for this choice. First, Afghanistan was overwhelmingly rural, and most of the students had roots in the peasantry, even if they once lived in Kabul. Second, after the Republican coup of President Daud in July 1973, most of the fundamentalist leaders in Kabul were forced to go underground and to flee the capital.

An endeavor in 1975 to stir up the peasantry against the Daud regime in the name of Islam was a complete failure. Most of the peasants did not discern a difference between "Islamic" revolutionaries and "communist" revolutionaries and thus handed over to the government the militants who tried to enlist them in their jihad. The bulk of the traditional clergy did not follow the movement, because they did not see how a genuine jihad could have as its goal the ouster of a leader who claimed to be a good Muslim. After this failure the young fundamentalists went into exile in Pakistan. There the more radical of them, including Gulbuddin Hikmatyar, were recruited by the Pakistani military intelligence, which was eager to use the fundamentalists as a tool against a nationalist Afghanistan which had laid claim to the western part of Pakistan populated by the same Pashtun ethnic group that was dominant in Kabul. Fundamentalism was thereby used by Pakistan as a counterweight against Afghan nationalism.

The situation within Afghanistan changed dramatically when the Marxist-oriented People's Democratic Party of Afghanistan (PDPA) seized power on 27 April 1978. It did not take long for the peasants to rise up and for the ulama to call a jihad against the "infidel" regime. The causes of the peasant upheavals were not directly linked with religion, but Islam provided the intellectual framework that allowed the peasants to articulate and legitimize their grievances against the new regime. The main reason for the upheavals was the state's encroachment on the traditional way of life and its social, economic, and cultural patterns. The agrarian reform program introduced by the PDPA, without providing a viable alternative to it, threatened the social structure which was based on a landowner/tenant relationship that politically and socially functioned as a patron/client relationship. Other reforms—the abolition of the dowry, the enforcement of compulsory literacy courses, the appointment of young, inexperienced, and dogmatic urbanites as local administrators, followed by mass arrests of popular local leaders labeled "feudalists"—antagonized rural communities and rekindled defiance toward state and government encroachments.[10]

The ulama were more concerned about the openly secular, if not atheistic, propaganda of the new regime. They began to preach against the regime in the months following the April coup and found a receptive audience among peasants. Unlike the new rulers, whose incomprehensible ideological speeches were fueled with neologisms borrowed from foreign languages (*fiudal, dimukratik, imperialist*), the ulama spoke the familiar language of religion, of simple right and wrong. They condemned the agrarian reform as "non-Islamic" and the literacy campaign as atheistic propaganda. In the countryside, the ulama preached jihad against the *kafir* (nonbelievers, or, here, "renegades"). Assisted by the local petty notables who were able to escape the mass arrests, the ulama ignited people's resentment against the new regime and led hundreds of local assaults against government posts and buildings. Without organization, a political party, or instructions from a central authority, a general insurrection, conducted under the slogans of "*Allahu Akbar!*" and "Long live Islam!" liberated two-thirds of the Afghan territory during the period from summer 1978 to fall 1979.

In this insurrection, the defense of a traditional society was expressed in the garb of a defense of Islam, because Islam was inextricably bound to tradition in the worldview of the Afghan peasantry. But the ulama added their own brand of fundamentalism to this popular expression. One of the common topics of the preachers was: "If the Communists have been able to take power, it is because we were forgetting true Islam, and specifically Shari'a." In the liberated areas, the ulama acted as fundamentalists by replacing state law, and even common law, by Islamic law.

At first the insurrection was an expression of the traditionalism which has been recurrent through the different jihad campaigns of the past; it was not yet a revolutionary movement to implement a new society. This partly explains why the insurrection was thought doomed to failure by most foreign analysts. But soon the new fundamentalist intellectuals, who had gone underground or fled to Pakistan between 1975 and 1979, made their return to the same countryside they had failed to ignite four years earlier. These people brought some elements alien to the traditional jihad spirit: a sense of political organization and ideology which does not simply reject modernization but advocates an "Islamicization" of modernity, in both its technological and its intellectual benefits. They generally had some scientific background and political experience, from the militant years on the Kabul campuses, where they studied mainly in scientific universities and high schools. They fought against the Marxists but also engaged in dialogue with them.

Through their studies and especially their commitment to militancy, the new fundamentalists had a knowledge of modern political ideologies and of the workings of the modern state. Thus, they were in many regards able to modernize the traditional patterns of fighting the regime by crafting modern political structures (e.g., discrete parties, a chain of command) and by making use of communications technology, especially radio. In these ways the Muslim insurrection—and the traditional jihad—was given a more modern and "revolutionary" look. In the forming of this fundamentalist political consciousness and in the acquisition of technological knowledge, the Pakistani army did not play a direct role but instead confined its help to basic military training until 1985; direct Western training did not commence until 1986. The Islamic fundamentalists had been nurtured in Afghanistan universities and radical cells.[11]

In December 1979, the Soviets invaded Afghanistan, thus antagonizing urban and secular categories of the population which until then had been reluctant to join either the ulama or the new fundamentalists. The bulk of these new recruits now joined the resistance but, despite some attempts (mainly by former Maoists), were unable to provide a secular and nationalist alternative to the Islamic resistance against the Soviets. From that time everybody and everything in the resistance had to be "Islamic." Islam was the only banner. But under it, the Afghan society did not relinquish its diversity and antagonisms.

The Organization of the Resistance

From the beginning a whole range of political entities participated in the Afghan resistance. The first demarcation line was between Shi'ites and Sunnis, the second line between "moderates" (more exactly, traditionalists) and "fundamentalists."

The Afghan Shi'ites have traditionally identified themselves with Iran, whatever the regime. Three years after the Iranian Revolution of 1979, Tehran sought to unify the Afghan Shi'ites under its control by expelling the moderate Shi'ite groups. Most of the Afghan Shi'ites belong to the Hazara ethnic group, living in central Afghanistan (and not on the Iranian border). The Hazara society, more hierarchically structured than the other Afghan ethnic groups, was once very conservative and not a fertile ground for revolution, whether Islamic or not. To achieve its aim, Iran relied on two categories of young Afghan Shi'ites, the clerics educated in Najaf and Qom under the authority of Imam Khomeini, who resented the monopolization of power in Hazarajat by traditional notables like *sayyad* and landlords, and young lay students and workers who had emigrated to Iran to find a job and had come under the influence of the revolutionary movement. However, Tehran never succeeded in establishing and controlling a common organization for the Shi'ites. Eight Shi'ite parties, all claiming to follow Imam Khomeini, formed a coalition based in Qom. These parties control most of the Hazarajat, under the banner of a common organization, Hezb-i Wahdat ("Unity Party"). But in fact Afghan Shi'ites were less ideologically minded than their Iranian counterparts and did not implement a real revolution in Hazarajat. The alignment of the Shi'ite Hazaras with Iran had more to do with the traditional will to lean on Iran and the emergence of a younger educated generation opposed to the local establishment. The Shi'ite groups remained aloof and distant from the Sunni ones.

There has never been military cooperation, let alone coalition building, between Shi'ite and Sunni fundamentalists. Religious sectarianism (Shi'ite versus Sunni) and ethnic antagonism (Hazara versus Pashtun) proved to be stronger than ideological proximity. More than that, both Shi'ites and Sunnis tended to adopt their patrons' sets of strategic alliances: the Sunni fundamentalists tended to side with the Saudis and the Muslim Brothers, who see Iranians as almost heretical, while the Shi'ites tended to side with Iran against the Arabs.

Among the Sunni majority of Afghanistan, the political landscape is more contrasted. The merging of a traditional Muslim revivalist movement with an elite fundamentalist vanguard made the Afghan resistance unique among both other liberation movements and other Islamist movements. At the time of the communist coup, the Muslim Youth movement split into three parties. The more radical, the Hizb-i-Islami, is headed by Gulbuddin Hikmatyar, a layman, a former student in engineering, and the most extreme of all the Afghan resistance leaders. Hikmatyar recruits mainly among uprooted Pashtuns of the Ghilzay tribal confederation. Given the relative conservatism of the ulama's brand of fundamentalism, it is not surprising that the most radical fundamentalist movement is headed by the sole layman among the seven Sunni leaders in exile. The second party, a splinter group also called Hizb-i-Islami, is headed by Mawlawi Khalis, one of the few traditional clerics to join the Islamist movement; he recruits mainly in tribal eastern Pashtun areas. The third party is the Jamiyyat-i Islami, headed by Burhanuddin Rabbani, a former professor at the State Faculty of Theology and the only native Persian speaker of the Sunni parties. Rabbani is far more moderate than is Hikmatyar. From these three examples, it is obvious that no party could be particularized by a single ideological issue: ethnic criteria are always combined with political ones. It is sometimes difficult to understand what is the watershed of political affiliation, ethnicity or ideology? A fourth "radical" party, for example, the Ittihad of Sayyaf, was in fact a creation of the Saudi Wahhabis.

The other three Sunni parties are "moderate" (in fact "traditionalist") parties created in Peshawar in the wake of the communist coup. Most of their members have no previous political experience. These parties embody both the former secular establishment and the bulk of the traditionalist ulama. Typically, most of the ulama, despite their strong opposition to the process of secularization initiated by the monarchy in the past, have preferred to side with the monarchists and not with the young fundamentalists. The Harakat-e enqela, the umbrella for all the clerical networks, is a clerical but moderate organization recruiting mainly among Pashtuns and Uzbeks. The Harakat advocates implementation of Shari'a but rejects the idea of an Islamic revolution.

The Islamic Front is headed by Sayyad Gaylani, the head of a religious brotherhood but himself not a cleric. It is the party of the former royalist and tribal establishment. Finally, the National Liberation Front, the smallest party, is led by a respected religious figure, Sebghatullah Mujaddidi. Both Gaylani's and Mujaddidi's families, despite their clerical background, are largely Westernized. These three parties, all of them headed by religious figures, are in fact opposed to the idea of an Islamic revolution and even advocate the return of former king Zaher. It is worthy of note, then, that Islamic radicalism is not primarily a product of the ulama.

The Sunni parties established a "Seven Parties Alliance" in 1985, based in Peshawar, Pakistan. In February 1989, after the Soviet withdrawal, they formed an "Afghan Interim Government" in order to replace the pro-Soviet regime in Kabul, which was not supposed to last after the Soviet withdrawal. But in fact this Afghan Interim Government was never able to draw a blueprint for governing. The differences among the Sunni parties have proven an obstruction to the forging of a common platform as the basis of an acting government. After ten years of war, the ideological differences led in 1990 and 1991 to a standoff between the increasingly radical and anti-Western Hizb-i-Islami of Hikmatyar, protected by Pakistan and Saudi Arabia, and all the other groups. The Jamiyyat, antagonized by the strongly pro-Pashtun bias of both Pakistan and Saudi Arabia, shifted slowly toward a more moderate stance and became the "middle of the road" party during this period, but its development was hampered by the fact that it is seen as a mainly *Tajik* (or Persian-speaking) party, a fact which antagonizes most of the traditionally dominant Pashtuns, whether monarchists or fundamentalists.

In Afghanistan, then, beyond fierce ideological slogans, ethnic issues remain the key for political alignment. All-encompassing Islam, with its appeal to the *umma*, or community of believers whatever their origins, was in effect unable to supersede the ethnic fragmentation in a durable and politically effective way. Just when the Afghan Interim Government seemed viable, tribal and ethnic affiliations penetrated the party structures, transforming even the supposedly modern political parties, as the fundamentalist parties were supposed to be, into networks of patron/client relationships based on common traditional identities. Thus, whatever impact the new fundamentalism could have had on Afghanistan or its neighboring countries has now been diluted by a return to traditional segmentation. The glue holding the factions together was apparently not a common Islamic ideology or vision, however varied in expression, but the threat posed by an ideologically monolithic superpower opponent. The withdrawal of the Soviet troops in February 1989 removed the only common objective of all these groups: to fight a jihad against a foreign and infidel intruder. Once the jihad's immediate objectives had been achieved, the question of how this jihad was to be interpreted—as a full-scale revolution leading to an Islamic government and the imposition of Shari'a from above (the radical fundamentalist view), or as a defensive war presaging a "return to normalcy" (the traditionalist view, held by a majority of the ulama)—returned in all of its divisiveness.

The most one can say regarding the contribution of the new fundamentalists to this jihad is that the modern cadres of fighters they formed were more effective than the traditionalist forces in opposing the Soviets militarily. The fundamentalist leaders and trainers of these cadres were graduates of engineering programs and had learned about modern weaponry and communications, the uses of propaganda, and the exigencies of political organization—often from their Marxist colleagues at the university. The traditional ulama had no knowledge of these modern developments and no interest in pursuing them.

Despite their impressive military success, however, the fundamentalists were unable to provide the model for a state. Indeed, during the course of the war itself, most of the local fundamentalist commanders adopted the traditional practice of exercising local power by fostering the traditional patron/client relationship. By doing so they reinforced a pattern that has historically served to fragment rather than to unite a society struggling to move from tribalism to statism.

Thus, the fundamentalists effectively, if not intentionally, abandoned their initial dream of transforming society from above, that is, by control of the state apparatus.[12] This "retraditionalization" of the new fundamentalist intellectuals narrowed the gap between them and the traditional notables and ulama. This was perhaps a necessary move, given the exigencies of a common armed resistance to the Soviets. But it also deprived the resistance of any efficient modern Islamic political model once the jihad proved successful. This situation also exposed a dilemma of the would-be "modern fundamentalists" in a tribal society. Drawing upon a traditionalist population through the use of Islamic slogans, symbols, and ideology, the modern fundamentalists in this case were ultimately captive to that traditionalist population and were unable to transform its deeply rooted social and cultural patterns. "Transformation from above" proved impossible without sufficient preparatory "transformation from below."

The two notable exceptions to this general trend are explored below for what they tell us about Islamic fundamentalism, for better and for worse. Masud, the only military commander able to adapt the efficient Maoist guerrilla model to a Muslim society, did so precisely by sing Islam as an ideology. On the other hand, the well-organized Hikmatyar Hizb-i-Islami party is gradually becoming a "modern" terrorist organization. But before analyzing this development and its impact of the Afghan war, let us look at the militancy and type of violence that characterize it.

War and Organization

For the last decade, three models of warfare have competed for prominence among the Mujahidin: traditional tribal warfare, the jihad, and the Maoist war of liberation.

In traditional tribal warfare, it does not make sense to actually take the target or to destroy the enemy's forces. The aim is to achieve a balance of power in favor of a given group, not to destroy the other groups or the state. The war is part-time and is never total; civilian society is not involved. The objective is to take booty from the enemy, to avenge the dead, and to obtain guarantees against state encroachments. A battle is seen as a kind of transaction: is the investment (in human terms) worth the result (in booty)? If not, it is wiser to negotiate the surrendering of the post or even the payment of an allowance. Traditional warfare is aimed not at destroying the state but at negotiating with it. Warfare's purpose is to obtain a favorable balance of power, not to destroy the state, because there is no alternative state.

Jihad, on the contrary, is the levy en masse of all the Muslim folk, whatever their tribal and ethnic affiliations, against an outsider. The leadership is made up of ulama, not of tribal leaders. In theory, the aim of jihad is the effective destruction of the enemy and the establishment of a new state power. But in fact jihad's tactics are similar to those used in traditional tribal warfare: it is waged in discontinuity, with a respect for civilian life; it is a battle of demonstration more than of annihilation. Jihad warriors evince a taste for plundering, and rivalries between the *khans* (clan leaders) are often sufficient to prevent victory. Generally the jihad army disbands once decisive victory is in sight. Partial victories are never exploited by a quick and decisive move. One never tries to strike at the core of the enemy. Jihad is not waged according to Clausewitz's rules of war. There is no obligation of result and effectiveness in jihad, for jihad is ultimately between God and man, not between a Mujahid and his enemy. Jihad is an auto-da-fé, not a strategy aimed at wiping out the enemy. The temporality of jihad is that of salvation and eternity, not of history. Jihad breaks with tribal warfare only in terms of the means by which it is legitimated and the larger (cosmic) scale in which it operates.[13]

In fact, in employing the rhetoric of jihad, most of the Afghans fought to liberate the territory of their own "communal group," or *qawm*.[14] The warriors tried to take over local government outposts: communists were killed, other civil servants or soldiers sent home, and government buildings destroyed. The destruction of the state buildings and apparatus was meant to purify and symbolize the reappropriation of the "communal territory," that is, the territory the warriors used to consider their own; these patterns of fighting have nothing to do with a global strategy of isolating and destroying the state. Local victories are not exploited. There is no march on Kabul. The Afghan resistance is thus characterized by a strategic immobility.[15]

This strategic immobility is embodied in the *markaz* (a center), or military base of the Mujahidin, which is protected by antiaircraft weapons. The markaz does not exist in traditional tribal warfare, where the warrior continues his life as a farmer and never goes far from his home. Establishing the markaz was the first consequence of facing a total war, but it still fitted in with a traditional pattern of Muslim warfare, the *ribat*, seen as both a cloister and a stronghold.[16] The markaz was almost always held by a single political party. Sometimes, like the ribat, it was associated with a *madrasa* (religious school) held by a Sufi religious leader (*pir*) or one of his disciples; in this case the markaz can extend beyond the qawm.[17]

From the markaz, mobile units patrolled the communal territory and permanently or occasionally besieged the few remaining government outposts in the area. Military operations, thus, occurred in a space defined not by strategic constraints (e.g., geography, or enemy defense structure) but by qawm affiliations. To operate outside communal territory would require first a cultural revolution rather than technical progress or better weapons. Afghan commanders generally explain their lack of strategic initiative by the lack of weapons or communication devices. But the real reason was cultural, not technical. The more the weapons, the more the immobility: in Paktya, where the best weapons were available, provided by U.S. money and distributed by the Pakistani military intelligence (ISI), the Afghans tended to fight a conventional war as far as tactics were concerned, but from a tribal strategic perspective, which meant no strategy at all, no destruction of the enemy forces, no discussions or negotiations.

A surprising aspect of the Afghan resistance when compared to other liberation movements is its attitude toward the civil society. In Afghanistan, the resistance authorities interfered as little as possible with everyday life: men and goods could circulate freely, privacy was respected, and the law was in the hands of the ulama, not of the Mujahidin. The Mujahidin of course levy taxes on the people, sometimes exorbitantly, but without providing a real administration. But even if everything had to be called "Islamic," this war was in fact not very ideologically minded.

Despite the central role of the fundamentalists in the resistance, traditional modes of warfare prevailed in most of Afghanistan. So why did the Soviets fail? First, because 80 percent of the country was in the hands of the Mujahidin. Second, because some fundamentalists, like Masud, were able to wage war in a more modern and efficient way.

A New Model of Guerrilla Warfare or a Return to Tribalism?

The first step in establishing modern guerrilla warfare, the development of a strategy aimed at taking state power and destroying the enemy forces, requires a professional army mobilized for action beyond the boundaries of the communal territory and prepared to threaten the enemy in a way that is meaningful to that enemy. This means going beyond the traditional segmentation in qawm and using jihad as a way to legitimate modern guerrilla warfare. Such a process entails changing the relations between the Mujahidin and the traditional society, without alienating this society. It is a narrow path, but it is the only way to avoid being worn down in a long-term was of attrition.

The personal innovation of Masud was to establish a military apparatus designed according to the Vietnamese model, not the traditional, tribal one. Its tactics were those of a modern guerrilla army: training, professionalization, a commando attack not just to demonstrate bravado but to take the target. In two years Masud captured about a dozen local government bases, suffering few losses. His actions lasted from two hours to one day, far from the interminable and ineffective fireworks of Paktya. Militarization was on display: uniform, fatigues, and the *pakul*, or woolen hat, by contrast with the turban of traditional tribal warriors.[18]

But the essential problem was how to expand beyond the traditional communal territories without alienating the traditional society. After an initial major mistake in 1983, in which the overtaking of Andarab valley resulted ultimately in losing the valley to the government, Masud drew upon a new generation of young and educated commanders, the same people frowned upon by traditional and ineffective local leaders. In 1985 Masud established a "supervisory council of the North" (*shura-ye nazar*) to provide a political framework for his expansion outside his original communal territory. Couching an essentially political move in a Qur'anic framework, he invoked the concept the *shura,* or consultation, that is, the necessity for the ruler to consult an advising body prior to taking any decision. Although these consultations are not binding, they are the only way to religiously justify the appointment of a consultative body, however it may be elected or nominated. Masud's knowledge of Islam was essential to this move. Only a reference to the umma can bypass the segmentation of the qawm, and the traditional understanding of jihad was insufficient to justify the military modernization Masud had in mind. Thus, the Qur'anic shura was a useful means of implementing the new strategies within an Islamic framework; it provided the new ideology with a new political framework, and thus opened the possibility of a new military strategy.

It took six years for Masud to expand beyond his original communal territory and to establish a professional, albeit small, army. Masud's groups are now multiethnic. Masud became the emir, that is, a political and military commander who is neither a khan nor a purely military commander; he is above the traditional segmentation, so that a khan or an *alim* (sing., ulama) could pay respect to him, a younger man from a middle-class family, without being humiliated. In this way, by giving an Islamic terminology and legitimation to what was an adaptation to modern guerrilla warfare, Masud was able to establish such a system in most of the Northeast of Afghanistan.

The rival Islamist party, Hizb-i-Islami of Hikmatyar, followed a different path. It slowly shifted in the late 1980s from a liberation movement to a terrorist organization, with connections, both domestic and international, far removed from the purity of Islamic ideology. Although the Hizb-i-Islami was the main recipient of American military assistance, it carefully avoided confronting the Soviet or the government military directly; instead, it stockpiled the weaponry in anticipation of the inevitable showdown among Mujahidin after the Soviet withdrawal. From the beginning of the war Hizb-i-Islami had harassed the other parties, mainly by ambushing supply caravans. In 1985, Hikmatyar initiated an assassination campaign, whose victims were either Westernized intellectuals living in Peshawar or rival Jamiyyat commanders. Under a tough and uncompromising ideology, the Hizb-i-Islami formed multiple and sometimes strange connections. Hikmatyar is of the same tribe (Kharruti), for example, as the hard-line former general secretary of the communist party, Hafizullah Amin. But Hizb-i-Islami also has close connections with Libyan president Muammar Qaddafi, the ISI, the fundamentalist Jama'at party of Pakistan, the conservative Saudi Wahhabi milieu, and the hard-liners of the Muslim Brothers movement. But until 1989, the bulk of its money and weapons were provided by the CIA.[19] Hizb-i-Islami is well implanted among the educated middle class in exile and among the refugee camps, but has recently lost a lot of ground inside Afghanistan due to its intransigence. If the political decline of Hizb-i-Islami continues, the party could easily turn into a terrorist organization whose real alliances would have little to do with its avowed ideology, as is the case with the Palestinian Abu Nidal group.[20]

The story of the Hizb-i-Islami is full of lessons on revolutionary fundamentalism; for example, it shows that some of the more radical factions are in fact closer to the

Communists than to the traditional clerics. On 6 March 1990, a communist hard-liner in Kabul, the defense minister Shahnawaz Tana'y, attempted a coup against the pro-Soviet president Najibullah, in close cooperation with Hikmatyar. The coup failed and Tana'y joined Hikmatyar. The purely religious content of fundamentalism faded away in favor of the anti-Western and revolutionary trends which were at work from the beginning. The shift of Hikmatyar in the direction of terrorism originated in the shrinking of his popular base in Afghanistan. As in others countries, the existence of a well-trained hard core of committed workers with a shrinking popular base led the leaders, whatever their avowed ideological aims, toward state-supported terrorism.

The fall of the Kabul regime in May 1992 proved to be less a victory for the Mujahidin—for a popular-based Islamic fundamentalism—than a further step toward factionalism. With the exception of the Hizb-i-Islami and Masud organizations, both of which were "modern" organizations, the Afghan jihad lost its momentum after the Soviet withdrawal and Afghanistan seems destined to return to tribalism or descend into Lebanonization—situations, that is, in which ideological factors will have little importance.

Clearly, after the Soviet withdrawal, most of the Mujahidin groups and command-ers inside Afghanistan, especially the petty ones, returned to traditional tribal warfare. Thus, we may conclude that it was the Soviet invasion that converted a rather conser-vative and traditionalist nation *temporarily* into an Islamist mass movement. And it was the Soviet withdrawal that broke the alliance between a peasant movement and a small, revolutionary Islamic fundamentalist nucleus. From 1988, local Mujahidin commanders even made local deals with the Kabul authorities, among whom family, tribal, and ethnic ties are more important than ideological commitments. Most of the military operations waged after the Soviet withdrawal were directed from Pakistan, with U.S. consent, under the direct auspices of the Pakistan military, which was eager to reap the fruits of ten years of support for the Mujahidin.

The International Impact

The Afghans attempted to export their jihad to the USSR. There are many ethnic and historical links between Soviet Central Asia and Afghanistan; the same ethnic groups (Turkmens, Tajiks, and Uzbeks) are living on both sides of the border. During the thirties, hundreds of thousands of Muslims fled the Soviet Union to avoid collectiv-ization. The Afghan Mujahidin adopted initiatives toward Central Asia aimed at weakening the USSR. They launched a propaganda war by smuggling religious and political booklets (in Russian) into the Soviet Union. They also took some commando actions, mainly in 1986. A strange phenomenon underlined by the Soviet press was the appearance, in the USSR, of political Muslim activists with exactly the same pro-file in age, occupation, and social background as the Afghan fundamentalists. In March 1987, Abdullah Saïdov, an engineer in his thirties and the son of a middle-ranking apparatchik, was imprisoned in Kurgan Tyube (Tajikistan) for having claimed solidarity with the Afghan Mujahidin. He was labeled "Wahhabi" by the Soviet press.[21] The term does not seem to refer to Saudi Arabia but to have been used as a generic term for all fundamentalist movements, just as the British had used the term in the subcontinent. It would be an exaggeration to suggest that the Afghans triggered the upheavals in Central Asia in 1990 and 1991; they had their own local causes. But the Afghan resistance movement was clearly a source of inspiration for Muslims in the Central Asian republics and contributed significantly to the trend in the region toward the self-reassertion of Muslim identity. In Afghanistan, the message went, the Red Army was beaten by Muslims. This victory marked the end of a century of fatalism.

But today, after ten years of war, it is obvious that the Afghan jihad has lost its momentum and has become a stake and a tool in the rivalry between Saudi Arabia and Iran to control the fundamentalist movements among the Muslim countries. Until 1990 a Saudi and Arab Muslim Brotherhood joint venture gained great influence over the fundamentalist movement in the non-Arab Muslim world. But the 1990–91 Gulf war disrupted this joint venture. The more radical Afghan fundamentalist leaders, namely Hikmatyar and Sayyaf, endorsed the Iraqi position, while moderate fundamentalists, such as Rabbani, supported the Saudis. This split among the fundamentalists weakened the jihad spirit.

The Afghan jihad had little repercussion in the Arab world before 1985. The Palestinian struggle was seen as more important in Arab public opinion, but after 1985 the Arab milieu played an increasing role in Peshawar. Except in Central Asia, the Afghans did not attempt to export their jihad; on the contrary, foreign fundamentalist movements tried to enlist the Afghan Mujahidin in their brand of fundamentalism, in the hope of opposing Iranian influence more than with an eye to fighting communism. The competition was mainly between the Iranians on one side, who in the late 1980s were still advocating an Islamic revolution, and the Saudi-sponsored Wahhabis and Muslim Brothers on the other side, who eschewed any revolutionary political program but were pushing for a renewal of the religious habits and lifestyle of the Afghans.

The paradox is that, in order to thwart Iranian Islamic revolutionary influence, Saudi Arabia decided to promote its own kind of conservative, but also strictly anti-Western, fundamentalism in a joint venture with the Egyptian, Jordanian, and Kuwaiti Muslim Brothers, who did not share the theological views of the Wahhabi religious school but needed the Saudi financial support. As regular Sunni, the Muslim Brothers were more acceptable to the Afghan religious scholars than the Wahhabi. A joint office was established in Peshawar as early as 1981, under the leadership of the Palestinian Abdallah Ezzam (who was mysteriously killed in November 1989). This office became very active in 1986. Thousands of Arabs volunteered to join the jihad in Afghanistan. They encouraged local commanders to become independent from the Peshawar parties and helped to establish two independent "fundamentalist" (called "Wahhabi" by other Afghans) "kingdoms" in the Kunar Province under the leadership of Mollah Afzal and Mawlawi Jamilurrahman (who both discarded the term "Wahhabi" and preferred to be called "Salafi," that is, followers of the four first successors of the Prophet Muhammad). The Saudis and the Muslim Brothers, after some hesitation, decided to back Gulbuddin Hikmatyar, not only because he was seen as a strong fundamentalist (there were other groups of this kind) but also because he was of the Pashtun ethnic group. The Arabs and the Pakistanis were suspicious of the Shi'ites, of course, but also of the Persian-speaking Sunni (the Tajiks), who, although they were as anti-Shi'ite as the Pashtuns, could preserve some potential cultural links with Persian-speaking Iran. In addition, many of the Pakistani officers of the military services and of the fundamentalist Jama'at party were Pashtuns (from Pakistan) and favored their ethnic brethren. For all these reasons, Arabs and Pakistani military backed the Pashtun fundamentalists, that is, mainly Hikmatyar. The line which divides the Muslim world between Sunni Arabs and Iranian Shi'ites was thus drawn across Afghanistan, where it also took an ethnic shape.

At the same time, the Wahhabis considered that Afghan Islam was not pure enough, being too much influenced by Sufism and local customs. They launched a predication campaign, with huge financial incentives, to bring the Afghans back into "true" Islam. This campaign had some very negative effects, triggering internecine feuds and alienating the urban population. In that regard the campaign backfired, as it pushed the urban population toward a position of neutrality between the government and the Mujahidin and away from a position of outright support for the latter.

For the Saudis and the Pakistanis, however, the geopolitical and strategic stakes were not only Afghanistan but the whole of Central Asia, whose door had been opened by the Afghan war and by perestroika. In 1988 Saudi Arabia and the Pakistani military became concerned about the crumbling of the Soviet empire; both powers feared that Islamic fundamentalism in Soviet Central Asia might fall under the influence of Iran. They decided not only to use the Mujahidin as a tool to influence the Soviet Muslims but also to send official teams to the Soviet Union to establish direct links with the Soviet Muslim clergy. In May 1990 Saudi Arabia shipped tens of thousands of Qur'ans into the USSR; in June 1990 one thousand Soviet Muslims performed the *hajj* in Mecca. They were not chosen by the officials; for example, Abdullah Saïdov, who was jailed in 1987 after demonstrating in favor of the Afghan Mujahidin (see above) and released in 1989, was a member of the Tajik pilgrims.[22]

The Iranian danger has been overestimated by the Saudis. Iran's influence was confined to the Shi'ite minority. It tried to bargain this influence in order not to be excluded from any political settlement. After the end of the Persian Gulf war with Iraq (1980–88), Iran's policy was purely strategically motivated, without any ideological considerations. Iran's fear was to have a Saudi, thus American, sponsored regime in Kabul. Once the Soviets were out, Iran stressed its support for a broad-based coalition government around the ex-communist regime rather than for a military victory of the pro-Arab coalition based in Peshawar.[23] After the fall of Kabul in 1992, Iran supported the Shi'ites.

Conclusion

The Afghans have no means by which to pursue a "Central Asian dream" because of the confused and uncertain situation that will prevail in Afghanistan for the next decade. They have likely lost the means to establish an Islamic state in Afghanistan due to the opposition between the Shi'ites and Sunnis and the pervasive strength of ethnic and tribal rivalries. Instead of exporting their jihad, the Afghans must deal with the side effects and consequences of the rifts and feuds within the Muslim world. The hopes for Sunni Arab fundamentalism rest primarily with Saudi Arabia and the Arab Muslim Brothers; the Afghans' return to tribalism has taken them out of the picture. The Afghan war was thus not the anticipated dawn of a new kind of Islamic fundamentalism in Central Asia. It has been a war of liberation which found in fundamentalist Islam its best expression and means of modernization, but this common ideology was not able, after the Soviet withdrawal, to supersede the traditional fragmentation, or to provide a model of a central state, which could prevent the Lebanonization of Afghanistan. Fundamentalism's future in Afghanistan thus may be as a reactive ideology and as a compromise between genuinely modern politics and traditional Islam.

On the other hand, upheavals in Central Asia will likely be waged mainly along ethnic and national lines. As in Afghanistan, the common Muslim identity, and even a organized fundamentalist movements, will probably be unable to supersede national feelings and ethnic feuds. But in case of a failure of the national, ethnic, and democratic movements to provide an alternative to the discredited Communist parties in Uzbekistan, Tajikistan, and Turkmenistan, the fundamentalist trend, reshaped and backed by the Saudis, could become a dominant factor, as it was in Algeria after the local elections of June 1990. By becoming more conservative under Saudi influence, the trend toward Islamic fundamentalism did not prove to be more prone to compromise with a secular outlook, either from the West or from the East. The paradox is that the United States gave full support to the Pakistanis and the Saudis during the Afghan war, support by which the Pakistanis and Saudis promoted and controlled their own brand of Islamic fundamentalism.

The Persian Gulf crisis of 1990-91 seemed to change the nature of the relations among the major players in Central Asia. Iraq, which supported the Kabul regime, took some discrete steps in early 1990 toward Hikmatyar's Hizb-i-Islami through the mediation of Yasser Arafat. When Iraq invaded Kuwait in August 1990, Hikmatyar was the only Afghan Mujahidin leader not to condemn the invasion. For the Saudis, the disillusionment was enormous as it became clear that they had subsidized movements which were not loyal despite the fact that five of the seven Peshawar-based parties, including Hikmatyar's, went to Saudi Arabia in early September 1990 to pledge support against Iraq. In addition, the Saudis were angered by the Arab Muslim Brothers, who also supported Saddam Hussein in the Gulf war. These "betrayals" reinforced the Saudi tendency to shun the more radical Islamic movements, including the Islamic Salvation Front (FIS) in Algeria, and to channel support exclusively to conservative fundamentalist movements in Central Asia and elsewhere. This shift in policy had the unintended consequence of radicalizing Islamic movements that were no longer restrained in their zeal by Saudi influence. For example, the Algerian fighters who made their jihad in Afghanistan with Hikmatyr's party returned to Algeria to form the armed wing of the FIS. (This *takfir wa hijra* group was subsequently dismantled by the Algerian army in the summer of 1991.) Meanwhile, the Pakistani military and conservatives, who ousted of Prime Minister Benazir Bhutto in early August 1990, continued to support Hikmatyar's party. After the fall of Kabul (May 1992), the Pakistani army went along with direct support for Hikmatyar, apparently without Saudi objection.

Despite these setbacks to radical fundamentalism in the region, there were signs in 1991 that the fundamentalist ideology would continue to exercise a powerful appeal in the Central Asian republics, as it had in the early phases of the Afghanistan conflict. In Soviet Central Asia a traditionalist clergy nurtured Islam during seventy years of communist rule. With the collapse of the Soviet Union there were signs of radicalization of elements of this formerly clandestine clergy, which is called "wahhabi" by the official press. Thus, even if the ideological dimension of the Afghan war was fading away in favor of tribal, ethnic, and national interests, fundamentalism as an ideology advocating the return to Shari'a seemed to have a future in Central Asia.

APPENDIX

The Resistance Parties

Sunni parties

Islamists

Hizb-i Islami: radical Islamists, led by Gulbuddin Hikmatyar. Its recruits are amongst those who are educated in the secular government schools and also some ulama from the Kabul region. Mainly Pashtun.

Hizb-i Islami (Khalis): moderate Islamists, led by Mawlawi Yunus Khalis. Its recruits come from those educated in the government schools and the ulama of the Khugiani and Jadran tribes as well as in the region of Kabul and Kandahar. Pashtun.

Jam'iyyat-i Islami: moderate Islamists, led by Burhanuddin Rabbani. Its recruits come from amongst those educated in the government schools (both religious and secular), the ulama in the north and naqshbandi in the north. Mainly Tajik.

Traditionalists

Harakat-i inqilab-i Islami: moderate clerical party, led by Muhammad Nabi Muhammadi. It gains recruits from the ulama educated in private madrasa. Mainly Pashtun.

Jabha-yi nejat- milli (National Liberation Front): secular, led by Sebghatullah Mujaddidi. Its recruits come mainly from the tribes, the establishment of the old social order and the naqshbandi in the south.

Mahaz-i Islami (Islamic Front): royalist, led by Pir Sayyad Ahmad Gaylani. Its recruits come from the establishment of the old social order, the tribes and the qadiri in the south. Mainly Pashtun.

Shi'ite parties

Shura-y- ittifagh-Islami: traditionalist, led by Sayyad Beheshti. Its recruits come from the Hazara peasantry, officered by the sayyad.

Nasr: radical Islamists, led by a council. It gains recruits from young Hazara educated in Iran.

Harakat-i Islami: moderate Islamists, led by Shaykh Asaf Muhseni. Its recruits are educated Shi'a from all ethnic groups.

Pasdaran (Guardians of the Revolution): radical Islamists who depend very much on Iran. Led by Akbari of Turkman and Saddiqi of Nili.

Source: Olivier Roy, *Islam and Resistance in Afghanistan* (Cambridge: Cambridge University Press, 1986), pp. 219–20.

Notes

1. On this point in the case of Egypt, see R. Hrair Dekmejian, *Islam in Revolution* (Syracuse University Press, 1985).

2. For historical examples, see Akbar Ahmed, *Millennium and Charisma among Swat Pathans* (London: Routledge and Kegan Paul, 1979).

3. On the traditional jihad waged from 1879 to the 1930s, see Ahmed, *Millennium and Charisma among Swat Pathans*.

4. See Hassan Kakar, *Government and Society in Afghanistan: The Reign of Amir Abd al-Rahman Khan* (University of Texas Press, 1979).

5. There was a numerous Hindu population among the Pashtun tribesmen until 1947, and the Pashtun tribes were more in favor of Gandhi's Congress party than of the Muslim League before the partition of India.

6. Amanullah was a reformist and enlightened monarch who ascended to the throne in 1919. Although a devout Muslim, he tried to modernize the country along the same patterns as had Reza Shah of Iran: doing away with the requirement that women wear veils, imposing Western dress in the capital, enhancing a reform of the judicial system, etc. He was defeated by a double insurrection: an uprising of Pashtun tribes on the eastern borders and a Tajik fundamentalist upheaval in northern of Kabul headed by Bacha-ye Saqqao, who took Kabul before being executed by the tribes in 1928.

7. Olivier Roy, *Islam and Resistance in Afghanistan*, 2d ed. (Cambridge University Press, 1990), chap. 4.

8. Ibid.

9. There are almost no books written by Afghan Islamists and ulama on these subjects. These analyses are based on interviews and articles published by Jamiyyat-i Islami *(Afghan News)* and Hizb-i-Islami.

10. For field studies see R. Canfield and N. Shahrani, eds., *Revolution and Rebellions in Afghanistan* (University of California Press, 1984).

11. Since the creation of Pakistan in 1947, the government in Kabul advocated the independence of Pashtunistan, the Pachtun-populated northwest frontier province of Pakistan. This claim was used by Kabul as a way to forge and consolidate an Afghan nationalism based on Pashtun identity. Hence the Pakistani support for a religious fundamentalism that was theoretically opposed to ethnic nationalism among Muslims. Biographical data on the Afghan Islamist leaders are taken from my own field researches. Biographies of Jamiyyat commanders were regularly published in 1989 and 1990 in the biweekly *Afghan News* (Peshawar, Pakistan).

12. See Roy, *Islam and Resistance in Afghanistan*, chap. 14.

13. Nineteenth- and twentieth-century colonial histories are full of accounts of these unsuccessful jihads, though they may have made the colonial rulers hesitate at the immensity of the task, like the British in Afghanistan in 1841 and 1880; in both instances, anyway, the colonial army was technically victorious.

14. I use the word "qawm" to describe the communal group most Afghans belong to, whatever its sociological basis: in tribal areas, it is the clan *(kheyl)*; elsewhere it can be the extended family with its dependents, the ethnic group, the occupational group (*mollah,* craftsmen), the caste *(sayyad* in a Shi'a area), or a mixed kinship and territorial group (like the inhabitants of a village or a valley). See Roy, *Islam and Resistance in Afghanistan*, p. 12.

15. See Olivier Roy, "Afghanistan, War as a factor of Entry into Politics," *Central Asian Survey* 8, no. 4 (1989): 43–62.

16. On the ribat, see Jean Paul Charnay, *L'Islam et la guerre* (Paris: Fayard, 1986), pp. 232, 250.

17. For instance, in the markaz of Myandarrah, south of Maymana, Faryab Province, a madrasa is headed by a *naqshbandi pir,* Shamsuddin, whose son-in-law, Mawlawi Yusuf, is the regional emir of the Jamiyyat-i

Islami; the *murid,* both Tajiks and Uzbeks, are organized around this madrasa (personal observation, August 1983).

18. Personal observations in Panjshir Valley, September 1981, August 1985, September 1987.

19. There in lies a mystery. Was the CIA manipulated by its Pakistani counterpart, the ISI, to support the most radical of the fundamentalist groups, or did the CIA have a master plan to support Sunni fundamentalism against the Shi'ites? Or was the CIA's stance an example of simply ineffectiveness and bureaucratic blunder?

20. For a somewhat overzealous report on Hikmatyar's links with terrorism, see the report for the House Task Force on Terrorism and Unconventional Warfare written by V. S. Forrest and Y. Bodansky, *Afghanistan Forum* 18, no. 3 (May 1990). But contrary to this report, there is no connection between Hikmatyar and the Shi'ites.

21. *Central Asia Newsletter,* London: Society for Central Asian Studies, Marie Broxup, ed. July 1987, p. 4.

22. For a regular report on Islamic activities in Central Asia, see *Central Asia and Caucasus Chronicle,* formerly *Central Asia Newsletter.*

23. Declaration of Foreign Minister Velayati and President Rafsanjani at the Second International Seminar on Afghanistan, 2–4 October 1990, Tehran.

Militancy and Religion in Contemporary Iran

Nikki R. Keddie and Farah Monian

Historical Background

In recent years it has been Muslims in the Middle East, and specifically Shi'ites in Iran and Lebanon, who have seemed to be the most militant and violent of religious groups.[1] The word "militant" is used in this essay to denote those who advocate or follow beliefs or ends in uncompromising ways that may include the use of physical violence. The idea that Lebanese or Iranian Shi'ites are especially militant or violent is one that has developed only since the 1978–79 Iranian Revolution, however, and attempts to link the violence of that revolution with past Shi'ite violence have limited validity.

To be sure, the early Shi'ites, those who believed that succession to Muhammad was inherited, starting with Muhammad's cousin and son-in-law 'Ali, were often rebellious. Indeed, the earliest religious revolts in Islamic history, if we exclude civil wars over the caliphate, were carried out by the first sectarian movements, the Shi'ites and the Kharijites,[2] both of whom had a totalizing and alternative view of Islam to that of the majority, who came to be called Sunni. While the earliest Shi'ites were Muslim Arabs with a largely political claim to succession, justifications of a more religious nature entered with the conversion of non-Muslims, some of whom had messianic religious ideas. Leadership of the Shi'ite community then became sacred, and religiopolitical revolt in favor of the Shi'ite leaders, or Imams, was often advocated. On the other hand, after the earliest centuries most Shi'ites opted for a nonviolent approach. Specifically, the line which became the Twelver Shi'ites, who are the majority of the Shi'ites worldwide as well as in Iran, Lebanon, and elsewhere, developed an ideology of political quietism. With this theory went a de facto acceptance of temporal rulers, whether Sunni or Shi'ite, which ended the early period of Shi'ite revolts.[3]

It was the other main line of Shi'ites, the Sevener or Isma'ili, which kept alive a more militant tradition. They organized and fought to set up a caliphate with messianic overtones, which became the Fatimid caliphate, beginning in the tenth century in North Africa and Egypt. Once they came to power, however, they lost much of their militancy. The Qarmatians, a related radical group, were able briefly to set up radical states in or near Arabia, centering on the Persian Gulf island of Bahrain, not far from Iran. The Qarmatians had communal ideas and practices regarding property. There is no proof that they directly influenced later Twelver Shi'ites in Iran, but radical religious movements do have a considerable history and fame in Iran, and the early radical movements, whether Isma'ili or not, probably had some long-lasting influence.

The Isma'ili states were generally formed when disciples were won over, organized, and then sent into battle, as was the case with both the Fatimids and the Qarmatians. A more contemporary-sounding form of militancy was pioneered later by a branch of the Fatimid Isma'ilis which came to be known in the West as the Assassins. Setting themselves up primarily in fortresses in Iran and Arab Asia, they battled against Sunni rulers and Crusaders. One of the methods they used was assassination of prominent figures. The name "assassin," which came from their reputed use of hashish, was given to them as a pejorative nickname. In the West the word took on its contemporary meaning.[4] They were suppressed by Mongol invaders in the thirteenth century, after which they largely went underground. They may have influenced certain trends in Twelver Shi'ism in Iran.

For some centuries both Twelver Shi'ites and Sunnis believed that existing rulers were to be obeyed and that no doctrinal justification for revolt existed. After 1500, with the formation of the Safavid state in Persia and the conversion of that heretofore Sunni land to Shi'ism, a more hierarchical and independent clergy arose in Iranian Shi'ism, along with the later doctrine that all believers must follow the rulings of a leading cleric (*mujtahid*). Only then was a doctrinal basis gradually laid for resistance to the government, provided it was authorized by leading clerics.

Today within the Muslin world the word "Shi'ite" is generally reserved for the Twelvers, while the Ismai'lis (and the Zaidis) are known by other names and not generally considered Shi'ite. There is no feeling of identification between the Twelvers and Isma'ilis, and probaby never has been. Similarities we may perceive in assassination techniques between today's Twelver militants and the medieval Assassins are due mostly to common assessments of the effectiveness of assassination in a given situation, and not imitation.

Today it is widely believed that Shi'ites are more inclined to violence than non-Shi'ites. This greater propensity to violence and death is supposedly the result of a Shi'ite martyr complex. It is true that the Shi'ites, whose first and third Imams, 'Ali and Husayn, were killed violently, came to believe that all the Imams were so killed and that there was special holiness in martyrdom. Twelver Shi'ite holidays commemorate the deaths of the Imams, with that of Husayn being the most important. However, recent scholarship has indicated that Husayn's martyrdom was not, until the late 1970s, generally taken as a model for rebellion or assassinations but rather as an occasion to ask for his intervention with God.

The beliefs that may be said to have encouraged the Shi'ites to holy war and vio-lence go back to early all-Islamic tenets rather than to tenets that are specifically Shi'ite. There is nothing specifically Shi'ite about the belief that warriors in a jihad go straight to paradise, but it is a Muslim belief that may encourage violence in what is believed to be a holy war.[5] Another means in Islam for justifying what we would call a revolt was for one to claim to be a renewer of Islam, the precursor of the Mahdi (a messianic figure believed in by Sunnis as well as Shi'ites), or the Mahdi himself. These means have both been used many times, sometimes at once. It should be stressed that these models were used by both Sunnis and Shi'ites. It is widely but mistakenly be-lieved that Shi'ism had more ideological justification for revolt than Sunnis and that past Shi'ites justified revolts by appealing to the model of Imam Husayn's battle against the unjust Umayyad caliph and Husayn's resulting martyrdom.[6] In fact, al-though bits of the Karbala/martyrdom paradigm may be detected in earlier Shi'ite revolts, most of these were dominated by the Mahdist paradigm, as were many Sunni revolts.[7] In the eighteenth and nineteenth centuries there was a rise in the number of revolts that used the renewer or Mahdist model, often along with the jihad model. These revolts, like the early rise of Islam, occurred mainly in areas that lacked states, or lacked strong ones, and occurred in the context of a state-formation movement, for which religio-ideological unity and Islamic law were useful.[8] The incidence of Islamic revolts in West Africa closely followed the movement of the slave trade. In South Asia the so-called Wahhabi revolts were even more clearly tied to British po-litical and socioeconomic influence. What is significant about these revolts is that they demonstrate that the supposed Islamic horror of revolt was rather easily overcome, given changed socioeconomic circumstances. And this could be done without any explicit change in old ideological attitudes toward revolt by claiming that, for ex-ample, the nominally Muslim rulers of West Africa or Sumatra were not true Muslims, and that fighting them was holy war.[9]

Except in the Sudan, there is little identification between the recent movements and those of the past. What is important, given this general lack of direct ties or influence, is the uninfluenced revival of themes found in the earlier movements, a fact which demonstrates how widespread in time and place a "fundamentalist" view of Islam can be. Nearly all of today's Islamists put as much stress on Islamic mores and morals as did earlier militants: the covering of women, sexual segregation, modest dress for men, no gambling, no alcohol, and enforcement of the Shari'a and Islamic punishments. There has been a strong revival of the themes of jihad in the sense of fighting those considered unbelievers, and at least among the Shi'ites, a kind of mahd-ism or messianism. Indeed, in revolutionary Iran, not only was the language of jihad heard again but also a messianic approach was taken to the leader Khomeini, who was called by the messianic title, Imam.

Today's Muslims have words which equate with the Western words "revolution," "revolt," and "uprising," and these words are used by Islamists, but it is striking how much they have resorted to an older Islamic vocabulary, which was once the only usable vocabulary for those who participated in revolts. This does not mean that the modern revivalist movements are close replays of eighteenth- and nineteenth-century movements. The world has changed too much for such parallelism, modern technology has largely obviated the concepts of center and periphery, Western economic penetration is no longer a new phenomenon, and the problems caused by Israel and by Western interest in maintaining control of oil are now the dominant considerations. The similarity of all the post–1800 Islamist stages, apart from their common culture and vocabulary, lies in all being in part responses to disruptions caused by interactions with the West.[10]

In the last few years many Islamists have become less militant. There is less emphasis on revolution (or, in the case of some movements, on assassination) and more on gaining political power. In one way or another Islamists have been running for political office, especially in Egypt, Turkey, Jordan, and Algeria, and have proved very strong, especially in the last two. This development has meant a decline in both the traditional and the modern vocabulary of revolt and a stress on extending democracy (which will let them campaign more extensively), majority decisions about the law, and the like. Whether this is a new phase will not become clear until and unless some of these groups gain power and either do or do not continue to allow democratic elections and laws contrary to Shari'a if the majority wants them. The majority of Muslims today are not Islamists, but the appeal of Islamism is strong in societies undergoing socioeconomic and cultural crises.

In turning to specific incidences of modern Shi'ite militance, we must keep in mind the important fact that religion and state were not as inseparable in Islamic history as is often stated. While revolt was considered illegitimate, there were ideological ways to get around this illegitimacy that cannot be too strongly stressed: the declaration of jihad against rulers characterized as un-Islamic, and the taking on of all or part of the religious identity of the messianic Mahdi. Such jihad and mahdist movements generally failed, but they did influence long-term state formation and Muslim ideology. During the past century this militant trend was in decline until about 1967, when militant Islamism began its spectacular rise. Although it owes little to movements of the last two centuries, contemporary Islamism uses many of those movements' concepts and key words. Further, many of the tactical approaches of earlier movements, such as assassination (which by no means is restricted to the Islamic world), have been utilized as well.

Iran's First Modern Shi'ite Militants: The Fida'iyan-i Islam

To turn to post–World War II Iran, the first group to include assassination as a major part of its activities was the Fida'iyan-i Islam, a small group of very young men espousing a then-rare Islamist politics on the order of the Egyptian Muslim Brotherhood. They considered the government, and some of its members in particular, to be traitorous foreign agents and felt that unbelieving foreign influences must be obliterated and true Islam restored. The early wrath of the group's founder, Navvab Safavi, was directed against the leading intellectual, Ahmad Kasravi, who had strongly criticized Shi'ism and clerical power as a source of moral and political corruption in Iran. He had thus become the target of angry attacks by clerics. Ruhollah Khomeini's first major published tract, the 1941 *Kashf al-Asrar* (Uncovering of secrets), had been in part a counterattack on Kasravi and his followers. Navvab Safavi's disciples assassinated Kasravi in an open courtroom in 1946. Pressure in their favor in clerical and bazaar circles brought the release of the perpetrators.[11]

The next clearly Fida'iyan assassination was of minister of court and former prime minister Abdul Husain Hazhir in 1949. Hazhir was seen as tied both to foreigners and to Baha'is.[12] More sensational was the March 1951 assassination of the prime minister, General Ali Razmara, who was trying to negotiate a compromise with the British in the dispute over Iranian oil and was accused of having ties with the British and the Americans.[13] Razmara's assassination, which occurred while nationalist feelings over control of Iranian oil were running high, was followed by the premiership of Muhammad Musaddiq, nationalization of the oil industry, and confrontation with the British government. In this atmosphere of radical nationalism, reinforced by death threats against present or future "traitors," Razmara's assassin, Khalil Tahmasbi, was released in 1952 via a bill passed by the Majlis. The Fida'iyan, however, soon broke with Musaddiq and even with their former patron, the activist anti-British Ayatollah Abul Qasim Kashani. They were responsible for a failed attempt to kill Musaddiq's foreign minister, Husain Fatimi, in 1952. After the overthrow of Musaddiq the Fida'iyan tried to assassinate Prime Minister Husain Ala in 1955, just before he left for Baghdad to represent Iran in the Baghdad Pact negotiations. Navvab Safavi and the Fida'iyan's three other top leaders were then executed, after which the group dispersed or went underground until the 1978–79 revolution. Remnants of the group are often considered responsible for the assassination of Prime Minister Hasan Ali Mansur in January 1965.[14] During the 1978–79 revolution a few men who had been with the early group identified themselves as Fida'iyan-i Islam, as did some newer converts to their ideology. The Fida'iyan did not become an important organization, however.

The Fida'iyan had an importance beyond their small numbers—a few thousand at most—mainly because of their assassinations of several prominent personalities. There was considerable public approval and organized political support for their actions. While previous Iranian political figures who called for a politicized "return to Islam" had been ulama—notably Shaikh Fazlullah Nuri in the constitutional revolution of 1906–11 and Sayyid Hasan Mudarris in the interwar Reza Shah period—the Fida'iyan followed the more contemporary pattern of modern Islamist groups by being an organization of laypersons. Almost all of Fida'iyan's members were from lower-middle-class bazaari families and had little education.[15]

The Fida'iyan represented a novel and influential pattern in their use of assassination. Assassination had been utilized earlier in modern Iran primarily by people to the political left of the targets they were attacking. An attempted assassination of Nasir al-Din Shah in 1852 by a small number of followers of the new and persecuted Babi religion brought about far worse persecution and was not imitated by later Babis. Nasir al-Din was assassinated in 1896 by a close disciple of Sayyid Jamal al-Din al-Afghani, the militant advocate of reformist self-strengthening in the Islamic world. The assassin gave essentially political reasons for his act, seeing it as a blow against tyranny. During the Constitutional Revolution there were several assassinations, as well as an attempt against Muhammad Ali Shah. The most important assassination, that of the chief minister (Amin al-Sultan) Atabeg, was carried out in 1907 by a member of a leftist group but was apparently also plotted by the shah. In 1910, the conservative constitutional leader Sayyid Muhammad Bihbihani was assassinated by an extreme leftist.[16]

Hence, in the century before the Fida'iyan-i Islam, assassinations had not been a tactic associated with those who wanted to restore the rule of Islam. Ideologically the Fida'iyan were close to members of the ulama who advocated a Shari'a-based government. But the Fida'iyan never presented well-worked-out and coherent ideological positions or a specific program for an Islamic government. Like many Islamically oriented activists they called for a reversal of changes in the status of women that they considered un-Islamic. Unlike some later Islamist movements, they did not reject monarchy in principle although they came to oppose Shah Muhammad Reza Pahlavi. A failed assassin of the shah in 1949 was found to have both Fida'iyan and Tudeh (Communist) Party documentation. His true affiliations were never proven.

While the Fida'iyan were certainly Shi'ite religious militants, most of the internal violence in the postwar years was perpetrated by the shah's government, with many killings after the government's reoccupation of Azerbaijan and Kurdistan in 1946 and again after the military overthrow, with U.S. and British aid, of Musaddiq in 1953. The frequent tortures and executions of political prisoners contributed to the widespread and growing discontent with the shah's dictatorship. With the replacement of Great Britain by the United States as the main outside supporter of the shah, antiforeign feelings, both religious and nationalist, came to focus on the Americans. Religious and national feelings combined to cast Israel as a persecutor of Muslims and an ally of the shah.

The Mujahidin-i Khalq, Khomeini, and the Formation of a Modern Islamic Revolutionary Discourse and Practice

The militant rhetoric and violent acts associated with Twelver Shi'ism after the 1978–79 Iranian Revolution came into being during the two decades preceding the revolution. Reinterpretation of Shi'ism as a revolutionary ideology of mass mobilization was a project first launched by modern educated intelligentsia and only later by Khomeini and a section of the ulama who were willing and able to lead a revolutionary movement. It is necessary briefly to review the political context of, and the forces involved in, the development of a revolutionary Shi'ite movement in Iran.

From 1953 to 1960 relations between the court and the country's religious establishment were peaceful. In 1960, however, new tensions arose when Iran's highest-ranking cleric (*marja' al-taqlid*), Ayatollah Husain Burujirdi, voiced opposition to the government's proposals for land reform. With Burujirdi's death in 1961 began a period of rivalry for the position of the highest marja' in a highly charged political atmosphere. It was at this point that Khomeini, who did not hold the very highest religious credentials, emerged as the most popular marja', as he took an increasingly militant posture vis-à-vis the shah. In the course of 1962, Khomeini's proclamations grew bolder as he moved from attacking the prime minister to criticizing, and eventually directly challenging, the shah.[17] The shah's counterattack on the oppositionist ulama and the killing of several religious students at Qom's Faiziyeh seminary by paratroopers led to proclamations by Khomeini in 1963 that were even more defiant.[18] On 4 June 1963 Khomeini and some other high-ranking clerics were arrested. The following day antigovernment demonstrations broke out in several cities. Hundreds, perhaps thousands, of unarmed demonstrators were killed by the shah's security forces.[19] After his release from prison, Khomeini spoke out against a bill proposing diplomatic immunity for the U. S. military. He strongly condemned the shah and was exiled to Turkey in 1964, whence he went to Iraq.

Contemporary students of Iran now agree with observers at the time, who saw the regime's massive use of violence in 1963 as a turning point which made peaceful political change appear impossible to many and set the stage for the emergence of a powerful undercurrent of revolutionary and violent opposition.[20] Faced with the impossibility of open opposition, a younger generation of militants began organizing underground cells and developing a new eclectic revolutionary theory and practice which drew on both Marxist and Shi'ite elements. These younger militants were also inspired by the ideology and practice of armed revolutionary movements in China, Vietnam, Algeria, Palestine, and Latin America.

There were also important domestic intellectual influences on the militant movement. These included Third Worldist anti-Western critiques, notably Jalal Al-i Ahmad's *Gharbzadigi* (Westoxication). In the same period religious oppositionists, whether leftist or not, began to reinterpret familiar religious concepts in new radical terms. The most important religious radical intellectual was 'Ali Shari'ati. The son of a cleric who belonged to a religious socialist organization, he early took on a similar orientation. As a student in Paris, he was active in the oppositional Confederation of Iranian Students, supported the Algerian revolution, and translated works by Ernesto (Che) Guevara and Frantz Fanon. In the late 1960s, he became famous as a lecturer in a reformist-oriented religious foundation, the Husainiyih Irshad, and was in contact with leaders of the Mujahidin-i Khalq guerrilla organization. His publications, which are mostly transcriptions of his lectures, show an effort to reinterpret Islam and Shi'ism in a populist and activist direction, rejecting the views of both the established clergy and the government.[21]

The Organization of the Iranian People's Mujahidin, often referred to as the Mujahidin (literally meaning those waging jihad), exemplifies the most systematic attempt at developing a revolutionary Shi'ite ideology prior to the 1978–79 revolution. While the Mujahidin's ideas were developed independently and prior to Shari'ati's, Shari'ati's writings were better known, because the Mujahidin were an underground group. It was the Mujahidin who first provided a radical revolutionary interpretation of Qur'anic concepts like *tawhid* (divine unity), *jihad* (holy war), *shahid* (martyr), and *mustaz'afin* (the dispossessed).[22] Many of their and Shari'ati's innovations, including the new use of such terms, were later adopted by Khomeini.

If the Fida'iyan-i Islam had a style reminiscent of the Muslim Brotherhood in Egypt, including attacks on imperialist powers, Zionists, and foreigners in the name of a "traditionalist" version of Islam, the Mujahidin-i Khalq represented a much more original phenomenon. This originality is notable not only for Iran but for the Muslim world as a whole. It combined a secret society with an activist program, conceived of as guerrilla warfare, but legitimated the killing of individual representatives of the Iranian government and of the United States, with a political program stressing a leftist interpretation of Islam.

Post-1963 armed actions against the regime began with the 1965 assassination of Prime Minister Hasan-Ali Mansur by an Islamic organization and an attempt on the shah's life in the same year, attributed to a Marxist circle of British-educated intellectuals. These actions were followed by the formation of more armed underground cells (both Marxist-Leninist and Islamist), laying the grounds for an intense campaign of guerrilla warfare in the early 1970s. The most prominent guerrilla groups were the Marxist Fida'iyan-i Khalq and the left-Islamic Mujahidin-i Khalq. Members and early leaders of the Mujahidin were mostly sons of traditional, provincial, and religious bazaari middle classes with a university education, particularly in engineering or other technical fields.[23] Important to the rise of militant groups in the 1960s and 1970s was a shift in the numbers and social composition of those who attended schools and universities. University education expanded dramatically in this period, and far more children of the lower middle class attended.

The Mujahidin claimed adherence to a "purified" Islam, which they saw as a revolutionary ideology. This interpretation of Islam was based partly on Marxism and partly on the history of revolutionary movements worldwide. The extent of this dependence on Marxism became obvious in 1975 when the Mujahidin declared their conversion to Marxism-Leninism. In fact, however, there had been a split in the organization and a minority of the leadership, maintaining their original ideas, survived and were later able to reclaim the Mujahidin-i Khalq's name and re-form as an Islamic organization. The Marxist Mujahidin soon abandoned this title and continued their activities under a different name.[24]

The Mujahidin's campaign of "armed struggle" began in 1971, right after the Marxist Fida'iyan-i Khalq officially declared their existence and began engaging in guerrilla operations. Both organizations had spent years in training and preparation. The Mujahidin had collected money from antiregime bazaaris and, between 1970 and 1979, sent thirty members to PLO camps in Jordan and Lebanon for military training. Before the Mujahidin could launch their first major operation, however, government security forces arrested about one hundred of their members, including most of the top leadership. In 1972, sixty-nine of the arrested were tried in military courts, where eleven were sentenced to death and the rest to imprisonment terms ranging from several years to life. The Mujahidin launched a systematic campaign of bombings and assassinations when the government began the execution of their captured members in 1972. They attacked police stations, blew up offices of American companies, and assassinated Iranian and U.S. military personnel. The United States was a principal target of Mujahidin's violence because of its support for the shah's regime and its role against revolutionary movements in Vietnam, Oman, and Palestine.[25] The Mujahidin's use of violence in pre-revolutionary years, however, did not match that of the Marxist guerrillas in either scope of intensity. As the leading expert of the Iranian guerrilla movement has noted:

> The various Marxist organizations active during this period outdid all the Muslim groups combined with a ratio of three to one in terms of sacrificing themselves, assassinating officials, robbing banks, and bombing governmental buildings. This may come as a surprise to outsiders subjected since the Islamic Revolution to the constant theme that Shi'ite Islam has a "martyrdom complex," preaches religious crusades [jihad], and inspires the faithful to sacrifice themselves for the divine cause.[26]

Despite its dramatic impact, Iran's guerrilla movement failed to attract a mass following. By the mid-1970s, government security forces had managed to bring the movement under control through the massive use of torture, execution, and imprisonment. Whether justified in Marxist or Shi'ite terms, the guerrillas' violent confrontations with an oppressive power did not lead the people to opposition and protest as long as the political situation was not conducive to such mass action.

From 1965 to 1978 Khomeini, in exile in Iraq, was important to the opposition, but not dominant. A book of his lectures as *Vilayat-i Faqih* (*The Guardianship of the Jurisprudent*, 1971), was innovative chiefly in calling the monarchy un-Islamic and in claiming that a leading clerical jurist should rule. Khomeini did not call for violence or holy war, however, and seems not to have expected victory soon.[27] In 1972 and 1974 Mujahidin representatives met with him but failed to get his endorsement of their views or of armed struggle.[28] However, Khomeini and his clerical followers did adopt many elements from the rhetoric and ideology of the Mujahidin and Shari'ati, especially those that they saw as useful in mass mobilization. Hence, there were ideological ties between the Islamic left and Khomeini's Islamic revolution. Khomeini's practice of assigning new meanings to Islamic terms was pioneered by the Mujahidin: among the terms with new meanings were *mustaz'afin*, the oppressed or dispossessed; and *mustakbarin*, the oppressors. To these, Khomeini added his own favorite terms of condemnation, including *taghuti*, idolater, and *shaitan*, devil. This terminology reflected a "Manichaean" division of the world into absolutely good and evil forces that was characteristic of both Khomeini and the secular and religious guerrilla groups. Although such a division does not always involve violence, it does mean an absolute and militant attitude toward opponents, who are seen as embodiments of evil oppressing the virtuous majority. While these views are based partly on the good-versus-evil divisions found in Shi'ite martyrology, they are also responses to a long history of foreign, particularly Western imperialist, domination, which made many Iranians, and not only religious or radical militants, believe that the virtuous majority was held back only because of foreign control exercised through puppet shahs. In a period of rising discontent, when the shah was associated both with foreign control and with secularism, it is not surprising that more and more people turned to an Islamic version of the Manichaean ideology, which placed the shah in the camp of the hated infidel. Such an ideology was also better able to mobilize the masses than were concepts found in Western-style secular nationalism.

Militancy and Violence during the Revolution

In 1978, Khomeini and his followers were able to assume the leadership of a growing movement of mass protest in Iran. While militantly rejecting compromises with the shah, Khomeini rejected the use of violence until after the shah's regime was brought down in February 1979.

Like most revolutions, the 1978–79 revolution was not expected to occur when it did, and it began with a series of rather minor events. The guerrillas had been much weakened by systematic government trials and executions, and Khomeini's strength was not obviously growing before 1978. A combination of economic dislocations and arbitrary government policies in the late 1970s added to the discontent, but not in a dramatic way. The immediate background of the revolution came in 1977 when, as a response to the Carter administration's human rights campaign, secular middle-class intellectuals voiced a variety of open protests, which the shah for the first time allowed. Some violent acts of government oppression also encouraged a growth in protests.

In the fall of 1977 Khomeini gave a speech from Iraq urging the ulama to join the protests: "Today in Iran, an opening has appeared and you must take advantage of this opportunity. . . . Now the writers of political parties criticize, protest, and write and sign letters; you too must write and a few of the ulama should sign."[29] The moderate and pragmatic tone of this whole speech casts light on Khomeini's behavior throughout the revolution. Khomeini during the revolution was militant in that he was uncompromising regarding the need to overthrow the shah, and rejected the large group of ulama and secularists who wanted, or were willing to settle for, a return to the constitutional monarchy intended by the 1906–7 Iranian constitution. He followed his own vision and would not compromise with the various groups, such as the liberal democratic National Front, which tried to enlist him in significant parts of its cause. On the other hand, he was pragmatic. For example, he went along with those among his lieutenants who played down the theocratic program and anti-Jewish bias of works like *Vilayat-i Faqih,* and even endorsed concepts he had once eschewed, such as that of a republic.

During most of 1978, Khomeini spoke favorably of constitutionalism, but remained vague and evasive about his own ideas of Islamic government. For example, on 6 September he declared: "The shah and his government are in a state of armed rebellion against the justice-seeking people of Iran, against the constitution, and against the liberating decrees of Islam."[30] In an interview with the foreign press in the fall of 1978 he said: "The Islamic government is a democratic government in the real sense . . . every one can express his views . . . and the Islamic government will respond to reason with reason. I shall not have any function in the government, having, as I do at the present, a guiding role when the Islamic government is established."[31]

Khomeini had an excellent feel for the realities of a revolutionary situation and must have seen that an endorsement of violence or assassination would weaken the revolutionary forces. He grasped that the best hope for victory lay in winning over large parts of a conscript military. Hence, we find no direct calls for violence by Khomeini and his lieutenants, not because they opposed violence in theory but because they saw it as counterproductive. Not until after the final victory of the revolution did Khomeini make use of the potentially powerful tool of calling for a jihad against his "unbeliever" enemies.[32] That this was a tactical restraint rather than a commitment to avoid violence is suggested by his dramatic shift toward violence in the post-revolutionary period.

Any violence that took place during the mass demonstrations of 1978 was overwhelmingly the result of police action. There was some significant violence against property, usually of those considered foreign agents, but very little against people. When there was oppositional violence, it was usually difficult to determine who was responsible for it, but it was unlikely that the major "militant" opposition groups, all of which during the revolution basically avoided violent tactics, were behind it.

During 1978, moderate oppositionists were pushed aside and Khomeini emerged as the undisputed leader of the opposition. This trend began with a major miscalculation by the court, almost certainly endorsed by the shah. On 7 January 1978, an article in the official newspaper, Ettela'at, attacked Khomeini in scathing and scurrilous terms. This attack set off the first of a series of militant demonstrations with mainly religious leadership that were one of the most important factors in bringing about a revolutionary situation. Thousands were killed as the armed forces fired on the demonstrators throughout 1978.[33]

In addition to the Ettela'at attack on Khomeini, three later incidents intensified the atmosphere of violence, frustrating moderate solutions and helping Khomeini impose his militant leadership. These three incidents, all of which involved violence, were probably the three main turning points propelling the revolutionary victory. First, on 19 August 1978, in the southern city of Abadan, a fire set in a movie house killed over four hundred people. Cinemas and banks in a number of cities had been set on fire during anti-shah demonstrations, but the perpetrators had been careful not to hurt people. The burning to death of hundreds of innocent people was an unprecedented act of violence that drove an already enraged population to depths of anger and frustration. The government and the opposition immediately blamed each other, but in mass demonstrations across the country people blamed the regime. They accepted Khomeini's declaration that "the evidence points to the criminal hand of the tyrannical regime, which wishes to distort the image of the humane Islamic movement of our people. . . . All indications are that the heart-rending incident in Abadan has the same origin as the massacres that have taken place in other cities . . . the regime may commit similar savage acts in other cities of Iran."[34]

In the wake of this incident, on 27 August, the shah appointed a new prime minister, Ja'far Sharif-Imami, who promised to talk to the opposition, to grant freedom of the press and to allow political parties, and to prosecute those responsible for the recent acts of violence. The victims' families continued pressing for inquiries during and after the revolution, staging sit-ins and demonstrations to overcome the reluctance of the new regime to investigate the incident. The pressure finally led to a public trial in which ten persons received death sentences. A religious fanatic named Husain Takbalizadeh confessed to having ignited the fire. But the court refused to probe the obvious involvement of his associates, who were connected to the Khomeinist movement, trying instead to uphold the official version by executing a number of individuals who were said to be the SAVAK agents who instigated the arson.[35]

The burning of the Rex Cinema in Abadan was the only important violent incident during the revolution instigated by Islamic militants. It was a major turning point at a time when the cycle of protest demonstrations had died down some and when many liberals were accepting the shah's promises of greater democracy. After the burning of the cinema, mass protests recommenced on a large scale. It is difficult to say what general conclusion may be drawn from the incident. The perpetrators were Khomeinists in politicoreligious spirit who did not follow Khomeini's nonviolent tactics. Their success in arousing the country was entirely due to the fact that most people believed that the act had been perpetrated by SAVAK or the shah or both. Yet we know too little about the perpetrators to know whether they were clever agents provocateurs who knew their act would stir up the people or whether, as seems more likely, they were just carrying to an extreme (perhaps not knowing that people were locked in the theater) earlier religious burnings of empty cinemas. The main relevant conclusion seems to be that trust in the regime had fallen so low that most people were prepared to believe the worst. The act was both violent and militant but was not evidence of the widespread adoption of violent tactics, nor did its agent provocateur aspect have any important parallels in other revolutionary events.

The second major act of violence of 1978 was the "Black Friday" incident. On 5 September over a million people took part in a peaceful demonstration in Tehran. On Friday, 8 September, the government declared martial law so early in the morning that many did not hear of it, and later in the day soldiers opened fire on a crowd of demonstrators in Tehran's Jaleh Square, killing several hundreds.[36] This incident doomed Sharif-Imami's "government of national reconciliation," which was replaced in November by a military government. By this time, however, the regime's use of violence was clearly counterproductive since demonstrations were growing larger and more defiant while the armed forces had begun to show increasing signs of wavering and disobedience when ordered to shoot on demonstrators. Finally, in January 1979, the shah appointed a National Front leader, Shapour Bakhtiar, prime minister and left the country on an extended vacation.

On 1 February, Khomeini made his triumphant return to Iran and the following day rejected Bakhtiar's government: "I'll appoint a government with the support of the nation . . . and I'll slap the Bakhtiar government in the mouth."[37] On 13 January, Khomeini announced the official formation of a rival government, the Council of the Islamic Revolution. However, the third important violent event, the armed uprising of 9–11 February that put a final end to monarchy, occurred contrary to Khomeini's explicit decree that he had not ordered a jihad. The rising took place as Khomeini and his Council of Revolution were engaged in behind-the-scenes negotiations with the shah's generals and American officials for a smooth transfer of power.[38] Meanwhile, on the evening of 9 February, an armed clash between monarchist and revolutionary elements at a military base in central Tehran took place involving both the Mujahidin and the Marxist Fida'iyan-i Khalq guerrillas. The fighting soon spread, and army barracks and police stations in Tehran and the surrounding provinces were attacked by thousands of people, led by the guerrillas and revolutionary defectors from the armed forces. On 11 February, the army chiefs of staff accepted the triumph of the revolution by declaring their political neutrality and calling the troops back to the barracks.

The political temper of the revolutionary authorities is indicated by their reaction to the 14 February 1979 seizure of the U.S. embassy and its personnel, including Ambassador William Sullivan, by leftists unconnected to Khomeini. This "mini hostage crisis" ended the day that Khomeinist forces, led by revolutionary council member Ibrahim Yazdi, rescued the hostages. Khomeini later sent personal envoys to apologize for the act.[39]

The revolution, which is most often dated January 1978–February 1979, saw an extensive use of mass demonstrations and strikes, but Khomeini and those around him deliberately minimized violence in order to win over the armed forces and the population. The use of violence by the religious right in August 1978 and by leftist guerrilla groups in February 1979 was a minority phenomenon, timed to be effective in both cases, but not tied to Khomeini.

The Post-Revolutionary Period

Revolutionary Iran's record on militancy and violence, under Khomeini's leadership in the decade from 1979 to 1989 decade, can be divided into two phases. In the first phase, from 1979 to 1984, militant rhetoric and officially sponsored violence increasingly became characteristic of the new regime in its domestic and foreign policies. This officially sponsored violence included executing opponents, taking hostages, conducting the war with Iraq, and attempting to export the revolution to Lebanon and the Persian Gulf region. This was followed by a second phase, beginning in 1984, in which Iranian leaders, including Khomeini himself, appeared to have realized the limited usefulness of such policies and began experimenting with a more pragmatic strategic approach, while continuing the militant rhetoric and making occasional tactical moves in line with their previous radicalism. In this period, Iran's involvement in the region's Shi'ite "liberation struggles" became more cautious and less overt, the political and military conduct of the war between Iran and Iraq became more pragmatic—eventually a cease-fire was accepted from a position of weakness—and systematic moves were made to mend fences with former adversaries, including major Western governments and even the United States. The Islamic Republic remained inflexibly uncompromising and violent in its treatment of organized political opposition.

The Revolution's Radical Phase: Confrontationist Foreign Policy and the Domestic Reign of Terror (1979–84)

A great potential for large-scale revolutionary violence had developed in 1978 and was released with the February 1979 armed uprising and its aftermath. Neighborhood revolutionary committees, already active around the country, were now armed because people had stormed army barracks during the chaos of power transfer in February 1979. Hundreds of thousands of guns were in the hands of an aroused populace, now engaged in acts of revenge and retribution. The new authorities were responsible for many executions, but they often tried to control or contain the unofficial use of violence. The first official acts of violence occurred amidst popular demands for the punishment of those responsible for large-scale killings during the revolution. Hundreds of military personnel, police, and SAVAK officials were summarily tried and executed in the first months of 1979 with Khomeini's approval. But following protests from moderate circles, Khomeini eventually ordered that only those directly involved in murder should receive death sentences.[40]

A public mood of anxiety and insecurity was intensified by the sporadic counter-revolutionary terrorism of monarchist elements, plus the widespread fear of foreign intervention, as had happened in 1953 when the American and British governments had helped reinstall an exiled shah through a military coup d'etat. Chaos and insecurity reigned during the first months of the revolutionary government. The radical left—the Mujahidin and the Marxist Fida'iyan-i Khalq—had emerged from the underground and was rapidly growing; Kurdistan was controlled by armed and organized local groups, while other regionalist movements were active in Khuzistan, Baluchistan, and the northern provinces. Meanwhile, terrorist attacks on revolutionary leaders by monarchists and especially the mysterious Forqan group had intensified. General Gharani, the first chief of staff of the Islamic Republic, and Ayatollah Mortaza Motahhari, a prominent modernist Shi'ite ideologue and one of Khomeini's favorite disciples, were assassinated in spring 1979, and revolutionary council member Hojja-tulislam Ali-Akbar Hashimi Rafsanjani barely escaped assassination. Terrorist attacks on government officials continued unabated in early 1979. Prime Minister Mehdi Bazargan's provisional government was paralyzed, and the nucleus of the future state was organized by a clerical group close to Khomeini.[41] Later to form the Islamic Republican Party under Ayatollah Muhammad Husain Beheshti's leadership, this group had a theocratic state (*wilayat al-faqih*) as their program and gradually took control of the Revolutionary Guards, the armed militia based on revolutionary committees. The more dramatic events of 1979–80, the hostage crisis and war with Iraq, occurred in the context of an intense power struggle between this clericalist group and all other factions. Regionalist forces such as the Kurds and Azerbaijanis (supporters of Ayatullah Kazim Shar'iatmadari), liberals (secular and Islamic), and the left (Mujahidin and Marxists) formed an incoherent but strong opposition that, had they stuck together, might have seriously challenged the passage of the new constitution proposed by the clericalist faction.[42]

In this explosive domestic situation, Iran's leaders exploited an emotional foreign policy issue when the shah was admitted to the United States for treatment of his cancer. Former U.S. ambassador William Sullivan had warned that admitting the shah to the United States would certainly lead to the seizure of the embassy in Tehran.[43] Anti-American sentiments were on the rise, especially after May 1979, when a U.S. Senate resolution strongly condemned arbitrary executions in Iran. This triggered angry demonstrations in Iran and was seen as a hostile gesture by the U.S. government—which had not protested when shah's opponents were killed by his regime. The second seizure of the U.S. embassy, in November 1979, was supervised by Khomeini's son, Ahmad, and directed by Hojjatulislam Muhammad Khu'iiniha, head of the Tehran University Revolutionary Committee, who chose groups of students from various universities for the task.[44] Khomeini soon declared his approval of this action, saying that the embassy seizure had triggered a "revolution bigger than the first."[45] Far from an act of blind fanaticism, the hostage taking was a shrewd political move, allowing the clericalist faction to pose as the champion of popular sentiments in direct confrontation with the shah and the United States, thereby outmaneuvering—and eventually defeating—all of its opponents, who were branded traitors and U.S. collaborators, and winning overwhelming support for the new constitution.[46]

In the midst of the hostage crisis, the Islamic Republican Party in April 1980 launched a "cultural revolution," forcibly removing "un-Islamic" groups, especially secular leftists and the Mujahidin, from university campuses in a series of violent clashes resulting in thirty-eight deaths and several hundred injuries.[47] In the same month Khomeini called on the Iraqi army to overthrow its leaders.[48] Meanwhile, in Paris, Shapour Bakhtiar announced the formation of a National Council of Resistance and called for the overthrow of the Iranian regime.[49] In May, Iran announced the uncovering of several military plots against the regime, some of which were linked to Bakhtiar. More executions followed.[50]

On 22 September 1980, following weeks of border clashes, Iraq invaded Iran. Iraq's objective was to occupy Khuzistan, set up a republic headed by Bakhtiar and the royalist Iranian general Ghulam-Ali Oveisi, and bring down the regime.[51] Khomeini declared this an invasion by the United States: "Due to her desire to completely end all relations with this great Satan, Iran is now burdened by these imposed wars; the U.S. has forced Iraq to shed the blood of our youths. . . . Muslim nations must know that Iran is a country officially at war with the U.S. and that our martyrs and these youths and brave soldiers and revolutionary guards are defending Islam against the U.S."[52]

On 20 January 1981, Iran released the fifty-two American hostages without having obtained any of its much publicized demands from the United States. The hostage crisis, however, had helped consolidate Khomeini's and his clerical followers' monopoly of power in Iran. In addition, it had scored at least one major victory for Khomeini's foreign policy. He personally and publicly called on the American people to reject Carter in the 1980 presidential elections.[53] This objective was achieved, with the help of the hostage crisis, which, more than anything else, doomed Carter's second term.

Throughout 1981, domestic power struggles intensified as the Islamic Republican

Party fought various factions, most notably the coalition led by Iran's president Bani-Sadr and the Mujahidin leader Mas'ud Rajavi. The Islamic Republican Party declared this struggle a "third revolution": yet another struggle against American-sponsored schemes. In June 1981, the regime was shaken by a Mujahidin armed uprising, followed by a bomb blast which killed almost the entire leadership of the Islamic Republican Party. The Mujahidin were now embracing violent tactics after having eschewed them since the revolution. Hundreds and eventually thousands of executions followed as the regime responded to the most serious attempt yet against its existence. Bombings and assassinations of the regime's leaders also continued throughout the year. In August the president and prime minister were assassinated, and in September Western sources reported an average of one hundred executions were taking place per day.[54] Iran's chief justice announced that any opponent of the regime could be executed upon arrest if two witnesses testified against him. In 1984 the Mujahidin published a list of names of those executed by the regime, mostly Mujahidin, numbering close to eleven thousand.[55] Except for the war with Iraq, this was the Islamic Republic's most violent campaign. Its victims were not infidel foreigners but Iranians who considered themselves truly revolutionary Shi'ites.

During 1982 the war tide turned as Iran recovered most of its lost territory and its armies crossed into Iraq. Iran was now fighting an offensive war, rejecting a United Nations resolution for a cease-fire and asking instead for Iraqi acceptance of war guilt, the punishment of Saddam Hussein, and payment of $100 billion in reparations to Iran, as conditions for cease-fire.[56] On the domestic front, too, the Islamic Republic appeared to be in control, having crushed the opposition by a reign of terror unprecedented in modern Iranian history. In December 1982, however, Khomeini issued an eight-point decree calling for restraint in dealing with the opposition and guaranteeing certain basic individual rights. Some judges were removed, and certain committees were purged. Universities were reopened after having been purged of "un-Islamic" students and professors.[57]

Iran's campaign of exporting the Islamic Revolution dramatically intensified in the early 1980s. Following the revolution's success in 1979, the Revolutionary Guards had set up a special Liberation Movements unit, directed by Mehdi Hashemi, a former theology student and activist of the Khomeinist movement with family and political ties with Ayatollah Husain-Ali Montazeri, member of the revolutionary council and later Khomeini's designated successor as Iran's supreme politicoreligious leader. Under the shah's regime, Mehdi Hashemi, who was said to have received military training at PLO camps in Lebanon, had been accused of murdering an ayatollah and condemned to death. Clerical intervention led to the mitigation of his sentence to life imprisonment, and he was freed during the revolution. As director of the Liberation Movements section of the Revolutionary Guards, he established contact with a number of armed groups active in Lebanon and Iran's neighboring countries. When the Liberation Movements office was dissolved due to intergovernmental conflicts, Hashemi continued his activities in cooperation with Ayatollah Montazeri's office.[58]

In March 1982 the Association of Militant Clerics and the Revolutionary Guards invited participants from Kuwait, Bahrain, Saudi Arabia, and Lebanon to attend a

"Seminar on the Ideal Islamic Government" in Tehran. Participants in this seminar agreed to struggle for true independence by returning to Islamic roots, to accord Shi'ites a larger role in the fight against foreign powers, and not to separate religion and politics or rely on any outside power. With Iranian inspiration and assistance, these men were to launch a coordinated offensive against the foreign presence in their countries. An umbrella organization, the Council of the Islamic Revolution, was set up under the supervision of Ayatollah Montazeri. Most of the council's members were clerics, but it also included secular members and "advisers" from Syrian and Libyan intelligence agencies. Its annual budget of reportedly over $1 billion came from the Iranian government and other sources.[59]

By June 1982, Iran had become involved in the Lebanese civil war, sending one thousand revolutionary guards to Baalbek in the Syrian-controlled Shi'ite Bekaa Valley in response to the Israeli invasion of Lebanon. The Iranians helped Husain Musawi, a defector from Lebanon's largest Shi'ite movement, Amal, to set up a rival Shi'ite organization, Islamic Amal. A few months later, another group formed around the local Shi'ite clerics of the Iranian-controlled region. Known as Hizbullah, the "Party of God," this was a politico-ideological movement dependent on the personal appeal of several religious leaders and their followers. Even more amorphous, and possibly no more than a name, was the mysterious "Islamic Jihad," which espoused a pro-Khomeini ideology and claimed responsibility for a series of deadly and effective terrorist acts in Lebanon.[60]

On 19 October 1983 a car bomber on a suicide mission drove into the U.S. Marine headquarters in Beirut, killing 241 Americans. A second bomb that day killed 58 French paratroopers in Beirut. The Islamic Jihad claimed responsibility, while the U.S. government suggested Iranian involvement and pointed to Musawi—who denied any responsibility on his part or by Iran, while approving the use of violence in retaliation for acts of violence by foreign forces in Lebanon. Ten days later another bomb killed 29 Israeli troops and over 30 Palestinian and Lebanese prisoners at the headquarters of the Israeli occupation forces in the city of Tyre. Six months earlier a similar attack had killed 63 at the U.S. Embassy in Beirut. It was never established who the attackers in these incidents really were. The increased activism of Lebanon's Shi'ite population, however, had more to do with the reaction to Western interference in the civil war than it did to Iranian instigation.[61]

The appearance of a pro-Iranian Shi'ite movement in Lebanon was the greatest success of Iran's campaign to export its revolution. Shi'ite terrorist tactics in Lebanon were successful insofar as they were followed by the departure of American forces. The Lebanese Shi'ite movement was largely the product of a series of complex domestic and foreign factors. The influence Iran had in Lebanon it used more in pursuit of pragmatic foreign policy interests than of ideological commitments. The subordination of ideology to pragmatism in the Islamic Republic's foreign policy was best exemplified in Iran's secret dealings with Israel, which began shortly after the revolution and culminated in the "Irangate" scandal.

The Persian Gulf was another region where Shi'ite militancy and violence, connected to Iran, broke out during the 1980s. In Bahrain, where there is an absolute

Shi'ite majority, in December 1981 the government arrested a group of Shi'ite conspirators belonging to the Islamic Front for the Liberation of Bahrain, with headquarters in Tehran. Bahraini and Saudi officials announced that Iran had trained and equipped this group, which had planned to overthrow the Bahraini government.[62] In Saudi Arabia's Shi'ite region of Hasa unrest began as early as 1979, when banned Ashura ceremonies were held that turned into violent confrontations with Saudi security forces. Radio Tehran was openly calling on the Saudi Shi'ites to rebel against the royal family.[63]

Truck bombings and hijackings were also carried out by Shi'ite groups in Kuwait. In December 1983, suicide bomb attacks by Shi'ite militants against the U.S. Embassy and the French consulate resulted in extensive destruction and were followed by the arrest of seventeen alleged conspirators, three of whom were sentenced to death. A year later, on 5 December 1984, another Shi'ite group, perhaps from Lebanon's Hizbullah, hijacked a Kuwaiti airliner to Tehran, demanding release of the radical Shi'ite prisoners in Kuwait. The hijackers' demands were not met, and they eventually surrendered to Iranian authorities.[64] While we do not have the details of any official Iranian collaboration with militant movements in Lebanon, Bahrain, Kuwait, and Saudi Arabia, existing information leaves no doubt that such collaboration was important.

Iran's offensive war against Iraq was seen as another means of exporting the Islamic Revolution. Pushing inside Iraqi territory in 1982, Iran officially declared as its war objective the liberation of Jerusalem via the road of the Iraqi holy city of Karbala. This was to say that Iran was to overthrow the Iraqi regime and to engage Israel militarily, spearheading a Shi'ite-led general Islamic uprising.[65] In this period Iran relied heavily on unconventional warfare, based on "human wave" offensives and the ideology of martyrdom. This strategy, which had been successful in recapturing Iranian territory occupied by Iraq, proved a failure as Iraq, which was backed by conservative Arab regimes as well as by the United States and France, withstood repeated Iranian offensives. Meanwhile, international pressure on Iran had been building up. This was led by the United States, which had become increasingly supportive of Iraq. In January 1984, Saddam Hussein admitted that U.S. pilots based in Saudi Arabia were providing Iraq with intelligence reports via AWACS.[66] In the same month, the United States listed Iran among the nations it believed were supporting international terrorism, warning that it would use preemptive military force to prevent Iranian attacks on U.S. targets. In November 1984, the United States restored diplomatic relations with Iraq.

Toward Accommodation and Normalization (1984–89)

Under mounting political and military pressure, and realizing the rapid depletion of Iran's human and economic resources, the Iranian leadership began in 1984 to move toward a more flexible policy. The shift toward pragmatism occurred not due to a sudden reversal of ideological commitments but as a gradual adjustment to new realities. It also evolved slowly and through a contradictory process, which retained certain features of the previous radical and extremist phase.

A number of developments were involved in bringing about a strategic change in Iranian policy. Initially, the war had been widely perceived as a defense of Iran's popular revolution and territorial integrity against foreign aggression. It had therefore served to create a powerful national consensus helping the Islamic Republic's state building and political mobilization projects. But after 1982 the nature of Iran's war effort began to change from a popular revolutionary national struggle to an offensive war against an enemy which seemed ready for peace and a return to the pre-war status quo. Hence, popular support for the war began to wane, even more so as it gradually became clear that despite massive human and material losses, Iran could not win the war, given the regional and international support for Iraq. Politically the continuation of an inconclusive war could only exhaust the very limited resources of the Iranian regime, already in a dangerous situation of total international isolation and facing the erosion of its domestic base of support. The clericalist faction organized in the Islamic Republican Party had managed to eliminate all opposition groups during the early defensive phase of the war, but factions and intense factional conflicts over domestic and foreign policy, including the war effort, reappeared from within the ruling party's ranks and intensified to the point of its official dissolution by 1987. All of these factors combined to exert growing pressure on the Iranian leadership to adopt a more flexible approach to war and foreign policy. Both the evolution and the implementation of this new approach came through an inherently contradictory process which was reflected in an apparently inconsistent and "irrational" behavior in Iranian policies.

As far as policy toward the United States was concerned, both the militancy and the inconsistencies of Iranian behavior in this period were predicated upon a deep-seated hostility, mistrust, and fear due to real grievances against past American interference in Iran, such as the United States' role in Musaddiq's overthrow in 1953 and consistent American support for the shah. There was also a strong popular perception that Iran was at war not merely against Iraq but, at a more fundamental level, against a coalition of hostile international forces under American hegemony. This perception denied the Islamic Republic's responsibility for Iran's problems and international isolation. Despite its distorted premise, this view was logical in stressing the United States' role, since the military stalemate meant that even an American "tilt" toward either belligerent could decide the war's outcome. The Islamic Republic's secret dealing with the Reagan administration was therefore not an irrational reversal of previous anti-Americanism but an attempt to get needed arms and to neutralize a much stronger adversary, the "Great Satan," the United States, while trying to defeat a smaller one, Iraq, the "little Satan." Finally, American policy toward revolutionary Iran, especially under the Reagan administration, also included widely inconsistent agendas from direct and indirect support for the Iraqi war effort to clandestine attempts at restoring relations with and arming Iran.

The development in the Islamic Republic of a more flexible and pragmatic approach to international relations is of particular interest in this chronicle of militance. A succession of policies adopted by Khomeini and other leaders in relation to the war and to the increasingly direct American involvement in the Iran-Iraq conflict led to this development.

The first significant indications of a new course appeared in late 1984. In a speech on 28 October 1984, Khomeini rejected isolationism as the "satanic" suggestion of those who wanted to destroy the Islamic Republic and said relations were possible even with the United States if the latter "corrects its behavior and stops its aggression from the other side of the world toward the Persian Gulf and Lebanon."[67] This was followed by official declarations rejecting violent means of exporting the Islamic revolution. Iranian prime minister Husain Musawi said: "We do not want to export armed revolution to any country. That is a big lie. Our aim is to promote the Islamic Revolution through persuasion and by means of truth and courage. These are Islamic values." Early in 1985, Iran also announced a major shift in military strategy aimed at minimizing casualties through use of conventional warfare.[68]

The most dramatic breakthrough in Iran's foreign policy, however, occurred in 1985, as secret negotiations led to the restoration of an arms-supply relationship with the United States. Meanwhile, Iranians toned down their anti-Americanism. In December 1984 Iranian commandos stormed a Kuwaiti plane that had been hijacked to Tehran by Arab terrorists, freeing two Americans. In June 1985, Rafsanjani called for restoration of relations with the United States and helped to free thirty-nine American hostages in Beirut and also to end a TWA hijacking.[69] In August 1985, 508 TOW antitank missiles were sent to Tehran via Israel, and more shipments came later in November. In July, Richard Murphy, U.S. assistant secretary of state, sharply attacked the Mujahidin-i Khalq organization, calling them antidemocratic and anti-American. This signaled a change in the United States' stance (there had been some congressional support for Mujahidin) as the clandestine U.S.–Iranian negotiations were making progress.[70] On 25 May 1986, a U.S. delegation, headed by Robert McFarlane, flew to Tehran on a secret mission to deliver an arms shipment and President Reagan's personal message of goodwill. On 4 November, however, Rafsanjani publicly acknowledged McFarlane's trip, apparently in reaction to its disclosure in the Lebanese press, which had received the information via the Iranian radical faction of Mehdi Hashemi. American officials, including Reagan, first denied and finally admitted these reports. Khomeini, too, tried to minimize the incident's damage, forbidding its discussion and claiming that the United States had come meekly to Iran's gates, begging to restore relations. Meanwhile, the Islamic Republic dealt severely with the so-called radicals who had sabotaged its newly developing policy toward the United States. Mehdi Hashemi and a group of his followers were arrested and put on trial and charged with, among other things, "illegal clandestine activities" and "diversion of minds and sowing discord." Khomeini personally called for the persecution of the Hashemi group, saying they had published falsehoods. In August 1987, Mehdi Hashemi was executed.[71] These events marked the most important departure from the militant export of revolution to pragmatism in Iran's foreign policy.

By 1987, even though a channel of communications was kept open, U.S.–Iran relations deteriorated and the United States was again tilting toward Iraq in the Gulf War. Iran resumed its anti-American rhetoric, while being careful not to engage the

U.S. forces in the gulf. In fact, the most damaging attack on the United States in the gulf came from Iraq, which, on 17 May 1987, scored a direct missile hit on the *U.S.S. Stark,* killing thirty-seven Americans. The Iraqi government apologized for this "error." The incident was played down in the United States, while President Reagan blamed Iran. In the summer of 1987, tensions between the United States and Iran increased as the United States reflagged Kuwaiti oil tankers while Iran deployed mines in the Persian Gulf. In August, Iran seemed to provoke another regional crisis when, following Khomeini's instructions, Iranians demonstrating during hajj ceremonies clashed with Saudi police and over three hundred of them were killed. In Tehran, crowds attacked the Saudi and Kuwaiti embassies.[72] Khomeini's attempt to disturb the hajj ceremony was of little political cost to Iran, while it was a major embarrassment to the Saudis, who were a main pillar of the anti-Iranian coalition in the Iran-Iraq war. Further, Khomeini's contention that in an earlier and purer Islam the hajj was an important political occasion, with the umma gathered to discuss the questions vital to the day, found validation in the actions of Iranian and other pilgrims gathered in Mecca.[73]

In 1988 Iran and Iraq hit each other's major population centers with long-range missiles and aerial bombardments (War of the Cities) as skirmishes between the United States and Iran in the gulf continued. Iran's acceptance of the cease-fire, however, came soon after Iranian officials declared that the United States was now in direct military engagement against Iran.[74] A tragic incident seemed to confirm this claim and exacerbate Iranian fears of further confrontation with the United States. On 2 July, the *U.S.S. Vincennes* fired on an Iranian airbus, killing 290. On 18 July, Iran accepted U.N. resolution 598 for a cease-fire in the war. Khomeini called this cease-fire worse than taking poison, saying it had to be accepted for reasons that could not be made public. With Iran militarily hard pressed by Iraq and facing increasing and direct American intervention, its leaders appear to have concluded that continuing the war could seriously endanger the regime's survival.[75]

In 1988–89, while Khomeini had become gradually less visible, the official discourse of Iranian leadership reflected more flexibility, emphasizing peace, reconstruction, and normalization in both domestic and foreign policies.[76] The war had been the most potent and enduring project sustaining the Islamic Republic's militant and radical tendencies. Hence, the 1988 cease-fire was followed by what appeared to be a sudden collapse of militancy to the point that moderate, and even severely critical, protests against the regime's handling of the war, corruption, and repressive policies began to surface openly. The rapid ascendancy of the moderates, however, received a partial setback with a wave of executions following an invasion of Iranian territory by the Mujahidin-i Khalq, now based in Iraq, and by the resignation of Ayatollah Montazeri from the position of Khomeini's successor, after being reprimanded by the latter for alleged "liberal" leanings. Also in February 1989, following riots in Pakistan protesting the British author Salman Rushdie's portrayal of Islam and the Prophet Muhammad in his book *The Satanic Verses,* Khomeini issued a decree condemning Rushdie to death. This decree caused an uproar in the West and led to the breaking of diplomatic relations between Iran and the United Kingdom. Khomeini died on

3 June 1989. Since his death the predominent direction of Iran under President Raf-sanjani has been toward greater pragmatism, moderation, and restoration of ties with countries like Great Britain and France.

The decree against Rushdie may be regarded as an act by Khomeini himself rather than as part of a general trend then operative in the revolution. It was sparked not by events within Iran but by mass and sometimes bloody demonstrations among South Asian Muslims both in their home countries and in Great Britain. It was not part of a Shi'ite movement, unlike earlier Iranian encouragement of militant acts among Shi'is in Lebanon and the gulf countries, but one that took an all-Islamic stance. It built upon Islamic law and traditions against what the West calls blasphemy, but it was certainly not required even by a strict interpretation of Islam—many say it went beyond such an interpretation in calling for an assassination. In terms of Iranian history it may be said to indicate how far Khomeini was prepared to go both in enforcing his interpretation of Islam and in using his position to champion a cause raised by Sunni and Shi'ite Muslims of other countries, thus supporting his claims to be a world Islamic leader.

In terms of the trends seen in Iran in the past few years, however, the Rushdie incident, and the antiforeign activities resulting from it, was something of an aberration. These years, and particularly 1991 and 1992, have seen the long-predicted evolution toward moderation in what may be called a delayed "Thermidor" of the Iranian revolution. Although a more militant faction retains some power and could slow the movement to moderation favored by President Rafsanjani, the latter trend has been dominant. The improvement of relations with Western countries—particularly the restoring of diplomatic relations with Britain despite the nonwithdrawal of the decree calling for Rushdie's death—has been dramatic. By June 1991 even the United States was allowing some business with Iran and Iran was hosting a large international congress.

The chief motivation of this trend toward pragmatism by is clearly economic; Iran needs foreign trade, investment, and help in secondary and tertiary recovery of oil even if it is to regain the economic status it had before the war with Iraq. Although Khomeini once indicated that the revolution was not being fought to increase people's economic well-being, there are limits to what even the most ideologically motivated will stand for in terms of worsening conditions. Although the revolution has done rather well in terms of maintaining or even improving conditions for the urban and rural poor, there has been a fall in the GNP that affects many sectors of the population. The government is now concerned with reversing this, and finds that Western aid and cooperation are needed for economic development and that these can be had only with a more Western-style politics. Hence, there has been a notable decline in internal and international militancy, particularly after the final batch of post–Iran-Iraq war executions. Once again it is possible to explain much of Iranian politics without constant reference to Iranian brands of Islam and their supposed intrinsic ties to militancy. Without denying that there are Shi'ite elements in Iranian militancy, one may say that these elements are too often used to explain developments that have parallels both in Western revolutions and in non-Shi'ite and non-Muslim Third World countries where various movements have tried to free their nations from Western control and from Western-oriented autocracies.

Conclusion

Militance in Iran goes back in history at least to the time of a number of radical medieval religious groups, especially the Assassins. In modern times, assassination of leading figures was used mainly by various kinds of "opponents on the left." Only after World War II, however, were groups founded combining a new type of Islamic ideology with an authorization of assassinations and violence as tactics. The two most important such groups were the Fida'iyan-i Islam of the 1940s and 1950s and the Mujahidin-i Khalq from the 1960s to today. The former had what may be termed a neotraditionalist or fundamentalist ideology. The group was small and could be broken up by the execution of its main leaders. The Mujahidin-i Khalq were the first significant militant leftist Islamic group in the Muslim world, and their tactics changed with the circumstances. In their early years they carried out a number of assassinations, but during the Islamic Revolution they generally went along with Khomeini's nonviolent tactics, until their participation in the violent transfer of power. In 1981 they stopped cooperating with the Islamic Republic and launched a campaign of killings against it, which resulted in the execution of far more of their members and other leftists than could have been involved in the killings. Like some of the conservative opponents of the Islamic regime, they sided with Iraq in the Iran-Iraq war. They had considerable success in keeping adherents even after their organization's decimation by executions, and their viability suggests that their militant Islamic leftism continued to have appeal, even though their Islam has always been unorthodox.

If Iran pioneered in militant Islamic leftism, so did it pioneer in effective Islamic revolutionary doctrine. Khomeini's reinterpretation of traditional Islam to the effect that clerics should rule directly created the basis for a militant theocracy. In addition, Khomeini was much more politically uncompromising than most clerics. As the 1978–79 revolution began, however, Khomeini was pragmatic enough to see that winning allies from all sectors of the population, and especially neutralizing the armed forces, required an essentially nonviolent policy. Violence would only have brought out the military against unprepared popular forces. Hence, there was not significant violence on the revolutionary side except during the final takeover.

Once Khomeini took power, however, there was considerable violence, first against partisans of the old regime and then against revolutionary opponents, especially on the left. This violence helped the Khomeini forces achieve a monopoly of power, which they did within two years. Executions of opponents continued sporadically, partly owing to the invasion by Iraq in 1980.

Another aspect of militance appeared in foreign policy. Although Khomeini spoke of Islam and not of Shi'ism, in practice the new revolutionary philosophy appealed far more to Shi'ites than to other Muslims. The only important international incidents owing to ties to Iran occurred among Shi'ite groups in Lebanon, Bahrain, Kuwait, and Saudi Arabia. In addition, Iran sent military support to Shi'ite groups fighting in Afghanistan against their government and the Soviet Union. Most of this militant activity occurred in the early 1980s; by the late 1980s Iran was often trying to settle hijackings and the outcomes of earlier militant acts.

In Iran, while many Shi'ites have always rejected violence, the frequent oppositional role of many others has provided a background for religious militance not duplicated in other Islamic countries. Khomeini's militant Islamic ideology combined a new reading of old texts with the militant activism and populism found in groups like the Mujahidin-i Khalq. This ideology proved effective for taking and holding power, and has also been adapted to nonviolent and pragmatic ends. It has yet to be seen whether it can meet the economic and social demands of the people, not to mention the demands of many Iranian men and women for basic rights and freedoms.

Notes

1. Thanks to Rudi Matthee for his excellent assistance in research. Many interviews and discussions over the years have contributed to this project, especially, in 1981, with Mas'ud Rajavi near Paris and in 1989, with Jahangir Behrooz, Ahmad Jalali, Baqer Mo'in, and Sadeq Zibakalam in Great Britain and Amir Farmanfarmaian in Cambridge, Massachusetts.

2. The Kharijites, a radical secessionist party in early Islam, first supported the party of 'Ali and then broke with him, holding that succession to the caliphate should be solely on the basis of election by the consensus of the community rather than by descent either from the family of the Prophet or from the Umayyad party. Interpretations of the Kharijites may be found in Ira M. Lapidus, *A History of Islamic Societies* (New York: Cambridge University Press, 1988), p. 58, and Marshall G. S. Hodgson, *The Venture of Islam*, vol. 1 (Chicago: University of Chicago Press, 1974), pp. 215–16.

3. According to Twelver Shi'ites, Muhammad al-Baqir became the fifth Imam in 712–13. After his death in 735, his son, Ja'far al-Sadiq, held the title of the sixth Imam until his death in 765. See S. H. M. Jafri, *The Origins and Early Development of Shi'a Islam* (New York and London: Longmans, 1979), pp. 246, 255, 312. Early

Shi'ite history is discussed in the above source as well as in the following: Said Amir Arjomand, *The Shadow of God and the Hidden Imam: Religion, Political Order, and Societal Change in Shi'ite Iran from the Beginning to 1890* (Chicago: University of Chicago Press, 1984), chaps. 1–3. See also the introductions by Nikki R. Keddie in idem, ed., *Religion and Politics in Iran: Shi'ism from Quietism to Revolution* (New Haven: Yale University Press, 1983), pp. 1–18, and by Nikki R. Keddie and Juan R. I. Cole in idem, eds., *Shi'ism and Social Protest* (New Haven: Yale University Press, 1986), pp. 1–29.

4. In the late nineteenth and early twentieth centuries assassination on a world scale was associated primarily with atheistic Western anarchists, whose ideology shows hardly any affinity for that of the Shi'ites. Assassination may more usefully be seen as a response of some activist minority movements to conditions where it is seen as a way to increase their influence than as the outcome of a particular political or religious doctrine. On the Assassins, see Marshal G . S . Hodgson, *The Order of the Assassins: The Struggle of the Early Nizari Isma'ilis against the Islamic World* (The Hague: Mouton, 1955); and Bernard Lewis, *The Assassins: A Radical Sect in Islam* (New York: Basic Books, 1968).

5. In modern times the jihad approach has looked especially to the medieval thinker Ibn Taymiyya in his attack on the (converted) Mongol rulers of Iran as unbelievers against whom jihad was licit.

6. See especially Mary Hegland, "Two Images of Husain: Accommodation and Revolution in an Iranian Village," in Nikki R. Keddie, ed., *Religion and Politics in Iran,* pp. 218–37.

7. Ibid. Also, from a conversation with Mansoor Ehsan, who is studying martyrdom and the Husain paradigm as bases for revolts in Shi'ism.

8. See Christine Dobbin, *Islamic Revivalism in a Changing Peasant Economy: Central Sumatra, 1784–1847* (London, 1983).

9. In the extensive literature on West African jihad movements, see especially Peter B. Clarke, *West Africa and Islam* (London: Edward Arnold, 1982), and David Robinson, *The Holy War of Umar Tal* (Oxford: Clarendon Press, 1985).

10. For a fuller elaboration of this point, see Nikki R. Keddie, "Can Revolutions Be Predicted; Can Their Causes Be Understood?" *Contention: Debates in Society, Culture, and Science* 1, no. 2 (Winter 1992), pp. 159–82.

11. For Fidi'yan-i Islam's assassination of Kasravi, see Farhad Kazemi, "The Fada'iyan-e Islam: Fanaticism, Politics and Terror," in Said Amir Arjomand, ed., *From Nationalism to Revolutionary Islam* (Albany: State University of New York Press, 1984), pp. 158–76. Studies of Fida'iyan-i Islam are found in *Encyclopedia of Islam,* 2d ed., s.v. "Fidaiyyan-i Islam"; Adele K. Ferdows, "Religion in Iranian Nationalism: The Study of the Fadayan-i Islam" (Ph.D. diss., Indiana University, 1967); Sayyid Husain Khush Niyyat, *Sayyid Mujtaba Navvab-i Safavi: Andishiha, mubarizat va shahadati U* (Tehran: 1360/1981–82); Yann Richard, "L'Organization des feda'iyan-e eslam, mouvement integriste musulman en Iran (1945–1956)," in Olivier Carré and Paul Dumont, eds., *Radicalismes islamiques,* tome 1, Iran, Liban, Turquie (Paris: L'Harmattan, 1985), pp. 23–82.

12. *Khandaniha* 11, no. 56, March 1951, pp. 8–12.

13. *Khandaniha* 11, nos. 56–60, Esfand 1329/March 1951.

14. Bizhan Jazani, *Tarikh-i si salih-yi Iran,* vol. 2 (Tehran: Maziar, 1979), p. 64.

15. Ervand Abrahamian, *Iran between Two Revolutions* (Princeton: Princeton University Press, 1982), p. 259. See Nikki R. Keddie, "The Assassination of the Amin as-Sultan (Atabak-i A'zam), 31 August 1907," in C. E. Bosworth, ed., *Iran and Islam: In Memory of the Late Vladimir Minorsky* (Edinburgh: Edinburgh University Press, 1971), pp. 315–30.

16. See Nikki R. Keddie, "The Assassination of the Amin as-Sultan," pp. 315–30. Information on the assassination of Bihbihani was given to N. Keddie in 1960 in Tehran by Sayyid Hasan Taqizadeh.

17. For texts of Khomeini's proclamations, see Sayyid Hamid Ruhani, *Barrasi va tahlili az nihzat-i Imam Khomeini* (Tehran, n.d.), pp. 152–58, 195–204.

18. Ibid., pp. 263–66, 376–77.

19. For example, Marvin Zonis, in *The Political Elite of Iran* (Princeton: Princeton University Press, 1971), p. 63, cites "many thousands" of casualties.

20. Ervand Abrahamian, *The Iranian Mojahedin* (New Haven: Yale University Press, 1989), pp. 84–85; Mohsen M. Milani, *The Making of Iran's Islamic Revolution: From Monarchy to Islamic Republic* (Boulder and London: Westview Press, 1988), chap. 5; Dehnavi, *Qiam-i khunin-i panzdahom-i khurdad-i Chihil-u-du* (Tehran, 1982).

21. For Shari'ati's life and ideas, see, for example, Mehdi Abedi and Gary Legenhausen, eds., *Jihad and Shahadat: Struggle and Martyrdom in Islam* (Houston: Institute for Research and Islamic Studies, 1986), pp. 32–35 and chaps. 5–8; Sharough Akhavi, "Shari'ati's Social Thought," in Nikki R. Keddie, ed., *Religion and Politics in Iran* (New Haven and London: Yale University Press, 1983), pp. 125–44; Abrahamian, *The Iranian Mojahedin,* chap. 4.

22. Abrahamian, *The Iranian Mojahedin,* pp. 103–4. Abrahamian's work remains the only scholarly study of the Mujahidin-i Khalq. The Mujahidin's accounts of their

own history can be found in *Sharh-i ta'sis va tarikhchih-i vaqayi'-i sazman-i Mujahidin-i Khalq-i Iran az sal-i 1344 ta sal-i 1350* (Tehran: Organization of the Iranian People's Mujahidin Publications, 1979) and in *Tarikhchih-i jariyan-i kudita va khat-i mashy-yi Kununi-yi sazman-i Mujahidin-i Khalq-i Iran* (Tehran: Abuzar Publications, 1979).

23. Abrahamian, *The Iranian Mojahedin,* p. 90. Founders of the Fidai'yan-i Khalq came from a similar background. See Maziar Behrooz, "Iran's Fadayan, 1971–1988: A Case Study in Iranian Marxism," *Jusur* 6 (1990): 1–39.

24. *Tarikhchih-i jaryan-i kudita ,* pp. 7–8.

25. Abrahamian, *The Iranian Mojahedin,* pp. 127–28, 140–42.

26. Ibid., p. 152.

27. Ruhollah Khomeini, *Vilayat-i faqih* (Tehran, 1979), for an English version, see Ruhollah Khomeini, *Islam and Revolution: Writings and Declarations of Imam Khomeini,* Hamid Algar, trans. (Berkeley: Mizan Press, 1981).

28. In 1980 Khomeini discussed this meeting and his rejection of the Mujahidin's views including their advocacy of armed struggle; see *Kalam-i Imam,* vol. 13 (Tehran, 1984), pp. 247–48.

29. Quoted in Mehdi Bazargan, *Inqilab-i Iran dar du harikat* (Tehran: Naraqi, 1984), p. 26.

30. Ruhollah Khomeini, *Islam and Revolution,* p. 235.

31. Quoted in Bazargan, *Inqilab-i Iran dar du harikat,* p. 55.

32. For Khomeini's response to the use of violence by the government in this period, see Khomeini, *Islam and Revolution,* pp. 212–30; see also Khomeini's interviews with the international news media in the fall of 1978, where he systematically rejected the use of violence, in *Nida-yi haq* (Tehran, n.d.), pp. 31–113.

33. One source, William A. Dorman and Mansur Farhang, *The U.S. Press and Iran* (Berkeley and Los Angeles: University of California Press, 1987), p. 165, estimates that about ten thousand were killed, while

another, Ahmad Ashraf and Ali Banuazizi, "The State, Class and Modes of Mobilization in the Iranian Revolution," *State, Culture and Society* 1, no. 3 (Spring 1985): 3–40, gives a lower figure of about three thousand.

34. Khomeini, *Islam and Revolution,* pp. 233–34.

35. *Kayhan International,* 22, 23, 27, 28, and 29 August 1978. For the trial. see *Kayhan Tehran,* 6 September 1980 and, Mustafa Abkashak, *Musabbibin-i vaqi'i-yi faji'ih-i hulnak-i sinima-yi Abadan chih kasani hastand?* (Los Angeles, 1989).

36. Government figures were 58 dead and 205 wounded, while the opposition claimed casualties reaching hundreds or even several thousands. See H. Muvahhid, *do sal-i akhir: riform ta inqilab* (Tehran, 1984), pp. 169–71.

37. Dilip Hiro, *Iran under the Ayatollahs* (London: Routledge and Kegan Paul, 1985), pp. 90–91.

38. On 7 February, during the armed uprising in Tehran, Khomeini issued a declaration saying: "Even though I have not ordered a holy jihad, wanting to preserve peace and acting according to the people's will and legal norms, I cannot bear these violent acts and I warn that if this fratricide is not stopped, if the imperial guard division does not return to its base and army officials do not prevent these violations, I shall, God willing, make my final decision on with whom the responsibility lies, the aggressors and transgressors." See Muvvahid, *Do sal-i akhir: riform ta inqilab,* p. 311; for the three-sided negotiations between Khomeini's inner circle, Iranian army generals, and U.S. representatives in Paris and Tehran, see William H. Sullivan, *Mission to Iran* (New York and London: W. W. Norton and Company, 1981), chaps. 20–21, 23–24.

39. Sullivan, *Mission to Iran,* pp. 254–67.

40. *New York Times,* 14 May 1979, and *Ettela'at,* 8 Farvardin 1358/28 March 1979, p. 5.

41. Dadgustari-yi Jumhuri-yi Islami-yi Iran, *Gha'ilih-yi chahardahum-i isfand-i 1359* (Tehran, 1985), pp.96–100.

42. *The Christian Science Monitor,* 3 January 1980; *Tehran Mussavar,* no. 11, 17 Farvardin 1357/6 April 1979, pp. 8–13.

43. Robin Wright, *Sacred Rage: The Wrath of Militant Islam* (New York: Linden Press/Simon and Schuster, 1982), p. 76.

44. James A. Bill, *The Eagle and the Lion: The Tragedy of American-Iran Relations* (New Haven: Yale University Press, 1988), pp. 283–84.

45. *Gha'ilih-yi chahardahum-i isfand-i 1359,* p. 218.

46. Hiro, *Iran under the Ayatollahs,* pp. 136–38; for the clericalist faction's use of this occasion to attack Bazargan's government, see *Gha'ilih-yi chahardahum-i isfand-i 1359,* pp. 240–41.

47. *Daily Telegraph,* 27 April 1980.

48. Hiro, *Iran under the Ayatollahs,* pp. 166–67.

49. *Christian Science Monitor,* 30 April 1980; *Gha'ilih-yi chahardahum-i isfand-i 1359,* pp. 234–37.

50. *Los Angeles Times,* 28 May 1980, reported eight hundred executed since February 1979.

51. MERIP reports, July–August 1981, pp. 3–4.

52. Speech of 12 September 1980, in *Kalam-i Imam,* vol. 2, p. 26.

53. As was his style, Khomeini had personalized the U.S.–Iranian confrontation by directly attacking Carter. On different occasions he urged Americans not to elect Carter to a second term. A clear statement of his anti-Carter campaign can be found in his long interview published by *Time* magazine, 7 January 1980, pp. 26–28. *Time* had chosen Khomeini as "Man of the Year."

54. *Sunday Times,* 21 June 1981; *New York Times,* 1 July, 1 September, and 29 December 1981.

55. *List of Names and Particulars of 10,930 Victims of Khomeini Regime's Executions,* compiled and published by the Organization of the Iranian People's Mujahedin, 1984.

56. Hiro, *Iran under the Ayatollahs,* p. 212.

57. *Iran Times,* 11 February 1983, p. 2.

58. *Iran Press Digest,* Tehran, vol. 5, no. 43, 4 November 1986, pp. 2–5.

59. Wright, *Sacred Rage,* pp. 26–30, 32–33.

60. Augustus Richard Norton, *Amal and the Shi'a: The Struggle for the Soul of Lebanon* (Austin: University of Texas Press, 1987), pp. 88, 100–104.

61. Wright, *Sacred Rage,* pp. 72–75, 83.

62. R. K. Ramazani, "Iran's Resistance to the U.S. Intervention in the Persian Gulf," in Nikki R. Keddie and Mark J. Gasiorowski, eds., *Neither East nor West* (New Haven: Yale University Press, 1990), pp. 48–49.

63. Jacob Goldberg, "The Shi'i Minority in Saudi Arabia," in Cole and Keddie, *Shi'ism,* pp. 240–43.

64. "Introduction," in Cole and Keddie, *Shi'ism,* pp. 13–14.

65. Gary Sick, "Trial by Error: Reflections on the Iran-Iraq War," *Middle East Journal* 43, no. 2 (Spring 1989): 235–36.

66. *Financial Times,* 12 May 1984.

67. Khomeini also mentioned how, while in Paris, he had met with U.S. representatives, some of whom he thought evil and others acceptable; see *Iran Times,* 2 November 1984, pp. 1, 14.

68. Gary Sick, "Trial by Error," p. 237.

69. *Los Angeles Times,* 3 July 1985.

70. *Iran Times,* 2 August 1985, p. 15, and 30 August 1985, pp. 15–16.

71. *Iran Press Digest,* vol. 5, no. 44, 11 November 1986, pp. 5–8, and *FBIS,* 18 August 1987.

72. *Kayhan-i Hava'i,* 27 April 1988, pp. 2, 11, 32.

73. Ruhollah Khomeini, *Islam and Revolution,* pp. 130–31. "The first Muslims, on the other hand, used to accomplish important business on the occasion of the hajj or at their Friday gatherings. . . . Entire armies used to be mobilized by the Friday sermon and proceed directly to the battlefield."

74. *Kayhan-i Hava'i,* 20 April 1988, pp. 8–9, and 27 April 1988, pp. 8–9.

75. Gary Sick, "Slouching toward Settle-

ment: The Internationalization of Iran-Iraq War, 1987–1988," in Keddie and Gasiorowski, *Neither East nor West,* pp. 240–42. Though supported by Khomeini, Iranian leaders were hard pressed for explanations of the cease-fire; see, for example, Rafsanjani's Friday sermons in *Kayhan-i Hava'i,* 27 July and 3 August 1988, and Khamenei's sermon in *Kayhani Hava'i,* 17 August 1988. Rafsan-

jani also said, "We still do not think it proper to explain the key reasons leading us to this position, since they may be used by our enemies"; quoted in *Kayhan-i Hava'i,* 24 August 1988, p. 8.

76. See headlines, editorials, and Friday sermons printed in almost every issue of *Kayhan International* in 1988 and 1989.

Hizbullah: The Calculus of Jihad

Martin Kramer

Of the many fundamentalisms that have emerged within Islam during recent years, perhaps none has had so profound an impact on the human imagination as Hizbullah—"the Party of God." This movement of Lebanese Shi'ite Muslims gained both fame and infamy within months of its first public appearance in 1982, by its resort to ingenious forms of violence. Hizbullah's progression from suicide bombings to airliner hijackings to hostage holding made it an obsession of the media and the nemesis of governments.

For a time, Hizbullah seemed invincible, dealing blow after blow to the "enemies of Islam" and creating islands of autonomous fundamentalism in Lebanon. Hizbullah held the attention of the world. Armies of journalists besieged the press secretaries of Hizbullah's leaders. Satellites crisscrossed the blackness of outer space above Hizbullah's bases, searching for the tracks of its adherents. Diplomats and mediators shuttled around the globe, seeking deals that would check or conciliate Hizbullah. More than any other fundamentalist movement in recent history, Hizbullah evoked the memory of the medieval Assassins, who had been feared in the West and Islam for their marriage of fierce militancy with destructive deeds. Like the Assassins, Hizbullah gave rise to an immense lore, and much confusion.

That Hizbullah owed its impact to its violence is beyond any doubt. Although it grew into a social movement, it never commanded the means or manpower necessary to seize power in Lebanon. Hizbullah's appeal remained limited to perhaps half of one sect, in a small and vulnerable state inhabited by many other sects. As for resources, Hizbullah disposed of an estimated annual budget of less than half that of the University of Chicago. The movement owed its reputation almost solely to its mastery of violence—a violence legitimated in the name of Islam. This legitimation may be fairly described as Hizbullah's most original contribution to modern Islamic fundamentalism. Hizbullah's vision of an Islamic state and society was derivative, but its methods for inspiring and rationalizing violence displayed a touch of genius.

This violence is subject to interpretation from any number of analytical and disciplinary vantage points, but any approach must necessarily settle on the core issues of cause, intent, and effect. Why and in what circumstances did the adherents of Hizbullah resort to force? What did they intend to achieve by their acts? What were the effects of their violence? These are large questions, and the evidence is scattered at best. The purpose here is not to provide confident answers but to chart the islands of existing knowledge where answers might be found. The point is to better understand the unique predicament of Hizbullah—unique even within contemporary Islam. Nevertheless, the experience of Hizbullah may illuminate the passage of other fundamentalist movements into violence, a passage for which there are examples in every great tradition.

Shi'ite Fundamentalism in the Lebanese Context

Hizbullah's militance must first be set in context. But which context? There is the 1,400-year legacy of Shi'ism, a legacy of martyrdom and suffering, resting on an ancient grievance: the belief that Islamic history was derailed when political power passed out of the hands of the family of the Prophet Muhammad in the seventh century. In the subsequent course of history, Shi'ism has sometimes erupted as a form of protest against the existing order in Islam; at other times it has retreated into an otherworldly preoccupation with messianic redemption. This inner tension in Shi'ism, and Lebanon's place in it, was explored in an earlier study in this series. The themes addressed there, especially the crisis that confronts all contemporary Shi'ism, are the necessary prelude to any appreciation of Hizbullah.[1]

Here it is more appropriate to dwell on the narrow but rich Lebanese context of Hizbullah. Many works of reportage and scholarship now attest to the power of modern grievance among Lebanon's Shi'ite Muslims. Their pattern of settlement reflected a history of persecution, from which they had found refuge in redoubts along the eastern shore of the Mediterranean. The Shi'ites felt secure and free in the mountains of what is now the south of Lebanon and the plains of the Bekaa Valley, tucked between two high ranges. But when the impact of the West struck Lebanon in modern times, the isolated Shi'ites felt it last, and they were slow to modernize. When Lebanon became independent in 1946, the Shi'ites became the despised stepchildren of a state governed by (and for) Maronite Christians and Sunni Muslims.[2]

The Shi'ites have been rushing breathlessly to catch up ever since. Demographically, they soon surpassed every other sect. In the thirty-five years between 1921 and 1956, the Shi'ite population had risen from 100,000 to 250,000, but its percentage of Lebanon's total population remained steady at about 19 percent. Yet, in the twenty years between 1956 and 1975, the Shi'ite population tripled, from 250,000 to 750,00, bringing the Shi'ites to about 30 percent of the total population.[3] The larger size of the Shi'ite families, coupled with Christian emigration, had produced a dramatic rise in the Shiʿite proportion of Lebanon's population. The Shiʿites had become Lebanon's largest single confessional community, surpassing the Maronite Christians and Sunni Muslims.

But the Shiʿites could not close the social and economic gap. Some did shake the legacy of poverty and ignorance, and forced open Beirut's worlds of commerce, administration, and education. But many more flocked from their villages to the great Lebanese capital to sweep the streets and hawk on corners. The angriest of the Shiʿites joined the revolutionary movements that swept Lebanon in the 1960s and 1970s, especially those founded and led by Palestinians, who were even angrier. Other Shiʿites who still held out hope for reform created their own communal movement to promote their interests, under the leadership of a progressive cleric and middle-class professionals. After the outbreak of the Lebanese civil war in 1975, this movement created a militia known as Amal ("Hope"), which adopted a largely defensive posture in the fighting.[4]

But geography trapped the Shiʿites in the withering crossfire of the shootout that pitted the Palestinian organizations in Lebanon against the Maronite-led Lebanese Forces and Israel. Hundreds of thousands of Shiʿites became refugees, first from Maronite-Palestinian fighting in 1976, then as the result of the Israeli invasion of South Lebanon in 1978. A quarter of a million refugees poured into the squalid southern suburbs of Beirut, which they transformed into a massive village, reeking of garbage and open sewage.[5] By 1982, the storehouse of Shiʿite grievance had filled to overflowing and Amal could scarcely manage it.

For some years before 1982, a few voices, mostly of Shiʿite clerics, had raised a slogan very different from Amal's call for reform. These voices pronounced the death of Lebanese confessionalism and urged the transformation of Lebanon into an Islamic state. Not only did they demand rule by Muslims, who now constituted a majority of the Lebanese, but they claimed that only an Islamic government could restore peace and independence to Lebanon.[6] Few persons in the jaundiced world of Lebanese politics took this promise of an Islamic utopia seriously, even within the Shiʿite community. But after the Islamic Revolution in Iran in 1979—a revolution that swept a white-bearded Shiʿite cleric to power on a tide of revolutionary rage—the idea of an Islamic state suddenly seemed real to many Shiʿites, and even urgent. The events of 1982, including the Israeli occupation of the Shiʿite south, the massacre of Palestinians by Maronite militiamen in league with Israel, and the deployment of American and French troops near the Shiʿite slums of Beirut, convinced many Shiʿites that they stood to become the victims of history once again.

As the vise closed ever tighter, the Shiʿite community finally cracked. A faction of Amal bolted, and the defectors left in the hundreds for the Bekaa Valley. They were accompanied by several fervent young Shiʿite clerics, whose minds burned with visions of a Lebanon purified by Islamic revolution. There the Lebanese Shiʿites joined hands with a contingent of a thousand Iranian Revolutionary Guards, who had come to do battle with the "enemies of Islam" now assembled in Lebanon and to spread the revolutionary message of the Imam Khomeini. Together they seized a Lebanese army barracks on a hill in the Bekaa Valley and transformed it into a formidable fortress, ringed by antiaircraft emplacements and bristling with antennae. This base, and several smaller installations in its vicinity, would become the nucleus of an autonomous zone, governed by the precepts of Islam. The new formation took the name of Hizbullah—the "Party of God"—after a verse in the Qur'an (V, 56): "Lo! the Party of God, they are the victorious."[7]

Hizbullah thus issued from a marriage of Lebanese Shi'ites and Islamic Iran, and grew to become the most influential Shi'ite fundamentalist movement outside Iran. Here lies a paradox. Iran's Islamic Revolution first targeted the Shi'ite populations of the countries immediately adjacent to Iran or across the Persian Gulf: Iraq, Kuwait, Saudi Arabia, Bahrain, and Afghanistan. Some of these states had large Shi'ite populations that were in ready reach. Yet Iran's revolution ultimately had its greatest impact in Lebanon, the most westward and remote outpost of the Shi'ite world, and home to only 2 or 3 percent of the world's Shi'ites outside Iran. Despite the distance from Iran, Lebanon seemed to magnify the signal of Iran's revolution many times over, generating a Shi'ite fundamentalism that marched stridently to Iran's cadence. (Lebanon also produced the only Sunni fundamentalist movement that unashamedly embraced Iran as its model, the Tawhid movement in Tripoli.)

The paradox had a ready explanation: Lebanon's civil war amplified the effect of Iran's revolution. The collapse of the state and the resulting violence had taken a tremendous toll on Shi'ite society, producing demographic, social, and economic dislocations that dwarfed the simple discrimination suffered by Shi'ites elsewhere. Many hundreds of thousands of Shi'ites had been made into destitute refugees, in a country without a functioning state, in a capital city without operational municipalities and services. On the scale of human distress, Lebanon's Shi'ites could not be surpassed by Shi'ites elsewhere, and their hopelessness made them the most receptive of all Shi'ites to the siren calls that issued from Iran.

Just as important, the gate to Lebanon lay wide open. Iraq and the Arab Gulf states, while closer to the torch lit by Khomeini, also had the will and means to extinguish local sparks of sympathy with Iran's revolution. Iraq went to war to do so; Saudi Arabia and Kuwait launched cold wars against Iran, which included the arrest and deportation of thousands of Iran's Shi'ite sympathizers. But in Lebanon, there was no one to arrest or deport those sympathizers, or even to keep Iran's zealots from entering Lebanon in force to join hands with their Shi'ite admirers. "The biggest obstacle to starting Islamic movements in the world is the people's attachment to governments," declared Islamic Iran's first ambassador to Lebanon. "But since the republic of Lebanon does not have much power, there is no serious obstacle in the way of the people of Lebanon."[8] Syria, which exercised a statelike authority in parts of Lebanon, was willing to accept any help against the hostile foreign forces entrenched in its Lebanese backyard: Syria allowed a supply line of support to run from Iran through Syria to Lebanon's Shi'ites. The absence of effective government, and the ease of Iranian access to Lebanon, created hothouse conditions for the rise of Iranian-inspired fundamentalist movements in Lebanon, a situation unique in the Middle East.

The Partisans of God

Those Lebanese Shi'ites who rallied around the banner of Islam in the summer of 1982 came from many different walks of life, but they all bore a double grievance. Not only did they feel threatened by outside enemies—the "satans" against whom Khomeini railed—but also they seethed with resentment against the Amal movement and its allies in the Shi'ite clerical establishment.

At the forefront of the new movement were young clerics, all drawn from the same narrow age group. They shared the stigma of inadequate preparation for their chosen profession. The fault was not theirs. Like their elders, they had gone to the Shi'ite shrine cities in Iraq to acquire the best credentials at the best theological academies. But in the 1970s the Iraqi security authorities decided to expel most foreign Shi'ite students, and several hundred returned to Lebanon empty-handed. The Shi'ite clerical establishment then spurned them, and they became a disgruntled mass, uncertain of their allegiance. When Iran's emissaries arrived in the Bekaa Valley in 1982 and issued the clarion call to make a revolution, these young clerics rushed to pledge their loyalty to Khomeini and assume positions of leadership in Hizbullah.

Iran's emissaries also reached out to the great Shi'ite clans of the Bekaa Valley. The Bekaa Shi'ites had long felt themselves excluded from the higher echelons of Amal, which drew its leaders from the south of Lebanon. Yet the Shi'ites of the Bekaa had recently enjoyed an unprecedented prosperity, the result of a trade in illicit drugs that had flourished since the collapse of central authority. They now sought a vehicle to legitimize their new status and found it in Hizbullah, which accorded them a disproportionate place in its leadership and turned a blind eye to the original source of their wealth. The first two incumbents of the office of secretary-general, Hizbullah's highest office, were clerics who hailed from the Bekaa Valley: Shaykh Subhi al-Tufayli and Sayyid 'Abbas al-Musawi.

Hizbullah also fed upon another grievance against Amal. Many young Shi'ites had joined Palestinian organizations during the 1970s, usually to escape poverty. When Israel forced the Palestinian organizations out of Lebanon in 1982, these Shi'ites lost their paymasters. In a blunder Amal would come to regret, it failed to make room for these Shi'ite orphans of the Palestinian revolution, scorning them for their service in a cause that had brought misery to South Lebanon. But Iran's emissaries held no grudge against them. Indeed, many of these same Iranians had been trained in Palestinian camps before the Islamic Revolution and they saw Palestinian service as a commendable credential. They now offered the unwanted Shi'ite militiamen jobs, weapons, and a sense of divine purpose. These Shi'ites joined enthusiastically and rose quickly through the ranks. The brilliant commander of the Islamic Jihad, Hizbullah's clandestine branch, would be a graduate of long Palestinian service: 'Imad Mughniyya.

Iran's emissaries even recruited successfully from within Amal. The established Shi'ite militia had grown brittle over the years, and some of its junior commanders concluded they had no prospects for advancement. When Iran offered Amal's malcontents some of the most senior command positions in the new movement, they jumped at the opportunity. Hizbullah even incorporated a faction called Islamic Amal, comprising disaffected Amal veterans and led by Husayn al-Musawi.

Finally, Hizbullah won followers among the many tens of thousands of Shi'ites who had no stake in existing communal institutions. Many were impoverished refugees from the south who had crowded into the southern suburbs of Beirut. They had suffered terribly, and they regarded Amal and the Shi'ite clerical establishment as ineffectual defenders of the Shi'ite interest. Iran's emissaries moved quickly to offer food, jobs, loans, medicine, and other services to the teeming masses of impoverished Shi'ites in Beirut's slums. In return, they gave Hizbullah their loyalty. The senior cleric often named as the spiritual mentor of Hizbullah, Sayyid Muhammad Husayn Fadlallah, personified their grievance. His native town in the south of Lebanon abutted Israel and had often been emptied by fighting. He relocated to a Shi'ite slum in East Beirut, but lost his first pulpit in Maronite-Palestinian fighting in 1976 and arrived as a refugee to Beirut's southern suburbs. There, like other refugees, he began anew, without the help of the Shi'ite establishment. The mosque he built and guided would become the hub of Hizbullah in the city.[9]

From this account, it is clear that Hizbullah met some very mundane needs among its adherents. Yet it also made some very severe demands. The most fundamental of these demands was the obligation to "strive in the path of God." This is the literal meaning of jihad, interpreted in Shi'ism as a willingness to sacrifice in defense of Islam. Hizbullah's strength resided in its ability to harness a hundred grievances to one sublime purpose and to persuade its downtrodden adherents of their own hidden strength—the strength of sacrifice.

To Right a World

One compelling idea forged a movement from these fragments of broken humanity, from the diverse grievances of thousands. It resided in a holistic vision that ingeniously transformed every kind of despair, injustice, and suffering into the product of one great crink in the world. Muslims had abandoned Islam. Seduced by the falsehoods of others, they had cast aside the only known certainty in this world: the divine revelation of the Prophet Muhammad. The more they doubted this revelation, the further they fell from grace. Now they had lost all power to defend themselves, and their enemies preyed on their wealth, territory, and lives. Only by returning to Islam could Muslims right the world and set human history on the course intended by God.

The great return to Islam was already under way, led by the Imam Khomeini. By his appearance, he had begun to banish the darkness that enveloped the believers. Beneath his evocation of Shi'ite symbolism, his message had a dualistic simplicity: all that was truly Islamic was pure; all that was demonstrably foreign was impure. If the pure did not root out the impure, then the impure would prevail. The message touched a deep chord in Iranian culture, amplifying more prosaic grievances. Ultimately Khomeini succeeded in turning the Iranian people into a caldron of righteousness. He promised to overturn the faithless regime of the shah, purge society of hypocrites and corrupters, and cut the tentacles of the foreign powers that gripped Iran's destiny. He kept his word. The shah fell, the accused hypocrites faced imprisonment or execution, and every trace of American influence vanished. Khomeini had created the first Islamic fundamentalist state.

Lebanon's Shi'ites watched his performance with amazement. Some began to believe that his medicine could cure Lebanon as well. Hadn't Lebanon's Muslims been corrupted by foreign ways? Didn't foreign powers control the destiny of the country? Hizbullah ultimately rested on an analogy between Lebanon and Iran—an analogy that defied vast disparities in the size and populations of the two countries, and in their geostrategic positions and resources. In the eyes of some, Lebanon now appeared to be some remote extension of Iran, linked by a shared fealty to one man. Hizbullah's program, conveyed in its "open letter" of February 1985, declared that the movement "abides by the orders of the sole wise and just command represented by the supreme jurisconsult who meets the necessary qualifications, and who is presently incarnate in the Imam and guide, the Great Ayatollah Ruhollah al-Musawi al-Khomeini." [10] Khomeini became the only source of legitimate authority, and by their allegiance to him the Shi'ites of Hizbullah ceased to be Lebanese. "Some say we are Muslim Lebanese," noted Husayn al-Musawi. "No! We are Muslims of the world, and we have close links with other Muslims of the world." [11] "We do not work or think within the borders of Lebanon," declared Shaykh Subhi al-Tufayli, "this little geometric box, which is one of the legacies of imperialism. Rather, we seek to defend Muslims throughout the world." [12]

Hizbullah's vision was as grand as Lebanon was small. Its goals exceeded even the transformation of Lebanon into an Islamic state. The establishment of an Islamic state in Lebanon "is not our demand," said Husayn al-Musawi. The aim was not Islam in one country but the creation of an "all-encompassing Islamic state" which would absorb Lebanon. [13] An almost apocalyptic messianism animated this vision of a sweeping triumph of Islam. Islamic revolution had first occurred in Iran, but it was not Iranian. As one of Hizbullah's leading clerics declared: "The divine state of justice realized on part of this earth will not remain confined within its geographic borders and is the dawn that will lead to the appearance of the Mahdi, who will create the state of Islam on earth." [14] This evocation of the Mahdi, the messianic figure in Islamic eschatology, suggested that the world had entered upon the last days and that redemption might be imminent.

In this vision, Hizbullah had the heroic role of purifying a province of Islam. "We are proceeding toward a battle with vice at its very roots," declared Hizbullah's manifesto. "And the first root of vice is America." The manifesto announced that "the Imam Khomeini, our leader, has repeatedly stressed that America is the cause of all our catastrophes and the source of all malice. . . . We will turn Lebanon into a graveyard for American schemes." [15] Once the Americans were ousted, their agents would fall as well. "We will bring down the Maronite regime just as we brought down the shah in Iran," promised the chief of staff of the Revolutionary Guards to his Lebanese listeners—although he could only address them in Persian. [16] And Hizbullah was finally charged with the most daunting task of all: driving Israel from Lebanon and then from existence. Israel was the "cancer of the Middle East," said Sayyid 'Abbas al-Musawi. "In the future, we will wipe out every trace of Israel in Palestine." [17]

This grandiose vision served the deepest needs of the most alienated of Lebanon's Shi'ites. Through their membership in Hizbullah, the clerics, commanders, and common followers of the movement could escape narrow allegiances and embrace a vast cause that transcended the boundaries of family, clan, sect, and state. Through an affiliation with Hizbullah, the individual ceased to be Lebanese, Shi'ite, Arab—a member of a disadvantaged sect in a small war-torn state populated by many different sects. Through the agency of Hizbullah, the poor village boy or slum-dweller became a true Muslim, a member of a religious-political community spanning three continents, and a soldier in a world movement led by the Imam Khomeini for redressing the imbalance between Islam and infidelity. This was a mission above human history, a task of eschatological significance. A sense of divine purpose accounted for Hizbullah's appeal and eased its resort to violence, not only in Lebanon but throughout the world.

But to remake the world, the adherents of Hizbullah first had to remake themselves. The adherents of Hizbullah had to undergo a spiritual transformation if they were to muster the inner strength necessary for sacrifice—the kind of sacrifice without which the weak could not overcome the strong. The Iranian Revolutionary Guards brought with them to Lebanon the fire that had made the revolution in Iran. Sayyid 'Abbas al-Musawi, Hizbullah's secretary-general from 1991 until his assassination by Israel in 1992, was a cleric who had passed some time in higher theological studies in Najaf. He also took the first training course offered by the Revolutionary Guards in 1982. Of the two experiences, his training with the Guards had the greater impact:

> I recall one of the sights I can never forget. We were awakened at night by the weeping of the brethren Guards during the night prayer. Is this not the greatest school from which one can graduate? I also recall when one of the brethren Guards gave a weapons lesson. Suddenly, after he had given all the explanations, he put the weapon aside and swore an oath saying: "All I have explained to you will not help you; only God can help you." He began to talk about belief and reliance on God. . . . When I joined the Guards and sat with the brethren in the first course they gave in the Bekaa Valley, I felt I derived immense benefit. I felt I had truly penetrated genuine Islam. If this is how I felt, as someone at an advanced level of schooling, then how must the other youths have felt who filled the ranks of the Guards? [18]

Fadlallah called this transformation the "rebellion against fear." The great powers inspired fear among the oppressed, who had no more than "children's toys" to mount their opposition. But by conquering their own fear, through acceptance of the virtue of martyrdom, the oppressed could evoke alarm and fear among their oppressors. [19] In a short span of time, the first adherents of Hizbullah had overcome that fear. "The school of the Islamic Revolutionary Guard made the Muslim youths love martyrdom," said 'Abbas al-Musawi. "We were not surprised at all when, shortly after the arrival of the Guards, a Muslim youth in Lebanon smiled at death while carrying with him 1,200 kilograms of explosives."[20]

The Revolutionary Guards passed the torch to Hizbullah's clerics. Their new role found symbolic representation in the arming of clerics at Hizbullah's rallies. They would stand in a row at the head of marches, awkwardly gripping AK-47s and M-16s, occasionally wearing the added accessory of an ammunition belt. They delivered funeral orations over dead fighters while brandishing rifles. In fact, clerics were not expected to bear arms in combat; the clips in the paraded weapons were probably empty. But the bearing of arms constituted a visual allusion to the preaching of the clerics. It reminded witnesses not that clerics sometimes took up arms but that they guided those who did.

Violence and Virtue

The blinding light of Lebanese Shi'ite anger, focused through the lens of Iran's Islamic zeal, set a fire. To understand the impact of that violence, it must first be characterized. A day-by-day chronology of the violence employed by Hizbullah during its first decade would be long indeed—too long to bear repetition.[21] But most of it fell into these four categories:

1. Campaigns meant to rid the Shi'ite regions of Lebanon of all foreign presence. Assassinations of individual foreigners later escalated into massive bombings, some of them done by "self-martyrs," which destroyed the American embassy and its annex in two separate attacks in 1983 and 1984; the barracks of American and French peace-keeping troops in two famous attacks on the same morning in 1983; and command facilities of Israeli forces in the occupied south in 1982 and 1983. Hundreds of foreigners died on Lebanese soil in these bombings, the most successful of which killed 241 U.S. Marines in their barracks. These operations, combined with other, lesser actions, forced American and French forces into a full retreat from Lebanon. As one Hizbullah leader put it, they "hurriedly ran away from three Muslims who loved martyrdom."[22] This violence also pushed Israeli forces back to a narrow "security zone" in the south.[23] "The Israeli soldier who could not be defeated was now killed, with an explosive charge here and a bullet there," said Fadlallah. "People were suddenly filled with power, and that power could be employed in new ways. . . . it deployed a small force and a war of nerves, which the enemy could not confront with its tanks and airplanes."[24] Hizbullah continued to launch frequent attacks against Israeli forces and their Lebanese ally, the South Lebanon Army, in the "security zone." "Our goal is not the liquidation of [South Lebanon Army commander] Antoine Lahad in the border zone," said Sayyid 'Abbas al-Musawi. "Our slogan is the liquidation of Israel."[25]

2. Operations intended to lend support to the efforts of Iran during the Iran-Iraq war. Before Hizbullah's emergence, its Shi'ite fundamentalist precursors launched a violent campaign against Iraqi targets in Lebanon, culminating in the destruction of the Iraqi embassy in Beirut in a 1981 bombing. The campaign later spread to Kuwait,

where Hizbullah's Islamic Jihad bombed the American and French embassies and other targets in 1983, in an effort to compel Kuwait to abandon its support of Iraq. This violence peaked in a series of paralyzing terror bombings in Paris in 1986 meant to force France to abandon its policy of supplying Iraq with arms. The cease-fire between Iran and Iraq in 1988 brought this campaign to an end.

3. Operations meant to free members and affiliates of Hizbullah who had been captured by enemy governments in the Middle East and Europe. These operations included the hijacking of an American airliner in 1985 to secure the freedom of Lebanese Shi'ites held by Israel, and two hijackings of Kuwaiti airliners in 1984 and 1988 to win freedom for Lebanese Shi'ites held by Kuwait for the bombings there. The hijackers killed passengers in each of these hijackings, to demonstrate their resolve. In addition, Islamic Jihad and other groups affiliated with Hizbullah abducted dozens of foreigners in Lebanon, mostly American, French, British, and German citizens, for the same purpose. Some of these foreigners would later be traded for American arms needed by Iran in the Gulf War, but the motive for the wave of abductions remained the release of Hizbullah's imprisoned fighters elsewhere. The longest-held hostage spent over six years in captivity. Most of the hostages were freed; a few died in captivity.

4. Battles waged against the rival movements over control of neighborhoods in Beirut and villages in the south. In 1986, Hizbullah clashed repeatedly with the Syrian Social Nationalist Party over control of routes leading from the Bekaa Valley to the south. And beginning in 1988, occasional skirmishes with Amal escalated into war. Several thousand Shi'ites, many of them noncombatants, died in this intra-Shi'ite fighting, which persisted despite numerous cease-fire initiatives. In the course of the battles, Hizbullah perpetrated several atrocities and assassinated two prominent leaders of Amal. Hizbullah usually enjoyed the upper hand in fighting, but it was denied the fruits of victory by Syrian intervention. The fighting ended in late 1990 with a cease-fire mediated by Syria and Iran.

In what way did this violence reflect its origins in a fundamentalist movement? Violence in Lebanon did not constitute a deviation. Indeed, it had become the norm. Long before the appearance of Hizbullah, Lebanon had become a land in which guns spoke louder than words. To do battle was not a matter of choice but of survival. And in some respects, this violence followed well-worn paths in Lebanon—paths blazed first by the Palestinians in the early 1970s and followed by various militias in the late 1970s. The commanders of Hizbullah were veterans of either Palestinian service or the Amal militia, and they often took pages from both books.

Nor could the "self-martyrdom operations," which Hizbullah pioneered, qualify as a strictly fundamentalist mode of operation. Groups in Lebanon that were not fundamentalist, religious, or Shi'ite quickly imitated this method. In terms of the number of casualties inflicted by such operations, Hizbullah undoubtedly deserved place of primacy. Hizbullah employed the method first and enjoyed the advantage of surprise. But in terms of the number of operations—and the number of "self-martyrs"—pride of place went to the imitators: the secular, nationalist organizations that operated in Lebanon under Syrian auspices. A study that summarized the major round of "self-martyrdom operations" from their inception in 1983 through the end of 1986 found that Shi'ite organizations perpetrated only seven of the thirty-one attacks. Pro-Syrian organizations carried out twenty-two attacks, most notably by the Syrian Social Nationalist Party (ten attacks) and the Ba'th Party (seven attacks). (These operations were all directed against Israel and the South Lebanon Army.)[26]

It was also obvious that Hizbullah's collective choices regarding the extent and intensity of its violence had a clear political rationale. Hizbullah was also a political movement and indeed saw politics as an inseparable part of religion. When it employed violence, it did so for political and not ritualistic purposes—to bring it closer to power. In making its choices, Hizbullah weighed benefits against costs. Violence drove enemies into retreat and created a zone of autonomous action for Hizbullah. But it simultaneously invited punitive retaliation and at times created political complications for Iran. Fadlallah fairly described the guiding principle of Hizbullah: " I believe that in all cases violence is like a surgical operation that the doctor should only resort to after he has exhausted all other methods."[27]

But the calculus of politics is not driven by a universal logic. It is conditioned by cultural values. Hizbullah did not simply seek power; it sought power in order to implement Islamic law. That goal had to be pursued within the law of Islam, as understood by its interpreters among the clerics. "The Muslim fighter needed answers to many questions," said Shaykh 'Abd al-Karim 'Ubayd, a Hizbullah cleric who would be made famous after his abduction by Israel in 1989. "Is resistance to the occupation obligatory on religious grounds? What about the question of self-martyrdom? The law has an answer to these examples, which therefore are not political questions so much as legal questions, and here lies the role of the cleric." Only he could provide answers; without his essential contribution, there could be no legitimate violence, since "these questions cannot be answered by the military commander, especially for the believing fighter, who must turn to a cleric who is enthusiastic, responsive, and committed to resistance."[28]

On the one hand, submission to Islamic law freed Hizbullah from non-lslamic moral constraints. Hizbullah felt no need to justify its acts by other codes. Its struggle was a jihad, a form of sacred warfare regulated solely by Islamic law (hence the choice of Islamic Jihad as the name for Hizbullah's clandestine branch). It made no difference to Hizbullah's adherents that jihad remained associated with fanaticism in the historical consciousness of the West. They did not seek the favor of world public opinion and addressed their justifications solely to Muslim believers.

On the other hand, jihad had its requirements. The Islamic law of war is the codification of a moral sensibility. While it is open to interpretation, it is not infinitely elastic. Some of its provisions compel violence—acts of punishment or resistance. But other provisions forbid violence against persons afforded protection by law. The believing public had to be persuaded that Hizbullah's actions were not criminal but "in the nature of a jihad, launched by the oppressed against the oppressors."[29] The clerics, as interpreters of law, constantly subjected Hizbullah's selection of targets and techniques to the judgment of this law.

In doing so, they forced Hizbullah to resist two powerful temptations of its Lebanese environment. First, Hizbullah sometimes threatened to deteriorate into one more sectarian militia devoted to battling other sectarian militias. "Parties and movements and organizations begin as great ideas," warned Fadlallah, "and turn into narrow interests. Religion starts as a message from God and struggle, and turns into the interests of individuals and another kind of tribalism."[30] That deterioration had to be fought. The clerics never ceased to remind the movement of its divine mission and to urge the expansion of the jihad to confront the "global infidelity" of foreigners. Second, Hizbullah occasionally seemed poised to imitate the sectarian militias, by employing wholly indiscriminate violence. The clerics never ceased to insist that the jihad not harm innocents. To be worthy of Islam, the struggle had to be global in conception but discriminating in execution.

In retrospect, some of Hizbullah's acts of violence met these demanding criteria, some did not. It soon became clear that in the real world, violence could rarely be pure. A few acts approximated the ideal, such as the earliest bombings by "self-martyrs" against foreign forces in Lebanon. These targeted armed, foreign intruders and so constituted legitimate jihad in the defense of Islam. And the use of "self-martyrs" assured that these attacks achieved pinpoint precision—an unusual technique for Beirut, where exploding cars usually killed indiscriminately.

Yet even here, a problem of Islamic law arose, since some innocents did die in these attacks: the "self-martyrs" themselves. Suicide is prohibited by Islam, and the question of whether their deaths did or did not constitute suicide tugged at the consciences of Hizbullah's clerics. As long as the attacks succeeded so dramatically, the clerics suppressed all doubt. But the question resurfaced when subsequent attacks began to produce lower yields in enemy casualties. "The self-martyring operation is not permitted unless it can convulse the enemy," said Fadlallah. "The believer cannot blow himself up unless the results will equal or exceed the [loss of the] soul of the believer. Self-martyring operations are not fatal accidents but legal obligations governed by rules, and the believers cannot transgress the rules of God."[31] The clerics ultimately banned such operations, and they gradually ended.

Other acts generated even more controversy. Abductions of innocent foreigners divided Hizbullah's clerics. Some came out clearly against the practice, which they criticized as a violation of Islamic law. Other clerics justified the hostage-holding as an unfortunate but necessary evil. But even these showed some hesitation, so that the hostage-holders often had to provide their own justifications, communicated through hand-scrawled missives to the press. Ultimately, the debate over the Islamic legality of hostage-holding did not produce a repentant release of hostages. They were usually freed when it served Iran's purposes, in moves governed by the ethic of the marketplace rather than Islamic law. But the debate did put the perpetrators of these acts in the moral docket, before the only constituency that mattered: believers in the primacy of Islamic law. And it is possible that hostage-holding would have been practiced even more extensively had this debate never taken place, although no one can say this for certain.[32]

Finally, some acts could not be defended from the point of view of Islamic law. True, France supplied Iraq with the weapons that killed Iran's faithful in the Gulf war. Striking at French interests would show the solidarity of true believers. But the bombings that shook Paris in 1986, and which killed at random in shops and trains, represented acts of sheer terror that Hizbullah's clerics could never have defended. And so the Lebanese Shi'ite plotters, who came from within Hizbullah, took care not to claim the bombings for Islam and even enticed a hapless Tunisian recruit to plant the bombs. Both distancing measures reflected a certain knowledge that the bombings constituted terror by *any* definition, Western or Islamic. Perhaps for this reason, the Paris bombings remained an isolated instance, although Hizbullah possessed the capability to launch similar campaigns abroad and was reported ready to do so on many occasions.

Hizbullah's war with Amal also caused deep anguish among the clerics, for it involved the killing of Shi'ites by Shi'ites. Of course it could be rationalized: Amal had conspired with the enemies of Islam, within Lebanon and abroad. It denied the global leadership of Islamic Iran and protected Israel by barring Hizbullah's way to the south. Yet Hizbullah's clerics were not completely persuaded that these deeds justified killing, and they persisted in calling the struggle a "dissension," a *fitna*, rather than a sacred war, a jihad. This did not stem the fighting. But if Amal had to be fought, then it had to be fought quickly and in a spirit of regret. At one point, at the height of the fighting, the clerics could no longer look away, for fighters in the field had taken to mutilating corpses in Lebanese fashion—a method used to inspire terror in the enemy. The men of religion issued a religious edict against the practice.

In the end, Hizbullah's violence could not help but demonstrate the movement's contradictory character. Hizbullah was Islamic by day, Lebanese by night. What seemed right in the mosques did not always work in the alleys. Hizbullah's clerics had to know when to avert their eyes from the compromises between the ideal and the real. Was this hypocrisy? There were some principles, even of Islam, that the poor could not afford. And if the poor did not have smart bombs, then who would deny them the blunt weapons at hand? "The oppressed nations do not have the technology and destructive weapons America and Europe have," said Fadlallah:

They must thus fight with special means of their own. . . . [We] recognize the right of nations to use every unconventional method to fight these aggressor nations, and do not regard what oppressed Muslims of the world do with primitive and unconventional means to confront aggressor powers as terrorism. We view this as religiously lawful warfare against the world's imperialist and domineering powers.[33]

But even Fadlallah drew a line: sacred ends could not be achieved *only* by profane means. There always had to be some aspects of Hizbullah's struggle that approached the exacting standards of the law. And usually there were. At one moment, a guard might beat a hapless foreign hostage to discourage thoughts of escape. But that could be rationalized if, at the same moment, a fighter of the jihad prepared himself to court death by assaulting an Israeli army patrol. "There is evil in everything good and something good in every evil," reasoned Fadlallah.[34] Even a fundamentalist movement preoccupied with purity had to acknowledge its own impurities—and strive to cleanse itself, even as it cleansed the world around it.

The Impact of Hizbullah

During the decade between 1982 and 1992, Hizbullah's violence made an indelible impression on the world and its name passed into common parlance. Yet Hizbullah's vision of a new age receded from grasp. By the end of the decade, the triumph of Islam in Lebanon, the further spread of Iran's revolution, and the liberation of Jerusalem all seemed more remote than ever. Lebanon inched toward a Syrian-guaranteed peace based on (revised) confessionalism—a reform, not a revolution. Islamic Iran, still smarting from wounds sustained in a failed war with Iraq, turned toward domestic reconstruction. And Arab states, Lebanon among them, sat down with Israel in direct talks to discuss a possible peace. Had Hizbullah chased the horizon?

No one could say for certain, but none could deny that Hizbullah had become one of the realities of Lebanon and the region. Hizbullah did not have the means to turn the world upside-down, but it had fought and bought its way into the hearts of perhaps as many as half of Lebanon's politically active Shi'ites. Hizbullah had played an instrumental role in driving foreign forces out of Lebanon and continued a tireless campaign against Israel in the south. It had rendered some service to Islamic Iran by its abductions of foreigners and had also secured the release of many of its own imprisoned members. It had defeated its Shi'ite rivals in one confrontation after another, earning the respect of friends and the fear of enemies. And above all, it had initiated a return to Islam—a gradual process of inner transformation whose results no one could predict.

Still, the world had changed in profound ways while Hizbullah made itself secure. Old ideologies broke under the weight of economics, old conflicts moved toward resolution. Even Islamic Iran turned a corner, moving from confrontation to cooperation with the West. Fadlallah helped his listeners accept the fact. "Like all revolutions, including the French Revolution, the Islamic Revolution did not have a realistic line at first," he said. "At that time it served to create a state, it produced a mobilization, a new religious way of thinking and living, with the aim of winning Muslim autonomy and independence from the superpowers." But "the new phase which should now be reached is the normalization of relations with the rest of the world."[35] To speak of the Islamic Revolution like any other revolution, to speak of accepting the world as it is—at first these ideas found little echo among Hizbullah's other clerics. But soon they also would concede that Hizbullah, too, would have to turn a corner. The release of nearly all the Western hostages in 1991 indicated that the reassessment was under way.

Fadlallah had warned against the limits of violence. The Palestinians in the 1970s had also stunned the world with their violence—and still had nothing to show for it. To avoid such an impasse, Hizbullah would have to move to a new phase: the struggle for ideas. This would be a different kind of jihad, requiring perseverance and patience, for Hizbullah had taken only a first step: "We work to arrive at a result from within the objective and actual circumstances, some of which we ourselves must work to create, while others we must await with the passage of time. We see that these conditions do not exist in the Lebanese reality at the present stage and in the immediate stages to follow—this, despite the spread of the Islamic spirit which transformed Islam into a pressure force on political reality."[36]

Hizbullah began to fashion a new strategy for this jihad over hearts and minds. At home in Lebanon, it would become more committed to grass-roots social activism and more willing to substitute the slogan of democracy for the slogan of revolution. Elsewhere in the region, Islamic movements bid for power as political parties, not as revolutionary conspiracies, and they enjoyed remarkable success. Might this not work in Lebanon? After all, Shi'ite and Sunni Muslims constituted a clear majority in the country. Hizbullah began to demand a general referendum on the question of an Islamic state. In an ironic twist, Hizbullah cast itself as a champion of democracy; the "Party of God" began to evolve slowly into a political party, a *hizb*, whose clerics spoke more like candidates.

Hizbullah also transformed its own vision of its regional role. During the 1980s, the movement had looked east toward Islamic Iran, anticipating a victory against Iraq and the creation of an "all-encompassing Islamic state." That dream had been shattered, but another arose to replace it. Hizbullah's leaders noticed how Mediterranean Islam began to gain social and political momentum in the 1980s—in Algeria, Tunisia, Egypt, Jordan, and among the Palestinians. Islamic movements in these countries also sought the transformation of secular state and society into Islamic state and society. Mediterranean Islamic activism is largely Sunni, as are the great majority of Muslims in the Mediterranean basin. But its attitude to Shi'ism was usually dispassionate, and it now contained pockets of open sympathy for Iran's revolution as a genuine expression of Islam, from Tunisia's "Renaissance" Islamic party to the Palestinian Islamic Jihad.

Hizbullah sat astride a point where two powerful winds of Islamic reassertion converged—one from the west, the other from the east. And it soon established itself as the mediating bridge between Mediterranean Islam—the Islam of the Algerian Islamists and the Palestinian Jihad groups—and the stalled but still potent Islam of Iran. In short, Hizbullah sought to play the classic Lebanese role of middleman—to stay afloat by mediating the contact between two parts of the Muslim world separated by language, culture, and space. This kind of mediation is precisely the Lebanese art, and it is the way Lebanon has found its place and livelihood in the world. Hizbullah bid to become the bridge between Shi'ism and Sunnism, Iran and the Arabs, the Gulf and the Mediterranean.

Were Hizbullah to become such a bridge, its role would change profoundly. The fighting vanguards of Islamic revolution would become the talking mediators of ideas. Lebanon would cease to be the ground of contention; instead, Hizbullah would assist the struggle of others, by becoming a regional amplifier of Islamic Iran's message.

It now remained to be seen whether Hizbullah would prove as adept in persuasion as in coercion, whether its words would topple the structures that its bombs had only shaken.

Notes

1. See Abdulaziz A. Sachedina, "Activist Shi'ism in Iran, Iraq, and Lebanon," in Martin E. Marty and R. Scott Appleby, eds., *Fundamentalisms Observed* (Chicago: University of Chicago Press, 1991), pp. 403–56 (includes select bibliography).

2. Many aspects of the history of the Shi'ites in what is now modern Lebanon remain obscure. For general appreciations, see Mounzer Jaber, "Pouvoir et société au Jabal Amel de 1749 à 1920 dans la conscience des chroniques chiites et dans un essai d'interprétation," thèse 3e cycle, Paris IV, 1978; Monika Pohl-Schöberlein, *Die schiitische Gemeinschaft des Südlibanon (Gabal 'Amil) innerhalb des libanesischen konfessionellen Systems* (Berlin: Klaus Schwarz, 1986); and Ghaleb el Turk, "The South," in Halim Said Abulzzedin, ed., *Lebanon and Its Provinces: A Study by the Governors of the Five Provinces* (Beirut: Khayat, 1963), pp. 49–71.

3. On the voluntary movement of Shi'ites to Beirut before the outbreak of the civil war in 1975, see Salim Nasr, "La transition des chiites vers Beyrouth: Mutations sociales et mobilisation communautaire à la veille de 1975," in CERMOC, *Mouvements communautaires et espaces urbains au Machreq* (Beyrouth: Editions du CERMOC, 1985), pp. 87–116.

4. For the history of the Shi'ite awakening in Lebanon, see Fouad Ajami, *The Vanished Imam: Musa al Sadr and the Shia of Lebanon* (Ithaca: Cornell University Press, 1986); Augustus Richard Norton, *Amal and the Shi'a: Struggle for the Soul of Lebanon* (Austin: University of Texas Press, 1987); and Andreas Rieck, *Die Schiiten und der Kampf um den Libanon: Politische Chronik, 1958–1988* (Mitteilungen des Deutschen Orient-Instituts, 33) (Hamburg: Deutsches Orient-Institut, 1989). Article-length studies that consider important aspects of the awakening include Thom Sicking and Shereen Khairallah, "The Shi'a Awakening in Lebanon: A Search for Radical Change in a Traditional Way," *CEMAM Reports,* no. 2: *Vision and Revision in Arab Society, 1974* (Beirut: Dar al-Mashreq, 1975), pp. 97–130; Talal Jaber, "Le discours shi'ite sur le pouvoir," *Peuples Méditerranéens* (Paris), no. 20 (July–September 1982), pp. 75–92; Salim Nasr, "Mobilisation communautaire et symbolique religieuse: L'imam Sadr et les chi'ites du Liban (1970–1975)," in Olivier Carré and Paul Dumont, eds., *Radicalismes Islamiques,* vol. 1: *Iran, Liban, Turquie* (Paris: L'Harmattan, 1985), pp. 119–58; Elisabeth Picard, "De la 'communauté-classe' à la Résistance 'Nationale.' Pour une analyse du rôle des Chi'ites dans le système politique libanais (1970–1985)," *Revue française de science politique* (Paris) 35, no. 6 (December 1985): 999–1027; and Shimon Shapira, "The *Imam* Musa al-Sadr: Father of the Shiite Resurgence in Lebanon," *Jerusalem Quarterly,* no. 44 (Fall 1987): 121–44.

5. On the forced movement of Shi'ite refugees to West Beirut and the southern suburbs after 1975, see Salim Nasr, "Beyrouth et le conflit libanais: Restructuration de l'espace urbain," in J. Metral and G. Mutin, eds., *Politiques urbaines dans le Monde Arabe* (Lyons, 1984), pp. 287–305.

6. On the emergence of this trend, see Chibli Mallat, *Shi'i Thought from the South of Lebanon* (Oxford: Centre for Lebanese Studies, 1988).

7. On the emergence of Hizbullah and the role of Iran, see these studies by Martin Kramer: *Hezbollah's Vision of the West.* (Washington, D.C.: Washington Institute for Near East Policy, Policy Paper no. 16, October 1989); "The Moral Logic of Hizballah," in Walter Reich, ed., *Origins of Terrorism: Psychologies, Ideologies, Theologies,*

States of Mind (Cambridge: Cambridge University Press, 1990), pp. 131–57; "Redeeming Jerusalem: The Pan-Islamic Premise of Hizballah," in David Menashri, ed., *The Iranian Revolution and the Muslim World* (Boulder: Westview Press, 1990), pp. 105–30; "Sacrifice and Fratricide in Shiite Lebanon," in Mark Juergensmeyer, ed., *Violence and the Sacred in the Modern World* (London: Frank Cass, 1992), pp. 30–47; and my annual essays for the *Middle East Contemporary Survey,* commencing with volume 8 (1983–84). See also R. K. Ramazani, *Revolutionary Iran: Challenge and Response in the Middle East* (Baltimore: Johns Hopkins University Press, 1986), pp. 175–95; Yves Gonzales-Quijano, "Les interprétations d'un rite: Célébrations de la 'Achoura au Liban," *Maghreb-Machrek* (Paris), no. 115 (January–March 1987): 5–28; Shimon Shapira, "The Origins of Hizballah," *Jerusalem Quarterly,* no. 46 (Spring 1988): 115–30; Andreas Rieck, "Abschied vom 'Revolutionsexport'? Expansion und Rückgang des iranischen Einflusses im Libanon, 1979–1989," *Beiträge zur Konfliktforschung* (Cologne) 20, no. 2 (1990): 81–104; and Augustus Richard Norton, "Lebanon: The Internal Conflict and the Iranian Connection," in John L. Esposito, ed., *The Iranian Revolution: Its Global Impact* (Miami: Florida International University Press, 1990), pp. 116–37.

8. Interview with Hojjat al-lslam Fakhr Rouhani, *Ettela'at* (Tehran), 9 January 1984.

9. On Fadlallah, see Martin Kramer, "Muhammad Husayn Fadlallah," *Orient* 26, no. 2 (June 1985): 147–49. Some of Fadlallah's theoretical writings, mostly from the 1970s, have been examined by Olivier Carré, "Quelques mots-clefs de Muhammad Husayn Fadlallah," *Revue française de science politique* (Paris) 37, no. 4 (August 1987): 478–501; and "La 'révolution islamique' selon Muhammad Husayn Fadlallâh," *Orient* (Opladen, West Germany) 29, no. 1 (March 1988): 68–84. Both have been reprinted in Olivier Carré, *L'Utopie islamique dans l'Orient arabe* (Paris: Fondation nationale des sciences politiques, 1991).

10. "Nass al-risala al-maftuha allati wajjahaha Hizbullah ila al-mustad'afin fi Lubnan wal- 'alam" ("Open Letter from Hizbullah to the Disinherited in Lebanon and the World") (Beirut), 16 February 1985, p. 6.

11. Interview with Husayn al-Musawi, *Kayhan* (Tehran), 27 July 1986.

12. Speech by Shaykh Subhi al-Tufayli, *Al-'Ahd* (Beirut), 10 April 1987. *Al-'Ahd* is the weekly newspaper of Hizbullah.

13. Interview with Husayn al-Musawi, *Al-Harakat al-Islamiyya fi Lubnan* (Beirut: Dar al-Shira', 1984), pp. 226–27.

14. Speech by Sayyid Hasan Nasrallah, *Al-'Ahd,* 7 February 1986.

15. *Nass al-risala al-maftuha,* pp. 9, 17.

16. Speech by the chief of staff of the Revolutionary Guards Corps, delivered in the Imam Ali Mosque in Baalbek, *Al-Anwar* (Beirut), 9 February 1988.

17. Interview with Sayyid 'Abbas al-Musawi, *La revue du Liban* (Beirut), 27 July 1985.

18. Interview with Sayyid 'Abbas al-Musawi, *Al-'Ahd,* 16 October 1987.

19. Interview with Fadlallah, *Al-Nahar al-'arabi wal-duwali,* 21 July 1986.

20. Interview with Sayyid 'Abbas al-Musawi, *Al-'Ahd,* 16 October 1987.

21. For chronologies of Hizbullah's campaign, see the section "Shiite Terrorism" in the annual *Middle East Military Balance,* published by the Jaffee Center at Tel Aviv University, and also the U.S. Department of State's annual *Patterns of Global Terrorism.* For a comprehensive account of Hizbullah's hostage-holding, see Maskit Burgin et al., *Foreign Hostages in Lebanon* (Jaffee Center for Strategic Studies Memorandum no. 25; Tel Aviv, August 1988). Hizbullah's violence is also described in a number of accounts by journalists from the Western countries targeted by Hizbullah's violence. From the American vantage point, see Robin Wright, *Sacred Rage: The Wrath of Militant Islam* (New York: Simon and Schuster, 1986); John Wolcott and David C. Martin, *Best Laid Plans: The Inside Story of America's War against Terrorism* (New York: Harper and Row, 1988); and Larry Pintak, *Beirut Outtakes: A TV Correspondent's Portrait of America's Encounter with*

Terror (Lexington, Mass.: Lexington Books, 1988). From the French vantage point, see Xavier Raufer, *La Nébuleuse: Le terrorisme du Moyen-Orient* (Paris: Fayard, 1987); Yves Loiseau, *Le grand troc: Le labyrinthe des otages français au Liban* (Paris: Hachette, 1988); and Gilles Delafon, *Beyrouth: Les soldats de l'Islam* (Paris: Stock, 1989). There are already many published firsthand accounts by former hostages.

22. Interview with Sadiq al-Musawi, *Al-Nahar al-'arabi wal-duwali*, 28 July 1986.

23. See W. A. Terrill, "Low Intensity Conflict in Southern Lebanon: Lessons and Dynamics of the Israeli-Shi'ite War," *Conflict Quarterly* 7, no. 3 (1987): 22–35.

24. Al-Sayyid Muhammad Husayn Fadallah, *Al-Muqawama al-Islamiyya fi al-Janub wal- Biqa' al-Gharbi wa-Rashayya: Tatallu'at wa-afaq* (Beirut, 1984), p. 11.

25. Speech by Sayyid 'Abbas al-Musawi, *Al-Safir* (Beirut), 23 September 1986.

26. Ariel Merari, "The Readiness to Kill and Die: Suicidal Terrorism in the Middle East," in Walter Reich, ed., *The Origins of Terrorism* (Cambridge: Cambridge University Press, 1990), pp. 204–5. These proportions are brought home vividly in the collection of obituaries reproduced in a Syrian-sponsored publication, *Al-'Amaliyyat al-istishhadiyya: Watha'iq wa-suwar* (The self-martyring operations: documents and photographs) (Damascus, 1985). While the volume covers all operations by all groups, it is clearly intended to emphasize Syrian preeminence in the employment of this technique, and opens with excerpts from remarks by Syrian president Hafiz al-Asad.

27. Interview with Fadlallah, *Monday Morning* (Beirut), 15 October 1984.

28. Interview with Shaykh 'Abd al-Karim 'Ubayd, *Al-Safir*, 28 July 1986.

29. Interview with Husayn al-Musawi, *Kayhan*, 29 July 1986.

30. Friday sermon by Fadlallah, *al-Nahar* (Beirut), 27 July 1985.

31. Speech by Fadlallah, *Al-Nahar*, 14 May 1985.

32. For the debate in Hizbullah over hostage-holding, see Kramer, "The Moral Logic of Hizballah," pp. 149–56.

33. Interview with Fadlallah, *Kayhan*, 14 November 1985.

34. Fadlallah Friday sermon, *Al-'Ahd*, 5 December 1985.

35. Interview with Fadlallah, *La Repubblica* (Rome), 28 August 1989.

36. Interview with Fadlallah, *Al-Shira'* (Beirut), 18 March 1985.

Saving America's Souls: Operation Rescue's Crusade against Abortion

Faye Ginsburg

The Lord Jesus Christ is the foundation and life source of Operation Rescue. We know that without Him we can do nothing. A personal relationship with Jesus Christ is essential to victory—both personally and corporately.[1]

Many came straight from the pew to the abortuary door saying to God, "Please forgive me for my apathy."[2]

At six o'clock in the morning on 28 November 1987, Randall Terry, a lanky, twenty-seven-year-old born-again Christian from upstate New York, led his first official "rescue," a blockade of an abortion clinic in Cherry Hill, New Jersey. Three hundred rescuers sealed off access to the building. As Terry describes it, "We sang, prayed, read psalms," and conducted a parachurch service "on the doorstep of hell for nearly eleven hours! No babies died. It was glorious, peaceful, and prayerful."[3] By the end of the day, 211 "mothers, fathers, grandmothers, grandfathers, and singles"[4] had been arrested, charged with trespassing, and released.

The event served as the trial demonstration of a militant anti-abortion organization, Operation Rescue, composed of fundamentalist and evangelical Christians. The group was formally established in the spring of 1988 by Randall Terry and quickly escalated its activities. By 1989, Operation Rescue had gained a prominent, if notorious, reputation, even among fellow travelers in the pro-life movement. By 1990, according to the group's figures, there had been over thirty-five thousand arrests, while sixteen thousand individuals had risked arrest in what they call "rescues."[5] Unlike those allied with other anti-abortion groups, which hold regular meetings, call upon political representatives, and in other ways operate as ongoing arenas of action, Operation Rescue relies on the existing infrastructure of independent fundamentalist churches and conservative Roman Catholic congregations and organizations as its base. For most members beyond the leadership, sporadic participation in "rescue" demonstrations constitutes the central activity. Focusing organizational energy into "rescues" takes maximum advantage of the publicity generated by dramatic confrontation.

The blockades carried out by Operation Rescue have been described variously as acts of "biblical obedience," civil disobedience, harassment, and terrorism, and even as a form of racketeering and antitrust action. The distinct positions represented by these terms suggest the complex and often ironic impact of this group.

Whatever the judgment of a particular observer, however, Operation Rescue's political tactics and philosophy distinguish it in two ways. First, it is the most confrontational and right-wing of the contemporary anti-abortion groups. Contrary to stereotypes that portray right-to-life activists as homogeneous and puritanical, a remnant of Victorian mores and family forms, the pro-life cause has generally tolerated a spectrum of practice, belief, and lifestyle through an overall commitment to moderation and single-issue politics. However, Operation Rescue's scorn for civil political process, its uncompromising interventionist tactics, and its absolutist Christian ideology have strained the alliances in the movement. For a decade after the 1973 *Roe v. Wade* decision legalizing abortion, right-to-life activism tended to take a civil approach, attempting to influence political action by working within the legislative and electoral systems. Since 1983, radical elements in the pro-life movement—from the Pro-Life Action League of ex-Benedictine monk Joseph Scheidler (whose work influenced Randall Terry) to individuals responsible for incidents of bombing and arson at abortion clinics—have become increasingly active and more visible than the moderate mainstream represented by the National Right to Life Committee. By the end of the 1980s, Operation Rescue had become the umbrella sheltering the more extreme activists.

As a second distinction, Operation Rescue is the first pro-life group not only to draw large numbers of conservative Protestants into ongoing, organized anti-abortion activity, but also to join them in action with conservative Roman Catholics. Terry himself has been heavily influenced by the teachings of the late evangelical Protestant author Francis Schaeffer, who viewed legal abortion as the epitome of twentieth-century decadence.[6] In his book, *A Christian Manifesto,* published in 1981, Schaeffer recommended civil disobedience in opposition to abortion as a way for evangelicals to "challenge the entire legitimacy of the secular modern state, withholding allegiance until the nation returns to its religious roots in matters like public prayer and religious education."[7] It is not surprising, then, that Terry judged an event like Cherry Hill as a turning point not only because of its impact on abortion politics but also because of the response it generated in the Christian community.[8] In this view, opposition to abortion is not the end so much as the means to a larger goal of returning America to "traditional Christian values." Terry has made this point with a combination of pastoral, industrial, religious, and military metaphors. "God is using us to separate sheep from goats . . . the wheat from the chaff," he writes. "There are a lot of people who believe this is going to be the seedbed of revival in the church, the locomotive to bring reformation in our culture. When the Lord put the vision in my heart, it was not just to rescue babies and mothers but to rescue the country. This is the first domino to fall."[9]

Operation Rescue has catalyzed fundamentalist and evangelical participation in political action that began in America in the mid-1970s, bringing thousands of conservative Christians into the anti-abortion movement and transforming them in the process. In addition to expanding the revival of fundamentalist and evangelical social action, Operation Rescue has had a number of ironic consequences. For example, it has unintentionally served as one stimulus for reinvigorating the organization and focus of the pro-choice movement. It has also introduced a new element of dissension within the right-to-life movement, pushing activism in a more confrontational and militant direction. Like an impatient and unruly youngster (only "born" in 1988), Operation Rescue has disturbed the more settled, mature, and moderate anti-abortion veterans who have been organizing for twenty years.

The Rise of the Right-to-Life Movement

Every year on the anniversary of the 22 January 1973 *Roe v. Wade* ruling that legalized abortion, leaders of the right-to-life movement, often at odds, come together for a "March for Life." Held in Washington, D.C., it draws anywhere from twenty to fifty thousand pro-life supporters from around the country and, since the 1980s, has merited a speech from, and sometimes a meeting with, the president. These annual displays are a reminder of the legalization of abortion as well as the transformation of a small pro-life effort into a national, well-organized social movement. For many activists, the Supreme Court ruling stands as a turning point. In response to it, large numbers of "ordinary citizens," especially women,[10] have become involved in the right-to-life movement. Through their participation, the cause has become a grass-roots movement that draws its strength from local-level activists.[11]

While pro-life activism includes a multitude of organizations, the largest and oldest of these, the National Right to Life Committee (NRLC), represents the mainstream of the movement. The NRLC grew out of the U.S. Catholic Conference Family Life Bureau in the late 1960s when the bureau, along with ad hoc groups, organized to oppose efforts to repeal anti-abortion laws. By the 1980s it claimed over ten million members in three thousand grass-roots groups around the country. Although those membership figures have been questioned, the NRLC is distinguished from most other pro-life groups by its commitment to maintaining a diverse constituency, united around the single issue of the "right-to-life."[12]

The increasing national political strength of the pro-life movement was dramatically marked in the 1977 congressional passage of the Hyde amendment and the U.S. Supreme Court ruling in *Doe v. Poelker,* which allowed the federal government and the states to prohibit the use of public funds (Medicaid) to pay for poor women's abortions, except to save the mother's life.[13] That year, a loose coalition of right-wing politicians and religious leaders known as the New Right adopted a strategy to broaden their influence by developing a "pro-family" campaign.[14] In an effort to gain support for their conservative agenda, leaders targeted fundamentalist churches and single-issue groups concerned with the "traditional" social roles of family, church, and school. Their hope was to engage them in politics and create a "winning coalition" that would bring electoral success to their candidates and programs.[15] Abortion was just the sort of single-issue the New Right was looking for: a populist, cross-class social concern that had not been (to that point) allied to right-wing causes more generally. New Right leaders hoped to recast the right-to-life position in its most conservative interpretation, linking it to their vision of the proper role of government, family, and sexuality in American society.[16] However, for the leadership of the National Right to Life Committee (NRLC), to ally with the New Right would undercut one of the primary benefits of single-issue organizing, which, by tolerating multiple interpretations of opposition to abortion, encompasses a large and various membership. Regardless of stereotypes that cast anti-abortion positions in the same mold as conservative political, economic, and religious philosophies, pro-life activists link their views on the single issue of abortion to a surprisingly diverse range of ideologies, from the "seamless garment"[17] Catholic argument on the left to classic right-wing views like those of Phyllis Schlafly. Because right-to-lifers are inclined to single-issue voting patterns, such distinctions are not always apparent to those focused on the political arena. And, regardless of a right or left orientation, all players share a critique of American culture as in a state of moral decline, symbolized by the acceptance of abortion, which they regard as the devaluation of human life.

In the popular media, the anti-abortion movement was increasingly associated with both the religious and the political dimensions of the New Right, a distortion which, judging by the responses, was making the moderate right-to-life leadership uneasy. The NRLC made a point of publicizing the liberal/Democratic races that they supported were anathema to the conservative program.[18] The liberal evangelical Christian magazine *Sojourners* warned against an "unholy alliance between the anti-abortion movement and the right-wing."[19] The U.S. Conference of Catholic Bishops, by clearly linking its "human life" position to support of a nuclear freeze and increases in social welfare, further distanced a large part of the pro-life movement from other conservative interests. In short, despite the hopes and plans of the New Right leadership to create what would have been an unprecedented joining of Catholics, liberal Protestants, conservative politicians, and Protestant fundamentalists over the abortion issue, the reality of such an alliance has been ephemeral at best. By 1979, the New Right leaders, frustrated at their inability to win over the mainstream pro-life movement, had set up right-to-life groups to rival the NRLC.[20]

While their broader agendas and specific tactics differ, both NRLC and New Right activists choose to work within the existing political system and gain legitimacy in the public eye. In that sense, they accept the same "rules of the game" as their opponents and the shared aim of winning over the American public. The more general point to be understood here is that abortion is a powerful political symbol, in contention not only between the pro-life and the pro-choice movements. Those opposed to abortion also have been struggling with each other to gain material and ideological control over abortion's larger meaning and practice, a battle that became even more dramatic as groups that were more militant emerged in the pro-life camp.

The Rise of Right-to-Life Militance

While the stated raison d'être of the right-to-life movement has been to overturn the Supreme Court ruling through a constitutional amendment, activism has focused increasingly on local-level conflicts and events. By the 1980s, some pro-life groups were adopting direct action techniques—harassing local abortion providers, picketing facilities, or staging sit-ins at clinics—not unlike those used by their radical opponents in the abortion rights struggle in the late 1960s. In both cases, the intent was to disrupt the status quo on abortion by challenging the law and forcing judicial clarification of areas left unclear in the Court's ruling on abortion.[21] It was only a matter of time before these areas would be brought before the Supreme Court for resolution, as was the case in the 1989 ruling on a Missouri case, *Webster v. Reproductive Health Services*.[22] However, with two exceptions, the high court declined to rule on any of them until 1983.[23] In June of that year, the Supreme Court ruled that a variety of state and local ordinances designed to restrict abortion practice were unconstitutional, underscoring the position it had taken supporting elective abortion in the 1973 rulings.[24] Soon after, an additional blow was dealt the pro-life cause when two different pro-life proposals for a constitutional amendment to restrict abortions lost in Congress. Together, the events of the summer of 1983 served as an endorsement of the pro-choice status quo and a setback for the right-to-life cause.

Despite the fact that the right-to-life movement was well organized, maintained a large membership, and had become quite sophisticated regarding political action, it had achieved only modest successes in gaining direct political victories through legislative or judicial channels. The mainstream right-to-life leadership that had managed to prevail over the more radical elements of the movement by arguing that direct action would undercut public sympathy for pro-life efforts began to lose its credibility.[25] Thus, the relatively moderate philosophy and strategy of the NRLC could no longer contain a diverse movement through its efforts to bring about change within the political system. The NRLC lost its hold as a centripetal force binding a divided movement.

This conclusion seems to be supported by the fact that the setbacks of 1983 for the right-to-life movement were followed by a dramatic escalation in violence directed against abortion clinics.[26] According to the National Abortion Federation (NAF), a trade association for U.S. abortion providers, "acts of violence" include invasions of clinics, vandalism, death threats, bomb threats and bombings, assaults, arson attempts and arson, and kidnappings. Using this definition, the NAF documented 115 violent incidents over five years involving 46 clinics between 1977 and 1982. By contrast, during the next two years (March 1983 to March 1985), there were 319 acts of violence affecting 238 clinics. By the end of 1985, 92 percent of abortion clinics had reported harassment, ranging from picketing of clinics to vandalism, an increase of approximately 60 percent from 1984.[27] One of the more prominent incidents took place on Christmas morning of 1984 in Pensacola, Florida. The Ladies Center abortion clinic and the offices of two doctors who offered abortions were bombed with homemade explosive devices made by two young men active in the Assemblies of God who had seen right-to-life films but had never participated in any kind of political action, and who willingly took credit for their actions.[28]

Their case is typical of the histories of those apprehended for such actions between 1983 and 1985. This phase of destructive violence was carried out mostly by individuals who were often peripheral to the mainstream of pro-life activism, both locally and nationally.[29] All but two of them identified themselves as fundamentalist or evangelical, and all of them justified their actions through some version of the "Higher Laws" argument: God's law supersedes human law, and the saving of life (by interfering directly with abortions) takes precedence over the preservation of property. Thus, one possible explanation for the increase in violence after 1983 is the increasing political activism among fundamentalist Christians in the early 1980s. This general shift toward increased involvement in political activism seems to have encouraged particular individuals to act violently on their anti-abortion sentiments.[30]

The rise in violent incidents captured widespread media attention and evoked ambivalent reaction from moderate pro-life activists. Dr. Jack Willke, then NRLC president, for example, condemned the 4 July 1984 firebombing of the NAF headquarters in Washington, D.C., by two radical pro-lifers who called themselves the "Army of God." Willke was concerned that the resort to violence by radicals would only hurt his own organization's image and future efforts. Nonetheless, he seemed to be praising with faint damnation when he used the opportunity to equate abortion itself with violence: "Every second living human being that goes through [an abortion clinic's] front door is killed."

Observers both inside and outside the pro-life movement view the rise in such activity as a reaction by more radical pro-lifers to a number of related events. In addition to the two-pronged defeat of right-to-life efforts in 1983, that same year, then president Reagan published an influential anti-abortion essay, *Abortion and the Conscience of the Nation.* In response to the bombings, he claimed that the alarming increase in attacks on abortion clinics did not constitute terrorism because they were not carried out by an "organized group" that claimed responsibility for them.[31] A number of the perpetrators interpreted Reagan's words as a sign of his support.[32] Only in January 1985 did the president finally speak out against these "violent anarchistic activities" and promise to throw the weight of federal law enforcement efforts behind apprehending the criminals.[33]

Interestingly, after 1985, there was a small but significant decline in the most extreme forms of violence against clinics. The number of arsons and bombings dropped by over a third from the previous years.[34] This may have been due not only to Reagan's shift in position but also to the arrest and conviction of over a dozen offenders, as well as calls by other government officials[35] and pro-life leaders for a halt to violence.[36]

From interviews it appears that most of the bombers had not been officially active in right-to-life activities; yet their marginality in relation to the movement as a whole did not diminish the significance of their actions. These extremists represented an exaggerated expression of a more general shift taking place in pro-life protests. By the mid 1980s, groups that advocated direct action bordering on violence and terror—

harassing patients, holding sit-ins, intimidating abortion providers—emerged with new confidence. The most notable of the direct action groups were Scheidler's Pro-Life Action League and, by 1988, Operation Rescue. Although the direct action groups distinguished their activities from the bombings and arson that attracted so much attention, it was not altogether clear in their rhetoric where or whether the line between direct action and violence was sharply drawn.

Indeed, direct action tactics of these two organizations have a variety of manifestations, which typically include accosting women entering abortion clinics and blocking their access to the abortion facility, confronting them verbally and physically, and following them or even tracing their license plate numbers and calling them at home. Physicians and clinic personnel have had their homes picketed and have received threatening letters and phone calls. As security grows more precarious at clinics, leases are lost and insurance costs escalate. Private guards, bomb checks, and escorts for patients are now considered essential for most facilities. Proponents claim that direct action is rooted in traditions of American civil disobedience, whereas opponents believe their behavior verges on terrorism in its effects, much like the Ku Klux Klan.[37] The threat of greater destruction began to loom over clinics, creating an atmosphere of chronic fear of physical and emotional assault for both personnel and clients. This is the background from which Operation Rescue emerged.

The Emergence of Operation Rescue

For those who had long scorned the more or less civil tactics that had dominated the pro-life movement's political style since 1973, the disarray after 1983 became an opportunity. Two groups in particular began to gain strength, convinced that restraint and civility had been ineffective: Joe Scheidler's Pro-Life Action League, established in 1980, and Randall Terry's Operation Rescue, officially launched in 1988. Scheidler and Terry, whose contempt for the "mainstream style" was openly expressed in epithets such as "wimps for life," focused their efforts on dramatic demonstrations directed at abortion users and providers. Some observers identified this strategy as a "male" tendency, in terms of both the gender of the participants and the aggressive and militant style of their actions.

For example, Randall Terry's methodical "rescues" are embellished with "covert" and "intelligence" operations, requiring the stealthy maneuver of "troops" and a solemn "chain of command."[38] He speaks of "organizing for war" and calls participants "warriors."[39] Reliance on male pastors in the movement led to the privileging of a traditional male perspective and adherence to conventional gender roles. "It takes leadership that can inspire confidence and women can do this. But most people, men and women included, are more comfortable following men into a highly volatile situation," Terry explained. "It's just human nature. It's history."[40] One observer of rescues noted the consequences of this division of labor: "A mostly male vanguard stands shoulder to shoulder on the frontlines, attempting to push past the linked arms of feminists guarding the clinic. Off to the side, the mostly female auxiliary, Operation

Rescue's "Prayer Support Column," is chanting hymns."[41] Actions generally include blockading clinic entrances so that no one can gain access, entering clinics and stopping procedures, pouring glue into door locks, and otherwise disrupting activities.

While Operation Rescue has drawn between forty and fifty thousand individuals into such events,[42] there is no documentation as to the continuing commitment of demonstrators and there is actually some evidence of a decline in commitment after the initial rescue experience.[43] Long-term research in the field with members of these organizations has not been carried out, partly because the groups are so new, but mostly because of the mercurial nature of the organizing, which focuses on sporadic and dispersed demonstrations rather than building bases in communities over time. Other anti-abortion groups rest on well-run local and national bases, regular meetings and events, and similar ongoing activities, such as "problem pregnancy counseling," that provide some indication of their influence on the lives of grass-roots members. Lacking such structures, Operation Rescue and the Pro-Life Action League are difficult to assess in the same way. These groups are unlike organizations such as the NRLC that have elections and a relatively decentralized, democratic organization. Rather, they are built around the particular visions and charismatic personalities of their founders, who have developed very effective forms of political display. Because of the critical role played by the leaders of direct action anti-abortion movements, this essay focuses on Randall Terry (and Joseph Scheidler to a lesser extent).

For this new style of right-to-life activist, the preoccupation of moderates with building or maintaining a public image as reasonable, good citizens is simply beside the point. These activists are succeeding on their own terms by immediately disrupting abortion services and gaining media attention for their cause. Like hijackers, they amplify their effect through dramatic tactics that attract television cameras and news reporters in a way that more moderate right-to-life activity has never been able to do. They have a shrewd sense of the potential the mass media have for aggrandizing the impact of small numbers.

Joseph Scheidler, founder (in 1980) of the Chicago-based Pro-Life Action League and author of *Closed: 99 Ways to Stop Abortion,* appears to have inspired and given crucial support to Randall Terry's work in developing Operation Rescue. Scheidler and Terry are open in their contempt for letter writers and lobbyists. They justify their actions by the "doctrine of necessity"—a view that violence is permissible as a last resort when it must be used to stop or prevent greater violence (i.e., in their view, abortion)—to justify actions such as illegally entering clinic operating rooms and disrupting abortions in progress. Terry's philosophy also involves the strict fundamentalist notion of "biblical obedience" in which scriptural passages are understood as mandates to action: "The next time you study your Bible, use a concordance to look up verses containing words like justice, judgment, rescue, deliver, vindicate, innocent, needy, weak, fatherless, and widow. You will find an overwhelming number of verses commanding *action* from God's people on behalf of the needy."[44]

Scheidler, as a Catholic, is less concerned with literal readings of the Bible. He claims adherence to a philosophy of nonviolence and blames the media for linking his actions with those of violent extremists. He nonetheless makes public his sympathy for and identification with those more radical than he.[45] Until the mid-1980s, the zealotry and controversial actions he advocates had consigned him to the fringe of the pro-life movement. He was seen as disruptive of efforts to gain the moral and political high ground through legislative actions. However, as the pro-life movement attempted to regroup after its 1983 defeats, people like Scheidler gained at least some temporary legitimacy with the mainstream. Scheidler was invited to speak at their annual convention in 1984 and was among a handful of national pro-life leaders who met with President Reagan in 1984 during the annual 22 January "March for Life" in Washington, D.C. (After Scheidler asked the president to pardon "pro-life political prisoners"—i.e., those found guilty of bombing clinics—he was not invited back to the White House.)[46]

In 1984, around the time Scheidler was moving into a position of some visibility in the pro-life movement, Randall Terry had a threefold "vision":

> First, to do everything possible to rescue babies and their mothers from the nightmare of abortion on the very doorstep of local abortion clinics. Second, to show the love of Christ to women in crisis pregnancies by providing whatever help they need to carry their child to term. Third, to re-educate the public and the church to the value of human life from a Bible-based, Christian perspective and to expose the horrors of abortion.[47]

Randall Terry's story of divine inspiration seems appropriate for one raised in upstate New York's "Burned-Over district," so named because of the widespread evangelical revivals that caught fire there in the nineteenth century.[48] Like many of the young men caught up in the religious enthusiasms of the past, Terry grew up in a middle-class, liberal, church-going family (that includes some strong feminists); yet he found himself attracted to the social turbulence of the 1960s, although he grew up in the 1970s.[49] He describes himself as "a young rebel. I was in some aspects, I imagine, a holdout. . . . The sixties in many ways was an era of searching. People wanting to know the answers, wanting to know truth. In the seventies, people just wanted to get high, but I wanted to know answers."[50] An honors student and a talented musician, Terry left high school early and hitchhiked south, getting involved with drugs as he unsuccessfully sought his fortune in rock and roll. Shortly after he returned home, at age seventeen, he was "saved," joined a charismatic independent church, and began preaching first to his family, then on the street and in malls. Two years later he entered the "transdenominational" Elim Bible Institute, with plans to become a missionary in Central America.

After leaving Elim in 1981,[51] he married a fellow student, Cindy Dean, and began working in a variety of jobs, from serving customers at fast-food outlets to selling cars, eventually moving to Binghamton, New York. The couple, who had been struggling with infertility problems for several years (a problem they later overcame), was "called to the mission field of abortion clinics." In 1984, Cindy began demonstrating in front of Southern Tier Women's Services, a Binghamton abortion clinic. Later Randall joined her, then replaced her and started what he called Project Life. Although by the summer of 1984 he had opened the Crisis Pregnancy Center to "offer women free pregnancy tests, confidential counseling, baby clothes, baby furniture, and other services,"[52] that nurturant part of the vision never went much further as he concentrated on "the war." In 1985, when the clinic responded by providing escorts to clients, Terry mobilized thirty people from his home church, the Church at Pierce Creek, for a protest at Southern Tier.

Over a year later, in January 1986, Terry called Joseph Scheidler and invited him to Binghamton to hear the anti-abortion songs Terry had been composing and performing. During the visit they discussed plans to blockade clinics across the country, incite mass arrests, and thus disrupt the business of abortion and gain mass media coverage.[53] Apparently inspired and perhaps directly encouraged by Scheidler, Terry organized his first "rescue mission" at the Binghamton clinic the next week. In this first effort, Terry and seven others gained access to one of the inner rooms of the clinic.[54] In the words of an unsympathetic reporter, "They locked themselves in the counseling room, ripping out the phone system, smashing furniture, wedging the door so tight the police had to break it down with a crowbar."[55] All were arrested for criminal trespass and resisting arrest. Only Randall Terry refused to pay his fine and went to jail. This experience led to future developments in his tactics. "By the end of my jail term in the summer of 1986," he writes, "I had a more definite idea of what it was going to take to secure justice again for the children. . . . I also realized that the pro-life movement was not creating the tension and upheaval necessary to produce political and social change. We were being too nice."[56] As a result of the agitation, the clinic lost its lease and had to relocate.

Terry continued to meet with other pro-life advocates of direct action, ranging from Joe Scheidler to leftist "seamless garment" Catholic organizers, such as John Cavanaugh-O'Keefe and Joan Andrews,[57] and Feminists for Life leader Juli Loesch Wiley.[58] These activists, disturbed by the escalation in arsons and bombings of abortion clinics that had been taking place, called the meetings in order to "coordinate their activities and adopt standards of behavior."[59] At a 1987 meeting, Terry reportedly presented a plan to expand the movement's reach by organizing nationwide "rescues," with demonstrations planned for the 1988 Democratic National Convention. Terry's strategy of blockades at clinics (rather than invasions of them), arrests, and noncooperation with police in the name of the "doctrine of necessity" and "higher law" showed the influence of Scheidler's philosophy and tactics, and was generally well received.[60]

Encouraged to test these tactics on a smaller scale before the Democratic National Convention, Terry led a series of assaults on clinics in New York (modeled on the 1987 Cherry Hill blockade), generating a few hundred arrests and a smattering of local press coverage. In the process, he put together a dedicated team of nine organizers, all in their thirties. While the members of this group included one Catholic, two ordained ministers, and two women, the group's style "is decidedly male, lay, young and clamorously pious in evangelical style."[61]

In February 1988, the Operation Rescue team launched a series of trial actions in New York City, blockading three sites where abortions were offered and preventing them from conducting any business for one day. The goal was to gain publicity and support, and familiarize "rescuers" with Terry's distinct direct action approach that borrowed from both Scheidler and Cavanaugh-O'Keefe. Over sixteen hundred of these mostly white, middle-aged evangelicals who had come from thirty-five states were arrested. At the end of the week, federal judge Robert Ward issued a temporary restraining order banning them from blocking entrances to medical services and threatened them with a $25,000-a-day fine for violations.[62]

On 30 April 1988, Terry officially formed Operation Rescue. Because of its avowed commitment to breaking the law, and also to avoid financial disclosure, it was established as a business.[63] The NRLC said they were not associated with the effort and declined comment.[64]

Operation Rescue became national news (as was intended) when it descended on Atlanta abortion clinics during the 1988 Democratic National Convention, beginning what Terry called the "Siege of Atlanta." Over thirteen hundred demonstrators, including Terry, were jailed for trespassing between July and October. To replace those arrested, hundreds of people poured in on buses, summoned via Terry's appearance on Pat Robertson's television show, the "700 Club." Many followed instructions not to give their names, identifying themselves as "Baby Doe" (in solidarity with the unborn); the intention and result were to clog the jails and courts, since they could not be released without identification.[65]

Despite much negative response from other pro-life groups and prominent Christians, the publicity attracted a flood of financial contributions, including $10,000 from Jerry Falwell.[66] Before the "siege," Operation Rescue had about $5,000 coming in a month; by December 1988, the monthly income had jumped to $60,000.[67] Legal action escalated as well. The Atlanta courts forbade protestors from blocking access to clinics; in turn, Operation Rescue accused the Atlanta police department of the excessive use of force.

Just after the "siege" ended in October, the group organized a "National Day of Rescue": 2,631 people were arrested in thirty-two cities, nineteen states, and Canada. In addition, 2,019 risked arrest while 5,443 provided "Prayer Support columns." Relations with the police were considerably better than they had been in Atlanta. Protestors walked to paddy wagons and gave their legal names, while police officers were careful not to give injury.[68] On the second National Day of Rescue, 26 April 1989, sixty-four cities participated in rescues, twice the number that had participated less than six months prior.[69] A "Holy Week of Rescue" in Los Angeles during Easter of 1989 engaged 300 police in riot gear; more than 700 people were arrested, bringing the total number of arrests to 20,000 in less than a year.[70] Pro-choice sources estimate that from May 1988 to May 1989 there was at least one local Operation Rescue blockade every weekend.[71] The movement was mushrooming. It seemed, indeed, that Randall Terry's statement to the press was accurate:

We have been completely successful. We have shut down abortion facilities, we have rescued babies, we have maintained a peaceful, prayerful atmosphere. We have injected new vision and hope into the pro-life movement. . . . This was a week of on-the-job training for future leaders. Now we will see a major turn in the battle toward more peaceful blockades. Every major political change in this country has been preceded by social upheaval and that has been the missing element of the pro-life movement.[72]

Operation Rescue's effectiveness was due not only to the scale and frequency of its demonstrations, but to the systematic organization of them.[73]

On 3 July 1989, the U.S. Supreme Court ruled on a Missouri case, *Webster v. Reproductive Health Services*.[74] The decision, which effectively allows states to impose restrictions on abortion, was regarded as a pro-life victory by activists on both sides. Randall Terry took the *Webster* decision as a sign to begin to expand his work toward his larger agenda. "We are launching a two-pronged offensive. Thousands will surround abortion mills to rescue children and mothers, and we will impact state legislatures with equal force."[75] Operation Rescue began holding week-long training camps in the Binghamton area near its headquarters, where would-be rescuers paid to hear lectures on the evils of feminism and liberal government as well as to learn practical political skills, from resisting arrest to electing conservative politicians.[76] Through these actions, the implicit differences between Operation Rescue and other pro-life groups became explicit. For Terry, mobilizing against abortion is only a means to the end. "What we *can* work for," he wrote, "is a nation where once again the Judeo-Christian ethic is the foundation for our politics, our judicial system, and our public morality; a nation not floating in the uncertain sea of humanism, but a country whose unmoving bedrock is Higher Laws."[77] His language makes clear his agenda: to refashion what he sees as a godless society according to the beliefs and values of his version of Christian fundamentalism.

Legal Setbacks

In the midst of this expansion, however, Operation Rescue's disdain for the law and legal process finally began to have its effect. In 1989, more than a dozen lawsuits were pending around the country, brought mostly by pro-choice groups and clinics in response to the effects of the dramatic demonstrations that had gained the group national attention. On 29 September 1989 an Atlanta jury found Terry guilty of trespassing and illegal assembly and charged him $1,000 (in lieu of two years in jail). Refusing to pay the fine, Terry was jailed on 5 October 1989.[78] Around the same time, a federal appeals court levied penalties of $50,000 against the group for violating court orders which barred protesters from blocking access to abortion clinics in the New York area.[79] Operation Rescue's appeal on the basis of First Amendment rights was denied; the court ruled that while protesters may make speeches, counsel women, and hand out pamphlets, "blocking access to public and private buildings had never been upheld as a proper method of communication in an orderly society."[80] Then the Supreme Court denied review of a case that found anti-abortion groups which act with the intent of closing down clinics and intimidate their clients liable under federal antitrust statutes and racketeering (RICO) laws.[81] In December 1989, the United States Attorney's Office in New York seized Operation Rescue's payroll accounts and financial information in an effort to collect the unpaid fines. In January 1990, when Terry was released from jail in Atlanta (after an anonymous donor paid his fine), he announced that he would be closing Operation Rescue's Binghamton headquarters due to the escalating fines, legal fees, and a $70,000 debt. (Both pro-choice and anti-abortion activists considered the decision a tactical strategy to avoid having money seized by the government.)[82] At his press conference, Terry announced that "the rescue is not through. There are more than one hundred [legally autonomous] rescue groups around the country. They will continue doing what they have been doing."[83]

However, less than a month later, the actions of Judge Robert Ward of New York's federal district court undermined Terry's strategy to decentralize Operation Rescue. Recognizing the activists' general disregard for the law, Judge Ward took the unusual step of imposing additional fines of $400,000 on ten *individuals* as well as the expected organizations, thus warning potential rescuers that they could be *personally* liable.[84] Commenting on his unusual decision and the high fines, Judge Ward acknowledged he resorted to such measures because prior rulings "were ignored and did not stop the protests. It was necessary to take coercive action."[85]

Operation Rescue's last resort, an appeal to a conservative U.S. Supreme Court, failed. In May 1990, the Court let stand decisions made in the Atlanta and New York areas prohibiting protesters from blockading abortion facilities or from abusing or harassing people entering or leaving clinics. After the Supreme Court rulings, Terry continued to invoke claims of religious legitimacy. "We're following God's law, and that's more important than man's law. . . . We as a nation are doomed to a severe chastening from the hand of God," he was quoted as saying. "Abortion is the symbol of our decline, the slaughter of the most innocent. What kind of justice is it when ten of us are fined $450,000 for trying to stop the murder of innocent babies while the homosexuals who entered St. Patrick's Cathedral and disrupted Mass are fined $100 each?"[86]

Unlike less radical fundamentalist activists, such as Falwell, who have learned to operate successfully within the political system, Terry seemed genuinely surprised that the American judicial system was unmoved by his appeal to "Higher Laws." After the 1990 court decision Terry continued to direct Operation Rescue, although he was nominally replaced by Reverend Keith Tucci. Terry began to develop new strategies to change what he considers to be the "anti-Christian bias of the nation's judicial system." Appropriating the rhetorical style and strategy of minority rights movements in their fights against discrimination, Terry has linked the prosecution of Operation Rescue to systemic discrimination against Bible-believing Christians in the United States:

> We want to train people to write letters, to lobby, to let the light shine on the steady diet of anti-Christian bigotry we're seeing. . . . When a Christian gets hammered with an unfair arrest or a huge fine or a two year jail sentence for trying to follow God's laws, the media and most of the Christian community

ignores it. We've got to learn to phone the sheriff, picket the judge's home, hold a press conference, or get the calls going to a prosecutor.[87]

In the summer of 1990, Terry organized a Christian Defense Council to educate Christians about "police oppression, judicial tyranny and political harassment."[88] By fall of 1990, there was a noticeable decline in the mention of abortion in Terry's rhetoric, and a former political liaison for Operation Rescue ran for a seat on the New York state assembly from the Binghamton area.[89]

It appeared that Operation Rescue's anti-abortion activities had been stymied by the multiple legal actions brought against the organization and its followers. According to a news report sent out by Terry in October 1990, federal marshals had seized the last Operation Rescue bank account the previous month. However, as Terry explained, his strategy was to "close our doors" and "go into a new phase" by turning the organizational weakness of Operation Rescue into a strength by decentralizing activities.

> Our enemies have never understood this movement, what makes us tick, or how we function. . . . They have believed (wrongly so) that Operation Rescue was a top-down bureaucracy; that we were somehow controlling from Binghampton all rescues around the nation! Hence, they have been preoccupied with closing down the "National Office" in the vain hope that this would end the rescue movement. . . . This is why from the beginning, we have been committed to *not* building an organization. We've desired fully autonomous, locally led and financed groups. That way, whatever happens in Binghampton, N.Y., the one hundred–plus rescue groups around the country will continue on. . . .
>
> Yes, it looks like we will have to lay off the remainder of our staff and close our doors. Does that mean we're through? No. Only *underground*.[90]

In November 1990, Operation Rescue sponsored its first national event in over a year, a three-day conference and rescue in Washington, D.C., entitled "D.C. Project II: Veteran's Campaign for Life." The meeting highlighted a strategy begun in June 1990 as a siege of an abortion clinic in the town of Dobbs Ferry, New York. The siege lasted for over six months. This technique of targeting a single clinic for long-term harassment was dubbed "Operation Goliath." A brochure described the tactic as "Phase II" of the Rescue Movement. "The goal [of this phase] is to unite all pro-life and rescue forces into one mighty army, with one specific focus: an all-out holy war on the child-killing industry—one mill at a time."[91]

The events of the summer of 1991 suggested that Phase II was succeeding. On 15 July 1991, hundreds of demonstrators began a siege of three abortion clinics in Wichita, Kansas, and actually succeeded in closing them for the first week of the siege. Operation Rescue leaders had chosen their site carefully: Wichita's mayor, police chief, and city manager, as well as the governor of Kansas, were staunchly pro-life. The behavior of local police did little to quell the clinic blockades.[92] On 29 July the siege made the national news when federal district judge Patrick Kelly called in federal marshals to enforce the restraining order he had issued to stop the demonstrators. In the restraining order Judge Kelly invoked the Civil Rights Act of 1871, a statute, originally intended to shield freed slaves from actions of the Ku Klux Klan, that declares it illegal for two or more people to conspire to deprive any person or class of persons from exercising their constitutional rights. The publicity intensified when the Justice Department filed an amicus brief on behalf of Operation Rescue's appeal of the injunction, arguing that its actions were merely trespassing and loitering and therefore were only subject to local legal authorities. While the drama of the protests brought the case into sharp focus, a similar test of the 1871 law, *Bray v. Alexandria Women's Health Clinic,* loomed on the horizon, scheduled to be heard during the next session of the predominantly conservative U.S. Supreme Court.[93]

As of this writing (September 1991) the protest continues with 2,661 arrests of fifteen hundred individuals to date, costing Wichita over $400,000.[94] According to reports, approximately 50 percent of the protestors were from Kansas; the leadership and half of the protestors were from other states. Some of the protestors called themselves "Lambs of Christ" or the "Victim Souls of the Unborn Christ Child."[95] They were part of a hard core of approximately two hundred devoted "rescuers" who have given up jobs and other commitments to travel around the country, blockade clinics, and risk arrest multiple times.[96] Published reports indicate that the majority of the protestors in Wichita were white blue-collar workers—schoolteachers, service workers, and technicians. The number included retired and unemployed people; approximately one-third of the demonstrators were reportedly over sixty years of age.[97] Catholics and Protestant fundamentalists were both out in force, dividing into separate groups for prayer sessions, with rosaries on one side and witnessing to Jesus on the other.[98]

Understandably, Operation Rescue leadership took heart from this turn of events. Terry declared the rescue movement "alive and well and in full strength. The challenge before us is to use the street-level momentum and take back the state legislatures all over the country." The comments of spokesperson Reverend Patrick Mahoney verified that the siege of Wichita represented a new strategy for Operation Rescue's anti-abortion activity. "The abortion battle is not going to be decided in the trendy urban centers," Mahoney proclaimed. "It will be decided street by street, town by town, village by village. . . . Wichita embodies what we will see in the next three or four years."[99]

A majority of local residents, however, disputed the Operation Rescue analysis of the impact of the protest. While there was support from clergy and some Kansas political leaders, a poll conducted by the local paper and TV station found that 78 percent of residents surveyed disapproved of the protestors' tactics.[100]

Nonetheless, the larger agenda of saving America's soul was not forgotten by the members of Operation Rescue. The April–June issue of *National Rescuer* advertised an October 1991 Joshua Project Leadership Summit in Washington, D.C., for pastors and church leaders. Hosted by Terry and several other Operation Rescue leaders, the Project's goal was to "sound the alarm, to install the vision, and to establish the leadership that will enable us to reclaim the heart of our culture."

The Impact of Operation Rescue

The Wichita siege has given Operation Rescue a new sense of power. Although the group did not succeed in closing down any of the clinics it attacked, Operation Rescue's harassment of administrators, doctors, patients, and local peacekeeping forces has been such that the *idea* of an Operation Rescue blockade coming to a clinic in a small city now has the capacity to cause considerable panic. Clearly, Wichita put Operation Rescue back in the public eye, although there is no clear evidence that public opinion turned in its direction, even with the Bush administration's amicus brief in its favor for the Supreme Court appeal on the *Bray v. Alexandria Women's Health Clinic* case discussed above. Certainly the position of the administration is contested by many federal judges, not only because of Operation Rescue's flagrant disregard of the law but also because of the tactics it uses, such as flooding the judge's chambers and prosecutor's office with protest calls.

Perhaps the most important effect of the 1991 blockades (now called the "Summer of Mercy" by Operation Rescue) has been financial. (Many fines incurred during the arrests in Wichita were dropped. Final legal resolution awaits the rulings of the Supreme Court for 1991–92.) According to those who have been closely monitoring the group, checks totaling approximately $150,000 with a memo line for Operation Rescue were deposited every day of the three-week siege in the bank accounts of other pro-life groups, thus circumventing the fines on Operation Rescue's accounts. As of fall 1991, it appears that the money is being translated into support for more demonstrations. In a letter to supporters dated 6 September 1991, the agenda for the coming year included: National Days of Rescue IV, scheduled for the week of 17 November and meant to encompass fifty to sixty cities; the Capitol Rescue, to be held 20–22 January 1992 in Washington, D.C.; and rescue events to coincide with the Democratic National Convention in New York City (13–16 July) and the Republican National Convention in Houston (17–20 August). The letter ends with a plea for "as large a gift as you possibly can [make] to help in the upcoming events."[101] Increased money collected in ways that circumvent fines could take on greater significance should *Roe v. Wade* be overturned by the now exceedingly conservative Supreme Court. In that case, the battle for abortion rights could be turned back to individual states and support for state-by-state lobbying could be crucial.

It is hard to judge whether the events in Wichita have actually mobilized new recruits sufficiently to turn around the decline in support that had occurred by 1990. In a letter to supporters written in the spring of 1990, Terry acknowledged the movement's decline. "We are in a lull. The number of rescues and the number of rescuers has decreased. Why? Rescuers are tired and battle-weary. The cost in many areas has gone up."[102]

Not every activist has the general personal commitment of a zealot like Randall Terry or his team members. Grass-roots participants appeared to be disillusioned on the basis of their own experiences. Orin Cooper, president of the Chicago chapter of Operation Rescue, commented, "People found out that when you start going back to court and losing work, it is quite heavy on the budget."[103] It appears that injunctions have hampered demonstrations, and holding people personally liable has tested even the most dedicated. As an indication of the decline in support, an effort for a 1990 Mothers' Day rally in Chicago drew one hundred people and resulted in twenty-six arrests; in 1989 there were fifteen hundred people and two hundred arrests.[104] According to Operation Rescue's figures, there was an average of eighty participants in ten rescues reported for spring and summer of 1991.[105]

In a September 1991 letter to supporters, Reverend Keith Tucci seemed to be declaring a reversal of this decline. "There is no doubt that the Summer of Mercy has sparked new and fresh passion and commitment into the pro-life movement. . . . The rescue movement is stronger than ever, and we cannot be stopped by the best efforts of Planned Parenthood, the N.O.W., the A.C.L.U., and various and sundry tyrannical judges."[106] Terry claims that Operation Rescue has had a much greater impact than the moderate groups. (Terry seems somewhat preoccupied with his place in history.)[107] "The pro-life movement has failed to learn the lessons of history, which show how the labor movement, the civil rights movement, Vietnam protest, and gay liberation all occurred because a group of people created social tension," he has argued.[108]

Terry is correct in his assessment that his movement brought the right-to-life cause renewed public attention. However, unlike the social movements he claims as models, Operation Rescue's actions often decrease public support for the pro-life cause. One unintended result of Operation Rescue's prominence has been the mobilization of a long quiescent opposition to the anti-abortion movement. But it is not only pro-choice activists who disagree with Operation Rescue. A second unintended consequence was the divisions that the direct action movements introduced into the ranks of Christians concerned about abortion's legality. Christians from various quarters expressed ambivalence about the group's ongoing active engagement with secular political processes and especially their intentional breaking of the law. While Jerry Falwell, Pat Robertson, and Charles Colson argued that Operation Rescue's tactics are permissible, other prominent Christian leaders, both liberal and conservative, argued that rescuers take too lightly the scriptural mandate to obey civil authorities (Romans 13:10–5, 1 Peter 2:13–15).[109] Terry retorted in true fundamentalist fashion by invoking Proverbs 24:11, which he has taken as his literal mission: "Rescue those who are unjustly sentenced to death; don't stand back and let them die. Some liberal theologians disagree, saying that such writings are not meant to be commands, 'but inductive generalizations about wisdom in this life.'"[110] Taking a conservative position, former president of the Southern Baptist Convention Charles Stanley attempted to distance himself and the Southern Baptists he represented from Terry's biblical readings. While he agreed that abortion is an "abomination before God," Stanley contended that Operation Rescue's approach does not meet the biblical criteria for civil disobedience. In a treatise issued in response to Terry's request for an endorsement during the "siege of Atlanta," Stanley wrote that such actions are justified only when the state "requires an act which is contrary to God's Word" or "prohibits an act which is consistent with God's Word." Stanley also describes women as "free moral agents responsible before Almighty God for their actions, including the exercise [*sic*] of the rights of their innocent, unborn child."[111] Terry responded:

> In order to obey many of these scriptures, we will have to leave the comfort and safety of our church pews. We are going to have to get our hands dirty and be *active* in society. . . . If Christians stay cloistered in their little groups, it's easy to keep unstained by the world. But when we go to the trenches of this life, when we reach out to help the unlovely, we run the risk of being defiled. Involving yourself in society rather than abandoning it, presents a far greater challenge to stay pure.[112]

It may seem paradoxical that right-to-life militants, who hope to repeal the "legislated social change" of the 1960s, consider the civil rights movement as a model for their activism. "In many, many ways, the rescue really is like the civil rights movement," Terry has said. "This is a civil rights movement, seeking to restore the civil rights of children, the right to life."[113] Indeed, Operation Rescue mirrors a certain consistency in the style of American social movements, regardless of their position on the ideological spectrum. Commenting on the conditions under which extremism has emerged in American social life, historian Thomas Rose has observed that "violence is a political resource when the bargaining process provides no other alternatives, or at least when some groups perceive no other alternatives. Political violence is an intelligible pattern of interaction that exists in America, but we refuse to understand and confront it as integral to our life."[114] Operation Rescue's resort to militant action may indeed be understood as a strategy to galvanize the larger anti-abortion movement stymied on the mainstream political level by the mid-1980s.

Yet it is this question of violence in Operation Rescue's tactics and strategies that has created the greatest dissension among right-to-life activists. Operation Rescue is not philosophically opposed to the use of violence, as many other pro-life groups, including many direct actionists are.[115] The influential NRLC has maintained its policy of silence on Operation Rescue's activities, but makes clear its differences with the group by underscoring the motives for its own commitment to legal and nonviolent action. "We will want people to obey the new abortion law we are working for, so it is important we let the nation know we are responsible people ourselves," Willke has said. "We will not win with violence. That is the tactic of the abortionist."[116] Indeed, the moderate center of the pro-life movement has tended in public pronouncements to deny the legitimacy of violence. Yet the moderate center has also used, and benefited from, the "antics" of the direct actionists; invariably, the moderates' public exposure, credibility, and relative level of public approval have grown with the rise of Operation Rescue. According to this interpretation, just as the bombings and arsons of even more militant groups made Operation Rescue appear less radical than it otherwise might have appeared, so Operation Rescue's advocacy of radical and sometimes violent behavior lends legitimacy to the moderate right-to-life movement. By contrast, the moderates appear civil, flexible, and representative.[117]

However, many right-to-life activists are skeptical that outsiders can make such fine distinctions, especially given the way right-to-lifers are represented by the secular media. Television and the press in general give disproportionate attention to dramatic political confrontation with little concern for distinctions between groups. News stories tend to conflate those who carry out controversial activities with the movement as a whole; and moderate activists are reluctant to discuss their differences for fear that divisions in the movement will work to the advantage of their opponents. It is not only that violence makes a good story and sells newspapers. Dave Andrusko, editor of the NRLC's newsletter, in an essay entitled "Zealots, Zanies, and Assorted Kooks: How the Major Media Interprets the Pro-Life Movement," writes that for the "media elite" "pro-lifers (and even more so pro-family people) are synonymous with repression, political and sexual. The buzz words practically leap off their typewriters: punitive, prudish, Victorian, rigid, repressed, hysterical, etc."[118] Andrusko is correct insofar as the profession of journalism is dominated by liberals who favor a pro-choice position.[119] Not surprisingly, the more extreme and reprehensible pro-life activities which paint the movement in the worst light, from their perspective, receive the most coverage. Taking advantage of the situation, Operation Rescue has managed to magnify the impact of their minority position in the right to life movement through dramatic, media oriented demonstrations. .

Part of Terry's importance thus has to do with his savvy management of image and performance, and his relatively sophisticated understanding of the means by which he can manipulate the media to do his work: "If we can get the press there, we don't need to send out a press release."[120] While the media attention has made people aware of Operation Rescue and catalyzed previously quiescent pro-life sympathizers to action, it is unlikely that the publicity has altered anyone's opinion on abortion, given the immobility of public opinion on this issue.[121] In fact former NRLC president Willke argued that Operation Rescue's publicity has had a negative impact because it is equated with the whole pro-life movement. He is concerned with what ethicists call the logic of "moral calculus": which strategy will save more lives? He draws a different conclusion regarding publicity than does Terry. "In the sixties, the media were behind the civil rights movement. They are not behind the pro-life movement. They portray those demonstrators as a bunch of kooks, religious fanatics." The sit-ins may stop a few abortions, "but if it postpones the reversal of *Roe v. Wade* for just one day by turning people off to the cause, that's 4,000 babies."[122]

In the view of most pro-life moderates, Operation Rescue has undercut one of the larger objectives of the right-to-life movement: to gain credibility for the pro-life position with the American people in order to gain support for a constitutional amendment banning abortion. And as long as public opinion is understood to be shaped by and reflected in the print and electronic media, pro-life activists of all stripes believe that they should pitch their efforts toward gaining favorable coverage. The jury is still out regarding public opinion outside the movement, but evidence suggests that Operation Rescue mobilized its opposition and generated hostility from those uninvolved in the issue. In a recent poll by Terry's hometown newspaper, 70 percent of county residents said they disapproved of Operation Rescue's demonstrating near abortion clinics, and 90 percent disapproved of the organization's blocking or entering the clinics illegally. Sixty-three percent of those polled had a positive impression of the pro-choice movement, while only 37 percent were favorably impressed with the pro-life movement. However, while the Southern Tier clinic of Binghamton is still in business after enduring multiple rescues, local doctors no longer provide abortions in the counties' two clinics. Some doctors, on rare occasion or in cases of therapeutic diagnosis, will do abortions in local hospitals.[123]

In the pro-choice camp, there has been in the last three years a resurgence in organizing formerly complacent activists. The most direct impact has been the multiple lawsuits discussed earlier, the product of sophisticated and strategic organizing on the part of feminist and pro-choice leaders against Operation Rescue. At the grassroots level, it is difficult to determine exactly what role Operation Rescue has played in that revitalization, since its period of greatest visibility has coincided with new conservative U.S. Supreme Court appointments. These developments, and especially the *Webster* decision, have also helped rouse a slumbering pro-choice movement, as was clear in the 1989 March for Women's Lives in Washington, D.C. One recently mobilized activist in her twenties explained that the *Webster* decision inspired her commitment. "I always figured someone else would fight the battle. But the Webster decision was such an affront. Before, I didn't pay much attention to Randy Terry. He was just some jerk chaining himself to things."[124] Of course, politically it is advantageous to paint the opposition in the darkest possible colors. As a strategist recently pointed out in a discussion of post-*Webster* pro-choice organizing, "From a tactical standpoint, the movement's most extreme opponents, like Operation Rescue, are its strongest allies."[125]

From a purely financial point of view, this seems to be the case. In the first three months of 1989, the National Abortion Rights Action League (NARAL) raised $300,000, ending the quarter with $347,000 in the bank; during that same three months, the NRLC raised $7,000, ending the quarter with $51,000 in the bank.[126] The ranks and annual budget of the National Organization for Women, which brought several of the legal suits against Operation Rescue, nearly doubled from 1988 to 1989.[127]

While the impact of Operation Rescue on the pro-choice and pro-life movements is important, to analyze the group only within the framework of the abortion debate is to misunderstand its significance. It is intent on mobilizing people not just to stop abortion but to impose on American society at large a conservative Christian culture. Until 1988, most direct action militants were Catholic. Terry has succeeded in catalyzing the direct participation of thousands of evangelicals and fundamentalists in anti-abortion politics who had never before been involved in political action. In his recruiting pitch, Terry addresses this "late arrival" of evangelicals to right-to-life activity with the quip, "There are no heroes in this movement; we are all fifteen years too late."[128] Charging Christians with apathy and their need to repent for the neglect of the abortion issue, he compares them to Christians who did not resist the Nazis in Germany during the Holocaust. He has managed to mobilize evangelical Christians through direct appeal, the mass media, and churches.[129] Some estimate that the pro-life movement is now anywhere from one-third to two-thirds evangelical-fundamentalist. Willke (a Catholic) described it as "an awakening from its slumber of literally millions of deeply committed Protestant folk. . . . This is no longer a Catholic movement. This is very much ecumenical [almost] to the point of being a Protestant Christian Movement."[130] Terry did not create the fundamentalist interest so much as "he caught the wave of evangelical involvement just as it began to crest."[131]

Garry Wills, in a provocative essay on Operation Rescue, suggests that these newly mobilized Christians represent a distinct group on America's religious and political landscape. They are not interested in the eschatological disputes that dominated fundamentalism in a prior generation but in issues that seem to shape their immediate world. All the key leaders and many of the rescuers are, like Terry, in their thirties, with a particular outlook that marks them as a distinct generation in the emergent world of conservative Christian activism in America. Many came of age during the mobilization of the Christian Right in the 1970s and accept that movement as a model of political action. As Wills notes:

> While paying their respect to elders who helped evangelicals get engaged in politics—to Jerry Falwell or Pat Robertson—the Operation Rescue leaders are also gently dismissive of them as armchair warriors, people resting on their laurels and not taking the heat of today's battle. . . . Terry's people talk of the televangelists as tied down to their assets, like bishops in their dioceses. They see themselves as roving carriers of a burning message . . . and the ties they form with other opponents of abortion speed the process, already noticed by sociologists, whereby evangelism has been losing its hostility to Jews, Catholics, blacks and Hispanics.[132]

Others have explored the generational location of Operation Rescue from the perspective of gender and class. Noting that 56 percent of arrested activists are men and half of Operation Rescue's active participants are in their twenties and thirties, author Susan Faludi sketches a profile of these fundamentalist men of the "late baby-boom generation" as sociological mirrors of Randall Terry, with an economic grudge against "careerist" women. They "not only missed the political engagement of the sixties but were cheated out of that era's affluent bounty," she observes. "They are downwardly mobile sons, condemned by the eighties economy to earning less than their fathers, unable to buy homes or support families. . . . These are men who are losing ground and at the same time see women gaining it."[133]

Terry has transformed this marginality into a virtue; his "rescuers" are the righteous remnant, opposed not only to unbelievers but also to many pastors he describes as "pillars of Jello." They "seek to upset no one, to step on no toes. . . . With an eye for the offering plate or having the biggest church in town, many seek to protect their own welfare and glory, rather than the welfare and glory of God's Kingdom."[134] Acting against what they see as the tepid Christianity of the mainstream, rescuers hope to "defeat the abortion holocaust, restore religious and civil liberties to individuals, bring justice to our judicial system, see common decency return, and the godless, hedonistic, sexually perverted mindset of today pushed back into the closet—and hopefully back to hell where it came from."[135]

Recriminalizing abortion is only the first domino to fall in the campaign to reverse the effects of the liberal hegemony of the 1960s and 1970s.

> The future of America . . . will depend . . . in part upon the rescue movement. If we do not bring this nation through rescues, through upheavals, through repentance, then America is not going to make it. We are launching a whole political wing. We have thousands of people who have risked their freedom, had their arms broken. For them to work a precinct to get a pro-life official elected is a piece of cake. We have an *army* of people. . . . Child killing will fall, child pornography and pornography will follow, euthanasia, infanticide—we'll totally reform the public education system . . . we'll take back the culture.[136]

Dramatic demonstrations bring these issues to the public by gaining media attention, but perhaps they are most significant for the participants themselves. Political performances reinforce for activists the righteousness of their own cause. Carrying a picket or blockading a doorway is a radicalizing event for the thousands of conservative Christians who follow Terry's lead. "Being dragged by the neck to a paddy wagon is an epiphany."[137]

Operation Rescue and Contemporary Fundamentalism

Whatever face Operation Rescue presents to the outside, it is clear from the writings and speeches of its founder and leader, Randall Terry, that he and those inspired by him see it as a vehicle for Christian social action. Terry puts no exclusive labels on Operation Rescue. His home church is an independent ministry; his training was nondenominational; he seems uninterested in discussing his theological position on the millennium. These characteristics, coupled with his embrace of Catholics and even a few non-Christians in the movement, and his emphasis on political involvement (including law breaking) are a break with the long-standing emphasis on separatism that has characterized American fundamentalism for nearly half a century.

However, if one looks at Operation Rescue historically, one sees parallels to the situation of seventy years ago when fundamentalism first emerged as a powerful presence on the American landscape.[138] Contemporary struggles over abortion, school prayer, and pornography draw fundamentalists (and others) into political battles in much the same way that opposition to the teaching of evolution in the schools mobilized fundamentalist reformers in the early part of the century. The militantly antimodernist fundamentalists of the 1920s had multiple cultural, theological, and organizational roots, but they shared a developing premillennial theology that recommended separation from the world.[139] Nonetheless, fundamentalists formed an active social movement opposed to both the increasing secularization of American life and the liberalizing trends in most Christian denominations. When the activists of the 1920s failed to halt the "modernizing" of American Protestantism and when the press and public reaction following the Scopes trial in 1925 made clear that fundamentalists were increasingly marginal to American culture, the fundamentalists retreated from active engagement in both secular arenas and mainline religion in order to develop their own networks of exclusive institutions.[140] Although there were some calls to activism in the 1940s and 1950s from both the right and the left, the central activity and strategy of fundamentalism for five decades was personal witnessing.[141]

By the 1970s, the expanding organizational structures and the increasing numbers of mainstream middle-class Americans attracted to evangelical Christianity had given fundamentalist activists the infrastructure, intellectual framework, social base, and membership to carry out successful political action. For some, crossing the boundary into the corrupt world undermined the legitimacy of people like Falwell and his organization, the Moral Majority.[142] Operation Rescue has gone much farther than Falwell in breaking the boundary of separation between Christian activists and the world. Fundamentalists who are strict about separatism in particular take Terry to task for making alliances and contact with those outside the group—including Catholics and Jews. Terry justifies this action in biblical terms: "We must serve fellow Christians in whatever way their need requires. But our duty does not stop there. The Lord commands His disciple to serve those *outside* the faith; those who might not value or appreciate our help—or those who might even despise it."[143]

Clearly, it is a mistake to think this movement is simply about abortion. Fundamentalist militance in America has never confined itself to a single issue, and Operation Rescue is the latest incarnation of the fundamentalist impulse to impose its religious culture on others. For "rescuers," fighting abortion is simply a first step in reversing America's "moral decline," much as opposition to the teaching of evolution was considered a way to fight secularization in the 1920s. For these new Christian soldiers, the boundaries of separation that restrained fundamentalist activism for half a century are virtually gone.

In fact, despite Terry's frequent references to the Bible and the ideological and theological basis of the movement in the writings of Francis Schaeffer, there has been a conscious attempt to avoid sectarianism within this activist sect. Operation Rescue has formed an identity rooted in a shared "orthopraxis" more than a shared "orthodoxy."[144] The fact that Roman Catholics and even Jews have joined with conservative Protestant participants—an alliance enabled by the low level of structural organization of the movement itself—has been crucial to the success of the rescues. As a result there is greater emphasis on ritual action than on dogmatic interpretation of the action; the rescues themselves are highly organized and ritualistic, although the ideology and the organizational structure are not. Participants share a sense of moral outrage at abortion, coupled with the conviction that they are together opposing the most brutal results of modern American secularization. There is no evidence to date that Operation Rescue is, as fundamentalist protest movements have been elsewhere in the world, a vehicle for conversion to a specific denominational or sectarian orientation. The point is not to render members more Christian but to render society more fundamentalist, in the larger Judeo-Christian sense. This activist, open fundamentalist movement is indeed a new hybrid on the religious horizon.

For this coalition of fundamentalist and conservative Christians and Catholics, taking action in the "real world" has had real world consequences. In the pluralist setting of America, displaying contempt for the rights of others and the legal system—even in the name of God—carries stiff penalties. However, for a movement that took a martyred and militant Christ, suffering at the hands of the Romans, as a primary image, the punitive actions of the state have been only confirmation of its righteousness.

Whether Operation Rescue manages to surmount the legal obstacles imposed on it and continue its blockades or whether it transforms itself into Terry's Christian Defense Council (with an agenda that, ironically, resembles that of the lobbyists and letter writers he disdains), there is no question that the movement has had a discernible impact. Through an organization committed to direct action, Randall Terry has revived long-term right-to-life loyalists who had become discouraged at the minimal gains of fifteen years of legislative efforts. While he has strengthened the pro-life cause by delivering thousands of new activists, he has also divided the movement because of his law-breaking tactics and the controversial media coverage he has attracted, which has seriously altered the public image of right-to-lifers in the late 1980s and early 1990s. Perhaps of greatest significance, he has offered a new generation of the ever-increasing number of young evangelical Christians in America an incontrovertible experience of militant fundamentalist social action. What the consequences of this transformation will be are difficult to predict. What *is* clear is that the future envisioned by these warriors, now rearming themselves with secular political knowledge, is nothing short of the "rescue" of a nation on fundamentalist Christian terms.

Acknowledgments

For their support and insightful comments on earlier drafts of this paper, I thank Fred Myers and R. Scott Appleby. I also thank Dick Norton for his patience and encouragement. I am grateful to a number of journalists who have sent me their articles and discussed ideas with me, particularly Susan Church, Jeff Davis, and Barbara Brotman. Thanks are due to documentary-maker Julie Gustafson for sharing her ideas with me and for letting me look at many hours of her videotapes for a work-in-progress on the abortion controversy, particularly her interviews with Randall Terry and her complete documentation of the October 1988 rescue in Vestal, New York. I also am grateful to Ann Baker of the 80 Percent Majority for comments and information resources, as well as Meg McLagan, my research assistant during 1989–90, for providing an excellent "clipping service." Some of the material on the background of the right-to-life movement is drawn from my book, *Contested Lives: The Abortion Debate in an American Community* (Berkeley: University of California Press, 1989).

Notes

1. Randall A. Terry, *Operation Rescue* (Springdale, Pa.: Whitaker House, 1988), p. 211.

2. Terry, *Operation Rescue,* p. 25.

3. Ibid, p. 24.

4. Ibid. Interestingly, over 25 percent of those arrested were single and in their thirties. Ann Baker, personal communication.

5. Randy Frame, "Rescue Theology," *Christianity Today,* 17 November 1989, pp. 46–48. Many activists have been arrested multiple times, so arrest numbers are larger than the number of protesters.

6. In an interview with Garry Wills ("Evangels of Abortion," *New York Review of Books,* 15 June 1989, pp. 15–21) Randall Terry told Wills, "You have to read Schaeffer's *Christian Manifesto* if you want to understand Operation Rescue" (p. 15), and that he considers Schaeffer "the greatest modern Christian philosopher" (p. 18).

According to Wills, in his studies at Elim Bible Institute, a homiletics teacher assigned three of Schaeffer's books and screened the film "What Ever Happened to the Human Race?" made in 1979 by Schaeffer with evangelical doctor C. Everett Koop who later served the Reagan administration as surgeon general. The film, which analyzes abortion as a symptom of the decline of Western civilization, "had a big impact on Terry" (p. 18).

7. Wills, "Evangels of Abortion," p. 15.

8. Terry, *Operation Rescue,* p. 25.

9. This quote is from Julie Gustafson's videotaped interview with Randall Terry in Operation Rescue's Binghamton offices, 27 October 1988.

10. Why women became the mainstay of the right-to-life movement in the 1970s may seem both obvious and puzzling to observers. My recent book *Contested Lives: The Abortion Debate in an American Community* (Berkeley: University of California Press, 1989) is a study of female activists on both sides of the debate. Briefly, I suggest that women's attraction to this cause is an expression of different social solutions to the felt contradiction between mothering and other kinds of labor in this society. I argue that this takes very specific form as consciousness emerges from the different experiences of historical generations of women and the dialectics between those generations.

11. Kristin Luker, *The Politics of Motherhood* (Berkeley: University of California Press, 1984), p. 137; Faye Ginsburg, *Contested Lives,* chap. 3.

12. For example, contrary to current popular stereotype, the NRLC included a vocal "progressive" component from the outset. Pro-lifers for Survival, an antinuke pacifist group, was founded in 1971, and Feminists for Life organized soon after. The "progressives" continue to have a minor influence and visibility within the movement. Their articles appear regularly in national NRLC publications, and they have urged and gained NRLC support of liberal candidates who are against abortion. For discussion of this, see Connie Paige, *The Right-to-Lifers* (New York: Summit Books, 1983), p. 223; and Ginsburg, *Contested Lives,* chap. 3.

13. The Hyde amendment, named for its sponsor Henry Hyde (R, Ill.), is attached to annual appropriations for the Department of Health and Human Services. First introduced in 1974, it catalyzed eleven weeks of congressional debate over the question of the government's obligations to provide support for abortion services. Since then, each Congress has accepted a version of the Hyde amendment.

14. I include in the term "New Right" both social and political conservatives who sought to be identified with the term itself, including Phyllis Schlafly and her Eagle Forum, Jerry Falwell and his Moral Majority, and Richard Viguerie and Paul Weyrich and their National Conservative Political Action Committee, to name some of the more prominent players.

15. There was little pretense as to the goals behind the New Right's "pro-family" agenda. As New Right political strategist Paul Weyrich commented in a special report on his movement in a 1979 issue of *Conservative Digest,* "The New Right is looking for issues that fit the bill . . . gun control, abortion, taxes and crime. . . . Yes, they're emotional issues but they're better than talking about capital formation."

16. See Alan Crawford, *The New Right and the Politics of Resentment* (New York: Pantheon, 1980); *Conservative Digest,* "The New Right: A Special Report," June 1979.

17. The "seamless garment" argument, identified with Cardinal Bernardin of Chicago, extends the pro-life position on abortion to include opposition to capital punishment, nuclear weapons, and child

abuse. This faction has been active in setting up centers to give mothers with "crisis pregnancies" support. For a discussion of this, see Wills, "Evangels of Abortion," p. 19, and "Save the Babies," p. 27. However, as Ann Baker points out (personal communication), "People are not being excommunicated from the Catholic Church because they publicly disagree with the Peace Pastoral or the Pastoral on Economic Justice. Disciplinary action is only taken against pro-choice Catholics."

18. Connie Paige, *The Right-to-Lifers*, p. 223.

19. Jim Wallis, "Coming Together on the Sanctity of Life," *Sojourners* 9, no. 11 (1980): 4.

20. In 1979, NRLC staff person Judie Brown left that organization and began working with New Right leader Paul Weyrich to set up the American Life Lobby (ALL), while her husband, Paul, set up the Life Amendment Political Action Committee (LAPAC). With aid from New Right fund-raiser and strategist Richard Viguerie, and with a mandate to organize fundamentalist Christians, ALL claimed sixty-eight thousand on its mailing lists by 1981.

21. In addition to efforts to simply ban the procedure, the bills and ordinances raised questions regarding requirements for parental or spousal consent; hospitalization for second- and third-trimester abortions; disposal of fetal remains; informing a woman of the "humanlike" characteristics of the fetus; a twenty-four-hour waiting period between the scheduling and carrying out of an abortion; municipal zoning and regulation of abortion clinics; and the presence of a second doctor during late abortions when the fetus could be viable.

22. The justices' ruling did not overturn *Roe v. Wade* since they declined to rule on phases regarding when human life begins. However, they decided that it was constitutional for states to set limits on abortion services, specifically the banning of the use of state facilities and the prohibiting of state employees from performing abortions. They also upheld a provision requiring physicians to perform viability tests on fetuses esti-

mated at twenty weeks' gestation. In effect, the Court gave a green light to state legislatures to place restrictions on abortion.

23. In July 1976, the Court ruled in *Planned Parenthood of Central Missouri v. Danforth* that it was unconstitutional for a husband or for parents to have veto power in a contested abortion. In 1977, in *Belotti v. Baird*, the Court ruled that states could require parental notification in the case of an abortion for a minor, provided that alternative means of obtaining consent were available, i.e., the approval of a judge if just cause were shown as to why parents should not be informed. See Eva R. Rubin, *Abortion, Politics, and the Courts* (New York: Greenwood Press, 1987).

24. The cases ruled on were challenges to local ordinances passed and challenged in Akron, Ohio, and Virginia, Minnesota. In brief, the court struck down as unconstitutional the following restrictions: abortions after twelve weeks of pregnancy must be done in hospitals only; physicians must inform patients of dangers of and alternatives to abortion; physicians must enforce a twenty-four-hour waiting period for abortions; and physicians must dispose of fetal remains in a "humane and sanitary" manner. See Rubin, *Abortion, Politics, and the Courts*, p. 149.

25. See Ginsburg, *Contested Lives*, pp. 46–54.

26. The figures cited are from a March 1985 report, "Summary of Clinic Violence as Reported to the National Abortion Federation," National Abortion Federation, 900 Pennsylvania Ave, S.E., Washington, D.C., 20003. Only about 40 percent of all the arsons and bombings since 1977 have been solved and the perpetrators convicted.

27. Jacqueline Forrest and Stanley Henshaw, "The Harassment of U.S. Abortion Providers," *Family Planning Perspectives* 19, no. 1 (1987): 9–13.

28. Dallas A. Blanchard and Terry J. Prewitt, "The Gideon Project: Religious Violence and Abortion in America Today" (unpublished manuscript).

29. For accounts of abortion bombers and arsonists, see Teresa Carpenter, "Four

Who Bombed in God's Name," *Village Voice,* 27 August 1985, pp. 19–26; Samuel Freedman, "Abortion Bombings Suspect," *New York Times,* 7 May 1987; and Martin Mawyer, "Bombing Clinics Causes Conflict within Pro-Life Movement," *Fundamentalist Journal,* March 1985, pp. 59–60.

30. Blanchard and Prewitt, *The Gideon Project,* p. 391.

31. Investigations were carried out by the Bureau of Alcohol, Tobacco, and Firearms Abuse. The FBI's jurisdiction is "true terrorism" that aims to "overthrow the Government."

32. Blanchard and Prewitt, *The Gideon Project,* p. 257.

33. Ibid, p. 87.

34. National Abortion Federation figures cited in Blanchard and Prewitt, *The Gideon Project,* p. 258.

35. For example, in March 1985, the National Association of State Attorneys General petitioned the Justice Department to investigate abortion clinic violence and "illegal harassment and intimidation of people who work in or visit abortion clinics." Ibid., p. 107.

36. Ted Robert Gurr, "Political Terrorism: Historical Antecedents and Contemporary Trends," in Ted R. Gurr, ed., *Violence in America,* vol. 2 (Newbury Park, Calif.: Sage Publications, 1989), p. 209.

37. I use the common dictionary definition of "terror" as an intense fear that is somewhat prolonged and may refer to imagined or future dangers.

38. Francis Wilkinson, "The Gospel according to Randall Terry," *Rolling Stone,* 5 October 1989, p. 91.

39. Terry, *Operation Rescue.* For example, chaps. 11 and 12 are entitled, respectively, "There's a War Going On" and "Called to the Front Lines."

40. Quote from interview with Francis Wilkinson in *Rolling Stone,* p. 86.

41. Susan Faludi, "Where Did Randy Go Wrong?" *Mother Jones,* November 1989, p. 24.

42. This is an estimate drawn from reports of the number of demonstrators at events listed in newspaper accounts, Operation Rescue newsletters, and pro-choice reports on counterdemonstrations.

43. See Tamar Lewin, "With Thin Staff and Thick Debt, Anti-Abortion Group Faces Struggle," *New York Times,* 11 June 1990; and Barbara Brotman, "Abortion Opponents Regroup," *Chicago Tribune,* 20 May 1990.

44. Terry, *Operation Rescue,* p. 35.

45. For example, in August of 1983, Scheidler led a protest demonstration in front to the Catholic hospital that had appointed Dr. Hector Zevallos, an abortion clinic owner who had been kidnapped and held at gunpoint for a week in 1982 by two pro-lifers who called themselves the "Army of God." En route to the protest, Scheidler stopped to visit the wife of the man convicted of that kidnapping and of bombing two clinics. Scheidler made a point of informing the media of this detour. See Theodore Roeser, "The Pro-Life Movement's Holy Terror," *Chicago Reader* 12, no. 44 (1983): 13–20.

46. Quoted in an interview with Garry Wills, in an article "Save the Babies," in *Time,* 1 May 1989, p. 27.

47. Terry, *Operation Rescue,* p. 11.

48. This idea was used by Susan Faludi in her essay "Where Did Randy Go Wrong?"

49. The following sketch of Randall Terry and Operation Rescue draws on a number of interviews and investigative pieces done on the movement since 1988. Much of the material is redundant. I used the following pieces for this section: Susan Church, "Abortion: A Community Speaks," *Binghamton Press & Sun Bulletin,* 19 November 1989, and "Abortion Battle Comes Home" and "Terry's Absence Raises Questions about Operation Rescue," ibid., 19 and 20 November 1989; Jeff Davis, "Randall Terry's Crusade," ibid., 22 January 1989, and "Terry's Fight Creates Family Feud," ibid., 24 January 1989; Susan Faludi, "Where Did Randy Go Wrong?"; Mary Suh and Lydia Denworth, "The Gathering Storm: Operation Rescue," *Ms.,* April 1989, pp. 92–94; Randall Terry, *Operation Rescue*

(Binghamton: Whitaker House, 1988); Francis Wilkinson, "The Gospel according to Randall Terry," pp. 85–92; Garry Wills, "Evangels of Abortion," pp. 15–21; "Save the Babies," pp. 26–28.

50. Quoted in Faludi, "Where Did Randy Go Wrong?" p. 25.

51. Elim is not a degree-granting institution, so completion of three years has no equivalent to an undergraduate degree or a master's of divinity for people preparing for the ministry. Rather, its curriculim focuses on proof-texting the Bible. Ann Baker, personal communication.

52. Terry, *Operation Rescue*, p. 17.

53. Faludi, "Where Did Randy Go Wrong?" pp. 61–62.

54. As Terry describes it, "A rescue mission happens when one or two, or a group of people go to an abortion clinic and either walk inside to the waiting room, offering an alternative to the mothers, or sit around the door of the abortion clinic before it opens to prevent the slaughter of innocent lives." When demonstrators refuse to leave, they are charged with criminal trespass and arrested. Usually they go limp, slowing down the police in order to "buy as much time as possible for the children."

55. Faludi, "Where Did Randy Go Wrong?" p. 61.

56. Terry, *Operation Rescue*, p. 22.

57. Wills, in his 1989 article "Save the Babies," describes Andrews as "the one authentic hero of the pro-life movement." She was jailed for over two years after attempting to disengage a suction machine used for abortions. In jail, she was put in solitary confinement because of her "loving noncooperation" with authorities (p. 27).

58. Wills. "Save the Babies, p. 28.

59. Wills, "Evangels of Abortion," p. 19.

60. Scheidler remains largely unacknowledged by Terry as an influence. Suh and Denworth interpret that fact as an indication that Terry became Scheidler's "front man" when Scheidler had to scale down his presence due to negative media coverage and a 1986 lawsuit against him by the National Organization for Women (NOW). As evidence, they cite Terry's involvements with Scheidler's protests in Pensacola in 1986. By contrast, Susan Faludi suggests that Terry usurped Scheidler's power, and implies that once Terry got the spotlight, he was unwilling to share it.

61. Wills, "Save the Babies," p. 28.

62. When the order became a permanent injunction early in 1989, Operation Rescue immediately incurred a $50,000 fine for two days of protests at New York's Margaret Sanger Clinic in January 1989. Nadine Brozan, "Effectiveness of Abortion Protests Is Debated," *New York Times*, 8 May 1989, p. 28.

63. Wilkinson, "The Gospel according to Randall Terry," p. 86.

64. Ibid.

65. "Days of Abortion Protest End with 40 More Atlanta Arrests," *New York Times*, 9 October 1988.

66. Wilkinson, "The Gospel according to Randall Terry," p. 86.

67. Wills, "Evangels of Abortion," p. 21. Between February and November 1989, Operation Rescue, Southern California, raised approximately $1.5 million, most of which was sent to Binghamton. Ann Baker, personal communication. Most of the information on Operation Rescue's finances and relations with other political organizations is drawn from depositions made by Lynn Schopf, the group's accountant, on 5 January 1989 and by Terry on 7 July 1988 for legal suits brought by NOW and other complainants.

68. Michelle Hiskey, "Thousands Join Rescue Movement around Nation," *Christianity Today*, 9 December 1988, p. 52.

69. Kim Lawton, "Operation Rescue," *Christianity Today*, 6 June 1989, p. 54.

70. Kathy Dobie, "With God on Their Side: Operation Rescue Hits L.A.," *Village Voice*, 11 April 1989, pp. 28–36.

71. Suh and Denworth, "The Gathering Storm: Operation Rescue," p. 92.

72. Quoted in Brozan, "Effectiveness of Abortion Protests Is Debated."

73. Garry Wills, the historian and scholar

of American culture observed in an essay written in the summer of 1989 that Terry's "contribution to the effort was not only his organizing on a larger scale but his disciplining of the movement by adoption of common tactics for all the demonstrations, which had been improvised and unpredictable (in the Scheidler manner) up to this point." Wills, "Evangels of Abortion," p. 19.

74. See n. 35 for details.

75. Quoted by Ronald Smothers, "Organizer of Abortion Protests Is Jailed in Atlanta," *New York Times,* 12 July 1989, p. A10.

76. Susan Church, "Tactics Change as Time Passes," *Binghamton Press & Sun Bulletin,* 20 November 1989, p. 5A.

77. Terry, *Operation Rescue,* p. 175.

78. Jerry Schwartz, "Abortion Protester Jailed after Objecting to Fine," *New York Times,* 6 October 1989.

79. Operation Rescue was found guilty of violating the civil rights of women seeking abortions on the basis of an 1871 law drafted to prevent Ku Klux Klan activity. Operation Rescue has challenged the ruling, and the case, *Bray v. Alexandria Women's Health Center,* will be heard before the U.S. Supreme Court during 1991–92.

80. Constance Hays, "Abortion Foes Lose Appeal on Protests," *New York Times,* 21 September 1989, p. A1.

81. The Racketeer Influenced and Corrupt Organizations (RICO) Law, written in 1970, was aimed at organized crime. The case against Operation Rescue, *NOW et al. v. Scheidler et al.,* using this law was brought by NOW, Planned Parenthood, NARAL, and a number of clinics. NOW claimed that Operation Rescue members were acting like racketeers, trying to frighten away pregnant women and health care workers from clinics. In that sense, they argued, Operation Rescue was engaged in extortion and the use of force to deny rights to others. Operation Rescue has been fined $150,000 in New York; other anti-abortion groups have been fined $350,000. Alan Dershowitz of Harvard Law School feels this application is too broad. "Whatever you can say about these demonstrators, they're not racketeers. They're not doing it for a financial motive. The idea that you can terrorize protestors with the threat of bankruptcy is an attack on democracy." See David Shribman, "NOW's Use of RICO against Attacks by Groups on Abortion Clinics Stirs Debate on Law's Intent," *Wall Street Journal,* 22 May 1990, p. A22. On 28 May 1991, district Judge James Holderman dismissed *NOW v. Scheidler* on the grounds that the defendants are not financially competitive with the plaintiffs. His decision will be appealed by the plaintiffs. See Ann Baker, "NOW v. Scheidler," *Campaign Report* 4, no. 13: 7.

82. "Rescue Bails Out," *Time,* 12 February 1990, p. 29.

83. Quoted in Kim Lawton, "Operation Rescue HQ Closed," *Christianity Today,* 5 March 1990.

84. The fines were for breaking injunctions preventing people from blocking women's access to abortion clinics.

85. Craig Wolff, "Judge Fines 10 for Protests over Abortions" *New York Times,* 28 February 1990.

86. Quoted in Tamar Lewin, "With Thin Staff and Thick Debt," p. A16. It should be noted that the protesters at St. Patrick's paid their fines and respected court orders, unlike the Operation Rescue activists. Violating the court order was the reason for the fine.

87. Ibid.

88. Ibid.

89. Personal communication, Susan Church, journalist at the *Binghamton Press & Sun Bulletin.*

90. Randall A. Terry, letter to supporters, 15 October 1990, Binghamton, N.Y.

91. D.C. Project II brochure, n.d., Greenbelt, Md.

92. Associated Press, "Judge Orders U.S. Marshals to Prevent Closing of Abortion Clinics," *New York Times,* 30 July 1991.

93. Gwen Ifill, "1871 Law at Issue in Abortion Dispute," *New York Times,* 11 August 1991.

94. Isabel Wilkerson, "Drive against Abortion Finds a Symbol: Wichita," *New York Times,* 4 August 1991.

95. In early 1989, Father Norman Weslin, a former lieutenant colonel in the U.S. Army paratroopers, joined with activists Joan Andrews and Randall Terry to form what he describes as a "rapid deployment force, a special group of 50–200 dedicated persons who will fly to any part of the nation on short notice to assist any rescue operations with needed reinforcements." Stanley Interrante, *Wanderer,* 16 February 1989. Originally he called this group the "Victim Souls of the Unborn Christ Child" and later the "Lambs of Christ."

According to Ann Baker, who runs a pro-choice watchdog organization called the "80% Majority," the group chose its own targets and hopes there will be local support. "Lambs" are supposed to identify with the fetus, giving as their name either Baby John or Baby Jane Doe. They refuse to give their names or walk anywhere from the time they are arrested until they are sentenced. The period of incarceration accomplishes several goals: it ties up local systems, it provides a focus for fundraising, and it allows the core group members—who have no jobs—free room and board. It appears that there are between fifty and one hundred dedicated itinerant militants who follow Weslin's leadership directly, although there are others who behave similarly who are not as extreme. Three other organizations—Victim Souls, Pro-Life Police, and Rescue Outreach—offer support and probably fundraising. In 1990–91, "Lambs" blockaded clinics in Burlington, Vt.; Pittsburgh, Pa.; Toledo, Ohio; Appleton, Wis.; Youngstown, Ohio; Lufkin, Texas; South Bend, Ind.; Dobbs Ferry, N.Y.; Asheville, N.C.; and Fargo, N.D. See Ann Baker, "A Report on the Direct Action Militants," *Campaign Report* 4, no. 9: 5–8.

What is particularly interesting from the perspective of this volume is that this group, made up of radically conservative Catholics, is cooperating so completely with the new breed of fundamentalists represented by Terry.

96. Don Terry, "Face of Protests in Wichita Is Religious and Undoubting," *New York Times,* 12 August 1991.

97. Ibid.

98. Ann Baker, personal communication, August 1991.

99. I. Wilkerson, "Drive against Abortion."

100. Don Terry, "Faces of Protest."

101. Keith Tucci, letter to supporters from Operation Rescue, 6 September 1991, Somerville, S.C.

102. Quoted in Lewin, "With Thin Staff and Thick Debt."

103. Barbara Brotman, "Abortion Opponents Regroup," p. 9.

104. *Rescue Report,* June 1990, Operation Rescue.

105. "National Rescue Recap," *Operation Rescue National Rescuer,* August–September 1991, p. 5.

106. Tucci letter.

107. When the writer, Francis Wilkerson, in his 1989 interview published in *Rolling Stone,* queried Terry about the comparisons made between him and Martin Luther King, Terry replied that he discourages it. "Moments later, however, Terry has the temerity to explain that his proper place will be a matter determined by history. 'The applause or contempt of contemporaries means very little,' he adds with a flourish" (p. 92).

108. Quoted in Lyn Cryderman, "A Movement Divided," *Christianity Today,* 12 August 1988, p. 48.

109. Such activities were also denounced by right-wing Christian reconstructionists because they are in violation of civil law, and because they "violate the Christian presupposition that change comes only through God's power." Ammerman, *Bible Believers,* p. 80. See also Randy Frame, "Atlanta Gets Tough," *Christianity Today,* 4 November 1988, p. 35.

110. David Coffin, director of the Berea Study Center, quoted in interview with Randy Frame, "Rescue Theology," *Christianity Today,* 17 November 1989, p. 48.

111. These quotes are from a two-page statement released by the staff of Stanley's

church, the First Baptist Church, the largest congregation in Atlanta after Terry sought Stanley's endorsement during Operation Rescue demonstrations in Atlanta. The treatise is entitled "A Biblical Perspective on Civil Disobedience." See Randy Frame, "Atlanta Gets Tough," *Christianity Today,* p. 35.

112. "By misinterpreting 2 Corinthians 6:17 ["Therefore come out from their . . . midst and be separate"] many have neglected their God-given commands to influence society and serve their fellow man. . . . When salt [the Christian influence] stops preserving a nation, that society is going to deteriorate. There's no way around it." Terry, *Operation Rescue,* p. 51.

113. Quote from videotaped interview with Julie Gustafson in the Operation Rescue offices, Binghamton, N.Y., 27 October 1988.

114. Thomas Rose, "How Violence Occurs: A Theory and Review of the Literature," in Thomas Rose, ed., *Violence in America* (New York: Vintage Books, 1969), p. 30.

115. For an interesting discussion of right-to-life positions on this issue, see Randy Frame, "Rescue Theology," *Christianity Today,* 17 November 1989.

116. NRLC president Jack Willke, quoted in Lyn Cryderman, "A Movement Divided," *Christianity Today,* 12 August 1988, p. 49.

117. These points are raised by Blanchard and Prewitt regarding abortion bombers in *The Gideon Project,* pp. 266 and 394.

118. Dave Andrusko, "Zealots, Zanies, and Assorted Kooks: How the Main Media Interprets the Pro-Life Movement," in Dave Andrusko, ed., *The Pro-Life Movement: A Handbook for the 1980s* (Harrison, N.Y.: Life Cycle Press).

119. See Robert S. Lichter and Stanley Rothman, "The Media Elite," *Public Opinion* 96 (1981): 117–25.

120. Terry, from taped interview with Julie Gustafson.

121. On the bases of analyses by the Na-

tional Opinion Research Center and Gallup Polls between 1973 and 1985, it appears that the level of approval for legalized abortion has remained stable since 1973. Approximately 23 percent believe that abortion should be legal in all cases, while 19 to 22 percent believe it should be illegal. The remainder believe it should be legal in some cases, such as rape, incest, or endangerment to a woman's life. For further analyses of these data, see Daniel Granberg, "The Abortion Issue in the 1984 Elections," *Family Planning Perspectives* 19, no. 2: 59–62.

122. Willke, quoted in Lyn Cryderman, "A Movement Divided."

123. Susan Church, "Poll Shows Terry's Tactics Disliked," *Binghamton Press & Sun Bulletin,* 20 November 1989, p. 1.

124. Ibid.

125. Ibid.

126. "Anti-Abortion Group Lacks in Raising Funds," *New York Times,* 30 April 1990.

127. Jane Gross, "At NOW Convention, Goal Is Putting More Women in Office" *New York Times,* 1 July 1989, p. A12.

128. Quoted in Wills, "Save the Babies," p. 28.

129. One observer noted that a single speaking engagement before an evangelical congregation, with the endorsement of the pastor, can reap a busload of volunteers. Wilkinson, "The Gospel according to Randall Terry," p. 86.

130. Kim Lawton, "Can the Prolife Movement Succeed?" *Christianity Today,* 15 January 1988, p. 36.

131. Wills, "Evangels of Abortion," p. 21.

132. Ibid.

133. Faludi, "Where Did Randall Terry Go Wrong?" p. 25.

134. Terry, *Operation Rescue,* p. 172.

135. Ibid., p. 175.

136. Wilkinson, "The Gospel according to Randall Terry," p. 92.

137. Ibid.

138. Many scholars use broad under-

standings of fundamentalism as opposed to narrower ones that are based on definitive characteristics such as separatism and the theology of dispensational premillennialism. Among those who use the broader reading are Nancy Ammerman, *Bible Believers: Fundamentalists in the Modern World* (New Brunswick, N.J.: Rutgers University Press, 1987); Steve Bruce, *The Rise and Fall of the New Christian Right* (New York: Oxford University Press, 1988); Susan Harding, "Casting Out the Fundamentalist Other: The Scopes Trial and the Modern Apotheosis," talk delivered at the Society for Cultural Anthropology annual meetings, May 1990; George M. Marsden, *Fundamentalism and American Culture* (New York: Oxford University Press, 1980); Martin Marty, "Fundamentalism as A Social Phenomenon," *Bulletin of the American Academy of Arts and Sciences* 42, no. 2 (November 1988): 15–29. Ernest Sandeen, in his book *The Roots of Fundamentalism* (Chicago: University of Chicago Press, 1970), espouses the more specific definition of fundamentalism based on doctrinal differences.

139. Marsden, *Fundamentalism and American Culture*, p. 5.

140. Ibid., p. 186; Nancy Ammerman, "North American Protestant Fundamentalism," *Fundamentalisms Observed* (Chicago: University of Chicago Press, 1991), pp. 1–65.

141. According to Ammerman in her essay "North American Protestant Fundamentalism," by the 1950s the "choice facing the movement was between cultural relevance and cultural separation." In 1948, the evangelical leader Carl Henry argued in his influential book *Remaking the Modern Mind* that Christians should be socially and politically active in an effort to reestablish claims in a civilization dominated by secular humanism, while the quintessential separatist was the anticommunist right-wing crusader Carl McIntire (p. 58). Ammerman notes: "A few fundamentalists had joined the anticommunist crusades of the fifties, but most had remained relatively inactive in politics, preferring instead to put energy into the churches and institutions that made their view of the world possible. Evangelism and missions far outweighed social reform on their agendas" (p. 61).

142. Ammerman, "North American Protestant Fundamentalism."

143. Terry, *Operation Rescue*, p. 48.

144. I am indebted to Scott Appleby for this phrasing.

24

Buddhism, Politics, and Violence in Sri Lanka

Stanley J. Tambiah

In this essay the main question I shall probe is the extent to which, and the manner in which, Buddhism as a "religion," espoused by Sri Lankans of the late nineteeth and the twentieth centuries, has participated in the current ethnic conflict and collective violence in Sri Lanka. If it has participated, have there been changes in the nature of that participation over time? And if there have been changes, how are we to describe the changing or the changed shape of Buddhism itself as a lived reality?

A major aspect of this difficult task is the manner and extent to which issues defined as "Buddhist" issues, and the actors, both monks and laity, who have espoused "Buddhist" causes, have contributed to the outbreaks of collective violence in the form of ethnic riots.

My investigation must, it seems to me, begin with what has come to be called the "Buddhist revival" that began in the latter part of the nineteeth century. What I propose to do is to cover the century of Sri Lanka's history from the 1880s to the 1980s, focusing on the main landmarks and watersheds that figure in the story of how Buddhism as a collective and public religion was interwoven with the changing politics of the island, and how that meshing contributed to ethnic conflicts, especially the occurrence of various episodes of violence in the form of civilian riots and insurrections.

The Period of Buddhist Revivalism, 1860–1915

The most vivid and consequential formulation of Sinhala Buddhist revivalism with nationalist overtones was the anti-Christian movement begun by monks like Gunananda and Sumangala in mid-nineteeth century, then given an institutional and propagandist basis by the Theosophists, notably Colonel Henry Steele Olcott as their leader in the 1880s, and taken to its ideological limits by the charismatic Anagarika Dharmapala (1864–1933). Fortunately, this phase of Buddhist revivalism during the latter phase of the British Raj has been thickly documented, and in this essay I need only sketch in the main points.[1]

There is no doubt that Sinhala Buddhist revivalism and nationalism, in the form we can recognize today, had its origin in the late nineteeth and early twentieth centuries. In this earlier period we see most clearly the very contours of a movement that acted as a major shaper of a Sinhala consciousness and of a sense of national identity and purpose. The most significant activity of the Buddhist revivalism stimulated and sponsored by Colonel Olcott and the Buddhist Theosophical Society, founded in 1880, was the establishment of Buddhist schools to counter the near monopoly that the Protestant missions (and to a lesser extent the Catholic church) had over the educational system. This issue would surface again in the 1940s and 1950s.

Dharmapala first found his vocation and acquired his propagandist skills in association with the Theosophists but later broke away to propagate Buddhist causes as he envisaged them. His revivalism has been dubbed "Protestant Buddhism"—a useful label to a point, that is, if not overly associated with a world-transforming, this-worldly asceticism.

The major features of his Buddhist revivalism are as follows: a selective retrieval of norms from canonical Buddhism; a denigration of alleged non-Buddhist ritual practices and magical manipulations (an attitude probably influenced by Christian missionary denunciation of "heathen" beliefs and practices); the enunciation of a code for lay conduct, suited for the emergent Sinhalese urban middle class and business interests, which emphasized a puritanical sexual morality and etiquette in family life; and, most important of all, an appeal to the past glories of Buddhism and Sinhalese civilization celebrated in the *Mahavamsa* and other chronicles as a way of infusing the Sinhalese with a new nationalist identity and self-respect in the face of humiliations and disabilities suffered under British rule and Christian missionary influence.

For our purposes it is most relevant to note that Dharmapala's brand of Sinhala Buddhist revivalism and nationalism was supported by and served the interests of a rising Sinhala Buddhist middle class and a circle of businessmen, and that some of these were implicated in the anti-Muslim riots of 1915 directed against their competitors in the shape of Muslim shopkeepers and businessmen, who were branded as exploiters of the Sinhalese consumer public at large.[2]

Politics and Constitutional Progress, 1915–46

The time of the twilight of the British Raj was also the seedbed of a number of developments, both contradictory and complementary. They foreshadowed things to come.

A remarkable feature of the Buddhist fundamentalist and Sinhala nationalist movement spearheaded by Anagarika Dharmapala is that after the British Raj's show of armed strength and suppression of the 1915 riots, and its incarceration of the temperance leaders (which included F. R. and D. S. Senanayake), and Dharmapala's pro-longed absences in India where he concentrated on the recovery of Buddha Gaya for Buddhism, the movement itself seemed to lose prominence and surrendered the lime-light to a different cast of Sinhalese and Tamil politicians, who were to initiate a phase of collaboration rather than confrontation in their dealings with the British.

It seems as if the trauma of the riots—during which British officials, the police, and volunteers took punitive and disgracing actions against many Sri Lankan leaders, per-sons of education and high social standing—energized these leaders first to protest[3] and then, in a mood of dialogue, to form political associations in order to negotiate with authorities.

These leaders were educated in English, were in distinct ways Westernized in dress and style of life, and were dedicated to a policy of gradualism in seeking more political rights for the Ceylonese through constitutional means. The Ceylon Reform League was formed in 1916 and was subsequently transformed into the Ceylon National Congress in 1919, which through a series of respectful "memorials" to the Governor and the Colonial Office sought an increased representation for its elite supporters in the administration of the colony.

In fact the older nationalist thrust, focused as it was on religious and cultural revivalism, identity, and "uplift" through a rejection of Christian privilege and a West-ern lifestyle, seemed to be upstaged by the newer movement led by the Ceylon Na-tional Congress. This movement was committed to a gradualist program of winning political independence through concessions relating to representative government.[4]

In their deliberations with the Raj, the politicians of the Ceylon National Congress did gain political concessions. The two most important political gains, stemming from the Donoughmore Constitution, were the granting of universal franchise in 1931 (a bonus granted by the liberal commission against the wishes of most members of the congress who advocated a more restricted franchise entailing property and literacy qualifications for the voters) and of a large measure of internal autonomy to a State Council consisting of sixty-one members, the majority of whom (fifty) were to be elected through universal suffrage from territorial constituencies.

Radical Monks and the Legitimation of Monks' Participation in Politics

Before and during the very first general election of 1947 a group of extremist, able, Marxist-oriented Buddhist monks exploded on the political scene in support of the leftist parties, which were explicitly dedicated to secular politics and to the devaluation of religion in human affairs. How was this possible?

Before this election of 1947, individual *bhikkhus* (monks) may have supported certain political candidates who as *dayakas* (lay patrons) may have sought their bless-ings and legitimation. Such participation by monks was limited and informal; and where a Christian candidate had to be overcome, the slogan of Buddhism had been effective.

But now appeared a group of highly educated, vocal, and activist monks who were to set several precedents which would influence the public posture of many future monks. One was the unclouded and self-conscious pronouncement of the right and responsibility of monks to participate in politics, in matters to do with the public weal, and in the nationalist movement and decolonization process. The second was their banding together as a pressure group engaging in political activism. Thus, in a sense this new band of monks, who were labeled the "Vidyalankara Group"[5] by virtue of their association with Vidyalankara Pirivena, one of the monastic colleges on the island, remind us of monk activists like Gunananda, who stimulated Dharmapala, whose own revivalist-nationalist movement espoused by the laity superseded the role of the monks. Now, in 1946–47, the political monk reemerged in a full-fledged form.

The years 1946 and 1947 are a landmark because they witnessed the trenchant articulation of the debate, Should monks participate in politics? Out of this polemic emerged the self-conscious "political monk" in Sri Lanka. Though tested, rebuked, and even reviled by certain conservative establishment monks within the *sangha* (brotherhood of monks) and by many members of the laity, both pious Buddhists and iconoclastic "leftists," the political monks established their niche and their right to participate in politics within certain limits. They became part of the regular political scene. They numbered in many hundreds, they were accepted members of the sangha, and as we shall see they mobilized for action. (We shall investigate as we proceed to what extent such political monks and their ideologies and activities actually fanned the fires of ethnic and religious violence in subsequent times, especially in 1956 and 1958.)

It is relevant to take account of the writings of two scholar monks who propounded radical ideas at this time. Walpola Rahula (who would later author scholarly books on Buddhism[6] and also increasingly become conservative and chauvinistic) wrote in 1946 a book called *Bhikkhuge Urumaya* (The heritage of bhikkhus) in which he sought to establish that monks had from earliest times played a significant political and social role in Ceylon. K. Pannasara, principal of Vidyalankara Pirivena, in a riposte entitled *Bhikkhus and Politics* (1946) to the charge by United National Party (UNP) politicians (including the Senanayakes) that monks should stay away from elections, declared that politics included all aspects of public welfare and it was the vocation of monks to direct efforts to that end.[7]

The radical monks stepped up their criticism and increased their following when various sections of the clergy and laity—such as the chief priests of the Malwatte chapter of the Siyam Nikaya and of Ramanna Nikaya (a *nikaya* is a sect), the Maha Bodhi Society (founded in 1891 by Dharmapala), and the press—sought to censure them. Even the All-Ceylon Buddhist Congress, composed of lay Buddhists committed to the restoration of Buddhism, felt obliged to declare that no monk should seek or exercise the rights of a voter and that no monk should seek election to a political office.

The radical monks at a meeting held on June 1946 determined to form the Lanka Eksath Bhikkhu Mandalaya (LEBM) (Ceylon Union of Bhikkhus). This body, now with a larger reach attracting many oppositional monks, declared its intention to protect the civil and political rights of the sangha, affirmed that monks should take part in politics, and aired its aim to overthrow the present UNP capitalist government.

The radical political mood of the LEBM can be gauged from these resolutions adopted in a meeting held in the following year (March 1947): the rejection of the Soulbury Constitution as falling short of Ceylon's desire to be a free and independent sovereign state; the support for a socialist program for the nationalization of transport, mines and estates; the necessity to control foreign investments; and the support for a scheme of free education.

The LEBM and the radical monks both proved to be ahead of their time but paved the path for things to come. Once the election of 1947 was over and the UNP was elected, they soon became defunct. Being politically radical, there was little to differentiate the LEBM political platform from that of the left parties,[8] who found it difficult to withstand the charge that Buddhism should be saved "from the flame of Marxism." The LEBM was tarred with the same brush.

The real significance of the LEBM was that it was the forerunner of forceful and effective participation of monks in the elections to come, most importantly in 1956, and that it voiced the powerful claims of Sinhala Buddhist nationalism. In time the "political bhikkhus" of the sort who joined the LEBM would progressively shed their left-wing affiliations and rhetoric and join a more congenial political coalition under the leadership of S. W. R. D. Bandaranaike. As we shall see, Sri Lankan politics would take an increasingly narrow path limited to a range of issues framed within the confines of a Sinhala Buddhist nationalism, and the major Sinhala political parties would by and large converge in a consensus.

The Betrayal and Restoration of Buddhism: Accusations and Remedies

What did the Buddhist (Sinhala) leaders, the activists and protesters, both lay and clerical, mean by such slogans as "the restoration of Buddhism to its rightful place" and "the betrayal of Buddhism" during colonial rule, especially under the British Raj?

The enumeration of wrongs committed, and the description and interpretation in detail by Buddhist activists of the restoration of due rights, is our best entry into understanding what the revival and restoration of Buddhism meant to the Sinhalese activists in substantive terms. This is one way to see how the cause of Buddhism entered, informed, and intervened in Sri Lankan politics, that is, to see the relationship between Buddhism and politics.

If we take this investigative and interpretive strategy, there is one text that was produced in the mid-1950s in Sri Lanka that could be said to act as the ideological charter of the Buddhist activists. It is *The Betrayal of Buddhism* (1956), a report published by the Buddhist Committee of Inquiry, which was set up in 1954 by virtue of a resolution passed by the All-Ceylon Buddhist Congress at its thirty-third annual conference held in December 1953. The committee's brief was "to inquire into the present state of Buddhism in Ceylon and to report on the conditions necessary to improve and strengthen the position of Buddhism, and the means whereby those conditions may be fulfilled."

The Betrayal of Buddhism

The professional and vocational backgrounds of the members of the Committee of Inquiry who wrote *The Betrayal of Buddhism* are instructive. The committee had seven Buddhist monks, six of whom could be identified as "scholar monks," most of them active as vice-principals or senior teachers at *pirivenas* (monastic colleges). The country's most famous pirivenas, such as Vidyodaya, Vidyalankara, and Balagalla pirivenas, and representatives from the major sects, Siyam, Amarapura, and Ramanna Nikayas, were represented. The lay members of the committee numbered seven, and four of them were well-known educationalists.[9] *The Betrayal of Buddhism* composed by this Committee of Inquiry thus reflected the views of some of the island's foremost Buddhist scholars and educators, both clerical and lay. It should come as no surprise that their cause concerned the system of education in the country, especially in the nineteenth and twentieth centuries, and the consequences of that system for Sinhala Buddhists as the majority category in the population.

The Betrayal of Buddhism in essence made two major comparisons between the status of the Christian missions and of the Buddhist sangha in Sri Lanka, especially during the British period (1796–1948) and the first years of independence. One comparison portrayed the missions as having a "corporate" organizational structure and enjoying special immunities and privileges from the Raj in order to pursue their activities, whereas the Buddhist sangha was fragmented. The component units of the sangha suffered from certain disabilities concerning the use of their economic resources and thereby were restricted in their activities. The second comparison, closely related to the first, focused on the successful educational (and proselytizing) activities of the Protestant missions, which always had highly favorable relations with the colonial government, as did the Roman Catholic church in more recent times. By comparison, the educational activities of the Buddhist sangha enjoyed little support from the British, and there were few Buddhist-Sinhalese schools compared with the Christian schools on the one hand and the Buddhist Sinhala majority population on the other. The report's conclusion and exhortation was as follows: "Education in Ceylon today should be oriented towards the bringing forth of a generation with an intimate awareness of its national language, history and culture and capable of enriching that national heritage."[10]

The report suggested two basic remedies for the two major disabilities suffered by Buddhism in comparison with Christianity. One remedy was that the government should pass a Buddha Sasana Act by which it "would create an incorporated Buddha Sasana Council to which may be entrusted all the prerogatives of the Buddhist kings as regards the Buddhist religion." (The Buddhist kings of the past in collaboration with certain "orthodox" segments of the sangha would regulate it and periodically purify it [*sasanavisodhana*].) The proposed council, to be composed of elected and appointed representatives of the sangha and the laity, would act as a "centralized authority" to prevent the disintegration of Buddhism in the face of competition from hostile Christian missions. Because of past colonial confiscations of sangha properties, temple lands, and income, a yearly sum of money would be given to the council by way of compensation for the conduct of educational activities on behalf of the sangha. Furthermore, the government would appoint a minister for religious affairs who would act to "rehabilitate the religions which had suffered under Colonial rule."

The second remedy proposed had as its purpose the withdrawal of grants-in-aid to Christian mission schools (and other "assisted schools") and the subsequent take-over of all assisted schools by the state. In due course the control and administration of schools would be transferred to central and local government agencies. The same policy of state takeover would be applied to all teacher training colleges. By having the state take over all the schools and teacher training colleges, the monopoly of English education enjoyed by Christian mission schools, and the advantage over the schools of other religions enjoyed by Christian teachers' colleges, would be removed. The Buddhist activists did not at all mind the government takeover of Buddhist schools, because they advocated religious education in state schools and were confident that government policy would favor the transmission of Buddhist values, Sinhalese language and literature, and "traditional culture."

The Social Revolution of 1956

Sinhala Buddhist nationalism remained latent for some time and began to gain momentum in the early fifties. In 1956 it achieved historic political success. A confluence of many concerns and aspirations had a cumulative effect upon the elections held at this time. The concerns were the rehabilitation and restoration of Buddhism to its former precolonial status; the shift from the English language as the medium of administration (official language) and education to indigenous mother tongues (especially Sinhalese); and the fostering by the Sinhalese of their "national identity" and their "national culture."

Moreover, the year 1956 was one of great expectations because it would be the time for staging the celebration of Buddha Jayanthi marking twenty-five hundred years since the death of the Buddha and the landing of the first Sinhalese, Vijaya, and his band of followers in Sri Lanka. The UNP government had appointed a body called the Lanka Bauddha Mandalaya to plan the celebration and to initiate projects for the compilation and translation of religious texts. There was much politics surrounding the nomination of members to this body.

In the preceding years the All-Ceylon Buddhist Congress had made certain demands. One was that the government should protect and maintain Buddhism and Buddhist institutions. Proposals were also made for the creation of a Buddha Sasana Department and for the appointment of a Buddhist commission to inquire into the state of Buddhism. Shunning government sponsorship, the Congress had appointed its own Buddhist Committee of Inquiry, which produced on the eve of the 1956 elections the explosive report discussed above, *The Betrayal of Buddhism,* an attack on Christian, especially Catholic, proselytization in schools. The report also assailed the UNP government as lukewarm toward Buddhist restoration. Finally, on the question of official language(s), there was adverse commentary on the government's vacillation regarding the declaration of Sinhalese as the *only* official language.

These issues led to the defeat of the UNP in the fateful elections of 1956 when that party's monopoly of power since independence came to a traumatic end. Organization and mobilization at the popular grass-roots level, involving both Buddhist monks and laity, contributed to the overthrow of the UNP and the success of the Mahajana Eksath Peramuna (MEP), headed by S. W. R .D. Bandaranaike, who was also the leader of the Sri Lanka Freedom Party (SLFP). Noteworthy in this regard were the efforts of a civil servant, N. Q. Dias, who first launched a Buddhist movement among the government administrative servants. In Sabaragamuwa Province, Dias and a monk, Gnanaseeha Thero, founded what came to be called Buddha Sasana Samiti, societies formed to look after the bhikkhus' needs, to manage *dhamma* schools, etc. These societies caught on and spread all over the country, numbering thirty-five hundred in the mid-1950s. Thereafter Dias, operating from Colombo in collaboration with L. H. Mettananda, the principal of Ananda College and a member of the Commission of Inquiry, established associations of monks called Sangha Sabhas in many electorates, numbering seventy-two by 1954. The importance of these efforts is that central government officials and local government servants used their positions and their networks to organize associations of monks at the local level. The seventy-two sabhas formed the Sri Lanka Maha Sangha Sabha (SLMSS), a national Colombo-based aggregation.

An even more dramatic development that raised the intensity level just before the 1956 election was the formation of the United Front of Monks.[11] This front was a potent combination of two monk organizations the SLMSS, and the All-Ceylon Congress of Buddhists (whose members mostly belonged to the LEBM, the movement of "progressive monks" of the 1940s).[12] The geographical and sectarian representation of the United Front of Monks is significant. Its leading lights were Colombo-based, and the leaders and the majority of the membership came from the Amarapura and Ramanna Nikaya—the so-called reform sects which were founded in the nineteenth century in the southwest urban coastal areas. By contrast, the establishment Siyam Nikaya, whose main chapters were located up-country in Kandy, was largely unrepresented. However, its low-country chapter, located in Kotte just outside Colombo, and the monks of the historic and wealthy temple at Kelaniya, also outside Colombo, who also belonged to the Siyam Nikaya, joined ranks with the United Front. Indeed, the forceful politician-monk Mapitgama Buddharakkhita, head *(viharadhipati)* of the Kelaniya temple, would be in the forefront of the election campaign. (He would gain notoriety a few years later for being implicated in the assassination of Premier Bandaranaike.)

The United Front of Monks was fiercely opposed to the UNP and listed ten points Buddhists should take into account in their voting, including the candidates' willingness to implement the proposals in *The Betrayal of Buddhism,* to make Sinhala the only official language, and to support the implementation of democratic socialism. The United Front was also anti-West, anti-Catholic. One of its slogans was "A vote for the United National Party is a vote for the Catholics; a vote for the MEP is a vote for the Buddhists."

The United Front monks, working through the network of local sangha sabhas, proved to be formidable and untiring election campaigners—making house-to-house visits and distributing pamphlets. It is said that about three to four thousand monks—about one-fourth of the national total—worked as campaigners. Although the UNP did enlist some establishment monks, including the leaders of leading pirivenas, who tried to prevent the monk activists from electioneering, its clerical support was not by and large effective. Thus, it is no exaggeration to say that the 1956 election which swept Bandaranaike and the MEP to power was the climactic and singular moment in the twentieth-century political life of Sri Lanka, the moment when a significant number of monks temporarily organized to win an election. Never again in the ensuing decades would the sangha show this much purpose and action. The United Front's decisive contribution lay in "its role in the support mobilization of the Buddhists and in providing a country-wide Bhikkhu cadre to a party [the MEP] with very little organization and projecting its image as the party of the common man."[13] At the same time, the United Front did not build a strong organizational structure that would provide the basis for systematic and long-term action.

The Riots of 1956 and 1958

In the years immediately following the 1956 elections, the ushering in of an alleged "social revolution" dedicated to the restoration of Buddhism, and the achievement by the Sinhalese of their due rights as a nation, there occurred two riots. To what extent can we say that revivalist Buddhism, the Buddhist component of Sinhalese nationalism, and the political activism of Buddhist monks contributed to these violent outbursts?

The first legislation submitted by the Bandaranaike government mandated Sinhalese as the sole official language. There were two indigenous languages used on the island: Sinhalese, the mother tongue of the Sinhalese majority, and Tamil, the language of the minority, who are mostly Hindu. The issue of contention was the role to be assigned the Tamil language (and thus Tamil-Hindu culture) in the public affairs of the country. Certain concessions to the Tamils were considered. These included the provision of opportunities for persons trained in English or Tamil to take examinations in those languages for entry into the public service, the right of local bodies to decide for themselves the language of their business, and the right of persons to communicate with the government in their own language. The turmoil over these concessions culminated in the first postindependence ethnic riots, which were initiated by elements of the Sinhalese civilian population against the Tamils. "Such explicit legislative guarantees would have gone a long way to reassure the bulk of Tamils, but the reactions of extremists among the Tamils and the Sinhalese were decidedly unfavorable," W. H. Wriggins has written. A group of Buddhist bhikkhus connected with the United Front of Monks protested the inclusion of a clause permitting individuals who had been educated in English or Tamil to take public examinations in that language until 1967 and urged the government to press ahead more rapidly with language changes. Their rally on the steps of the house of representatives culminated in a fast by a prominent university lecturer. Other concessional clauses appended to the legislation also incited organized protests. "Antagonism became so great that a Tamil sit-down demonstration, near the house of representatives, called by the Federalist leader the day the controversial legislation was submitted to parliament, led to bitter riots in which over one hundred people were injured. In a few days they spread to Eastern Province, where Tamils and Sinhalese lived intermingled; in Batticaloa and the Gal Oya Valley there was such violence that between twenty and two hundred persons were killed, depending on which side was doing the tallying."[14] In these first ethnic riots of the postindependence period the damage to life, limb, and property was relatively small compared to the scale of destruction that would occur in future riots.

If one wonders what could be the relationship between the official language controversy and the ethnic violence taking place at this time in the Eastern Province, the answer is that around this time the language issue was also becoming interwoven with the government's policy of peasant resettlement in the less populous parts of the island. Just as the first issue had implications for the educational and employment prospects of the Tamils, so would the second be construed as causing demographic changes in Sinhalese and Tamil (and Muslim) ethnic ratios in the Eastern Province and therefore as bearing on the politics of territorial control and of "homelands."

The 1956 riots did not delay the passing of the official language legislation (the Sinhala Only Bill): among the members present, the two main Sinhala parties, the MEP and the UNP voted for it, and the Tamil and Left parties voted against it.

The 1958 riots were much more serious. The slide to more acrimonious confrontation between the Tamils and the Sinhalese was quick. While the government proceeded to translate the Sinhala-only policy into action—by reserving a leading teacher training college for training Sinhalese only, by creating scholarships and distributing them on a quota basis six to one in favor of the Sinhalese, for example—the opposition Federal Party in turn in June 1956 proclaimed its objective of establishing an "autonomous Tamil linguistic state within a Federal Union of Ceylon" to protect the cultural freedom and identity of the Tamil-speaking people. The Federal Party committed itself to nonviolent direct action *(satyagraha)* to achieve its goal of a federal union.

For a while it seemed as if Bandaranaike and the Tamil leaders would reach an understanding on two fronts: the reasonable use of Tamil as the language of a minority, especially in the administration of the Northern and Eastern Provinces; and the creation of regional councils to correct the overcentralization of the administration and to enable Tamils to exercise some of control over local affairs through the devolution of powers. This was the substance of the famous Bandaranaike-Chelvanayagam pact, which might have settled the ethnic conflict. But it was precisely at this time that the Buddhist monk pressure groups, such as the United Front and the Sri Lanka Maha Sangha Sabha, in conjunction with their lay sponsors and allies, stepped up their protest against a "surrender" to Tamil demands and threatened to conduct their own satyagraha campaign unless the prime minister repudiated the agreement. A Kandyan organization, called the Tri Sinhala Peramuna, and the UNP, now in opposition, also protested any concession to the Tamils.

The about-face performed by the UNP under the influence of J. R. Jayawardene—who would some decades later lead the country and rue this manoeuvre—is worthy of note as marking the "first cycle in a pattern which has recurred as a central and poisonous feature of the political process at critical junctures. The party in power strives to foster communal accommodation. The major party in opposition manipulates Sinhalese parochialism to wreck that attempt."[15] This bipolar oscillation in the politics of the Sinhalese majority would also hereafter find its support among groupings within a divided sangha.

Other sporadic incidents occurred near the time Bandaranaike and Chelvanayagam met on 4 April to discuss the implementation of their pact. But the story belongs to the bhikkhus as the final destroyers of the pact. Several dozen bhikkhus staged a sit-down near the prime minister's home and refused to move until the pact was rescinded. After several unsuccessful attempts to persuade the monks to disband, Bandaranaike capitulated to their siege and drove to the radio station to announce that the pact was dissolved. Bandaranaike's biographer comments, "And so, in the most grievous blunder of his career, he caved in."[16] "The Tamil leaders retorted by preparing for a massive civil disobedience in protest, and planned to hold a conference in late May at Vavuniya, a town on the borderline between Tamil and Sinhalese settlements in the north."[17]

The political crisis between the Federalist Tamils and their Sinhalese opponents was then fatefully escalated by strikes among government workers directed by Communist and Trotskyite trade unions. In this atmosphere of the weakening of the law enforcement agencies, the riots of 1958 exploded around the time that the Federalists were preparing to hold their annual convention in Vavuniya in the north preparatory to launching a campaign of nonviolent protest.

The riots occurred in three overlapping phases in late May 1958. The first serious incidents occurred mainly in and around Polonnaruwa in the predominately Sinhalese area of the North Central Province and in Eravur in a mainly Tamil section of the Eastern Province. The second phase was marked by attacks, overwhelmingly against Tamils, throughout most of the Sinhalese majority areas. The third phase took place mainly in the Tamil-dominated Northern and Eastern Provinces. "The violence there was directed against Sinhalese and against government personnel and installations."[18] It is not necessary for us to know the actual details of these riots, except to remark that the worst violence occurred in the North Central and Eastern Provinces, especially in the Polonnaruwa region, the center of the largest peasant resettlement schemes.

The Restoration of Buddhism and the Transformation of Education in the 1960s and 1970s

When one scrutinizes the 1958 riots—the participants, their locations, and their nature—and considers them in relation to the preceding events and issues—such as the official language controversy, the Tamils' pressure for a federal solution to their underdog status, the demonstrations and fasts staged by the United Front monks and lay Buddhist nationalists to protest concessions to the Tamils, the labor strikes that had their origins in the rivalries of leftist parties and which weakened public order, and, finally, the fact that the worst riots occurred not in Colombo and Jaffna but in the far provinces of peasant colonization resettlement—one is puzzled how to identify in any meaningful way the "Buddhist" components of the riots in contrast to other components, be they economic, territorial, or political. Since these components are difficult to disaggregate, I approach the religious, social, and political aspects of Sri Lankan Buddhism differently. I will argue that as the energies of Sinhala Buddhist nationalism were translated into concrete policies and programs of language, education, employment, peasant resettlement, territorial control of the island, and so on, the substantively soteriological, ethical, and normative components of canonical doctrinal Buddhism qua religion were weakened, displaced, even distorted. As part of this same process, the religiopolitical associations of Buddhism as set out in the chronicles (e.g., the *Mahavamsa*) assumed an unprecedented primacy. This religiopolitical association linked Buddhism with the Sinhala people, with the territory of the entire island, and with a political authority dedicated to the protection of Buddhism. Thus, Buddhist fundamentalism and revivalism were progressively transformed into a Buddhist nationalism that in turn evolved into a political Buddhism in the late 1970s and 1980s. The religious core or inspiration of contemporary political Buddhism is either privatized or leached out in favor of a political collectivity that sees itself as homogeneous and majoritarian and for which doctrinal Buddhism is a possession owned as a legacy, an object that is appropriated—but a "Buddhism" that, for many of its members, no longer serves primarily as an ego-ideal and a mental discipline for personal salvation.

To put the matter another way, Sinhalese revivalist Buddhism with nationalist overtones that had an upsurge toward the end of the nineteenth century and the early decades of the twentieth contained an appeal to a selective scripturalism that placed an accent on certain doctrinal tenets and on the devaluation of "superstitious" accretions and practices. But inevitably this purification of the religious involved a process of popularization whereby the Buddhist doctrine and message were carried to the people in simplified catechistic terms leavened with mythohistorical claims culled from chronicles such as the *Mahavamsa*. This propagandization and popularization entailed the acquisition and use of modern communications media such as the printing press, the founding of new educational institutions (Buddhist schools for boys and girls) and organizational forms (the Buddhist Theosophical Society, the All-Ceylon Buddhist Congress, the Young Men's Buddhist Association), the deployment of effective techniques of dissemination like sermons and pamphlets in the vernacular, and the celebration on a national scale of Buddhist festivals such as the *Vesak*.

But these activities of revivalism and reform, including scripturalism, led progressively to the ideologization of religion as a charter which represented an increasing shift from "religiousness" to "religious-mindedness," from religion as moral practice to religion as a cultural possession. Finally, in developments since the 1950s, nationalism, which grew out of revivalism, advanced further by encompassing and then superseding it in substantive terms. Subsequently comes arguably the climactic phase of a political Buddhism or a Buddhist nationalism and chauvinism, which in its collective manifestation has few links with the major tenets of Buddhist ethics and, because of its hegemonic, preferential, and exclusive claims vis-à-vis other collectivities in its midst, erupts as periodic overflows of violence in its alleged defense.

This, however, is only one side of the story. There is another development which gives a substantive content and ideological potency to political Buddhism. While many of the truths of doctrinal Buddhism fade in urgency, a collectivist fundamentalist conception of "Buddhist nationalism" and "Buddhist democracy"—even of "Buddhist socialism"—sketched and preached by some prominent clerical scholar monks, ideologues, and activists suffuses the public consciousness. This in many ways is a "positive" ideological project despite its limitations and its "creative" misreadings of the past. It refers back to certain canonical *suttas* dealing with ideal righteous rulers in the form of *cakkavatti* and sees in them the attainment of glorious welfare-oriented rule. It also refers back to the regimes of great Sinhalese kings of *Mahavamsa* fame such as Dutthagamani and Parakrama Bahu, who allegedly constructed an egalitarian rural society focused on the triad of temple (*dagaba*), the irrigation tank (*vava*), and rice fields (*yaya*). It sounds a clarion call for Sinhalese unity and berates the contemporary Sinhalese for their divisiveness. It criticizes present-day divisive party politics, present-day hankering after West-inspired materialist, consumerist, and capitalist self-seeking goals, and proposes in their place a simpler harmonious "Buddhist way of life" in a "Buddhist democracy." This call to a Buddhist way of life does invoke some of the precepts and admonitions suitable for householders set out in doctrinal texts. Finally, it envisages a central role for monks at all levels of the Buddhist polity as advisers and counselors. Both trends elucidated above are interwoven in political Buddhism. Its trajectory informs and colors the episodes and developments that I shall now sketch.

Let us focus first on some relevant developments in the sixties and seventies. The mid-fifties constituted a watershed in the politics of postindependence Sri Lanka, when the arguments for a Buddhist restoration, for the dethronement of the English language and the elevation of the Sinhalese language, and for the recovery of Sinhalese majoritarian influence were accepted as legitimate through the electoral process, and entrusted to Bandaranaike and the MEP for implementation. The sixties and seventies represent a different trend by virtue of both major parties—the SLFP and the UNP—attempting to implement those objectives, and largely succeeding in the task (though there were many other issues of reform and reconstruction that had been stalled or evaded).

By the 1960s the UNP had accepted these objectives as essential planks in its party platform; therefore, the two major Sinhala political parties, the UNP and the SLFP, grew closer ideologically and became alternative choices at subsequent elections. Sri Lankan politics is enacted in an arena where the majority group, the Sinhalese, has a "bipolar" division within it and is ranged against a minority which, according to the situation, is regarded as an enemy or an ally.

Paralleling this process toward a dual balance was the progressive bifurcation of the support of the Buddhist monks for the two major parties. If in 1956 the enormous ground swell of monks led by the progressive monks of the United Front overshadowed the rest of the sangha and decided an election, in the 1960s and 1970s the monks of all sects, temples, and status tended toward a spectrum of parallel support for the two main Sinhala parties.

The Buddha Sasana Commission (which had been recommended in 1956 in *The Betrayal of Buddhism*) had made certain regulatory proposals regarding the reorganization and unification of various chapters of monks—a move designed to stem the alleged increased fragmentation of the sangha and to give it organizational strength to compete with the challenge of Christian missions—and regarding whether monks should receive salaries for filling certain positions, especially in schools. The SLFP government felt obliged to move toward the implementation of these proposals, and this generated a wave of resistance against government "interference." Thus, for instance, the All-Ceylon Buddhist Congress protested that "antireligious" and "antidemocratic" Marxists were influencing the government. It was clear that by now the SLFP of 1965 among some circles had tarnished its reputation as the knight in shining armor defending Buddhism.

This is one of the central obstacles in Sri Lanka (and Burma) to any return to governmental regulation and "purification" of the sangha's internal organization, which was achieved with varying efficacy in the precolonial political regimes and was abandoned by the British as part of their "disestablishment of Buddhism." Disestablishment entailed the withdrawal of state support and protection of Buddhism as the official religion of the state. The monks and laity might collaborate in general in "restoring" Buddhism to its previous preeminence, but would diverge sharply on the concrete need for administrative regulation of the sangha and its temporalities. And this issue would split the sangha itself, as well as create differences and tensions between lay Buddhist leaders and establishment monks.

So when large numbers of monks began to canvass in the March 1965 elections, there was parallel support for the UNP and SLFP, which signaled the emergence of a political dualism within the sangha matching the polarization between the two major political parties.[19] The modes of mobilization of support, through rallies, meetings, and pamphlet distribution were replicated. According to Phadnis, 1965 "could be termed as the point when the Bhikkhus' participation in electoral politics had turned full circle. Political polarization of the Bhikkhu community had reached its high water mark as both the major parties were supported by a conglomeration of Bhikkhu groups who, whatever their nomenclature, could be easily identified in their political alignments."[20]

In 1965 the UNP won the election. In 1970 it lost it again to Mrs. Bandaranaike, but it won yet again in 1977 under the leadership of Mr. J. R. Jayawardene, who was in power until 1987, having changed the government to a presidential form, maintaining control through referendums rather than elections. In 1987, elections were again held, and Mr. Premadasa and the UNP were elected to power.

The seesaw victories of the SLFP and the UNP between 1960 and 1977 did not change the now-established pattern of the monks' customary participation in electoral politics and their divided support for the two main parties. From 1960 to 1977 there were no anti-Tamil riots or any form of collective violence against ethnic minorities. The period was, however, punctuated by the 1971 insurrection of the Sinhalese youth (the Janatha Vimukthi Peramuna [JVP]) against an SLFP government which at that time was inspired more by grievances against the government than by grievances against the Tamils. (But as we shall see later, in 1977, and again in 1981 and 1983, there was a recurrence of anti-Tamil riots, those in 1983 being the worst.)

Why was there a period of quiescence in 1960–77 as far as ethnic violence and Buddhist militancy was concerned? Why in 1977 did ethnic riots resume and reach a level of violence never before witnessed, and thereafter plunge the country into a prolonged civil war?

Between 1960 and the early 1970s the aspirations and objectives of militant lay Buddhists and politically ardent Buddhist monks with regard to the restoration of Buddhism to a preeminent place had been largely addressed and fulfilled. The symbolic high point of this era, when both the SLFP and the UNP collaborated in its acceptance, was the inclusion in the country's constitution in 1972 of the formal declaration that Buddhism would have the "foremost place" as the religion of the majority. After the victory of Bandaranaike and the MEP in 1956 a Department of Cultural Affairs had been set up to sponsor Buddhism. The Buddha Jayanthi celebrations had been successfully staged with pomp, fervor, and piety in that same year— and the characteristic projects of all politically sponsored Buddhist revivals in the traditional Buddhist polities of Southeast Asia were undertaken. They were projects to collate and edit the texts of Pali canon, the Tripitaka, and to translate them into Sinhalese, to publish a number of Buddhist literary texts, to compile an encyclopedia in Sinhalese and English, and to restore the Dalada Maligawa (the temple in Kandy where the Buddha's tooth relic, the palladium of the precolonial Sinhala Kingdom, resided) and other famous Buddhist monuments in Anuradhapura, Polonnaruwa, and elsewhere. In the mid-fifties similar projects celebrating the restoration of Buddhism were undertaken in Burma by Premier U Nu.

Indeed, the architectural restorations of the ancient capitals and other famous monuments, accompanied by extensive Sinhalese peasant colonization and resettlement of the ancient lands that lay in their hinterland, and the popularization of pilgrimages to these restored sites must be judged to be important contributions to the stimulation as well as appeasement of Sinhalese desires to regain their past glories.

But it is education that has been at the heart of postindependence politics. Education is the umbrella term under which were grouped a set of interlocking issues and interests: the animus against the Christian schools, which taught in English and produced a largely Christian elite; the restoration of Sinhalese as the language of administration and education, thereby enhancing the social mobility of the lower classes, which could learn in the vernacular language; the restoration of Buddhist and other Orientalist studies to a position of preeminence in the universities; and so on.

A conspicuous step taken was the creation of two Buddhist universities—Vidyodaya and Vidyalankara—in 1959 by an act of Parliament at the very sites of the island's two most distinguished pirivenas which had dispensed education to monks. (The staff of the parent pirivenas were absorbed into the universities, and many other pirivenas were affiliated with the universities.) These two universities, as we have already seen, were the seat of and the breeding ground for the scholarly activist "progressive" monks who led the United Front. Indeed, the intensified political participation of the monks in the sixties was itself a barometer of their faith in achieving results through political participation; and their political relevance and strength as championing "Buddhist" social welfare issues were harnessed to the full by both the UNP and the SLFP during the 1965 and 1970 elections.

In both ideological and practical terms, probably the most important measures taken related to the school system and the teacher training colleges of the island. *The Betrayal of Buddhism* had warned that "what Buddhism has to protect itself from today is not the Catholic Church, but Catholic Schools" and had urged the nationalization of all schools. The SLFP promise to bring the schools under a central system that would give a national stamp to the education imparted was kept by Mrs. Bandaranaike in the sixties. All private schools had previously been assisted by the state. Now it was declared that all grade III assisted schools (primary and postprimary) would be taken over by the government; all grade I and grade II assisted schools would also be taken over, unless they chose to remain private and to forgo financial assistance. The net result was that the majority of schools so nationalized were those previously run by Christian organizations, though the latter did decide to retain some of their best secondary schools as private fee-paying schools. The Catholics were the major losers, especially the poorer amongst them. The beneficiaries in the private fee-paying Christian schools came mostly from the elite and wealthy families. Hence, Christian privilege, though diminished, was not eradicated. The majority of private teacher training colleges run by Christian bodies were also similarly surrendered to the government. By comparison with the Christian schools, the private schools run by Buddhist organizations readily participated in the takeover, because now under governmental sponsorship their Sinhala-Buddhist identity would be further enhanced.[21]

The takeover of the majority of schools, combined with the switch to the mother tongue as the medium of instruction, which was achieved in all primary and secondary schools by 1967, was perhaps the most substantial accomplishment of the program to restore the rights of the religion and language of the majority.

The 1970s and 1980s: The Deepening Crisis

If by the early 1970s the program of Sinhala Buddhist nationalism on which most segments of the laity and all the clergy could agree had been largely achieved, then why did the Sinhala-Tamil conflict flare up again and produce the riots of 1977, 1981, and 1983, the last being the most violent and destructive so far experienced? The answers are complex.

At the core of the Sinhala-Tamil ethnic conflict since the 1970s, which invoked and generated the passions of Sinhala Buddhist nationalism and the separatist claims of Tamils, are two clusters of interest-based issues. One cluster concerns the official language(s) of administration and the linguistic media of education, and their linkage with the issues of educational opportunities, including admissions to universities and places of higher learning and of recruitment to administrative services and the professions. In the long run the Tamils have lost out on these issues, decided in their favor by the Sinhalese majority, by the imposition of quotas and discriminatory policies.

The Sri Lankan Tamils living in the north and the east, regions which by distant location and poor resources were less economically developed than many other parts of the island, had pursued education in order to secure employment in administration and in the professions. The "Jaffna Tamils" in particular occupied a conspicuous place in the public life of the country, and their visibility and concentration in certain middle-class occupations had generated the charge among Sinhalese competitors that the Tamils were overrepresented in the envied positions.

The skewing of higher education in favor of the Sinhalese majority was a climactic step of discrimination against the Tamils. The Tamil politicians of the Federal Party, and later of the Tamil United Liberation Front (TULF), had stoutly complained but had not succeeded. Their failure to change anything by constitutional means finally drove the Tamil youth movement for Eelam (the Tamil homeland) to take up arms and engage in militant confrontation.

In Sri Lanka the facilities for training in the sciences, both theoretical and applied, are limited. There is heavy competition to enter the universities, especially in the natural sciences, engineering, and medicine. In the mid-1970s fewer than 9 percent of those taking the entrance examinations were admitted to the universities. A so-called standardization policy that adjusted the examination scores when test answers were written in the Sinhalese and Tamil languages and a quota system with special concessions for "backward" districts ultimately worked first against the educated Tamil youth of the north and second against the educated youth of Colombo.

The second cluster concerns "colonization schemes" of peasant resettlement in the sparsely populated "Dry Zone" of Sri Lanka, which covers regions in the North Central, Northern, and Eastern Provinces. This ongoing conflict involves the vexed and contested issues of devolution of powers from the central government to provincial/regional councils, the ethnic quotas to be allocated to colonization schemes under central and local control, the degree to which regional autonomy is to be granted in matters of local government, education, land alienation, and policing, and so on.[22]

While the colonization of the Dry Zone was begun before Independence, since the 1950s it has been continuously implemented on a large scale as the major form of agricultural development. Large capital-intensive multipurpose enterprises such as the Gal Oya Scheme and the Mahaweli Programme are part of this developmental trust. Many centuries ago, the Dry Zone was the site of a much glorified Sinhala Buddhist civilization centered in Anuradhapura and Polonnaruwa, and a return of Sinhalese peasantry to the area is seen as a re-creation of that past. But the Northern and Eastern Provinces currently have as their majority population Sri Lankan (and Indian) Tamils, with the Muslims the next largest category. Peasant resettlement has involved the migration and transplantation of poor peasants from the densely populated and land hungry parts of the country, which are located in the central, south, and southwestern parts of the island, where Sinhalese vastly predominate. And successive Sinhalese majoritarian governments have been preoccupied with catering to the needs of the Sinhalese peasantry, while either discriminating against or ignoring the interests and needs of the minorities, who are the major native populations of the Northern and Eastern Provinces. Given the ethnically preferential policy and the manner in which the Sinhala-Tamil conflict was developing, it was inevitable that the Sri Lankan Tamils would see the massive migrations of Sinhalese into the Dry Zone as an intrusion into their "homelands" and as an attempt to swamp them. The separatist claim to Eelam is the stance taken by the most radical and militant of the Tamil dissidents.[23]

From the Riots of the 1980s to the Indo–Sri Lanka Accord

Since 1956, mass violence in the form of riots has been launched seven times by segments of the Sinhalese population against the Tamils. The most destructive of these riots took place in 1958, 1977, 1981, and 1983. I have already discussed those that occurred in 1956 and 1958. Our concern here is with those that flared up in 1981 and 1983.

The riots perpetrated by the Sinhalese civilians upon the Tamils in 1981 and 1983 were a result of the collision between an emphatic but still unsatiated Buddhist Sinhala nationalism, which had nevertheless, as we have seen, secured since 1956 more and more benefits for the Sinhalese majority, and a rising, desperate, confrontational Tamil nationalism, which threatened secession and a separate state of Eelam, objectives which were bound to infuriate and inflame Sinhala chauvinists.

While at no time did the Tamil civilian public as such initiate riots against the Sinhalese public, armed insurgency began in the late seventies among Tamil youth. The Tamil Tigers formed as the end result of many developments. Their feeling of hopelessness was caused by the discrimination practiced against them in higher education, the TULF's intensified objections to the pace and magnitude of resettlement of Sinhalese peasants in the homelands of the Tamils, and finally the TULF's declaration of its commitment to Eelam.

The militants' first homicide victims were some Tamil politicians and policemen who were labeled collaborators. The government reacted by sending an army of occupation (the army is virtually a Sinhalese monopoly) to the north and the east to stamp out the insurgency.

The following chronology of events escalated to produce the riots of 1983. In 1977, after seven years of SLFP rule, the UNP was reelected under the leadership of J. R. Jayawardene. In 1979 this government passed the Prevention of Terrorism Act with its draconian provisions, such as defining certain acts as unlawful including the speaking or writing of words intended to cause religious, social, or communal disharmony; allowing confessions made to the police, possibly under duress, as admissible evidence; and permitting the army and police to arrest persons and hold them incommunicado for up to eighteen months without trial. This act allowed the security forces to take punitive actions in the north that would progressively alienate the Tamils there (e.g., arresting persons without a warrant, seizing possessions concerned with "unlawful activity," and indefinitely detaining persons). Then in 1981 the elections to the District Development Councils were seriously disturbed with violence by the Tamil insurgents and the burning of the Public Library in Jaffna by Sinhalese security forces (in this case the police). Thereafter a string of violent encounters between the army and the insurgents occurred: the Tamil insurgents detonated land mines and the army engaged in arrests and shooting reprisals. The atmosphere was further poisoned by random punitive actions of Sinhalese civilians against Tamil civilians in many towns throughout the country, including actual or threatened physical attacks on persons or their shops. These mounting tensions escalated into the riots of 1983. The riots were set off when Tamil insurgents ambushed thirteen Sinhalese soldiers in the north on 23 July. Their mangled bodies were subsequently displayed in Colombo's main cemetery.

The 1983 riots began in Colombo, the capital city, on 24 July and lasted until 5 August; the attacks on Tamils spread in widening circles to towns in the southwest, to the central tea plantation districts, and to Trincomalee in the Eastern Province. The death toll was between 350 (the government figure) and 2,000 (the Tamil estimate), and the refugees in the Colombo camps numbered from 80,000 to 100,000. Arson and property destruction were extensive. Properties methodically destroyed, burned, and looted in Colombo included Tamil homes in the city's middle- and lower-class residential wards; groceries; textile shops; tea shops owned by Tamils and located in the dense business districts, main thoroughfares, and residential wards; and over one hundred industrial establishments (textile mills, garment factories, rubber goods factories, and coconut oil distilleries). The main victims in Colombo were thus Tamil homeowners of the middle class, shopkeepers, large business owners and entrepreneurs, and merchants.

Although some monks were involved in inciting the crowds, the vast majority of the Buddhist monks and the sangha were not directly involved in the riots. Nor were they prominent in the immediately preceding events, when the issues that engaged the Sinhalese and the Tamils seemed to be more political and territorial—focused on secession and homelands, peasant colonization and discrimination—than directly religious, in the sense of the "restoration of Buddhism," as they had been in the late 1950s and the 1960s. Those previous Buddhist demands—recognizing Sinhalese as the official language, denying state aid to Christian schools, promoting the status of monastic colleges, and making Buddhism the foremost religion on the island—had been largely satisfied. But as we soon shall see, the explosive issues of the 1980s surrounding the claim by Tamils to their homelands, and the increasing toll Tamil insurgent violence would take on both Sinhalese security forces and civilians, would regalvanize the cause of Sinhala Buddhist nationalism, a cause in which Buddhist activist monks would once again become increasingly involved in the 1980s.

The years 1984 to 1987 saw the engagement of the government's army and security forces with the Tamil militants of the north and the east. Surely and unavoidably, however, the civilians on both sides became exercised. During these years certain incidents took place which would periodically inflame the Buddhist and nationalist sentiments of the public at large, including many sections of the Buddhist sangha. In 1985 Tamil militants took the fateful step of for the first time attacking Sinhalese civilians in the vicinity of the sacred Bo Tree in the historic city of Anuradhapura, a city that is not merely a reminder and repository of ancient glory, but also the focus of pious and celebrated pilgrimages. It also stands at the heart of the region of expanding peasant resettlement, and of the ancient kingdom immortalized by the *Mahavamsa*. Increasingly, Sinhalese civilians, monks, and Buddhist temples became targets of Tamil militant attacks. A particularly notorious case was the brutal killing at Arantalawa in 1986 of a busload of monks returning from a pilgrimage. The Sinhalese army previously not only killed many Tamil civilians but had also demolished Hindu temples and killed their priests. The army conducted these operations under the banner of a commitment to stamping out terrorism. While Sinhala Buddhist nationalism must have influenced many of the soldiers, the attack on temples as on schools was also motivated by the belief that they are places of refuge and hiding for the rebels. In the course of such actions civilians who seek refuge in these public institutions have been victimized. Now the Tamil rebels turned the tables, hitting the Sinhalese at their sacred sites, thereby making a statement that they were prepared to use the same kind of violence against civilians, bystanders, and nonmilitary targets as the armed forces did. The Sinhalese civilians themselves became directly implicated in the civil war in the Northern and Eastern Provinces when the government distributed arms to the Sinhalese Civilian Home Guards and encouraged them to engage with the Tamil dissidents, because the government army was unable to contain, let alone defeat, the Tamil militants.

Thus, by the mid-1980s, as we shall see in the following sections, various protest organizations and movements, made up of varying numbers of members of political parties, Buddhist monks, and concerned laymen, were being formed not only to support the war against Tamil separation but also to protest any tendency on the part of the UNP government to negotiate a peace with the Tamil insurgents on the basis of a devolution of powers to provincial councils. At the same time, the government of India supported the Tamil rebels and applied pressure on the Sri Lankan government to cease its economic blockade of Jaffna. The Sri Lankan army's determined last push to eradicate the rebels, the Vadamarachchi Operation, proved fruitless. These events finally pushed Jayawardene to sign the Indo–Sri Lanka Agreement (the Peace Accord) in July 1987.

The Peace Accord allowed for the entry into Sri Lanka of a large Indian army (estimated at its maximum to be around fifty-five thousand troops) to enforce the accord, to pacify the north and the east, and to achieve what the Sinhalese armed forces had hitherto failed to accomplish. The Sri Lankan government had on its side, apart from the threat of an armed Indian invasion, good reasons for signing the accord. The Janatha Vimukthi Peramuna (JVP), an opposition party which had been banned in Sri Lanka in 1983, had mounted its own illicit destabilizing and oppositional militancy in the core Sinhalese majority provinces (in central, southwestern, southern parts of the island). As a result, the government felt the need to withdraw its troops so as to deploy them against the insurrectionary threat in its own midst.

But the accord stirred the fears of Sinhalese nationalists on many grounds. While affirming the need to preserve the unity and integrity of Sri Lanka, the accord acknowledged that Sri Lanka was a "multiethnic and multilingual plural society," that each ethnic group had its "distinct cultural and linguistic identity," which had to be nurtured, and that "the Northern and Eastern Provinces have been areas of historical habitation of the Sri Lankan Tamil speaking peoples" while sharing their territory with other ethnic groups. This was tantamount to recognizing the north and east as the homelands of the Tamil, subject to the residential rights of other groups.

The accord also stated that once peace was restored a single provincial council consisting of both the Northern and Eastern Provinces would be formed; it was understood on the basis of previous negotiations that this provincial council would have all powers held by a state in the Indian Union. Elections to the council were to be held before the end of 1987. The president of Sri Lanka was authorized to hold a referendum in the Eastern Province in the course of the following year to determine whether the people in that area (the Muslims were nearly a third of the population) wished to remain united with the north or have a separate provincial council of their own.

The annexure to the accord provided for an Indian peacekeeping contingent, when requested by the Sri Lankan government, to help in terminating the hostilities and to implement the terms of the agreement. This agreement to an active Indian presence and intervention in Sri Lankan affairs (which in fact did happen subsequently) was further complicated by an agreement between the Indian and Sri Lankan governments in an exchange of letters that neither the port of Trimcomalee nor any other part of the island would be made "available for military use by any country in a manner prejudicial to India's interests."

While some ministers even within the UNP government (like Prime Minister Premadasa and Athulathmudali, minister for national security) thought that their leader, President Jayawardene, had conceded too much, opposition forces quickly coalesced, however tenuously and intermittently, to create an uproar. They were led by the SLFP, the main opposition party, and supported by the MEP and the JVP. The objections, which exploited the most unfavorable readings of the terms of the accord, were that the government had acceded to the Tamil extremists' demand for their separate homelands, that the island had thereby been dismembered and partitioned, and that Sri Lanka had become a pawn and a client state of India, which had geopolitical ambitions of exercising hegemony over the Indian Ocean. The actual presence of a large Indian army was an effective stick to beat the UNP with, and it played upon all the historic fears of marauding Hindu Tamils invading the island, and threatening the unity and sovereignty of a beleaguered but 2,500-year-old Sinhala Buddhist polity.

One of the complicating factors in Sri Lanka's current conflict is that "devolution" itself is a highly emotive and explosive term, carrying different meanings to different persons and groups. A separate state of Eelam; a federal union between Tamil and the

Sinhalese states; a unitary state with devolution of power to regional or provincial councils; the recognition of a merger between existing northern and eastern provinces, or portions of them, so as to constitute Tamil homelands; the exact powers and functions with regard to security, defense, taxation, peasant colonization, education, etc., that are to be reserved to the center and allocated to the regional or provincial councils—these are merely some of the many issues which have been periodically discussed by the Sri Lankan and Indian governments, with or without Tamil representatives of the TULF and the militants present. Between June 1985, when under Indian auspices the Sri Lankan government directly discussed issues with the Tamil insurgents in Thimpu, the capital of Bhutan, and July 1987, when the Indo–Sri Lankan Agreement was signed, there were talks at New Delhi (September 1985) between Indian and the Sri Lankan officials, at Colombo (July 1986) between an Indian delegation and Sri Lankan government, and at Bangalore (December 1986) between Rajiv Gandhi and Jayawardene. All these talks were concerned with specifying the terms of a devolutionary solution, and no doubt much progress had been made toward a solution that was finally embodied in the Indo–Sri Lanka Peace Accord. But this accord was an agreement between two governments. And the interpretation and implementation of its terms would provide plenty of contentious space for the Sinhalese parties and interest groups in opposition to the UNP government on the one hand and, on the other, to the Tamil dissidents and militants, whose participation in the negotiations was irregular, discontinuous, and not binding. In this situation of ambiguity, disagreement, misperception, mischievous exaggeration, and bad faith among the Tamil dissidents, the Sinhala political parties, and various pressure groups, "devolution" is a rallying cry of hope and reconciliation for some, a warning slogan of national division and dismemberment for others, and an occasion for stretching out the conflict and regrouping for still others.

The Mavbima Surakime Vyaparaya (MSV)

The Movement for the Protection of the Motherland

Schalk[24] and Amunugama[25] discuss how the Buddhist sangha engages in political action and exercises power through linkages with political parties and, indirectly, through monks' participation in intersecting, joint, intermediary militant movements composed of laity and monks. These movements and organizations, militantly Buddhist, increasingly proliferated in the 1980s and focused on the Sinhala-Tamil ethnic conflict allegedly in order to protect the rights of the "sons of the soil," the native Sinhalese, heirs to the island and protectors of the Buddhist religion. These movements harkened back to, and reactivated, on the one hand, the enduring slogans of the remote past enshrined in the *Mahavamsa,* such as Dhammadipa (the island of the Dhamma), the island's unification under King Dutthagamani, and the more recent Sinhala Buddhist nationalism and revivalism of Dharmapala. On the other hand, the movements addressed proximate and immediate events of the present-day ethnic conflict and its "murderous" Tamil separatism. They warned against the dangers of a devolutionary solution to the ethnic conflict, which they interpreted as the partition of a unitary island. Finally, they opposed the terms of the Indo–Sri Lanka Peace Accord of 1987, which they interpreted as an ignominious capitulation to the designs of imperialist India and its sponsorship of the Tamil cause. Seven leading *new* organizations have formed since 1979, with members drawn from political parties, lay circles, and the ranks of Buddhist monks. These organizations have as their principal purpose the promotion of the interests of Sinhala Buddhists as the true "sons of the soil."[26]

We are here primarily concerned with one of these organizations, the Movement for the Protection of the Motherland, or Mavbima Surakime Vyaparaya (MSV), founded in July 1986. It was a wide-ranging umbrella organization which included many of the new lay cum clerical Buddhist organizations such as the Sinhala Bala Mandalaya and the Jatika Peramuna.

The MSV's Membership and Organization

It is worth listing the organizational components and leading figures in the MSV, which is an amalgam both of laity and monks in their professed identity and unity as Buddhists and as non-Marxists and of anti-UNP political opponents. This broad coalition against the UNP is constituted of three entities: members of political parties, members of the sangha, and individual lay Buddhist enthusiasts and special cause activists.

From the political parties, we have in the forefront of the MSV the SLFP led by former prime minister Sirimavo Bandaranaike, the MEP led by Dinesh Gunawardena (the son of Philip Gunawardena, the founder), and a front organization of the banned JVP called the Sri Lanka Deshapremi Peramuna.[27] In understanding the participation of Buddhist monks, it is relevant to note that they have many organizational identities and, according to context and cause, they mobilize in terms of one or the other. At the same time it is noteworthy that these multiple memberships, identities, and interests sometimes work at cross purposes and thus sometimes lead to fragmentation, weak organizational structure, and lack of sustained activity.

Their first organizational identity is "sectarian" stemming from their *nikaya* (sect) membership in the Siyam, Amarapura, and Ramanna Nikayas, respectively, that are distributed in various strengths throughout the island. The next is the separate territorial groupings on a "district" basis of the monks belonging to each nikaya—these are smaller local groupings. Each of the three sects has its head monk (*mahanayake*) and a working committee (*karaka sabha*) to speak officially on the entire nikaya's behalf. The sect leadership appoints a monk to be head of each of its district groupings.

Leaving aside their sectarian membership, Buddhist monks belonging to all three nikayas may band together to form special interest associations with a political agenda. Their membership in these associations is therefore *trinikaya* (three-sect), and these associations transcending sect division have known links to political parties and may thus be acknowledged as branches or components of the UNP, SLFP, MEP, JVP, and so on. These special interest political associations of monks on a trinikaya basis may be organized at local, regional, or national levels and may be mobilized at all these levels to rally, to meet, and to launch movements.[28]

Three monks who in recent times have figured conspicuously as leaders of activist movements which are coalitions of both monk and lay organizations are Palipane Chandananda, the head monk of the Asgiriya chapter of the Siyam Nikaya; Sobhita Thero, the head monk of Naga Viharaya in Kotte, leader of a temperance movement, and a popular preacher; and Muruttetuve Ananda Thero, incumbent of Abhayarama, a temple located in Narempitiya on the immediate outskirts of Colombo, and the chaplain and president of the Nurses Union. All three have been vociferous opponents of the Indo–Sri Lanka Peace Accord and of the ruling UNP.

The members of the MSV, like many "patriotic" Sinhalese, deny the claim of the Tamil insurrectionists and politicians to their own homelands and are totally opposed to any devolutionary solution of the conflict (equating and exaggerating any notion of provincial councils as a division and partition of the country). The MSV's special Buddhist dimension comes from its plea that a division of the country and the weakening of its "sovereignty" would also diminish, even doom, Buddhism and the Sinhala culture that it supports. These are not specifically "monkish" preoccupations or slogans, but today's monks are proclaiming these views and waving these banners as participants of clearly political organizations, even as adherents of different political parties, while also keeping their membership in purely sangha-linked organizations.

To underscore the significance of the MSV, let me recapitulate the shifts that have taken place through time with regard to the issues that have exercised activist monks and the patterns of their political participation. The Vidyalankara monks of the 1950s were the first to assert the rights of the monks to engage in politics, and the United Front of Monks, as a canvassing phalanx of monks, largely won the elections for Bandaranaike in 1956. In the sixties and seventies we saw a bipolar division within the sangha paralleling the contest between the two political parties—the UNP and the SLFP. Today we see a further transformation of the sangha. The monks are more differentiated, having pluralistic affiliations, and participate not only in coalition groups of politicians, laity, and monks but also as members of branch units and wings of political parties.

As Schalk has demonstrated, the effectiveness and visibility of the MSV lay in its short-term spasmodic capacity to organize "colorful rallies all over the country led by famous and heart-stirring speakers who can stimulate and mobilize the masses."[29] In Sri Lanka the techniques for organizing and staging rallies, processions, demonstrations, and public meetings are well established and widely used in mass politics.

The campaign of the MSV, thus, in our era of participatory politics and crowd formations, has consisted in its devotion to and expertise in mobilizing masses for the holding of rallies and demonstrations. Emotive slogans, stirring rhetoric from impassioned speakers, the massing of people amidst flags and loudspeakers, the converging of linear processions in a central arena to fuse into a milling mass—these episodic short-lived spectacles have been effective in putting pressure on the leading politicians and their parties. They have the impact of opinion polls and instantaneous media transmission. In this context, it is noteworthy that the generalized battle cry on behalf of the motherland has been suitably (and humorously) adjusted to their needs by university students, secondary school students, and scholar monks in seminaries as "Motherland first, degree second"; "Motherland first, school second"; and "Motherland first, pirivena second."

Schalk reports that "between the end of August and the middle of September 1986 as many as sixteen rallies were planned—almost one daily" and that by November of the same year thirty rallies had been held. We can take the story beyond where Schalk leaves off—the story of how on the eve of the actual signing of the Indo–Sri Lanka Peace Accord on 29 July 1987, an accord which was seen by members of the MSV coalition as conceding to the Tamils and the Indian government the very "unity" and "sovereignty" of the country, a mass rally of protest organized by the MSV deteriorated into a horrible riot in Colombo.

On 28 July 1987, the major components of the MSV—the SLFP with Mrs. Bandaranaike and other leaders of that party, the MEP led by Dinesh Gunawardena, the banned JVP represented by university student supporters, and finally at least two hundred monks from virtually all their member organizations—staged a procession and assembled under the sacred Bo Tree in Pettah, Colombo's "native" commercial center. The location, adjacent to the central bus station and near the Fort Railway Station, was chosen so as to enable the commuting participants to congregate easily. A huge crowd had formed, and the monks as well as the lay leaders waving black flags urged the people to protect the motherland from division and to oppose the accord, which would pave the way for India to take control of the island. Jayawardene's government in turn was prepared to disperse the demonstration by the use of force. The police fired tear gas into the crowd, which went on a destructive rampage. According to one report, nineteen civilians were killed during this one-day riot and more than a hundred were wounded when the police fired into the crowds. The mobs set fire to eighty buses, scores of cars, and a number of buildings, including shops, hospitals, and other government property. The government sealed off the major entry points into the city when it heard that crowds were amassing in the immediate suburbs with the intent of marching to the city's center.

This political demonstration deteriorating into a riot was the climactic point in the political rallies mounted by the MSV as well as the beginning of its disarray. Many participants were put off by the violence. The monks had been publicly, rudely, and summarily put in vans and taken away. The JVP and its youthful enthusiasts would now turn to and intensify their own brand of insurgency, which was marked by terrorism and violence. The JVP, which had in recent years sporadically practiced violence, would now systematize it and become a mirror image of the Tamil youth insurgents, fighting the government for its alleged concessionary attitude to the Tamils and its signing of the Peace Accord, and for its alleged injustices and inability to address the grievances of the poor.

Monks and Violence Face to Face

The politically active monks of the 1980s, consisting of many established leaders known for their orthodox adherence to rules pertaining to the monastic life and, even more, the young monks, a great many of whom were at universities and pirivenas or had recently left them, were, by virtue of their political commitments, confronted with the question of having to come to terms with the violence generated by the Tamil-Sinhala ethnic conflict and later by the civil war unleashed within the Sinhala society itself by the JVP.

As stated before, Tamil guerrillas had attacked Buddhist temples and killed monks. Sacred pilgrimage sites were being made inaccessible. In this charged atmosphere, it was found possible to fling the ancient epithet of *mlecca* ("savage") at those committing heinous crimes against Buddhism.

By and large the Sinhalese army's operations in the north and the east, especially after 1983 when the Tamil insurgents themselves became committed to counterviolence, had been supported by the Sinhala public, and it can be said that, with some notable exceptions, the majority of monks explicitly or privately supported and condoned the Sinhalese army's killing of Tamil guerrillas. The cause of preserving Sri Lanka as a sovereign undivided Sinhala Buddhist state is so paramount that the main body of the sangha has not felt the moral imperative to object to the tribulations imposed on Tamil civilians.

In the late 1980s, as popular movements composed of politicians, lay enthusiasts, and activist monks increasingly formed for protesting the "murderous Tamil Eelamism" and the government's attempts to seek a devolutionary solution to the ethnic conflict, Buddhist ceremonial and ritual, and the preachings of monks invoking allegedly Buddhist concepts and justifications, informed, colored, and legitimated the public posture. How have the "sons of Buddha"—ideally dedicated to nonviolence and required by disciplinary rules not only to refrain from acts of killing but also to be nowhere near marching armies and the traffic in arms—taken on the more compelling identity of "sons of the soil," which entails militant and violent politics? The most dramatic illustration of this transformation was in a 1982 May Day parade when about a thousand young monks affiliated with the JVP "clad in their distinctive saffron red robes walked under the banner of the socialist Bhikkhu Front."[30]

In the charters and propaganda sheets of these movements, "Buddhist" aims and objectives are inserted and interpreted as consonant with the preoccupations of the sons of the soil. Monks recite *pirit* at the public ceremonies and rallies; they stage sermons which are given the inflated name of *dharmadesanaya;* the "commemoration" and recall of the Buddha's enlightenment itself may precede the campaign rhetoric of fighting Tamil terrorism; and, finally, the newly prominent *bodhipuja* ritual may again be a part of a rally to protect the motherland.[31] Moreover, bodhipujas were held in leading temples to seek the blessings of gods in ensuring the safety and success of military personnel. Monks officiated at military functions, and the central army cantonment at Panagoda saw the erection of an impressive *chaitya* (pagoda).[32] If in previous times prime ministers and ministers of state did this, now military commanders too worship at the Temple of the Tooth Relic in Kandy upon appointment, and obtain blessings from the head monks of the Asgiriya and Malwatte chapters.

The JVP Monks: Alienation and Violence

For the remaining years of the decade, or more accurately until the end of the year 1989, the story of the monks' involvement with militant politics is best told by reference to the JVP. Among all the Sinhala political parties it was the JVP that most systematically set out to mobilize monks as an essential militant support group. The JVP membership itself was primarily drawn from Sinhala Buddhist male youth of rural social origins. And the movement sought to infiltrate the universities, where young monks have increasingly come to constitute as important segment of the student population. The egalitarian, populist, nationalist, anti-Tamil (and notably anti-Indian estate labor) Sinhala-Buddhist charter of the JVP appealed to young monks. In fact, in the 1971 insurgency some Buddhist temples in the interior had been used to store arms and ammunition and as hiding places and outposts for the insurgents.[33]

But it was in the late eighties that monks became an integral component of the JVP. Accusing it of participating in the anti-Tamil riots of 1983, the Jayawardene government had banned the JVP, which thereafter had to operate through "front" organizations. Aside from lay university and upper school students, young Buddhist monks provided this shield and outlet.

The JVP attempted to operate through national committees and territorial organizations at zonal, district, and subdistrict levels, and it appears that an attempt was made to form a JVP monk branch at each territorial level.[34] Monks of all sects were invited to join the JVP. While other political parties had also, as we have seen, organized cohorts of monks across nikaya differences, it was the JVP that achieved the most effective and widest trinikaya formation of politically activist monks.

These monks were particularly useful in the canvassing of young people to ascertain their views on issues. They joined all opposition groups in calling for early general elections. They also gave voice to the increasingly visible "consumerism"—a negative judgment on the increased flow of Western goods into Sri Lanka and the intensified adoption of Western lifestyles and recreational patterns ensuing from the "liberalizing" of the economy, the establishment of the free-trade zone, and the expansion of tourism under the UNP regime. The Buddhist emphasis on muting worldly desires and the nostalgic fiction of a simple homogeneous precolonial Sinhala-Buddhist peasant society were the themes articulated against consumerism and against deepening the division between the rich and the poor.

The most crucial dilemma facing the JVP monks concerned their party's decision to engage in "revolutionary violence" to right these wrongs. Officially this violent activity was said to be the work not of the JVP but of another organization, the Deshapremi Janatha Vijayaparaya (DJV), which, despite its disavowal, the public knew to be an armed division of the JVP, implementing the latter's decisions.

The engagement in militant violence by the JVP—which in the event was directed not so much against the distant Tamil insurgents and the alien Indian army as against chosen targets among the security forces of the government, its administrators, and local as well as national political agents of the UNP, all Sinhalese in identity and living in Sinhalese majority areas—divided all the groups and parties which saw themselves as opposed to the UNP government in power.

Cracks began to appear in the MSV, the umbrella organization made up of a loose coalition of the major opposition parties—SLFP, MEP, JVP, and several lay and monk Buddhist organizations. The representatives of the SLFP and MEP, and leading monks such as Chandananda, the Mahanayake of Asgiriya, now saw the need to distance themselves from active involvement with the MSV first, and even more emphatically with the young monks committed to the JVP's brand of militant nationalism, which was now creating havoc within the Sinhala body politic. The argument of the JVP that its violence was a response to the government's prior use of force and repression against civilians provided no balm to those who were dissociating themselves from it.

Many of the JVP monks, faced with what they construed as abandonment, even betrayal, by their senior monks and sectarian leaders, and compelled by their political commitments, became condoners of, and even collaborators in, acts of violence against senior monks. Within their own temples and within their own sects, they mounted criticism against their elders and their clerical authorities; they advocated that the monks in authority should sever their political connections with the major Sinhala parties, the UNP and the SLFP, both of which were believed to be willing to live with the accord; they passively condoned, perhaps even collaborated in, the assassination of recalcitrant senior monks by JVP/DJV executioners.

The government forces and paramilitary agents counterattacked by killing suspected JVP insurgents. Their victims included many alleged JVP monks, who were treated unceremoniously, chased, degraded, arrested, and tortured, and in some cases killed. The JVP monks in reply organized many fasts and satyagrahas at Buddhist temples, the most massive of which was staged at the Temple of the Tooth to put pressure on the senior monks of the Asgiriya and Malwatte chapters, the highest establishments of the Siyam Nikaya. "Soon after this demonstration the highest decision making bodies (Karaka Sabha) of these two establishments passed resolutions condemning the Accord and seeking protection for the monks who had been taken into custody by armed services. When the JVP escalated their terror tactics, leading Buddhist monks were characterized as traitors and sent death threats. As a result some left the island and others drastically curtailed their religious and social activities."[35] The JVP radical monks' basic stand was that the religion of the Buddha and the language and culture of the Sinhalese cannot flourish without a sovereign territory which is the motherland of Sri Lanka, and the uncompromising judgment they pronounced on their elders was that the elders had been slothful in their patriotic obligations, and had become trapped in such worldly interests as property, rank, and temple building.

By late 1989 and 1990, the time of my writing, the wheel of fortune had turned against the JVP as a whole, and also therefore against the JVP monks. The UNP government of Premadasa has by the compliant use of the security forces and their paramilitary organs succeeded in killing the leadership (the "Politburo") of the JVP and, finally, in decimating and capturing the dispersed JVP rank and file. The JVP monks have paid the price of this awesome show of force by the state: being readily recognizable in their robes, many have been killed; many have surrendered, or been disrobed and become laymen; many have confessed and turned informers. Many have retreated with lay members to jungle camps and hideouts. The monk who has finally taken to the gun can no longer be considered a vehicle of the Buddha's religion; moreover, he is unlikely to survive physically as a rebel in the jungle, the same jungle that fostered the wandering, meditating renouncer of the world, the highest achiever in Buddhism.

APPENDIX

LIST OF PARTIES AND ASSOCIATIONS WITH ABBREVIATIONS

All-Ceylon Buddhist Congress (All-Ceylon Buddhist Congress)
Ceylon National Congress (CNC)
Communist Party (CP)
Lanka Sama Samaja Party (LSSP)
Lanka Eksath Bhikkhu Mandalaya (LEPM)
Eksath Bhikkhu Peramuna (United Front)
Sinhala Maha Sabha (SMS)
Mahajana Eksath Peramuna (MEP)
United National Party (UNP)
Sri Lanka Freedom Party (SLFP)
Mavbima Surakime Vyaparaya (MSV)
Deshapremi Janatha Vijayaparaya (DJV)
Janatha Vimukthi Peramuna (JVP)
Tamil United Liberation Front (TULF)
Liberation Tigers of Tamil Eelam (LTTE)

Notes

1. The following are examples: Kitsiri Malagoda, *Buddhism in Sinhalese Society, 1750–1900: A Study of Religious Revival and Change* (Berkeley: University of California Press, 1976); Sarath Amunugama, "Anagarika Dharmapala (1864–1933) and the Transformation of Sinhala Buddhist Organization in a Colonial Setting," *Social Science Information* 24, no. 4 (1985): 697–730; Ananda Guruge, ed., *Return to Righteousness: A Collection of Speeches, Essays, and Letters of Anagarika Dharmapala* (Colombo: Government Press, 1965); George Bond, *The Buddhist Revival in Sri Lanka: The Religious Tradition, Reinterpretation and Response* (Columbia: University of South Carolina Press, 1988); and Richard Gombrich and Gananath Obeyesekere, *Buddhism Transformed: Religious Change in Sri Lanka* (Princeton, N.J.: Princeton University Press, 1988).

2. The anti-Muslim riots of 1915 are well documented. For example, see *Journal of Asian Studies* 24, no. 2 (1970), in which there are three essays under the rubric, "The 1915 Riots in Ceylon: A Symposium," with

an introduction by Robert Kearney; Ameer Ali, "The 1915 Racial Riots in Ceylon (Sri Lanka), a Reappraisal of Its Causes," *South Asia* 4, no. 2 (1981): 1–20; and A. P. Kannangara, "The Riots of 1915 in Sri Lanka: A Study in the Roots of Communal Violence," *Past and Present,* no. 2 (1984), pp. 130–65.

3. See P. Ramanathan, *Riots and Martial Law in Ceylon, 1915* (London, 1915).

4. As R. Kearney (1967: 47–48) puts it: "Although originating in the same social and ideological discontents and sharing hostility toward colonial rule, the two streams of sentiment developed markedly different characteristics. The Congress was led by men who, although occasionally displaying a sentimental attachment to the Sinhalese past and idealized village life, used the English language for the home and the public platform and adopted Western dress, manner of living, and mode of thought. Whereas the Sinhalese traditionalists defined their social and cultural goals by reference to the Sinhalese past, the congressmen tended to seek their goals in a closer emulation of modern Britain."

5. Some of the prominent monks in the so-called Vidyalankara Group were Rev. Naravila Dhammaratana, Rev. Udankandawela Saranankara, Rev. Walpola Rahula (all three studied in Calcutta), Rev. Bambarenda Siriseevali (who studied in Varanasi), and Rev. Kalalalle Anandasagra.

6. Walpola Rahula authored these two standard works in English: *History of Buddhism in Ceylon* (Colombo: Gunasena, 1956); and *What the Buddha Taught* (Gordon Bedford: Fraser, 1967).

7. See Urmila Phadnis, *Religion and Politics in Sri Lanka* (London: C. Hurst, 1976), pp. 163–65.

8. Communist Party (CP) and Lanka Sama Samaja Party.

9. The most prominent of them were G. P. Malalasekera, professor of Pali and Buddhist civilization, dean of the Faculty of Oriental Studies at Peradeniya University, who served at the height of his career as the president of the All Ceylon Buddhist Congress, and later, as the President of the World Buddhist Congress; P. de S. Kularatne, at one time principal of Ananda College, the most famous of the Buddhist schools on the island, and later manager of the Buddhist Theosophical Society schools; and L. H. Mettananda, a strong critic of the Catholic church and its activities, also an important educationalist associated with BTS schools. Mettananda served as principal of Dharmaraja College in Kandy before becoming the head of the first Ananda College.

10. Rahula, *History of Buddhism in Ceylon,* p. 92.

11. Eksath Bhikkhu Peramuna.

12. Samastha Lanka Bhikkhu Sammalanaya (SLBS).

13. Phadnis, *Religion and Politics in Sri Lanka,* p. 187.

14. W. Howard Wriggins, *Dilemmas of a New Nation* (Princeton, N.J.: Princeton University Press, 1960), pp. 260–61.

15. James Manor, *The Expedient Utopian: Bandaranaike and Ceylon* (Cambridge: Cambridge University Press, 1989), p. 269.

16. Ibid.

17. Ibid., p. 287.

18. Ibid., pp. 286–87.

19. Thus, Phadnis writes that while the Lanka Eksath Bhikkhu Mandalaya (LEBM) and many teachers of the Vidyalankara and Vidyodaya universities supported the coalition of the SLFP and the LSSP (Marxists), the UNP drew support from newly formed Colombo-based monk organizations such as Maha Sangha and Maha Sangha Peramuna as well as from the chief monk of the Malwatte chapter of the Siyam Nikaya. *Religion and Politics in Sri Lanka,* pp. 19–92.

20. Ibid., p. 195.

21. The number of private Hindu schools was small by comparison with Christian and Buddhist schools, and most of the former were taken over by the government.

22. On the Bandaranaike–Chelvanayagam Pact of 1956–57 and subsequent discussions on devolution, see Stanley J. Tambiah, "Ethnic Fratricide in Sri Lanka: An Update," in Remo Guidieri, Francesco Pelizzi, and Stanley J. Tambiah, eds., *Ethnicities*

and Nations (Austin: University of Texas Press, 1988). Also see James Manor, *The Expedient Utopian: Bandaranaike and Ceylon,* chap. 8.

23. Two informative recent discussions on these issues are Patrick Peebles, "Colonization and Ethnic Conflict in the Dry Zone of Sri Lanka," pp. 30–55, and Amita Shastri, "The Material Basis for Separatism: The Tamil Eelam Movement in Sri Lanka," pp. 56–77, both in *Journal of Asian Studies* 49, no. 1 (February 1990).

24. Peter Schalk, "'Unity' and 'Sovereignty': Key Concepts of a Militant Buddhist Organization in the Present Conflict in Sri Lanka," *Temenos* 1988, pp. 55–82.

25. Sarath Amunugama, "Buddhaputra and Bhumiputra? Dilemmas of Modern Sinhala Buddhist Monks in Relation to Ethnic and Political Conflict," *Religion* (1991).

26. Other organizations concerned with politicoreligious causes are the All-Ceylon Buddhist Congress and the national branch of the World Fellowship of Buddhists.

27. There were two other smaller parties listed by Amunugama (1990), namely, Sinhala Bala Mandalaya led by Nath Amerakone, and Sinhala Janata Peramuna.

28. Amunugama names three such national organizations, two of which were JVP oriented and the third MEP oriented, They are Deshapremi Taruna and Bhikshu Sanvidayana (both JVP oriented), and Samastha Lanka Pragatisili Bhikshu Peramuna (MEP oriented). "Buddhaputra and Bhumiputra?"

29. Schalk, "'Unity' and 'Sovereignty,'" pp. 57–58. One document published by the MSV claimed that "these rallies have given to the country a correct understanding about the provincial council ordinance which has been proposed by the President, Mr. J. R. Jayawardena, and which aims to divide the Country."

30. Amunugama, "Buddhaputra and Bhumiputra?"

31. On the *bodhipuja* ritual, see H. L. Seneviratne and Swarna Wickremaratne, "Bodhipuja: Collective Representations of Sri Lanka Youth," *American Ethnologist* 7, no. 4 (1980): 734–43.

32. Amunugama, "Buddhaputra and Bhumiputra?"

33. See A. C. Alles, *Insurgency-1971* (Colombo: Colombo Apothecaries' Co., 1976).

34. Amunugama, "Buddhaputra and Bhumiputra?"

35. Ibid.

CHAPTER
25

Conclusion: Remaking the State:
The Limits of the Fundamentalist Imagination

Martin E. Marty and R. Scott Appleby

Fundamentalisms Observed, the first volume in this series, demonstrated that religious fundamentalisms thrive in the twentieth century when and where masses of people living in formerly traditional societies experience profound personal and social dislocations as a result of rapid modernization and in the absence of mediating institutions capable of meeting the human needs created by these dislocations. Occasioned by mass migration from rural to urban areas, by unsynchronized social, economic, and cultural transformations and uneven schemes of development, by failures in educational and social welfare systems, and ultimately by the collapse of long-held assumptions about the meaning and purpose of human existence, the experience of dislocation fosters a climate of crisis. In this situation people are needy in a special way. Their hunger for material goods is matched by a thirst for spiritual reassurance and fulfillment. If these needs are integrated and integral, so must be the power offering fulfillment. Religion presented as an encompassing way of life suggests itself as the bearer of that power.

Taken together, volumes 2 and 3 of The Fundamentalism Project—*Fundamentalisms and Society* and *Fundamentalisms and the State*—confirm the notion that religious fundamentalisms are concerned with defining, restoring, and reinforcing the basis of personal and communal identity that is shaken or destroyed by modern dislocations and crises. The individual finds her true self in communion with a reality that transcends time and space, be this a personal God or an impersonal Principle. In either case, the gift of a religious conversion carries with it an obligation to bind oneself (*religare*) to like-minded individuals. By dictating the codes of behavior that govern the lives of these individuals, fundamentalist leaders bind so that they may unleash. People are united in their common experience of oppression or dislocation, bound together in community by their obligation to uphold the will of the One who

620

has freed them, and sent forth into the laboratories and schools and political parties and militias in order to secure and expand the borders of the sacred community.

Unlike many of their nonfundamentalist coreligionists, fundamentalists demand that the codes of behavior be applied comprehensively—not only to family life and interpersonal relations but to political organizations and international economies as well. Fundamentalists struggle for completeness because, as modern people, they have learned that traditional life based in the home, school, village, or tribe is not sufficient to ward off the invasive, colonizing Other. The religious community must therefore reject artificial distinctions between "private" and "public" realms—distinctions too easily accepted by conservative or orthodox believers who prefer to "live and let live." Fundamentalists know that life itself depends on victory over the enemy in a war for the control not only of resources but of ideas—so they prepare true believers for placement in institutions at every level of society, including the state. The observances of a religious community should permeate the whole of life, an organic unity that the agents of secular modernity have wrongly segmented and compartmentalized. The boundaries that matter are not between the "private" and the "public," but between the believer and the infidel.

Fundamentalisms as Imagined Communities

As world-builders motivated by a fierce opposition to the status quo, fundamentalists are eager participants in an ongoing global process of national self-definition—a process that has occurred with a special intensity in periods following a major international war, with the ensuing prospects for realignment and the shifting of boundaries. Because they are essentially modern constructs, fundamentalist religious communities, like secular regimes, tend to appropriate the language of nationalism. Yet the fundamentalist nation is grounded firmly in a territorial and social space inherited from the premodern religious past.

Benedict Anderson has observed that the end of the era of nationalism is not remotely in sight; indeed, "nation-ness is the most universally legitimate value in the political life of our time." Once established in the sixteenth century, nationality, or nation-ness, became modular, Anderson argues, and is "capable of being transplanted with varying degrees of self-consciousness to a great variety of social terrains, to merge and be merged with a correspondingly wide variety of political and ideological constellations."[1]

Religious fundamentalism appears increasingly to be one such constellation. When social philosophers and political theorists describe the paradoxes of nationalism, the student of comparative fundamentalisms is reminded of modern religiopolitical ideologies that borrow the language of ultimacy found in a sacred text or tradition.[2] For example, while the bureaucratic and technocratic nation-state is, objectively speaking, a product of modernity, nationalists perceive it subjectively as being rooted in antiquity. The same may be said of Christian fundamentalists in the United States, who insist that their Enlightenment-era democratic republic is the modern political-philosophical expression of the ancient Judeo-Christian tradition; of Hindu fundamentalists, who define the modern Indian nation as "Hindustan," a vision drawn from the prehistorical past; or of the radical Jewish settlers on the West Bank, who imaginatively extend the nation of Israel's borders to the dimensions of the "Whole Land of Israel" as set forth in the Torah.

Other paradoxes are shared by nationalists and fundamentalists. While nationalists assume that nationality as a sociocultural concept is universal—everyone can, should, and will have a nationality—the concept is irredeemably particular in its concrete manifestations. By definition Spanish nationality is sui generis. In the same way, each fundamentalism recognizes and even expects that other peoples will react as they do by establishing precise boundaries for the sacred community and by developing and deepening the particularities of belief, behavior, dress, diet, and ritual that define a tribe. But this acknowledgment of the universal need for rootedness in a traditional soil and culture does not modify or soften the fundamentalist's insistence on exceptionalism: his claims to the land and cultural definition take priority over others, because his vision is authentic while others are imitations. The West Bank Jewish radicals do not pretend that their Palestinian Arab neighbors will one day accept the Jewish interpretation of history and the land. But the Palestinians will have to accept Jewish cultural and political hegemony because it is promised by God. North Indian Muslims and Sikhs actually live in Hindustan, according to the Rashtriya Swayamsevak Sangh (RSS) (the National Union of Volunteers), and must become "Hindu" by subordinating their particular rites and behaviors, when necessary, to the ethos of the dominant Indian culture. In the late twentieth century, "the most messianic nationalists do not dream of a day when all of the members of the human race will join their nation in the way that it was possible in certain epics for, say, Christians to dream of a wholly Christian planet."[3] Rather, they anticipate a time when the true believer will establish the rules of the game for believer and nonbeliever alike.

Thus, one may also juxtapose the political power of nationalisms (and fundamentalisms) and their "philosophical poverty and even incoherence."[4] What Ernest Gellner attributes to nationalisms may be said, mutatis mutandis, of many fundamentalisms: "Nationalism is not the awakening of nations to self-consciousness; it *invents* nations where they do not exist."[5] The establishment of national borders has indeed been an arbitrary process, taken to absurd extremes in the segmentation of the Middle East after the Allied defeat of the Ottoman Empire. Why does this river or that line of hills serve as the national dividing line, when the people across the river or over the hills are of the same bloodline or religious faith? If, as historian Tom Nairn has written, nationalism is the pathology of modern developmental history, fundamentalists are equally "pathological" when they redraw the dividing lines by imagining and seeking to govern a "Land of Purity" (e.g., the Sikh Khalistan) set off and secured from nonbelievers.[6]

The fundamentalist land of purity may coincide with, exist within, or transcend existing national boundaries. That is, fundamentalisms may, strictly speaking, be subnational, national, or transnational in orientation. In any case, the fundamentalist homeland is an imagined political community that extends beyond local or regional groupings. A member of the Jamaat-i-Islami, which numbers in the millions, will never know all of his fellows; nor do the one million members of the RSS function as a discrete unit. Each individual or group acts with a sense of his or her belonging to a larger whole that supercedes all other national or regional configurations. Even in the smaller groups such as the Jewish Gush Emunim, or the American Christian Operation Rescue, in which members may well know one another intimately, there is a sense of unity with a silent and faceless mass of passive believers who are waiting for the vanguard to plant the seed of the new Israel or the restored Christian America.

In Islamic fundamentalisms, for example, there has been a rejection of Arab nationalism and a rhetorical embrace of the *umma,* the universal community of Muslims. In practice, however, fundamentalist movements have experienced factionalism and shifting alliances across national borders, as Olivier Roy points out in his chapter on Islamic movements in Afghanistan. Alluding to the patterns of Saudi funding of movements before and after the 1990–91 Gulf War, Roy notes that the Saudis were angered and disappointed when certain of the groups they had supported financially, including the Afghan resistance movement Hizb-i-Islami headed by Gulbuddin Hikmatyar, backed Saddam Hussein's invasion of Kuwait. After the war, the Saudis altered their pattern of funding, deepening a split between radical fundamentalist movements and the more conservative or moderate movements favored by the Saudi monarchy. Indeed, the range of responses by fundamentalist groups to the Gulf Crisis demonstrated the fluidity of fundamentalist alliances and the distance to be traveled before Muslim fundamentalists can claim the realization of a pan-Islamic vision.[7] Nonetheless, a period of intense collaboration among movements on either side of the moderate-radical divide seemed possible in 1992. Reports that the Sudan had inherited Lebanon's role as home for international terrorists, including Shi'ite cadres financed by Iran, were one sign that previous barriers to pan-Islamic fundamentalist collaboration among radical movements may have fallen in the wake of the Gulf War, the collapse of the Soviet Union, and the loose talk of a new world order, interpreted by Islamic radicals as a code for a return to Western control of Arab resources.

However fundamentalists come to define the "nation," the similarities between nationalist and fundamentalist imaginings are not merely coincidental. The concept of the sovereign nation was born in an age in which enlightenment and revolution were destroying the legitimacy of the divinely ordained, hierarchical dynasty. The nation was invested with ultimacy, even as traditional religion fell into eclipse, only to reemerge, transformed and modernized, in the late nineteenth and twentieth centuries as a competitor with secular ideologies of all kinds. The nation has finite, if elastic, boundaries, which are contested by outsiders; the same may be said of fundamentalisms. But both the nation and the fundamentalist community are conceived of as deep horizontal comradeships, "sacred" fraternities for which people may die or kill other people. Like nationalisms, fundamentalisms possess hegemonic political ambitions and demand colossal sacrifices from their devotees.

National communities are to be distinguished, then, not by the credentials or status of their founders but by the "style in which they are imagined."[8] *Fundamental-*

isms and the State offers insights regarding the "style" of fundamentalists' imaginings, and the ways in which these imagined communities have been realized in local and state governments, in domestic and international economies, and in wars of attrition and conquest.

A Religious Imagination

As the preceding chapters demonstrate, fundamentalists have been successful in attracting attention to themselves and to their causes, with the result, in some cases, that they have become viable players in the structuring of polities and the ordering of economies. Fundamentalists have earned the fear and grudging respect of their secular and religious opponents. The limits of this success require careful analysis, as do the reasons for it.

Part of the explanation for their success in mobilizing followers is found in the ostensibly religious character of fundamentalisms. Not all of the people who are involved in fundamentalist movements, or who benefit from them, are devout. Indeed, fundamentalisms in every tradition attract their share of charlatans and manipulators who cloak themselves in religious orthodoxy for the sake of political or financial gain. And, as we shall see, fundamentalisms often exploit economic and social discontent more skillfully and readily than they tap religious idealism. To put it another way, religious idealism is often a convenient form by which to express and channel the outrage of the economically or politically marginalized.

Analysts commit a serious error, however, if they assume that fundamentalism is, as one former State Department official put it during a public conference, "essentially a sociopolitical protest movement sugarcoated with religious pieties." Standing behind some of the most spectacular blunders of the foreign policy establishment have been a number of errors in judgment, including the smug assumption that secular rationality is the system underlying all forms of discourse; the tendency to underestimate the capacity of well-educated people for religious sensibilities; and the unwillingness or failure to appreciate the genuine alterity of the religious consciousness. To put the matter directly: many influential leaders in the world genuinely believe in and live by religious doctrine taken in its most literal meaning. When the late Iranian Shi'ite Ayatollah Ruhollah Khomeini issued a *fatwa* sentencing the Pakistani expatriate/British citizen/former Muslim Salman Rushdie to death for apostasy, and promised paradise to his executioner, many Western analysts focused on the possible political, economic, and diplomatic rationales for Khomeini's move. By dramatically condemning a prominent author whose novel, *The Satanic Verses,* had disgraced the memory of the Prophet, the Ayatollah was sending a signal of support to the hardliners in the Iranian regime. Or, other commentators suggested, Khomeini was reasserting his position as the leader of revolutionary Islam in the Middle East and South Asia. These were cogent and valid explanations, imputing a certain amount of shrewd political calculation to Khomeini. But they also tended to overlook a simple and basic explanation, one more scandalous to Western sensibilities but also more useful to an understanding of the likely course of events in the years that followed the sentencing.[9] Khomeini was the genuine article: he saw the world through the eyes of a Muslim *marja'al-taqlid*, a "source of imitation," who believed himself to be the Supreme Jurist, obligated to govern the Islamic Republic in the absence of the Hidden Imam. By this reckoning such refined Western notions as the independent sovereignty of Great Britain and the rights of its citizens, including former Muslims, were not recognized. Khomeini acted on faith—a faith shared by millions of Muslims who perpetuated the calumny on Rushdie long after the Ayatollah passed from the scene. This shared faith remains a legitimating principle for putatively Islamic regimes, as well as for the post–Khomeini Islamic Republic of Iran.

The religious character of fundamentalisms provides a cause whose importance outweighs the value of the believer's life or liberty. As David Rapoport points out in his chapter on fundamentalist militancy, religious rituals of self-sacrifice, like the self-flagellation of Shi'ites commemorating Ashura, or the prayers of Operation Rescue members lying in a fetal position before the doors of abortion clinics, locate the believer in a sacred cosmos that rewards martyrdom or imprisonment in the service of God. The dramatic examples of suffering welcomed in the cause of righteousness divert attention from the less sensational but no less "heroic" daily self-sacrifices of fundamentalists who seek to remake the world. The suicide missions of Hizbullah truck bombers and the armed battles of the Intifada between Jewish settlers and Palestinian Arabs make the headlines, but they are eruptions of private lives characterized, in the Islamic case, by the "greater jihad," the daily struggle to win control over one's life in the face of the temptation to seek material gain and physical comfort, and, in the Jewish case, by the observation of one mitzvah, or religious commandment, that takes precedence over the others—the wearying responsibility to cling tenaciously to the Land of Israel.

The ability of fundamentalisms to inspire heroism and self-sacrifice stems in part from a belief in the possibility of personal or collective immortality. The expectation of an afterlife, although understood in its particulars in very different ways by the religious groups studied in this volume, gives fundamentalist leaders an important psychological advantage in mobilizing people for dangerous assignments and in retaining them as active members in the long-term operations of a movement. Andersen points out that there is no Tomb of the Unknown Marxist or cenotaph for fallen liberals. "The reason is that neither Marxism nor liberalism are much concerned with death and immortality," he observes. "If the nationalist imagining is so concerned, this suggests a strong affinity with religious imaginings."

> The great merit of traditional religious worldviews has been their concern with man-in-the-cosmos, man as species being, and the contingency of life. The extraordinary survival, over thousands of years, of Buddhism, Christianity, or Islam, in dozens of different social formations attests their imaginative response to the overwhelming burden of human suffering, disease, mutilation, grief, age, and death. Why was I born blind? Why is my best friend paralyzed? Why is my daughter retarded? The religion is an attempt to explain. The great weakness of all evolutionary progressive styles of thought not excluding Marxism is that such questions are answered with impatient silence.[10]

In the attempt to explain, or at least account for, the mysteries of human suffering and the sacred meaning of history, fundamentalists often draw on eschatalogical, or end-time, thought. Muslims, Christians, Jews, and Sikhs have in recent decades emphasized messianic and millenarian themes within their respective religious traditions. Expectations of an imminent, sweeping, divinely led victory over their enemies have informed the self-understandings and operational strategies of the Sikh radicals of the Damdami Taksal, the Gush Emunim in Israel, the Hizbullah of Lebanon, and other militant groups studied in this volume. The resort to violence by these groups, prompted in part by the failure of purely political means of persuasion, occurs within and is conditioned by the moral framework of apocalypticism.

In many cases in which militance is seen as a necessary means of achieving divine ends, the religious imagination envisions a "nation" that transcends existing borders. Martin Kramer quotes one of Hizbullah's leading clerics' prediction that "the divine state of justice realized on part of this earth will not remain confined within its geographic borders." Similarly, Harjot Oberoi notes, Sikhism possesses the most advanced paradigm of millennial thought and practice of all the indigenous religious communities in India. "For much of their history, at least since the rise of the Khalsa, Sikhs have opted to deal with major social crises—state oppression, economic upheavals, colonialism, collapse of semiotic categories—by invoking the millenarian paradigm," he writes. "Central to this entire model has been a prophetic figure of extraordinary charisma with the will to establish an alternative social system in which oppression would cease and people would lead a life of harmony, purity, and good deeds." In 1982 the Sikh fundamentalist leader, Jarnail Singh Bhindranwale, led the *dharma yuddh,* or righteous battle, which he characterized as an epic war in which good was pitted against evil and only one side was to be victorious. Bhindranwale expected the Sikhs "to rule Delhi, rule the world."

The religious imagination of fundamentalists is not, however, captured solely by grisly scenes of holy war and self-immolation for the cause; it is also a vision of mercy. Compassion for the suffering of others finds concrete expression in the thousands of health care clinics, orphanages, hospitals, schools, and service agencies sponsored by fundamentalist movements or individuals around the world. The good done by these institutions is at least as important in winning recruits for the cause as are the rallies and riots. In both cases the success of fundamentalisms stands as an indictment of the weaknesses of secular systems in providing for human psychological and social needs.

A Political Imagination

Fundamentalists inform their religious critique of society with shrewd observations of the political culture that resonate with economically or socially aggrieved peoples. The years of observing their secular opponents at close range enable fundamentalists to imitate their ways and adopt their means—fundamentalists are increasingly at ease in parliaments and press conferences, and adept at mass-mail lobbying and computer-driven technologies. Politics informed by fundamentalist religion is in many ways like politics-as-usual: in all but the most oppressive dictatorships, compromise and negotiation are its lifeblood, and adaptation to changing political realities its mode of response. But fundamentalist politics also proceeds by its own internal rhythms, dictated by the particular organizational and ideological requirements of the movement. Fundamentalists may attempt, as the Islamists did for a time in Algeria, to overcome or minimize the reluctance of voters by projecting an image of moderation. But they may also follow a strategy of polarization designed to provoke their opponents and scandalize the world outside the national community, thereby hoping to tap xenophobic energies of the masses and to awaken previously politically somnolent sympathizers.

The politics of crisis born of the religious imagination of fundamentalism was strikingly on display on the Indian subcontinent in late 1991 and early 1992. On 11 December 1991, an extraordinary caravan of trucks, jeeps, and a few customized Toyotas embarked on a "sacred journey" from the southernmost tip of India with the goal of reaching the city of Srinagar, some fifteen hundred miles away, on the northwestern border with Pakistan. Riding in the caravan were prominent members of the the Bharatiya Janata Party (BJP), the opposition party in India which is closely aligned with the Hindu activist movement RSS—the National Union of Volunteers. Riding atop the lead Toyota, protected by a bullet-proof shield, was the president of the BJP, Murli Manohar Joshi, a former professor of physics. Organized as a display of Indian "unity," the caravan was an expression of the singular nationalist vision of the BJP-RSS-VHP front that Robert Frykenberg describes in this volume.

The BJP and RSS believe that what they call "Hindu-ness" is the authentic source of unity in the sprawling, multiethnic, multilingual, multireligious Indian nation, governed presently by a secular constitution that favors no one religion but ensures the right of each to worship as it pleases. The BJP and RSS seek to alter that constitution by defining citizenship on the basis of "Hindu-ness." They seek to "Hinduize" all of India, which they refer to as "Hindustan," the sacred Hindu nation. All citizens of Hindustan, including Sikhs, Muslims, Christians, Jains, Buddhists, and Marxists, must put aside ethnic, religious or ideological beliefs and practices that conflict with the dominant Hindu ethos—an ethos that is not spelled out with great precision but is nonetheless spread through the newly revitalized Hindi language and through textbooks filled with Hindu mythology and politics that are being urged upon Indian schoolchildren.[11]

The three-month trek across India involved thousands of Hindus and featured the full repertoire of fundamentalist agitants. The BJP eagerly anticipated that a symbolic journey of Hindu militants through contested regions of northern India would scandalize not only the Sikh and Muslim separatists living there who reject Hindu hegemony, but the secularists of the governing Congress party as well. The BJP president's vow to raise the Indian flag in Srinigar, the capital of the Muslim-dominated region of Kashmir, was calculated to provoke a crisis leading to Muslim riots and the consequent assertion of Indian state control over the contested region.

Like the radical Jewish settlers on the West Bank profiled by Charles Liebman and Ehud Sprinzak, or the Sinhalese Buddhist militants in Sri Lanka described by Stanley Tambiah, the RSS and BJP cadres forming the Hindu caravan saw themselves as a sacred vanguard bent on inducing a reluctant state to declare its true affinities and endorse a religious imagining of the nation. In cases like these, in which a religious fundamentalist group is the provocateur setting the terms of the engagement, any responsive action of a secular government to defend national integrity against a rebellious minority is liable to be interpreted as an affirmation of a particular ethnoreligious identity for the entire nation. The imagined community narrows to a monolith when fundamentalists lead or shape the imagining. Fundamentalists provoke a crisis, identify their cause with the nation's cause, and challenge the government to do the enforcing. When Jewish religious nationalists succeed in provoking state action against Palestinian Arabs on the West Bank, when Sinhalese Buddhists inflame the campaign against Tamil Hindus in northern Sri Lanka, when Hindu militants incite state retaliation against Sikhs in the Punjab or Muslims in Kashmir, the fundamentalist identification with the sovereign nation is deepened. Fundamentalists shrewdly perceive, exploit, and draw strength from the absolutism implied in the very concept of a sovereign nation; they drink at the same wells and are eager to give a name to the principle of sovereignty, whether that name be Rama, Allah, Yahweh, or God.

The Hindu provocateurs sought to reinterpret and rename the boundaries of India. Congress party officials viewed the procession as "unnecessarily provocative" but were at a loss as to how to stop it without seeming to acknowledge that India is ungovernable. One of the clear conclusions of this volume is that fundamentalist activism yields intended and unintended consequences, both for the fundamentalists and for the people they seek to influence. As in nonfundamentalist politics, there is little or no linear progression from intention to result; other players have a way of reacting in unpredictable ways that ensure that fundamentalist designs are either frustrated or complicated in the unfolding. The complex impact of the BJP caravan on India's Sikh, Muslim, and Hindu enclaves provides a case in point.

The first violent reaction came from Sikh militants, who ambushed a bus carrying BJP workers as it entered the Punjab. The gunmen, disguised as police officers, killed five people and wounded forty—the first act in a cycle of violence that continued for days. Sikh radicals came to the fore in Punjab in 1983, when members of the moderate Sikh political party Akali Dal abandoned the party to swell the ranks of Jarnail Singh Bhindranwale, the afore-mentioned charismatic leader of the radical Damdami Taksal party. Oberoi explains that the moderates had failed to translate the demography of Punjab into a permanent political power for the Sikh majority. The radicals charged that the democratic option had only further weakened the Sikhs by making them susceptible to factionalism, political manipulation, and extended rule by the Congress party. Even when a moderate Sikh government ruled the Punjab, it failed to advance Sikh religious interests, because it almost always had alliances with other political parties, including Hindu parties. Bhindranwale took the road of violence. To the traditional symbols on the Sikh insignia—the unshorn hair, short pants, and sword—he added the motorcycle and the revolver.

In peripheral agrarian or partially industrialized societies such as the Punjab, Oberoi writes, fundamentalist movements address predicaments that are routinely addressed in the West by the welfare state and its socioeconomic programs. Yet

fundamentalists are seldom politically or economically capable of permanently addressing the systemic problems of the region. The movements remain simply reactive.
Denied political authority and engaged in a constant struggle for survival and legitimacy, Sikh peasants from the countryside swelled the ranks of the radicals but without
offering any concrete programs for reform, much less grand paradigms of social transformation. The cosmos of peasant societies is invariably parochial rather than national
or universal. Sikh fundamentalism is thus characterized by marginality, incoherence,
and disorder. In 1991 the police recorded 4,766 violent deaths in the Punjab related
to militant Sikh separatist activism intended to show the Punjab is ungoverned and
ungovernable.[12]

Thus, the caravan that rolled through the Punjab in January 1992 was assured of
provoking unrest. The sight of Hindu nationalists protected by Indian security forces
doubtless brought to mind the 1984 storming of the Sikh Golden Temple at Amritsar
which had claimed one thousand lives, made a martyr of Bhindranwale, and led to
more Sikh deaths in Hindu riots after Indira Gandhi's assassination by her Sikh bodyguards. Enraged by the return of Hindu militants to the Punjab, Sikh radicals raided
the BJP caravan and shortly thereafter warned that they would kill anyone voting in
the elections for parliament and the local legislatures scheduled for 19 February 1992.
Despite the presence of a quarter of a million Indian state soldiers, the death threats
kept away the vast majority (70 percent) of Punjab voters. In some villages, not a
single person came to vote. Those who did tended to be members of the Hindu
minority.[13]

The BJP caravan rolled on to Kashmir, where the Jammu Kashmir Liberation
Front has led Muslim separatists in their efforts to secede from India. In anticipation
of the arrival of the caravan, Muslim militants bombed the regional police chief's
office in Srinagar. On 25 January 1992, the BJP called off plans to drive a large
motorcade through the vale of Kashmir. But Joshi did hoist the Indian flag in Srinagar's town square—although to do so he required the presence of tens of thousands
of heavily armed troops and a total curfew in the Kashmir Valley.[14]

Across the border in Pakistan the Hindu caravan had its own unsettling impact.
On 13 February, with thousands of supporters trailing behind him, many of them
members of the Islamic fundamentalist party Jamaat-i-Islami, Amanullah Khan, the
Pakistani counterpart to Joshi, led a march toward Indian-controlled Kashmir. He
was ready to die for Allah. "It's not important who leads, but I hope that I will get
the first Indian bullet," he was quoted as saying. Pakistani police fired on the separatists trying to cross the border into India, and the Pakistani prime minister, Nawaz
Sharif, concerned about the possibility of a war with India, said that Amanullah's
action was "like throwing innocent people into the fire."[15]

Sharif's dilemma was instructive to observers of fundamentalist political influence.
His Democratic Alliance won the October 1990 election by defeating the Pakistan
People's Party of Benazir Bhutto. The first head of government drawn from the
middle class and not from the landowning aristocracy, Sharif implemented policies
designed to revive the national economy. His government removed most restrictions
on currency and trade, and began turning over many state-run companies and several

banks to private owners. The Pakistan rupee quickly surpassed the Indian rupee in value. Yet the new prime minister was caught in the middle between Pakistan's vocal and influential Muslim fundamentalists and the secular government of India. Thus, he referred to the Muslim marchers on India as "freedom fighters" even as he came under criticism from Islamic fundamentalists for halting the march. Sharif was also compromised, in Muslim fundamentalists' eyes, by his ongoing attempts at rapprochement with the United States. Indeed, his policies seemed to reflect a mild case of schizophrenia. In 1991 he courted the fundamentalists by introducing a so-called Shari'a Bill in the wake of the Gulf War. The Democratic Alliance claimed that the bill satisfied the demand for the legislation of Islamic law, but the Jamaat-i-Islami found it to be superficial and rejected it. In 1992, with Pakistan under an American aid embargo, Sharif attempted to rehabilitate Pakistan's image by abandoning the long-standing support of the Muslim fundamentalist fighters in neighboring Afghanistan. The move enraged the Islamic parties, which hold only 10 of the 217 seats in the National Assembly but form an important part of the governing coalition and wield enormous influence over the conservative and largely illiterate population.

What seemed schizophrenic was actually a carefully calibrated policy designed to appease Muslims on domestic issues while applying the principles of realpolitik on the international front—a policy also followed by Arab leaders in Egypt and Jordan besieged by fundamentalist demands.[16] But this policy carries a high risk of backfiring. As Timur Kuran documents in the present volume, "Islamic economics" has been a slogan rather than a serious policy in Pakistan. But in 1992 Sharif's policies, a mixture of Western-style modernization and Islamic moderation, incited the highest religious courts in Pakistan to order the government to suspend Western-style banking and abolish interest on bank deposits, loans, land acquisition, insurance, and cooperative societies—moves that would risk financial collapse, jeopardize international financial dealings, and thwart attempts to attract foreign investments. Sharif's finance minister initially said the government would appeal but backed off, temporarily at least, when the Jamaat threatened to bring down the ruling coalition by withdrawing from it. The story exemplifies the continuing pressure brought to bear by fundamentalists upon governments that claim to uphold Islam without actually implementing Islamic law.[17]

The Limits of the Fundamentalist Imagination

What lessons about "fundamentalist impact" are contained in the episode of the BJP caravan?

Fundamentalist leaders are effective in exploiting the ideological inconsistencies and policy failures of nonfundamentalist governments and in mobilizing large numbers of people for intense and highly visible short-term rallies or projects, and smaller numbers of very loyal workers to sustain the long-term life of the organization or movement. While zeal and increasing political sophistication have carried fundamentalist groups to power or to the brink of power in several nations, these groups have not yet proven themselves capable of actually governing effectively. The BJP's Hindu leadership had not formulated a viable economic program by the time of the election campaign of 1991. Thus, they seemed unprepared to lead India out of its worst economic crisis since independence. In this volume Deepak Lal describes BJP economic policies as "changing, vague, and incoherent." The Hindu nationalist movement rejects the "foreign" influences of Islam, Christianity, capitalism, and socialism alike as failed remedies to India's deep-rooted social and economic problems—but has posed no viable alternative. To varying degrees the same can be said of the Islamic, Jewish, Christian, Sikh, and Buddhist fundamentalists profiled in this volume: they have proven themselves skilled at discerning the problems of society and naming the perpetrators, but they have been far less impressive in posing workable solutions.[18]

Along with the impressive qualities of the fundamentalist political imagination, then, comes a severe limitation. Fundamentalists find it difficult to govern without resorting to the services of professional politicians and nonfundamentalist allies. "Authentic" fundamentalists—that is, men and women motivated primarily if not exclusively by religious considerations—are caught in a dilemma when they attempt to realize the world they have imagined. On the one hand, self-reliance can lead quickly to failure. Genuine fundamentalists are first and foremost men and women of religion rather than of government—even when, as in the case of Sunni Muslim groups, they are drawn from the ranks of engineers rather than clergy. This is not to say that all fundamentalists are ipso facto politically naive—this is hardly the case—but they do tend to be inexperienced in governance, especially in the delicate and all-important area of international relations. For a head of state or cabinet minister to be a novice in the ways of a world run according to secular-material rather than religious-spiritual values is to court disaster. On the other hand, reliance on sympathizers and advisers from outside the inner circle can lead just as quickly to the politics of compromise and the distillation of the fundamentalist sociomoral message. (This was precisely the possibility that Islamic fundamentalist hardliners feared in the temporizing regime of Iranian president Rafsanjani.) Or, conversely, rule by political or military professionals can lead to a despotic hardening of fundamentalist injunctions as a justification for the imposition of a police state (as in the case of the Sudan under General Omar Hussain al-Bashir and Hassan al-Turabi).

Many of the fundamentalist or fundamentalist-like groups examined in this volume seemed to be engaged in a third way of negotiating political influence. In this pattern fundamentalist leaders and secular politicians found that they shared temporal goals and so entered tacitly or openly into a mutually beneficial alliance. Fundamentalist leaders are willing to be carried along on a wave of socioeconomic or purely political resentment, while secular politicians provide financial and political support for the religious "pioneers" who will say and do things that a "mainstream" politician studiously avoids. When they are drawn into these types of alliances, fundamentalists may make rather modest political demands for themselves, in most cases asking for the retention or modest extension of privileges and exemptions that they already enjoy.

Three authors of the "Remaking Polities" part of the volume emphasize this point in describing fundamentalist groups which are in tacit alliance with (politically conservative) secular agents. John Garvey and Steve Bruce agree with many other observers that the "New Christian Right," which came to prominence in the 1980s in the United States, provided an example of a fundamentalist protest movement co-opted and used by a powerful and sophisticated secular political group—in this case, the ultraconservative wing of the Republican Party. The New Christian Right had a much more expansive political and legal agenda, Garvey points out, than did the Moral Majority or the Religious Roundtable.

Charles Liebman makes a similar point about the influence of religious Jews—the *haredi-leumi*, or "nationalist haredi," a recent convergence of two distinct strands of radical Judaism in Israel—on the Israeli political agenda. If one looks at their specific and unique political agenda, Liebman argues, rather than at their long-term cultural influence, one finds that their political demands have been relatively modest, and mostly designed to protect privileges they currently enjoy under Israeli law. Furthermore, the "success" of the radical Jews in pioneering settlements on the West Bank has been possible only with the approval of nonfundamentalist, nonreligious Israelis. The fundamentalists have proven to be useful agents of an expansionist policy of a secular government and an increasingly militant Israeli public which does not share the religious doctrine or ideology of the radicals.

For the purpose of analyzing the political impact of Jewish radicals on the Israeli political system, Liebman conflates the two major groups, the religious Zionist settlers of the Gush Emunim and the anti-Zionist "ultra-Orthodox" haredi Jews. But when one looks at these groups separately, as Ehud Sprinzak does in his chapter, one notices two distinct types of political-cultural impact on the Israeli population. The Gush Emunim activists, who believe that the time of redemption is nigh and that they are the agents of the Messiah, wish to serve as models for an Israeli public which they are hoping to incite to political action on God's behalf (that is, in their view, action in opposition to Palestinian Arabs living in the territories occupied by Israel since the 1967 Six Day War). Hoping to lend a religious zeal and ultimacy to what many perceive as an ethnic Arab-Israeli conflict, the Gush activists appeal to the religious heritage of the secularized Jews, who make up 80 percent of the Israeli population.

In this way the religious Zionists aspire to the type of role played by the Ulster Protestants profiled by Bruce. "In Northern Ireland," Bruce writes, "the basic structure of the ethnic conflict with Catholics means that, for Protestants, religion remains a vital part of their sense of identity, and even those people who are not committed 'born-again' believers find themselves turning back to conservative Protestant ideologies and languages to make sense of their apparently beleaguered position in the north of Ireland and to give purpose to their political agenda, which is dominated by a desire to remain part of the United Kingdom of Great Britain and Northern Ireland." Thus, fundamentalism takes on a political role and attracts a variety of adherents who do not necessarily accept many of the theological doctrines espoused by the Reverend Ian Paisley, a prominent leader of the Ulster Protestants.

In the same way, the haredi Jews of Israel, who enter politics reluctantly and then only in order to maintain the privileges of their subculture, are comparable to American Christian fundamentalists, who may employ a rhetoric of dominance but whose political actions suggest that they, too, are actually in the game primarily to protect the values of a distinctive religious subculture from further erosion.

Liebman argues that as long as the religious fundamentalists are politically accountable to the secularists upon whom they depend for protection and financing, they may continue to pay lip service to the demand for religious legislation but satisfy themselves with a defense of their narrower communal interests. "Democracy not only limits the achievements of the fundamentalists; it even moderates many of their demands." Sprinzak notes, however, that the escalating use of violence by both groups fosters a constant sense of crisis that has a destabilizing effect on Israeli society and thus poses a serious challenge for the long-term prospects of democracy. "For a democracy to survive decently, it is not enough that all the partners to the regime formally respect its institutions. A respect for its value and a positive orientation toward its legal order are also necessary," he writes. "This is today the Achilles' heel of Israel's democracy and the problem with the new religious radicalism. Even those ultranationalists and fundamentalists who say they are committed to democracy in their own way are a serious danger because their commitment is instrumental and their allegiance is conditional."

When one turns from secular democracies to sectarian states, however, the influence of fundamentalist extremism is less liable to be neutralized by the exigencies of political compromise. Stanley J. Tambiah's account of ethnic and religious conflict between Tamil Hindus and Sinhalese Buddhists on the island nation of Sri Lanka provides an example of the dynamic of violence between religious-ethnic communities in an unstable state. In struggling for political hegemony, the fundamentalist perpetrators of violence move beyond the parameters of the historic religious tradition they intend to defend. That the Buddhist tradition, committed historically to nonviolence, could produce a "fundamentalism" defined in recent years by "Buddhist nationalism" and anti-Tamil militance is no less troubling than the abandonment of *ahimsa* by the radical Tamils, Tambiah comments.

Similarly, there is no mistaking the scandalous aspect of the recent manifestations of Islamic fundamentalism in the Sudan and in Iran, two quite different regimes but comparable in their disregard for Western standards of human rights. Although the revolutionary fervor and radical fundamentalism embodied in Iran by Ayatollah Khomeini may have waned with his passing, the Islamic Republic was sustained and perhaps strengthened by what Said Arjomand calls a "pragmatic" ruling elite led by President Hashemi Rafsanjani. Despite its commitment to realpolitik, its tentative moves toward the reestablishment of open diplomatic relations with the United States, and its consequent relaxation of support for Islamic revolutionary movements elsewhere, the Iranian government remained committed to the "revolutionary traditionalism [which] has transformed the Iranian nation-state as fundamentally as it has Shiʻism." Though constitution-making in Iran does bear the distinct imprint of the legal logic of the modern state, Arjomand writes, "it has nonetheless transformed the latter into a veritable theocracy."

The National Islamic Front, led by the Western-educated legal scholar Hassan al-Turabi, has controlled the military government of General Omar Hussan al-Bashir since the 1989 coup that brought the military to power. The NIF wants to spread fundamentalism to the moderate Arab countries and the rest of Africa. In a 1992 interview al-Turabi described the march of fundamentalism as "inevitable" as it moves to fill the vacuum left by the failures of Western-inspired African socialism and Arab nationalism. Al-Turabi's vision of an Islamic world held together by religion and economic interdependence led him, a Sunni, to seek assistance from Iranian Shi'ites, who provided oil and military training in the early 1990s.[19] As Ann Mayer documents in her chapter, al-Turabi's brand of Islamic fundamentalism has emerged since the 1989 coup as antidemocratic, a violator of human rights, and a protector of international terrorist groups. According to Amnesty International and other human rights organizations, the military government has banned the Sudan's well-entrenched political parties, imprisoned suspected opponents, and tortured detainees.

With or without support from Iran or Saudi Arabia, their other major patron, Islamic fundamentalist movements vied for power in Algeria, Pakistan, Egypt, Afghanistan, Lebanon, Nigeria, Jordan, and the Sudan, among other places. As the present volume amply demonstrates, these movements have had "impact" on different levels of political society and through diverse strategies. Some, as in Algeria, Egypt, Nigeria, and Pakistan, formed as political parties which attempted to work within the confines of the social contract and "rules of the game" established by the regime in power. "Islamization" was attempted both through alliances with the ruler (e.g., Pakistan under Zia) and through initial openings toward democratic reform (e.g., Egypt, Jordan). Both developments provided Islamic groups with an expanded political arena in which to solidify and enlarge their constituencies. While the Islamic groups benefited from these developments in the short term, the developments also exposed flaws in the fundamentalist program to render Islam an ideological system—that is, to translate religious law and Qur'anic precept into a coherent modern political vision capable of inspiring the formulation of effective solutions for difficult or even intractable problems. Islam itself often seemed diminished by its direct politicalization. As Mayer puts it in describing Islamization programs in Pakistan, Iran, and the Sudan, frequently "considerations of political expediency were officially permitted to override Islamic criteria."

A similar statement may be made regarding Hizbullah's revolutionary program. Although Hizbullah has employed violence for political and not ritualistic purposes, Martin Kramer notes, the goal of Hizbullah activism is the creation of an Islamic state. That goal had to be pursued within the law of Islam, and Hizbullah clerics placed restrictions on violence that prevented the group from pursuing narrow sectarian interests and employing wholly indiscriminate violence. "To be worthy of Islam," Kramer writes, "the struggle had to be global in conception but discriminating in execution." Nonetheless, "some of Hizbullah's acts of violence met these demanding criteria, some did not." The suicide missions and the abduction of innocent foreigners divided Hizbullah clerics, some of whom adapted the teaching to the practice, others of whom railed against what they saw as a clear departure from Islamic principles. The salient point for our discussion is that the clerics in these instances reacted to, rather than shaped, the actions of the militants.

The limitations of the fundamentalist imagination are perhaps most apparent in the chapters on economics. In a pluralistic polity such as the one that exists in the United States, a nation in which Protestant Christian fundamentalists are increasingly assimilated into the mainstream political and economic culture, Laurence Iannaccone finds that fundamentalists have not developed an economic vision or program expressive of their distinctive theological views.[20] Furthermore, one cannot even generalize about Christian fundamentalists and conservative evangelicals who write about economics. Iannaccone rehearses the "myth" that such Protestants are always staunch defenders of market capitalism and advocates of free enterprise as the solution to virtually every economic problem. "The reality is both different and more complex," he writes. "Theologically conservative Protestant leaders espouse a variety of economic positions. . . . And, despite well-publicized and extensive lobbying of social and moral issues, even such avowedly conservative groups as the Moral Majority have never seriously attempted to implement an *economic* agenda."

Timur Kuran comes to a similar conclusion in surveying and evaluating "Islamic economics," which aims "to provide a comprehensive blueprint for all economic activity." Some Islamic economists are quick to admit that in most economic realms the nascent discipline has yet to make a significant contribution. But they generally agree that the fundamental sources of Islam harbor clear and definitive solutions to every conceivable economic problem. To find these, they suggest, we must turn to the Qur'an and to the wisdom of the earliest Islamic community in seventh-century Arabia, drawing wherever necessary on modern tools and concepts. In so doing, however, these economists must operate within market systems and international rules of banking, and compete with interest-driven systems. "In this scenario," Kuran points out, "the practitioners of Islamic economics serve as hidden agents of secularization, arbiters between the discipline's goals and the secular practices it now condemns."

In a chapter on Buddhist economics, Charles Keyes documents the ways in which "fundamentalists" in both Burma and Thailand have sought to shape debates about the relationship of the economies of these countries to a global system dominated by capitalism. "They have not, however, been notably successful in acquiring the power which would make it possible to translate their positions into effective public policy," he concludes. "This lack of success demonstrates how difficult it has been to make sufficiently militant a religion which stresses individual responsibility and nonviolence." Deepak Lal's account of the failures of BJP leaders to develop a sophisticated system of Hindu economics confirms the conclusion that the construction of a viable economic program has not been the first item on the fundamentalist agenda.

The Question of Moderation: The Case of Algeria

Keyes and Lal, writing about the lack of a developed economic program in either Buddhist or Hindu "fundamentalism," note that Eastern religious traditions which do not hold a linear or progressive view of history, and which do not embrace a revealed set of laws, must first identify, or even construct, the religious "fundamentals" that would justify political action. One might expect, then, that the "People of the Book"—Jews, Christians, and Muslims—are better poised for political action because each of the three monotheistic faiths has a code of law and/or behavior revealed through a sacred text. Yet even in these cases one finds a lack of consensus on political programs and an inability, even among various fundamentalist groups in the same religion, to agree upon a normative politics. Islam, with its code of Shari'a, is nonetheless "protean" and "imprecise" on a number of questions, including politics. James Piscatori writes:

> The believer says, "Look to the Qur'an," but, like all fundamental documents, it is what the reader makes of it. Ask, "Does it support polygamy or monogamy, socialism or capitalism, equality of women or inequality, birth control, parliamentary democracy?" and the answers hinge on what one hopes to find. Although scriptural interpretation is problematic in every religion, it is especially so in the case of Islam and for several reasons.[21]

> The problem with this way of arguing [that religion and politics are one in Islam] is that it treats religion and politics as ideal categories and takes no real account of them as social phenomena. It thus fails to see that their conduct is often in conflict because their motivations are in conflict. If we set aside the logic of faith, there is no reason why truth should triumph over power. But, more to the point, it is very rarely possible when speaking of motivations to make such simple equations of religions and truth, and of politics and power. The history of every civilization shows that both religious and political institutions operating in society are contenders, and very often competitors, for people's loyalties and hence for power. In this sense both are political, but in the process the religious most often ends up being subject to, or used by, the explicitly political—quite contrary to what a great deal of contemporary Muslim opinion holds.[22]

> Several political ideas grow out of the shahada and also seem unexceptionable; that all mankind constitutes one spiritual community but that there is also a temporal community of believers which may or may not coincide with the universal community; that God does not directly govern the community of believers but that its government is based on His revealed law (it is not a theocracy but a nomocracy), that governmental edicts and legislation must not contradict the revealed law; that obedience is owed to the guardians of the law—in the first instance, the Prophet himself and, later, his successors to temporal power, though not to prophetic power; and that the actions of the governors themselves must be judged by the standards of the revealed law. These ideas mark off the Islamic political field, but we can also see that it is a broad field in which many questions—such as who decides on the succession of the Prophet, what form of regime (monarchy or democracy, for example) is sanctioned, and exactly when political revolt is permissible—are left unanswered. In truth, this broad field is really a battleground where many other ideas, such as the permissibility of birth control or the prohibition on interest-taking, must contend.[23]

The situation in Algeria in 1992 demonstrated the challenges faced by Islamic fundamentalist movements which attempt to become viable as political parties in secular states. In January of that year the fundamentalist Islamic Salvation Front (FIS) was poised to assume a commanding majority in parliament when President Chadli Benjedid of the ruling National Liberation Front resigned, thereby delivering the government into the hands of the military and effectively ending Algeria's three-year experiment in democracy.

By winning 180 of 231 seats contested in the December 1991 election, the first free national election since Algeria gained its independence from France in 1962, the Islamists had surprised their secular opponents, who believed that the fundamentalists would falter as a result of voter dissatisfaction with their incompetent administration of the municipalities they had won in local elections held in June 1990. Yet the voters seemed not to notice; the FIS was better organized and much more popular than the forty other alternatives to the ruling party, including the Front for Socialist Forces, which took a mere 25 seats. Exploiting widespread disgust with the National Liberation Front, the Marxist party that controlled Algeria for thirty years despite a record of inefficiency and corruption, the Islamists mobilized the disgruntled and the zealous alike, including thousands of veiled Algerian women clad in traditional Islamic garb. With more than 200 additional seats in parliament to be decided in the 16 January 1992 election, the Islamists were only 28 seats short of a simple majority, and well within reach of the two-thirds majority that would allow them to rewrite Algeria's constitution on the model of an Islamic republic.

The government crackdown on the fundamentalists, engineered by the "High State Council" formed to rule the country into 1993, amounted to the cancellation of the Arab world's first full-fledged experiment in democracy. The military regime arrested hundreds of Islamic fundamentalists, along with Arab-language journalists who had criticized the military or printed fundamentalists' communiqués. The ruling body banned rallies and other political activities at mosques, a move widely interpreted as intending to taunt and provoke the poor and jobless young men who constitute the inner cell of FIS supporters.

In covering these developments in Algeria, the (secular) Western media perceived the crisis through interpretive lenses similar to those used by the (secular) Algerian government. The political flexibility of Islam, suggested by Piscatori in the passages quoted above, was forgotten in several accounts which portrayed the Islamists as eager to enforce the "chilling penal law known as Shari'a," as one journalist reported.[24] Evidently lost on the reporter was the fact that the penal code, including the *huddud* punishments for adultery, theft, and other crimes, comprises only a small portion of the Shari'a, the complex body of sacred law drawn from the Qur'an, the Traditions of the Prophet, and revered commentary on both. By the logic that prevailed in much of the media analysis, however, either the Algerian voters were unaware of the dozens of alternatives to the Islamic party, or they were duped by the Islamists, or they were simply irrational and hopelessly "backwards." The notion of Islamic fundamentalism as rebarbative found support in the chant of 100,000 Algerians at a stadium rally on election eve—"We recognize no constitution and no laws but the laws of God and Islam"—and in the call for the veiling of women and their retreat from the workplace.

Algerian supporters of the FIS, motivated more by a passion for Islam than for democracy, were not preoccupied with working out a long-term alliance between the two. But neither was such an alliance out of the question. Because the Qur'an and the Shari'a provide a sociomoral framework rather than a detailed blueprint for the political order, and allow a measure of adaptation and flexibility in state-building, it was not inevitable that the Islamists would take a radical fundamentalist position by which retaliation against secularists would be the first order of business.

Islamic fundamentalists have made great demands on their governments without yet developing coherent and sophisticated alternative economic and social policies; the emphasis to date has been on cultural and political authenticity and self-reliance. But the quest for sovereignty and self-reliance does not rule out a gradual process of incorporation and "Islamization" of Western structures and mechanisms, including mass participation in democratic procedures. (Indeed, this has been the pattern followed in the Islamists' appropriation of Western science and technology, a borrowing which they describe as, instead, an act of "repossession" of a mode of discourse and production that originated, they claim, in the golden age of Islamic civilization.)[25] Like any complex legal code developed over time, the Shari'a admits of many interpretations and diverse applications, each of which is unavoidably selective. Even "progressives"—by any Western standard—have styled themselves as fundamentalists dedicated to the proper interpretation and application of the Shari'a.

University of Khartoum professor Akmed An Na'im, a leader of an Islamic reform movement in the Sudan called the Republican Brothers, has argued that a "fundamentalist" retrieval of Islamic law may be reconcilable with Western notions of human rights in civil society. Imprisoned without charge in 1984 by then Sudanese president Numayri, a self-proclaimed fundamentalist, An Na'im protested that Numayri's brand of Islamic fundamentalism, shared by other Islamic radicals in the Middle East, was a mistaken attempt to impose the Shari'a as an antidote to Western neocolonialism and cultural domination. He argued that the elements of Shari'a invoked by Numayri (and Khomeini)—those prescriptions revealed to Muhammad in Medina dealing with penal law, civil liberties, and the treatment of minorities and women—promoted a "historically dated Islamic self-identity that needs to be reformed." Islamic economic and social justice and the exercise of legitimate political power depend upon the retrieval of the teaching of the Prophet in Mecca, which provided, in An Na'im's judgment, the "moral and ethical foundation" of the tradition. "The Medina message is not the fundamental, universal, eternal message of Islam. That founding message is from Mecca," he writes. "This counter-abrogation [of the Medina code] will result in the total conciliation between Islamic law and the modern development of human rights and civil liberties." Rare is the disputant in such a conflict who does not claim to be upholding the "fundamentals." Rather, the battle is often over what they are, where they are to be found, how and by whom they are to be interpreted. In demanding the retrieval of the Mecca prophecy, An Na'im concludes, "We [Republican Brothers] are the *super-fundamentalists.*"[26]

The possibility of a "progressive" fundamentalism-in-power does not ensure, of course, the existence of one. If the fundamentalists had won in Algeria, they may or may not have behaved in accord with the best interests of the West or of the Algerian people. Should the Islamists eventually come to power, the situation may allow, or necessitate, the kind of shrewd compromise with secular governments and economies that has characterized the "conservative fundamentalist" monarchy in Saudi Arabia. Or the situation in Algeria may eventually approximate that of Egypt, in which lip service, public ceremony, co-opted senior *ulama* (men of religion), and occasional deferential rulings of government (that is, secular) courts serve as a panacea in lieu of the actual implementation of the Islamic law.

The comparison with Egypt is instructive because Egypt has developed a carefully calibrated response to fundamentalist political activism. Egypt lives with the presence of many levels and varieties of Islamic fundamentalism within its borders, and over the course of forty years, since the Free Officers Revolution that brought Nasser to power in 1952, the secularized military state has gradually perfected the fine art of constraining and containing Islamic militancy. This it has done, in the Mubarak years, by a sophisticated policy combining partial appeasement, co-optation, ruthless repression, constant surveillance and infiltration of radical cells, and a crushing monopoly over the media. Nonetheless, the Islamic current endures, with monthly reports of firebombs hurled through the windows of liquor stores and bars, unveiled women harassed by young ruffians, and gun battles with one or more of the dozens of clandestine radical splinter groups that long ago rejected the moderation of the original fundamentalist movement, the Muslim Brotherhood. In 1992 the Brotherhood published a weekly newspaper, supported the Labor Party, and had representatives in the Egyptian Parliament. But young Islamic radicals have meanwhile taken over student organizations at most universities, and constantly denounce what they perceive as the rampant corruption and inefficiency of the ruling party—which is to be expected, they maintain, of a ruling elite which long ago abandoned Islam.

Many of the "mainstream" Islamic parties have radical counterparts in the underground. Abdel Azim Ramadan's chapter in this volume compares the strategies of the Egyptian Muslim Brotherhood with the radical *takfir* groups of the 1970s and 1980s. Whereas the former presently eschews violence and subversive activities and finds its greatest contemporary expression in political alliances with the Labor Party, the latter remain dedicated to an ideology which brands the government as atheistic and leads to physical confrontation with security forces.

Islamists throughout the Middle East and South Asia now recognize that a divine mandate to rule does not make the social and economic problems of the umma less intractable. In Algeria, if "Islam is the solution," it must become prepared to tackle a $25 billion foreign debt, a 30 percent unemployment rate, and severe shortages of health services and housing—and do so while avoiding charging *riba* (interest) and dealing with the International Monetary Fund and the World Bank, Western institutions that do not honor the economic prescriptions and proscriptions of the Islamic law. Kuran's comparative study of "Islamic economics" in the four nations in which Islamists have striven to implement the Shari‘a—Iran, Pakistan, the Sudan, and Saudi Arabia—demonstrates a wide and often inconsistent variety of practices in fulfillment of the religiously mandated *zakat* (voluntary tax system) and the religiously proscribed charging of interest. It seemed certain in 1992 that Islamists in Algeria or elsewhere would be required by the exigencies of governing to accept compromises between the ideal and the possible—a practice not unknown in the brief history of Islamic fundamentalisms come-to-power.

Conclusion

The limited but real impact of fundamentalisms is due in part to the fact that nations continually define themselves and are thus continually open to revisions in self-understanding. The present volume indicates, however, that the success of fundamentalisms in reimagining the nation and remaking the state have occurred primarily if not exclusively in states in which the public-private distinction, to use John Garvey's term, has not been written into the constitution and protected by laws and judicial rulings. To put the matter another way: in polities in which some form of church-state separation has been adopted, fundamentalism seems less likely to dictate the course of national self-definition—unless and until the fundamentalists undergo a process of moderation. This is most apparent in the case of Christian fundamentalism in the United States.

The privatization of religion, encouraged by the constitutional protection or the de facto practice of church-state separation, became a defining characteristic of Western democracies in large part because Christianity in the West experienced debilitating wars over religion in the sixteenth and seventeenth centuries. The modern doctrine of secularism developed as an antidote to the practice of using the coercive powers of the state to enforce religious orthodoxy.[27]

In Islam, on the other hand, where traditionally there is no such thing as heresy in the Christian sense of the term, the "privatization of religion" and the enforcement of a distinction between religious and political affairs became a central concern only in the twentieth century and then only in Turkey, the one Muslim nation which has formally legalized the separation of religion and state. Because the demand of Islam is not textual accuracy in belief, but loyalty to the community and its constituted leader, Bernard Lewis points out, the broad tolerance of deviation in Islam "ceased only at the point where it became disloyalty, easily equated with treason, or where it became seditious and subversive, a danger to the existing social and political order." When that happens, apostasy occurs and it becomes an issue of law, a matter for prosecution and punishment. Lewis comments:

> For Muslims, the state was God's state, the army God's army, and, of course, the enemy was God's enemy. Of more practical importance, the law was God's law, and in principle there could be no other. The question of separating Church and state did not arise, since there was no Church, as an autonomous institution, to be separated. Church and state were one and the same.
>
> For the same reason, though Islamic society very soon developed a large and active class of professional men of religion, these were never a priesthood in the Christian sense, and could only loosely be described even as a clergy. . . .
> It is only in Ottoman times, almost certainly under the influence of Christian

example, that an organization of Muslim religious dignitaries was developed, with a hierarchy of ranks and with territorial jurisdictions. The ayatollahs of Iran are an even more recent innovation, and might not unjustly be described as another step in the Christianization of Islamic institutions, though by no means of Islamic teachings. . . .

It was not only the theoretical and historical basis for separation that was lacking in Islam; it was also the practical need. The level of willingness to tolerate and live peaceably with those who believe otherwise and worship otherwise was, at most times and in most places, high enough for tolerable coexistence to be possible, and Muslims did not therefore feel the imperative need felt by Christians to seek an escape from the horrors of state-sponsored and state-enforced doctrine.[28]

Fundamentalists Muslims have openly rejected the attempts of earlier Islamic modernists and reformers to incorporate the Western principle of separation, and the practice of privatization, into Islamic political and religious discourse. Subsequently "a number of governments have begun to reintroduce Shari'a law, either from conviction or as a preemptive strike against the fundamentalist challenge. Even nationalism and patriotism, which, after some initial opposition from pious Muslims, had begun to be generally accepted, are now once again being questioned and even denounced as anti-Islamic."[29] In this volume Serif Mardin describes the efforts of the Nakshibendi order to challenge Kemalist secularism in this century, and Umar Birai discusses the tajdid movement as an attempt to renew the religiously divided Nigerian state on Islamic principles.

When one looks beyond the Christian and Muslim worlds, with their different approaches to the relationship between religion and the state, it becomes clear that the political imagination of fundamentalists is focused on the questions of constitutionalism and law in nations that seem not to have settled such foundational questions for the current generation. As we have seen, India is a case in point, with Hindus, Sikhs, Muslims, and Buddhists each forming viable fundamentalist-like movements which seek to define the national identity of India (and Sri Lanka) in religio-legal terms. The limited but real successes of Jewish fundamentalists in Israel have likewise come in times of national soul-searching regarding the foundational questions of ethnic and religious identity, in relation to the way Israel should define and protect its national borders.

The success or failure of fundamentalists' various attempts to realize the "imagined community," then, have depended largely on the sociopolitical environment and historical character of the land they sought to inherit or repossess. As a general rule fundamentalists in democratic or quasi-democratic societies could hope only for a piece of the pie; their imaginings were confined to the home, school, and ghetto. When they ventured into the larger, vibrantly plural world of political competition, fundamentalists found it necessary to compromise. In sectarian states susceptible to or manipulated by ethnic and religious extremisms, radical fundamentalism found its natural métier. There it stands the better chance of making a world of its imaginings.

Notes

1. Benedict Anderson, *Imagined Communities: Reflections on the Origin and Spread of Nationalism,* rev. ed. (London: Verso, 1983; reprint 1991), p. 4.

2. On theories of nationalism, see E. J. Hobsbawm, *Nations and Nationalism since 1780: Programme, Myth, Reality* (Cambridge: Cambridge University Press, 1990).

3. Anderson, *Imagined Communities,* p. 7.

4. Ibid, p. 5.

5. Ernest Gellner, *Thought and Change* (London: Weidenfeld and Nicholson, 1964), p. 161.

6. Tom Nairn, *The Break-up of Britain* (London: New Left Books, 1977), p. 359.

7. See the discussion in James Piscatori, ed., *Islamic Fundamentalisms and the Gulf Crisis* (Chicago: American Academy of Arts and Sciences, 1991).

8. Anderson, *Imagined Communities,* p. 6.

9. The expectation of the Western press was that the bounty on Rushdie's head would be lifted when Khomeini died and the "pragmatic" Rafsanjani came to power. Instead, Rafsanjani increased the bounty. See Malise Ruthven, *A Satanic Affair: Salman Rushdie and the Rage of Islam* (London: Chatto and Windus, 1990), pp. 104–25.

10. Anderson, *Imagined Communities,* p. 10.

11. Krishna Kumar, "Hindu Revivalism and Education in North Central India," in Martin E. Marty and R. Scott Appleby, *Fundamentalisms and Society: Reclaiming the Sciences, the Family, and Education* (Chicago: University of Chicago Press, 1992).

12. "Violence like Punjabs' Wheat Finds Fertile Soil," *New York Times,* 1 February 1992, p. A2.

13. "Punjab's Election Chilled by Threat," *New York Times,* 20 February 1992.

14. Edward A. Gargan, "Kashmir Caravan by Hindus Is Halted," *Chicago Tribune,* 26 February 1992. On the Jammu Kashmir Liberation Front, see Mumtaz Ahmad, "Islamic Fundamentalism in South Asia: The Jamaat-i-Islami and the Tablighi Jamaat" in Martin E. Marty and R. Scott Appleby, *Fundamentalisms Observed* (Chicago: University of Chicago Press, 1991), pp. 457–530.

15. *Chicago Tribune,* 14 February 1991, p. 22.

16. See Beverley Milton-Edwards, "A Temporary Alliance with the Crown: The Islamic Response in Jordan," and Gehad Auda, "An Uncertain Response: The Islamic Movement in Egypt," in Piscatori, ed., *Islamic Fundamentalisms and the Gulf Crisis,* pp. 88–108.

17. *New York Times,* 22 February 1992.

18. The case of Iran is a notable exception in that an Islamic government has been in power for over a decade, and its successes and failures by various standards are the subject of chapters in this volume by Said Arjomand, Ann Mayer, Nikki Keddie, and Timur Kuran.

19. "Fundamentalist Finds a Fulcrum in Sudan," *New York Times,* 29 January 1992, p. A3. Turabi who is fifty-nine years old, has degrees in law from Khartoum University, London University, and the Sorbonne, and is fluent in Arabic, English, and French, presents the Islamization of the Sudan in a milder way. He says the Shari'a, which calls for the amputation of limbs as the punishment for armed robbery, is being enforced in a responsible manner. He was the architect of Shari'a-based laws in Numayri's regime that resulted in a number of amputations that were carried out in public.

20. The Christian Reconstructionists, profiled by Nancy Ammerman in volume 1 of this series and dicussed by Iannaccone in the present volume, are a possible exception to this generalization.

21. James Piscatori, *Islam in a World of Nation-States* (Cambridge: Canbridge University Press, 1986), p. 3.

22. Ibid., p. 13

23. Ibid., pp. 14–15.

24. Jill Smolowe, "An Alarming No Vote," *Time,* 13 January 1992, p. 28.

25. See the discussion by Bassam Tibi, "The Worldview of Sunni Arab Fundamentalists: Attitudes Toward Modern Science and Technology," in Marty and Appleby, eds., *Fundamentalisms and Society.*

26. Abdullahi Ahmed An Na'im, "The Reformation of Islam," *New Perspectives Quarterly* (Fall 1987), p. 51.

27. Bernard Lewis, "Muslims, Christians, and Jews: The Dream of Coexistence," *New York Review of Books* 39, no. 6 (26 March 1992): 49.

28. Ibid., p. 50. "The character and extent of traditional Muslim tolerance should not be misunderstood. If by tolerance we mean the traditional Muslim state was not tolerant, and indeed a tolerance thus designed would have been seen not as a merit but as a dereliction of duty. No equality was conceded, in practice or even less in theory, between those who accepted and obeyed God's word, and those who willfully and of their own choice rejected it. Discrimination was structural, universal, imposed by doctrine and law and enforced by popular consent. Persecution, on the other hand, though not unknown, was rare and atypical, and there are few if any equivalents in Muslim history to the massacres, the forced conversions, the expulsions, and the burnings that are so common in the history of Christendom before the rise of secularism.

By a sad paradox, the adoption in the nineteenth and twentieth centuries of democratic constitutions, guaranteeing equal rights for all citizens, in the Ottoman Empire, in Iran, Egypt, and elsewhere, on the whole weakened rather than strengthened the position of minorities. On the one hand it deprived them of the limited but substantial and well-grounded rights and privileges which they enjoyed under the old Islamic dispensation. On the other, it failed to make good the new rights and freedoms offered to them by the newly enacted constitutions which, in this as in many other respects, proved a dead letter. It is easier to be tolerant from a position of strength than from a position of weakness, and in the age of overwhelming European superiority of wealth and power, the Christian and to an extent the Jewish minorities, suspected with some justification of sympathizing and even collaborating with European imperialists, were subject to increasing hostility. After the withdrawal of those imperialists in the postwar period, the surviving minorities were in an exposed and dangerous position."

29. Ibid., p. 52.

CONTRIBUTORS

R. SCOTT APPLEBY, the associate director of the Fundamentalism Project, is a historian of religion and currently a visiting research associate at the University of Chicago. He is the author of *Church and Age, Unite! The Modernist Impulse in American Catholicism* and is the coeditor, with Martin E. Marty, of *Fundamentalisms Observed.*

SAID AMIR ARJOMAND was born in Tehran, received his Ph.D. from the University of Chicago in 1980, and is professor of sociology at the State University of New York at Stony Brook. He is the author of *The Shadow of God and the Hidden Imam* and *The Turban for the Crown.* He has held visiting appointments at St. Antony's College, Oxford (1981-82), the University of California at Berkeley (1989), and the University of Freiburg (1990–91), and was a member of the Institute for Advanced Study at Princeton (1984–85).

UMAR M. BIRAI is senior lecturer in the Department of Political Science and dean of student affairs at the University of Abuja, Nigeria. He has written and lectured frequently on the Islamic revival in Africa.

STEVE BRUCE is head of the Department of Sociology at the University of Aberdeen, Scotland. He is the author of *Pray TV: A Sociology of Television Evangelism* and *The Rise and Fall of the New Christian Right: Protestant Politics in America, 1978–88.*

ROBERT ERIC FRYKENBERG is professor of history and South Asian studies at the University of Wisconsin at Madison. He is the author of *Guntur District, 1788–1848: A History of Local Influence and Central Authority in South India,* has published numerous articles, and is the editor of several volumes on India, including *Land Tenure and Peasant in South Asia, Delhi through the Ages,* and *Studies of South India.*

JOHN H. GARVEY is the Ashland Professor of Law at the University of Kentucky College of Law. He has served as assistant to the solicitor general of the United States and is the author of numerous articles on constitutional religious issues and coeditor of *Readings in Modern Constitutional Theory* and *The First Amendment: A Reader.*

FAYE GINSBURG is associate professor of anthropology at New York University where she is also the director of the Program in Ethnographic Film and Video. She is the author of the award-winning book *Contested Lives: The Abortion Debate in an*

American Community and coeditor, with Anna Tsing, of *Uncertain Terms: Negotiating Gender in American Culture*. In 1991–92, she received a Guggenheim Fellowship for her research and writing on the use of film and video by indigenous peoples. She is beginning a long-term ethnographic study of the Salvation Army.

LAURENCE R. IANNACCONE is associate professor of economics at Santa Clara University. He has written many articles and presented numerous papers on his research, which centers on economic models of religious behavior.

NIKKI R. KEDDIE is professor of history at the University of California at Los Angeles and editor of the journal *Contention*. She has published numerous articles and books on Iran and the Middle East, including *Roots of Revolution: An Interpretive History of Modern Iran* and, with Juan Cole, *Shi'ism and Social Protest*.

CHARLES F. KEYES is professor and chairman of anthropology and director of Southeast Asian studies at the University of Washington and has recently been a visiting senior research scholar at Chiang Mai University, Thailand. He is the author of *Thailand: Buddhist Kingdom as Modern Nation-State* and editor of *Reshaping Local Worlds: Rural Education and Cultural Change in Southeast Asia*.

MARTIN KRAMER is associate director of the Moshe Dayan Center for Middle Eastern and African Studies at Tel Aviv University. He is the author of *Islam Assembled: The Advent of Muslim Congresses* and editor of *Middle Eastern Lives: The Practice of Biography and Self-Narrative* and *Shi'ism, Resistance, and Revolution*.

TIMUR KURAN is associate professor of economics at the University of Southern California. His research focuses on the evolution of values and institutions. Several of his essays evaluate the economic doctrines associated with Islam. He is completing a book on the ideological, social, political, and economic consequences of preference falsification—the act of concealing one's wants under social pressure.

DEEPAK LAL is the James S. Coleman Professor of International Development Studies at the University of California at Los Angeles and professor of political economy at University College, London. He is the author of numerous articles and books on development, including *The Poverty of Development Economics* and *The Hindu Equilibrium*. He has advised a number of countries and has worked for various international organizations, most recently as research administrator at the World Bank.

CHARLES S. LIEBMAN is professor of political science at Bar-Ilan University in Ramat-Gan, Israel. He is the author of many articles and books on religion, politics, and society among Jews in the United States and Israel, including *Religion and Politics in Israel* and *Two Worlds of Judaism*.

ŞERIF MARDIN is a sociologist in the School of International Service at American University and the author of numerous studies on the Middle East including *The Genesis of Young Ottoman Thought*. He taught at Bogazici University, Istanbul, Turkey, from 1973 to 1990.

MARTIN E. MARTY is the Fairfax M. Cone Distinguished Service professor of the History of Modern Christianity at the University of Chicago, the director of the Fundamentalism Project, and a senior editor of *Christian Century*. A fellow of the American Academy of Arts and Sciences, Marty is the author of over forty books, including the four-volume history, *Modern American Religion*.

ANN ELIZABETH MAYER is associate professor of legal studies at the Wharton School of the University of Pennsylvania and the author of *Islam and Human Rights*. She has also written on the role of Islamic law in contemporary Middle Eastern societies.

HARJOT OBEROI holds the chair in Sikh and Punjabi studies in the Department of Asian Studies, University of British Columbia, Vancouver, Canada. He is associate editor of *Pacific Affairs* and is the author of a forthcoming book from Oxford University Press on the emergence of modern Sikh identity.

ABDEL AZIM RAMADAN is professor of contemporary history, Faculty of Arts, Monofiya University, Egypt. Recipient of the Egyptian Order of Sciences and Arts, Dr. Ramadan is an editor and writer for the political weekly *October*. He is the author of twenty-five books in Arabic on the social and political history of Egypt and the Arab world.

DAVID C. RAPOPORT is professor of political science at the University of California at Los Angeles and the editor of the *Journal of Terrorism and Political Violence*. He is the author of *Assassination and Terrorism* and editor of *Inside Terrorist Organizations*.

OLIVIER ROY is a researcher at CNRS (French National Center for Scientific Research). He has traveled with participants in Afghan resistance movements and is the author of numerous articles on Iran and Afghanistan and the book *Islam and Resistance in Afghanistan*.

EHUD SPRINZAK is associate professor of political science at Hebrew University of Jerusalem. He is the author of *The Ascendance of Israel's Radical Right, Illegalism in Israeli Society,* and many essays on political and religious extremism.

STANLEY J. TAMBIAH is professor of anthropology at Harvard University. He was president of the Association for Asian Studies (1989–90) and is a fellow of the American Academy of Arts and Sciences. He is the author of many books, among which are *Sri Lanka: Ethnic Fratricide and the Dismantling of Democracy* and *Buddhism Betrayed? Religion, Politics and Violence in Sri Lanka*.

INDEX

'Abduh, Muhammad, 153
Abdurrahman, Emir, 493
Abhidharma (Buddhist scripture), 375
abortion: in Britain, 56; in Ireland, 52; Protestant fundamentalists on, 22, 30, 32, 36, 46n.35, 64, 296, 352, 353, 356; in U.S., 35, 41–42, 59, 61, 440. *See also* Operation Rescue; *Roe v. Wade*
Abu Nidal, 503
Addis Ababa Agreement (Sudan), 133, 148n.61
Adolescent Family Life Act, 49n.74
Advani, Lal Krishan, 244, 245, 249, 250, 421
Afghanistan, 456, 623; war of, with Soviet Union, 434, 491, 492, 497, 499, 503, 504. *See also* Mujahidin; Sunni fundamentalism: in Afghanistan
AFRC, 188, 190, 192
Africa Watch organization, 150n.79
Afzal, Mollah, 505
Agency for International Development (AID): in the Sudan, 136
agricultural reform, 14; in Afghanistan, 496; and Hindu economics, 413, 420; in India, 263–64, 417. *See also* Green Revolution
Agudat Israel party, 70, 71, 75, 76, 82, 83, 86n.11
Ahmad, Jalal Al-i, 517
Ahmad, Khurshid, 315
Ahmadis: in Pakistan, 25, 125, 272
al-Ahram (Egyptian weekly), 156
AIDS, 17, 18, 19
Akali Dal, 259, 260, 262, 264, 266, 267, 268, 274, 275, 276, 280, 628
Akbar, Emperor, 235
Ak-Doğus group (Turkey), 230
Ala, Hussain, 515
alcohol, use of: and Islamic law, 113, 149n.67, 149n.69; in U.S., 30, 59
Algeria, 639; fundamentalist movements in, 4,

143, 491, 492, 627, 634, 635–38. *See also* elections: in Algeria
Ali Shah, Muhammad, 516
All-Ceylon Buddhist Congress, 592, 593, 595, 596, 600, 602
Alliance Party (Northern Ireland), 58
All-India Hindu Mahasabha. *See* Hindu Mahasabha
All-India Sikh Students Federation, 269, 279
alms, giving of: in Buddhism, 297, 299, 368, 371, 373, 377, 385, 390, 397. See also *zakat*
Amal (Hope), 431, 435, 527; and Hizbullah, 541, 543–44, 548
Amalekites, 449, 467
Amanullah Khan, King (Afghanistan), 493, 509n.6, 629
Amer, Ahmed Salih, 159
American Civil Liberties Union: on creationism, 62
American Coalition for Traditional Values, 60, 63
American Economic Association, 303, 345
American Family Association, 42
Amin, Hafizullah, 503
Aminu, Jibril, 190
Amish, 23
Amital, Rabbi Yehuda, 86n.21
Amlashi, Rabani, 92
Ammerman, Nancy, 345
Amnesty International, 145n.14, 147n.39, 149n.65, 151n.85, 634
Amrik Singh, Bhai, 262
Amritsar, 245, 258, 259, 273, 277, 284n.41, 629
Anandpur Sahib Resolution, 259, 274–79
Anderson, Benedict, 621, 625
animism: in Nigeria, 185; in the Sudan, 133
Ansar Sufi order, 132, 138
apocalypticism: and fundamentalism, 626
Apprentice Boys of Derry, 55

627; Islamic, 125, 186, 194, 327, 328; Israeli, 72, 76, 81
Eelam (Tamil homeland), 605, 606, 609, 614
Egypt: fundamentalist movements in, 4, 25–26, 630; and Israel, 157, 162, 169, 170, 471; and the Soviet Union, 156; and the Sudan, 141; and U.S., 169. *See also* Islamization: in Egypt
Eitan, General Raphael, 475
elections: in Algeria, 143, 507, 637; in Burma, 382; in Egypt, 162, 174; in India, 245, 249, 250–51, 262, 279, 418, 420, 629; in Iran, 90, 94, 122, 143; in Israel, 24, 70, 71, 75, 76–78, 85, 431, 462, 463, 478, 483; in Nigeria, 192, 198–99; in Northern Ireland, 54–56, 66n.9; in Pakistan, 129, 130, 146n.31; in Sri Lanka, 433, 591, 593, 596, 597, 602, 603, 607, 609, 612; in the Sudan, 138, 139, 144, 150n.74; in Turkey, 217, 218; in U.S., 59, 525
el-Nur, Farouk Ibrahim, 140
Emerald Buddha, 406n.91
Emerson, Ralph Waldo, 225
Enforcement of Shari'a Act 1991, 130
Enlightenment, Jewish, 469
Enlightenment, Scottish, 292
Episcopal Church of Ireland (in Ulster), 53
Epistle of Light, 218, 219, 220
Equal Access Act (1984), 38, 41
Equal Rights Amendment (U.S.), 37
Erbakan, Necmettin, 222
Erev Shabbat (Israeli religious weekly), 70
eschatology: and fundamentalisms, 626
Establishment Clause. *See* U.S. Constitution: Establisment Clause
Ettela'at, 521
Etzion, Yehuda, 474, 475, 476
European Economic Community (EEC): Turkey and, 223, 226–27
evangelicalism, 343, 352–56, 361n.7, 364n.53; in America, 23, 50, 51, 61, 63, 363–64n.42; in Buddhism, 394; in Northern Ireland, 53, 54, 55, 56–57. *See also* New Christian Right
evolution, 38, 39; and Islam, 140, 150–51n.80
Ezra movement, 70
Ezzam, Abdallah, 505

Fadlallah, Muhammad Husayn, 544, 546, 547, 549, 550, 551–52
Faisal, King (Saudi Arabia), 165
Falwell, Jerry, 19, 29, 31, 32, 35, 60, 345, 346; on economic matters, 347, 356, 357, 360
Family Law Ordinance 1967 (Pakistan), 128
Family Protection Act (U.S.), 37
Family Protection Act of 1967 (Iran), 116, 120

Fanon, Franz, 480, 481, 517
faqih, 114, 116, 118, 122
Faraj, Muhammad Abd al-Salam, 159–60
Farrakhan, Louis, 199
Fatimi, Husain, 515
Fatimids, 512
fatwa (legal ruling), 160, 315
FBI: and Kahane, 477–78
Federal Party (Tamil), 598, 599, 605
feminism: and fundamentalism, 25, 30; in Pakistan, 125, 127
Fida'iyan-i Islam, 434, 514–16, 518, 523, 524, 533
FIS. *See* Islamic Salvation Front
Five Pillars of Islam, 318
FLN. *See* National Liberation Front
Fodio, Usman Dan, 185, 186, 195
Forqan group, 524
France, 14; and Hizbullah, 550–51; influence of, on Islamic law, 118–19, 135; and Iraq, 528
freedom, religious, 14, 15, 21, 24, 25, 35, 36, 38, 39, 40, 42, 43
Freedom Movement (Iran), 98, 143
Free Exercise Clause. *See* U.S. Constitution: Free Exercise Clause
free market system: Christian fundamentalists on, 344, 346–47, 348, 356, 359, 363–64n.42; and Hindu economics, 410, 420, 422; in India, 417; in Iran, 121, 123; in Pakistan, 130
Free Officers Revolution (Egypt), 639
Free Presbyterian Church of Ulster, 18, 20, 26, 54–55, 56, 57
Free Presbyterian Party, 59
Friedman, Milton, 347
Front for Socialist Forces party (Algeria), 637
fundamentalism, characteristics of: Buddhist, 368, 369, 376, 399; Christian, 15, 28, 29–34, 35, 36, 37–38, 39, 50–51, 294, 343, 345, 361n.7, 365n.59, 623–33; general/comparative, 2–4, 5–7, 8n.4, 9n.7, 13, 15, 16–17, 19, 22, 23, 24–25, 204, 207–8, 236, 257, 429–30, 431, 442, 447, 450, 454–56, 463, 620–24, 631; Hindu, 410–11; Islamic, 6, 103, 113, 114, 121–22, 142–43, 430, 638; Jewish, 17, 72–73, 438; Sikh, 17, 257, 258, 629
fundamentalism, impact of: Buddhist, 384, 399–400; Christian, 30–31, 43–44, 50, 63–64, 65, 31, 298, 360–61, 457n.3, 621–22, 623, 635, 640; general/comparative, 624, 626–27, 628, 631, 634, 640, 641; Hindu, 240, 244, 248–49, 250, 251–53, 253, 622; Islamic, 112–15, 121–22, 132–33, 134, 139, 142, 143–44, 152–53, 154, 204–5, 217–18, 226, 228, 280, 553, 633, 638; Jewish, 68, 70, 73, 78–82, 300, 445,